DATE DUE

Architecture of the Early XX. Century

Architecture of the Early XX. Century

Selection and Commentary by Peter Haiko

RIZZOLI
NEW YORK

First published in the United States of America in 1989 by
Rizzoli International Publications, Inc.
300 Park Avenue South, New York, NY 10010

Copyright © 1989 by Ernst Wasmuth Verlag Tübingen

ISBN 0-8478-1083-6
LC 89-42691

Printed and bound in West Germany
by Universitätsdruckerei Dr. C. Wolf und Sohn, Munich

Inhalt	Table des matières	Contents

Publisher's Preface

The documentation of the foremost examples of the earliest twentieth–century architecture from 1901 to the First World War – in 14 volumes with a total of 1400 plates, each accompanied by a detailed commentary – was an enormous undertaking accomplished by the publishing house of Ernst Wasmuth in Germany. Selections from this important journal are now made available for all who share an interest in architectural history.

In selecting the material to reprint, the editors were careful to retain the original character of The Architecture of the 20th Century and to avoid any shift of emphasis. Thus, a number of early, well-known masterpieces of modern architecture, which some readers may miss, were apparently not considered significant enough for inclusion at the time of original publication. Nevertheless, this important reprint of selections from The Architecture of the 20th Century–Journal of Modern Architecture represents an essential contribution to the history of the earliest twentieth-century architecture, seen here as it was first chronicled in its own day.

The original journal appeared on a quarterly basis from 1901 to 1914 and provided descriptions in three languages during its first nine years of publication. Starting in 1910, however, it appeared in German only. In compiling this new selection of works, the text accompanying the illustrated buildings of the period from 1910 to 1914 has been translated into French and English. To preserve the stylistic continuity, these texts are also presented in Eckmann type. Many of the captions have been revised in all three languages to conform to today's terminology.

The journal originally appeared in a large folio of 32 × 48 cm (12½ × 18¾ in.), which is now reduced for this book. Limitation of space have prevented the inclusion of every plan, sketch, or plate for each building, but the book does include the illustrative material considered most essential and interesting for today's readers. The text has been abridged in only a few cases; the plans appear in a wide range of scale, as was the case in the original edition. Plan numbers or letters are explained in either the corresponding key or in the accompanying text. In addition, readers may consult the "Table Explaining the Ground-Plans", on page 20.

Each plate number, which also marks the corresponding text, is followed by the year of publication and are helpful when using this book for academic purposes. A geographical index has also been provided as a quick reference to the buildings documented in the text.

Peter Haiko

The Architecture of the 20th Century
Journal of Modern Architecture

Its Contribution to the Architectural History of Modernism

The Architecture of the 20th Century – Journal of Modern Architecture, a quarterly first published by Ernst Wasmuth in Berlin in 1901, announces in its title and subtitle the immense standards of the new periodical. For with this title, the journal postulates its ability to document the definitive examples of twentieth century architecture – virtually at the very start of the new epoch. Furthermore, it confidently suggests at this early date that its diagnosis of the seminal works of twentieth century architecture will be confirmed in the future as having been unquestionably accurate. This revealing self-assessment goes one step further in the subtitle; a strictly modern architecture is to make its presence felt in the journal.

Since The Architecture of the 20th Century does not represent one of the many publications sponsored by various circles of self-appointed Modernists, the journal claims to take a practically nonpartisan and objective approach toward the issue of Modernism. It therefore includes only those works of the new century in which contemporary architecture has made the transition to a truly modern one.

The validity of these claims applies not only to Germany, the country of publication, but, as evidenced by the trilingual format of the journal until the year 1909, to all of Europe, indeed to the rest of the world. Yet what supports these claims even more than the journal's trilingualism are the recurring examples, however sporadic, of works from outside Germany.

Contrary to the vehement debates of the 1890s which revolved around the concept of Modernism – one only has to recall Otto Wagner's book Moderne Architektur, as well as the concerted efforts of the many "Secessionist" movements – this journal's concept of Modernism is quite different, a fact which may surprise many of today's readers.

Conditioned by a particular conception of the avant-garde, today's readers, upon first leafing through the pages of a publication entitled The Architecture of the 20th Century – Journal of Modern Architecture, would expect to find the same milestones of modern architecture listed in recent reference works covering the architecture of the twentieth century. Illustrious names which dare not be omitted in any catalogue of modern architecture come immediately to the mind of today's architectural historians, who naturally wish to find them in this publication as well. It would seem that it is once again respectable to regard the familiar landmarks of Modernism with an air of reverence.

But this is by no means the case here. Entire lists could be filled with those architectural works of the early twentieth century missing from the pages of The Architecture of the 20th Century. How, then, are we to overcome the inevitable sense of frustration of today's faithful connoisseurs who consider themselves well-versed in this century's architectural history? Are we to assume the publishers simply left all of these names out of the publication to avoid competing with their simultaneously released Moderne Städtebilder (Modern Townscapes), which includes many modern masterpieces? Although this speculation cannot be dismissed, it is at best an oversimplification of the matter.

What the present journal does confirm, however, is that today's popular conception of the roots of Modernism at the beginning of the twentieth century is a far too

linear one based on a extremely limited number of model examples. This journal shows that what was considered modern around 1900 cannot and should not be measured with the yardstick of Modernism used in the 1920s; the idea of Modernism in 1900 was based on a much different, sometimes glaringly contradictory, conceptual meaning. Understood in this light, it does not always refer to that brand of Modernism recognized as the direct predecessor and pioneer of the avant-garde movement which arose after the First World War.

The Modernist debate conducted at the turn of the century was not dominated by the anticipated ideas of Adolf Loos, Walter Gropius, Mies van der Rohe or Le Corbusier, but by an architecture which superseded and deliberately distanced itself from the tradition of the nineteenth century. Clearly formulated in the introduction to the first issue of the 1901 volume, with its programmatic title "Ziele der Architektur im neuen Jahrhundert" (Goals of Architecture in the new Century), Modernism means an abandonment of Historicism and the limitations imposed by its strict doctrines. But Modernism here should also be understood as a rejection of Art Nouveau, which was considered as purely arbitrary.

The Architecture of the 20th Century shatters that portrait of early twentieth century Modernism so cherished by many historians of architecture. It is no longer possible to uphold the established notion of a unified Modernist movement, that is, a Modernism whose unbroken development from the 1900s to today – despite the present trend of the Postmodern countermovement – is regarded as the expression of an unwavering artistic will. The Architecture of the 20th Century exposes this presumptuous homogeneity of Modernism as a restorative utopia. A monolithic Modernism is suddenly replaced by many movements, some of which are motivated by completely different aims. All are united by one factor only – their renunciation of historicism, that style which so dominated the art of the second half of the nineteenth century. We should bear in mind that even as early as 1900, when it was still in its prime – the journal Ver Sacrum first appeared in the year 1898 – Art Nouveau was no longer undisputedly recognized as the chief exponent of the modern movement. It was denied this recognition not only by its strictest opponents, but by those who, although in agreement with the aims of Art Nouveau and in particular with its criticism of Historicism, categorically rejected the artistic solution it offered.

The author of the programmatic introduction mentioned above is none other than Cornelius Gurlitt, one of the leading art critics of his day. He characterizes the fin de siècle situation as follows: "The severity of scientific methods stood on the one side and militated against a caprice which can be restrained by no outward rules, but only by the temperate mind of the artist."[1] In describing the past epoch, Gurlitt metaphorically likens it to a "feast of old forms," which, although "rich and plentiful," was not able to satiate the "craving after real art." He contrasts the self-denial of the nineteenth century with the gluttony of the exponents of Modernism in the 1890s, whose opposition to Historicism required that, "every line must demonstrate the

1 Die Architektur des XX. Jahrhunderts – Zeitschrift für moderne Baukunst (The Architecture of the 20th Century – Journal of Modern Architecture), 1, 1901, p. 2

ubiquitous 'I', that not a stroke dare remind of another hand."[2] The ascetic orientation toward the past in Historicism, together with its accompanying loss of individuality and identity, is countered by the unbridled rejection of the past in Art Nouveau, a style whose loss of (artistic) self-control Gurlitt finds no less reprehensible.

In his introductory article, Cornelius Gurlitt lays down the journal's editorial line and, what is more, defines what he considers to be truly modern. For Gurlitt, the task of Modernism is to transcend historical forms, "to consider the antique as a ladder" which it may mount.[3] Its purpose – so the author concludes – is to "bring the Renaissance to an end."[4] As revolutionary as this might sound, as reminiscent of the various radical rejections of historicism à la Wagner, Loos, Muthesius and others, it is not actually meant to be so. For this postulated "entrance into the new land" proves upon closer interpretation to be more of a way of achieving a certain distance between the modern age and the past, a means for Modernism to step aside while being careful not to lose contact with the past altogether. The obligatory reverence for the past is to be replaced by a voluntary and independent approach, namely, that of transcending the historical form. Future masters are to be regarded as those "who use the antique . . . only as a fertile soil."[5]

For Gurlitt, the duty of the twentieth century is to fulfill the dreams of the nineteenth century in its own contemporary style. These dreams "dared not express themselves openly as they wished, dared not to be original" because they were incompatible with the flamboyantly heralded teachings of the Renaissance.[6] The style of the Renaissance revival, like that of any other revival, has become indisputably obsolete. The artist's path must be "clear for all independent achievements."[7]

Yet in this respect Gurlitt – strongly influenced by Otto Wagner's book Moderne Architektur, which was first published in 1896 – faithfully echoes Modernist criticism of Historicism. Gurlitt writes "that the demands of modern art" cannot be satisfied by "adhering to the old lines, and by creating with the spiritual guidance of the ancients alone."[8] This very thought had been formulated by Wagner several years previously as follows: "The task of art, and of modern art as well, remains the same as it has been at all times. Modern art must represent modern man, our ability, what we do and do not do, through forms created by us." And "It seem to me childish to see the 'be all and end all' in one style or another, or to put specific styles at the service of special architectural purposes, and the truly progressive artistic impulse will surely reject such onesidedness."[9] For Otto Wagner, Gurlitt's call for an end to the Renaissance has already been fulfilled. Yet in place of Historicism's revival of the Renaissance Wagner now substitutes his own rebirth of art and tersely remarks, "Today there is a larger gap between Modernism and the Renaissance than between the Renaissance and the Antique."[10] In the same spirit as Gurlitt's vision of a free treatment of art forms, regarded as the fertile soil from which new ones may sprout, Wagner asserts that the new style in architecture will be established by "further development and transformation, along with the utilization of all motifs and materials."[11]

Based on Otto Wagner's concept that every art form must reflect its times, the motto of the Vienna Secession, "to each age its art," is expressed by Gurlitt in terms of the widespread realization which emerged at the end of the nineteenth century, namely, that "no one style of those ages which have gone before" – meaning the various trends in Historicism – "is sufficient for the artistic demands of the present day."[12]

Nevertheless, the striking verbal affinity between the journal's proclaimed editorial line and the goals of Modernism as formulated by an Otto Wagner does not seem to match the stylistic congruity of the works selected for the journal. If these examples of contemporary architecture between 1901 and 1914, each with its own description and comprising a total of 1400 plates, were to be reduced to a common stylistic denominator – in itself practically a violation of the architectural historian's commitment to careful analysis – most of them would fall under the categories of "Late Historicism," "Architecture of the Wilhelmite Era," and "Early Regionalism".

This theoretical agreement, between the aims of Modernism and Otto Wagner, remains an ostensible one which fails to produce an architecture reflecting these aesthetic requirements. Yet in this respect, Gurlitt's postulate of transcending "historical forms" should be understood ultimately as something quite different – or at any rate more restricted – than that to which Wagner laid claim. History has bequeathed an inheritance, whereby the artist, whom Gurlitt considers a legitimate heir, is free to dispose of it as he pleases. In the final analysis, however, history is inalienable and as such, the artist remains bound to it. For a work to be included in The Architecture of the 20th Century, it must first meet the journal's prime criterion of demonstrating a free treatment of the past instead of a slavish orientation toward it. If the illustrated work also fulfills such criteria as practicality, it is then regarded as a prime example of modern architecture.

Complexity and contradiction – both in form and content – are the two qualities most prized by the journal in its evaluation of the architecture it chooses to present. For example, "This splendid building, thoroughly modern in construction, represents a felicitous marriage of motifs from the German Early Renaissance with those forms of the French and English Renaissance."[13] Or an apartment building designed by Berlage is noted for its "medieval architecture adapted to modern requirements, and medieval ornament modified and permeated by modern taste."[14] The "early medieval composition" of a bank building for example, can be clothed in "modern robes," thus resulting in an architecture which is entirely modern.[15]

Each of the three subsequent issues of the 1901 volume contains an introduction devoted to an appraisal of the architecture of a European country, namely, England, Austria and France. This series concludes in the first 1902 issue with the article "The Development of Architecture in Germany." Each article interprets the situation of architecture in its respective country along the same lines as those set forth in Gurlitt's introduction.

In England, for example, there is a certain group of disciples beyond the pale of Historicism to whom the word "'style' is like a red rag to a bull. They do not seek . . . to apply to their buildings features belonging intrinsically to other centuries; their aim is to evolve a truly modern architecture."[16] Yet an ambition bordering on "egotism which prompts some architects to attempt to set aside the examples of the past results in the production of buildings which are neither beautiful nor appropriate."[17] However, "the more moderate recognize that art and architecture are progressive developments." While they study the work of the past "in order to acquire the accumulated knowledge which it affords, they are not slaves to it, but are free to create new forms . . . ".[18]

In his article on the state of Viennese architecture at the start of the new century, Ferdinand von Feldegg, publisher of the influential "moderate" Viennese architectural journal Der Architekt, is convinced that the future of Austrian architecture will be neither a return to the "ancients" nor an enduring establishment of "all that is now understood under the term 'modern', as the blind followers of the present style confidently believe," but a synthesis of the old and the new. According to Feldegg: "lastly will remain with us the courage to dare – to dare to strike off the chains of the historical 'Tabulator' and of its most rigid adherents – the Philistines of art . . . But transitory will be the illusion that the architecture of our own time can only rise from the ruins of the older art, or that the entire destruction of what has gone before must be a necessary preliminary to the development of a style worthy of the time in which we live."[19]

In their essay on German architecture, the editors of The Architecture of the 20th Century also reject both the dogmatic style of Historicism and the nihilistic one of Art Nouveau. Instead, they call for a plurality of style, for designs which are created "according to taste and ideas"[20] and for an intensified regionalism. The article notes approvingly, "It is indeed a noticeable fact that German architects have taken upon their shoulders the beautification and general artistic construction of the streets and places of their cities, and where defects and deficiencies have occurred in the course of years, it is a labour of love for our architects to cover the one and improve the other."[21]

2   Ibid.
3   Ibid., p. 3
4   Ibid. This concluding sentence is missing from the original French and English translations.
5   Ibid.
6   Ibid.
7   Ibid.
8   Ibid., p. 2–3
9   Otto Wagner: Moderne Architektur. Vienna 1896, p. 31, and Otto Wagner: Sketches, Projects and Executed Buildings, London 1987, forward
10 Wagner, Moderne Architektur (cited in note 9), p. 39
11 Wagner, Sketches, Projects and Executed Buildings (cited in note 9)
12 Architektur des XX. Jahrhunderts, 1, 1901, p. 2

13 Ibid., 2, 1902, p. 4
14 Ibid., 1, 1901, p. 11
15 Ibid., 2, 1902, p. 12
16 Ibid., 2, 1901, p. 17
17 Ibid., p. 18
18 Ibid., p. 17f.
19 Ibid., p. 35f.
20 Ibid., 2, 1902, p. 4
21 Ibid., p. 2

Nationalism and regionalism in architecture are seen as the answer to the supraregional recourse to the past in Historicism, especially in its Renaissance revival phase, as well as to the internationalism of the fin de siècle movements which rebelled against it. "The incorporation of traditional folk motifs in modern buildings" is now given special emphasis in the journal's descriptions.[22] It is for this very reason that the "imitation of the early Romantic style of the northern Harz region" lends the villa of a factory owner a "charm of its own."[23] It is not the creation of entirely new forms that becomes the barometer of artistic invention, but the free and independent handling of older, historical ones. Architecture "provides us with a portrait of a revival of the German Renaissance taking place in a freer form," or an architecture which "makes free use of medieval forms or is based on them," as well as "the impression of the entire design, whose form evokes the older edifices of the city, is particularly delightful, and is not yet overgrown by alien elements,"[24] are but a few of the many epithets applied to buildings which, especially in the first few volumes, are presented as examples of modern architecture.

In no way does this recourse to the past, albeit unfettered and free, contradict the striving toward modernity. Quite the contrary, the buildings of Theodor Fischer are not the only ones which garner special praise for their "modern artistic forms," which "express themselves even in the oldest German ecclesiastical architecture."[25] A building of "late medieval form elaborated in the modern spirit" commands the same respect as a "beautiful building in modern Baroque style with a slight admixture of Rococo."[26]

The element of restraint exerted by Historicism's recourse of referring to the past is thus abandoned in favour of an apparently unconstrained treatment of a stylistic model. "Stylistically informal" is the proclaimed motto, but by no means should this be interpreted as "stylistically unfounded." The orientation toward omnipotent models is not abolished entirely, only the sense of obligation to them has been relaxed. History, which continues to be ever-present, is now shorn of its omnipotent sense of duty. We might say that, in a certain sense, history has become more manageable.

With this apparent casting aside of history's supremacy, which had become a permanent, almost compulsive fixture in Historicist architecture, an element of the "Hope Principle" becomes reality. At the same time, however, we must qualify the Hope Principle itself in terms of a Modernism which has broken away from history without losing sight of historicity. The axiom of architecture now becomes: reject the past, but do not sever its bonds to the present.

In some cases, the concept of what is modern is reduced to fulfilling the exigencies of the day. In keeping with the wishes of the building sponsor, a building was designed in architectural forms which were developed in their day for originally Gothic structures finished in a Renaissance style. These forms were heavily influenced by traditional designs of the Rhineland, particularly those of Cologne, as well as by elements found in wooden architecture, which by being incorporated into the main building, were "modified in form to suit modern taste." The entire plan of the house for a Cologne industrialist shows that "every provision was made to satisfy the demands of modern comfort and the house is, in this respect, of unusual completedness,"[27] rebutting evidence, as it were, to the critics of Historicism, who contend that it fails to respond to the needs of modern man. For contemporary demands of livability, comfort, etc. do not necessarily conflict with an orientation towards the past. "Traditional architecture" is completely capable of being "happily wedded to the requirements of modern comfort."[28]

One quality constantly emphasized by the descriptions is that of the picturesque. "We see new buildings rising which in charm and picturesqueness are among the best of yet produced in modern times."[29] "A picturesque building with much artistic individuality,"[30] "picturesque character of a country house,"[31] "in an attempt made to retain the picturesqueness of the street,"[32] "an artistic and picturesque appearance,"[33] a "picturesquely-grouped complex of buildings,"[34] "a touchingly picturesque sil-

houette with rich instrumentation,"[35] "In a simple manner and with little expense, the architect has yet produced an artistic group of buildings which add not a little to the picturesque effect of the street;"[36] – these and similar passages are echoed throughout the first five volumes of The Architecture of the 20th Century. In the later volumes, however, the accompanying text dispenses with evaluation in its commentary altogether and henceforth delivers a practically "value-free" description of the works presented.

With the publication of Camillo Sitte's book Der Städte-Bau nach seinen künstlerischen Grundsätzen (City Planning According to Artistic Principles, Vienna 1889), the picturesque, a topic long dealt with by art theory, suddenly became the main point of contention between Traditionalists and Modernists in the contemporary debate over architecture and city planning. Sitte sees in the "modern building-block system," a dominance of economic interests so preponderate that the limits of art are thereby reached and a humane relationship between the city and its inhabitants has ceased to exist. "The regular parcelling of city lots based on purely economic consideration" results in the total loss of those urban beauties which Sitte clearly associates with the concept of the pictorial.[37] Gone are the twisted streets, the irregularities developed over the years, all those characteristic features so vital to a city.

Sitte astutely foresees the very desolation of our cities caused by an orientation towards profit as will be formulated by Alexander Mitscherlich nearly one hundred years later. By raising the issue of the individual's relationship to his ambience, Sitte launches the debate concerning a "humane environment." "We do indeed comprehend . . . that a city must be so designed as to make its people at once secure and happy. In order to realize this, city planning should not be merely a technical matter, but should in the truest and most elevated sense be an artistic enterprise."[38] Sitte's remarks are based on the observation that older cities possessing what he emphasizes as the positive characteristics of the picturesque have a beneficial psychological effect on the observer.

By regarding the picturesque as an integral component in its understanding of Modernism, the journal once more takes a stand against the innovators – and thus against the advocates – of the concept of the modern city. For it is they who state that "we should always keep in mind that a modern metropolis neither can nor should have the appearance of ancient Rome or medieval Nuremberg."[39] Otto Wagner, for example, holds that "the desired picturesque effect, with its major points of perspective, well-placed arrangement of thoroughfares, vistas, etc.," will develop of its own accord; to "execute it in a frequent and deliberate manner has no justification whatsoever."[40]

The dilemma of the situation in the early 1900s is also clearly reflected in the debate on the picturesque. The wish to remedy the aesthetic deficit caused by the growth of large cities must be conceded to both camps, the Traditionalists as well as the Modernists. While the former chooses to undo the loss by means of an almost magical invocation of the past, the latter attempts to blaze new trails – in a figurative sense – through the thickets of the cities and line them with a new architecture. Half a century later, their self-designated successors (most of them erroneously so) will – to state quite succinctly – land at this debate's very point of departure, namely, the problem of the desolation of cities and their architecture.

In its own fashion The Architecture of the 20th Century attempts now to square the circle. By virtually cutting itself off from both artistic extremes, by strictly rejecting the examples of both Art Nouveau and late Historicism, it hopes to show the way to a more moderate, and thus a genuinely contemporary, trend-setting Modernism. It is for this very reason that it features such architects as Berlage, Sullivan, Fabiani, Dülfer, Fischer and even Messel, Behrens and many others. Yet it consistently selects only those solutions from among these architects which can be more easily linked, so to speak, into an unbroken chain of historical development from Historicism to Modernism. The Architecture of the 20th Century is anything but a compilation of individual works of heroic brilliance. It is a vividly illustrated history of architecture from the years 1901 to 1914.

This, however, is accomplished without the journal ever once revealing where its actual preferences lie. Nothing can demonstrate this better than the examples selected

22 Ibid., p. 17
23 Ibid., p. 21
24 Ibid., p. 24 f., 41
25 Ibid., 3, 1903, p. 2 f.
26 Ibid., p. 5 f.
27 Ibid., 2, 1902, p. 57
28 Ibid., 1, 1901, p. 7
29 Ibid., 2, 1902, p. 54
30 Ibid., p. 22 f.
31 Ibid., p. 26
32 Ibid., p. 40
33 Ibid., p. 44
34 Ibid., p. 55

35 Ibid., p. 6
36 Ibid., 3, 1903, p. 6
37 Camillo Sitte: City Planning According to Artistic Principles in: George R. Collins & Cristiane Crasemann Collins: Camillo Sitte: The Birth of Modern City Planning. New York 1986, p. 254
38 Ibid., p. 141
39 Wagner, Moderne Architektur (cited in note 9), p. 84
40 Otto Wagner: Erläuterungs-Bericht zum Entwurfe für den General-Regulierungs-Plan über das gesamte Gmeindegebiet von Wien. Wien ²1894, p. 21

from the Chicago school of architecture. In principle, the journal states that the skyscrapers of North American cities, "though very interesting to the building engineer, are rarely interesting to the artist in architecture."[41] If the "Medinah Temple" in Chicago is chosen not only for its remarkable skeleton construction but primarily for its "rich Moorish architecture," then the Auditorium Building built by Sullivan and Adler is selected as an "exception to the rule" because its "architectural details are not only on the lower and upper stories, where they are most noticeable, but on the entire façade, being from a distant view very effective." The adjoining Studebaker Building is evaluated more euphorically, for here the architects – according to the text – have "succeeded in avoiding the barrack-like appearance of most business houses and … happily achieved a satisfactory result."[42] It is probably no accident that the photograph chosen to illustrate the building prominently displays in its foreground the Chicago Club House, "built in Romanesque forms, the so-called 'Richardson style'."[43]

As for those works illustrated in the journal which actually do correspond to our understanding of the historical emergence of Modernist architecture, The Architecture of the 20th Century places all of them in a broad artistic context, whereby they are suddenly relativized. Some of the formerly prized works prove to be less eccentric models of Modernism; the once erratic block has now become a link in a chain of development. And rightly so, for only in this way – and this is the essential contribution of The Architecture of the 20th Century – will the hitherto accepted history of the Modernist genius give way to a history of Modernist architecture; only in this way will the history of architects and artists be replaced by a history of art and architecture.

With this in mind, it will come as less of a surprise that while Adolf Loos's house on Michaelerplatz in Vienna is included in the journal, it has simply been placed among 99 other examples. As a practically arbitrary plate, this work is suddenly threatened by the loss of its aura and runs the risk of becoming merely one example among many. Suddenly, its traditional features seem to dominate; the lack of ornamentation stands out less than the unsullied, puritanical whiteness, an effect which is largely due to the reproduction method of the plates. Yet one cannot resist the impression of having seen this traditional façade design, with its elevated socle zone at the shop level, repeated in a number of photographs. Moreover, can it be that the various façade inscriptions in the Loos house have unobtrusively assumed the role formerly assigned to ornamentation in the other examples?

On the whole, The Architecture of the 20th Century forces us to free ourselves from the paradigm of epoch-making events so that we may at last be able to write a true history of the rise of Modernist architecture with all its contradictions. It should be emphasized that in order to accomplish this, we would have to interpolate all those examples missing from the journal which up to now have been the sole and exclusive determinants of our concept of Modernism before the First World War.

In the course of analyzing The Architecture of the 20th Century – Journal of Modern Architecture, one question begins to assert itself with increasing persistence. The free and unbound treatment of the past, the deliberate complexity and inconsistency as an artistic method, the intended "picturesque" effect, and above all the basic rejection of a former style felt to be too doctrinaire – does all of this represent anything more than merely a superfluous parallel to the so-called Postmodern movement? Is not their most important task also one of "building bridges between today's current needs and concepts of design taken from the historical experiences of our architectural traditions?"[44] Is not history to be defined now as well as then, as a possible source of learning for the present?

In order for the past to be effective in the present as well as in the future, Historicism makes use of quotations in such a manner that the historical form being quoted can be recognized as such in the quotation. The past is put to the task of pointing out precisely this association. In Historicism, the past, as a legitimation of a collective ideal, becomes the basis of a world view.

In The Architecture of the 20th Century, and similarly in the Postmodern movement, the past made present is confronted by the remembrance of the past and the motto "to the present – its own past." Unlike Historicism, the level of collective reassurance has been abandoned where refuge is sought in selected sacrosanct ideals of the past and their future exploitation for selfish ends. What is expressed now is the artist's own sense of self-esteem and his personal relationship with the past. Tradition is no longer seen as a prescribed and unavoidable obligation, but as a creative possibility open to each individual.[45]

The process of dehistorization so obviously manifested in the journal is brought to a close in the Postmodern movement, where the collective social obligation to the past is now replaced by a personal relationship to it. No longer quoted word for word, the past, now stripped of history, becomes part of the artistic present as a rather vague and indistinct memory. Recognizability – the hallmark of Historicism – yields to the present demand for the cognizance of blurred forms. Relieved of the ballast of its original content, form is now free to take on any new interpretation.

In the same way that the journal's idea of Modernism attempts to free itself from the dictates of Historicism, so too does Postmodernism try to break away from the Modernism of the 1920s; "Architects can no longer afford to let themselves be intimidated by the puritanical mores of conventional modern architecture."[46] Both early Modernism and Postmodernism are attempts to recover a banished sensuousness, a creative artistry.

The position taken by The Architecture of the 20th Century could be ostensibly likened to the "everything goes" philosophy of Postmodernism, and in this sense it offers a wealth of material to be happily plagiarized. Yet Postmodernism, with its concept of irony, rarely has anything really adequate to offer which suggests a potential of fantasy in treating the past. In its creatively constructive way of dismantling the past, the period of the early 1900s – as documented in The Architecture of the 20th Century – confronts Postmodernism with standards of quality that are once again almost doctrinaire in nature.

41 Architektur des XX. Jahrhunderts, 3, 1903, p. 20
42 Ibid., p. 7
43 Ibid., 3, 1903, p. 20

44 Paolo Protoghesi, quoted in B. Schmidt: Postmoderne – Strategien des Vergessens. Darmstadt-Neuwied 1986, p. 191
45 Concerning the relationship between Historicism and the Postmodern movement, see: Peter Haiko and Mara Reissberger: Vom gebundenen Zitat der Historie im Historismus zum ungebundenen Umgang mit Geschichtlichkeit in der Postmoderne. In: Festschrift für Hans-Joachim Kunst. Marburg 1989 (Marburger Jahrbuch für Kunstwissenschaft, 22), p. 247ff.
46 Robert Venturi: Komplexität und Widerspruch in der Architectur. Braunschweig 1978, p. 23

Ziele der Architektur im neuen Jahrhundert.

Le but de l'architecture au nouveau siècle.

The aim of Architecture in the New Century.

Der Baukunst des XX. Jahrhunderts sollen diese Blätter gewidmet sein!

Was werden sie bringen? Was wird der Inhalt dieser Hefte sein?

Wenn vor hundert Jahren ein ähnliches Werk herausgegeben worden wäre, hätte selbst der Größte seiner Zeit voraussehen können, wohin die Kunst ihre Wege lenken, welche Wege sie einschlagen, wo sie im Jahre 1900 enden werde?

Anzeichen waren da, auf denen er seine Schlüsse hätte aufbauen können. In Frankreich war man zu der Erkenntnis gekommen, daß allein eine feste Gesetzmäßigkeit die Kunst aus den Banden des schon tief verachteten Rokoko reißen könnte. Man arbeitete wie im politischen Leben so in der Baukunst an der Feststellung der vernunftgemäßen Regel, an dem Gesetz, das die Willkür beseitigen solle, an der Einreihung des Einzelnen unter die planmäßig aufgebaute Gesamtheit, die dort der Staat, hier, in der Baukunst, die Säulenordnung darstellte.

In England suchte man in die Starrheit der Regel und in die Einseitigkeit des klassischen Gesetzes dadurch Breche zu legen, daß man eine Kunst der Empfindung, des Gemütes, eine solche des seelischen Erfassens der Schönheit erstrebte. Sie führte hinaus in die Gotteswelt, sie offenbarte sich in schwärmerischem Entzücken über deren Schönheit, sie suchte die Natur in der Kunst, das Schlichte, Ländliche, Gemütstiefe, Schwermütige: und sie entdeckte damit den Wert des mittelalterlichen Schaffens, sie schuf die Romantik.

Beide Strömungen begegneten sich in Deutschland. Dies wurde zum eigentlichen Kampfgebiet zwischen Klassizität und Romantik. Aber schon entstanden hier die Männer, die beides in sich zu vereinen wußten: an ihrer Spitze Goethe.

Die führenden Architekten erfaßten nun die klassische Welt mit dem Gemüt, sie versenkten sich mit romantisch gestimmten Sinnen in die große Zeit von Hellas und es schien zu Anfang des XIX. Jahrhunderts, als sehe Deutschland seine höchste Aufgabe darin, sich geistig ganz an Hellas hinzuopfern. Des deutschen Künstlers Vaterland war Griechenland.

Das Jahrhundert erfüllte die Forderungen seiner Jugend: Mit einem bisher unerreichten Eifer wendete es sich der Erforschung dessen hin, was früher geschaffen worden ist. Indem der Fuß der Kunst mit der Zeit vorwärts zu wandeln gezwungen war, blieb das Auge nach den rückwärts liegenden Zielen gerichtet. Von Jahrzehnt zu Jahrzehnt erkannte man aufs neue, daß die Vorhergegangenen trotz ihres geschichtlichen Strebens die alten Zeiten ungenügend oder falsch verstanden hätten, und vertiefte man sich aufs neue in das Wesen einstiger Jahrhunderte, in der Hoffnung, aus diesem heraus das allen Zeiten Gemeinsame, mithin auch das unserer Zeit Eigene schöpfen zu können. Die, welche bewußt Neues zu schaffen strebten, die Modernen, wurden mit mißtrauischen Augen betrachtet. Mehr und mehr erkannte man in allen Arten alter Kunst die ihnen eigentümliche Schönheit: Eine nach der andern trat auf dem Markte der Entwürfe hervor und sprach in das Schaffen des XIX. Jahrhunderts mit herrischen Worten hinein. Es fügte sich an die Wiedergeburt der Antike, die nun seit dem XV. Jahrhundert die Welt beschäftigt, die Wiedergeburt des Mittelalters, der Renaissance in allen ihren Gestaltungen: Also eine Neubelebung des vor 400 Jahren Neubelebten.

Und so reich das Mahl an alten Formen war, das dem Schaffenden geboten wurde, so

C'est à l'architecture du XXe siècle que sont dédiées ces feuilles!

Que nous apporteront-elles? Quel sera le contenu de ces livraisons?

S'il y a cent ans, un ouvrage semblable avait été entrepris, est-ce que même le plus grand génie de cette époque aurait pu prévoir où l'art allait se diriger, où chercherait ses voies et où elles le conduiraient en l'an 1900?

Il y avait bien quelques indices dont il aurait pu tirer certaines conséquences: En France on en était arrivé à la conviction que l'art ne pouvait être dégagé de l'influence du style Louis XV, déjà tombé en discrédit, que par une réglementation sévère.

Comme dans la vie politique, on travaillait dans l'art de bâtir à l'établissement de règles conformes à la raison, à la loi qui devait supprimer l'arbitraire, à l'asservissement de l'unité à un plan d'ensemble et ce principe fondamental de l'état était représenté dans l'architecture par l'ordonnance classique de la colonne.

En Angleterre on s'efforçait de battre en brèche la raideur de la règle et l'uniformité de la loi classique en cherchant un art de sentiment et d'impression, une sorte de beauté puisée du fond de l'âme. Cette recherche conduisait au culte de la nature, on se pâmait sur sa beauté, on demandait à l'art la simplicité, le champêtre, la sentimentalité, la mélancolie, et on trouva tout cela dans l'art du Moyen-âge, on créa le romantisme.

Ces deux conceptions de l'art se rencontrèrent en Allemagne qui devint le champ de bataille du classicisme et du romantisme, mais là déjà se trouvaient des hommes capables de concilier les deux principes, à leur tête Goethe.

Les maitres de l'architecture saisirent l'art classique par le coeur, ils se plongèrent avec une sentimentalité romanesque dans les grands souvenirs de la Grèce et il semblait au commencement du XIXe siècle que le rôle de l'Allemagne fût de se sacrifier au génie de la Grèce; ce pays devenant la patrie de l'artiste Allemand.

Le siècle tint les promesses de ses débuts, il se voua avec un zèle inconnu jusqu'alors à l'étude de ce qui avait été créé avant lui. Tandis que l'art était forcé de marcher en avant avec le temps, le regard restait attaché sur le passé.

D'année en année on apprenait à nouveau que les prédécesseurs n'avaient, malgré leurs recherches historiques qu'imparfaitement compris les styles passés et les avaient faussement interprétés.

On reprit alors l'étude des siècles passés et on espéra y découvrir le caractère commun à toutes les époques et en même temps particulier à la nôtre. Les modernes, ceux qui le sachant et le voulant s'efforçaient de créer quelque chose de nouveau étaient vus d'un oeil méfiant. De plus en plus on reconnaissait dans chaque style des temps anciens la beauté qui lui est particulière. L'un après l'autre, chacun trouva son application dans l'art du XiXe siècle et s'y affirma dans de magnifiques compositions. Après la résurrection de l'antique qui préoccupait le monde depuis le XVe siècle on vit renaitre le Moyenâge et la Renaissance sous toutes ses formes. Et l'on assistait ainsi à la résurrection d'un art déjà restustifé 4 siècles auparavant.

Mais quelque abondante que fût pour l'artiste la moisson de formes anciennes, elle ne réussissait par à satisfaire ses aspirations. La fin du siècle ne produisit pas d'unité dans l'effort créateur.

This work is dedicated to the architecture of the 20th Century. What shall it bring? And what can we expect from its pages?

Had such a work appeared 100 years ago, could the greatest architect of his time have foreseen into which paths Art would wander, have predicted which turnings she would take, and what would be her aims and ends at the close of the century?

Certain portents were there from which such an observer might have come to certain conclusions. In France, one had already learnt that the only way out of the rapidly declining Rococo was to be found by strict conformity to the old historical traditions of art. As in political life, so in architecture, men were anxious to return to the rule of pure reason, were striving to inaugurate the reign of law which should curb every attempt at caprice, and were insisting on the subordination of the special to general rules by law established; as in the State, so in architecture, all was to be ordered with the regularity of the colonnade.

In England, an attempt was made to storm the classic citadel, fortified as it was by the impregnable rules of art, by the weapons of sentiment, of feeling, and of the susceptibility of the soul to the sense of beauty. This art led man forth into God's world and showed herself in an intoxicating delight in the beauties of Nature; she strove after the simple, the rural, the sentimental, the melancholy; — in doing so, she brought to light the beauties of the mediaeval artists, in a word, she created the Romantic.

Both streams met in Germany, which became the battlefield of the struggle between the classic and the romantic. Men arose who knew how to combine the two, at their head stands Goethe.

The leading architects of this time brought sentiment and feeling and all that one understands under the term „romantic" to their study of ancient Greek models, and the beginning of the 19th Century seemed to indicate that Germany would bring her Art to sit at the feet of Greece. Greece was to be the Fatherland of the German artist.

The century fulfilled the promise of its youth. „The child was father to the man". With unprecedented industry, search was made among the works of former masters. And although the feet were forced to march in the paths of progress, the eyes were faithfully kept fixed on the great masters of the past.

From decade ot decade it was seen with ever increasing clearness that earlier efforts to interpret the meaning of the old masters had been insufficient and therefore unsuccessful. Renewed efforts were made to become one with the spirit of the medieval artists, in the hope that from the study of general rules which had been proved eternally fit, a new and distinctive German art might arise. Those who were audacious enough to produce anything strictly new, strictly modern, were regarded with suspicion. Everywhere the peculiar beauty of the old forms was acknowledged, and gratefully accepted. The old masters rose from their graves and spoke again with voices of authority in all the schools of design. It was a new birth of the antique which had held mankind in thrall since the 15th century — the Renascence of the middle ages, the Renascence of that which 400 years before was itself a Renascence.

wenig vermochte es den wahren Hunger nach Kunst zu sättigen. Das Ende des Jahrhunderts brachte kein einheitliches Schaffen. Gegenüber stehen sich wieder wissenschaftliche Strenge und eine nur von innerlichem Werte gebändigte Willkür. Wissenschaftliche Strenge, wie sie am schönsten bei unseren Erneuerungen an alten Bauwerken sich äußert! Der Künstler schult sich dahin, daß er ganz dem alten Meister entspreche; sein Ziel ist, daß man nichts davon merke, daß er am Bau die Hand im Spiel hatte; er verzichtet völlig auf sein Ich zu gunsten eines Meisters, der vor Jahrhunderten lebte. Und von hier die Abstufungen der Strenge: Von jenen, die nur im Stil einer Zeit schaffen, bis zu jenen, die mit Sorgfalt das gesamte wissenschaftliche Werkzeug benutzen und im Stil jeder Zeit zu schaffen wissen und dadurch der in Vielgestalt endenden Renaissance entsprechen.

Daneben Willkür! Leute, die der Ansicht sind, daß des Nachahmens genug geschehen ist und daß man endlich anfangen müßte, grundsätzlich das Alte zu vermeiden. Die nur dann recht zu schaffen glauben, wenn jeder Strich ihr Ich verrät und nichts an einen Anderen mahnt; die ihre ganze Kraft daran setzen, in jeder Linie neu zu sein, und mögen die Altgläubigen noch so sehr darüber klagen, daß diese Absicht zur Gewaltsamkeit führt; wenn die neue Form auch noch so fremd der Menge, den an alte Form gewohnten, entgegentritt.

Das XIX. Jahrhundert unterschied sich von den vorhergehenden darin, daß es den Begriff der Renaissance weiter faßte: Nicht nur Wiedergeburt der alten, sondern aller vergangener Kunst. Es sah seine Aufgabe darin, durch kunstgeschichtliches Erkennen unseren Blick für die Schönheit jeder Art menschlichen Schaffens zu schärfen, es schulte die Hände und Geister im erneuten Herausbilden der so erkannten Schönheit. Aber es erdrückte die Renaissance älterer Art durch die Fülle des Neuen; sie erfüllte ihre Aufgabe nur zu sehr, so daß man am Schlusse des Jahrhunderts erkannte, keine von all' diesen gewesenen Künsten könne unserer Zeit völlig gerecht werden. Zuerst fiel das vornehmste Vorbild, Hellas, von dem man einst hoffte, daß es allein herrschen und die höchsten Freuden bringen werde. Die anderen Vorbilder folgten. Es giebt keinen Künstler mehr, der sagen möchte: Im Nachahmen dieser oder jener Kunst, ja selbst im Nachschaffen aus ihrem Geist heraus werdet ihr die wahrhaft eigene Zeitkunst erringen. Wir haben durch die Ueberfülle der Renaissance erkannt, daß die Renaissance uns nicht mehr zu fördern vermag, daß wir den Sprung ins Neuland wagen müssen.

Das XX. Jahrhundert scheint demnach die Aufgabe zu haben, die gewaltige Bewegung zu beenden, die im XV. Jahrhundert von Italien ausging. Schwerlich wird es, so sehr das auch die Dränger nach dem Neuen von sich selbst wünschen, das, was das XIX. hinterläßt, nämlich den ungeheuren Reichtum an Formenkenntnis einfach über Bord werfen. Denn Wissen kann man nicht durch einen Willensentschluß aufgeben, es ist unveräußerlich. Aber wir werden lernen müssen, die Verehrung für das Alte mit der Erkenntnis zu vereinen, daß wir notwendiger Weise uns als ü b e r der geschichtlichen Form stehend zu betrachten haben. Diese ist unser Erbe, über die wir als rechtmäßigen Besitz frei schalten.

In der Mitte des XIX. Jahrhunderts wurde die Klage laut, daß der Zeit der eigene Stil fehle. Ihn zu suchen, zeigen sich hier und da bescheidene Ansätze. Solche großen Absichten sind nie rasch erfüllbar: Das XX. Jahrhundert hat die Träume seines Vorgängers zu verwirklichen. Dieser, gefesselt in geschichtliche Banden, ertrug die Erfüllung der eigenen Wünsche, jener Regungen des selbständigen Kunstgewissens, nicht, weil sie mit der so laut verkündeten Renaissance-

La règle scientifique se trouve de nouveau en conflit avec un arbitraire modéré seulement par la valeur individuelle de l'artiste. Nous voyons d'une part: Sévérité scientifique qui trouve sa plus belle expression dans la restauration des monuments anciens.

L'architecte tâche de s'identifier avec le maître ancien, il ne veut pas que l'on remarque qu'il a mis la main à l'ouvrage, voilà son but! il fait entièrement abstraction de sa personnalité au profit d'un maître qui vivait il y a cent ans et puis viennent tous les degrés des adeptes de la règle, depuis celui qui ne travaille que dans un style, jusqu'à celui qui, utilisant avec soin tout l'appareil scientifique sait composer dans le style de chaque époque et rappelle l'éclectisme de la Renaissance à son déclin.

D'autre part: arbitraire: des gens qui trouvent que l'on a assez imité et copié et qu'il est temps de répudier systématiquement les anciens styles, qui croient ne produire que lorsque chaque trait dénonce leur individualité et que rien ne rappelle quelqu'un d'autre, qui concentrent toute leur force à être nouveaux dans chaque ligne sans se préoccuper des adeptes de l'ancien régime qui se plaignent de ce que cette recherche du nouveau conduit à la violation du goût; sans avoir égard au public, qui habitué à des formes connues considère avec étonnement les productions nouvelles.

Le XIXe siècle s'est distingué de ses prédécesseurs en ce qu'il a saisi d'une façon plus large l'esprit de la Renaissance: non pas seulement renaissance d'un art unique, mais de tous les arts passés, il a compris sa mission dans l'éducation de notre oeil qu'il a rendu capable de saisir les beautés de chaque période de la culture humaine et cela par la connaissance de l'histoire de l'art, il procéda ensuite à l'éducation de la main et de l'esprit en leur faisant reconstituer les beautés ainsi découvertes. Mais ce siècle étouffait en même temps le vrai esprit de la Renaissance sous la masse d'éléments nouveaux, et lorsqu'il toucha à sa fin, on reconnut qu'aucun des styles essayés ne suffisait aux besoins de notre époque.

On vit d'abord s'effondrer la glorieuse image de la Grèce dont on attendait autrefois le salut et qui devait nous doter des biens les plus précieux. La chute des autres illusions suivit et il n'y a plus un artiste qui oserait dire: C'est dans l'imitation de tel ou tel style ou même dans l'interprétation de son esprit qu'on arrivera à la vraie expression d'un art contemporain. Les exagérations et les dévoiements de la Renaissance nous ont montré que ce style ne pouvait pas nous porter plus avant et que nous devions risquer le saut dans l'avenir.

Le XXe siècle semble donc avoir la mission de mener à bonne fin le puissant mouvement qui partit au XVe siècle de l'Italie. Malgré toute l'ambition des novateurs de ne créer que de nouveau, il sera difficile de jeter par dessus bord l'énorme trésor de connaissance de formes que nous lègue le XIXe siècle.

En effet, il n'est pas donné à l'homme de se débarrasser par un décret de ses connaissances, ce bien est inaliénable. Mais il nous faudra apprendre à concilier le respect du passé avec la conviction que nous devons nécessairement nous considérer comme dominant les formes historiques. Voilà l'héritage dont nous avons le droit de disposer comme d'une propriété légale.

Au milieu du XIXe siècle on se plaignait de ne pas avoir de style propre. On fit quelques modestes efforts pour en chercher un. De si grandes aspirations ne peuvent être rapidement contentées: c'est le XXe siècle qui aura à réaliser les rêves de son devancier.

But though the feast of old forms set before the waiting artists was rich and plentiful, it failed to satisfy their craving after real art. The end of the century brought no uniformity of style. The severity of scientific methods stood on the one side and militated against a caprice which can be restrained by no outward rules, but only by the temperate mind of the artist.

The scientific severity is best seen in our restoration of old buildings. The artist has schooled himself to follow obediently the design of the old master; his aim is that no one shall see the other hand at work in the architecture; he effaces himself entirely to let the master who has lain so long in his grave continue to speak. From this height downwards are many steps, from the architect who will only create in one style, to him, who, making careful use of the means and implements at his disposal, knows how to create a style embracing all epochs, a Renascence of all previous models. On the other side stands the despotism of caprice represented by artists who consider that enough has been done for the past, and that one must at last turn one's back one the ancients, — that every line must demonstrate the ubiquitous „i" —, that not a stroke dare remind of another hand — that originality must be attained at any cost, let the orthodox complain ever so loudly, and let the strangeness of the conception awake ever so much consternation among the uninitiated whose eyes have delighted to rest on the old forms.

The 19th century therefore differed from its predecessors in this — that it strove after a Renascence not only of medieval forms but of the art of all previous times. It took for its task the bringing into prominence all that was worthy among every style of creative art; it schooled the hand and spirit to reproduce these acknowledged beauties in new and original forms. But the antique was eclipsed, or at least lost sight of, in the multitude of novel forms; so that the work of the century has only brought us to the conclusion, that no one style of those ages which have gone before, is sufficient for the artistic demands of the present day. The first idol to fall was the oldest of gods — Hellas, who was to be absolute and from whom all joys were to spring. The others followed. There exists no longer an artist who dare say that by adhering to the old lines, and by creating with the spiritual guidance of the ancients alone, he is able to satisfy all the demands of modern art. The Renascence has then nothing more to ask of us, we have acknowledged it and used it, now for the entrance into the new land.

The XX century seems destined to put an end to that powerful influence which came forth from Italy in the 15th century. But even the most earnest apostle of novelty will find it difficult to throw overboard the rich legacy of form that the 19th century has bequeathed to us. Knowledge cannot be forgotten at will. We must however learn that reverence for the old forms must no longer be slavish worship, and that we must consider the antique as a ladder from which we are to mount, as an inheritance whose riches we are to spend in the best way.

In the middle of the 19th century the complaint arose that the century had not made for herself her own distinctive style.

A few modest efforts in this direction are arising here and there, but such a great consummation as the formation of a style cannot be rapid.

The XX century must fulfil the dreams of the 19th. These, still in the fetters of the con-

lehre nicht übereinftimmten. Wir haben dafür zu forgen, daß den Regungen, die auf Selbftändigkeit zielen, die Bahn frei werde, daß in kommenden Zeiten vor allen der als ein Meifter gelte, dem die Form vergangener Zeiten nur als frucht-bringender Boden dient, aus dem heraus er fich felbft auszugeftalten und auszuwachfen vermag. Und wenn er den Boden dabei mit Füßen tritt!

Das XX. Jahrhundert fcheint die Aufgabe zu haben, die Renaiffance zu beenden.

Cornelius Gurlitt.

Ce dernier, enchaîné dans la tradition his-torique ne put accomplir son propre vœu ni satisfaire ses aspirations artistiques; car elles ne s'accordaient pas avec les principes si haut proclamés de la Renaissance. C'est à nous à préparer la voie libre aux aspirations d'indé-pendance, à veiller à ce que dorénavant celui là seul soit proclamé comme maître, qui ne considère le passé que comme une terrain fertile dont il peut tirer ce qui lui convient, et qu'il peut même au besoin fouler aux pieds.

Cornelius Gurlitt.

ventional, dared not express themselves openly as they wished, dared not to be original.

We must therefore strive to keep the road clear for all independent achievement, so that in future times he shall be considered a master who uses the antique not with uplifted eyes of adoration, but only as a fertile soil which he treads with his feet if necessary, from which to bring forth new and beautiful cultures.

Cornelius Gurlitt.

Architektur in England.

Will man sich eine Vorstellung von dem augenblicklichen Stand der englifchen Archi-tektur und ihrer vorausfichtlichen Entwicklung im XX. Jahrhundert verfchaffen, fo ist es em-pfehlenswerth, sich die Hauptentwicklungsftufen, die dem vergangenen Jahrhundert das Gepräge aufdrücken, vor Augen zu führen.

Ganz zweifellos ist der heutige Stand der Architektur bei weitem befriedigender, als er es vor 100 Jahren war; denn im Beginn des XIX. Jahrhunderts stagnierte das fchon an fich fchwächliche innere Leben völlig, während augen-blicklich mehrere fehr ausfichtsvolle Bewegungen im Gange sind.

Im vergangenen Jahrhundert feierten grie-chifcher, romanifcher und gotifcher Stil, die Renaiffance, und fchließlich das ganze Kunst-gewerbe ein Wiedererwachen. Sie alle hinter-ließen einen Eindruck, der zur Folge hatte, daß heute die Architekten fich zu verfchiedenen Parteien bekennen; trotz alledem macht fich eine Bewegung bemerkbar, deren Endziel ein natio-naler englifcher Stil ift.

Zum Klaffizismus bekennen fich viele Männer von hervorragendem Ruf, aber ein Mangel an Tradition hemmt fie, ein Mangel, der fich vor allem in einer fehlenden maßgeblichen Auf-faffung über die Verhältniffe der Säulenordnung äußert; auf der anderen Seite können fie fich im Entwurf von umfaffenden Gebäudemaffen nicht mit der franzöfifchen Schule meffen.

Auch der gotifche Stil hat feine Jünger, aber fie befchränken fich faft ausfchließlich auf Kirchenbauten. Ganz allgemein kann man fagen, daß Monumentalbauten in England die Formen der Renaiffance zeigen, während die Kirchen zum größten Teil im gotifchen Stil erbaut find. Neben diefen beiden Richtungen geht das Kunst-gewerbe feine eigenen und neuen Wege.

Auf manche feiner Jünger wirkt das Wort „Stil" wie das rote Tuch auf den Stier. Sie wollen nicht in toten Sprachen reden, fie wollen ihren Gebäuden keine Formen geben, die ihrer Natur nach anderen Jahrhunderten angehören, fie wollen eine durch und durch moderne Archi-tektur fchaffen. Zu diefem Zweck wollen die einen den Begriff „Stil" völlig über Bord werfen, während die gemäßigten Elemente einfehen, daß Kunst und Architektur eine fortfchreitende Ent-wicklung bedeuten; fie ftudieren Werke früherer Zeiten, um das darin aufgefpeicherte Wiffen fich anzueignen, ohne aber fklavifch daran zu hängen, fie bewahren fich vielmehr genügend Freiheit zur Schaffung neuer Formen, die ihrer ureigenen Perfönlichkeit entfpringen, und diefe muss ja

L'architecture en Angleterre.

Si l'on veut se faire une idée de l'état actuel de l'architecture en Angleterre et de son développement probable au XXme siècle, il est nécessaire de passer en revue les degrés successifs par lesquels elle a passé pendant le siècle dernier.

Il est hors de doute que l'état actuel de l'architecture est de beaucoup plus satisfaisant qu'il ne l'était il y a cent ans, car au commen-cement du XIXme siècle, le peu de vie propre qui s'était maintenu jusqu'alors avait cessé d'être, tandis qu'aujourd'hui, on peut constater des tendances dignes d'éveiller de grandes espé-rances. Au siècle dernier, les styles grec, roman et gothique, la renaissance et finalement l'art décoratif dans son ensemble faisaient peau neuve. Tout ce travail eut pour résultat de grouper les architectes en différents partis, malgré tout on remarque un mouvement qui est le style na-tional anglais. Beaucoup d'hommes d'une ré-putation considérable appartiennent à l'école classique, mais il sont entravés par un manque de traditions, lacune qui se traduit surtout par l'absence du sens des proportions dans les ordres de colonnes. D'autre part, ils ne peuvent se mesurer pour l'ampleur du plan de grandes masses monumentales avec les maîtres de l'école française.

Le style gothique a aussi ses adeptes, mais ils bornent presque exclusivement leur activité à la construction d'édifices religieux. On peut dire d'une façon générale que le style monu-mental en Angleterre emploie les formes de la renaissance tandis que la plupart des églises sont bâties en style gothique. En dehors de ces deux courants principaux, l'art décoratif suit sa voie propre et nouvelle. Le mot style fait à beaucoup de disciples de la nouvelle école l'effet du drap rouge au taureau. Ils ne veulent pas parler une langue morte, ils se refusent à donner à leurs édifices des formes qui appartiennent à des siècles passés, ils veulent créer une ar-chitecture moderne de toutes pièces. C'est pour cela qu'ils s'efforcent de rejeter définitivement l'idée de style, tandis que les éléments modérés conviennent que l'art et l'architecture sont sou-mis aux lois d'un développement progressif, ils étudient les œuvres des âges passés pour s'as-similer les connaissances qui y sont accumulées, sans cependant les copies servilement, ils se réservent au contraire suffisamment de liberté pour créer des formes nouvelles qui correspon-dent à leur individualité et c'est cette dernière qui doit finalement imprimer son sceau aux styles d'architecture.

Architecture in England.

In forming an estimate of modern English architecture and an idea of its possible development during the twentieth century it will be hepful to remember the chief phases which characterised the past century. There can be no doubt that the position of architecture to-day is far more satisfactory than it was a hundred years ago, for, whereas at the commencement of the nineteenth century its life was feeble and stagnant, there are at present in progress several movements capable of effecting much good. The past century was one of revivals — Greek, Roman, Gothic, Renaissance and, lastly, the revival of the arts and crafts. All these left their mark and at the present time architects are divided into several factions, though there is an ever-increasing movement towards the evolution of a national British architecture. The Classicists count among themselves many men of distinction, but they are hampered by their loss of tradition, which especially results in the absence of any definite conception of proportion in the Orders; while in regard to large blocks of buildings the planning does not exhibit that mastery which characterises the French school. The Gothic still has its ad-herents, but these mainly concern themselves with ecclesiastical architecture; in fact it may be stated that almost without exception the mo-numental buildings erected in England to-day follow Renaissance models, whereas the great majority of the churches are in the Gothic style. Besides these two schools there is that which is the outcome of the arts and crafts. To many of its members „style" is like a red rag to a bull. They do not seek to speak in dead lan-guages nor to apply to their buildings features belonging intrinsically to other centuries; their aim is to evolve a truly modern architecture. Some affect to eschew all „style", but the more moderate recognise that art and architecture are progressive developments; so that while they study old work in order to acquire the accu-mulated knowledge which it affords they are not slaves to it, but are free to create new forms of their own embodying principles which must govern all styles of architecture. That there is a danger in the study of old work of becoming

ſchließlich alle Architektur-Stile meiſtern. Die
Furcht, infolge des Studiums der Werke früherer
Zeiten pedantiſch zu werden, iſt nicht unbe-
gründet, aber auf der anderen Seite iſt zu bedenken, daß die Meiſter Griechenlands und
Roms nebſt ihren Epigonen ungewöhnlich be-
fähigte Geiſter waren. Wenn alſo manche Architekten mit an Egoismus ſtreifendem Ehrgeiz es
verſuchen, das Althergebrachte völlig zu ver-
laſſen, ſo ſchaffen ſie Gebäude, die weder
äſthetiſchen noch praktiſchen Anſprüchen genügen.

Unzweifelhaft würde hierin durchgreifend
Wandel geſchaffen werden, wenn man mehr Gelegenheit zum Studium der Architektur bieten
würde.

Die Architekten Englands verfügen über
2 Haupt-Organiſationen „the Royal Inſtitute of
British Architects" und „the Society of Architects".
Die zahlreichen, über das ganze Königreich ver-
ſtreuten Vereinigungen ſind Tochtervereine der
beiden erſtgenannten. The Royal Inſtitute iſt
von beiden bei weitem die bedeutendſte und
die dort beſtandenen Prüfungen ſind eine vorzügliche Empfehlung. Bis auf den heutigen Tag
iſt der Begriff „Architekt" geſetzlich nicht feſt-
gelegt, und es beſtehen keine Staatsprüfungen.
Jedermann kann ſich Architekt nennen, ob er
dazu qualifiziert iſt oder nicht, deshalb wünſcht
man immer ſehnlicher eine offizielle Feſtlegung.

Auf den Univerſitäten wird wenig Wert auf
Architektur gelegt — University College und
Kings College in London und Viktoria Univerſity
in Liverpool ſind die einzigen, die eine Fakultät
dafür beſitzen. In dieſer Beziehung iſt man in
verſchiedenen andern Ländern weiter, beſonders
in Amerika, wo man ſich eine vorzügliche Ausbildung verſchaffen kann.

Selbſt die London University hat keine beſondere Fakultät für Architektur. Aber auch in
dieſer Beziehung eröffnet ſich eine Ausſicht auf
Beſſerung, und die nächſten Jahre bringen
vielleicht ſchon eine erhebliche Erleichterung für
den, der ſich eine Ausbildung in der Architektur
aneignen will.

Zahlreiche wichtige Angelegenheiten, die
augenblicklich Englands Architekten beſchäftigen,
muß ich hier leider aus Raummangel unter-
drücken, nur das architektoniſche Hauptereignis
des Jahres 1900 möchte ich mit einigen Worten
andeuten.

Die Londoner Stadtverordneten-Verſammlung
hatte beſchloſſen, von Holborn nach the Strand
eine neue Straße durchzuführen. Die Baukoſten
waren auf 5 000 000 £ veranſchlagt, und ein
Wettbewerb wurde ausgeſchrieben. Die neue
Straße ſoll 100 Fuß breit werden und gabelt
ſich bei „the Strand", wo ein großer halbmond-
förmiger Abſchluß projektiert war. Dieſer Abſchluß bildete die ſpezielle Aufgabe für den Wettbewerb, zu dem 8 Architekten aufgefordert
waren. Jeder erhielt für ſeine Mühe 250 £. Die
eingelieferten Entwürfe waren hochintereſſant,
aber man kann nicht behaupten, daß der Wettbewerb gerade einen Erfolg bedeutet hätte. Der
Hauptgrund dafür mag wohl darin zu ſehen
ſein, daß die Stadtverordneten-Verſammlung
keine Garantie dafür übernehmen wollte, daß
einem der Beteiligten auch die Bauausführung
übertragen werden würde.

Mr. Norman Shaw war ſachverſtändiger
Beirat der Jury, aber aus irgend welchen
Gründen iſt ſein Urteil nicht veröffentlicht worden.

Die Abſicht der Stadtverordneten-Verſammlung in dieſer Angelegenheit iſt überhaupt nicht
ganz klar, und es bleibt nur zu hoffen, daß
man eine ſo günſtige Gelegenheit für eine her-
vorragende architektoniſche Aufgabe nicht unbe-
nutzt vorübergehen läßt, wie das bis jetzt bei
Neuanlagen von Straßen in der Hauptſtadt des
Landes geſchehen iſt.

Ce n'est pas sans raison qu'on craint de
tomber dans le pédantisme en étudiant les
oeuvres des siècles passés, mais d'autre part,
on ne peut nier que les artistes de la Grèce, de
Rome et leurs disciples ne fussent des esprits
d'élite. Si donc certains architectes essayent avec
un amour-propre voisin de l'égoisme, d'abandonner
entièrement la tradition, ils élèvent des constructions qui ne satisfont ni au sens esthétique,
ni aux exigences pratiques.

Il est certain qu'il pourrait être remédié à
cet état de choses en offrant plus d'occasions
d'étudier l'architecture.

Les architectes anglais disposent de deux
institution principales: "The Royal institute of
British Architects" et "The Society of Architects."
Les nombreuses associations répandues dans
tout le royaume sont des ramifications de ces
deux sociétés.

Le Royal Institute est de beaucoup le plus
important et le diplôme qu'il délivre constitue
une recommandation de premier ordre. Jusqu'à présent, la qualité d'architecte n'est pas
définie légalement et l'état ne délivre pas de
diplômes. Chacun peut se nommer architecte,
qu'il en ait les qualités ou pas, c'est ce qui fait
désirer ardamment une qualification officielle.

L'enseignement universitaire ajoute peu
d'importance à l'étude de l'architecture. L'University College et le Kings College à Londres
ainsi que la Victoria University à Liverpool sont
les seuls qui aient une faculté d'architecture.
Sous ce rapport on est plus avancé dans
d'autres pays, particulièrement en Amérique où
on peut faire d'excellentes études.

La London University, elle même, n'a pas
de faculté pour l'architecture. Mais sous ce
rapport aussi ou peut prévoir une amélioration
et peut-être verrons nous sous peu de nouvelles
facilités offertes à celui qui veut étudier l'architecture. Je dois malheureusement, faute de
place, laisser de côté de nombreuses et importantes questions lui préoccupent actuellement les
architectes anglais, je voudrais cependant mentionner en quelques mots l'évènement architectural le plus important de l'année 1900.

L'édilité Londonienne a décrété une nouvelle artère de Holborn an Strand. Les frais
étaient devisés à 5 000 000 de livres et un concours fut ouvert. La nouvelle rue doit avoir
100 pieds de large et déboucher dans le Strand
en formant une vaste place en forme de demi-
cercle.

C'est ce point de jonction qui formait le
sujet du concours, au quel huit architectes furent
invités à prendre part.

Chacun d'eux reçut comme honoraires 250 £.
Les projets livrés étaient très intéressants,
mais on ne peut pas dire que ce concours fût
précisément un grand succès; ce qui s'explique
par la raison que la municipalité n'avait pas
pris l'engagement de confier l'exécution du projet
à un des architectes invités à prendre part au
concours. M. Wonnau Shaw était membre rap-
porteur du jury, mais pour une raison quelconque,
son rapport n'a pas été publié.

Les intentions de la municipalité ne sont
au reste pas absolument claires dans cette
affaire et on ne peut que se borner à espérer
qu'une occasion aussi exceptionnelle ne sera pas
perdue, comme cela a été le cas jusqu'à présent lors de la création de nouvelles artères
dans la capitale.

Pour terminer, resumons les conditions qui,
selon nos prévisions doivent influencer le développement de l'architecture en Angleterre; on

pedantic we have ample proof, yet on the other
hand it must not be forgotten that the Greek,
Roman and succeeding masters were men of no
ordinary calibre and the egotism which prompts
some architects to attempt to set aside the
examples of the past results in the production
of buildings which are neither beautiful nor
appropriate.

No doubt a great change will be effected
when the opportunities for architectural education
are improved. In England there are two chief
architectural societies, the Royal Institute of British
Architects and the Society of Architects, with
which the numerous other societies throughout
the kingdom are affiliated. The Royal Institute
is by far the more important of the two and
the examinations which it holds are most commen-
datory. At the present time however there is no
legal recognition of the architect and hence no
government examinations. Anyone may practise as
an architect, whether he is qualified or not, and
for this reason there is a growing desire for
official registration. The universities give architecture little consideration — it is dealt with
only by University College and King's College,
London, and the Victoria University at Liverpool.
In this respect we are far behind several
other countries, notably America, where such
excellent tuition is obtainable. Even the London
University does not include architecture among
its faculties. Here again however there is
prospect of a change for the better, and the next
few years may witness a great improvement in
the facilities for architectural education.

It is impossible in the space now at my
disposal to deal with many other matters of importance with which architects in Great Britain
are at present concerned, but a brief reference
should be made to what was undoubtedly the
chief architectural event of 1900. This was the
competition in connection with the new street
from Holborn to the Strand which the London
County Council propose to form at a cost of about
£ 5,000,000. This new street will be 100 ft. wide
and at the Strand end will bifurcate, forming a
large crescent. It was in connection with this
crescent that the competition was held. Eight
architects were invited to compete, each being
paid £ 250 for his services. The designs sub-
mitted were of considerable interest, but it cannot
be said that the competition has been a success,
for, in the first place, the Council would give
no guarantee that the authors of any of the
designs would be employed to carry out the
work. Mr. Norman Shaw acted as assessor,
but for some reason his award has not been
made public; in fact it is most difficult to
ascertain what is the Council's intention in
the matter, though it is hoped that such an
opportunity for a fine architectural treatment
will not be thrown away, as has hitherto
been the case with other new streets in the
metropolis.

In conclusion a few indications of possible

Zum Schluß fassen wir die Bedingungen zusammen, die voraussichtlich die zukünftige Entwicklung beeinflussen werden. Wie falsch es ist, alte Gebäudeformen in die Bedürfnisse der Neuzeit hineinzwängen zu wollen, ist eine weit verbreitete Erkenntnis. Die Zeiten haben sich geändert, die Forderungen, wie sie vor 3 Jahrhunderten bestanden, sind mit den heutigen überhaupt nicht zu vergleichen. Die heute bestehenden Regeln des Entwurfs für Kirchenbau sind, wie wohl jeder einsieht, reformbedürftig, man muß die Gebäude mehr den Forderungen anpassen, die die bedeutenden Mengen von Kirchgängern in großen und kleineren Städten mit sich bringen. Die Forderung der Feuersicherheit birgt in sich einen neuen Zwang zu Aenderungen, einen Zwang, dem auch schon heutzutage die Konstruktionen gefolgt sind und es in Zukunft noch mehr thun werden.

Der Entwurf wird sich der Anwendung von Stahl und Eisen anpassen müssen, wenn man auch nicht annehmen kann, daß die beiden Metalle Mauer- und Werksteine völlig verdrängen werden.

Hygienischen Anforderungen wird heutzutage vollauf genügt, und die Zukunft wird nicht viel neues bringen, aber die Ventilation, die jetzt noch sehr im Argen liegt, wird sich neuen Bedürfnissen anpassen müssen und sicherlich bedeutende Fortschritte machen.

Das moderne Büreau, das Mietshaus, das Hotel, das Privathaus, sie alle werden sich erweitern, ein Bedürfnis wird zum andern kommen, und der Architekt wird kompliziertere Arbeit zu leisten haben, als heutzutage.

Zum Schluß können wir vielleicht die Hoffnung aussprechen, daß die architektonische Erfindung selbst Fortschritte zeigen wird, aber diese sind nicht zu suchen in der Wiederholung alter Formen, sondern in der Schaffung neuer, die dem jeweiligen Zweck möglichst entsprechen.

R. Randal Phillips.

reconnaît généralement aujourd'hui que c'est une faute de vouloir imposer aux besoins modernes les formes anciennes. Les temps sont changés, les exigences que l'on avait il y a trois siècles ne peuvent plus être comparées aux nôtres.

Les principes réglant de nos jours la disposition d'une église, ont ainsi que chacun en convient, besoin d'être réformés, il faut tenir compte dans une plus large mesure des exigences de la masse des fidèles, qui dans les grandes et les petites villes se pressent pour assister au culte. La nécessité de diminuer les dangers d'incendie exerce aussi son influence sur les formes, cette influence se fait sentir déjà dans les constructions et se fera sentir encore davantage à l'avenir. Les projets devront tenir compte, de l'emploi de fer et d'acier, même si l'on est en droit d'admettre que ces deux métaux ne remplaceront pas complètement la pierre et la brique.

Les lois de l'hygiène sont déjà complètement observées et l'avenir ne nous donnera plus beaucoup de nouveauté sous ce rapport, mais la ventilation, qui n'en est encore qu'à ses débuts, aura de nouvelles exigences à satisfaire et fera certainement de grands progrès. Le bureau moderne, la maison à loyer, l'hôtel, la maison privée vont s'elargir, une exigence en appellera une autre et l'architecte aura des problèmes plus difficiles a résondre que maintenant. Pour terminer, qu'il nous soit permis d'exprimer un désir, c'est que l'esprit d'invention fasse aussi des progrès en architecture, ces progrès ne doivent pas consister dans la répétition de formes connues, mais dans la création de nouvelles formes dictées dans chaque cas par les circonstances spéciales.

R. Randal Phillips.

developments in the future may be mentioned. It is very widely recognised that the practice of adapting old types of buildings to modern needs is a bad one, because the times have changed and the requirements of to-day are totally different to what they were, say, three hundred years ago. It seems probable that some revision of the present methods of church planning will be effected in order that the buildings may be more adapted to the large congregations in towns and cities; fireproof construction is another factor of change — it has already altered construction largely and will render further changes necessary. The increasing employment of iron and steel in buildings will considerably alter their design, though it is not probable that these metals will supplant brick, stone and similar building materials. Sanitation is now almost perfect and will effect few further changes, but ventilation — a science little understood — will no doubt be greatly improved, with consequent new requirements.

The modern office, flat, hotel, lodging-house, will all undergo extension, and here again additional needs will tend to render the work of the architect even more complex than it is to-day.

Finally, we may hope for an improvement in architectural design itself — and this hope lies not in the duplication of old forms but in the creation of new ones exactly fitted to the tasks they have to perform.

R. Randal Phillips.

Die moderne Architektur in Oesterreich.

Es ist ja schon ausgesprochen worden: die moderne Architektur weist, was ihre künstlerische Grundtendenz, zumal ihren Gegensatz zu dem ihr Voraufgegangenen anbelangt, eine entschiedene Aehnlichkeit mit der Frühgothik auf.

Hier wie dort eine weit stärker gewollte als klar erkannte, weit mehr der allgemeinen Zeitrichtung als einem legitimen künstlerischen Drange entspringende Losfagung vom Ueberkommenen, bis dahin in Uebung Befindlichen, hier wie dort eine nach Verinnerlichung strebende, bis zu einem gewissen Grade selbst volkstümlichnaiv gemeinte Grundtendenz. Dem herrschenden Schema, der traditionellen Autorität wird der Krieg erklärt; was der Geist an Neuem, noch nicht Dagewesenem zu erdenken vermag, wird als willkommene Eingebung betrachtet und an sich schon, um seiner Neuheit willen, hochgeschätzt. Mit einem Worte: Ein heuristischer Zug, ein großer Wille nach Erfindung beherrscht den neuen künstlerischen Geist beider Zeiten.

Rund dem Lustrum haben nunmehr auch wir in Oesterreich diesem Walten des neuen Geistes zugesehen, — teils mithelfend da, wo er uns

L'architecture moderne en Autriche.

On l'a déjà dit: l'architecture moderne présente une certaine ressemblance avec le gothique primitif, en ce qui concerne sa tendance artistique fondamentale, surtout par son contraste avec ce qui la précède.

Ici comme là un renoncement à la tradition et aux principes jusqu'alors pratiqués, désistement plus fortement voulu que clairement compris, désistement provenant plutôt du cours général des temps que d'un besoin artistique légitime. Ici comme là, une tendance conçue jusqu'à un certain point dans un sentiment naïf et populaire. La guerre est déclarée à la règle régnante et à l'autorité de la tradition. Ce que l'esprit tend à imaginer de nouveau, d'original est considéré comme une inspiration bienvenue et par cela même est très apprécié. En un mot une inspiration nouvelle, un grand désir d'inventer domine le nouvel esprit artistique des deux époques.

Depuis environ cinq ans nous avons aussi assisté en Autriche à ce mouvement du nouvel esprit — tantôt en y coopérant lorsqu'il paraissait être méritant et répondre à nos aspirations, tantôt

Modern Architecture in Austria.

It has been often said, that in its fundamental tendency, and in its sharp contrast to the art of the time immediately preceding it, modern architecture shows a decided leaning towards the Early Gothic.

Now as then, it may be noticed that the intention was sincere, though it often fell short in the performance; and it was often more a powerless drifting with the times than a real artistic impulse towards freedom from conventionality. Now as then, there was a striving after what one may call "inwardness," which manifested itself in an almost naive popular form. War was declared against all tradition. Every effort towards novelty, towards originality at any price was welcomed with joy just because it was new. In a word, a strictly modern spirit, a strenuous endeavour towards invention ruled then, as now, all the art of the time.

For about the space of a lustre, we in Austria have also watched the streaming of the current towards novelty; going with it whenever we saw what we considered congenial and valuable, striving against it when we found it

Verwandtes und Wertvolles zu fördern schien, teils abwehrend da, wo er das uns Widerwärtige und Falsche begünstigte. Wir Oesterreicher kommen auch hier später als alle Andern — England, Frankreich, Deutschland waren uns vorangegangen. Aber diese zeitliche Verspätung hat für uns keineswegs Abhängigkeit bedeutet. Wer hinter einem Vordermann schreitet, braucht nicht immer in dessen Fußstapfen zu treten. Und auch wir traten in keines Anderen Fährte.

Wir hatten — um einen hier festzustellenden historischen Vorgang einmal in Hegels Sprache auszusprechen, — wir hatten unsere eigene Thesis, unsere eigene Antithesis, und so werden wir auch unsere eigene Synthesis haben.

Welches war unsere Thesis? Wohl keine andere als die Wiener Baukunst der siebziger Jahre, eine bis zum Ueberdrusse sich üppig gebende, vollbusige Kunst, ein patrizierhaft-protziges Rennaissancefühlen im Sinne und Wesen unseres, wie kein zweiter Künstler neben ihm uns repräsentierenden — Hans Makart. Unsere Thesis war also: die „Wiener Kunst". Sie war es, so wie unser — unser Oesterreicher — Typus das Wiener Weib ist.*) Wollen wir Oesterreicher als Gesamtheit irgendwie gelten, als Gesamtheit in Vergleich treten wieder mit Gesamtheiten, so müssen wir es eben schlechterdings als Wiener thun. Unser völkerreicher Staat hat, da ihm die nationale Einheit fehlt, nur eine lokale Einheit, — (oder er hat überhaupt keine). Und diese lokale Einheit ist uns Oesterreichern Wien.

Wiens Kunstleben der siebziger Jahre also war unsere Thesis. Eine gewisse Größe wird man ihr niemals absprechen dürfen.

Kühle Palastluft weht uns entgegen, sobald wir uns in jene Zeiten versetzen. Was der „vornehme Gallerieton" in der Malerei, das bedeutete diese Luft in der Baukunst. Palastluft überall: Echt in den wirklichen Palästen jener monumentalen Periode, gefälscht in den Afterpalästen der ihr unmittelbar folgenden Zeit. Echt in den Werken eines Hansen, Schmidt, Ferstel, Hasenauer — gefälscht in den Warenhäusern Rothberger oder Schein.

So vergingen die achtziger Jahre, so kamen die neunziger Jahre.

Noch im vollen Schwunge erreichte sie das Rad, dessen Bahn wir eben kurz charakterisierten. Da wich plötzlich der Boden. Nicht nur, daß in rascher Folge die Großen der Künstlergeneration dahinsanken, auch die Aufgabe, die dieser Generation gestellt war, erwies sich als vollzogen. Wien hatte seine „Renaissancebauherren" und seine „Renaissancebaumeister" (dieses Wort nicht in einseitiger Stilbeschränkung verstanden) mit einem Schlage und zugleich verloren. Eine „Zeit" lag hinter uns, und vor uns das — Leere.

Wenn je in der Geschichte die Thesis (das Gewesene, das Gesetzte) eine Antithesis zeitigte und je das „Eine" ein „Anderes" bedingte, so mußte in diesem Augenblicke in Wiens Kunstleben die Antithesis, das „Andere" eintreten. Und es trat ein.

„Erruptiv" nannte gelegentlich Otto Wagner den Beginn der neuen Richtung in einem an mich gerichteten Briefe. Und dieses Wort besagt nicht zu viel. Erruptiv, fast revolutionär setzte die neue Zeit, die neue Generation ein. Eine kühne Verachtung alles dessen, was uns bis dahin als Dogma galt — um eben deswillen, weil es als solches galt — verband sich bei den Talenten — und solche waren in diesem Augenblicke gleichsam aus dem Boden gestampft — mit einer begreiflichen Sucht, das Neue um seiner selbst willen zu erküren. In der Kunst begann die Mode ein gewichtiges Wort,

*) Das Wort von der gesunden Blutmischung dürfte sich in ihm erfüllen; in ihm und vielleicht auch in unserer Kunst.

en lui résistant lorsqu'il favorisait le faux et le laid. Dans ce domaine, nous arrivons, nous Autrichiens, plus tard que les autres, — l'Angleterre, la France, l'Allemagne nous avaient devancés. Toutefois ce retard ne signifie en aucune manière pour nous dépendance ou assujettissement. Celui qui marche derrière un autre n'est pas pour cela forcé de suivre ses traces; nous ne marchons donc pas dans les traces des autres.

En nous exprimant dans le language de Hegel — pour parler d'un fait historique ici bien établi: — nous avons eu notre propre thèse, notre propre antithèse et nous aurons aussi notre propre synthèse.

Quelle était notre thèse? Aucune autre assurément que l'art viennois de 1870—1880, un art exubérant, voluptueux, développant jusqu'au degoût l'exagération des formes, une interprétation de parvenu du sentiment de la renaissance, incarné dans la personne et l'esprit de Hans Makart, plus qu'en aucun autre artiste. Notre thèse était donc celle-ci: „art viennois". Elle était à nous: aussi bien que la femme viennoise représente pour nous le type autrichien*). Si nous voulons, nous Autrichiens, former en quelque sorte un ensemble, une unité et marcher dans ce sens-là en parallèle avec les autres, ce n'est que comme Viennois que nous pouvons le faire. Notre peuple, composé de tant de races diverses, possède sinon une unité nationale, du moins une unité locale (ou peut-être pas même celle-ci); et cette unité locale pour nous Autrichiens c'est Vienne.

La vie artistique de Vienne de 1870—1880, voilà quelle est notre thèse. Personne n'osera dénier à cette vie artistique une certaine grandeur.

Lorsque nous nous reportons a cette époque, nous éprouvons un sentiment de froideur; cette impression est à l'art architectural ce que le ton des musées est à la peinture. Partout règne un air froid: authentique dans les véritables palais de cette époque monumentale, faux dans les imitations de l'époque suivant immédiatement; pur dans les œuvres d'un Hansen, d'un Schmidt, d'un Ferstel, d'un Hasenauer, faux dans les grands magasins Rothberger ou Stein.

Ainsi se passèrent ces dix années de 1880—1890, de même vinrent les dix dernières années du XIXe siècle. Encore en plein élan elles atteignirent l'art dans sa course dont nous caractérisons justement le chemin. Soudain le sol lui manqua: non seulement parce que les grands hommes de la génération artistique s'étaient éteints, mais encore parce que la tâche imposée à cette génération se trouvait accomplie. Vienne avait perdu en même temps et d'un seul coup ses mecènes et ses architectes de l'art renaissance (ne prêtons pas à ce mot le sens étroit du style).

Derrière nous une époque, devant nous le vide.

Si jamais dans l'histoire une thèse (ce qui est passé, ce qui est établi) devait engendrer une antithèse et si jamais l'une devait avoir l'autre pour conséquence, c'est à cette époque de la vie artistique de Vienne que l'antithèse devait apparaître: et elle apparut.

Dans une lettre qu'il m'adressait une fois, Otto Wagner appelait „éruptif" le commencement de cette nouvelle tendance. Ce mot n'est pas exagéré.

Eruptive, presque révolutionnaire s'annonçaient la nouvelle époque, la nouvelle génération. Un mépris audacieux de tout ce qui jusqu'alors nous avait servi de dogme — et justement parce qu'il

*) La théorie de l'avantage d'un heureux mélange de races peut trouver ici son application, comme peut-être aussi dans notre tempérament artistique.

false and inartistic. We Austrians have held back longer than any other country in this forward movement, England, France and Germany have all been before us. But this apparent going with the stream is nowhere shown in a blind following, or in a want of independence. Whoever marches behind the Vanguard is not obliged to tread exactly in his footprints, and we Austrians have not followed obediently in the exact path of any pioneer.

We had, to use a Hegelian form for our historical purpose, our own Thesis, our own Antithesis, and we shall also have our own Synthesis.

What was our Thesis? Surely no other than the Vienna architecture of the seventies, an art rich and florid almost to satiety, a voluptuous full-bosomed art, as shown in the creations, half patrician, half pompous, and embued with much of the spirit of the Renascence, of our Hans Makart, the most representative Austrian artist.

Our Thesis then, was Vienna art; that was our fundamental idea, just as female beauty as shown in the Viennese is our recognised artistic type.*) If we Viennese then wish to show ourselves or our art as distinctive as compared with the distinctive art of other nations we must come forward in the first place as Viennese.

Our State with its various peoples and languages has no national unity; there can be only local unity, and, if there be any unity at all, that local unity is for us Austrians — Vienna.

The artistic life of Vienna in the seventies then was our Thesis. That it possessed a certain grandeur no one can deny. We breathe the royal air of palaces when we transport ourselves back to these times. What we call in painting the „aristocratic gallery tone" strikes us in the architecture of the period. Everywhere — palatial air. Real palatial air in the palaces built in this monumental period, — false in those baser imitations built in the time immediately following. Real in the works of a Hansen, a Schmidt a Ferstel and a Hasenauer, and false in the bazaar buildings of Rothberger or Schein.

So passed the eighties away, and then came the nineties. Vienna art, now in full swing, caught and held fast the advancing wheel whose path we have briefly described. But suddenly, the earth gave way under our feet. Not only did the great artists of this time disappear in rapid succession, but the generation itself on whom the task of continuing their work devolved, suddenly folded its hands — no progress was made. Vienna lost at one stroke her Renascence architects and builders, Renascence here not to be understood in its restricted sense. Behind us lay an „Age", before us lay — a void. But to return to our historical parallel — the thesis, the „has been" the conventional disappears, and the antithesis takes its place. The „one" necessitates the „other". This then was the moment for the antithesis in the life of Vienna art — the time for the „other". And this time came.

In a letter of Otto Wagner to me at the beginning of this new era he called it „eruptive", and the word was not ill-chosen. „Eruptive", one may almost say revolutionary was the tendency of art at the beginning of this epoch. A bold disdain of all that had hitherto been accepted as dogma, just because it was dogma, marked the work of this period, and all talented artists (and they sprang up at this time like mushrooms) strove for novelty at any price. Fashion began to speak with a voice of authority, in fact, she

*) The advantage of a healthy mixture of races is exemplified in this type of beauty, in this, and perhaps also in our Art.

beinahe das entscheidende mitzureden. Das Bestreben, es möglichst individuell der Allgemeinheit gleichzuthun — dieses lebendige Paradoxon wurde zum leitenden Prinzip der jungen heranwachsenden Schule.

Um Wagner an der Akademie sammelte sich diese Schule; anfänglich (und verhältnismäßig nur sehr kurz) vom Meister geführt — später ihn führend, beinahe verführend, wie ein freies, gegnerisches Wort jener Tage lautete.

Mehr instinktiv (im fanatischen Glauben an die eigene Mission) als mit ruhigem Zielbewußtsein brach sich der künstlerische Nachwuchs seine Bahn; hie und da das Alte auch die Alten mitreißend, meist aber in bitterem Gegensatze alles gewaltsam zur Seite schiebend, was neben ihm allenfalls noch Anspruch auf Geltung erhob.

Nichts vielleicht kennzeichnet das erruptive Wesen unserer Modernen, ihren Mangel an kritischer Besonnenheit besser, als der Umstand, daß ein Versuch, wie Wagners Schrift über die „Moderne Architektur", gemacht und eine zeitlang wirklich als die „Bibel" der neuen Lehre von Freund und Feind ernstgenommen werden konnte.

In Wahrheit ist dieser theoretische Versuch Wagner's mit seiner grob-materialistischen Grundtendenz Alles eher als ein Ausdruck der neuen Richtung, ein Versuch, der, gesetzt diese Richtung verstünde sich selbst, von ihr entrüstet zurückgewiesen werden müßte. In Wahrheit auch ist diese Richtung alles eher als materialistisch, — eher superidealistisch, romantisch, selbst mystisch. — Ihre kritischen Apostel, so ungeschickt, ja durch ihre lächerlichen Uebertreibungen selbst verderblich sie die Sache auch geführt haben, geben doch ausnahmslos gerade dafür beredtes Zeugnis. Von Hermann Bahrs trotz allem Ueberschwang immer geistreichen Ausbrüchen bis zu den dreisten Apologieen Hevesi's spannt sich ein kühner Bogen romantisch-mystischer Dialektik. Wenn ein leitender Grundgedanke hier gesucht und auch gefunden werden kann, so ist es der: Lossagung nicht nur von aller Convention, sondern auch von allem, was dem schlichten Verstande bisher geläufig gewesen. Das Untertauchen in einer von allem Ausgemachten freien, neu aus sich selbst geborenen, gleichsam an sich selbst entflammten starken, ich möchte sagen: Böcklin'schen Empfindung — das ist es, was gleichermaßen die junge Schule für die zu lösende künstlerische Aufgabe und die deren Wesen nachspürende Kritik als das zu lösende dialektische Problem ansieht. Wie weit aber dergleichen von den Feststellungen nüchterner baumechanischer Wahrheit — diesem einzigen Thema der baukünstlerischen „Construction" — entfernt ist, bedarf wohl erst keines Beweises. Und so sehen wir denn in der That in den künstlerischen Werken der jungen Richtung — in den wenigen von ihr ausgeführten Bauten*) nicht minder als in ihren zahlreichen Publikationen — Alles eher, denn eine „constructive" Architektur.

Hier sind wir auch auf den Punkt gestoßen, in welchem sich unsere, die „österreichische" Moderne von den analogen Bestrebungen der andern, z. B. der deutschen unterscheidet. Ein Stück „Romantik" wird ja wohl auch hier nachzuweisen sein, — ja, wenn wir diesen Begriff historisch fassen, sogar deutlicher vielleicht als in unserer — wieder historisch genommen — mehr antikisierenden österreichischen Moderne. Aber die neue deutsche Richtung ist doch andererseits so unverkennbar stark durchsetzt mit historischen und nationalen Elementen, zeigt eine so unverkennbare Hinneigung zur Gothik, daß die freie Empfindungsform gleichsam erst ins Konstruktive-

*) Z. B. dem Secessionsgebäude Olbrich's.

nous avait servi de dogme, forma un lien entre les hommes de talent — (et à ce moment là ils sortaient du sol) — qui éprouvaient le besoin compréhensible de proclamer la nouvelle doctrine pour l'amour d'elle-même. La mode commence à jouer dans l'art un rôle important, presque décisif. La tendance à faire admettre à la masse sa propre individualité, ce paradoxe vivant, devint le principe dirigeant de la nouvelle école.

C'est à l'académie, autour de Wagner, que se groupe cette école, conduite d'abord par le maître (relativement peu de temps), puis le conduisant, le déroutant presque, ainsi que l'a dit librement un adversaire de cette époque.

La nouvelle génération se fraye son chemin plus instinctivement et avec la croyance fanatique en sa propre mission qu'en connaissance sûre de son but; parfois elle détruit l'ancien et aussi les Anciens, mais le plus souvent, en opposition acharnée, elle repousse tout ce qui, à côté d'elle, prétend valoir quelque chose.

Rien peut être ne caractérise mieux cette époque que l'esprit éruptif de nos modernes et leur manque de raisonnement critique, que le fait d'un essai qu'écrivit Wagner sur l'architecture moderne, écrit qui put être accepté comme l'évangile de la nouvelle école par ses amis et par ses ennemis.

En vérité cet essai théorique de Wagner avec sa tendance grossièrement matérialiste est tout plutôt qu'une expression de la nouvelle époque, un essai qui, étant donné que cette tendance se comprit d'elle-même, devait être repoussé par elle avec indignation. En vérité cette tendance est tout plutôt que matérialiste, elle est plutôt idéaliste, romantique en même mystique. Ses apôtres critiques en donnent la preuve convaincante par la manière si inhabile, dangereuse même par les exagérations ridicules dont ils ont mené la campagne. Un pont hardi est jeté de Hermann Bar entre les théories spirituelles malgré leur exubérance et les apologies effrontées de Hevesi, et ce pont hardi, c'est la dialectique romantique et mystique. Si une pensée dominante peut être cherchée et trouvée ici, la voici: désistement non-seulement de toutes conventions, mais encore de tout ce qui jusque là avait été accessible au simple bon sens. Ce que la jeune école considérait comme capable de lui permettre de résoudre les problèmes artistiques, et à la critique d'en étudier l'essence, de lui permettre enfin de résoudre le problème dialectique qui lui sera posé, ce devait être de se plonger dans l'oubli de toute tradition, de se sentir né à une vie nouvelle, et de sentir en soi brûler le feu sacré. Il n'y a pas besoin de prouver combien de telles fantaisies sont éloignées de l'assurance de la vérité scientifique, principe unique de la construction artistique. Et nous le voyons en effet dans les oeuvres artistiques de la nouvelle école, dans le peu de constructions érigées par elle*) et encore plus dans ses nombreuses publications. C'est tout ce qu'on voudra, mais pas de l'architecture constructive.

Ici, nous arrivons au point où notre art moderne autrichien se distingue des efforts analogues des autres pays, par exemple de ceux de l'Allemagne. On pourra même prouver la présence d'un peu de romantisme, surtout si nous prêtons à ce mot un sens historique, voir même plus précis que celui de notre art moderne autrichien, imitant l'antique et que nous pouvons de nouveau considérer comme historique. Mais cette nouvelle tendance allemande est, d'autre part, si évidemment mélangée d'éléments nationaux et historiques, elle montre un penchant si indéniable pour le gothique, que la libre composition paraît d'abord se traduire dans une

*) Par exemple le bâtiment de la Secession d'Olbrich.

often spoke the decisive word. The endeavour to be as original as possible and yet to conform to the existing fashion, this, paradoxical as it may sound, was the leading principle of the young and growing school. They gathered round Wagner at the Academy, led at the beginning by the master, but only for a very short time; later they led him, and not only led him, but led him away, as the opponents of the school wittily expressed it at the time.

Instinct with a fanatical belief in its own mission, the new art broke its way; sometimes carrying with it the old school and its representatives but generally pushing on one side in bitter opposition every other form of art that attempted to exist beside it.

In nothing perhaps did our modern „eruptive" school show their plentiful lack of critical discretion, more than in the manner in which Wagner's book on „Modern Architecture" was received as the Gospel of the new doctrine by friend and foe alike. In actual truth, this theoretical attempt of Wagner, with its underlying tendency of coarse materialism; is everything else except an exposition of the doctrines of the new school, and one, which if it understands its own nature, it must repudiate with indignation. In truth, this new movement is everything else, but not materialistic, rather super-idealistic, romantic, even mystical. Its apostles unwittingly prove this in their awkward and even laughable exaggerations; they actually destroy what they wish to create. From Hermann Bahrs (in spite of all his bombast always full of inspiration) to the bold and almost daring works of Hevesi, there stretches a broad arch of romantic — mystic dialectic. If one seeks in these works for a leading idea and finds one, it is this: — the rejection not only of everything conventional, but of everything which up to this time seemed the outcome of simple Reason. The effort to obtain perfect freedom from all established laws brought forth a newly-born, self-illuminated, I may almost say „Böcklin-like" perception of art, and this it is that the young school considers as the problem given it to solve; the efforts of the critics are directed naturally to solve the dialectic problems which follow out of it.

It will not be necessary to point out here how far these ideas are removed from the sober truth of building construction; we see in the artistic productions of the new school — in the few representative buildings,*) not less than in their numerous publications, everything except constructive architecture.

At last we have arrived at the point where the work of our Austrian moderns differs from similar endeavours in other lands, e. g. in Germany. Here too, we see remains of the Romantic, perhaps even more than among our Austrian artists of the same school. But the current of new German art is unmistakeably coloured with historical and national elements; and remains so true to Gothic traditions, that all free perceptions of form seem to be first regulated by constructive historical laws before they come to the light of day. „Frozen" was the word which Otto Wagner applied to it, and it was not inappropriate.

*) e. g. The Secessions buildings of Olbrich.

Hiltoriſche überſetzt erſcheint, bevor ſie zu Tage tritt. „Erſtarrt" hat Otto Wagner dies gelegentlich genannt, und er hat auch hiermit in ſeiner Weiſe kein ganz unrichtiges Wort geſprochen.

Das alſo iſt — man nehme Alles nur in Allem — unſere „Theſis", die Theſis unſerer, der öſterreichiſchen Moderne.

Zur „Syntheſis" (um ausklingend noch einmal Gegels Worte zu gebrauchen) ſind wir heute noch nicht gelangt. Aber vorahnend läßt ſich wohl vermuten, daß dieſe Syntheſis weder (etwa ſich ſelbſt verleugnend) eine Rückkehr zum „Alten" ſein wird, wie die Gegner der Moderne voreilig triumphieren, noch auch eine dauernde Etablierung alles deſſen, was bei uns heute in Erſcheinung tritt, wie die blinden Anhänger der Moderne glauben.

Bleiben wird uns der große vorurteilsloſe Blick für das individuelle Weſen eines Kunſt‑ zumal Bauwerks, für ſeinen von allem Geweſenen zunächſt freien, weil in jedem einzelnen Falle neuen Empfindungsinhalt. Bleiben wird uns die — wie Semper ſich ausdrückte — „objektive Beherrſchung" deſſen, was man „Stil" nennt, aber nicht bloß in dem eingeſchränkten Sinne Vignolaiſcher „Ordnungen", ſondern in dem erweiterten Sinne, in welchem Stil die Ueber‑ einſtimmung der Teile mit dem Empfindungs‑ inhalt eines Werkes bedeutet. Bleiben wird uns endlich der Mut des Wagniſſes, des Wagniſſes, gleicherweiſe uns loszumachen von der „Tabulatur" der Biltorik und von deren getreueſtem „Merker", dem Philiſtertum in der Kunſt. Das alles wird uns bleiben. Vergehen aber wird der Wahn, daß die Baukunſt unſerer Zeit nur auf den Trümmern der ihr voraufgegangenen Bauſtile erſtehen kann, daß deren gänzliche Vernichtung die Vorausſetzung eines unſerer Zeit würdigen neuen Stils iſt.

F. v. Feldegg.

---

forme constructive et historique, avant même d'avoir vu le jour. Otto Wagner l'a appelée une fois pétrifiée, en cela il a, à sa manière, employé un mot assez juste.

C'est donc notre thèse, au bout du compte, la thèse de notre style moderne autrichien.

Nous ne sommes pas encore arrivés au‑ jourd'hui à la synthèse, pour employer en ter‑ minant la langue de Hegel. Mais encore une fois, il est à présumer, que cette synthèse (se reniant elle‑même) ne sera, ni un retour à l'„ancien", comme les adversaires du style mo‑ derne le prétendent en triomphant trop vite, ni un établissement durable de tout ce qui surgit aujourd'hui chez nous, ainsi que le croient les adeptes aveugles de l'art nouveau.

Ce qui nous restera, ce sera le coup d'oeil impartial, pour juger de l'individualité de l'œuvre d'art, pour son contenu, libre de toute tradition, puisqu'il aura puisé son inspiration dans chaque cas particulier. Ce qui nous restera, c'est, comme s'exprimait Semper: le jugement „objectif" de ce qu'on appelle le „style" non simplement dans le sens borné des ordres de Vignole, mais dans un sens plus large, un style, dans lequel l'har‑ monie des parties offre une signification avec le sentiment intime de l'œuvre. Ce qui nous restera, enfin, ce sera le courage d'avoir osé nous défaire des règles de l'histoire et de son fidèle satellite, la „bourgeoisie" dans l'art. Tout cela nous restera. Mais ce qui passera, c'est l'illusion que l'architecture moderne ne peut naître que des ruines des styles qui l'ont pré‑ cédée, et que son anéantissement complet est le précurseur d'un art nouveau, qui permettra à notre époque de voir surgir un style digne d'elle.

F. v. Feldegg.

Speaking then generally, this was our thesis — the thesis of modern Austrian art.

To our Synthesis (to use again Hegel's form) we have not yet attained. But we may safely prognosticate that it will not deny its parentage and return to the „ancients", as its opponents, somewhat prematurely, triumphantly prophesy. Neither will it take for its enduring foundations all that is now understood under the term „modern", as the blind followers of the present style confidently believe.

One thing will certainly remain with us — the wide impartial view which will rightly value every strenuous individual endeavour after real art, whether it be new or not. As Semper ex‑ presses it, the „objective mastery" of that which one designates as style will remain with us, not in the limited sense of the Vignola "Regulations"; but in the wide sense in which the various parts of a work of art unite with the perception which called it forth to form one harmonious whole. Lastly will remain with us, the courage to dare — to dare to strike off the chains of the historical „Tabulator" and of its most rigid adherents — the Philistines of art. All that will surely remain to us. But transitory will be the illusion that the architecture of our own time can only rise from the ruins of the older art, or that the entire destruction of what has gone before must be a necessary preliminary to the development of a style, worthy of the time in which we live.

F. v. Feldegg.

Die franzöſiſche Architektur im 20. Jahrhundert.

Als am 31. Dezember 1900 die La Critique den Anfang des 20. Jahrhunderts bei einem Diner feſtlich beging, ergriff der franzöſiſche Architekt Hector Guimard im Namen der anweſenden Künſtler das Wort um den Wunſch auszuſprechen, daß die neue Aera eine moderne Architektur zeitigen möge, die unſeren Bedürf‑ niſſen und dem Geſchmack des Tages, den hygieniſchen Einrichtungen, einer ſchönen Ein‑ fachheit, in Gemeinſchaft mit Baukunſt und Ingenieurwiſſenſchaft entſpreche.

Weder die Worte „neue Kunſt" noch „neuer Stil" wurden ausgeſprochen, da die ſich gegenwärtig vollziehende Umwälzung, deren Zeuge wir ſind, noch nicht beendet iſt und noch nicht die Grundſätze erkennen läßt, welche erforderlich ſind, um die an ſich berechtigte, moderne Bewegung zu charakteriſieren.

Das kommt daher, weil die Architektur des XX. Jahrhunderts ſich in Frankreich wie im Auslande noch in der Periode des Werdens befindet: heute bringt ſie Werke hervor, die originell bleiben werden, morgen vielleicht ſchafft ſie das Meiſterwerk, daß die wirkliche Schön‑ heit beſtimmen und infolgedeſſen den Stil, für den ſich die Zukunft begeiſtern wird.

L'architecture française au XXe siècle.

Au dîner du 31 décembre 1900, où La Critique fêta l'aurore du XXe siècle, l'architecte français Hector Guimard prit la parole, au nom des artistes présents, pour sou‑ haiter que l'ère nouvelle donnât une architecture moderne plus conforme à nos besoins et au goût du jour, des constructions hygièniques, d'une belle simplicité, en accord avec l'art du constructeur et la science de l'ingénieur.

Il ne fut prononcé ni les mots art nouveau, ni style nouveau, l'évolution qui s'accomplit actuellement et dont nous sommes témoins n'étant pas achevée et n'ayant pas encore permis de donner les bases nécessaires à l'établissement du style bien défini qui doit caractériser l'époque où nous entrons.

C'est que l'architecture du XXe siècle, — qu'on l'appelle ainsi ou autrement, — en France comme à l'étranger est dans une période de tâ‑ tonnement: elle produit aujourd'hui des oeuvres qui resteront originales, elle donnera demain peut‑être le chef d'oeuvre qui déterminera la vraie beauté et parconséquent un style dont l'avenir s'inspirera.

French Architecture in the XX. Century.

On the 31st December 1900 "La Critique" celebrated the beginning of the XX. cen‑ tury by a banquet, on which occasion the French architect Hector Guimard, speaking in the name of the assembled artists, expressed the hope that the new era might inaugurate a new modern school of architecture, which would embody at once the taste and the necessities of the age, and which, while displaying a beautiful simplicity, would unite in itself the latest sanitary impro‑ vements with the most advanced discoveries in architectural and engineering science. The words "new art" and "new style" were not used, and advisedly, as we are still in the period of revo‑ lution, and there is at present no settled foun‑ dation on which we can ground so important a certainty as the characterization of a new style.

In France, as well as in other countries, the architecture of the XX. century is coming into being, today shows us much original work, tomorrow perhaps may bring us the master‑ piece fulfilling all the requirements of modern art, and which may so embody the spirit of the age, as to be the model to which future gene‑ rations may look for precedent and precept.

In Frankreich hat sich ein kleiner Kreis von Vorläufern, anknüpfend an die Bewegung in Belgien und Deutschland seit 5 oder 6 Jahren, vor allen anderen die schwierige Aufgabe gestellt, eine nationale Architektur in die Wege zu leiten. Sie verdienen, daß ihre Namen mit goldenen Lettern in dem Marmor des zukünftigen Palastes der Architektur verewigt werden. Hector Guimard marschiert an der Spitze der Schar der Neuerer mit seinen Villen in Auteuil, seinen Schweizerhäuschen in Sèvres, Garches und Lion-sur-mer, dem Magazin Coutolleau in Angers, dem Castel Béranger, wo zum ersten Mal die Kunst mit bescheidenen Mitteln in Wohnräume eingedrungen ist; Castel Béranger ist das erste interessante Gebäude, das im neuen Geiste geschaffen wurde.

Inzwischen hat Niermans, dessen Spezialität Cafés und Musikhallen sind, eine Dekoration versucht, in der er den Reiz der Flora wieder zur Geltung bringen wollte. Wir müssen die Ausschmückung des Casino de Paris, der Olympia, der Parisiana, des Café Mollard, des Restaurant Pousset und des Wiener Restaurants anführen. Niermans hat vielleicht, indem er die Idee zum Luxus und Reichtum gab, die Dekoration gemißbraucht, aber hier ist nicht der Ort die ersten Arbeiten derjenigen zu kritisieren, die ihre Existenz einer so edlen Sache gewidmet haben.

L. Majorelle hat mehrere Salons im Café de Paris, G. Serrurier einen Salon im Hôtel Chatam, Sonnier die Cafés Maxim und Lapré eingerichtet. Louis Martin, ein geschickter Architekt, hat Modebazare auf der Place de la Madeleine und der avenue de l'Opéra ausgeführt.

Staatsarchitekt Gustave Rives hat das reizende Theater des Automobil-Club gebaut.

Besonders thut sich ein junger Architekt unmittelbar durch seine einfachen und eleganten, in einem gut französischen Geschmack gehaltenen Bauten hervor, es ist Charles Plumet, der ein Miethaus in der rue de Tocqueville, ein Privathaus in der avenue Malakoff und unter Mitarbeit von Tony Selmersheim zahlreiche Läden, das Restaurant Edouard, das Magazin Roddy, ein Hôtel Vestibule in der rue d'Amsterdam, Wäschegeschäfte in der Chaussée d'Antin und rue Saint-Dominique, ein Konfiturengeschäft auf dem boulevard des Capucines etc. gebaut hat.

Xavier Schoelkopf baute 1899 ein Wohnhaus in der avenue d'Jéna und führte das Haus der Yvette Guilbert auf dem boulevard Berthier auf.

Dann kam 1900 die Pariser Ausstellung, die so viele Anstrengungen krönte und das Interesse für eine neue Architektur zeitigte. Fast alle Architekten versuchten, in ihren Gebäuden frische und neue Motive zum Ausdruck zu bringen, und für viele wurde dies ein wirkliches Vorbild. Man wird sich der von Sorel, Felix Aubert, Benouville, Franz Jourdain, R. Binet, J. Weber etc. ausgeschmückten Abteilungen wohl erinnern.

Einige Arbeiten fielen auf der 1900er Ausstellung auf: das großartige aber vergängliche Palais der Land- und Seetruppen von Auburtin, das Theater der Loie Fuller von H. Sauvage, Pierre Roche und Francis Jourdain, das Restaurant zur schönen Müllerin von G. Tronchet, die Billethäuschen und verschiedenen Pavillons von Louis Martin.

Als die Ausstellung beendigt war, begann strahlend das von Robida geträumte 20. Jahrhundert.

Die Eisenbahngesellschaften wurden durch das Ministerium veranlaßt, neues, in hygienischer und bequemer Beziehung besseres Material anzuschaffen. Neue Bahnhöfe sind im Entstehen — der kleine Bahnhof von Boulainvilliers von Barré kam zuerst, dann die großen Bauwerke, der Bahnhof am Quai d'Orsay von Laloux und der Bahnhof Paris-Lyon von Toudoire. —

En France, un petit noyau de „précurseur,, s'inspirant un peu des belges et des allemands, a, depuis cinq ou six ans, tenté cette tache difficile entre toutes de rénover l'architecture nationale. Ils méritent l'inscription de leurs noms en lettres d'or sur le marbre du futur palais de l'architecture.

Hector Guimard marche en tête de la phalange des novateurs avec ses villas d'Auteuil, ses chalets à Sèvres, à Garches, à Lion-sur-mer, le magasin Coutolleau à Angers, le Castel Béranger où, pour la première fois, une note d'art a pénétré dans les appartements à prix modiques; le Castel Beranger a été la première maison de rapport conçue dans l'esprit nouveau.

Entre temps, Niermans qui s'était fait une spécialité des cafés et music-halls y a essayé une décoration où il a voulu évoquer le charme de la flore. Nous devons citer la décoration du Casino de Paris, de l'Olympia, de Parisiana, du café Mollard, de la brasserie Pousset et de la brasserie Viennois.

Niermans, en donnant l'idée de luxe et de richesse, a peut-être abusé du décor, mais nous ne devons pas à cette place critiquer les premières oeuvres de ceux qui ont consacré leur existence à une aussi noble cause.

L. Majorelle a installé plusieurs salons au Café de Paris, G. Serrurier un salon à l'Hôtel Chatam, Sonnier les Cafés Maxim et Lapré. Louis Martin, un architecte habile, a agencé des magasins de modes place de la Madeleine et avenue de l'Opéra.

Gustave Rives, architecte officiel, mais qui ne demande qu'à innover, a construit le gracieux théâtre de l'Automobile-Club.

Mais un jeune architecte s'est immédiatement imposé par ses constructions simples et élégantes, dans un goût bien français, c'est Charles Plumet qui a construit une maison de rapport rue de Tocqueville, un hôtel privé avenue Malakoff, avec la collaboration de Tony Selmersheim de nombreux magasins: le restaurant Edouard, le magasin Roddy, un vestibule d'hôtel rue d'Amsterdam, des chemiseries chaussée d'Antin et rue Saint-Dominique, une confiserie boulevard des Capucines, etc.

Xavier Schoelkopf, en 1899, construisit un hôtel privé avenue d'Jéna et entreprit l'hôtel de Mme Yvette Guilbert boulevard Berthier.

Vint alors, en 1900, l'Exposition de Paris qui couronna tant d'efforts et montra l'intérêt d'une architecture nouvelle. Presque tous les architectes essayèrent de mettre une note jeune et gaie dans la décoration de leurs édifices et pour beaucoup ce fut un véritable apprentissage. On se rapellera les Sections décorées par Sorel, Félix Aubert, Benouville, Frantz Jourdain, R. Binet, J. Weber, etc.

Quelques oeuvres s'imposèrent à l'Exposition de 1900: le magistral mais éphémère Palais des Armées de terre et de mer d'Auburtin, le théâtre de la Loie Fuller de H. Sauvage, Pierre Roche et Francis Jourdain, le restaurant de la Belle Meunière de G. Tronchet, les douanes et pavillons divers de Louis Martin.

L'Exposition terminée, le vingtième siècle rêvé par Robida s'est ouvert radieux.

Les compagnies de chemins de fer à qui un ministre avisé impose un matériel plus conforme à l'hygiène des voyageurs ont commencé par construire de nouvelles gares: la petite gare de Boulainvilliers, par Barré d'abord; puis les

Since 5 or 6 years, a small band of French pioneers have joined their brethren in Belgium and Germany in their endeavours to bring again into fashion a national architecture. They deserve to have their names inscribed in letters of gold on the marble palaces of the future. At the head of these, marches Hector Guimard with his villas in Auteuil, his Swiss cottages in Sèvres, Garches, and Lion-sur-mer, the establishment of Coutolleau in Angers, the Castel Béranger, where Art has penetrated for the first time, it is true modestly, into the dwelling rooms, and which is the first really interesting building in the new style.

In the meantime Niermans whose specialities are cafés and music halls, has in his use of floral decoration sought to revive a half-forgotten art. As examples we give the decorations of the Casino de Paris, the Olympia, the Parisiana, the restaurant Pousset and the Vienna restaurant. Perhaps Niermans has overdone the use of this luxurious and expensive style of decoration, but it would be out of place here to criticize an effort which has sprung from so noble and praiseworthy a motive.

L. Majorelle, has decorated several saloons in the Café de Paris; G. Serrurier one in the Hotel Chatham, Sonnier the cafés Maxim and Lapré. Louis Martin, a clever architect, has carried out the bazaars on the Place de la Madeleine, and the Avenue de l'Opera.

The architect of government Gustave Rives has built the charming theatre of the Automobil Club. But there is one young architect whose work, at once simple, elegant and distinctly French is coming gradually to the front. It is Charles Plumet, who has an interesting house in the rue de Tocqueville, a private house in the Avenue Malakoff, with Tony Selmersheim numerous shops, the Restaurant Edouard, the establishment Roddy, a Hotel Vestibule in the rue d'Amsterdam, underclothing establishments in the Chaussée d'Antin and the rue Saint Dominique, a confectioner's shop in the boulevard des Capucines etc.

Xavier Schoelkopf in 1899 built a dwelling house in the avenue d'Jéna, and carried out the house of Yvette Guilbert in the boulevard Berthier.

The Paris Exhibition of 1900 saw the culmination of much upward effort, and interest for the new architecture was awakened on all sides. Nearly all architects strove after freshness and novelty in their designs, and many of these can serve as examples worthy of imitation. It is only necessary to call to remembrance the works of Sorel, Felix Aubert, Benouville, Franz Jourdain, R. Binet, J. Weber etc.

Certain buildings of the Exhibition of 1900 were specially noticeable; the splendid, but evanescent Palace of the military and naval troops of Auburtin, the theatre of Lois Fuller by H. Sauvage, Pierre Roche, and Francis Jourdain, the Restaurant "Zur schönen Müllerin", by G. Tronchet, the ticket office and several pavilions by Louis Martin. As soon as the Exhibition was at an end, the dawn of the XX. century as dreamed of by Robida began to shine. The Railway companies were obliged by the State to provide carriages more in consonance with modern hygiene and comfort.

New stations are being constructed, the small station of Boulainvilliers of Barré came first, then the large buildings, the station on the Quai d'Orsay of Laloux and the station Paris—Lyons by Toudoire.

Die Stadtbahn-Gesellschaft hat die äußere Architektur ihrer Pariser Bahnhöfe Hektor Guimard übertragen. Seine Entwürfe sind unter sich verschieden und passen sich der Lage des Ortes genau an: die an der Place de l'Etoile sind kleine Gebäude von einer vollendeten Leichtigkeit; die Bahnhöfe an der Porte-Maillot und den Champs-Elysées sind einfache Treppenaufgänge oder Balustraden, die auch genügen.

Ungefähr zur selben Zeit vollendete Guimard in der rue des Belles-Feuilles einen Saal für Kammermusik.

Lavirotte, der in der rue Sédillot ein kleines Einfamilienhaus errichtet hat, vollendet soeben in der Avenue Rapp und Square Rapp zwei bedeutende Häuser, bei welchen zum größten Teile Steingutornamente von Bigot in verschwenderischer Weise angewandt wurden. Dieser glasierte Stein tröstet uns für einige in Cement aufgeführte, triste Häuser, die gewisse Unternehmer bei uns einführen wollten.

Ein anderer Architekt, der einfache und interessante Formen anwendet, ein Freund schöner Linien mit nur absolut notwendiger Dekoration, ist Lefranc, der auf dem boulevard du Temple, einer besonders reich bevölkerten Gegend, ein großes nennenswertes Gebäude für kleine Mieter gebaut hat, welches als das Haus der Zukunft gewissermaßen gelten kann. Lefranc hat mit einem Meistertreffer in der neuen Architektur debutiert.

In Passy, rue de l'Yvette, baut der Bildhauer Gaudissart ein Haus, das mit Steingutreliefplatten bekleidet ist, die das Familienleben und die Freuden des Heims darstellen.

In Nancy legen H. Sauvage und L. Majorelle die letzte Hand an ein Privathaus, das nach ihren Plänen erbaut wurde.

Endlich hat in Paris der Maler Mucha für den Juwelier Georges Fouquet einen Laden ausgeführt, der eine der Zierden der rue Royale ist.

Die Jugend ist es, von der man erwartet, daß sie die französische Architektur wieder neu beleben wird. Kaum der Ecole des Beaux-Arts entwachsen, haben sich schon mehrere mit Versuchen, die etwas für die Zukunft versprechen, bemerkbar gemacht: Abel Landry mit seinen Villen und Läden in Paris, Réchin mit Bauten in Angers, Bacard & Klein mit dem Casino in Enghien u. s. w.

Auch muß man eine so bald wie mögliche Umgestaltung der Lehrprogramme an der Ecole des Beaux-Arts, an der Ecole spéciale d'architecture und sogar an der Ecole des Arts décoratifs wünschen; endlich einen Kursus für angewandte Kunst in der Industrie an der zukünftigen Ecole des Arts et Métiers de Paris.

Anläßlich des großen Römischen Preises 1901 hat ein Mitbewerber Tony Garnier auf seinem Entwurf (Eine Industriestadt) den revolutionären Gedanken ausgesprochen: „Wie alle Architekturen auf falschen Principien beruhen, so ist auch die antike Architektur ein Irrtum." Diese Offenbarung hat in der Ecole des Beaux-Arts einen Entrüstungssturm hervorgerufen.

Stanislas Ferrand hat sich damit befaßt, die Verteidigung des Kühnen in seinem Journal „Le Bâtiment" und im Parlament zu übernehmen: „Die Lehre, daß die Architektur ausschließlich auf den Prinzipien der Antike basiert, ist ein Fehler, man muß sie verjüngen, modifizieren und den Fortschritten der Wissenschaft und der Civilisation Rechnung tragen. Man muß in unseren Schulen die Kunst lehren, die morgen durch den Staat selbst, durch unsere Departements, durch unsere großen Städte und durch alle diejenigen, die sich der Architektur als eines mächtigen Mittels sozialer Thätigkeit bedienen, ins Praktische umgesetzt wird."

grands monuments, la gare du Quai d'Orsay par Laloux et la gare de Paris-Lyon par Toudoire.

La compagnie du chemin de fer métropolitain a demandé la partie extérieure de ses gares parisiennes à Hector Guimard. Les modèles ont été variés à l'infini, suivant les emplacements: ceux de la place de l'Etoile sont de petits édifices d'infinie légéreté; les gares de la Porte-Maillot et des Champs-Elysées sont de simples abris d'escaliers ou des ballustrades nécessaires et suffisantes.

Vers la même époque, Guimard a achevé une salle de concerts classiques, rue des Belles-Feuilles.

Lavirotte qui avait érigé un petit hôtel rue Sédillot vient d'achever avenue Rapp et square Rapp deux maisons importantes, recouvertes en grande partie en grès céramique de Bigot, avec une profusion de décor. Le grès vernissé, d'une exhubérante galté, nous console des tristes maisons en ciment armé que certains entrepreneurs voudraient implanter chez nous.

Un autre architecte, de conceptions simples et sages, un ami des belles lignes avec la décoration strictement nécessaire, Lefranc a terminé tout récemment au boulevard du Temple, quartier essentiellement populeux, une grande maison de rapport qui donne certainement l'indication précise de l'architecture de demain. Lefranc a débuté par un coup de maître dans l'architecture nouvelle.

A Passy, rue de l'Yvette, le sculpteur Gaudissart construit une maison extérieurement revêtue de carreaux de grès en relief qui représenteront la vie en famille et les joies de foyer.

A Nancy, H. Sauvage et L. Majorelle mettent la dernière main à un hôtel particulier, établi sur leurs plans.

Enfin à Paris, le peintre Mucha a fait, pour le joaillier Georges Fouquet, un magasin qui est l'un des ornements de la rue Royale.

C'est des jeunes qu'il faut attendre l'effort qui rénovera l'architecture française. A peine sortis de l'Ecole des Beaux-Arts, plusieurs se sont déjà fait remarquer par des tentatives qui promettent pour l'avenir: Abel Landry, des villas et magasins à Paris, Réchin, des maisons à Angers, Bacard et Klein, le casino d'Enghien, etc.

Aussi faut-il souhaiter au plus tôt le remaniement des programmes d'enseignement à l'Ecole des Beaux-Arts, à l'Ecole spéciale d'Architecture, et même à l'Ecole des Arts décoratifs, enfin un cours d'art appliqué à l'industrie à la future Ecole des Arts et Métiers de Paris.

A l'occasion du grand Prix de Rome 1901, un concurrent Tony Garnier a inscrit sur son envoi (une cité industrielle) la pensée révolutionnaire: „Ainsi que toutes les architectures reposant sur des principes faux, l'architecture antique est une erreur".

Cette manifestation a fait scandale à l'Ecole des Beaux-Arts et à l'Institut. Stanislas Ferrand, architecte doublé d'un député, s'est chargé de prendre la défense de l'audacieux dans son journal Le Bâtiment et au Parlement: „L'enseignement de l'architecture exclusivement basé sur les principes de l'antique est une erreur, il faut le rajeunir, le modifier, tenir compte des progrès de la science et de la civilisation. Il faut enseigner dans nos écoles l'art qui, demain sera mis en pratique par l'Etat lui-même, par nos départements, nos grandes villes et par tous ceux qui se servent de l'architecture comme d'un moyen puissant d'activité sociale".

The town railway has entrusted the exterior of their Paris station to Hektor Guimard. His designs possess great variety, and are always adapted to the special requirements of the building. The erections on the Place de l'Etoile are small and of exquisite lightness; the stations on the Porte-Maillot and the Champs Elysées are simple staircases or balustrades which however sufficient for the purpose.

About the same time Guimard completed a hall for Chamber Music in the rue des Belles Feuilles.

Lavirotte who has built in the rue Sédillot a small house for one family has just completed two important houses in the Avenue Rapp and the Square Rapp, in which coloured flintware from Bigot has been used in a truly lavish manner. This glazed stone consoles us a little for some miserable looking cement houses which certain builders are forcing upon us in some places.

Another architect, whose forms are at once simple and interesting, who is a friend of the simple line with only absolutely necessary decoration, is Lefranc. He has built in the thickly populated Boulevard du Temple large and important buildings for small families which may be designated the House of the Future. Lefranc has made a brilliant debût, and bids fair to hold a permanent place in architecture.

In Passy, rue de l'Yvette, the sculptor Gaudissart has built a house, ornamented with square sandstone reliefs depicting family life and the joys of home. In Nancy, H. Sauvage and L. Majorelle, are putting the finishing touches to a private house built after their plans; lastly, in Paris the painter Mucha has erected for the jeweller Georges Fouquet, a shop which is an ornament to the Rue Royale.

It is from the young architects that we expect the rejuvenation of national French architecture. Some just fresh from the Ecole des Beaux Arts, have put forth efforts which promise much for the future: Abel Landry with his villas and shops in Paris, Réchin with buildings in Angers, Bacard and Klein with the Casino d'Enghien etc.

An alteration in the curriculum of the Ecole des Beaux Arts, of the Ecole speciale d'Architecture and even of the Ecole des Arts décoratifs, is devoutly to be wished; and a course of art study as applicable to industrial works, is to be recommended to the projected Ecole des Arts et Métiers de Paris.

One of the competitors of the Grand prize of Rome for 1901 Tony Garnier has in his design (an industrial town) shown a decidedly revolutionary leaning „As all architecture is based on false principles, antique architecture is also a mistake."

This manifesto has raised a storm of indignation in the Ecole des Beaux Arts. Stanislas Ferrand, in his journal "Le Bâtiment" has undertaken to defend the temerity of this rash innovator and says: „To teach that architecture must be based entirely on antique principles is a mistake: one must rejuvenate and modify, one must keep in sight the progress of science and the requirements of modern civilization. That art must be taught in our schools which tomorrow will be disseminated throughout the entire State, through our departments, through our large towns, in fact in every place where architecture can be made a mighty factor in social progress".

The façade competition of the town of Paris

Die Fassaden-Concurrenzen der Stadt Paris müssen in viel weiterem Geist gefaßt werden; die Architekten müssen ihren Einfällen freien Lauf lassen, wenn sie aufgefordert werden, die neuen Pariser Stadtteile im Quartier des Invalides und auf dem Champ-de-Mars zu bauen.

Die Architektur des XX. Jahrhunderts soll nicht suchen als neue Kunst bezeichnet zu werden, sie soll einfach, ökonomisch, hygienisch, rationell sein, dem Geschmack und den Bedürfnissen unserer Zeit angepaßt. — So wird sie eine Etappe in der Baukunst markieren: Einen Stil.

Georges Bans.

Les concours de façades de la Ville de Paris devront être compris dans un esprit plus large; les architectes devront donner libre cours à leur inspiration quand ils seront appelés à construire les nouveaux quartiers de Paris, aux Invalides et au Champ-de-Mars.

L'architecture du XXe siècle ne doit pas chercher à être qualifiée „art nouveau", elle doit être simple, économique, hygiénique, rationnelle, conforme aux goûts et aux besoins de notre époque. Ainsi elle marquera une étape nouvelle dans l'art de construire: un style.

Georges Bans.

will, it is hoped, show much that is based on broader lines. The architects must give free scope to their ideas, and show what they can do when they are entrusted with the construction of the new quarter of the town in the Quartier des Invalides and the Champ de Mars.

The architecture of the XX. Century shall not strive after a new name, such as the "new Art" but it shall be simple, economical, hygienic and rational, suitable to the taste and requirements of the time. Then will a great forward step be taken in architectural progress — that will be the formation of a new style.

Georges Bans.

Die Entwickelung der Architektur in Deutschland.

Mit klaren Worten entwickelt Professor Cornelius Gurlitt in dem Aufsatz „Ziele der Architektur im neuen Jahrhundert" in allgemeinen Umrissen die Bewegung, die im verflossenen Jahrhundert auf architektonischem Gebiete hauptsächlich in Deutschland sich abspielte, und die Folgerungen, welche im allgemeinen als Ergebnis der stattgehabten Kämpfe, im neuen Jahrhundert sich daran knüpfen lassen. Die Betrachtungen über die unserer heutigen gleichartige Bewegung in England, Oesterreich und Frankreich schildern uns, daß in ersterem Lande es an einer staatlichen Organisation des Architekturunterrichtes durchaus gebricht und wie man bestrebt sei, diesem Mangel abzuhelfen, obgleich auch dort viele Architekten jeden „Stil" verabscheuen. Die Aeußerungen aus Frankreich hingegen besagen, daß „Schüler" der Pariser Ecole des Beaux-Arts, die bislang als die beste und vornehmste der Welt angesehen ward, „der Architektur" den Fehdehandschuh hingeworfen haben, da „alle Architekturen auf falschen Prinzipien beruhten und demnach auch die antike Architektur ein Irrtum sei!" Sie fordern die vollständige Umgestaltung des Lehrprogramms sämtlicher baukünstlerischen Schulen. Aus dem Berichte über die moderne Architektur in Oesterreich hinwieder ersehen wir, daß in Wien die durch Professor Wagner begründete und nach ihm benannte moderne Schule erruptiv, ja sogar revolutionär aufgetreten ist. Und in allen diesen Berichten aus verschiedenen Ländern müssen wir uns sagen lassen, daß Deutschland in der Neuentwickelung der Dinge den Reigen eröffnet habe. Viele Deutsche glaubten das bisher nicht, weil hier alle Wandlungen sich ganz in der Stille vollzogen hatten. Und viele, vor allem unsere Fachgenossen in anderen Ländern möchten es kaum glauben, daß unsere sämtlichen Bahnbrecher Zöglinge unserer staatlichen Schulen und daß diese insgesamt sich wohlbewußt sind, wie sehr ihr eingehendes Studium der Antike sowohl als des Mittelalters und der Renaissance für sie die Grundlage bildete zu neuartigem Schaffen und zwar zu einem solchen, das sie noch lange nicht als abgeschlossen ansehen, das sie um deswillen als durchaus entwickelungsfähig erachten müssen, weil sie Irrgänge zu vermeiden wußten. Auch unsere Schulen mögen nicht ganz frei sein von Altherkömmlichem, das recht wenig in unsere heutige Zeit paßt. Aber wir dürfen hoffen, daß allmählich auch darin Wandel eintreten wird, wie schon so vieles, das der freien künstlerischen Entwickelung der jugendlichen Architekten, ebenso

Développement de l'architecture en Allemagne.

C'est en paroles lumineuses que le professeur Cornelius Gurlitt dans son étude „Buts de l'architecture dans le nouveau siècle" développe en traits généraux le mouvement qui se produisit pendant le siècle passé dans le domaine de l'architecture particulièrement en Allemagne et les résultats qu'on peut en général attendre pour le nouveau siècle, des combats qui ont eu lieu. Les considérations sur les tendances analogues aux nôtres et qu'on peut également constater en Angleterre, en Autriche et en France nous apprennent que dans le premier de ces pays il manque absolument une organisation de l'état pour l'enseignement de l'architecture et quels sont les moyens qu'on veut employer pour remédier à cet état de choses, quoiqu'il y ait là aussi nombre d'architectes qui ont horreur de tout style.

Les renseignements qui nous viennent de France par contre, nous apprennent que certains élèves de l'Ecole des Beaux-arts de Paris, qui était considérée jusqu'à présent comme la meilleure et la plus distinguée du monde, ont jeté le défi à l'architecture, parce que „toutes les architectures reposent sur des principes faux, par conséquent l'architecture antique aussi serait une erreur". Ils demandent le remaniement complet du programme d'enseignement de toutes les écoles artistiques d'architecture.

Nous apprenons par contre par les rapports sur l'architecture moderne en Autriche qu'à Vienne, l'école moderne fondée par le professeur Wagner et qui porte son nom a eu un effet irruptif et même révolutionnaire. Et d'après ces renseignements de différents pays, nous devons apprendre que c'est l'Allemagne qui a ouvert la marche dans cette joute de la modernité artistique.

Il y a beaucoup d'Allemands qui n'y croyaient pas encore, parce que la transformation s'est opérée chez nous en toute tranquillité. Il y en a beaucoup et surtout parmi nos collègues de l'étranger qui pourront à peine croire que tous nos innovateurs sont des élèves de nos écoles du gouvernement et que tous savent parfaitement combien leur profonde étude de l'antique, du Moyen-âge et de la Renaissance leur a facilité la création d'œuvres nouvelles, ils savent aussi que la nouvelle tendance est absolument susceptible de développement parce qu'ils ont su éviter les errements. Il se peut bien que nos écoles ne soient pas entièrement dépourvues d'anciennes traditions qui ne s'accordent plus avec l'esprit de notre époque, mais nous pouvons espérer que là aussi des temps meilleurs

Development of Architecture in Germany.

In his Essay on the "Aims of Architecture in the new Century", Professor Cornelius Gurlitt has given a clear general account of the development of architecture in Germany during the last century, and has foreshadowed the approaching struggle of the various schools which will be a probable consequence of that development during the present century. When we contemplate the same period in England, Austria and France we come to the conclusion that in England at all events state organisation for architectural training has not been successful, although it must be owned that every effort has been made to cover this deficiency. We find however architects in England who abominate any given style. From France we see that the scholars of the Paris Ecole des Beaux-Arts, long looked upon as the best and most distinguished of schools, have thrown down the gauntlet to architecture with the cry, "All architecture rests on false principles, therefore antique architecture is also faulty." These scholars demand the thorough reorganisation of the curriculum of every architectural school. From the accounts of this development in Austria we see that the school founded in Vienna by Professor Wagner and named after him has declared itself at once "eruptive" in fact "revolutionary." But from all these different reports from various lands we can gather that it was in Germany that all these movements originated, that Germany was the pioneer. Up to this time many Germans have not believed this, as the changes have all been made silently. Many others too, particularly our foreign fellow-workers can scarcely believe that these pioneers have all of them been students at our state schools; that their reverent and thorough study of the antique as well as of medieval and Renaissance architecture has laid for them a foundation on which their own new creations may rest, and from which still more and still greater works may develop themselves; and this because their firm faith will always prevent them from being led into the wrong road, and from following false lights.

fehr in ihrem Studium als im fpäteren Wirken hinderlich war, dem Anfturme der zu einem „Verbande" vereinten deutfchen Architekten- und Ingenieurvereine hat weichen müffen. Eine neue Architekturrichtung auf der Schule zu lehren, fcheint uns folange ein Irrweg, bis es fich um eine ausgebildete, durch Erfolg als nützlich bewiefene Lehre handelt; man würde zu leicht dem Fehler verfallen, eines einzelnen Lehre zu einem Dogma zu erheben. Die Erfolge, die wir erzielt haben, beruhen alle auf felbftändigem Vorgehen der einzelnen, das fich wieder auf Erziehung zur Selbftändigkeit gründet, und die, wenn fie nicht zur Dreffur, zur „Abrichtung" führen foll, nur durch reiches Wiffen und Können erreicht werden kann.

Auf unferen Technifchen Hochfchulen, die eine gleiche Verfaffung genießen wie unfere Univerfitäten, denen fie im übrigen gleichgeftellt find, ift es einem jeden „Künftler" möglich als „Privatdozent" fich zu habilitieren, und zeigt fich feine Lehre von Erfolg, fo wird ihm kaum die Berufung als „Profeffor" ausbleiben. Das ift unferes Erachtens das befte Korrektiv gegen Ueberwuchern veralteter Lehren; wenigftens hat fich dies bei allen deutfchen Univerfitäten im Laufe der Jahrhunderte beftens bewährt. In Verbindung damit ift — wie den Profefforen — den angehenden Architekten nicht nur eine, fondern es find ihnen neun deutfche und die Schweizerifche in Zürich, als gleichberechtigend geöffnet. Paßt dem Einzelnen der Vortrag der Dozenten an der einen Schule nicht, fo fucht er fich diejenige, an welcher etwas freiere Lehre herrfcht. Neben dem fteht den angehenden Baukünftler noch eine große Zahl von „Kunftakademien" und (diefen gleichgeftellte) Kunftinftitute offen, auf denen er eine — freilich nur in befchränktem Maße für den Eintritt in den Staatsdienft berechtigende — künftlerifche Ausbildung in der Architektur finden wird.

Diefe Vielgeftaltigkeit des Unterrichtes, die Verbreitung der Schulen über ganz Deutfchland (nur im äußerften Often beftehen noch Lücken) in den verfchiedenften Einzelftaaten, die teilweife fogar befondere Eigenheiten auch in künftlerifcher Richtung fich gewahrt haben, fowie fie eigenartig typifche Denkmäler älterer Baukunft aufweifen, fichern vor Einfeitigkeit, vor dem Unitarismus des Unterrichtes. Und fo fehen wir denn auch Architekten aus Norddeutfchland in Süddeutfchland und füddeutfche im Norden wirken und fich auszeichnen, ohne daß dadurch das künftlerifche Gepräge der einen oder anderen Landfchaft oder Stadt beeinträchtigt werden könnte.

Das ift fogar eine der hauptfächlichften Aufgaben, derer fich die Architekten Deutfchlands befleißigen: den Landfchaften, den Städten ihr künftlerifches Gepräge, „das Städtebild", zu erhalten oder, wo es verftümmelt oder in der Entwickelung gefährdet erfcheint, wieder aufzubeffern und zu fchmücken. In diefer Beziehung hat fich auch der realiftifcht und modernft wirkende deutfche Architekt den vollen Idealismus erhalten, und ift wohl fein größtes Streben, darin feine Künftlerfchaft zu bekunden.

Dabei ift felten eine in ftreng hiftorifcher Treue gefaßte Nachbildung beabfichtigt, dagegen wird höchfter Wert auf charakteriftifche Silhouette und Gefamterfcheinung gelegt.

Befondere Vereine, nicht allein die archäologifchen und Gefchichtsvereine, fondern hauptfächlich die örtlichen Architektenvereine wirken in diefem Sinne anregend fowohl bei den Staats- als den Verwaltungen der Städte, und fie haben fchöne Erfolge erzielt.

Ein einziger, durchaus gemeinfamer Grundzug beherrfcht die gefamte deutfche Architektur in Nord und Süd, in Oft und Weft, in den

viendront peu à peu, de même que déjà, tant d'obstacles qui se dressaient sur le chemin du jeune architecte, tant pendant ses études que pendant sa pratique ont dû céder le pas à l'opposition des sociétés allemandes d'architectes et d'ingénieurs réunies en société centrale. L'enseignement d'une nouvelle doctrine d'architecture dans nos écoles nous paraîtrait une aberration, tant qu'il ne s'agira pas d'un enseignement dont l'utilité aura été confirmée par le succès. On courrait trop facilement le risque d'élever à la hauteur d'un dogme la doctrine d'un seul. Les résultats que nous avons obtenus sont tous dus à l'initiative d'artistes isolés qui doivent leur individualité au genre d'éducation qu'ils ont reçue. Cette individualité pour éviter de dégénérer en originalité forcée, ne peut être que le fruit d'un vaste savoir et d'une grande puissance de création.

Il est loisible à chaque vrai artiste de monter en chaire comme professeur libre (Privatdocent) dans nos écoles polytechniques, qui jouissent de la même organisation que nos universités et qui sont du reste placées sur le même rang. Si son enseignement est couronné de succès, il est presque certain qu'il obtiendra la place d'un professeur définitif. C'est là à notre avis le meilleur correctif contre la prédominance d'un enseignement suranné; ce système a du moins fait ses preuves pendant des siècles dans toutes les universités allemandes. C'est ainsi que les jeunes architectes de même que les professeurs ont à leur disposition non pas une seule, mais neuf écoles polytechniques auxquelles il faut encore ajouter l'école suisse de Zurich placée sur le même pied.

Si l'enseignement des professeurs ne convient pas à l'élève dans telle ou telle de ces écoles il n'a qu'à chercher ailleurs une doctrine plus libre et qui selon ses aspirations; à part cela l'élève architecte a encore à sa disposition un grand nombre d'académies des beaux-arts et d'autres instituts analogues où il peut étudier le côté artistique de l'architecture mais dont les études n'ouvrent pas aussi facilement l'accès aux fonctions publiques.

Cette variété dans l'enseignement, cette profusion d'écoles dans toute l'Allemagne (il n'y a de lacunes que dans les provinces orientales) et dans tous les états d'Allemagne, ayant en partie leurs caractères particuliers et leurs tendances artistiques, les caractères différents que présentent les anciens monuments, tout cela est une garantie contre la monotonie et contre l'esprit unitaire de l'enseignement.

C'est ainsi que nous voyons des architectes de l'Allemagne du nord pratiquer dans le midi et s'y distinguer et vice versa sans que cela nuise au caractère artistique de l'une ou de l'autre contrée ou ville. C'est même un des buts les plus élevés que se soient fixés les architectes d'Allemagne, de conserver aux villes et aux paysages leur caractère distinctif, leur physionomie propre ou là, où cette physionomie a été modifiée, où elle paraît être en danger de disparaître, de la rétablir et de l'embellir.

Dans ce domaine, l'architecte allemand a su à côté de ses dispositions d'esprit éminemment pratiques et modernes conserver l'étincelle idéale et c'est certainement sa plus grande ambition de montrer là sa valeur artistique. À l'intention rare imitation fidèle de styles historiques est prévalante une recherche marquée de silhouette caractéristique de l'ensemble. Certaines associations et non seulement les sociétés d'histoire et d'archéologie, mais surtout les sociétés locales d'architectes rendent dans ce sens de grands services, elles agissent auprès de l'état et des municipalités et ont obtenu de beaux résultats.

It is possible that our schools must plead guilty to the charge of having retained much of the conventional which suits ill with the requirements of the present day, but this fault can be, it is to be hoped, gradually mended. Our young architects in the course of their artistic development have already stormed the citadel of conventionality, as may be seen by the formation of Architects' and Engineers' Unions. To found a new school of architecture on the teaching of the schools seems on the face of it an error; first experience must prove it to be of general utility and beauty, before it can be elevated to the height of a dogma. The successes we have achieved have been the outcome of independent thought founded on such thorough knowledge and power of performance as can only result from careful study and which can never be achieved by "cram" or by mechanical imitation. Our technical High Schools which are in all respects equal in rank to our univerfities appoint any artist who distinguishes himself as univerfity tutor. Is his teaching successful he is appointed professor. This is surely a sufficient corrective to obsolete methods and out-of-date teaching, and it is a plan which has proved itself successful on German universities for nearly a century. The young German architectural student has the choice of nine of these German High Schools, together with one in Zurich; all of equal value. If the teaching on one of these is not free enough for him, he can seek another where the teaching is freer. As well as these institutions, there are numerous Art Academies and Art Institutes at which a young student may qualify himself within certain limits for the state service. These various methods and schools of instruction, the spread of these schools throughout the length and breadth of Germany (only in the extreme east do we find any lack), the fact that many of these have already made themselves a name for certain special studies of which memorials exist in various great towns, all these things protect the teaching from monotony and the German architect from one-sidedness. So we see the works of North German architects in South Germany and vice-versa, and this without any detriment to the artistic appearance of either landscape or city.

It is indeed a noticeable fact that German architects have taken upon their shoulders the beautification and general artistic construction of the streets and places of their cities; and where defects and deficiencies have occurred in the course of years it is a labour of love for our architects to cover the one and improve the other. Even the most realistic and modern of German architects never sacrifices his ideal so far as to forget this; in fact most of them strive to prove their real artistic power in the degree in which they are successful in this respect. Strict historical truth is perhaps seldom intended in these buildings, but great stress is laid on a characteristic silhouette and an effective general appearance.

The archeological and historical unions have of course their word to say in such matters, but they are largely supported by the local

Städten und auf dem Lande: es ist die Lossagung vom Kasernenmäßigen, von allem, was
dem Palazzo ähnelt, von allem Kastenmäßigen,
von unschön gezwungener Symmetrie und un-
endlichen, langweiligen Wiederholungen. Bei
den städtischen Bauten wird ebensowohl malerische
Wirkung in den Vordergrund gestellt und daher
die lange vernachläßigt gebliebene Ausbildung
des Daches gepflegt, und selbst auf Kirchenbauten
dehnt sich das Bestreben zu malerischer Gestaltung aus. Das ist der starke, nur scheinbar
unterdrückt gewesene germanistische Zug, der
wieder zum Durchbruch gekommen ist, der Auf-
gezwungenes nicht duldet!

Und selbst bei den Staatsbauten, wie z. B. den
Gerichtsbauten, selbst bei den Kasernen-Neubauten,
bei Staats- und städtischen Schulen, Kranken-, Waisen-
und Alters-Versorgungshäusern und sogar bei Ge-
fängnissen wird eine malerische Wirkung an-
gestrebt. Bei Museenbauten ist z. B. eine
malerisch gruppierte eingebäudige Anlage bei dem
„Bayerischen Nationalmuseum für volkstümliche
Kunst" in München durch Gabriel Seidl und bei
dem „Märkischen Museum" der Stadt Berlin
durch Ludwig Hoffmann durchgeführt worden,
weil die inneren Erfordernisse einer einheitlichen
Architektur der verschiedenen Baukörper wider-
sprechen. Die malerische Wirkung ist bei den
neuen Staatsmuseen in Berlin in drei getrennten,
nur durch offene, bedeckte Wandelgänge verbundenen Einzelbauten erzielt worden.

Ein mächtiger Anstoß zu einer innigeren
Anteilnahme weitester Bevölkerungskreise an
Architekturbestrebungen erwuchs uns durch einige
Stadterweiterungen und die Anlage von Villen-
kolonien in Umgebung der größeren Städte.
Hier war dem Künstler vergönnt, seiner Phantasie
freieren Lauf zu lassen als in dem so vielfach beengten Rahmen der binnenstädtischen Bebauung.

Die „Behaglichkeit", welche ehemals in
der deutschen bürgerlichen Wohnung geherrscht
hatte, war unter einem steifen Formalismus zu
Grunde gegangen. In den neugeschaffenen
Landhausbezirken konnte diese Behaglichkeit
wieder aufleben — man brauchte nur auf die
teilweise in England und mehr noch in Amerika
gepflegte, der Bequemlichkeit der Bewohner an-
gepaßte Raumausbildung und -Verteilung zurück-
zugreifen. — Daß derartige Wohnanlagen auch
einst deutsche waren, sogar die einzig ur-
deutschen, — davon hat man sich erst später über-
zeugt. Derartige Belehrungen haben aber auch
wieder eine recht nachhaltige Wirkung ausgeübt,
indem man sich dem Studium des altdeutschen
Bürger- und des Bauernhauses zugewandt
und in den spärlichen, von der sogenannten
„Kultur" des 18. und 19. Jahrhunderts nicht bis zur
Unkenntlichkeit verstümmelten, verunstalteten
oder verwischten Ueberresten, herrlichste Spuren
einer ehemals das gesamte Volk beherrschenden
Kunstrichtung wiederentdeckt hat, auf deren
Wiedererweckung einige Meister neuerer Richtung
(vielleicht unbewußt?) ihre Lehren aufbauen.
Vielfach läßt diese altdeutsche „Volkskunst" sich
nur aus den in jenen vom großen Verkehr ab-
geschiedenen Gegenden stammverwandter nor-
discher Völker (Norwegen, Schweden u. s. w.) er-
haltenen Ueberresten primitiver Kunstleistungen
zu richtiger Wertschätzung ergänzen.

Aber die größten Errungenschaften der Bestrebungen der deutschen Architekten haben wir
darin zu erblicken, daß die Staaten wie auch die
bis dahin im staatlichen Gängelbande geführten
Großstädte sich wieder einer volkstümlichen
Architektur zugewandt haben.

Im Kirchenbau werden bald romanische, bald
gotische Anlagen oder Ausbildungsweisen — je
nach Belieben und Auffassung der Gemeinden
— bevorzugt, und das gilt für alle Bekenntnisse.

Un trait unique et général domine dans
toute l'architecture allemande, que ce soit au
nord ou au sud, à l'est ou à l'ouest, dans les
villes ou à la compagne: c'est le renoncement
au genre caserne, à tout ce qui ressemble soit
au palazzo, soit au caisson, à toute symétrie
forcée, aux répétitions innombrables et ennuyeuses.
Dans les constructions urbaines on recherche avant
tout les ensembles pittoresques et on retourne
aux grandes et belles silhouettes de toits si
longtemps négligées; ce besoin de groupement
pittoresque de l'ensemble s'étend aussi aux édifices
religieux. C'est là le relèvement de l'esprit
d'indépendance germanique, qui a paru quelque
temps étouffé mais qui reprend tous ses droits
et ne souffre aucune contrainte.

On recherche maintenant un emsemble
intéressant pour les édifices publics comme par
exemple pour les palais de justice, même pour
les casernes et pour les écoles, les hôpitaux,
les orphelinats, les asiles de vieillards et jusqu'aux prisons.

Dans les nouvelles constructions de musées
par exemple comme au musée national d'art
populaire à Munich par Gabriel Seidl et au
Musée des Marches de la ville de Berlin par
Ludwig Hoffmann, il a été recherché un groupement pittoresque des différents corps du bâtiment
parce que les exigences de l'aménagement intérieur ne s'accommodaient pas d'une architecture
uniforme pour les différentes parties de l'édifice.
L'effet pittoresque a été obtenu pour les nouveaux musées de l'état à Berlin en reliant par
des passages couverts trois bâtiments séparés.

Une puissante impulsion a été donnée à
l'intérêt général et profond que porte la population aux questions de l'architecture, par quelques
agrandissements de villes et par l'étude de colonies de villas dans les environs des grandes
villes. Ici l'artiste pouvait laisser à son imagination un cours plus libre que cela n'est généralement le cas dans le cadre étroit de l'intérieur des cités.

Le comfortable intime qui autrefois caractéri-
sait le logement de la bourgeoisie allemande
avait fait place au formalisme et à la raideur.
Dans les nouveaux quartiers de villas, cette intimité pouvait reparaître, on n'avait qu'à étudier
l'agrément et le comfort en usage dans les
maisons anglaises et plus encore dans celles
de l'Amérique ou la disposition et l'arrangement
des pièces sont dictés par la commodité des
habitants. Ce n'est que plus tard qu'on s'est
convaincu que de telles dispositions avaient
été allemandes et mêmes les seules en usage en
Allemagne autrefois. Cette expérience a eu un
durable effet, en poussant à l'étude des anciennes
habitations allemandes du bourgeois et du campagnard ainsi que de celles du paysan, on a
découvert d'admirables restes d'un art autrefois
généralement répandu dans le peuple, et cela
en fouillant les maigres débris que nous a
épargnés la soi-disant culture des 18me et 19me
siècles, lorsque ces débris ne sont pas dé-
figurés et rendus méconnaissables. C'est sur
ces vertiges que quelques maîtres de la nouvelle
école basent leurs innovations, peut-être sans
s'en rendre compte eux-mêmes. Souvent, il
n'est possible de se faire une idée exacte de ce
qu'a dû être le vieil art populaire allemand qu'en
faisant des recherches en dehors des chemins
battus, chez les peuples du nord parents des
Germains (en Suède, en Norwège etc.).

Mais le plus grand mérite des efforts des
architectes allemands consiste dans le résultat
obtenu, que les monuments élevés par le gouvernement et par les grandes villes autrefois
menées en lisière par le gouvernement sont
maintenant empreints d'un caractère populaire.
Dans les constructions religieuses on choisit tantôt

architectural unions, by the State and by the
town administrations, all of which encourage and
stimulate the architects and help to bring about
such satisfactory results.

One general feature may be noticed in the
whole of German architecture whether it is from
North, South, East or West, whether it is in
town or country and that is the effort to be
free from the barrack style, from everything
which looks like a "palazzo" or a "box", from
unbeautiful and forced symmetry, and from
tiresome endless monotonous repetitions. For
city buildings the picturesque is also demanded;
the roof so long neglected, has been made to
show its capabilities of beauty and variety, and
even ecclesiastical edifices must not fail in being
picturesque. This impatience of forced conventionality is a strong Germanic feature which
has always existed and which was only partially
suppressed. Government buildings and others,
where as a rule utility was the only consideration,
must now be beautiful as well as useful, and
this applies to barracks, hospitals, orphanages,
almshouses and even prisons. As an example of
museum buildings, we may cite the picturesquely
grouped edifice for the "Bavarian National
Museum for popular Art" in Munich by Gabriel
Seidl, and the "Museum of the Mark Brandenburg" in the city of Berlin by Ludwig Hoffmann;
the requirements of a museum cannot of course
permit of a symmetrical interior architecture.
The new State Museum of Berlin achieves
its picturesque effect by the union of the
three detached buildings by open covered
colonnades.

An immense impetus to architecture generally
was given by the rapid growth of many large
cities, and by the formation in their suburbs
of villa colonies, this has been the work of the
people. Here the architect could let his fancy
wander at its own free will, unhemmed by the
exigencies of the streets of large cities. The
home comfort which formerly existed in German
citizens' houses, had disappeared and was replaced
by stiff comfortless formality; but these new
villas have afforded scope for the realization of
the artist's ideas as to comfort and snugness,
and we find the English and American idea of
a comfortable home in many cases imitated.
That this comfort was originally German, and
was in fact in olden times the chief idea of a
German house many existing examples prove to
us, and these have proved of great value as
teachers to the new generation. These old
citizens' and peasants' homes, many of which
were defaced and altered by the „culture" of
the 18th and 19th centuries, yet retain traces of
an art which was at one time to be found in
every German home, and many features of
which are seen in the works of the most modern
artists, perhaps unconscious imitations. Many
of these houses are found in retired spots in
Germany and in remote parts of Sweden and
Norway countries, which in primitive art have
much in common with old Germany. The
greatest victory has however been won in the
great towns, where architecture has freed itself
from the leading strings of the state, and
flourishes in characteristic popular forms.

Bald ist die streng archaische, bald eine freiere malerische Durchbildung bevorzugt, bald giebt man einer ganz modernen Auffassung Raum, wie z. B. die dekorative Ausbildung in allermodernstem Sinne bei der Kreuzkirche in Dresden durch Schilling & Gräbner durchgeführt worden ist.

Für die Verwaltungsgebäude oberer und niederer Staatsbehörden kommen durchweg nur mehr örtliche Rücksichten in Betracht, die nahe verwandt sind mit den vorgeschilderten, wobei nunmehr ebenfalls Bezugnahme auf die geschichtliche Entwickelung der betr. Städte und das Städtebild im Vordergrund steht.

Die „Architektur des XX. Jahrhunderts", die es sich zur Aufgabe stellt, alle neueren hervorragenden Erscheinungen und Bewegungen zu verfolgen und in Wort und Bild zu schildern, hat im vorigen Jahre eine Reihe von Veröffentlichungen gebracht, die das oben Gesagte unterstützen.

Der Erfolg, den wir mit diesen Veröffentlichungen erzielt haben, sei uns denn ein Sporn, auf dem bisher betretenen Wege weiter zu wandeln:

So beabsichtigen wir, in diesem Jahre denjenigen deutschen Städten, in denen sich ein besonderes Aufblühen der Architektur bemerkbar macht, ausführlichere Sonderbetrachtungen zu widmen.

Den Reigen wird Berlin eröffnen, und hier sollen dann auch die Schöpfungen des jetzigen Stadtbaurats Ludwig Hoffmann (Erbauer des Reichsgerichts in Leipzig) eingehend gewürdigt werden, der es verstanden hat, dem Städtischen Bauwesen frisches, blühendes Leben einzuhauchen. Von seinen Bauten, die übersichtlich in der „Berliner Architekturwelt" *) erscheinen, enthält bereits das vorliegende Heft einen Beitrag.

So soll auch der zweite Band Zeugnis ablegen von dem ernsten, erfolgreichen Wirken der deutschen Architektenschaft.

Die Redaktion.

le style et la disposition des églises romanes ou gothiques selon le goût ou la manière de voir des communautés, et cela pour toutes les confessions. Tantôt on préfère la disposition sévèrement archaïque, tantôt une composition plus libre et plus pittoresque, tantôt même, on emploie les formules les plus modernes pour la décoration, comme par exemple à l'église de la Croix à Dresde restaurée par les architectes Schilling & Gräbner. Pour les bâtiments d'administrations des ressorts plus au moins élevés, on ne s'inspire guère que des conditions locales qui dépendent en grand partie du développement historique et de l'aspect général des villes en question.

L'architecture du XXme Siècle qui s'est donné la mission de suivre et de décrire par le texte et par l'illustration toutes les nouvelles et importantes manifestations de l'art de bâtir a déjà publié l'an passé une série de constructions qui confirment ce que nous venons d'avancer.

Le succès que nous avons obtenu avec ces publications sera pour nous un encouragement à continuer dans la voie que nous nous sommes tracée.

Nous avons l'intention de consacrer cette année des articles spéciaux aux villes allemandes chez lesquelles on peut constater une floraison architecturale particulièrement développée.

C'est avec Berlin que nous commencerons et nous rendrons d'abord hommage aux créations de l'architecte en chef actuel de la ville, Ludwig Hoffmann, l'auteur du tribunal suprême à Leipsic c'est à lui que nous devons le souffle de fraîcheur et de liberté qui a rajeuni l'architecture de l'édilité de la Ville de Berlin.

Le numéro présent contient déjà un exemple de ces constructions qui sommairement se publient dans la „Berliner Architekturwelt" *)

Ainsi notre présent second volume témoignera des aspirations sérieuses et fructueuses du monde des architectes allemands.

La Rédaction.

In ecclesiastical architecture, we see now Romanesque, now Gothic, according to the taste and ideas of the parish, and independent of any confession. Here one may see the most severe archaism, and there a free picturesqueness. The interior decoration of the old Kreuz Kirche in Dresden (Schilling and Gräbner) is strictly modern. For Government buildings of all kinds the local requirements are first considered, and these can be, and are as a rule, made to harmonize with the general appearance of the town and its historical development.

The "Architecture of the XXth Century" has set itself the task of chronicling all new and important works and movements, and to illustrate these by words and pictures. In this work we find all that has been said above exemplified. The success which has hitherto attended our efforts, encourages us to pursue the same path that we have hitherto done. We intend during the coming year to devote special articles to these German towns, in which the development of architecture is specially to be noticed. Berlin will open the series, and the works of the city Baurath Hoffmann (the talented architect of the Reichsgericht in Leipsic) will receive special and deserved attention. This artist may be said to have infused new life and vigour into the city architecture. The present number contains specimens of Hoffmann's buildings which appear more detailed in the "Berliner Architectur Welt" *).

It is to be hoped that this second volume will give evidence of the earnest and successful efforts of German architects.

The Publishers.

Erläuterungstafel für die Grundrisse
Table explicative des plans
Table explaining the ground-plans

№	Deutsch	Français	English
1	Portal	Portail	Portal.
2	Eingang	Entrée	Entrance.
3	Vestibül	Vestibule	Vestibule.
4	Diele, Halle	Hall	Hall.
5	Haupttreppe	Grand escalier	Grand staircase.
6	Nebentreppe	Escalier de service	Staircase.
7	Flur	Corridor	Floor.
8	Vorraum	Hall	Waiting-room.
9	Empfangszimmer	Antichambre, salon	Parlour.
10	Salon	Salon	Drawing-room.
11	Speisezimmer	Salle à manger	Dining-room.
12	Musikzimmer	Salon de musique	Music-room.
13	Rauchzimmer	Fumoir	Smoking-room.
14	Billardzimmer	Salle de Billard	Billiard-room.
15	Wintergarten	Jardin d'hiver	Winter-garden, palm-house.
16	Terrasse	Terrasse	Terrace.
17	Veranda	Véranda	Veranda.
18	Balkon	Balcon	Balcony.
19	Loggia	Loggia	Loggia.
20	Arbeitszimmer	Cabinet de travail	Workroom, study.
21	Bibliothek	Bibliothèque	Library.
22	Herrenzimmer	Chambre de Monsieur	Gentlemen's-room.
23	Damenzimmer	Chambre de Madame	Ladies'-room.
24	Kinderzimmer	Chambre d'enfants	Nursery.
25	Wohnzimmer	Salle de séjour	Sitting-room.
26	Schlafzimmer	Chambre à coucher	Bed-room.
27	Badezimmer	Salle de bains	Bathing-room.
28	Closet	Cabinet d'aisance	Watercloset.
29	Garderobe	Vestiaire	Wardrobe.
30	Ankleidezimmer	Cabinet de toilette	Dressing-room.
31	Fremdenzimmer	Chambre d'amis	Room for guests.
32	Küche	Cuisine	Kitchen.
33	Spülküche	Lavoir	Rinsing-room.
34	Anrichtezimmer	Office	Serving-room.
35	Speisekammer	Garde-manger	Provisions-room (larder).
36	Kammer	Débarras	Room for china.
37	Plättzimmer	Lingerie	Linen-room.
38	Waschküche	Buanderie	Washing-room.
39	Mädchenzimmer	Chambre des domesti-	Servant's-
40	Dienstbote	ques.	room.
41	Kohlenkeller	Dépôt de combustible	Coal-cellar.
42	Keller	Cave à vin	Wine-cellar.
43	Boden	Grenier	Larder.
44	Heizung	Chauffage	Central-heating appa-ratus.
45	Hof	Cour	Court.
46	Wirtschaftshof	Cour de service	Outhouse.
47	Garten	Jardin	Garden.
48	Gewächshaus	Serre	Green-house.
49	Stall	Ecurie	Stable.
50	Wagenremise	Remise	Coach-house.
51	Laden	Magasin	Shop.
52	Geschäftsraum	Comptoir	Office.
53	Lagerräume	Lieu de dépôt	Room of business.
54	Privatkontor	Bureau privé	Private-office.
55	Sprechzimmer	Parloir	Parlour.
56	Aufzug	Elévateur	Lift.
57	Kasse, Kassierer	Caisse	Cash-office.
58	Tresor	Trésor	Treasury.
59	Bureau	Bureau	Office.
60	Lichthof	Cour vitrée	Court with sky-light.
61	Oberlicht	Toiture vitrée	Sky-light.
62	Café	Café	Coffee-house.
63	Restauration	Restaurant	Restaurant.
64	Buffet	Buffet	Buffet.
65	Orchester	Orchestre	Orchestra.
66	Galerie	Galerie	Gallery.
67	Bühne	Théâtre	Theatre.
68	Kegelbahn	Jeu de quilles	Skittle-ground.
69	Maschinenraum	Salle de machines	Machinery.
70	Foyer	Foyer	Foyer.
71	Vorhalle	Vestibule	Vestibule.
72	Erker	Cabinet saillant	Bow.
73	Vorplatz	Esplanade	Landing place.
74	Frühstückzimmer	Salle du petit déjeuner	Breakfast-room.
75	Waschraum	Cabinet de toilette	Wash-room.
76	Lichtschacht	Cour vitrée	Light-shaft.
77	Dachgarten	Toit-terrasse	Dormer-garden.
78	Pförtner	Concierge	Porter.
79	Direktor	Directeur	Director.
80	Bote	Messager	Messenger.
81	Konferenzzimmer	Salle des conférences	Painted chamber.
82	Kanzlei	Chancellerie	Chancery.
83	Registratur	Greffe	Registry.
84	Archiv	Archives	Archives.
85	Aktenraum	Etude	Acts-room.
86	Altan	Plate-forme	Plat-form.
87	Aula	Salle des actes	Assembly-hall.
88	Saal	Salle	Parlour.
89	Lehrerzimmer	Salle de professeurs	Professor-room.
90	Turnhalle	Gymnase	Gymnastic-hall.
91	Durchfahrt, Durch-gang	Passage	Passage.
92	Brunnen	Puits, fontaine	Well.
93	Spielplatz	Terrain des jeux	Play-ground.
94	Windfang	Tambour	Wind-screen.
95	Atelier	Atelier	Work-shop.
96	Laboratorium	Laboratoire	Laboratory.
97	Magazin	Magasin	Magazine.
98	Ausstellungsraum	Salle d'exposition	Exhibition.
99	Vorratsraum	Magasin	Store-room.
100	Vorstand	Direction	Chief.
101	Warteraum	Salle d'attente	Waiting-room.
102	Publikum	Public	Public.
103	Hausmeister	Concierge	Intendant.
104	Sitzungssaal und -zimmer	Salle de réunions	Session-room.
105	Sekretär	Secrétaire	Secretary.
106	Buchhalterei	Tenue des livres	Book-keeping.
107	Expedition	Expédition	Expedition.
108	Schalter	Guichet	Wicket.
109	Klasse	Classe	Classe.
110	Untersuchungsraum	Chambre préventive	Inquiry-room.
111	Dienstzimmer	Local de service	Service-room.
112	Kasino	Casino	Casino.
113	Loge	Loge	Box.
114	Auto- und Farräder-Garage	Garage-automobile	Auto-garage.
115	Requisiten	Accessoires, décors	Requisite.
116	Packraum	Salle de conditionnement	Packing-room.
117	Ausgang	Sortie	Egress.

Zu den Tafeln.

Explication des planches.

Description of Plates.

1 [1901; 1—3]

Für die Civilabtheilungen des Landgerichts I und Amtsgerichts I in Berlin war ein Neubau nöthig geworden, bei deſſen äußerer Geſtaltung auch künſtleriſche Intereſſen berückſichtigt worden ſind, die bisher in Berlin bei Gerichtsgebäuden vernachläſſigt worden waren. (Tafel 1—3). Nachdem ein Entwurf im Miniſterium der öffentlichen Arbeiten aufgeſtellt worden war, wurde die weitere Ausarbeitung den Bauinſpektoren Rudolf Moennich und Otto Schmalz übertragen, die die Façaden und die Haupträume des Innern, beſonders die große Treppenhalle in der Mitte des Vorderbaus, in den Formen des ſüddeutſchen Barockſtils ausbildeten. Die ungünſtige Lage des Bauplatzes, der an der Oſtſeite von der dicht vorüberführenden Stadtbahn, an der Nord- und Weſtſeite von zwei auch nicht ſehr breiten Straßen eingeſchloſſen wird, während die Südſeite an Privathäuſer grenzt, beſtimmte die Architekten, das Hauptgewicht auf die Geſtaltung der Nord- und Weſtſeite zu legen. Die Nordſeite iſt die Hauptfront geworden, die in der Mitte durch ein monumentales Portal und einen maleriſchen Dachaufbau ausgezeichnet und an den Ecken von zwei hohen Thürmen flankirt iſt. Trotz der Anlehnung an hiſtoriſche Stilformen haben ſich die Architekten in der Bildung der Einzelheiten in voller Freiheit bewegt. Beſonders iſt die Ornamentik in durchaus modernem Geiſt behandelt worden. Für die Façaden konnte echtes Material (Sandſtein) nur an den Haupttheilen verwendet werden. Die übrigen Flächen ſind abwechſelnd glatt und rauh verputzt worden. Durch dieſe Abwechslung wurden maleriſche Wirkungen von großem Reiz erzielt, die auch ſchon von den Architekten der Barockzeit erprobt worden ſind. Die Hauptfront iſt 83 Meter, die weſtliche Seitenfront 220 Meter lang. Die Baukoſten werden etwa 6 Millionen Mark betragen.

1 [1901; 1—3]

Une nouvelle construction était devenue indispensable pour les services des tribunaux civils de première instance du district de Berlin et il fut tenu compte à cette occasion de certains intérêts artistiques qui jusqu'à présent avaient été négligés dans la capitale pour ce genre d'édifices. (Planches 1—3).

Après que le ministère des travaux publics eût fait un projet, l'étude définitive en fut confiée aux inspecteurs des travaux Rudolf Moennich et Otto Schmalz, qui traitèrent les façades et les salles principales entre autres la grande cage d'escalier du milieu de l'avant-corps dans les formes baroques caractéristiques pour l'Allemagne du Sud. La situation défavorable de la place qui est bordée à l'est par une ligne de tramway très rapprochée; au nord et à l'ouest par deux rues d'une largeur fort restreinte, tandis que le côté sud est borné par des maisons particulières, détermina les architectes à ne traiter d'une façon monumentale que les façades nord et ouest. La façade nord est devenue la façade principale, elle est flanquée aux angles de deux hautes tours et décorée au centre d'une porte monumentale et d'un décrochement pittoresque du toit; quoique s'inspirant des formes d'un style historique, les architectes ont cependant composé le détail en pleine liberté. L'ornementation en particulier est traitée dans un esprit tout-à-fait moderne. On ne put employer la pierre de taille que pour les parties principales des façades. Les surfaces ont été crépies, le crépissage étant en partie lisse, en partie rugueux. Cette variété dans l'apparence des surfaces produit des effets très heureux qu'ont déjà pratiqués les architectes du XVIIIe siècle.

La façade principale mesure 83 mètres, la façade occidentale 220 mètres. Le coût de l'édifice sera d'à peu près 6 millions de Marcs.

1 [1901; 1—3]

A new building was required for the Civil department of Landgericht I and Amtsgericht I in Berlin. Up to this date there had been very little artistic taste displayed in the buildings appointed for the Law Courts in Berlin, utility having been the only point considered. The new Law Courts were to be not only useful but artistic, and a plan for the same was designed in the office of the Ministry of Public Works. The carrying out of the design was entrusted to the building inspectors, Rudolf Moennich and Otto Schmalz. The south German barock style has been adopted for the facade, the principal rooms of the interior, and especially for the great central hall in the middle of the front building. The unfavourab'e site, hemmed in as it is by the town railway on the East, enclosed on the North and West by two narrow streets, while private houses come close up on the south side, necessitated the principal approaches to be laid on the north and west sides. The north side is the principal front, and is distinguished by a centre portal of noble proportions with a picturesque erection on the roof, flanked at the corners by two high towers. Though keeping in the main to historical forms, the architects have allowed themselves full freedom in the elaboration of the details, the ornament especially being strictly modern. Only the principal parts of the facade are of real sandstone; the other parts are alternately rough and smooth plaster. These effective alternations, of which ancient and modern barock architects have always availed themselves, give a special charm to this style of architecture. The principal front is 83 metres — the west side 220 metres long. The approximate cost of the building is 6 000 000 Marks.

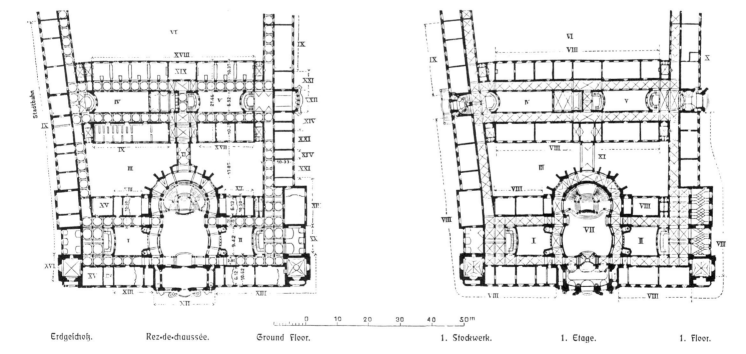

Erdgeſchoß.   Rez-de-chaussée.   Ground Floor.   1. Stockwerk.   1. Etage.   1. Floor.

I—VI. Höfe.	I—VI. Cours.	I—VI. Courtyards.
VII. Haupteintrittshalle.	VII. Grand hall.	VII. Great entrance-hall.
VIII. Kaſſe.	VIII. Caisse.	VIII. Cash-office.
IX. Bureaux und Schreibſtuben.	IX. Bureaux et chambres de greffiers.	IX. Bureaux and offices.
X. Poſtamt.	X. Bureau de poste.	X. Post-office.
XI. Brücke über den Hof.	XI. Passerelle au-dessus de la cour.	XI. Foot - bridge over the courtyard.
XII. Plenariaal.	XII. Grande salle d'audience.	XII. Great Judgment-hall.
XIII. Berathungs- und Sitzungszimmer.	XIII. Salles de conseil et de séance.	XIII. Council rooms.
XIV. Direktor.	XIV. Chambre du directeur.	XIV. Room for the governor of court.
XV. Präſidialrath.	XV. Salle de conseil des présidents.	XV. Council room for the presidents of court.
XVI. Präſident.	XVI. Chambre du président.	XVI. Room for the president of court.
XVII. Bibliothek.	XVII. Bibliothèque.	XVII. Library.
XVIII. Rechtsanwälte.	XVIII. Chambre des avocats.	XVIII. Room for the attorneys.
XIX. Bibliothek der Rechtsanwälte.	XIX. Bibliothèque des avocats.	XIX. Library of the attorneys.
XX. Wartehalle.	XX. Salle d'attente.	XX. Waiting-room.
XXI. Terminzimmer.	XXI. Salles d'audience.	XXI. Judgment - chambers.
XXII. Leſezimmer.	XXII. Cabinet de lecture.	XXII. Reading-room.

Die moderne Richtung in der Architektur, die auf einen völligen Bruch mit der Ueberlieferung oder doch auf den Ausdruck des modernen Lebens in den überlieferten Bauformen dringt, ist in den letzten Jahren auch in Dresden in den Vordergrund getreten. Es ist bezeichnend, daß sich ihr nicht nur die Mehrzahl der jüngeren Architekten, sondern auch einige ältere Meister angeschlossen haben, die mit den Mitteln ihrer reifen Kunst nach neuen, lebendigen Ausdrucksformen suchen. Zu ihnen gehören Schilling und Graebner, die bei dem Bau der Sächsischen Handelsbank (Tafel 4—5) in der Behandlung der Rustika-Façaden neue Wege eingeschlagen haben.

Bei der Verlegung und Bearbeitung der Quadern ist jede Symmetrie vermieden und nur auf eine kräftige malerische Wirkung gesehen worden.

Völlig unabhängig von der Ueberlieferung ist auch die Ornamentik behandelt, die sich in ihrer frischen Ursprünglichkeit dem rauhen Quaderwerk glücklich anpaßt.

2, 3 [1901: 4, 5]

Le goût moderne dans l'architecture, qui tend à rompre ouvertement avec toute tradition, ou tout au moins à imprimer l'expression de la vie moderne aux formes transmises par les styles antérieurs, s'est aussi implanté ces dernières années à Dresde et s'y est placé au premier rang. Il est intéressant de constater, que ce n'est pas seulement la majorité des jeunes architectes qui tend vers l'innovation mais que quelques maîtres d'un âge plus mûr, se soignent à eux et viennent mettre au service de la nouvelle école les ressources de leur expérience. C'est ainsi que Schilling et Graebner dans la construction de la banque commerciale saxonne (Sächsische Handelsbank) (Planche 4—5) ont cherché de nouvelles voies dans la manière dont ils ont traité les bossages de la façade. Dans la pose et la facture des blocs de pierre, toute symétrie a été évitée et il n'a été tenu compte que d'un effet puissant et pittoresque. Dans la décoration sculpturale toute tradition a été complètement abandonnée et l'ornement d'un sentiment primordial et plein de fraîcheur se marie agréablement à la rudesse des bossages.

2, 3 [1901: 4, 5]

The modern tendency in architecture, either to break with all tradition, or to adapt all traditionary forms to the aspects and uses of modern life has been frequently displayed in the architecture of Dresden during the last few years. It is characteristic too, that this striving after modern types is not only noticeable among the younger architects, but even older masters have brought their ripe experience to aid in the development of newer and more living forms of art.

To these belong Schilling and Graebner, who in the „Sächsische Handels Bank" (Plate 4—5) have taken a novel direction in the handling of the Rustic facade. In the erection and working of the square stone all symmetry has been avoided, and a strikingly picturesque effect is the result. The ornament too, is quite independent of all tradition, and with its fresh originality harmonizes well with the rustic masonry.

Unter den holländischen Architekten der Gegenwart, die während des letzten Jahrzehnts die meisten Großstädte des Landes mit einer stattlichen Anzahl eigenartiger, charaktervoller Bauwerke bereichert haben, herrscht bei der Gestaltung der Fassaden eine starke Neigung zum Alterthümlichen. Sie knüpfen mit Vorliebe an die strengen Formen der mittelalterlichen Baukunst an, von der sich nur noch spärliche Denkmäler, im Gegensatz zu den zahlreichen der Renaissance, erhalten haben. Auch in der Wahl des Baumaterials — Backstein mit verhältnißmäßig geringer Verwendung von Sandstein — hängen sie eng mit der Vergangenheit zusammen, so daß durch die Neubauten in die Farbenstimmung der älteren holländischen Bauten kein neuer Ton hineingebracht wird. Das moderne Element tritt nur in der Detaillierung einzelner Formen, der Giebelabschlüsse und Balkonbrüstungen, der Pfeilerkapitäle und Konsolen u. dergl. m. hervor. Ein charakteristisches Beispiel dafür ist die auf unserer Tafel 15 dargestellte Fassade des Bankgebäudes der „Twentsche Bankvereeniging" in Amsterdam von A. L. van Gendt & Söhnen, die mit an der Spitze der modernen Bewegung in der holländischen Architektur stehen. Von künstlerischem Interesse sind auch die ebenfalls in mittelalterlichem Geiste erfundenen, zum Theil höchst phantastischen Bildwerke, die meist nach Modellen des Bildhauers Zyl oder von ihm selbst unmittelbar in Stein ausgeführt sind.

Die Baukosten betrugen 200000 holländ. Gulden.

4 [1901: 15]

Parmi les architectes hollandais contemporains, qui depuis dix ans ont enrichi les villes principales de leur pays de nombreuses constructions particulières pleines de caractère, il règne quant à la composition des façades un goût prononcé pour les styles anciens. Ils s'attachent de préférence aux formes sévères du moyen-âge dont on n'a conservé que de rares monuments, tandis qu'il reste de nombreux édifices datant de l'époque de la Renaissance. Il en est de même pour le choix des matériaux de construction — briques avec un peu de grès — avec les quels ils témoignent de leur goût pour le passé, si bien que leurs nouvelles constructions n'apportent aucune note nouvelle dans l'ensemble des anciennes constructions hollandaises. Ce n'est que dans les détails de certaines formes, des pignons et balustrades de balcon, des chapiteaux à piliers et consoles etc., que l'élément moderne s'affirme. Un exemple caractéristique pour ce que nous venons de dire est la façade de la banque „Twentsche Bankvereeniging" à Amsterdam, représentée sur notre planche 15, et construite par MM. A. L. van Gendt & Fils, ces architectes marchent à la tête du mouvement moderne parmi leurs collègues hollandais. Les sculptures composées également dans l'esprit du Moyen-âge et en partie très fantaisistes, sont aussi d'un grand intérêt, elles ont été en majeure partie exécutées d'après les modèles de M. Zyl, sculpteur, ou directement taillées sur la pierre par lui-même. Les frais de la construction s'élèvent à 200000 Florins hollandais.

4 [1901: 15]

Among the great number of interesting and characteristic buildings with which Dutch architects have enriched most of the large towns of the country during the last decade, one can detect a strong tendency towards antique forms.

They prefer the severe lines of mediaeval architecture of which so few monuments remain to us, and do not care to imitate the Renaissance style of which comparatively numerous examples are to be found.

They transfer their ideas also to the material — mostly brick, seldom sandstone, — so that the modern buildings do not even with respect to colour bring a new tone into the effect of the old Dutch architecture. Only certain details show a modern influence, such as the termination of gables, the cornices, the capitals of pillars etc.

Our plate 15 gives a characteristic example in the façade of the bank building of the „Twentsche Bankvereeniging" in Amsterdam by A. L. van Gendt & Sons, who are reckoned among the leaders of the present movement in Dutch architecture.

The statuary is interesting from an artistic point of view, being designed after the models of the sculptor Zyl, or even hewn in stone by the master him self. Part of the statuary is most fantastic in form, and one can clearly see the influence of the mediaeval spirit.

The cost of building amounted to 200000 Dutch Gulden.

Das von Mervyn Macarthly erbaute Wohnhaus in London, Queen's Gate 167, ist charakteristisch für das Geschick der englischen Architekten, mit dem sie auch bei schmaler Front jedem Miethshause eine individuelle Physiognomie zu geben wissen. Durch den Gegensatz zwischen den rothen Backsteinen der oberen Façadentheile und dem hellen Portlandstein, worin die Loggia und der Erkerbau ausgeführt sind, ist zugleich eine kräftige Farbenwirkung erzielt worden.

Zur Erbauung eines Warenhauses im großen Stile hatte der Großkaufmann Tietz im Jahre 1898 am östlichen Ende der Leipziger Straße in Berlin eine Häusergruppe erworben, die, an der Südseite der Straße gelegen, in enger

5 [1901: 18]

La maison d'habitation Queen's Gate 167 à Londres bâtie par Mervyn Macarthly témoigne de l'habileté des architectes anglais à donner un cachet individuel même à la façade étroite d'un immeuble locatif. Le contraste entre la brique rouge des étages supérieurs et la pierre claire de Portland avec laquelle sont construits la loggia et la tourelle offre un vigoureux effet de couleurs.

6 [1901: 8]

M. Tietz, négociant de Munich, avait acquis en 1898 à l'extrémité orientale de la rue de Leipsic à Berlin un groupe de maisons, pour y faire construire un bazar de grand style. Ces maisons, situées au côté sud de la rue,

5 [1901: 18]

The ingenuity of English architects is characteristically shown in the house of 167 Queen's Gate London. Their special talent of giving to houses with only a small frontage an individual physiognomy is here cleverly displayed. The contrast between the red brick of the upper part of the facade, and the light Portland stone of the loggia and bow windows is pleasing and effective.

6 [1901: 8]

A group of houses, situated at the east end of the Leipziger Strasse in Berlin was bought in 1898 by Mr. Tietz, merchant of Munich. The complex lay on the south side of the street, and was in close connection with some houses with

Verbindung mit einigen Vorderhäufern an der Nordfeite der Kraufenftraße ftand. Nachdem diefe ebenfalls angekauft worden, ergab fich nach der Niederlegung der alten Gebäude, von denen das hauptfächlichfte, das Concerthaus, für Berlin eine hiftorifche Bedeutung hatte, ein umfangreicher Bauplaß, der nicht nur die Anlage eines allen Anforderungen eines hochgefteigerten Verkehrs entfprechenden Warenhaufes, fondern auch eine bedeutfame künftlerifche Ausbildung an zwei Straßenfronten geftattete. Mit der Grundriß-difpofition beauftragte der Bauherr die Firma Lachmann & Zauber, die fpäter auch die Bau-ausführung übernahm, mit der Ausbildung des architektonifchen Theils der Aufgabe den Archi-tekten Bernhard Sehring, der fich durch mehrere Privatbauten, vornehmlich aber durch den Bau des Theaters des Weftens einen Namen gemacht hat. Als technifche Berather ftanden dem Bauherrn die Architekten Cremer & Wolffen-stein zur Seite.

communiquaient avec quelques maisons bordant au nord la rue Krausen.

Par l'achat et la démolition de ces vieux édi-fices, dont le principal, le Concert - Haus (Salle de Concerts), avait eu pour Berlin une importance historique, on avait créé un vaste emplacement qui devait permettre non-seulement la construction d'un grand bazar, répondant aux exigences d'un commerce développé au plus haut degré, mais encore la composition artistique de deux façades.

Le projet fut confié par le propriétaire à Messieurs Lachmann & Zauber, qui par la suite se chargèrent également de la construction de l'édifice, tandis que la partie artistique distingué fut remise a M. Bernhard Sehring, architecte distingué, qui s'était déjà fait un nom par plusieurs constructions particulières, entre autres par celle du „Theater des Westens" (théâtre de l'ouest). Enfin les architectes MM. Cremer & Wolffenstein avaient été choisis comme experts par le propriétaire.

street frontages on the north side of the Krausen-strasse. These houses were also bought, the idea of Mr. Tietz being to build a large retail Warehouse (Bazaar) on a grand scale.

When these houses (one of which, the old Concert-House, had a historical interest for Berlin) were pulled down, it was found that space remained for the construction of a building with a frontage in each street, which would not only satisfy all the demands of utility, but which would be of great architectural beauty.

The ground-plan was designed by Lach-mann and Zauber, the same firm being em-ployed to construct the building itself. The archi-tect was Mr. Bernhard Sehring, a gentleman al-ready well known in his profession as the designer of several private houses, and more especially of the "Theater des Westens". The firm Cremer and Wolffenstein acted as technical experts.

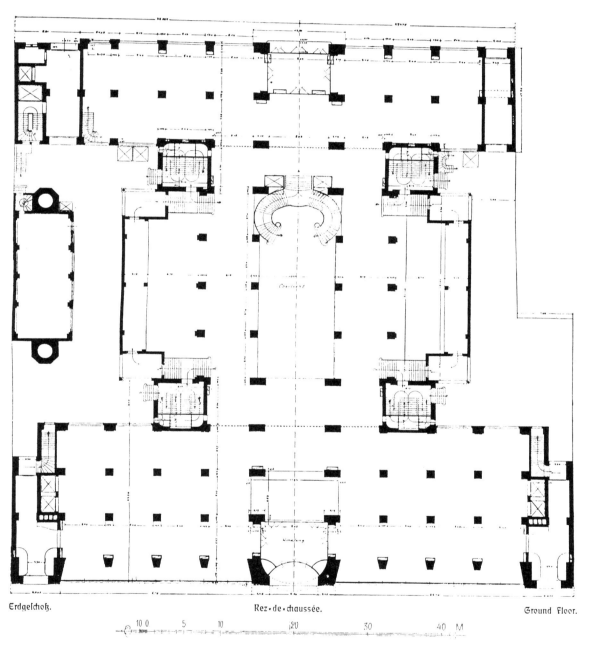

Erdgeschoß.   Rez-de-chaussée.   Ground Floor.

10 0   5   10   20   30   40   M

Bei der Grundrißbildung follte das Haupt-gewicht auf die größtmögliche Ausnußung des Raumes, auf die Anlage heller Verkaufsräume und auf eine gute Lage der Haupt- und Neben-treppen gelegt werden. Es gelang in der That, alle notwendigen Treppen — diefe find dreiarmig angelegt — fo glücklich anzuordnen, daß fie leicht gefunden werden können. Die Haupt-difpofition ift derartig erfolgt, daß an der Leipzigerftraße rechts und links vom Haupt-eingang ein Gebäudetrakt von je 22 Metern Tiefe, an der Kraufenftraße ein folcher von je

les principales exigences dont il fallait tenir compte en dressant les plans étaient l'utilisation absolue de l'espace disponible, la création de magasins très-éclairés et la disposition de l'escalier principal et des escaliers de dégagement. On réussit en effet à ménager tous les escaliers nécessaires — ils ont été disposés à trois rampes — si habilement qu'on les trouve tous sans la moindre difficulté. La disposition générale de l'édifice a été choisie de telle façon que les deux côtés de l'entrée princi-pale à la rue de Leipsic sont flanqués par un

The ground-plan was constructed to fulfil the following conditions:
1. The most economical and expedient use of the allowed space.
2. The erection of light shops.
3. The most suitable position for the princi-pal and secondary staircases.

The principal staircase, divided into 3 flights, is so placed as to be easily accessible to the public.

The details of the building plan are, in short, as follows:

15 Metern Tiefe angeordnet ist. Beide werden durch einen Mitteltrakt von 27 Metern Tiefe verbunden.

Die nothwendigen Treppen, die in den vier Ecken des Mitteltrakts Platz gefunden haben, vermitteln den Verkehr zwischen den fünf Stockwerken des Gebäudes. Dem Hauptverkehr des Publikums soll eine Prachttreppe dienen, die in dem im Mitteltrakt gelegenen Oberlichthofe angeordnet worden ist. Um die Besucher zu veranlassen, alle Theile des Gebäudes zu durchwandern, ist diese Treppe einmal nach dem

système de constructions de 22 m de profondeur chacun et celle qui donne sur la rue Krausen par des ailes de 15 m de profondeur chacune. Les deux ailes communiquent entr'elles par un corps intermédiaire de 27 m de profondeur. Les escaliers nécessaires, qui ont été pratiqués aux quatre coins de l'aile intermédiaire, établissent la communication entre les cinq étages du bâtiment. Un escalier monumental, établi dans la cour vitrée qui se trouve dans l'aile du milieu, sert à la circulation principale du public. Afin d'engager les visiteurs à

In the Leipzigerstrasse, on the right and left side of the chief entrance are two parallel wings of a depth of 22 metres; in the Krausenstrasse is one wing of 15 metres. Both are connected by a centre wing with a depth of 27 metres.

The secondary staircases between the five storeys are placed at the four corners of the centre wing.

For use of the public a grand staircase is constructed in the sky-lighted hall of the centre wing. In order that no part of the building

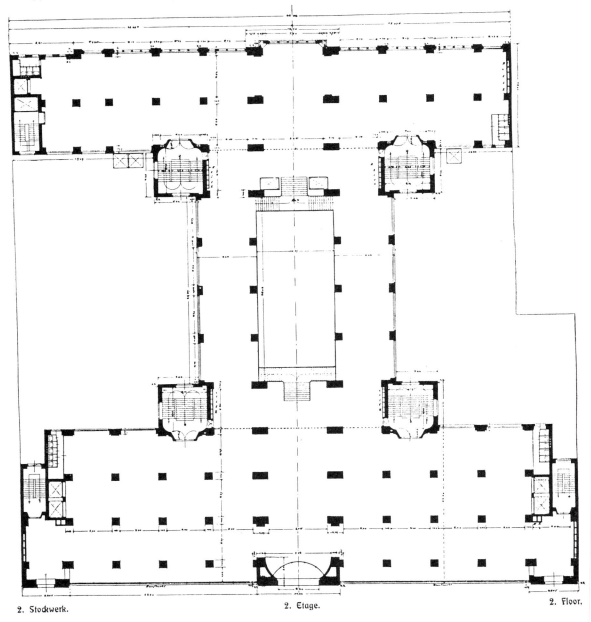

2. Stockwerk.   2. Étage.   2. Floor.

Trakt an der Krausenstraße, einmal nach dem an der Leipzigerstraße gewendet. — Bei der Ausgestaltung des Erdgeschoßgrundrisses ist die Hälfte der Hofflächen als glasüberdeckte Höfe zur Erweiterung des Mitteltraktes links und rechts hinzugezogen worden.

Die Hauptfront an der Leipziger Straße (Tafel 8) zeigt barocke Anklänge. Für die Formengebung der Fassade an der Krausenstraße (Tafel 9) sind mittelalterliche Formen mit derber, fast überkräftiger Ornamentik maßgebend gewesen, zum Theil mit jener Neigung zum Malerisch-Romantischen, der Sehring auch bei den Hinter- und Nebengebäuden des Theaters des Westens nachgegeben hat. — Eine in Deutschland noch nicht zur Anwendung gekommene Neuerung ist die zusammenhängende Anlage der Schaufenster an der Leipziger Straße, die zwischen Eck- und Mittelrisalit eine Breite von je 25½ Metern und durch drei Stockwerke hindurch reichend, eine Höhe von 17½ Metern hat. Diese Anlage ist auf besonderen Wunsch des Bauherrn gewählt worden.

parcourir toutes les pièces du bazar, cet escalier tourne alternativement du côté de la rue de Leipsic et de la rue Krausen. En construisant le rez-de-chaussée on a eu soin d'élargir l'aile centrale en y ajoutant des deux côtés la moitié de la surface de la cour, transformée ainsi en une halle énorme à toiture en verre.

La façade principale sur la rue de Leipsic (planche 8) est de formes baroques. Dans la façade du côté de la rue Krausen (planche 9) dominent les formes du moyen-âge d'une ornementation vigoureuse, presque trop lourde, en partie avec ce penchant au pittoresque, auquel a cédé M. Sehring en décorant les arrière-corps et les annexes du Théâtre de l'Ouest.

Une nouveauté, inconnue jusqu'à présent en Allemagne, sera l'installation des devantures contiguës, donnant sur la rue de Leipsic. Elles auront entre les l'avant corps et d'angle central des deux côtés une largeur de 25,5 m sur 17,5 m de hauteur; prise sur trois étages. Cette disposition est due à un désir spécial du propriétaire.

may escape the eye of the public, this staircase is so constructed that one flight ascends in the direction of the Krausenstrasse wing, and the other to that of the Leipzigerstrasse.

In the construction of the ground floor, half of the courtyard is connected with the middle wing right and left, and roofed with glass.

The principal front on the Leipzigerstrasse (plate 8) is composed in Barock style. The Facade on the Krausenstrasse side (plate 9) is in mediaeval style with solid, one might almost say too solid, ornamental lines; partly in that romantic-picturesque manner which Sehring has used in the back and side buildings of the "Theater des Westens".

A novelty for Germany is the construction of connected shop windows used on the Leipzigerstrasse frontage. They show between corner and centre "risalto" a breadth of 25,5 metres, and a height of 17,5 metres, reaching through three storeys. This was done at the special wish of the owner.

Im Innern find bei den großen Abmessungen nur Werksteinpfeiler als Träger der durchweg massiven, aus Eisen und Stein hergestellten Decke verwendet worden. Die Architekturtheile der Fassade an der Leipziger Straße sind in weißem Mainsandstein, die Fassade an der Krausenstraße ist in schlesischem Sandstein mit eingesetztem Maßwerk aus künstlichem Sandstein ausgeführt worden.

Zur Erzeugung der Kraft für die elektrische Beleuchtung, den Betrieb der Fahrstühle u. s. w. ist im östlichen Hof ein Kesselhaus mit zwei hohen Schornsteinen erbaut worden, in welchem zu ebener Erde vier Borsig'sche Dampfmaschinen von je 400 Pferdekräften und über ihnen vier Röhren-Dampfkessel aufgestellt sind.

Die Baukosten — ohne Grunderwerb — betragen etwa 4½ Millionen Mark.

Vu les grandes dimensions de l'intérieur de l'édifice, on n'a fait usage que de piliers de pierre de taille servant de points d'appui à la voûte massive en toutes ses parties et entièrement construite en fer et en pierre. L'architecture de la façade, de la rue de Leipsic, a été faite en grès blanc du Mein, celle de la rue Krausen en grès de Silésie avec meneaux encastrés de grès artificiel.

Afin de produire la force motrice nécessaire au service des ascenseurs et à la marche des dynamos pour l'éclairage électrique de la maison, on a érigé dans la cour orientale un bâtiment pour les chaudières avec deux hautes cheminées. Au rez-de-chaussée de cette dépendance, on a installé quatre machines à vapeur de Borsig, de 400 chevaux chacune, et au-dessus d'elles quatre générateurs tubulaires. Les frais de construction (prix du terrain non - compris) s'élèvent à environ quatre millions et demi Marks.

Having regard to the enormous size of the building only stone columns are used to support the ceiling which is massively constructed of brick and iron.

The sculptural parts of the façade of the Leipzigerstrasse are made of white sandstone, coming from the Main; on the Krausenstrasse side, Silesian sandstone, with tracery of artificial sandstone, is used.

For generating the power for the electric light, lifts etc. a boiler and engine house is constructed with two high chimneys, and provided with four Borsig steam engines each 400 H. P. above which are four multitubular boilers erected.

The cost of building, exclusive of the price of the site, amounted to 4½ million marks.

7 [1901: 14]

Unter den offiziellen Monumentalbauten der Pariser Weltausstellung kann das an der Westseite des Concordienplatzes nach den Plänen von René Binet erbaute Hauptportal, das den Hauptzugang von der inneren Stadt vermittelte, allein den Anspruch auf die Bedeutung eines von modernem Geiste erfüllten Bauwerks erheben. Ueber einem etwa gleichseitigen Dreieck baut sich auf drei Doppelpfeilern, von denen zwei an den Seiten des 27 Meter breiten Hauptbogens stehen, während der dritte in der Hauptachse liegt, eine mächtige Kuppel auf. Der dritte Doppelpfeiler enthält in der Mitte ein Eingangsthor, das nur zu besonderen festlichen Gelegenheiten geöffnet wurde. Das große Publikum wurde durch die beiden Bogen rechts und links eingelassen, von denen auf jeder Seite 16 strahlenförmig angeordnete Schalter in die Ausstellung führten. Der vordere Bogen war zu einem Triumphbogen ausgebildet worden, der in einem Postament gipfelte, auf dem eine farbig behandelte Kolossalstatue, die Stadt Paris in Gestalt einer modernen, die Gäste begrüßenden Pariserin, ein Werk des Bildhauers Moreau-Vauthier, aufgestellt war. Die Gesammthöhe des Portals bis zum Scheitel der Figur betrug 49 Meter. Von beiden Seiten des Triumphbogens ziehen sich im Viertelkreis niedrige Anbauten, deren Vorderseiten mit Friesen geschmückt sind, zu zwei Obelisken hinüber, die einen wirksamen Abschluß der Baugruppe bilden. Unter dem oberen, von dem Bildhauer Guillot geschaffenen Friese, der in lebensvollen Figuren aus dem modernen Leben den Triumph der Arbeit feierte, zog sich am Unterbau noch ein zweiter Fries von Thierfiguren in orientalischem Stil hin, der nach den Modellen des Bildhauers Jouve von Bigot und Muller in farbig glasirtem Steingut ausgeführt war. Bei der farbigen Gesammtwirkung war das Hauptgewicht auf die Mitwirkung des elektrischen Lichts gelegt worden. Tausende von Glühlampen in blauen, grünen und gelben Glashüllen besetzten nicht nur die Kanten und Hauptlinien der Architektur und die ornamentalen Theile, sondern auch alle Flächen. Die Ausführung ist in der Zeit von sieben Monaten in Eisenkonstruktion mit Holzverkleidung und darauf befestigtem Gips erfolgt. Die Kosten betrugen 570000 Frcs.

7 [1901: 14]

Parmi les monument officiels de l'exposition universelle de Paris on ne peut citer que la porte principale de René Binet, située à l'ouest de la place de la Concorde et formant la communication la plus directe avec le centre de la capitale, comme conçue dans un esprit vraiment moderne.

L'édifice se compose d'une importante coupole portée par trois piliers doubles, disposés sur un plan triangulaire, deux de ces piliers flanquent le grand arc d'entrée qui mesure 27 mètres d'ouverture, tandis que le troisième est placé dans l'axe de la même ouverture. Ce dernier pilier est percé d'une porte d'entrée qui ne s'ouvre qu'à certaines occasions solennelles. Le public pénètre dans l'exposition par les deux arcs de droite et de gauche, lesquels contiennent chacun 16 guichets disposés en éventail.

L'arc de front affectant la forme d'une arche triomphale se termine par un socle sur lequel se dresse une statue colossale et polychrome. Cette figure oeuvre du sculpteur Moreau-Vauthier représente sous les traits d'une femme moderne, la ville de Paris souhaitant la bien venue à ses hôtes. La hauteur de la porte monumentale jusqu'au sommet de la figure est de 49 mètres. Des deux côtés du grand arc d'entrée s'étendent en forme de quart de cercle deux ailes basses qui relient le monument à des obélisques; ces derniers terminent d'une façon harmonieuse l'ensemble de la silhouette. La façade des ailes est ornée de deux frises superposées, celle du haut modelée par le sculpteur Guillot représente en groupes modernes, pleins d'animation le triomphe du travail. Celle du bas décorant le socle est composée d'une suite d'animaux de style assyrien, exécutée en grès céramique polychrome d'après les modèles du statuaire Jouve par Bigot et Muller. Pour l'effet polychrome de l'ensemble, un rôle capital a été attribué à la lumière électrique. Des milliers de lampes à incandescence dans des cloches de verre bleu vert et jaune recouvrent non seulement les arêtes et les lignes principales de l'architecture et les décorations, mais encore toutes les surfaces.

L'exécution de cet édifice construit en fer avec revêtements de bois sur lequel fut appliqué le plâtre dura sept mois.

7 [1901: 14]

Of all the official buildings in connection with the Paris Exhibition, the principal portal built on the west side of the Place de la Concorde after designs by Rene Binet, is the only one which deserves to be considered an important work of modern tendency. Over an equilateral triangle a majestic dome is erected.

It rests on three double pillars, two of which are placed parallel to the side of the chief arch (27 metres broad), while the third pillar is placed in the main axis. The third double pillar contains in the middle a portal which is only opened on certain ceremonial occasions. The general public enter through the two arches right and left, from each of which 16 entrances radiate towards the exhibition.

The front arch is formed as a triumphal arch, on the top of which, placed on a sockel, is a colossal statue with decorative colouring. It represents the town of Paris in the form of a modern Parisienne bidding her guests welcome, and is the work of the sculptor Moreau-Vauthier. The entire height of the portal measured to the top of the figure is 49 metres. Both sides of the triumphal arch are flanked by smaller buildings which range round the quarter of a circle. Their fronts are ornamented with friezes and two obelisks at the two extremities give an effective finish to the whole group of buildings. Below the upper frieze (by the sculptor Guillot) which celebrated in life-like figures, the triumph of work, is a second frieze in oriental style, representing figures of animals and carried out in coloured glazed tiles after the designs of the sculptors Jouve von Bizot and Muller. The decorative colouring of the whole was so managed that the greatest effect was produced by the aid of electric light.

Thousands of electric lights with blue, green, or yellow glasses decorated not only the edges and chief lines of the architecture, but also the surfaces.

Iron girders covered with wood were used in the construction of the building, the wood being covered with plaster of Paris. It took 7 months in erection, and the cost amounted to 570000 francs.

8 [1901: 37]

Bei dem Bau des Apollotheaters in Düsseldorf (Tafel 37—38) war dem Architekten Hermann vom Endt die Aufgabe gestellt worden, ein Gebäude zu errichten, das sowohl den Zwecken eines Variététheaters und eines Cirkus, als auch Konzertaufführungen, öffent-

8 [1901: 37]

L'architecte du théâtre Apollon à Dusseldorf (Pl. 37—38), M. Hermann vom Endt, avait à satisfaire à un programme complexe. Le bâtiment devait se prêter aux représentations de théâtre de variétés et de cirque, il devait aussi servir

8 [1901: 37]

The architect of the Apollo Theatre in Dusseldorf, Hermann vom Endt, was entrusted with the task of designing a building which should serve as a Theatre of Varieties and a Circus, and also as a hall for concerts, meet-

lichen Verſammlungen und Ausſtellungen dienen ſollte, weshalb auch ausreichendeTagesbeleuchtung vorgeſehen werden mußte. Die Lage des Grund-ſtücks an einer Straßenecke geſtattete eine ſehr vorteilhafte und künſtleriſch wirkſame Geſtaltung des Grundriſſes, deren Hauptvorzug in der be-quemenVerbindung allerRäume liegt. Das Theater (cf. Grundriß a, b), das insgeſamt 3500 Perſonen faſſen kann, enthält über dem Parkettraum zwei Ränge. Die lichte Saalhöhe beträgt 20 Meter, die Geſamthöhe des Gebäudes 57 Meter. Die den Saal krönende, in Eiſen konſtruierte Kuppel hat in der Diagonale eine Spannweite von 40 Metern. Die hinten dreieckig abgeſchloſſene Bühne iſt 20 Meter breit und 22 Meter tief. Wenn das Theater in einen Cirkus verwandelt werden ſoll (cf. Grundriß c), wird der Fußboden des Parkett-raumes, der aus einzelnen Tafeln beſteht, entfernt und dadurch die untenliegende Manège mit Waſſer-gräben freigelegt. Die Sitze werden dann von der Manège aus amphitheatraliſch bis zum erſten

à des concerts, à des réunions publiques et à des expositions, ce qui exigeait un éclairage spécial. Le terrain à bâtir situé à l'angle de deux rues permit une disposition très avanta-geuse et artistique du plan, dont le principal mérite consiste en une communication facile de tous les locaux entre eux. Le théâtre (cf. plans a, b), qui peut contenir 3500 personnes possède deux galeries au dessus du parterre.

La hauteur de la salle est de 20 m, la hauteur totale de l'édifice est de 57 m. La coupole de fer couronnant la salle mesure 40 m en diagonale. La scène se terminant en arrière en forme de triangle a 20 m de largeur et 22 m de profondeur. Pour transformer le théâtre en cirque, (cf. plan c) on enlève le plancher du parterre et on découvre le manège entouré de fossés. Les sièges sont alons disposés en amphithéâtre du manège à la première galerie. — La scène devient le point de départ des artistes, elle se

ings, exhibitions etc. For this latter purpose, it was of course necessary to secure good daylight. The position of the site at the corner of a street gave good scope for an advantageous and artistic design of the ground plan, one noticeable merit of which is, the convenient connection between the various apartments. The theatre (cf. ground plans a, b), built to hold 3500 persons contains two circles over the ground floor. The height of the theatreroom is 20 metres, the entire height of the building is 57 metres. The cupola, constructed of iron, surmounting the central theatre measures diagonally 40 metres; the triangular stage is 20 metres broad and 22 deep. When the theatre is to serve as a circus, (cf. ground plan c) the floor of the stalls, consisting of separate blocks, is removed, and a circus, with a large water receptacle is thus laid free. The seats are then ranged in an amphitheatre, tier above tier to the first

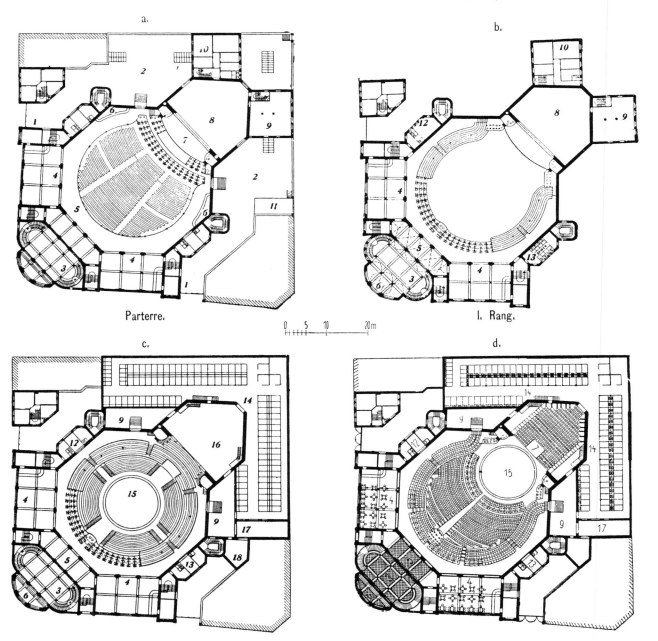

a.

Parterre.

b.

I. Rang.

0   5   10   20m

c.

d.

Range aufſteigend angeordnet. Die Bühne dient als Sattelplatz und Aufſteigeraum für die Künſtler, mit dem die 1½ Meter in den Erdboden vertieft angelegten Stallungen und die darunter gelegenen Ankleideräume unmittel-bar verbunden ſind.

Urſprünglich hatte der Architekt beabſichtigt, Manège und Bühne in ſo enge Verbindung zu bringen, daß beide zu gleicher Zeit für große Ausſtattungsſtücke benutzt werden konnten (cf. Grundriß d). Die Ausführung dieſes Planes

trouve en communication directe avec les écuries et les garderobes qui sont situées à 1½ m de profondeur en sous-sol.

L'architecte voulait dans le principe relier le manège à la scène de façon à ne former qu'une grande salle pour représentations popu-laires (cf. plan d). — Ce plan se heurta cependant à l'opposition de la direction du cirque qui y voyait des difficultés techniques insurmontables.

circle. The stage is then used as a saddle place for the artists; the horse-stalls and dres-sing-rooms lie 1½ metres below the stage, with which they have convenient communication. The original intention of the architect was to unite circus and stage so that the two could be used together for large spectacular entertainments (cf. ground-plan d). The idea however was not carried out, as the circus directors who were con-

scheiterte aber an praktischen Bedenken der um Rat befragten Cirkusdirektoren. Inzwischen hat aber ein englischer Architekt, dem H. vom Endt seinen Plan mitgeteilt, diesen in dem neuerbauten Hippodrom in London zur Ausführung gebracht.

Die Baukosten des Theaters betrugen bei einfacher Ausführung in Putzbau 850000 Mark, wozu noch 350000 Mark für die innere Einrichtung kommen.

9 [1901: 20]

In der Villenkolonie Grunewald bei Berlin, in der die Architekten der Reichshauptstadt ihre Phantasie und ihre Originalität am glänzendsten bewährt haben, findet man neben umfangreichen palastartigen Anlagen, neben Burgen und Schlössern im Stile des Mittelalters und der Renaissance auch eine beträchtliche Anzahl kleiner Bauten, in denen der einfache Landhaus-Charakter desto stärker betont ist. Zu ihnen gehört die Villa Wilhelm Wertheim, ein schlichter Fachwerksbau, den Professor Alfred Messel, der Architekt des großen Waarenhauses Wertheim in der Leipzigerstraße in Berlin, entworfen hat. Der ländliche Charakter ist auch darin zur Erscheinung gekommen, daß die Giebelseiten des Dachgeschosses und ein Theil des Erdgeschosses mit Schindeln bekleidet sind.

Depuis lors cependant, un architecte anglais a communiqué à M. de Endt son même plan exécuté à l'hippodrome nouvellement construit à Londres.

La simple construction du théâtre en maçonnerie crépie a coûté 850000 M. auxquels il faut ajouter 350000 M. pour les aménagements intérieurs.

9 [1901: 20]

Le quartier de villas de Grunewald près Berlin où les architectes de la capitale ont prouvé d'une façon éclatante la richesse de leur imagination et de leur originalité, possède non seulement des résidences qui sont de vrais palais, des châteaux et des manoires de style gothique et renaissance, mais encore une quantité de constructions plus modestes dans lesquelles le caractère champêtre a trouvé son expression la plus parfaite. Nous comptons parmi ces dernières la villa Wilhelm Wertheim, une simple construction en pans de bois, oeuvre du professeur Alfred Messel, l'auteur des grands magasins Wertheim dans la rue de Leipsic à Berlin. Le caractère champêtre de cette villa est aussi accentué par l'emploi de bardeaux recouvrant les pignons du comble ainsi qu'une partie du rez-de-chaussée.

suited could not be convinced of the practicability of the scheme. In the meantime however, Mr. vom Endt's plan has been used by an English architect in the construction of the newly-erected Hippodrome in London.

The cost of building the theatre amounted to 850000 Marks, with an additional 350000 Marks for interior fittings.

9 [1901: 20]

The architects of the German capital have displayed their originality and fancy in the most brilliant manner in the villa colony of the Grunewald, a forest near Berlin. One sees in this charming locality examples of every style, from the modern palatial mansion (many with castellated turrets in medieval style), to the simplest form of country house. To these latter belongs the villa W. Wertheim (Plate 20), a simple framework house, designed by Professor A. Messel, the architect of the well-known bazaar Wertheim in the Leipziger Street, Berlin. The rustic style of the house is emphasized by the use of shingle for the gables of the roof and for a part of the basement.

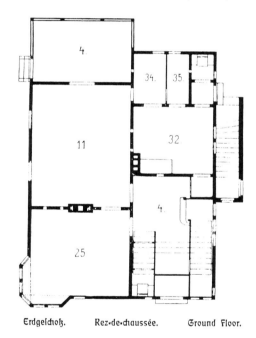

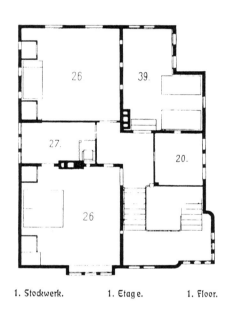

Erdgeschoß.   Rez-de-chaussée.   Ground Floor.

1. Stockwerk.   1. Etage.   1. Floor.

10 [1901: 23]

In der modernen Architektur Stuttgarts herrscht sowohl bei Monumentalbauten wie bei größeren Wohnhausanlagen der Barockstil vor, den auch die Architekten Eisenlohr und Weigle für die Ausbildung der Façaden des von allen Seiten freistehenden Wohnhauses von Simolin (Tafel 22—23) gewählt haben. Auf die im Barockstil

10 [1901: 23]

Le style baroc domine à Stuttgart dans les constructions monumentales aussi bien que dans les édifices privés de quelque importance. C'est aussi ce style qu'ont choisi les architectes Eisenlohr & Weigle pour la villa de Simolin dont les quatre façades sont à découvert. (Planche 22—23).

10 [1901: 23]

The modern architecture of Stuttgart is distinguished by the frequence of the barock style, both in the monumental buildings, and in dwelling houses. This style has been adhered to by the architects Eisenlohr and Weigle for the facade of the house Simolin (plates 22—23), the four sides of which are free and unenclosed.

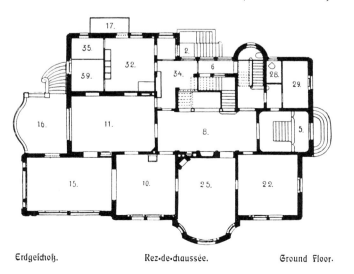

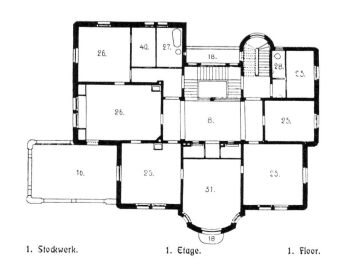

Erdgeschoß.   Rez-de-chaussée.   Ground Floor.

1. Stockwerk.   1. Etage.   1. Floor.

ionit übliche Verwendung reichen plaitiichen Schmucks ift verzichtet worden, damit das ichöne Sanditeinmaterial (aus Hall) zur vollen Geltung kommt. Nur die Straßenfront ift mit einer ipär-lichen Ornamentik bedacht worden. Das Dach, das an der Südieite von einer kleinen Kuppel überragt wird, ift mit Kupfer eingedeckt.

Pour laisser à la belle pierre de Hall tout son effet, on a renoncé ici à l'emploi de la riche décoration sculpturale usuelle dans le style baroc. Il n'y a que la façade principale du côté de la rue qui ait été décorée d'une façon très sobre. Le toit que domine une coupole dans sa partie méridionale est recouvert de cuivre.

The architects have avoided the usual orna-mentation, restricting themselves to simple sculptural effects on the facade; by this means the splendid sandstone from Hall is shown in all its beauty.

The roof, ornamented on the south side by a small cupola, is covered with copper.

11 [1901: 21]

Wie das auf Tafel 15 wiedergegebene Bank-gebäude ift auch das von H. P. Berlage in Amiterdam erbaute Wohn- und Geichäfts-haus (Tafel 21) charakteriitiich für die Be-itrebungen der modernen holländiichen Architekten, die mittelalterlichen Bau- und Zierformen wieder zu beleben, ie aber auch zugleich den modernen Bedürfniien anzupaien und die Einzelheiten der architektoniichen Glieder und der Ornamentik mit modernem Geiite zu durchdringen. Das mittelalter-liche Element zeigt ich beonders in den Giebel-bauten, in der maleriichen Belebung der Façaden durch Eckthürmchen, durch Standbilder unter Baldachinen, durch Koniolen mit figürlichem Schmuck u. . w. Der bildneriiche Schmuck chmiegt ich eng dem Charakter der Architektur an. Gleich den Architekten haben auch die holländiichen Bildhauer, die für die Dekoration von Façaden thätig ind, von der Kunit des Mittelalters den großen Zug angenommen, der den Linien der Architektur folgt. Die Bildwerke an den Façaden diees Haues, deen Fronten in Sanditein aus Oberkirchen und in blauem belgiichen Stein aus-geführt ind, haben B. van Hove und L. Zyl geichaffen. Die Baukoiten betrugen 200000 Mk.

11 [1901: 21]

Ainsi que la banque représentée sur notre planche 6., la maison d'habitation et de commerce bâtie par H. P. Berlage à Amsterdam témoigne de la tendance qu'ont les architectes hollandais à remettre en honneur les formes architecturales et ornementales du Moyen-âge, tout en tenant compte des exigences actuelles et en animant d'un souffle de modernité les dé-tails d'architecture et de décoration. Le style du Moyen-âge s'affirme dans les frontons, dans la disposition pittoresque des façades, dans les tourelles d'angle, dans les statues recou-vertes de baldaquins, dans les consoles ornées de figures etc.

La décoration plastique se lie intimément au caractère de l'architecture. Les sculpteurs hollandais qui travaillent à la décoration de façades ont, ainsi que les architectes, saisi le grand trait de l'art du Moyen-âge, qui se subor-donne aux lignes de l'architecture.

B. van Hove et L. Zyl sont les auteurs des statues ornant les façades de cet édifice. Les façades sont en grès de Oberkirchen et en pierre bleue de Belgique. Les frais de cette construction s'élèvent à 200 000 Mk.

11 [1901: 21]

The dwelling and business house on plate 22, built by H. P. Berlage in Amsterdam, is like the Bank building represented on plate 6 characte-ristic of the tendency of all the modern Dutch architects. One sees medieval architecture adapted to modern requirements, and medieval ornament modified and permeated by modern taste. The medieval element is particularly noticeable in the gables, in the picturesque ornamentation of the facade with corner towers, by statues under baldachins, and by various sculptural effects. The ornamental paintings harmonize in character with the general style of the architecture. The Dutch sculptors too, in the decoration of the facade have been mainly guided by the same medieval spirit as the architects, with the result that a harmonious whole has been achieved. The sculpture of the facade (carried out in sandstone from Oberkirchen, and in blue Belgian stone) is the work of B. van Hove and L. Zyl. The cost is 200 000 Marks.

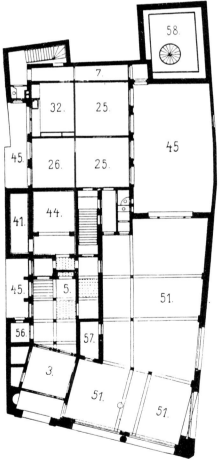

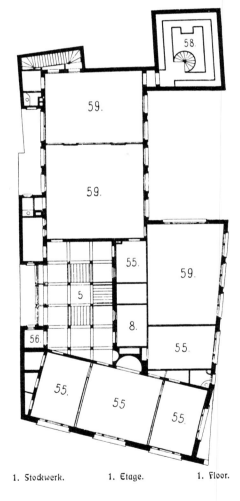

Erdgeichoß.   Rez-de-chanssée.   Ground Floor.   1. Stockwerk.   1. Etage.   1. Floor.

12 [1901; 29]

Der Architekt der Free Library in London, Bishopgate (Tafel 29), Charles Harrison Townsend, hatte sowohl bei der Geitaltung der Façade des zwiichen Häuern eingeklemmten Gebäudes wie bei der für den Leeiaal nötigen Lichtzuführung mit großen Schwierigkeiten zu kämpfen. Es ift ihm aber gelungen, die Façade, die nur in roten Backiteinen mit Verwendung von

12 [1901; 29]

Monsieur Charles Harrison Townsend archi-tecte de la librairie libre de Bishopgate à Londres (Pl. 29) avait de grosses difficultés à surmonter, tant pour la composition de sa façade resserrée entre des maisons, que pour donner à la salle de lecture la lumière nécessaire — il a réussi à créer une façade de briques rouges avec ornements de terra cotta d'un

12 [1901; 29]

Mr. Charles Townsend, the architect of the Free library in Bishopgate, London, has grappled successfully with many difficulties in the composition of his design.

The facade had to be crowded in between two houses, and much care had to be taken to

Terrakotta für die ornamentalen Teile ausgeführt ist, so eindrucksvoll und individuell zu gestalten, daß ihm selbst ein so anspruchsvoller Kritiker wie der jüngst verstorbene Maler Burne-Jones seine Anerkennung, namentlich wegen der feinen koloristischen Wirkung der Façade, ausgesprochen hat. Das Gebäude enthält eine 80 engl. Fuß lange und 40 Fuß breite Halle für Vorlesungen u. s. w., die Raum für 520 Personen gewährt und, durch Oberlicht erhellt, auch zu Gemälde-Ausstellungen benutzt werden kann. Die Bibliothek ist für eine Aufnahme von 30000 Bänden berechnet. Der im ersten Stock gelegene Lesesaal bietet Plätze für 200 Leser. — Die Baukosten betrugen (ohne Grunderwerb) 30000 Pfd. Sterling, wozu noch 3000 Pfd. für die innere Ausstattung kamen.

caractère si individuel, qu'il eut le bonheur de recueillir de la bouche même d'un critique aussi sévère que Burn-Jones, le célèbre peintre dernièrement décédé, des paroles élogieuses pour cette façade et particulièrement pour l'harmonie de ses couleurs. Le monument contient une salle de conférences de 80 pieds anglais de longueur sur 40 de large. Cette salle qui contient 520 personnes est éclairée par le haut et peut aussi servir à des expositions de peinture. La bibliothèque est destinée à recevoir 30000 volumes, la salle de lecture située au premier étage est suffisante pour 200 visiteurs. Le bâtiment coûta sans le terrain 30000 livres sterling, aux quelles il faut ajouter 3000 livres pour les aménagements intérieurs. —

secure sufficient light for the reading-room. The architect has succeeded in giving the facade (of red limestone with terra-cotta for the ornamental details) so individual a character, that even so fastidious a critic as the late Burne-Jones acknowledged the artistic beauty of the effective colouring. The building contains a hall, lighted from the top, 80 feet long and 40 feet broad, capable of accommodating 520 persons; this is used for lectures and if necessary for picture exhibitions. The library is constructed to contain 30000 volumes. The reading-room on the first floor can accommodate 200 readers.

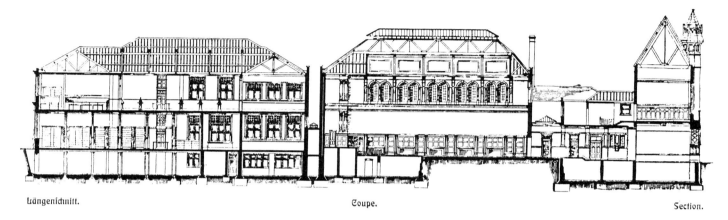

Längenschnitt. Coupe. Section.

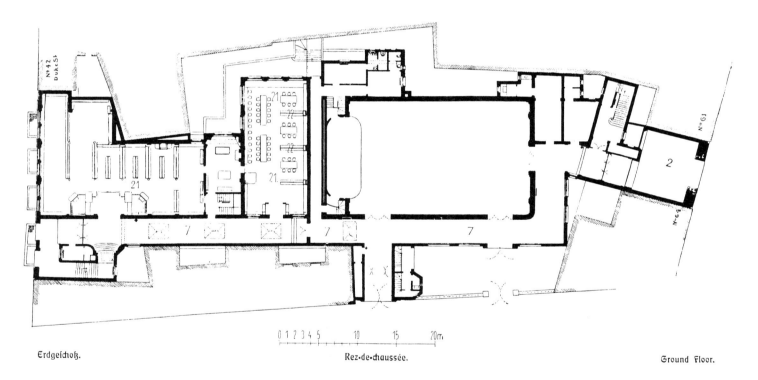

Erdgeschoß. Rez-de-chaussée. Ground Floor.

Bei dem Bau großer Strombrücken waren seit Jahrzehnten die Gesichtspunkte einer zweckmäßigen Eisenkonstruktion so stark in den Vordergrund getreten, daß die Lösung dieser Aufgaben ausschließlich den Ingenieuren überlassen und die künstlerische Seite der architektonischen Gestaltung völlig außer acht gelassen wurde. Erst seit einigen Jahren ist die Notwendigkeit einer künstlerischen Gestaltung der Brücken, wo sie durch die Bedeutung des Stromes oder durch die landschaftliche Umgebung gefordert war, zu allgemeinem Bewußtsein gekommen. Mit der Rheinbrücke bei Bonn ist der Anfang gemacht worden, und ihr sind zwei Rheinbrücken bei Worms gefolgt, die im Jahre 1900 der Benutzung übergeben worden sind. Die eine dient dem Eisenbahnverkehr, die andere als Straßenbrücke für Wagen

Jusqu'à nos jours, on n'avait tenu compte pour la construction des grands ponts en fer que des nécessités constructives. Les ingénieurs exclusivement chargés de ce travail, négligeaient complètement le côté artistique et architectural dans ces constructions. Il n'y a que peu d'années que l'on a compris l'importance de la composition esthétique des ponts, les mettant en rapport avec la majesté du fleuve qu'ils ont à traverser ou avec le caractère du paysage. —

Le premier pas dans cette direction fut fait pour un pont du Rhin à Bonn; vinrent ensuite deux ponts franchissant également le Rhin à Worms, ces derniers furent livrés en 1900 à la circulation. — L'un sert au chemin de fer, l'autre aux voitures et piétons. —

Of late years, in the construction of river bridges everything has been left to the engineer, who has given much attention to utility and strength, but who has entirely lost sight of the demands of architectural beauty. But during the last few years, bridges built over an important river, or at a point where the beauty of the landscape made it a necessity, have shown much more artistic beauty.

The bridge over the Rhine at Bonn was the first of these, and this was followed by two more Rhine bridges at Worms, which were opened for traffic in 1900. One of them is a railway bridge and the other for carriages and footpassengers. The architectural part of these two

und Fußgänger. Der architektonische Teil beider Brücken ist nach den Plänen des Geheimen Oberbaurats Professor K. Hofmann in Darmstadt in den massigen und doch malerisch wirkenden Formen des romanischen Baustils, in Uebereinstimmung mit den mittelalterlichen Bauwerken der Stadt Worms, ausgeführt worden. Die Straßenbrücke (Taf. 42), deren Gesamtansicht die Abbildung oben auf der Tafel wiedergiebt, ist durch zwei monumentale Thorthürme ausgezeichnet worden, deren Einzelformen den alten, zu Anfang des 11. Jahrhunderts erbauten, 1689 zerstörten Stadtthoren von Worms nachgebildet worden sind. Der Turm an der Wormser Seite, den unsere Tafel in großem Maßstabe zeigt, ist 57,5 m hoch und reicher gestaltet als der nur 56,6 m hohe Turm am jenseitigen Ufer, wo nur eine kleine Häusergruppe gelegen ist. Als Baumaterial sind Bruchsteine für das Mauerwerk, Grauwacke für die Flächen und roter Mainsandstein und Pfälzer Sandstein für die Gliederungen verwendet worden. Die Dächer sind mit rheinischem Schiefer gedeckt. Außer den Räumen für die Brückengeld-Erhebung sind in den Thorthürmen vier Beamten-Wohnungen untergebracht.

La partie architecturale de ces ponts a été exécutée d'après les plans du professeur K. Hoffmann, architecte à Darmstadt, dans les formes puissantes et pittoresques du style Roman, s'accordant bien avec les monuments Moyen-âge de la ville de Worms. —

Le pont pour voitures (Pl. 42), dont nous donnons une vue d'ensemble au haut de la planche, est marqué par deux portes monumentales dont les détails rappellent les anciennes portes de la ville construites au commencement du XIme siècle et détruites en 1689. La tour du côté de Worms représentée sur une planche à grande échelle, a 57,5 m de haut et est plus richement décorée que celle de l'autre côté du fleuve où il ne se trouve qu'un petit groupe de maisons; cette dernière a 56,6 m de haut.

Comme matériaux de construction, on a employé le grès rouge du Main et du Palatinat pour les lignes d'architecture et le moellon pour la maçonnerie.

Les toits sont recouverts en ardoise rhénane, à côté des bureaux pour les droits de péage, ces portes contiennent quatre logements d'employés.

bridges is the work of Oberbaurat Professor R. Hofmann in Darmstadt. The architect has adhered mainly to the temperate, yet picturesque Romanesque style, which corresponds well with mediaeval architecture of Worms.

The street-bridge (plate 42), a survey of which may be seen on the above plate, is distinguished by two monumental portals, the architecture of which is an exact copy of the old town gates of Worms, built at the beginning of the 11th century, and destroyed in 1689. The tower on the Worms side (reproduced on a large scale by one of the plates) is 57.5 metres high, and is larger and more important than the tower on the opposite bank which is 56.6 metres high, and the surroundings of which are only a small group of insignificant houses. The building materials are freestone for the brickwork, gray stone for the walls, and red sandstone from the Main and the Palatinate. The roofs are covered with Rhine slate. The gate doors contain rooms for the convenience of the toll-collectors, and four dwellings for the necessary officials.

---

14 [1901: 41]

Aus altem städtischen Besitz und durch Vermächtnisse kunstsinniger Bürger waren die kunstgewerblichen Sammlungen der Stadt Köln, die seit 1887 zu einem Kunstgewerbemuseum vereinigt worden waren, derart angewachsen, daß der Bau eines eigenen Hauses zur Aufnahme der in verschiedenen Gebäuden untergebrachten Gegenstände notwendig geworden war. Das Grundkapital für den Neubau stellte ein Bürger der Stadt, Geheimer Kommerzienrat Otto Andreae, im Betrage von 400000 M. zur Verfügung, unter der Bedingung, daß die Stadt einen geeigneten Bauplatz hergeben und die Mehrkosten tragen würde. Der Bauplatz wurde am Hansaring gefunden, und die Ausführung des Gebäudes ist nach den Plänen des Architekten Franz Brantzky vom Frühjahr 1897 bis Ende des Jahres 1899 erfolgt. Die Baukosten betrugen 665000 M. Nach den Erfahrungen, die für eine zweckmäßige Aufstellung kunstgewerblicher Sammlungen gemacht worden sind, ist der Grundriß so gestaltet worden, daß die Ausstellungssäle in zwei Geschossen um einen noch von Galerien umgebenen Lichthof gruppirt sind. Dem baulichen Charakter Kölns entsprechend ist die Architektur des Aeußeren in den Formen der Spätgotik gehalten (Tafel 41). Die Façaden sind in Heilbronner Sandstein unter Verwendung von Tuffstein für die Flächen ausgeführt, und ebenso ist auch das Innere einschließlich der Gewölbe und Treppen in Heilbronner Sandstein hergestellt. Der Lichthof ist mit einer Kuppel aus Eisen und Glas überdeckt. Für alle Einzelheiten hat der Architekt selbst die Entwürfe und Detailzeichnungen geliefert. Die Bildhauerarbeiten haben Rothe & Barutzky und Degner & Albermann ausgeführt.

14 [1901: 41]

Les collections d'art décoratif de la ville de Cologne réunies depuis 1887 en un musée d'art décoratif avaient, grâce à d'anciennes collections municipales et à la générosité de quelques citoyens, atteint de telles proportions que la construction d'un musée central destiné à recevoir les collections disséminées était devenue nécessaire. Un citoyen de Cologne, le conseiller intime Otto Andreae offrit à cet effet une somme de 400000 M. à condition que la ville livrât la place et prît à sa charge ce que le bâtiment coûterait en plus de son don.

La place fut trouvée au Hansaring et le monument élevé du printemps 1897 à la fin de 1899 d'après les plans de l'architecte Frantz Brantzky.

Le coût total est de 740000 M. Tenant compte des expériences faites pour une exposition rationnelle d'objets d'art industriel, le plan a été combiné de telle sorte que les salles d'exposition sont groupées en deux étages autour d'une cour carrée entourée de galeries. — Les façades du nouveau musée sont traitées en harmonie avec l'architecture dominante de Cologne, dans l'esprit des formes du gothique tardif (Pl. 41).

Les lignes d'architecture des façades sont exécutées en grès de Heilbronn, les surfaces en tuf. Pour l'intérieur, y compris les voûtes et les escaliers, on a aussi employé le grès de Heilbronn. La cour est recouverte d'une coupole en fer et en verre. L'architecte a livré les projets et détails de toutes les parties de l'ensemble. — La décoration plastique a été exécutée par les sculpteurs Rothe & Barutzky et Degner & Albermann.

14 [1901: 41]

The valuable collection of art-treasures belonging to the town of Cologne has been gradually o enriched by the gifts of art-loving citizens that a Museum was founded in 1887. It consisted of a collection of buildings, which had become however quite intufficient for the purpose, and it was decided to build an Art-Museum worthy of the town. The capital necessary for the undertaking, a sum of 400000 Marks, was offered by a Cologne citizen, Geheimer Kommerzienrat Otto Andreae, on the condition that the town authorities should give a suitable site, and undertake to pay any sum over and above the 400000 Marks which the building might cost. A site was found on the Hansa Ring, and the Museum was built according to the designs of the architect Franz Brantzky, from the spring of 1897 till the end of the year 1899. The entire cost was 740000 Marks.

The ground-plan has been arranged in the manner which experience has shown to be the most suitable for the advantageous exhibition of objects of art; the exhibition rooms are grouped round a skylighted centre containing four galleries. The building contains two storeys.

In order to correspond with the prevailing Style of Cologne architecture, the exterior follows the form of late Gothic (Plate 41).

The facades are of Heilbronn sandstone, and tuff stone (calcareous tufa) is used for the surfaces. The interior, including the vaulted roof and stair-case is too of Heilbronn sandstone. The skylighted centre is roofed with a cupola of glass and iron. The architect himself has provided the plans and drawings for all the details. The sculptural ornament is the work of Rothe and Barutzky, and Degner and Albermann.

---

15 [1901: 43]

Die überwiegende Mehrzahl der von französischen Architekten für die Pariser Weltausstellung von 1900 errichteten Bauten, insbesondere die beiden Kunstpaläste, die auch ferner als Ausstellungsgebäude dienen sollen, haben gezeigt, daß die französische Architektur bei Errichtung von Monumentalbauten an ihrer ruhmvollen Ueberlieferung festhält, namentlich an den Stilen der Spätrenaissance bis zur Zeit Ludwig XV. Was ihr dabei an neuen Baugedanken mangelt, sucht sie durch eine lebendige Gestaltung der Einzelformen und durch einen Reichtum des

15 [1901: 43]

La grande majorité des constructions élevées par des architectes français pour l'exposition universelle de Paris, en particulier les deux palais qui doivent par la suite servir à des expositions, ont prouvé que l'architecture française s'en tient pour les monuments, à ses glorieuses traditions, en particulier aux styles de Louis XIII à Louis XV.

Elle s'efforce de suppléer par l'expression vivante du détail et par la richesse de la sculpture, à ce qui lui manque d'esprit novateur dans l'ensemble. Cette richesse se trouve être

15 [1901: 43]

The greater number of the buildings erected for the international Exhibition of 1900 show that French architects have for the most part remained true to those traditions on which the fame of French architecture has been founded. The style of the late Renaissance up to the time of Louis XV. is noticeable in all, particularly in the two palaces of Art, which are intended for future use as exhibition buildings. The architects strive to compensate for what they want in novelty of ideas by a more spirited composi-

plaſtiſchen Schmuckes zu erſeßen, der in ſcharfem Gegenſaß zu der geſuchten Einfachheit des modernen Stils ſteht. Dieſe Neigungen ſind auch bezeichnend für die äußere Geſtaltung des Hippo-droms an der Place de Clichy in Paris (Taf. 43), der, nach den Plänen der Architekten Cambon, Durey und Galeron erbaut, am 1. Oktober 1900 eröffnet worden iſt. Das Gebäude, das etwa 8000 Zuſchauer faſſen kann, ſoll für ge-wöhnlich für Zirkusvorſtellungen dienen, iſt aber auch als Reitbahn und dergl. m. eingerichtet.

en opposition avec la recherche de simplicité qui caractérise l'architecture moderne.

Ces tendances sont caractéristiques pour l'aspect extérieur de l'hippodrome à Paris (Pl. 43) Cet édifice construit d'après les plans des architectes Cambon, Durey et Galeron a été inauguré le 1. octobre 1900. Cet hippodrome sera généralement utilisé pour des représentations de cirque, il est cependant aussi destiné à servir de manège.

tion of single parts, and by a wealth of sculp-tural ornament; their work thus standing in sharp contrast with the studied simplicity of the modern style. The exterior of the Paris Hippo-drome (plate 43) is an example of this tendency. It is built according to the plans of the architects Cambon, Durey, and Galeron, and was opened October 1. 1900. The building is intended specially for circus performances, but can also be used for a riding school and for similar purposes.

16 [1901: 52]

Die Anlage öffentlicher Bäder beginnt in den modernen Großſtädten dieſelbe Bedeutung zu gewinnen wie im alten römiſchen Reich. Die großartigſte dieſer Anlagen, das am 1. Mai 1901 eröffnete Volksbad in München, erinnert auch in ihrer monumentalen Geſtaltung, in ihrem Umfang und in ihrer inneren Einrichtung an die römiſchen Thermen, die dem Erbauer, dem Profeſſor Karl Hocheder, auch als Vorbild gedient haben. Der größte Teil der Baukoſten iſt durch eine Stiftung von 1500000 M. beſchafft worden, die der Ingenieur Karl Müller der Stadt München zur Verfügung geſtellt hatte. Nachdem am rechten Ufer der Iſar, dicht bei der Ludwigsbrücke, ein geeigneter Bauplaß gefunden worden war, wurde 1897 mit der Ausführung begonnen. Nach ſeiner im Anfang des Jahres 1901 erfolgten Vollendung ſtellt ſich das Volksbad als ein zwar einfacher, aber doch wirkungsvoller Monumentalbau in den Formen des ſüddeutſchen, ſogenannten bürgerlichen Barockſtils dar.

Das Gebäude enthält außer einer Vorhalle und einem das Treppenhaus umfaſſenden Lichthofe drei Baſſinräume, das Schwimmbad für Männer, das Schwimmbad für Frauen und den Bade- und Douche-Raum des römiſch-iriſchen Bades, die dazugehörigen Kabinen zum An- und Auskleiden

16 [1901: 52]

Les bains publics commencent à prendre dans les grandes villes modernes une importance semblable à celle qu'ils avaient autrefois dans l'empire romain.

Le bain populaire de Munich est le plus grandiose de ces établissements, il rappelle dans sa disposition monumentale les thermes romains, dont s'est inspiré du reste le professeur Karl Hocheder l'architecte de ce bain, tant pour l'ampleur du plan que pour les arrangements intérieurs. La plus grande partie des frais de construction a été couverte par la fondation de l'ingénieur Karl Müller de 1 500 000 M. que ce dernier a mis à la disposition de la ville de Munich. Après avoir trouvé un emplacement convenable sur la rive droite de l'Isar on put en 1897 se mettre aux travaux.

L'édifice qui fut terminé au commencement de l'année 1901 est traité dans les formes monumentales du style baroc, tel qu'il fut appliqué dans le sud de l'Allemagne au XVIII. siècle aux constructions d'utilité publique. Le bâtiment contient un vestibule et une cour dans laquelle se trouve l'escalier, en outre trois bassins, celui des hommes, celui des femmes servant tous deux à la natation, puis la salle de bain et de douche du bain romain-irlandais, ainsi que les cabinets de toilette qui

16 [1901: 52]

The institution of public baths begins to oc-cupy in modern cities a position of as much importance as it did in ancient Rome. Perhaps the most magnificent building erected in modern times for this purpose was opened at Munich on the 1th May 1901. This splendid edifice, in its monumental architecture, in its extent and in its equipment is similar to the Roman Thermal Baths, in fact Professor Karl Hocheder took this ancient model for his design.

Herr Karl Müller Engineer placed a sum of 150000 Marks at the disposal of the town to defray the cost of the building. After a suitable site (on the right bank of the Saar, adjoining the Ludwig Bridge) had been decided upon, the building was begun in 1897. In the beginning of 1901 it was completed, and is an imposing building in the south German barock style (Pl. 51—52).

The building contains an entrance hall with staircase lighted from the roof, three halls for baths, the swimming bath for men, that for women, the bath and douche rooms for the Roman-Irish baths, the dressing rooms and 85

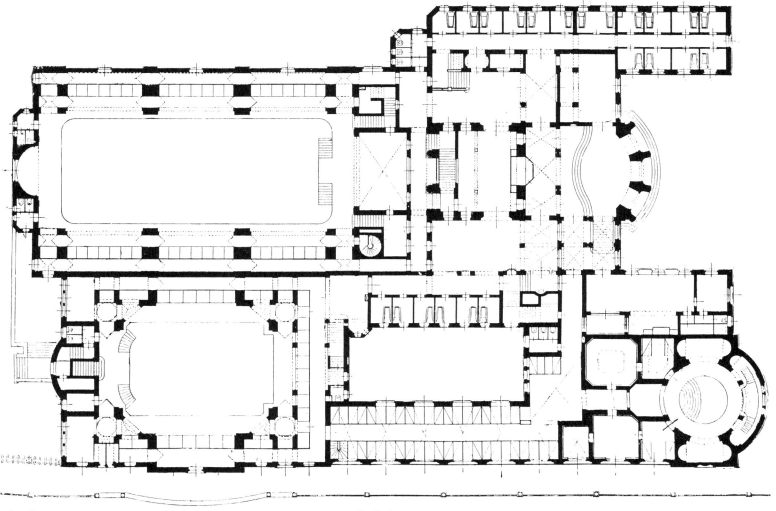

Erdgeſchoß.   Rez-de-chaussée.   Ground floor.

Männerschwimmbad.   Bassin de natation des hommes.   Men's swimming bath.

Vorhalle und Treppenhaus.   Vestibule et cour d'escalier.   Entrance hall and staircase.

und 85 Kabinen für Wannen- und 25 Kabinen für Braufebäder. Ein befonderer Wert ift auf eine bequeme Verbindung fämtlicher Räume durch Korridore oder Gänge gelegt worden.

Das Männerfchwimmbad, das 33 Meter in der Länge und 19 Meter in der Breite mißt, wird durch fieben mächtige, dreigeteilte Bogenfenfter erhellt. Dazu gehören 75 Ankleidekabinen. Die Schwimmhalle für Frauen ift kleiner (19 zu 11 Mtr.) und mit nur 59 Kabinen verfehen, aber fonft von gleicher Anlage wie das Männerbad. Ganz anders geftaltet ift das römifch-irifche Bad, zu dem 27 Kabinen gehören. Es ift ein kreisrunder Saal mit kaffettierter Kuppel, deren Scheitel durch-brochen und von einer Laterne überhöht ift, durch die das Tageslicht gedämpft einfällt.

Unter Verzicht auf reiche Ornamentik hat der Architekt nur nach einer monumentalen Geftaltung der inneren Räume geftrebt, die ganz in lichten, weißen und grauen Tönen gehalten find.

Die Größenverhältniffe des Volksbades über-treffen die aller ähnlichen Anlagen aus neuerer Zeit.

---

en dépendent; il s'y trouve en outre 85 cabines pour bains de baignoire et 25 cabines pour bains de douche.

On a mis un soin tout particulier à établir des communications commodes entre tous les locaux. Sept immenses fenêtres cintrées partagées en 3 parties éclairent le bassin de natation des hommes qui mesure 33 m de long et 19 m de large. 75 cabinets de toilette y sont adjoints. La piscine des dames est plus petite: 19 m sur 11 m et ne possède que 59 cabines, à part cela, elle est disposée comme celle des hommes. — Le bain romain-irlandais auquel sont annexées 27 cabines est disposé d'une façon toute diffé-rente, il est construit sur un plan rond recouvert d'une coupole à cassettes percée au sommet d'une lanterne élevée qui répand dans la salle une lumière voilée.

L'architecte a renoncé à une riche décoration pour ne rechercher qu'un effet monumental des salles qui sout traitées en tons clairs, blancs et gris.

Les dimensions de ce bain dépassent celles des établissements analogues construits ces der-nières années.

---

separate cabins for ordinary baths, with 25 cabins for shower baths. Much thought has been ex-pended to make a convenient connection between the whole of the rooms by means of corridors.

The men's swimming bath is 33 meters long 19 meters wide and is lighted by 7 large triplet windows. To this belong 75 dressing rooms.

The swimming bath for the women is smaller (19 meters by 11 meters) and has 59 dressing rooms. The equipment and fittings are the same as the men's bath.

The Roman-irish bath contains 27 cabins. It is a circular hall, with a cupola surmounted by a glass lantern through which the softened daylight enters.

The architect has only sought to attain solid simplicity in the interior arrangements, and has avoided every kind of ornament. The colouring is throughout light, either white or grey. In ex-tent and importance these baths are superior to any other modern establishment.

---

17 [1901: 44]

Aus den in neuefter Zeit mit großem Eifer gepflegten Beftrebungen der holländifchen Architekten, die heimatlichen Stilformen des 14. und 15. Jahrhunderts auf Gebäude für moderne Zwecke zu übertragen, ift auch die Façade des Bankhaufes Heerengracht 579—599 in Amsterdam erwachfen, das Eduard Cuypers in der Zeit vom Juni 1895 bis Juni 1897 erbaut hat, ohne daß der Gefchäftsbetrieb während des Baus unter-brochen wurde (Tafel 44). Der für diefe Richtung befonders bezeichnende Giebelaufbau ift maffiv in Oberkirchener Sandftein ausgeführt worden; die übrigen Façadenteile wurden mit demfelben Material verblendet. Mit welcher Freiheit die gotifchen Zierformen im modernen Geifte behandelt worden find, zeigt vornehmlich die ornamentale Ausbildung des Treppenhaufes. — Die Baukoften betrugen 350 000 Gulden.

---

17 [1901: 44]

La façade de la banque Heerengracht 579 à 599 à Amsterdam construite de Juin 1895 à Juin 1897 par Eduard Cuypers sans que les affaires de banque aient été interrompes pendant la construction, témoigne du souci qu'ont les architectes hollandais contemporains s'adapter les formes de l'architecture nationale des XIV et XV siècles aux exigences modernes — (Pl. 44). Le fronton qui caractérise particulièrement cette tendance est construit en grès de Oberkirchen; les autres parties de la façade seront revêtues de la même pierre.

La décoration de l'escalier montre surtout avec quelle liberté les motifs gothiques ont été traités pour obtenir un effet des plus modernes.

---

17 [1901: 44]

The Dutch architects have lately made great efforts to preserve the ancient style of the 14th and 15th centuries, at the same time cleverly modifying it to suit the requirements of modern life.

The facade of the bank house Heerengracht 579—599 Amsterdam is an example of this. It was built from June 1895 to June 1897 by Edward Cuypers, without disturbing the conduct of the business (Plate 44). The additional building of the roof is carried out in solid Oberkirchen sandstone and is a good example of the style above mentioned. The same material is used for the other parts of the facade. The Gothic ornamental style has been treated with much freedom and with good effect in the decoration of the staircase. The cost of building was 350000 gulden.

---

18 [1901: 54]

Das im Herbft 1898 vollendete Warenhaus Wertheim in Berlin, deffen Erbauer Alfred Meffel darin einen klaffifchen Typus des modernen Kaufhaufes gefchaffen hat, der zum Ausgangspunkt einer großen Bewegung auf diefem wichtigen Gebiete des architektonifchen Schaffens unferer Zeit geworden ift, hat während des Jahres 1900 eine beträchtliche Erweiterung erfahren. Die Façade an der Leipzigerftraße ift um ein Drittteil, bis zur Breite von 100 Metern, ausgedehnt worden, und zugleich wurde der Bau bis zur Voßftraße durchgeführt, fodaß er jetzt eine Grundfläche von 7800 Quadratmetern be-deckt. An der Leipzigerftraße wurde das Pfeiler-fyftem des älteren Baues mit feinen weiten Schaufenfterflächen beibehalten. An der Voß-ftraße, die den Charakter eines vornehmen, von palaftartigen Wohnhäufern eingefaßten Verkehrs-weges trägt, mußte dagegen auf die Anlage von Schaufenftern verzichtet werden, und der Architekt hat fich bei der 50 Meter breiten Façade für eine Steinarchitektur mit horizontalen Stockwerks-teilungen entfchieden, die fpätgotifche Formen in freier Behandlung zeigt (Taf. 54). Die Ge-ftaltung des Dachgefchoffes mit feinen Giebeln ift durch die umgebenden Häufer bedingt worden. Das Baumaterial der Façade ift gelbgrauer Kalk-ftein aus Ober-Dorla in Thüringen.

---

18 [1901: 54]

Le grand magasin Wertheim à Berlin terminé en automne 1898, oeuvre de l'archi-tecte Alfred Messel est un type devenu classique de ce genre d'établissements, il a été le point de départ d'un grand mouvement dans ce domaine si important de l'activité architecturale de notre époque. Cet édifice a été consi-dérablement agrandi en 1900. La façade de la rue de Leipzig a été prolongée d'un tiers, elle mesure maintenant 100 m de front, tandis que la construction s'étendit en profondeur jusqu'à la rue Voss couvrant ainsi une super-ficie totale de 7800 m². Le système de piliers et de larges fenêtres de l'ancienne façade fut maintenu pour la rue de Leipzig; par contre l'architecte renonça aux devantures de magasin pour la façade de la rue Voss, cette dernière étant bordée de maisons de maîtres d'un caractère de palais; il divisa donc la façade de 50 m de longueur en étages superposés en ligues horizontales nettement accentuées. Cette façade en pierre est traitée dans l'esprit du gothique tardif librement inter-prété (Pl. 54). L'arrangement du toit avec ses pignons a été motivé par les maisons avoisinantes. La façade est construite en pierre calcaire jaunâtre de Ober-Dorla en Thuringe.

---

18 [1901: 54]

The bazaar Wertheim, completed in 1898 by Alfred Messel represents a truly classic type of the modern bazaar. In the year 1900 this building was considerably enlarged. The façade on the Leipziger Strasse side is extended by one third to an entire length of 100 metres. The building is carried through to the Voss-Strasse, so that the entire area now measures 7800 square metres. In the Leipziger Strasse, the façade of the new building is like the old one, entirely of glass; but on the Voss-Strasse (a street consisting for the most part of palatial private houses,) this style was not allowed and the architect has constructed a façade 50 metres broad, which corresponds in character with the surrounding architecture. The style is late Gothic with considerable freedom of treatment (Plate 54). The construction of the roof story with its gables was rendered necessary in order to accord with the adjoining houses. The material used is a yellow-grey limestone from upper Doria in Thuringia.

Jn Paris, dem Ausgangspunkte aller Neuerungen auf dem Gebiete der bildenden Künste, hat sich die Architektur allein gegen die moderne Bewegung in der großen Mehrzahl ihrer Vertreter bisher ablehnend verhalten. Jn keinem anderen Lande Europas ist die künstlerische Entwicklung seit den Zeiten der römischen Herrschaft in so engem Zusammenhang geblieben wie in Frankreich, und daraus erklärt sich der konservative Zug, der die Architektur und die ihr dienenden dekorativen Künste durchdringt und sie in der Nachahmung der glänzendsten Epochen der französischen Kunst, der Stile Ludwigs XIV., XV. und XVI. beharren läßt. Ganz und gar fehlt es aber doch nicht an Künstlern, die mit der Ueberlieferung gebrochen und sich namentlich mit Entschiedenheit gegen die unzweckmäßige Ueberladung der modernen Bauten mit plastischem Schmuk gewendet haben. Der selbständigste unter ihnen ist Charles Plumet, der die Reform mit der Umgestaltung des Mobiliars begann, indem er die Schönheit nur in der anmutigen Bewegung der Linien suchte und Ornamente nur da anbrachte, wo sie die Linie beleben oder stärker betonen können. Diese Grundsätze hat er auch, als ihm die Ausführung von städtischen und ländlichen Wohnhäusern anvertraut wurde, auf die Gestaltung der Façaden übertragen. Am umfassendsten hat er sie an dem stattlichen Baue an der Ecke der Avenue du Bois de Boulogne und der Avenue Malakoff bewährt. Der Versuchung, die Ecke nach herkömmlicher Weise durch einen Thurmaufbau zu betonen, ist er aus dem Wege gegangen, indem er sich damit begnügt hat, den letzten der Dachgiebel an der Avenue Malakoff über die benachbarten emporzuziehen und ihm einen Erker vorzulegen (Taf. 56). Um eine Harmonie zwischen beiden Fronten zu erzielen, hat er die Giebel an der Avenue du Bois de Boulogne (Taf. 57) ebenfalls steil gezogen, so daß sich der Uebergang von der einen Façade zur anderen in angemessener Abstufung vollzieht. Die in den Dachgiebeln stark hervortretende Höhentendenz wird durch die zwischen ihnen angeordneten Bogen sehr glücklich ausgeglichen, und in gleicher Absicht ist dem zweiten Geschoß eine offene Galerie vorgelegt worden.

An die Wohnhausgruppe schließt sich an der Avenue Malakoff ein zweistöckiges Nebengebäude an, das die Wirtschaftsräume enthält und mit dem Hauptgebäude durch überdeckte Galerien in Eisenfachwerk und einen gleichfalls nur aus Glas und Eisen -hergestellten Wintergarten darüber verbunden ist.

C'est à Paris, le point de départ de toute innovation dans le domaine des beaux-arts, que seule l'architecture, dans la personne de la plupart de ses représentants, fait opposition aux tendances modernes.

Dans aucun pays d'Europe, comme en France, le développement artistique ne s'est effectué depuis la domination romaine avec autant de conséquence et d'unité. C'est ce qui explique l'esprit conservateur imprégnant l'architecture et les arts décoratifs qui en dépendent et qui les fait persister dans l'imitation des époques les plus brillantes de l'art français, les styles Louis XIV., Louis XV. et Louis XVI.

Jl ne manque cependant pas entièrement d'artistes, qui ayant brisé avec la tradition, protestent hautement contre l'abus des décorations sculpturales dans l'architecture.

Le plus indépendant de ces artistes est Charles Plumet, celui qui commença par la réforme du mobilier en cherchant la beauté dans l'harmonie des lignes et en n'employant l'ornement que là où il pouvait animer la ligne on lui donner un accent plus vif. Jl a également appliqué ces principes à la composition des façades lorsque l'exécution de maisons de ville on de campagne lui fut confiée.

C'est à l'importante construction qu'il eut l'occation d'élever à l'angle de l'avenue du Bois de Boulogne et de l'avenue Malakoff qu'il les appliqua le plus largement.

Jl a évité l'idée banale de planter une tour sur l'angle, en se contentant de développer particulièrement la dernière lucarne sur l'avenue Malakoff, de lui faire dominer les autres et de lui placer une tourelle en avant.

Pour créer une harmonie entre les deux façades il a également surélevé les lucarnes du côté de l'avenue du Bois de Boulogne, de telle sorte que la transition d'une façade à l'autre a lieu d'une façon agréable.

La tendance à l'élévation fortement accentuée dans les lucarnes est mitigée heureusement par les arcs qui les relient l'une à l'autre. C'est dans le même but qu'une galerie ouverte a été placée en avant du second étage.

Une maison à deux étages est annexée sur l'avenue Malakoff au bâtiment principal, elle contient les dépendances et est reliée à la maison de maîtres par une galerie couverte construite en fer sur la quelle se trouve un jardin d'hiver également construit en fer et en verre.

Paris, long the acknowledged centre of all that is new in Art, has yet held back up to the present from every innovation in the form of architecture. In no country of Europe has the continuity of Art from the time of the Roman occupation to the present day been so marked as in France. This explains the conservative nature of French architecture, of her taste and in all those decorative arts which are the handmaidens of architecture. This it is which still makes French artists linger in the most brilliant epoch of French art — the time of Louis XIV., Louis XV. and Louis XVI.

There are, however, artists who have broken with the ancient traditions, and whose work is a protest against the overloading of modern buildings with sculptural ornament. The most independent of these is Charles Plumet. This artist was in the first instance a pioneer in the reform of furniture; in his work he showed the importance of beauty of line, keeping ornament as a subordinate, and only using it to enliven, or to emphasize the lines.

He has carried out this principle in the façades of the houses and villas he has built. The beautiful house at the corner of the Avenue du Bois de Boulogne and the Avenue Malakoff is a good example of his work. He has avoided the temptation of the conventional tower at the corner, and has substituted an original construction of the gables. He has made the last of the gables at the Avenue Malakoff higher than the neighbouring ones and has added a bay (Plate 56). In order to obtain a certain harmony between the two fronts, he has constructed the same steep gable at the Avenue du Bois de Boulogne (Plate 57); the harmonious effect being increased by the gradual diminishing of the height of the gables. Steep gables are apt to give an idea of great height; to obviate any disproportionate effect, the architect has joined them by arcs by which this impression is avoided. For the same reason, the first floor shows an open gallery running round it.

Another two-storied building in the Avenue Malakoff joins the principal house, and is intended for household purposes. It is connected with the principal building by covered galleries of iron frame work, with which a winter garden roofed with iron and glass is also connected.

Dresden, die klassische Stadt des Rokokostils, steht jetzt, neben München, an der Spitze der modernen Bewegung. In keiner Stadt hat freilich die Macht der historischen Ueberlieferung so stark auf die Regungen des jetzigen Künstlergeschlechts gedrückt, das eigene Kräfte in sich spürt und den Drang empfindet, moderne Baugedanken auch in neuen Bauformen zu zeigen. Unter den Dresdener Architekten, die diese Ziele mit größter Energie verfolgen, steht F. R. Voretzsch in erster Reihe. Von seinen beiden Wohnhäusern, die unsere Tafeln 58 und 59 wiedergeben, zeigt das an der Bürgerwiese gelegene in der Komposition der Façade bereits einen völlig modernen Zug, der sich ebenso entschieden auch in dem größten Teile der plastischen Ornamentik offenbart. Nur die Atlanten, die den Erker tragen, erinnern in ihrer stürmischen Bewegung noch an die Zeit des klassischen Dresdener Barock- und Rokokostils. Die Façade ist in Elbsandstein ausgeführt. Die Baukosten betrugen 320 000 M.

Dresde, la ville classique du style Roccoco se trouve actuellement avec Munich à la tête du mouvement moderne. Jl est vrai que dans aucune autre ville la puissance de la tradition historique n'a pesé aussi lourdement sur les aspirations de l'école moderne, qui sent sa propre force et qui veut montrer de nouvelles formes en architecture. Parmi les architectes de Dresde qui poursuivent ce but avec le plus d'énergie, se trouve F. R. Voretzsch en tête. Des deux maisons que représentent nos Planches 58 & 59, celle qui se trouve à la Bürgerwiese nous montre dans la composition de la façade un esprit tout à fait nouveau qui se manifeste egalement dans la plupart des ornements plastiques, il n'y a que les cariatides supportant la lanterne qui rappellent dans leur allure tumultueuse l'architecture dresdoise du XVIIIme siècle.

La façade est construite en grès de l'Elbe. Les frais de cet édifice s'élevèrent à 320 000 M.

Dresden, the classic city of the rococco style, stands with Munich in the front of the modern architectural movement. Perhaps, in no town however, has historical tradition kept so firm and restraining a hand on the fancy of the young architect, filled with inspiration, and aspiring to clothe modern ideas in new forms. Among the Dresden architects there is none who strives so energetically in this new direction as F. R. Voretzsch. Of the two houses represented by our plates 58 and 59 that built on the „Bürgerwiese" shows in the façade and in the sculptural details a thoroughly modern tendency. Only the Atlas pillars on which the bay rests, are somewhat stormy in expression, recalling the old classic Dresden. The façade is of sandstone from the Elbe. The cost was 320 000 Marks.

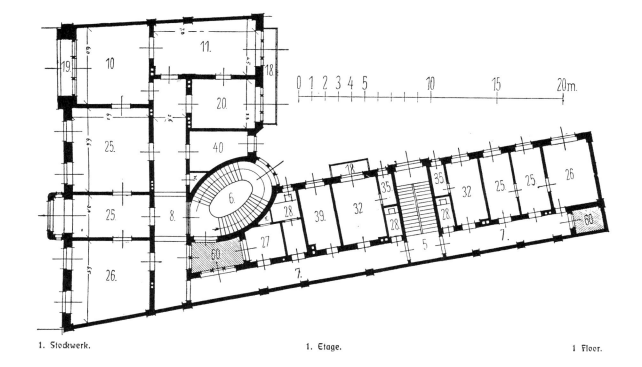

1. Stockwerk.   1. Étage.   1 Floor.

21 [1901; 63]

Im Gegenſaß zu den belgiſchen Architekten, die den modernen Stil vertreten, ſuchen die holländiſchen Architekten gleicher Richtung den modernen Geſchmack und die Anforderungen des modernen Geſchäftsbetriebes und Wohnungs- bedürfniſſes mit den Ueberlieferungen ihrer heimiſchen Baukunſt, insbeſondere der des Mittel- alters zu vereinigen. Einer der erfolgreichſten Vertreter dieſer Beſtrebungen iſt H. P. Berlage, der mit H. Bonda das Haus Raadhuisſtraat 30—34 in Amſterdam von 1897—1898 erbaute, das in ſeinem Erdgeſchoß Geſchäftslokale, in den oberen Stockwerken Wohnungen enthält. Obwohl die Façaden ganz in Sandſtein aus Oberkirchen in Verbindung mit blauem belgiſchen Stein aus- geführt ſind, betrugen die Baukoſten nur 130 000 M.

21 [1901; 63]

Les architectes hollandais en opposition à leurs collègues belges qui cultivent le style moderne, s'appliquent à concilier la tradition des styles historiques du pays avec le goût mo- derne et les exigences des affaires et du pro- gramme des appartements contemporains. Un des représentants les plus autorisés de cette tendance est H. P. Berlage qui a construit de 1897 à 1898 en collaboration avec H. Bonda la maison Raadhuisstraat 30—34 à Amsterdam. Cette maison contient au rez-de-chaussée des locaux de commerce et des logements aux étages supérieurs. Quoique les façades soient entièrement en grès d'Oberkirchen et en pierre bleue de Belgique, les frais ne d'élevèrent qu'à M. 130 000 (Pl. 63).

21 [1901; 63]

The Belgian architects, it may be remarked, are almost universally of the modern school; the Dutch architects, on the contrary, while not leaving out of sight the demands of modern comfort and of modern business, yet endeavour to preserve as much as possible their national architecture, particularly that of the Middle Ages. Perhaps the most successful exponent of this style is H. P. Berlage, who together with H. Bonda has built the house Raadhuisstraat 30—34 in Amsterdam. The ground-floor contains shops, the upper stories are dwellings. Although the facades are of Oberkirchen sandstone and of blue Belgian stone, the cost of building only amounted to 130 000 Marks.

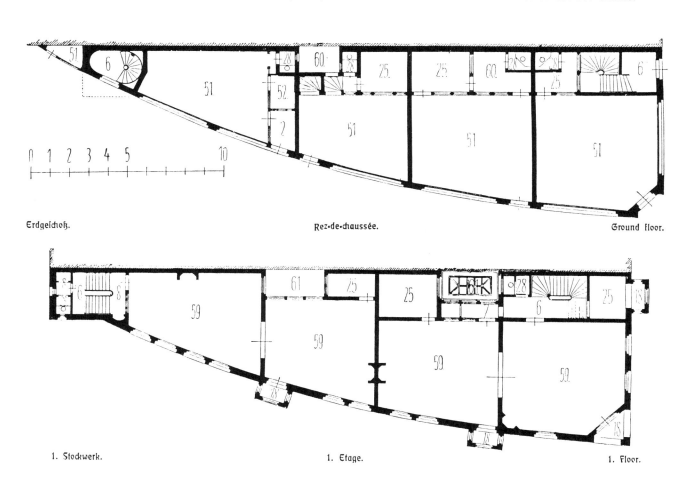

Erdgeſchoß.   Rez-de-chaussée.   Ground floor.

1. Stockwerk.   1. Étage.   1. Floor.

Ein charakteriftifches Beifpiel des modernen Stils in Deutfchland, der hier in ftrenger Folgerichtigkeit durchgeführt worden ift, bietet ein von Gottfried Wehling im Jahre 1899 erbautes Haus in der Schadowftraße in Düffeldorf (Taf. 66). Die Façade ift farbig behandelt. Das Erdgefchoß, das zwei Gefchäftslokale enthält, ift in poliertem Mahagoniholz ausgeführt, die oberen Stockwerke in Puß mit eingelegten irifierenden Plättchen. Der plaftifche Schmuck, der fich am reichften an dem das Dach völlig verdeckenden Halbgefchoß ausbreitet, ift nach den detaillierten Zeichnungen des Architekten und unter deffen Leitung von den Modelleuren Zobus und Eifenmenger ausgeführt worden. — Die Schaufenfter find 6 Meter weit in den Flur hineingeführt, wodurch die Ausftellungsfläche verdoppelt worden ift. Die Thür, die während der Nacht den Flur abfchließt, ift zum Verfenken eingerichtet. — Die Baukoften beliefen fich auf etwa 150 000 M.

22 [1901: 66]

Une maison construite à Dusseldorf par Gottfried Wehling en 1899 dans la rue de Schadow, présente un exemple caractéristique du style moderne en Allemagne, il a été appliqué ici avec toutes ses conséquenses (Pl. 66). La façade est traitée en couleur. Le rez-de-chaussée qui contient deux magasins est exécuté en acajou poli, les étages supérieurs en enduit avec incrustation de carreaux irisés.

La riche décoration plastique qui s'épanouit particulièrement sur le demi-étage qui cache entièrement le toit a été exécutée par les modelleurs Zobus et Eisenmenger d'après les dessins et sous la direction de l'architecte. Les devantures ont été prolongées de 6 mètres dans le vestibule, ce qui double la surface d'étalage. La porte qui ferme le vestibule pendant la nuit s'abaisse en sous-sol. Cette maison a coûté environ M. 150 000.

22 [1901: 66]

The modern style of architecture in Germany is characteristically shown in a house built in 1899 in the Schadowstrasse Düsseldorf (Plate 66) by the architect Gottfried Wehling. The façade is coloured. The ground floor containing two shops, is of polished mahogany and the upper stories of plaster with inlaid ornaments. The rich sculptural ornament is most striking on the half story which quite hides the roof, and is the work of the modellers Zobus and Eisenmenger carried out from the detailed designs of the architect. The shop windows are carried for 6 metres inside the door way by which the space available for exhibiting purposes is doubled. The door, which is so constructed as to shut the premises at night is made to sink into the cellar. The cost of building amounted to 150 000 Marks.

Wie auch in anderen Ländern hat die einzig malerifch wirkende „moderne" Richtung noch lange nicht eine vollftändige Vorherrfchaft erlangt. Viele halten an den blühenden Renaiffanceformen feft, welche feit Duban's Zeiten in der Privatarchitektur des letzten Kaiferreichs immer weiter gebildet und in der neueften Zeit verfeinert und fich feither immer üppiger und fprudelnder entfaltet haben.

Namentlich bei den fogenannten kleinen Hôtels (Einzelwohnhäufer) wohlhabender, kunftfinniger Befitzer und an ruhigen Plätzen gelegenen, für eine geringe erlefene Mieterzahl beftimmten Zinshäufern ift das giltig.

Von erftgenannter Gattung bringen wir hier die Faffade und zwei Grundriffe des prachtvollen von Jules Lavirotte erbauten Haufes: Rue Sédillot 12 zur Anfchauung, das Anfang 1901 vollendet, nur 15 Monat Bauzeit und 152 000 Mark Koften erfordert hat. Nur im Gitterwerk der Fenfter, Balkone und Treppen machen fich wirklich moderne Ausbildungsformen geltend. Splendid wie das Äußere ift auch der innere Ausbau gehalten.

Die Faffade ift ganz in franzöfifchem Schnittftein verfchiedenen Urfprungs, mit fichtbaren weißen burgundifchen und farbigen Kunftziegeln von Bigot (fog. grès flammé) aufgebaut. Aus letzterem

23 [1901: 94]

En France, comme dans d'autres pays, la tendance moderne n'a pas encore remporté une victoire complète. Beaucoup d'architectes continuent la tradition de Duban, en cultivant les formes élégantes de la Renaissance telles qu'elles furent pratiquées sous le second empire tout en les affinant et en les enrichissant et les exagérant comme elle a bien fuit depuis quelquetemps.

Ce style particulièrement admis pour les petits hôtels de particuliers riches et amis des arts situés dans des quarties tranquilles et pour les maisons à loyer destinées à un petit nombre de locataires choisis.

Nous publions ici comme exemple de la première catégorie la façade de la magnifique maison Rue de Sédillot 12 terminée au commencement de l'année 1901 n'a exigé que 15 mois de construction et M. 152 000 de frais.

On ne remarque de formes modernes qu'aux fers forgés des fenêtres, des balcons et des escaliers. L'intérieur est traité d'une façon aussi splendide que l'extérieur. La façade est composée entièrement de pierre de taille française de diverses provenances, avec des grès flammés de Bigot et des briques blanches de Bourgogne. Les balustres et les plaques décoratives du cheneau sont également en céramique Bigot.

La hauteur d'étage comporte de planches à plan-

23 [1901: 94]

In France, as in other lands, the modern style in its only really picturesque form has not yet come to its full development. Many still hold fast to the florid Renaissance forms which, since Duban's time, became more and more popular in the private architecture of the Second Empire and which in the present day has developed itself in a refined form with ever-increasing luxuriance. This may be seen in the so called small hôtels or detached houses built by wealthy art lovers in quiet spots for a few select tenants. Of the first-named style we bring the facade of the beautiful house situated 12 Rue Sédillot of Mr. Jules Lavirotte.

The house Rue Sédillot 12, finished at the beginning of 1901, only occupied 15 months in building and cost 152 000 Marks. The only modern feature is the trellis work of the windows, balconies and stairs. The interior decoration is of the same splendid character as the exterior. The facade is entirely of French carved stone from various parts, with an effective use of white and coloured Art-tiles (so-called grès flammé) of Bigot. This latter material is used too in the balustrades, and for decorative purposes on the roof.

The height of the different stories, measuring between the floor and the strong stone — iron

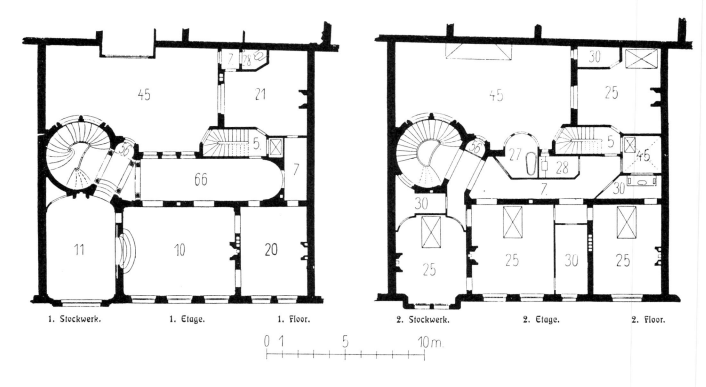

1. Stockwerk.　　1. Etage.　　1. Floor.　　2. Stockwerk.　　2. Etage.　　2. Floor.

0　1　　　5　　　10 m.

Material beitehen auch die Baluitern und Schmuck-
platten namentlich der Dachrinne.

Die Stockwerkshöhen betragen zwiichen Fußboden und den durchweg 30 cm itarken Stein-
Eiiendecken im Keller 2,6, im rd. 0,4 m ein-
geienkten Erdgeichoß 3,0, im I. Stock 3,95, im
II. Stock 3,6 und im Dachgeichoß 2,9 m. Der
Keller enthält nur Vorratsräume und die Räume für
Heizung und die elektriichen Aufzüge. Im Erdgeichoß befindet iich neben der Vor- und Treppenhalle die Küche nebit Abwaichküche und Leinen-
kammer, eine große Plättitube und Dieneritube.
Das Dachgeichoß enthält zwei Zimmer in der Front
und drei Dienerituben.

ches pour la cave 2,6 m, pour le rez-de-chaussée
3 m, pour le Ier étage 3,95 m, pour le IIme 3,6
et pour l'étage du toit 2,9 m. Le rez-de-chaussée
est de 0,4 m en sous-sol et les pontraisons
de fer et pierre sont de 0,30 m d'épaisseur.

La cave ne contient que des locaux pour
provisions, pour le chauffage et pour les lifts
électriques.

Au rez-de-chaussée se trouvent outre le vestibule et l'escalier la cuisine, la buanderie, la lingerie,
une grande chambre à repasser et la chambre des
gens. L'étage du toit comprend outre deux
chambres en façade, trois chambres de domestiques.

ceilings (everywhere 30 centimetres in thickness)
is in the cellars 2.6 m, in the basement (about
0.4 m underground) 3.0 m, in the first floor
3.95 m, in the second floor 3.6 m and in the
roof story 2.9 m. In the cellar are only store
rooms and the apparatus for the heating and
electric light. In the basement, by the side
of the staircase is the kitchen with the adjoining
scullery and linen closet, a large ironing room,
and servants' room. The roof story contains
2 rooms in front, and 3 servants' rooms.

24, 25 [1901: 98, 99]

Bei dem durch die Architekten Schilling &
Graebner in Dresden, Hähnelitraße 13,
während eines Zeitraums von 7 Monaten mit 4 Wohn-
geichoiien für den Preis von 13400 Mark errichteten, landhausartigen Eckgebäude wirkt die
Einfügung moderner Ornament- und Gitterformen
im Rahmen eines nachmittelalterlichen Aufbaues
ebeniowenig auffällig als die aus ⌐ Eiien
beitehenden Säulchen an dem Runderker mit
ihrer unverhüllten ⊥ Eiien-Überdeckung. Das
ericheint alles io künitleriich zwanglos, daß es
kaum „modern" erıcheint.

24, 25 [1901: 98, 99]

L'emploi d'ornements et de fers forgés de
style moderne dans la construction de la
maison d'angle Hähnelstrasse 13 à Dresde ne
lui donne pas un caractère trop excentrique.
Cet édifice, œuvre de M. M. Schilling et Graebner
à Dresde est bâti en 7 mois et se compose
de 4 étages; il a coûté 13400 Mark; il est
tenu en style fin moyen-âge, caractère villa.
Les petites colonnes en fers à ⌐ et les
fers à ⊥ formant lintaux à la tourelle ronde sont
apparents. Tout cela est traité d'une façon si

24, 25 [1901: 98, 99]

A corner building in the villa style has been
in buildig by the architects Schilling and
Graebner at 13 Hähnelstrasse Dresden. The
house contains four stories arranged as
dwellings; the cost of building was 13400
Marks. The style is end-medieval, with
the introduction of modern ornament, but
the pillars of ⌐ iron on the bow with their
undisguised ⊥ iron coverings appear to harmonize so well with the whole, that it can
scarcely be said to have a modern effect.

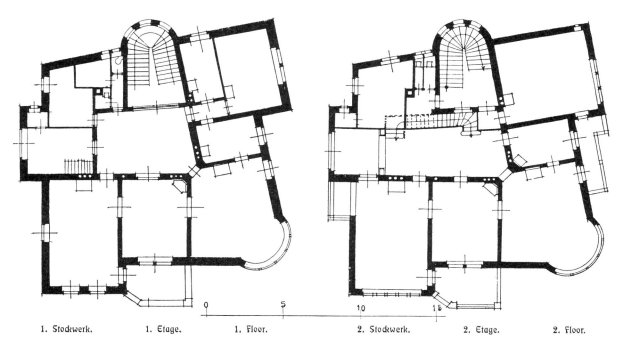

1. Stockwerk.   1. Etage.   1. Floor.   2. Stockwerk.   2. Etage.   2. Floor.

Die eine Hälfte des dritten Obergeichoiies
iit zur Hälfte mittels einer die ganze Höhe einnehmenden Diele des zweiten Obergeichoiies zu
einer einzigen größeren Wohnung zuiammen-
gezogen.

Der Bau iit in Backitein gepußt, mit Sand-
iteinumrahmung ausgeführt.

Namhafte Künitler haben an der Ausführung mitgewirkt; io haben u. A. Bildhauer
Offermann in Dresden den Fries und Profeiior Groß ebenda das Portal hergeitellt; das
bunte Feniter der Diele entitammt dem Atelier von
Urban & Goller in Dresden, das des Erkers
dem von Profeiior Chriitianien in Darmitadt.

libre et si artistique qu'on a à peine l'impression
d'art nouveau.

La moitié du troisième étage est reliée à
celle du second par un hall montant de fond
et forme ainsi un seul grand appartement. La
construction est en briques crépies avec encadrement de pierre. Des artistes de renom ont
pris part à l'exécution; ainsi, le sculpteur
Offermann de Dresde a exécuté la frise, et le
professeur Gross le portail. Le vitrail peint
du hall est l'œuvre de M. M. Urban et Goller
à Dresde, celui de la tourelle est dû au
professeur Christiansen à Darmstadt.

One half of the third floor is connected with
one half of the second floor to form one larger
dwelling. The building is of plastered brick
with sandstone mouldings. Well known artists
have taken part in the erection — e. g. the
sculptor Offermann in Dresden designed the
frieze, Professor Gross also of Dresden designed
the portal; the coloured window of the square
hall is from the „atelier" of Urban and Goller in
Dresden, that of the bow from Professor Christiansen
in Darmstadt.

26 [1901: 62]

In Wilhelmshöhe bei Kaiiel hat Georg
Kegel am Endpunkte der von Kaiiel nach
dem Parke führenden elektriichen Straßenbahn
ein Stationsgebäude errichtet, das mit großem
Geichick der landichaftlichen Umgebung angepaßt

26 [1901: 62]

Monsieur Georges Regel a construit à Wilhelmshöhe près de Cassel à l'extrèmité
du tram électrique conduisant de Cassel au
parc une gare qui se marie admirablement au
paysage (Pl. 62).

26 [1901: 62]

In Wilhelmshöhe near Cassel, an electric street
tramway runs from Cassel to the Park, and
at the terminus of this line, Georg Kegel has
erected a station building, which he has with
great taste made to harmonize with its pictures-

worden ist (Taf. 62). Das Untergeschoß, das einen Raum für das Dienstpersonal, die Aborte, den Keller und die Waschküche enthält, ist in rotem Sandstein ausgeführt, das obere Geschoß in Backstein mit Ecken und Fenstergewänden aus weißem Sandstein, das Dachgeschoß in Fachwerk. Da das Gelände an der Parkseite etwa 3 Meter höher liegt als das an der Straßenseite, wurde die Anlage einer großen Treppe erforderlich, die zu den Wartezimmern im ersten Obergeschoß führt. Im zweiten Obergeschoß befindet sich die Wohnung des Stationsbeamten. — Die Baukosten betrugen 34 783 M.

le rez-de-chaussée qui contient une chambre pour le personnel de service, les commodités, la cave et la buanderie est construit en grès rouge. Le premier étage est en briques avec angles et encadrements de fenêtres en pierre blanche. L'étage sons le toit est en pans de bois. Comme le terrain est de trois mètres plus haut du côté du parc que de celui de la rue, on installa un escalier qui conduit aux salles d'attente au 1er étage. — Au 2me étage se trouve l'appartement du chef de gare.

Les frais de construction se sont élevés à 34,783 Marks.

que surroundings. (Plate 62). The lower floor contains a room for the attendants, lavatories, cellars, and wash house, and is built of red sandstone. The upper floor is of brick, with corners and window coping of white sandstone; the roof story is of frame work. As the site on the park side is 3 metres higher than on the street side, a wide stair-case was necessary which leads to the waiting-room on the first floor. On the next floor is the dwelling of the station officials. The cost was 34 783 Marks.

27 [1901; 88]

Die „Münchener Allgemeine Zeitung" hat von April 1900 bis Mai 1901 durch Architekt Martin Dülfer sich ein neues Geschäftshaus Bayerstraße 57/59 in München, erbauen lassen, dessen Gesamtkosten einschließlich Architekten-Honorar 550 000 M. betragen haben.

Vom Hauptgebäude dient im Erdgeschoß nur der linksseitige Laden den Zwecken der Zeitung; die übrigen Läden sind vermietet. Das Zwischengeschoß ist für die Redaktion und Bureauräume bestimmt; die Obergeschosse enthalten je zwei geräumige Mietwohnungen.

Die seitlichen Flügelbauten wie der mächtige hintere Querbau dienen lediglich dem Geschäftsbetriebe der Zeitung; im Erd- und Obergeschoß als Druckerei und Setzerei u. s. w. und im Keller und in den oberen Geschossen zu Lagerräumen. Der Fassadenaufbau der oberen Geschosse stützt sich auf eiserne, mit Zement geputzte Pfeiler, wobei jedoch eine Auflagerung von größeren Mauerwerksmassen vermieden ist. Alle Flächen sind in Zement mit Kalkmörtelüberzug geputzt, die ornamentalen Teile in Antragarbeit aus-

D'avril 1900 à mai 1901, le journal „Münchener Allgemeine Zeitung" a fait construire par M. Martin Dülfer, architecte, une nouvelle maison Bayerstrasse 57/59 à Munich. Les frais, y compris les honoraires de l'architecte, se sont élevés à M. 550 000.

Au rez-de-chaussée du bâtiment principal, il n'y a que le magasin de gauche qui serve au journal, les autres magasins sont loués. L'entresol est occupé par la rédaction et les bureaux, les étages supérieurs contiennent chacun deux appartements spacieux.

Les ailes du bâtiment ainsi que la vaste annexe de derrière sont entièrement consacrés au service du journal. Au rez-de-chaussée et à l'étage supérieur se trouvent l'imprimerie et la composition tandis que les caves et les autres étages servent de depôts et magasins. La façade repose sur des piliers en fer revêtus de ciment; on a eu soin d'éviter la charge de trop fortes masses de maçonnerie pour ces piliers. Toutes les surfaces sont en ciment revêtues d'un enduit de mortier de chaut, les ornements sont

The architect Martin Dülfer has built new business premises for the "Münchener Allgemeine Zeitung" at 57—59 Bayer Strasse, Munich. The cost, including the architect's fee was 550 000 Marks. The ground floor of the principal building contains shops, only the left side being retained for the use of the publishers. The first floor contains the Editor's room and the publishing offices of the paper; the upper floors contain each of them two large private dwellings. The side and back wings are used for the printing offices of the paper, compositors rooms etc. as well as store rooms in the cellars and upper stories. The fronts of the upper stories are supported by iron pillars with cement plastering. This has prevented a too clumsy use of brick work. All the surfaces are of plastered cement, the ornaments being put on separately. The colouring is vivid; the less prominent surfaces being in deep yellow and black, the architectural tracery in light stucco,

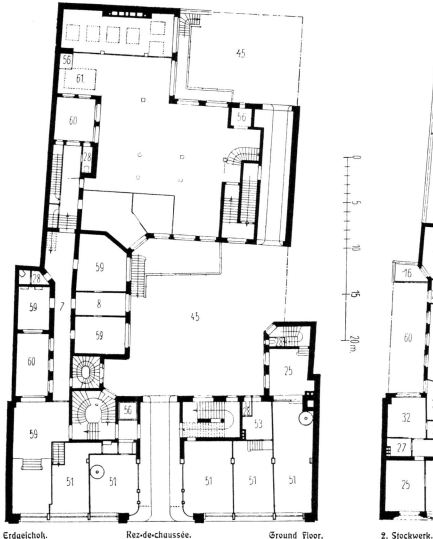

Erdgeschoß.   Rez-de-chaussée.   Ground Floor.

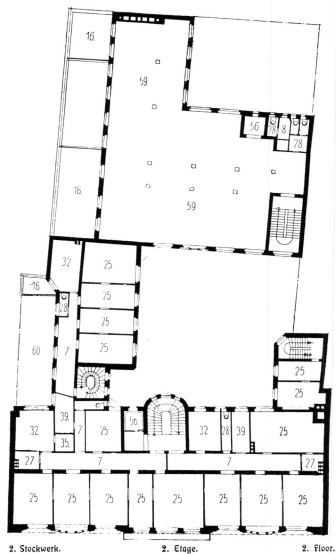

2. Stockwerk.   2. Etage.   2. Floor.

geführt. Bei der sehr kräftig gehaltenen Tönung sind die untergeordneten Flächen in sattem Gelb und Schwarz gehalten, die tragenden Architekturglieder in hellem Putz, die ornamentalen Teile in lebhaften Farben mit Gold hervorgehoben.

Von den Ausführenden sind besonders zu nennen: Joh. Grübel für den Rohbau, für Stuck- und Bildhauerarbeit Cornelius Hauer, für Malerarbeit Schmidt & Co., Balkongitter Wolfgang Domproff, Elektrische Einrichtung Allgemeine Elektrizitäts-Gesellschaft, sämtlich in München, für die Aufzüge und Rohrpost Gebr. Weißmüller, bezgl. Wagner & Brandt in Frankfurt a. M.

modelés en mortier. Le tout est peint en couleurs très vives, les surfaces en jaune et noir, les membres d'architecture en clair et les parties ornementales en couleurs brillantes rehaussées d'or.

Comme entrepreneurs nommons particulièrement: Joh. Grübel pour le gros œuvre, Cornelius Hauer pour la sculpture, Schmidt et Cie. pour la peinture, Wolfgang Domproff pour les balustrades de balcon, Allgemeine Electricitäts-Gesellschaft pour les installations électriques; tous à Munich. Les maisons Gebr. Weissmüller et Wagner et Brand à Francfort ont exécuté les ascenseurs et la poste pneumatique.

and the ornaments in bright colours with gold bosses.

Of the firms employed in the construction, the following deserve especial notice. Joh. Grübel for the brick work, for stucco and sculpture Cornelius Hauer, for painting Schmidt & Co. The balcony iron work is by Wolfgang Domproff, the electric light installation by the "Allgemeine Elektizitäts-Gesellschaft" — all these firms are in Munich. The lifts and pneumatic post are by Brothers Weissmüller, and Wagner and Brandt in Frankfurt on Main.

Für die israelitische Gemeinde in Straßburg i. E., die während des schnellen Aufschwungs der Stadt nach dem deutsch-französischen Kriege auf über 4000 Seelen angewachsen war, war schon in den achtziger Jahren der Neubau einer Synagoge nötig geworden, der aber erst in den Jahren 1895—1898 nach den Plänen des Architekten Professor Ludwig Levy in Karlsruhe ausgeführt werden konnte, nachdem die Stadt einen geeigneten Bauplatz am Stadtgrabenkanal geschenkt hatte. Auf diesem Gelände konnte das Gotteshaus in reicher Gruppierung nach allen Seiten freiliegend entwickelt werden (Taf. 67). Für die Außen- und Innenarchitektur hat der Architekt streng romanische Formen gewählt, die bei großer monumentaler Wirkung auch eine gewisse Freiheit in der malerischen Bewegung gestattet haben, die bei dem durchbrochenen Eckturm noch durch die Verwendung frühgotischer Elemente gesteigert worden ist. Die Außenarchitektur ist in hellem Vogesensandstein hergestellt. Die Gewölbe des Innern, das sich durch feierliche Raumwirkung auszeichnet, sind in Tuffstein mit Backsteingurten, der Orgelprospekt ist in Sandstein ausgeführt. Die Säulen der Estraden sind aus farbigem Marmor, die der Emporen aus Granit. Wände und Gewölbe sind verputzt, in sogenanntem Besenwurf, auf dem die Malereien sehr gut wirken. — Der Bau besteht aus zwei Teilen, dem eigentlichen Synagogenbau, der mit seiner Hauptachse von Westen nach Osten orientiert ist, und dem an der Nordwestseite angrenzenden Gemeindehaus. Die

Dès 1880, la construction d'une nouvelle synagogue s'imposait à la communauté israélité de Strasbourg, laquelle pendant le rapide développement de la ville après la guerre franco-allemande comptait plus de 4000 âmes. Ce ne fut qu'en 1895 qu'on put procéder à l'exécution du projet d'après les plans du professeur Ludwig Levy de Karlsruhe, après que la ville eût fait don d'une place auprès du fossé des remparts. Le temple pouvait sur ce terrain développer de tous côtés la riche silhouette de ses différentes parties (Pl. 67). L'architecte s'est servi pour l'architecture extérieure et intérieure des formes du style roman qui se prêtaient à une grande monumentalité jointe à un groupement pittoresque du monument. La tour d'angle percée à jour montre quelques traces de gothique primitif qui augmentent encore le charme de la composition. — Les façades sont construites en grès clair des Vosges. L'intérieur, de dimensions imposantes, est recouvert de voûtes en tuf à arêtes en briques (Pl. 68). La façade de l'orgue est exécutée en grès.

Les colonnes des estrades sont en marbre de couleur, celles des galeries en granit. Les parois et les voûtes sont recouvertes d'un crépissage rugueux sur lequel les peintures font le meilleur effet. L'édifice se compose de deux parties: la synagogue proprement dite dont l'axe principal est orienté de l'ouest à l'est et la maison de la communauté qui borde la synagogue au Nordouest.

A new synagogue for the Jewish community in Strassburg in Alsace, which, owing to the rapid growth of the town after the Franco-German war, now numbers 4000 souls, has long been a necessity. It was already projected in the eighties, but was only built in 1895—1898 from the designs of Professor Ludwig Levy of Carlsruhe. The town presented a suitable site on the Stadt-graben canal. On this site it was possible to build the synagogue so that it lies, admirably grouped, and free on all sides (Plate 67). For both exterior and interior, the architect has mostly kept strictly to the Romanesque style, with however an occasional freedom which has had the most happy results, a considerably heightened effect being obtained by the lattice-work stone corner tower, designed in the Early Gothic style. The exterior is of sandstone from the Vosges. The vaulted roof of the interior, whose oast-proportions produce an effect of great solemnity (Plate 68) is carried out in tuff stone with brick work girders — the niche for the organ loft is of sandstone. The pillars of the estrade are of coloured marble those of the gallery of granite. The walls and roof are plastered in a kind of rough cast on which the paintings show with good effect. The building is in two parts, the actual synagogue lying with its central nave from west to east, and the house of the community which is built on the northwest side.

The synagogue on the ground floor contains two entrance halls or porches; the principal

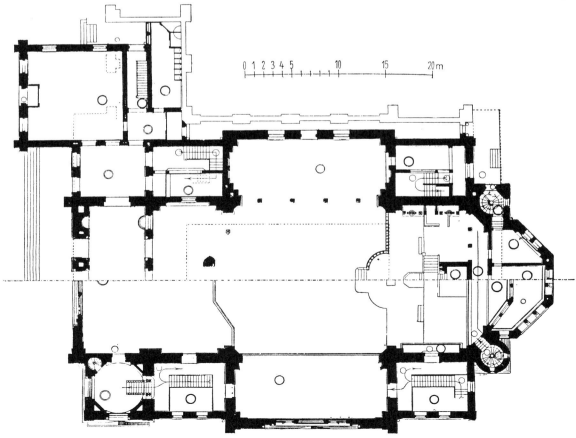

Synagoge enthält im Erdgeichoß zwei Vorhallen, den Hauptraum mit 825 Sitzplätzen für Männer und eine Eitrade mit den Sißen des Koniiftoriums, der Synagogenverwaltung und dem Vorbeterfiich. Darüber und dahinter erheben fich die Kanzel, das Allerheiligite und die Sängerempore. Vier Treppen führen zu den Emporen, die, nach jüdiichem Ritus ausichließlich für Frauen beitimmt, 654 Siße enthalten. — Das dreigeichoifige Gemeindehaus enthält im Erdgeichoß eine Werktags-Synagoge mit 100 Pläßen und die Loge des Kaitellans, im eriten Obergeichoß einen Sißungsiaal mit Verwaltungsräumen für das Koniiftorium und im zweiten Obergeichoß die Wohnung des eriten Kantors. — Die Baukoiten betrugen etwa 700 000 M.

La synagogue contient au rez-de-chaussée deux porches, la salle principale avec 825 places pour hommes, puis une estrade avec les sièges du consistoire, des membres du conseil de synagogue et la table du prieur; au dessus et au fond de la salle s'élèvent la chaire, le sanctuaire et les galeries du choeur — quatre escaliers conduisent aux galeries, qui selon le rite juif sont exclusivement réservées aux femmes et contiennent 654 places. La maison de la communauté se compose de trois étages, elle contient au rez-de-chaussée une synagogue de semaine avec cent places et la loge du concierge, au premier étage se trouve une salle de conseil avec chambres d'administration pour le consistoire, au deuxième étage l'appartement du premier chantre. Les frais s'élevèrent à environ M. 700000.

building contains 825 seats for men, a dais (estrade) for the seats of the consistory, of the synagogue authorities and for the Prayer Table. Over and behind the chancel, are the Holy of Holies, and the singer's gallery. Four staircases lead to the galleries, which according to the Jewish rite, are used exclusively for women, and which contain 654 seats. The three storied house adjoining, contains on the ground floor a synagogue for week-days with 100 seats, and the lodge of the sacristan. The next story contains a committee room with adjoining offices for the Consistory and Administration, and the next floor the dwelling of the first Cantor. The cost of building was about 700000 Marks.

Als hervorragendes Beiipiel der zweitgenannten Gattung iit das Miet-Haus, Square Rapp 3, ebenfalls eine der neueiten Schöpfungen des Architekten Jules Lavirotte, anzuiehen. Noch auffälliger als bei voritehendem Bau knüpfen die hier als „moderne" anzuiehenden Formen an die der uriprünglichiten Frührenaiiance, beionders der „niederländiichen" an. Bei 18 monatiger Bauzeit hat das Haus nur 310 000 Mark gekoitet. Es zählt acht durch feuerfeite Decken von 0,3 m Dicke geichiedene Geichoiie, deren lichte Höhen betragen: im Keller 2,8, Erdgeichoß 2,8, I. Stock 3,4, II. Stock 3,0, III. Stock 2,9, IV. (Dach-Balkongeichoß) 3,1, im V. (Obermaniarde) 2,85 und im oberiten Dachgeichoß 2,6 m.

Eigentümlich iit die Ausnüßung des Gebäudes, das im Erdgeichoß und I. Stock von der Eigentümerin bewohnt iit. Der II. und III., dem I. Stock gleichgeitaltet, jedoch eine Küche habend, find je für fich vermietet; im IV., der ebenfalls gleich diefem, und im hinteren Teil des V. iit ein kleines Hotel eingerichtet, während der vordere Teil diefes und des oberiten Dachgeichoifes als Wohnung und Atelier des Architekten ausgebildet find.

Das Material iit im allgemeinen dasielbe wie vor, jedoch treten dazu noch rote Ziegel aus

Un remarquable exemple de la seconde catégorié que nous avons mentionnée est la maison à loyer Square Rapp 3, également une des dernières créations de l'architecte Jules Lavirotte. Les formes modernes se rattachent ici d'une façon plus frappante encore que dans l'exemple précédent à celles de la Renaissance primitive particulièrement à celles des Pays-Bas. Ce bâtiment a coûté 18 mois de construction et 310 000 Mark, il compte 8 étages séparés par des pontraisons incombustibles de 0,3 m d'épaisseur. Les hauteurs mésurées dans le vide comportent pour la cave 2,8 m, rez-de-chaussée 2,8 m, Ier étage 3,4 m, IIme étage 3,0 m, IIIme étage 2,9 m, IVme étage avec balcons 3,1 m, Vme étage, mansardes supérieures, 2,85 m et chambres hautes 2,6 m.

La disposition générale du bâtiment dont le propriétaire occupe le rez-de-chaussée et le Ier étage est originale. Les second et troisième étages, semblables au premier mais ayant chacun une cuisine, sont loués séparément. Au quatrième, semblable aux précédents, et sur le derrière du cinquième est installé un petit hôtel, tandis que le devant de ce dernier étage et de l'étage supérieur est aménagé en appartement et en atelier de l'architecte.

Les matériaux sont en général les mêmes que dans le cas précédent; il faut cependant y ajouter des briques rouges de Vaugérard et des

A good example of the second kind is the dwelling house Rapp Square 3, one of the latest works of the architect Jules Lavirotte. One sees here still more plainly than in the former building, how modern forms have been added gradually to the Early Renaissance, particularly to the Dutch style. The time occupied in building was 18 months, the cost only 310 000 Marks. There are 8 different stories, separated by fire-proof ceilings, 0.3 metres in thickness. The height of the stories is as follows: the cellars 2.8 m, basement 2.8, 1st floor 3.4, 2nd floor 3.0, 3rd floor 2.9, 4th floor (roof-balcony story) 3.1, 5th floor (upper gable) 2.85, and in the garrets 2.6 m.

The arrangement of the building is however peculiar; the basement and first floor are inhabited by the ladyowner. The second and third floors are like the first, but with a general kitchen, and are let to two different tenants. The fourth floor and the back part of the fifth are occupied by a small hotel; the front part of the fifth and the highest roof story is the dwelling and "atelier" of the architect.

The material is in general the same as in the last-mentioned house with the addition of

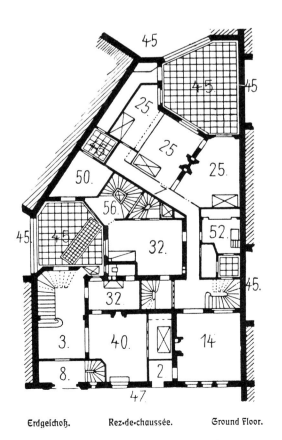

Erdgeichoß.   Rez-de-chaussée.   Ground Floor.

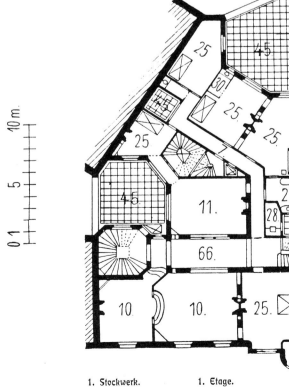

1. Stockwerk.   1. Etage.   1. Floor.

— 48 —

Vaugirard und emaillierte von Bigot. Decken und Dächer sind durchaus feuerfest, letztere mit Bigotschen Ziegeln gedeckt. Das Haus hat eine eigene, durch Heißluftmaschine betriebene Wasserversorgung für Klosets und Antrieb der Aufzüge. Das Sammelbecken steht in einem Türmchen über der Haupttreppe.

fayences émaillées de Bigot. Les pontraisons et les toits sont incombustibles, ces derniers sont couverts en tuiles Bigot.

La maison a une conduite d'eau spéciale actionnée par une machine à air chaud pour les closets et les lifts. Le réservoir se trouve dans une tourelle au dessus de l'escalier.

red tiles from Vaugirard and enamelled tiles by Bigot. The ceilings and roofs are everywhere fire-proof, the latter are roofed with Bigot's tiles. The house is furnished with a hot air engine for pumping the water, and for driving the lifts; the water basin is in a small tower over the principal staircase.

31 [1901: 10]

Unter geschickter Benutzung der Bodenverhältnisse, die für die die Altstadt Stuttgarts einschließenden, vorzugsweise für den Villenbau geeigneten Höhenzüge charakteristisch sind, hat der Erbauer der Villa Eitel, (Tafel 10) Albert Eitel, mit einfachen Mitteln eine reizvolle, malerische Anlage geschaffen, deren architektonische Ausbildung in Renaissanceformen mit Fachwerkbau sich an heimische Baugewohnheiten anschließt. Für den Unterbau, der die Wirthschaftsräume u. s. w. enthält, und für einzelne Architekturtheile ist weißer Sandstein verwendet worden. Die Flächen sind verputzt, die Dächer mit rheinischem Schiefer eingedeckt.

Bei der Ausbildung der Dächer ist der Architekt leider durch die baupolizeilichen Vorschriften beeinträchtigt worden, weshalb die Firsthöhe geringer bemessen werden mußte, als der Komposition des Ganzen zuträglich war.

Die Baukosten betrugen ohne die Stützmauer 85000 Mark.

31 [1901: 10]

Mettant habilement à profit la formation du sol, caractéristique pour les collines environnant la ville de Stuttgard et qui se prêtent fort bien à la construction de villas, Mr. Albert Eitel, l'architecte de la Villa Eitel (Planche 10) a créé avec des moyens bien simples une charmante et pittoresque maison, dont les formes du style Renaissance avec pans de bois ont été inspirées par les traditions locales. Dans la construction du sous sol, contenant les pièces de ménage, ainsi que dans quelques parties architecturales on a employé le grès blanc. Les murs sont crépis et les toits couverts d'ardoise rhénane. — Malheureusement les ordonnances de la police des constructions ont lié l'architecte relativement à la construction de la toiture, de sorte que la hauteur du faîte est inférieure à ce qu'elle devrait être en proportion du reste de l'édifice.

Les frais de construction, le mur de soutènement non-compris, s'élèvent à 85000 Marks.

31 [1901: 10]

The "Altstadt" Stuttgart is surrounded by hills which offer sites especially suited for building villas. Mr. Albert Eitel, the architect of the Villa Eitel (Plates 10) has cleverly availed himself of this circumstance, and has erected with simple means, a beautiful picturesque building. The architectural composition shows the Renaissance style, and yet with its frame work resembles in many respects the home style of building. The basement (sockel) which contains kitchen and offices is built of white sandstone, which material is used too for other parts of the house. The surfaces are plastered, and it is roofed with slate from the Rhine. In constructing the roof, the architect has been bound by the exigencies of the police regulations, consequently the height of the ridge is lower than it should be according to the composition of the whole.

The cost of building, exclusive of the supporting wall, amounted to 85000 Marks.

32, 33 [1901: 96, 97]

Castel Beauveau-Craon auf der Höhe von Garches bei Paris ist eines der im Leitartikel des Herrn Bans unter den jüngsten Schöpfungen des Architekten Hector Guimard hervorgehobenen Werke, das wir nach dessen Handzeichnung zur Anschauung bringen. Die Ausführung dauerte nur 14 Monate, und die Kosten betrugen 49500 Mark. Mr. Baudouin in Garches führte die Maurer- und Steinhauer-, Mr. Neubort ebenda die Eisenarbeiten und Mr. Normand in Suresnes die Zimmer- und Tischlerarbeiten aus.

Als Materialien dienten Bausteine aus der Umgebung, Backstein, und für das Füllmauerwerk Mühlstein in kleinen unregelmäßigen, porigen Stücken. Das in einem herrlichen Park gelegene Schlößchen gewährt von seinen Terrassen und Balkonen aus eine herrliche Aussicht auf das Seinethal.

Von demselben Architekten geben wir hier noch dessen eigenhändige Entwurfsskizze zu einem Castel Eclipse benannten, kleinen eingebauten Wohnhause in Versailles, die wohlgeeignet ist, die stilistische Auffassung und Weise dieses Künstlers darzulegen.

32, 33 [1901: 96, 97]

Le castel Beauveau-Craon situé sur la hauteur de Garches près Paris est un des derniers ouvrages de M. Hector Guimard architecte cités dans l'article par cette livraison M. Bans.

Nous publions cet édifice d'après un dessin original de l'artiste. La construction dura 14 mois et coûta 49500 Mark. Les travaux de maçonnerie et de taille furent exécutés par M. Baudoin à Garches, les constructions en fer par M. Neubort, la charpente et la menuiserie sont de M. Normand à Suresnes.

La pierre provient des environs, on employa aussi des briques et pour le gros oeuvre de la meulière. Ce petit chateau situé dans un parc magnifique offre de ses terrasses et balcons une vue splendide sur la vallée de la Seine.

Nous publions une esquisse pour une petite maison du même artiste, nommée Castel Eclipse qui se trouve à Versailles, elle se prête fort bien à caractériser le style et le genre du maître.

32, 33 [1901: 96, 97]

Castel Beauveau-Craon on the hill of Garches near Paris is one of the latest creations of the architect Hector Guimard, to which allusion has been made in the leading article of this number, and of which we give the artist's illustration in the accompanying sketch. The whole building was completed in only 14 months, and the cost was 49500 Marks. The brick and stone work was carried out by Mr. Baudouin of Garches, the iron work by Mr. Neubort of the same place and the carpenter's and joiner's work by Mr. Normand of Suresnes.

The materials used are hewn stone from the neighbourhood, brick and burr-stone for the filling broken into small irregular porous pieces. The mansion lies in a splendid park and commands from its terrace balconies a lovely view over the valley of the Seine.

We give an artist's sketch from the same architect of the Castel Eclipse, a small dwelling house in Versailles, which is a happy illustration of this artist's style and manner.

34 [1902: 19]

Von den Architekten Berninger & Krafft in Straßburg i. E. ist daselbst in der Ruprechtsauer Allee 76 das schöne Landhaus des Herrn O. Schützenberger aus französischem

34 [1902: 19]

Mrs Berninger et Krafft architectes ont construit à Strasbourg l'allée de Ruprechtsau No 76 la belle maison de M. O. Schützenberger, en pierre de Savonnières fran-

34 [1902: 19]

The architects Berninger and Krafft in Strassburg in Alsace have built in the Ruppt rechtsauer Allee 76 the beautiful villa o Mr O. Schützenberger. The house is built of French

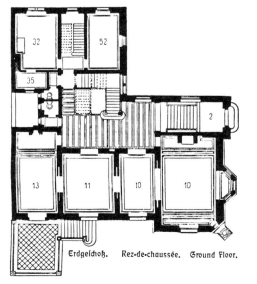

Erdgeschoß.   Rez-de-chaussée.   Ground Floor.

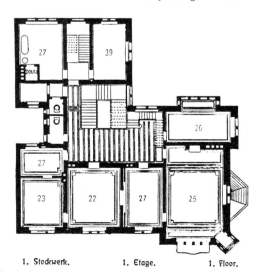

1. Stockwerk.   1. Etage.   1. Floor.

(Savonnières-) Kalkstein erbaut worden. In der Gesamtanlage an italienische Villenbauten erinnernd, zeigt die feinfühlige und glänzende, durchaus moderne Detail-Formgebung zwar verwandte Züge mit der des Baues am Broglieplatz (Taf. 14), ist jedoch durchaus der ruhig würdigen Aufbauerscheinung des vornehmen Landsitzes angepaßt.

çaise. La disposition générale rappelle celle des villas italiennes, mais si la façon brillante et toute moderne dont est traité le détail montre quelque parenté avec la maison de la place de Broglie (Pl. 14), elle est admirablement adaptée à l'aspect tranquille et digne d'une habitation de campagne distinguée.

limestone (Savonnières) and a while as a whole recalling the Italian villa style, it shows much fine feeling and thoroughly modern form details. It is in many respects similar to the building on the Broglieplatz (see plate 14), but the idea of a restful quiet home is never lost sight of.

35 [1902: 1]

Architekt Franz von Hoven errichtete von Oktober 1899 bis April 1901 in den Taunusanlagen 18 das Geschäftsgebäude für die „Frankfurter Transport - Unfall - und Glasversicherungs - Aktiengesellschaft" in Frankfurt a. M.

Der durchaus modern aufgefaßte Prachtbau zeigt eine glückliche Verbindung der Motive deutscher mit französischer und englischer Frührenaissance. Der Unterbau ist aus Bergsträßer Granit, der Aufbau aus hellem Burgreppacher Sandstein der Firma Ph. Holzmann & Co. ausgeführt. Untergeschoß und Erdgeschoß dienen als Geschäftslokal der Eigentümerin, der I. Stock ist als Geschäftslokal vermietet. Der II. Stock enthält zwei vornehme Wohnungen. Die Rohbauarbeiten wurden von Schuffner & Albert, die Kunstschlosserei durch Gebr. Armbrüster in Frankfurt, die Bildhauerarbeiten von Fritz Klimsch in Charlottenburg, und die Zentralheizung von Gebr. Sulzer in Winterthur ausgeführt.

35 [1902: 1]

Monsieur Franz von Hoven architecte à Francfort s. M. a construit d'octobre 1899 à avril 1901 dans les Taunusanlagen No 18 la maison de la „Société francfortoise par actions, d'assurance contre les accidents et la brisure de glaces".

Ce palais conçu dans un esprit tout moderne montre un heureux mélange de Renaissance allemande, française et anglaise. Le socle est construit en granit clair de la Bergstrasse, les étages en pierre claire de Burgreppach de la maison Ph. Holzmann & Co. Le sous-sol et le rez-de-chaussée servent de bureaux à la société, le 1er étage est loué à une maison de commerce. Le second étage contient deux appartements de maîtres. Le gros-œuvre a été exécuté par Mrs Schuffner & Albert, la ferronnerie d'art par les frères Armbrüster à Francfort, la sculpture par Fritz Klimsch à Charlottenbourg et le chauffage central par les frères Sulzer à Winterthour.

35 [1902: 1]

The architect Franz von Hoven built from October 1899 to April 1901 the business premises of the "Frankfurter Transport-, Unfall- and Glasversicherungs - Aktien-Gesellschaft".

This magnificent edifice which has a thoroughly modern aspect is a happy union of the German with the French and English early Renaissance. The lower part is of Bergsträsser granite, the upper part of light Burgreppacher sandstone was carried out by the firm Ph. Holzmann and Co. The ground floor and basement are the business premises of the owners, the first floor is let as business premises, the second floor contains two superior dwellings. The masonry was carried out by Schuffner and Albert, the iron work by the Brothers Armbrüster in Frankfurt, the sculptural details by Fritz Klimsch in Charlottenburg and the hot air heating apparatus by the Brothers Sulzer in Winterthur.

36 [1902: 9]

Das in Wien, Nordbergstraße, Ecke Althanplatz 4, von den Architekten und k. k. Hofbaumeister Ferd. Dehm & F. Olbricht vom 20. November 1899 bis 9. März 1901 errichtete Zinshaus, kann als typisch für die Gestaltung der großen städtischen Gebäude in neuester Entwicklungsstufe der Wiener „Modernen" Schule gelten, insofern die Aufbauverhältnisse des bisher geltenden Barocks durchweg beibehalten und an Stelle dessen konstruktiven Zierformen das rein äußerlich aufgeheftet aus dem „Empirestil" u. a.

36 [1902: 9]

La maison à loyer construite à Vienne, Nordbergstrasse, à l'angle de la place Althan No. 4 par les architectes de la cour Ferd. Dehm et F. Olbricht du 20 novembre 1899 au 9 mars 1901, peut être considérée comme un type de la disposition de grandes maisons de ville au dernier degré de développement de l'école moderne viennoise, en ce sens que les proportions des façades baroques jusqu'à présent usuelles, ont été conservées pour ce monument, mais, qu'au lieu du détail de ce style a pris place une

36 [1902: 9]

The dwelling house arranged in flats built in Vienna, Nordbergstrasse at the corner of Althanplatz 4 by the architect and Government building master Ferd. Dehm and F. Olbricht from 20 Nov. 1899 to March 1901, may be considered as a type of the new Vienna modern school.

The erection is the conventional barock style, but instead of using barock ornament, we find the "Empire" and other styles added for this purpose.

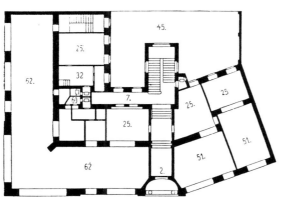

Erdgeschoß.   Rez-de-chaussée.   Ground Floor.

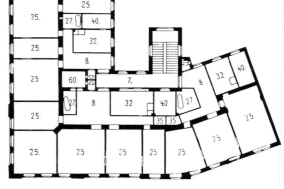

1. Stockwerk.   1. Étage.   1. Floor.

entnommene Schmuckwerk getreten ist. Die Tunnelöffnung (Eckbauerdgeschoß), die Vergoldung der Kuppelrippen- und Bekrönung, vollständige Vergoldung der Balkongitter, erhöhen den angestrebten theatralisch-pomphaften Eindruck. Pomphaft ist auch das Innere, z. B. mit Treppenstufen von gelbem ungarischen Marmor ausgestattet, während die Fassade sich als Putzbau kennzeichnet.

Die Bauausführung und Leitung lagen in den Händen der Baumeister Eduard Dücker und Architekt E. Liebmann. Die Bildhauerarbeiten sind von Ed. Kubesch, die Tischlerarbeiten von den Brüdern Schlesinger, die Arbeiten der Schlosser von Anton Teische, und die der Maler von Sim. Seemann ausgeführt.

décoration extérieure empruntée au style empire. L'entrée en forme de tunnel au rez-de-chaussée de l'aile d'angle, la dorure des arêtes de la coupole et de son couronnement, les grilles de balcon entièrement dorées, rehaussent l'impression intentionnée de faste pompeux et théâtral.

L'intérieur est aussi fastueux avec ses marches d'escalier en marbre jaune de Hongrie; les façades sont crépies. La conduite et l'exécution des travaux ont été confiées à l'entrepreneur Edouard Dücker et à l'architecte E. Liebmann. Les sculptures son dûes à Ed. Kubesch, la menuiserie aux frères Schlesinger, la serrurerie à Antoine Teische et la peinture à Sim. Seemann.

The opening to the tunnel (corner house basement), the gilding of the ribs of the cupola and of the garlands round it, the entire gilding of the balcony iron work help to enhance the theatrical pompous effect of the whole. The interior is equally magnificent with steps of yellow Hungarian marble; the facade is of plaster work. The superintendence lay in the hands of the building master Edward Dücker and the architect E. Liebmann. The sculpture is by Ed. Kubesch, the wood work by the Brothers Schlesinger, the iron work by Anton Teische and the painting by Sim. Seemann.

Von Mai 1900 bis November 1901 hat Architekt W. Martens (weltbekannt durch die vielen von ihm ausgeführten stolzen Bankbauten) in Berlin zwischen Behren- und Rosmarienstraße, Ecke der Charlottenstraße 42, das Haupt-Geschäftsgebäude der „Berliner Bank" errichtet. Um genügendes Tageslicht zu sichern, mußten die Fassaden an der engen Charlotten- und der noch engeren Rosmarienstraße um einige Meter gegen die alte Baufluchtt zurückgesetzt werden, und um für die im Erdgeschoß liegenden Hauptkassenräume eine gesteigerte Helligkeit zu erzielen, ist auch der obere mittlere Teil der Front an der Charlottenstraße noch weiter eingerückt worden.

Der untere Sockel der Fassaden besteht aus feingestocktem, hellgrauem Oberstreiter Granit; im Untergeschoß und in den Dachaufsätzen ist geschliffener, hellgelber Friedersdorfer und im übrigen heller Alt-Warthauer Sandstein verwendet. Die Fassade an der Rosmarienstraße ist geputzt. Die Dächer sind mit blaurotem Schiefer eingedeckt. Die Architektur nähert sich dem Berliner Barock der Zeit Friedrichs des Großen,

Monsieur W. Martens architecte à Berlin, bien connu pour les importantes et nombreuses maisons de banque qu'il a construites, a élevé à Berlin de mai 1900 à novembre 1901 entre les Behren- et Rosmarienstrasse, à l'angle de la Charlottenstrasse No 42, le bâtiment principal de la Berliner Bank. Pour garantir un jour suffisant, les façades sur la Charlottenstrasse et la Rosmarienstrasse plus étroite encore, ont été reculés de quelques mètres de l'alignement et pour donner aux salles de la caisse principale situées au rez-de-chaussée une clarté plus grande encore, on a retiré davantage la partie supérieure centrale sur la Charlottenstrasse.

Le socle des façades est en granit gris clair de Oberstreit finement piqué, pour le rez-de-chaussée et pour les parties supérieures on a employé du grès jaune clair de Friedersdorf et pour le reste, de la pierre claire de Alt-Warthau. La façade sur la Rosmarienstrasse est crépie. Les toits sont couverts en ardoise bleue. L'architecture rappelle le Barocco Berlinois

The architect W. Martens, already well known by his splendid Bank buildings has built in Berlin between the Behren- and the Rosmarienstrasse (corner of the Charlottenstrasse 42) the principal building of the Berliner Bank. In order to secure sufficient day-light, the building was obliged to be set a few meters back from the usual line of frontage in the narrow Charlottenstrasse and the still narrower Rosmarienstrasse. For the principal Cash entrance on the ground floor in the middle, the building is set still farther back for the same reason.

The base is of light grey Oberstreiter granite, the lower story and the roof story is of carved light yellow Friedersdorfer sandstone, for the remaining part of the building Alt Warthauer sandstone. The facade on the Rosmarienstrasse is of plaster, the roofs are of slate. The style is Berliner barock of the time of Frederick

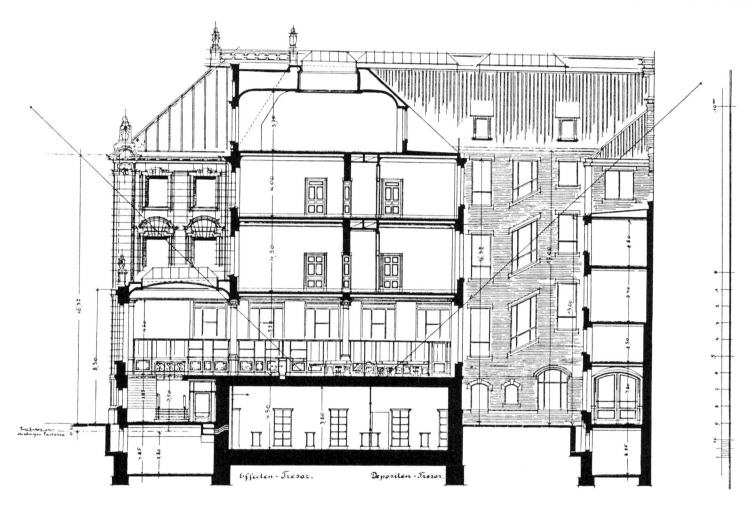

Effecten-Tresor.   Depositen-Tresor.

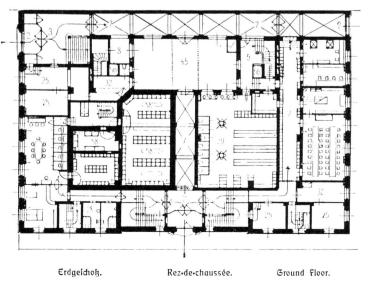

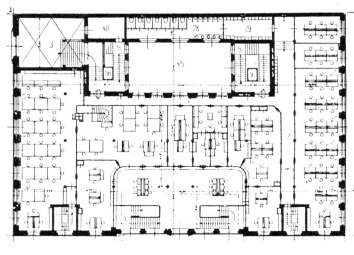

Erdgeschoß.   Rez-de-chaussée.   Ground Floor.   1. Stockwerk.   1. Etage.   1. Floor.

das noch frei war von der Ueberladung späterer Zeiten. Indes ist diese ältere Auffassung hier nicht sklavisch nachgeahmt, sondern sie ist in ganz modernem Sinne durchgeführt und sie weist auch durchaus moderne Züge auf, die besonders ausgeprägt in den Ziergiebeln, dem Portal und an dem eingeschossigen Vorhallenbau an der Charlottenstraße zum Ausdruck kommen.

Es braucht kaum gesagt zu werden, daß die Bank mit doppelten elektrischen Personenaufzügen und nach neuesten Systemen durchgebildeten Stahlkammern mit für die Kundschaft vermietbaren Abteilen eingerichtet ist.

Der figürliche Schmuck des Giebelfeldes ist von Professor Brütt, der ornamentale Teil des Inneren und Aeußeren vom Bildhauer Gerschel, die Malerarbeit von M. J. Bodenstein ausgeführt; das Kunstschlosserwerk lieferten Ed. Puls und Baechler & Paasche, die Tischlerarbeit G. Olm und G. Kuhnert und die Möbel der Direktionsräume Kimbel & Friederichsen, sämtlich in Berlin.

sous Frédéric le Grand, alors pas encore surchargé comme il le fut plus tard. Cette application du style baroque n'est cependant pas une imitation servile, mais elle est bien traitée dans un esprit entièrement moderne, qui s'affirme particulièrement dans les frontons, le portail et le hall d'entrée du côté de la Charlottenstrasse.

Il est à peine besoin de dire que cet établissement est pourvu de lifts doubles électriques et de trésors construits d'après les systèmes les plus modernes et dont une partie est louée à la clientèle de la banque.

Les figures qui ornent le fronton sont l'œuvre du professeur Brütt; la décoration de l'intérieur et de l'extérieur est due au sculpteur Gerschel; M. J. Bodenstein a exécuté les travaux de peinture. Les fers forgés sont de Ed. Puls et de Baechler et Paasche, la menuiserie de G. Olm et G. Kuhnert, enfin les meubles des salles de la direction sont de Kimbel et Friederichsen, toutes ces maisons à Berlin.

the Great, which was then simpler and less overloaded than it became afterwards. It is by so means a slavish imitation, a thoroughly dans modern spirit pervading the whole. Many details, such as the ornamental gables, the portals, and the portico in the Charlottenstrasse are distinctly modern. There are two double electric lifts, and safety chambers of the newest construction for the use of the clients.

The sculptural decoration of the gables is by Professor Brütt, the other ornamental parts by the sculptor Gerschel, the painting by M. J. Bodenstein, the iron and lock work by Ed. Puls, Baechler and Paasche, the woodwork by G. Olm and G. Kuhnert, and the furniture of the Director's rooms by Kimbel and Friederichsen all of them in Berlin.

38 [1902: 5]

Der „Medinah-Tempel" benannte Riesenbau in Chicago ist binnen 15 Monaten durch die Architekten Beers, Clay & Dutton für den Preis von 3 000 000 Mk. errichtet worden. Das Gebäude enthält im Erd- und I. Obergeschoß Kaufläden mit Schaufenstern und in den hierauf folgenden acht Stockwerken je 22 große kaufmännische Bureaux und Comptoirs, die teilweise mit Tresoranlagen versehen sind. Für die beträchtliche Anzahl von Rohrzügen für Dampf etc. sind besondere Räume x x angelegt. Die gleich den Portalen in reichen maurischen Formen durchgeführten Oberstockwerke dienen der Besitzerin, einer Freimaurerloge, als Heim und enthalten außer den üblichen Arbeits- und Festräumen einen Bankettsaal für 2000 Personen. Der Titel der Loge: „The Ancient Arabic Order of Majestic-Shrine" gab den Anlaß zur Wahl der maurischen Ausbildungsformen und er erklärt auch die obige Benennung des Bauwerks.

Auf Pfeilern fundiert, ist das Skelett des Aufbaues aus gußeisernen Säulen und Stahlträgern, durchaus feuersicher hergestellt; alles Eisenwerk ist mit Streckmetall in 3,8 cm starkem Cementputz eingehüllt; das Mauerwerk besteht aus hartgebrannten Backsteinen, die Zierteile aus harter Terracotta, die Dachdeckung aus rotglasierten Falzziegeln.

38 [1902: 5]

Le gigantesque édifice de Chicago nommé le „Temple de Medinah" a été construit en 15 mois par les architectes Beers, Clay et Dutton pour le prix de 3 000 000 Marks. Le bâtiment contient au rez-de-chaussée et au premier étage des magasins avec devantures tandis que les huit étages qui se trouvent au dessus contiennent chacun 22 grands bureaux et comptoirs qui sont en partie pourvus de trésors. On a disposé des locaux spéciaux x x pour le grand nombre de tuyaux à vapeur et autres qui traversent les étages.

Les étages supérieurs traités ainsi que les portails en style mauresque servent à la propriétaire, la loge maçonnique: „The Ancient Arabic Order of Majestic-Shrine". Il s'y trouve outre les salles usuelles de travail et de fête, une salle de banquet pour 2000 personnes.

Le nom de la loge donna lieu au choix du style mauresque et explique la dénomination populaire du monument. Le squelette de l'édifice formé de colonnes de fonte et de poutres d'acier reposant sur une fondation de piliers est absolument incombustible, toutes les constructions en fer sont revêtues de ciment et métal-réticulaire en 3,8 cm d'épaisseur. La maçonnerie est en briques dures, les ornements en terra-cotta également dure, la toiture en tuiles à recouvrement rouges vernies.

38 [1902: 5]

The gigantic building called the "Medinah Tempel" in Chicago was erected during fifteen months by the architects Beers, Clay and Dutton at a cost of 3000000 Marks. The building contains on the ground and first floors business premises with shop windows; the eight stories above contain each 22 large mercantile offices which are in places furnished with patent safes. For the considerable amount of piping necessary for heating, water etc. separate apartments have been constructed. The first floor which like the portals is of rich Moorish architecture is reserved as the Freemasons' lodge to which society the whole building belongs. This floor contains in addition to the usual necessary rooms a banquetting hall capable of seating 2000 persons. The title of the lodge „The Ancient Arabic Order of Majestic Shrine" suggested the selection of the Moorish style of architecture, and the name of the abovementioned temple. The foundation rests on pillars, the frame-work of the house is of cast iron pillars and steel girders. All the iron work is covered with a thick coating of streehedmetal and cement, the brick-work is of rough bricks, the ornamental parts of hard terra-cotta, the roofing of red glazed tiles.

39 [1902: 7]

Eine mächtige künstlerische Begabung bekunden die Karlsruher Architekten Curjel & Moser in ihrem jüngsten Meisterwerke, der protestantischen Pauluskirche in Basel. Es ist das ein Werk, das fast eigens dazu geschaffen erscheint, einerseits die Notwendigkeit oder doch die Vorteile streng wissenschaftlicher Durchbildung der Architekten in Konstruktion wie in geschichtlicher, architektonischer und formalistischer Beziehung darzulegen, andererseits den Beweis zu liefern, wie sehr wohl selbst die als archaistisch, vollständig abgeschlossen geltenden romanischen Bauweisen einer weiteren Fortbildung in ganz modernem Sinne sich leihen, ohne in ihrem hehren Charakter dadurch Einbuße zu erleiden. Freilich setzt das immer voraus, daß solches „Unterfangen" nur einem Meister der Kunst ansteht, der nicht durch Stil und stilistische Bedenken sich beherrschen läßt, sondern die gestellte Aufgabe und darin sich häufende Stilfragen zu „bemeistern" versteht.

Die Zentralanlage, mit der Kanzel in der Mitte, davorstehendem Altartische und da-

39 [1902: 7]

Les architectes Curjel et Moser de Carlsruhe témoignent dans leur dernier chef d'œuvre, l'église protestante la „Pauluskirche" à Bâle d'une puissante originalité artistique. C'est une œuvre qui paraît expressement devoir servir à la démonstration, d'une part de la nécessité, ou du moins des avantages pour l'architecte d'une instruction approfondie, scientifique en construction et en matières historiques, architectonique comme des formes artistiques spéciales; d'autre part de prouver combien même les éléments archaïques, absolument limités en apparence, de l'architecture romane, sont susceptibles de développement dans un esprit entièrement moderne sans perdre pour cela de leur caractère austère. Convenu, qu'une telle entreprise ne peut être tentée que par un maître qui non seulement ne se laisse pas dominer par un style et des scrupules de stilistique mais qui possède son programme à fond et qui saura maîtriser les questions de style qui s'y pressent.

Le système central: la chaire au milieu, la table-autel devant, l'orgue et le chœur derrière correspond le mieux aux exigences du

39 [1902: 7]

Very high artistic gifts are shown in the last masterpiece of the Carlsruhe architects Curjel and Moser, the protestant Paulus church in Basel. This is a work which seems created to show on the one side the absolute necessity of a thorough technical training of the architect in construction viewed in its architectural and historical sense; on the other side it is a proof that churches professedly archaic and complete in all details of the Romanesque style can yet bear the addition of modern touches, without sacrifiing any of their sacredness. As a matter of course these touches must be from the hand of a master; — a master who does not let himself be coerced into a blind obedience to style but who harmonizes the various crowding diversities and forces them into subservience to his own original idea.

The central nave with the chancel in the middle at the end, with the altar in front and the organ and choir behind, fulfils the great

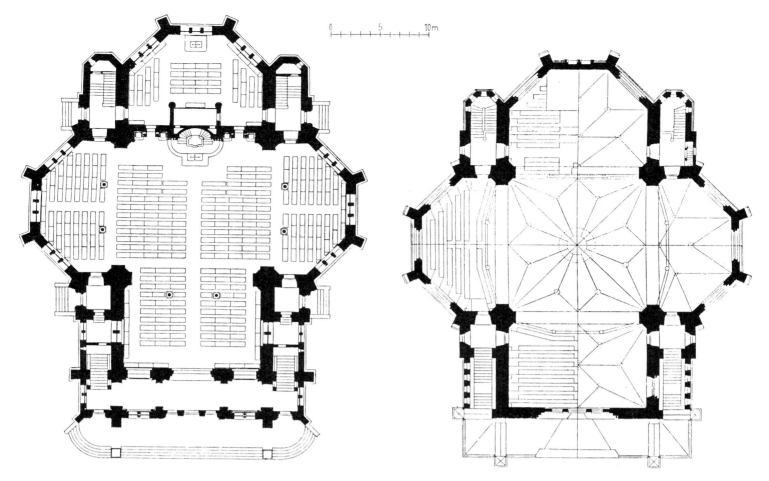

hinter liegender Orgel und Sängerchor entspricht den Anforderungen, welche das protestantische „Gemeindehaus" als „Predigtkirche" erfüllen soll, am besten, indem der Blick sämtlicher Gemeindeglieder unverwandt, beständig auf Kanzel, Altar und Orgel gerichtet bleibt. Auch die Verwendung des Erdgeschoßraumes unter der Orgelempore (im Chor) als Confirmanden= saal ist den rituellen Ansprüchen durchaus ange= paßt, und sie sichert am besten eine vollkommene Akustik. Durch die äußerlich klar gekennzeichnete Anlage der Emporentreppen ist in einfachster Weise allen Verkehrsstockungen und Störungen beim Betreten und Verlassen der Kirche vorge= beugt und damit ein Moment gewonnen, das natürlich die malerische Wirkung und gleich= zeitig die Standfestigkeit des Baues zu erhöhen beiträgt. Das ist von besonderem Wert, da der Vierungsturm vollständig ohne Eisen kon= struiert ist.

Der Bau, bei welchem Architekt W. Mund mit der Bauführung betraut war, dauerte von Juni 1898 bis November 1901 und erforderte einen Aufwand von 640000 M. Sockel, Treppen und Säulenschäfte bestehen aus Gotthardgranit, die äußeren Quadern aus weißgelbem Sandstein aus Hartenburg i. d. Pfalz (von Gebr. Schmitt). Zu dem äußeren Schichtenmauerwerk sind Bruch= steine (Moëllons) aus Fels in Luxemburg, zum innern dagegen weißgelber Sandstein aus Luxeuil verwendet worden. Bildhauer Kiefer in Ett= lingen führte die Michaelstatue, die Kanzel wand und das Eingangsportal aus, Binz in Karlsruhe die Evangelistenzeichen und Hyer in Basel die ornamentalen Skulpturen. Von Maler Asal in Karlsruhe rühren die Turmfiguren her und die Figurenfenster von Professor Laenger in Karlsruhe.

culte protestant qui a besoin d'une église de paroisse, d'une salle de prédicateur dans laquelle le regard de tous les fidèles se porte sans entraves et continuellement sur la chaire, l'autel et l'orgue. De même l'adaptation du local en rez=de=chaussée sous la galerie de l'orgue dans le choeur comme salle de confirmants cor= respond absolument aux exigences rituelles et assure le mieux une acoustique parfaite.

En exprimant clairement à l'extérieur les escaliers des galeries on a empêché tout en= combrement et désagrément pour les fidèles tant à l'entrée qu'au sortir du service divin et en même temps on a obtenu un motif qui contribue à rehausser le côté pittoresque de l'édifice et à en augmenter la stabilité.

On conviendra que cela est un avantage tout particulier si l'on songe que la tour quadrilatérale est construite en exclusion de absolue feraille.

La construction dont la conduite a été con= fiée à Mr W. Mund architecte a duré de juin 1898 à novembre 1901 et a coûté Marks 640000. Le socle, les escaliers et les futs de colonnes sont en granit du St. Gothard, les pierres de taille des façades sont d'un grès jaune clair de Hardenbourg dans le Palatinat (Frères Schmitt). La maçonnerie extérieure est composée d'assises de moëllons de Fels en Luxembourg, on a employé par=contre de la pierre blanche de Luxeuil à l'intérieur. La statue de (St.) Michael, la paroi de la chaire et le portail d'entrée ont été exécutés par le sculpteur Kiefer d'Ettlingen. Binz de Carlsruhe a sculpté les figures des Evangelistes et Hyer de Bâle les décorations ornementales.

Le peintre Asal de Carlsruhe a composé les figures de la tour, celles des fenêtres sont du professeur Laenger à Carlsruhe.

requirement of all protestant churches, that the eyes of the congregation shall be always fixed on chancel, altar and organ. The room under= neath the organ gallery is arranged as a con= firmation room; this is strictly canonical and has the advantage of securing the best possible acoustic. The staircase to the gallery is visible and is calculated, though simple in construction to ensure the easiest possible means of ingress and egress, so that no stoppage or disturbance can take place. This one detail enhances the effect of the whole and bears witness to the substantiality of the building. This is a matter of great moment as the quadrilateral tower is built entirely without iron. The building, the superintendence of which was entrusted to the architect W. Mund was erected from June 1898 to November 1901 at a cost of 640 000 Marks. The base, steps, and pillars are of Gotthard granite, the outside square stones are of yellow= white sandstone from Hartenburg in the Pala= tinate (Broth. Schmitt). For the outer masonry free stone from Fels in Luxemburg, for the interior yellow white sandstone from Luxeuil. The statue of (St.) Michael is by the sculptor Kiefer in Ettlingen, the same artist composed the chancel wall and the entrance porch; the Evangelists a reby Binz in Carlsruhe; the orna= mental sculpture by Hyer in Basel. The figures on the tower are by Asal in Carlsruhe, and the window designs by Professor Laenger in Carls= ruhe.

40 [1902: 44]

Von Curjel & Moser wurde in Karls= ruhe das zweigeschossige kastellartige, gänz= lich freistehende Wohnhaus Hoffstraße 2 von Mai 1900 bis August 1901 bei einem Kostenauf= wande von ca. 200000 M. aus gelblichem Sand=

40 [1902: 44]

Ce sont les architectes Curjel et Moser qui ont construit à Carlsruhe de mai 1900 à août 1901 pour la somme de 200000 M. la maison à deux étages, à l'aspect de château, tout à fait isolée Hoffstrasse 2. Cette maison a été construite

40 [1902: 44]

By the architects Curjel and Moser was built the castellated detached house 2 Hoff= strasse Carlsruhe from May 1900 to August 1901 at a cost of 200000 Marks. It is built of yellow sandstone from Brothers Schmidt in

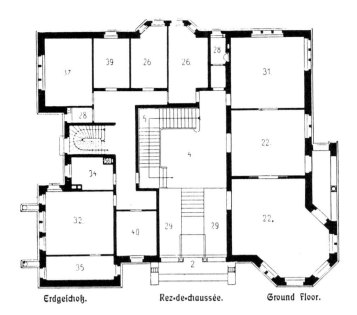

Erdgeſchoß.　　　　Rez-de-chaussée.　　　　Ground Floor.

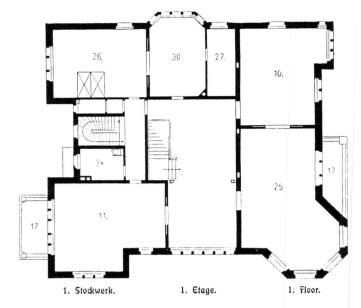

1. Stockwerk.　　　　1. Etage.　　　　1: Floor.

ſtein der Gebr. Schmidt in Hartenberg und mit reich ausgeſtattetem inneren Ausbau hergeſtellt. Bauführer Greulich und die Bildhauer Bing und Schach waren mit der Ausführung betraut.

en pierre jaune des frères Schmidt à Hartenberg; l'interieur est traité avec luxe. Le conducteur de travaux Greulich et les sculpteurs Bing et Schach ont été chargés de l'exécution.

Hartenberg. The interior is finely built. The building master Greulich and the sculptors Bing and Schach were entrusted with the carrying out of the architects design.

41 [1902; 58]

Das Neue Hauptpoſtgebäude am „Nieuwe Zijds Voor Burgwal" in Amſterdam, durch Architekt C. H. Peters errichtet, hat trotz der ſehr ſchwierigen Gründungsarbeiten nur dreieinviertel Jahre Bauzeit, bei einem Aufwande von rd. 1526000 Mark in Anſpruch genommen. Das Gebäude liegt an drei Seiten frei, die Vorderfront am genannten Voorburgwal, links begrenzt von der Radhuisſtraat, die Hinterfront an der Spuiſtraat, rechts anſtoßend an ein Privatgebäude (zum Hafen von Cleve).

Der einzige dem Publikum zugängliche Haupteingang I, durch die Pförtnerloge a beherrſcht, führt nach der im Erdgeſchoß liegenden Schalterhalle A A, um welche ſämtliche Räume für den öffentlichen Dienſt gruppiert ſind. An ſie ſchließen ſich mit ihren Schalterwänden links das Verſendungs- (Abfertigungs-) Bureau G, das Frankierungsamt F und das Ankunfts- (Ausgabe-) Bureau E an. Eine Ausbuchtung B wird durch die dort aufgeſtellten vier Geſtelle von ſog. „Lock-Boxes" gebildet, aus deren verſchließbaren Fächern die Empfänger der ankommenden Briefe

41 [1902; 58]

Le nouvel Hôtel Central des Postes au Nieuwe Zijds Voor Burgwal à Amsterdam élevé par monsieur C. H. Peters architecte, n'a demandé que trois ans et un quart de construction malgré les conditions particulièrement défavorables de fondation.

Ce bâtiment qui a coûté 1526000 Marks est dégagé de trois côtés, la façade principale au Voor Burgwal déjà nommé, celle de gauche bornée au Radhuisſtraat, la façade postérieure se trouve sur le Spuistraat tandis qu'à droite l'édifice est bordé par une maison particulière (au port de Cleve). La seule entrée I ouverte au public et surveillée par la loge du portier a, conduit à la halle aux guichets A A située au rez-de-chaussée et autour de laquelle se groupent tous les locaux destinés au service public. C'est ici que s'ouvrent les guichets à gauche du bureau d'expédition G, le bureau d'affranchissement F et le bureau d'arrivée E. Un dégagement B contient les quatre rayons de "Lock Boxes" dont les casiers fermés à clef sont à la disposition des locataires qui viennent y chercher eux-mêmes

41 [1902; 58]

The new General Post-Office on "Nieuwe Zijds Voor Burgwal" in Amsterdam, was built by the architect C. H. Peters in $3\frac{1}{2}$ years at a cost of Mk. 1,526,000. The fundament presented many difficulties which were however overcome in a comparatively short time. The building is free on three sides, the front faces the Voorsburgwal, the left side faces the Radhuisstraat, the back of the building is in the Spuistraat, and the right side joins a private building (zum Hafen von Cleve).

The principal entrance I, the only one available for the public leads to the great, hall for letter boxes A A, guarded by a porters lodge a and situated on the ground floor. Round this are grouped the various official apartments. Here lie the expedition bureau G, the stamp office F and the receiving and despatching office E. The recess B is occupied by 4 cases containing "Lock Boxes" from which the owners can take their own letters. On the right are two rooms

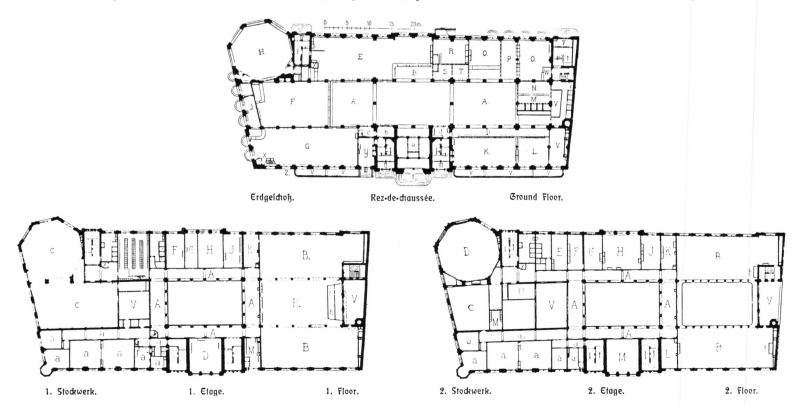

Erdgeſchoß.　　　　Rez-de-chaussée.　　　　Ground Floor.

1. Stockwerk.　　　　1. Etage.　　　　1. Floor.　　　　　　2. Stockwerk.　　　　2. Etage.　　　　2. Floor.

diese selbst entnehmen. Rechts schließen sich daran zwei Räume S u. T für den Postwert-zeichen-Verkauf, dahinter der Depositenraum R, die Postsparkasse Q. Der Gang P nimmt die Schalter der Telegrammannahme O auf. Für den Nachtdienst dieser ist der Schalterraum W von der Treppe V aus zugänglich gemacht. N ist das Bureau für Telephonie, mit Raum für das Publikum M und fünf Sprechzellen.

Die Schalter für Postanweisungen liegen bei D mit dem Bureau K und dem für die Quittungen L sowie dem Botenraume V. Die Treppe II führt nach dem Amtszimmer des Postdirektors Y mit Wachtkammern b u. c, sowie nach seiner Wohnung im I. u. II. Stock. Die Treppe III mit dahinter liegendem Sprechzimmer d ist für die Telegraphen-beamten im I. u. II. Stock bestimmt, während die Treppe V den Telegraphenboten und Treppe IV den Briefbestellern vorbehalten ist.

V, V sind Lichtschächte, X, X Aufzüge (in sämtlichen Grundrissen gleich bezeichnet).

Der Gang J verbindet die Unterfahrt H mit den Räumen F und G. Im Untergeschoß liegt unter dem obengenannten Raum G, an der Vorderfront der drei Fensterjoche umfassende Abstempelungsraum, in dessen Vorderwand bei Z drei Briefeinwürfe für den Stadtverkehr und drei solche für Fernsendungen angelegt sind. An der Front rechts schließt sich daran die Haus-meisterwohnung, deren Zugang Treppe VI bildet. Hinter dem Stempelraum ist der Raum für die Briefbeutel u. s. w.

Die übrigen Räume des Untergeschosses dienen als Magazine für die Post und Telegraphie, als Accumulatorenkammer, Kessel und Maschinen-räume für Wasser- und Luftpumpen und für deren Wärter, sowie ein großer vier Joche umfassender Raum als Aufenthalt der Telegraphenboten u. s. w.

Im I. Stock umgeben die Galerien A, A den zentralen Oberlichtraum, der die Halle des Erd-geschosses erleuchtet. Die Apparatesäle B, B, B mit dem Leitungsschacht b b dienen der binnen-ländischen Telegraphie. M ist der Kleiderraum für die Damen und L der für die Herren. F und G sind Bureau und Sprechzimmer des Tele-graphendirektors, H und I die zugehörigen Ver-waltungsbureaux, K Bureau des T. Ingenieurs. D enthält die Postverwaltung; die Räume a, a (nebst gleichartigen darüber im II. Stock gelegenen) die Wohnung des Postdirektors und C, C sind Briefträgersäle.

Im II. Stock reihen sich wieder rechts an die Galerien A, A die beiden Apparatesäle B, B, der eine für Ausland- der andere für Nacht-telegraphendienst mit Leitungskasten b b, dazu L, Raum für den Leitungswärter. C ist der Telephonsaal, M ist die Kantine, G ist Ingenieur-, H Verwaltungsbureau der Telegraphie, I für den Instrumentenmacher, K für den Aufsichtsbeamten bestimmt. An die Wohnräume des Postdirektors a, a schließt sich der Telephonsaal an, mit Damen-kleiderraum M. O sind Magazine, D der In-struktionssaal und E und F Bureaux des Telephon-aufsehers und des -Ingenieurs.

Der Bau ist in allen Teilen mit Dampf-heizung und reichlicher Warm- und Kühl-Druck-Luftzuführung, mit Trink- und Spülwasserleitung u. s. w. versehen. Die Fassaden sind aus Fein-ziegeln mit Oberkirchner und Bentheimer Sand-stein aufgeführt; die Bauausführung war den Unter-nehmern D. Cerlyn & Sohn und A. J. de Haan, die Bildhauerarbeiten an E. Bourgognon vergeben.

leur correspondance. A droite de la halle s'alignent les locaux S & T destinés à la vente des timbres et cartes, en arrière le bureau de dépôt R de la caisse d'épargne postale Q. Dans le passage P se trouve le guichet de réception des télégrammes O. Pour le service de nuit, le bureau W est accessible par l'escalier V. Le bureau N est celui du téléphone avec salle pour le public M et cinq cabinets de téléphone.

Les guichets pour mandats de poste sont en D avec le bureau K et le bureau L pour les quittances et la chambre V pour les facteurs. L'escalier II conduit au bureau du directeur des postes Y et aux chambres de garde b et c ainsi qu'au logement du directeur au 1er et 2nd étage.

L'escalier III avec le parloir d, en arrière est destiné aux employés du télégraphe des 1er et 2me étages, tandis que l'escalier V sert aux porteurs de télégrammes et l'escalier IV aux facteurs postaux. V V sont des courettes X X des lifts ainsi désignés dans tous les plans d'étages.

Le corridor J relie le passage souterrain H avec les locaux F et G. Au sous-sol se trouve au-dessous du local G, du côté de la façade principale la salle d'oblitération à trois fenêtres de front: cette dernière communique avec la rue par trois boîtes aux lettres Z pour le service local et trois autres pour l'étranger. Du côté droit se trouve l'appartement du concierge dont l'entrée est formée par l'escalier VI. Derrière la salle d'oblitération se trouve la salle pour les sacoches de lettres etc.

Les autres localités du souterrain servent de magasins pour les postes et télégraphes, de chambres d'accumulateurs, de salles pour les chaudières et machines, pour pompes à eau et à air; cet étage contient en outre une salle de 4 travées de fenêtres pour les facteurs du télé-graphe etc.

Au premier étage les galeries A A entourent la cour vitrée centrale éclairant la halle du rez-de-chaussée. Les salles d'appareils B B B avec l conduites des fils b b, servent à la télégraphie du pays. M est le vestiaire des dames, L celui des messieurs. F et G sont le bureau et le parloir du directeur des télégraphes, H. et I les bureaux d'administration dépendants de ce service. K bureau de l'ingénieur. D contient l'administration des postes. Les locaux a a ainsi que ceux qui leur correspondent au 2me étage servent de logement au directeur des postes, c c sont les salles des facteurs de poste.

Au deuxième étage les salles d'appareils B B s'ouvrent à droite sur les galeries A A, l'une pour le service télégraphique à l'étranger, l'autre pour le service télégraphique de nuit. b b sont les armoires à conduites, L est la chambre du gardien des conduites. M est la can-tine, G le bureau l'ingénieur, H de l'administration de la télégraphie, I celui du mécanicien, K celui du fonctionnaire surveillant.

La salle du téléphone avec vestiaire des dames M rejoint l'appartement du directeur des postes a a. O sont des magasins, D la salle d'instruction E et F les bureaux du gardien et de l'ingénieur des téléphones. Le bâtiment est pourvu dans toutes ses parties de chauffage à vapeur, d'abondante ventilation à pression pour air frais et chaud, d'eau potable et d'eau de lavage etc.

Les façades sont construites en briques avec du grès d'Oberkirch et de Bentheim. L'entreprise fut confiée à Mrs D. Cerleyn et fils et A. J. de Haan. E. Bourgognon a exécuté les travaux de sculpture.

S & T for post cards and stamps, behind this the deposit bureau R of the Post office Savings Bank Q. The corridor P contains the office for the receipt of telegrams O. For the telegraphic night service is appointed the office W reached by the staircase V; N is the Telephone bureau with accommo-dation for the public M and 5 speaking cells.

The money order office is situated at D with the bureau K, for receipts L and the messenger's room V. The stair case II leads to the bureau of the Post Director Y and the watchman's rooms b & c, as well as to the private dwelling of the Director in the I and II stories. The staircase III with the room d lying behind it, is for the Telegraph officials in the I and II story, and staircase V is for the telegraph messengers and staircase IV for the letter carriers.

V V are light courts X X are lifts seen in all ground plans.

The corridor J connects the porch H with the rooms F and G. In the ground floor lying under the room G in the front of the building is a three-windowed stamping room, on the front wall of which by Z are three openings for letters, for town post, and three for distant post service.

To the right, in front is the dwelling of the house porter with an entrance from staircase VI. Behind the stamping room is the room for letter bags &c. The remaining rooms of the ground floor are used as magazines for post and tele-graphy, as accumulator chambers, boiler and machine rooms hot water and air pumps and for the attendants of the same, as well as a large 4 windowed room for the telegraph messengers &c.

In the I floor the galleries A A surround the central sky-light, which lights the hall on the ground floor. The apparatus rooms B B B with a shaft for the conductors b b are for inland tele-graphy. M is the Ladies' Cloak room and L that for gentlemen. F and G are the office and consulting room of the Telegraph director, H and J the administrative offices, K the office of the Telegraph Engineer. D contains the Postal administration; the rooms a a (as well as similar rooms on the second floor) form the dwelling of the Post Director and c c are the postmen's rooms.

In the second floor round the galleries A A are the apparatus rooms B B, one for night telegraph service, the other for foreign telegraph service with the cableshafts b b, with a room L for the attendant. M is the canteen, G is engineers bureau, H the administration of the telegraph service, J for the instrument maker, K for the superintending officials. By the side of the private dwelling of the Director a a is a telephone hall with adjoining ladies' cloak room M. O are magazines, D is the instruction room, E and F the bureau of the telephone superintendent and the engineer.

The building is everywhere heated by steam with warm and cool air apparatus, it contains a complete water supply. The facades are of fine tiles with Ober-Kirchner and Bentheim sandstone. The builders were D. Cerlyn and Son and A. J. de Haan, the sculpture is by E. Bourgognon.

Eine ganz neue Tonart schlägt Architekt Max Fabiani in Wien bei dem von ihm dort Starhemberggasse 47, Ecke Favoritenplatz, errichteten Miets-Wohn- und Geschäftshause an.

L'architecte Max Fabiani à Vienne, a touché une note toute nouvelle dans la maison à loyer qu'il a construite en cette ville à l'angle de la Starhemberggasse 47 et place des Favorites.

A new note has been struck by the architect Max Fabiani in Vienna in the large dwelling and business house built by him at the corner of the Starhemberggasse and Favo-

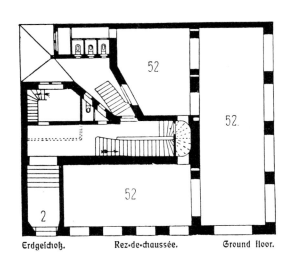  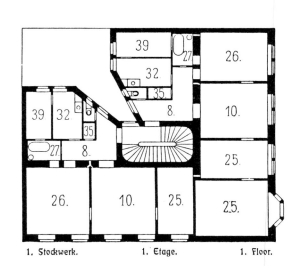

Erdgeschoß.   Rez-de-chaussée.   Ground floor.   1. Stockwerk.   1. Étage.   1. Floor.

Er bildet dasselbe als Pfeilerbau, dessen Füllungswände berankt und aus welchen die nötigen Fensteröffnungen ausgeschnitten erscheinen. Das als dünne, weit ausladende Platte in Erscheinung tretende Dach ruht auf vorgestreckten I Trägern, die teilweise durch ein unterliegendes Dreieck, und über den Pfeilern durch paarige eiserne Konsolträger unterstützt sind. Das ganze ist als Putzbau mit angetragenem Ranken-Ornament durchgeführt.

Il figure une construction à piliers, entre lesquels les panneaux couverts de branchailles sont découpées les baies des fenêtres

La saillie du toit apparaît comme une mince et large dalle qui repose sur des fers à I saillants, lesquels sont en partie soutenus par des triangles et au dessus des piliers par des consoles accouplées. Le tout est exécuté en maçonnerie crépie avec ornements modelés en mortier de chaux.

ritenplatz. It is a pillared edifice with wreathed panels between, in which the necessary window openings are cut. The roof projects far out with a thin edge and rests on I girders which are partly supported by under-lying triangular supports and by consoles forming the capitals to the pillars. The whole building is of plaster-work with ornaments modeled in mortar.

Als hervorragenden Versuch frühmittelalterliche Aufbaumotive bei modernen Profanbauten und in modernem Gewande zu verwenden, kann das in Karlsruhe, an der Karlstraße, Ecke Akademiestraße, von April 1898 bis Oktober 1901 durch die Architekten Curjel & Moser (Conf. Pauluskirche in Basel, Taf. 7—8), für den Preis von 700000 Mk. errichtete Bankgebäude von Veit L. Homburger gelten. Es ist aus weiß-gelbem Spessartsandstein von Gebr. Adelmann, durchaus massiv hergestellt.

La maison de banque de Mr Veit L. Homburger à Carlsruhe, Karlstrasse, à l'angle de la Akademiestrasse construite d'avril 1898 à octobre 1901 par les architectes Curjel et Moser (voyez Pauluskirche à Bâle Pl. 7—8) a coûté 700000 Marks. C'est un essai des plus importants d'application d'une façade du Moyen-âge primitif à un édifice moderne profane avec une décoration moderne.

L'édifice a été construit massif en pierre blanche du Spessart par les frères Adelmann.

The bank building of Veit L. Homburger in Carlsruhe Karlstrasse at the corner of the Akademiestrasse built from April 1898 till Oct. 1901 by the architects Curjel and Moser (see Paul's Church in Basel plate 7—8) at the cost of 700000 Marks, may be considered as a meritorious and successful attempt to reproduce early medieval church architecture and apply it to ordinary modern purposes. It is massively built of yellowish white Spessart sandstone and was carried out by the Brothers Adelmann.

Erdgeschoß.   Rez-de-chaussée.   Ground Floor.   1. Stockwerk.   1. Étage.   1. Floor.

Mit der Bauführung war der Architekt R. Bischoff betraut; die Bildhauerarbeit hat O. Kieffer in Ettlingen ausgeführt. Die Schlosserarbeiten stammen von Sauer, Nagel & Weber in Karlsruhe, die inneren Marmorverkleidungen aus Schachermühle bei Straßburg i. E.

Les travaux ont été conduits par l'architecte R. Bischoff; O. Kieffer à Ettlingen a exécuté la sculpture. Sauer, Nagel et Weber à Carlsruhe ont livré les ouvrages de serrurerie. Les revêtements intérieurs de marbre proviennent de Schachermühle près de Strasbourg en Alsace.

The direction of the building was in the hands of the architect R. Bischoff, the sculpture is by O. Kieffer in Ettlingen, the iron work by Sauer, Nagel and Weber in Carlsruhe, the interior marble panelling was from Schachermühle near Strassburg in Alsace.

Das von Architekt Lefranc in Paris, Boulevard du Temple 7 und 9, erbaute Zinshaus gewährt ein recht glückliches Bild von den Bestrebungen der Pariser Architekten, ihrer Stadt ein freundlicheres Straßenbild zu schaffen, als es unter der Geltung des im Haussmann'schen Regime bedingten auch die Baukunst knebelnden Schematismus sich entwickeln konnte.

Befreiend wirkten vor allem die Aufhebung der alten Fenstersteuer und die Freigabe der Anlage von Erkern und Loggien, welche wie alle größeren Vorsprünge an Privatbauten aus „strategischen Gründen" untersagt waren. Die Bildsamkeit und Tragfähigkeit des prachtvollen dortigen Steinmaterials erlaubt die, an anderen Orten kaum durchführbaren, höchst praktisch ausgekragten Bogenanlagen, welche wesentlich die reizvolle Erscheinung unserer Fassade begünstigen. Zeigt die Anlage der Kaufläden auch keinerlei Fortschritte, wie sie in den benachbarten Staaten längst zur Durchführung kamen, so ist das lediglich in der konservativen Eigenwilligkeit der Pariser Kleinkaufleute begründet, gegen welche der Architekt nicht anzukämpfen vermag. Die Anlage von Dachgaupen nahe an der First ist deshalb geboten, weil die durchweg dem Gesinde zugewiesenen oberen Bodenkammern nicht mehr wie früher durch schiefliegende Fenster erhellt werden dürfen.

La maison à loyer construite par M. Lefranc architecte, à Paris Boulevard du Temple 7 et 9 offre un heureux exemple des efforts faits par certains architectes parisiens pour donner aux rues de leur ville un aspect plus riant que ne le permettait la règle imposée par le régime Haussmann et qui avait pour but de baillonner l'architecture. La suppression de l'ancien droit des portes et fenêtres ainsi que la permission accordée d'établir des bow-windows en saillie et des loggias permet à l'architecte de se mouvoir plus librement, ces derniers appendices étaient auparavant interdits aux constructions particulières „pour des raisons de stratégie".

La force de résistance et la souplesse de l'admirable pierre du pays permet l'exécution à peine possible ailleurs d'arcs en saillie d'une grande utilité pratique, ces saillies contribuent largement à l'aspect séduisant de cette façade. Si la disposition des magasins ne montre aucun des progrès que nous constatons dans ce domaine chez les nations voisines, cela tient surtout à l'obstinément conservateur des boutiquiers parisiens, que l'architecte ne pourra que vainement combattre. Les lucarnes proches du faîte éclairent les chambres pour des combles qui généralement sont réservées aux domestiques et ne doivent plus comme autrefois être éclairées par des chassés en pente.

The dwelling house built by the architect Lefranc in Paris, Boulevard du Temple 7 and 9, is a particularly good example of the efforts of French architects to construct more cheerful-looking streets than it was possible to do under the "Haussmann régime", a régime which not only regulated the direction of the streets; but which forced all architecture to be of the same monotonous character. A great step towards freedom was the repeal of the window-tax, and the permission to use loggias and bows; ornaments which had been formerly forbidden on "strategical grounds". The exceedingly plastic quality of the splendid stone material found in the neighbourhood in great abundance renders it eminently workable into a variety of useful and beautiful architectural forms. The Paris architects therefore have a comparatively easy task in constructing charming facades. And when we cannot note a corresponding progress in the architecture of the public shops, it is principally owing to the conservative obstinacy of the small shopkeepers; against which the most enthusiastic architect struggles in vain. The erection of straight corners nearly to the summit of the building has been a necessity for lighting the garrets, the old slanting window in the roof being forbidden as a means of lighting servants' bedrooms.

Als würdiges Seitenstück zu der in Nr. IV 1901 auf Taf. 82—84 gebrachten Hofapotheke und dem hier auf Taf. 12 abgebildeten Bau ist das von Herrm. Walder in Karlsruhe, Ecke der Kaiser- und Karlstraße errichtete Geschäfts- und Wohnhaus anzusehen.

Der Aufbau gemahnt mit seinen zweigeschossigen Bogenöffnungen, dem hohen Wartturm und den breiten Söllern an alte Kauf- und Gewerkshäuser. Mit seinem durchaus volkstümlichen, von Künstlerhand ausgeführten Bildwerk ist der Bau eine Zierde der Stadt geworden.

Freudig berührt es, daß auch der davor stehende, schmiedeeiserne Licht- und Stromträgermast eine entsprechende künstlerische Ausbildung in modernen Formen gefunden hat.

On peut considérer comme un digne pendant de la pharmacie de la cour publiée dans le No IV 1901 Planches 82—84 et du bâtiment représenté ici Planche 12, la maison d'habitation et de commerce à l'angle de la Kaiserstrasse et de la Karlstrasse à Carlsruhe construit par Mr Herrmann Walder, architecte à Carlsruhe.

La façade rappelle avec ses arcades à deux étages, sa haute tour et ses larges balcons, les anciennes maisons de commerce et des métiers. Cette construction avec ses décorations sculptées d'un caractère absolument populaire et artistique constitue un ornement pour la ville. On est aussi agréablement surpris de voir le mât en fer forgé pour la lumière électrique etc. traité d'une façon artistique en style moderne.

The house built by Hermann Walder in Carlsruhe at the corner of the Kaiser- and Karlstrasse partly as business premises and partly as dwellings, may be considered a worthy companion to the Court Pharmacy illustrated in No IV (1901) on plates 82—84 and in this number on plate 12. The imposing archway stretching upwards through two stories, the high tower, and two large terraces remind us of the merchant's and guild houses of ancient times. While the architecture is thoroughly characteristic of the country and people, it yet shows the hand of a master and is one of the greatest ornaments of the town. An agreeable impression is made by the suitable artistic design of the electric mast standing before the house.

In Straßburg i. E. bauten die Architekten Berninger & Krafft am Broglieplatz, Ecke der Blauwolkengasse, vom 1. Juli 1900 bis zu dem 1901 für den Eigentümer H. Flach ein Geschäfts- und Wohnhaus in ganz moderner Stilfassung. Die von aller Schulmäßigkeit sich lossagende Aufbau-Komposition der ausgebauten Loggien, der Dacherker und des Erkerturmes, wie der gesamten ornamentalen Durchführung des Eisenwerkes, gewähren dem Bau einen eigenartigen Reiz, der gegenüber den meist monotonen älteren und neueren Bürgerhäusern an einem der wichtigsten Verkehrsplätze des inneren Straßburgs recht vorteilhaft zur Geltung kommt. Das Material ist vornehmlich Eisen und französischer (Morlaix-) Kalkstein mit Backstein für die Zwischenpfeiler.

Mrs Berninger et Krafft architectes ont tbâti du 1er juillet 1900 au 1er juillet 1901 à la place Broglie au coin de la Blauwolkengasse à Strasbourg pour M. H. Flach une maison d'habitation et de commerce en style entièrement moderne. La composition de la façade avec ses loggias en saillie, ses lucarnes et sa tourelle ainsi que l'ensemble de la décoration de la construction en fer, n'a rien d'académique et donne à l'édifice un charme particulier. Cette maison située sur une des places les plus importantes et les plus animées de l'intérieur de Strasbourg contraste avantageusement avec les maisons bourgeoises, tant anciennes que modernes, qui sont généralement fort monotones.

The architects Berninger and Krafft in Strassburg in Alsace have built on the Broglieplatz at the corner of the Blauwolkengasse from 1st July 1900 to the summer of 1901 a business and dwelling house for Mr. H. Flach. The house is distinctly modern; the unconventional composition of the loggias, of the roof gables and of the towers as well as of the ornamental iron work lend an exceptional charm to the building which stands out in advantageous contrast to the monotonous architecture of the old and new surrounding houses in one of the most important centres of Strassburg. The material is principally iron and French (Morlaix-) limestone with brick for the supports.

In Zürich, in prachtvollster Lage am Seefeldquai, mit reizendster Aussicht auf den See und die Alpen, hat Architekt Alexander Koch in London für Herrn Ruegg-Honegger eine nach englischer Auffassung malerisch gruppierte, dem Landschaftsbilde wohlangepaßte Villa erbaut, die auch in der Grundrißausbildung den äußersten

M. Alexandre Koch architecte à Londres à construit pour M. Ruegg-Honegger à Zurich, dans une situation admirable sur le Seefeldquai avec vue délicieuse sur le lac et les Alpes, une villa conçue dans l'esprit anglais, avec groupement pittoresque des différentes parties et se mariant bien avec le paysage. Le

In Zurich, on a splendid site on the Seefeld quai with a charming outlook on the lake and the Alps the architect Alex. Koch of London has built a villa for Mr Ruegg-Honegger. The house is English in form and fashion and is so grouped as to command the best possible view of the

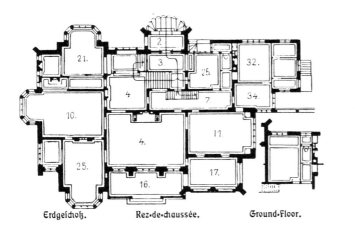
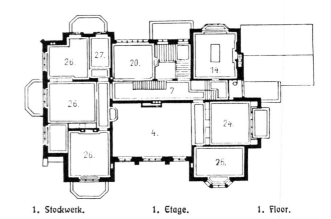

Erdgeschoß.   Rez-de-chaussée.   Ground-Floor.   1. Stockwerk.   1. Etage.   1. Floor.

Anforderungen vornehm-behäbiger Wohnlichkeit Rechnung trägt.

Darunter ist besonders hervorzuheben, wie die große, durch zwei Stockwerke durchgehende Halle, in der das gesellschaftliche Familienleben seinen Mittelpunkt findet, und die vorgelegte Terrasse, auch gegen die schärfsten Seewinde durch die seitlich vorspringenden Gebäudeteile geschützt, jederzeit den Genuß des reizenden Panoramas unbehindert gewähren. So bewegt die ganze Anlage sich dem Auge bietet und die Ausblicke unbehindert läßt, zeigt sie doch im Innern die Geschlossenheit, die einen bequemen Zusammenhang der Räume und Schutz gegen das Einspielen der Winde sichert.

48 [1902; 29]

In den kontinentalen Großstädten, in welchen das Reihen-Etagenmiethaus vorwaltet und die Höhenentwickelung so manchen Beschränkungen unterliegt, ist dem Architekten zur Aufgabe gestellt, durch eine kräftige Gliederung der einzelnen Gebäudeteile dem Hause und dem Straßenbilde ein malerisches Gepräge zu schaffen. In denjenigen Städten der Niederlande und in England, besonders in London, wo mit guter Absicht schmale Baustellen vorherrschen und, den örtlichen Bedürfnissen entsprechend, kaum andere als Dreifenster-Häuser Käufer oder Mieter finden würden, wird dem Architekten die entgegengesetzte Aufgabe: durch Zusammenfassung einer Zahl von Einzelhäusern eine Gruppe zu schaffen, um der bizarr wirkenden Zerrissenheit des Straßenbildes zu steuern. Jedoch muß dann jedem Hause die vollständige Selbständigkeit (auch im äußeren erkennbar) gewahrt bleiben. Das ist also wieder durchaus verschieden von dem vornehmlich in Wien herrschenden System: mehrere Miethäuser zu einem Mietskasernenpalast zusammen zu kuppeln.

Ein recht schönes Beispiel aus London zeigen die vier von dem Architekten E. W. Stephens errichteten, zu einer Häusergruppe vereinigten Gebäude an dem neu angelegten „Hans Place" Nr. 11—14, Herbert Crescent, Chelsea, S.W. Wie wenig Zwang ein solches Vorgehen dem Architekten auferlegt, wird durch die im Vorbau und die in drei Geschossen durchgeführte zweiachsige Fensterteilung des Hauses Nr. 11 ohne weiteres ersichtlich; eine Störung in der Gesamterscheinung der Gruppen ist dadurch nicht hervorgerufen, sondern es hat nur die malerische Wirkung gewonnen.

49 [1902; 30]

Die im vornehmsten Viertel Londons (am Hydepark) durch Architekt A. H. Kersey, F. R. J. B. A. errichteten fünf Wohnhäuser, Parkstreet 2—10, sind in einheitlicher Architektur zu einem Block gruppiert. Alle Innen- und Außendetails sind vom Architekten selbst entworfen.

Unsere Abbildung zeigt das Eckhaus (Nr. 10) an der Aldfordstreet. Die Fronten wurden aus

plan de cette maison se plie aux exigences d'une habitation réunissant la grande élégance à l'extrême comfort.

Remarquons en particulier le grand hall montant de fond et formant le centre de la vie de famille et la terrasse placée devant, protégée par les corps de bâtiments avancés contre les âpres vents du lac et offrant de tous temps la jouissance du grandiose panorama des montagnes. Malgré la diversité qu' offre le coup d'œil de l'ensemble et la variété des points de vue dont on jouit, l'intérieur montre cependant ce caractère de „chez soi" que donne la suite des chambres communiquantes et protégées contre le jeu des vents.

48 [1902; 29]

Dans les grandes villes du continent où dominent les grandes maisons à loyer et où les règlements imposent certaines limites pour les hauteurs, les architectes ont reconnu la nécessité d'employer des motifs d'architecture vigoureux pour distinguer certaines parties des façades et donner un caractère pittoresque aux rues.

Dans certaines villes des Pays-Bas et d'Angleterre, particulièrement à Londres où dominent les terrains étroits et où d'accord avec les habitudes du pays on ne trouve guère d'acheteur ou de locataire que pour la maison à trois fenêtres de front, l'architecte a un programm opposé; il s'efforce de grouper en un seul corps un certain nombre de maisons pour mitiger l'aspect décousu des rues. Chaque maison doit cependant à l'extérieur conserver entièrement sa physionomie propre. Voici donc un système absolument contraire à celui de Vienne qui consiste à grouper plusieurs maisons en un type de palais-caserne à louer.

Un bel exemple du système anglais est le groupe de quatre maisons construits par l'architecte E. W. Stephens sur la place nouvellement créée, dite „Hans Place" No. 11—14. Herbert Crescent, Chelsea, S.W.

La disposition de fenêtres à deux axes dans l'avant corps et les trois étages de la maison No. 11 nous montre du premier coup de combien de liberté jouit l'architecte. Cela ne trouble en aucune façon l'aspect général du groupe, mais en augmente au contraire l'impression pittoresque.

49 [1902; 30]

Dans le plus beau quartier de Londres, longeant Hydepark, cinq maisons nouvellement érigées par l'architecte Mr A. H. Kersey, F. R. J. B. A. Parkstreet 2—10 paraissent groupées en un seul bloc, d'architecture similaire; tous les détails d'intérieur et d'extérieur sont dûs au crayon de l'architecte même.

Nous représentons ici la maison à l'angle de l'Aldfordstreet.

landscape in which it is itself an interesting object. The hall, which extends upwards through two stories is particularly noticeable and is so arranged as to be the centre of social and family life; the terrace in front, protected from the sharp sea wind, is at all times available as an agreeable point from which to view the lovely surrounding panorama. Wide and free to the winds of heaven as the house is on the outside, so carefully and snugly is the interior of the house arranged; and the greatest possible comfort is secured.

48 [1902; 29]

In the large cities of the continent the architect who is subject to various restrictions as to the height of the houses is obliged to construct flats extending through one enormous story. And the house itself occupying a wide area forms an important feature in the picturesque development of the street. In the Netherlands and in England, particularly in London where the building sites are for the most part narrow, and seldom afford room for more than three windows, the architect has another task before him; he has to construct a number of single houses so as to form a harmonious group in the line of the street, and yet to preserve for each its individuality both of interior and exterior. This is in striking contrast to the Vienna fashion, where several houses are grouped together into a kind of palatial barracks.

A fine example from London is shown in the four houses by E. W. Stephens at the "Hans Place" newly laid out, No. 11—14, at Herbert Crescent, Chelsea, S.W.

The architect has shown great freedom in his treatment of the porch and in the window framing of the three stories, of the house No. 11, and yet the harmony of the whole is not disturbed, on the contrary, a most picturesque effect has been thereby achieved.

49 [1902; 30]

The architect of the residences 2—10 Park Street, London W., is Mr A. H. Kersey, F. R. J. B. A. Red brick and Portland stone were used for the exterior. The ornamental plasterwork has been executed by Mr Sidney Elms, the ironwork by White and the glazing by Mrs Warrington & Co. The roofs are covered with Broseley tiles.

roten Ziegeln und Portlandſtein hergeſtellt, die Dächer mit Broſeley-Ziegeln gedeckt. Die Bildhauerarbeiten ſind durch Mr. Sidney Elms, das Schmiedewerk durch White und die Verglaſungen von Mrs Warrington & Co. ausgeführt. Zum inneren Tiſchlerwerk ward weſentlich gebeiztes Eichenholz verwendet, für die Geſellſchaftsräume aber Zeder- und amerikaniſches Nußholz und für die mit Atlas tapezierten Boudoirs Walnuß mit Ahorn. Die maſſiven Decken ſind mit Eichenholzparket, die Treppenſtufen mit Teakholz belegt.

Les façades sont en brique rouge avec pierre du Portland, les toitures couvertes en tuiles Broseley. Les sculptures sont exécutées par Mr Sidney-Elms, les ferronneries par White et les vitrages par Mrs Warrington & Co.

Les boiseries intérieures sont généralement en chêne macéré, celles des salles de réception en cèdre et noyer d'amérique et en noyer érable dans les boudoirs, dont les pans hauts sont tapissés en satin.

Les plafonds massifs sont couverts de parquets en chêne et les marches des escaliers en bois-teak.

The interior woodwork is chiefly fumigated oak, with the exception of the drawing-rooms, where pencil cedar and American walnut have been employed, and the boudoirs, which are panelled in satin walnut and maple. The floors are of parquet oak laid on solid boarding. The stairs have teak treads and risers.

A feature of this large block of residences, in the most fashionable part of London, is that all the details were designed by the architect.

50, 51 [1902: 21, 22]

Eins der auffälligſten aber auch am klarſten durchgebildeten Werke der „Wagnerſchule" iſt der „Königsbazar" am Franzensplaß in Budapeſt. Die Architekten Aladar Kármán und Julius von Ullmann haben den ausgedehnten, in allen Teilen fein durchgebildeten Bau vom 5. September 1899 bis 1. November 1900 für den Preis von rd. 1110000 Mk. aus Backſtein in Putzbau mit Granitpfeilern und zwiſchen genieteten Trägern ausgewölbten Decken ausgeführt. Wie der Aufbau, ſo zeigt auch der Grundriß eine bemerkenswert glückliche Löſung in der äußeren Zuſammenfaſſung von zwei Eckgebäuden mit einem zwiſchenliegenden zu einem großen von der Paſſage durchzogenen Prachtbau, ohne Beeinträchtigung der Selbſtändigkeit der einzelnen Bauten.

50, 51 [1902: 21, 22]

Le Königs-Bazar, Place François à Buda-Pest est une des œuvres les plus imposantes et aussi les plus claires de l'école du profeſſeur Wagner. Les architectes Aladar Kármán et Julius von Ullmann ont élevé cette construction étendue si bien étudiée dans tous les détails, du 5 septembre 1899 au 1er novembre 1900 pour le prix de 1110000 Marks. L'édifice est en maçonnerie de briques crépies, avec des piliers en granit et des plafonds voûtés entre traverses en fer rivées.

Le plan montre ainsi que l'élévation une heureuse solution du programme demandant un ensemble monumental formé par trois maisons de location, separées, dont deux d'angle, flanquant une de milieu, les trois traversées par un passage commercial.

50, 51 [1902: 21, 22]

One of the most noticeable and at the same time one of the clearest exponents of the Wagner school is the "Königsbazar" on the Franzensplaß in Budapest. The building, carried out in all its details in the sincerest and most artistic manner, was erected by the architects Aladar Kármán and Julius von Ullmann from 5th Sep. 1899 to 1st Nov. 1900 at a cost of 1110000 Marks. It is of brick with plasterwork, the pillars are of granite and the vaulted roofs are supported by iron girders. The ground plan as well as the erection shows a particularly happy solution of a difficult problem; the two corner buildings being connected with a third by a magnificent arcade, and yet each separate building is complete in itself.

---

52 [1902: 23]

Martin Dülfer, der Architekt des Geſchäftshauſes der „Münchener Allg. Zeitung" (vergl. Jahrg. 1901, Heft IV, Taf. 91), errichtete von April 1899 bis März 1900 das hier abgebildete Landhaus in München-Sendling, Wolfrathshauſerſtr. 31½, für den Preis von nur 58000 Mark. Faſt allen äußeren Schmuckwerkes entbehrend — nur die Balkongitter des Giebelbaues ſind in blendend reizvoller Schmiedetechnik und das tragende Holzwerk der Freihalle wie die Ortſparren durch einfache Bemalung oder charakteriſierende Bearbeitung hervorgehoben — zeichnet ſich der vornehme Bau durch eine freundlich anmutende, poeſie- und ruhevolle Stimmung aus, die durch eine ungekünſtelte Silhouette gehoben, auch weit in der Ferne zur Geltung kommt. Bis zur Sockelóberkante iſt der Bau in Beton, der Aufbau in verpußtem Ziegelmauerwerk ausgeführt, das Dach mit Ziegeln (Biberſchwänzen) gedeckt.

Der Grundriß und die geſamte Einrichtung geſtatten, daß das Haus ungeteilt oder auch durch zwei Familien bewohnt werden kann.

52 [1902: 23]

Martin Dülfer, l'architecte de l'immeuble du journal „Münchener Allgemeine Zeitung" (voyez No IV 1901 Planche 91), a construit d'avril 1899 à mars 1900 la maison de campagne représentée ici. Cette villa qui se trouve Wolfrathshauserstrasse 31½ à Sendling Munich n'a couté que 58000 Marks; elle est presque dépourvue de tout ornement. Seules les balustrades des balcons du fronton sont d'un travail charmant en fer forgé et les bois de construction de la verandah ainsi que les chevrons de front sont rehaussés d'une peinture simple et d'une décoration caractéristiques. Cet édifice d'un caractère si distingué commande l'attention par son aspect gai et poétique ainsi que par sa calme fraicheur; sa silhouette pleine de naturel se distingue de fort loin. La construction est en beton jusqu' à la hauteur du socle, en briques crépies pour les étages; le toit est recouvert en tuiles. Le plan et la disposition générale sont composés de façon à permettre par d'habiter la maison une seule famille ou par deux.

52 [1902: 23]

Martin Dülfer the architect of the business premises of the "Münchener Allgemeine Zeitung" (see No IV plate 91 year 1901 of this periodical) built from April 1899 till March 1900 the country house here represented in Munich-Sendling Wolfrathshauserstrasse 31½ at a cost of only 58000 Marks. The ground-plan and arrangement of the rooms make the house convenient for the use of one or of two families. The lower part is of beton the upper part of plastered brick-work; it is roofed with flat tiles. Avoiding nearly all external ornament, with the exception of the extremely artistic iron work of the balcony and of the tastefully coloured and carved wood work, the architect has succeeded in creating a noblelooking house at once homelike and restful, and which stands out, an effective silhouette, in the surrounding landscape.

---

53 [1902: 41]

Das von Architekt Edw. T. Hapgood in Hartford, Conn. (U. S. A.) in der Farmington Avenue im Jahre 1901 für Herrn Theodore B. Dickerſon erbaute Landhaus kann als klaſſiſches Beiſpiel für die praktiſche und maleriſch reizvolle Anlage nordamerikaniſcher Wohnhäuſer gelten. Die durchaus einfache und ungekünſtelte Grundrißanlage begünſtigt den bequemſten Zuſammenhang der Räume und bietet reiche Ausſchau auf die Umgebung.

Das Kellergeſchoß iſt mit roten, genau ſchichtmäßig aber in den Köpfen nicht bearbeiteten Sandbruchſteinen verkleidet. Die Außenwände des Erdgeſchoßes ſind aus Klinkern hergeſtellt, deren vom Brand bunt gefärbte Köpfe die Flächen in unregelmäßiger Muſterung beleben. Das Obergeſchoß aus Fachwerk hat gleich den Dächern eine mit Papier überdeckte Verſchalung und darüber eine Schindelverkleidung erhalten, die mit vandyckbrauner „Cabot"ſcher Schindel-

53 [1902: 41]

La maison de campagne construite en 1901 dans Farmington Avenue par Mr Edw. T. Hapgood à Hartford, Conn. (Etats-Unis) pour Mr Theodore B. Dickerson, peut être citée comme exemple classique d'habitation américaine unissant le plus grand comfort à l'extrème élégance. La disposition du plan favorise une communication commode des pièces et offre une vue splendide sur les environs.

L'étage des caves est revêtu de pierres rouges en assises régulières traitées en bossage. Les façades du rez-de-chaussée sont construites en briques dures dont les bouts surcuits à différentes couleurs forment des surfaces à dessins irréguliers.

L'étage supérieur est en pans de bois et a ainsi que les toits un revêtement en feuillets recouverts de papier et bardeaux pardessus, peints d'une peinture spéciale brun Van-Dyck dite de Cabot.

53 [1902: 41]

A classical and charming example of North American house architecture at once picturesque and practical is the house built by the architect Edw. T. Hapgood in Hartford. Conn. (U. S. A.) in the Farmington Avenue in 1901 for W. Theodore B. Dickerson. The simple ground plan allows of the most comfortable arrangement of the rooms, from which one has wide views of the surrounding country. The underground basement is panelled with sandstone; the outside walls are of "clinkers" whose burnt surfaces give an agreeable element of colour. The upper story is of framework and has, as well as the roofs a patent covering painted vandyke brown "Cabot". The panels of the frieze and of the corner towers are of

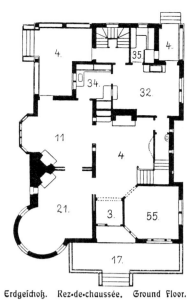  

Erdgeschoß. Rez-de-chaussée. Ground Floor.   1. Stockwerk. 1. Étage. 1. Floor.

farbe geftrichen ift. Die Flächen der aus Stuck hergeftellten Panele des Friefes und des Erker-turmes find mit Zement angetragen und mit hellen Kiefeln und Glasfplittern gefpickt, wodurch fie einen achatähnlichen, bunten Schiller erhalten haben. Die Stockwerkhöhen betragen nur: im Keller 2,20, Erdgeschoß 3,14, I. Stock 2,73, Dach-geschoß 2,51 m. (a. Sc. Am. 1901.)

Les surfaces des panneaux de la frise et de la tourelle sont crépies en ciment et lardées d'éclats de verre et de cailloux clairs, ce qui leur donne un reflet d'agate et un riche chatoiement. La hauteur d'étages est pour la cave de 2,20 mètres, pour le rez-de-chaussée de 3,14, pour le premier étage de 2,73 et pour les chambres hautes de 2,51 mètres. (Sc. Am. 1901.)

cement and are ornamented with fragments of glass and with light-coloured pebbles, the whole having the effect of agate. The height of the various stories is as follows: basement 2,20 m, ground floor 3,14 m, 1st floor 2,73 m, roof story 2,51 m. (Sc. Am. 1901.)

54, 55 [1902: 27, 28]

Als beftätigenden Beitrag zu der im Auffatze „Die Entwickelung der Architektur in Deutschland" (vergl. Seite 1 und ff. diefes Jahr-gangs) auf Seite 4 angeführten Thatfache, daß in Deutschland auch bei den Bauten der ver-fchiedenen Verwaltungsbehörden die örtlichen Rückfichten mit Bezug auf gefchichtliche Ent-wickelung und Städtebild in Vordergrund geftellt werden, bringen wir hier zwei Anfichten vom Aeußeren und eine vom Inneren der foeben er-öffneten Schalterhalle des „Neuen Haupt-bahnhofes in Danzig".

Kaum eine unferer großen Seehandelsftädte hat eine wechfelvollere Gefchichte aufzuweifen — felbft das in fo vielen Beziehungen ähnliche Venedig nicht! Aus einer dänifch-flavifchen Niederlaffung entftanden, unter der Herrfchaft des Deutfchherren-Ordens zu weltbedeutender Blüte entwickelt, als deutfche Hanfaftadt, alsdann Republik unter polnifchem Protektorat u. f. w., bis es 1793 wieder unter preußifche Herrfchaft zum deutfchen Stammlande kam, bezeugt auch feine eigentümlich entwickelte Architektur unverkennbar die Einflüffe folch wechfelnder Gefchicke. Bezeugt uns die Baugefchichte, daß die reichen Kauf-herren feinerzeit ganze Paläfte aus Venedig, aus Portugal herangefchafft und hier wieder auf-bauen ließen, fo läßt fich leicht ermeffen, daß die heimifchen Architekten bei eigenem Schaffen fich den Einflüffen folcher Vorbilder nicht ent-ziehen konnten. So entftand denn in Danzig, dem „Venedig der Weichfelmündung an der Oftfee", die eigentümliche, an orientalifche oder venetianifche Pracht mahnende, ftolztroßende „Danziger Renaiffance", der baltifch-nordifchen fehr nahe verwandt und doch vollftändig ihre felbftändige, nirgend wiederkehrende Eigenheit wahrend. Das allgemein zur Geltung kommende Material befteht aus tiefbraunroten, hand-geftrichenen, aber fehr regelmäßigen Backfteinen und hellgrauem fchwedifchen Granit, deffen Textur der ftraffen Führung des auf Fernwirkung berechneten Ornaments angepaßt ift. Die Dächer find mit Falzziegeln, die Türme mit Kupfer gedeckt.

54, 55 [1902: 27, 28]

Comme preuve de ce qui a été dit dans notre article sur le développement de l'architecture en Allemagne (voyez p. 1 et suivantes de cette année) et de ce que nous avons affirmé p. 4, qu'on tenait compte en Allemagne pour les divers bâtiments d'administation des conditions locales et historiques, nous publions ici deux vues extérieures et une intérieure de la spacieuse halle aux guichets de la „Nouvelle gare cen-trale à Dantzig".

Il existe à peine un port de mer qui ait subi un sort plus varié dans son histoire que Dantzig, pas même Venise, qui lui ressemble sous tant de rapports.

Issue d'une colonie slavo-danoise, elle attint un développement inouï sous la domination de l'Ordre des chevaliers teutons, comme ville de la Hanse allemande. Elle fut ensuite république sous le protectorat de la Pologne, jusqu'à ce qu'en 1793 elle retourna à son pays d'origine sous le règne de la Prusse. Le singulier déve-loppement de son architecture trahit indubitable-ment la variété de ses destins politiques: L'histoire nous apprend qu'autrefois de riches marchands firent venir de Venise et de Portugal des palais entiers qui furent élevés ici, il est donc facile-ment admissible que les architectes du pays furent, dans leur travaux, influencés par de tels modèles. C'est ainsi que se développa à Dantzig, la „Venise de l'embouchure de la Vistule sur la Baltique", cette étonnante Renaissance dantzicoise rappelant par sa pompe et son origina-lité l'Orient et Venise: elle est parente de l'archi-tecture des pays baltiques mais a bien ses caractères propres qu'on ne retrouve nulle part ailleurs.

Les matériaux généralement employés sont les briques rouges formées à la main mais très régulières et le granit gris clair de Suède dont le grain demande une ornementation raide, propre à ètre vue de loin.

Les toits sont couverts en tuiles à recouvre-ment, les tours en cuivre.

54, 55 [1902: 27, 28]

As a proof of the statements enlarged upon in our Essay "The development of Archi-tecture in Germany" (compare page 1 and fellowing pages) we read on page 4: that all official buildings are designed with regard to both local requirements and to historical association. We bring as examples of this two views of the exterior and interior of the newly opened booking-office of the "New Railway Terminus in Dantzic".

There is scarcely a large seaport in the world that can look back on such a changeful past as Dantzic, not even Venice which it greatly resembles. Founded by a Danish-Slavish colony and raised to a great height of prosperity by the order of "Deutschherren" as a German Hanse town, then a republic under a Polish protectorate and then in 1793 again a German town under the Prussian flag. The peculiarities of its most interesting architecture show the vicissitudes of its history. We learn that the rich Dantzic merchants transported whole palaces from Venice and from Portugal and had them re-erected in their own town, and we can imagine how great an influence this imported architecture had on the native builders of the day. In this way arose in the "Venice on the Vistula" what was called the Dantzic Renaissance, an original style half Oriental half Venetian and wholly proud and magnificent; related it is true to the North Baltic home style, but yet thoroughly independent and peculiar to this city alone.

The principal material used in the new booking-office is dark red-brown brick laid with great regularity and light grey Swedish granite; the com-bination is most effective and ornamental, parti-cularly in the distance. The roofs are covered with Falztiles, and the towers are covered with copper.

Die durch die Architekten Schmohl & Stähelin in Stuttgart während nur 13 monatiger Bauzeit in der Neckarstraße 56 errichtete „Stuttgarter Bürgerhalle" giebt uns ein schönes Bild der in freierer Fassung wieder auflebenden Deutsch-Renaissance.

Der stolze Bau, der im Erdgeschoß nur Restaurationsräume, im I. Stock Säle zu Festlichkeiten und Konzerten birgt, enthält in den oberen Stockwerken größere Mietwohnungen.

Die Fassade besteht aus Hochdorfer Sandstein. Sämtliche Entwürfe für Bildhauer, Maler, Kunstschmiedewerke und Ausstattung sind ausführlich von den genannten Architekten durchgearbeitet und unter deren persönlicher Leitung zur Ausführung gebracht worden. Das macht die geringe Kostensumme, die nur 400 000 M. betragen hat, wohl erklärlich.

Ein ganz eigenartig malerisches Gepräge kennzeichnet das vom Architekten (Maurer- und Zimmermeister) Wilh. Gebhardt in der Prinzenstraße 42 zu Berlin von Februar bis Ende September 1901 errichtete Geschäfts- und Wohnhaus. Die Grundrisse sind vom Erbauer in Gemeinschaft mit dem Architekten Kolb, die Fassaden von den Architekten Schweitzer und Eberhardt, die innere Ausstattung von dem Letztgenannten entworfen.

Zu der Vorderfront sind lederfarbene Siegersdorfer Verblendsteine und Kunststandstein (von Gebr. Friesecke) verwendet worden; der Sockel besteht aus Granit. Die grauweißen Putzflächen und die in Stuck ausgeführten Antragarbeiten wurden durch Bildhauer Otto Pobig ausgeführt. Die Kunstschmiedearbeiten entstammen den Werkstätten von Semmler und Bleyberg.

An der Herstellung des Baues, der einen Gesamtaufwand von rund 200 000 Mark (d. i. 640 Mark für 1 qm) erforderte, sind namentlich noch nachfolgende Firmen beteiligt gewesen: für das Zimmerwerk: die des Erbauers, das Mauerwerk: Chr. Neumann, Marmor- und Granitarbeit: Wilh. Sasse Nachflg., die Dächer: Fr. Hieke, elektrische Anlagen: Allgemeine Elektrizitäts-Gesellschaft und Fr. Wiegel, den Fahrstuhl: Berliner Aufzug-Fabrik (P. Müller), Zentralheizung: Th. Lepthin, sämtlich in Berlin.

In Zürich, an der breiten Bahnhofstraße 69, auf einem spitzwinklig durch die schmale Sielgasse begrenzten Gelände, dessen scharfe Spitze durch die hier ebenfalls abzweigende Seidengasse abgestumpft ist, stand bisher ein baufälliges Gebäude, „zur Trülle" benannt, weil hier einst eine jener mittelalterlichen Martereinrichtungen stand: ein aus eisernen Stangen gebildeter, um seine senkrechte Achse drehbarer Käfig, in welchem

La „Stuttgarter Bürgerhalle", Brasserie construite à Stuttgart, Neckarstrasse 56 par les architectes Schmohl et Stähelin dans l'espace de 13 mois nous donne un bel exemple de libre interprétation de renaissance allemande renouvelée.

Cette belle construction occupée au réz-de-chaussée par un restaurant et au Iᵉʳ étage des locaux de fêtes et de concerts, contient aux étages supérieurs de grands appartements à louer.

Les façades sont en pierre de Hochdorf. Tous les projets pour sculpteurs, peintres, serrurerie artistique et mobilier ont été étudiés en détail par les architectes et exécutés sous leur direction immédiate; cela explique le prix très bas de cet édifice qui ne s'est élevé qu'à 400 000 Marks.

La maison de commerce et d'habitation élevée de février jusqu'à fin septembre 1901 par l'architecte et entrepreneur de maçonnerie et de charpente Wilh. Gebhardt, Prinzenstrasse 42 à Berlin fait une impression tout à fait particulière et pittoresque. Les plans ont été élaborés par le constructeur en collaboration avec l'architecte Kolb, les façades sont des architectes Schweitzer et Eberhardt les installations intérieures ont été composées par ce dernier.

La façade principale est en briques couleur de cuir de Siegersdorf et en pierre artificielle de Frieseke frères. Le socle est en granit. Les surfaces crépies et les décorations en stuc ont été exécutées par Mr Otto Pobig sculpteur. Les fers forgés sortent des ateliers de Semmler et Bleyberg.

A l'exécution des travaux, qui a nécessité une dépense de 200 000 Marks, soit 640 Marks par mètre carré, ont pris part outre les maisons sus-nommées: Wilh. Gebhardt pour la charpente, pour la maçonnerie: Chr. Neumann, les travaux de marbre et de granit: Wilh. Sasse successeur, la toiture: Fr. Hieke, l'installation électrique: la Allgemeine Elektrizitäts-Gesellschaft et Fr. Wiegel, l'ascenseur: la fabrique berlinoise d'ascenseurs (P. Müller), le chauffage central: Th. Lepthin, tous à Berlin.

A Zurich, bordant la large rue de la Gare No. 69, sur un terrain en forme d'angle aigu, borné par l'étroite Sielgasse, dont l'angle aigu est ici coupé par la Seidengasse qui aboutit également à ce point dans la rue de la gare, s'élevait jusqu'à nos jours une bâtisse branlante, nommée „au pilori" du nom d'un de ces instruments de supplice placé à cet endroit au Moyen-âge. C'était une sorte de cage en fer fixée

The German Renaissance has received a new and beautiful example in the "Stuttgarter Bürger Halle", built in Stuttgart, Neckarstrasse 56 by the architects Schmohl and Stähelin in a period of 13 months. The imposing building contains on the ground and first floor only restaurants and halls for concerts etc.; the upper floors are large dwellings arranged in flats. The facade is of Hochdorfer sandstone. The designs of the sculptor, of the painter, of the artistic iron work, in fact the entire equipment were worked out thoroughly under the personal superintendence of the architects. This explains the comparatively small cost of the building, which was only 400 000 Marks.

The house in the Prinzenstrasse 42, Berlin erected by the architect and builder Wilh. Gebhardt from February till the end of September 1901 is a picturesque building with much artistic individuality. The ground plan was constructed by the builder together with the architect Kolb, the facades are by Schweitzer and Eberhardt, the inside equipment by the last-named firm. The front is of leather-coloured Siegersdorfer stone and artificial sandstone by Brothers Friesecke, the basement is of granite, the grey-white plasterwork and the stucco is by the sculptor Otto Pobig; the artistic iron work is by Semmler and Bleyberg. The following firms were employed in the building which cost about 200 000 Marks (640 Marks per square metre) woodwork — the builder; brickwork: Chr. Neumann; marble and granite work: Wilh. Sasse; the roofs: Fr. Hieke; electric installation: Allgemeine Electrizitäts-Gesellschaft and Fr. Wiegel; the lifts: Berliner Aufzug-Fabrik (P. Müller); central heating apparatus: Th. Lepthin, all in Berlin.

In the broad Bahnhofstrasse 69 Zurich, there stood till lately a dilapidated building on a piece of land which formed an acute angle with the narrow Sielgasse; the sharp corner of this angle is cut off by the Seidengasse and here stood the building known as "Zur Trülle". It was probably used in the Middle Ages as a place of torture, and the iron cage was evidently

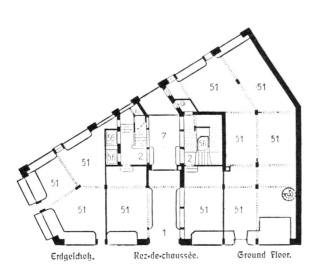

Erdgeschoß. Rez-de-chaussée. Ground Floor.

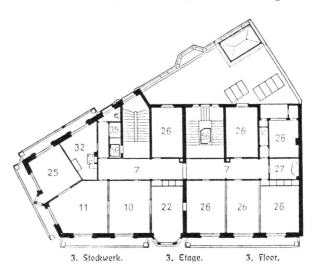

3. Stockwerk. 3. Etage. 3. Floor.

„arme Sünder" öffentlich zur Schau gestellt und von der lieben Gassenjugend durch Umdrehen des Käfigs u. s. w. geneckt wurden. Auf diesem Gelände haben die Architekten Pfleghardt und Häfeli ein modernes Zinshaus errichtet, das im Erdgeschoß und den beiden unteren Obergeschossen große Geschäftsräume und in den oberen je zwei größere Wohnungen enthält, während in dem ausgebauten Dachgeschoß nur Fremdenzimmer, zu den unteren Wohnungen gehörig, angelegt werden durften.

Die ausgezeichnete Lage bedingte eine Hervorhebung des Baues über die nachbarlichen Gebäude, was durch die Anlage des Turmes und Emporführung des Ziergiebels an der Ecke wirksam erfolgte. In diesem Giebel erscheint denn auch die Benennung des Hauses durch figürliche Darstellung ihres Ursprunges versinnbildlicht: der darüber angebrachte lächelnde Narrenkopf soll die Thorheit der alten Zeit, die derartige Einrichtungen als „Weisheit" erachtete, aussprechen.

Nach der schmalen Sielgasse durfte das Gebäude nur in beschränkter Höhe aufgeführt werden; das Dach des niedrigen Teiles ist als Garten angelegt. Die Fassaden sind aus ostschweizerischem Sandstein hergestellt; alle freiliegenden Eisenstützen und Träger sind mit Kieselguhr zwischen Asbest ummantelt, die Decken über Keller und den drei Geschäftsgeschossen in Stein-Eisenkonstruktion ausgeführt, die Dächer mit Bieberschwänzen gedeckt, die Türme mit Kupfer. Das Bildhauerwerk des Giebels führte Siegwart in Luzern aus, das der übrigen ornamentalen Teile Paul Abry in Zürich. Das Kunstschmiedewerk wurde Illi von Arx und Theiler in Zürich übertragen. Die Baukosten betrugen ca. 33,6 M. für einen cbm umbauten Raum, von der Kellersohle bis zum Dachkranz gerechnet.

61 [1902: 42]

Zu den Werken, mit welchen Architekt F. R. Voretzsch in Dresden die neuzeitliche Architekturrichtung des XX. Jahrhunderts einleitete (vergl. Jahrg. 1901, S. 30, 41 u. 42, bez. Taf. 50, 58 u. 59), gehört u. a. auch das große Mietwohnhaus Reichenbachstraße 57. Das Bildwerk der im ganzen sehr schlicht gehaltenen Sandsteinfassade ist von Prof. Rr. Rentsch ausgeführt. Die Herstellung des ganzen Baues beanspruchte nur 8 Monate bei einem Aufwande von 102 000 M.

62 [1902: 50]

In Berlin ist durch Architekt Georg Rathenau binnen Jahresfrist, bis zum 1. April 1902, das in der Leipziger Straße 92 gelegene „Verwaltungsgebäude der Singer Co., Nähmaschinen Akt.-Ges." errichtet und fertiggestellt worden. Der sehr schmale Bau fesselt durch seine vornehm ruhigen Verhältnisse und seine fein durchgeführten Skulpturen. Die Fassade ist aus schlesischem Sandstein mit Sockel aus schwedischem Granit von Wimmel, während die Skulpturen von Bildhauer Pobig ausgeführt wurden. Die Decken sind nach System „Kleine" (Backstein mit Bandeisen-Einlage zwischen ⊥ Trägern) hergestellt. Um im Laden Pfeilervorlagen zu vermeiden, wurden die Deckenstützen aus Eisen mit Kreuzverankerung gebildet. Beide Fahrstühle sind nach System „Otis". Die Mauerarbeiten führte Carl Bäsell, das Kunstschmiedewerk die Firma Golde & Raebel aus. Die Gesamtkosten beliefen sich auf rund 200 000 M., das sind rund 690 M. für 1 qm überbauter Fläche oder 26,5 M. für einen 1 cbm umbauten Raum.

63 [1902: 47]

In der Berliner Grunewaldkolonie wurde bei einjähriger Bauzeit am 1. Oktober 1901 die von Architekt Agathon Reimann an der

---

sur un axe vertical et dans laquelle de pauvres délinquants étaient exposés à la risée publique et aux plaisanteries de la jeunesse des rues qui s'amusait à faire tourner la cage. C'est sur cette place que les architectes Pfleghardt et Häfeli ont élevé une maison de rapport moderne, contenant de grands locaux de commerce au rez-de-chaussée et aux deux premiers étages ainsi que deux grands appartements par étage pour les étages supérieurs. Dans l'étage du toit ont été aménagées des chambres d'amis dépendant des appartements.

L'excellente situation de cet immeuble exigeait un signe marquant qui le distinguât des maisons voisines, c'est ce qui fut obtenu au moyen d'une tour et d'un fronton élevé dominant l'angle. Dans ce fronton un groupe rappelle l'origine du nom de l'ancienne maison; au dessus se trouve une tête de fou qui doit rappeler à quelles aberrations étaient sujets les ancêtres qui considéraient comme sages des institutions inhumaines.

Du côté de l'étroite Sielgasse, la maison ne devait avoir que peu de hauteur; le toit de la partie basse est disposé en jardin. Les façades sont construites en grès de la Suisse orientale. Tous les supports en fer sont revêtus de masses isolantes. Les plafonds des caves et des trois étages de comptoirs sont construits en fer. Les toits sont recouverts en tuiles, les tours en cuivre.

La sculpture du fronton a été exécutée par Siegwart de Lucerne, les autres décorations plastiques sont l'œuvre de Paul Abry à Zurich. Les ouvrages en fer forgé sortent des ateliers de Illi von Arx et Theiler à Zurich. Les frais de construction comportent Marks 33,60 par mètre cube d'espace compté du sol des caves jusqu' à l'entablement principal.

61 [1902: 42]

La grande maison à loyer Reichenbachstrasse 57 fait partie des oeuvres avec lesquels Mr F. R. Voretzsch architecte inaugurait à Dresde la nouvelle direction dans l'architecture du XXme siècle (Voyez l'année 1901 p. 30, 41 et 42, Pl. 50, 58 et 59). La sculpture de la façade traitée du reste d'une façon très sobre est du Professeur Rr. Rentsch. La construction de toute la maison n'exigea que 8 mois et une dépense de 102000 M.

62 [1902: 50]

La maison d'administration de la société par actions pour la fabrication de machines à coudre „Singer Co." a été élevée et terminée dans l'espace d'un an jusqu'au 1er avril 1902 à la Leipzigerstrasse 92 à Berlin par Georges Rathenau architecte. L'étroite façade séduit par ses proportions nobles et tranquilles ainsi que par la finesse de ses sculptures. La façade est en grès de Silésie, le socle en granit de Suède de Wimmel, les sculptures sont dûes au sculpteur Pobig. Les plafonds sont construits d'après le système „Kleine" (Briques enjointées de fers à cerceau entre fers ⊥). Pour éviter de gros piliers dans le magasin, les supports du plafond furent exécutés en fer. Les deux ascenseurs sont du système „Otis". Les travaux de maçonnerie furent exécutés par Carl Bäsell, les fers forgés par la maison Golde & Raebel. Le coût de la construction fut de 200000 M. ce qui représente 690 M. par m² de surface bâtie ou 26,50 M. par mètre cube de construction.

63 [1902: 47]

Mr Agathon Reimann architecte a terminé après un an de travaux la „villa Heil" à l'angle des rues Fontane 8—10 et Bettina

---

a pillory in which "poor sinners" were exposed to the insults of the populace. On this site, the architects Pfleghardt and Häfeli have erected a modern house containing on the ground and first floors large business premises and on the upper floors dwellings; the roof story contains additional rooms belonging to the dwellings. The imposing site has been advantageously used to erect a noticeable building, the towers and the architecture of the roof being particularly striking. On the gables is an allegorical figure emblematic of that which formerly stood there; above this is a Fool's Head representing Modernity laughing contemptuously at what was considered the wisdom of medieval times.

The side fronting the narrow Sielgasse could not be carried up very high, and the roof of the lowest part is laid out as a garden. The facades are of sandstone from East Switzerland all free lying iron parts are covered with a preparation of asbestos; the ceilings of the cellars and of the business premises are of stone and iron, the roofs are of tiles, and the towers roofed with copper. The sculpture of the gables is by Siegwart of Lucerne, the other ornamental parts by Paul Abry of Zurich, the artistic iron work is by Illi of Arx and Theiler of Zurich. The cost of building amounted to 33,6 Marks pr. 1 cubic metre of building reckoned from the floor of the cellar to the capital cornice.

61 [1902: 42]

The large dwelling house in the Reichenbachstrasse 57, Dresden built by the architect F. R. Voretzsch must be considered as one of those works by which this architect illustrates the modern tendency of the 20th Century (compare year 1901 page 30, 41 and 42 with plates 50, 58 and 59). The sculpture of the exceedingly simple sandstone facade is by Prof. Rr. Rentsch. The entire building only occupied 8 months and cost 102000 Marks.

62 [1902: 50]

The architect George Rathenau is building in the Leipzigerstrasse 92, Berlin the „Verwaltungsgebäude der Singer Co. Nähmaschinen Aktien-Gesellschaft" in one year ending April 1902. The very narrow building attracts by its distinguished and restful character and by the finely executed sculpture. The facade is of Silesian sandstone, the basement of Swedish granite by Wimmel, the sculpture by Pobig. The ceilings are consructed after the system "Kleine" (brick with band iron between ⊥ girders). In order to avoid the inconvenience of pillars in the shops the roof supports have a specially fitted iron construction. The lifts are according to the system "Otis". The brickwork is carried out by Carl Bäsell, the artistic iron work by the firm Golde and Raebel. The entire cost amounted to 200000 Marks, or 690 Marks per square metre of building site; or 26,5 Marks per cubic metre of building.

63 [1902: 47]

In the Grunewald colony near Berlin was built the villa Heil in the Fontanestrasse 8—10 corner of the Bettinastrasse from

Fontaneſtraße 8—10, Ecke Bettinaſtraße erbaute „Villa Heil" fertiggeſtellt, die in vier Stockwerken ſechs Familienwohnungen enthält, aber in ihrer ganzen Erſcheinung und Einrichtung vermöge ihrer bewegten Grundriß- und Silhouettenausbildung den für Bauten dieſer Kolonie bedingten maleriſchen Landhauscharakter wahrt.

Das Faſſadenmaterial beſteht aus roten Handſtrich-Backſteinen, unbehauenem Kalkſtein und Zementputz. Die Dächer ſind teils mit holländiſchen Pfannen, teils mit Falzziegeln eingedeckt.

dans la colonie de villas Grunewald près Berlin. Cette villa contient en quatre étages six appartements, mais sa disposition et son aspect s'accordent parfaitement avec le caractère pittoresque exigé pour les constructions dans cette contrée, grâce à son plan mouvementé et à sa silhouette.

Les façades sont en briques rouges, en pierre calcaire non taillée et en crépissage de ciment. Les toits sont recouverts en partie avec des tuiles hollandaises, en partie avec des tuiles à recouvrement.

October 1. 1900 to October 1901 by the architect Agathon Reimann. The house has four stories containing 6 flats for family dwellings; it is however in its arrangement and architecture suitable to the position which it occupies in the villa colony. The material of the facade is red brick with limestone and cement work. The roofs are covered with tiles partly hollandish form and partly from the Rhine.

64 [1902: 52]

Jn Berlin, Caubenſtraße 16—18, haben die Architekten Solf und Wichards für die in Magdeburg domizilierte „Allgemeine Verſicherungsgeſellſchaft Wilhelma" ein großes Geſchäftshaus errichtet, das im Dezember 1901 fertiggeſtellt wurde.

Für die Plangeſtaltung war zwiſchen mehreren der hervorragendſten Architektenfirmen ein Wettwerben ausgeſchrieben worden, demzufolge obengenannten Architekten im April 1900 der Sieg und damit der Bauauftrag zufiel. Die Bedingungen zielten weſentlich dahin, auf dem bis 1. September noch mit mehreren älteren Häuſern bebauten Gelände, deſſen Erwerb allein 1225000 M. koſtete, ein vornehmes, der hohen geſchäftlichen Stellung der „Wilhelma" entſprechendes Repräſentativ-Geſchäftshaus zu errichten, in welchem das 1. oder 2. Obergeſchoß für Geſchäfts- und Repräſentationsräume ihrer Berliner Niederlaſſung entſprechende zuſammenhängende Räume bieten müſſe, während die übrigen Räume an einige vornehme Geſchäftsfirmen oder als erſtklaſſige Wohnungen so vermietbar ſeien, daß deren Zinsertrag einen Ueberſchuß über die übliche Verzinſung des aufzuwendenden Geſamtkapitals mit Sicherheit ergebe.

Unſere Grundriſſe zeigen die ſehr weit ausgedehnte Raumausnußung, die nur durch eine vorſichtige Anordnung der Höfe erzielbar war.

64 [1902: 52]

Mrs Solf et Wichards architectes ont construit à Berlin, Caubenstrasse 16 à 18, une grande maison commerciale pour la „Société d'assurances générales Wilhelma", domiciliée à Magdeburg; cette construction fut terminée en décembre 1901.

Pour obtenir le plan il avait été fait un concours entre plusieurs des premiers architectes et c'est à la suite de ce concours que les architectes sus-nommés obtinrent le succès et l'exécution en avril 1900. Le but principal était d'élever un monument distingué et digne de la haute importance commerciale de la Wilhelma sur un terrain occupé encore jusqu'au 1er septembre par de vieilles maisons et dont l'acquisition avait à elle seule absorbé 1225000 Marks.

Le premier ou le second étage devait contenir une suite de locaux destinés au service de la succursale de Berlin, tandis que les autres parties de l'édifice devaient être louées à des maisons de premier ordre ou servir de logements à des familles distinguées pour assurer d'une façon certaine un interêt supérieur à une rente normale, du capital reposant sur cet immeuble.

L'espace disponible a été utilisé aussi complètement que possible, ainsi que le montrent nos plans; cette utilisation n'a été obtenue que grâce à une disposition spéciale des cours. Remarquons

64 [1902: 52]

The architects Solf and Wichards have built business premises at the Caubenstrasse 16—18 Berlin for the Magdeburg „Allgemeine Versicherungs-Gesellschaft Wilhelma". Jt was completed in December 1901.

For the design an open competition took place, and the prize was awarded to the above firm in April 1900. The conditions were mainly to construct on a site with several old houses standing and which alone cost Mk. 1225000 an imposing building in every way representative of the important company "Wilhelma". The 1st or 2nd floor were to be reserved for the offices of the Berlin branch of the Company. And the other part was to be constructed as superior flats or as first-class business premises; thus affording a prospect of good interest on the capital invested in the building. Our ground plan shows the very careful distribution of the various rooms, which was only achieved by a thoughtful consideration of the courts. Jt will

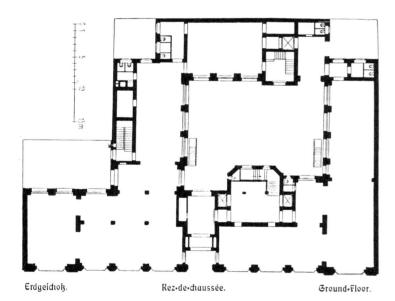

Erdgeſchoß.   Rez-de-chaussée.   Ground-Floor.

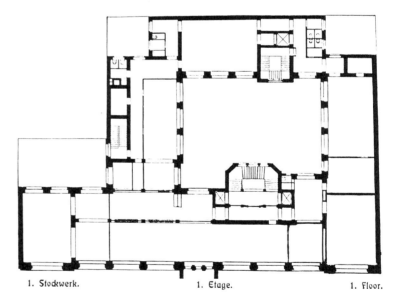

1. Stockwerk.   1. Étage.   1. Floor.

Dabei iſt zu bemerken, daß die Nebenhöfe und -Treppen durch die im Haupthofe rechts und links angeordneten Kellertreppen zugänglich und die Keller ſelbſt durch große Einfallichte gut erhellt ſind. Das Erdgeſchoß iſt als vornehmes Ladenlokal für Luxuswaren (Möbel und Stoffwaren?) beſtimmt. Das erſte Obergeſchoß dient der Wilhelmageſellſchaft, während die darüber liegenden Geſchoſſe an die „Deutſche Spiritusverwertungsgeſellſchaft" (ſog. Spiritusring) als Geſchäfts- und Ausſtellungslokale vermietet ſind.

Die Faſſade aus gelbweißem Wünſchelberger Sandſtein, deren Bildwerk nach Modellen von Profeſſor G. Riegelmann ausgeführt, von einer Jdealfigur der „Wilhelma" von Günther-Gera

en passant que les cours secondaires sont accessibles par les escaliers de cave situés à droite et à gauche de la cour principale et que les caves elles-mêmes sont bien éclairées par de grands soupiraux.

Le rez-de-chaussée est disposé pour magasins d'objets de luxe, meubles et étoffes. Le premier étage sert à la société Wilhelma, tandis que les étages supérieurs sont loués comme bureaux et salles d'exposition à la Société allemande pour l'exploitation de l'esprit-de-vin (Spiritusring).

Les façades sont en pierre jaune clair de Wünschelberg, leur décoration sculpturale est due au professeur G. Riegelmann qui en a livré les modèles; une figure représentant la Wilhelma,

be noticed that the adjoining courtyards and steps are connected with the right and left basement steps; the basement is efficiently lighted. The ground floor is occupied by a business for artistic furniture stuffs, the first floor contains the "Wilhelma" offices and over this are the premises of the German Spirit Company (so called "Spiritus-Ring").

The facade is of yellowish-white Wünschelberger sandstone, the sculpture is according to the models of Prof. Riegelmann and is crowned

gekrönt, bringt den baulichen Gedanken klar zu vornehmstem Ausdruck.

Die Hoffronten sind sehr einfach aber höchst stattlich mit weißglasierten Backsteinen und Einfassungen von Warthauer Sandstein ausgeführt. Ebenso stattlich ist das Innere, dessen künstlerische Antragarbeiten von Thiele & Tschinkel herrühren. Besonders prächtig ist das Treppenhaus ausgeführt, mit einer bis zu Schulterhöhe reichender Täfelung von schwarzbraun geädertem, mit grünadrigem weißen Marmor umrahmt, die Treppe selbst nebst Brüstungen aus gelblichem Marmor, das Geländer aus Aluminbronce, die Fenster in heller Kunstverglasung von J. Scheerer. Die verglasten Trennwände der Vorräume sind Kunstschnitzwerke. Die Dacheindeckung besteht aus braunglasierten Marienburger Pfannen. Das ganze Gebäude wird mit einer Niederdruck-dampfheizung erwärmt und ist reich elektrisch erleuchtet. Die elektrisch betriebenen Fahrstühle sind nach Otissystem gebaut.

œuvre de Günther-Gera couronne l'édifice.

Les façades sur la cour sont exécutées très simplement, mais d'une façon digne de l'ensemble, en briques blanches émaillées avec encadrements de pierre de Warthau. Les intérieurs sont également traités avec le plus grand soin, on y remarque entre autres des ornements modelés sur place par Thiele & Tschinkel. L'escalier est disposé d'une façon particulièrement somptueuse, il est bordé d'un revêtement de marbre noir brun encadré de marbre blanc veiné de vert; ce revêtement atteint la hauteur de l'épaule. Les marches d'escalier et les balustrades sont en marbre jaune, avec treillis en bronze d'aluminium. J. Scheerer a exécuté les fenêtres en vitraux clairs. Les parois vitrées des vestibules sont artistiquement sculptées.

Les toits sont couverts en tuiles de Marienburg brunes émaillées. Tout le bâtiment est chauffé au moyen d'un calorifère à vapeur à basse pression et abondamment pourvu de lumière électrique. Les lifts électriques sont construits d'après le système Otis.

in an appropriate manner by an ideal figure of „Wilhelma" the work of Günther of Gera. The sides facing the courtyards are of effective simplicity with their white glazed tiles and Warthauer sandstone. The interior is stately, the artistic ornaments are by Thiele and Tschinkel. The stair-case is especially magnificent, it is richly panelled to a considerable height with finely-veined marble. The stairs are of yellowish marble, the balustrades of aluminium bronze, the windows are of light glass of artistic design by J. Scheerer. The glass partitions in the front rooms are of artistically cut glass. The roof is tiled with brown glazed tiles from Marienburg. The whole building is heated by steam, and is well illuminated with electric light. The electric lifts are according to the system "Otis".

Das Hotel Central in der Hybernergasse 17 in Prag-(Neustadt), das nach ungefähr dreijähriger Bauzeit im Frühjahr 1902 eröffnet wurde, ist mit allen neuesten Einrichtungen von dem Prager Architekten Bélsky nach einem in Gemeinschaft mit dem Oberbaurat und Professor Friedrich Ohmann (Architekt des Hofburg-baues in Wien) verfaßten Grundriß ausgeführt worden. Nach ursprünglichem Fassadenentwurf von Ohmann ist unter dessen Einfluss die weitere Bearbeitung durch Ohmanns ehemalige Schüler, die Prager Architekten Al. Dryack und Fr. Bendelmayer erfolgt, denen auch Entwurf und Ausführung der Innendekorationen u. s. w. selbständig anvertraut waren.

Die Fassade ist in Backstein ausgeführt und geputzt, das Ornament freihändig modelliert, das Portal aus lichtgelbem Karstmarmor hergestellt.

Das die Stelle des Hauptgesimses einnehmende Vordach ist in Eisenkonstruktion mit zwischen-liegenden farbigen Glastafeln ausgeführt, das des Erkers aus Zinkblech getrieben und mit goldgelbem Oelfarbeanstrich versehen.

An der Ausführung waren Bildhauer und Stuckateur Simanowsky und Schlossermeister Nyedly beteiligt.

L'Hôtel Central dans la Hybernergasse No. 17 à Prag-Neustadt qui fut ouvert au printemps de l'an 1902 après une période de construction de trois ans à peu près, est l'œuvre de l'architecte Bélsky de Prague qui l'a édifiée avec toutes ses installations les plus modernes d'après un plan étudié en collaboration avec le professeur Frédéric Ohmann architecte de la résidence impériale à Vienne.

Les architectes Al. Dryack et H. Bendel-mayer à Prague, anciens élèves de monsieur Ohmann ont terminé l'étude des façades sous la direction du maître et d'après ses projets primitifs, ces deux architectes ont aussi été chargés du projet et de l'exécution des décorations intérieures qui est leur œuvre personnelle. La façade est en briques avec enduit, les ornements sont modelés sur place, le portail est construit en marbre de Karst jaune clair.

L'avant-toit qui tient la place de corniche est exécuté en fer avec panneaux de verre de couleur; celui de l'encorbellement est repoussé en zinc et verni en couleur d'or.

Le sculpteur stucateur Simanowsky et le maître serrurier Nyedly ont contribué à la décoration de cet édifice.

The Hotel Central in the Hybernergasse 17 Prague (Neustadt) has been built in about 3 years by the Prague architect Bélsky with the cooperation of Oberbaurat Professor Friedrich Ohmann, the architect of the Hofburg in Vienna, who was consulted as to the ground plan. The hotel was opened in the spring of 1902 and is equipped with every modern appliance. The original of the facade was the work of Ohmann, but it was carried out by his former pupils the Prague architects Al. Dryack and Fr. Bendel-mayer, who also designed the interior decoration. The facade is of brick and is plastered, the ornaments are of free-hand modelling, the portal is of light yellow Karst marble. The glass roof in the place of which runs the chief moulding is of ironwork with coloured glass panes. The bow window is roofed by hammered zinc, painted with oil of a golden yellow.

The sculptor Simanowsky and the iron-worker Nyedly were entrusted with the carrying out of the work.

Das in Wien am Alois Drasche Park 5, Ecke Kolschitzky-Gasse von der Baufirma Holzmann & Co. unter Architekt Carl Holzmann erbaute, ein bewohnbares Unter- und fünf Obergeschosse umfassende Miethaus hat trotz schwieriger Gründung nur 10 Monate Bauzeit (bis Mai 1901) bei rd. 278500 Mark Baukosten erfordert. Das aus Backstein von Wiener Berg mit Putzfassaden und mit Dach aus englischem Schiefer ausgeführte Gebäude ist mit Treppenstufen aus Karstmarmor und eichenem Brettchenboden versehen. Die Fundierung besteht aus einer 2 m starken, mit Eisen gegürteten Platte von Portlandzementbeton und hat bisher keinerlei Senkung ergeben.

Die Bildhauerarbeiten wurden durch Sandor & Frühauf, die Malerarbeiten durch J. Böhm ausgeführt; die Schlosserarbeit war an Joh. Loukotzky, das Tischlerwerk an Joh. Küttag, die Zimmerarbeit an E. Pollack und der Anstrich an H. Berkefeld vergeben.

La maison à loyer Alois Drasche Park 5, angle de la rue Kolschitzky à Vienne, contenant un sous-sol habitable et cinq étages a été construite par la maison Holzmann & Cie sous la direction de Mr Charles Holzmann architecte dans l'espace très court de 10 mois, jusqu'en Mai 1901 malgré de grandes difficultés de fondation.

Les frais de construction se sont élevés à M. 278500.

Le bâtiment est construit en briques de la tuilerie Wiener Berg, les façades enduites, le toit est recouvert d'ardoises anglaises; les escaliers sont en marbre du Karst et les planchers en bois de chêne. La fondation consiste en une assiette de béton de ciment de Portland de deux mètres d'épaisseur; ces dalles sont armées de fer et il ne s'est produit jusqu'à présent aucun tassement. Les travaux de sculpture furent confiés à Sandor et Frühauf, ceux de peinture artistique à J. Böhm. L'entrepreneur de serrurerie était Joh. Loukotzky, celui de menuiserie Joh. Küttag, celui de charpente E. Pollak, celui de peinture H. Berkefeld.

The building firm Holzmann & Co. under the superintendence of architect Carl Holzmann have built in Vienna, Alois Drasche-Park 5, corner of Kolschitzky-Gasse a dwelling house consisting of a ground floor and five upper stories. The fundament caused much difficulty, but the time occupied in building was only 10 months (till May 1901) and the cost was 278500 Marks.

The house is built of brick from Vienna Berg, the facades are plastered, and it is roofed with English slate. The stairs are of Karst marble and the floors of oak boards. The foundations are strengthened by iron bound plates of Portland-cement beton and up to the present have not sunk in the least.

The sculptural work has been done by Sandor and Frühauf, the painting by J. Böhm, the locks and iron work by Joh. Lou-kotzky, the carpenter's work by Joh. Küttag, the joiner's work by E. Pollack and the outside painting by H. Berkefeld.

Nur durch die Perczel utcza (Gasse) von vorstehendem Bau getrennt, haben die Architekten Aladár Kármán und Julius von Ullmann in Budapest gleichzeitig an demselben Platze, Szabadsay-tér, die bis zur Kiss Erüss utcza reichende Gebäudegruppe No. 12, 11 und 10 errichtet.

Das mittlere Haus, Szabadsay-tér No. 11, ist im Erd- und Zwischengeschoß als Kaufladen ausgebildet, während die oberen Geschosse große Mietswohnungen enthalten, deren grosse Loggien, namentlich die des IV. Stockwerks mit seinen aus Stabeisen gebildeten Pfeilern und dem zeltartig vorladenden Sonnendach wesentlich zur stattlichen Erscheinung des Baues beitragen.

Les architectes Aladár Kármán et Jules de Ullmann à Budapest ont construit en même temps et sur la même place Szabadsay-tér un groupe de maisons No. 12, 11 et 10 s'étendant jusqu'à la Kiss Erüss utcza et qui n'est séparé du bâtiment décrit plus haut que par la rue Perczel.

La maison du milieu, Szabadsay-tér No. 11 est distribuée en magasins au rez-de-chaussée et à l'entresol, tandis que les étages supérieurs sont aménagés en grands appartements à louer. Les grandes loggias de ces derniers, en particulier celle du quatrième étage avec ses piliers en fer et son avant-toit saillant en forme de tente contribuent puissamment à l'apparence majestueuse de l'édifice.

The architects Aladár Kármán and Julius von Ullmann of Budapest have erected on the site Szabadsay-ter a group of buildings No. 12, 11 and 10 reaching to Kiss Erüss utcza and separated from the named herebefore buildings by the Perczel utcza.

The middle house No. 11 is equipped, on the ground and intermediate stories as shops; the upper stories contain private dwellings. The large loggias on the IV floor with their ornamental iron pillars and their tent-like roof add much to the stately appearance of the building.

Das Neue Stadthaus in Zürich, an der Einmündung des Zürichsees in die Limmat, an Stelle der alten ungenügenden Baulichkeiten errichtet, ist ein Werk des Stadtbaumeisters Prof. Gust. Gull, von dem wir auf Taf. 2 dieses Jahrganges die schöne Schule an der Lavaterstraße daselbst mitgeteilt haben. Ganz in hellem Sandstein erbaut, wirkt es durch seine auffälligen, nur sparsam geschmückten Massen recht glücklich weit in die Ferne, sodaß es von den am See, wie den an den Berghängen gelegenen Stadtteilen gesehen, im Bilde der Stadt beherrschend auftritt. Besonders erfreulich berührt die an ältere Bauwerke der Stadt anklingende Auffassung der gesamten Formgebung, die noch von landesfremden Elementen nicht überwuchert war. Das war aber auch eine Bedingung bei Wiederherstellung des durch so manche geschichtliche Reminiscenzen geweihten Verbindungsbaues des Stadthauses mit der alten Fraumünster Kirche, die auf unserem Bilde rechts erscheint.

Einen wirksamen Gegensatz bildet das neue Postgebäude, das in italienischer Renaissance aufgeführt, zu dem interessanten Städtebilde auch nach der Seeseite hin den rahmenden Abschluß bildet.

Le nouvel Hôtel de Ville de Zürich, à l'embouchure du lac de Zürich dans la Limmat, élevé sur l'emplacement d'anciennes constructions insuffisantes, est l'œuvre de l'architecte de la Ville, Mr le Professeur Gustave Gull. Nous avons déjà publié Pl. 2 de cette année la belle école de la rue Lavater qui est du même artiste.

Cet Hôtel de Ville construit entièrement en pierre blanche brille par la disposition de ses masses décorées avec réserve et discernement, on le voit de fort loin, et il domine la ville, vue du lac ou des hauteurs avoisinantes. On constate avec une satisfaction toute particulière que cet édifice est décoré dans le goût d'anciens monuments de la ville, lesquels n'ont pas encore été modifiés par des influences étrangères. Cette condition était du reste exigée pour la reconstruction du bâtiment historique, consacré par tant de souvenirs, reliant l'Hôtel de Ville à l'ancienne église de Fraumünster, visible á droite sur notre planche.

La nouvelle poste construite dans le style de la Renaissance italienne forme un contraste intéressant dans la perspective qu'elle termine du côté du lac.

The new Town Hall in Zürich placed on a site near the confluence of the Lake Zürich with the Limmat is the work of the town architect Prof. Gust. Gull of whose work we have given an illustration (Plate 2 of this year's issue) in the beautiful school buildings in the Lavaterstrasse.

The town hall replaces an old building which was insufficient for the requirements, and is built entirely of light sandstone; the ornamentation, though sparely used, is so effective that the building forms a conspicuous and attractive landmark in the town placed so picturesquely on the side of the mountain. The form is admirably suited to the old architecture of the town, a style which was never overloaded with foreign ornament. The same reverence has been displayed in the rebuilding of the edifice connecting the town hall with the Fraumünster Church which is hallowed by so many historical reminiscences. The edifice appears on the right of our illustration.

An effective contrast is made by the new Post office, built in the Italian Renascence, and forming an interesting feature in the view of the town from the lake.

Wohl eine der originellsten Schöpfungen neuzeitlicher niederländischer Privatarchitektur ist das Wohnhaus, das Architekt Ed. Cuypers sich in der Jan Luykenstraat 2 in Amsterdam erbaut hat. So wie die Grundrisse mit Rücksicht auf äußerste Bequemlichkeit und Behaglichkeit sorgfältigst durchgebildet sind, so zeigt sich auch in den Fassaden eine vollständige Befreiung von jeglicher Schultradition: nur Zweck-

Une des plus originales créations de l'architecture privée contemporaine des Pays-Bas est bien la demeure que s'est élevée à la Jan Luykenstraat 2 à Amsterdam l'architecte Ed. Cuypers. De même que les plans étudiés dans leurs moindres détails en vue de la commodité et de l'agrément, les façades témoignent d'un abandon complet de toute tradition d'école. Dans leur composition ainsi que dans leur exé-

Perhaps the most original creation of modern Netherlands private architects is the house built by Ed. Cuypers in the Jan Luykenstraat 2 in Amsterdam. The ground plan shows that extreme comfort and convenience were kept in view; and the facade shows an utter freedom from all tradition and conventio-

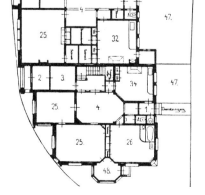

mäßigkeit und künstlerisch-malerische Erscheinung haben bei deren Entwurf und Ausführung bestimmend gewirkt. Die Ausführung, zu der Backstein und harter Sandstein verwendet wurden, hat nur ein Jahr erfordert.

cution, il n'a été tenu compte que de nécessités constructives et d'un aspect artistique et pittoresque.

La construction exécutée en briques et en grès dur n'a duré qu'un an.

nality. Only utility and artistic picturesqueness have been allowed to influence the design and completion of this building. The house is of brick and hard sandstone and occupied one year in building.

Die Durchführung befferer Wegfamkeit und gefundheitlicher Maßnahmen in überbevöl-kerten Stadtteilen von London, namentlich der City, die dadurch verminderten Bauflächen zwingen unabweislich dazu, das bisher faft all-gemein herrichende Syftem der Einzelfamilien-häufer aufzugeben und zu dem der in kontinen-talen Großftädten üblichen Etagenhäufer, mit einer oder mehreren Wohnungen in jedem Stock, überzugehen. Gleichwohl ift man beflifen, das maleriiche Straßenbild des alten London auch unter den neuen Verhältniffen fortzuführen, aber der Zerriffenheit deffelben durch gleich hochgeführte Gefimslinien nebeneinanderliegender Bauten vorzubeugen.

Ein hervorragendes Beifpiel für ein der-artiges Vorgehen bieten uns die in der FitzGeorge Avenue durch Architekt Delissa Joseph eben fertiggeftellten Miethäufer, von welchen das größere (das linke Haupt- und einem ausgebauten Dachgeichoß je zwei größere Mietwohnungen enthält. Das Material und die Ausführung ift die allgemein übliche: roter Backftein mit iparfamer Einichaltung von ein-heimiichem Hauftein, rote Ziegelbedachung und Schiebefenfter.

In ähnlicher Weife geht man vor bei Beichaffung von Arbeiter- und Werkleute-wohnungen. Dafür tritt befonders die Stadt-verwaltung ein. So hat fie jüngft durch das Stadt-Bauamt auf dem bis dahin durch das „Mill-bankgefängnis" befetzt geweienen, in Weft-minfter hinter der Tate-Bildergallerie gelegenen großen Befitztum mehrere Blocks von Arbeiter-wohnhäufern errichten laffen, die nach bedeutenden britiichen Künftlern benannt wurden. Der hier abgebildete, „Millais-Buildings" benannte Block birgt in vier Hauptgeichoffen und dem ausgebauten Dachftock je vier Wohnungen, die im ganzen 120 Perfonen beherbergen iollen. Diefer Bau und der gegenüberliegende gleichzeitig und ganz gleich errichtete „Leighton Buildings" kofteten zuiammen 250000 Mark. Gegenwärtig find durch die Stadtverwaltung auf der genannten Befitzung in diefer Art Wohnungen für 5000 Per-ionen geichaffen worden.

Natürlich find die Bauten mit knappeftem Aufwande, aus Backftein, mit iehr wenig Kalk-ftein und mit roten Ziegeln ausgeführt. Nur ein Teil hat Schiebefenfter, der andere Teil nach außen aufichlagende Flügel. Der maleriiche Effekt ift unvergleichlich glücklicher, als er bei ähnlichen Unternehmungen mit unzulänglichen künftleriichen Mitteln zu erzwingen veriucht wird.

Auf Taf. 1 diefes Jahrganges ericheint neben dem dort dargeftellten Gebäude (rechts an-ichließend) das Geichäftshaus der „Frankfurter Verficherungs-Gefellichaft Providentia", Taunusanlage 20 in Frankfurt a. M., deffen in blühender italieniicher Hochrenaissance mo-derner Auffafiung uniere gegenwärtige Abbildung zeigt. Der mit reichem allegoriichen Figuren-ichmuck ausgeftattete, auch durch feine vornehmen, in größtem Maßftabe durchgeführten Verhältnifie auffallende Bau ift von dem dortigen Architekten Hermann Ritter ausgeführt. Dem iehr einfach klaffiich-überfichtlich entwickelten Grundriß ent-fpricht auch der klaffiiche Aufbau. Am linken Rande uniere Tafel ericheint wiederum der rechte Flügel des eingangs genannten ungefähr gleich-zeitig errichteten Bauwerks.

In Karlsruhe i. B. haben die Architekten Billing & Mallebrein — von denen wir bereits in vorhergehenden Heften eine Reihe

---

L'amélioration des voies de communication et les mesures d'hygiène à prendre dans les quartiers trop populeux de Londres et princi-palement de la cité, la réduction de la surface à bâtir qui en résulte, forcent d'une façon inéluctable à abondonner le système jusqu'alors presque unique des maisons à une famille et de se mettre à construire comme on le fait déjà dans les grandes villes du continent, des maisons à plusieurs étages avec un ou plusieurs appar-tements par étage. En même temps, on s'efforce de conserver avec ces modifications le caractère pittoresque du vieux Londres, tout en remédiant à son aspect décousu, en donnant l'uniformité de hauteur aux corniches des maisons voisines l'une de l'autre.

Les maisons à loyer élevées à l'avenue Fitz George par Mr Delissa Joseph architecte nous offrent un exemple remarquable de cette innovation. La plus grande de ces maisons, celle de l'angle gauche, contient deux grands logements à louer dans chacun des quatre étages et dans l'étage du toit. Les matériaux de con-struction et l'exécution sont ceux générale-ment en usage: brique rouge avec un peu de pierre du pays, toit de tuiles rouges et fenêtres à guillotine.

Il en est de même pour la création d'habi-tations pour ouvriers et artisans. C'est surtout l'administration communale qui s'occupe de cette question. C'est ainsi qu'elle a fait élever dernièrement par le bureau de construction de la Ville sur le grand terrain occupé jusqu'à présent par la prison de Millbank à West-minster derrière la galerie de tableaux de Tate, plusieurs blocs de maisons ouvrières, portant les noms d'artistes anglais célèbres. Le bloc nommé "Millais-Buildings" représenté ici contient dans chacun de ses quatre étages et son toit, quatre appartements, pouvant abriter en tout 120 per-sonnes. Ce bâtiment et celui qui lui fait vis-à-vis, "Leighton Buildings" élevé en même temps et semblable en tous points ont coûté ensemble 250000 Marks. En ce moment, la Ville a fait construire de cette façon sur le dit terrain des logements pour 5000 personnes.

Il va sans dire que ces constructions sont élevées avec la plus grande économie, en briques avec très peu de pierre et recouvertes en tuiles rouges. Une partie seulement des fenêtres est à coulisses, les autres s'ouvrent en dehors.

On a obtenu ici un effet pittoresque infini-ment plus satisfaisant que dans la plupart des tentatives du même genre où les ressources artistiques font défaut.

La Planche 1 de ce volume représente à côté de l'édifice qui y est figuré, le bordant à droite, l'immeuble de la „Société Francfortoise d'Assurance Providentia", Taunusanlage 20 à Francfort sur Main, que nous publions main-tenant séparément pour en montrer le trait mo-derne appliqué aux formes d'une riche Renaissance italienne. Ce bâtiment frappant par la richesse de sa décoration sculpturale, et de ses figures allégoriques ainsi que par la noblesse et la grandeur de ses proportions est l'œuvre de l'architecte H. Ritter. A gauche de notre planche on aperçoit l'aile droite de l'édifice nommé plus haut et qui a été élevé à peu près à la même époque que la Providentia.

Les architectes Billing et Mallebrein à Carlsruhe, dont nous avons déjà publié une série de bâtiments remarquables dans les

---

The necessity for more convenient com-munication and for more complete sanitary organisation has compelled the authorities of large over-populated cities such as London, to abandon the plan of the one family house, and to erect large buildings of great height arranged in flats. One sees however that an attempt is made to retain the picturesqueness of old London, and an idea of uneformity is seen by the com-parative similarity of the mouldings on buildings lying near together.

A striking example of this is seen in the Fitz George Avenue, built by the architect Delissa Joseph. The large left corner house contains four stories and a roof or attic story, each floor containing two lodgings. The material is as usual, red brick with a spare use of English hewn stone, red tiles for the roof, and sash windows.

Workmens' and mechanics' lodgings are too now built in a similar fashion, the County Council have the superintendence of this archi-tecture. As good examples may be mentioned the blocks of buildings erected on the site of the old Millbank prison behind the Tate Picture Gallery and named after celebrated English artists.

We give an illustration of the "Millais buildings" which contains four stories and a roof story, and which is built to accommodate 120 persons. This building, and its exact counterpart lying opposite and called the "Leighton buildings", cost together Mk. 250000. On this same site, it is proposed to erect similar buildings sufficient to accommodate 5000 inhabitants.

The buildings have been erected with the greatest economy; they are of brick with a little lime-stone and are roofed with red tiles. The windows are partly sash-windows and partly the so-called French-windows. The general effect of these simple buildings is more pictu-resque than if the architect had attempted anything like artistic ornament with insufficient means.

On plate 1 of this year's issue next to the house there illustrated (on the right) are the premises of the Frankfurt Insurance Com-pany "Providentia", Taunus-Anlage 20 in Frankfurt on Main. This forms, with its fresh and modern interpretation of the Italian High Renascence, the subject of our present illustration. The building is richly ornamented with allegorical figures and is altogether so nobly proportioned as to be a striking point in the architecture of the street. The architect is H. Ritter. On the left side of the plate is the right wing of the building mentioned above, which was built at the same time.

The architects Billing and Mallebrein, of whose work we have given examples in previous numbers, have built in Carlsruhe

bemerkenswerter Bauten mitteilten — vom 1. Mai 1901 bis 1. Mai 1902 das vornehme Wohnhaus des dortigen Augenarztes Dr. Ellinger, Stephanien-Straße 66, erbaut, das auch dessen Klinik enthält.

Die Fassaden bestehen aus weißem Mainthäler Sandstein; die Modelle der figürlichen Bildhauerarbeiten sind von Professor Pietsche ausgeführt, die Kunstschlosserarbeiten von Fr. Lang und die Ausstattung der Halle von der Möbelfabrik M. Reutlinger & Co., sämtlich in Karlsruhe.

Die innere Ausstattung des Hauses, auch die mit elektrischem Licht u. s. w. entspricht der vornehmen Gestaltung der Fassade, wie das auch die in Taf. 78 und 79 mitgeteilten Ansichten der Halle erkennen lassen.

livraisons précédentes, ont construit du 1 mai 1901 au 1 mai 1902 la demeure distinguée de l'oculiste docteur Ellinger, Stephanien - Strasse 66. Cette maison contient la clinique du médecin.

Les façades sont en grès blanc de la vallée du Main; les modèles pour la décoration plastique ont été exécutés par le professeur Pietsche, les fers forgés par Fr. Lang et la décoration du Hall par la fabrique de meubles M. Reutlinger et Co. tous à Carlsruhe.

L'aménagement intérieur ainsi que les installations de lumière électrique etc. sont en rapport avec la noble ordonnance des façades ainsi qu'en témoigne la vue du Hall que nous publions Pl. 78 et 79.

in Baden a beautiful house for the oculist Dr. Ellinger at 66 Stephanien-Strasse. The house, which was built from May 1901 to May 1902, contains the consultation rooms of the doctor.

The façade is of white sandstone from the Mainthal; the models for the statuary are by Professor Pietsche, the ornamental iron-work is by Fr. Lang and the furnishing of the hall is by the firm M. Reutlinger and Co., all of Carlsruhe.

The interior equipment of the house, the electric light installation etc. correspond to the superior appearance of the exterior, Plate 78 and 79 gives a view of the hall which will corroborate our opinion.

74 [1902; 76]

Die Schulgebäude der Stadt Berlin wurden längere Jahre als mustergiltig angesehen und sind auch an anderen Orten vorbildlich gewesen. Einer vielfach beklagten, zu häufigen schematischen Wiederholung in Grundriß und Aufbau ist seit dem Amtsantritt des Stadtbaurats Ludwig Hoffmann in anerkennenswertester Weise ein Ziel gesetzt: ein jeder Schulbau wird nunmehr individuell behandelt, ohne Hintansetzung der reichen Erfahrungen, die bei den bisherigen Bauten gewonnen wurden, und ohne die charakteristische Erscheinung als „Schulhaus" zurückzudrängen. Als ein bemerkenswertes Beispiel hierfür kann die XIII. Realschule am Schleswiger Ufer 9 gelten. Der Entwurf und die Detaillierung dieses Baues stammen von Stadtbauinspektor V. Dylewsky, der unter Oberleitung des Stadtbaurats Hoffmann den Bau ausführte, während Architekt Zeisberg die Bauleitung hatte.

Der Bau der ca. 8 m tiefen Fundamente, die aus Stampfbeton 2,5 m unter Grundwasser reichen, ward um Mitte September 1900 mit Absenkung des Grundwasserspiegels begonnen; der Aufbau dauerte von Mitte April 1901 bis Ende März 1902. Das Gebäude ist aus Backsteinen hergestellt, mit Verkleidung des Untergeschosses aus Ettringer Tuffsteinen und der oberen Teile aus Rathenower roten Handstrichsteinen (von Mathes & Sohn) und Cottaer und Nesselberger Sandstein; die Decken der Flure sind auf Eisenträgern als preußische Kappen gewölbt, die übrigen als Holzbalkendecken auf eisernen Unterzügen hergestellt. Das Dach ist mit roten Biberschwänzen eingedeckt.

Die Schulsäle sind mit Rettig'schen Bänken ausgerüstet. Die gesamten Baukosten der drei Gebäude einschließlich ihrer Ausrüstung betrugen 500 000 Mark. Das Schulhaus enthält im Untergeschoß neben dem Durchgang für die Direktorwohnung (links) und der Hofeinfahrt (rechts) die aus drei Stuben und Küche bestehende Wohnung des Schuldieners und die reichlich bemessenen Heiz- und Luftkammern nebst Kohlenraum. Im Erdgeschoß liegen neben dem Haupteingang rechts das Konferenz- und links das Amtszimmer sowie vier Klassensäle. Im sonst gleichgebildeten I. Obergeschoß ist der über dem Amtszimmer liegende Raum disponibel, während der über dem Konferenzzimmer liegende, über den Eingangsflur hin ausgedehnt, ein fünftes Klassenzimmer bildet. Im II. Obergeschoß ist auch der disponible Raum an der Front mit letzterem zu einem Zeichensaale zusammengefaßt, und im III. Obergeschoß entsteht unter Hinzunahme des Flures die Aula, deren Tribünen durch die kleinen eisernen Treppen (an den Enden des Flures) zugänglich sind. Rechts und

74 [1902; 76]

Les bâtiments scolaires de la ville de Berlin passèrent pendant de longues années pour des modèles du genre et servirent de types pour d'autres villes. L'entrée en fonctions de l'architecte conseiller de la ville, Ludwig Hoffmann mit heureusement un terme à des répétitions trop fréquentes qui s'étaient cependant peu à peu introduites dans la composition du plan et des élévations. Maintenant, chaque école est traitée d'une façon individuelle tout en faisant large part aux nombreuses expériences faites dans les constructions précédentes et sans renoncer à donner au bâtiment l'aspect d'une „école". On peut considérer comme une preuve remarquable de ce que nous avançons, la XIIIme école réale au Schleswiger Ufer 9. Le projet et le détail de cet édifice sont de l'inspecteur de la ville V. Dylewsky qui l'exécuta sous la direction de Monsieur Hoffmann, tandis que Mr. Zeisberg architecte était chargé de la conduite des travaux.

La construction commença au milieu de septembre 1900 par les travaux nécessaires a faire baisser les eaux, les fondations ont 8 m de profondeur dont 2,5 m au dessous du niveau de l'eau souterraine, ces fondations sont en béton comprimé. Le bâtiment d'école fut construit du milieu d'avril 1901 jusqu'à fin mars 1902. Les façades tout en briques revêtues au rez-de-chaussée avec du tuf de Ettringen et aux étages supérieurs avec des briques rouges de Rathenow (Maison Mathes & fils) ainsi qu'avec du grès de Cotta et de Nesselberg. Les corridors sont couverts en voûtes à la prussienne posées sur poutres en fer, les autres plafonds sont en solives de bois posées sur des poutres en fer. Le toit es couvert avec des tuiles rouges.

Les salles d'école sont pourvues de bancs système Rettig. Le coût total des trois bâtiments y compris les installations fut de 500 000 Marks. La maison d'école contient au sous-sol, outre le passage pour la maison du directeur à gauche et la porte cochère de la cour à droite, l'appartement du concierge, composé de trois chambres et d'une cuisine ainsi que de spacieux locaux pour le chauffage, la prise d'air et le combustible. Au rez-de-chaussée se trouvent à droite de l'entrée principale la salle de conférences et à gauche le bureau d'administration plus 4 salles d'étude. Le premier étage a la même disposition que le rez-de-chaussée, avec la différence que le local situé au dessus de la chambre d'administration est disponible, tandis que celui qui ce trouve au dessus de la salle de conférence, augmenté de la surface de l'entrée forme une cinquième salle d'étude. Au second étage, le local disponible en façade est joint à la classe voisine et au 3me étage, ces locaux augmentés du vestibule forment la aula dont les tribunes sont accessibles par les petits es-

74 [1902; 76]

The school-buildings of Berlin have been considered for many years to be the most perfect of their kind, and have been imitated in many other towns. This has naturally led to a stereotyped style of school-building, where all individuality was lost, and where no use was made of the teachings of experience. This has been altered by the Town Baurat Ludwig Hoffmann who has built the school premises of the XIII. Real School, Schleswiger Ufer 9. The design and details of this building are by the town building inspector V. Dylewsky who carried out the building under the superintendence of the Baurat Hoffmann. Other work was carried out by the architect Zeisberg.

The building of these 8 metres deep foundations (stampf-beton 2,5 metres below underground water) was begun in the middle of September 1900, and the remainder of the building took from April 1901 till the end of March 1902. The building is of brick, the lower part covered with Ettringer tuffstone, the upper part with Rathenow red stone (from Mathes and Son) and Cotta and Nesselberger sandstone. The ceilings of the entrance are vaulted and supported on iron girders the others are supported by wooden beams with iron supports. The roof is of red tiles.

The school rooms are fitted up with „Rettig" school seats. The entire cost, including the interior equipment amounted to 500000 Marks. The school-house contains in the lower part a passage to the directors dwelling on the left; the yard entrance, on the right and the lodging of the school-porter (consisting of 3 rooms and a kitchen) and extensive accommodation for wood and coal, for heating, and for ventilation machinery. On the ground floor, at the side of the principal entrance are on the right the Conference hall and on the left the Committee Room, as well as four class-rooms. The first floor is similarly constructed, with a class room extended over the entrance, the second floor is the same, but the three rooms are jointed to a drawing room; white on the third floor is the "Aula" the tribune of which is reached by small iron steps. Right and left

links der Aula liegen Bibliothek und Natur-historische Sammlung, während an der Hinterfront die Physikklasse, deren Apparatenkammer und eine Reserveklasse liegen. Die kleinen Treppen führen auch nach dem Dachboden und geben durch eine mittlere eiserne Treppe Zugang zu den Turmkammern und der darüber liegenden, mit Steinboden versehenen Terrasse, die dem meteoro-logischen und astronomischen Unterricht dient.

Im Dachboden sind die Entlüftungsschlote zu-sammengeschleift, die in den kleinen achtseitigen Türmchen über Dach münden. An der Ausfüh-rung waren in hervorragendem Maße beteiligt: die Bildhauer Latt und Westphal, die Maler Boguth und Bodenstein für die Aula; die Tischler Wolff, Seeling, Thiemich & Sohn und Zahn. Die Turngeräte führte Buczilowski aus, während die Schlosser- und Kunstschmiedearbeiten von A. W. Krause und Schulz & Holdefleiß ge-leistet wurden. Die Fundierungen wurden durch Th. Moebus, die Maurerarbeiten durch Hoffmann & Wüstenhagen, die Zimmerarbeiten durch G. A. L. Schultz & Co. die Steinmetzarbeiten durch Körner & Plöger und die Heizanlage durch Janeck & Vetter, sämtlich in Berlin, ausgeführt.

75 [1902: 82]

Freudiges Erstaunen erweckte in der gesamten Kunstwelt die Veröffentlichung von „Mo-derne Städtebilder" Abteilung I: „Brüssel", die die ganz eigenartigen Schöpfungen von Saintenoy, Hankar und Horta weiteren Fachkreisen zur Anschauung brachte. Namentlich der beiden letzten, höchst feinfühlig und anmutig kecke Gestaltungen erfreuten sich der allgemeinsten Anerkennung, und sie haben nicht wenig bei-getragen zu der freundlich-heiteren Auffassung, die in der modernen Architektur allenthalben durchgedrungen ist. Hankar ist leider frühzeitig hingeschieden, aber er sowohl als Horta haben be-geisterte Schüler und Anhänger gebildet, unter denen Architekt E. Blérot zu nennen ist, von dessen jüngsten Schöpfungen wir auf Taf. 82 das von ihm Rue Monastère 34 in Brüssel erbaute Wohn-haus mitteilen. Es zeigt ganz die künstlerische Auffassung, die Hortas Werke auszeichnet: frei von allem Schwulst und falschem Prunk, doch reich, vornehm-prächtig wirkend.

76 [1902: 88]

In Frankfurt a. M., am Roßmarkt 15, 17, 19 Ecke Salzhaus 6, haben die Architekten Rindsfüßer und Kühn vom Mai 1901 bis März 1902 drei Häuser, welche bisher schon zu dem alten Gasthofe „Englischer Hof" gehörten, neu erbaut. Es war gefordert, daß die drei an dem vornehmsten Platze der Stadt gelegenen Gebäude zwar äußerlich ein einheitlich Ganzes bilden und in den Obergeschossen als Fremden-zimmer des Gasthofes benützt oder je für sich vermietet werden können, so wie die drei Läden in den Erdgeschossen durch Feuermauern getrennt gehalten sein mußten. So sind denn auch in den oberen Geschossen die Feuer-mauern (natürlich mit den nötigen Verbindungs-öffnungen) durchgeführt, die übrigen Raumscheide-wände jedoch nur in leichter Konstruktion her-gestellt. Zur Ausführung, welche 300 000 Mark kostete, ward für die breiten Fassadenpfeiler im Erdgeschoß schwedischer Granit, für die oberen Fassadenteile Burgreppacher Sandstein, für die Decken sogenannte Müller'sche Voutenplatten (Stampfbeton zwischen Eisenträgern), für die Dächer Schiefer und für die Türme Kupfer verwendet. Die Fensterrahmen im Erd- und im Zwischen-geschoß sind aus Eisen.

---

caliers en fer qui se trouvent à l'extrémité du corridor. A droite et à gauche de la aula se trouvent la bibliothèque et la collection d'histoire naturelle, tandis que la salle de physique avec la salle de préparation et une classe de réserve ont été placées sur la façade postérieure. Les petits escaliers conduisent aussi dans les combles et donnent accès grâce à un escalier central en fer, dans la tour (deux étages en pignon) et sur la terrasse qui la surmonte, cette terrasse couverte en pierre sert à l'enseignement de la météorologie et de l'astronomie.

Dans le toit, les canaux de ventilation ont été rassemblés dans les petites tours octogonales qui surmontent le toit. Ont pris part à l'exécution: les sculpteurs Latt et Westphal, les peintres Boguth et Bodenstein pour la aula; les menuisiers Wolff, Seeling, Thiemich & fils et Zahn. Les engins de gymnastiques furent livrés par Buczilowski, tandis que A. W. Krause et Schulz & Holdefleiss livrèrent la serrurerie et les travaux en fer forgé. Les travaux de fondation furent exécutés par Th. Moebus, ceux de maçonnerie par Hoffmann et Wüsten-hagen, ceux de charpente par G. A. L. Schultz & Cie, ceux de pierre de taille par Körner et Plöger, le chauffage par Janeck & Vetter, tous à Berlin.

75 [1902: 82]

Lorsque les "Vues de villes modernes" dans leur première livraison, Bruxelles, pu-blièrent les originales créations de Saintenoy, de Hankar et Horta et les portèrent à la connaissance des architectes, ce fut une joyeuse surprise dans le monde des arts tout entier. Ce sont surtout les oeuvres des deux derniers, d'une finesse et d'une hardiesse peu communes, qui conquirent tous les suffrages, elles n'ont pas peu contribué à la tendance plus gaie qui partout se fait jour dans l'architecture moderne. Hankar est malheureusement mort jeune, mais Horta ainsi que lui, ont formé des disciples enthousiastes parmi lesquels nous nommerons en première ligne E. Blérot. Parmi les dernières créations de ce maître, citons la maison d'habitation Rue Monastère 34 à Bruxelles, représentée Pl. 82. Elle montre tout à fait l'esprit qui distinguait les oeuvres de Horta, libre de toute exagération de formes et de tout clinquant, elle produit cependant un effet riche et distingué.

76 [1902: 88]

Les architectes Rindsfüßer et Kühn ont rebâti à Francfort (Main) sur le Rossmarkt No. 15, 17, 19 à l'angle du Salzhaus 6, du mois de mai 1901 au mois de mars 1902 trois maisons, qui jusqu'alors avaient fait partie de l'hôtel „Englischer Hof". Il était sousentendu que ces trois bâtiments étant situés sur la place la plus distinguée de la ville devaient tout en ayant une façade commune, fournir des chambres d'étrangers à l'hôtel, ou être loués à part et que les trois magasins du rez-de-chaussée devaient être séparés par des murs mitoyens.

Dans les étages du haut les murs mitoyens sont pourvus des ouvertures nécessaires à la communication, tandis que les cloisons inter-médiaires sont construites en matériaux légers. On employa dans cette construction qui coûta 300 000 Marks du granit de Suède pour les larges piliers de la façade, pour les parties du haut du grès de Burgreppach, pour les plafonds des hourdis système Müller (béton dammé entre les poutres en fer), pour les toits des ardoises et pour les tours du cuivre. Les cadres des fenêtres au rez-de-chaussée et dans l'entre-sol sont en fer.

---

of the Aula lie the Library and Natural history collection. On the same floor is the laboratory for instruction in physics and a reserve class room. Small steps lead to the roof and lead by another stair-case to the tower-rooms and a terrace with a stone floor from which astronomical and meteoro-logical instruction can be given. On the roof are the ventilation canals, all of which open into the small octagonal turrets over the roof. The following firms were specially employed. Sculptors Latt and Westphal, painters Boguth and Bodenstein for the Aula, joiners Wolff, Seeling, Thiemisch and Son and Zahn. The gymnastic apparatus is by Buczilowski, the ornamental iron work by A. W. Krause and Schulz and Holdefleiss. The foundation work was done by Th. Moebus. The brick work by Hoffmann and Wüstenhagen, the carpentry G. A. L. Schultz and Co., the stone-work by Körner and Plöger and the heating apparatus by Janeck and Vetter, all of Berlin.

75 [1902: 82]

The whole artistic world has been agreeably surprised and greatly delighted by the wonderful productions of Saintenoy, Hankar and Horta now offered to the public in the first part (Brussels) of "Moderne Städte-bilder". In the case of the two last men-tioned artists the fine feeling, the fresh charm, and the bold originality of their work cannot fail to excite admiration. The early death of Hankar is deeply to be deplored, but he has left behind him an enthusiastic band of disciples as followers of him and of Horta. Among these may be mentioned the architect E. Blérot whose latest work, a house built at 34 Rue Monastère, Brussels, we publish on plate 82. We see in this, the artistic leanings of Horta, free from all glaring ornament and meretricious pomp, and yet rich, distinguished and splendid.

76 [1902: 88]

The architects Rindsfüßer and Kühn have built in Frankfort-on-the Main, Ross-Market 15, 17, 19 at the corner of the Salz-haus 6, three houses. These houses formerly comprised the hotel "Englischer Hof" and they have been rebuilt; the time occupied being from May 1901 to March 1902. As the situation is the best in the city, it was desirable that a certain uniformity of design should be kept in view; at the same time the upper parts can be united and used for hotel accommodation, or separated and let as private dwellings. On the ground floor the houses are separated by fire-proof walls, these are carried throughout the building, the other walls are of lighter con-struction, but in all cases provision is made to unite the three houses as easily as possible into one.

The cost of construction was Marks 300 000; for the broad pillars on the façade of the ground floor, Swedish granite is used; for that of the upper parts Burgreppacher sandstone; for the ceilings, the so-called "Müller Voutenplatten" (beton between iron girders); for the roofs slate, and for the towers copper. The window frames on the ground and intermediary floor are of iron.

Die gesamte Bauausführung lag in Händen des Unternehmers Carl Junior; die Bildhauerarbeiten lieferten Ph. Holzmann & Cie., die ornamentalen Modelle L. Brosius und die figürlichen Bildhauer Balz. Die Kupferarbeiten sind von C. Knodt, das Kunstschmiedewerk von Gebrüder Armbrüster (sämtlich in Frankfurt) ausgeführt.

Mr. Charles Junior entrepreneur exécuta la bâtisse, Mr. Ph. Holzmann et Co. fournirent les sculptures, Mr. L. Brosius les modèles des ornements, Mr. Balz sculpteur ceux des figures. Les travaux en cuivre ont été faits par Mr. C. Knodt, les fers forgés artistiques par Mrs. Armbrüster frères, (tous de Francfort).

The work was placed in the hands of the contractor Carl Junior; the sculpture was entrusted to Ph. Holzmann & Co., the ornamental models were made by L. Brosius, the figures by the sculptor Balz. The copper work was done by C. Knodt, the ornamental iron work by Bros. Armbrüster, all in Frankfort.

77 [1902; 92]

In Straßburg i. E. führte Architekt Gustav Oberthür an Stelle der Am Hohen Steg bestandenen, „Kleine Metzig" benannten alten Baulichkeiten vom Januar 1900 bis Oktober 1901 ein neues Kaufhaus auf, das im II. Obergeschoß im mittleren Teil des Frontbaues zwei Wohnungen enthält, während beide Seitenflügel wie im I. Obergeschoß zu Lagerräumen dienen. Das Untergeschoß hat nur Lager-, Haus- und Maschinenkeller für die elektrischen und hydraulischen Aufzüge sowie für die Heizanlage. Durch das in deutscher Frührenaissance unter Anlehnung an die Formen alt-straßburglicher Bauten errichtete Gebäude führt ein bei Tageszeit öffentlicher, reich gewölbter und ausgemalter Durchgang, der in gebrochener Richtung auf den ebenfalls öffentlichen Durchgang in dem alten sogenannten Aubettehause mündet. Die Statuen beiderseits des Portales stellen 1. den Städtemeister Sturm von Sturmeck, 2. den Festungs- und Stadtbaumeister des 16. Jahrhunderts Specklin dar; sie sind Werke des Bildhauers Margolff in Straßburg.

Der Bau ist in weißem Vogesensandstein aufgeführt; die Stützen und Decken sind nach „System Hennebique" hergestellt, die Fußböden haben Linoleumbelag auf Cementestrich. Die Dampfheizanlagen wurden von Bechem & Post in Hagen und die reichen Schmiedearbeiten von der Firma Unselt in Straßburg ausgeführt. Die gesamten Baukosten haben sich auf rund 600 000 Mark belaufen.

77 [1902; 92]

Mr. Gustave Oberthür architecte à Strassbourg a construit de janvier 1900 à octobre 1901 à la place des vieilles masures dites „Kleine Metzig" sur le „Hohe Steg" un nouveau bâtiment qui contient au second étage, dans la partie centrale de la maison de front, deux appartements, les deux ailes ainsi que le premier étage servent de magasins. Le sous-sol ne contient que des magasins, des caves et les machines des ascenceurs électriques et hydrauliques et le chauffage.

Un passage voûté et richement peint ouvert pendant la journée traverse l'immeuble construit en Renaissance allemande primitive rappelant les vieilles batisses strassbourgeois, ce passage aboutit en face du passage public de la vieille maison dite Aubette. Les statues flanquant l'entrée exécutée par Mr. Margolff sculpteur à Strassbourg représentent le maire Sturm von Sturmeck et l'architecte de la ville et des fortifications du 16ème siècle Specklin.

L'édifice est en grès blanc des Vosges, les piliers et les plafonds sont construits d'après le „système Hennebique", les planchers sont couverts de linoléum sur ciment. Mrs. Bechem et Post à Hagen fournirent le chauffage central à vapeur et Mr. Unselt à Strassbourg les riches fers forgés. Les frais s'élevèrent en tout à 600 000 Marks.

77 [1902; 92]

A new business house has been built in Strassburg in Alsace by the architect Gustav Oberthür on the site of the so-called "Kleine Metzig" in the street "Am Hohen Steg". The time occupied was from January 1900 to October 1901.

The middle part of the front building contains in the second floor, two lodgings, while the two side wings are built for store rooms. The basement contains storage room, cellarage and machine rooms for the electric and hydraulic lifts as well as for the heating apparatus. The style is Early German Renascence with a blending of the old local Strassburg architecture.

A vaulted and painted thoroughfare, open to the public, leads through the house and goes into another public archway leading through the so-called "Aubette house". The statues on each side of the portals represent the town celebrities Sturm of Sturmeck and Specklin an architect of the XVI Century. They are the work of the sculptor Margolff in Strassburg.

The building is carried out in white sandstone, the supports and ceilings are constructed according to the "System Hennebique" the floors are covered with cement with a layer of linoleum. The steam heating apparatus is by Bechem and Post in Hagen, and the ornamental iron work by Unselt in Strassburg. The entire cost was Marks 600 000.

78 [1902; 90]

Die Villa Siebel, Mainzerstraße 70 in Coblenz ist ebenfalls von Architekt Otto Nebel von August 1900 bis 1. April 1902 erbaut.

78 [1902; 90]

Citons encore la villa Siebel, Mainzerstrasse 70 à Coblenz également construite par Mr. Otto Nebel de août 1900 au premier avril 1902.

78 [1902; 90]

The villa Siebel, Mainzerstrasse 70 Coblenz, was built by the architect Otto Nebel from August 1900 to 1 April 1902.

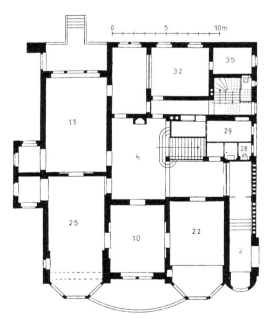

Erdgeschoß.   Rez-de-chaussée.   Ground Floor.   1. Stockwerk.   1. Etage.   1. Floor.

Dem äußerst malerisch gruppierten Aufbau entsprechen die reich durchgebildeten Fassaden; sie sind unter Verwendung von Haustein und altem Eichenholz teils in glattem, teils in rauhem Putz — in teppichartiger Stipparbeit — hergestellt, wie letztere Art der Ausführung, besonders die flache Seitenfront neben dem großen Erkervorbau erkennen läßt.

Les façades richement décorées correspondent à la silhouette extrêmement pittoresque de l'ensemble; elles sont traitées en crépissage avec emploi de pierre de taille et de vieux chêne. Ce crépissage est en partie lisse, en partie rugueux et imitant un dessin de tapis, ainsi qu'on peut le voir particulièrement à la façade latérale nue près du pignon d'avant-corps.

The richly and well-built facade is fitly crowned by a picturesquely-grouped upper building. The architect has used rough stone and old oak wood, partly in rough plaster work and partly smooth, in all cases contrasting the different processes with much taste.

Vor langen Jahren konnte man in Deutschland in Gebirgsthälern, so namentlich am Mittelrhein, an der Mosel und auch an der Wupper, nicht allein in Dorfschaften, sondern selbst in aufstrebenden Städten, wie Trarbach, Bernkastel, Barmen, Elberfeld u. s. w., eine Mehrzahl von Patrizierhäusern sehen, deren ganze äußere Architektur und malerischer Reiz durch gelegentliche Zu- und Anbauten von Erkern u. s. w. und in einer Beschieferung der wetterseitigen Wände zum Ausdruck kamen. Ein anderes Moment, das die malerische Wirkung von im Putzbau ausgeführten Gebäuden wahrte, war die Ausführung in grobem Mörtel, indem an Stelle des Sandes ein mittelgrober Kies beim letzten Antrage verwendet und das Ganze mit frischer Kalkmilch getüncht wurde. Während in Deutschland eine beklagenswerte, sogenannte „klassische" Richtung diese malerische Auffassung bürgerlicher Baukunst zurückgedrängt hatte, trieb sie in England und Amerika reiche Blüten.

In der Reihe von Landhäusern aus London-Hampstead sehen wir auf Tafel 97 an dem von Architekt Amos F. Faulkner erbauten „Cricklewood House", das im Erdgeschoß aus gefugten Backsteinen nur eine sparsame Haustein-Architektur aufweist, die Wände des Obergeschosses nur beschiefert, die Gewandungen der Fenster in Holz. Bei dem links davon stehenden Baue, „The Homestead" von den Architekten Real & Macdonald, das ebenfalls bei allgemein einfacher Gestaltung in seinem Portalbau schon mehr aufwändig erscheint, bewirkt die durch den rauhen Kiesputz erzielte warme Tönung der Wände vornehmlich die behagliche Erscheinung des Gebäudes. An dem wiederum links von diesem Bau erscheinenden Haufe sehen wir das Obergeschoß mit Schuppenziegeln verkleidet, deren Schuppenendung neben ihrem halbrunden Abschluß einen etwa 1 cm breiten wagerechten Steg aufweisen, demzufolge lediglich das Schuppennetz zur malerischen Wirkung gelangt.

Il y a bien des années, on pouvait voir en Allemagne, et particulièrement dans les contrées rhénanes, dans les vallées de la Moselle, et de la Wupper, et non seulement dans les villages, mais même dans des villes florissantes comme Trarbach, Bernkastel, Barmen, Elberfeld etc. une quantité de maisons patriciennes dont toute l'architecture et le charme pittoresque consistait dans l'emploi d'encorbellements et d'appentis et dans le revêtement en ardoise des façades du côté de la pluie. Un autre élément de pittoresque pour ces constructions crépies était l'emploi, pour le crépissage de mortier à gros grain dans lequel entrait au lieu de sable, du petit gravier, cet enduit était blanchi à la chaux; tandis qu'en Allemagne cette intéressante expression de l'architecture privée cédait malheureusement le pas à la tendance dite „classique" elle portait des fruits en Angleterre et en Amérique.

Parmi les nombreuses maisons de campagne de Hampstead à Londres, nous voyons sur la Pl. 97 la maison „Cricklewood House" construite par l'architecte Amos F. Faulkner, le rez-de-chaussée est en briques jointoyées, la pierre n'y est employée qu'avec modération. Les murs de l'étage supérieur sont recouverts en ardoises, les encadrements de fenêtres sont en bois. A gauche de cette maison s'élève „The Homestead", bâti par les architectes Real & Macdonald aussi fort simple un peu plus riche grâce à son portail, et un aspect chaud et comfortable grâce à son crépissage à gros grain. La maison suivante, également à gauche, montre un étage supérieur recouvert de tuiles en écailles arrondies dans le bas avec interstice horizontal de 1 cm, ce qui donne à toute la surface écaillée un aspect des plus pittoresques.

Many years ago, there were to be seen in the mountain-valleys of Germany, on the middle Rhine, on the Moselle, on the Wupper not only in villages but in growing towns such as Trarbach, Bernkastel, Barmen, Elberfeld etc. a number of old patricien houses the external architecture of which was occasionally altered by an additional bow or corner-or by tiling the weather-side of the house. Later on, one saw the picturesque effects of various kinds of ornamental mortar on plasterwork, the whole embellished with fresh lime wash. In Germany his interesting and charasteristic style has been unfortunately put into the background by the so-called "classical" school, but in England and America it has flourished with everincreasing success.

Among the country houses at Hampstead near London, we wish to draw attention to "Cricklewood House" by the architect Amos F. Faulkner an illustration of which is given on plate 97. The ground floor is built of brick with a slight mixture of rough stone, the walls of the upper stories are only stated, the framework of the windows is of wood. The house on the left, "The Homestead", is from Mrs. Real & Macdonald, architects; although the details are much simpler, yet the portal makes a more important appearance, and this is principally attained by the warm tone of the walls which are of rough plaster. On the left of this second villa is a house the upper part of which is covered with tiles overlapping in scale form. The scales are so arranged as to present with their semicircular finish, a horizontal line of about 1 centimetre in breadth which has a very picturesque effect on the whole appearance.

Das Hauptgebäude der I. Internationalen Ausstellung für moderne dekorative Kunst in Turin 1902. Bei allen bedeutenderen Ausstellungsbauten hatte man bisher wohl versucht, für diese eine künstlerische, dem Zwecke der betreffenden Bauten Ausdruck gebende Lösung zu finden. Die großen und wesentlichen Verschiedenartigkeiten der zur Ausstellung gelangenden Gegenstände bedingten verschiedenartige Bauanlagen von entsprechend verschiedenartiger Charakteristik und wehrten damit der Durchführung eines durchschlagenden künstlerischen Grundgedankens. Das war auch der Grund dafür, daß die großartigen Kunstleistungen der Säkular-Ausstellung in Paris 1900 ernsteren, rein-künstlerischen Anforderungen nur in ihren Einzelheiten Befriedigung gewähren konnten.

Weit leichter ließ ein einheitlicher Gedanke sich zum Ausdruck bringen bei der unter Führung des Professors Jos. M. Olbrich in Darmstadt 1901 von der dortigen Künstlerkolonie veranstalteten Ausstellung für moderne Kunst. *) War deren Erfolg zwar gewiß ein glänzender zu nennen, so galt er doch nur einem schüchternen Versuch einer an Zahl und Mitteln sehr beschränkten lokalen Künstlergenossenschaft, die Ausstellungsbauten selbst, so zu deren ferneren persönlichen Zweckzielen errichtet.

Bei der gegenwärtigen, im Mai d. J. eröffneten I. Internationalen Ausstellung für moderne dekorative Kunst in Turin war durch ihre Benennung selbst schon ein klares, scharf umrissenes Programm vorgeschrieben. Dank

Le bâtiment principal de la première exposition internationale d'art décoratif à Turin 1902. Pour tous les bâtiments importants d'exposition on avait jusqu'à ce jour bien cherché une solution artistique et une forme exprimant la destination de ces constructions. La grande diversité et l'incohérence des produits exposés exigeaient divers groupes de bâtiments et de différents caractères pour ces batisses, et empêchaient ainsi l'exécution d'un plan d'ensemble unique et conséquent.

C'est la raison pour laquelle à la grandiose exposition séculaire de Paris en 1900 on ne rencontra que dans certaines créations séparées, des solutions sérieuses et purement artistiques.

Il fut beaucoup plus facile de donner un caractère d'unité à l'exposition pour d'art moderne *) à Darmstadt en 1901, exposition organisée par la colonie d'artistes de cette ville, sous la direction du Professeur Jos. M. Olbrich. Quoique le succès de cette entreprise ait été brillant, il ne s'agissait cependant que d'une modeste tentative d'un groupe d'artistes local, peu nombreuse et ne disposant pas de grandes ressources, puisque les maisons exposées devaient par la suite servir d'habitation à ces mêmes artistes.

Pour la première exposition internationale d'art décoratif à Turin actuelle, ouverte en Mai de cette année, un programme clair et nettement déterminé était déjà fixé par la dénomination de l'exposition. Grâce à l'habile direction de l'architecte Raimondo d'Aronco le programme a été résolu d'une façon aussi claire que brillante dans l'exécution du bâti-

The principal building of the First International Exhibition for Modern decorative Art in Turin 1902. The demands made upon the designers of Exhibition buildings of any importance are not only artistic, but utilitarian, — the building must by its exterior appearance and internal equipment, fulfil the purpose for which it is intended. The great number and variety of the exhibits necessitate a corresponding variety and fitness in the rooms for their reception, and the whole must be the result of a carefully designed and well carried out plan. This want of harmony in the design was the reason why the great Exhibition in Paris of 1900 was disap pointing to the serious, purely artistic spectator, although the charm and distinction of the several details could not be denied.

This harmony of design was much more happily expressed by the Exhibition of Modern Art in Darmstadt 1901,*) erected under the superintendence of the designer Prof. Jos. M. Olbrich of the artists' colony of that city. When one considers that the exhibition was only a modest attempt by a small and comparatively poor artistic union, we may call the result exceedingly satisfactory. The exhibition buildings are to be the permanent home of art for painters working in Darmstadt. The present International Exhibition for decorative art in Turin opened in May of this year, gave by its name the leading idea to the architect in a clear and simple manner. This idea, thanks

der glücklichen Leitung durch Architekt Raimondo d' Aronco ist es so wie in dem Hauptgebäude, auch bei den vielen, ebenfalls von ihm selbst und seinen ehemaligen Studiengenossen und Schülern entworfenen und ausgeführten Nebengebäuden ebenso klar wie glänzend durchgeführt worden! Das wird besonders erklärlich durch den Hinweis, daß d'Aronco ein Schüler von Prof. Otto Wagner in Wien ist, gleich wie Prof. Olbrich in Darmstadt und Prof. Baumann in Wien, der die österreichischen Bauten, die einzigen fremdländischen Sonderbauten der Ausstellung ausgeführt hat; ferner: daß Architekt Rigotti, von dem ein wichtiges Begleitwerk der Ausstellung, die Wein- und Oelhalle, herrührt, d'Aroncos Strebensgenosse ist. Das ist nun die erste Regung einer ausgesprochen modernen Architekturrichtung in Italien, in dem bisher die Tra-

ment principal ainsi que dans celle des nombreuses annexes projetées et élevées par lui, par ses anciens camarades d'étude et par ses élèves. Notons en passant que d'Aronco est l'élève du Professeur Otto Wagner à Vienne, de même que le Professeur Olbrich à Darmstadt et le Professeur Baumann à Vienne, celui qui exécuta les pavillons autrichiens, les seuls d'une puissance étrangère à l'exposition de Turin; notons de plus, que Mr. Rigotti, architecte, l'auteur de la halle des vins et des huiles, une importante annexe est un émule de d'Aronco. Ceci n'est qu'une première tentative d'architecture moderne en Italie, pays où la tradition de la Renaissance classique s'est jusqu'à ce jour opposée à tout essai de modernisme, seules la peinture et la sculpture, et particulièrement l'art décoratif faisaient exception et se modernisaient tout en

to the designer, the architect Raimondo d'Aronco, has been brilliantly carried out. Not only the principal building, but the supplementary erections designed either by him or by his colleagues and pupils all show the same harmony of design and unanimity of intention. The reason for this is clearly seen, when it is known that d'Aronco, as well as Prof. Olbrich of Darmstadt and Prof. Baumann of Vienna are all pupils of the Vienna master Prof. Otto Wagner. Professor Baumann has designed the Austrian department of the Exhibition, the only foreign building present; the wine and oil Hall, an important supplementary building is the work of the architect Rigotti, one of d'Aroncos colleagues who strives with him to introduce the

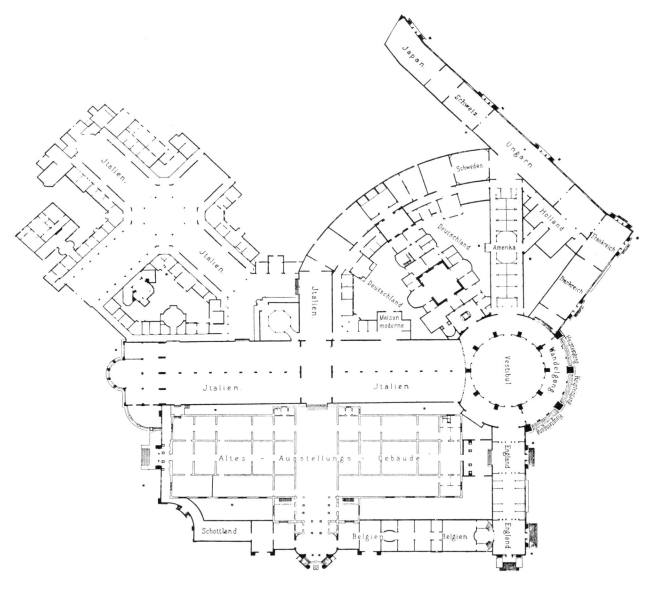

ditionen klassischer Renaissance allen Neuerungsversuchen entgegenstanden: nur bezüglich der Malerei und Plastik, namentlich aber der Kleinkunst bestanden Ausnahmen, die zu nicht unwesentlichem Teil von altpompeianischen Vorbildern ihren Ausgang ableiteten.

Wir müssen uns hier auf d'Aronco's Hauptwerk: das Hauptgebäude, beschränken, das in der schwierigen und doch übersichtlichen Grundrißlösung wie im Aufbau durchaus sein eigenes Werk ist. Eine besondere Schwierigkeit entstand dadurch, daß der Bau in eine Ecke des Geländes gedrängt und in bequeme Verbindung des mitbenutzten älteren Ausstellungsbaues zu bringen war. Der äußerst geschickten Grundrißentwickelung, welche diesen Verhältnissen unverblümt Rechnung trägt, verdankt der ganze Bau zu nicht geringem Teil seinen allgemein befriedigenden, großartigen Erfolg. Um eine auf zehn Pfeilern errichtete

s'inspirant d'une façon frappante des modèles pompéiens.

Nous devons nous borner ici au bâtiment principal, œuvre capitale de d'Aronco, qui, par la solution difficile et claire du plan et de l'élévation est absolument sienne. Le fait que le bâtiment dût être relégué dans un angle du terrain et dût enclure en communication facile l'ancien bâtiment d'exposition également utilisé, créait une grande difficulté. Le succès éclatant et général qu'obtient ce bâtiment est dû en grande partie à l'extrème habilité avec laquelle le plan fut aménagé en tenant compte des exigences mentionnées plus haut. Tout autour d'une haute, coupole portée par dix piliers, s'étend une halle circulaire plus basse, ces deux halles formant ensemble la salle principale de représentation. Aux piliers intérieurs correspondent les piliers, formant contreforts saillants, dont quatre en façade

modern style. This may be considered the first important attempt to supplant the traditional classical Renascance in Italy by decidedly modern architecture; painting and sculpture have always been exceptions to this tradition, a considerable number of examples showing unmistakeably their old Pompeian origin.

Here, we must limit ourselves to a description of the principal building, which is entirely the work of d'Aronco, the solution of the difficulties of the ground-plan, and the accomplishment of the building was his unaided work. One special difficulty to be surmounted was the fact that the new building was crowded into a corner that it might join on and utilize an old Exhibition building. The exceedingly clever way in which the two buildings are united is mainly the reason

hohe Kuppelhalle zieht lich eine niedrigere breite Ringhalle, mit erlterer den Hauptrepräsentations-raum bildend. Den inneren Pfeilern entlprechen nach außen weit vortretende Widerlagspfeiler, von denen drei in der Fallade die drei Haupt-eingänge einrahmen. Strahlenförmig entwickeln lich aus den nächltgelegenen Pfeileröffnungen zwei konvergierende Seitenflügel. Zwilchen dielen entfalten lich wieder, teils ebenfalls strahlen-förmig, teils auf erlterer lenkrecht, weitere Ausitellungsgalerien. Ein größerer Teil dieler Hallen ilt der italienilchen Kunlt und Kunlt-indultrie überwielen, der übrige Teil den anderen ausltellenden Ländern. Für Deutlchland war in dem einen Zwickel des Hallenkomplexes Platz zu eigenen, nicht in äußere Erlcheinung tretende Bauten gelallen, in denen es, ganz leinen Eigen-tümlichkeiten entlprechend, lich einrichten konnte. Oelterreich errichtete, wie lchon bemerkt, abge-londerte Bauten im Park.

Von dem Inneren ilt hier die große zwei-lchiffige Halle der italienilchen Kunltindultrie gegeben, die ganz in der Wagnerlchen Richtung lich bewegt. Tafel 99 giebt uns ein Bild des die linke Seitenfallade bildenden Hallenbaues, welcher den alten, der italienilchen Kunlt vorbehaltenen Bau gelchickt verdeckt und dafür den Haupteingang bildet.

Von dem Itolzen Kuppelbau (Tafel 98) lei noch erwähnt, daß die gelchwungenen Vordächer über den Kuppelfenltern nicht blos dekorativen Zwecken dienen, londern dem Eindringen Iteiler Sonnen-Itrahlen vorbeugen und gleichzeitig eine Gegen-wirkung auf den Schub der Kuppel ausüben. Das noch auffälligere Anklingen des Kuppel-baues an orientalilche Bildungsweile, als lonlt lchon der Fall ilt bei Bauten Wagnerlcher Richtung, will man aus den Einflüllen herleiten, welche die tägliche Anlchauung der prachtvollen altbyzantinilchen Molcheen, namentlich der Hagia Sophia, auf den Architekten ausübte: d'Aronco wohnt nämlich in Konltantinopel, wolelblt er die Stelle eines erlten Architekten des Sultans bekleidet.

---

82 [1903; 5]

Die Evangelilche Erlölerkirche in München-Schwabing (bisheriger Vorort von München) wurde nebit zugehörigem Pfarr-haule durch Profellor Theodor Filcher in München (jetzt in Stuttgart) vom März 1900 bis Oktober 1901 erbaut.

Der im Aeußeren und Inneren gleich Itim-mungsvolle Kirchenbau, der in leiner Anlage und Durchbildung an die altromanilche Balilika anknüpft, hat ein breites, nördliches Seitenlchiff, das über und unter der Empore günltigen Ausblick auf Altar und Kanzel gewährt, während das lchmale, lüdliche Seitenlchiff welent-lich nur einen Verbindungsgang bildet. Die Orgel ilt in einem belonderen, an leßteren an-Itoßenden Kapellenbau aufgeltellt derart, daß lie und der Sängerchor der Gemeinde und dem Prediger überlichtlich bleiben. Der aus Itatilchen Gründen erforderliche Chorumgang verleiht der Anlage eine belonders weihevolle Stimmung; hier nehmen die Kommunikanten Platz, um Störungen des Gottesdienltes zu vermeiden. Diele Rücklicht ilt überhaupt bei der ganzen Anlage und belonders bei Anordnung der Vor-hallen durchgeführt. Das Pfarrhaus, das auch Wohnung für den Hilfsgeiltlichen und den Kirchen-diener enthält, nimmt auch den Saal für den Vorbereitungsunterricht der Konfirmanden auf.

Für den Kirchenbau wurden rund 210 000 und für den des Pfarrhaules 40 000 Mark auf-gewendet. Beide Bauten lind aus Backltein, mit ganz dünnem Kalkmörtel (mit der Kelle auf-gezogen) geputzt, sodaß das Fugenneß noch deutlich erkennbar bleibt. Zu Bildhauerarbeiten

---

encadrent les trois entrées principales. Deux ailes latérales convergentes se développent en rayonnant des ouvertures suivantes. Entre ces dernières s'étendent d'autres galeries d'exposition, en partie rayonnantes, en partie perpendiculaires sur les premières. La plus grande partie de ces galeries est consacrée à l'art et à l'art appliqué italiens, les autres parties aux pays étrangers exposants. La section allemande avait trouvé place dans un angle des bâtiments; là elle pouvait s'organiser suivant ses besoins particuliers toute-fois sans obligation de s'affirmer par des façades à l'extérieur. L'autriche éleva ainsi que nous l'avons déjà dit des constructions séparées dans le parc.

Nous donnons ici, comme vue d'intérieur la grande halle à deux nefs de l'art appliqué italien, qui est tout à fait dans la direction de l'école de Wagner. La Pl. 99 représente la construction de la halle formant façade latérale qui masque adroitement l'ancien bâtiment destiné à l'art italien et en forme l'entrée principale. Quant à la magni-fique coupole Pl. 98 notons encore que les avant-toits recourbés qui couronnent les fenêtres de la coupole n'ont pas seulement un but décoratif, mais qu'ils servent à protéger l'intérieur contre les rayons du soleil et en même temps à con-trebuter la poussée de la coupole. Le profil de la coupole encore plus surprenant qu'il ne l'est dans les constructions de l'école de Wagner, peut-être expliqué par l'influence que la vue quotidienne des magnifiques anciennes mosquées byzantines et particulièrement celle de Ste Sophie exerce sur l'architecte: d'Aronco habite Constantinople où il occupe la place de premier architecte du Sultan.

---

82 [1903; 5]

L'église protestante du Rédempteur à Schwabing-Munich (jusqu'à ce jour faubourg de Munich) fut bâtie ainsi que la cure qui en dépend, par le professeur Theodor Fischer de Munich du mois de mars 1900 au mois d'octobre 1901.

Cette église aussi imposante à l'intérieur qu'à l'extérieur rappelle, par sa disposition et ses détails, l'ancienne basilique romane; elle a une large nef latérale au nord, laquelle offre un coup-d'œil favorable sur l'autel et la chaire, tandis que le bas côté sud est étroit et ne sert que de passage. L'orgue est placée dans une petite chapelle annexe spéciale, touchant au bas côté sud et située de façon à rester, ainsique le chœur des chanteurs, visible au public et au prédicateur. Le bas côté entourant le chœur, nécessaire pour les raisons de statique, donne à l'ensemble un caractère particulièrement solennel; c'est ici que se placent les commu-niants pour éviter de troubler le service divin. Pareil soin a du reste été observé dans toutes les parties de l'édifice et particulièrement dans la disposition des porches. La maison du pasteur qui contient en même temps les logements du suppléant et du sacristain est occupée également par une salle servant au cours préparatoire des cathéchumènes.

On dépensa la somme ronde de 210 000 Marks pour l'église et de 40 000 pour la cure. Ces deux bâtiments sont en briques recouvertes d'un très léger crépissage de mortier de chaux, appliqué à la truelle et qui laisse apparent l'appareil des joints. Pour les travaux de sculpture on employa

---

why the effect of the whole is so satisfactory, one may say magnificent. A high central Hall surmounted by a cupola on 10 pillars, is sur-rounded by a broad low second hall, which form with the first-mentioned, the chief reception rooms. The inside pillars correspond with outside pillars with abutments which stand prominently forward, and four of which in the façade form a frame for the three principal entrances. From the next openings of the pillars, two radial converging side wings extend. Between these, are other exhibition galleries, partly radial, partly vertical. The greater amount of space is devoted to the exhibition of Italian art, and artistic in-dustries, the remainder is divided among other countries. Germany was allotted a corner of the Hall in which it could most suitably display its characteristic exhibits. Austria built separate halls in the Park. We give here the great Hall with its two naves in which Italian in-dustries were exhibited. This is entirely in Wagner's style. Plate 99 gives us a view of the hall which forms the left side front, and which, while it ingeniously hides part of the old buil-ding, forms the principal entrance. Respecting the stately cupola (Plate 98) it may be mentioned that the bold projecting roof over the cupola windows is not only ornamental, but serves to divert the direct rays of the sun, and to soften the light from the cupola. The greater promi-nence given to the cupola than is generally the case in the buildings of the Wagner school may be attributed to the influence of the daily ob-servation of the magnificent Byzantine mosques, particularly the Hagia Sophia: d'Aronco lives in Constantinople where he occupies the post of first architect to the Sultan.

---

82 [1903; 5]

The Evangelical Church of the Redeemer in Munich-Schwabing (a suburb of Munich) was built, together with the parsonage adjoining, by Professor Theodor Fischer of Munich from March 1900 till October 1901.

Both the exterior and interior of the church show the reverent spirit of the architect. The design as a whole, is based on the old Roman basilica, the interior has one broad north aisle from which, both over and under the gallery, is seen to great advantage the altar and chancel; the narrow south side aisle is only intended to be a means of communication. The organ is placed in a special chapel built on to the church, and the organ loft and choir are visible to the preacher and to the congregation. The place round the choir — a necessity for the stability of the building — adds to the solemnity of the interior and is used as a seating-place for communicants by which means all unnecessary disturbance of the Service is avoided. This latter fact has been specially borne in mind in the whole design, particularly in the position of the entrance porches. The parsonage contains also apartments for the accommodation of cu-rates and for the verger; a hall is reserved for the instruction of Confirmation candidates.

The church cost 210 000 Marks and the par-sonage 40 000 Marks. Both buildings are of brick with a thin plastering of lime so that the

ward Muschelkalk, zum Altar und zur Kanzel aber gelber Veroneser Marmor verwendet. Sie sind sämtlich ohne Modell lediglich nach den Zeichnungen des Architekten Professor Fischer durch Bildhauer Neumeister unmittelbar aus dem Stein ausgemeißelt.

Es darf hier wohl darauf verwiesen werden, wie bei diesem Bau ganz moderne Kunstbestrebungen in dem Formengewande älterer deutsch-christlicher Baukunst zum Ausdruck kommen oder sich damit decken.

du calcaire et pour l'autel et la chaire du marbre jaune de Vérone. Ces travaux de sculpture furent exécutés sans modèles, taillés directement dans la pierre par le sculpteur Neumeister d'après les dessins du professeur Fischer.

Il est bon d'attirer ici l'attention sur le fait que dans ce monument, des tendances toutes modernes sont exprimées dans l'esprit de la plus ancienne architecture chrétienne germanique et que ces deux tendances se complètent et s'accordent.

lining of the bricks is plainly visible. The sculptural parts are of Muscle lime, for altar and chancel yellow Veronese marble has been used. They were carved by the sculptor Neumeister in stone direct from the drawings of Professor Fischer without any previous casting.

In contemplating this building one cannot help being struck by the manner in which modern artistic forms express themselves even in the oldest German ecclesiastical architecture.

83 [1903; 9]

Die neue Rheinwerftanlage in Düsseldorf ist eine derjenigen modernen Verkehrsanlagen, bei welcher durch einträchtiges Zusammenwirken von Architekt und Ingenieur, vielfach bei ähnlichen Leistungen beklagte Anomalien glücklich vermieden wurden: Eine seltene Harmonie der überwiegend technischen Leistungen mit den künstlerischen ist hier erzielt worden.

Es handelt sich um die Verbindung und einheitliche Gestaltung der bei dem Bau der festen Rheinbrücke 1896—98 angelegten Werft mit der des stromaufwärts angelegten Hafens.

83 [1903; 9]

L'établissement des Nouveaux Quais à Düsseldorf représente un bel exemple de viabilité moderne, d'autant plus remarquable, que grâce à la collaboration intelligente de l'architecte et de l'ingénieur, maintes inconveniences à plaindre ailleurs en pareil cas, ont été evitées, mais encore: Il a été obtenu ici une rare harmonie entre la partie technique dominante et l'oeuvre purement artistique.

Il s'agit du raccordement et de la composition d'ensemble du quai construit lors de l'établissement du pont fixe sur le Rhin de 1896 à 1898 avec celui du port construit en amont du fleuve.

83 [1903; 9]

The new Rhine wharf plant in Düsseldorf is an example of modern traffic improvement in which architect and engineer, by working together with one aim, have avoided the anomalies so often to be seen when this harmony of intention has not existed.

In this case, where the architectural ornament has sensibly given way to the more important technical requirements we have a satisfactory result which is rarely attained.

The task was to connect the wharf, laid out at the building of the Rhine bridge (1896—1898) with the up-stream harbour.

Das Werk ist unter Mitwirkung und Kostenbeteiligung des Preußischen Staates und der Stadtverwaltung von Düsseldorf entstanden und ausgeführt worden wie folgt: Der Vorentwurf der Anlage stammte von dem verstorbenen Stadtbaurat Frings in Gemeinschaft mit der ausführenden Firma Ph. Holzmann & Co. in Frankfurt a. M., bezw. deren Oberingenieur W. H. Lauter, bezüglich des technischen Teiles, und für die architektonische Ausgestaltung von Architekt Eberlein (jetzt in Köln). Die weitere Bearbeitung in Entwurf und Ausführung des erfolgte unter Leitung des Wasserbauinspektors Stadt Düsseldorf). Die Ausführung der Uferbauten des Königl. Baurats Radke (Beigeordneter der Ganzen lag auch in den Einzelheiten in Hand

L'oeuvre a été accomplie solidairement et à frais communs par l'état prussien et la municipalité de Düsseldorf. Le projet primitif es dû à feu le conseiller des travaux de la ville Frings collaborant avec la maison d'entreprise Holzmann et Cie. à Francfort s. M. représentée par son ingénieur W. H. Lauter pour ce qui concerne la partie technique et par l'architecte Eberlein, actuellement à Cologne, pour la partie artistique. — L'étude définitive du projet et son exécution furent confiés au conseiller royal des bâtiments Radke (adjoint de la ville de Düsseldorf), qui fut aussi chargé de tous les détails. Les travaux riverains furent exécutés par la maison Holzmann et Cie. sous la conduite de l'inspecteur des ponts et eaux, Mr. Ottmann, durèrent du printemps 1899 jusqu'en mars 1902.

The work was carried out jointly by the Prussian government and by the town of Düsseldorf in the following manner. The first design of the whole plant was by the town building councillor Frings (since deceased) together with the contractors Ph. Holzmann & Co. of Frankfort on Main. The first engineer of this firm W. H. Lauter was entrusted with technical part, and the architectural part was given to the architect Eberlein (at present in Cologne). Certain details, both of design and of building were placed in the hands of the building councillor Radke of Düsseldorf. The water "Bau-Inspektor" Ottmann was entrusted with the superintendence of the work, which occupied from Spring 1899 to March 1902.

Ottmann durch vorgenannte Firma; fie erfolgte in der Zeit von Frühjahr 1899 bis März 1902.

Die vom Staate getragenen Koften für die wafferbaulichen Arbeiten betrugen rund 2 Millionen Mark, die von der Stadt für die Straßen- und Geleifeanlagen, Betriebseinrichtungen, Ausftattung, Gas-, Waffer- und Elektrizitätsanlagen fowie Baumpflanzungen rund 1½ Millionen Mark.

Wie hier die einfache Verkehrsanlage zu einer wirklich hochbedeutfamen, architektonifchen Schmuckanlage geftaltet worden ift, würdig der rheinifchen Kunftmetropole, davon legen unfere Bilder reichlich Zeugnis ab.

Les frais supportés par l'état pour les travaux hydrauliques se montèrent à deux millions de Marks, ceux de la ville pour les travaux des quais, de la rue des lignes de chemin de fer, de décoration, d'installations de gaz, d'eau et d'électricité ainsi que pour les plantations d'arbres furent d'un million et demi de Marks.

Nos planches donnent la preuve indiscutable qu'en ce cas, on a su faire d'une simple question de voirie une question hautement artistique: l'architecture de toute cette installation se trouve ainsi digne de la métropole artistique des provinces rhénanes.

The Government bore the cost of that part of the work connected with the water and which amounted to about 2 Millionen Marks while the cost of the formation of the roads, the railway, the offices, the equipment, the gas, water, and electricity plants, as well as the planting of the trees, was borne by the town of Düsseldorf, and amounted to 1½ Millionen Marks.

Our illustrations will show how this simple place of traffic has been metamorphosed into an important ornamental quarter, worthy of the Rhine art metropolis.

84 [1903; 100]

Nachdem die aus verfchiedenen Bauperioden des XII.—XV. Jahrhunderts ftammende, auf einer Anhöhe des rechten Donauufers von Budapeft (der Alt-Ofener Baftei) gelegene Sankt Mathiaskirche mit ihrem 80 m hohen Turm im Jahre 1896 durch Profeffor Schulek wieder hergeftellt war, handelte es fich darum, dem prachtvollen Bilde der gefchichtlich wie künftlerifch hochbedeutenden Krönungskirche der ungarifchen Könige einen entfprechenden, würdigen Rahmen zu geben und dazu einen monumentalen Aufgang von der Herzog Albrechtftraße zu fchaffen, von dem man das fich bietende herrliche Panorama ungeftört genießen kann.

Profeffor Friedrich Schulek ward mit der Planung und Ausführung in Stilformen betraut, die denen des X.—XI. Jahrhunderts entfprechen, um damit eine Anknüpfung an die Zeit des heiligen Stefan, des großen Ungarkönigs (998 bis 1031) zu finden.

84 [1903; 100]

Après que l'église de Saint Mathieu située sur une élévation de la rive droite du Danube à Budapest (ancien bastion de Ofen) en 1896, avec sa tour de 80 mètres de hauteur eut été restaurée par le professeur Schulek, il s'agissait de donner à l'admirable aspect de cette église de couronnement des rois de Hongrie, un cadre dègne et un accès monumental montant de la rue de Herzog Albrecht; cette construction devait offrir des points de vue sur le panorama splendide qui se déroule au pied de l'église.

Vu que l'église, importante comme monument historique et artistique, date des époques du XII au XV siècle, le professeur Frédéric Schulek fut décidé l'exécution à en formes correspondantes au stile du Xme et du XIme siècles, pour y trouver un accord avec le temps de Saint Etienne, le Grand Roi Hongrois (998—1031).

La construction pour laquelle l'architecte exécuta tous les dessins et modèles d'ornement de

84 [1903; 100]

In 1896 Professor Schulek had restored the St. Mathias church of Budapest. The church which dates from various periods of the XII. to XV. centuries is situated on an eminence on the right bank of the Danube (the Alt-Ofener Bastei). The task now presented to the architect was to form a worthy frame for this artistically important "Krönungskirche" of the Hungarian kings, and at the same time to construct a monumental mount from the Herzog Albrechtstrasse from which the eye can enjoy undisturbed the magnificent panorama.

Professor Friedrich Schulek was entrusted with the planning and carrying out of this task, and has adopted for his purpose the style of the X. and XI. centuries, thereby linking the buildings with the memory of the holy Stefan the great Hungarian king (998 to 1031).

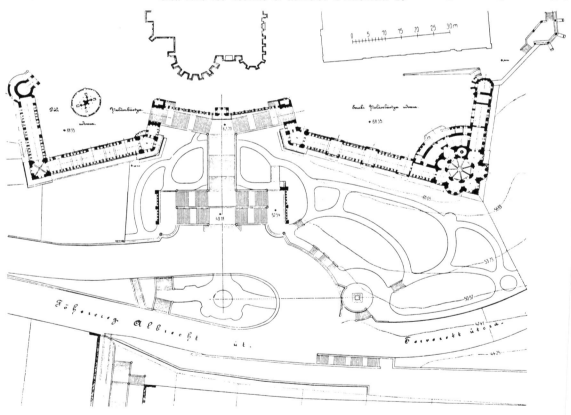

Der Bau, zu dem der Architekt alle Entwürfe und ornamentalen Modelle eigenhändig ausführte, dauerte von September 1899 bis Mai 1902.

Die in unfrer Bildtafel dargeftellte Treppenanlage umfaßt: 7 + 2.2.12 + 3.15 + 2.15 + 16 = 146 Stufen zu je 14 cm Höhe; fie erfteigt alfo zufammen eine Höhe von 20,44 m.

Die örtliche Bauleitung führte Architekt Jánosz Schulek. Die Koften haben insgefamt rd. 1340000 Mark betragen. Alle Konftruktionen find nach mittelalterlicher Weife durchgeführt. Als Material diente der dortige harte, weiße Süßwafferkalk.

sa propre main, dura du mois de septembre 1899 jusqu' en mai 1902.

L'ensemble des escaliers représentés sur notre planche comprend: 7 + 2.2.12 + 3.15 + 2.15 + 16 = 146 marches de 0,14 cm chacune, cet escalier franchit donc une hauteur totale de 20,44 mètres.

La direction des travaux fut confiée à l'architecte Jánosz Schulek. Les frais s'élevèrent en tout à 1340000 Marks. Toutes les constructions furent exécutées d'après les principes du moyen-âge. On employa comme matériaux le calcaire d'eau douce blanc et dur de la contrée.

The building, for which the architect drew with his own hand all designs and ornamental models, lasted from September 1899 to May 1902.

Our illustration gives the ornamental steps: 7 + 2.2.12 + 3.15 + 2.15 + 16 = 146 steps each 14 centimeters high; together therefore the steps reach a height of 20,44 meters.

The local superintendent was the architect Jánosz Schulek. The cost amounted to 1340000 Marks. The style is in every part medieval; the material is the local hard white "Süsswasser" limestone.

85, 96 [1903: 14, 13]

Die durch Profeſſor Martin Dülfer in München, Kaulbachſtraße 22, 22a, 24 und 26 nach ſeinen Entwürfen ausgeführte Gruppe kleiner Wohnhäuſer zeigt eine äußerſt glückliche Löſung einer der ſchwierigſten Aufgaben des modernen Städtebaues: Durch die Zuſammenlegung der einzelnen Höfe, die ſich teilweiſe (wie zwiſchen No. 20 und 22 und zwiſchen No. 24 und 26) nach der Straße hin öffnen, gewinnen die Gebäude günſtigſte Beleuchtung und Beſonnung, wie eine ſtets wirkſame Durchlüftung. In künſtleriſcher Beziehung iſt hier in

85, 96 [1903: 14, 13]

Le groupe de petites maisons d'habitation construites à Munich, Kaulbachstrasse 22, 22a, 24 et 26 d'après ses plans par professeur Martin Dülfer, montre une solution particulièrement heureuse d'un des problèmes les plus difficiles de l'édification urbaine moderne. Grâce à la combinaison des différentes cours qui s'ouvrent en partie sur la rue, comme entre les No. 20 et 22 et entre les No. 24 et 26, les bâtiments profitent d'un éclairage et d'une ventilation extrêmement favorables, tandis qu'ils sont entièrement

85, 96 [1903: 14, 13]

A group of small dwellinghouses has been built by Professor Martin Dülfer at Kaulbachstrasse 22, 22a, 24 and 26, Munich. The design proves that Professor Dülfer has solved successfully one of the most difficult problems of modern town architecture. The courtyards at the back of the houses, are not altogether separated and are partly open to the street (between 20 and 22 and between 24 and 26). By this means the houses get more sun, are

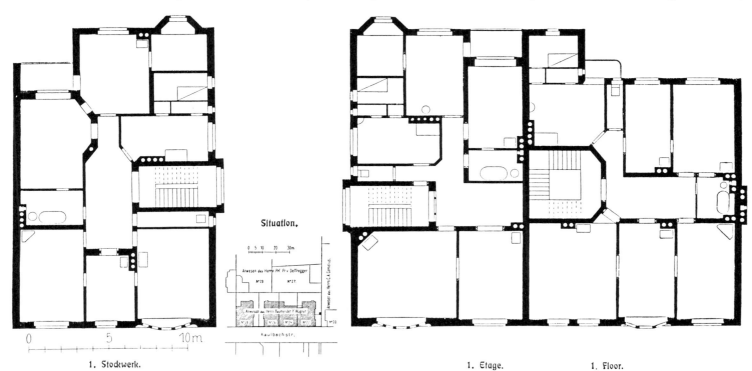

Situation.

1. Stockwerk.

1. Etage.

1. Floor.

natürlicher Weiſe und mit wenig Aufwand ein durchaus künſtleriſch wirkendes, ruhiges und doch maleriſch belebtes Straßenbild geſchaffen: Die vier Gebäude haben zuſammen nur rund 200 000 Mark Baukoſten erfordert. Es ſind Backſteinbauten mit Kalkputz, in den Wandflächen gekämmt (gerifſelt) und abgefärbt, die Architekturteile glatt mit angetragenem, in den Gründen farbig ausgelegtem Ornament.

Die Dächer ſind mit roten Bieberſchwänzen hergeſtellt, die Turmhauben, Abdeckungen, Rinnen u. ſ. w. aus Kupfer. Die Gitter ſind vergoldet.

exposés aux rayons du soleil. Au point de vue artistique, il a été créé ici d'une façon absolument naturelle et avec peu de dépenses un ensemble perspectif parfaitement satisfaisant, formant une silhouette tranquille et sans être monotone. La construction des quatre bâtiments ensemble n'a coûté que 200 000 Marks. Ce sont des édifices en briques crépies à la chaux; les surfaces des murs sont striées et teintes; les parties architecturales sont lisses avec des ornements à fonds de couleur.

Les toits sont recouverts de briques rouges; les tourelles, les couvertures, les cheneaux etc. sont en cuivre. Les fers forgés sont dorés.

better lighted and better ventilated. In a simple manner, and with little expense, the architect has yet produced an artistic group of buildings which add not a little to the picturesque effect of the architecture of the street. The whole expense of the four buildings was only about 200 000 Marks. They are of brick, with plaster surfaces, the walls are roughened in small grooves and coloured, the architectural parts are smooth with coloured ornament.

The roofs are of flat red tiles; the cupolas of the towers, the gutter pipes etc. are of copper. The iron railings are gilded.

86 [1903: 21]

Die Heilmannſche Grundbeſitz-Verwaltung (Geſ. m. b. H.) in München hat daſelbſt vom Oktober 1901 bis Auguſt 1902 durch Architekt Oskar Deliſle das große Zinshaus Herzog Wilhelmſtraße 19 ausführen laſſen, das im 4,3 m hohen Erdgeſchoß nur Kaufläden enthält und in den oberen Geſchoſſen zu Zwecken der Augenheilanſtalt des Profeſſors Dr. Schlöſſer ausgebaut iſt.

Nach dem urſprünglichen Entwurfe ſollten zwar die Obergeſchoſſe je zwei, alſo zuſammen acht größere Mietwohnungen enthalten; jedoch um eine anderweitige Ausnutzung zu ermöglichen (wie ſie jetzt durchgeführt iſt), wurde der geſamte tragende, innere Aufbau in Eiſen, nach Art des amerikaniſchen „Steel framing"-Syſtems derart durchgebildet, daß die ſämtlichen Scheidewände aus Schwemmſteinen hergeſtellt werden konnten und bei etwaigem Bedürfnis unbedenklich entfernt oder verſchoben werden können.

Im Erdgeſchoß iſt das Veſtibül nebſt Fahrſtuhl.

86 [1903: 21]

L'administration des biens immobiliers Heilmann (Société à garantie limitée) à Munich a fait construire du mois d'octobre 1901 jusqu'en août 1902 par Monsieur Oscar Delisle architecte, la grande maison de rapport Herzog Wilhelmstrasse 19; cet immeuble ne contient au rez-de-chaussée haut de 4,3 m que des magasins et dans les étages supérieurs les locaux destinés à la clinique de l'oculiste Docteur Professeur Schlösser.

Il est vrai de dire que d'après le projet primitif les étages supérieurs devaient être divisés chacun en deux appartements, ce qui représentait en tout huit grands logements, cependant, pour pouvoir, suivant les exigences disposer de ces locaux en toute liberté (ainsi que cela a lieu maintenant) toute la construction fut exécutée en fer d'après le système américain „Steel framing", de façon à ce que les cloisons intérieures (en pierre ponce) puissent, suivant les besoins, être éloignées ou changées de place.

Au rez-de-chaussée se trouvent le vestibule avec lift et une loge pour son desservant.

86 [1903: 21]

The Administration of the Heilmann property (L. L. Co.) in Munich has built in that city Herzog Wilhelmstrasse 19 from October 1901 till August 1902 a large dwelling house. The architect is Mr. Oscar Delisle. In the ground-floor, 4,3 metres high, are only shops, and the upper storeys are occupied by the Eye Hospital of Professor Dr. Schlösser.

According to the original design, the upper part was to consist of 8 large private dwellings; but, in order that the building could be easily adapted to other purposes (and this has actually taken place), the whole of the interior was carried out on the American steel framing system. The separating walls of schwemm stone could be at once and without difficulty removed.

On the ground-floor is a vestibule containing a lift and a room for the lift-attendant.

The hospital, with its extensive clinical accommodation, can house 80 patients. It contains

Die Heilanstalt umfaßt neben ausgedehnter Klinik für 80 Kranke, die Räume für ein Ambulatorium A im erften Stockwerk, zugleich Demonftrations- und Hörfaal nebft Dunkelraum a, dem Warteraum b für Studierende mit gefonderter, gedeckter Treppe c und dem Garderoberaum d nächft der Haupttreppe, dem fämtlichen Gefchoffe miteinander verbindenden, elektrifch betriebenen Fahrftuhl gegenüber. Die Garderobe hat ein großes Oberlicht und fcheidet die Ambulanz von der Klinik ab, der die fämtlichen übrigen Räume angehören. Im 1. und 3. Stock find die Zimmer für Kranke 3. Kl., im 2. Stock die für Kranke 1. Kl. und in den nach der Straße zu gelegenen Räumen des 4. Stockwerkes die Zimmer der Kranken 2. Kl., zufammen 80 Krankenbetten.

L'établissement de l'oculiste contient à part une grande clinique pour 80 malades, salle de clinique A au premier étage, servant d'auditoire et salle de démonstration, avec chambre obscure a, la salle d'attente b, pour les étudiants, avec escalier séparé et couvert c et le vestiaire d dans le voisinage de l'escalier principal, vis-à-vis de l'ascenseur électrique reliant tous les étages les ceux aux autres. Le vestiaire à plafond vitré, sépare l'ambulance de l'hôpital qui comprend tous les autres locaux. Au premier et au 3me étages sont les chambres des malades de 3me classe, au 2me étage celles des malades de première classe tandis que les chambres du 4me étage donnant sur la rue, sont destinées aux malades de 2me classe; ces chambres contiennent en tout 80 lits.

Ambulatorium A on the first floor containing demonstration and lecture rooms with darkened room a, the waiting room for students with a separate covered stair case c and the cloak room d adjoining the principal stair case. The lift, worked by electricity, connects all storeys with each other. The cloak room has a sky-light and is placed between the ambulance and the hospital to which latter the whole of the upper rooms are devoted. In the first and third storey are the rooms for patients of the third class. The second floor contains the first class patients. The rooms facing the street of the fourth floor are reserved for second class patients, altogether there are 80 beds.

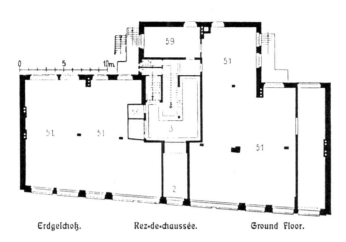

Erdgefchoß.   Rez-de-chaussée.   Ground Floor.

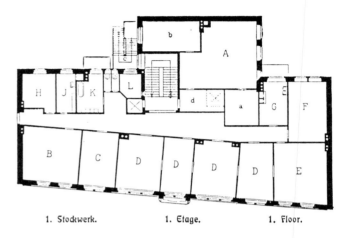

1. Stockwerk.   1. Étage.   1. Floor.

Die Beftimmung der Räume ift folgende: Im 1. Stock: B für Schwerkranke, C Arbeitszimmer, D Krankenzimmer, E Tageraum, F Arbeitszimmer und Apotheke, G Anrichte (mit Aufzug zur Küche), H Zimmer der Krankenfchweiter, J Wäfche- und Gefchirrkammer, K Bade- und Wafchraum, L Buchhalterei.

La destination des locaux est la suivante: au premier étage: B pour gravement malades, C chambre de travail, D chambre de malades, E chambre de société, F chambre de travail et pharmacie, G office (avec ascenseur de la cuisine), H chambre de la sœur de charité, I lingerie et vaisselerie, K bain et lavoir, L comptable.

The rooms are further subdivided into: first floor B Severe cases, C Work room, D Patients room, E Day room, F Work room and surgery, G room for food preparation (in connection with the kitchen by lift), H Nurses room, I Linen and china room, K Washing and Bath room, L Book-keeping department.

87 [1903; 24]

Ganz im Rahmen der Aufbauformen einer edlen Renaiffance zeigt das durch die Architekten Gebr. Schauppmeyer in Köln am Deutfchen Ring 42 erbaute Wohnhaus die Durchbildung in höchft wirkfamen, modernen Schmuckformen.

87 [1903; 24]

La maison d'habitation au Deutscher Ring 42 à Cologne construite par les frères Schauppmeyer architectes, montre des formes modernes d'un effet extrèmement frappant dans un cadre général d'aspect renaissance.

87 [1903; 24]

The noble style of the Renascence is shown in a house build at Deutschen Ring 42, Cologne by the architects Brothers Schauppmeyer. The effect is exceedingly striking and shows a judicious use of modern ornament.

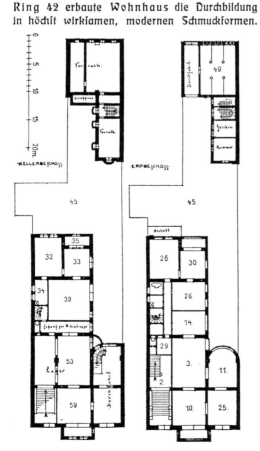

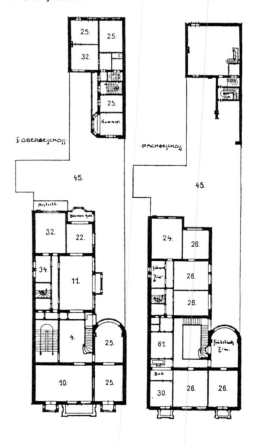

Das Haus hat zwei Wohnungen, deren eine, das Unter- und Erdgeschoß einnehmend, auch einige Geschäftsräume (Lager und Bureau) zu kaufmännischen Zwecken enthält. Die andere, opulentere umfaßt das 1. und 2. Obergeschoß. Die Zentralheizung nebst Kohlen- und Vorratsräumen liegt in einem Tiefkeller, der die ganze Gebäudefläche einnimmt. Der Bodenraum ist zu Kammern, Waschküche und Trockenboden eingerichtet.

Das im Jahre 1900 fertiggestellte Gebäude hat rund 288 500 Mark und das zugehörige Stallgebäude 30 800 Mark gekostet. Die Bildhauerarbeiten der gänzlich in Haustein hergestellten Faßade sind durch Erwin Haller in Köln ausgeführt.

La maison contient deux appartements, dont l'un situé dans le sous-sol et au rez-de-chaussée, comprend aussi quelques pièces pour bureaux et magasins. L'autre, bien plus opulent, occupe les premier et deuxième étages. Le calorifère, la soute à charbon et les caves à provision sont situés dans une cave qui s'étend sous toute la maison. Dans les combles sont disposés des chambres, des galetas, la buanderie et la lingerie.

Cet édifice fini en 1900 a coûté 288 500 Marks et l'écurie qui en dépend 30 800 Marks. Les travaux de sculpture des façades entièrement construites en pierre de taille ont été exécutées par Erwin Haller à Cologne.

The house contains two dwellings; one, comprising the ground floor and basement, contains certain rooms used for business purposes (store rooms and bureau); the other, more handsomely finished, occupies the first and second floors. The hot air heating apparatus, together with coal and storage rooms, lies in a deep cellar which extends under the whole building. The garret storey contains the laundry with drying room and some small chambers.

The house, which took a year to build, was finished in 1900; it cost about 288 500 Marks, the stabling an additional 30 800 Marks. The facade is entirely of rough stone, the sculptural parts are the work of Erwin Haller of Cologne.

88 [1903: 46]

In Budapest an der Vaczi-Körut 61 erbauten die Architekten Weinreb & Spiegel*) ein Geschäfts- und Wohnhaus, das in seiner Frontausbildung Schönheiten der Wiener Wagnerschule mit denen italienischer Palastarchitektur verbindet.

Die vornehm auffällige Gestaltung dieser Putzfassade ist erzielt, ohne von der aus praktischen Gründen bedingten Gleichteilung der Pfeiler und Oeffnungen u. s. w. abzugehen, lediglich durch die äußerst gewandte ornamentale Behandlung der Flächen. Eine reich und künstlerisch entwickelte, auf die geschäftliche Thätigkeit der Ladeninhaber bezügliche Emblematik verleiht der Fassade ein volkstümliches Gepräge, in wirksamem Gegensatze zu der meist unverständlichen Symbolik ähnlicher, gleicher Schule entsprossener Bauwerke.

88 [1903: 46]

Les architectes Weinreb & Spiegel*) construisirent à Budapest, rue Vaczi Körut 61 une maison de commerce et d'habitation montrant dans sa façade les beautés de l'école de Wagner unies à celles de l'architecture de palais italiens.

L'aspect distingué et surprenant de cette façade crépie est obtenu surtout par la façon extrêmement habile dont sont décorées les surfaces, mais sans renoncer à l'écartement égal des axes des piliers et des ouvertures, exigé par des raisons pratiques. Une décoration emblématique abondante et artistique se rapporte à l'activité commerciale des propriétaires des magasins et donne à l'édifice un caractère individuel en opposition à la plupart des décorations symboliques appliquées sans jugement aux bâtiments de même destination et provenant de la même école.

88 [1903: 46]

The architects Weinreb and Spiegel*) have built on the Vaczi Körut 61, Budapest business premises and a dwelling house, the facade of which is a fine example of the beauties of the Vienna Wagner School combined with the palatial architecture of Italy.

The exceedingly distinguished appearance of this ornamental elevation is mainly achieved by the clever handling of the decoration of the surfaces; at the same time utility has not been lost sight of, as one may see by the regular arrangement of the pillars and the different openings. The ornament is rendered specially attractive to the general public by emblematic devices applicable to the business carried on in the various shops, a happy contrast to the usual incomprehensible symbols which accompany this style of architecture.

89 [1903: 20]

Architekt Rudolf Bislich erbaute vom Juni 1901 bis März 1902 das „Landhaus Will" in der Kolonie Grunewald bei Berlin, Dunkerstraße No. 4, für den Preis von 70 000 Mark.

Der Sockel des Gebäudes ist bis zu den Fenstern des Erdgeschosses mit roten Rathenower Steinen verblendet, der übrige Teil der Fassaden mit Graukalk (in Rieselbewurf) geputzt, das Holz der Fachwerke mit Silikatfarbe gestrichen. Die Dächer haben Deckung in roten Rathenower Dachsteinen erhalten. Die Außenwände sind mit Isolierschlitzen ausgeführt, die mit Kieselguhr ausgefüllt wurden. Die Erwärmung des Hauses erfolgt mittels Wasserheizung. Die Innenwände der Haupträume sind nach besonderer Angabe und Detailzeichnungen des Architekten in Leimfarbe gestrichen, die Decken durchweg weiß gehalten, davon einige mit Balkenteilung.

89 [1903: 20]

Monsieur Rudolf Bislich architecte construisit de juin 1901 à mars 1902 la maison de campagne Will dans la colonie de Villas de Grunewald près de Berlin, Dunkerstrasse 4, pour le prix de 70000 Marks.

Le socle de cette construction est revêtu jusqu'aux fenêtres du rez-de-chaussée de pierre rouge de Rathenow, les autres parties des façades sont crépies au mortier; le bois des pans est peint à la couleur de silicate. Les toits sont recouverts de tuiles rouges de Rathenow. Les parois extérieures sont construites avec intervalles isolateurs, remplis de Kieselguhr. Le chauffage de la maison s'effectue au moyen d'un calorifère à eau chaude. Les parois des pièces principales sont peintes à la détrempe d'après les indications et dessins spéciaux de l'architecte; les plafonds sont tous blancs, quelques uns d'entre eux avec divisions marquées par des poutres.

89 [1903: 20]

The architect Rudolf Bislich built from June 1901 to March 1902 the "Villa Will" in the villa colony Grunewald near Berlin, Dunkerstrasse 4. The cost amounted to 70 000 Marks.

The basement up to the windows is faced with red Rathenow stone, the remaining parts of the facade are of grey lime; the wood and frame work is painted with silicate colour. The roofs are of red Rathenow tiles. The out-side walls have "Isolier" apertures which are filled up with silicate guhr. The house is warmed by hot water. The inside walls of the principal rooms are coloured according to special design of the architect; the ceilings are every where white, some are divided by beams at regular intervals.

90 [1903: 30]

Das von Architekt Carl Stief in Karlsruhe i. B. an der Eisenlohrstraße 27 erbaute Einfamilienhaus gewährt in seinem naiven, auf rechteckigem Grundriß entwickelten, sehr bewegten Aufbau einen eigenartig malerischen Reiz. Alle Erker ruhen auf Steinvorkragungen ohne Eisenträger oder -Anker. Dadurch, daß die Küche ins Untergeschoß gelegt werden konnte, mit dem Fußboden auf Höhe des Bürgersteiges, war neben großer Bequemlichkeit erzielt worden, nur den einen Teil des Gebäudes dreistöckig aufführen zu müssen, wodurch die ganze Anlage noch an Reiz gewonnen hat. Über dem Bruchsteinmauerwerk sind die Flächen geputzt; die Dächer sind beschiefert, ebenso die Wetterseite des in Fachwerk ausgebauten seitlichen Erkers. Die Baukosten stellten sich auf 26 000 Mark.

90 [1903: 30]

La maison pour une famille bâtie par Monsieur Carl Stief architecte à Carlsruhe, Eisenlohrstrasse 27, offre avec son plan carré et son élévation mouvementée, finement développée par sa naiveté, un charme tout particulier. Toutes les saillies reposent sur des consoles en pierre, sans secours de constructions en fer. Par le fait que la cuisine a été placée au rez-de-chaussée avec son sol à la hauteur du trottoir, on a obtenu, outre les avantages pratiques que présente une telle disposition, de n'élever qu'une partie du bâtiment en trois étages, ce qui augmente considérablement le charme de l'ensemble. Au dessus de la maçonnerie en moellons, les surfaces sont crépies: les toits sont recouverts en ardoises, de même que la façade en pans de bois de l'appentis latéral, exposée à la pluie. Les frais de construction s'élevèrent à 26 000 Marks.

90 [1903: 30]

The house, intended for the accommodation of one family and built by the architect Carl Stief at Eisenlohrstrasse 27 Carlsruhe in Baden has a strikingly effective elevation, and the whole building has a picturesqueness which lends it a peculiar charm. All the bows rest on stone cornices without iron girders or supports. The kitchen is situated in the basement, the floor is even with the ground, an arrangement, which besides adding to the convenience of the house, necessitated only one part of the upper building being carried up three storeys; this too has added much to the external appearance. The walls are of freestone plastered, the roofs are of slate, slate is also used for the weather side of the frame work balcony built out on the side. The cost of building was 26,000 Marks.

Die von Architekt Aug. Stürzenacker in Karlsruhe i. B. am neuen Rheinhafen ausgeführten Hochbauten sind sämtlich in verwandtschaftlichem Charakter in Anlehnung an die Formgebung der altrheinischen Bauten romanischer Zeit ausgebildet. Wir geben hier das Wohnhaus des Hafendirektors. Es ist trotz sehr schwieriger, hier nicht zu erwähnender Gründung, in Jahresfrist erbaut. Die Grundrisse zeigen besondere Freitreppenanlage zu den beiden Diensträumen und zu der Wohnung.

Die Innenräume sind mit großer Sorgfalt in der Art großstädtischer Villen ausgestattet, ein Teil in Anlehnung an tirolisch-gotische Formen. Die Fassaden sind aus winkelrecht gefügten, sonst hammerrecht bearbeiteten, gefugten, roten Pfinzthäler Sandbruchsteinen und Maulbronner rotem Sandstein für die Architekturteile, hergestellt. Die Dachdeckung besteht aus rheinischem Schiefer. Die Wappenschilde sind in heraldischen Farben bemalt.

Das Bildwerk ist durch Bildhauer Sieferle in Karlsruhe ausgeführt. Die Gesamtkosten belaufen sich auf 60 000 Mark.

In der Emser Allee 38 in Dresden-Blasewitz haben die Architekten Schilling und Graebner in der Zeit von Juli 1902 bis 1. April 1903 die Villa des Herrn Landrichter Doehn zum Preise von 65000 Mark erbaut.

Zu bemerken ist, daß die Diele der Wohnung im I. Stock sich im Dachgeschoß fortsetzt und dies mit ersterem wohnlich verbindet.

Die Fassaden sind als Putzbau durchgeführt, die ornamentalen Arbeiten in dem Putz ca. 3 mm vertieft und farbig ausgemalt.

In bevorzugtester Lage von Dresden, an der Wienerstraße 13, wo diese an der Einmündung der Pragerstraße zu einem Vorplatz des Hauptbahnhofes sich verbreitert, erbaute Architekt Kurt Diestel vom September 1901 bis Oktober 1902 für die „Landwirtschaftliche Feuerversicherung im Königreich Sachsen" ein großes Geschäftshaus, das allgemein nach dem darin angelegten „Kaiser-Café" benannt wird.

Die ausgezeichnete, freie Lage des Gebäudes erforderte eine größere Höhenentwickelung und die Wahl eines Baustiles, der zwar in der Durch-

Les constructions élevées par Monsieur Aug. Stürzenacker pour le nouveau port du Rhin près Carlsruhe sont toutes traitées dans un même caractère parent aux constructiones romanes des pays rhénans. Nous publions ici la maison du Directeur du port. Ce bâtiment a été élevé dans le cours d'une année, malgré des difficultés considérables rencontrées dans la fondation et que nous ne pouvons pas décrire ici. Les plans montrent les dispositions d'entrées bien distinctes pour les deux salles de service et pour le logement.

L'intérieur est traité avec beaucoup de soin dans le genre des villas de grandes villes, une partie s'inspire des formes gothiques tiroliennes. Les façades sont construites en assises régulières de pierre rouge des carrières de Pfinzthal, tandis que les lignes d'architecture sont en grès rouge de Maulbronn. La couverture est en ardoises du Rhin. Les écussons sont peints en couleurs héraldiques.

La sculpture a été exécutée par le sculpteur Sieferle à Carlsruhe. Les frais se sont élevés en tout à 60000 Marks.

A la Emser Allee 38 à Dresde-Blasewitz, les architectes Schilling et Graebner ont construit du mois de juillet 1902 au premier avril 1903 la villa du juge Mr. Doehn pour le prix de 65000 Marks.

Il est à noter que la halle de l'appartement du premier étage se prolonge dans l'étage du toit, reliant ainsi ces deux appartements.

Les façades sont exécutées en crépissage, les décorations ornementales sont gravées dans le crépissage à environ trois centimètres de profondeur et peintes en couleur.

Dans la situation la plus favorite de Dresde, Wienerstrasse 13, à l'endroit ou dans cette rue débouche la Pragerstrasse elle s'élargit pour former parvis de la gare centrale, Monsieur Kurt Diestel construisit de septembre 1901 à octobre 1902 une grande maison de commerce; cet immeuble appartenant à l'Assurance Agricole contre l'incendie pour le Royaume de Saxe, porte généralement le nom de „Kaiser-Café", d'après un établissement qui s'y trouve logé.

La position excellente et très en vue de cet édifice exigeait une grande hauteur et le choix

The buildings on the new Rhine wharf near Carlsruhe in Baden have been carried out by the architect Aug. Stürzenacker. All of them correspond in style with the old Rhine buildings of the Romanesque time. They were built in the space of one year, although there were great difficulties in the foundation which cannot be entered into here. Our illustration represents the residence of the Director. The groundplan shows the outside steps leading to the two offices and to the house.

The interior is carried out in a superior manner in the style of a large villa, partly decorated in the Tyrolese-Gothic style. The facades are of rectangular red Pfinzthäler sandfreestone and Maulbronn red sandstone for the architectural parts. The roofing is of Rhine slate. The armorial bearings are painted in heraldic colours.

The sculpture is by the sculptor Sieferle in Carlsruhe. The entire cost was 60 000 Marks.

The architects Schilling and Graebner have built in Dresden-Blasewitz, Emser Allee 38 from July 1902 to 1 April 1903 the villa of Mr. Doehn, Landrichter, at a cost of 65 000 Marks.

A noticeable feature of the interior is that the hall of the first floor is extended upwards to the roof, annex of the first floor.

The facades are of plaster-work, the ornamental work is carved 3 millimetres deep in the plaster-work and painted in colours.

The architect Kurt Diestel has built in Dresden Wienerstrasse 13 large business premises for the Agricultural Fire Insurance Company of the Kingdom of Saxony. The site, where the Pragerstrasse joins the Wienerstrasse and forms a spacious square before the principal Railway Terminus, is a fine one; the café which occupies part of the building gives its name to the house which is called the "Kaiser-Café". The time occupied was from September 1901 to October 1902.

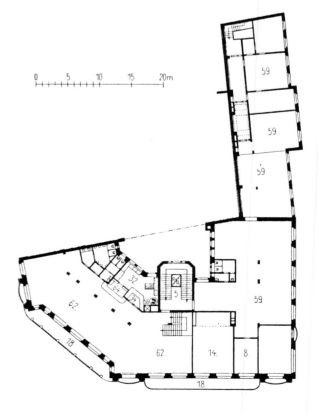

bildung modern ist, in großen Zügen jedoch an altsächsische Bauweise anknüpft. Das gab dann Gelegenheit zur Anlage von Aussichtsterrassen, die eine herrliche Rundsicht gewähren.

Im Erdgeschoß sind an der Hauptfront acht schmale Kaufläden sowie ein Teil des Cafés angelegt, während an der an einem Hofe sich hinziehenden Seitenfront Bureauräume liegen.

Das I. Stockwerk wird an der Hauptfront durch die großen Caféräume und dessen Nebenräume eingenommen; ein Teil der letzteren liegt in einem Zwischengeschoß. Nur ein nächst der rechtseitigen Ecke gelegener Raum gehört nebst den sämtlichen Räumen an der Seitenfront zu den Bureaus der Feuerversicherung.

Im II. Stockwerk liegen ebenfalls Bureaus. Das III. Stockwerk enthält zwei vornehme Wohnungen und zwei Einzelzimmer unmittelbar an der Treppe; der hintere, abgetrennte, zwischen Hof und Seitenfront durchgehende Raum dient als Archiv zu den Bureaus im II. Stock; eine kleine Treppe bildet den einzigen Zugang.

Die Fassade ist im Erdgeschoß aus Postelwitzer Elbsandstein und in den oberen Teilen aus Cottaer Sandstein hergestellt; der Dachreiter hat Kupferverkleidung.

Alle Deckenkonstruktionen bestehen aus Zementdielen zwischen Eisenträgern, die auf eisernen Unterzügen und Stützen ruhen. Bauleiter war Architekt Ostrinski; die Bildhauerarbeiten der Fassaden und des Cafés sind nach den Entwürfen des Architekten Diestel der Hauptsache nach von Bildhauer Reinhold König, das Kunstschmiedewerk von der Firma Böhme & Heunen, der kupferne Dachreiter von Georg Pöschmann, sämtlich in Dresden, ausgeführt.

d'un stile, qui quoique moderne dans le détail s'inspirât cependant dans ses grandes lignes de l'ancien art de bâtir saxon; ainsi on arrivait à la création de terrasses qui offrent une vue splendide.

Au rez-de-chaussée se trouvent sur la façade principale huit magasins étroits et une partie du café, tandis qu'une aile s'étendant sur une cour contient des bureaux.

Le premier étage est occupé sur la façade principale par les grandes localités du café et par ses dépendances; une partie de ces dernières est placée dans un entresol. Un seul local situé à l'angle droit forme avec toutes les salles de la face latérale, les bureaux de la société d'assurance contre l'incendie.

Au deuxième étage se trouvent également des bureaux. Le troisième étage contient deux appartements de maîtres et deux chambres séparées donnant sur le palier. Le local de derrière séparé, situé entre les cours, dans l'aile latérale, sert d'archives pour les bureaux du second étage; ce local n'est accessible que par un petit escalier.

La façade est au rez-de-chaussée construite en pierre de Postelwitz sur Elbe, dans les parties supérieures en pierre de Cotta. La tour en cavalier est recouverte en cuivre.

Tous les planchers sont construits en dalles de ciment posées entre solives en fer, qui reposent sur des poutres et des piliers en fer. L'architecte Ostrinski fut chargé de la conduite des travaux. Les travaux de sculpture de la façade et du café ont été exécutés d'après les projets de l'architecte Diestel principalement par le sculpteur Reinhold König, les fers forgés par la maison Böhme & Heunen, la tourelle en cuivre par George Pöschmann, tous de Dresde.

The splendid free site demanded a lofty building, and gave scope to the development of a style which though in many respects modern, yet in its principal features is Old Saxon. This allowed the construction of various terraces and balconies from which a magnificent view can be obtained.

The principal front contains on the ground-floor 8 small shops and a part of the Café, towards the court-yard are bureaus and offices.

The I floor is entirely occupied by the Café, part of the subsidiary rooms are in an intermediate storey. Only one corner on the right is occupied with the offices of the Insurance Company to which is devoted the whole of the side wing.

The II floor contains offices. The III floor contains two superior dwellings, and two separate single rooms on the staircase. Rooms between the courtyard and the side wing are occupied with the archives of the bureaus on the II floor, a small staircase being the only access thereto.

The facade on the ground floor is of Postelwitz Elbe sandstone, the upper part is of Cotta sandstone, the ornaments of the roof are faced with copper.

All ceilings are of cement — planks with iron girders and supports. The manager was the architect Ostrinski, the sculptural parts of the facade and the Café are from the designs of the architect Diestel; the principal parts by the sculptor Reinhold König, the artistic iron work by the firm Böhme and Heunen, the copper turret by Georg Pöschmann, all of Dresden.

Aus London brachten wir in Jahrg. II auf Tafel 63 die Abbildung einer Häusergruppe aus Fitz George Avenue, die von Architekt Delissa Joseph F. R. J. B. A. erbaut war, in dem ersichtlichen Bestreben, da wo die hohen Grundstückspreise zum Bau von Etagenhäusern zwangen, seinen mit mäßigen Mitteln ausgeführten Gebäuden, trotz Durchführung der Gesimsteilungen, ein malerisches, künstlerisches Gepräge zu verleihen. Die beifällige Aufnahme dieser Leistungen bezeigt das vorliegende Bild, ein ebenfalls von Delissa Joseph errichteter Häuser-

Nous avons publié dans la seconde année Pl. 63, un groupe de maisons situées à Londres Fitz George Avenue construites par l'architecte Delissa Joseph F. R. J. B. A.; le groupe témoignait de la tendance à donner un caractère artistique et pittoresque, même à des maisons très hautes où le prix élevé des terrains force à distribuer les apartements par étages et où la fuite des corniches est donnée. La planche ci-contre témoigne du bon résultat de ces essais; un bloc de maisons également

In our second volume we brought on plate 63 an illustration of a group of houses from Fitz George Avenue, built by the architect Delissa Joseph F. R. J. B. A. It could be seen that the aim of the architect had been to construct picturesque artistic buildings with a small outlay, and that though the high price of building sites compelled architects to design houses in flats yet they need not be extravagant or ugly. The present illustration shows how successful the experiment was. It is

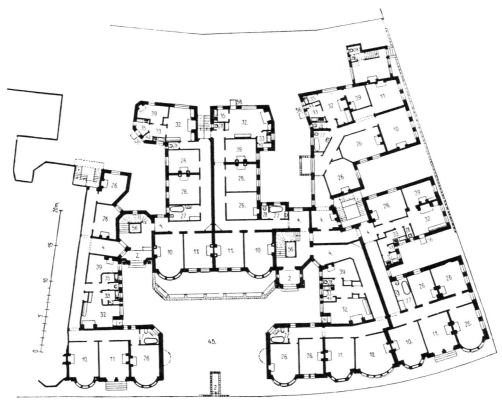

block der Fitz James Avenue in London W. Hier erreichen die Gebäude sogar die Höhe von fünf Wohnstockwerken über dem hohen Erdgeschoß; teilweise erscheinen die obersten Stockwerke als Mansarden und steigern so das malerische Straßenbild, das durch die glückliche Grundrißanordnung und die zahlreichen Erker und Balkone äußerst belebt erscheint.

construit par Delissa Joseph sur la Fitz James Avenue à Londres W. Ici, les bâtisses atteignent même la hauteur de cinq étages au dessus du haut rez-de-chaussée. Les étages supérieurs sont en partie traités en mansardes et augmentent ainsi l'aspect pittoresque qui du reste est dû à l'heureuse disposition du plan et aux nombreux bow-windows et balcons.

a block of houses by the same architect Delissa Joseph built in Fitz James Avenue London W. Here the houses are five storeys high above the high ground floor.

The storeys are partly gabled which adds to the picturesque appearance of the whole street. The numerous bows and balconies add to the cheerful and harmonious aspect of the facade.

95 [1903; 55]

Am Augustusplatz 8 in Leipzig errichtete Architekt H. P. Berlage in Amsterdam ein Geschäftsgebäude für die „Niederländische Lebens-Versicherungsgesellschaft" in der Zeit von November 1901 bis April 1903 zum Kostenpreis von rund 400 000 Mark. Die Fassade ist in Backstein mit Sandstein für besondere Konstruktionsteile und Granit zu Pfeilern und Abdeckungen, ausgeführt. Das Treppenhaus ist ganz in glasierten Ziegeln aufgeführt, nur die Stufen und Pfeiler bestehen aus Granit.

In dem Grundriß bedeuten: A, a bis f zu vermietende Räume, B Vorsaal, C Warte-, D Sprech-, E Direktorzimmer, F Kassenraum, G Buchhalterei, H Organisations-, J Expeditions-, K Schreibmaschinenabteilung, L Tresor, M Garderobe. Der Hof ist ganz unterkellert; in einem dieser Kellerräume liegt die Heizung. Die oberen Geschosse enthalten je zwei größere Wohnungen.

95 [1903; 55]

Monsieur H. P. Berlage architecte à Amsterdam éleva Augustusplatz 8 à Leipzic de novembre 1901 à avril 1903 une maison de commerce pour la „Société néerlandaise d'assurance pour la vie" pour la somme en bloc de 400000 Marks. La façade est en briques avec pierre de taille pour certaines parties de construction et granit pour les piliers et les couvertures. L'escalier est entièrement construit en briques émaillées, les marches et les piliers seuls sont en granit.

Voici la signification des lettres dans les plans: A, a à f locaux à louer, B antichambre, C salle d'attente, D parloir, E chambre de la direction, F caisse, G tenue de livres, H section d'organisation, J d'expédition, K des machines à écrire, L trésor, M vestiaire. La cour est entièrement excavée. Dans une des caves se trouve le chauffage central. Les étages supérieurs contiennent chacun deux grand appartements.

95 [1903; 55]

The Amsterdam architect H. P. Berlage has built at the Augustusplatz Leipsic business premises for the Netherlands Life Insurance Company. The time occupied was from November 1901 till April 1903, and the cost was about 400000 Marks. The facade is of brick with sandstone for certain parts of the construction with granite for the pillars and slopes. The staircase is entirely of glazed tiles only the steps and pillars are of granite.

The following is a key to the ground-plan. A a to f are premises to be let, B entrance hall, C waiting room, D Consultation Room, E Director's Room, F Cash, G Bookkeeping department, H Organisation, J Expedition, K typewriters, L Tresor, M Cloak Rooms. There is cellarage under the whole of the court-yard, part of which is occupied with the heating apparatus. The upper storeys have each two large dwellings.

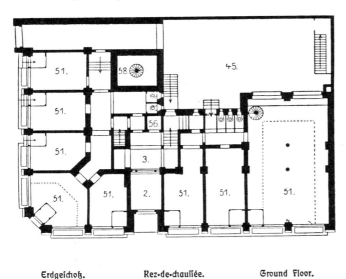

Erdgeschoß.   Rez-de-chaussée.   Ground Floor.   1. Stockwerk.   1. Étage.   1. Floor.

Bildhauer Zyl aus Amsterdam führte das Skulpturwerk aus, Zimmermeister Lenie aus Leipzig den inneren Ausbau und Schlossermeister Fritsche das Schmiedewerk.

Le sculpteur Zyl d'Amsterdam a exécuté les travaux de sculpture, le maître charpentier Lenie de Leipzic les intérieurs et le maître serrurier Fritsche les fers forgés.

The sculptor Zyl of Amsterdam has carried out the ornamental details, the joiner Lenie of Leipsic the interiors and the smith Fritsche the iron work.

96 (s. 85, 96)   96 (cf. 85, 96)   96 (s. 85, 96)

97 [1903; 63]

Das burgartig an der Wernerstraße auf der Rheininsel „Oberwerth" zu Koblenz sich erhebende Haus Castenholz ist unter Benutzung von Teilen eines älteren Baues durch Architekt Otto Nebel (conf. II, 3, S. 54, Taf. 89, 90, 91) mit einem Aufwand von rund 100000 Mark neu aufgebaut worden.

Fundamente und Kellermauern sind aus Bruchsteinen, das Aufgehende aus Backstein mit sparsamer Verwendung von Haustein, die Flächen sorgfältig geputzt, teilweise dekorativ mit Antragarbeiten, teilweise mit Malerei geschmückt. Das sichtbare, teilweise geschnitzte Holzwerk ist aus Eichen. Wie im Ganzen ein Wiederaufleben altrheinischen Kunsthandwerkes zu erkennen ist, so ist es namentlich in den Beschieferungen an der Nordseite der Fall. Dachdeckermeister Andreas Schmidt in Pfaffendorf a. Rh., hat sie in deutschem

97 [1903; 63]

La maison Castenholz s'élevant en forme de château à la Wernerstrasse sur l'île du Rhin „Oberwerth" à Coblence a été construite à neuf, mais en utilisant certaines parties d'un ancien édifice, par Mr. Otto Nebel architecte (voyez Vol. II, p. 54, Pl. 89, 90, 91). Les frais ont été de 100000 Marks en bloc.

Les fondations et les murs des caves sont en moellons, les parties supérieures en briques, avec un emploi restreint de pierre de taille. Les surfaces crépies avec soin sont décorées en partie d'ornements modelés dans le crépissage, en partie de peintures. Les constructions en bois visibles et dans certaines parties sculptées sont en chène. On retrouve avec plaisir dans ce bâtiment, le réveil d'anciennes traditions des artisans rhénans, et c'est surtout dans les ardoiseries du côté nord que cette tendance est

97 [1903; 63]

The house Castenholz, built in a castellated style in the Wernerstrasse on the Rhine island "Oberwerth" at Coblenz, is the work of the architect Otto Nebel (compare Vol. II, No. 3, page 54, plates 89, 90, 91) and cost about 100000 Marks.

The architect has made use of part of the old building; the foundations and cellar walls are of freestone the supporting walls are of brick with a slight addition of stone, the surfaces are carefully plastered partly decorated with relief work, and partly with painting. The woodwork, occasionally carved, is of oak. The whole building suggests a revival of the old Rhenisch artistic hand work and this is specially noticeable in the slating on the north side of the house. Mr. Andreas Schmidt of Pfaffendorf on Rhine had carried out it with dark blue slate

Art, mit dunkelblauem Schiefer aus Clotten a. Mosel und hellblauem von der Lahn und aus Belgien, grünem von der Lahn und rotem vom Main hergestellt.

Die Bildhauerarbeiten sind durch Wenzel Tina, die Stuckarbeiten durch G. Schichtel, die Malereien durch Joh. Kraef und die Warmwasserheizung durch Angrick in Frankfurt a. M. ausgeführt.

frappante. C'est maître Andréas Schmidt à Pfaffendorf sur Rhin qui les a exécutées en ardoise bleu foncé de Clotten sur Moselle et bleu clair de la Lahn et de Belgique, ardoises vertes de la Lahn et rouges du Main.

La sculpture est l'œuvre de Mr. Wenzel Tina, des stuccatures sont de G. Schichtel, la peinture de Joh. Kraef et le hydrocalorifère de Angrick à Francfort s. M.

of Clotten on Mosella, light blue of the Lahn and of Belgicum, green of the Lahn and red of the Main.

The sculptural details are by Wenzel and Tina, the plaster work by G. Schichtel, the painting by Joh. Kraef and the warm-water heating apparatus by Angrick in Frankfort on Main.

98 [1903; 80]

Die Villa des Architekten W. Lossow in Dresden, Tiergartenstraße 52, ist im Jahre 1902 durch die Architekten Lossow und Viehweger mit Fassaden in Sandstein und Putz ausgeführt worden. Die Kosten sind noch nicht ermittelt, da der sehr reiche, innere Ausbau noch nicht abgeschlossen ist.

Die lichten Geschoßhöhen betragen im Erdgeschoß 3,80 Meter, im I. Obergeschoß 3,60, im Dachgeschoß 3,25 Meter.

98 [1903; 80]

La villa de l'architecte W. Lossow à Dresde Tiergartenstrasse 52 a été construite en 1902 par les architectes Lossow et Viehweger; les façades sont en pierre de taille et en maçonnerie crépie. On ne connaît pas encore le coût de cette construction parce que l'intérieur très riche n'est pas encore terminé.

Les hauteurs d'étages comportent dans le vide: pour le rez-de-chaussée 3,80 mètres, pour le premier étage 3,60 mètres, pour l'étage des combles 3,25 mètres.

98 [1903; 80]

The villa of the architect W. Lossow, Tiergartenstrasse 52, Dresden, was built in 1902 by the architects Lossow and Viehweger. The facades are sandstone and plaster. The cost cannot yet be given as the interior decoration which is very beautiful, is not yet completed.

The height of the storeys is 3,80 meters on the ground floor, 3,60 meters on the first floor and 3,25 meters on the roof storey.

99 [1903; 3]

Das idyllische Landhaus Curry in Riederau b. Diessen am Ammersee, von November 1899 bis Juli 1900 durch Professor Martin Dülfer

99 [1903; 3]

L'idyllique maison de campagne Curry, à Riederau près Diessen au lac d'Ammersee construite par le professeur Dülfer de Munich,

99 [1903; 3]

The idyllic cottage "Curry" in Riederau near Diessen on the Ammersee was built by Professor Martin Dülfer of Munich,

Erdgeschoß.   Rez-de-chaussée.   Ground Floor.

1. Stockwerk.   1. Etage.   1. Floor.

in München erbaut, kostete nur 45 000 Mark. Es ist auf einem Unterbau von Beton in Ziegelmauerwerk aufgeführt und grobkörnig rauh verputzt; das glatte Ornament ist farbig ausgelegt. Die Dächer haben rote Bieberschwanzdeckung, die Giebel eine Verkleidung von kleinen Schindeln. Die Grundrisse zeigen, wie die im Aeußern sich aussprechende zwanglose Behäbigkeit auch im Innern durchgeführt ist.

de novembre 1899 à juillet 1900 ne coûta que 45 000 Marks. Cette maison s'élève sur un soubassement de béton et est construite en maçonnerie de briques grossièrement crépie au mortier. Les ornements lisses sont en couleur. Les toits sont recouverts en tuiles rouges, les pignons sont revêtus de petits bardeaux en bois. Les plans montrent combien l'aspect comfortable et libre de l'extérieur est également bien exprimé à l'intérieur.

from November 1899 to July 1900. The cost amounted to 45 000 Marks. The basement is of beton, the building itself of tiled brick work, and rough plastered. The ornament is flat and coloured. It is roofed with flat red tiles, and the gables are covered with small shingle. The ground plan shows that the same simple comfort which the outside displays is carried out in the interior arrangements.

100 [1903; 94]

In München hat man in verschiedenen Epochen größerer Bautätigkeit sich bemüht, bei Anlage größerer geradliniger Straßenzüge eine einheitliche Architektur für Wohnhäuser durchzuführen. Die unter Ludwig I. und Maximilian II. gepflegten derartigen Bestrebungen: hellenistisch-antikisierende, mit italisch-romanisierenden Elementen durchsetzte oder gar mittelalterlich-romanische und gotische Formen in die Zwangsschablone moderner Bedürfnisse und Ausführungsweisen einzupassen, haben, wie bekannt, recht wenig günstige Erfolge gehabt. Man darf heute wohl behaupten, daß die damals begonnenen Irr-

100 [1903; 94]

A différentes époques de grande activité dans la construction, on s'est efforcé à Munich, d'obtenir une certaine uniformité dans l'architecture des maisons à loyer pour les rues tracées en ligne droite. Les essais de cette sorte tentés sous les règnes de Louis 1 et Maximilien II; consistant à faire entrer de force les exigences de la vie moderne et les nouvelles manières de construire dans des formes antiques grecques ou italo romanes, ou même romanes moyen-age et gothiques, ont eu comme on le sait, des résultats fort peu réjouissants. On peut bien dire aujourd'hui, sans

100 [1903; 94]

During the various periods of architectural activity in Munich, attempts have always been made to secure a certain uniformity for the architecture of dwelling-houses. In the reigns of Ludwig I and Maximilian II efforts were made to combine the Greek-antique with the Italian-romanesque, and even to force medieval-romanesque and Gothic forms into the service of the conventional modern house and its various requirements; these efforts were attended with little success. One can only sur-

tümer wesentlich in der allgemein zu wenig verbreiteten eingehenderen Kenntnis der Bauten früherer Epochen begründet waren. Besseren Erfolg scheinen heutige, gleichartige Unternehmungen zu versprechen, bei denen einzelnen Straßen glücklicherweise verschiedenartige Typen unterlegt werden. Von der in der Franz Josephstraße durch Architekt F. Trump nach einheitlichem Schema ausgeführten Gruppe von 16 Reihenhäusern, jedes in vier Geschossen je zwei größere Wohnungen an der Front und eine im ausgebauten Dachgeschoß enthaltend, geben wir ein Gruppenbild der Häuser Nr. 32, 34 und 36, sowie Nr. 34 auf besonderem Blatt. Man kann daraus erkennen, daß hier nur Aufbau- und Schmuckelemente der gesunden Münchener Putzarchitektur verschiedenster Epochen, freilich in modernem Gewande auftreten. Zur Kennzeichnung und Unterscheidung der einzelnen Gebäude dienen (außer der Nummerbezeichnung) nur die Bildwerke auf den Mittelpfeilern der Erker über der Haustür jedes zweiten Bauwerkes. Durch das Verbot der Anlage von Kaufläden usw. in diesen Wohnstraßen, wird die Entstellung der Fassaden durch Schildereien verhütet und den Straßen ihre ruhige Vornehmheit gesichert.

exagération, que les erreurs commises alors provenaient en grande partie du manque de connaissance approfondie des monuments des époques passées. Des entreprises analogues de nos jours pour lesquelles on propose heureusement différents types pour la même rue, semble promettre un meilleur résultat. Nous publions ici un groupe de maisons No. 32, 34 et 36 ainsi que le No. 34 sur planche spéciale, construites à la Franz Josephstrasse à Munich par Monsieur F. Trump architecte. Il s'agit d'un groupe de 16 maisons construites d'après un système uniforme, les immeubles ont chacun deux grands appartements sur la rue en leurs quatre étages et un logement dans l'étage du toit. On peut voir d'après ces modèles, qu'ici il n'y a pour produire de l'effet que les parties élevées et les ornements d'une saine architecture munichoise empruntée à différentes époques, mais traitées dans un esprit moderne. Pour distinguer les différentes maisons les unes des autres, il n'a été employé (à part les numéros) que des décorations sculpturales sur le pilier central des avant-corps au-dessus de la porte d'entrée alternant d'une maison à l'autre. Comme il est défendu d'établir des magasins, comptoirs etc. dans cette rue, la défiguration des façades par les enseignes est évitée et la rue est sûre de conserver son aspect discret et distingué. —

mise that the designers had little or no real knowledge of architecture of pasted epochs. At the present time, the same aims appear to be more success fully achieved and some streets have good examples of various kinds. In the Franz Josephstrasse the architect F. Trump has built a group of 16 houses according to a uniform scheme. Each house contains 4 storeys with two large dwellings in the front and one in the roof-storey. We give illustrations of No. 32, 34 and 36, that of 34 on a separate sheet. One can see from these that the ornamental details and the elevation are really Munich ornamental architecture but in a modern dress. In order to distinguish the various houses there are, in addition to the house numbers, differences in the statuary placed on the middle pillar of the bow. Through the prohibition of shops &c. in the street, the facades are not defaced by business plates and such-like disfigurements so that the street has a quiet and distinguished appearance.

101 [1903: 98]

Architekt F. R. Voretzsch in Dresden erbaute dort Lindengasse 14 vom 15. April 1901 bis 15. März 1902 zum Preise von 100000 Mark das vornehme Miet-Wohnhaus, dessen Grundriß

101 [1903: 98]

Monsieur F. R. Voretzsch architecte à Dresde construisit dans cette ville, Lindengasse 14, du 15 avril 1901 au 15 mars 1902 pour le prix de 100000 Marks la belle maison

101 [1903: 98]

In the Lindengasse 14 in Dresden, the architect F. R. Voretzsch has built a dwelling-house of much distinction. The time occupied was from 15. April 1901 to 15. March 1902 and the cost

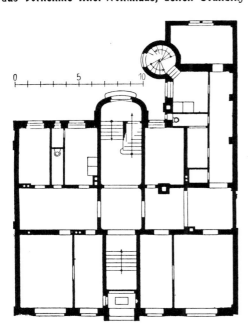

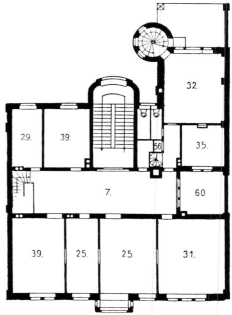

vom allgemeinen Schema weit abweicht. Im I. Obergeschoß ist unter dem Lichthofe ein Rauchzimmer mit Oberlicht angeordnet; das I. und II. Obergeschoß sind zu einer einzigen Familienwohnung verbunden.

Die Fassade ist in weißem und gelbem Elbsandstein ausgeführt.

Die Geschoßhöhen betragen sämtlich je 4 Meter, jedoch im I. Obergeschoß 4,20 Meter.

à loyer dont le plan diffère sensiblement du type général. Au premier étage se trouve sous la cour un fumoir avec plafond vitré. Le premier et le second étages forment ensemble un seul appartement pour une famille.

La façade est exécutée en pierre blanche et jaune de l'Elbe.

Les hauteurs d'étages sont toutes de 4 mètres, excepté pour le premier étage qui compte 4,20 mètres.

was 100000 Marks. The ground plan shows great originality. On the first floor under the skylight a smoking-room has been arranged with windows above — and the first and second floors are connected and form a comfortable family dwelling.

The facade is of white and yellow Elbe sandstone.

The height of the rooms is 4 meters, those of the first floor 4,20 meters.

102 [1903: 61]

Im Westend von London sind in jüngster Zeit, namentlich an Park Lane, von hervorragendsten Architekten palastartige Wohnhäuser für den englischen Hochadel erbaut worden, von denen wir gegenwärtig das durch Architekt F. B. Wade an der Ecke von Mount Street 54 als Residenz des Lord Windsor erbaute zur

102 [1903: 61]

Ces derniers temps, d'éminents architectes ont élevé à l'ouest de Londres et particulièrement dans les environs de Park Lane des demeures de grand style pour la haute noblesse anglaise, nous publions ici un de ces palais bâtis par l'architecte F. B. Wade, à l'angle de Mount Street 54 comme résidence de Lord

102 [1903: 61]

Certain neighbourhoods in the Westend of London have been lately enriched by the erection of palatial dwelling-houses by celebrated architects. These have been built mainly in Park Lane for the English aristocracy. We give an illustration of the residence built for Lord Windsor at the corner of Mount Street 54

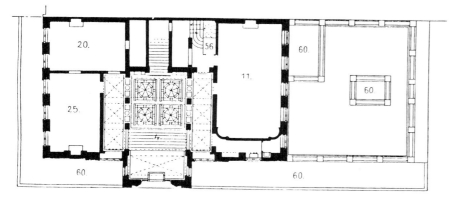
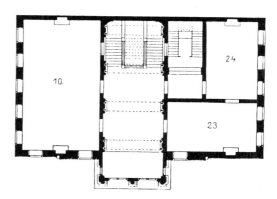
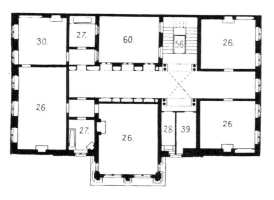
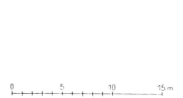
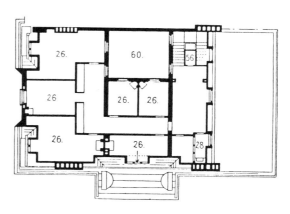

Schau bringen; es ist in Portland-Stein und Bracknellbackstein von rd. 23:11,5:5 cm ausgeführt. Der Bau zeichnet sich durch seine wohl durchgebildeten Verhältnisse und Formen vorteilhaft gegenüber anderen in der Umgebung jüngst errichteten Bauwerken aus.

Windsor. La construction est en pierre de Portland et en briques de Bracknell de 0,23 de longueur, 0,115 de largeur et 0,05 de hauteur. Cet édifice se distingue avantageusement d'autres constructions élevées dernièrement dans les environs par la beauté de ses proportions et de ses formes.

by the architect F. B. Wade. The building is of Portland stone and Bracknell bricks measuring 23:11,5:5 centimetre side length. The house contrasts favorably in its forms and proportions with other buildings lately erected in the neighbourhood.

Im Inneren sind die Halle und Treppen in Marmor ausgeführt, die Halle mit Rahmungen von Alabaster aus Lord Windsor's Brüchen in Penarth (Süd-Wales). Aus Rot-Zedernholz bestehen die Täfelungen im Morgen- oder kleinen Wohnzimmer, aus italienischem Walnußholz im Arbeitszimmer und in der Vorhalle, während geflecktes Eschenholz dazu größtenteils in den Schlafzimmern und deren Fluren verwendet ist. Gemaltes Tannenholz ist in den Empfangsräumen im 1. Stockwerk angewendet. Die Fußböden haben Parkett von einfacher Zeichnung erhalten.

Alles Bildhauerwerk des Äußeren und Inneren wie die Stuckarbeiten der Decken sind besonders sorgfältig und zwar durch Mr. H. M'Carthy ausgeführt.

A l'intérieur, la halle et les escaliers sont exécutés en marbre, la halle est décorée d'encadrements d'albâtre provenant des carrières de Lord Windsor à Penarth dans la Galle du sud. Les boiseries du petit salon ou salle de matin sont en bois de cèdre rouge, celles de la chambre de travail et de l'antichambre sont en bois de noyer italien, tandis qu'un bois de frène tacheté trouve son emploi dans la plupart des chambres à coucher et dans leurs antichambres. On employa du bois de sapin peint dans les salles de réception du premier étage. Les parquets sont d'un dessin simple.

Toute la sculpture de l'extérieur et de l'intérieur, ainsi que les travaux de stuc des plafonds ont été exécutés d'une manière particulièrement soignée par Mr. H. M'Carthy.

The hall and stairs of the interior have been carried out in marble, in the principal hall is a cornice of alabaster from Lord Windsor's quarry at Penarth, South-Wales. The morning room is panelled with red cedar wood, the study with Italian walnut which has also been used for the entrance hall, stained ash has been used for the bed-rooms and floors. Painted pine wood has been used for the reception rooms on the first floor, the floors are parquetted in a simple design.

All the sculptural work of the exterior and interior as well as the ceilings, has been carried out with special care by Mr. H. M'Carthy.

103 [1903; 15]

Die Architekten Hart und Lesser, von denen wir im Jahrgang II das große Geschäftshaus der Druck- und Verlagsfirma Ullstein veröffentlichten, haben Berlin wieder ein glänzendes Werk in ihrer eigentümlichen, an Rokoko streifenden Behandlung der modernen Barockarchitektur gebracht: Das Geschäftshaus der Firma Trunck u. Co., Kronenstraße 10, weist in seiner sehr einfachen Grundrißgestaltung nur Ausstellungs-, Verkaufs- und Aufbewahrungsräume nebst zubehörigen Werkstätten und Bureaus auf, soweit solche zu der Firma eignem Bedarfe der Fabrikation von feineren und Kunstmöbeln erforderlich sind. Die Fassade ist in hellgelblichem Sandstein, das sie krönende Belvederedach in Kupfer ausgeführt. Das Haus ist im Laufe des Jahres 1902 erbaut.

104 [1903; 37]

Architekt Dr. Max Fabiani hat beim Bau des Geschäftshauses der Firma Portoix und Fix (Kunstmöbelfabrik) in der Ungargasse 51, 53 zu Wien die Lehren der von ihm eifrig ver-

103 [1903; 15]

Les architectes Hart et Lesser, dont nous avons publié dans la seconde année le grand immeuble de rapport de la maison Ullstein imprimeur et éditeur, ont de nouveau doté Berlin d'une brillante composition traitée dans leur manière particulière, sorte d'architecture baroque moderne s'inspirant quelque peu du roccoco.

La maison de commerce Trunck & Co., Kronenstrasse 10 ne contient dans son plan d'une extrême simplicité que des salles de vente et d'exposition, des magasins, des ateliers et des bureaux, en un mot tous les locaux nécessaires aux besoins particuliers de cette raison sociale qui s'occupe spécialement de la fabrication de meubles d'art. Cette maison a été construite dans le courant de l'année 1902.

104 [1903; 37]

L'architecte Docteur Max Fabiani a appliqué dans ses plus extrêmes conséquences les principes de l'école de Wagner, qu'il a si ardemment défendus, dans la construction de la

103 [1903; 15]

The architects Hart and Lesser, of whose work we gave an example in our second volume (the large business house of the printing and publishing firm Ullstein) have lately enriched Berlin by another of their characteristic works, a beautiful building in barock style with a slight admixture of rococo.

The business house of the firm Trunck and Co., Kronenstrasse 10. The ground plan is exceedingly simple and is divided into the necessary sale rooms, exhibition rooms and store rooms together with the usual workshops and bureaus. Every provision is made for the production of such Art furniture as the firm has already made its speciality. The house was built during the year 1902.

104 [1903; 37]

The architect Dr. Max Fabiani in Vienna has built the business premises of the firm Portoix and Fix (artistic furniture factory) in the Ungargasse 51, 53. The building is

fochtenen „Wagnerschule" in äußerster Folgerichtigkeit zur Durchführung gebracht: die Faßade
ist im unteren Teil mit dunklem Marmor und
hellem schwedischen Granit verkleidet und nach

maison de commerce Portoix et Fix, (fabrique
de meubles d'art) dans la Ungargasse 51, 53
à Vienne. La façade est dans sa partie inférieure revêtue de marbre et de granit clair de

a correct example of the Wagner school of which
this architect is an earnest champion. The lower
part is faced with dark marble and light Swedish

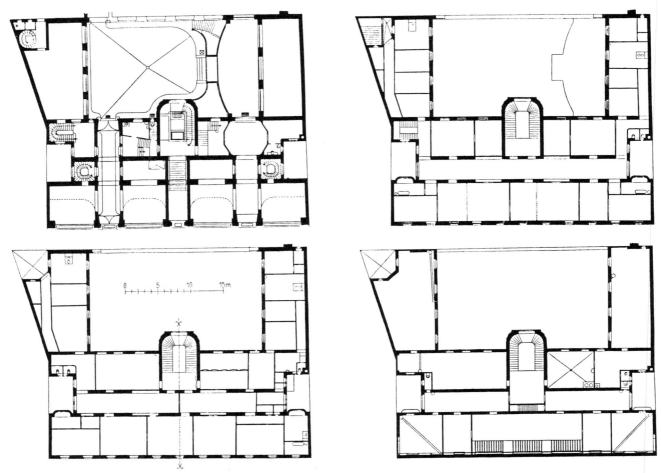

oben nur mit einem leichten, wulstartigen Bande abgeschlossen. Der obere Teil der Front einschließlich der Fensterlaibungen ist gänzlich mit Kacheln
aus sogen. „Pyrogranit" (von Szolnay in Fünfkirchen) in abgestuft dunklen und hellen stumpf-
grünen Tönen vertäfelt. An Stelle eines Hauptgesimses ist die Faßade nur mit einer nach hinten
abgerundeten (nicht vorspringenden) Platte abgeschlossen. Die Rinne ist in einem reich verzierten, durch wellenförmige Stäbe getragenen
Korbe gelagert, der an dem mittelst Docken
ausgekragten, reich geschmiedeten Dachgitter be-
festigt ist.

Die seitlichen Teile des Daches sind in dem
vorderen, bogenförmigen Stück mit Theerfilz, und
im oberen, flachen Teil mit Holzzement gedeckt.
Der mittlere Teil ist indeß als Atelier verglast
und kann mittelst Stabrollläden beschattet werden.

Die Baldachine der Sonnenblenden der
Faßadenfenster bestehen aus Rotguß. Der Wechsel
der Färbungen, auch der teilweise in Kupfer und
Messing ausgeführten Gitter u. s. w., bringt
einen frohen Einklang in die ganze farben-
freudige Erscheinung. Ein Vorteil dieser Ausführung ist die fast unbegrenzte Haltbarkeit, und
daß die Front nicht durch Staub und Ruß ver-
schmutzen kann. Das Gebäude, von dem unser
Bild nur sieben Teilungsfelder aufweist, hat deren
elf; der linke Eingang ist für die im hinteren
Teil beschäftigten Arbeiter u. s. w., der mittlere
als Eingang zu den Ausstellungs- und Verkaufs-
räumen, der rechte (hier nicht sichtbare) für herr-
schaftliches Fuhrwerk bestimmt. Die oberen Räume
des Vorderhauses dienen zu Lager- und Aus-
stellungszwecken in Zimmeranordnung, um erforderlichen Falles zu Wohnzwecken vermietet
werden zu können.

Die Baukosten stellen sich einschließlich Zentralheizung, Wasser- und elektrischen Anlagen auf
rund 400000 Mark.

Suède et couronnée dans le haut par un léger
cordon de profil arrondi. La partie supérieure
de la façade, y compris les tableaux des fenêtres
est entièrement revêtue de plaques céramiques,
appelées „pyrogranit" (de la maison Szolnay
à Fünfkirchen) elles sont de tons dégradés,
foncés et clairs, d'un vert effacé. A la place
d'une corniche, la façade porte simplement une
assise non saillante et arrondie en arrière.
Le chéneau est posé dans une sorte de berceau
richement décoré, porté par des barreaux de
forme ondulée, il est fixé à une balustrade du
toit forgé d'un riche travail.

Les parties latérales du toit sont dans la
partie arrondie du devant couvertes avec du
feutre goudronné, et la partie plate avec du
papier goudronné, recouvert de terrasse. La
partie centrale est disposée en atelier et vitrée,
elle peut être abritée contre le soleil par une
jalousie.

Les baldaquins des jalousies des fenêtres
de la façade sont en cuivre rouge. La variété
des couleurs, les balustrades exécutées en partie
en cuivre et en laiton etc. mettent une note
gaie dans l'aspect festival et coloré du tout.
L'avantage de cette exécution sont la durée
presque illimitée et la propreté de la façade qui
ne peut être salie ni par la poussière, ni par
la fumée. L'édifice, dont notre planche ne donne
que sept travées en compte onze. L'entrée de
gauche est réservée aux ouvriers occupés dans
la partie postérieure de la maison etc.; celle du
milieu donne accès aux locaux d'exposition et
de vente, celle de droite (non visible ici) sert
de passage aux équipages de maîtres. Les
pièces supérieures de la façade servent de
magasins et de chambres d'exposition, elles peuvent aussi au besoin être louées comme appartements.

Les frais de la construction s'élevèrent y compris le chauffage central et installation électrique
à 400000 Marks.

granite finished at the top with simple ovolo
mouldings. The upper part of the front including the window frames is entirely faced with
tiles of so-called "Pyrogranit" (from Szolnay in
Fünfkirchen) arranged in alternate layers of light
and dark dull green. In place of the principal
moulding, the facade is rounded off at the
back with a non projecting band. The gutter
is laid in a richly ornamented basket supported
by undulating bars and fastened to the richly
wrought roof railing by projecting balusters.

The side part of the roof is, in the front
arched plaster work, covered with tarfelt, the
upper flat part with so called "Holzcement." The
middle is glazed and shall be used as a studio,
being protected from the sun by wooden revolving
shutters.

The baldachins which protect the windows are
of tombac. The variety of colouring, the railing
partly in copper and partly in brass gives
a cheerfulness of tone which taken together with
the other details has a most agreeable effect.
One great advantage is the almost unlimited
durability of this arrangement, and another is,
that the front is protected from dust and smoke.
The building, of which our illustration gives
only seven divisions, has really eleven. The
left entrance is for the workmen employed in
the back premises; the middle serves as entrance
to the exhibition and sale rooms, the right entrance (here not visible) is for carriages. The
upper storeys of the front house are used as
store and exhibition rooms, and can, if necessary
be used as dwellings.

The cost of building including central heating,
water and electric installation amounted to
400000 Marks.

Am Brauhausberge zu Potsdam, auf einer die Umgebung weit beherrschenden, prachtvolle Aussicht über die Stadt mit ihren Schlössern, Gärten und Seeen gewährenden Platte über dem linken Havelufer, errichtete Geheimer Baurat Professor Franz Schwechten in Berlin den Neubau für die Königliche Kriegsschule.

Das Gebäude erforderte eine seiner Gegenüberstellung zu den königlichen Schlössern am rechten Havelufer und auf dem Babelsberge, sowie seiner Lage an dem mit mächtigen Eichen bestandenen Waldesrande, entsprechende charakteristische, malerische Ausgestaltung. Diese fand ihre natürliche Hebung in der Anlage eines zu Unterrichtszwecken erforderlichen hohen Aussichtsturmes mit Umgängen u. s. w.

Unsere Bilder zeigen den Bau noch ohne den figürlichen Schmuck von Statuen, die sich über den Portalen erheben werden.

Sur un plateau du Brauhausberg à Potsdam, situé sur la rive gauche de la Havel et offrant une vue incomparablement belle sur la ville avec ses châteaux, ses jardins et ses lacs, le conseiller intime, professeur Franz Schwechten a élevé la nouvelle Ecole Royale de Guerre.

Cet édifice exigeait une architecture caractéristique et pittoresque, en harmonie avec les châteaux royaux situés vis-à-vis sur la rive droite de la Havel et sur le Babelsberg et avec la lisière voisine d'un bois d'anciens et puissants chênes. Cette exigence fut facilitée par l'installation d'une tour élevée, entourée de galeries etc. nécessaire aux études.

Nos vues montrent le monument sans la décoration de statues qui doivent s'élever au dessus des portails.

Les plans indiquent le système de distribution des pièces dans le bâtiment principal. Remarquons en passant que dans le premier

The Geheimer Baurat Professor Franz Schwechten of Berlin has built the new premises for the Imperial Military School in Potsdam. The building is erected on the Brauhaus Berg on a site which commands a splendid view of the town with its castles, its gardens and lakes and with the left bank of the Havel.

Standing as it does opposite the Royal castles on the right bank of the Havel, within view of Babelsberg, and surrounded by mighty oaks which form the fringe of the adjacent woods, it was necessary that the building should be at the same time imposing and picturesque. This it certainly is, and the lofty tower added for educational purposes adds not a little to the grandeur of the general effect.

Our illustrations give no example of the sculptural figures which are eventually to ornament the portal.

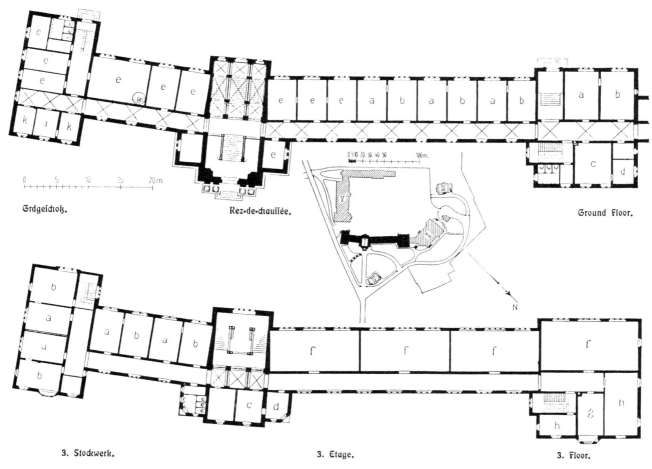

Grdgeschoß. Rez-de-chaussée. Ground Floor.

3. Stockwerk. 3. Etage. 3. Floor.

Die Grundrisse geben das System der Raumverteilung im Hauptgebäude an. Dabei ist zu bemerken, daß im I. und II. Stock die Räume des linken (östlichen) Flügels der Einteilung folgen, die im Grundriß des III. Stockwerks gegeben ist, während im rechten (westlichen) Flügel die Räume der Einteilung des Erdgeschosses folgen. Nur für Bibliothek und Waffensaal waren im I. Stock unwesentlich veränderte Einteilungen erforderlich.

Es bezeichnen in den Grundrissen: a Schlaf-, b Wohnzimmer der Kriegsschüler, c, d die der Leutnants, e die Geschäfts- und Konferenzsäle, f die Hörsäle, g das Lehrerzimmer mit h, h der Modellsammlung; i ist Zimmer des Arztes mit k, k Krankenzimmern, und l sind die Räume für die Handwerker und Ordonnanzen.

Die Ausführung war der Militär-Bauverwaltung unterstellt. Die Maurerarbeiten sind durch Lihi, das Zimmerwerk durch Krüger, Potsdam ausgeführt; die Zwischendecken nach System Donath durch Beyerth, Potsdam, die nach System Förster durch Remmler, Magdeburg. Zu dem Cyklopenmauerwerk des Unterbaues ward grauer

et le second étages, les localités de l'aile gauche ou orientale suivent la disposition indiquée dans le plan du troisième étage, tandis que dans l'aile droite ou occidentale, les localités sont groupées comme dans le plan du rez-de-chaussée. Ce n'est qu'au premier étage qu'une disposition spéciale était nécessitée par la bibliothèque et la salle des armes.

Dans les plans, les lettres a indiquent les dortoirs, b les chambres d'habitation des élèves, c, d celles des lieutenants, e les salles d'administration et de conférences, f les auditoires, g la salle des professeurs avec h, h la collection des modèles, i la chambre du médecin avec k, k l'infirmerie, enfin l sont les pièces pour les ouvriers et les ordonnances.

L'exécution du bâtiment a été soumise à l'administration des constructions militaires; les travaux de maçonnerie ont été exécutés par Lihi, ceux de charpente par Krüger à Potsdam; les planchers du système Donath ont été exécutés par Beyerth de Potsdam, ceux du système Förster, par Remmler de Magdebourg. Pour l'appareil rustique du soubassement, on employa de la pierre grise calcaire de la contrée de Nord-

The ground-plan shows the distribution of the rooms in the principal building. It must be noticed that the first and second storeys of the left (east) wing follow the ground-plan of the third storey, while the right wing (west) is divided like the ground-floor. The library and the armoury on the first floor required for their construction a slight alteration in the plan.

The ground plan is as follows: a Bed, b Living rooms of the pupils, c, d those of the lieutenants, e business and committee rooms, f auditories, g teachers' rooms with h, h collection of models, i doctor's room with k, k infirmary, l rooms for workmen and servants.

The building was superintended by the military building administration. For the masonry of the lower building grey Musche lime from Nordhausen was used. This part was entrusted to Lihi, the joiners work was by Krüger of Potsdam, the inserted ceilings system Donath by Beyerth of Potsdam, those according to

Mufchelkalk aus der Gegend von Nordhaufen verwendet; für die oberen Mauerflächen dienten rote Rathenower Backfteine großen Formates (von Mathis) und für Thür- und Fenfterfäumungen wie zu den Ecken Kunftfandftein von Große & Vockeroth in Küftrin; die Dächer find mit roten Falzziegeln durch Schönemann, Potsdam gedeckt. Mufchelkalk und Cottaer Sandftein lieferte Schilling, Berlin. Das Bildwerk führte Bildhauer Hauer, das Kunftfchmiedewerk Ferd. Paul Krüger aus, beide in Berlin. Die Niederdruckdampfheizung des Hauptgebäudes und der Speifeanftalt ift durch Rietfchel & Henneberg, Berlin ausgeführt.

hausen, pour la maçonnerie du haut, on se servit de briques rouges de grand format de Rathenow, de la maison Mathis et pour les encadrements de portes et de fenêtres, ainsi que pour les angles, de pierre artificielle de Grosse et Vockeroth de Cüstrin; les toits sont recouverts en tuiles à recouvrement rouges par Schönemann à Potsdam. La pierre calcaire et le grès de Cotta fut livré par Schilling à Berlin. Les travaux de sculpture furent exécutés par le sculpteur Hauer; les fers forgés par Ferd. Paul Krüger, tous deux à Berlin. L'appareil de chauffage à vapeur à basse pression pour le bâtiment principal et pour la messe a été construit par Rietschel et Henneberg à Berlin.

system Förster by Remmler of Magdeburg. The upper part is of red Rathenow bricks of large size (Mathis); for door and window frames and for the corners, artificial sandstone from Grosse and Vockeroth in Cüstrin; the roofs are of red gutter tiles from Schönemann of Potsdam. The sculptural parts are by sculptor Hauer of Berlin. The Musche lime and Cotta sandstone was provided by Schilling of Berlin. The artistic iron-work is by Ferd. Paul Krüger of Berlin. The low pressure steam heating apparatus of the principal building and of the dining hall is by Rietschel and Henneberg, Berlin.

106 [1903; 75]

Die Werfthalle ift zur Lagerung der zu Schiff oder Eifenbahn und umgekehrt ein- und abgehenden Güter, auch der zollficher verfchloffenen, eingerichtet. Sie ift durch eine Brandmauer in zwei gleiche Hälften zerlegt und hat ein gegen Eindringen von Waffer abgedichtetes Kellergefchoß, das mit Koenenfcher Voutendecke abgedeckt ift. Die an den Endtrakten eingebauten kleinen Räume find links für die Arbeiter und die Wafferbehörde, rechts für die Zollabfertigung und die Betriebsbureaux beftimmt. A A find die Aufzüge, W W die Wagen, B B die zugehörigen Bureaux.

106 [1903; 75]

La halle d'entrepôt est disposée pour le dépôt des marchandises arrivant ou partant par bateau ou chemin de fer ainsi que pour celles sous plombe douanière. Elle est partagée en deux parties égales par un mur de refend et possède, un étage de caves protégé contre l'infiltration de l'eau et couvert de plafonds à gorges du système Koenen. Les petits locaux bâtis aux deux extrémités sont destinés, à droite aux ouvriers et à l'administration des eaux, à gauche, au service des douanes et aux bureaux du mouvement. A A sont les ascenseurs, W W les balances, B B les bureaux qui en dépendent.

106 [1903; 75]

The large building of the wharf is arranged to store goods coming or going either by water or by rail, also for those which are not to be opened for Custom-house examination. It is divided into two equal spaces by a fire-wall, the cellarage is constructed so as to keep the water out and is supplied with Koenen Vouten ceilings. The small rooms at the extremities of the building are, on the left for the workmen and the water-police; those on the right are for the Custom-house, and for the general working of the wharf.

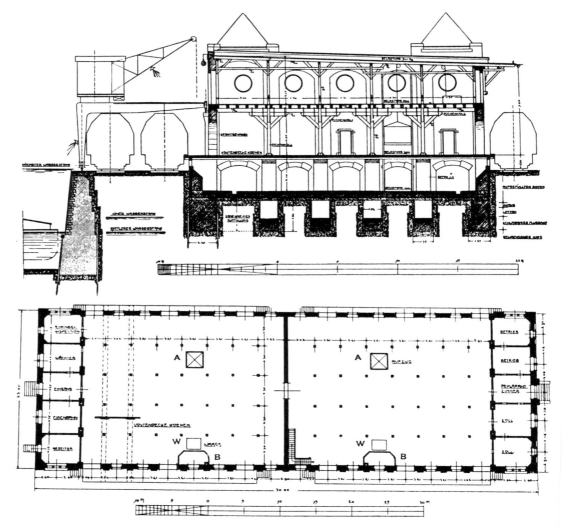

Die Stützen des oberen Lagerbodens beftehen aus Eichenholz, das Dach ift in Holzcement abgedeckt, jedoch find die Ecktürme mit Deckung in grünglafierten Ziegeln verfehen.

Das Material der Faffaden ift roter Sandbruchftein mit Maulbronner Sandfteinquadern. Die Koften betrugen einfchließlich der fchon beregten fchwierigen Gründung rd. 236000 Mark.

Les supports de l'étage supérieur sont en bois de chêne, le toit est couvert en papier goudronné avec terrasse; les tours d'angle sont recouvertes en tuiles vertes émaillées.

Les façades sont construites en moellons de grès rouge avec pierre de taille de Maulbronn. Les frais s'élevèrent, y compris les fondations difficiles dont nous avons déjà parlé, à 236000 Marks.

A A are lifts, W W the weighing apparatus, B B the bureaus belonging to the same.

The supports of the upper store rooms are of oak the roof is covered with wood-cement, the corner towers are roofed with green glazed tiles.

The facade is of red sand-stone with Maulbronn sand-stone squares. The cost, including the expensive and difficult foundation before referred to, amounted to 236000 Marks.

Das Elektrizitätswerk der Stadt Karlsruhe i. B. verleiht sowohl den Hafen wie die Stadt selbst mit elektrischem Strom.

An die große, mittlere, hochragende Maschinenhalle lehnt sich links ein zweistöckiger Anbau mit Aufgangsturm, der im Erdgeschoß Arbeitsräume und ein Magazin enthält; das Obergeschoß ist als Schaltraum eingerichtet mit Schalttafel innerhalb der Maschinenhalle, letztere durch die eingebaute Galerie zugänglich. Rechts an den Maschinenraum lehnt sich das Kesselhaus; weiter rechts befinden sich die angebauten Räume für die Wasserreinigung und den Vorwärmer, ferner drei Räume für Arbeiter und ein großer Kohlen-

La centrale d'électricité de la ville de Carlsruhe en Bade, fournit aussi bien le port que la ville de courants électriques.

Une annexe de deux étages, qui contient au rez-de-chaussée des salles de travail et un magasin, s'appuie à gauche contre la grande et haute halle aux machines. L'étage supérieur est disposé pour recevoir les appareils avec indicateur du côté de la halle, ce dernier est accessible par une galérie en saillie, à droite de la halle aux machines s'appuie la halle aux chaudières; plus loin à droite se trouvent les locaux pour le nettoyage des eaux et le chauffage, en plus, trois chambres pour les ouvriers et un grand magasin

The electrical Works of the town of Carsruhe supplies the wharf and the town with electric fluid.

On the left side of the centre machine hall, a large and lofty building, there is a two-storied annexe with entrance-turret, the ground floor contains work-rooms and a magazine, the upper floors are equipped as circuit rooms, a switchboard is placed inside the machine hall, which is connected therewith by a gallery. On the right of the machine room is the boiler house, farther to the right are the additional buildings for the water purification and warming, next are three rooms for workmen and a large coal

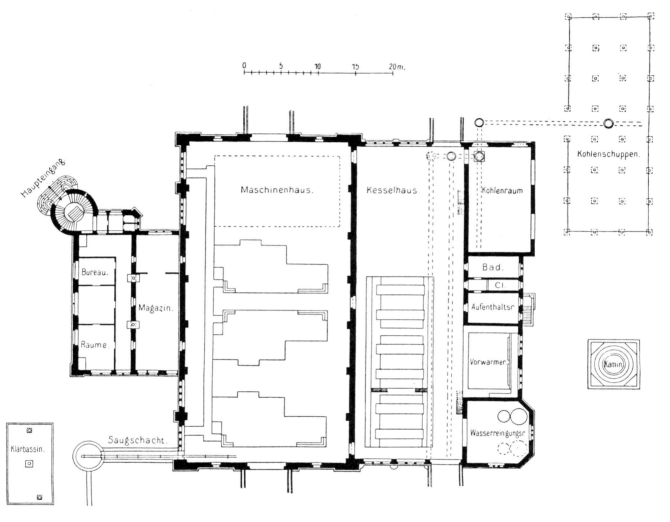

raum. Ganz rechts stehen der hohe Schlot und dahinter ein offener Kohlenschuppen.

Das Material und seine Behandlung sind gleich wie bei den vorangeführten Bauten; hervorzuheben ist nur eine reichere Verwendung von grauem Schwarzwald-Granit für Sockel und Portal.

Auch die Schuppenbauten haben im ganzen eine ähnliche Behandlung erfahren, wie der in der nachstehenden Skizze abgebildete Geräte- und Werkschuppen mit überhängendem, rotem Ziegeldach zeigt. I ist der zugehörige Hof, II Geräteraum, III, IV sind Werkstätten für Schlosser und Schreiner, V, IIa Magazine, VI ist Wagenremise.

store house. On the extreme right stands the high chimney, and behind that the open coal bunkers.

The material and the working of the same is similar to that of the before-mentioned buildings, one sees however a more profuse use of Schwarzwald granite for the sockel and portal.

The store house buildings are also very similar as may be seen from the accompanying sketch of tool and apparatus house with overhanging red-tiled roof. I is the courtyard, II Apparatus room, III and IV work-rooms for engineers and carpenters, V, IIa magazines, VI carriage house.

pour la houille. Tout à droite se trouve la haute cheminée et derrière, un hangard ouvert pour le charbon.

Les matériaux et leur mise en œuvre sont les mêmes que pour les bâtiments précédents, il est bon de mentionner qu'on a fait ici un plus grand emploi de granit gris de la Forêt-Noire pour le socle et le portail.

Les hangards ont d'une façon générale été traités de la même façon, ainsi que cela se voit dans le hangard pour les outils et ateliers, représentés sur l'esquisse ci contre. I, représente la cour, II, le dépôt d'outillages III et IV, les ateliers de serrurerie et de menuiserie V et IIa, les magasins, VI, la remise aux voitures.

Das Bestreben, reine Nutzbauten künstlerisch auszubilden, beschränkt sich nicht auf die öffentlichen, im Inneren und in der Umgebung der Großstädte errichteten Bauten. Das Fabrikgebäude der Firma Stiller & Sohn in Seifersdorf b. Sorau (in der südöstlichen Ecke der Mark Brandenburg), jüngst durch die Architekten Erdmann und Spindler (in Berlin) errichtet, gibt uns dafür ein glänzendes Zeugnis.

La tendance à donner un caractère artistique aux constructions purement utilitaires ne se borne pas aux édifices publics élevés à l'intérieur et aux environs des grandes villes. C'est ce que prouve d'une façon éclatante la fabrique construite pour la maison Stiller & fils à Seifersdorf près Sorau (dans l'angle sud est de la Marche de Brandebourg) par les architectes Erdmann et Spindler de Berlin.

The endeavour to construct buildings of real utility in an artistic appearance is not confined to town and suburb buildings; we have a splendid example of this in the factory erected for the firm Stiller & Sons in Seifersdorf near Sorau (in the south-east corner of the Mark Brandenburg) by the architects Erdmann and Spindler of Berlin.

Das Gebäude ist in hellroten, weißverfugten Ziegelsteinen, mit dekorativ ausgekratzten, weißen Putzflächen errichtet. Die Dächer sind mit roten Ziegeln doppelt eingedeckt; das sichtbare Zimmerwerk ist aus Kiefernholz, braungebeizt. Der langgestreckte linke Teil des Gebäudes ist das Kessel- und Maschinenhaus; der Eckbau enthält Bureaus, die Werkmeisterwohnungen u. s. w., woran sich rechts die mit Sägedächern gedeckten Werkstättenräume anschließen.

L'édifice est construit en briques rouges claires, jointoyées en blanc, avec des surfaces décoratives de crépissage blanc rehaussées d'ornements gravés en creux. Les toits sont recouverts de tuiles rouges doubles; la charpente visible est en bois de pin bruni. L'aile gauche allongée du bâtiment est la halle aux machines et aux chaudières; le bâtiment d'angle contient les bureaux, les appartements des contre-maîtres etc., les ateliers couverts en sheds s'y raccordent à droite.

The building is of light red tiles with white jointing, and with white scraped decorating plastered surfaces. The roofs are doubly covered with red tiles, the external wood-work is of pine wood, stained brown. The left side of the building in its long extent is occupied with the boiler and machine rooms, the corner building contains bureaus, the foremens dwellings etc. to which are annexed the workshops roofed with sheds.

109 [1903; 82]

Das in Frankfurt a. M. an der Gallusanlage, Ecke der Kronprinzenstraße, durch Architekt Oskar Heußner vom 1. März 1901 bis 1. Juni 1902 ausgeführte Hotel Fürstenhof (auch Palasthotel genannt) kostete (ausschließlich der Baustelle) im ganzen 1 200 000 Mark. Die Fassaden sind ganz aus gelbweißem Sandstein aufgeführt; das Dach ist mit Cauber Schiefer gedeckt; der Turm, die Abdeckungen und Dachfenster sind mit Kupfer verkleidet; die Zwischendecken sind feuerfest aus Eisen und Beton hergestellt; der zum Wirtschaftsbetrieb benutzte breite Vorplatz ist mit Mettlacher Platten belegt und mit glasgedeckten zeltartigen Hallen ausgerüstet.

Im Kellergeschoß befinden sich die Weinkellerei, die Küchen- und zubehörigen Räume, sowie Heizung und Maschinenanlage usw.

Das Erdgeschoß umfaßt zunächst links neben dem großen Vestibül eine Trinkstube A (American bar) mit anschließendem Rauchzimmer B und einen großen Restaurationssaal C mit Orchesterbühne; ein Saal für Kuriere D schließt sich an die Durchfahrt E an; hofwärts liegen Büfett und Aborte.

Rechts an der Front liegen zwei Salons F, G, in Verbindung mit dem großen Fest- und Speisesaal H, dessen hinterer Teil durch Deckenlicht o-o erleuchtet ist, mit Anrichte J, ferner hofwärts das Schreib- und Lesezimmer K und neben der Treppe

109 [1903; 82]

L'hôtel Fürstenhof aussi nommé Palasthôtel, construit à Frankfort sur Main sur la Gallusanlage par Monsieur Oscar Heussner du premier mars 1901 au premier juin 1902 coûta sans le terrain 1 200 000 Marks. Les façades sont entièrement exécutées en pierre jaune clair. Le toit est recouvert en ardoises de Caub. La tour et les lucarnes sont recouverts en cuivre. Les planchers sont incombustibles en fer et béton. La large avant-cour consacrée au service du restaurant est pavé de dallages de Mettlach et pourvu de halles vitrées en forme de tentes.

En sous sol se trouvent les caves pour le vin, les locaux nécessaires à la cuisine et dépendances, ainsi que ceux du chauffage central, des machines etc.

Le rez-de-chaussée contient d'abord à gauche, près du grand vestibule une buvette A (bar americain) avec fumoir adjacent B et une grande salle de restaurant C avec tribune pour l'orchestre. Une salle pour les courriers D communique avec le passage E. Du côté de la cour se trouvent le buffet et les water closets.

A droite, sur la façade, se trouvent deux salons F, G, en communication avec la grande salle des fêtes qui sert aussi de salle à manger H. Sa partie postérieure est éclairée par le vitrage o-o, elle possède une office J; du côté de la cour se trouvent la chambre de lecture et de correspondance K et près de l'escalier, le bureau L. Un ascenseur

109 [1903; 82]

The architect Oscar Heussner has erected from 1. March 1901 to 1. June 1901 the Hotel Fürstenhof (Palasthotel) on the Gallusanlage at the corner of the Kronprinzenstrasse Frankfort on Main. The cost, exclusive of the site, amounted to 1 200 000 Marks. The facades are entirely of yellow-white sandstone, the roof is covered with Cauber slate, the tower the bow roofing and the gables are covered with copper. The ceilings are fireproof, and are constructed of iron and beton. The broad place in front, used as a restaurant is laid with Mettlach tiles, and is equipped with tent-like, glass-covered halls.

In the basement are the wine cellars, the kitchen and adjoining rooms, as well as the heating and machine fittings and apparatus.

The ground floor contains, on the left beside the great vestibule, a drinking room (American bar) with a smoking room B and a large restaurant saloon C with an orchestrastage, a saloon for couriers D lies near the entrance E, towards the court yard lies the buffet and the lavatories.

On the right of the front are two saloons F, G, connected with a large dining and banquetting hall H, the back part of which is lighted by a skylight o-o; a serving room J, farther towards the court yard is a writing and reading room K

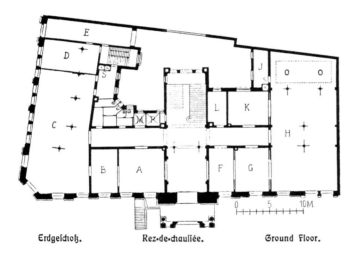

Erdgeschoß.   Rez-de-chaussée.   Ground Floor.

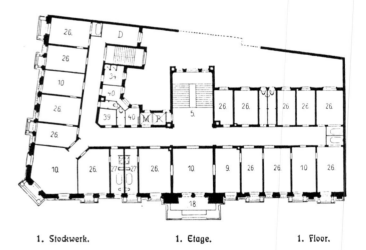

1. Stockwerk.   1. Étage.   1. Floor.

das Bureau L. Ein Aufzug für Gepäck M, einer für Personen P und drei Speisenaufzüge S dienen dem Betrieb.

Die Einteilung des I. und II. Obergeschosses ergibt sich aus dem Grundriß (die eingeschriebenen Buchstaben haben gleiche Bedeutung wie im Erdgeschoß); sie wechselt nur wenig in den oberen Geschossen. Es ist darauf Bedacht genommen, daß in den Hauptgeschossen eine größere Zimmerflucht mit einem oder mehreren Salons unter einem einzigen Abschluß zusammenhängend vergeben werden kann. Deshalb sind sowohl die Zwischentüren, wie die nach dem Flur gehenden mit äußerer Polster- und innerer Holztür versehen. Die Schlafzimmer der Dienerschaft liegen in dem oberen Dachraum.

pour le bagage M, pour personnes P et trois monteplats desservent l'établissement.

La disposition du premier et second étages est indiquée par le plan (les lettres inscrites ont la même signification qu'au rez-de-chaussée), elle ne varie que peu pour les étages supérieurs. Il faut remarquer que dans les étages principaux un certain nombre de chambres avec un ou plusieurs salons forment appartement et peuvent être loués séparément. C'est ce qui explique que les portes d'une chambre à l'autre aussi bien que celles qui conduisent dans les corridors sont doubles: les uns en bois, à l'intérieur et capitonnées à l'extérieur. Les chambres à coucher des domestiques sont situées dans l'étage supérieur des combles.

and near the stair-case the bureau L. A lift for luggage M, a passenger lift P and 3 dinner lifts S are also provided.

The division of the I. and II. floors can be seen from the ground plan (the letters on the ground floor apply equally to these floors); the upper floors are not quite the same. Provision has been made that in the principal floors suites of rooms larger or smaller, with one or more saloons can be arranged with one private entrance door; for this reason all rooms are provided with doors upholstered on out side and wood doors on the other. The bedrooms of the servants are in a upper roof storey.

Im ganzen enthält das Haus 100 Fremden-zimmer und 32 Bäder. Der Ausbau aller Räume ist mit einem dem Titel des Hauses entsprechenden Luxus durchgeführt; so bestehen z. B. die Säulen und Täfelungen des Vestibüls, des Treppenhauses und der Säle aus kostbarem Marmor, dessen Pracht durch reiche Vergoldung noch gehoben ist, usw.

Die Höhen betragen einschließlich der Decken: im Keller 3,5 Meter, im Erd- und den folgenden Geschossen 5,3, 4,1, 3,8, 3,5, 3,5, 3,5 Meter und im Dienergeschoß i. l. 2,0 Meter. An der Aus-führung waren nur in Frankfurt ansässige Firmen beteiligt.

L'hôtel contient en tout 100 chambres d'étran-gers et 32 salles de bains. L'installation de toutes les chambres est faite avec un luxe cor-respondant au titre de la maison; ainsi par exemple, les colonnes et les pannelages du vestibule, de la cage d'escalier et des salles sont de marbre précieux dont la splendeur est encore rehaussée par de riches dorures etc.

Les hauteurs d'étages comprennent avec les poutraisons: pour la cave 3,50 mètres, pour le rez-de-chaussée et les étages suivants 5,30, 4,10, 3,80, 3,50, 3,50, 3,50 et pour l'étage des domestiques 2,00 mètres. L'exécution ne fut con-fiée qu'à des maisons résidant à Frankfort.

The house contains 100 bedrooms and 32 baths. The interior decorations and equipment are suitable and representative of the name of the house; e. g. the pillars and panelling of the vestibule, of the staircase and of the saloons, are all of costly marble, &c. made still more magnificent by rich gilding.

The height of the rooms is as follows: Cellar 3,5 meters, ground and following floors 5,3, 4,1, 3,8, 3,5, 3,5 3,5 and in the servant's quarters 2,0 meters. Frankfort firms were exclusively employed in the construction and equipment of the house.

110 [1903; 91]

Am Elisabethplatz in München erbaute Professor Theodor Fischer (jetzt in Stutt-gart) von Oktober 1900 bis September 1902 das malerisch durchgeführte Schulgebäude, das unsere Abbildungen zeigen und dessen Kostenbetrag einschließlich vollständiger Einrichtung sich auf 661 000 Mark belaufen hat.

Es ist als Backsteinbau mit Kalkmörtel geputzt, nur der Sockel ist in Beton und die Portale sind in Marktbreiter Muschelkalk ausgeführt. Die Decken bestehen aus Eisenbalken mit Betonaus-stampfung und sind mit Linoleum bedeckt. Die Dächer sind mit Ergelsbacher Tonplatten einge-deckt. Die Treppen sind aus Beton, mit Thorralit belegt.

Der Uhrturm, auf allen vier Seiten mit Ziffer-blatt versehen, dient als Abzugschlot für die Ab-luft sämtlicher Lehrsäle u. s. w. Das aus Keller-, Erd- und Obergeschossen bestehende Gebäude ent-hält in den zweiseitig an den Mittelgängen auf-gereihten Sälen: 10 Knaben-, 11 Mädchen- und 9 Handwerksklassen, 1 Beschäftigungs- und 1 Spiel-saal für den Kindergarten, 2 Turnsäle, 3 Lehr-mittel- und 1 Konferenzzimmer, 4 Karzer, 4 Schülerwerkstätten (2 für Holz-, 2 für Metall-arbeiten), 1 Suppenküche, 1 Suppensaal, 1 Brause-bad, 32 Garderoben, 11 Aborte, 2 offene Loggien und 2 Oberlehrerzimmer.

Die Zeichnungen zu den Putzdekorationen der Erker und Blenden sind nach Skizzen des Archi-tekten von Herrn S. v. Suchodolski gezeichnet.

Monsieur le professeur Theodor Fischer maintenant à Stuttgart, bâtit à la place Elisabeth à Munich le bâtiment scolaire pittoresque que représentent nos planches. La construction dura d'octobre 1900 à septembre 1902 et exigea la somme de 661000 Marks, y compris l'installation complète.

Le bâtiment est exécuté en briques crépies de mortier de chaux; le socle seul est exécuté en béton et les portails en pierre calcaire de Marktbreit. Les planchers sont formés de poutres en fer et remplissage de béton recouvert de linoleum. Les toits sont recouverts en tuiles plates de Ergelsbach. Les escaliers sont en béton, recouverts de Thorralit.

La tour d'horloge, pourvue de cadrans sur ses quatre faces, sert de souche de ventilation pour toutes les salles etc. Le bâtiment composé d'une cave, d'un rez-de-chaussée et des étages supérieurs, contient dans les salles disposées des deux côtés des corridors centraux, 10 classes de garçons, 11 de filles et 9 de métiers, une pour les occupations et jeux de jardins d'enfants, deux de gymnastique, trois chambres pour les moyens d'instructions et une de con-férences, quatre cellules d'incarcération, quatre ateliers pour élèves (deux pour travaux en bois et deux pour travaux en métal), une cuisine, à soupe, une salle à manger la soupe, un bain à douches, 32 vestiaires, 11 cabinets d'aisance, 2 loggias ouvertes et deux chambres des maitres supérieurs.

Les décorations du crépissage des panneaux et des avant-corps ont été dessinées par Monsieur S. v. Suchodolski d'après les es-quisses de l'architecte.

110 [1903; 91]

The new schoolbuildings on Elisabethplatz in Munich, which have a strikingly pictu-resque appearance, have been built from October 1900 to September 1902 by Professor Theodor Fischer (now of Stuttgart). The cost of the buil-ding, of which we give an illustration amounted to 661000 Marks.

It is a brick building with mortar plaster, the sockel is of beton and the portals are of Markt-breiter Musche lime. The ceilings are of iron girders with beton, and are covered with linoleum. The roofs are covered with Ergelsbacher tiles. The stairs are of beton, with a covering of Thorralit.

The clock tower, which has four dials, serves as a ventilating shaft for the various schoolrooms &c. The building consists of basement, ground and first floors, and contains 10 boys' schoolrooms, 11 girls' rooms, 9 work-rooms for mechanical occupations an employment and play-room for the Kinder-garten, 2 gymnasia, 3 school apparatus rooms, 1 committee room, 4 rooms for solitary confine-ment, 4 school work shops (2 for wood and 2 for metal work), 1 soup kitchen, 1 dining hall, 1 shower bath, 32 cloak rooms, 11 waterclosets, 2 open balconies and 2 headteachers' rooms.

The drawings for the plaster decorations of the balconies &c. are from sketchets by the architect, drawed by Mr. S. v. Suchodolski.

111 [1903; 25]

Dresden ist in der Zeit vom Februar 1899 bis März 1901 durch ein Bauwerk be-reichert worden, das in technischer Beziehung als das erste seiner Art in Europa, in künst-lerischer Hinsicht einzig dasteht: Es ist das nach den technischen Vorentwürfen des Geh. Baurats Temper und nach dem Fassadenentwurf der Architekten Lossow und Viehweger in der Nähe des Hofopernhauses erbaute Fernheiz- und Elektrizitätswerk.

Es liegen dort am linken Elbufer, auf einer Strecke von rd. 1,5 km, in fast gerader Linie verteilt, 18 größere und kleinere Hof- und Staats-gebäude, die meistenteils eine größere Zahl vereinzelter Feuerstellen enthielten; so hatte u. a. das Hofopernhaus deren 24. Der größere Teil dieser Bauten, schon als geschichtliche Kunstwerke kaum ersetzlich, birgt die unschätzbaren Samm-lungen von Kunstwerken verschiedenster Art, die Dresden zu einem Wallfahrtsorte der Künstler und Kunstliebenden der Welt werden ließen.

Die eminente Feuersgefahr, die überhand-nehmende Entwickelung von Rauch und Staub bedrohten diesen Bestand, und der Verkehr zeigte

La ville de Dresde a été enrichie du mois de février 1899 au mois de mars 1901 d'un édifice qui au point de vue technique est le premier de son espèce en Europe, et qui au point de vue artistique est unique en son genre. C'est la centrale de chaleur et d'électricité élevée dans le voisinage de l'opéra royal d'après les projets techniques du conseiller intime des constructions W. Temper et d'après le projet de façades des architectes Lossow et Viehweger.

Il se trouvent dans cette contrée, sur la rive gauche de l'Elbe, sur une longueur d'un kilomètre et demi à peu près et presque en ligne droite 18 monuments de plus ou moins d'importance, appartenant soit à l'Etat soit à la couronne, les-quels contenaient pour la plupart de nombreux foyers de chauffage. L'opéra entre autres en avait 24. Le plus grand nombre de ces monu-ments d'une valeur artistique et historique in-calculable par eux mêmes, contiennent en outre les collections inestimables d'oeuvres d'art de tout genre, faisant de Dresde un lieu de pélerinage des artistes et des amateurs du monde entier.

Le danger imminent d'incendie, l'augmentation continuelle de fumée et de poussière menaçaient

111 [1903; 25]

In the period from February 1899 to March 1901 Dresden has been enriched by an edifice technically speaking the first in Europe, and which viewed artistically must be considered as unique; it is the Electrical Works for heating and lighting built in the neighbourhood of the Royal Opera house after the technical designs of Baurat Temper, and the architec-tural designs of the architects Lossow and Viehweger.

On the left bank of the Elbe, there stretches a site extending for about 1,5 kilometres in a nearly straight line, and on which are built 18 larger and smaller court and state buildings, containing a large number of separate fire stations. The greater number of these buildings, in themselves most valuable as memorials of historical architecture, contain the priceless collection of art treasures of various kinds to which the artist and art-lover make pilgrimages from all parts of the world.

lich durch Anfuhr des Brennmaterials beläftigt; dazu kam noch der Umftand, daß eine unmittelbare Heizung der katholifchen Hofkirche fich als unmöglich erwiefen hatte. Der Gedanke, den Geh. Baurat Temper (damals im königl. fächf. Finanzminifterium) faßte: ein mit Dampf zu betreibendes Fernheizwerk für diefe fämtlichen Bauten zu errichten und es mit einem Elektrizitätswerk zu verbinden, erfchien um fo mehr berechtigt, als die meiften diefer Bauten in den Abendftunden elektrifcher Beleuchtung bedürfen, zu einer Zeit, in der in der Regel der geringfte Aufwand an Wärme ftattfindet. So kann das Werk auch äußerft wirtfchaftlich arbeiten. Eine in diefer Beziehung günftige Bauftelle fand fich am Elbufer neben dem Packhof und Steuerverwaltungsgebäude, durch Geleife an fämtliche Eifenbahnen angefchloffen.

Schwierigkeiten technifcher Natur boten nur die Anlage der Rohrkanäle unter dem Straßenpflafter und zweckmäßiger Wärmefchutz der Dampfrohre, fowie Sicherung der in den blanken Kupferleitungen in den Kanälen geführten, hochgefpannten elektrifchen Ströme.

Um fo größere Schwierigkeiten bot die architektonifche Ausgeftaltung des Gebäudes in unmittelbarer Umgebung der hochbedeutfamen Bauwerke, die Dresdens anmutigem Städtebild das Gepräge verleihen, namentlich des Opernhaufes, des Mufeums, des Zwingers, der Katholifchen Hofkirche und des Königlichen Schloffes. Jeglicher Verfuch, in irgend welche Anklänge an deren Architektur einzugehen, mußte zu den fchreiendften

ces trésors, le transport des matériaux de chauffage incommodant la circulation, il fut en outre constaté qu'un chauffage immédiat de l'église catholique de la cour n'était pas praticable. La proposition du conseiller intime des constructions Temper (alors fonctionnaire au ministère des finances de Saxe) d'établir une centrale de chaleur obtenue par la vapeur pour tous ces édifices et de la relier avec une usine électrique, parut d'autant plus digne d'être prise en considération, que la plupart de ces monuments ont besoin d'éclairage pendant la soirée, dans un moment où en général on réclame moins de chaleur. C'est ce qui fait que cette installation peut travailler d'une façon tout à fait économique. Une place favorable à cet établissement fut trouvée sur la rive de l'Elbe près la douane et administration des impôts, qui est reliée à toutes les lignes de chemin de fer.

Il ne se présentaient des difficultés techniques que pour l'établissement des canaux sous pavé des rues et dans les précautions efficaces à prendre contre la déperdition de chaleur des tuyaux à vapeur et pour la sécurité des courants électriques à haute tension, conduits par des fils de cuivre apparent dans les canaux.

La composition architecturale du bâtiment présentait par contre de beaucoup plus grandes difficultés, vu son emplacement avoisinant les monuments de haute importance qui donnent à la ville de Dresde son caractère si particulier, notamment l'opéra, le musée, le Zwinger, l'église catholique de la cour et le château royal. Toute tentative, de chercher à rappeler l'architecture d'un de ces monuments, devait produire les dissonances les plus criardes. Il était nécessaire d'agir avec

The great danger of fire, and the smoke and dust incident to the ordinary modes of heating have long been subjects of anxiety to the authorities. In addition, it has been found almost impossible to heat the Catholic Court Church. These circumstances suggested to the Geheimer Baurat Temper (then a member of the Royal Saxon Finance ministry) the idea of a central power plant driven by steam for this collection of buildings. To combine this with electric works seemed specially suitable, as all these buildings require electric light at a time when the least degree of heating is required. Through this, the arrangement becomes an economical one. A most suitable site was found on the banks of the Elbe near the goods office, the Tax administration office, and in connection with the lines of the various railways.

The only technical difficulties were the laying of the necessary tubes under the streets, the protection of the steam pipes from cold, and the security of the electric current which is sent into the canals through pure copper.

On the other hand, the architectural difficulties were great. To erect any building in the neighbourhood of those important edifices to which Dresden owes its charming aspect — the Opera House, the Museums, the Zwinger, the Catholic Court Church and the Royal Castle, was in

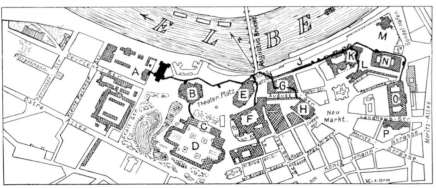

Situation   Plan de situation   General plan

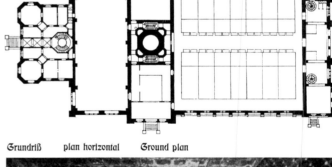
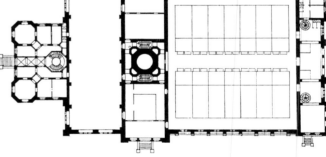

Grundriß   plan horizontal   Ground plan

A. Zoll- u. Steuer-Direktion	A. Douane et administration des impôts	A. Goods and tax administration offices
B. Hofopernhaus	B. Opéra royal	B. Royal Opera House
C. Bildergalerie	C. Musée	C. Museum
D. Zwingergebäude	D. Zwinger	D. Zwinger
E. Kath. Hofkirche	E. Eglise catholique de la cour	E. Catholic Court Church
F. Residenzschloß	F. Château royal	F. Royal Castle
G. Neues Ständehaus	G. Conseil d'états	G. State house
H. Johanneum (hift. Sammlung)	H. Collection historique	H. Historical Collection
J. Bibliothek	J. Bibliothèque	J. Library
K. Kunftakademie und -Ausstellung	K. Académie d'art	K. Academy of art
L. Altes Polizeigebäude	L. Ancien bâtiment de police	L. Old police office building
M. Belvedere	M. Belvedere	M. Belvedere
N. Albertinum (Sculpturen- sammlung, Staatsarchiv)	N. Collections de sculptures archives de l'Etat	N. Collection of sculptures state archives
O. Neues Polizeigebäude	O. Bâtiment neuf de police	O. New police office building
P. Landhaus	P. Bâtiment de l'administration régionale	P. Administration building

Leitungskanal   Canal sous pavé   Transmission canal

Mißklängen führen. Befondere Vorficht war geboten bei Ausgeftaltung der hohen Effe, die zur Förderung der durchgeführten rauchfreien Verbrennung ungewöhnliche Abmeffungen erforderte und im Städtebilde um fo eher unangenehm wirken konnte, als fie felbft vom jenfeitigen Ufer gefehen, dominiert. Die architektonifchen Pläne wurden im Wege eines befchränkten Ideenwettbewerbs erlangt, bei dem die Architekten Lossow und Viehweger den Preis errangen. Die Ausführung gefchah unter Oberleitung des Geh. Baurats Temper, durch Landbauinfpektor Schmiedel, und für den mafchinen- und heiztechnifchen Teil durch Baurat Trautmann, unter Mitwirkung der erften fächfifchen Heiz-, Mafchinen-, Keffel- und Elektrizitätsfirmen.

une extrême susceptibilité dans la conception de la haute cheminée, qui pour arriver à la combustion absolue franche de fumée, exigeait des dimensions exeptionelles; cette cheminée pouvait dans la vue d'ensemble produire un effet d'autant plus déplorable que même de l'autre côté du fleuve, elle domine tout le tableau. Les plans d'architecture furent obtenus dans un concours restreint, dans lequel les architectes Lossow et Viehweger obtinrent le prix. L'exécution fut sous la direction générale de Geheimer Baurat Mr. Temper, confiée à l'inspecteur Schmiedel. Les machines et installations techniques de chauffage, furent exécutées selon les projets et directions de Mr. Baurat Trautmann, secondé par les premières maisons pour machines, chaudières électricité et chauffage de Saxe.

itself a difficulty. To attempt anything like similarity would have been a terrible blunder. Great care was necessary in the construction of the high chimney which on account of the smoke-consuming apparatus required to be of large dimensions, and which seen from the opposite bank could not fail to be a prominent object. A limited competition was resorted to, to gain various ideas, and the architects Lossow and Viehweger were the prize-winners. The work was carried out by the Geheimer Baurat Temper and the building inspector Schmiedel. The machine and technical heating department was entrusted to Baurat Trautmann together with

Das Gebäude hat im vorderen Teile Wohn- und Bureauräume, dann folgen die Maschinenräume, der für Akkumulatoren und der für 14 Keſſel (von denen dermal nur zehn aufgeſtellt), und zum Schluß Werkſtätten u. ſ. w.

Die Faſſaden ſind aus hellgelbem Elbſandſtein (durchbindend) hergeſtellt, die Decken aus Stampfbeton bezw. Monierwerk, die Dächer aus Eiſen mit Holzſparren und Zinkpfannen auf Holzſchalung über dem Maſchinenhauſe, ſonſt mit glaſierten Biberſchwänzen gedeckt. Die Anlage hat insgeſamt nur rd. 3 Millionen Mark gekoſtet.

Hier oben iſt ein Einblick in die Leitungskanäle gegeben: links die Dampfrohre, von denen das obere ſchon ſeinen Wärme-Iſolierungsmantel erhalten hat; unten die Kondens-Waſſerrückleitungsrohre, rechts hinter dem Drahtgitter die elektriſchen Leitungen.

112 [1903: 36]

Aus der noch wenig bebauten Umgebung von Chicago (U. S. A.) ſeien hier Anſichten zweier Landhäuſer mitgeteilt, die in ihrer höchſt maleriſchen Anordnung und Ausbildung für nordamerikaniſche Landhausbauten charakteriſtiſch ſind. Bei dem von J. L. Cochran zum Verkauf erbauten Landhaus iſt mit Abſicht in ſeiner äußeren Erſcheinung alles vermieden, was an das ſtädtiſche Wohnhaus anklingt. Nur im Unterbau und an dem großen Schornſtein tritt Steinkonſtruktion zutage — und dieſe nur als Zyklopenmauerwerk aus Steinen verſchiedenſter Färbung mit teils rohen, teils geſlächten Häuptern. Die Wandflächen ſind im Erdgeſchoß mit übergreifenden Brettern und im Giebel, gleich wie die Dächer, mit Schindeln verkleidet. Die wenigen, in vorzüglicher Technik ausgearbeiteten Architekturgebilde heben ſich von dem dunklen Grunde ganz ſelbſtändig frei ab.

Das zweite Landhaus erſcheint in noch viel einfacherer, rein maleriſcher Geſtaltung. In ländlich naiver Technik beſchränkt ſich der Aufwand in Architektur auf den polygonalen Treppenturm, deſſen Flächen, ebenſo wie die des ganzen Gebäudes, in ihrer Schindelverkleidung erſcheinen.

113 [1903: 99]

Das große Geſchäftshaus Friedrichſtraße 231 in Berlin wurde durch Architekt Paul Jaßow von Oktober 1900 bis April 1902 als reiner Pfeilerbau errichtet. Die für Berliner Verhältniſſe etwas lange Bauzeit wurde durch ungemein ſchwierige Gründung verurſacht, die für das Vorderhaus an den Grenzen der Nachbargebäude bis auf 14 Meter unter Straßengleiche hinabgeführt werden mußte, da ſich hier ein alter, verſchütteter Graben vorfand, über dem das hier geſtandene, alte Gebäude auf Pfählen ruhte.

Der Sockel der Faſſadenpfeiler beſteht aus Granit, der darüber liegende Teil aus Warthauer Sandſtein und von dem Bande ab aus ſächſiſchem Sandſtein.

Die durch Kunſtſchloſſer F. Stahl & Sohn hergeſtellten Erker ſind aus gebräuchlichen Eiſenprofilen (Rund-, Flach- und Winkeleiſen) ausgeführt und vergoldet. Bildhauer Weſtphal fertigte das Bildwerk, während die Sandſteinarbeiten durch Hofſteinmetzmeiſter Karl Schilling geliefert wurden. Die Maurerarbeiten führte Maurermeiſter Krüger aus.

114 [1903: 33]

Die turmartig hochgeführten Rieſenhäuſer der nordamerikaniſchen Großſtädte, die ſo ſehr das Intereſſe der Bauingenieure verdienen, wecken nur ausnahmsweiſe künſtleriſches Aufmerken.

Le bâtiment contient sur le devant des locaux pour bureaux et logements, ensuite viennent les salles de machines et celle pour 14 chaudières (dont 10 sont pour le moment installées) et enfin les ateliers etc.

Les façades sont construites en grès jaune clair de l'Elbe, les plafonds sont en béton comprimé et en construction monier, les toits sont en fer avec des chevrons en bois couvertes en tuiles de zinc sur voliges en bois sur la halle aux machines; les autres parties de l'édifice sont recouvertes en tuiles vernissées. Tout l'établissement a coûté rond 3 millions de marks.

Ci-haut une vue dans les canaux sous pavé: à gauche les conduites de vapeur, dont la supérieure est déjà pourvue de son manteau isolateur, au dessous les tuyaux de retour de l'eau de condensation, à droite, derrière le treillis de fil de fer, les conduites électriques.

112 [1903: 36]

Nons publions ici les vues de deux maisons de campagne des environs encore peu habités de Chicago aux Etats-Unis, qui dans leur arrangement et leur architecture extrêmement pittoresques, sont caractéristiques pour les villas américaines. Dans la maison bâtie pour la vente par J. L. Cochran tout a été soigneusement évité à l'extérieur, de ce qui pourrait rappeler la maison d'habitation en ville. Ce n'est qu'au soubassement et aux grandes cheminées que la pierre a trouvé quelque emploi, et cela, seulement comme appareil cyclopéen de pierres de différentes couleurs avec des surfaces en partie brutes, en partie travaillées. Les surfaces des murs sont garnies au rez-de-chaussée de planches posées à joints couverts, tandis que le fronton est comme le toit recouvert de bardeaux. Les quelques rares motifs d'architecture d'un travail très soigné se détachent d'une façon remarquable du fond foncé.

La seconde maison de campagne paraît encore beaucoup plus simple dans son architecture entièrement pittoresque. L'appareil architectural se borne à la tour d'escalier polygonale d'une structure naive et champêtre, ses surfaces sont ainsi que celles de toute la maison recouvertes en bardeaux.

113 [1903: 99]

La grande maison de rapport Friedrichſtraße 231 à Berlin fut construite par Monsieur Paul Jaßow architecte, d'octobre 1900 à avril 1902; c'est une construction reposant entièrement sur des piliers. La durée de la bâtisse qui paraît un peu longue par rapport aux habitudes berlinoises, fut occasionnée par des travaux de fondation extrêmement difficiles. Ces travaux s'étendent pour la maison de devant, aux lisières des maisons voisines jusqu'à 14 mètres au dessous du niveau de la rue, parce qu'il se trouvait à cette place un ancien fossé comblé, sur lequel la vieille maison qui se trouvait à cette place, etait posée sur pilotis.

Le socle des piliers de la façade est en granit, la partie supérieure est en grès de Warthau et au dessus du cordon en grès de Saxe.

Les devantures, exécutées par les serruriers F. Stahl & fils sont construits en fers profilés se trouvant dans le commerce (fers plats, ronds et à cornières); elles sont toutes dorées. Le sculpteur Westphal fut chargé de la sculpture, tandis que les travaux de pierre de taille furent livrés par la maison Carl Schilling. Les travaux de maçonnerie furent exécutés par l'entrepreneur Krüger.

114 [1903: 33]

Les maisons géantes montées comme des tours, des grandes villes de l'Amérique du Nord, et qui méritent à plus d'un titre d'éveiller l'intérêt des ingénieurs ne possèdent qu'exceptionnellement une valeur artistique.

---

the first Saxon heating, machine, boiler and electric firms.

The building has in the front dwellings and bureaus, then come the machine rooms, those for the accumulators, and room for the 14 boilers (of which 10 are erected) and last, come the workshops etc.

The facades are of light yellow Elbe sandstone, the ceilings of beton or monierwork, the roofs of the machine house are of iron with wooden ruſters and zinctiles, the other roofs of glazed tiles. The whole plant has only cost 3 Millionen Marks.

Therebefore shows a view of the transmission canal; on the left the steam pipes — the upper is already jacketed in its warm isolating cover, below is the condensed water pipe, on the right under the wire fence is the electric wire.

112 [1903: 36]

We have here two views of villas built outside Chicago, the neighbourhood of which is at present very little built over. These cottages however in their highly picturesque design and situation are eminently characteristic of North American country houses. The one, built for sale by J. L. Cochran, is noticeable as avoiding every detail which might remind the spectator of the city houses. Stone is only visible for the chimneys and for the basement and here only as Cyclops masonry with stones of various colours with partly rough and partly hewen surfaces. The wall surfaces of the ground floor are faced with overlaying planks, and the walls of the gables and the roofs are shingled. The few, but splendidly executed architectural details stand out most effectively from the dark shingled found.

The second cottage is much simpler, but is still of picturesque appearance. The style is extremely countrified, and the only attempt at architecture is the polygonal staircase tower, the surfaces of which as well as those of the whole house are covered with shingles.

113 [1903: 99]

The large business house Friedrichstrasse 231 in Berlin was built by the architect Paul Jutzow from October 1900 to April 1902. It is entirely arranged in pillars. The comparatively long time occupied in building was occasioned by the exceedingly difficult foundation which, for the front house, had to be carried 14 meters under the level of the street at the side of the adjoining house; an old filled-up ditch was discovered in building on which the old house supported by pillars, had to been built.

The base of the pillars on the facade is of granite, the upper part of Warthau sandstone, and over the bands of Saxon sandstone.

The bow, by the artistic iron work firm F. Stahl & Sons, is constructed of ordinary iron parts (round, flat, corners) and afterwards gilded. The sculptor Westphal carried out the sculptural decorations, the sandstone work was done by Carl Schilling, and the brick work by the builder Krüger.

114 [1903: 33]

The tower-like gigantic houses of the large towns of North America though very interesting to the building engineer are rarely interesting to the artist in architecture.

Als eine solche Ausnahme war im Jahrg. II auf Bl. 5 das Gebäude des „Medinah-Temple" in Chicago mitgeteilt. Auf Tafel 33 des vorliegenden Heftes geben wir die Ansicht einer Reihe solcher, nicht an enger Straße, sondern an einem freien Platze, dem Castle-Square, errichteter Bauten wieder, an denen die tektonische Ausbildung also nicht nur an den unteriten und den oberiten, weithin wirkenden Geschossen, sondern an der ganzen Fassade von jedem nicht allzu nahen Standpunkt aus zur Geltung kommt.

Das nur teilweise sichtbare Gebäude links, das Hotel-Auditorium, erbaut von den Architekten Adler und Sullivan, ist dadurch auffällig, daß es in allen Fensterachsen der Fassade durch fünf übereinanderliegende Stockwerke ausgebaute Glaserker hat. Das durch einen breiten Hof davon getrennte zweite Gebäude von denselben Architekten erbaut, wird als Annex zum Hotel-Auditorium bezeichnet. Im Ganzen denselben Aufbauorganismus — jedoch ohne die Erker — aufweisend, gibt es von den Bestreben der Architekten Kunde: die unschönen, aber durch Bedürfnisforderungen bedingten Verhältnisse fast gleicher Stockwerkshöhen und Pfeilerteilungen zu günstiger Erscheinung zu zwingen.

Künstlerisch weit überlegen zeigt sich das mittlere, noch höher geführte Gebäude von gleicher Stockwerkszahl, das von dem Architekten S. S. Beman errichtete Studebaker-Building. Die hinteren Teile dieses Geschäftshauses sind als Theater ausgebaut, in dem die Aufführungen der Castle Square Opera Co. stattfinden. Bei diesem Bau ist es dem Architekten gelungen, das Kasernenartige, den Charakter eines gewöhnlichen Lagerhauses, mit Glück zu vermeiden und schöne Verhältnisse zu erzielen.

Das daran angelehnte, in romanisierenden Formen — dem sogenannten Richardson-Stil — durchgeführte Chicago Club House, von den Architekten Burnham und Rost erbaut, ist niedrig, mit nur drei Obergeschossen aufgeführt, um der Seitenfront des Theaterbaues nicht alles Licht zu entziehen.

Sur la planche 5 de la 2me année nous avons publié une de ces exceptions: le bâtiment du „Medinah-Temple" à Chicago. La planche 33 de la livraison présente montre la vue d'une série de ces constructions élevées sur une place libre, le Castle-Square, et non pas sur une rue étroite, ces édifices ne sont par conséquent pas décorés architecturalement seulement aux étages superieurs visibles de loin, et aux parties inférieures, mais sur toute la surface des façades, de sorte que chaque partie produit son effet, vue d'un point pas trop rapproché.

La maison de gauche, visible en partie seulement est l'hôtel-auditorium bâti par les architectes Adler et Sullivan, il est remarquable par les bowindows vitrés, placés sur toutes les axes de fenêtres sur une hauteur de cinq étages superposés. Le second bâtiment séparé du premier par une large cour, bâti également par les mêmes architectes est désigné comme annexe de l'hôtel-auditorium. En somme, c'est le même organisme constructif, mais sans les bowindows; ces deux édifices témoignent du désir des architectes, de présenter d'une façon favorable la proportion peu avantageuse que donne la répétition monotone d'étages et de piliers égaux exigés par les circonstances.

La maison du milieu, du même nombre d'étages, mais d'une élévation plus considérable encore, est d'une beaucoup plus grande valeur artistique, c'est le Studebaker-Building, construite par S. S. Beman. Les parties postérieures de cette maison de commerce sont disposées pour un théâtre, dans lequel ont lieu les représentations de la Castle Square Opéra Compagnie. Dans cet édifice, l'architecte a réussi parfaitement à éviter le caractère caserneal ou de magasin d'entrepôt, et d'obtenir de belles proportions.

La maison contiguë, du Chicago Club, construite dans les formes romanisantes, dites Style Richardson, a été élevée par les architectes Burnham et Rost; elle est basse et ne compte que trois étages supérieurs pour ne pas priver de lumière l'aile latérale du théâtre.

An exception to this rule was an illustration of the "Medinah-Temple" in Chicago given on the 5th plate of our second volume. On plate 33 of the present number we give an illustration of a row of such buildings not situated in a narrow street but in a free place Castle Square. It will be noticed that the architectural details are not only on the lower and upper storeys where they are most noticeable but on the entire facade, being from a distant view very effective.

The building on the left only partially visible is the Hotel Auditorium built by the architects Adler and Sullivan. A noticeable feature is in five consecutive storeys the windows are built in the form of glass bows. The second building, separated from the first by a broad courtyard, and built by the same architect is designated the Annex to the Hotel Auditorium. It is built in much the same style as the auditorium without the glass bows, and is a proof of the artistic efforts of the architect to make as beautiful a building possible while being restricted, on utilitarian grounds, to the monotonous arrangement of design and details.

A far more artistic result must be conceded to the middle and still higher building by the architects S. S. Beman and called the Studebaker building. The back part of this business house is arranged as a theatre in which are given the performances of the Castle Square Opera Company. The architect has succeeded in avoiding the barrack-like appearance of most business houses and has happily achieved a satisfactory result.

The Chicago Club House adjoining, built in Romanesque forms, the socalled "Richardson style" built by the architects Burnham and Rost is low, with only three upper storeys, in order to allow sufficient light for the side front of the theatre.

115 [1903; 69]

Das in Stuttgart von den königl. Bauräten Eisenlohr und Weigele daselbst für Herrn Breuninger erbaute Kaufhaus „Zum Großfürsten" ist in zwei Bauperioden errichtet worden:

115 [1903; 69]

La maison de commerce dite: „Zum Großfürsten" batie à Stuttgart par les architectes Eisenlohr et Weigele a été élevée en deux périodes, du printemps 1901 au printemps

115 [1903; 69]

The Royal building Councillors Eisenlohr and Weigele have built business premises in Stuttgart for Mr. Breuninger. The house is called "Zum Grossfürsten" and was built

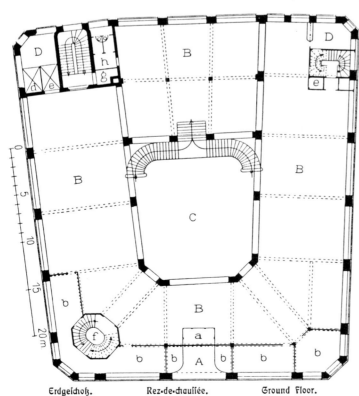

Erdgeschoß.   Rez-de-chaussée.   Ground Floor.

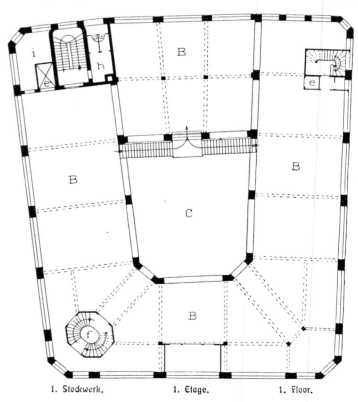

1. Stockwerk.   1. Étage.   1. Floor.

von Frühjahr 1901 bis Frühjahr 1902 und von da ab bis Februar 1903. Unsere Abbildung zeigt die Fassade des ersterbauten Teiles. Der von vier Straßen umgebene Bau kostete im ganzen rd. 650 000 Mark. A ist der Haupteingang, der durch den Windfang a in die Verkaufsräume B B führt. Diese umgeben einen großen, mit Glas abgedeckten Lichthof C und sind neben dem Eingang mit eingebauten Auslagen (Schaukästen) b ausgestattet. D D sind Nebeneingänge, letztere für den Waren-Ein- und -Ausgang, mit Hebebühne d (zum Keller) und Warenaufzügen e e zu den oberen Geschossen führend; f ist Personenaufzug, g Pförtnerraum, h Waschraum. Diese Bezeichnungen gelten für beide Grundrisse, h im 1. Obergeschoß als Kleiderraum für Angestellte.

Die Decken sind als „Könensche Voutenplatten" ausgeführt, die Fassaden aus weißem Keupersandstein.

1902, puis de ce moment au mois de février 1903. Notre planche montre la façade de la première partie. Cette bâtisse entourée de 4 rues a coûté en tout 650 000 Marks. A, est l'entrée principale, qui conduit par le porche a dans les magasins B B. Ces derniers entourent une grande cour vitrée C, et sont pourvus près de l'entrée de grandes devantures b. D, D, sont des entrées secondaires, ces dernières pour l'entrée et la sortie des marchandises avec plateau de descente d, pour la cave et ascenseurs pour les marchandises e e, conduisant aux étages supérieurs, f, est un lift pour personnes, g, loge du portier, h, toilette. Ces définitions sont valables pour les deux plans, h, à l'étage supérieur est un vestiaire pour les employés.

Les plafonds sont exécutés en fer et béton système Könen, les façades sont en grès blanc.

in two periods from Spring 1901 to Spring 1902 and from then till February 1903. Our illustration is of the facade of the part built first. The building, which has frontages on four streets cost 650 000 Marks. A is the principal entrance, which leads through the passage a to the sale rooms B B. These enclose a large skylighted hall C which, by the side of the entrance is furnished with shop windows b. D D are side entrances, the latter for the entrance and exit of goods, with hoisting apparatus d for the cellar and goods lifts e e to the upper floors; f is passenger lift, g porter's room, h washing room. These illustrations refer to the both ground-plans, h in the first upper storey being the cloak-room for the employes.

The ceilings are of so called "Könen voute plates", the facades of white Keuper sandstone.

116, 117 [1903; 1, 2]

Der Letteverein in Berlin, eine langjährig bestehende Stiftung zur Hebung der Erwerbsfähigkeit junger Mädchen, besaß bis dahin ein eigenes Heim, das den anschwellenden Bedürfnissen nicht mehr genügte. Das neue Heim des Lettevereins ist nun durch Professor Alfred Messel auf einem sehr tiefen Gelände am Viktoria-Luiseplatz 6 in der westlichen, mit Berlin vollständig verwachsenen Stadt Schöneberg vom Oktober 1901 bis Oktober 1902 erbaut worden.

Das Gelände von unregelmäßiger Gestaltung weist eine zweite Fassade an der Neuen Bayreuther Straße auf. Behufs seiner günstigen, wirtschaftlichen Ausnützung wurden an beiden Straßenfronten Mietwohnhäuser (Tafel 1) errichtet, während das eigentliche Vereins- und Schulhaus (Tafel 2) als Quergebäude mit seinen Flügelbauten einen größeren Schmuckhof umfaßt.

Sämtliche Fassaden sind, unter Verwendung von Cottaer Sandstein zu den durch Bildhauer Ernst Westphal ausgeführten bildnerischen Arbeiten, in hydraulischem Mörtel verputzt. Die Malerarbeiten führte M. J. Bodenstein aus.

116, 117 [1903; 1, 2]

La société Letteverein à Berlin, une ancienne fondation pour faciliter aux jeunes filles les possibilités de gagner leur vie possédait jusqu'à aujourd'hui une maison à elle, qui ne suffit plus aux besoins toujours croissants de cette institution. La nouvelle maison du Letteverein a été construite par le professeur Alfred Messel sur un terrain très profond à la place Victoria-Louise 6, d'octobre 1901 à octobre 1902 dans la ville de Schöneberg située à l'ouest de Berlin et maintenant complètement reliée à la capitale.

Le terrain d'une forme irrégulière présente une seconde façade sur la Neue Bayreuther Strasse. Pour utiliser d'une façon absolument rationelle cette propriété, on se décida à établir des maisons à loyer sur les deux rues (Pl. 1) tandis que la maison d'école et de société fut installé dans un bâtiment central, qui avec ses ailes entoure une grande cour d'agrément.

Toutes les façades sont crépies au mortier de chaux hydraulique avec emploi de grès de Cotta pour les travaux de sculpture exécutés par le sculpteur Ernst Westphal. Les travaux de peinture furent exécutés par M. J. Bodenstein.

116, 117 [1903; 1, 2]

The Lette-Verein of Berlin, an old and exceedingly useful Society for the education and improvement of young women, has so increased its sphere of usefulness that the premises hitherto occupied have been found insufficient for the numerous claims of the Society. A new home has therefore been built by Professor Alfred Messel on an extensive site in the Victoria-Luiseplatz 6. It is situated in the west of Berlin where that city joins the suburb of Schöneberg now continuous with Berlin. The time occupied was from October 1901 to October 1902.

The somewhat irregular site possesses a second frontage on the Neuen Bayreuther Strasse, and in order to secure the necessary interest on the capital expended, both frontages are occupied with dwellings let at remunerative rents while the actual premises of the Society are situated in the courtyard with its side wings, an open ornamented space. (See Plates 1 and 2.)

All the facades are of Cotta sandstone with hydraulic mortar plaster. The sculptural work is by Ernst Westphal and the painting by M. J. Bodenstein.

118 [1903; 77]

Das neue Rathaus in Dessau wurde von den Architekten Reinhardt und Süßenguth in Charlottenburg von 1899 bis Oktober 1901 auf der erweiterten Baustelle des alten Rathauses, mit schmaler (nördlicher) Hauptfront an dem Kleinen Markt und Nebenfassaden an der ziemlich engen Schloßstraße (links) und der verbreiterten Zerbsterstraße (rechts) errichtet.

Die Entwürfe wurden in einem wiederholten Wettbewerb gewonnen, in dem genannte Architekten Sieger blieben. Ihnen wurde die gesamte Ausführung und künstlerische Leitung übertragen; nur die Geschäftsführung blieb in Hand der städtischen Bauverwaltung; mit der örtlichen Leitung war Architekt Möbius betraut.

Die Gesamtkosten, ausgenommen für Honorar und Bauleitung, betrugen 1 024 000 Mark, oder für 1 cbm umbauten Raumes von Kellerfußboden bis Oberkante Dachfußboden 26 Mark. Dabei ist jedoch der 3512 cbm Raum umfassende Turm mit 30 Mark für 1 cbm in Anrechnung gebracht. Bei 1640 qm bebauter Grundfläche ergeben sich für 1 qm 624 Mark. Überdies wurden noch 50 000 Mark für Möbel und Beleuchtungskörper verausgabt.

Die Raumverteilung ist folgende: Im Untergeschoß erstrecken sich an der Kopfseite bis zu den Durchfahrten an den Nebenfronten, der Ratskeller nebst Räumen für den Wirt, Wohnung für den Heizer und den Pförtner. Die dahinter

118 [1903; 77]

Le nouvel Hôtel-de-ville de Dessau a été construit par les architectes Reinhardt & Süssenguth de Charlottenbourg de 1899 à octobre 1901 sur l'emplacement agrandi de l'ancien hôtel-de-ville. Le monument a sa façade principale étroite, au nord sur la petite place du marché et ses façades latérales, à gauche sur la rue assez étroite, Schlossstrasse, et à droite sur la Zerbsterstrasse élargie.

Les plans furent obtenus à la suite d'un concours répété dans lequel les architectes susnommés restèrent vainqueurs. L'exécution entière et la direction artistique leur furent confiées, seule la direction des affaires resta en main de l'administration urbaine. La conduite des travaux sur place fut confiée à Monsier Möbius, architecte.

La somme totale des dépenses, non-compris les honoraires d'architectes et de conducteurs des travaux a été de 1 024 000 Marks, soit, de 26 Marks par mètre cube de construction mesurée du sol des caves à la poutraison du plancher du toit. Dans cette somme se trouve cependant la tour mesurant 3512 mètres cubes comptés à 30 Marks le mètre cube. Sur une surface bâtie de 1640 mètres carrés, le mètre revient à 624 Marks, à part cela, on dépensa encore 50 000 Marks pour mobilier et appareils d'éclairage.

Les locaux sont répartis comme suit: Dans le sous-sol s'étendent en façade jusqu'aux passages des ailes, le restaurant et l'appartement du tenancier, ainsi que les logements du chauffeur et du

118 [1903; 77]

The new Guildhall in Dessau has been built by the architects Reinhardt and Süssenguth of Charlottenburg from 1899 to October 1901. On an enlarged building site of the old hall with a narrow principal frontage (north) on the Kleinen Markt and side facades on the rather narrow Schlossstrasse (left) and the broadened Zerbsterstrasse (right).

The designs were the result of a repeated open competition in which the above-named firm remained the victors. To this firm the entire technical and artistic work was entrusted, the business arrangements remained in the hands of the town administration; the local superintendence was in the hands of the architect Möbius.

The entire cost, exclusive of fees and superintendence, amounted to 1 024 000 Marks or for 1 cubic meter built space from cellar to roof 26 Marks. With this is included the 3512 cubic meters space of the tower which was reckoned with 30 Marks per cubic meter. With 1640 square meters of built surface the cost of 1 square meter amounted to 624 Marks. For furniture and lighting apparatus 50 000 Marks were expended.

The distribution of room is as follows: The basement contains the "Ratskeller" with rooms for the landlord, the dwellings of the firemen and

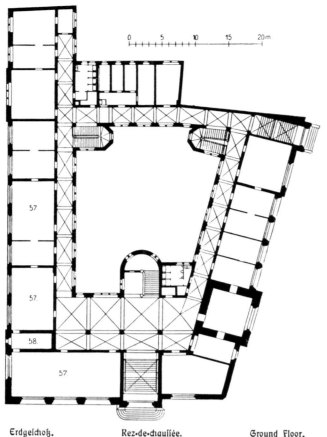
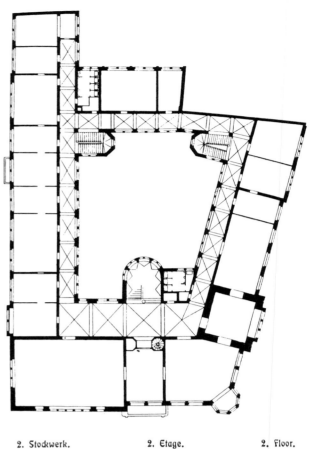

Erdgeſchoß. Rez-de-chauſſée. Ground Floor. 2. Stockwerk. 2. Étage. 2. Floor.

liegenden Teile ſind nebſt den im Erdgeſchoß liegenden Räumen des Quergebäudes der Feuerwehr und der Polizei eingeräumt. Im Hauptteil des Erdgeſchoſſes liegen die Räume der Kaſſenverwaltung. Das I. Obergeſchoß wird von der Zentral- und der Armenverwaltung, ſowie dem Standesamt eingenommen, deſſen Trauſaal im Turm liegt, während dem Oberbürgermeiſter als Zentralraum der Erkerſaal über dem Hauptelngange nebſt dem anſtoßenden Erkerſaal beſtimmt iſt; letzterer enthält auch die Magiſtratsbibliothek. In dem II. Obergeſchoß liegen an der Hauptfront der Sitzungsſaal der Stadtverordneten nebſt Vorſaal, derjenige für das Gewerbegericht, ferner anſchließende Kommiſſionsſäle und nachfolgend die Volksbibliothek nebſt Leſeſaal. Die geſamten Räume im linken und Querflügel ſind von dem Stadtbauamt eingenommen; der Saal des Stadtbaurates liegt neben dem großen Sitzungsſaale. Das Dachgeſchoß iſt ganz zu Aktenräumen ausgebaut. Im tiefen Unterkeller liegt die (gemiſchte) Warmwaſſer-Niederdruck- und Niederdruck-DampfLuftheizung. Die Faſſaden ſind aus Warthauer und Rackwitzer Sandſtein, mit Flächenverblendung aus Bernburger Rogenſtein in natürlichen Bruchflächen, und der Sockel aus Granit, während an Hoffronten roter Mainſandſtein die blaugrau geputzten Mauerflächen umrahmt. Sämtliche Decken ſind in Schlackenbeton hergeſtellt, mit Fußboden aus Parkett, Terrazzo oder Linoleum; in den Hallen und Fluren ſind ſie ein viertel Stein ſtark unterwölbt.

Die Höhen betragen einſchließlich Decken: im Unterkeller 2,65 Meter, im Untergeſchoß 4,35, im Erdgeſchoß, I. und II. Obergeſchoß 4,50, 4,25 und 4,70, im Dachgeſchoß 3,75 und darüber bis zum Firſt 10,75 Meter.

119 [1903; 78]

Profeſſor Martin Dülfer in München erbaute dort Bayerſtraße 43 das große, mit Nebengebäude ſich nach der Mittererſtraße ausdehnende Haus des Terminus-Hôtels.

Die Bauzeit währte nur vom 1. Juli 1902

concierge. Les locaux situés en arrière servent, avec ceux qui sont situés au rez-de-chaussée du bâtiment transversal, au service des pompes à incendie et à la police. Dans la partie principale du rez-de-chaussée se trouvent les bureaux de la caisse. Le premier étage est occupé par l'administration centrale et par celle des pauvres, ainsi que par l'État civil dont la salle des mariages est placée dans la tour; la salle dominante avec son avant corps l'entrée principale, est — comme pièce centrale — destinée au bourgmestre, ainsi que la salle adjointe à tourelle d'angle, qui contient la bibliothèque municipale. Le second étage contient en façade la salle des séances du conseil municipal avec antisalle, la salle du conseil des prud'hommes, les salles adjacentes pour commissions et la bibliothèque populaire avec salle de lecture. Tous les locaux des ailes gauche et transversale sont occupés par l'administration des travaux publics; le bureau de l'architecte conseiller est situé près de la grande salle des séances. Le toit contient les locaux des archives. Dans la basse cave se trouve le chauffage, système combiné, eau et vapeur à basse pression. Les façades sont construites en pierre de Warthau et de Rackwitz avec surfaces de moellons d'oolithe de Bernburg, le socle est en granit, tandis qu'aux façades des cours de la pierre rouge du Main encadre les surfaces crépies et teintées en bleu gris. Tous les planchers sont construits en beton d'escarbille avec sols de parquet, terrazzo ou linoleum. Les halles et corridors sont recouverts de voutes en briques.

Les hauteurs sont y compris les poutraisons, pour la cave 2,65 mètres, pour le sous sol 4,35 mètres, pour le rez-de-chaussée, le premier et le second étages 4,50, 4,25 et 4,70 mètres, pour l'étage du toit 3,75 mètres, de là jusqu'au faite 10,75 mètres.

119 [1903; 78]

Monsieur Martin Dülfer Professeur à Munich éleva dans cette ville, Bayerstrasse 43, le grand bâtiment de l'hôtel Terminus, lequel s'étend avec ses dépendances jusqu'à la Mittererstrasse.

the porter; these occupy the front. In the back the room is reserved for the fire-extinguishing apparatus and service and for the Police. The principal part of the ground floor contains the rooms of the cash administration. The first floor contains the administration of the central commission for Poor Relief, as well as a Registrar's office, the hall for the solemnization of marriages lying in the tower. For the Mayor the central rooms over the chief entrance are reserved, where is also placed the magistrate's library. On the second floor of the principal front are the committee rooms of the town councillors with an entrance room, rooms for the trade courts, with adjoining commission rooms, and following this — the public library with reading-room. The whole rooms of the left and transverse wings are occupied by the town building offices, the office of the town "Baurat" lying next to the large committee room. The roof storey is equipped entirely as archive room. In the deep under-cellar lies the low pressure warm water and steam heating apparatus. The facades are of Warthau and Rackwitz sandstone, the surfaces of Bernburger Rogen stone, and the sockel is of granite. The fronts of the courtyards are of red Main sandstone with blue grey plastering. All ceilings are of beton, the floors are parquetted and partly of Terrazzo and linoleum; in the halls and passages they have a firm layer of stone underneath.

The height including ceilings is as follows: under cellar 2,65, basement 4,35, ground floor, first and second upper floors 4,50, 4,25 and 4,70, roof storey 3,75 and from there to the extreme top 10,75 meters.

119 [1903; 78]

Professor Martin Dülfer has built in Bayerstrasse 43 Munich the new house of the Terminus Hotel.

The time occupied was from 1. July 1902

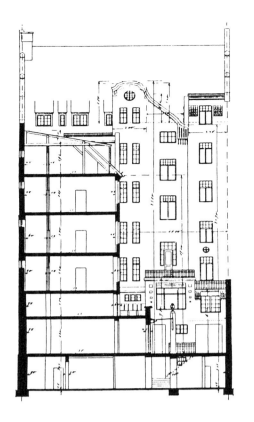

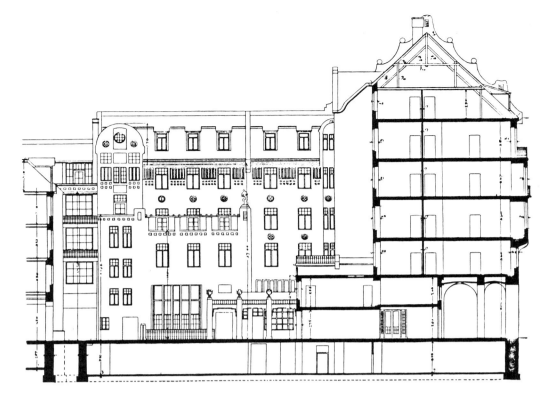

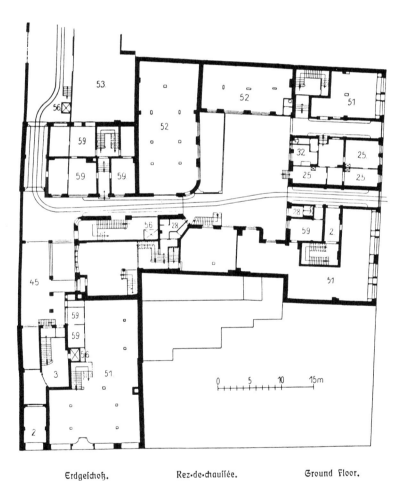

| Erdgeschoß. | Rez-de-chaussée. | Ground Floor. | 2. Stockwerk. | 2. Etage. | 2. Floor. |

bis 15. Mai 1903, und die Koften beliefen fich einfchließlich der für das Nebengebäude auf 1020000 Mark und die der Inneneinrichtung auf 200000 Mark.

Der Bau ift in Backftein mit Kalkmörtelputz ausgeführt, das Dach mit roten Biberfchwänzen. Die Decken find von Wayß & Freytag als Zellendecken hergeftellt.

Das Gebäude ift durchweg mit Zentralheizung und mit eigner Elektrizitätsanlage verfehen; es hat einen Perfonen- und einen Laftenaufzug.

Das ganze Gebäude ift einfchließlich der Höfe (zum Teil doppelt) unterkellert; diefe fämtlichen Räume find zu Lager- und Gefchäftsräumen verwertet.

Le temps de la construction dura du 1er juillet 1902 au 15 mai 1903 et les frais s'élevèrent, y compris les dépendances à 1020000 Marks, les installations intérieures coûtèrent 200000 Marks.

La construction est exécutée en briques avec crépissage de mortier; le toit est recouvert en tuiles rouges; les planchers sont construits par Wayss & Freytag d'après le système dit „à cellules".

Le bâtiment est pourvu dans son ensemble d'un chauffage central et d'une installation électrique propre, il possède un ascenseur et un montecharges.

Toute la construction, y compris les cours est placée sur caves (en partie doubles); tous ces locaux servent de magasins, dépôts et ateliers.

to 15. May 1903, the cost including the adjoining building amounted to 1020000 Marks and the interior decoration to 200000 Marks.

The building is of brick with mortar plastering the roof of flat red tiles. The ceilings are cellular-system by Wayss & Freytag.

The whole building is heated with hot air, and lighted by electric light, and has passenger and luggage lifts.

The whole building has extensive cellarage which extends under the court yards; these are used for storage and business premises.

Das Vorderhaus an der Bayerstraße enthält im Erd- und Zwischengeschoß Kaufläden, und in den oberen Geschossen sowie in sämtlichen Geschossen des anstoßenden Seitengebäudes die Räume des „Hotel Terminus". Die anderen Rückgebäude sind in beiden unteren Stockwerken zu Geschäftsräumen ausgebildet; die übrigen Teile enthalten Wohnungen mit verschiedener Zimmerzahl.

Die Bildhauerarbeiten der Fassaden sind von Anton Neumair, die Figuren derselben von E. Beyrer, die Malerarbeiten von Arnold Geschwind, die Gitter und Tore von Ludwig Rueff, die Inneneinrichtungen von den Möbelfabriken Workmann & Co., M. Ballin und Schücker & Sohn, die Beleuchtungskörper von Steinicken & Lohr, sämtlich in München.

Im Hauptgebäude betragen die Lichthöhen im Keller 3,08, im Erdgeschoß 2,95, im Zwischengeschoß 2,65 Meter, die Höhen von Fußboden, Oberkante Erdgeschoß bis desgleichen I. Obergeschoß 6,14, darüber bis desgleichen II. Obergeschoß 3,90, desgleichen im III. und IV. Obergeschoß 3,67 bzw. 3,80, im ausgebauten Dachgeschoß im Lichten 2,90 Meter. Die Oberkante des Hauptgesimses liegt 21,08 Meter über Straßengleiche.

120, 121 [1904; 3, 2]

Die Römisch-Katholische Westminster-Kathedrale in London, nach den Plänen von Architekt John F. Bentley im Aufbau vollendet, ist jüngst in Gebrauch genommen worden, obgleich weder der innere Ausbau noch die geplante musivische Ausschmückung der Böden, Wandungen und Gewölbe fertig gestellt sind, dieselben vielmehr noch längere Jahre in Anspruch nehmen werden. Mit Ausnahme zweier Kapellen: der der Heiligen Gregor und Augustin, steht das ganze Innere noch im Rohbau von unverputzten, ungefugten Backsteinen scheckiger Färbung.

Den ersten Gedanken zum Bau der Kirche hatten schon Kardinal Wieseman und sein Nachfolger, Kardinal Manning gefaßt. Kardinal Vaughan konnte ihn erst in den letzten acht Jahren zur Ausführung bringen lassen. Der Architekt John F. Bentley konnte leider die Vollendung seines Werkes nicht erleben; er verschied im März 1902. Behufs Anstellung der Vorstudien nahm er wiederholt während längerer Zeiten Aufenthalt im Orient, woselbst er sich weniger mit Aufnahmen beschäftigte als mit eifrigen Studien, namentlich bezüglich der räumlichen und der farbigen Wirkung der altbyzantinischen Kirchenbauten.

Die byzantinische Stilfassung ward hauptsächlich gewählt, um die Kirche in möglichstem Gegensatz zu den anglikanischen Kirchen und vor allem zu der nahe gelegenen, alten Westminsterkirche erscheinen zu lassen. Im weiteren erachteten die drei Kardinäle byzantinische Bauweise als die dem reinen, unbeeinflußten Römischkatholizismus geschichtlich und nach ihrer Raum- und Formenbildung am meisten (wenn nicht allein) entsprechend. Auch noch ein praktischer Grund soll für diese Wahl mitbestimmend gewesen sein: nämlich die Rücksicht auf möglichst kurze Ausführungszeit und auf die Möglichkeit, den Bau — wie geschehen — gebrauchsfähig aufzuführen, konstruktive Schmuckformen möglichst zu vermeiden und somit die ganze innere Ausschmückung als Vertäfelung nachträglich, mit dem Zufluß an finanziellen Mitteln fortschreitend herzustellen. Nur die monolithen, polierten Säulen aus prachtvollen Buntmarmorarten aus den alten Justinianischen

Le bâtiment principal sur la Bayerstrasse contient au rez-de-chaussée et à l'entresol des magasins, aux étages supérieurs ainsi qu'à tous les étages de la construction latérale, les locaux de l'hôtel Terminus. Les autres bâtiments de derrière sont disposés dans leurs étages inférieurs en bureaux et comptoirs; les autres parties contiennent des appartements avec un nombre variable de chambres.

Les travaux de sculpture des façades sont de Anton Neumair, les figures de E. Beyrer, les travaux de peinture ont été exécutes par Arnold Geschwind, les grilles et portails par Ludwig Rueff, les décorations intérieures par les fabriques de meubles Workmann & Co., M. Ballin et Schücker & fils, les lustres et appareils d'éclairage par Steinicken & Lohr, tous de Munich.

Dans le bâtiment principal, les hauteurs d'étage comportent, pour la cave 3,08, pour le rez-de-chaussée 2,95, pour l'entresol 2,65 mètres; la hauteur du plancher du rez-de-chaussée au plancher du premier étage comporte 6,14 mètres, du 1er au 2me étage mesuré de la même façon 3,90, de là au 3me 3,67, de là au 4me 3,80 mètres, l'étage du toit mesure dans le vide 2,90 mètres. Le dessus de la corniche se trouve à 21,08 mètres au dessus du niveau de la rue.

120, 121 [1904; 3, 2]

La cathédrale catholique romaine de Westminster à Londres, terminée en son gros œuvre d'après les plans de l'architecte John F. Bentley, a été dernièrement livrée au culte, quoique ni les aménagements intérieurs, ni la décoration de mosaïque projetée pour le sol, les parois et les voûtes ne fussent encore terminées, et que bien au contraire, ces travaux doivent exiger encore de longues années. A l'exception de deux chapelles, celles des Saints Grégoire et Augustin, tout l'intérieur est encore à l'état brut, de maçonnerie de briques non crépissée, non jointoyée et de couleur bigarrée.

Le cardinal Wieseman et son successeur, le cardinal Manning avaient déjà eu la première idée de cette construction. Le cardinal Vaughan ne put se décider à entreprendre l'exécution de la cathédrale que dans les huit dernières années. L'architecte John F. Bentley ne put malheureusement voir son œuvre achevée; il mourut en mars 1902; pour ses études préparatoires il séjourna souvent et longtemps en Orient où il s'occupa moins de faire des relevés, que d'étudier assidûment les effets de proportion des masses et de couleur des anciennes constructions sacrules byzantines.

Le style byzantin fut choisi surtout pour produire un contraste aussi grand que possible avec toutes les églises anglicanes et surtout avec l'ancienne abbaye de Westminster qui se trouve dans le voisinage. D'autre part les trois cardinaux considéraient la structure byzantine comme convenant le mieux, sinon seule, historiquement et artistiquement parlant, par sa forme et son esprit au culte catholique romain pur et libre de toute influence étrangère. Une raison pratique doit aussi, avoir contribué à faire choisir ce style: c'est-à-dire la possibilité de construire le plus vite possible, de livrer, ainsi que cela a eu lieu, le monument à l'exercice du culte sans attendre son achèvement complet, d'éviter toute forme décorative et de procéder à toute la décoration intérieure par revêtements pouvant être appliqués successivement et au fur et à mesure de l'obtention des ressources financières. Seules, les colonnes monolithes polies, de magnifique marbre de couleur provenant des antiques carrières de Justinien sur l'île d'Eubée et en Thessalie, furent placées pendant la con-

The front house has shops on the ground and intermediate floors; the upper floors and those of the entire side buildings being occupied by the rooms of the Hotel Terminus. The backbuildings are in the lower storey let as business premises the upper parts contain flats of various sizes.

The sculpture of the facades is by Anton Neumair, the statuary by E. Beyrer, the painting by Arnold Geschwind, the railings and doors by Ludwig Rueff, the interior equipment by the firms Workmann & Co., M. Ballin and Schücker & Son, the lighting apparatus by Steinicken & Lohr, all of Munich.

The height of the rooms is as follows: In cellar 3,08, ground-floor 2,95, intermediary floor 2,65 meters. From floor of ground-floor, to floor of first storey is 6,14, from there to second storey 3,90, third and fourth 3,67 and 3,80, in roof storey 2,90 meters. The moulding of the roof lies 21,08 meters above the level of the street.

120, 121 [1904; 3, 2]

The Roman Catholic Cathedral in Westminster, London, designed by the late John F. Bentley architect, has been opened for public worship although only the erection is completed. The interior, the floors, the walls and vaulted roof will take several years to complete with mosaïcs according to the architects design. The whole of the interior at present is of unplastered coloured brick-work.

The first idea of the cathedral was in the time of Cardinal Wieseman, his successor Cardinal Manning was also interested in the matter; unfortunately the architect John F. Bentley died in 1902 before the completion of the work. Mr. Bentley had devoted many years to the study of old Byzantine architecture in the East with the idea of adapting the space and colouring of the Cathedral to this style. It was not until the time of Cardinal Vaughan that the plans of the designer could be realised.

The Byzantine ecclesiastical style was decided upon in order to present as strong a contrast as possible to the Anglican churches, more particularly to Westminster Abbey which is close by. In general too, the three Cardinals were agreed that the Byzantine style is more in harmony with pure uninfluenced Roman Catholicism, and that the forms and arrangement of space of this style are historically more, if not exclusively in keeping with Romish traditions. Another practical reason for this choice existed. This was the comparatively short time required for the erection, the possibility of using so to say, the shell of the building for public worship while decorations and completions were added as time and money permitted. By the erection however the splendid monolith polished pillars of coloured marble were placed in their perma-

Brüdien auf Euböa und in Theſſalien, (die ſdion der Sagia Sophia dienten und jetzt von der Firma W. Brindley ausgebeutet werden), mußten beim Aufbau mitverſetzt werden, ebenſo wie ihre aus je einem einzigen Block weißen, karrariſchen Marmors gebildeten Kapitäle, von denen jedes verſdiedene Ausbildung erhielt. Im Äußeren war nur ein Moſaikbild in der großen Bogen-niſdie über dem Sqaupteingang auszuführen, das bereits fertiggeſtellt iſt, während die ſämtlichen übrigen Teile des Äußeren in roten, ſauber-gefugten Feinziegeln und weißem Portland-Kalk-ſtein auszuführen waren.

Da der Bauplatz durch umgebende Säuſer, beſonders in der Länge, zur Anlage einer äußeren Vorhalle ſehr eingeſdiränkt war, ſudite man durch den großen Portalbogen (A) nebſt den beiden Kuppeltürmen für die Weſtfront die entſpredhend großartig feierlidie Erſdheinung zu erzielen. Unter demſelben führen drei Eingangshallen a mit Windfängen b zur inneren Vorhalle (Narthex) B. Eine ſoldie Eingangshalle führt auf der Nord-ſeite ebendahin, und eine weitere mit Windfang auf derſelben Seite und eine auf der Südſeite führen nadi dem Tranſept.

(Zwar ließ ſidi die Orientierung des Baues rituell nidit genau durdiführen, ſondern ſie weidit

struction. Ces matériaux qui trouvèrent déjà leur emploi dans l'église de Sainte Sophie à Constan-tinople sont exploités maintenant par la maison W. Brindley. On monta également de suite les chapitaux de marbre blanc de Carrare d'un seul bloc et traités chacun d'une manière décorative différente. A l'extérieur, il n'y avait à exécuter qu'un seul grand sujet en mosaïque dans le tympan dé l'arcature de l'entrée principale; il est déjà fini, tandis que toutes les autres parties de l'extérieur sont construites en briques rouges finement jointoyées et en pierre calcaire blanche de Portland.

Comme la place etait trop réduite, surtout dans le sens de sa longueur, par les maisons environnantes pour y établir un porche extérieur, on s'efforca d'obtenir sur la façade occidentale, un effet solennel et en rapport avec l'importance du monument, au moyen du grand portail à cintre A, avec les deux tours à coupoles. Sous le grand portail, conduisent trois entrées a avec tambours b dans le porche intérieur B (Narthex). Un porche semblable du côté nord conduit égale-ment à l'intérieur; une autre entrée avec tambour du même côté et une autre encore du côté sud conduisent au transept.

(Il est vrai de dire que l'orientation du mo-nument ne pouvait pas être établie strictement

nent position. These are from the old Justinian quarries in Eubia and Thessaly (formerly in the Haga Sophie) and dug out by the firm W. Brindley. The capitals, each of one single block of white Carrara marble, and each with a separate design, are also placed in position. On the exterior only one mosaic decoration has been carried out on the thympanum of the great arch over the principal entrance. The other parts of the exterior are of red, finely jointed tiles and white Portland limestone.

As the length of the site was very much cramped by the surrounding houses, it was difficult to afford an entrance porch; but a worthy and imposing effect has been achieved by the large portal arch A and the two cupola-crowned towers on the West front. Under this, three entrancess a with porches b lead to an inner porch the Narthex B. Another entrance leads to the North side, another with porch on the same side, and one on the South side, lead to the transept.

(It is true that the position of the east wall is not, as the ritual demands due east, but

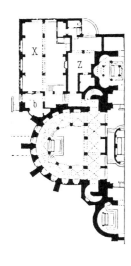
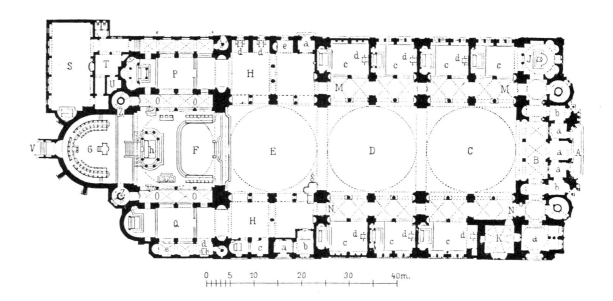

0 5 10   20   30   40m.

bedeutend nadi Südoſt ab. Dodi des leidhteren Verſtändniſſes halber bleibt hier die rituelle Be-zeidinung beibehalten!)

Der Narthex ſdiließt ſidi das aus drei, mit vollen, aus den Zwiðeln der Gurte aufſteigenden Kuppeln überdeðten Feldern C, D, E gebildete Sdiiff (mit Kanzel g) an, das ſeitlidi von den Neben-ſdiffen M, M und N, N begleitet iſt, die wiederum im Tranſept H, H münden, an die wiederum eine Reihe größerer und kleinerer Kapellen c, c von geringerer Sqöhe angelehnt ſind; mit d, d ſind die Beidhtſtühle, mit e Gebetlogen bezeidhnet.

J iſt Taufkapelle; K das Turmgelaß, enthält das Einſdreibebudi. In Fortſetzung des Sdiffes liegt der Sqohe Chor F (Sanctuary), um ſedis Stufen erhöht, mit dem um weitere drei Stufen erhöhten Platz für den Sqochaltar h. Audi dieſer Raum iſt von einer Kuppel überdeðt, die aber durdi adit Fenſter mit Stidikappen helles Licht einfallen läßt; da audi die ſeitlidien Gänge O, O im Oberen hohe Stidibogenfenſter haben, ſo iſt dieſer Raum der hellſte der Anlage. Dahinter folgen die Apſis G, die wiederum um 16+2 Stufen erhöht liegt, und darunter eine geräumige, helle Krypta, von den Wendeltreppen aus zugänglidi.

Von der Apſis führt ein bedeðter Gang V zum Kloſter bezw. dem erzbiſdhöflidien Palais.

d'après les règles du rite, mais que l'axe dévie sensiblement du côté du sud-est. Cependant, pour faciliter la compréhension de la description, nous conserverons la désignation rituelle!)

La grande nef formée par les trois champs C, D, E couverts de coupoles pleines, portées par les pendentifs et les arcs fait suite au narthex. La grande nef où se trouve la chaire g, est bordée par les bas côtés M, M et N, N qui débouchent dans le transept; une ligne de petites chapelles c, c de peu de hauteur est adossée aux bas côtés; les confessionaux sont indiqués par d, d, les prie-Dieu par e.

J est la chapelle baptismale, K la salle de la tour qui contient le livre d'inscriptions. Dans le prolongement de la grande nef se trouve le sanctuaire ou chœur de six marches avec le maître-autel plus élevé lui-même de trois marches. Cette partie est aussi voutée d'une coupole, qui percée de huit fenêtres en capuches, laisse pénétrer une vive lumière. Comme les passages latéraux O, O ont aussi de hautes fenêtres à arc surbaissé dans leur partie supérieure, cette partie est la plus claire de l'église. En arrière suivent l'abside G qui est élevée de 16+2 degrés, au dessous une crypte vaste et bien éclairée, accessible par escaliers tournants.

actually nearly South East, but it is considered to be the East end of the cathedral.)

The Narthex joins the nave (with chancel g) divided into three parts each roofed by a cupola rising from the spandrels of the string-courses; the aisles are M, M and N, N which lead to the transept H, H and which also lead to a number of larger and smaller chapels c, c not very lofty; d, d are the confessional boxes and e the prayer chambers.

I is the baptistery, K the Tower which contains the registration volume. In the continuation of the nave is the High Choir, the Sanctuary raised on six steps — a further ascent of three steps leads tho the high altar h. This space is roofed by a cupola through the light windows of which clear daylight falls; as the side aisles O, O have too, high segmental arched windows this space is the best lighted of the whole cathedral. Behind this is the apsis G, which is raised by 16 + 2 steps, and under which a roomy light crypt is reached by winding stair-cases.

From the apsis a covered way V leads to a cloister and thence to the archbishop's Palace.

Neben F bezüglich den Gängen O,O liegen südlich P die Herz-Jesu- und nördlich Q die Madonnen-Kapelle. Durch einen niedrigen Seitengang f,f gelangt man zur Vorsakristei T mit dem Schatzschrank U und dann zur Hauptsakristei S. Letztere hat im Untergeschoß den Raum X für Arbeitsleistungen und einen Lagerraum Z mit Schatzkammer.

Die ganze Kirche umzieht eine Empore auf Bogenstellung; im seitlichen Abschluß des Hohen Chors erhebt sich über dieser wieder eine zweite, engere Arkadenstellung.

Das Schiff allein soll 10000 Andächtigen ungehinderten Ausblick auf den Hochaltar gewähren, auch wenn die Seitenschiffe gleichzeitig zu feierlichen Umgängen benutzt werden.

Un passage couvert V, conduit de l'abside au cloître dépendant du palais archiépiscopal. Près de F ou des passages O, O se trouvent au sud la chapelle du Sacré Cœur P, et celle de la Vierge Q. Un passage latéral bas f, f conduit à l'avant sacristie T avec le trésor U et ensuite à la grande sacristie S. Cette dernière possède en sous-sol la salle X destinée aux travaux de parage et un magasin Z avec trésor.

Une galerie sur arcades entoure toute l'église, sur les côtés du chœur élevé monte une seconde étroite galerie à arcades.

La grande nef seule doit offrir à 10000 fidèles un coup d'œil libre sur le maître-autel, même que les collatéraux sont occupés par des processions solennelles.

By F from the aisles O,O lie on the S the chapel Blessed Sacrement and to the north the Lady chapel. A low side aisle f,f leads to the first vestry I with the treasure chamber U and then to the principal sacristy S. Under this is in the lower story a workroom X and a store-room Z with treasure-chamber.

The whole of the church is surrounded by an arched gallery; on the side of the Sanctuary a second pillared gallery with narrow arches is erected.

The nave affords an uninterrupted view of the High Altar to 10000 worshippers, even when the side aisles are used for ceremonial processions.

122, 123, 124 [1904: 4, 5, 6]

Die durch Architekt H. P. Berlage erbaute, im Mai 1903 eröffnete Neue Börse in Amsterdam, hat, wesentlich durch die Schwierigkeit ihrer Fundierung veranlaßt, einen Aufwand von 2 160 000 Mark und die Regulierung ihrer Umgebung weitere 140 000 Mark, also zusammen rund 2 300 000 Mark erfordert. Zur Gründung an Stelle der alten Börse und über dem Dam Rak waren über 5000 Pfähle erforderlich.

Der ganze Bau ist in Backstein mit Architekturstücken aus Sandstein und Granit hergestellt, die Pfeiler von poliertem Granit, die innere Verkleidung der Wandflächen in den Oberlichtsälen größtenteils aus glasierten Steinen. An der Ausführung waren beteiligt: für Bildhauerwerk: L. Zyl und H. Mendes da Corta, für Dekorationsmalerei: A. J. Derkinderen, J. Torop und R. Roland Holst.

122, 123, 124 [1904: 4, 5, 6]

La nouvelle Bourse d'Amsterdam bâtie par Monsieur H. P. Berlage architecte et ouverte en mai 1903 a exigé une dépense de 2 160 000 Marks, occasionnée en grande partie par la difficulté de sa fondation. Le dégagement de ses alentours a coûté de plus 140 000 Marks ce qui fait en tout 2 300 000 Marks. On employa plus de 5000 pilotis pour la fondation à la place de l'ancienne bourse et sur le Dam Rak.

Tout le monument est construit en briques avec les lignes d'architecture de grès et de granit; les piliers sont en granit poli; les revêtements intérieurs des parois dans les salles éclairées par le haut sont pour la plupart en briques émaillées. Ont pris part à l'exécution: pour la sculpture: L. Zyl et H. Mendes da Corta; pour la peinture décorative: A. J. Derkinderen, J. Torop et R. Roland Holst.

Le bâtiment s'étend du Dam (la grande

122, 123, 124 [1904: 4, 5, 6]

The new Bourse in Amsterdam has been built by the architect H. P. Berlage, and was opened in May 1903. The cost amounted to 2 160 000 Marks; a considerable part of this was occasioned by the difficulties of the foundation. The regulation of the surrounding site cost a further sum of 140 000 Marks, so that the total cost was 2 300 000 Marks. In the foundation on the site of the old Bourse and over the Dam Rak more than 5000 piles were necessary.

The whole building is of brick with architectural details in sandstone and granite, the pillars are of polished granite, the interior panelling of the wall surfaces in the sky-lighted halls is principally of glazed stones. The work was carried out by L. Zyl and H. Mendes da Corta for the sculpture, and A. J. Derkinderen,

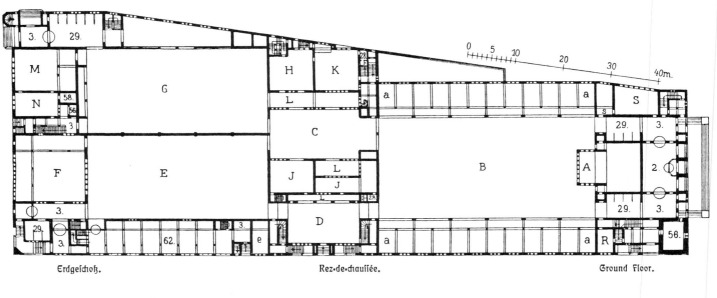

Erdgeschoß. Rez-de-chaussée. Ground Floor.

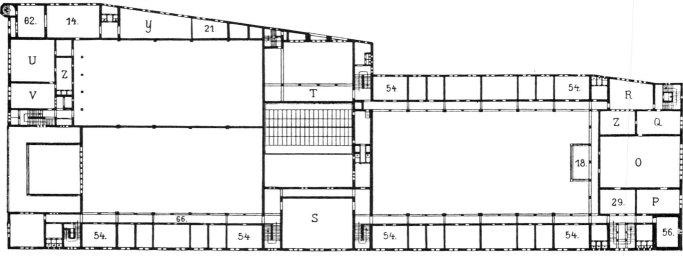

1. Stockwerk. 1. Etage. 1. Floor.

Das Gebäude erſtreckt ſich vom Dam (dem großen Platz vor dem Palais) zwiſchen ziemlich engen Straßen, in nördlicher Richtung nach dem „Y" zu, ſüdlich begrenzt von dem Überreſt des alten Dam Rak, und ſeine dortige Faſſade iſt dem Zentralbahnhof zugekehrt.

An der Nordfaſſade liegen über dem Haupt-eingang die Räume der Handelskammer, deren große Fenſtergruppe nebſt bezüglichen allegoriſchen Reliefs das Hauptfaſſadenmotiv abgeben; den Eck-ſtein des Turmes, gleichſam als ein neues Wahr-zeichen der Stadt, bildet die Statue ihres Be-gründers: Gysbrecht (Gisbert) van Amstel.

Die Raumverteilung iſt folgende*): Im Erd-geſchoß, zunächſt des Eingangs an der Hauptfaſſade, von den Vorräumen umgeben, liegt der „Nach-richtenſaal" A mit einem in den Saal der „Waren-börſe" B vorſpringenden, oben mit Glasplatten ab-gedeckten Erker. Die an den Seitenfronten, unter den Galerien des Börſenſaales ſich bildenden Kojen a, a gewähren Raum für 68 Händler- und Makler ſtände. Nördlich grenzt an den Saal B der ebenfalls mit Glasdach überdeckte „Durch-gangsſaal" C. An dieſem, rechts und links: H Staats- und I Orts-Telephon, J Telegraph und K Poſtbureaus nebſt Schalterräumen L, L. An der Faſſade links: die „Schifferbörſe" D. Saal E nebſt dem unbedeckten, jedoch an zwei Seiten von ge-deckten Hallen umgebenen Hof F bilden die Ge-treidebörſe; dazu gehört noch e das Abrechnungs-zimmer. Der „Effektenbörſe" gehören der Saal G nebſt dem Notierſaal M und dem Loſeſaal N. R iſt eine Rettungswache.

Im I. Obergeſchoß bilden die Säle O, P, Q, R, Z die Räume der Handelskammer, S Verſammlungs-ſaal der Getreidehändler, T desgl. der Effekten-händler und U, V Saal und Bureau für den Verein der Geldhändler. Z ſind die Archive bezeichnet, Y iſt ein Leſeſaal.

Im II. Obergeſchoß liegen an den Straßen-fronten vermietbare Privatkontors gleichwie im I. Obergeſchoß, außerdem noch kleine Verſamm-lungsſäle und eine Anzahl Archive.

Im III. Obergeſchoß befinden ſich noch ein größerer und ein kleinerer Verſammlungsſaal und die Wohnungen der Hauswarte.

Im Untergeſchoß liegen unter den Räumen der Nordfront Bureaus einer Depoſitenanſtalt, deren Schatzkammer ſich unter dem Börſenſaale B in Länge von rd. 34 m bei rd. 6,5 m Breite hin erſtreckt, ringsum von hell erleuchteten, wohl-bewachten Räumen umgeben. Sonſt enthält das-ſelbe außer den Keſſelräumen und der Börſen-druckerei, eine Hauswartwohnung und vermiet-bare Keller an den Straßenfronten.

Place devant le palais) entre des rues passa-blement étroites, du côté du nord vers le „Y", bordé, au sud par les restes de l'ancien Dam Rak, sa façade de ce côté là est tournée vers la gare centrale.

Sur la façade nord, au dessus de l'entrée principale, se trouve la chambre de commerce, dont le grand groupe de fenêtres ainsi que les reliefs allégoriques forment le motif principal de la façade. La statue du fondateur de la ville: Gysbrecht (Gisbert) van Amstel forme la pierre d'angle de la tour, nouvelle silhouette caractéris-tique de la ville.

La disposition des locaux est la suivante*): Au rez-de-chaussée, près de l'entrée de la façade principale, entourée de vestibules, se trouve la salle des nouvelles A, avec un pavillon à plafond vitré, faisant saillie dans la bourse des marchandises B. Les compartiments a, a situés sur les côtés, au dessous des galeries de la salle de la bourse offrent la place à 68 comptoirs de marchands et agents de bourse. La salle de passage C, également recouverte d'un toit vitré, borde au nord la salle B. A droite et à gauche de cette salle C se trouvent: les téléphones d'état H et local I, le télégraphe J et le bureau de poste K avec les guichets L, L. Sur la façade à gauche: la bourse des „bateliers" D. La salle E avec la cour F découverte, mais entourée de deux côtés de halles couvertes forment la bourse des grains, dont fait encore partie la chambre des comptes e. La salle G avec la salle des notes M et la salle de lots N font partie de la bourse des effets. R est un corps de garde de sauvetage.

Au premier étage, les salles O, P, Q, R, Z forment les locaux de la chambre de commerce, S la salle de réunion des marchands de céréales, T celle des marchands d'effets et U, V la salle et le bureau pour la société des changeurs. Z sont les archives, Y la salle de lecture.

Au deuxième étage se trouvent sur les rues de même qu'au premier étage, les comptoirs particuliers à louer, ainsi que de petites salles de comités et un certain nombre de locaux pour archives.

Au troisième étage se trouvent encore une grande et une petite salle de réunion et les appartements des gardiens.

Le sous-sol contient au dessous des locaux de la façade nord, une administration de dépôts dont le trésor s'étend sur une longueur de 34 mètres et une largeur de 6,5 mètres au dessous de la salle de bourse B; ce local est tout entouré de salles bien claires et bien gardées. A part cela, le sous-sol contient des locaux pour chaudières, une imprimerie de la bourse, un appartement de concierge et des caves à louer sur les faces des rues.

J. Torop and R. Roland Holst for the deco-rative painting.

The building extends from Dam (the large square in front of the Palace) between rather narrow streets in a northerly direction towards the "Y", on the south it is bounded by the remains of the old Dam Rak and the facade on this side faces the Central Railway Station.

In the north facade, over the principal en-trance are the rooms of the Chamber of Com-merce; the large group of windows, with emble-matic allegorical reliefs, form the principal feature of the front facade; the corner stone of the tower is carved into the statue of the founder of the town Gysbrecht (Gisbert) van Amstel, and serves in addition as a town emblem.

The distribution of the room is as follows*): In the ground floor, next to the entrance on the principal facade, and surrounded by the entrance halls is the "News Hall" A with a bay ceiled with glass, and extending into the "Ware Bourse" B. The apartments a a on the side fronts, under the galleries of the Hall of Exchange afford accommodation for 68 sellers and brokers. The "Thoroughfare Hall" C also roofed with glass joins on its north side the Hall B. On this, right and left are H state- and I local-Telephone. J Tele-graph, K Postbureaus with booking offices L L. On the facade to the left is the "Shipping Bourse" D. Hall E together with the uncovered court-yard F surrounded by covered halls, forms the Corn Bourse; to this belongs e the settling room. The "Securities Bourse" is in Hall G and in the Hall for Quotations M. The lots-room is N. R is a assistancy-station.

In the first upper storeys the Halls O, P. Q, R, Z are the rooms of the Chamber Of Commerce. S is the meeting room of the Corn merchants, T that of the effects merchants and U, V are hall and bureau for the money merchants. Z are reserved for archives, Y is a Reading room.

In the second upper storey on the street front are rentable private offices as in the first upper storey, in addition are small meeting rooms and some of the archives.

In the third upper storey are a large and a small meeting hall, and the lodging of the custodian.

In the basement under the bureaus on the north front is a deposit room, the treasure chamber of which extends under the Bourse Hall in length 34 metres and in breadth 6,5 metres, surrounded by well lighted carefully watched premises. In the same basement are boiler-room, the Bourse printing-press, a lodging for the porter and ren-table cellars facing the street.

125 [1904; 7]

Der Neubau des Geſchäftshauſes „Rudolf Moſſe" in Berlin SW., Jeruſalemer-ſtraße 46—47 und Schützenſtraße 20—25, iſt in Zeit von 2³/₄ Jahren durch die Architekten Cremer und Wolffenſtein ausgeführt und im September 1903 beendet worden. Die Koſten belaufen ſich auf 1 150 000 Mark, ausſchließlich der bisher von ſieben älteren Gebäuden einge-nommenen Bauſtelle.

Das Gebäude zerfällt in zwei, äußerlich wie im Innern genau ſich kennzeichnende Teile: in das den Hof I umſchließende Eckgebäude, den Re-daktionsbau und den in der Flucht der Schützen-ſtraße ſich anſchließenden Teil mit den Höfen II und III, die Druckerei.

Im Eckgebäude liegen: im Untergeſchoß links die Räume für die Expedition, rechts die für Ver-kauf der Verlagswerke, im Erdgeſchoß links die

125 [1904; 7]

Le nouvel établissement „Rudolf Mosse" Jerusalemerstrasse 46-47 et Schützen-strasse 20-25 à Berlin SW. a été construite dans l'espace de deux ans et trois quarts par les architectes Cremer et Wolffenstein et terminée en septembre 1903. Les frais s'élevèrent à 1 150 000 Marks, non compris l'achat du terrain occupé auparavant par sept anciennes construc-tions.

Le bâtiment se compose de deux parties distinctes à l'intérieur comme à l'extérieur. Dans le corps de bâtiment d'angle entourant la cour I, se trouve la rédaction, et dans l'aile adjacente longeant la Schützenstrasse et comprenant les cours II et III, l'imprimerie.

Le bâtiment d'angle contient au sous-sol à gauche, les locaux pour l'expédition, à droite ceux pour la vente des livres, au rez-de-chaussée à gauche les bureaux pour les annonces, à droite ceux pour le commerce d'édition. Tout le premier

125 [1904; 7]

The new building of the business house "Rudolf Mosse" Berlin SW., Jerusa-lemerstrasse 46—47 and Schützenstrasse 20—25 has been built by the architects Cremer and Wolffenstein during a period of 2³/₄ years ending in September 1903. The cost amounted to 1 150 000 Marks exclusive of the site which was formerly occupied by seven old buildings.

The building, both in its exterior and interior is in two separate parts. In courtyard I sur-rounded by the corner building are the editorial offices, and the second part is in the Schützen-strasse with the courtyards II and III, and is devoted to the printing offices.

In the corner building lie the following rooms: In the basement are the rooms for the expedition office, on the right the sale rooms for the pub-lished works; on the ground floor to the left are the Advertisement bureaus, on the right the

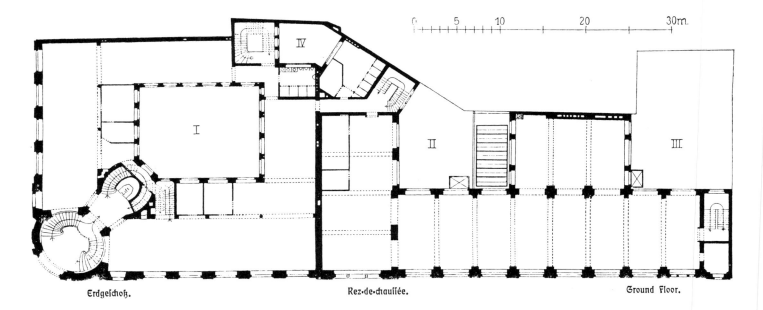

Erdgeschoß.   Rez-de-chaussée.   Ground Floor.

Bureaus für den Annoncenverkehr, rechts desgleichen für das Verlagsgeschäft. Das ganze erste Obergeschoß wird von den verschiedenen Zeitungs-Redaktions-Abteilungen beansprucht, deren Bibliothek im rechten Seitenflügel liegt. Im II. Obergeschoß liegen die Verwaltungsbureaus, und im III. die der Redaktion des Reichsadreßbuches. In dem Teil rechts der Brandmauer liegen: im Untergeschoß die Schnellpressen, im Erdgeschoß die Buchbinderei, im I. Obergeschoß der Setzersaal und (zwischen den Höfen II und III) der Stereotypierraum. Das II. und III. Obergeschoß wird von den Rotationsmaschinen eingenommen.

Äußerlich ist das Redaktionsgebäude als das eines Welthauses recht wirksam durch die über dem Eingang angelegte Warte mit den beiden Pilonen (als Nachrichtenempfangsstation) und den sinnigen Darstellungen des schönen Bronzereliefs gekennzeichnet. Die Fassaden sind aus hellgelbem schlesischen Sandstein von Steinmetzmeister Schilling, das Bildwerk durch Bildhauer Westphal ausgeführt, nach dessen Modell auch das Bronzerelief in der Kunsttreiberei von Lind Nachfolger (Kriga) hergestellt worden ist. Held & Franke führten das Mauerwerk aus, Tischler Klempau und Aschenbach die Schreinerarbeit, Kimbel & Friederichsen die Kunsttischlerei. Das Kunstschlosserwerk stammt von Puls, Marcus und Franke; die Malerarbeiten sind von Walter & Senftleben ausgeführt.

étage est occupé par les services des rédactions des journaux, dont la bibliothèque se trouve dans l'aile latérale droite. Au deuxième étage se trouvent les bureaux d'administration et au troisième la rédaction de l'Annuaire commercial de l'Allemagne. La partie à droite du mur mitoyen contient: au sous-sol les presses rapides, au rez-de-chaussée les ateliers de reliure, au premier étage la salle de composition et entre les cours I et II le local pour la stéréotypie. Le deuxième et le troisième étages sont occupés par les machines à rotation.

A l'extérieur, le bâtiment de rédaction est, comme maison universelle, caractérisé par la tour avec les deux pilones (effigie station de réception des nouvelles) et par les représentations ingénieuses du beau relief de bronze. Les façades sont en pierre de grès jaune clair de Silésie, livrées par le maître tailleur de pierres Schilling; la sculpture a été exécutée par le sculpteur Westphal; c'est d'après ses modèles que fut exécuté le relief de bronze dans l'établissement artistique de Lind successeur (Kriga). Held & Franke exécutèrent la maçonnerie, les maître menuisiers Klempau et Aschenbach la menuiserie, Kimbel & Friederichsen furent chargés de l'ébénisterie artistique. La serrurerie artistique est l'œuvre de Puls, Marcus et Franke. Les travaux de peinture sont de Walter & Senftleben.

publishing offices. The whole of the first floor is occupied by the different editorial departments of the newspapers, the library lying in the right side wing. In the second upper storey lie the administrative bureaus and on the third the editorial office of the German Directory. On the right side of the fire-wall: in the basement are the printing presses, on the ground floor is the book-binding department, in the first upper storey the type-setting rooms and (between courtyards II and III) the stereotyping department. The second and third floors are occupied by rotation machines.

The exterior of the editorial building is, as befits a house of world-wide reputation, very effectively carried out. Over the entrance are figures which represent the watch of a sentinel with two obelises (Pilonen) as "News Receivers"; the beautiful bronze reliefs add not a little to the general effect. The facades are of light yellow sandstone from the stone-mason Schilling, the sculpture is by Westphal who also supplied the model of the bronze relief in the Art Department by Lind successor (Kriga). Held & Franke carried out the brick work, Klempau and Aschenbach the wood work, Kimbel and Friederichsen the artistic carving. The iron work is by Puls, Marcus and Franke, the painting by Walter & Senftleben.

126 [1904: 13]

Der „Industriepalast" in Berlin, Lindenstraße 3, ist vom 1. Oktober 1902 bis 1. Oktober 1903 durch Baumeister Kurt Berndt, mit Fassade von Architekt A. F. M. Lange, mit einem

126 [1904: 13]

La maison „Industriepalast" Lindenstrasse 3 à Berlin à été construite du premier octobre 1902 jusqu'an premier octobre 1903 par l'entrepreneur Kurt Berndt pour la somme

126 [1904: 13]

The "Industrie Palast" in Berlin, Lindenstrasse 3 was built from 1 October 1902 to 1 October 1903 by the building master Kurt Berndt with a facade by the architect A. F. M.

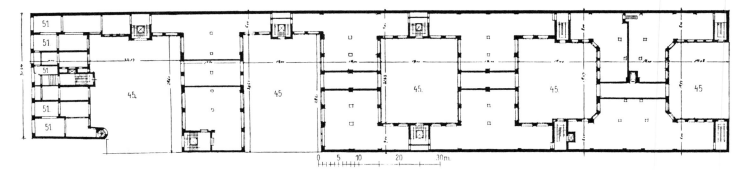

Kostenaufwande von 2 000 000 Mark erbaut worden. Die Fassade des Erdgeschosses ist aus Cottaer Sandstein hergestellt, die der oberen Geschosse und des Giebels aus bräunlichgrauen Verblendern in Blockverband mit Architektur- und Zierteilen, sowie den Figuren aus Terrakotta gleicher, aber lichterer

de 2 000 000 Marks. La façade a été composée par Monsieur A. F. M. Lange architecte; au rez-de-chaussée, elle est en pierre de Cotta, aux étages supérieurs et au fronton en briques apparentes d'un gris brunâtre; les lignes d'architecture et les ornements ainsi que les figures

Lange. The cost amounted to 2 000 000 Marks. The facade of the ground floor is of Cotta sandstone the upper storeys and the gables are of browngrey facing stones ornamented with architectural details, the terra-cotta figures are of

Färbung. Die Schaufensterausbauten sind in echter Bronze, die Gitter in reicher Vergoldung aus Schmiedeeisen ausgeführt.

Das Bildhauerwerk stammt aus den Werkstätten von Robert Schirmer, die Malereien sind von Maler Schwarz, die Schlosserarbeiten von R. Blume ausgeführt. Die Verblendsteine und Terrakotten wurden von den Siegersdorfer Werken geliefert.

Der Giebelschmuck soll darauf hinweisen, daß außer den Wohnungen an der Fassade, das Bauwerk in seinen hinteren Teilen wesentlich industriellen Betrieben und großen Buchdruckereien dient, so z. B. der Druckerei der „Nationalzeitung".

sont en terre-cuite de même couleur, mais d'une nuance plus claire. Les devantures de magasin sont en vrai bronze; les balustrades en fer forgé sont richement dorées.

La décoration sculpturale sort des ateliers de Robert Schirmer; les peintures sont du peintre Schwarz, la serrurerie a été exécutée par R. Blume. Les briques et les Terre-Cuites ont été livrées par la tuilerie de Siegersdorf.

La décoration du fronton doit indiquer que derrière les appartements situés sur la façade, l'édifice contient sur ses derrières, surtout des installations industrielles, et de grandes imprimeries, ainsi par exemple celle de la „Nationalzeitung".

the same colour of a lighter shade. The shop-window extensions are of bronze, the railings of wrought iron are richly gilded.

The sculpture is by Robert Schirmer, the paintings by the painter Schwarz, the iron work by R. Blume. The facing-stones and terra-cotta are from the Siegersdorfer works.

The ornaments of the gables are so arranged as to give notice of the business premises at the back of the building. The facade is devoted to dwellings, but in the back premises are large printing offices etc. e. g. the printing office of the "National Zeitung".

127 [1904: 50]

Da das an der Lindenstraße 20—21 in Berlin gelegene ältere Geschäftshaus der Allgemeinen Versicherungs · Aktien · Gesellschaft

127 [1904: 50]

Comme l'ancienne maison de la société générale d'assurances par actions Victoria Lindenstrasse 20—21 à Berlin ne suffisait plus

127 [1904: 50]

The old business house of the "Allgemeine Versicherungs-Aktien-Gesellschaft Victoria" situated in the Lindenstrasse 20 and 21

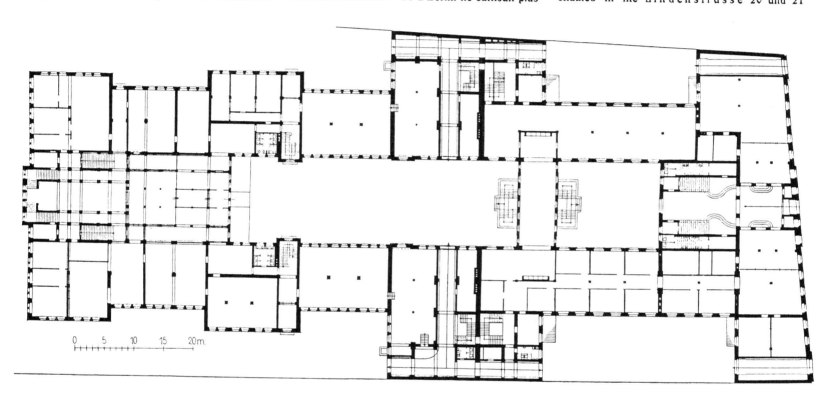

0 5 10 15 20m.

Victoria dem ausgedehnten Betrieb nicht mehr genügte, erwarb die Gesellschaft das bis zur Alten Jakobstraße reichende Hinterland und ließ nach Abbruch der Häuser Alte Jakobstraße 130—132 nach den Plänen des Regierungsbaumeisters Wilhelm Walther in den Jahren 1902—1904 ein neues Gebäude errichten, dessen Front der zuletzt genannten Straße zugekehrt ist. Die ganz in bayerischem Kalkstein ausgeführte Fassade bewegt sich in kräftigen Barockformen mit reichem plastischen Schmuck, der sich besonders auf das Mittelrisalit und die beiden Eckrisalite konzentriert. Im Mittelrisalit treten die beiden oberen Geschosse hinter vier Säulen zurück, deren Schäfte mit Bossagenbändern umschnürt sind. Darüber steigt ein Giebelbau empor, dessen Gebälk von vier Atlanten getragen wird.

Sämtliche vier Stockwerke enthalten Geschäfts- und Bureauräume. Im Erdgeschoß (siehe den Grundriß) sind links von dem geräumigen Vestibül der Raum für das Publikum, die Hauptkasse, die Buchhalterei und die Registratur, rechts vom Vestibül Bureauräume angeordnet. Weitere Bureauräume und die Tresors gruppieren sich um den Hof des Neubaues, von dem man durch einen zweiten Hof zu dem älteren Gebäude an der Lindenstraße gelangt.

à l'accroissement des affaires, la société se rendit acquéreuse des terrains situés en arrière de ses immeubles et s'étendant jusqu'à l'ancienne Jacob-strasse; elle fit élever sur ces terrains, d'après les plans de l'architecte du gouvernement Wilhelm Walther, pendant les années 1902 et 1903 un nouveau bâtiment dont la façade principale est située sur cette dernière rue. La façade principale toute en pierre calcaire de Bavière est traitée dans les formes puissantes de l'architecture baroque avec une riche décoration plastique lequel se concentre particulièrement sur le corps central et les deux ailes. Au corps central, les deux étages supérieurs sont situés en retrait de quatre colonnes dont les fûts sont cerclés de cintres de bossage. Au dessus de ces colonnes s'élève un fronton dont la corniche est portée par quatre atlantes.

Tous les quatre étages contiennent des locaux pour comptoirs et bureaux. Au rez-de-chaussée (voyez le plan) se trouvent à gauche du vaste vestibule, l'espace pour le public, la caisse principale, la tenue des livres et la régistrature, à droite du vestibule sont disposés les bureaux. D'autres bureaux et les trésors sont groupés autour de la cour du nouveau bâtiment duquel on peut atteindre l'ancienne maison de la Lindenstrasse en passant par une seconde cour.

Berlin, has been found insufficient for the greatly increased business of the Company. To provide further accommodation, the Company has acquired the back premises reaching down to the Alte Jakobstrasse, numbers 130—132 of which street had to be pulled down to make room for the new buildings. The design is by the Regierungsbaumeister Wilhelm Walther, it was built from 1902 to 1904; and the principal frontage is now in the Alte Jakobstrasse. The facade is entirely of Bavarian limestone, is of barock style with rich sculptural ornamentation. Particularly noticeable are the ornamental parts of the centre risalto and the two corner risaltos. In the middle risalto, the two upper stories are partially hidden by four pillars, the shafts of which are embossed. From this rises the gables, the timber-work of which is ornamented by four "Atlas" figures.

All four stories are used for business and bureau purposes. On the ground floor (see ground-plan) left from the spacious vestibule, are the rooms for the public, the principal cash, the bookkeeping department and the registry; on the right of the vestibule are bureaus. Other bureaus and the tresors are arranged round the courtyard of the new building, through which one can go to a second courtyard, belonging to the old building and thence to the Lindenstrasse.

In allen Stockwerken ausschließlich Geschäftszwecken dient das Haus in der Lindenstraße 69 in Berlin, das vom 1. Oktober 1901 bis Ende September 1902 durch Baumeister Kurt Berndt, mit Fassade von Architekt A. F. M. Lange, mit einem Kostenaufwande von 700000 Mark erbaut wurde. Die Fassaden des Erdgeschosses und des ersten Obergeschosses sind in Cottaer Sandstein, die der übrigen Geschosse in Zementputz mit Zementguß ausgeführt. Der plastische Schmuck ist aus der Bildhauerwerkstatt von Robert Schirmer.

Das hinter dem Vorderhaus gelegene Grundstück, das eine beträchtliche Tiefe hat, ist für Hintergebäude ausgenutzt worden, die ebenfalls meist geschäftlichen und industriellen Zwecken dienen.

La maison de la Lindenstrasse 69 à Berlin, construite du 1 octobre 1901 à fin septembre 1902 par l'entrepreneur Kurt Berndt avec les façades composées par Monsieur A. F. M. Lange architecte, a coûté 700000 Marks, elle est occupée exclusivement dans tous ses étages par des locaux de commerce. Les façades du rez-de-chaussée et du premier étage sont en grès de Cotta, aux autres étages en maçonnerie crépie au ciment avec ornements en stuc. La décoration plastique sort des ateliers de sculpture de Robert Schirmer.

Le terrain situé derrière la maison de devant a une grande profondeur, il a été utilisé pour une maison qui sert presque entièrement à des emplois industriels et commerciaux.

The house, situated Lindenstrasse 69 Berlin, built from 1 October 1901 to September 1902, is entirely devoted to business premises. It was built by the building-master Kurt Berndt (the facades by the architect A. F. M. Lange) at a cost of 700000 Marks. The facades of the ground floor and of the first upper story are of Cotta sand-stone, the other parts are of cement plaster. The statuary is by Robert Schirmer.

The site lying behind the front house is of considerable depth and has been utilized for the back premises, all of which are equipped for business or industrial purposes.

Das von Architekt Oskar Marmorek in Wien, an der Wienstraße 28, am Zusammentreffen mit der Wienzeile erbaute Haus Rüdigerhof ist ganz in moderner Wiener Putzarchitektur mit Sgraffitoornamenten ausgeführt,

La maison Rüdigerhof, bâtie à Vienne, Wienstrasse 28, au point de confluence avec la Wienzeile, par Monsieur Oscar Marmorek architecte, a été exécutée en crépissage, style moderne viennois, avec des ornements en Sgraffito. Les surfaces crépies du rez-de-chaussée et du

The house "Rüdiger Hof" built by architect Oscar Marmorek in Vienna at the junction of the Wienstrasse 28 with the Wienzeile, is an example of modern Vienna plaster architecture with Sgraffito ornaments.

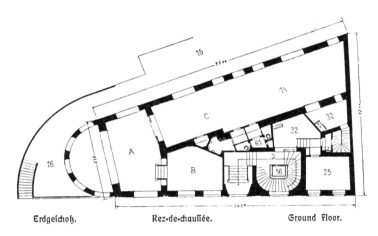

Erdgeschoß.   Rez-de-chaussée.   Ground Floor.

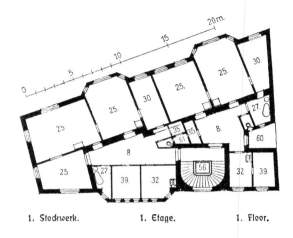

1. Stockwerk.   1. Etage.   1. Floor.

das Erd- und Zwischengeschoß mit wellig gekämmten Putzflächen.

Das mit breiter Terrasse ausgestattete Café im Erdgeschoß hat einen großen Lesesaal A mit einerseits anstoßendem Spielzimmer B, andrerseits den Billardsaal C; die Wirtschaftsnebenräume usw. sind durch die Nebentreppe an der Nachbargrenze zugänglich; die kleine Wohnung an der Wienstraße ist die des Hausbesorgers. Die oberen Geschosse haben je zwei kleine Wohnungen eine von zwei, die andre von drei Stuben und Kabinett, kleiner Küche, Mädchenkammer, Bad usw.

premier étage sont traitées au peigne et en ondulations.

Le café du rez-de-chaussée, pourvu d'une large terrasse, a une grande salle de lecture A, avec une salle de billard adjacente d'un côté C et de l'autre côté la salle de jeu B. Les dépendances du café etc. sont accessibles par l'escalier de service sur la limite voisine; le petit logement sur la Wienstrasse est celui du concierge. Les étages supérieurs contiennent chacun deux petits appartements, l'un de deux, l'autre de trois chambres avec cabinet, petite cuisine, chambre de bonne, bain etc.

The ground and intermediate storey are of ribbed plaster surfaces.

The café on the ground floor has a large reading room A with an adjoining card-room B on the other side is a billiard room C. The household offices etc. are reached by a secondary stair-case; the small lodging in the Wienstrasse is intended for the house porter. The upper storeys have each two small lodgings one with two rooms the other with three rooms each with cabinet, small kitchen, servant's bedroom, bath etc.

Auf Grund eines engeren Wettbewerbes zwischen den Wiener Theaterarchitekten Fellner und Helmer und dem Berliner Heinrich Seeling, der sich ebenfalls bereits durch eine Reihe von Bauten in diesem Spezialfach bewährt hatte, wurde letzterem die Ausführung eines neuen städtischen Schauspielhauses in Frankfurt a. M. übertragen, da das alte den Bedürfnissen der Gegenwart und dem Wachstum der Bevölkerung längst nicht mehr genügte. Das Programm forderte ein Haus für Schau- und Lustspiel und für die kleine Spieloper; der Zuschauerraum sollte nicht mehr als 1200 Plätze enthalten, deren Zahl sich bei der Ausführung auf 1226 erhöht hat (davon 1120 Sitzplätze und 106 Stehplätze). Um den zur Verfügung gestellten Bauplatz am Gallustor nach Möglichkeit auszunutzen, hat der Architekt, wie aus dem Grundriß ersichtlich ist, das Theater rechts an der Untermain-Anlage und links eine Gruppe von Miethäusern (V) für Wohn- und

A la suite d'un concours restreint entre Fellner et Helmer de Vienne, architectes spécialistes pour théâtres d'une part, et Henry Seeling architecte à Berlin d'autre part, la construction du théâtre de la ville de Francfort s. M. fut confiée à ce dernier, lequel s'est aussi déjà distingué comme spécialiste dans de nombreuses constructions de ce genre. L'ancienne salle de Francfort ne suffisait plus, ni aux exigences modernes, ni à l'accroissement de la population. Le programme exigeait un théâtre pour la tragédie et la comédie, ainsi que pour les petits opéras; la salle ne devait pas contenir plus de 1200 spectateurs, dont le nombre s'est cependant élevé pendant la construction à 1226 (dont 1120 places assises et 106 debout). Pour utiliser le plus avantageusement possible le terrain situé au Gallustor, l'architecte a, ainsi que le montre le plan, disposé son bâtiment avec le parc du Main à droite et un groupe de maisons à loyer

The old theatre in Frankfort on Main had been for some time insufficient for modern requirements and for the largely increased population of the town. An open competition for the design of a new theatre resulted in a choice between the design of the Vienna theatre architects Fellner and Helmer, and that of. Heinrich Seeling of Berlin an architect already celebrated in this special branch, and to whom the preference was given. The requirements were, a house suitable for the representation of tragedy, of comedy and of operettas; the auditorium was not to contain more than 1200 places. (The actual number is 1226; of which 1120 are seats and 106 standing places.) In order to utilize the site on Gallustor to the utmost the architect, as may be seen from the ground-plan, has provided for the erection of dwelling-houses (V) on the right by the Untermain place and on the left, of which some are

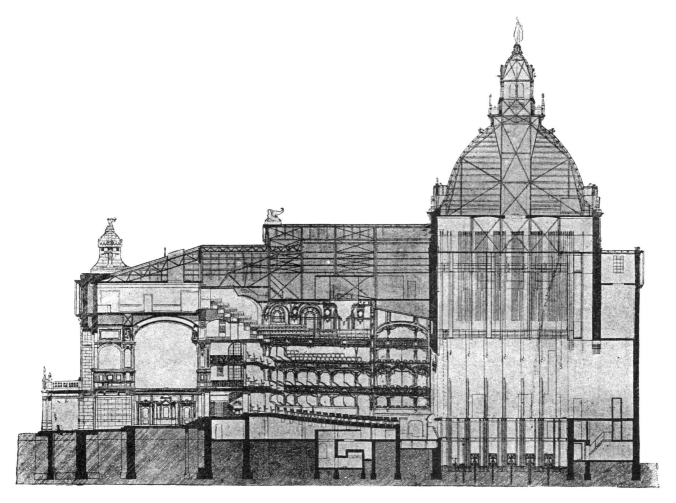

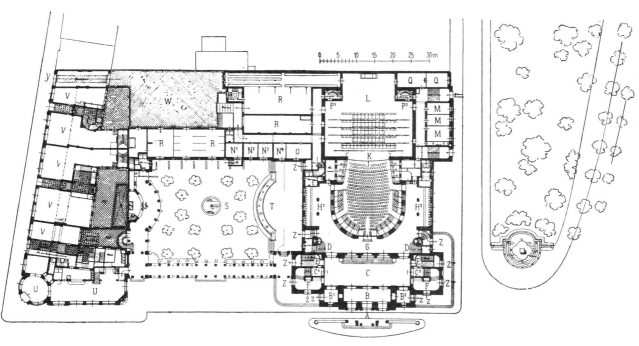

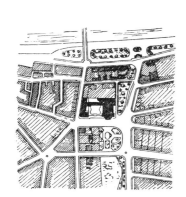

Situation.

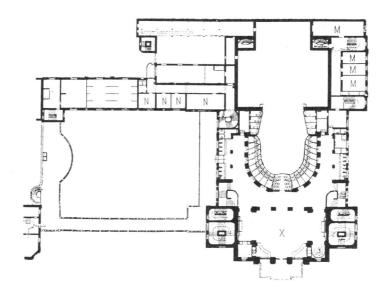

Geſchäftszwecke angeordnet. Beide Baugruppen umſchließen einen Garten (S), der ſowohl vom Theater wie von dem im linken Eckhauſe gelegenen Reſtaurant (U) zugänglich iſt und gegen die Straße durch eine Säulenhalle begrenzt wird. An der Gartenſeite des Theaters iſt eine große erhöhte Terraſſe (T) für die Beſucher des Parketts angelegt worden, und über ihr befindet ſich in der Höhe des erſten Ranges ein Balkon von etwa 25 Metern Länge und 5 Metern Tiefe.

Da das Grundſtück ſich mit der Rückſeite gegen ein Nachbargrundſtück lehnt, konnte der rückwärtige Teil für die Zwecke des Bühnenbetriebs in bequemer Weiſe ausgenußt werden. Längs des Gartens wurde ein Seitenflügel für die Magazine (R) bis an die Miethäuſer vorgeſchoben und hinter dieſem ein Wirtſchaftshof für den Bühnenbetrieb (W) angelegt, zu dem eine breite Durchfahrt (V) von der Neuen Mainzer Straße führt.

Der Zuſchauerraum enthält über dem Parkett drei Ränge. Das Parkett iſt in drei Abteilungen gegliedert und auf jeder Seite von zwölf Logen umgeben. Der erſte Rang, der nur Logen enthält, iſt durch zwei Treppen (D) vom Umgang des Parketts aus zugänglich; die Zugänge zu den Treppen, die zum zweiten und dritten Rang führen (E u. F), befinden ſich an den Schmalſeiten der Eintrittshalle.

Das Foyer (Erfriſchungsraum) ſchließt ſich unmittelbar an den Umgang des erſten Ranges an (X). Von den Umgängen des zweiten Ranges führen beſondere Treppen zum Foyer hinab, und auch der Umgang des dritten Ranges iſt gegen das Foyer geöffnet. Für die Galerie iſt über dem Foyer ein großer Vorſaal mit Büfett angeordnet.

Der Zuſchauerraum hat eine Breite von 18,14 Metern, in Parketthöhe bis zum Vorhang eine Länge von 23 Metern und eine mittlere Höhe von 15 Metern; die Bühnenöffnung iſt 10,5 Meter weit. Die Bühne (K) iſt 24 Meter breit, 15,75 Meter tief und mit einer 14,30 Meter breiten und 8 Meter tiefen Hinterbühne (L) verſehen.

Die in frei behandelten Renaiſſanceformen ſich bewegende Außenarchitektur iſt teils in Sandſtein aus Schönbrunn in Baden, teils in Pußbau ausgeführt. Die über dem Bühnenraum bis zu einer Höhe von 54 Metern aufſteigende Kuppel hat dem Stadtbilde von Frankfurt a. M., das an hervorſtechenden Punkten nicht reich iſt, einen charaktervollen Zug hinzugefügt.

An der bildneriſchen Ausſchmükung des Theaters waren zahlreiche künſtleriſche Kräfte beteiligt. Varneſi in Frankfurt a. M. fertigte die Gruppen der Poeſie an der Vorderfront, die beiden Relieffiguren des Luſtſpiels und der Tragödie an den Mittelpfeilern oberhalb der Einfahrt, die Reliefs an der rechten Seitenfront und den hauptſächlichſten ornamentalen Frontſchmuck. Das Relief des Giebeldreiecks iſt von Fritz Klimſch in Berlin, das Modell des den Hauptgiebel krönenden, in Kupfer getriebenen Panthergeſpanns und die Koloſſalbüſten von Goethe und Schiller an der Vorderfront ſind von Ferdinand Krüger in Berlin ausgeführt worden. Das Modell der in Kupfer getriebenen und vergoldeten Figur der die Kunſt beſchirmenden Stadt Frankfurt, die ſich auf der Laterne der Kuppel erhebt, hat Bildhauer Herold gefertigt. Profeſſor Hausmann in Frankfurt a. M. hat die Gruppe der Wahrheit an der Vorderfront, die Reliefs an der linken Seitenfront und den figürlichen und ornamentalen Schmuck des Foyers geſchaffen.

Nach dreieinhalbjähriger Bauzeit iſt das Theater, das einen Koſtenaufwand von etwa 2575000 Mark erfordert hat, am 1. November 1902 eröffnet worden. In die Koſten einbegriffen iſt eine nachträglich unter dem Wirtſchaftshof des Bühnenhauſes angelegte elektriſche Umformer-Akkumulatorenſtation, die der Stadt gehört.

(V) avec logements et magasins à gauche. Les deux groupes de bâtiments encadrent un jardin (S) accessible aussi bien du théâtre que du restaurant (U) situé dans la maison d'angle; il est séparé de la rue par une colonnade. Du côté du jardin, le théâtre possède une terrasse élevée (T) pour les spectateurs du parquet; au dessus de cette terrasse se trouve à la hauteur du premier rang, un balcon de 25 mètres de longueur sur 5 mètres de profondeur.

Comme le terrain touche sur ses derrières à une place voisine, on pouvait utiliser cette partie d'une façon très pratique pour les dépendances de la scène. Le long du jardin on plaça une aile latérale pour les magasins (R) qui s'étend jusqu'aux maisons de rapport; derrière cette aile se trouve une cour de service (W); un large passage couvert (V) y conduit de la nouvelle Mainzerstrasse.

La salle contient trois galeries au dessus du parterre. Le parterre est divisé en trois parties et est entouré de chaque coté de douze loges. La première galerie qui ne contient que des loges, est praticable par deux escaliers, (D) montant du pourtour du parterre. Les entrées des escaliers conduisant à la deuxième et à la troisième galerie (E et F) se trouvent sur le petit côté de la halle d'entrée.

Le foyer (X), en même temps buffet pour rafraîchissements, s'ouvre immédiatement sur le pourtour du premier balcon. Des escaliers spéciaux conduisent du pourtour de la seconde galerie au foyer; le pourtour de la troisième galerie lui-même est ouvert sur le foyer. Pour l'amphithéâtre on a disposé au dessus du foyer un grand vestibule avec buffet.

La salle a une largeur de 18,14 mètres et une profondeur de 23 mètres, mesurés du haut du parquet jusqu'au rideau et une hauteur moyenne de 15 mètres. L'ouverture de la scène est de 10,50 mètres. La scène (K) a 24 mètres de largeur, 15,75 de profondeur, elle possède une arrière-scène (L) de 14,30 mètres de largeur et de 8 mètres de profondeur.

L'architecture extérieure qui s'inspire librement des formes de la Renaissance, est en partie en pierre, en partie en maçonnerie crépie. La coupole située au dessus de la scène et qui s'élève à la hauteur de 54 mètres a donné une silhouette caractéristique à la ville de Francfort qui n'est pas riche en points saillants.

De nombreux artistes ont prêté leur concours à la décoration plastique au théâtre. Monsieur Varnesi de Francfort exécuta les groupes de la Poésie à la façade principale, les deux figures en relief de la Comédie et de la Tragédie sur les piliers du centre, au dessus de la porte cochère, les reliefs de la façade latérale de gauche, ceux de la façade latérale de droite et la plus grande partie de la décoration ornementale de la façade. Le relief du fronton est de Fritz Klimsch à Berlin; le modèle du chariot tiré par des panthères, groupe en cuivre repoussé, couronnant le grand fronton, ainsi que les bustes colossaux de Goethe et de Schiller sur la façade principale, ont été exécutés par Ferdinand Krüger à Berlin. Le sculpteur Herold a composé le modèle de la ville de Francfort protégeant les arts, groupe doré en cuivre repoussé qui se trouve au dessus de la lanterne de la coupole. Monsieur le professeur Hausmann à Francfort a créé le groupe de la Vérité sur la face principale, les reliefs de la façade latérale à gauche et la décoration figurale et ornementale du foyer.

Le théâtre coûta 2575000 Marks, il fut inauguré le premier novembre 1902, après trois ans et demi de construction. Dans cette somme est comprise une installation électrique avec des accumulateurs transformeurs, située sous la cour de service; cette installation appartient à la ville et a été décrétée après coup.

designed as business houses. Both building-groups are surrounded by a garden (S), which can be reached from the theatre itself, as well as from the restaurant situated in the left corner house (U) and which has a colonnade separating it from the street. On the garden side of the theatre is a raised terrace (T) for the use of the stalls, over this, on the first floor is a large balcony 25 meters long and 5 meters broad.

The back part of the site is conveniently placed for the erection of all the plant necessary for the conducting of the theatre performances and for the necessary premises of the employees. Along the length of the garden is a side wing containing theatre appurtenances (R). Reaching to the dwelling-houses and behind them is a courtyard containing all the equipment for stage-working (W) to which a wide thoroughfare (V) enters from the Neue Mainzer Strasse.

The auditorium contains three tiers of seats over the stalls. The stalls have three divisions and on each side twelve boxes. The dress circle containing only boxes, is reached by two staircases from the corridor of the stalls, the entrances to the staircases leading to the second and third tiers are on the narrow side of the entrance hall (E and F).

The refreshment rooms (X) are near the corridor of the dress-circle. From the corridors of the second tier a special staircase leads down to the refreshment room, the same accommodation is afforded to the third tier. For the gallery is a special refreshment room built over the Foyer.

The auditorium is 18,14 meters broad, from the highest end of the stalls to the stage the length is 23 meters, the height from the middle of the stalls is 15 meters. The stage (K) is 24 meters broad 15,75 deep with a back stage of 14,30 meters broad and 8 meters deep (L).

The exterior is Free Renaissance in style, partly of sandstone and partly plastered. The cupola which reaches a height of 54 meters over the stage room, forms a characteristic feature in the town architecture which is not very rich in such striking buildings.

Many artists were employed in the sculptural decoration of the theatre. Varnesi in Frankfort on Main has formed the group "Poesy" on the front centre, as well as the two figures in relief of Comedy and Tragedy on the middle pillars above the entrance, the reliefs on the right side entrance, and all the principal ornamental statuary of the front. The relief on the three-cornered gable is by Fritz Klimsch of Berlin. The harnessed panthers of hammered copper crowning the principal gable, and the colossal busts of Goethe and Schiller on the middle front are by Ferdinand Krüger of Berlin. The figure of the town of Frankfort as the protectress of Art is of hammered copper and gilded, and was modelled by the sculptor Herold. Professor Hausmann of Frankfort on Main has modelled the group of "Truth" on the middle front, the reliefs on the side entrance (left) and the figures and ornaments of the "foyer".

After a building time of three and half years, and at a cost of 2575000 Marks the theatre was opened on 1 November 1902. Included in the cost is the electric installation, situated under the stage premises, and which belongs to the town.

Die Baukosten des Eckhauses, das mit den beiden sich anschließenden Miethäusern zu einer einheitlichen Architekturgruppe zusammengefaßt ist, der Hallen- und Gartenanlage und der Terrasse betragen etwa 560000 Mark.

An der technischen Ausführung waren hauptsächlich folgende Firmen beteiligt: Aktiengesellschaft Holzmann (Mauer- und Steinmetzarbeiten), Aktiengesellschaft Humboldt in Kalk (Eisenarbeiten), Dyckerhoff & Neumann in Wetzlar (Marmorarbeiten), C. Hoppe in Berlin (maschinelle Bühneneinrichtung), Gebrüder Körting in Hannover (Heizung und Ventilation), Allgemeine Elektrizitätsgesellschaft in Berlin (elektrische Beleuchtung), Schulz & Holdefleiß in Berlin und Wirth in Frankfurt a. M. (Kunstschlosserarbeiten), Glückert in Darmstadt, Niederhofer, Prösler, Abt, Grumbach und H. Jacquet Sohn (Kunsttischlerarbeiten), G. Knodt und H. F. A. Schmidt in Frankfurt a. M. (Kupfertreibarbeit der Bedachung).

Im Grundriß bedeuten: A die Unterfahrt, B die Windfanghalle mit den Windfängen B¹ und B², C die Kassenhalle mit den Kassen C¹ und C², G den Zuschauerraum mit den Kleiderablagen H¹ und H², J das Orchester, M die Herrenankleidezimmer, N die Damenankleidezimmer, O das Konversationszimmer, P¹ und P² die Arbeitertreppen, Q den Requisitenraum und Z die Ausgänge.

La maison d'angle qui forme un ensemble architectural avec les deux maisons de rapport, a coûté avec la colonnade, le jardin et la terrasse 560000 Marks environ.

Les maisons qui ont pris une part particulièrement importante à l'exécution technique de cet édifice sont les suivantes: Holzmann pour la maçonnerie et la pierre de taille; la société par actions Humboldt à Kalk pour les constructions en fer; Dyckerhoff & Neumann à Wetzlar pour les travaux de marbrerie; C. Hoppe à Berlin pour la machinerie de la scène; les frères Körting au Hannovre pour le chauffage et la ventilation; la Allgemeine Electricitätsgesellschaft à Berlin pour l'éclairage électrique; Schulz & Holdefleiss à Berlin et Wirth à Francfort s. M. pour les travaux de serrurerie artistique; Glückert à Darmstadt, Niederhofer, Prösler, Abt, Grumbach et H. Jacquet fils pour la menuiserie artistique; G. Knodt et H. F. A. Schmidt à Francfort s. M. pour les travaux de cuivre repoussé des toitures.

Dans le plan: A signifie entrée pour les voitures, B le tambour avec les portes B¹ et B², C la halle aux guichets de caisse C¹ et C², G la salle de spectacle avec les vestiaires H¹ et H², I l'orchestre, M les garderobes pour messieurs, N les garderobes pour dames; O le salon de conversation, P¹ et P² les escaliers pour les ouvriers, Q les magasins d'accessoires et Z les sorties.

The building of the corner house (which forms with the two adjoining dwelling houses a uniform architectural group), the building of the colonnades, the laying out of the gardens and terrace, cost altogether about 560000 Marks.

In the technical equipment the following firms were employed: Comp. Lim. Holzmann (brick and stone work), Comp. Lim Humboldt in Kalk (iron work), Dyckerhoff & Neumann in Wetzlar (marble-work), C. Hoppe in Berlin (machine stage equipment), Gebrüder Körting in Hannover (heating and ventilation), A. E. G. Berlin (electric light), Schulz & Holdefleiss in Berlin and Wirth in Frankfort on Main (artistic iron work), Glückert in Darmstadt, Niederhofer, Prösler, Abt, Grumbach and H. Jacquet Sohn (wood work), G. Knodt and H. F. A. Schmidt in Frankfort on Main (hammered copper work of the roofing).

The lettering of the ground plan is as follows: A the lower entrance, B the ventilating shaft room with the ventilators B¹ and B², C the booking-offices, with the counters C¹ and C², G the auditorium with the wardrobe corridors H¹ and H², J the orchestra, M Gentlemen's dressing room, N Ladie's dressing room, O Conversation room, P¹ and P² workmen's staircases, Q room for requisites, Z Exits.

132, 133, 134 [1904: 30, 29, 31]

Im Gegensatz zu der malerischen Gruppe des Schauspielhauses in Frankfurt a. M. ist das ebenfalls von Heinrich Seeling erbaute fürstliche Theater in Gera ein geschlossener, auf allen Seiten freistehender Bau. Hier war die Aufgabe dadurch kompliziert worden, daß außer dem Theater noch ein besonderer Konzertsaal nebst Probesaal und Orchesternische, der mit jenem unter einem Dache vereinigt werden sollte, und eine fürstliche Loge mit gesondertem Zugang gefordert waren. Aus den Grundrissen geht hervor, wie der Architekt diese Aufgabe gelöst hat.

Die Mitte des unter dem Konzertsaale (W) liegenden Raumes dient als Eintrittshalle (C) und enthält auch die Kasse (D). Rechts liegt der Saal für Gesang- und Musikproben (G¹), links ein Tagesrestaurant (G), das mit dem davorliegenden Park in Verbindung steht, wo im Sommer Konzerte stattfinden. Die Treppe rechts vom Windfang (E) ist bei Konzerten für den Fürsten vorbehalten, die Treppe links (F) führt zur Galerie des Konzertsaals, der in Saalhöhe 700 Sitzplätze und 114 Stehplätze, in Balkonhöhe 307 Logenplätze und 45 Stehplätze, in den oberen Logen 30 Sitzplätze und 30 Stehplätze enthält, also insgesamt 1226 Zuhörer fassen kann (Tafel 31). Die zum ersten Rang führenden Treppen (H) dienen bei Konzerten zugleich als Hauptzugänge für die Saalhöhe. Der Umgang des ersten Ranges (K) ist an der der Bühne gegenüberliegenden Seite zu einem Foyer (Z) erweitert worden, das bei Konzerten als Vorraum des Saals benutzt wird. Letzterer hat bei einer Breite von 17,30 Metern eine Länge von 45 Metern und eine Höhe von 12,50 Metern. Das Orchesterpodium ist 12 Meter breit und 9,50 Meter tief.

Der Zuschauerraum hat eine Breite von 15,50 Metern und in Parketthöhe eine Tiefe von 19,50 Metern. Er enthält im Parkett 348, im ersten Rang 177 und im zweiten Rang 203 Sitzplätze, wozu noch 90 Sitzplätze und 150 Stehplätze

132, 133, 134 [1904: 30, 29, 31]

Le théâtre princier de Gera, également construit par Henry Seeling, est en opposition avec le groupement pittoresque du théâtre de Francfort, un bâtiment ramassé, libre de tous cotés. Ici, le programme était compliqué par le fait qu'à part le théâtre, une salle de concert avec salle de répétitions et niche pour l'orchestre devaient être logés sous le même toit et que la loge princière devait être accessible par un passage particulier. On voit dans les plans comment l'architecte a résolu ce problème.

Le milieu de l'espace situé sous la salle de concert (W) sert de vestibule (C) et contient aussi la caisse (D). A droite se trouve la salle pour les répétitions de musique et de chant (G¹), à gauche un restaurant de jour (G²), qui est en communication avec le parc situé devant ses fenêtres; en été, il y est donné des concerts. L'escalier à droite du tambour (E) est réservé pour le prince en cas de concert, l'escalier de gauche (F) conduit à la galerie de la salle de concert, celle-ci contient au parterre 700 places assises et 114 places debout, à la hauteur des balcons 307 places de loges et 45 places debout, dans les loges supérieures, 30 places assises et 30 places debout, donc ensemble 1226 auditeurs (Pl. 31). Les escaliers (H) conduisant au premier rang servent également, en cas de concert, de communication principale pour les parties élevées. Le pourtour de la première galerie (K) a été élargi de façon à former un foyer (Z) dans la partie faisant face à la scène; ce foyer sert de vestibule de la salle quand il y a un concert. La salle a une largeur de 17,30 mètres, une longueur de 45 mètres et une hauteur de 12,50 mètres. L'estrade de l'orchestre est large de 12 mètres et profonde de 9,50 mètres.

La salle de spectacle a une largeur de 15,50 mètres et une profondeur mesurée au haut du parquet de 19,50 mètres; elle contient au parterre 348, à la première galerie 177, à la seconde 203 places assises, il faut encore y ajouter 90 places assises et 150 places debout

132, 133, 134 [1904: 30, 29, 31]

The Court theatre in Gera also designed by Heinrich Seeling is a great contrast in its enclosed building standing on all sides free, to the picturesque grouping of the Frankfort theatre. The requirements of the design were here more complicated, for as well as the theatre, there was to be a concert hall with rehearsal saloon and orchestra niche all under one roof, and a box for the court with a separate entrance. The ground-plan shows how the architect has solved the problem.

The middle of the space lying under the Concert-hall (W) serves as entrance hall (C) and contains the booking office (D). On the right is the saloon for singing and playing rehearsals (G¹), on the left a restaurant day (G) connected with the gardens lying in front, in which concerts are given in summer. The staircase to the right of the ventilator (E) is reserved at concerts for the Prince, the staircase left (F) leads to the gallery of the concert hall, which contains on the first floor 700 seats and 114 standing places, on the balcony floor 307 box places and 45 standing places, and in the upper boxes 30 seats and 30 standing places, altogether accommodating 1226 auditors (see plate 31). The staircase leading to the dress circle (H) serves at concerts as the entrance to the first floor of the concert room. The corridor round the dress circle (K) is on the side opposite to the stage, broadened out into a foyer (Z) which serves at concerts as entrance room to the concert hall. This latter has a breadth of 17,30 meters, a length of 45 meters and a height of 12,50 meters. The orchestra podium is 12 meters broad and 9,50 meters deep.

The auditorium has a breadth of 15,50 meters and a depth in the stalls of 19,50 meters. It contains in the stalls 348 seats, in the dress

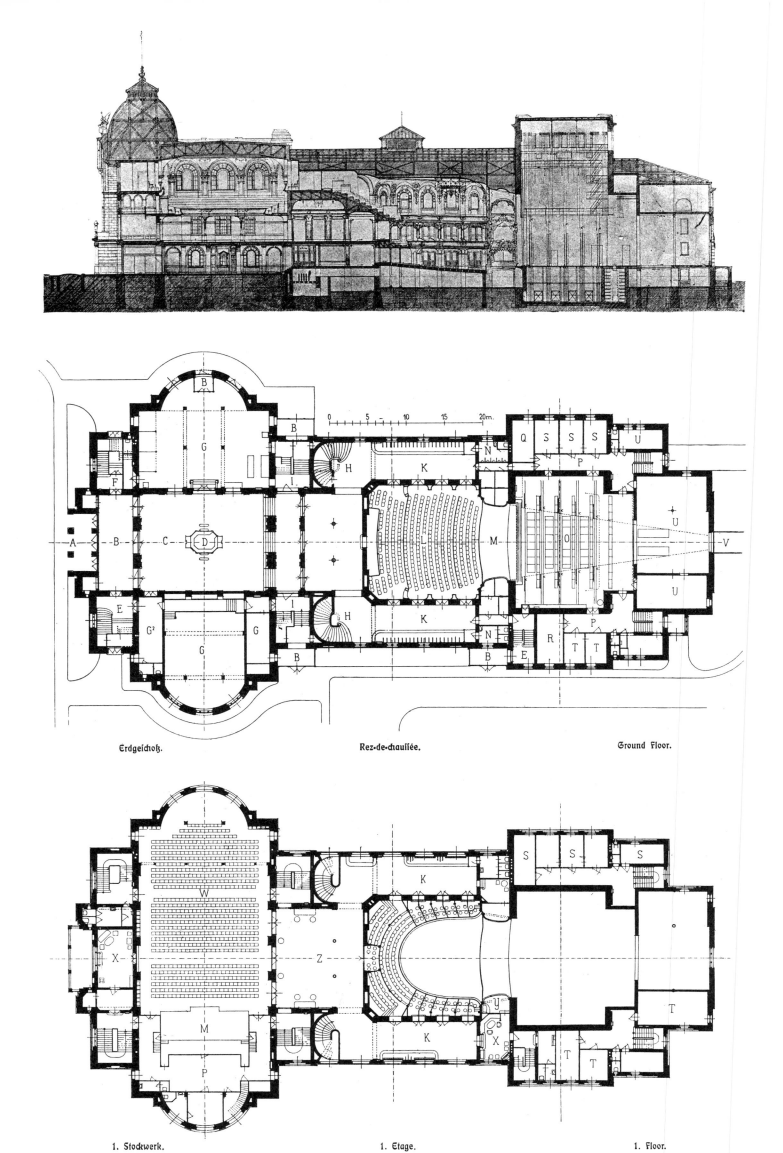

Erdgeſchoß.   Rez-de-chauſſée.   Ground Floor.

1. Stockwerk.   1. Etage.   1. Floor.

in der Galerie des zweiten Ranges kommen, im ganzen alſo 968 Plätze. Die Bühnenöffnung iſt 10,50 Meter weit, die Bühne iſt 18 Meter breit, 15,50 Meter tief und ohne Unterbühne 20,50, mit dieſer 25,50 Meter hoch.

Im Frühjahr 1900 begonnen, iſt das Theater am 18. Oktober 1902 eröffnet worden. Bei Ausführung der Faſſaden in Putzbau mit Verwendung von Sandſtein und Kunſtſtein für die Geſimſe betrugen die Baukoſten 1067349 Mark.

Das Modell für den geflügelten Genius auf dem Hauptgiebel hat Bildhauer A. Meißner in Friedenau gefertigt. Die bildneriſchen Arbeiten im Zuſchauerraum hat Ernſt Weſtpfahl in Berlin, die im Konzertſaal haben Gebrüder Bieber in Berlin ausgeführt. Im übrigen waren an der Ausführung faſt ausſchließlich einheimiſche Kräfte beteiligt.

In den Grundriſſen bedeuten: A Vorhalle, B Windfänge, C^2 Garderobe für die Muſiker, C^3 Notenzimmer, I die Treppen zum zweiten Rang, L Zuſchauerraum, M Orcheſter, N die Toiletten, O die Bühne, P die Korridore, Q Direktorzimmer, R Konverſationszimmer, S Damen-, T Herren-Ankleideräume, U Hinterbühne, Kuliſſenmagazin und Requiſitenraum, V die Rampe, X die fürſtlichen Salons und Y die Fürſtenloge.

de l'amphithéâtre de la seconde galerie, on peut donc compter en tout 968 places. L'ouverture de la scène est de 10,50 mètres de largeur; la scène a 18 mètres de largeur, 15,50 mètres de profondeur et une hauteur de 25,50 mètres.

La construction du théâtre commença au printemps de 1900 et le bâtiment fut ouvert le 18 octobre 1902. Les frais s'élevèrent à 1 067 349 Marks, les façades sont en maçonnerie crépie avec emploi de pierre de taille et de pierre artificielle pour les profils.

Le sculpteur A. Meissner à Friedenau a exécuté le modèle pour le génie ailé qui couronne le fronton principal. Les travaux décoratifs de la salle de spectacle sont de Ernest Westpfahl à Berlin, ceux de la salle de concert sont des frères Bieber à Berlin; à part cela, on n'employa à l'exécution presque exclusivement que des maisons de l'endroit.

Dans les plans: A signifie vestibule, B tambours, C^1 vestiaire pour les musiciens, C^2 chambre des notes, I les escaliers pour la deuxième galerie, L la salle de spectacle, M l'orchestre, N les toilettes, O la scène, P les corridors, Q la chambre du directeur, R le salon de conversation, S garderobe pour dames, T garderobe pour messieurs, U arrière scène, magasin des décors et magasin des accessoires, V la rampe, X les salons princiers et Y la loge princière.

circle 177, in the second tier 203 seats, a gallery contains 90 seats and 150 standing places together 968 seats. The stage opening is 10,50 meters deep, without the under stage 20,50 high, with this, 25,50 meters high.

The theatre was begun in spring 1900 and opened on 18 October 1902. The facades are of plaster with sandstone and artificial stone mouldings, the cost amounted to 1067349 Marks.

The model for the winged "Genius" on the principal gable is by sculptor A. Meissner in Friedenau. The sculptural work in the auditorium is by Ernst Westpfahl of Berlin, that in the concert hall is by Gebrüder Bieber of Berlin. The rest of the work was done by local artists and workers.

The ground plan shows the following lettering: A Entrance hall, B ventilator, C^2 cloakroom for musicians, C^3 Music room, I staircase to second tier, L auditorium, M Orchestra, N Lavatories, O the stage, O the corridors, Q Directors Room, R Conversation room, S Ladies-, T Gentlemens Cloak room, U Backstage, Scene and requisite rooms, V the ramp, X the court saloons, Y the court box.

---

135 [1904; 60]

In Budapeſt machen ſich die Beſtrebungen der Architekten, eine moderne, von der Überlieferung völlig unabhängige Ausdrucksweiſe zu ſchaffen, mit beſonders großer, dem Volkscharakter entſprechender Lebhaftigkeit geltend. Ein bezeichnendes Beiſpiel dafür iſt der von Oedon Lechner aufgeführte Neubau der Königlich ungariſchen Poſtſparkaſſe (Tafel 60). Um die Monotonie des fünfgeſchoſſigen Baues, der in allen Stockwerken Kaſſenzimmer, Bureaus, Verwaltungsräume u. dgl. m. enthält, wirkſam zu bekämpfen, hat der Architekt die drei unterſten Stockwerke und die beiden oberſten durch eine einheitliche Dekoration zuſammengefaßt und beide Gruppen durch einen geſimsartig abgeſetzten, wellenförmigen Streifen geſchieden. Die lebhafte

135 [1904; 60]

La tendance des architectes, de créer une expression nouvelle, entièrement libérée des traditions, adaptée au caractère spécial du peuple est particulièrement accentuée à Budapest. Le nouveau bâtiment des de la Caisse d'épargne de la Post royale construit par Oedon Lechner en donne une preuve caractéristique (Pl. 60). Pour rompre la monotonie inévitable d'un édifice de cinq étages, contenant dans chacun d'eux des comptoirs, des bureaux, des chambres d'administration, l'architecte a embrassé les trois étages du bas d'une part, les deux du haut d'autre part, dans une décoration d'ensemble, puis il a séparé ces deux systèmes par une sorte de bandeau en forme de corniche, orné de lignes ondulées.

135 [1904; 60]

The architects of Budapest seem to be all striving in the one direction of abjuring all conventionality and of adapting their style more and more to the individuality of the Hungarian people. An example of this is the new building of the Royal Hungarian Savings' Bank (plate 60) designed by Oedon Lechner. In order to avoid the monotony inevitable in a 5 storied building each floor of which must contain cash-rooms, bureaus, administration rooms &c, the architect has designed a uniform decoration for the three lower stories and has connected it with that of the two upper stories by a moulding of waving stripes. The facade is

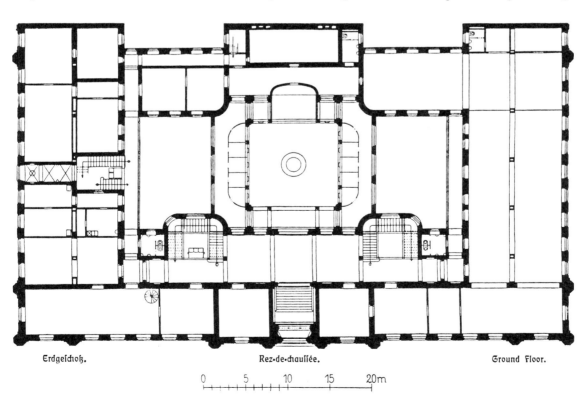

Erdgeſchoß.   Rez-de-chaussée.   Ground Floor.

0   5   10   15   20m

Bewegung der Faſſaden wird noch ſtärker akzentuiert durch die giebelartigen Dachaufſätze mit ihren phantaſtiſchen Endigungen.

Le mouvement très vif des façades est encore accentué par les annexes du toit en forme de pignons avec leurs couronnements phantastiques.

further characteristically decorated by the gable additions to the roof, which give an effective finish to the whole.

136 [1904: 17]

Die Architekten Kármann Aladár & Ullmann Gyula in Budapest erbauten dort binnen Jahresfrist das große Zinshaus Leopoldring 12. Das Haus ist in Backstein mit Steinsandputz zum Preise von 306000 Mark hergestellt. Die Fassade kann als ein glänzendes Beispiel für die reiche Entwicklungsfähigkeit und dekorative Wirkung der aus der Wagnerschule hervorgegangenen Behandlung einfacher Putzarchitektur gelten.

137 [1904: 79]

Rein künstlerische Bestrebungen im Miethäuserbau von Berlin und seiner Nachbarschaft sind immer noch so seltene Erscheinungen, daß eine jede ernster Beachtung würdig ist. Eine solche haben wir in dem von Albert Geßner entworfenen und ausgeführten Miethause in Charlottenburg, Mommsenstraße 6, zu begrüßen, das in der Zeit vom 1. Oktober 1903 bis 1. September 1904 mit einem Kostenaufwande von 396000 Mark erbaut worden ist (Tafel 79).

Durch ihre warme Tönung wie durch ihre individuelle Behandlung hebt sich die Fassade vorteilhaft von ihrer Umgebung ab, obwohl sich das Haus mit seinen vier Stockwerken im übrigen nicht von dem in jener Gegend üblichen Typus unterscheidet. Der warme Ton ist durch mit gelbem Ocker gefärbten Putz erzielt worden, mit dem der in graugelbem Cottaer Sandstein ausgeführte Erker vor dem ersten und zweiten Obergeschoß der linken Fassadenhälfte und die in gleichem Material hergestellte Portaleinfassung und Brüstung des Treppenaufgangs gut zusammengestimmt sind. Dem Hochparterre der rechten Fassadenhälfte ist ein in der Mitte durch einen Balkon durchbrochener Erker vorgelegt, der mit Kupfer gedeckt ist. In Kupfer sind auch die über dem Erker aufsteigenden Säulen und die Blumenbretter der oberen Stockwerke ausgeführt. Das Hauptdach ist mit Rathenower Biberschwänzen eingedeckt.

Bei der großen Tiefe des Grundstücks schließt sich an den Seitenflügel des Vorderhauses ein Gartenhaus, das herrschaftlich eingerichtete Wohnungen von fünf bis sechs Zimmern enthält. Mit Rücksicht darauf haben auch die Fassaden des Seitenflügels und des Gartenhauses eine künstlerische Durchbildung erfahren, deren malerische Wirkung durch grün gestrichene Treillagen am Erdgeschoß und durch eine Brunnenanlage vor dem Gartenhause erhöht wird.

Die Modelle für die Bildhauerarbeiten und die Antragearbeiten hat Richard Kühn ausgeführt.

138 [1904: 80]

Für den Kunsthändler D. Heinemann in München hat Professor Emanuel Seidl in der Zeit vom 1. März 1903 bis 15. Februar 1904 am Maximiliansplatz 3 ein Gebäude von sechs Etagen errichtet, dessen beide unteren Geschosse den Geschäftszwecken des Besitzers dienen, während die drei oberen und das Dachgeschoß Wohnungen enthalten. Im Erdgeschoß befinden sich das Empfangsbureau (A), ein Ausstellungsraum (B) und in der Rücklage ein zweiter Ausstellungsraum (C) für Skulpturen (D), an den sich noch ein Bureau (D) anschließt. Das erste Geschoß enthält ein Kabinett (E) und einen größeren Raum zu Ausstellungen (F) und rückwärts einen großen Saal mit Oberlichtdach (G), das in Eisen konstruiert ist.

Die Decken sämtlicher Etagen sind massiv als Hohlsteindecken zwischen T-Trägern ausgeführt. Alle Stockwerke sind durch einen elektrischen Personenaufzug mit Druckknopfsteuerung verbunden. Außerdem geht noch ein elektrischer Aufzug für Lasten bis zum ersten Obergeschoß.

---

136 [1904: 17]

Les architectes Kárman Aladár et Ullmann Gyula à Budapest ont bâti dans cette ville, dans l'espace d'une année la grande maison de rapport Leopoldring 12. Cette construction est en briques avec crépissage; elle a coûté 306 000 Marks. La façade peut être considérée comme un brillant exemple de la richesse et de l'effet décoratif extraordinaire que l'on peut obtenir avec architecture de surfaces crépies, traitées selon les principes de l'école de Wagner.

137 [1904: 79]

Les maisons à loyer de Berlin et de ses environs témoignent si rarement de véritables aspirations artistiques, que lorsqu'une exception se présente, il faut s'empresser de la signaler. C'est ainsi que nous pouvons saluer la maison à loyer projetée et exécutée par Albert Gessner à Charlottenbourg, Mommsenstrasse 6, du premier octobre 1903 au premier septembre 1904 pour la somme de 396000 Marks. (Pl. 79.)

Grâce à sa chaude coloration et à son caractère individuel, la façade se distingue avantageusement de son entourage, quoique le type de la maison à quatre étages soit le même que celui des autres immeubles de la contrée. Le ton chaud a été obtenu au moyen d'un crépissage coloré d'ocre jaune; la tourelle du premier et du second étage de la moitié gauche de la façade construite en pierre jaune grise de Cotta ainsi que l'encadrement du portail et le contre-cœur de la fenêtre d'escalier de même pierre s'accordent très bien avec le crépissage. Une tourelle interrompue par un balcon et recouverte en cuivre a été placée en avant et au milieu de la moitié droite de la façade. Les colonnes surmontant la tourelle et les balcons à fleurs des étages supérieurs sont exécutés en cuivre. Le toit est recouvert en tuiles de Rathenow.

La grande profondeur du terrain a permis d'élever en prolongation de l'aile latérale du bâtiment principal, un pavillon de jardin contenant de riches appartements de maître de cinq et six chambres. Par égard pour ce pavillon, on a traité les façades de l'aile latérale d'une façon artistique; leur aspect pittoresque a été augmenté par l'emploi de treillages peints en vert au rez-de-chaussée et par une fontaine devant le pavillon.

Les modèles pour les travaux de sculpture et de modelage ont été livrés par Richard Kühn.

138 [1904: 80]

Monsieur le Professeur Emanuel Seidl a construit du premier mars 1903 au quinze février 1904, pour le marchand d'œuvres d'art D. Heinemann à Munich, Maximiliansplatz 3, une maison de six étages dont les deux étages inférieurs servent au commerce du propriétaire, tandis que les trois étages supérieurs et le toit contiennent des appartements. Au rez-de-chaussée se trouvent: le salon de réception, une salle d'exposition, et en arrière une seconde salle d'exposition pour la sculpture à laquelle touche un bureau. Le premier étage contient un cabinet et une grande salle d'exposition, sur le derrière se trouve une grande salle éclairée par le haut avec construction en fer.

Les poutraisons de tous les étages sont massives et construites en hourdis creux entre fers à T. Tous les étages sont reliés entre eux par un lift électrique à simple pression de bouton. Un autre monte-charges électrique monte en outre jusqu'au premier étage.

---

136 [1904: 17]

The architects Kárman Aladár and Ullmann Gyula in Budapest have built in that city in the course of a year the large dwelling house situated in the Leopoldring 12. The house is of brick, with stone-sand plaster and cost 306000 Marks. The facade may be considered as a splendid example of the capability of development and decorative effect of simple plaster architecture as practised by the Wagner school of architects.

137 [1904: 79]

Endeavours to give an artistic character to large dwelling houses in Berlin are still so rare, that any effort in this direction must be hailed with pleasure. Such we have in the house built by Albert Gessner at Mommsenstrasse 6, Charlottenburg from 1 October 1903 to 1 September 1904 at a cost of 396000 Marks. (See plate 79.)

The house with its warm colouring and characteristic style contrasts advantageously with the neighbouring buildings, although it consists of four floors as do most of the surrounding houses. The colouring is of yellow ochre plaster, with which the grey-yellow Cotta sandstone used for the bays of the first and second floors and for the porch and entrance floor, harmonizes extremely well. The bay of the first floor of the right side of the facade has a covered balcony roofed with copper. The same material is used for the pillars and for the flower stands of the upper stories. The principal roof is of Rathenow red tiles.

The site of the house is of great depth, and gave opportunity for the building of side wings which contain lodgings of 5 and 6 rooms. Here the same artistic design may be noticed, and a happy ornamental effect has been achieved by the green colouring of the ground floor and by a fountain in the garden.

The models for the statuary and sculptural details are by Richard Kühn.

138 [1904: 80]

Professor Emanuel Seidl has built in Munich premises for the picture-dealer D. Heinemann. The house is in Maximiliansplatz 3, and was built from 1 March 1903 to 15 February 1904. It has six stories, the two lowest are occupied by the business of the owner, the three upper and the roof story contain dwellings. On the ground floor is a reception bureau, rooms for exhibitions, in the back parts rooms for the exhibition of sculpture with an additional bureau. The first floor contains a cabinet and a large hall suited for exhibition purposes, extending to the back of the house is a large sky lighted gallery constructed of iron.

The ceilings of each story are massive and have T girders. All floors have electric lifts for passengers; an electric lift for goods is also up to the first floor.

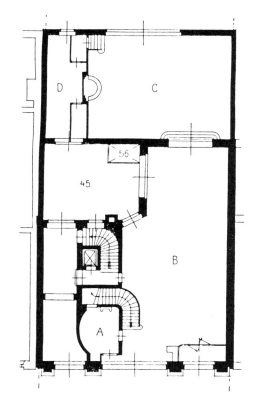

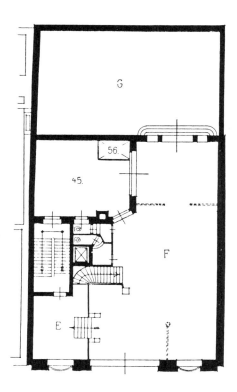

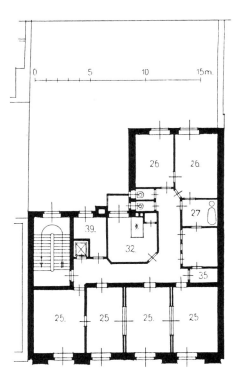

Mit Rückſicht auf die Nähe des Wittelsbacher Brunnens iſt die Faſſade (Tafel 80) im Renaiſſanceſtil komponiert, aber in modernem Sinne detailliert. Der Sockel iſt in Granit, die Faſſade in grauem Mainſandſtein ausgeführt. Der ſich unter dem Hauptgeſims hinziehende plaſtiſche Fries hebt ſich von einem ſchwarzen Untergrund aus venezianiſchem Glasmoſaik ab.

Die Fenſter im erſten Obergeſchoß haben Umrahmungen aus Kupfer mit Meſſingkapitälen, die Balkone im zweiten Obergeſchoß in Kupfer getriebene Brüſtungen. Die Eingangstüren ſind aus gebeiztem und poliertem Eichenholz mit glatten Meſſingbeſchlägen.

Die geſamte Bauausführung hat die Firma E. Seidl & O. Steinbeis beſorgt. Die figürlichen Arbeiten an der Faſſade und die Bildhauer- und Stuckarbeiten des Innern haben die Hofbildhauer Rappa & Co. ausgeführt.

Die Baukoſten betrugen 340 000 Mark.

Par égard pour la fontaine de Wittelsbach, la façade (Pl. 80) est traitée dans l'esprit de la Renaissance mais le détail est moderne. La frise qui s'étend au dessous de la grande corniche est en mosaïque vénitienne et se détache sur un fond noir.

Les fenêtres du premier étage ont des encadrements en cuivre avec chapiteaux de laiton. Les balcons du second étage sont pourvus de balustrades en cuivre repoussé. Les portes d'entrée sont en bois de chêne ciré et poli avec garnitures en cuivre poli.

Toute l'exécution a été faite par la maison E. Seidl et O. Steinbeis. Les sculpteurs de la cour Rappa & Co. ont exécuté les décorations figurales de la façade ainsi que les travaux plastiques de stuc de l'intérieur.

Les frais de construction s'élevèrent à 340 000 Marks.

In order to correspond with the Wittelsbach fountain the facade (see plate 80) is of Renaissance style, with a modern touch. The sockel is of granite, the facade of grey sandstone. The sculptural frieze extending under the principal moulding stands out in relief from a black background of Venetian glass mosaic.

The windows of the first floor are framed in copper with brass ornaments, the balconies of the second floor have hammered copper balustrades. The entrance doors are of stained and polished oak, with plain brass plates.

The whole building was carried out by E. Seidl & O. Steinbeis. The sculptural details of the facade and interior are by Rappa & Co.

The cost of building amounted to 340 000 Marks.

139 [1904: 61]

Das Kaufhaus N. Israel in Berlin iſt in den Jahren 1899—1902 von Ludwig Engel in Berlin erbaut worden. An drei Seiten freiliegend, kehrt es ſeine Hauptfront der Spandauerſtraße

139 [1904: 61]

La maison de commerce N. Israel à Berlin a été construite dans les années 1899 à 1902 par Ludwig Engel architecte dans la même ville. Cet édifice est libre de trois côtés et dresse sa façade principale sur la

139 [1904: 61]

The business house of N. Israel in Berlin was built in the years 1899 to 1902 by Ludwig Engel of Berlin. The building is free on three sides and has its principal front

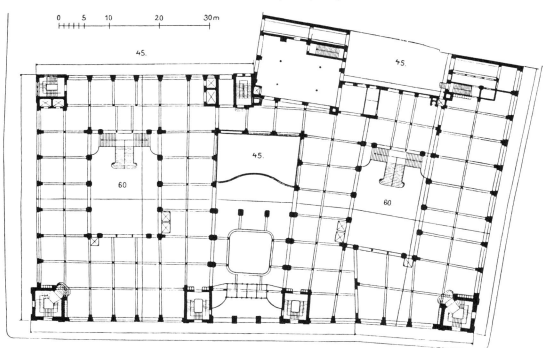

zu. Unfere Tafel 61 gibt den Mittelbau diefer Hauptfront mit dem Haupteingang wieder. Rechts und links davon liegen zwei Nebeneingänge, von denen aus Treppen unmittelbar zu den oberen Gefchoffen führen. Dem Hauptverkehr mit diefen follen jedoch die beiden Freitreppen in den glasgedeckten Lichthöfen rechts und links von dem großen Mittelhof dienen. Die beiden Freitreppen find mit Abficht etwas weit vom Haupteingang angeordnet worden, damit das Publikum Gelegenheit hat, einen größeren Teil des Erdgefchoffes zu durchfchreiten und dabei die ausgeftellten Waren zu befichtigen. Die Faffaden find ganz in Sandftein ausgeführt.

Spandauerstrasse. Notre Planche 61 reproduit le corps central de cette façade avec l'entrée principale. A droite et à gauche de l'entrée principale se trouvent deux entrées secondaires, lesquelles conduisent directement par des escaliers aux étages supérieurs. Leur principale communication est cependant établie par les deux escaliers libres situés dans les cours vitrées à gauche et à droite de la grande cour centrale. Ces deux escaliers ont été intentionnellement placés un peu loin de l'entrée principale, pour donner au public l'occasion de traverser une plus grande partie du rez - de - chaussée et en même temps d'y considérer les marchandises exposées. Les façades sont entièrement construites en grès.

In the Spandauer Strasse. Our plate 61 shows the middle building of this principal front with the principal entrance. Right and left of this, are two side entrances which lead by staircases immediately to the upper stories. The principal means of access, however, to these upper stories is from the glass-roofed hall right and left from the great middle hall, by means of open stair-cases which are purposely placed at some distance from the principal entrance; the public is thus compelled to go through the whole shop and to view the goods exhibited there. The facades are entirely of sandstone.

140 [1904: 84]

Von der Häufergruppe in Dresden, Lindengaffe 2, 4, 6, die unfere Tafel 84 wiedergibt, find die beiden rechts gelegenen (Nr. 2 und 4) von F. R. Voretzfch, das dritte (Nr. 6) von Louis Voigt erbaut worden. In der Anordnung wie in der Ornamentik der Faffaden find diefe Häufer ein bezeichnendes Beifpiel für die modernen Beftrebungen, die in der Dresdener Architektur mehr und mehr zum Durchbruch kommen.

Die Faffaden der Häufer Nr. 2 und 4, deren jedes 95000 Mark gekoftet hat, find in gelbem Cottaer Sandftein ausgeführt. Die Modelle zu den Verzierungen hat Bildhauer Peter Henfeler, die fchmiedeeifernen Balkonbrüftungen Hermann Müller geliefert. — Die Faffade des Haufes Nr. 6 ift in weißem Elbfandftein ausgeführt. Die Modelle und die Steinbildhauerarbeiten find von Hugo Hahn, die Geländer der Balkone von Schloffermeifter Ernft Schöne.

Die Baukoften betrugen 97500 Mark.

140 [1904: 84]

Dans le groupe de maisons de la Lindengasse Nr. 2, 4, 6 à Dresde que représente notre Planche 84 les deux situées à droite (Nr. 2 et 4) ont été bâties par F. R. Voretzsch, la troisième (Nr. 6) par Louis Voigt. La disposition générale, ainsi que la décoration des façades de ces maisons livrent un exemple significatif de la tendance moderne qui se fait de plus en plus jour dans l'architecture de Dresde.

Les façades des maisons Nr. 2 et 4 qui ont coûté chacune 95000 Marks, ont été construites en grès de Cotta. Les modèles des ornements ont été livrés par le sculpteur Pierre Henseler, les balustrades de Balcon en fer forgé sont l'œuvre de Hermann Müller. — La façade de la maison Nr. 6 est construite en grès blanc. Les modèles et la sculpture sont de Hugo Hahn, les balustrades des balcons du maître serrurier Ernest Schöne.

Les frais de construction s'élevèrent à 97500 Marks.

140 [1904: 84]

The group of houses in Dresden, Lindengasse 2, 4 and 6, represented on our plate 84 were built (No. 2 and 4) by F. R. Voretzsch and (Nr. 6) by Louis Voigt. The style, arrangement and ornamentation of these facades form a good example of the efforts of modern architects to adhere to a characteristic style; this is specially noticeable in Dresden architecture.

The facades of No. 2 and 4, each of which cost 95000 Marks, are of yellow Cotta sandstone. The models for the ornamentation are by Peter Henseler, the wrought-iron balcony balustrades are by Hermann Müller. The facade of the house No. 6 is of white Elbe sandstone. The models and the statuary are by Hugo Hahn the iron work of the balcony by the Smith Ernst Schöne.

The building cost 97500 Marks.

141 [1904: 14]

Profeffor Hermann Billing in Karlsruhe in Baden, dem wir fchon fo viele Beiträge zu verdanken haben, hat jüngft dort die „Baifchftraße" auf dem Hinterlande des Doppelhaufes Stephanienftraße 84 und 86 angelegt, die ihren einzigen Zugang durch einen zwifchen beiden Bauten angeordneten hohen Torbogen hat. Das Gelände hat eine Breite von nur rd. 31 Metern, der Fahrdamm 5 Meter und die beiderfeitigen Bürgerfteige je 1,5 Meter, fo daß alfo beiderfeitig der Straße je 11,5 Meter breite Bauftellen entftanden, von denen die linksfeitige mit drei freiftehenden, villenartigen, an die Nachbargärten angrenzenden Einzelfamilienhäufern, Nr. 1, 3 und 5, und rechtsfeitig mit einem dergleichen, Nr. 2, und zwei aneinander gebauten, Nr. 4 und 6, befetzt wurden, die alle das den Billingfchen Bauten eigentümlich malerifch reizende Gepräge zeigen.

141 [1904: 14]

Monsieur le professeur Hermann Billing de Carlsruhe en Bade, a qui nous sommes redevables de tant de communications intéressantes a crée dernièrement dans cette ville la „Baischstrasse", derrière la maison jumelle Stephanienstrasse 84 et 86; cette nouvelle rue a son seul accès par un large passage voûté entre ces deux maisons. Le terrain a une largeur de 31 mètres en tout, la chaussée a 5 mètres et les trottoirs de chaque côté, chacun 1,5 mètres de sorte qu'il reste à droite et à gauche de la rue une profondeur de 11,5 mètres pour bâtir. Du côté gauche, il furent élevées trois villas isolées, pour une famille chacune, touchant les jardins voisins; ce sont les Nos. 1, 3 et 5 et du côté droit, une maison isolée, No. 2 et deux maisons mitoyennes Nos. 4 et 6. Toutes du caractère si original et si charmant des créations de maître Billing.

141 [1904: 14]

Professor Hermann Billing in Carlsruhe in Baden, to whom we already are indebted for so many contributions, has lately laid out in that city the "Baischstrasse" on a site behind the double house Stephanienstrasse 84 and 86. The only entrance to the street is through a lofty archway between the two houses. The site is only about 31 meters broad, the street 5 meters and pathway on each side 1,5 meters. By this means building sites 11,5 in breadth are parcelled out; on those on the left are erected 3 detached villa residences for single families nos 1, 3 and 5. The right side has another similar villa no 2 and two semi-detached houses nos 4 and 6. All of the houses have the charming distinctive picturesqueness which always characterizes Professor Billing's work.

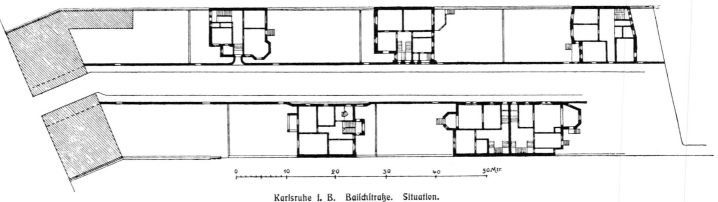

Karlsruhe i. B. Baifchftraße. Situation.

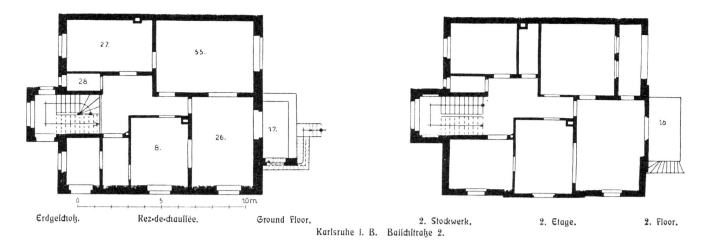

Erdgeſchoß. Rez-de-chauſſée. Ground Floor. 2. Stockwerk. 2. Etage. 2. Floor.

Karlsruhe i. B. Baiſchſtraße 2.

Die Villa Baiſchſtraße Nr. 2 iſt zum Preiſe von 32000 Mark errichtet; das Faſſadenmauer-werk beſteht aus grünem Sulzfelder Sandſtein, das Holzwerk iſt verſchindelt.

La villa Baischstrasse No. 2 construite pour le prix de 32 000 Marks. La maçonnerie des façades est en grès vert de Sulzfeld, le bois est recouvert de bardeaux.

Villa Baischstrasse No 2 cost 32000 Marks; the facade brick work is of green Sulzfeld sand-stone. The wood work is shingled.

142 [1904: 69]

Auf den das Tal von Stuttgart einſchließenden Höhenzügen hat ſich in den letzten Jahr-zehnten eine eigenartige Villenarchitektur ent-wickelt, bei der das Hauptgewicht auf einen kräftig wirkenden Umriß gelegt wird, da die in ziemlich weiten Abſtänden voneinander liegenden Villen ſonſt in dem weit ausgedehnten Land-ſchaftsbilde verſchwinden würden. Mit Rückſicht darauf haben die Architekten Lambert und Stahl bei der von ihnen in der Zeit vom Juli 1901 bis Juli 1902 erbauten Villa an der Birken-waldſtraße 97a (Tafel 69) nach energiſcher, ein-druckſvoller Gliederung der Faſſaden geſtrebt und außerdem die Wirkung in die Ferne noch durch ein ſteiles Dach in Pyramidenform geſteigert. Da man von der auf dem Kriegsberg gelegenen Villa einen ſchönen Blick auf die Stadt und das

142 [1904: 69]

Il s'est développé ces dernières années sur les montagnes qui entourent la vallée de Stuttgard, une architecture particulière pour les villas; cette particularité consiste en une silhouette très prononcée qui permet aux maisons isolées ou séparées de leurs voisines par de grands espaces de maintenir leur valeur dans un paysage étendu où elles risqueraient de se perdre. C'est en tenant compte de cette nécessité, que les archi-tectes Lambert et Stahl ont construit depuis le mois de juillet 1901 au mois de juillet 1902 une villa à la Birkenwaldstrasse 97a (Pl. 69). Ils ont cherché une division énergique et vivante des façades et ont encore augmenté l'effet de l'édifice, vu de loin, en le couronnant d'un toit élevé en forme de pyramide. Comme on jouit de la montagne où se trouve la villa (Kriegs-

142 [1904: 69]

On the range of hills, which surround the valley of Stuttgart, have been built during the last decade groups of villas which owe their effectiveness to the striking style of their archi-tecture. This style was necessary, or the houses would have been lost in the widely-extending grounds in which they have been built. This point has been kept in mind by the architects Lambert and Stahl in their design of a villa built by them in the Birkenwaldstrasse 97a (plate 69) in the time from July 1901 to July 1902. The villa is picturesque owing to the energetic, im-pressive arrangement of the facade, and the effect in the distance is enhanced by the steep roof in a pyramidal form. The house stands on the Kriegsberg and from thence a beautiful view is obtainable of the town and of the Neckar valley;

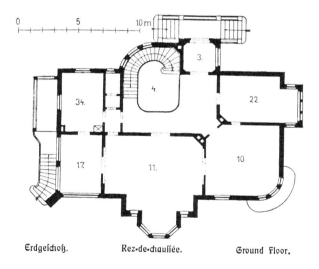

Erdgeſchoß. Rez-de-chauſſée. Ground Floor.

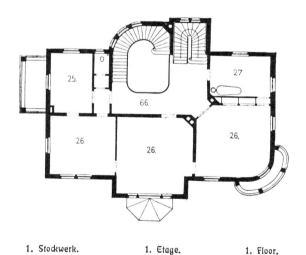

1. Stockwerk. 1. Etage. 1. Floor.

Neckartal genießt, wurde für reichliche Anlage von Balkons, Erkern, Erkertürmchen und Veranden geſorgt. Die Außenarchitektur der Faſſaden, die in weißem Mainſandſtein ausgeführt ſind, iſt in modernen Formen mit Anlehnung an den Schloß-bau der Renaiſſancezeit gehalten. Das Dach iſt mit roten Biberſchwänzen eingedeckt. Den plaſtiſchen Schmuck der Faſſaden hat Bildhauer Brülmann geſchaffen.

Im Erdgeſchoß ſind um die Halle ein Speiſe-zimmer, ein Anrichtezimmer, ein Salon, ein Herrenzimmer und eine Veranda gruppiert. Im Obergeſchoß liegen ein Wohnzimmer, drei Schlaf-zimmer, ein Ankleide- und ein Badezimmer. Die Halle und das Speiſezimmer ſind reich mit Tiſchlerarbeit ausgeſtattet. Die Baukoſten betrugen einſchließlich der Einfriedigung und der An-lage der Zufahrt, aber ohne die Gartenanlage 133000 Mark.

berg) d'une vue étendue sur la ville et la vallée du Neckar, on eut soin de pourvoir la maison de balcons, de terrasses et de verandas. L'archi-tecture des façades est en pierre blanche du Main, les formes sont modernes en s'inspirant du style des châteaux de l'époque de la Renaissance. Le toit est recouvert en tuiles rouges; la décoration plastique des façades a été exécutée par le sculpteur Brülmann.

Au rez-de-chaussée sont disposés autour de la halle une salle à manger, une office, un salon, la chambre du propriétaire et une veranda. Au premier étage sont situés un salon, trois chambres à coucher, un cabinet de toilette et un cabinet de bain. La halle et la salle à manger sont pourvues de riches travaux de menuiserie. Les frais de construction com-portèrent avec la grille et la route d'accès, mais sans le jardin, 133000 Marks.

for this reason there are numerous balconies, bays, corner towers and verandahs. The exterior architecture of the facade is of white Main sand-stone, the old castle style of the Renascence time has been kept in mind, but the forms are modern. The roof is covered with flat red tiles; the sculptural decoration is by the sculptor Brül-mann.

On the ground floor, round the hall are a dining-room with a serving-room, a drawing-room, a smoking room and a veranda. On the upper floor are a living-room, three bed-rooms, a dressing room and a bath-room. The hall and the dining room are richly decorated with wood-work. The cost of building, including the palings and the construction of the entrance drive, but exclusive of the laying out of the garden, amounted to 133000 Marks.

Auf einem in Hamburg vom Alsterdamm bis zur Ferdinandstraße hindurchreichenden Grundstück haben die Architekten Lundt und Kallmorgen 1902 ein Doppelhaus mit zwei Straßenfronten erbaut, das zu seinem größeren Teil Geschäftszwecken dient (Tafel 56—57). Die in modernisierten Barockformen komponierte Fassade am Alsterdamm ist in Cudowa-Sandstein ausgeführt. Die Säulen des Erdgeschosses sind aus Labradorgranit. Das Dach ist mit Kupfer eingedeckt. Die Front an der Ferdinandstraße ist bis auf das in Putz ausgeführte Untergeschoß mit weißen, glasierten Verblendziegeln bekleidet.

Les architectes Lundt et Kallmorgen ont construit à Hambourg en 1902 une maison double avec deux façades, sur un terrain s'étendant du Alsterdamm jusqu'à la Ferdinandstrasse; cet immeuble sert surtout à des usages commerciaux (Pl. 56—57). La façade sur le Alsterdamm composée en formes baroques modernisées est construite en pierre de Cudowa. Les colonnes du rez-de-chaussée sont en granit de Labrador. Le toit est recouvert en cuivre. La façade sur la Ferdinandstrasse est construite en briques blanches émaillées, à l'exception du rez-de-chaussée qui est crépi.

On a site reaching from the Alsterdamm to the Ferdinandstrasse in Hamburg, the architects Lundt and Kallmorgen have built in 1902 a double house with two street frontages, for the most part devoted to business purposes (plates 56—57). The facade on the Alsterdamm is of modern barock style and is built of Cudowa sandstone. The pillars of the ground floor are of Labrador granite. The roof is covered with copper. The frontage in the Ferdinandstrasse is faced with white glazed tiles except in the lower story which is plastered.

Die Anlage der von Professor Hermann Billing in der Zeit vom 1. Juli 1902 bis 1. August 1903 erbauten Häusergruppe in Karlsruhe, Stephanienstraße 94 u. 96, ist durch eine das Grundstück durchschneidende Privatstraße bedingt worden. Für die Durchfahrt nach dieser Straße, der die Hoffronten zugekehrt sind (Tafel 77—78), ist ein Torbogen von einer lichten Spannung von sieben Metern konstruiert worden. Dadurch sind zwei Flügelbauten von gleicher Größe entstanden, die in der Höhe des zweiten und dritten Stocks durch einen Mittelbau verbunden werden, der Loggien für die angrenzenden Wohnungen enthält.

Die Fassade (Tafel 76), deren Detaillierung sich in modernen Stilformen bewegt, ist ganz in weißem Haustein aus Klingenmünster ausgeführt. Einzelne Architekturglieder sind zum Teil vergoldet, zum Teil farbig behandelt. Die eine Haustür ist mit Kupfer, die andere mit Neusilber bekleidet. Die Seitenfassaden sind einfacher gehalten. Nur das Erdgeschoß ist in Haustein ausgeführt; die oberen Stockwerke sind verputzt.

Das Gebäude enthält in allen Etagen herrschaftlich eingerichtete Wohnungen von sechs bis sieben Zimmern, die mit Zentralheizung und elektrischem Licht versehen sind. In den Dachgeschossen befinden sich Ateliers.

Die Baukosten betrugen 260 000 Mark.

La disposition du groupe de maisons construites par Monsieur le Professeur Hermann Billing à Carlsruhe, Stephanienstrasse 94—96, du premier juillet 1902 au premier août 1903, fut dictée par une rue privée qui traverse le terrain à bâtir. Cette rue, sur la quelle sont tournées les façades des cours, est fermée par une porte cochère de sept mètres d'ouverture (Pl. 77—78). Il est résulté de cette disposition deux ailes de même grandeur, qui à la hauteur du deuxième et du troisième étage sont reliées par un corps central, ce dernier contient des loggias pour les appartements adjacents.

La façade (Pl. 76) dont le détail est tenu dans l'esprit des formes modernes est entièrement construite en pierre blanche de Klingenmünster. Quelques membres d'architecture sont en partie dorés, en partie polychromes. Une des portes d'entrée est recouverte en cuivre, l'autre en argent. Les façades latérales sont traitées plus simplement. Seul le rez-de-chaussée est en pierre de taille, les étages supérieurs sont en maçonnerie crépie.

L'immeuble contient à tous ses étages des appartements de maîtres de six et sept chambres, ils sont pourvus de chauffage central et de lumière electrique. Dans le toit se trouvent des ateliers.

Les frais de construction furent de 260000 Marks.

A group of houses was built by Professor Hermann Billing from 1 July 1902 to 1 August 1903 at Stephanienstrasse 94—96 Carlsruhe. The position of the houses was determined by a private street which cuts through the building site. For the thorough-fare to this street (which is faced by the courtyards of the house) an arched doorway with a span of 7 meters has been constructed. By this means two side buildings of equal size have been built which on the second and third floors are united by a middle floor containing the loggias for the adjoining dwellings.

The facade (see plate 76) of modern style as to its details, is of white stone from Klingenmünster, certain architectural details are gilded, others coloured. One house door has platings of copper, the other of German silver. The side facade is of greater simplicity. The ground floor only is of stone, the other floors are plastered.

The house contains on each of its floors dwellings of from six to seven rooms, which are fitted with central heating apparatus and electric light. In the roof story are artists' studios.

The cost of building amounted to 260 000 Marks.

Durch Zusammenfassung dreier Miethäuser in der Franz Josefstraße in München (Tafel 81—83) zu einer Baugruppe, die in Jahresfrist, von 1902 bis 1903 erbaut worden sind, hat der Architekt Martin Dülfer einen gewissen Grad von monumentaler Wirkung erreicht, auf die bei Miethäusern gewöhnlich verzichtet werden muß. Zu dieser Wirkung hat auch die Höhe der Geschosse wesentlich beigetragen, die durch die Notwendigkeit bedingt worden ist, im Dachgeschoß jedes Hauses Künstlerateliers mit nach der Straße gerichteten Fenstern unterzubringen. Diese haben gewissermaßen den Maßstab für die Gestaltung der Fassaden gegeben.

Abgesehen von einigen Anklängen an den Stil Ludwigs XVI., sind die Fassaden in modernem Sinne ausgebildet und dekoriert. Sie sind mit Rautputz versehen, und die Ornamente sind teils in Zement gegossen und eingesetzt, teils freihändig aufgetragen.

Monsieur Martin Dülfer architecte à Munich a obtenu par le réunion de trois maisons à loyer, dans la Franz Josefstrasse à Munich, un certain degré de monumentalité qui ne se trouve généralement pas dans ce genre de constructions. Les travaux furent exécutés de 1902 à 1903 (Pl. 81—83). La hauteur d'étages a contribué d'une façon sensible à l'effet monumental, cette dernière a été imposée par la nécessité d'installer dans le toit de chaque maison un atelier de peintre, avec vitrage situé sur la rue. Les vitrages ont dans une certaine mesure donné l'échelle pour la composition des façades.

A part quelques réminiscences du style Louis XVI. les façades sont traitées et décorées dans un esprit moderne. Elles sont crépies et striées au peigne; les ornements sont en partie coulés en ciment, en partie modelés à main libre sur place.

The architect Martin Dülfer in Munich, Franz Josefstrasse has connected three dwelling houses so as to form one group of buildings (see plates 81—83). The time occupied was one year 1902—1903. By this plan, the architect has achieved almost a monumental effect which one generally fails to see in this kind of house. The height of the different stories has contributed not a little to this effect, this height was a necessity, as the roof stories in each house have been arranged as artists studios with windows on the street front. These windows have to a certain extent been the standard for the arrangement of the other parts of the facade.

If we except a few details which remind us of the style of Louis XVI we may say that the facades are essentially modern in construction and decoration. They are covered with rough plaster, the ornaments are partly cast in cement and partly hand work.

Unter den Architekten, die den neu entstandenen Villenvierteln von Karlsruhe in Baden ein charakteristisches Gepräge gegeben, haben Curjel & Moser eine besonders rege Tätigkeit entfaltet. Wie sie mit möglichst geringen Baukosten eine schlicht vornehme, aber echt künstlerische Erscheinung zu erzielen wissen, zeigt

Parmi les architectes qui ont su donner un caractère artistique aux nouveaux quartiers de villas de Carlsruhe en Bade, il faut nommer en première ligne Messieurs Curjel & Moser. La villa double construite par eux à la Bachstrasse 2 et 4 montre combien ils savent à peu de frais obtenir un ensemble simple mais

The architects Curjel & Moser have done much to give the new villa colony of Carlsruhe in Baden its characteristic and picturesque charm. A double villa in the Bachstrasse 2 and 4 shows how these architects are able to design a simple, distinguished

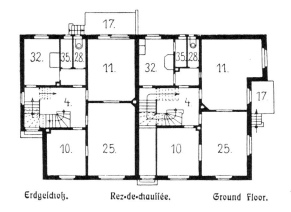

Erdgeſchoß.

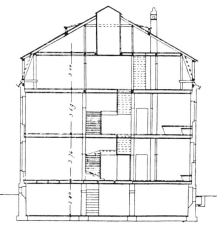

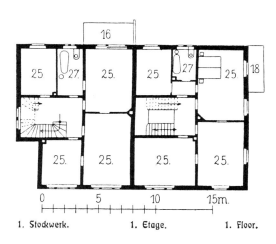

Rez-de-chauſſée.　　　Ground Floor.

0　　　5　　　10　　　15m.

1. Stockwerk.　　　　　1. Etage.　　　　　1. Floor.

die Doppelvilla an der Bachſtraße 2 und 4, die in zwei Geſchoſſen vier Wohnungen enthält, von denen je zwei um eine Diele gruppiert ſind. Die Faſſaden ſind in Putzbau ausgeführt, die Steilwände des Dachgeſchoſſes, das die Schlafräume für die Dienſtboten u. dgl. mehr enthält, teils mit Brettern verkleidet, teils wie die Dächer mit Ziegeln gedeckt. Die Baukoſten betrugen etwa 66000 Mark.

de bon goût. Cette villa double contient en deux étages quatre appartements dont deux sont groupés autour d'un hall. Les façades sont exécutées en maçonnerie crépie; les pans du toit qui contiennent les chambres à coucher des domestiques et d'autres locaux sont en partie recouverts en planches, et en partie comme les autres surfaces du toit, en tuiles. La dépense fut de 66 000 Marks.

and artistic house at the least possible cost. The house contains four dwellings arranged on two floors, two dwellings being arranged round each central hall. The facades are of plaster, the steep walls of the roof story, containing servants rooms are boarded partly, and partly tiled like the roof. The cost amounted to 66000 Marks.

148 [1904: 32]

Die zweigeſchoſſige Villa in Coblenz, die Baurat Otto March in Charlottenburg für den Arzt Sanitätsrat Dr. Timme erbaut hat, hat einen Koſtenaufwand von 163000 Mark erfordert, d. i. 26,30 Mark für den Kubikmeter umbauten Raumes. Der Sockel und Teile der aufgehenden Flächen ſind mit roten Ziegeln verblendet; die übrigen Flächen haben einen hellen Putz von Trierer Kalk erhalten, der ohne Anſtrich eine warme, grau - gelbliche Färbung hat. Der Erkerbau iſt in Sandſtein ausgeführt, das Fachwerk der Giebel von Eichenholz; das Dach iſt mit Ziegeln gedeckt.

148 [1904: 32]

La villa à deux étages que l'architecte conseiller Otto March de Charlottembourg à construit à Coblence pour Monsieur le Docteur Timme médecin, à occasionné une dépense de 163000 Marks, soit de 26,30 Marks par mètre cube de construction. Le socle et une partie des façades sont revêtus de briques rouges; les autres surfaces ont été crépies avec de la chaux claire de Trèves qui, sans peinture à une chaude couleur naturelle gris jaune. La tourelle est en pierre, les pans de bois en chêne; le toit est recouvert en tuiles.

148 [1904: 32]

The two-storied villa in Coblentz, built by the Baurat Otto March of Charlottenburg for Dr. Timme, Sanitätsrat, cost 163000 Marks, that is to say 26,30 Marks per cubic meter of built space. The sockel and part of the surfaces are covered with red tiles; the other surfaces are covered with light plaster of Trier lime, which is naturally of a warm grey-yellowish colour. The bay is carried out in sandstone, the frame-work of the gables is of oak, the roof is covered with tiles.

149 [1904: 64]

Für den Bau der Villa Gerſtenberg, der in dem an Schmargendorf grenzenden Teil des Grunewalds bei Berlin in der Zeit vom 1. März 1903 bis 1. Mai 1904 von Landbauinſpektor C. Vohl errichtet worden iſt, wurde dem Architekten ein umfangreiches Gelände zur Verfügung geſtellt, das einerſeits eine reiche Gruppierung des Baues und eine maleriſche Belebung der Baugruppe durch Terraſſen und Anbauten ermöglichte, andrerſeits aber auch zur Beherrſchung des Geländes eine beträchtliche Höhenentwicklung des Baus verlangte. Dies hat der Architekt, ohne im übrigen über eine zweigeſchoſſige Anlage auf hohem Sockelgeſchoß hinauszugehen, vornehmlich durch die Anordnung eines Rundturms erreicht, der dem Bau das charakteriſtiſche Gepräge gibt. (Tafel 64.)

Das Sockelgeſchoß enthält nicht nur die Räume für die Zentralheizung und für die Brennmaterialien, zwei Weinkeller und einen Pflanzenkeller, ſondern es iſt auch durch Anlage eines

149 [1904: 64]

Un vaste terrain se trouvait à la disposition de Monsieur C. Vohl, inspecteur des bâtiments, pour l'érection de la villa Gerstenberg dans la partie de Grunewald près Berlin, qui se trouve près de Schmargendorf. La construction eut lieu depuis le premier mars 1903 jusqu'au premier mai 1904. Le terrain permettait d'une part un riche groupement des parties et un développement de terrasses et d'annexes qui augmentaient le charme pittoresque de l'ensemble, mais d'autre part, il exigeait une grande extension des hauteurs pour arriver à dominer la contrée. Ce but a été atteint par l'architecte, sans dépasser du reste le nombre de deux étages situés sur un sous-sol élevé, au moyen d'une tour ronde qui donne au bâtiment son aspect caractéristique. (Pl. 64.)

Le sous-sol ne contient pas seulement les locaux pour le chauffage central et pour le combustible, deux caves à vin et une cave pour les plantes, mais il sert encore à l'habitation

149 [1904: 64]

The building inspector C. Vohl has built from 1 March 1903 to 1 May 1904 the villa Gerstenberg which is situated in that part of the Grunewald (near Berlin) bordering Schmargendorf. An extensive site afforded the architect the opportunity of erecting a picturesque building with terraces and bays, on the other hand it necessitated its being taken to a considerable height so as not to look insignificant. The architect has built a two storied house on a high sockel and has given an importance to the appearance by constructing on one side a round tower. (See plate 64.)

The basement contains the rooms for the heating apparatus and fuel, two wine cellars, a plant cellar, as well as a laboratory and adjoining

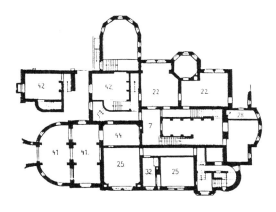

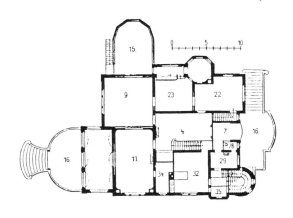

Laboratoriums und zweier Arbeitszimmer für die Zwecke des Besitzers bewohnbar gemacht worden. — Von der Vorderterrasse gelangt man durch den Eingangsflur in das Erdgeschoß, das, um die Diele angeordnet, die Empfangs- und Gesellschaftsräume enthält: das Zimmer des Herrn und das Zimmer der Frau, die beide durch Zugänge mit dem gemeinsamer Benutzung dienenden Erker verbunden sind, das Empfangszimmer, an das sich der Wintergarten anschließt, und das Speisezimmer, das sich nach einer Gartenhalle öffnet, der eine zum Garten führende Terrasse vorgelagert ist. An das Speisezimmer grenzen der Anrichteraum, die Küche und die Speisekammer.

Im Obergeschoß liegen das Schlafzimmer der Eltern, das Schlafzimmer und das Wohnzimmer der Tochter, das Badezimmer, drei Fremdenzimmer und ein Schrankzimmer.

Das Sockelgeschoß ist in Kalkstein ausgeführt, im übrigen sind die Fassaden mit hydraulischem Kalk verputzt. Bei der Ausarbeitung der Details stand dem Architekten Regierungsbaumeister Dammeier zur Seite.

du propriétaire, qui y a installé un laboratoire et deux chambres de travail. On pénètre de la terrasse de devant, par la porte d'entrée dans le rez-de-chaussée, le quel contient, groupées autour de la halle les salles de réception et de société: La chambre de Monsieur et celle de Madame, ces deux pièces communiquent toutes deux avec le bow window qui leur est commun; le salon de réception lequel communique avec le jardin d'hiver et la salle à manger s'ouvrant sur une halle ouverte, devant cette halle s'étend une terrasse qui donne accès au jardin. L'office, la cuisine et le garde-manger sont contigus à la salle à manger.

A l'étage supérieur, nous trouvons la chambre à coucher des parents, la chambre à coucher et le salon de leur fille, la chambre de bains, trois chambres d'amis et une chambre à armoires.

Le socle de l'étage en sous-sol est construit en pierre calcaire, les autres parties de l'édifice sont en maçonnerie crépie. Monsieur Dammeier architecte du gouvernement a prêté la collaboration pour l'étude des détails.

dwelling rooms fitted up for the use of the owner. From the front terrace one reaches the entrance, and comes into the ground floor which contains, arranged round the hall, the reception rooms, the smoking room, the boudoir (which last two are connected by a balcony accessible to both), the drawing room opening into a conservatory, and the dining room which opens into a veranda leading to a garden terrace. Adjoining the dining room is the serving-room, the kitchen and the pantry.

On the upper story are the bedrooms of the family, a sitting room, a bath-room, three spare-bedrooms and a wardrobe room.

The lower story is of lime-stone, the facades are plastered with hydraulic lime. The builder was assisted in the architectural details by the architect Dammeier.

---

150 [1904: 48]

Im Stadtgarten zu Köln hat Architekt Otto Welsch nach dem Entwurfe des Stadtbauinspektors Friedrich Bolte einen Musikpavillon erbaut, der, wie es in neuerer Zeit üblich geworden, auch noch anderen Zwecken dienstbar gemacht worden ist. Der Unterbau enthält nämlich ein vollständig eingerichtetes Büfett (A) für den Betrieb der Gartenwirtschaft,

150 [1904: 48]

Monsieur Otto Welsch architecte à Cologne a construit dans le jardin de cette ville un pavillon de musique; ce bâtiment élevé d'après le projet de l'architecte inspecteur de la ville Friedrich Bolte peut servir aussi à d'autres usages, ainsi que cela a lieu pour plusieurs autres pavillons construits ces dernières années. Le soussol contient un buffet complète-

150 [1904: 48]

In the public gardens at Cologne, the architect Otto Welsch has built a music pavilion according to the design of the town building-inspector Friedrich Bolte. As is the custom in these days, the building has to serve several purposes; the basement is equipped as a superior refreshment buffet. A is the premises of the

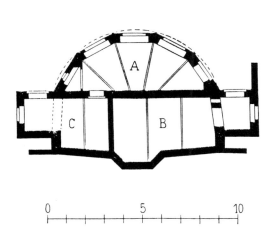

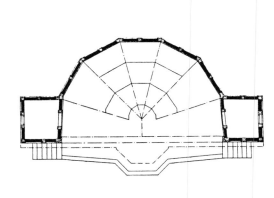

einen isolierten Bierkeller (B) und die Garderobe für die Kellner (C). Der Pavillon ist in Tannenholz mit Eichenholzbekleidung, das innere Gewölbe in Monierkonstruktion ausgeführt, die Dächer sind mit Biberschwänzen eingedeckt. Auf beiden Seiten des Orchesters ist eine Garderobe für die Musiker und eine Instrumentenkammer angelegt. Die Beleuchtungskörper hat Kunstschlosser Clemens Pretsch in Köln angefertigt. Baukosten: 8300 Mark.

ment organisé (A) pour le service du restaurant du jardin, une cave à bière isolée (B) et le vestiaire pour les garçons (C). Le pavillon est en bois de sapin avec revêtement de bois de chêne, la voûte de l'intérieur est en construction Monnier; les toits sont recouverts en tuiles. Sur le côté de l'orchestre se trouve un vestiaire pour les musiciens et une chambre pour les instruments. La maison de serrurerie artistique Clemens Pretzsch à Cologne a construit les appareils d'éclairage. Les frais de la construction s'élevèrent à 8300 Marks.

garden administration, B is an isolated beer cellar, C is the cloak-room for the waiters. The pavilion is of pine-wood panelled with oak, the interior vaulting is of Monier construction, the roofs are of red flat tiles. On the side of the orchestra is a cloak-room for the musicians together with an instrument room. The chandeliers are the work of Clemens Pretzsch in Cologne. The cost amounted to 8300 Marks.

---

151 [1904: 20]

In den Umgebungen der Geschäftszentren englischer Großstädte finden sich stille, vornehm bewohnte Straßen, die mit Bauten von äußerster Schlichtheit besetzt sind.

Wir bringen hier zwei solcher, von Architekt C. R. Ashbee in London, Cheyne-Walk 74 und 75 erbaute. Beide Häuser stehen nur mit ihrem niedrigen Erd- und Zwischengeschoß in der Straßenflucht, während das einzige Ober-

151 [1904: 20]

Dans le voisinage des grands centres de commerce et d'industrie des villes anglaises, on trouve des rues tranquilles et distinguées, bordées de maisons d'une extrême simplicité.

Nous publions ici deux de ces dernières, construites à Londres, Cheyne-Walk 74 et 75 par Monsieur C. R. Ashbee architecte. Les deux immeubles n'ont que leur bas rez-de-chaussée et leur entresol sur l'alignement de la

151 [1904: 20]

In the neighbourhood of many of the great business centres of England, one meets with quiet distinguished streets in which are houses of great simplicity and elegance.

We give here examples of two built by the architect C. R. Ashbee in 74 and 75 Cheyne-Walk London. Only the low ground and intermediate floor of both houses is in a line with

geſchoß zurückgeſetzt iſt; in die hohen Dachräume ſind dann wieder zwei Geſchoſſe eingebaut.
Die Wände ſind in gefugtem Backſtein, mit wenig
Hauſtein ausgeführt, und im Zwiſchengeſchoß mit
Grobmörtel gepußt. Die Steilwände der Dach-
geſchoſſe ſind ebenſo wie die Dachflächen ein-
geſchiefert.

Über dem Vorbau des Hauſes Nr. 75 iſt eine
Gartenterraſſe angelegt. Eine vornehme Ausbildung zeigen nur die Türen mit ihren Beſchlägen.
Dieſe und der kleine Weltgenius auf dem Vor-
kopf der Brandmauer zwiſchen beiden Gebäuden
ſind die einzigen Gebilde, die im Aufbau über
das notdürftige hinausgehen — und doch iſt die
ganze Anlage gerade in ihrer ſchlichten Ruhe
einfach vornehm maleriſch.

rue, tandis que le seul étage supérieur est en
retrait; deux étages sont encore construits dans
la haute toiture. Les façades sont en briques
jointoyées avec un peu de pierre de taille,
elles sont crépies de gros mortier à l'entresol.
Les parties verticales des étages du toit sont
de même que les surfaces du toit revêtues
d'ardoises.

Un jardin en terrasse a été établi sur l'avant-
corps. Seules les portes et leures ferrures
témoignent d'un certain luxe; ces portes et le
petit genie place sur le mur mitoyen entre les
deux maisons sont les seules parties de la
construction qui sortent du strict nécessaire — et
rependant, l'ensemble est justement dans sa
noble tranquillité d'un caractère pittoresque et
distingué.

the street the only upper storey is set back.
In the roof storeys of which there are two, are
high rooms. The walls are of pointed brick with
a slight addition of freestone; the intermediate
storey is plaster, rough cast the steep sides of
the roof storey are like the roof, slated.

In front of the house No. 75 over the porch
a garden terrace has been laid out. The doors
with their ornamental details and the small
statue on the projecting part of the fire wall
between the two houses, are the only parts of
the building which are not of the extremest
simplicity and yet the whole effect is exceedingly restful and elegant.

152 [1904: 21]

Das jüngſt eröffnete neue „Amerikaniſche
Hotel, Café und Reſtaurant", das von den
Architekten H. G. Janſen & W. Kromhout CZN.
in Amſterdam, am Leydenſchen Tor, zwiſchen
Marnixquai und Marnixſtraße, an Stelle des
alten Amerika-Hotel errichtet worden iſt, ändert
das altniederländiſche Stadtbild dieſer Gegend
in gleich einſchneidender Weiſe, wie der Bau des
Staatsbahnhofes und der neuen Börſe das Gepräge
der nördlichen Seite der Stadt umgeſtaltet haben.

Das Gebäude hat im Erdgeſchoß an der linken
(kurzen) Seitenfront ein prachtvolles Veſtibül, mit
dem Hauptaufgang zum Hotel und daran an-
ſchließend einen Empfangsſalon, dem ein großer
Speiſeſaal (ganz in Marmor verkleidet) folgt.

152 [1904: 21]

L'hôtel Américain, Café et Restaurant
dernièrement ouvert à Amsterdam, à la
Porte de Leyde, entre le quai Marnix et la
rue Marnix, a été élevé par les architectes
H. G. Jansen & W. Kromhout CZN. à la
place de l'ancien America-Hôtel. Ce bâtiment
modifie l'aspect vieux hollandais de cette partie
de la ville, d'une façon aussi radicale que la
construction de la gare de l'Etat et de la nouvelle
bourse ont modifié le caractère des quartiers nord
de la ville.

L'édifice contient au rez-de-chaussée, sur la
courte face latérale, un magnifique vestibule avec
l'entrée principale conduisant à l'hôtel et à côté,
un salon de reception, auquel fait suite une
grande salle à manger, toute revêtue de marbre.
Au milieu de la façade principale se trouve un
second vestibule avec loge de portier; c'est l'entrée

152 [1904: 21]

The newly opened "American Hotel, Café
and Restaurant" on the Leyden Tor,
between Marnix Quay and Marnixstrasse
Amsterdam has been built by the architects
H. G. Jansen & W. Kromhout CZN. of
Amsterdam, on the site of the old America Hotel.
By this building the old Netherlands appearance
of this part of the town has been entirely altered,
just as the entire face of the northern part of
the city has been changed by the building of
the State Railway terminus and the new Bourse.

On the ground floor on the short left side
front of the building is a splendid vestibule with
the principal entrance to the hotel; this approaches a reception saloon which leads into a large

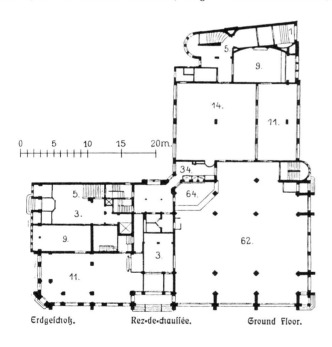

Erdgeſchoß.   Rez-de-chauſſée.   Ground Floor.

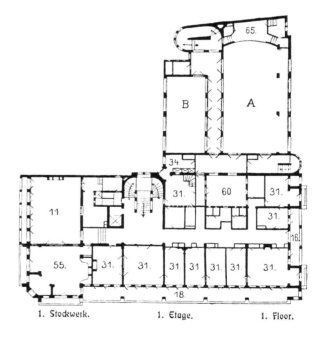

1. Stockwerk.   1. Etage.   1. Floor.

In der Mitte der Vorderfront iſt ein zweites
Veſtibül mit Portierloge; es iſt der Haupteingang
zum Café der den großen Eckſaal rechts einnimmt. An dieſen reihen ſich ein Billard- und
ein zweiter Speiſeſaal und dahinter ein zweiter
Empfangsſaal, der namentlich bei Feſtlichkeiten
in den oberen Lokalen dient. Endlich folgt die
beſondere Feſttreppe.

Im I. Obergeſchoß liegt an der kurzen Front
der Speiſeſaal des Hotels mit einem prachtvollen
Konverſationsſaale an der Ecke. Das Veſtibül
mit der zweiarmigen, nach den oberen Geſchoſſen
führenden Haupttreppe, vermittelt den Verkehr
nach den Fremdenzimmern und den Feſtſälen,
von denen der rechtsliegende größere mit Orcheſter-
bühne ausgerüſtet iſt.

Badezimmer und Kloſetts ſind an paſſenden
Stellen um den Lichthof gruppiert.

principale du café qui occupe la grande salle
d'angle à droite. Après ces locaux vient une
salle de billard et une seconde salle à manger
et derrière, un second salon de réception qui sert
particulièrement lorsqu'il y a des fêtes dans les
appartements du haut. Vient enfin l'escalier
d'honneur spécial.

Au premier étage, on trouve sur la façade
latérale, la salle à manger de l'hôtel avec une
superbe salle de conversation sur l'angle. Le
vestibule, avec l'escalier principal à deux rampes
conduisant aux étages supérieurs, dessert la circulation avec les chambres d'étrangers et les salles
des fêtes, dont la plus grande à droite est pourvue
d'une tribune pour orchestre.

Des chambres de bains et des water-closets
sont disposés d'une façon ingénieuse autour de
la cour.

dining Hall entirely panelled in marble. In the
middle of the front is a second vestibule with
porter's office; this is the principal entrance to
the Café which occupies the large corner saloon
on the right. This is followed by a billiard-
room and a second dining room with a second
reception room which is used for entertainments
and dinners given in the upper floors. Following
this is a special staircase for occasional use.

On the first upper storey on the short front
is the dining room of the hotel with a splendid
conversation saloon at the corner. The vestibule has a staircase leading in two broad divisions to the rooms and saloons above-that on
the right, the larger, has an orchestra stage
equipment.

Bathrooms and lavatories are grouped round
the courtyard in convenient positions.

Das von Architekt Julius Deininger in Wien, Maßlindorferstraße 6 erbaute Zinshaus zeigt in seiner Putzfassade eine neue, auf Einfachheit zielende Richtung der Jünger der Wagnerschule und ist wohl geeignet, mit dem auf Blatt 10 dargestellten, deren gegenwärtige Bestrebungen allgemein zu kennzeichnen, während Blatt 17 wieder die auf reicheren Schmuck ausgehende Tendenz verfolgt. Sehr lehrreich ist unser vorliegendes Fassadenbild durch den Gegensatz der fast nüchternen Erscheinung der Deiningerschen Fassade zu der mit Ornament überladenen Fassade des Nebenhauses, von der ein Teil (links) auf unsrem Bilde miterscheint.

La maison de rapport Matzlindorferstrasse 6 à Vienne bâtie par Monsieur Jules Deininger architecte, montre dans sa façade crépie une nouvelle tendance cherchant son effet dans la simplicité, cultivée par les disciples de Wagner. Cette oeuvre ainsi que celle représentée sur la Pl. 10 sont de nature à caractériser d'une manière très évidente cette tendance nette, tandisque la Pl. 17 vise plutôt à une décoration plus riche. La vue de notre façade est fort instructive grâce au contraste que forment la façade presque nue de Deininger et la façade de la maison voisine dont une partie apparaît à gauche sur notre planche; cette dernière est surchargée d'ornements bouffus.

The dwelling house situated at Maßlindorferstrasse 6 Vienna was built by architect Julius Deininger; the facade is of plaster and the whole building in its admirable simplicity is a good example of the tendency of the Wagner school. No. 10 gives an illustration of this building. The illustration No. 17 is on the other hand an example of a more richly ornamented style. Our facade picture is rendered still more instructive by the contrast with the neighbouring house of which one part (left) appears on our illustration. The sober simplicity of the Deininger facade is a fine contrast to the pretentions overloaded ornament of its neighbour.

Das „Liberaal Volkshuis" (Freie Volkshaus) rue du Peuple in Antwerpen ist im Auftrage der dortigen Société coopérative „Help U Zelve", als deren Geschäfts- und Gesellschaftshaus, durch Architekt Jan van Asperen erbaut und im vorigen Jahre eröffnet worden. Die Kosten betrugen rd. 320000 Mark.

Die Architektur ist in allen Teilen in den, in Belgien als volkstümlich-national angesehenen, „Neuen Formen" durchgeführt, als deren vornehmste Vertreter einst Bankar und Horta galten.

Sämtliche inneren und Rahm-Konstruktionen des vornehmen Baues sind in Eisen mit reichem Zierschmiedewerk, die Fassadenwände aus grauem Backstein und mit blauem Kohlenmuschelkalk (sog. petit granite) hergestellt. Die dekorativen Felder der Fassade sind in venezianischer Glasmosaik ausgeführt.

Ebenso wie die gesamten Konstruktionen, sind auch alle dekorativen Arbeiten unter persönlicher Leitung und nach eigenen Entwürfen und Skizzen des Architekten zur Ausführung gekommen.

Le „Liberaal Volkshuis" (Maison libre du peuple) rue du Peuple à Anvers a été construit au compte de la Société coopérative de cette ville „Help U Zelve", pour lui servir à ses agencements et réunions; c'est l'architecte Jan van Aspersen qui a été chargé des travaux; ces derniers ont été terminés dans le courant de l'anné dernière, les frais s'élevèrent à 320 000 Marks en bloc.

L'architecture de cet édifice est traitée dans toutes ses parties selon l'esprit des „Formes nouvelles" considérées en Belgique comme une sorte de style national populaire, et dont les représentants les plus distingués furent Maîtres Hankar et Horta.

Toutes les constructions intérieures de ce noble bâtiment sont en fer avec de riches ornements forgés; les façades sont en briques grises et en pierre calcaire bleue (petit granit). Les panneaux décoratifs de la façade sont exécutés en mosaiques de verre vénitiennes.

De même que toutes les constructions, tous les travaux décoratifs ont été exécutés sous la direction personnelle et d'après les esquisses et projets de l'architecte.

The "Liberaal Volkshuis" (Free People's House) situated in rue du Peuple in Antwerp has been built by the architect Jan van Aspersen under the auspices of the local cooperative society "Help U Zelve". The house, which was opened last year, cost about 320 000 Marks; it is intended as a business and meeting house for the above society.

The architecture is of the national popular Belgian type, called "New Forms", the most distinguished representatives of which were Hankar and Horta.

The erection and the interior construction of this imposing edifice are framed in iron, with rich ornamental wrought iron work, the facade is of grey brick with blue mountain limestone, the socalled "petit granite". The decorative surfaces of the facade are of Venetian glassmosaic.

The entire construction and all the decorative details have been carried out according to the designs and sketches of the architect and under his personal superintendence.

Mit einer älteren Villa in Copseham (Surrey) in England haben die Architekten E. Guy Dawber und Crawley Boevey in London im Jahre 1902 drei wirtschaftlichen Zwecken dienende Gebäude zu einer malerischen, durch eine Gartenanlage zusammengefaßten Gruppe vereinigt. Zwei davon dienen den sportlichen Neigungen des Besitzers: ein Stallgebäude mit Wagenremise, Geschirrkammer und Ständen für mehrere Pferde, und ein Gebäude, das zur Aufnahme von Fahr-

Les architectes E. Guy Dawber et Crawley Boevey à Londres ont dans l'année 1902 réuni en un groupe pittoresque une ancienne villa à Copseham (Surrey) et trois bâtiments servant à un des emplois économiques, ce groupe est entouré d'un jardin. Deux de ces constructions servent aux goûts sportifs du propriétaire, une comme écurie et remise à voitures, sellerie et boxes pour plusieurs chevaux; l'autre bâtiment est destiné à recevoir les bicyclettes, les auto-

The architects E. Guy Dawber and Crawley Boevey of London have in 1902 taken an old villa in Copseham, Surrey, England and transformed it into three buildings which serve various economic purposes, the whole forming a picturesque group with surrounding gardens. Two of these buildings are used by the owner (of sporting proclivities) for the various requisites. First are stables, with carriage house, harness room, and stalls for

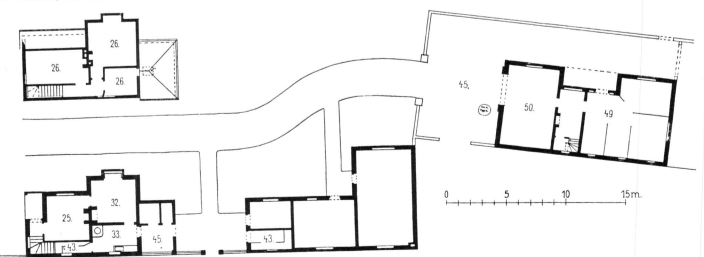

rädern, Automobilen und den zugehörigen elektrischen Batterien bestimmt ist. Das dritte Gebäude enthält die Gärtnerwohnung mit einer Wohnstube, Küche und Abwaschraum im Erdgeschoß und drei Schlafzimmern im Obergeschoß. Die Gebäude sind

mobiles et les batteries électriques. La troisième maison contient l'appartement du jardinier avec une chambre, une cuisine et une toilette au rez-de-chaussée, et trois chambres à coucher au premier étage. Les bâtiments sont en briques

several horses; secondly is a building for the accommodation of bicycles and automobiles and the necessary electric batteries; the third building contains the gardener's dwelling consisting of sitting room, kitchen and scullery on the ground

in roten Bakſteinen, zum Teil mit rauhem Kalk-
bewurf, ausgeführt und mit roten Ziegeln eingedeckt. Die Fenſterrahmen ſind weiß, die Außen-
ſeiten der Tore und Türen grün mit ſchwarzen
Einfaſſungen geſtrichen.

Bei der Wahl des Bauplaßes für ſein eignes
Wohnhaus, genannt „Der Lindenhof“, das
ſich Profeſſor Max Littmann in München in
der Vorſtadt Bogenhauſen, in den Gaſteiganlagen an der Jſar, von 1902—1903 erbaut hat,
war der Umſtand beſtimmend geweſen, daß das
Grundſtück mit ſeiner Front nach Norden zeigte und
dadurch die Möglichkeit gegeben war, alle Wohn-
und Schlafzimmer nach Süden und dem ruhig
gelegenen Garten zu verlegen. Die Wohn- und
Geſellſchaftsräume ſind von den Wirtſchaftsräumen
getrennt, die in einem eignen Trakt, und zwar
mit Rückſicht auf die in München vorherrſchenden
Südweſtwinde, auf der Oſtſeite des Hauſes untergebracht worden ſind. Dieſer wurde durch Ein-
ſchiebung eines Zwiſchengeſchoſſes dreigeſchoſſig
geſtaltet, während der Hauptbau nur zwei Geſchoſſe
hat. An der Straßenfront (Tafel 89) liegen außer
dem zur Diele führenden Haupteingang einerſeits
die Küche, andrerſeits das Zimmer des Herrn,
für das ein unmittelbarer Verkehr von der Straße
her erwünſcht iſt.

Sein Hauptaugenmerk hat der Architekt auf
eine wohlorganiſierte Raumentwicklung, ſelbſt des
untergeordnetſten Zimmers, gerichtet. Die Höhe
des Erdgeſchoſſes wurde durch das 9:6 Meter

rouges en partie recouvertes d'un crépissage
grossier, ils sont recouverts en tuiles rouges.
Les cadres de fenêtres sont blancs, le côté
extérieur des portails et des portes est peint en
vert avec des lignes noires.

Ce qui détermina le choix de la place sur la
quelle le professeur Max Littmann éleva
sa propre demeure appelée le Lindenhof dans
le faubourg de Bogenhausen à Munich,
dans la promenade de Gasteig sur la Jsar,
fut l'orientation de la façade sur la rue au nord,
ce qui permit d'orienter les chambres à coucher
et à habiter du côté du sud et de jouir de la
tranquillité du jardin. La construction dura de
1902 à 1903. Les chambres d'habitation et de
réception sont séparées des locaux de service,
ces derniers se trouvant dans une aile spéciale
située du côté est de la maison, à cause de la
direction dominante des vents à Munich, qui
viennent du sud-ouest. Cette aile fut élevée de
trois étages, grâce à un entresol, tandis que la
maison n'a que deux étages. Sur la façade
donnant sur la rue (Pl. 89), se trouvent, à part
le vestibule conduisant à l'escalier principal, d'un
côté la cuisine, de l'autre la chambre du propriétaire, pour la quelle une communication directe
de la rue était désirée.

Le soin principal de l'architecte a été d'obtenir
une disposition pratique du plan, dans lequel
même la chambre la moins importante doit
être à sa juste place. La hauteur du rez-

floor, with three bedrooms above. The buildings
are of red brick, partly with rough plastering,
and are roofed with red tiles. The window
frames are white, the outside of gates and
doors are green outlined in black.

In choosing the site for his own dwelling
house, Professor Max Littmann of
Munich was careful so to construct the design
that all the living and sleeping rooms faced
south, while the front had a northern aspect.
The house is situated in the suburb Bogenhauſen on the Gaſteiganlagen on the banks
of the Jsar and was built from 1902—1903.
The dwelling and reception rooms are separated
from the household offices, which, in consideration of the prevailing south-west wind of
Munich, extend along the east side. By the
building of an intermediate story this part of
the house consists of three floors while the
remaining part of the house is of only two stories.
On the street frontage (plate 89) there are entrances to the kitchen and to the private room
of the owner as well as the principal entrance
to the hall of the house.

The architect has kept in view in a special
manner the arrangement of the rooms so as to
give the greatest possible cubic measurement

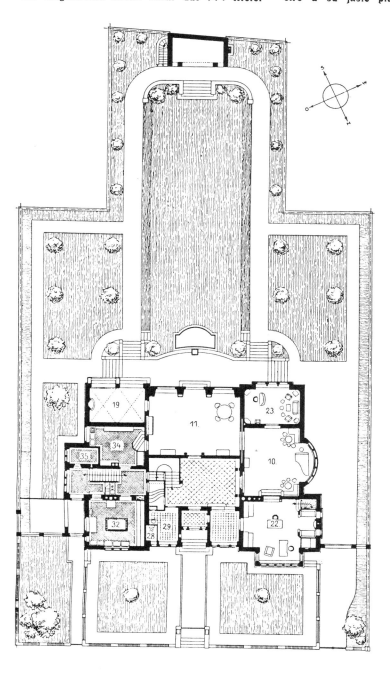

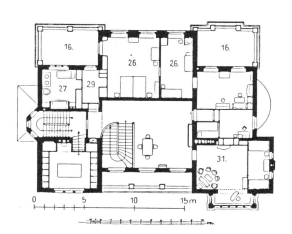

große Speisezimmer auf 4,65 Meter im Lichten bestimmt. Der angrenzende Salon, der zugleich als Musikzimmer dient, hat die gleiche Höhe, erscheint aber durch eine aus akustischen Gründen tief kassettierte Decke niedriger. Das kleinere Herrenzimmer ist noch niedriger geworden durch die Höherlegung des Fußbodens, die durch die unter ihm angeordnete Wohnung des Hausmeisters bedingt war.

Bei der Ausstattung des Innern ist die Verwendung irgendwelcher Surrogate grundsätzlich vermieden worden. Obwohl die Wohn- und Gesellschaftsräume des Erdgeschosses durch künstlerischen Schmuck bevorzugt worden sind, hat der Architekt seine Sorgfalt auch der künstlerischen Durchbildung aller Nebenräume zugewendet.

Das Äußere ist ganz aus dem inneren Organismus entwickelt. Der Sockel ist in Muschelkalk, alle architektonischen Gliederungen sind in Mainsandstein ausgeführt, die Flächen mit weißem Kalkmörtel verputzt. Das Haus ist nur bis zu der baupolizeilich unbedingt nötigen Höhe über das Terrain emporgehoben, damit die Parterreräume mit dem Garten möglichst zusammenwachsen. Aus demselben Grunde ist der Vorgarten vor dem Hause, der durch eine niedrige Balustrade gegen die Straße abgeschlossen ist, gehoben worden. Zu beiden Seiten des Einganges sind die Bronzefiguren eines Hirsches und eines Elches von den Bildhauern Düll und Pezold aufgestellt. Das die Architektur darstellende Fresko über der Eingangstür hat R. von Seitz, den plastischen Schmuck des Erkers Professor Waderé ausgeführt.

de-chaussée fut fixée à 4,65 mètres mesurés dans le vide à cause de la grande salle à manger, la quelle mesure 9:6 mètres. Le salon adjacent qui sert de salle de musique a la même hauteur mais paraît moins haut à cause du plafond à profondes cassettes disposées dans un but acoustique. La chambre plus petite de Monsieur a été réduite de hauteur par l'élévation du sol, cette disposition est motivée par l'appartement du concierge qui se trouve en dessous.

Pour les aménagements intérieurs, il a été fait abstraction par principe de toute espèce de pastiche. Quoique les chambres d'habitation et de réception au rez-de-chaussée aient été privilégiées dans leur décoration, l'architecte a cependant apporté le plus grand soin à l'exécution de tous les locaux secondaires.

L'extérieur est absolument dicté par l'organisme intérieur. Le socle est en pierre calcaire, toutes les parties architecturales sont en grès du Main, les surfaces sont crépies en mortier clair. La maison n'est élevée au dessus du terrain, qu'autant que l'exigent les prescriptions de police, afin que les chambres du rez-de-chaussée se trouvent le plus intimement possible reliées au jardin. Pour la même raison, le jardin devant la maison qui est séparé de la rue par une balustrade basse, a été légèrement élevé. Des deux côtés de l'entrée ont été placées les statues en bronze d'un cerf et d'un élan, modelées par les sculpteurs Düll et Pezold. La fresque au dessus de la porte d'entrée, représentant l'architecture, est l'œuvre de R. von Seitz, la décoration sculpturale de la tourelle est due au ciseau du professeur Waderé.

of space. The height of the ground floor was regulated by that of the dining room (9×6 meters) and is 4,65 meters. The saloon adjoining, which also serves as a music-room, is of the same height although it appears lower on account of the construction of the ceiling which has deep hollows for acoustic reasons. A small smoking room is lower on account of a slightly higher floor necessitated by the dwelling of the steward placed beneath.

In the construction of the interior all imitations have been carefully avoided, and although the reception rooms have specially beautiful artistic decoration, the other less seen apartments have not been forgotten in this respect.

The exterior corresponds to the interior. The sockel is of Muschel limestone, all architectural details are of Main sandstone, the surfaces plastered with white. The house has only been carried to the height above the surface which the police regulations enforce, so that the ground floor rooms have easy access to the garden; for the same reason the front garden, separated from the street by a low railing, has been raised. On each side of the entrance are bronze figures of a stag and an elk by the sculptors Düll and Pezold. The fresco over the entrance is by R. von Seitz, the sculptural decoration of the bay is by Professor Waderé.

157 [1905; 1]

Das Warenhaus Wertheim in Berlin ist im Laufe des Jahres 1904 durch einen Erweiterungsbau vergrößert worden, der sich im Anschluß an den älteren Bau bis an die Ecke des Leipziger Platzes und in diesen hinein noch an dessen Westseite in einer Länge von 38,13 m erstreckt, so daß auch nach dieser Seite hin eine stattliche Frontentwicklung möglich war. Die Front an der Leipzigerstraße ist durch den Erweiterungsbau, der sich hier streng an das bekannte System von bis zum Dache durchgehenden Granitpfeilern anschließt, auf eine Länge von 147,50 Meter gebracht worden.

Für die Ecke und die Front am Leipziger Platz hat sich der Architekt, Professor Alfred Messel, zu einer anderen Lösung seiner Aufgabe entschlossen. Um die Fassade zu einer den Platz beherrschenden Geltung zu bringen, hat er sie in zwei Geschosse von beträchtlichen Höhenabmessungen gegliedert und darüber ein mit schwarzbraunen holländischen Pfannen gedecktes, hoch ansteigendes Mansardendach aufgebracht. Dem unteren Geschoß ist eine Halle vorgelegt, die sich gegen den Leipziger Platz durch vier Bogen, gegen die Leipziger Straße durch einen Bogen öffnet. Das obere Geschoß ist durch vier, durch Stabwerk senkrecht geteilte Fenster durchbrochen. Die abgeschrägte Ecke am Leipziger Platz und die Felder zwischen den Bogen sind von den Bildhauern Josef Rauch und Floßmann in München und Ernst Westpfahl und A. Vogel in Berlin reich mit Figuren und Reliefs geschmückt worden. — Die Front am Leipziger Platz ist in fränkischem Muschelkalkstein ausgeführt.

157 [1905; 1]

La maison de commerce Wertheim à Berlin a été augmentée dans l'année 1904, d'une aile supplémentaire qui, ajoutée à l'ancien bâtiment, le prolonge jusqu'à l'angle de la place Leipzigerplatz et s'étend encore sur cette dernière d'une longueur de 38,13 mètres, de sorte que de ce côté aussi, on obtient un développement imposant de façade. La façade sur la Leipzigerstrasse a été, grâce à cet accroissement, portée à une longueur de 147,50 mètres, la nouvelle partie se raccorde exactement à l'ancienne, en adaptant le principe connu des piliers de granit montant de fond jusqu'au toit.

Pour l'angle et la façade sur le Leipzigerplatz l'architecte, professeur Alfred Messel, a pris le parti d'une autre solution. Pour faire dominer la façade sur la place, il l'a divisée en deux étages d'une hauteur considérable, qu'il a couronnées d'un haut toit mansard recouvert de tuiles hollandaises brun-noires. Il a placé devant le rez-de-chaussée une halle s'ouvrant par quatre arcades sur le Leipzigerplatz et par une sur la Leipzigerstrasse. L'étage supérieur est percé de quatre fenêtres divisées par des meneaux verticaux. Le pan coupé sur le Leipzigerplatz et les champs entre les arcs ont été richement décorés de figures et de reliefs par les sculpteurs Rauch et Flossmann de Munich et Ernest Westpfahl et A. Vogel de Berlin. La façade sur le Leipzigerplatz a été exécuté en pierre calcaire de Franconie.

157 [1905; 1]

The bazaar Wertheim in Berlin has been further enlarged during 1904 by an additional building which joins the former house and extends to the corner of the Leipzigerplatz and down the westside of this for 38,13 meters. This site made it possible for the architect to design a stately building; the front on the Leipzigerstrasse measures 147,50 meters, and the additional building is in strict keeping with the original part, granite pillars extending from ground floor to roof.

The corner and the Leipzigerplatz frontage have been designed by the architect Professor Alfred Messel in a different style. In order to render this corner more effective he has constructed two very lofty stories and over them a mansard roof extending to a great height and faced with black-brown Dutch tiles. The lower story has a sort of arcade opening to the Leipzigerplatz through four arches, and to Leipzigerstrasse through one arch. The upper story contains four windows with perpendicular divisions. The corner to the Leipzigerplatz is chamfered, and has been richly ornamented with figures and reliefs by the sculptors Joseph Rauch and Flossmann of Munich and Ernest Westpfahl and A. Vogel of Berlin; the same artists have ornamented the surfaces between the arches. The front on the Leipzigerplatz is of shell-limestone from Franconia.

158 [1905; 2]

Nach dem Pavillonsystem hat Professor Martin Dülfer in der Zeit von August 1903 bis April 1904 an der Gedonstraße 6 in München ein Doppelhaus erbaut, das in allen seinen Teilen Mietwohnungen von vier bis sieben

158 [1905; 2]

Monsieur le Professeur Martin Dülfer a construit à Munich Gedonstrasse 6, du mois d'août 1903 à celui d'avril 1904 une maison double en système de pavillons. Cet immeuble contient dans toutes ses parties des

158 [1905; 2]

Professor Martin Dülfer, in the time from August 1903 to April 1904 has built a double-house in the Gedonstrasse 6 in Munich, containing flats of four to seven rooms

Zimmern enthält (Tafel 2). Die ganz in Putzbau hergestellte Fassade wirkt vornehmlich durch den Wechsel der in sogenanntem Kammputz ausgeführten Flächen mit den glatt verputzten Fensterumrahmungen und sonstigen Gliederungen. Die Ornamentik bewegt sich in den eigenartig modernen

appartements à louer de quatre à sept chambres (Pl. 2). La façade entièrement construite en maçonnerie crépie obtient son effet par le contraste de surfaces traitées au peigne et des encadrements de fenêtres ainsi que d'autres membres d'architecture traitées lisses. L'orne-

(see plate 2). The facade, entirely of plaster, has an agreeable effect by the contrast of socalled "comb" plastering in wavy ridges with smooth surfaces framing the windows and such

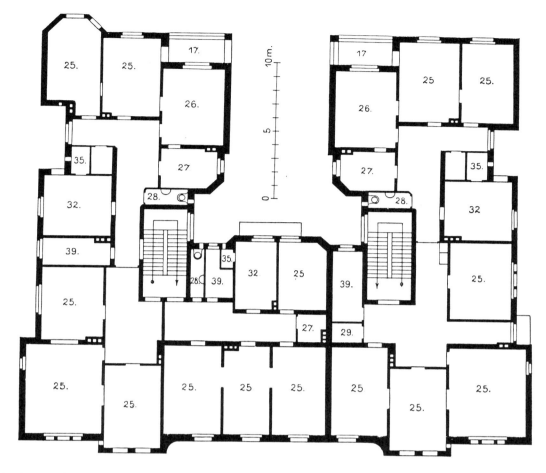

Formen, die der Architekt aus der Antike abgeleitet hat.

Das Dachgeschoß ist in der Mitte zu einem Atelier ausgebaut.

mentation se meut dans le domaine des formes modernes que l'architecte fait dériver de l'antique.

Le toit a été construit de façon à donner place à un atelier dans son milieu.

like parts. The ornament is that peculiar modern form of the antique for which this architect is justly celebrated.

In the roof story is an artist's studio.

159 [1905: 18]

Durch die wirksame Verbindung von gelben, unregelmäßig behauenen Tuffsteinquadern mit grau verputzten Flächen hat die Villa an der Studtstraße 21a in Freiburg im Breisgau, die Rudolf Schmid 1903 mit einem Kostenaufwande von 45000 Mark erbaut hat, einen burgartigen Charakter erhalten. Dieser Eindruck

159 [1905: 18]

La villa bâtie par Rodolphe Schmid Studtstrasse 21a à Fribourg en Brisgau, en 1903 a l'aspect d'un château fort, grâce à l'emploi judicieux de pièces de tuf jaune irrégulièrement taillées et de surfaces crépies de ton gris; cette construction a coûté 45000 Marks. L'impression de château est encore augmenté par le double

159 [1905: 18]

The villa in the Studtstrasse 21a in Friburg in Brisgow was built by Rudolph Schmid in 1903 at a cost of 45000 Marks. By an effective combination of yellow, irregularly hewn tufa square stones with grey plastered surfaces the architect has given the building the appearance of a castle. This effect is heigh-

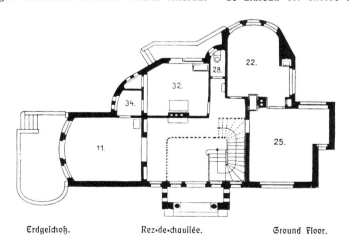

Erdgeschoß.　　　　Rez-de-chaussée.　　　　Ground Floor.

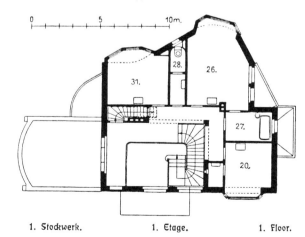

1. Stockwerk.　　　1. Etage.　　　1. Floor.

wird noch durch das doppelte Mansardendach verstärkt, dessen Scheitel durch einen tambourförmigen Aufbau durchbrochen wird (Tafel 17—18).

Das Erdgeschoß enthält ein Wohnzimmer, das Herrenzimmer und das Eßzimmer, das durch die Anrichte mit der Küche in Verbindung steht. Im Obergeschoß liegen ein Arbeitszimmer, ein Schlafzimmer, der Baderaum und ein Fremdenzimmer.

toit mansard dont le faîte est interrompu par une surélévation en forme de tambour (Pl. 17—18).

Le rez-de-chaussée contient une chambre d'habitation, la chambre de Monsieur et la salle à manger, laquelle est reliée à la cuisine par une office. A l'étage supérieur se trouvent une chambre de travail, une chambre à coucher, la chambre de bain et une chambre d'amis.

tened by the double mansard roof the crown of which is ornamented by a tholobate erection (see plate 17—18).

The ground floor contains a living-room, a smoking-room and the dining-room which latter is connected with the kitchen by a serving-room. The upper story contains a study, a bed-room, bath-room and spare bed-room.

Nach einer Bauzeit von drei Jahren ist das neue Justizgebäude in Berlin, das das Landgericht I und das Amtsgericht I aufgenommen hat, auch in dem an der Neuen Friedrichstraße gelegenen Teil vollendet worden. Wie an der Grunerstraße, die den Eingang zum Landgericht vermittelt, ist auch hier der zum Amtsgericht führende Haupteingang durch einen Portalbau ausgezeichnet, der von reich bewegten Giebelaufbauten und einem hinter ihnen aufsteigenden Turm gekrönt wird. Dieser ganz in gelbgrauem Sandstein von warmer Tönung ausgeführte Mittelbau ist noch reicher gegliedert und noch reicher mit ornamentalem und figürlichem Schmuck versehen als der Mittelbau in der Grunerstraße. Unter Verwendung der schönsten Motive des süddeutschen Barockstils hat der Architekt, Otto Schmalz, eine Schöpfung von großartiger Wirkung zustande gebracht, die in allen Einzelheiten von modernem Geiste erfüllt ist (Tafel 6).

Auch das Erdgeschoß der angrenzenden Fronten ist mit Sandstein verkleidet. Die oberen Flächen sind verputzt.

Die Front an der Neuen Friedrichstraße hat nach der Vollendung des ganzen Baues eine Länge von rund 220 Metern.

Le nouveau palais de Justice de Berlin contenant le tribunal civil de première instance et la justice de paix, a aussi été terminé dans sa partie située sur la nouvelle Friedrichstraße après une période de construction de trois ans. De même qu'à la Grunerstraße sur laquelle se trouve l'entrée du tribunal de la justice de paix, ici, l'entrée principale conduisant au tribunal civil de première instance, est aussi marquée par un portail monumental couronné par de riches pignons très mouvementés, derrière lesquels s'élève une tour. Ce corps central, entièrement exécuté en pierre jaune-grisâtre, d'un ton très chaud est encore plus riche dans ses divisions et dans sa décoration ornementale et figurale que l'avant corps situé sur la Grunerstraße. L'architecte Otto Schmalz a, tout en employant les plus beaux motifs du style Baroc de l'Allemagne du Sud, produit une création grandiose, d'un effet imposant, animé dans toutes ses parties d'un esprit moderne (Pl. 6).

Le rez-de-chaussée des façades adjacentes est également revêtu de pierre. Les surfaces supérieures sont crépies.

La façade de la nouvelle Friedrichstraße a, après le parachèvement de tout le monument, une longueur de 220 mètres.

After a period of three years, the new Law Courts in Berlin have at length been finished. They include "Landgericht I" and "Amtsgericht I" as well as the courts lying in the Neue Friedrichstrasse. As in the Grunerstrasse, which contains the entrance to the "Landgericht", the principal entrance to the "Amtsgericht" is through an imposing portal, with an ornamental roof erection, the back of which is crowned by a tower. This part of the edifice is of yellow grey sandstone of a warm tone and forms the middle of the building. It is more elaborately articulated and more ornamentally decorated with statuary than the middle building in the Grunerstrasse. The architect Otto Schmalz has chosen the most beautiful features of the south German barock style, has imbued these in every detail with the modern spirit, and the result is a magnificently effective creation (see plate 6).

The ground floor of the adjoining facade is faced with sandstone. The upper surfaces are plastered.

After the completion of the whole building the frontage on the Neue Friedrichstrasse measures about 220 meters.

Ein bezeichnendes Merkmal des modernen Villenbaus in Deutschland ist die zunehmende Farbenfreudigkeit, die sich aber meist von allzu grellen Wirkungen fernzuhalten weiß. Ein Beispiel

Un signe caractéristique de l'architecture moderne des villas allemandes est la tendance marquée à l'emploi de couleurs, lesquelles sont du reste pour la plupart tenues

A characteristic distinction of modern villa architecture in Germany is the growing taste for colour, — a taste which fortunately seldom degenerates into exaggeration. An example of

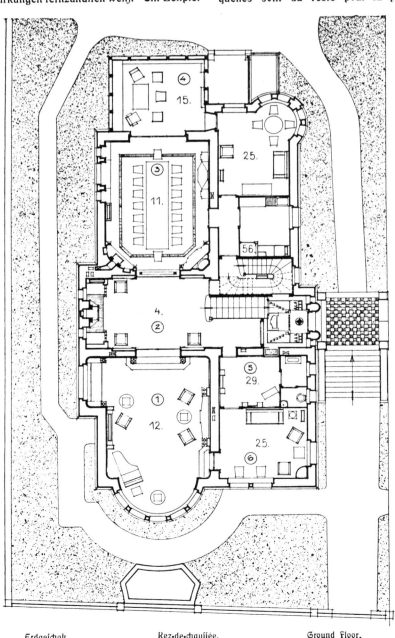

Erdgeschoß.   Rez-de-chaussée.   Ground Floor.

1 Stockwerk.   1. Etage.   1. Floor.

feinfinnigen Maßhaltens ift die von Wehling und Ludwig von September 1901 bis April 1903 erbaute Villa Beltgen am Deutfchen Ring in Köln. Das Sockelgefchoß ift in gelblich-grauem Sandftein ausgeführt; die Flächen darüber find hell verpußt; die Eifenteile find blau und die Holzteile weiß geftrichen; die Säulen am Portal find mit farbigem Glasmofaik bekleidet (Tafel 10).

Das Erdgefchoß enthält, um die Diele gruppiert, einen Mufikfalon, ein Wohnzimmer, das Speife-zimmer in Verbindung mit einem Wintergarten und das Frühftückszimmer. Im Obergefchoß liegen ein Wohnzimmer, ein Arbeitszimmer, vier Schlafzimmer und das Bad.

Die beiden Figuren auf dem Dach hat Bild-hauer Adolf Simatfchek in Düffeldorf aus-geführt.

Die Baukoften betrugen 165000 Mark.

162 [1905: 7]

Zur befferen Verzinfung des von der Kaufmann-fchaft in Wien aufgebrachten Stiftungsfonds hat der Architekt Ernft von Gotthilf in der Zeit vom 1. Oktober 1903 bis 1. September 1904 ein Miethaus erbaut, bei deffen Grundriß-geftaltung der Architekt hauptfächlich darauf Wert gelegt hat, daß fich das Haus für alle eventuell vorkommenden Bedürfniffe eigne. Jedes Stock-werk ift fo disponiert, daß es entweder als ganzes, oder in zwei bis drei Wohnungen oder in mehrere Bureaus geteilt vermietet werden kann, ohne daß durch diefe Teilungen große Koften entftehen.

Die Faffade (Tafel 7) ift zum Teil mit rot-grünen irifierenden Majolikafliefen von Zsolnay in Fünfkirchen bekleidet. — Eine technifche Neuerung find die hier zum erften Male ange-wendeten Fensterverdachungen, die aus fchmiede-eifernen Rahmen mit Verglafung beftehen.

Die Baukoften betrugen etwa 300000 Kronen.

163 [1905: 11]

In der kurzen Frift von März 1903 bis Ende September 1903 haben die Architekten Heil-mann und Littmann an der Theatiner-ftraße 38/39 in München ein fünfftöckiges Gebäude errichtet, deffen zwei untere Gefchoffe Gefchäfte enthalten, während die drei oberen zu Mietwohnungen von je fieben Zimmern mit Zubehör eingerichtet find (Tafel 11). Da das Grundftück bei beträchtlicher Tiefe nur eine geringe Frontentwicklung hat, ift auf eine reiche Gliederung der Faffade mit möglichft ftarker Reliefwirkung Gewicht gelegt worden. Ein weit-ausladendes Gefims fcheidet die beiden unteren Stockwerke von den oberen.

Die Faffade ift ganz in gelbem Sandftein aus Königsbach hergeftellt. Die Friefe zwifchen dem dritten und vierten Gefchoß find vom Bildhauer Seidler in München ausgeführt.

Zur Erhöhung der Feuerficherheit find die Decken zwifchen eifernen Trägern mit Beton eingewölbt und die eifernen Ständer in den unteren Gefchoffen mit Rabißpuß umhüllt.

164 [1905: 12]

Norman Shaw, dem Begründer des neuen Stils im englifchen Wohnhaus-Bau, ift die Mehrzahl der englifchen Architekten gefolgt, weil in dem entfchiedenen Anfchluß an die heimifche Bauweife eine überzeugende Wahrheit lag, die fchnell allgemeinen Eingang fand. Wenn auch feine Nachfolger im einzelnen eigne Wege ein-gefchlagen haben, fo haben fie doch an dem Grund-

---

dans une gamme peu vive. La villa Bestgen au Deutscher Ring à Cologne, construite de septembre 1901 à avril 1903 par Messieurs Wehling et Ludwig donne un exemple de cette délicate réserve. Le socle est exécuté en pierre grise jaunâtre; les surfaces au dessus sont crépies en clair; les parties en fer sont peintes en bleu, celles en bois en blanc; les colonnes du portail sont revêtues de mosaïques de verre polychromes (Pl. 10).

Le rez-de-chaussée contient groupées autour du hall, une chambre de société, la salle à manger, reliée à un jardin d'hiver et la chambre à déjeûner. A l'étage supérieur se trouvent une chambre de société, une chambre de travail, quatre chambres à coucher et le bain.

Les deux figures sur le toit ont été exé-cutées par le sculpteur Adolph Simatscheck à Düsseldorf.

Les frais de construction s'élevèrent à 165000 Marks.

162 [1905: 7]

Afin d'obtenir un plus haut intérêt d'un fonds de fondation, créé par la corporation des marchands de Vienne, Monsieur Ernest von Gotthilf, architecte a construit du premier oc-tobre 1903 au premier septembre 1904, une maison de rapport; dans la composition de son plan, l'architecte s'est particulièrement appliqué à ce que la maison se prêtât à toutes les exigences qui pourraient être posées. Chaque étage est disposé de façon à pouvoir être loué dans son ensemble, ou partagé en deux ou trois apparte-ments ou en plusieurs bureaux, sans que de grands frais soient occasionnés par ces divisions.

La façade (Pl. 7) est en partie revêtue de plaques de faïence vert-rougeâtres, irisées, de Zsolnay à Fünfkirchen. Les avant-toits des fenêtres sont une nouveauté technique appliquée ici pour la première fois, ils consistent en un cadre de fer forgé et vitré.

Les frais de construction s'élevèrent à 300000 couronnes.

163 [1905: 11]

Les architectes Heilmann et Littmann ont élevé dans le temps restreint de mars 1903 à fin septembre de la même année, une maison de cinq étages à la Theatinerstrasse 38/39 à Munich; ses deux étages inférieurs contiennent des locaux de commerce, tandis que les trois supérieurs sont disposés en appartements à louer de sept chambres chacun avec dépendances (Pl. 11). Comme le terrain à bâtir n'avait que peu de front sur la rue, mais une profondeur considérable, on a tenu à faire une façade riche-ment divisée avec des saillies aussi fortes que possible. Un profil très saillant sépare les deux étages inférieurs des supérieurs.

La façade est entièrement construite en pierre jaune de Königsbach. Les frises entre le troi-sième et le quatrième étages ont été exécutées par le sculpteur Seidler de Munich.

Pour augmenter la sécurité contre l'incendie, les plafonds sont construits en béton entre poutres en fer; les colonnes en fer des étages inférieurs ont été entourées d'un manteau de construction Rabiß.

164 [1905: 12]

La plupart des architectes anglais suivit l'exemple de Norman Shaw, le fondateur du nouveau style de la maison d'habitation d'Angleterre. En effet, il existe dans le principe de la continu-ation du style national une vérité convaincante qui trouva partout un écho sympathique. Quoique quelques uns de ses successeurs aient suivi leurs voies propres, ils ont cependant tous

---

the temperate use of this decoration is the villa Bestgen on the Deutscher Ring in Cologne built by Wehling and Ludwig from September 1901 to April 1903. The ground floor is of yellow grey sandstone, the surfaces above are of light plaster, the iron parts are painted blue, and the wood-work is painted white (see plate 10).

The ground floor contains a square hall round which are grouped a music room, a drawing room, the dining room leading to a winter-garden and a breakfast room. In the upper story are a sitting room, a study, four bedrooms and a bath room.

The two figures on the roof are by the sculptor Adolf Simatschek of Düsseldorf.

The cost of building amounted to 165000 Marks.

162 [1905: 7]

In order to increase the income of the pension fund of the Commercial Union of Vienna the architect Ernest von Gotthilf has built a house from 1 October 1903 to 1 September 1904. The ground plan shows that the aim of the architect was to construct a house which should fulfil every purpose. Every story is so arranged that it can be one or more dwellings, or one or more bureaus as the necessity arises; the changes can be made at very little cost.

The facade (see plate 7) is partly faced with redgreen iridescent majolica tiles by Zsolnay at Fünfkirchen. A technical novelty has been adapted to the windows which are for the first time roofed with glazed wrought iron frames.

The cost of building amounted to 300000 Kronen.

163 [1905: 11]

In the short period from March 1903 to the end of September of the same year, the architects Heilmann and Littmann have built a five-storied house in the Theatiner-strasse 38/39 in Munich. The two lower stories are arranged as business premises while the three upper floors are divided into flats of seven rooms each (see plate 11). As the site, though of considerable depth, has only a narrow frontage, the facade is so articulated as to afford the strongest possible relief effects. The widely projecting moulding separates the two lower stories from the upper ones.

The facade is of yellow sandstone from Königsbach. The frieze between the third and fourth floors is by the sculptor Seidler of Munich.

In order to render the building secure against fire, the ceilings are of iron girders with beton; in the lower stories the iron pillars are clothed in Rabiß plaster.

164 [1905: 12]

Norman Shaw, the pioneer of the new style of English dwelling house architecture has been followed by the greater number of English architects, to all of whom the truth seems to have been made clear that this style is the one most in sympathy with the peculiar native archi-tectural conditions. It is true some of his follo-

satze festgehalten, daß für das nordische, ins-besondere für das englische Klima das Fenster das belebende Element der Fassade ist und die Bildung der Fassade zu bestimmen hat. Von diesem Grundsatze ist auch das auf unserer Tafel 12 wiedergegebene Landhaus in Sun-dridge Park beherrscht, bei dem das Haupt-gewicht auf reichen Lichteinfall von allen Seiten gelegt ist. An den beiden Längsfronten ist das beliebte englische Motiv: der weit herausgebogene Erker mit ringsherumgehenden Fenstern, an-gewendet worden.

respecté ce principe: que, étant donné le climat des pays septentrionaux et particulièrement de l'Angleterre, la fenêtre devait être l'élément vivi-fiant de la façade, et qu'elle avait à déterminer la composition de cette dernière. C'est de cette règle qu'est dominée la maison de campagne au Sundridge Park, pour la quelle il a été ajouté une importance capitale à ce que la lumière fût répartie à profusion de tous côtés. Sur les deux longues faces on a adopté le motif préféré de l'architecture anglaise, la tourelle très saillante, toute entourée de fenêtres (Pl. 12).

wers have deviated slightly into paths of their own, but in doing so they have kept fast to the main principle — that for a northern, and specially for the English climate, the window must be the dominating feature of the facade and must decide its construction. This is the leading idea of the house built in Sundridge Park; the principal noticeable feature is the abundant provision made for the entrance of light on all sides. On the two principal frontages one sees the favourite English bay window, large and widely projecting.

165 [1905: 19]

Die Fassade des fünfstöckigen Miethauses am Kurfürstendamm Nr. 8 in Berlin (Tafel 19), das die Architekten Hart und Lesser in der Zeit vom 15. November 1903 bis 1. Oktober 1904 erbaut haben, läßt in dem Wechsel von Loggien und Erkern und in der Mannigfaltigkeit der Fensterausbildungen das Bestreben erkennen, von dem Typus der einförmigen Mietkasernen abzuweichen, der leider auch in jener bevorzugten Gegend Berlins vorherrscht. Der Umstand, daß das Gebäude auf allen Seiten freiliegt, hat den Anlaß zur Anlage eines seitlichen Turmes gegeben, der die Umgebung wirkungsvoll beherrscht.

165 [1905: 19]

La façade de la maison à loyer de cinq étages au Kurfürstendamm No. 8 à Berlin (Pl. 19) que les architectes Hart & Lesser ont bâtie du 15 novembre 1903 au premier octobre 1904 témoigne par la variété de l'arrange-ment des fenêtres, ainsi que par l'alternance de loggias et de tourelles, du désir de renoncer au type monotone de casernes à loyer; type qui malheureusement domine dans cette contrée favorisée de Berlin. Comme cet immeuble est dégagé de tous côtés, on en a profité pour élever une tour latérale qui domine d'une manière caractéristique la contrée.

165 [1905: 19]

The dwelling house Kurfürstendamm No. 8 Berlin (see plate 19) was built by the architects Hart and Lesser from 15 No-vember 1903 to 1 October 1904. The house is five storied, and the numerous loggias and bays as well as the variety in the design of the windows show that the architects have striven to avoid the type of the monotonous barrack-like buildings which are unfortunately only too common even in this, the best part of Berlin. The building is detached on all sides, this afforded an opportunity for the erection of a tower which is an effective object in the neighbourhood.

166 [1905: 22]

An Stelle eines im November 1901 abge-brannten, alten Gasthauses in Traben an der Mosel hat Bruno Möhring in Berlin von Mai 1902 bis September 1903 für den Hotel-besitzer Clauß-Feist einen Neubau errichtet, der in seinen Einzelheiten vielfach an die in den Moselgegenden heimische Bauweise anklingt, aber in seinen stattlichen Abmessungen die alten Bau-werke weit übertrifft (Tafel 22). Am Ufer der Mosel gelegen, beherrscht der Bau nicht nur seine Umgebung, sondern er wirkt auch durch die Aus-bildung des steil ansteigenden Daches und den Eckturm mit seinem schlanken Helm in die Ferne. Das Sockelgeschoß ist in blauem Schieferbruchstein hergestellt; die Architekturteile sind in Sandstein aus Wallerfangen ausgeführt, die Flächen verputzt.

Im Erdgeschoß liegen die zum Hotel- und

166 [1905: 22]

Monsieur Bruno Möhring architecte à Berlin a construit du mois de mai 1902 à celui de septembre 1903, un immeuble pour l'hôtelier Clauss-Feist à la place d'une ancienne auberge brûlée en novembre 1901 à Traben sur la Moselle. Cette construction rappelle en bien des points l'ancienne architecture de la contrée, mais elle surpasse de beaucoup par ses dimensions les vieilles maisons (Pl. 22). Situé au bord de la Moselle, le nouvel hôtel ne domine pas seulement son entourage, mais il s'annonce encore de loin par la disposition de sa haute toiture raide et de sa tour d'angle couronnée d'une flèche élancée. L'étage du socle est construit en pierre d'ardoise bleuâtre, les membres d'architecture sont en pierre de Wallerfangen; les surfaces sont crépies.

166 [1905: 22]

On the site of an old hotel which was burnt down in November 1901 at Traben on the Moselle, Bruno Möhring of Berlin has built a new hotel for the owner Mr. Clauss-Feist from May 1902 to September 1903. In many of its details the new hotel retains the old traditional style of the Moselle neighbour-hood, but its stately proportions by far exceed the modest limits of the old building (see plate 22). Situated on the banks of the Moselle, the hotel is not only the most prominent feature of the immediate neighbourhood, but with its perpendi-cular roof and corner tower surmounted by a slender cupola, it can be seen far in the distance. The basement story is of blue slate quarried stone, the architectural parts are of sandstone from Wallerfangen, the surfaces are plastered.

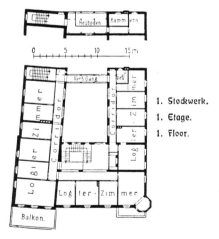

Erdgeschoß.
Rez-de-chaussée.
Ground Floor.

1. Stockwerk.
1. Etage.
1. Floor.

Restaurationsbetrieb nötigen Räume, hinter der offenen Terrasse und der geschlossenen Veranda zunächst ein Gastzimmer, dann das Lesezimmer, das Frühstückszimmer und der Speisesaal. In den beiden Obergeschossen liegen die Logierzimmer, die sämtlich von Korridoren zugänglich sind, die um den offenen Hof gelegt sind.

Von hervorragenden Mitarbeitern sind Maler C. Bisse in Karlsruhe (Wandbild im Speisesaal), O. Eckardt in Berlin (dekorative Malereien), V. Hillmer in Berlin (Metallarbeiten) und W. Knodt in Traben (Holzarbeiten) hervor-zuheben.

Die Baukosten betrugen 120000 Mark.

Au rez-de-chaussée se trouvent les localités nécessaires au service de l'hôtel et du restaurant, derrière la terrasse ouverte et la veranda fermée, une chambre de restaurant, puis la salle de lec-ture, la chambre de déjeûner et la salle à manger. Aux deux étages supérieurs sont placées les chambres d'étrangers qui sont toutes acces-sibles par les corridors situés sur la cour ouverte.

Ont pris part à la construction: Messieurs C. Bisse peintre de Carlsruhe: peinture de la salle à manger, O. Eckardt de Berlin: peintures décoratives, V. Hillmer de Berlin: travaux de métaux et W. Knodt de Traben: travaux de bois. Les frais s'élevèrent à 120000 Marks.

On the ground floor are the rooms necessary for the hotel offices and the restaurant; behind the open terrace and a closed verandah come a guest room, the reading room, the breakfast room and the dining room. In the two upper stories are the bed rooms, all accessible from the corridors and facing the open court yard.

The most important firms and artists employed were painter C. Bisse in Carlsruhe (wall pain-ting in dining room), O. Eckardt in Berlin (deko-rative painting), V. Hillmer in Berlin (metal work) and W. Knodt in Traben (wood work).

The cost of building amounted to 120000 Marks.

Zur Erlangung eines Entwurfs für ein Stadttheater in Dortmund hatte der Magistrat
im Juni 1901 einen Wettbewerb ausgeschrieben,
zu dem alle in Dortmund tätigen Architekten
zugelassen und außerdem eine Anzahl anderer
Architekten eingeladen worden waren, die sich
bereits im Theaterbau bewährt hatten. Das
Ergebnis dieses Wettbewerbs war, daß zwischen
den Herren Moritz, Dülfer und Fellner & Helmer
ein engerer Wettbewerb veranstaltet wurde, aus
dem Professor Martin Dülfer in München als
Sieger hervorging. Nach seinen Plänen ist der
Bau in der Zeit vom 15. Januar 1903 bis
15. September 1904 ausgeführt worden. Sowohl
in der Anordnung und Ausbildung der inneren
Räume wie in der Gestaltung des Äußeren bietet
er so starke Abweichungen von dem überlieferten
Theatertypus, daß er als eine bedeutsame Erscheinung in der Entwicklung des modernen
Theaterbaues bezeichnet werden muß.

Auf die eigenartige Ausbildung des Grundrisses hat zunächst natürlich die Gestalt des Bauplatzes eingewirkt, der von drei sich unter schrägen
Winkeln schneidenden Straßen begrenzt wird.
Aus dieser wenig günstigen Gestalt hat Dülfer
aber einige Vorteile gezogen, die es ermöglicht
haben, daß auch die zum Bühnenbetrieb erforderlichen Nebengebäude mit dem Hauptgebäude in
unmittelbare Verbindung gebracht werden konnten.
So ist das Kulissenhaus durch eine Nebenbühne
an die Bühne direkt angeschlossen, und seitwärts
schließt sich an das Bühnenhaus in bogenförmigem
Grundriß ein Flügel an, der die Räume für die
Verwaltung enthält. Diesem Verwaltungsflügel
(Tafel 24) sollte auf der andern Seite (Westseite)
ein zweiter, gleichartiger Flügel für Wohnungs-
zwecke entsprechen, dessen Ausführung aber vor-
läufig aufgegeben worden ist.

Auch der Zuschauerraum zeigt eine vom Herkömmlichen abweichende Gestaltung. Die Decke,
die sich wie ein Zelt ohne Stützen über den
ganzen Raum spannt, fällt von der Rückwand
des dritten Ranges stark nach vorn ab, so daß
sie sich unmittelbar an die Wand des Proszeniums
anschließt. Dadurch hat der Architekt eine geschlossene Wirkung des Zuschauerraums erzielt
und die Aufmerksamkeit des Publikums auf das
Bühnenbild konzentriert. Zu diesem Zwecke ist
auch der Fußboden des Parketts nach der Mitte
muldenförmig vertieft worden. Da die Decke
des Zuschauerraums direkt auf der Wand lastet,
konnten auch bei den Rangbalkonen alle störenden
Stützen vermieden werden.

Pour obtenir un projet de théâtre de la
ville, la municipalité de Dortmund avait
en juin 1901 publié un concours auquel pouvaient
prendre part les architectes établis à Dortmund
et un certain nombre d'architectes étrangers ayant
déjà acquis une notoriété dans la construction
de théâtres et qui furent spécialement invités.
Le résultat de ce concours fut une seconde
épreuve restreinte entre Messieurs Moritz, Dülfer
et Fellner & Helmer, dont Monsieur le professeur
Martin Dülfer de Munich sortit vainqueur.
C'est d'après ses plans que le monument fut
élevé du 15 janvier 1903 au 15 septembre 1904.
Ce théâtre présente dans l'aménagement intérieur
aussi bien que dans son aspect extérieur, une
différence si grande du type habituel de ces
sortes d'édifices, qu'on peut le considérer comme
faisant époque dans l'histoire du développement
du théâtre moderne.

Il va sans dire que c'est d'abord la forme
du terrain, limité par trois rues se coupant à angles
inégaux, qui a surtout influencé la composition
du plan. Dülfer a su tirer de ces conditions,
plutôt génantes du terrain, certains avantages,
entre autres celui de placer en rapport direct
avec le bâtiment principal, les dépendances indis-
pensables au service de la scène. C'est ainsi
que le magasin des décors est directement relié
par une arrière-scène à la scène principale;
et sur le côté, une aile dont le plan est en
forme d'arc et qui contient les bureaux de l'administration rejoint également la scène. De
l'autre côté (à l'ouest) devait s'élever une aile
semblable à celle de l'administration et lui faisant
pendant, elle aurait servi à l'habitation (Pl. 24),
on a cependant pour le moment renoncé a son
exécution.

La salle de spectacle montre aussi des sin-
gularités qui la distinguent des types connus.
Le plafond qui s'étend comme une tente sur
toute la salle sans supports, s'abaisse rapidement
depuis la paroi postérieure de la troisième galerie
sur le devant, de façon à se relier directement
avec la facade de l'avant-scène. De cette manière,
l'architecte a obtenu un effet simplifié et harmonieux, il concentre en même temps l'attention
du public sur la scène. Dans le même but, le
plancher du parquet a été creusé en forme de
vallon sur le milieu. Comme le plafond repose
directement sur les murs de la salle, tous les
appuis génants pouvaient être supprimés pour
les galeries.

In order to obtain a design for the town
theatre of Dortmund, the town authorities
in June 1901 offered an open competition, in
which all Dortmund architects were invited to
compete as well as many others who were
known to be experienced in designing theatres.
The result was the choice of three designs,
those of Messrs Moritz, Dülfer and Fellner
& Helmer. Of these three designs the prize
fell to Professor Martin Dülfer of Munich.
The building was carried out according to his
designs from 15 January 1903 to 15 September
1904. In the distribution and equipment of the
interior as well as in the erection of the exterior,
this artist has shown such marked individuality,
and has struck out such new paths differing
completely from the old conventional types, that
he must be considered as a most important
figure in the development of modern theatre-
building.

The peculiar design of the ground plan was
of course the result of the nature of the site
which is bounded by three street frontages
crossing at acute angles. From these rather
unfavourable circumstances Professor Dülfer has
made it possible for an advantage to be gained,
that of having all the necessary secondary
buildings for the stage management under one
roof. Thus we find the scenery house directly
connected with the stage by a secondary stage,
at the side of the stage, is a circular wing in
which are situated the rooms for the administration. This wing (see plate 24) was originally
to be repeated on the other (west) side and to
be used for dwelling rooms but at present that
has not been carried out.

The auditorium differs materially from the
conventional type. The ceiling, like a tent
without supports, spans the whole space, and
from the wall of the third tier slopes abruptly
forward so that it directly joins the walls of the
proscenium. By this means the architect has
achieved an effect by which the whole attention
of the audience is concentrated on the stage.
For this same reason, the floor of the stalls
about the middle has a trough-like depression.
As the ceiling of the auditorium rests directly
on the walls, all disturbing supports and pillars
are rendered unnecessary.

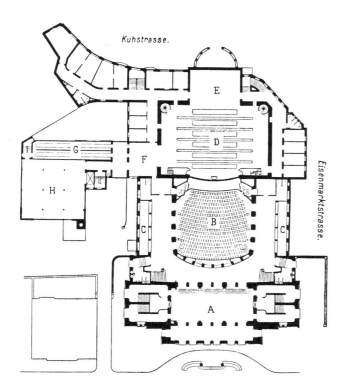

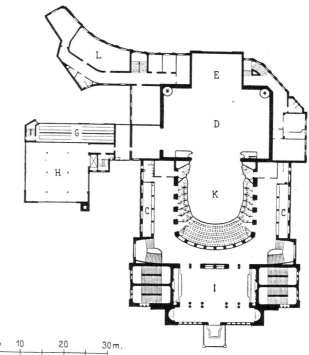

0 5 10   20   30 m.

Bei der Ausbildung der Hauptfront (Tafel 23) ist der Architekt von dem Gedanken ausgegangen, daß ein Theater seinen Hauptzweck nur in den Abendstunden zu erfüllen hat, und demnach ist er auch hier von dem herkömmlichen Typus abgewichen, indem er mit der Anlage von Fenstern sehr sparsam gewesen ist. Er hat Lichtöffnungen nur da angebracht, wo der Einlaß des Tageslichts erforderlich war, und dadurch größere Mauerflächen gewonnen, die zum Eindruck einer feierlichen Monumentalität wesentlich beitragen.

In der Detaillierung hat Dülfer wieder die von ihm eigenartig ausgebildete Formensprache angewendet, die er aus der Antike abgeleitet hat.

Die Hauptfront ist in Tuffstein mit Sockel aus Basaltlava, die Nebenfronten sind in Münchener Putztechnik ausgeführt. Zu den beiden Genien an der Hauptfront ist zu bemerken, daß sie vergoldete Lorbeerkränze emporhalten, die zur Zeit unserer photographischen Aufnahme abgenommen waren.

Die Baukosten betrugen 1 200 000 Mark einschließlich der Bühneneinrichtung, der Möblierung und des Architektenhonorars.

Pour la disposition de la façade principale (Pl. 23) l'architecte est parti du principe qu'un théâtre étant surtout en activité de nuit, il fallait faire le moins de fenêtres possibles, s'écartant en cela de nouveau du type usuel. Il n'a fait d'ouvertures que là où la lumière du jour était indispensable, il a de cette façon gagné de grandes surfaces de mur qui contribuent singulièrement à augmenter l'impression de monumentalité solennelle de cet édifice.

Dans la composition du détail, Dülfer a de nouveau employé son style particulier pour lequel il s'inspire de l'antique.

La façade principale est exécutée en tuf avec socle de lave de basalt; les façades latérales sont exécutées en crépissage selon la manière de Munich. Les deux génies de la façade principale portent des palmes dorées qui manquaient au moment où nous avons photographié l'édifice.

Les frais de construction s'élevèrent à 1 200 000 Marks, y compris l'installation de la scène, le mobilier et les honoraires de l'architecte.

In the construction of the principal front the architect has been dominated by the idea that a theatre is principally built for use at night, for this reason he has departed from the conventional rule and windows are very scarce. Openings for light only occur where they are really necessary by this means large surfaces have been won which add not a little to the imposing effect of the edifice.

In details, Professor Dülfer has expressed himself in those now well-known but characteristic forms which he has modernized from the antique.

The principal front is of tufa stone, the socle of basalt lava, the side fronts are of Munich plaster. It is to be remarked that the two genii on the principal front are holding up golden bay wreaths, these had been taken away at the time of our photographic illustration.

The cost of building amounted to 1 200 000 Marks including the equipment of the stage, the furniture and the architects' fees.

168 [1905; 25]

Die Erläuterung und die Grundrisse der von Geh. Oberbaurat Professor Hoffmann erbauten Nibelungenschule in Worms werden wir in Heft 2 folgen lassen.

Anmerkung des Verlages zur vorliegenden Neuausgabe 1989: Die Erläuterungen und die Grundrisse der von Geh. Oberbaurat Professor Hoffmann erbauten Nibelungenschule wurden in der Originalausgabe irrtümlicherweise nicht veröffentlicht und fehlen daher auch in der Neuausgabe.

168 [1905; 25]

Le texte explicatif et les plans de la Nibelungenschule à Worms, construite par Mr. le professeur Hoffmann, seront publiés dans la livraison prochaine.

Remarque de la maison d'édition sur la nouvelle parution 1989: Les explications et les plans de l'école „Nibelungenschule", conçue par l'architecte professeur Hoffmann, ayant été involontairement omis de l'édition originale, ils ne figurent pas par conséquent dans notre réédition.

168 [1905; 25]

The explication and the groundplans of the Nibelungenschule at Worms, built by the Geheime Oberbaurat Hoffmann, shall be published in the next number.

Publisher's note to the 1989 reprint: The descriptions and plans of the Nibelungen School (designed by privy architect Professor Hoffmann) were mistakenly omitted from the original edition and therefore cannot be presented here.

169 [1905; 58]

Nach dem Vorgang der Bauverwaltung der Deutschen Reichspost hat auch die Bauverwaltung der preußischen Staatseisenbahnen in neuerer Zeit den rühmenswerten Grundsatz befolgt, sich bei dem Neubau von Bahnhofsgebäuden den Baugewohnheiten der betreffenden Gegenden anzupassen. Ein schönes Beispiel dafür ist der vom Regierungsbaumeister Hüter erbaute Bahnhof in Cochem an der Mosel, der sich in den Details seiner Außenseiten an die Grundmotive des Hausbaues in den Moselgegenden anschließt. Die Fassaden (Tafel 58) sind teils in Hau- und Bruchstein, teils in Putzbau in Verbindung mit Fachwerkbau ausgeführt. Auch in der Belebung der Fassaden mit Türmen, Giebeln und Erkern und in der malerischen Gestaltung des Daches ist der Architekt den alten, noch zahlreich vorhandenen Vorbildern gefolgt.

Suivant l'exemple de l'administration des postes impériales allemandes, l'administration des chemins-de-fer d'état prussiens a pris le louable parti de se conformer, pour la construction de nouvelles gares, aux traditions architectoniques de la contrée où elles devaient s'élever. Un bel exemple de cette tendance est la gare de Cochem sur Moselle construite par l'architecte du gouvernement Hüter, lequel s'inspira des motifs fondamentaux de l'architecture des maisons du bassin de la Moselle pour le détail de ses façades. Ces dernières sont en partie en moëllons et pierre de taille, en partie en maçonnerie crépie combinée avec la construction de pans de bois apparents, elles sont aussi agrémentées de tours, de frontons et de tourelles et l'architecte a aussi suivi l'exemple des anciens en donnant aux toits un groupement pittoresque.

Following the example of the building administration of the German Imperial Post, the building authorities of the Prussian State Railways have latterly adopted the praiseworthy idea of suiting the architecture of the new station buildings to that of the surrounding neighbourhood. An admirable example of this is the railway station at Cochem on the Moselle, built by the Regierungsbaumeister Hüter; this in the details of the exterior, is of the same character as the houses built in the neighbourhood of the Moselle. The facades (see plate 58) are partly of hewn and partly of freestone, and are partly of plaster and partly of frame work. In the use of turrets, gables and bays for the facade, the architect has taken the numerous examples at his disposal and has made admirable use of them.

170 [1905; 33]

In dem Landhause eines Gärtners in Chestrut Hill, Mass. (Vereinigte Staaten von Nordamerika), das die Architekten Coolidge und Carlson in Boston erbaut haben, bieten wir ein bezeichnendes Beispiel amerikanischen Villenstils, der sich mit großem Geschick der landschaftlichen Umgebung wie den klimatischen Verhältnissen anzupassen und zugleich den besonderen Charakter eines jeden Bauwerkes scharf zu betonen weiß (Tafel 33). Schon das Eingangstor mit seinem Schindeldach und seinen rustikalen Säulen bereitet auf den ländlichen Charakter des zugehörigen Gebäudes vor. Unter dem ganzen Haus zieht sich ein Keller hin, der den Heizapparat, die Feuerungsmaterialien, die Kühlräume, die Waschküche u. a. m. enthält. Die Außenwände und das Dach, das das obere Geschoß enthält, sind mit Schindeln bekleidet und moosgrün bemalt.

En publiant la maison de campagne d'un jardinier à Chestrut Hill, Mass. (Etats Unis de l'Amérique du Nord) construite par les architectes Coolidge et Carlson de Boston, nous faisons connaître un exemple caractéristique du style de villas américaines qui sait admirablement s'adapter au caractère du paysage ainsi qu'aux conditions climatériques, et qui exprime en ontre avec précision le caractère de chaque construction (Pl. 33). La porte d'entrée déjà avec son toit en bordeaux et ses colonnes de bosses rustiques prépare au caractère campagnard de la maison dont il dépend. Au dessous de toute la maison s'étend une cave contenant l'appareil de chauffage, le local réfrigérant, la buanderie etc. Les façades et le toit qui contient l'étage supérieur sont recouverts en bordeaux et peints en vert mousse.

The architects Coolidge and Carlson of Boston U. S. America have built a country house for a gardener in Chestrut Hill, Mass. This villa is a typical example of American villa architecture, and shows how American architects understand the art of taking into consideration scenic charm, climatic peculiarities, and architectural individuality. (See plate 33.) The entrance, with its shingled roof, gives at once a rustic character to the whole which is carried out in the same style. Under the whole house is a large cellar which contains the heating apparatus the fuel accomodation, the ice cellar, the washhouse etc. The outside walls and the roof are faced with shingle and painted mossgreen.

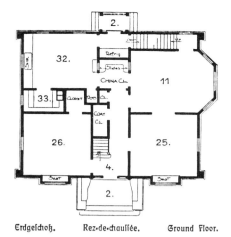

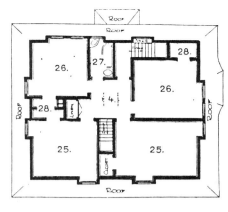

| Erdgeſchoß. | Rez-de-chaußée. | Ground Floor. | 1. Stockwerk. | 1. Étage. | 1. Floor. |

Die den Mittelpunkt des Hauſes bildende Halle enthält eine ornamentierte, zum oberen Stockwerk führende Wendeltreppe, unter der eine Garderobe angelegt iſt. Rechts vom Eingang liegt das Wohnzimmer mit einem Fenſterſitz und auf der anderen Seite, aber mit ihm in Verbindung ſtehend, das Speiſezimmer mit einem Erker. Von ihm führt eine zweite Treppe zum oberen Stockwerk, neben der die Kellertreppe liegt. Zu der mit allen modernen Einrichtungen verſehenen Küche gehören eine Speiſekammer und ein Nebenraum für das Eisſpind. An der Vorderſeite, dem Wohnzimmer gegenüber, liegt ein Schlafzimmer mit einem geräumigen Wandſchrank. Das obere Stockwerk enthält vier Schlafzimmer und die Badeſtube.

Un hall forme le centre de la maison, il contient un escalier tournant décoré, conduisant à l'étage supérieur, au dessous, on a disposé un vestiaire. À droite de l'entrée se trouve la chambre d'habitation avec un bowendow et de l'autre côté, mais communiquant avec elle, la salle à manger avec une tourelle, de cette dernière un second escalier conduit à l'étage supérieur; à côté se trouve l'escalier conduisant à la cave. La cuisine est pourvue de toutes les installations les plus modernes, elle possède un garde-manger et un local pour la glacière. Sur le devant, vis-à-vis de la salle à manger se trouve une chambre à coucher avec une armoire spacieuse. L'étage supérieur contient quatre chambres à coucher et la chambre de bains.

In the hall, which forms the middle of the house is an ornamental winding staircase, cender which is a cloak room. On the right of the entrance is a dwelling room with a window seat and on the other side, but in connection with it, the dining room with a bay window. From this a second staircase leads to the upper story by the side of which the cellar staircase is placed. The kitchen is equipped with every modern convenience adjoining it is a pantry, with ice cupboard accomodation leading from it. In the front of the house opposite the sitting room is a bed room with a spacious wall cupboard. The upper story contains four bed rooms and the bath room.

171 [1905: 49]

Im Villenbau Münchens und ſeiner Vororte hat die Neigung zu einer möglichſt ſchlichten, dem einfachen Bürgerſinn entſprechenden Geſtaltung der Faſſaden ſeit geraumer Zeit die Oberhand gewonnen. Auf reichen plaſtiſchen Schmuck wie auf maleriſche Gruppierung der Bauteile wird verzichtet. Nur die Mitwirkung der Farbe wird mehr oder weniger herangezogen. Daß ſich trotz dieſer Beſchränkung ein ſehr vornehmer Eindruck erzielen läßt, zeigt die Villa Schneider an der Möhlſtraße 27, die Heilmann und Littmann von Mai 1902 bis April 1903 erbaut haben (Tafel 49). Die Faſſaden ſind in Kalkmörtel geputzt und haben nur an einzelnen Stellen einen ſparſamen plaſtiſchen Schmuck erhalten. Dazu kommt ein Fries in der Hohlkehle des Hauptgeſimſes, den der Maler Möſſel in Fresko ausgeführt hat.

Im Erdgeſchoß gruppieren ſich um die Diele Herrenzimmer, Speiſezimmer, Salon, Wohnzimmer und eine Terraſſe, von der eine Treppe zum Garten hinabführt. Im Obergeſchoß liegen ein Schlafzimmer, ein Toilettezimmer, ein Schrankzimmer und zwei Fremdenzimmer.

Depuis longtemps, la construction des villas à Munich et dans ses environs a adopté comme système dominant, la tendance à une extrême simplicité dans la composition des façades, simplicité correspondant au bon sens d'une société bourgeoise. On renonce à une riche décoration plastique, ainsi qu'à un groupement pittoresque des différentes parties de la construction. On ne fait appel qu'à l'aide plus ou moins efficace de la couleur. La villa Schneider à la Möhlstrasse 27 construite par Heilmann et Littmann du mois de mai 1902 a celui d'avril 1903, montre que l'on peut obtenir un effet très distingué avec ces éléments réduits (Pl. 49). Les façades sont crépies au mortier de chaux et ont été ornées, à certaines places d'une modeste décoration plastique. Il faut encore y ajouter une frise que le peintre Mössel a peint à fresque dans la gorge de la corniche.

Au rez-de-chaussée, les pièces suivantes se groupent autour du hall: chambre de Monsieur, salle à manger, salon, chambre d'habitation et une terrasse d'où un escalier conduit au jardin. À l'étage supérieur se trouvent une chambre à coucher, une chambre de toilette, une chambre d'armoires et deux chambres d'amis.

The villa architecture of Munich and its suburbs has during the last years shown a decided tendency to simplicity of style as being the most suitable for the citizen's dwelling house. We find very little sculptural ornament, even picturesque grouping of the different parts seems to be avoided. Only the help of colour has been more or less employed: and that this is capable of producing a distinguished impression may be seen by the Villa Schneider in the Möhlstrasse 27, built by Heilmann and Littmann from May 1902 till April 1903 (see plate 49). The facades are of lime plaster and have only in certain parts a very unimportant sculptural ornament. Round the principal moulding is a frieze carried out in fresco by the painter Mössel.

On the ground floor grouped round the hall are the study, dining room, drawing room, breakfast room and a terrace leading to the garden. In the upper story are a bed room, a dressing room, a wardrobe room and two spare bed rooms.

172 [1905: 62]

Für einen Arzt haben die Architekten Lambert und Stahl an der Leſſingſtraße Nr. 12 in Stuttgart in der Zeit von April 1903 bis Juli 1904 eine Villa erbaut, die in ihrem Erdgeſchoß zunächſt dem Eingang das Warte- und Sprechzimmer und im übrigen die Geſellſchaftsräume (Zimmer der Frau des Hauſes, Speiſezimmer uſw.) enthält. Im Obergeſchoß liegen die Wohn- und Schlafzimmer, im Dachgeſchoß Fremdenzimmer und die Räume für die Dienerſchaft.

Das Untergeſchoß iſt mit Hauſtein verkleidet; die oberen Geſchoſſe ſind in Backſteinmauerwerk aufgeführt, das verputzt iſt, bis auf die Einrahmungen der Fenſter und Türen, die in Werkſtein hergeſtellt ſind. Das Dach iſt mit Schiefer gedeckt. Die Baukoſten betrugen 95000 Mark.

Les architectes Lambert et Stahl à Stuttgart ont construit pour un médecin à la Lessingstrasse No. 12 du mois d'avril 1903 à celui de juillet 1904 une villa, contenant au rez-de-chaussée près de l'entrée les chambres d'attente et de consultation, ainsi que les pièces de réception: chambre de Madame, salle à manger etc. L'étage supérieur contient une chambre d'habitation, et les chambres à coucher; dans le toit se trouvent les chambres d'amis et de domestiques.

Le socle est construit en pierre, les étages supérieurs en maçonnerie de briques crépie; les encadrements de fenêtres et de portes sont en pierre de taille. Le toit est recouvert en ardoises.

Les frais de construction s'élevèrent à 95000 Marks.

The architects Lambert and Stahl have built at Lessingstrasse 12, Stuttgart a villa for a doctor. The time occupied was from April 1903 to July 1904. On the ground floor is the entrance to the surgery and consulting room, as well as the principal rooms of the house, such as dining room, morning room etc. On the upper story are dwelling and bed rooms in the roofstory spare bed rooms, and accommodation for servants.

The lower story is faced with stone, the upper part is of brick which is plastered except in the framing of windows and doors, these are of stone. It is roofed with slate.

The cost of building was 95000 Marks.

Das Wohnhaus in Brüssel, Rue de la Vallée Nr. 45, ist ein bezeichnendes Beispiel für den unter dem Einfluß der modernen Bewegung entwickelten Wohnhausbau in der belgischen Hauptstadt. Unter Vermeidung aller aufdringlichen Ornamentik wird nur nach dem Eindruck ruhiger, einfacher Vornehmheit gestrebt, die jedem Hause ein eigenartiges Gepräge gibt. Haufteinflächen wechseln mit Backsteinflächen ab, die durch das zierliche Linienspiel der schmiedeeisernen Balkongitter angenehm belebt werden.

La maison d'habitation construite à Bruxelles, Rue de la Vallée No. 45 est un exemple caractéristique de l'influence exercée par la direction moderne sur l'architecture privée dans la capitale de la Belgique. Tout en évitant toute ornementation prétentieuse il n'a été cherché ici que l'impression de simplicité distinguée, capable de donner à chaque maison un cachet particulier. Les surfaces de pierre alternent avec des champs de briques et sont agrémentées par l'élégante lignes des balcons de fer forgé.

A dwelling house built at Rue de la Vallée 45 Brussels is an excellent example of the influence at work in the development of modern house architecture in the Belgian capital. Avoiding every unnecessary ornament, the architect strives only to attain simple, quiet excellence; and thus each house has its own distinguishing characteristics. Hewn stone alternates with brick in the facades, to which a certain elegance is given by the graceful lines of the iron work balconies.

In einem in der Nähe von Lüttich gelegenen Park hat der Architekt Gustav Serrurier eine zweigeschossige Villa erbaut, deren Detaillierung sich in den modernen Stilformen bewegt, die sich während der beiden letzten Jahrzehnte in Belgien unter der Führung von Horta und Hankar herausgebildet haben (Tafel 86 und 87). Die Fassaden sind in blaugrauem Zement verputzt unter Verwendung von blau emaillierten Backsteinen und grauem Haustein.

Im Erdgeschoß, dessen Eingang von einem schmiedeeisernen Bogen überspannt ist, gelangt man aus dem Vestibül in eine geräumige Halle, aus der einerseits der Zugang zu einem Salon mit angrenzender Terrasse und zu dem Speisesaal, andrerseits zu der Küche und ihren Nebenräumen erfolgt. Im Obergeschoß liegen ein Salon, ein Wohnzimmer, zwei Schlafzimmer mit Toiletteraum und das Badezimmer.

Monsieur Gustave Serrurier a construit dans un parc situé dans le voisinage de Liège une villa à deux étages. Le détail de cette maison se meut dans l'esprit des formes modernes, telles qu'elles se sont développées en Belgique dans les dix dernières années sous l'influence de Horta et de Hankar (Pl. 86 et 87). Les façades sont crépies en ciment gris-bleu avec emploi de briques émaillées et de pierre grise.

Au rez-de-chaussée, dont l'entrée est couverte d'un arc en fer forgé, on parvient par un vestibule dans un hall spacieux, qui donne accès d'un côté à un salon avec terrasse adjacente, de l'autre côté, à une cuisine et à ses dépendances. A l'étage supérieur se trouvent un salon, une chambre d'habitation, deux chambres à coucher avec toilette et chambre de bain.

In a park in the neighbourhood of Liege, the architect Gustavus Serrurier has built a two storied villa, the details of which are all in modern style; a style, which during the last 20 years has been largely represented by such men as Horta and Hankar (see plates 86 and 87). The facades are of blue grey cement plaster with a mixture of blue enamelled bricks and grey hewn stone.

On the ground floor, which is entered by a wrought iron arch, one enters a spacious vestibule, from one side of this is the entrance to the drawing room; with an adjoining terrace, and to the dining room; on the other side are the kitchen and domestic offices. In the upper story is a saloon, a sitting room, two bed rooms with dressing rooms and a bath room.

Der Palazzo Castiglione in Mailand (Tafel 37) ist in der Zeit vom 1. Dezember 1901 bis zum 20. Juni 1904 von dem Architekten Giuseppe Sommaruga erbaut worden, der sich durch Bauten gleichen Stilgepräges auch in England und Nordamerika bekannt gemacht hat. Das Sockelgeschoß und das erste Stockwerk bilden eine zusammenhängende Wohnung, die von dem Besitzer des Palastes eingenommen wird. Im Sockelgeschoß liegen links vom Eingang vier Räume, die als Arbeits- und Geschäftszimmer des Besitzers dienen und durch eine besondere Treppe mit dem darüber liegenden Stockwerk in Verbindung stehen. Rechts vom Eingang liegt die Pförtnerwohnung, und im rückwärtigen Teil sind die Wirtschaftsräume — Küche, Waschküche, Bügelzimmer usw.

Le palais Castiglione à Milan (Pl. 37) à été construit dans l'espace du 1 décembre 1901 au 20 juin 1904 par l'architecte Giuseppe Sommaruga, qui par des constructions analogues de style a su se faire aussi un nom en Angleterre et en Amérique. Le rez-de-chaussée et le premier étage forment ensemble un appartement occupé par le propriétaire du palais. Au rez-de-chaussée se trouvent quatre pièces à gauche de l'entrée, ils servent au propriétaire de chambres de travail et d'affaires et sont mises en communication avec l'appartement du dessus au moyen d'un escalier spécial. A droite de l'entrée est l'appartement du concierge et en arrière les locaux de service, cuisine, buanderie, chambre de repassage etc. ainsi que les chambres de domestiques. Sur l'angle droit

The Palazzo Castiglione in Milan (see plate 37) has been built from 1 December 1901 till 20 June 1904 by the architect Giuseppe Sommaruga who is already well-known by several buildings of the same style both in England and America. The ground floor and first floor comprise one dwelling which is inhabited by the owner of the palace. On the ground floor on the left of the entrance lie four apartments which are used as the study and business bureau of the owner, and which are connected with the floor above by a special staircase. On the right of the entrance is the porter's lodging, in the back part are the domestic offices (kitchen, washhouse, laundry etc.) and accommodation for

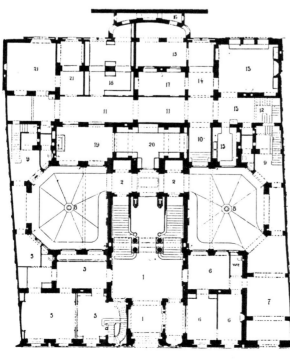

Erdgeschoß. Rez-de-chaussée. Ground Floor.

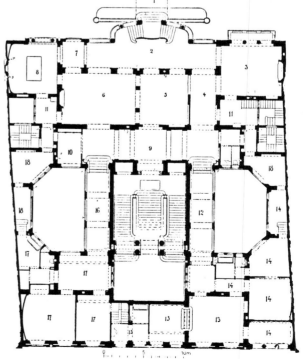

1. Stockwerk. 1. Etage. 1. Floor.

— und die Dienstbotenstuben angeordnet. An der rechten Ecke der Fassade befindet sich noch ein besonderer Eingang für das Dienstpersonal.

Im oberen Stockwerk befinden sich die Wohn- und Gesellschaftszimmer des Besitzers. Das zweite und dritte Stockwerk enthalten vier herrschaftlich eingerichtete Mietwohnungen. Ein Personen- und ein Lastenaufzug vermitteln den Verkehr zwischen den Etagen.

Der Sockel und das Untergeschoß sind mit Kalkstein aus Sarizzo Ghiandore, die ganze übrige Fassade mit Stein aus Ceppo di Brembate bekleidet. Die beiden Figuren am Haupteingang sind von dem Bildhauer Ernesto Bazzaro in Marmor ausgeführt, die übrigen dekorativen Bildwerke von Pirovano, sämtlich nach Zeichnungen und Modellen des Architekten.

Im Innern sind die Hauptpfeiler aus Granit. Die Wölbungen und Decken sind in Zement nach Hennebique-System ausgeführt. Die innere Treppe ist aus Veroneser Marmor; die Säulen der Vorhalle sind aus Labrador-Marmor hergestellt.

Die Baukosten betrugen 1 080 000 Lire.

de la façade on voit une entrée spéciale pour le personnel de service.

A l'étage supérieur les chambres d'habitation et de société du propriétaire ont trouvé place. Le second et le troisième étages contiennent quatre appartements à louer distribués en logements de maîtres. Le transport des personnes et des fardeaux se fait entre les étages au moyen de deux ascenseurs.

Le socle et le rez-de-chaussée sont recouverts de pierre calcaire de Sarizzo Ghiandore, le reste des façades de pierre de Ceppo di Brembate. Les deux figures de l'entrée principale ont été exécutées en marbre par le sculpteur Ernesto Bazzaro; les autres sculptures décoratives par Pirovano, toutes d'après des dessins et modèles de l'architecte.

A l'intérieur les piliers principaux sont en granit. Les voûtes et plafonds sont construits en ciment d'après le système Hennebique. L'escalier intérieur est en marbre de Vérone, les colonnes du vestibule sont en marbre de Labrador.

Les frais de construction s'élevèrent à 1 080 000 Lire.

the servants. At the right hand corner of the facade is a special entrance for servants.

In the upper floor are the dwelling and reception rooms of the owner. The second and third floors contain four superior lodgings which are let to tenants. Two lifts (for persons and for goods) are in use between the several stories.

The sockel and the basement are of limestone from Sarizzo Ghiandore, the whole of the rest of the facade is faced with stone from Ceppo di Brembate. The two figures at the entrance are by the sculptor Ernesto Bazzaro, and are of marble, the remaining sculptural decoration is by Pirovano, all of it from the designs and models of the architect.

In the interior the principal pillars are of granite. The vaulting and ceilings are of cement, constructed according to the Hennebique system. The inside staircase is of Veronese marble, the pillars of the vestibule are of Labrador marble.

The cost of building amounted to 1 080 000 lire.

176 [1905; 44]

An der Ecke der Kronen- und Markgrafenstraße in Berlin haben die Architekten Hoeniger und Sedelmeier in der Zeit vom 1. April 1904 bis 15. Februar 1905 ein fünfstöckiges Gebäude errichtet, das in allen seinen Stockwerken Geschäftszwecken dient (Tafel 44).

176 [1905; 44]

Messieurs Hoeniger et Sedelmeier ont construit à Berlin, à l'angle des rues Kronen- et Markgrafenstrasse un immeuble de cinq étages servant dans toutes ses parties à des comptoirs et magasins (Pl. 44). Cet édifice a été élevé du 1 avril 1904 au 15 février 1905. Par égard pour la destination de cet

176 [1905; 44]

The architects Hoeniger and Sedelmeier have built a five storied house at the corner of the Kronen- and Markgrafenstrasse Berlin, from 1 April 1904 till 15 February 1905. The house is intended for business premises, and each story is arranged for this purpose (see

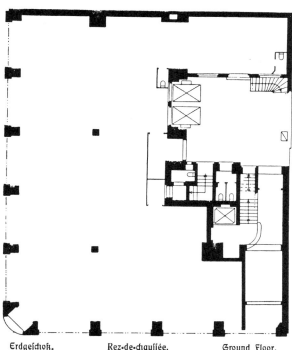

Erdgeschoß.   Rez-de-chaussée.   Ground Floor.

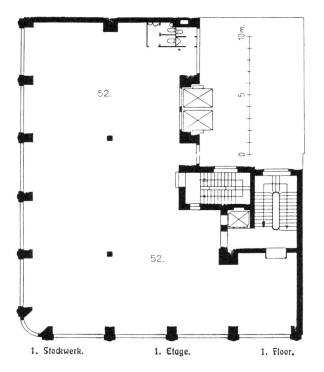

1. Stockwerk.   1. Etage.   1. Floor.

Mit Rücksicht auf diese Bestimmung des Gebäudes haben die Architekten den für solche Geschäftshäuser typisch gewordenen Pfeilerbau gewählt, der nur an der Straßenecke durch eine breitere Masse unterbrochen wird. Oberhalb des Dachgesimses sind die Endigungen der Pfeiler durch Obelisken betont worden. Die Architektur ist in hellgrauem Nesselberger Sandstein ausgeführt. Der reiche bildnerische Schmuck ist von dem Bildhauer Moeller geschaffen worden.

Die Baukosten betrugen 450 000 Mark.

immeuble, les architectes ont adopté le système devenu typique pour ce genre de maisons d'une suite de piliers interrompue seulement à l'angle des rues par une large masse. Au dessus de la corniche, les sommets des piliers ont été couronné d'obélisques. L'architecture est exécutée en pierre gris-claire de Nesselberg. La riche décoration plastique est l'œuvre du sculpteur Moeller.

Les frais de construction s'élevèrent à 450 000 Marks.

plate 44). For this reason too, the architects have chosen the typical style "Pfeilerbau" which is now used for all such buildings, the corner only being varied by a broader architecture. The ends of the pillars above the roof moulding are finished by obelisks. The material used is light grey Nesseberger sandstone. The elaborate sculptural decoration is by the sculptor Moeller.

The cost amounted to 450 000 Marks.

177 [1905; 50]

Im Auftrage der Direktion des Privat- und Familienfonds des Herrscherhauses Habsburg haben die Architekten Korb und Giergl in der Zeit vom 1. April 1900 bis 1. August 1902 in

177 [1905; 50]

Les architectes Korb et Giergl ont bâti pour la direction du fond privé et familial de la maison souveraine de Habsbourg un immeuble monumental à Budapest. Cet édifice a été

177 [1905; 50]

The Directors of the private and family funds of the Royal House of Habsburg have caused a monumental building to be erected for the necessary accommodation. It was built in

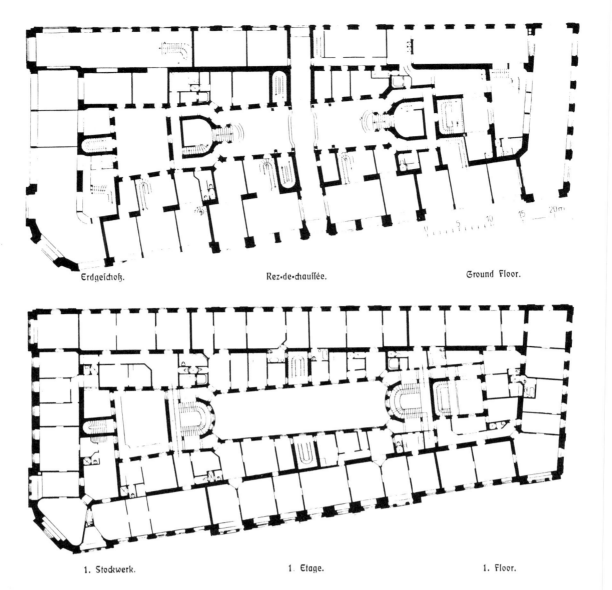

| Erdgeídhoß. | Rez-de-chauííée. | Ground Floor. |

| 1. Stockwerk. | 1. Etage. | 1. Floor. |

Budapeít einen Monumentalbau erriditet, deííen Erdgeídhoß für Geídháftslokale beítimmt iít, während das darüber liegende Mezzanin und die drei oberen Stockwerke Mietwohnungen enthalten (Tafel 50). Die Pfeiler des Erdgeídhoííes und des Mezzanins, die dem Regenwaííer ausgeíetzten Geíimíe, die Deckplatten und die Brüítungen der Balkone íind in Kalkítein aus Sütto ausgeführt, die übrigen Teile der Faííaden in Sandítein aus Soskut. Die Dädher der beiden mittleren Türmdhen íind mit Zinkbledh, die übrigen Dädher mit grünem Sdhiefer eingedeckt.

Die Bildhauerarbeiten an den Faííaden, die in reidhítem Barockítil geítaltet íind, hat Anton Scabó ausgeführt.

Die Baukoíten belieíen íidh auf 1500000 Kronen.

élevé du 1 avril 1900 au 1 août 1902; son rez-de-chaussée est destiné à des magasins, tandis que l'entresol et les trois étages supérieurs contiennent des appartements à louer (Pl. 50). Les piliers du rez-de-chaussée et de l'entresol, les profils exposés à l'eau de pluie, les couvertures et les balustrades de balcons sont construits en pierre calcaire de Sütto; les autres parties des façades en pierre de Soskut. Les toits des deux tourelles du milieu sont recouverts en zink, les autres toits en ardoise verte.

Monsieur Antoine Scabó a exécuté les travaux de sculpture qui sont tenus dans le genre baroque le plus riche.

Les frais de construction s'élevèrent à 1500000 Couronnes.

Budapest by the architects Korb and Giergl from 1 April 1900 to 1 August 1902. The ground floor is destined for business premises, the intermediate story and the three upper stories contain lodgings let to tenants (see plate 50). The pillars of the ground and intermediate floors, the mouldings exposed to the rain-water, the coping and the parapets of the balconies are of limestone from Sütto, the remainder of the facades are of sandstone from Soskut. The roofs of the two middle small towers are covered with zinc; the other roofs are slated with green slate.

The sculptural work of the facades, of a rich barock style has been carried out by Antony Scabó.

The cost of building was 1500000 Kronen.

178 [1905: 54]

Auf die ítarke Höhenentwicklung des Baues Am Markt 4 in Pforzheim, das in íeinem Erdgeídhoß außer einem Laden den Ausídhank der Brauerei Beckh mit drei großen Gaíträumen enthält, iít die Lage an einem freien Platze von entídheidendem Einfluß geweíen. Die ganz in rotem Mainíandítein ausgeführte Faííade (Tafel 54) hat Profeííor Hermann Billing in Karlsruhe entworfen, der dabei wieder íeine Virtuoíität in der völlig modernen Behandlung hiítoriídher Stilmotive bewährt hat. Im eríten Stockwerk befindet íidh nodh ein zur Wirtídhaft gehöriger Geíellídhaftsíaal. Im übrigen enthalten die oberen Stockwerke elegant eingeridhtete Wohnungen.

Die Grundriííe hat Ardhitekt Ernít Maler aufgeítellt; die Bildhauerarbeiten íind von W. Gerítel in Karlsruhe ausgeführt.

Die Koíten des Gebäudes, deííen Erridhtung die Zeit von Frühjahr 1902 bis Auguít 1904 in Aníprudh genommen hat, belieíen íidh auf 245000 Mark.

178 [1905: 54]

Dans la composition de la maison Am Markt 4 à Pforzheim et pour son développement en hauteur, la situation de cet immeuble sur une grande place a été d'une influence définitive; il contient au rez-de-chaussée, outre un magasin, le débit de la brasserie Beckh avec trois grands locaux. La façade (Pl. 54) complètement exécutée en pierre rouge du Main a été dessinée par Monsieur le professeur Hermann Billing à Carlsruhe qui a de nouveau témoigné ici de son talent à traiter d'une façon toute moderne les styles historiques. Au premier étage se trouve encore une salle de société dépendant du restaurant. D'élégants appartements ont été disposés dans les étages supérieurs.

Les plans ont été composés par l'architecte Ernst Maler; les travaux de sculpture sont l'œuvre de W. Gerstel à Carlsruhe.

Les frais de la construction qui a duré du printemps 1902 au mois d'avût 1903 se sont élevés à 245000 Marks.

178 [1905: 54]

A building has been erected by Professor Hermann Billing, Am Markt 4 in Pforzheim, in which the free-standing site allowed the architect to carry the house to a considerable height. The ground-floor contains a shop and a beer-house for the Brewery Beckh with three large drinking saloons. The facade is of red Mainland sandstone (see plate 54) and is another example of the modern handling of historical style which distinguishes this accomplished artist. The first floor contains a hall for entertainments etc. belonging to the beer-house and the upper stories are arranged as superior flats.

The ground plan was by the architect Ernst Maler, the sculptural work by W. Gerstel of Carlsruhe.

The cost of the building amounted to 245000 Marks, and the time occupied was from the spring of 1902 till August 1904.

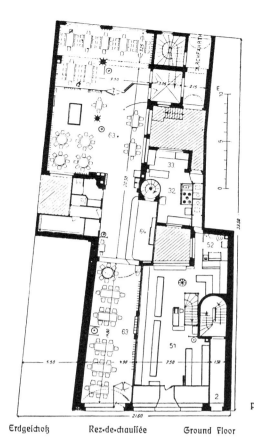

Erdgeſchoß   Rez-de-chauſſée   Ground Floor   1. Stockwerk   1. Etage   1. Floor

Pforzheim. Am Markt 4.

179 [1905; 52]

Für die Faſſaden des in Mainz, Kaiſer-
ſtraße 76 und 78, an der Ecke der Albiniſtraße gelegenen Miethauſes hat der Architekt
A. Greifzu in Mainz die Entwürfe geliefert, die
ſich in modern behandelten Barockformen bewegen
(Tafel 52). Die Fronten ſind in weißem Kunſt-
zementſandſtein ausgeführt. Die Grundriſſe hat
der Bauunternehmer Ernſt Zehrlaut aufgeſtellt,
von dem auch die Bauausführung herrührt, die
die Zeit vom 15. April 1902 bis 1. April 1903
beanſprucht hat.

Das Erdgeſchoß enthält an der der Kaiſer-
ſtraße zugekehrten Seite zwei Läden, zu deren
jedem ein Wohnzimmer gehört, und an der an
der Albiniſtraße gelegenen Seite eine Wohnung
von drei Zimmern mit Zubehör; die drei Obergeſchoſſe enthalten je zwei Wohnungen von vier
und fünf Zimmern.

Die Baukoſten betrugen rund 200000 Mark.

180 [1905; 51]

Für die Ortskrankenkaſſe in Düſſeldorf hat
der Architekt Hermann vom Endt an der
Kaſernenſtraße in der Zeit von März 1904 bis
Februar 1905 ein viergeſchoſſiges Gebäude errichtet, das außer den Geſchäftsräumen für die
Kaſſe im Erdgeſchoß zwei Läden und in den
oberen Geſchoſſen Mietwohnungen enthält. Durch
Vertrag mit der israelitiſchen Gemeinde, deren
Synagoge unmittelbar angrenzt, war die Höhe
des Gebäudes ſtark beſchränkt worden, ſo daß
die Verhältniſſe etwas gedrückt erſcheinen.

Die Faſſade (Tafel 51) iſt in Sandſtein aus
der Pfalz, der Sockel in Granit ausgeführt. Die
Einbauten der Schaufenſter ſind aus Tombak
hergeſtellt.

Die Baukoſten betrugen 140000 Mark.

181 [1905; 53]

Das vom Architekten Richard Bauer in
Düſſeldorf, Steinſtraße 13d, in der Zeit
von Oktober 1903 bis Juni 1904 erbaute, drei-
geſchoſſige Wohnhaus enthält in ſeinem Erdgeſchoß Bureauräume, deren Zugang getrennt

179 [1905; 52]

Monsieur A. Greifzu architecte à Mayence,
a choisi pour les façades des maisons
à loyer Kaiserstrasse 76 et 78 à l'angle de
la Albinistrasse, dont il a livré les projets, les
formes du style baroque moderne (Pl. 52). Les
façades sont construites en pierres blanches
artificielles de ciment. Les plans sont l'œuvre
de l'entrepreneur Ernest Zehrlaut qui s'est
aussi chargé de l'exécution, laquelle a duré du
15 avril 1902 au 1 avril 1903.

Le rez-de-chaussée contient deux magasins
du côté de la Kaiserstrasse, chacun d'eux
est relié à une chambre; du côté de l'Albinistrasse se trouve un appartement de trois
chambres avec dépendances. Les trois étages
supérieurs sont occupés chacun par deux appartements de quatre et cinq pièces.

La dépense s'éleva à 200000 Marks en bloc.

180 [1905; 51]

Monsieur Herman vom Endt à Düsseldorf, a construit dans cette ville, à la
Kasernenstrasse du mois de mars 1904 à
celui de février 1905, une maison à quatre étages
pour la caisse locale des malades. Ce bâtiment
contient outre les bureaux de la caisse au rez-
de-chaussée deux magasins, et aux étages supérieurs des appartements à loyer. Par suite d'une
convention conclue avec la communeauté israëlite
dont la synagogue est immédiatement voisine,
la hauteur de l'édifice avait été fortement limitée,
ce qui fait paraître les proportions un peu écrasées.

La façade (Pl. 51) est construite en pierre
du Palatinat, le socle en granit. Les installations
des devantures de magasin sont en Tombak.

Les frais de construction s'élevèrent à 140000
Marks.

181 [1905; 53]

La maison à trois étages construite par
Monsieur Richard Bauer architecte, Steinstrasse 13d à Dusseldorf a été élevée du
mois d'octobre 1903 à celui de juin 1904; elle
contient au rez-de-chaussée, des bureaux dont

179 [1905; 52]

The architect A. Greifzu of Mayence has
furnished the designs for the facade of a
house built in that town at 76 and 78 Kaiserstrasse, the corner of the Albinistrasse. The
style is the modern barock form (see plate 52)
and the material is of white artificial cement
sandstone. The ground plan is by the builder
Ernest Zehrlaut, who also superintended the
building; the time occupied was from 15 April
1902 till 1 April 1903.

On the ground floor facing the Kaiserstrasse
are two shops each with a dwelling room; on
the Albinistrasse is a lodging of three rooms
with offices. The three upper stories have each
two lodgings of 4 and 5 rooms.

The cost of building amounted to about
200 000 Marks.

180 [1905; 51]

For the local Sick Relief Society of Düsseldorf, the architect Hermann vom Endt has
built in the Kasernenstrasse from March 1904
to February 1905 a four storied house that, in
addition to the business premises of the Society
on the ground floor, contains two shops, and
on the upper floors, lodgings. The Jewish
congregation, whose synagogue is adjoining,
made a contract with the builder that the house
should not exceed a certain height, and this
has partly spoiled the effect.

The facade is of sandstone from the Palatinate (see plate 51), the sockel is of granite.
The framing of the shop windows is of Tombak.

The cost of building amounted to 140000
Marks.

181 [1905; 53]

The architect Richard Bauer has built in
Düsseldorf, Steinstrasse 13d from
October 1903 till June 1904 a three storied
house, containing on the ground floor bureaux
which have a separate entrance from the street.

von dem Eingang zur Wohnung von der Straße angelegt ist. Außerdem liegen im Erdgeschoß die zur Wohnung gehörigen Wirtschaftsräume, die wiederum von den Bureauräumen getrennt angeordnet sind. Die Wohnung des Besitzers nimmt die beiden oberen Geschosse ein. Im ersten liegen drei Wohnzimmer, ein Erkerzimmer und das Speisezimmer nebst Wintergarten, die sich um eine Diele gruppieren. Die mit einer großen Kaminnische ausgestattete Diele trägt den Charakter eines behaglichen Wohnraums. Da die Dielentreppe durch eine Nebentreppe entlastet ist, konnte die Deckenöffnung auf das Mindestmaß beschränkt und dadurch auch für die Zimmer des zweiten Obergeschosses ein großer Vorraum geschaffen werden. Das zweite Obergeschoß enthält drei Wohnzimmer, zwei Schlafzimmer, das Badezimmer und ein Fremdenzimmer.

Die Fassade (Tafel 53) ist zum Teil in glattem, zum Teil in graublauem Spritzputz ausgeführt, unter Verwendung von dunkelblauen, wetterfesten Platten und Einlagen von Opaleszentglas. Das an der Fassade verwendete Holzwerk ist ebenfalls von blauer Farbe mit gelben Ornamenten. Das Dach ist mit roten Biberschwänzen eingedeckt, der Erker und die Überdachung der Eingangstür mit Kupfer.

Die Baukosten betrugen 70000 Mark.

182 [1905; 64]

Bei dem Hause Königsallee Nr. 25 in Düsseldorf handelt es sich um den Umbau eines älteren Hauses, dem der Architekt Hermann vom Endt eine neue Fassade (Tafel 63—64) gegeben hat. Sie ist teils in Stampfbeton, teils in Kammputz ausgeführt, mit Keimschen Mineralfarben farbig behandelt und teilweise vergoldet. Die Ornamente sind ebenfalls in Stampfbeton ausgeführt. Die Rahmen und Stützen der Schaufenster sind aus Tombak hergestellt.

183 [1905; 56]

Das Erdgeschoß und das darüber gelegene Zwischengeschoß des Hauses Alter Weinmarkt Nr. 24 in Straßburg i. E., das die Architekten Brion und Haug in den Jahren 1900 und 1901 mit einem Kostenaufwande von rund 440000 Mark erbaut haben, dienen den Zwecken eines Bankgeschäftes. Durch den in der Mitte der Fassade gelegenen Haupteingang gelangt man rechts durch ein Vorzimmer in das Zimmer des Effektenvorstandes. Geradezu ist der Eingang zu der für den Verkehr des Publikums bestimmten Halle, an deren linker Seite die Hauptkasse liegt, während sich rechts die Effektenabteilung befindet. Links vom Haupteingang liegt das Zimmer der Direktion nebst einem Vorzimmer. Zwei Treppen

l'entrée séparée de celle de l'appartement est située sur la rue. D'autre part, les locaux de service dépendants de l'appartement se trouvent au rez-de-chaussée et sont séparés des bureaux. Le logement du propriétaire occupe les deux étages supérieurs. Au premier sont trois chambres d'habitation, une chambre à tourelle, la salle à manger avec jardin d'hiver; ces pièces sont groupées autour d'un hall. Le hall décoré d'une grande cheminée située dans une niche a le caractère d'un lieu de réunion intime. Comme l'escalier du hall est déchargé par un escalier de service, on a pu réduire à son minimum l'ouverture du plafond et gagner de cette façon un grand vestibule pour les pièces du second étage; cet étage contient trois chambres d'habitation, deux chambres à coucher et une chambre d'amis.

La façade (Pl. 53) est exécutée en partie en crépissage lisse, en partie en crépissage rugueux gris bleu avec emploi de plaques de verre opalescent enchassées, ces dernières sont bleu foncé, à l'abri des intempéries. Le bois employé dans les façades est également peint en bleu avec des ornements jaunes. Le toit est recouvert en tuiles rouges; la tourelle et l'avant toit au dessus de l'entrée sont recouverts en cuivre.

Les frais de construction s'élevèrent à 70000 Marks.

182 [1905; 64]

Königsallée No. 25 à Düsseldorf, une ancienne maison a été transformée et c'est à cet immeuble que Monsieur Herman vom Endt a donné une nouvelle façade (Pl. 63—64). Elle est en partie en béton comprimé, et en partie en maçonnerie crépissée au peigne, peinte en couleurs minérales de Keim et en partie dorée. Les ornements sont également exécutés en béton comprimé. Les cadres et soutiens des devantures de magasins sont construits en Tombak.

183 [1905; 56]

Le rez-de-chaussée et l'entresol de la maison Alter Weinmarkt No. 24 à Strassbourg en Alsace construite dans les années 1900 et 1901 par les architectes Brion et Haug, pour la somme de 440000 Marks, sert aux bureaux d'une maison de banque. Passant par l'entrée principale située au milieu de la façade, on pénètre à droite par une antichambre dans la chambre du directeur des effets. En face, se trouve l'entrée du Hall destiné au public; à gauche de cette pièce est placée la caisse principale, tandis qu'à droite on voit le rayon des effets. A gauche de l'entrée principale est disposée la chambre de la direction avec antichambre. Deux escaliers conduisent du rez-de-

In the ground floor also are the domestic offices belonging to the lodging above; these too have a separate entrance. The lodging of the owner is contained in the two upper stories. In the first are three living rooms, a corner room, the dining room with conservatory all of which are grouped round a hall. The hall has a large chimney corner and is a comfortable sitting room. Only a small staircase was necessary from the hall, as there is a secondary staircase; for this reason the opening in the ceiling is comparatively small; this has allowed more room for the apartments in the second storey. The second upper storey contains three sitting rooms, two bedrooms, the bathroom and a spare bedroom.

The facade (see plate 53) is partly in smooth and partly in greyblue rough plaster, together with dark blue weatherproof tiles, and inlaid with opalescent glass. The wood work of the facade is also coloured blue with yellow ornaments. It is roofed with flat red tiles, the bay and the roofing of the entrance door are of copper.

The cost of building amounted to about 70000 Marks.

182 [1905; 64]

In the house Königsallee 25 Düsseldorf, it was the task of the architect to remodel an old building, and the architect Hermann vom Endt has given it a new facade (see plate 63—64). It is partly of beton and partly in rough plaster, coloured with Keim mineral colours, and in some parts gilded. The ornaments are of beton; the frames and supports of the shop windows are of Tombak.

183 [1905; 56]

A house has been built by the architects Brion and Haug at Alter Weinmarkt 24, Strassburg in Alsace, from 1900 to 1901 at a cost of 440000 Marks. The ground floor and intermediary story are used as the offices of a Bank. The principal entrance, in the middle of the facade, leads on the right through an entrance room into the bureau of the Shares Department. The door in the centre leads straight into the public room of the bank on the left side of which is the principal cash, on the right is the Shares Department. Left of the principal entrance is the office of the directors with a waiting room. Two staircases lead from

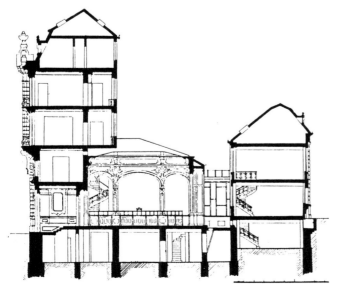

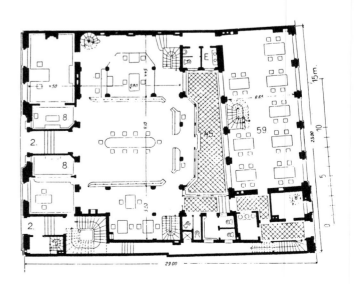

führen aus dem Erdgeſchoß zu den Treſors im Untergeſchoß. An der Hofſeite ſind ein großer Bureauſaal, die Waſchräume und die Aborte für die Beamten angeordnet. Im Zwiſchengeſchoß liegt an der Vorderſeite links ein Sitzungsſaal nebſt Vorſaal, rechts die aus zwei Zimmern und Küche beſtehende Wohnung eines Hausmeiſters. An der Hofſeite liegen Bureauräume und die aus einem Zimmer und Küche beſtehende Wohnung eines zweiten Hausmeiſters. Im erſten und zweiten Stock liegt eine zuſammenhängende Wohnung, zu der ein beſonderer Zugang an der rechten Seite der Faſſade führt. Im erſten Stock befinden ſich ein großer und ein kleiner Salon, ein Speiſezimmer und ein Rauchzimmer, im Seitenflügel der Anrichteraum und die Küche, dahinter die Waſchküche und ein Trockenboden. Der zweite Stock enthält ein Schlafzimmer, ein Toilettezimmer und zwei Mädchenzimmer.

Zu der in reichem franzöſiſchen Barockſtil geſtalteten Faſſade, die in hellrotem Sandſtein ausgeführt iſt (Tafel 56), hat der Architekt Frieſé in Paris die Skizze geliefert.

chaussée aux trésors en sous-sol. On a disposé du côté de la cour une grande salle de bureau, les toilettes et les cabinets d'aisance pour les employés. A l'entresol se trouvent sur le devant: à gauche une salle de conférences avec antichambre, à droite l'appartement d'un concierge, comprenant deux chambres et une cuisine. D'autres bureaux et le logement d'un second concierge consistant en une chambre et une cuisine se trouvent du côté de la cour. Le premier et le second étages sont reliés entre eux pour former un appartement auquel on parvient par une entrée spéciale, située du côté droit de la façade. Au premier étage on a placé un grand et un petit salon, une salle à manger et un fumoir, dans l'aile latérale, l'office et la cuisine, en arrière, la buanderie et un séchoir. Le second étage contient une chambre à coucher, une toilette et deux chambres de bonnes.

Monsieur Friesé architecte à Paris, a livré les dessins de la façade exécutée en riche style baroque français et construite en pierre rouge claire (Pl. 56).

the ground floor to the tresors in the basement. On the side facing the courtyard are a large bureau, and the lavatories for the officials. In the intermediate story, lie on the left in the front a committee room with a room adjoining, on the right is the dwelling of the house steward consisting of two rooms and a kitchen. On the side facing the courtyard are bureaus and a second dwelling of one room and a kitchen for the second house steward. In the first and second floors is one large dwelling to which an entrance leads from the right side of the facade. On the first floor is a large and small drawing room, a dining room and smoking room; in the side wing is the serving room and kitchen, behind this the washhouse and drying room. The second floor contains a bed and dressing room and two servants' bed rooms.

The architect Frieze of Paris furnished the sketches for the facade which is of a rich French barock style and carried out in light red sandstone (see plate 56).

184 [1905; 65]

Für den Verlagsbuchhändler Arthur Lang in Karlsruhe i. B. hat der Architekt Theodor Trautmann an der Waldſtraße 13 ein viergeſchoſſiges Gebäude errichtet, das in ſeinem

184 [1905; 65]

The architect Theodor Trautmann has built for the publisher Arthur Lang a four-storied house at Waldstrasse 13, Carlsruhe in Baden. The ground floor contains two shops, the upper

184 [1905; 65]

Monsieur Theodor Trautmann a construit Waldstrasse 13 à Carlsruhe en Bade, pour le libraire éditeur Arthur Lang, une maison à quatre étages qui contient deux magasins au

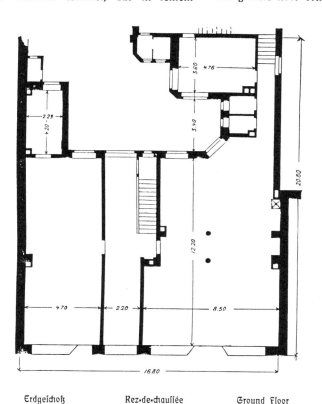

Erdgeſchoß   Rez-de-chauſſée   Ground Floor   1. Stockwerk   1. Etage   1. Floor

Erdgeſchoß zwei Läden, in den oberen Stockwerken Wohnungen enthält. Die Pfeiler des Erdgeſchoſſes ſind mit belgiſchem Granit verkleidet; im übrigen iſt die Faſſade in grünem Sandſtein aus Sulzfeld ausgeführt. Unter dem Hauptgeſims zieht ſich ein Fries aus glaſierten Tonplatten aus der Tonwarenfabrik von Profeſſor Läuger hin. Die Faſſade (Tafel 65) haben die Architekten Curjel und Moſer entworfen.

Die Bauzeit dauerte von Auguſt 1902 bis Juni 1903.

Die Baukoſten betrugen einſchließlich eines Hintergebäudes, das eine Druckerei enthält, rund 144000 Mark.

rez-de-chaussée et des appartements dans les étages supérieurs. Les piliers du rez-de-chaussée sont revêtus de granit belge, le reste des façades est exécuté en pierre verte de Sulzfeld. Une frise de plaques céramiques émaillées provenant des ateliers de céramique du Professeur Läuger se développe sous la corniche. Messieurs Curjel et Moser architectes ont composé la façade (Pl. 65).

La construction a duré du mois d'août 1902 au mois de juin 1903.

Les frais de construction, y compris une arrière maison contenant une imprimerie s'élèvent en bloc à 144000 Marks.

stories are arranged as flats. The pillars of the ground floor are faced with Belgian granite, the rest of the facade is of green sandstone from Sulzfeld. Under the principal moulding is a frieze of glazed tiles from the manufactory of Professor Läuger. The facade (see plate 65) is by the architects Curjel and Moser.

The time occupied was from August 1902 to June 1903.

The cost of building, including the back premises which contains a printing office, amounted to about 144000 Marks.

185 [1905; 81]

Mit dem Warenhauſe „A l'Innovation" in Brüſſel hat Victor Horta, der Führer der modernen Bewegung in der belgiſchen Archi-

185 [1905; 81]

Dans la construction du grand magasin „A l'Innovation" à Bruxelles, Victor Horta, le chef du mouvement novateur dans

185 [1905; 81]

In the bazaar "A l'Innovation" in Brussels, the architect Victor Horta, a well known leader in the modern movement in

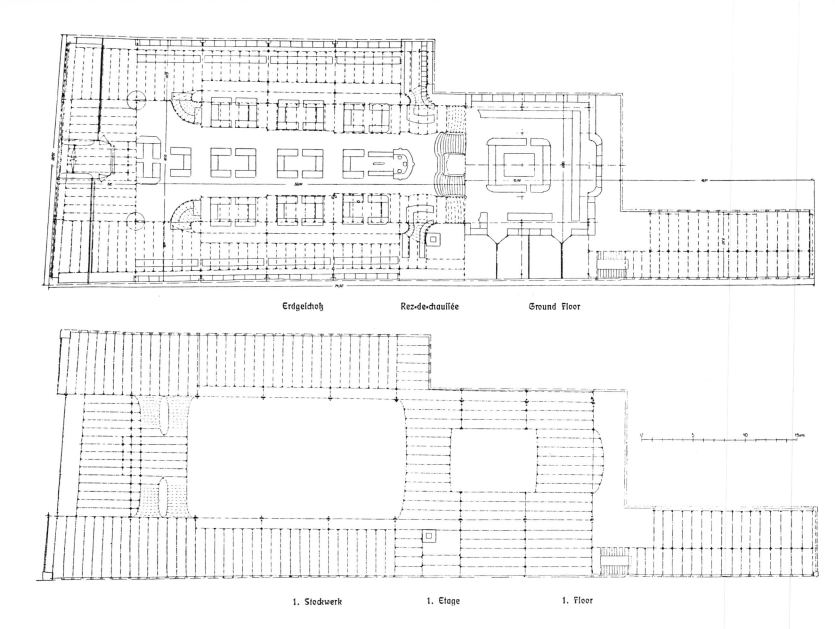

Erdgeſchoß   Rez-de-chauſſée   Ground Floor

1. Stockwerk   1. Étage   1. Floor

tektur, einen ſtarken Schritt auf dem Wege, der Eiſenkonſtruktion auch äſthetiſche Reize abzugewinnen, vorwärts getan (Tafel 81). Das bei dem modernen Warenhausbau herrſchende Syſtem großer Schauflächen, die nur durch die Pfeiler und Stäbe der Eiſenkonſtruktion geteilt werden, iſt hier bis zur äußerſten Konſequenz durchgeführt worden, ſo daß dem Steinbau nur die Rolle der äußeren Umrahmung übrig geblieben iſt. Dadurch iſt das ſonſt oft fühlbare Mißverhältnis zwiſchen Stein- und Eiſenpfeilern nach Möglichkeit ausgeglichen worden.

Im Gegenſatz zu der in anderen Ländern verbreiteten Gewohnheit, das Eiſen mit anderen Stoffen zu verkleiden und dadurch einen falſchen Schein hervorzurufen, vertritt Horta das Prinzip, Eiſen und Stahl ſichtbar zu laſſen, damit der wahre Charakter des Materials zum Ausdruck kommt. Auch wird dadurch an Raum geſpart und dem Licht freierer Zutritt geſchaffen, ohne daß die Feuersgefahr erhöht wird.

Außer Eiſen und Stahl iſt bei dem Bau franzöſiſcher Granit zur Verwendung gelangt.

l'architecture Belge, a fait un grand pas en avant dans la recherche du progrès esthétique dans la construction ru fer (Pl. 81). Le système dominant dans le grand magasin moderne, des grandes fenêtres de devanture qui ne sont séparées que par les piliers et les meneaux de fer, a été poussé ici à ses extrêmes conséquences, de sorte qu'il n'est resté à la pierre que le rôle de l'encadrement extérieur. De cette façon, la disproportion qui existe si souvent entre les piliers de pierre et de fer a été évitée dans la mesure du possible.

Au contraire de l'habitude répandue dans les autres pays, de revêtir le fer avec d'autres matériaux et de lui prêter de cette façon une fausse apparence, Horta préconise le principe de laisser le fer et l'acier visibles afin d'en exprimer le véritable caractère. Cette façon de faire présente en outre l'avantage de gagner de la place, de donner plus de surface à la lumière, sans pour cela augmenter le danger de feu.

A part le fer et l'acier, on a employé pour cette construction du granit français.

Belgian architecture, has taken a decided step forward in the adaptation of iron for beautiful architecture (see plate 81). The modern system of building bazaars simply as palaces of iron and glass has been carried out here to its fullest extent, stone being only used as the exterior frame work. By this, the want of harmony between iron and stone pillars, so often noticed, is avoided.

Again in contradistinction to the use prevalent in many countries of clothing iron in stone to give the impression of a solid stone pillar, Horta has kept to the principle of leaving iron and steel visible, so that the real nature of the material is seen. Other advantages are, the saving of space, the freer entrance of light and the immunity of danger from fire.

French granite is used in addition to iron and steel in the construction of the building.

186 [1905; 88]

Der Grundriß des Hotel Briſtol in Koblenz, das die Architekten Gebrüder Friedhofen von Mai 1904 bis Mai 1905 erbaut haben, iſt durch die Lage des Grundſtücks an einer ſtumpfen Ecke bedingt worden. Das Erdgeſchoß enthält links zwei Läden, rechts zwei große, zuſammenhängende Gaſtzimmer, die zum Hotelbetrieb gehören. Die Fremdenzimmer liegen in den Etagen. Außerdem iſt noch in der erſten Etage die Hotelküche untergebracht.

186 [1905; 88]

Le plan de l'hotel Bristol à Coblence, construit par les frères Friedhofen architectes, du mois de mai 1904 à celui de mai 1905 a été déterminé par la situation du terrain formant un angle obtus. Le rez-de-chaussée contient à gauche deux magasins, à droite deux grandes chambres communiquant entre elles et faisant partie de l'hôtel. Les chambres d'étrangers sont situées dans les étages. La cuisine de l'hôtel a été installée au premier étage.

186 [1905; 88]

The situation of the Hotel Bristol in Coblentz, built by the architects Brothers Friedhofen, from May 1904 till May 1905, necessitated the arrangement of the ground-plan round an obtuse angle. The ground floor contains on the left two shops, on the right two reception rooms leading into each other and belonging to the hotel. The bedrooms all lie in the upper stories. The hotel kitchen is on the first floor.

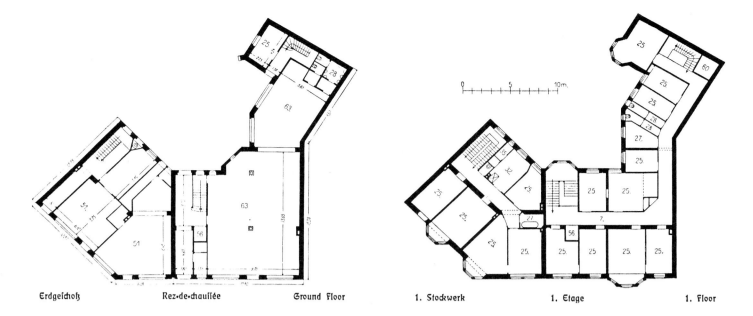

| Erdgeichoß | Rez-de-chauffée | Ground Floor | 1. Stockwerk | 1. Étage | 1. Floor |

Die in Kammputz mit reicher Ornamentik ausgeführten Faffaden (Tafel 88 und 89) haben eine blaugrüne Färbung mit Gold erhalten.

Die Baukoften beliefen fich auf 300 000 Mark.

Les façades de crépissage au peigne, décorées de riches ornements (Pl. 88 et 89) ont été peintes d'un ton gris-vert et rehaussées d'or.

Les frais de construction s'élevèrent à 300 000 Marks.

The facades (see plates 88 and 89) are of plaster richly ornamented, of a blue green colour with a little gilding.

The cost of building was 300 000 Marks.

187, 188 [1905; 82, 83]

Im Kiefernwald am Schlachtenfee bei Berlin hat Arthur Biberfeld in den Jahren 1904 bis 1905 mit einem Koftenaufwand von 150 000 Mark ein Sanatorium erbaut, deffen Befuchern der ftärkende Genuß der Waldluft auf alle Weife ermöglicht werden foll. Diefem Zwecke ift der Charakter des Gebäudes (Tafel 82—83) an-

187, 188 [1905; 82, 83]

Monsieur Arthur Biberfeld a construit dans les années 1904 et 1905 avec une dépense de 150 000 Marcs un sanatorium dans la forêt de pins au lac Schlachtensee près de Berlin. Les pensionnaires de cet établissement doivent pouvoir de toute manière jouir de l'air fortifiant de la forêt. Le caractère de l'édifice a été déterminé par cette condition (Pl. 82 et 83). Au

187, 188 [1905; 82, 83]

In the pine woods around Schlachtensee, near Berlin, Arthur Biberfeld has built, in the years 1904 and 1905, a sanatorium at cost of 150 000 Marks. The sanatorium is intended for those persons who are in need of the strengthening air of the pine woods, and the design of the building allows of this curative

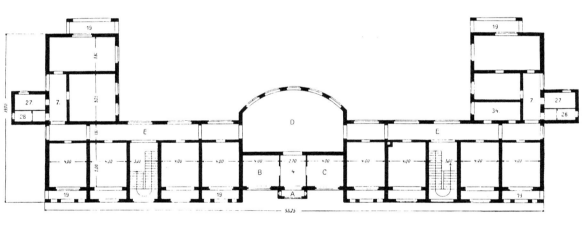

| Erdgeichoß | Rez-de-chauffée | Ground Floor |

gepaßt. Im Untergeichoß liegen links und rechts von der Eingangshalle das Zimmer des Arztes und das der Oberin, außerdem zu beiden Seiten je vier Krankenzimmer, in den anftoßenden Seitenflügeln je zwei Krankenzimmer, je ein Zimmer für den Wärter und die Wärterin, Badezimmer und Toilette. Das Obergeichoß enthält ebenfalls zwölf Krankenzimmer. Das Dachgeichoß wird in der Mitte durch eine große Terraffe durchfchnitten, fo daß nur vier Krankenzimmer an der Front liegen.

Getrennt vom Sanatorium liegt rückwärts eine Villa mit der Wohnung des Arztes, deren Bau 50 000 Mark gekoftet hat.

Die Ausführung der Faffaden erfolgte in Pußbau mit braunen Verblendfteinen und farbigem Holzwerk.

rez-de-chaussée se trouvent à droite et à gauche de la halle d'entrée la chambre du médecin et celle de la directrice, à part cela, de chaque côté quatre chambres de malades; dans chacune des ailes adjacentes sont placées deux chambres de malades; une chambre pour la garde-malade et pour l'infirmier, une chambre de bains et un cabinet de toilette. L'étage supérieur contient également douze chambres de malades. L'étage au toit est interrompu au milieu par une grande terrasse, de sorte que quatre chambres de malades seulement ont trouvé place sur la face principale.

En arrière du sanatorium et séparé de ce dernier se trouve une villa avec l'appartement du médecin, ce bâtiment a coûté 50 000 Marcs.

Les façades ont été construites en maçonnerie crépie avec des briques de revêtement brunes et des pans de bois en couleur.

agency being used to the fullest extent (see plate 82 and 83). On the ground floor, right and left, lie the rooms of the doctor and the lady superintendent; in addition, on each side are four rooms for the use of patients. In each of the side wings are two patients' rooms a room each for the male and female nurse, a bath-room and lavatory. The upper story contains twelve patients' rooms. The roof story is divided into two by a large terrace, but in the front are four rooms available for patients.

At the back of the sanatorium, but quite detached from it, is the residence of the doctor, a villa which cost 50 000 Marks. — The facades are of plaster faced with brown stone, and coloured wood work.

An das im Jahre 1857 für das Germaniſche Nationalmuſeum in Nürnberg angekaufte ehemalige Kartäuſerkloſter hat ſich im Laufe der Jahre ein umfangreicher Komplex von verſchieden gearteten Baulichkeiten angegliedert, der durch einen dreigeſchoſſigen, die geſamte Gebäudemaſſe überragenden Bau an der Südweſtecke einen vorläufigen Abſchluß gefunden hat. Dieſer Bau, der vom Oktober 1898 bis Mai 1902 nach den Plänen und unter der Leitung des erſten Direktors des Muſeums, Guſtav von Bezold, ausgeführt worden iſt, enthält in ſeinem Erdgeſchoß die Waffenhalle, einen das ganze Gebäude nach Länge und Breite einnehmenden Saal (Tafel 69), im erſten Obergeſchoß bäuerliche Hauseinrichtungen und im zweiten Obergeſchoß bäuerliche Trachten. Eine breite, an der Oſtſeite angelegte Treppe verbindet die drei Stockwerke untereinander und mit den angrenzenden Teilen des Muſeums.

Mit Rückſicht auf die maſſigen Formen der nahegelegenen, nur durch eine ſchmale Straße von der Südfront des Muſeums getrennten, alten Stadtmauer mit ihren Türmen, die an dieſer Stelle noch völlig unverſehrt erhalten iſt, mußte ſich der Architekt zu einer ſtarken Höhenentwicklung entſchließen, die in einem ſchlanken Dachreiter über dem Giebeldach an der Südweſtecke ausklingt (Tafel 67—69).

Für die Außenarchitektur, die in rötlichem Keuperſandſtein aus der Gegend von Nürnberg ausgeführt iſt, ſind zum Teil gotiſche Stilformen Nürnbergiſchen Charakters gewählt worden. Die Detailbearbeitung des Äußeren und der Treppe rührt vom Bauführer Heinrich Meickler her.

Un ensemble considérable de constructions de toute espèce s'est dans le cours des années, ajouté à l'ancien cloître des chartreux de Nuremberg, acheté en 1857 pour le Musée national germanique. Cet ensemble a trouvé son terme actuel dans la construction d'une aile de trois étages, située à l'angle sud-ouest et dominant le tout. Cette partie du musée construite du mois d'octobre 1898 jusqu'à celui de mai 1902, d'après les plans et sous la direction de Monsieur Gustave de Bezold directeur du Musée, contient la halle des armures au rez-de-chaussée, une salle occupant toute la longueur et toute la largeur du bâtiment; le premier étage est destiné à l'ameublement des paysans et le second aux costumes des campagnes. Un large escalier situé au côté oriental rejoint entre eux les trois étages et le nouveau bâtiment avec les parties voisines du musée.

Les lourdes formes du mur d'enceinte avec ses tours, situé à peu de distance et séparé du côté sud du musée par une étroite rue seulement, engagèrent l'architecte à régler ses formes d'après ces anciennes fortifications, encore entièrement conservées à cet endroit; il dut à cause de cela se résoudre à un grand développement des hauteurs; le bâtiment est couvert par un toit à pignon, lequel est couronnée à l'angle sud-ouest par une flèche élancée (Pl. 67 –69).⁵

Pour l'architecture extérieure qui a été exécutée en pierre de grès rouge des environs de Nuremberg, on a choisi en partie le style gothique caractéristique de Nuremberg. L'étude du détail de l'extérieur et de l'escalier a été confiée à Henry Meickler conducteur des travaux.

In the year 1857 the former Carthusian monastery was bought for the "Germanische National Museum" in Nuremberg. In the course of years a number of additional buildings of various kinds have grown up round it, and to these have been added during the last years (from October 1898 to May 1902) a three-storied lofty house on the south-west side, which overtops the other buildings, and which will probably be the last additional building. The edifice, constructed according to the plans and under the superintendence of the director of the Museum Gustav von Bezold, contains on the ground floor the armoury; on the first floor, a hall, comprising the entire length and breadth of the space at disposal, for old country house furniture, and on the second floor the same space is dedicated to the exhibition of old national costumes. A broad staircase on the last side gives access to these halls as well as to the other parts of the museum.

The museum is only separated from the massive city wall with its towers, which on this, the south side, is in good preservation; it was therefore necessary that the architect should carry the building to a considerable height, this he has done, finishing of the roof with a slender turret over the roof gable (see plates 67—69).

The exterior architecture is Gothic, with the Nuremberg characterization. The material is of reddish sandstone from the neighbourhood of Nuremberg; the details of the exterior and of the staircase are by the "Bauführer" Heinrich Meickler.

Den Charakter einer mittelalterlichen Burg hat Profeſſor Dr. ing. Bruno Schmitz in Berlin der von ihm in der Zeit von Mai 1902 bis Februar 1904 erbauten Villa Stollwerck in Köln gegeben, deren Beſitzer in Verehrung für den erſten Kanzler des Deutſchen Reiches ſeinen Wohnſitz „Bismarckburg“ getauft hat. Dieſer burgartige Charakter kommt beſonders in dem Aufbau der Hauptfront wie in der Bekleidung der Faſſaden mit Ruſtikaquadern aus graugelbem Heilbronner Sandſtein und Tuffſtein zum Ausdruck (Tafel 90), während die dem Rhein zugekehrte Seite, die von einer maleriſchen Pergola abgeſchloſſen wird, einen villenartigen Charakter trägt

Monsieur le professeur Docteur Bruno Schmitz de Berlin a donné un caractère de château du Moyen-âge à la villa Stollwerck à Cologne qu'il a bâtie du mois de mai 1902 à celui de février 1904. Le propriétaire de cette villa l'a appelée en témoignage d'admiration pour le premier chancelier de l'empire Allemand „Bismarckburg“. Le caractère de château Moyen-âge trouve surtout son expression dans la partie supérieure de la façade principale, ainsi que dans le revêtement des façades en appareil rustique de pierre jaune-grise de Heilbronn et en tuffe (Pl. 90), tandis que le côté qui regarde le Rhin et qui est bordé d'une pittoresque pergola a le caractère de villa

Professor Bruno Schmitz Dr. ing. of Berlin has given the character of a medieval castle to the villa Stollwerck in Cologne, built by him in the period from May 1902 to February 1904. The villa has been named by the owner "Bismarckburg" in honoured memory of the great Chancellor, the first of the German Empire. This castellated character is particularly striking on the principal front, which is faced with rustic square stones of greyish yellow Heilbronn sandstone and tuffstone (see plate 90). The side facing the Rhine is finished off with a picturesque pergola, and is of a villa-like style

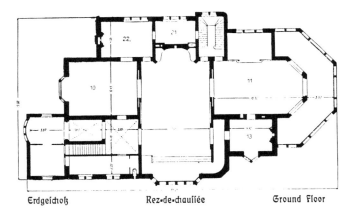

Erdgeſchoß   Rez-de-chauſſée

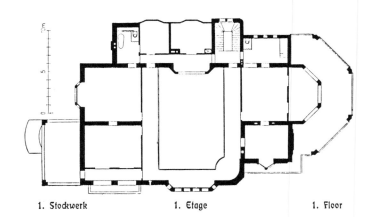

Ground Floor   1. Stockwerk   1. Étage   1. Floor

Der Sockel iſt in Baſalt ausgeführt, die Gartenfronten teilweiſe in Eichenholzfachwerk. Das Relief am Giebel der Hauptfront, das den Fürſten Bismarck in mittelalterlicher Rüſtung darſtellt, hat Profeſſor Chriſtian Behrens in Breslau geſchaffen.

Le socle est exécuté en basalt, la façade du jardin est en partie en pans de bois de chêne. Le relief du fronton de la façade principale qui représente le prince de Bismarck en armure du Moyen-âge est l'œuvre du professeur Chrétien Behrens à Breslau.

The sockel is of basalt, the frontage to the garden partly of oak wood-work. The statue of Bismarck, in relief on the gable of the principal front, represented as a medieval knight, is by Professor Christian Behrens.

Im Erdgeſchoß gruppieren ſich um die Diele ein Salon, zwei Geſellſchaftszimmer, das Zimmer des Herrn, die Bibliothek, das Speiſezimmer und das Rauchzimmer. Im Obergeſchoß liegen ſechs Wohn- und Schlafzimmer.

Die Baukoſten betrugen 460000 Mark.

191 [1905; 66]

Für die Firma A. Gerngroß in Wien haben die Architekten Fellner und Helmer an der Mariahilfer Hauptſtraße in den Jahren 1903 und 1904 ein Modewarenhaus erbaut, das in ſeiner äußeren und inneren Geſtaltung von den großen Warenhäuſern in Berlin mehrfach abweicht. Den Architekten war die Aufgabe geſtellt worden, dem Bauplatze die größtmögliche Fläche für den Betrieb abzugewinnen, was bei der äußerſt ungünſtigen Geſtaltung des Bauplatzes ungemein ſchwierig war. Trotzdem ſind von der 2090 Quadratmeter betragenden Geſamtfläche 1880 Quadratmeter bebaut worden. Ferner war

Au rez-de-chaussée, un salon, deux chambres de société, la chambre de Monsieur, la bibliothèque, la salle à manger et le fumoir se groupent autour du hall. A l'étage supérieur se trouvent six chambres à coucher et d'habitation.

Les frais de construction s'élevèrent à 460000 Marks.

191 [1905; 66]

Les architectes Fellner et Helmer ont élevé à Vienne à la Mariahilfer Hauptstrasse, dans les années 1903 et 1904, pour la maison A. Gerngross, un grand magasin pour confections qui diffère en plusieurs points, dans son extérieur et dans ses dispositions intérieures des grand magasins de Berlin. On avait posé aux architectes le problème de gagner la plus grande surface possible pour le service; ce qui était fort difficile à résoudre à cause de la forme particulièrement défavorable du terrain. Malgré cela, on a utilisé pour la bâtisse 1880 mètres carrés de la surface totale de 2090. Il était

On the ground floor are grouped round the hall a drawing-room, two saloons, a study, a library, the dining and smoking rooms. On the upper story are six living and bed rooms.

The cost of building amounted to 460000 Marks.

191 [1905; 66]

The architects Fellner and Helmer have built for the firm A. Gerngross, Mariahilfer Hauptstrasse in Vienna a bazaar during the years 1903 and 1904. Both in its external architecture and in its interior equipment it differs considerably from the same kind of building in Berlin. It was the task of the architect to arrange as large a space as possible for the public part of the business, a task which the awkward nature of the site rendered extremely difficult. In the spite of this, architect

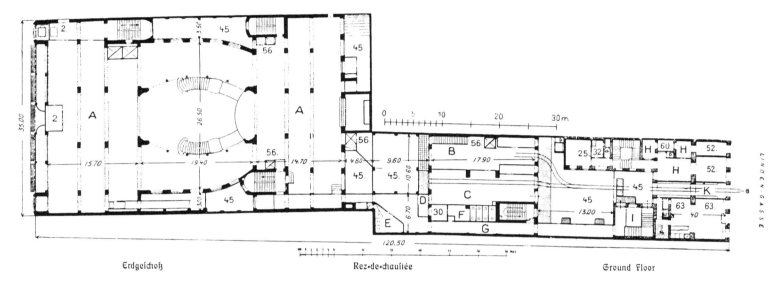

Erdgeſchoß — Rez-de-chauſſée — Ground Floor

es notwendig, dem Hauſe die möglichſte Durchſichtigkeit zu geben, damit ſämtliche Geſchäftsräume von jedem Punkte des Hauſes überblickt werden können, was einerſeits für das Publikum von größter Wichtigkeit, andrerſeits für den Eigentümer zur Überwachung des Geſchäftsbetriebes erforderlich iſt. Zu dieſem Zweck mußte der Anlage der Haupttreppe die größte Aufmerkſamkeit zugewendet werden. Im Gegenſatz zu den meiſten Warenhäuſern entſchieden ſich die Architekten dafür, die Haupttreppe nicht in die Mittelachſe des Gebäudes, ſondern mit zwei Anfangsarmen neben die Achſe zu legen. Dadurch iſt nicht nur eine reizvolle Anordnung gewonnen, ſondern auch eine Entwicklung des Parterrelokals in der ganzen Tiefe des Grundſtücks erreicht worden.

Um eine möglichſt große Feuerſicherheit einerſeits und eine möglichſt große Raumerſparnis andrerſeits zu erzielen, iſt der Bau in armiertem Beton ausgeführt worden.

In bezug auf die äußere Geſtaltung des Gebäudes war von dem Bauherrn „gemäßigt moderner Stil" verlangt worden. Demgemäß wurde mit der Ausarbeitung der architektoniſchen Skizzen und Details Architekt Ferdinand Fellner jun. betraut, der in Brüſſel bei Horta und in London Studien auf dieſem Gebiete gemacht hat (Tafel 66).

An das neue Warenhaus ſchließt ſich unmittelbar ein älteres Haus derſelben Firma an, deſſen Erdgeſchoß und erſtes Stockwerk mit dem Faſſadenſyſtem des Neubaues in Einklang gebracht worden ſind.

Die Koſten des Neubaues beliefen ſich bei 57000 Kubikmetern umbauten Raums auf 24,50 Kronen für den Kubikmeter.

en outre nécessaire de donner à la maison la plus grande transparence possible, a fin de pouvoir de chaque point apercevoir tous les locaux; ce qui est d'une part d'une grande importance pour le public et d'autre part nécessaire au directeur pour pouvoir surveiller facilement les opérations. Dans ce but, il était indispensable de prêter la plus grande attention à la disposition de l'escalier principal. Au contraire de ce qui se fait dans la plupart des grands magasins, les architectes prirent le parti de ne point placer leur escalier principal dans l'axe de l'édifice, mais de le disposer en deux branches à côté de l'axe. Cet arrangement a non seulement donné lieu à un motif charmant, mais il a encore permis un développement des localités du rez-de-chaussée dans toute la profondeur du terrain.

Pour obtenir d'un côté la plus grande sécurité contre les dangers d'incendie et de l'autre le moins de perte de place, le bâtiment a été conſtruit en béton armé.

Pour ce qui est de la composition des façades, le propriétaire avait exigé un „style moderne modéré". Pour répondre à ce vœu, on chargea de la composition et des détails architecturaux Monsieur Ferdinand Fellner cadet, qui a fait des études spéciales de cette partie chez Horta à Brussel et à Londres (Pl. 66).

Un ancien immeuble touchant directement aux nouveaux magasins et appartenant également à la maison Gerngroß a été accommodé de telle sorte, que son rez-de-chaussée et son premier étage ont été mis d'accord avec le système de façades du nouveau bâtiment.

Les frais de construction du nouvel immeuble s'élevèrent pour 57000 mètres cubes d'espace bâti à 24,50 couronnes par mètre cube.

has succeeded in reserving 1880 square meters out of 2090 square meters for the purpose required. It was further a matter of great importance that the whole building should be so built that a complete survey of each department was possible from all points, a matter no less agreeable to the public, than important for the business director whose eye can thus be over the whole building. In order to ensure this result, great attention was given to the principal staircase. Contrary to the general rule of having a central staircase in the middle nave of the building, he has constructed two side approaches which not only have a charming effect, but which allow a complete use of the whole ground floor for the business.

In order to secure on the one side economy of space, and on the other, security from fire the whole building is carried out in beton.

As regards style, the owners requested "a temperate modern style"; for this purpose the designs of Ferdinand Fellner jun. who has studied in Brussels under Horta, and in London, were used (see plate 66).

Adjoining the new bazaar is an old house belonging to the same firm, the ground floor and first story of which, have been made to correspond, as far as the facade is concerned, with the new building.

The cost of the new building of 57000 cubic meters, amounted to 24,50 Kronen per cubic meter.

Das alte Rathaus in Bensheim an der Bergstrasse ist von Professor Heinrich Metzendorf einem Umbau unterzogen worden, der sowohl die Fassade (Tafel 2) wie das Innere (Tafel 3—4) vorteilhaft umgestaltet hat. Die Fensteröffnungen sind im großen und ganzen unverändert geblieben; völlig neu sind der Giebel mit dem Ornament und das Portal. Das Erdgeschoß ist in rotem Sandstein aus dem Odenwald ausgeführt, die Flächen der oberen Geschosse sind grau verputzt. Das Dach ist mit roten Biberschwänzen eingedeckt.

L'ancien hôtel-de-ville de Bensheim à la Bergstrasse a été modifié par le Professeur Henri Metzendorf, qui a sû changer avantageusement les façades (Pl. 2) ainsi que l'intérieur (Pl. 3—4). Les ouvertures de fenêtres en général restées ce qu'elles étaient, il n'y a de complètement neuf que le fronton avec sa décoration et le portail. Le rez-de-chaussée est construit en pierre rouge de l'Odenwald, les surfaces des étages supérieurs sont crépis en gris. Le toit est recouvert en tuiles rouges.

The old Guildhall in Bensheim on the "Bergstrasse" has been rebuilt by Professor Heinrich Metzendorf; both the facade (see plate 2) and the interior (see plates 3—4) have been most advantageously altered. The window openings have, as a rule, been left as they were, but the gables, with the ornamentation, and the portal are quite new. The ground floor is of red sandstone from the Odenwald, and the surfaces of the upper storeys are of grey plaster. The roof is covered with flat red tiles.

Für das Haus Nachodstraße 30 in Berlin hat Arthur Biberfeld die Fassade gezeichnet, die in Putzbau ausgeführt ist (Tafel 5). Sonst ein entschiedener Vertreter der modernen Richtung, der gern eigene Wege geht, hat er sich hier an die Ornamentik der Biedermeierzeit angeschlossen, d. h. der Zeit von etwa 1815—1850, deren Schöpfungen wegen ihrer einfachen Zweckmäßigkeit in neuester Zeit vorbildlichen Wert gewonnen haben. Danach hat das Haus nach alter deutscher Sitte den Namen „Zum Biedermeier" erhalten. Es enthält in jeder Etage zwei Mietwohnungen, deren Grundrisse Baumeister Silber aufgestellt hat.

Monsieur Arthur Biberfeld a composé la façade de la maison Nachodstrasse 30 à Berlin, cette façade a été executée en maçonnerie crépie (Pl. 5). L'architecte qui est en général un représentant convaincu de l'école moderne et qui a l'habitude d'aller son propre chemin, s'est inspiré ici dans son ornementation du style dit „Biedermeier" c'est-à-dire du goût régnant de 1815 à 1850 à peu près, dont les créations ont ces derniers temps été imitées à cause de leur simplicité et de leur bon goût. C'est dans le même esprit que cette maison a été baptisée „au Biedermeier" d'après l'ancienne mode allemande. Cette immeuble contient à chaque étage deux appartements dont l'entrepreneur Silber a fait les plans.

The facade of the house Nachodstrasse 30 Berlin has been designed by Arthur Biberfeld, and has been executed in plaster work (see plate 5). This artist is, as a rule, a strict adherent to the modern style of architecture, and an advocate for individuality; but in this case he has gone back to the "Biedermeier" time, something between 1815 and 1850, ("Biedermeier" a simple straightforward citizen) and has shown that there is much to imitate in this simple utilitarian style. The house is named after this old German custom "Zum Biedermeier". On each floor are two flats; the ground-plans of which were designed by the Baumeister Silber.

In Charlottenburg haben die Architekten Hart & Lesser auf dem bis zur Bismarckstraße durchgehenden Grundstücke Berlinerstraße 146 (Tafel 14) in der Zeit vom 1. November 1904 bis 1. Oktober 1905 ein vierstöckiges Wohnhaus errichtet, dessen Fassaden die vornehmen Formen und Verhältnisse zeigen, die den Architekten eigen sind. Im Erdgeschoß befinden sich Geschäftsräume, an die sich kleinere Wohnräume anschließen; in den oberen drei Stockwerken befinden sich je zwei Mietwohnungen von sieben resp. fünf Zimmern.

Les architectes Hart et Lesser ont construit à Charlottenburg une maison d'habitation à quatre étages sur le terrain à bâtir situé Berlinerstrasse 146 et s'étendant jusqu'à la Bismarckstrasse (Pl. 14). Cet immeuble élevé du 1 novembre 1904 au 1 octobre 1905, montre dans ses façades, les formes distinguées et les belles proportions dont ces architectes ont le secret. Au rez-de-chaussée se trouvent des locaux d'affaires, les quels sont reliés à de petits appartements; dans chacun des trois étages supérieurs ont été installées deux appartements, l'un de sept, l'autre de cinq pièces.

The architects Hart and Lesser have built in Charlottenburg a four-storied house from 1 November 1904 to 1 October 1905. The site extends through from the Berlinerstrasse 146 to the Bismarckstrasse (see plate 14), and the facade displays the same distinction of style for which these architects have so long been celebrated. On the ground-floor are business premises with small dwelling rooms adjoining, on each of the three upper stories are two flats containing respectively seven and five rooms.

In Koblenz, am Kaiser Wilhelm-Ring Nr. 48, haben die Architekten Gebrüder Friedhofen in einem Zeitraum von elf Monaten ein dreigeschossiges Miethaus erbaut, dessen Fassade teils in Kammputz ausgeführt, teils mit reicher Ornamentik überzogen ist (Tafel 18). Das Erdgeschoß enthält eine Wohnung von drei Zimmern mit Zubehör, die Etagen je eine Wohnung von fünf Zimmern. In den oberen Stockwerken des Hofflügels, dessen Erdgeschoß Geschäftszwecken dient, liegen ebenfalls Wohnungen von je drei Zimmern. Die plastischen Arbeiten an der Fassade hat Bildhauer Ramminger ausgeführt.

Les frères Friedhofen, architectes ont élevé à Coblence au Kaiser Wilhelm-Ring No. 48, dans l'espace de mois une maison à loyer de trois étages, dont les façades sont en partie exécutées en crépissage au peigne, en partie recouvertes de riches ornements (Pl. 18). Le rez-de-chaussée contient un appartement de trois chambres avec dépendances, les étages contiennent chacun un logement de cinq chambres. Dans les étages superieurs de l'aile de la cour dont le rez-de-chaussée sert à des comptoirs, sont également situés des appartements de trois chambres. Le sculpteur Ramminger à exécuté les décorations plastiques de la façade.

Les frais de construction s'élevèrent à 72000

A three-storied house arranged in flats has been built at Kaiser Wilhelm-Ring 48 in Coblenz by the architects Bros. Friedhofen in the period of mouths the facade is partly of ribbed plaster and partly richly ornamented (see plate 18). The ground floor contains a lodging of three rooms with offices, the upper stories each a five-roomed lodging. In the upper stories of the side courtyard wing are also lodgings of each three rooms, the lower stories are let as business premises. The sculptural ornament of the facade is by the sculptor Ramminger.

Wie eine Putzfassade mittelst moderner, aus den Bedingungen des Materials hervorgegangener Ornamentik und farbiger Belebung derselben zu künstlerischer Wirkung gebracht werden kann, tritt an dem Wohnhause Kaiser Wilhelm-Ring 50 in Koblenz in Erscheinung (Tafel 46). Die Fassade wurde von den Architekten Gebrüder Friedhofen in Koblenz entworfen, etwa im Laufe eines Jahres für die Baukostensumme von 60000 Mark ausgeführten Hauses ist mit Zement geputzt, und aus demselben Material ist die im flachen Relief modellierte Ornamentik hergestellt. Die Zementputzflächen haben im allgemeinen den grauen Naturton beibehalten, da-

La maison d'habitation Kaiser Wilhelm-Ring 50 à Coblence prouve quel effet artistique on peut obtenir au moyen d'une façade crépie dans le goût moderne avec une ornementation soumise aux conditions des matériaux et rehaussée de couleurs (Pl. 46). La façade de cet immeuble construit dans l'espace d'une année à peu près, d'après les plans des frères Friedhofen architectes, pour la somme de 60000 Marks, a été crépie au ciment, dans lequel on a modelé les ornements en bas relief. Les surfaces crépies au ciment ont en général conservé leur ton gris naturel, tandis que les surfaces des piliers des

How much artistic attractiveness may be given to an ordinary plaster facade by a successful application of coloured ornament may be seen by the dwelling house Kaiser Wilhelm-Ring 50, Coblenz (see plate 46). The design of the facade is by the architects Brothers Friedhofen of Coblenz, the time occupied was one year, and the cost 60000 Marks. The material is cement, and the ornament is of the same material modelled in flat relief. The surfaces have retained the natural grey colour of the cement, as a rule, but in the upper stories the pillars and the foundation of the

gegen find die Pfeilerflächen der oberen Geschofie und der Grund des Giebels gelb gefärbt. Das grauweiße, grüne oder rote Ornament hebt sich meist von einem tiefblauen Grunde ab, während die Rofetten in den Brüstungstafeln der Fenster des zweiten Obergeschofies in blauer und roter Farbe abwechseln.

Das Haus besteht aus einem Erdgeschoß und drei Obergeschofien, von denen jedes eine Wohnung mit Nebenräumen enthält. Die in ein Oval eingebaute Haupttreppe führt vom Keller bis zum Dachboden.

199 [1906; 8]

Bei dem Entwurf der St. Johanniskirche nebst Pfarrhaus in Mannheim, die von Curjel und Mofer in Karlsruhe von September 1901 bis Mai 1904 erbaut worden ift, haben die Architekten das Ziel verfolgt, durch engen Zufammenfchluß beider Gebäude eine praktifche Anlage im Innern und einen wirkungsvollen Gruppenbau im Äußern zu fchaffen. Durch diefen Zufammenfchluß ift eine praktifche Verbindung der einzelnen Gebäude errichtet worden, die für einen bequemen Dienst notwendig ift. Unfere Tafel 8 gibt die Hauptfaffade der Kirche wieder und zugleich einen Überblick über die gefamte Gebäudegruppe. Links von der Hauptfaffade, die in weißem Sandstein aus der Pfalz ausgeführt ift, biegt fich der Konfirmandenfaal weit hinaus; rechts erhebt fich der mit einer Steinpyramide abgefchloffene Glockenturm, an den fich eine Vorhalle für die Unterfahrt von Wagen anfchließt. Durch drei von zwölf Säulen getragene Rundbogen erfolgt der Zugang zu der offenen Vorhalle und zur Kirche. Über dem mittleren Rundbogen vertieft fich die Mauer der Faffade zu einer Nifche, die ein Reliefbild des Evangeliften Johannes, von zwei Engeln umgeben, von Profeffor Friedrich Dietfche in Karlsruhe enthält. Statt des an diefer Stelle fonst üblichen Rofenfenfters ist ein gefchloffenes Feld gewählt worden, weil fich hinter der Giebelwand die Orgel befindet, von der atmofphärifche Einflüffe möglichst fernzuhalten find. In der Spitze des Giebelfeldes ift eine geflügelte Figur mit Pofaune angebracht, die die Gläubigen zur Andacht einladet.

étages supérieurs et le fond du fronton ont été teints en jaune. La décoration gris-blanchâtre, verte ou rouge, se détache sur un fond généralement bleu foncé, tandis que les rosaces des contrecœurs de fenêtres du deuxième étage alternent de couleur bleue et rouge.

La maison se compose d'un rez-de-chaussée et de trois étages supérieurs, dont chacun contient un appartement avec dépendances. L'escalier principal construit sur un plan ovale conduit de la cave aux mansardes.

199 [1906; 8]

Dans le projet de l'église de Saint Jean avec presbytère à Mannheim, que Messrs. Curjel et Moser, architectes à Carlsruhe ont élevés du mois de septembre 1901 à celui de mai 1904, ces architectes ont eu en vue d'obtenir une disposition pratique à l'intérieur et un effet imposant de groupement à l'extérieur, grâce à la liaison intime des deux édifices. Il a été obtenu par ce rapprochement, une communication pratique des deux constructions, laquelle est nécessaire à un service commode. Notre Planche 8 représente la façade principale de l'église et présente en même temps un coup d'œil d'ensemble sur tout le groupe. A gauche de la façade principale qui a été exécutée en pierre blanche du Palatinat, la salle des cathécumènes fait une forte saillie, à droite s'élève le clocher surmonté d'une flèche, contre ce dernier s'appuie un porche abritant l'arrivée des voitures. L'entrée dans le vestibule et dans l'église a lieu par trois arcs en plein cintre, supportés par douze colonnes. Au dessus de l'arc central, s'enfonce dans l'épaisseur du mur de façade, une niche qui contient une image en relief de l'Évangéliste Saint Jean entouré de deux anges, œuvre du professeur Frédéric Dietsche à Carlsruhe. Au lieu de la fenêtre en rose habituelle à cette place, on a préféré un panneau fermé, parce que derrière ce mur de pignon se trouvent les orgues qui doivent autant que possible être préservées des influences athmosphériques. Au sommet du pignon a été placée une figure ailée sonnant de la trompette, invitant les fidèles au culte.

gables are coloured yellow. The grey white, green or red ornament stands out effectively from a back ground generally of deep blue; the rosettes on the panels of the window sills of the first and second stories are alternately blue and red.

The house consists of a ground floor and three upper stories each containing a dwelling with the usual offices. The principal staircase, built in an oval form, leads from the basement to the roof.

199 [1906; 8]

The church of St. John and the adjoining parsonage in Mannheim was built by the architects Curjel and Moser of Carlsruhe from September 1901 to May 1904. The aim of the architects was to construct buildings lying as nearly as possible together, so as to be of practical utility in the interior and to form, as to the exterior, an effective group. The result is a most convenient arrangement of the various parts for the purposes of Divine service. Our plate 8 gives a view of the chief facade and a survey of the whole building. On the left of the principal front, which is of white sandstone from the Palatinate, stretches a large hall for confirmation candidates; on the right rises the bell-tower, finished off with a stone pyramid; under this is an entrance for carriages. Three arches supported by twelve pillars lead to the entrances of the open vestibule and to the church. Under the centre arch is a recess in the wall forming a niche in which is a relief of the evangelist St. John guarded by two angels; this is the work of Professor Friedrich Dietsche in Carlsruhe. Instead of the usual rose window in this place, is a plain surface, because behind this in the wall of the gable, is the organ loft, it being advisable not to subject the instrument to the variations of the atmosphere. At the summit of the gable is a winged figure with a trumpet, inviting the congregation to Divine service.

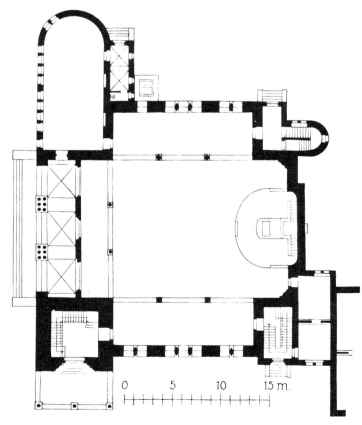

0   5   10   15 m.

Der Konfirmandenfaal ift fowohl von der Vorhalle als von der Nordfeite zugänglich und ift außerdem durch eine Tür mit der Kirche ver-

La salle des cathécumènes est aussi bien accessible du porche que du côté nord et a été en outre reliée à l'église par une porte, de sorte

The hall for confirmation candidates can be entered from the north side as well as from the vestibule, an additional entrance leads into

bunden, fo daß bei hohen Feften noch über 100 Kirchenbefucher darin dem Gottesdienft folgen können.

Der Kirchenraum ift auf der einfachen Kreuzform aufgebaut. Der Blick des Eintretenden wird fofort auf die in der Achfe liegende Kanzelwand gelenkt, auf die der künftlerifche Schmuck konzentriert worden ift (Tafel 9). Die Kanzel liegt über dem Altar, und die Wand hinter der Kanzel ift mit der Reliefgruppe der Kreuzigung gefchmückt, die fich von ornamentiertem, tiefblauem Grunde abhebt. Sie ift von Profeffor Dietfche modelliert und in den von Profeffor Läuger gegründeten Tonwerken von Kandern in farbiger Terrakotta hergeftellt. Kanzel, Altar und Rückwand find in weißem Sandftein ausgeführt. Die Kirche enthält etwa 1200 Sitzplätze.

Vom Altarraum führt rechts eine Tür zur Sakriftei, die durch ein Wartezimmer mit dem Pfarrhaus in Verbindung fteht. Letzteres enthält im Erdgefchoß drei Zimmer, Küche und Speifekammer, im Obergefchoß vier Zimmer und ein Badezimmer und im Dachgefchoß noch drei bewohnbare Räume.

Die Baukoften betrugen rund 390000 Mark, wovon 37000 Mark auf das Pfarrhaus entfallen.

200, 201 [1906; 88, 89]

Das Beftreben, Neues an die Stelle der traditionellen Bauformen zu fetzen, wird im Kirchenbau erfolgreich durch die Architekten Schilling und Graebner-Dresden vertreten. Die Kirche in Strehlen, auf einer Bodenerhebung des linken Elbufers ftehend, in den Umfaffungsmauern und Türmen aus Hauftein her-

qu'à l'occasion de fêtes solennelles, cent fidèles de plus peuvent, à cette place, assister au culte.

La nef est construite en simple forme de croix. Le regard de celui qui entre est de suite attiré sur la paroi de la chaire située dans l'axe, c'est sur cette paroi qu'a été concentré la décoration artistique (Pl. 9). La chaire est placée au dessus de l'autel et la paroi derrière la chaire est décorée d'un groupe en relief, représentant le crucifiement, ce relief se détache sur un fond bleu foncé couvert d'ornements, il a été modelé par le professeur Dietsche et exécuté en fayence de couleur dans les ateliers de poterie de Kandern fondés par le professeur Läuger. La chaire, l'autel et la paroi postérieure ont été exécutées en pierre blanche. L'église contient environ 1200 places assises.

A droite de l'autel, une porte conduit dans la sacristie qui est reliée au presbytère par une salle d'attente. Le presbytère contient trois chambres, la cuisine et un garde-manger au rez-dechaussée, à l'étage supérieur, quatre chambres et une chambre de bain et dans l'étage du toit encore trois pièces habitables.

Les frais de construction s'élevèrent à 390000 Marks, dont 37000 furent consacrés au presbytère.

200, 201 [1906; 88, 89]

La tendance à remplacer dans l'architecture religieuse les formes traditionelles par des formes nouvelles est poursuivi avec succès par les architectes Schilling et Graebner à Dresde. L'église de Strehlen, située sur une élévation du sol de la rive gauche de l'Elbe, appartient à la nouvelle école, elle est construite en pierre

the church, so that, on occasions, accommodation can be found for 100 worshippers who can take part in the service.

The body of the church is a simple cross; the eye of the beholder on entering the church is at once directed to the chancel where all the artistic ornament is concentrated (see plate 9). The chancel lies over the altar, and the wall behind the chancel is ornamented with a relief group of the Crucifixion, standing out from a decorated deep blue ground. It was designed by Professor Dietsche, and has been modelled in coloured terra cotta in the works of Professor Läuger in Kandern. Chancel, altar and back wall are all of white sandstone. The church contains 1200 seats.

From the altar on the right a door leads to the vestry from which through an entrance hall one can reach the parsonage. The parsonage contains on the ground floor three rooms with kitchen and pantry, the upper floor has four rooms and a bath-room; in the roof story are three rooms.

The cost of building amounted to about 390000 Marks, of which 37000 Marks were spent on the parsonage.

200, 201 [1906; 88, 89]

The architects Schilling and Graebner of Dresden have built a church at Strehlen in which they have successfully attempted to introduce modern art into the traditional architectural forms. The church stands on a raised site on the left bank of the Elbe; the outside

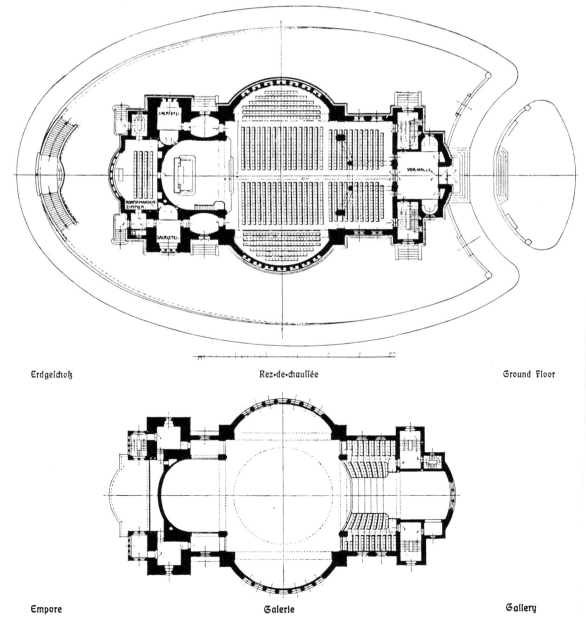

| Erdgefchoß | Rez-de-chauffée | Ground Floor |

| Empore | Galerie | Gallery |

geftellt, ift ein Werk der vorgenannten Architekten und gehört der neuen Richtung an.

Die Kirche bildet einen Zentralbau mit vier kurzen Anfätzen an einen mittleren quadratifchen Kuppelraum. In der Längsachfe fchließen fich einerfeits ein Arm in der vollen Breite des letzteren und eine Vorhalle an, beide find von einer Empore überbaut; andererfeits find ein eingezogener, halbkreisförmig gefchloffener Altarraum, zwei feitwärts gelegene Sakriffeien und hinter dem Altarraum ein Konfirmandenfaal angeordnet. In der Querachfe find dem Kuppelraume, in gleicher Breite mit diefem, beiderfeits im Segment- bogen ausgefchwungene Anbauten hinzugefügt. Sämtliche Raumteile find gewölbt; Holzdecken find nur unter der Orgelempore und in den Sakriffeien zur Verwendung gekommen.

Der Außenbau ift reich gegliedert; fo wird die Vorhalle von zwei kleineren Türmen ein- gefaßt, welche die Emporentreppen enthalten, und über den Sakriffeien erhebt fich ein hohes Turm- paar für die Glocken. Diefe Türme wie die vorigen find mit maffiven Spitzkuppelhelmen bekrönt. Die bildnerifchen Schmuckformen, eine Chriftusfigur über und zwei Engelsfiguren neben dem Haupteingange u. a., find von Bildhauer Pöpelmann-Dresden, die Reliefs über den Seiten- eingängen von Bildhauer König-Dresden, die Ornamente von Prof. Groß-Dresden gearbeitet. Der Altar ift mit Figuren von Bildhauer Hudler- Dresden, Lefepult und Kanzel find mit Reliefs von Bildhauer Kramer-Dresden geziert, während die Ornamente von Prof. Groß und die gemalten Fenfter fowie die Freskomalereien an den Ge- wölben von Prof. Gußmann-Dresden herrühren. Die gemalten Fenfter der Sakriffeien find von Maler Bothe-Dresden gefchaffen.

de taille, tant dans ses façades que dans sa tour; elle est l'œuvre des architectes sus-nommés.

L'église est de disposition centrale, elle possède un espace carré surmonté d'une coupole, auquel se rattachent quatre bras court. Dans l'axe principal se trouvent d'une part une nef et un porche aussi large que le corps central, tous deux contiennent une galerie, d'autre part un chœur fermé en forme demi-circulaire con- tenant l'autel, deux sacristies situées de côté, et derrière le chœur, une salle de confirmation. Dans l'axe transversal ont été disposés, de même largeur que le corps central, des nefs terminées en forme de segment. Toutes ces parties sont voûtées; on n'a employé des plafonds de bois que sous la galerie des orgues et dans les sacristies.

L'extérieur est d'une silhouette très mouve- mentée, le porche est flanqué de deux petites tours contenant les escaliers des galeries; au dessus des sacristies s'élève un couple de hautes tours contenant les cloches. Ces tours ainsi que les tourelles du porche sont couronnées de bonnets massifs. La décoration sculpturale con- siste en une figure du Christ au dessus de l'entrée principale et de deux figures d'anges à côté de cette même entrée et en reliefs au dessus des portes latérales, ces derniers sont dûs au sculpteur König de Dresde, tandis que les figures sont l'œuvre du sculpteur Pöpel- mann de Dresde; le professeur Gross de la même ville a fait les ornements. L'autel est décoré de figures du sculpteur Hudler de Dresde, le lutrin et la chaire portent des reliefs du sculpteur Kramer de Dresde, les ornements sont du professeur Gross. Le professeur Guss- mann de Dresde a exécuté les vitraux peints ainsi que les peintures à fresque des voûtes. Les fenêtres peintes de la sacristie sont l'œuvre du peintre Bothe à Dresde.

walls and towers are of hewn stone, and the work is of a decidedly modern type.

Above a central quadrilateral edifice is a cupola, and on each corner is a projecting abutment. From the middle aisle on one side is a side aisle of the same breadth leading to a vestibule; over these is a gallery. On the other side is a semi-circular enclosed chancel, two side sacristies and behind the chancel a hall for the preparation of confirmation candidates. In the transept is the space under the cupola from which aisles lead in the same breadth to the abutments, where they finish in segmental arched projections. All the spaces are vaulted; wood roofing is only used under the organ loft and in the vestries.

The exterior is richly treated; the vestibule has two small towers from which one reaches the gallery by a staircase. Over the vestry is the belfry, which consists of two towers; these, as well as the other towers have pointed cupolas. The sculptured figures, a figure of Christ over the principal entrance and two figures of angels at the side are by the sculptor Pöpelmann of Dresden; the reliefs over the side entrances are by the sculptor König of Dresden, and the orna- ments by Professor Gross, also of Dresden. The figures on the altar are by Hudler of Dresden, and the reading deck and pulpit are adorned with reliefs by Kramer of Dresden. The ornaments are by Professor Gross, and the stained glass windows and fresco paintings on the vaulted roofs are by Professor Gussmann of Dresden. The stained windows of the vestry are by the painter Bothe of Dresden.

202 [1906; 15]

Das Warenhaus Old England in Brüffel (Tafel 15) ift aus der gemeinfamen Arbeit des Architekten Paul Saintenoy, der die Faffade entworfen hat, und der Ingenieure Jules De- becker und Mykowski hervorgegangen. Der Befitzer, ein Schmiedemeifter, hatte eine Kon- ftruktion ganz aus Eifen verlangt, und demnach find alle anderen Materialien außer Eifen und Stahl ausgefchloffen worden. Nur die Decken find in Beton mit Eifenarmierung ausgeführt, und an der Faffade find dekorative Friefe in farbig

202 [1906; 15]

Le grand magasin „Old England" à Bruxelles (Pl. 15) est le résultat de la collaboration de Monsieur Paul Saintenoy architecte qui a composé les façades et des ingénieurs Jules Debecker et Mykowski. Le propriétaire, un maître de forges, avait exigé une construction toute en fer, et c'est pour cela que tous les matériaux, excepté le fer et l'acier ont été exclus de cette construction. Seuls les planchers ont été construits en béton avec arma- ture de fer et aux façades on a employé des

202 [1906; 15]

The bazaar "Old England" in Brussels (see plate 15) is the combined work of the architect Paul Saintenoy who has designed the facade, and the engineers Jules Debecker and Mykowski. The owner, a master smith, wished for a building entirely of iron, for this reason iron and steel have been exclusively used. Only the ceilings are of beton with iron

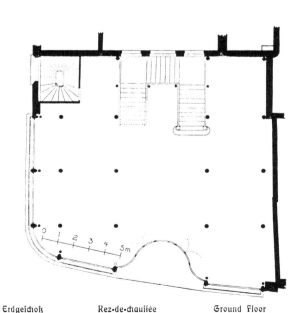

Erdgefchoß — Rez-de-chauffée — Ground Floor

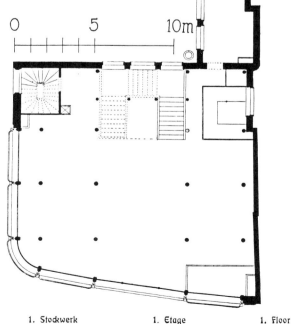

1. Stockwerk — 1. Etage — 1. Floor

glafierter Terrakotta verwendet worden. Die Kunftfchmiedearbeiten hat Pierre Desmedt aus- geführt.

frises décoratives de terra cotta émaillée poly- chrome. Les fers forgés artistiques ont été exécutés par Pierre Desmedt.

girders, and on the facade are terra-cotta coloured glazed tiles designed as an ornamental frieze. The artistic iron-work is by Pierre Desmedt.

Das Bahnhofsgebäude der Station Traben-Trarbach an der Mosel (Tafel 22) ist ein weiteres Beispiel der überaus feinsinnigen Art, mit der der Schöpfer dieser Neubauten, Regierungsbaumeister Hüter in Malstatt-Burbach, diese den Ansprüchen des modernen Verkehrs dienenden Nutzbauten dem romantischen Charakter der Landschaft und den einheimischen Bauüberlieferungen anzupassen weiß. Die von den alten, zum Teil noch aus dem 15. und 16. Jahrhundert stammenden Holz- und Fachwerksbauten gebotenen Motive hat er mit großem Geschick verwertet, daneben aber die moderne Bestimmung der Gebäude zu charakteristischem Ausdruck gebracht.

In freier Anlehnung an die alten Holzbauten hat man in neuerer Zeit besonders an Landhäusern den gelungenen Versuch gemacht, den Fachwerkbau in Verbindung mit überstehenden Dächern wieder neu zu beleben. Die Doppelvilla in Lüttich, Avenue des Ormes 3 u. 5, von dem Architekten Paul Tischmeyer entworfen und in etwa elf Monaten für die Bausumme von 42000 Frs., ohne Einbeziehung des Bodenwertes in diesen Betrag, zur Ausführung gebracht, gibt ein bezeichnendes Beispiel dieser gemischten Bauweise (Tafel 36).

La gare de la station Traben-Trarbach sur Moselle (Pl. 22) est un nouvel exemple de l'extraordinaire délicatesse avec laquelle, l'auteur de constructions analogues, l'architecte du gouvernement Hüter à Malstatt-Burbach a sû faire harmoniser des bâtiments d'utilité pratique, destinés à la circulation moderne, avec le caractère romantique de la contrée et avec les traditions locales d'architecture. Il a utilisé avec beaucoup d'habileté les anciens motifs de construction en pans de bois, datant encore en partie des 15me et 16me siècles, tout en donnant aux édifices le caractère de leur destination moderne.

On s'est efforcé depuis quelque temps de reprendre la tradition des constructions en pans de bois apparents avec toits à grandes saillies, en s'inspirant librement des anciens édifices en bois. La villa double, Avenue des Ormes 3 et 5 à Liège construite d'après les plans de Monsieur Paul Tischmeyer architecte, dans l'espace de onze mois environ, pour la somme de 42000 Francs, somme dans la quelle n'est pas compris le prix du terrain, donne un exemple caractéristique de ce mode mixte de construire (Pl. 36).

The Regierungsbaumeister Hüter of Malstatt-Burbach has built the Railway Station at Traben-Trarbach on the Moselle (see plate 22) and has there given another good example of the possibility of combining utility with beauty in these buildings, the one in question being suited in its style to the romantic character of the landscape and to the architecture of the district. The leading idea was given by the old wood and frame-work buildings of the 15ht and 16th centuries and this idea has been made use of with much ingenuity.

Many recently built villas show a return to the old style of wood buildings; it is true the imitation is somewhat free, but the use of framework and the overhanging roof has resulted in producing very attractive buildings. Of this happy combination of building materials an excellent example may be seen in the double villa Avenue des Ormes 3 and 5, Liege, designed by the architect Paul Tischmeyer and built in about 11 months for the sum of 42000 Francs exclusive of site (see plate 36).

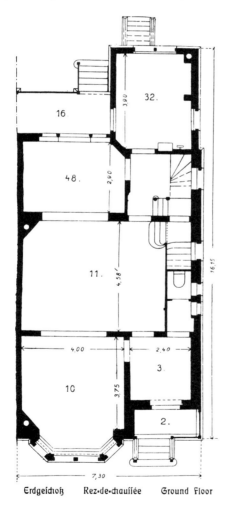

Erdgeschoß   Rez-de-chaussée   Ground Floor

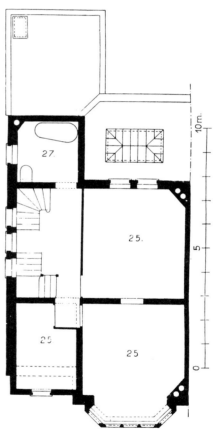

1. Stockwerk   1. Etage   1. Floor

Die beiden Villen bestehen jede aus einem Erdgeschoß, dem Ober- und dem ausgebauten Dachgeschoß. Das Erdgeschoß enthält den Salon mit Erkerausbau, den Wintergarten, den Speisesaal, aus dem zugleich die Etagentreppe aufsteigt, dann die Küche, die Anrichte mit der Kellertreppe, das Vestibül und die Toilette. An den Wintergarten schließt sich eine offene Terrasse an. Im Ober- und im Dachgeschoß liegen die Wohn- und Schlafzimmer.

Zu den Umfassungsmauern sind verwendet: grüne Bruchsteine im Kellergeschoß, rote, gefugte Backsteine in beiden oberen Geschossen, blauer Granit zu den Erkern und Türeinfassungen des

Chacune des deux villas se compose d'un rez-de-chaussée, d'un premier étage, et d'un étage dans le toit. Le rez-de-chaussée contient le salon avec avant-corps, le jardin d'hiver, la salle à manger, dans laquelle se trouve le départ de l'escalier pour l'étage supérieur, ensuite la cuisine, l'office située sur l'escalier conduisant aux caves, le vestibule et la toilette. Une terrasse découverte est reliée au jardin d'hiver. Au premier étage et dans le toit, sont situées les chambres à coucher et d'habitation.

On a employé pour les façades des moellons de pierre verte au sous-sol, des briques rouges jointoyées aux deux étages supérieurs, du granit bleu pour la tourelle et les encadrements de

Both villas consist of a ground floor with an upper and a roof story. The ground floor contains the drawing room with a bay, a conservatory, a dining room from which the staircase ascends, the kitchen, the serving room over the cellar steps, a vestibule and a lavatory. From the conservatory an open terrace is reached. In the upper and roof stories are living and sleeping rooms.

Green free stone has been used for the walls of the basement, red pointed brickwork for the upper stories, blue granite for the bays and door frames of the ground floor; the wood

Erdgeschosses, Holzfachwerk mit rotem und braunem Anstrich und verputzten, weißen Fachen für die Erker im Obergeschoß und die Giebel. Die vortretenden Dächer sind mit dunkelgrauem Schiefer eingedeckt.

205 [1906: 42]

Backsteinmauerwerk mit weißen Putzflächen, roter Sandstein und Holzfachwerk ergeben die Bestandteile für den malerischen Aufbau der von den Architekten Schilling und Gräbner entworfenen Doppelvilla Renz in Freiburg i. Br., Turmseestraße 72. Die Baukosten beider Gebäude betrugen 90000 Mark (Tafel 42).

Erdgeschoß und Obergeschoß sind in den Umfassungen massiv und verputzt, ebenso der seitlich vorspringende Turm in ganzer Höhe; nur der Sockel und einzelne Gebäudeecken sind aus rauhem und die Einfassungen und Teilungen der Fenster aus glatt bearbeitetem Haustein hergestellt. Das Holzfachwerk mit verputzten Fachen ist für eine Fenstergruppe im Obergeschoß, für die Giebelaufbauten und Dachluken zur Verwendung gekommen. Die vortretenden steilen Dächer sind mit Biberschwänzen eingedeckt.

206 [1906: 27]

Ein Bauwerk von entschieden modernem Zuschnitt und ausgeprägter Individualität, die Villa Düren in Godesberg, Kaiserstraße 5a, ist nach dem Entwurfe der Architekten Erdmann & Spindler in Berlin etwa im Verlaufe eines Jahres zur Ausführung gekommen (Tafel 27—28).

205 [1906: 42]

La maçonnerie de briques avec surfaces crépies en blanc, la pierre de taille rouge et les pans de bois apparents donnent les éléments constructifs et décoratifs de la double villa Renz Turmseestrasse 72 à Fribourg en Brisgau. Ce pittoresque édifice a été élevé pour la somme de 90000 Marks par les architectes Schilling et Gräbner (Pl. 42).

Les murs de façade du rez-de-chaussée et du premier étage sont massifs et crépies, de même que la tour latérale, saillante sur toute sa hauteur. Seuls le socle et quelques angles de la maison sont en pierre rugueuse, tandis que les encadrements et meneaux des fenêtres sont en pierre de taille lisse. On a employé pour un groupe de fenêtres au premier étage, pour les pignons et pour les lucarnes, la construction en pans de bois avec surfaces crépies. Les toits très inclinés et saillants sont recouverts en tuiles.

206 [1906: 27]

Un édifice de caractère décidément moderne et d'une individualité très forte, la villa Düren à Godesberg Kaiserstrasse 5a a été exécuté dans l'espace d'un an environ, d'après le projet des architectes Erdmann et Spindler à Berlin (Pl. 27—28). Le rez-de-chaussée contient

205 [1906: 42]

The picturesque elevation of the double villa Renz Turmseestrasse 72, Friburg in Breisgau, designed by the architects Schilling and Gräbner shows, as material used, brickwork with white plaster, red sandstone, and wood framework. The cost of both villas was 90000 Marks (see plate 42).

The ground floor and upper story are massive brickwork with plaster, the projecting tower on the side is in its entire height of the same material; the base and some corners are of rough lime stone, and the framing and articulations of the windows of smooth lime stone. Wood framework has been used for a group of windows in the upper story, for the projecting gables and roof windows. The steep overhanging roofs are covered with red flat tiles.

206 [1906: 27]

The villa Düren at Kaiserstrasse 5a, Godesberg after the design of the architects Erdmann and Spindler of Berlin. Built in one year it is a building of decidedly modern type and of striking individuality (see plate 27—28). The ground floor contains the

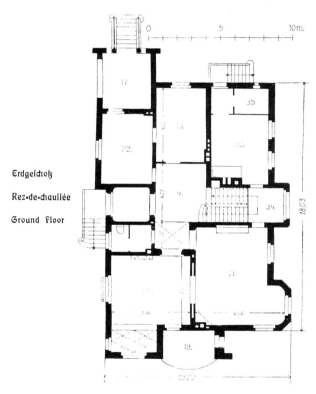

Erdgeschoß

Rez-de-chaussée

Ground Floor

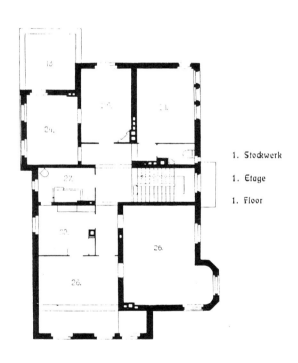

1. Stockwerk

1. Étage

1. Floor

Das Erdgeschoß enthält die Wohnzimmer um eine Diele gruppiert, in bequemer Verbindung mit der Küche und der nach dem Oberstock führenden Treppe. Das Wohnzimmer ist mit einem Erker ausgestattet und steht in Verbindung mit einer Loggia; das Speisezimmer ist ebenfalls durch einen Erker erweitert, und an das Herrenzimmer schließt sich eine bedeckte Veranda, aus welcher eine Freitreppe in den Garten hinabführt. Der Haupteingang des Hauses liegt an der Seitenfront. Im Kellergeschoß hat außer den Wirtschafts- und Heizräumen eine Trinkstube Platz gefunden. Im Obergeschosse sind die Schlafzimmer, Kinderzimmer und ein Fremdenzimmer untergebracht. Das Schlafzimmer der Eltern ist durch einen breit entwickelten Ausbau erweitert.

les chambres d'habitation groupées autour du hall et habilement reliées à la cuisine et à l'escalier conduisant à l'étage supérieur. La chambre d'habitation est décorée d'une tourelle et est en communication avec une loggia. La salle-à-manger est également augmentée de la surface d'une tourelle et une veranda couverte communique avec la chambre de Monsieur; un escalier conduit de cette veranda dans le jardin. L'entrée principale se trouve sur la façade latérale. On a placé en sous-sol, outre les locaux de service et le chauffage central, une chambre à boire. A l'étage supérieur se trouvent les chambres à coucher, les chambres d'enfants et une chambre d'amis. La chambre à coucher des parents se trouve agrandie par un large avant corps.

dwelling rooms grouped round a square hall in convenient connection with the kitchen and with a staircase leading to the upper story. The drawing room has a bay leading to a loggia, the dining room too is enlarged by a bay, and from the smoking room a covered verandah is reached from which steps lead into the garden. The principal entrance is at the side of the house. In the basement, as well as the domestic offices and heating apparatus, is a drinking room arranged. On the upper stories are bed rooms, nurseries and spare rooms; the principal bed room is enlarged by a broad projection of the building.

Das Äußere der Villa wird durch eine mäßige, durchweg aus dem Bedürfnis des Inneren hergeleitete Gruppierung wirkungsvoll belebt. Die Faſſaden ſind aus rötlichem Pfälzer Sandſtein und rauhem, naturfarbenem Mörtelputz ausgeführt; ein turmartiger Dacherker mit geſchwungener Haube iſt in den Flächen beſchiefert. Die Ornamentik iſt teils in Sandſtein gearbeitet, teils in Mörtel eingekratzt; die Loggia iſt farbig ausgemalt. Die Bauausführung geſchah durch die Firma Th. Wilh. Düren; als künſtleriſche Mitarbeiter ſind zu nennen: Bildhauer Richard Gerſchel in Berlin, die Maler Lichtermann und Wilmann in Düſſeldorf.

L'architecture extérieure de la villa reçoit son élément décoratif d'un groupement modéré des différentes parties, groupement correspondant exactement aux nécessités de l'intérieur. Les façades sont construites en pierre rougeâtre du Palatinat et en maçonnerie crépie grossièrement et de couleur naturelle du mortier. Les surfaces d'une tourelle et son toit en forme de bonnet renflé sont recouverts en ardoises. La décoration des façades est en partie en pierre, en partie creusée dans le mortier; la loggia est peinte en couleurs vives. Les travaux furent exécutés par la maison Th. Wilh. Düren. Comme collaborateurs artistiques nous nommons le sculpteur Richard Gerschel à Berlin et les peintres Lichtermann et Wilmann à Düsseldorf.

The exterior of the building is distinguished by an architectural grouping entirely in accordance with the interior and is everywhere simple in design. The facades are of red Palatinate sandstone and plastered with rough uncoloured plaster; a roof turret with a cupola is slated over the surfaces. The ornament is partly of sandstone and partly of furrowed mortar; the loggia is painted in colours. The firm Th. Wilh. Düren carried out the building operations; as artistic assistants may be mentioned the sculptor Richard Gerschel of Berlin, and the painter Lichtermann and Wilmann in Düsseldorf.

207 [1906: 48]

Zu den ausſchließlich nur für Handelszwecke beſtimmten Gebäuden gehört das Geſchäftshaus W. Henckel in Berlin, Lindenſtraße 86. Dieſer einheitliche Charakter des Innern kommt auch in der Faſſade klar zum Ausdruck. Architekt Rob. Weber in Dresden iſt der Urheber des Entwurfs, deſſen Ausführung zehn Monate in Anſpruch genommen hat. Die Baukoſten betrugen 210000 Mark (Taf. 48).

An der Faſſade zeigen ſich im Erdgeſchoß drei große mit Korbbögen überſpannte Öffnungen, von denen die eine ſeitliche als Eingang und Einfahrt dient; darüber ſteigen, durch drei Geſchoſſe gehend, abgerundete Pfeiler auf, welche zwiſchen ſich die in flacher Rundung erkerartig vortretenden Gruppenfenſter einſchließen. Ein kräftiges Geſims bildet den Abſchluß des mittleren Faſſadenteils; und über demſelben folgt noch ein niedrigeres Geſchoß mit geteilten Korbbogenfenſtern, welches von dem Dachgeſims und dem pavillonartig geſtalteten Manſardedach bekrönt wird. Zur Faſſade iſt weißer Cottaer Sandſtein verwandt, mit Ausnahme der Pfeiler im Erdgeſchoß, welche aus Lauſitzer Granit beſtehen. Die verzierten Konſolen an den Köpfen der oberen Pfeiler ſind aus getriebenem Kupfer hergeſtellt, die Firmenſchilder in Stiftmoſaik mit Glasbuchſtaben. Das Dach iſt mit roten Biberſchwänzen eingedeckt.

Die möglichſt ungeteilt gehaltenen Räume ſämtlicher Geſchoſſe, einen mittleren Lichthof umſchließend, haben Zementdielendecken zwiſchen Eiſenträgern erhalten; die durchgehenden Faſſadenſchäfte zur Verſtärkung der Steinpfeiler beſtehen aus Eiſen, ebenſo iſt der Dachſtuhl in Eiſen konſtruiert. Die dekorativen Bildhauerarbeiten der Faſſade ſind von Hugo Hahn in Dresden ausgeführt.

207 [1906: 48]

La maison de commerce W. Henckel, Lindenstrasse 86 à Berlin, appartient au groupe d'édifices entièrement destinés aux affaires. Le caractère dominant de l'intérieur s'affirme également à l'extérieur. Monsieur Rob. Weber architecte à Dresde est l'auteur du projet, dont l'exécution exigea un temps de dix mois; les frais de construction s'élevèrent à 210000 Marks. (Pl. 48).

En façade, on voit au rez-de-chaussée trois grandes ouvertures recouvertes d'arcs en anse de panier; l'une d'elles, de côté, sert d'entrée et de porte cochère, au dessus de cette ouverture s'élèvent, traversant trois étages, des piliers arrondis, entre lesquels font saillie des groupes de fenêtre de genre bow-windows en forme d'arcs. Un profil vigoureux couronne la partie centrale de la façade; au dessus s'élève encore un étage bas avec des fenêtres doubles, couvertes en anse de panier, cet étage est surmonté de la corniche et d'un toit mansard en forme de pavillon. On a employé de la pierre blanche de Cotta pour la façade, à l'exception des piliers du rez-de-chaussée qui sont en granit de la Lausitz. Les consoles décorées formant la tête des piliers supérieurs sont en cuivre repoussé, les enseignes des raisons sociales ont été composées en mosaïque avec des lettres en verre. Le toit est recouvert en tuiles rouges.

Les locaux de tous les étages sont le moins divisés possible, ils entourent une cour centrale, ils sont recouverts de plafonds en hourdis de ciment posés sur poutres en fer. Les grands cadres de façade servant à consolider les piliers en pierre de la façade tiennent toute la hauteur et sont en fer; la construction du toit est également en fer. Les sculptures décoratives des façades sont l'œuvre du sculpteur Hugues Hahn à Dresde.

207 [1906: 48]

The business house of W. Henckel Lindenstrasse 86, Berlin, has been built entirely for commercial purposes; both the exterior and interior are of this uniform character. The architect Rob. Weber of Dresden designed the building which took ten months to build and cost 210000 Marks (see plate 48).

The facade on the ground floor shows three arched openings, one of which on the side is used as entrance for foot-passengers and the other for vehicles; over this rise circular pillars extending through three stories and between these are arranged the window groups in the form of bays. A massive moulding is used as finish to the middle division of the facade; over this a comparatively low story with arched windows which is crowned by the roof moulding and by the pavilion-shaped mansard roof. For the facade white Cotta sandstone has been used, with the exception of the pillars on the ground floor which are of granite from the Lausitz. The ornamental capitals of the upper pillars are of hammered copper. The names of the firms are in mosaic with glass letters. The roof is of flat red tiles.

The rooms in the interior, arranged round a skylighted hall, are divided as little as possible, the ceilings are cement with iron girders; iron shafts extending through the centre of the pillars on the facade have been used for additional stability, and the roof beams are also of iron construction. The decorative sculpture of the facade is by Hugh Hahn of Dresden.

208 [1906: 33]

Die Herrenhäuſer der engliſchen Landſitze zeichnen ſich in der Regel vor gleichartigen Anlagen des Feſtlandes durch die größere Ausdehnung des ebenerdigen Grundriſſes aus, und verbinden ſich deshalb intimer mit der umgebenden Landſchaft. So ſind auch in Nether Swell Manor, in der Nähe von Stow-on-the-Wold gelegen, die Hauptwohnräume, in Verbindung mit der Küche, dem Küchenhofe und anſchließenden Nebenräumen ebenerdig zu einem lang entwickelten Gruppenbau inmitten umfänglicher Gartenanlagen vereinigt (Tafel 33).

Das von dem Architekten E. G. Dawber entworfene Herrenhaus umſchließt im Erdgeſchoß die von einem Vorflur aus zugängliche Halle, an welche ſich die Treppe, das Bibliothekzimmer, der Salon und das Speiſezimmer unmittelbar anſchließen; weiterhin folgen die meiſt einſtöckigen Küchenräume uſw., während der Hauptbau ein Obergeſchoß beſitzt. In dem letzteren ſind die Schlafzimmer, Fremdenzimmer und anderes untergebracht.

208 [1906: 33]

Les châteaux des propriétés anglaises se distinguent généralement des constructions analogues sur le continent par une plus grande étendue du plan du rez-de-chaussée et se marient par cela même plus intimement avec le paysage environnant. L'est ainsi que les pièces d'habitation principales de Nether Swell Manor dans le voisinage de Stow-on-the-Wold, en relation avec la cuisine, la cour de cuisine et les localités dépendantes, sont réunies au ras du sol en un groupe de constructions étendu et situé au milieu d'un vaste jardin (Pl. 33).

Le château dont le plan a été établi par l'architecte E. G. Dawber, contient au rez-de-chaussée un hall précédé d'un vestibule, immédiatement autour du hall se groupent l'escalier, la bibliothèque, le salon et la salle-à-manger; en arrière se trouvent les dépendances, cuisine etc., les quelles n'ont qu'un étage, tandis que le bâtiment principal en a deux. A l'étage supérieur sont situées les chambres à coucher; les chambres d'amis et autres localités.

208 [1906: 33]

The country houses on English estates differ as a rule from similar buildings on the Continent in one respect that the ground plan shows a much more extended use of the ground floor; the house consequently is much more open to, and dependent upon the surrounding landscape. This may be noticed in the house Nether Swell Manor near Stow-on-the-Wold; the principal reception rooms, the kitchens, the offices and adjoining premises are all arranged on the ground floor in a long extended group arranged among gardens and terraces (see plate 33).

The house designed by the architect E. G. Dawber, is entered by a vestibule leading to a hall from which is access to the staircase, the library, the drawing room and dining room; the kitchen rooms are mostly on the first floor, the principal centre of the building has an upper story in which are bedrooms of various sizes.

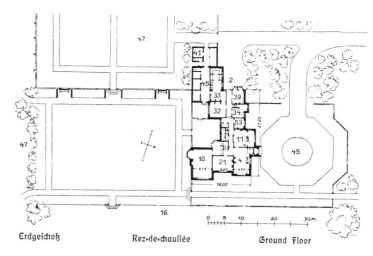

Die rauhen Bruchſtein-Umfaſſungswände ſind aus dem in der Nähe brechenden Roggenſtein hergeſtellt, die Quaderecken der Gebäudeteile, die Einfaſſungen und Teilungspfeiler der Fenſter aus Sandſtein; die Dächer ſind mit Glouceſter-ſhire-Schiefer eingedeckt. Das Hauptportal und noch entſchiedener die Innenräume ſind in Renaiſſanceformen ausgebildet.

Les murs sont de mœllons rugueux extraits de carrières d'oolithe situées dans le voisinage; les chaînes d'angle des bâtiments, les encadre-ments et meneaux des fenêtres sont en pierre de taille; les toits sont recouverts en ardoises de Gloucestershire. L'entrée principale et plus encore les intérieurs sont traités dans le goût de la Renaissance.

The boundary walls are of lime stone from the neighbourhood, the square corner stones of the house, the window frames and pillars are of sandstone, and the roofs are of Gloucestershire slate. The principal entrance and more decidedly the interior are of Renaissance style.

209 [1906: 34]

Als ein langgeſtreckter Gruppenbau von be-wegter, durch die Form des bebauten Grund-ſtücks bedingten Umrißlinie erſcheint das Gebäude des neuen Friedrichs-Gymnaſiums zu Frei-burg i. Br. Der von Oberbaurat Profeſſor Dr.-Ing. Joſef Durm in Karlsruhe entworfene Bau hat zur völligen Herſtellung eine Zeit von drei Jahren in Anſpruch genommen (Tafel 34). Die Klaſſenzimmer und Säle liegen ſämtlich in einſeitiger Aufreihung an einer Front, ſo daß an denſelben ein in allen Teilen hellbeleuchteter

209 [1906: 34]

Le bâtiment du nouveau gymnase Friedrich à Fribourg en Brisgau apparaît comme une longue masse de silhouette mouvementée, nécessitée par la forme du terrain sur lequel elle s'élève. L'édifice dont les plans ont été livrés par le Professeur Dr.-Ing. Joseph Durm conseiller supérieur des bâtiments de Carlsruhe a exigé une période de bâtisse de trois ans jusqu'à son achèvement complet (Pl. 34). Les classes et salles se trouvent toutes situées d'un même côté, sur une façade, de sorte qu'on put

209 [1906: 34]

The new Friedrich's Gymnasium at Frei-burg in Breisgau, an extended group of buildings whose form has been determined by the available boundary line, was designed by the Oberbaurat Professor Dr.-Ing. Josef Durm of Carlsruhe, and occupied three years in building (see plate 34). The class rooms and halls lie all on one side so that each has an entrance from a long and well-lighted corridor. The principal entrance A in the middle of the front

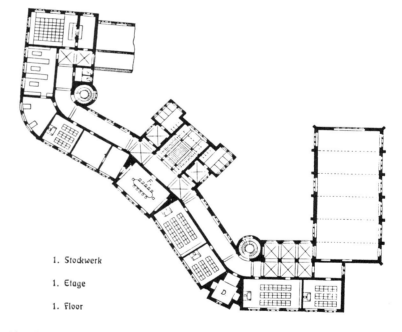

Flurgang durchgeführt werden konnte. Der Haupteingang A in der Mitte der Vorderfront mündet in eine geräumige Vorhalle B und führt weiter zu der breiten, doppelläufigen Haupt-treppe C, an welche ſich beiderſeits die Abort-anlagen mit ihren vom Flur zugänglichen Vor-plätzen anſchließen, eine Einrichtung, die ſich in allen drei Geſchoſſen wiederholt. Rechts vom Eingange iſt die Gebäudeecke durch einen vier-eckigen, mit ſchlankem Helm bekrönten Turm D ausgezeichnet. An der Hofſeite ſind in den Winkeln der Front zwei runde Treppentürme ein-gebaut, welche Ausgänge nach den Spielplätzen E enthalten. Das Konferenzzimmer F iſt über der Vorhalle im erſten Obergeſchoß untergebracht, darüber im zweiten Obergeſchoß liegt der Singe-

les relier toutes à un corridor largement éclairé dans toutes ses parties. L'entrée principale A, située au milieu de la façade sur la rue, conduit dans un vestibule spacieux B, et plus loin au large escalier à deux rampes C. A droite et à gauche de la cage d'escalier se trouvent les commodités avec leurs vestibules, communiquant avec le corridor; disposition qui se répète aux trois étages. A droite de l'entrée, l'angle du bâtiment est marqué par une tour D, couronnée d'une flèche élancée. Sur la façade de la cour, se trouvent dans les angles deux cages d'escaliers rondes qui contiennent des sorties sur les préaux E. La chambre des conférences F a été placée au premier étage, au dessus du vestibule; au dessus, au deuxième étage, se trouve la salle de chant et à la même hauteur, la salle de dessin. La

block leads into a spacious vestibule B and this leads to the broad double staircase C, from which are passages in connection with lavatories. This arrangement is repeated on each of the three stories. On the right of the principal en-trance, the corner of the building is continued upwards into a quadrilateral tower, crowned with a slender cupola D. On the courtyard side in the angles of the front are two round towers built, which contain staircases leading to the play grounds E. The Conference room F is on the first floor over the entrance vestibule; over this, in the second story is the singing room and on the same level the drawing hall. The

faal und in gleicher Höhe der Zeichenfaal. Die geräumige, im rechten Winkel an das Haupt-gebäude fich anfchließende Turnhalle G dient bei feftlichen Gelegenheiten als Aula und fteht fowohl mit dem Hauptbau als mit dem Spielhofe in unmittelbarer Verbindung.

Die Umfaffungsmauern des Gebäudes find mit Quadern aus rotem Sandftein, zum Teil aus den Brüchen der Umgegend von Freiburg, zum Teil aus dem Maintal ftammend, ver-blendet. Flurgänge, Treppenräume, Toiletten und Aborte find mit Eifenbetondecken überwölbt; die Treppenftufen beftehen aus Granit, in den Dienfttreppen freitragend, in der Haupttreppe auf Eifenkonftruktionen ruhend. Die Decken-gebälke der Säle liegen parallel zur Umfaffungs-mauer und ruhen auf einem Syftem eiferner Unterzüge. Das Gebäude ift mit elektrifcher Beleuchtung, Gaseinrichtung und Wafferleitung verfehen. Die Dächer find mit Schiefer einge-deckt; Säle und Gänge find mit Niederdruck-dampfheizung ausgeftattet. Die örtliche Bau-leitung lag in den Händen des Regierungsbau-meifters Jofef Graf in Freiburg.

Die Faffade ift in den Formen deutfcher Frührenaiffance einfach und fchlicht, dem Charakter eines Schulbaues entfprechend, ausgebildet, die Fenfter find durch Kreuzftöcke geteilt und gerad-linig, flachbogig oder im Vorhangsbogen über-deckt. Nur das den Haupteingang und darüber zwei Säle enthaltende Mittelrifalit hat eine reichere Architektur aufzuweifen.

An der Ausftattung des Gebäudes waren beteiligt: die Bildhauer Seiß und Müßle und für die Herftellung der Glasgemälde im Treppen-haufe und in der Turnhalle Profeffor F. Geiges in Freiburg. Die Baukoften betrugen 702 574 Mark, wobei der Bauplatz, die Herrichtung des Spiel-platzes, die innere Einrichtung der Schulfäle, fowie das Architektenhonorar nicht in Rechnung geftellt find.

210 [1906: 37]

Für den Turnverein in Mannheim hat A. Lang-heinrich eine Turnhalle erbaut, bei deren äußerer Geftaltung er den nüchternen Eindruck, der fonft derartigen Gebäuden anzuhaften pflegt, glücklich vermieden hat (Tafel 37). Der durch

salle de gymnastique G est grande, elle est située à angle droit sur le bâtiment principal auquel elle est reliée, elle sert d'Aula aux occasions solennelles et est en communication directe avec le bâtiment principal, ainsi qu'avec les préaux.

Les façades du bâtiment sont revêtues de pierre de taille rouge provenant en partie des carrières des environs de Fribourg, en partie de celles de la vallée du Main. Les corridors, les cages d'escaliers, les toilettes et les commodités sont recouverts de plafonds en béton armé. Les marches d'escalier sont en granit, suspendues dans les escaliers de service, posées sur fer dans l'escalier principal. Les poutraisons des salles sont posées parallèlement aux façades et reposent sur un système de sommiers en fer. L'édifice est pourvu d'éclairage électrique, ainsi que de conduites de gaz et d'eau. Les toits sont recouverts en ardoises. Les salles et corridors sont chauffés à la vapeur à basse pression. La conduite locale des travaux fut confiée à l'architecte du gouvernement Joseph Graf à Fribourg.

La façade a été traitée dans l'esprit de la Renaissance allemande primitive, simple et modeste, correspondant au caractère d'une école; les fenêtres sont séparées en meneaux et à couverte droite, en arc surbaissé ou pendant. Seul le corps central, contenant l'entrée princi-pale et deux salles au dessus a été traité d'une façon plus riche.

Ont pris part à l'exécution du bâtiment: les sculpteurs Seitz et Müssle, le peintre verrier Professeur F. Geiges à Fribourg pour l'établisse-ment des vitraux de la cage d'escalier et de la salle de gymnastique. Les frais de construction s'élevèrent à 702 574 Marks; dans cette somme ne sont pas compris: le prix du terrain, l'arrange-ment du préau, l'installation intérieure des salles de classe, non plus que les honoraires de l'architecte.

210 [1906: 37]

Monsieur A. Langheinrich architecte, a construit pour la société de gymnastique de Manheim une salle de gymnastique. Il a sü heureusement éviter pour les façades l'im-pression de sécheresse qu'ont généralement les

spacious gymnasium, which lies in the right angle of the principal building, and marked G serves on special occasions as Aula and is in connection with the play grounds and with the principal building.

The boundary walls of the building are of faced square stones of red sandstone partly from the quarries in the neighbourhood of Frei-burg and partly from the Main valley. The corridors, staircases and lavatories have all vaulted ceilings of iron beton; the steps of the staircase are of granite, which in the secondary staircases lie free, and in the principal staircase rest on iron work. The beams of the ceilings in the halls lie parallel to the boundary wall and rest on a system of iron bearers. The building is lighted with gas and electric light and is well supplied with water. The roofs are covered with slate, the halls and corridors are heated with low pressure steam apparatus. The local superintendence of the building was entrusted to the Regierungsbaumeister Josef Graf of Freiburg.

The facade is of German Early Renaissance, simple and severe, and suitable to a school; the windows are divided by cross bars and are arched partly by flat and partly by projecting arches. Only the windows of the principal en-trance, and of the two saloons over this have the frame work of the windows more elaborated.

The following artists were employed in the equipment of the building; the sculptors Seitz and Müssle, and for the stained glass of the stair-case and Aula Professor F. Geiges of Freiburg. The cost of the building amounted to 702574 Marks which does not include the site, the equipment of the play grounds, the interior equipment of the school rooms, nor the architect's fees.

210 [1906: 37]

A. Langheinrich has built a gymnasium for Mannheim, and has succeeded in giving the building an attractive exterior an ad-vantage seldom sonsidered in such things (see

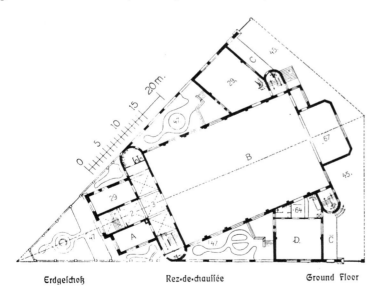

| Erdgeschoß | Rez-de-chaussée | Ground Floor | 2. Stockwerk | 2. Étage | 2. Floor |

Türme, Erker und Giebelaufbauten ungemein malerifch geftaltete Hauptkörper des Gebäudes enthält den großen, durch zwei Gefchoffe reichen-den Turnfaal, der fich rückwärts zu einer Bühne erweitert. Links fchließt fich an den Turnfaal eine Garderobe für die Turner, rechts ein Büfett, hinter dem ein Vereinszimmer liegt. Der Zugang erfolgt durch das Hauptportal, aus dem man zunächft in einen Vorraum gelangt, neben dem

édifices de ce genre (Pl. 37). Le corps principal divisé d'une façon extrêmement pittoresque grâce à l'emploi de tours, de tourelles et de pignons, contient la grande salle occupant la hauteur de deux étages; cette salle s'élargit au fond en forme de scène. A gauche, un vestiaire pour les gymnastes communique avec la salle, à droite un buffet, derrière le quel se trouve la chambre de société. L'entrée est formée par le portail principal, duquel on pénètre dans un

plate 37). The principal part of the building, which is ornamented in an uncommonly pictu-resque manner with towers, bays and gables, contains a large hall for athletics extending through two stories, this is extended at the back to from a stage. On the left are cloak rooms, on the right a restaurant behind which is a com-mittee room. The entrance is through the

links die Garderobe für die Turnerinnen, rechts ein Sitzungszimmer für den Vorstand angeordnet ist. Aus dem Vorraum tritt man in ein durch die ganze Breite des Gebäudes reichendes Vestibül, aus dem man unmittelbar in den Turnsaal tritt.

Im Obergeschoß des vorderen Teils befindet sich noch ein kleiner Turnsaal nebst Vorsaal, und ein Teil des Kellergeschosses ist ebenfalls körperlichen Übungen eingeräumt, da es eine Schießbahn und zwei Kegelbahnen enthält. Außerdem enthält es den Wein- und Bierkeller, die Küche für den Restaurationsbetrieb und die Keller für die Mietwohnungen, die sich in den Seitenflügeln des Quergebäudes befinden, das in geschickter Ausnutzung des Baugeländes dem Hauptgebäude angegliedert ist.

Die Außenarchitektur ist teils in rotem Mainsandstein, teils in grauem Terranovaverputz in Verbindung mit Fachwerk ausgeführt.

Die Baukosten betrugen rund 300000 Mark.

vestibule; à gauche de ce dernier s'ouvre le vestiaire des dames gymnastes, à droite, la salle des séances du comité. De ce vestibule on pénètre dans un second vestibule qui occupe toute la largeur du bâtiment, ce local donne directement accès dans la salle de gymnastique.

Au premier étage de la partie antérieure, se trouve encore une petite salle de gymnastique avec vestibule; une partie du sous-sol est également consacré à des exercices corporels, car il contient un jeu de tir et deux jeux de quilles. Le sous-sol contient en outre les caves à vin et à bière, la cuisine pour le restaurant et les caves pour les appartements à louer, lesquels se trouvent dans les ailes latérales du corps transversal; ce dernier a été habilement annexé au corps principal pour tirer parti le plus possible de la forme du terrain.

L'architecture extérieure est en partie en pierre rouge du Main, en partie en pans de bois, encadrant des surfaces crépies en Terranova grise.

Les frais de construction s'élevèrent à 300000 Marks.

principal portal, from which one comes first into an ante room, on the left is the cloak room for ladies, on the right a committee room. From this ante room one enters a large vestibule extending the whole breadth of the building and from there into the hall for athletics.

In the upper story is a small hall for practice with an ante room; part of the basement too is set apart for athletic exercise and contains a shooting-gallery and a skittle-ground. The basement contains also a wine and beer cellar, the kitchen for the restaurant, and cellars belonging to flats which have been arranged for letting in the side wings.

The exterior architecture is partly of red Main sandstone, partly in grey Terranova plaster with a mixture of frame work.

The cost of building amounted to 300000 Marks.

211 [1906: 41]

Das von drei Seiten freiliegende Gebäude der Universitäts-Bibliothek in Heidelberg, einen Hof umschließend, ist von Oberbaurat Professor Dr.-Ing. Josef Durm in Karlsruhe entworfen und unter seiner Oberleitung vom Sommer 1901 bis 1. November 1905 zur Aus-

211 [1906: 41]

Le bâtiment de la bibliothèque de l'Université à Heidelberg, dégagé de trois côtés et entourant une cour, est l'œuvre du conseiller Professeur Docteur Josephe Durm, à Carlsruhe, qui en a aussi dirigé la construction de l'été 1901 au premier novembre 1905. Hock

211 [1906: 41]

The new university library in Heidelberg occupies a site which is open on three sides and surrounds a courtyard. It was designed by Professor Dr.-Ing. Joseph Durm of Carlsruhe and was built under his superintendence from the summer of 1901 till November 1905. The building

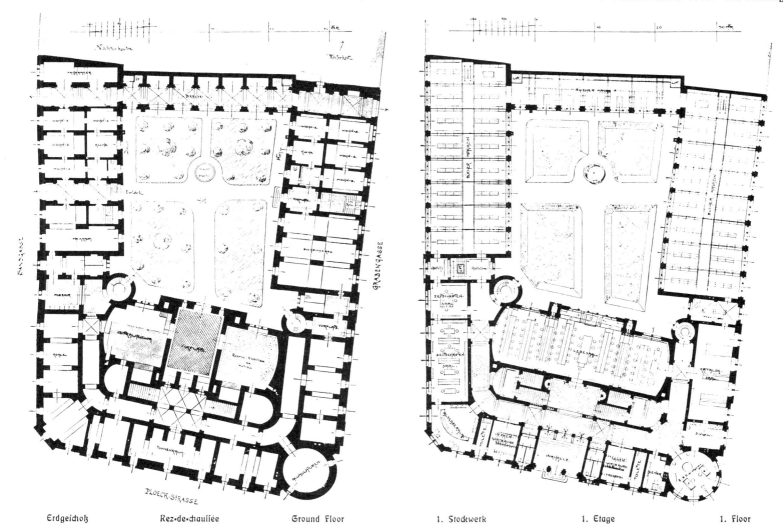

| Erdgeschoß | Rez-de-chaussée | Ground Floor | 1. Stockwerk | 1. Etage | 1. Floor |

führung gekommen. Als Bauführer waren Hock und Weinbrenner beschäftigt. Die Baukosten betrugen 1327967 Mark, ohne Bauplatz und Architektenhonorar einzubeziehen. Die innere Einrichtung erforderte 120000 Mark, die apparative Ausstattung 25000 Mark; der Bauplatz kostete 350000 Mark (Tafel 41).

Das vordere Verwaltungsgebäude enthält die dem Publikum zur Benutzung offenstehenden

et Weinbrenner occupaient le poste de conducteurs de travaux. Les frais de construction s'élevèrent à 1327967 Marks, non compris le terrain et les honoraires d'architecte. L'installation intérieure coûta 120000 Marks, les appareils contèrent 25000 Marks; le prix du terrain fut de 350000 Marks (Pl. 41).

Le bâtiment d'administration de devant contient les locaux ouverts au public et les chambres de

contractors were Hock and Weinbrenner. The cost of the building was 1327967 Marks, exclusive of the site and the architect's fees. The interior equipment cost 120000 Marks, the fittings and apparatus 25000 Marks, and the site 350000 Marks (see plate 41).

The administrative buildings in front contain the public rooms, and the official's rooms; the

Räume und die Arbeitszimmer der Beamten, während in den Seitenflügeln sowie in dem rückwärts gelegenen Hofflügel die Büchermagazine untergebracht sind. Das stattliche Portal in der Mitte der Vorderfront führt zur Vorhalle, an welche sich beiderseits die Garderoben und Toiletten, die Flurgänge und die zwischen festen Wangen aufsteigenden Haupttreppen anschließen; geradeaus gelangt man in den großen, durch zwei Geschosse geführten, mit Oberlicht und nördlichem Seitenlicht versehenen Lesesaal. In den Flügeln sind die Zimmer der Bibliothekare, der Katalogsaal und die Zeitschriftensäle untergebracht. Die Flurgänge endigen mit runden Diensttreppen. Die Räume des Obergeschosses sind einesteils für die Benutzer der Spezialsammlungen, sonst zu Diensträumen bestimmt.

Sämtliche Decken sind in Stampfbeton zwischen Eisenträgern ausgeführt; die Dächer sind mit Schiefer bzw. mit Kupfer eingedeckt, die Dachstühle über dem Treppenhause und den Magazinräumen in Eisen konstruiert. Die Beleuchtung geschieht durch elektrische Lampen, ebenso werden die Aufzüge elektrisch betrieben. Die Erwärmung der Räume erfolgt durch Niederdruckdampfheizung, außerdem ist überall Wasserversorgung eingerichtet.

Die Fassaden des vorderen Verwaltungsgebäudes, an denen Vergoldungen und Bildhauerarbeiten bedeutend zur Geltung kommen, sind reich in Spätrenaissanceformen ausgebildet und durch Ecktürme und Giebel belebt, während die Magazinflügel einfacher gehalten sind. Das Material für die Fassaden ist durchweg roter Maintaler Sandstein; die Treppen bestehen aus Granit, die Säulen, Pfeiler und Wandsockel des Innern aus poliertem Marmor. Außerdem ist das Innere mit Mosaiken und figürlichen Stuckarbeiten künstlerisch geschmückt. Bildhauer Professor Volz und Maler Hellwag sind als Urheber der figürlichen Ausstattungsstücke zu nennen.

212, 213 [1906; 44, 45]

Das Wohnhaus an der Ecke der Kriegs- und Hübschstraße in Karlsruhe hat durch mannigfache Gruppierung der Baumassen einen heiteren Charakter gewonnen. Autor der Fassaden ist Prof. Herm. Billing, während die Anordnung des Grundrisses sowie die Bauleitung

travail des fonctionnaires, tandis que les magasins de livres sont placés dans les ailes latérales et dans le corps postérieur. Le beau portail du milieu de la façade principale conduit dans le vestibule, duquel on parvient des deux côtés aux vestiaires et toilettes, aux corridors et aux escaliers principaux, montant entre des girons massifs. En face, on entre dans la grande salle de lecture éclairée par le haut et par le côté nord et montant de fond à travers deux étages. Dans les ailes se trouvent les chambres des bibliothécaires, la salle du catalogue et les salles des publications périodiques. Les corridors se terminent par des escaliers de services circulaires. Les locaux de l'étage supérieur sont d'une part destinés aux visiteurs des collections spéciales, d'autre part au service.

Tous les plafonds sont construits en béton comprimé entre poutres en fer; les toits sont recouverts en ardoise et en cuivre, les fermes du toit, au dessus de la cage d'escalier et des magasins à livres, sont en fer. L'éclairage se fait au moyen de lampes électriques; les lifts sont aussi mis par l'électricité. Le chauffage est opéré par un appareil de vapeur à basse pression; l'eau a été conduite partout.

Les façades du bâtiment de devant sont composées dans le goût de la Renaissance tardive, elles sont richement décorées de dorures et de sculpture, des tours d'angle et des frontons les animent en outre, tandis que les ailes des magasins sont traitées plus simplement. Les façades sont entièrement construites en pierre rouge du Main; les escaliers sont en granit, les colonnes, piliers et socles des parois intérieures sont en marbre poli. L'intérieur est en outre décoré de mosaïques et de représentations figurales en stuc. Nommons comme auteurs des décorations figurales, le sculpteur professeur Volz et le peintre Hellwag.

212, 213 [1906; 44, 45]

La maison d'habitation située à l'angle des rues Kriegs- et Hübschstrasse à Carlsruhe a un aspect de gaité grâce au groupement des masses. L'auteur de la façade est le professeur Herman Billing, tandis que Monsieur Théodore Trautmann

side wings and the courtyard wings at the back are used for the storage of books. A stately portal in the middle of the front leads to a vestibule which leads to the corridors and to the principal staircase, and also gives access to the cloak rooms and lavatories. Opening straight from the vestibule one enters the spacious reading room, extending upwards through two stories, lighted from the roof and supplied with a north window at the side. In the wings are the rooms of the librarian, the catalogue room and the journal saloon. At the end of the corridors are circular secondary staircases. In the rooms of the upper stories are apartments for special collections and their readers, and rooms for the officials.

All the ceilings are beton with iron girders; the roofs are partly of slate and partly of copper, the roof story over the staircase and the store rooms is of iron construction. The lighting is by electricity, the lifts are also electric; the heating is low pressure steam system and every where water is laid on.

The facades of the chief administrative building in front are richly ornamented with gilding and sculpture; the style is late Renaissance enlivened by the use of gables and corner turrets; the other wings are simpler in design. The only material used for the facade is red Main valley sandstone; the stairs are of granite, the pillars and postament of the interior are all of marble. The interior is further decorated with mosaic and sculptural ornament. The sculptor Professor Volz and the painter Hellwag may be specially mentioned in connection with the ornamental details.

212, 213 [1906; 44, 45]

An attractive character has been given to the house at the corner of the Kriegs- and Hübschstrasse in Carlsruhe by the varied grouping of the elevation. The designer of the facade is Professor Herm. Billing, and the ground plan and general superintendence of the

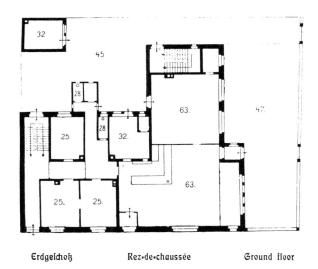

Erdgeschoß   Rez-de-chaussée   Ground floor

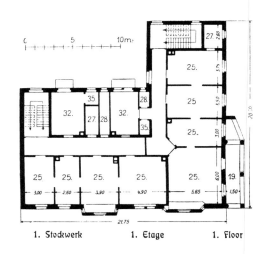

1. Stockwerk   1. Etage   1. Floor

in den Händen des Architekten Theodor Trautmann lag. Die Bauzeit nahm etwa 15 Monate in Anspruch; die Baukosten mit Inventar betrugen 129000 Mark (Tafel 44—45). Das Erdgeschoß enthält an der Ecke das Wirtschaftslokal „Zur roten Taube" mit geräumigem Nebenzimmer. Den übrigen Raum des Erdgeschosses nimmt die Wohnung des Wirts und ein besonderer an die Seite gerückter Eingangsflur mit der Treppe ein. Unmittelbar vom Hofe aus

architecte se chargea de la disposition du plan et de la conduite des travaux. La construction dura à peu près 15 mois; les frais de bâtisse, y compris l'inventaire, s'élevèrent à 129000 Marks (Pl. 44 et 45). Le rez-de-chaussée contient sur l'angle, le restaurant „à la colombe rouge" avec des chambres séparées spacieuses. Le reste de la place du rez-de-chaussée est occupé par l'appartement du tenancier et par une entrée spéciale reléguée sur le côté et conduisant à l'escalier. On pénètre directement de la cour à un escalier

building was entrusted to the architect Theodor Trautmann. The time occupied was 15 months, the cost of building and fittings amounted 129000 Marks (see plate 44 and 45). The ground floor contains at the corner, the public house "Zur roten Taube" with extensive secondary rooms; the other part of the ground floor is occupied by the residence of the landlord, and contains also a staircase reached through an entrance hall. Directly from the courtyard another

iſt eine Nebentreppe zugänglich. Das erſte und zweite Obergeſchoß umſchließen je eine geräumige Wohnung mit den erforderlichen Nebenräumen; auch die Dachaufbauten und Giebel ſind zur Anlage von Zimmern ausgenutzt.

Der untere Teil der Faſſaden, ebenſo die Säulen, Konſolen und Fenſtereinfaſſungen ſind aus grünem Hauſtein hergeſtellt, ſonſt zeigen ſich weiße Putzflächen; Dachaufbau und Giebel ſind mit Schindeln bekleidet und das Dach iſt mit Schiefer eingedeckt.

Im Wirtſchaftslokal iſt der untere Teil der inneren Wandflächen in Holz getäfelt; die oberen Wandteile und die Decke ſind mit gemaltem Linienornament mäßig verziert.

de service. Le premier et le second étage contiennent chacun un appartement spacieux avec les dépendances nécessaires. Les parties surélevées du toit et le fronton ont aussi été utilisés pour des chambres.

Les parties inférieures des façades, ainsi que les colonnes, les consoles et les encadrements de fenêtres sont en pierre de taille verte, le reste est en maçonnerie crépie claire. La mansarde et le fronton sont revêtus en bardeaux, le toit est recouvert en ardoise.

Dans le restaurant, la partie inférieure des parois est garnie de boiseries; la partie supérieure des parois et le plafond sont décorés sobrement d'ornements linéaires peints.

staircase leads to the upper stories. The first and second floors contain each a spacious dwelling with the necessary domestic offices; the roof story and gables are also utilized and contain rooms.

The lower part of the facade, the pillars, brackets and window frames are of green hewn stone, the other parts are plastered white, the roof elevation and the gables are shingled and the roof is of slate.

In the public house the lower part of the walls is panelled with wood, the upper part and the ceilings have a slight ornamentation in coloured lines.

214 [1906: 49]

Auf Grund ihres aus dem Wettbewerb von 1894 preisgekrönt hervorgegangenen Entwurfs zum neuen Rathauſe in Stuttgart wurde 1898 die Ausführung des Baues an die Architekten J. Vollmer und H. Jaſſoy übertragen, allerdings in einer gegen früher weſentlich erweiterten Anlage. Im Oktober 1901 konnte der rückwärts gelegene Teil des Baues in Gebrauch genommen werden, während der zweite Teil am 1. April 1905 eingeweiht wurde (Tafel 49).

214 [1906: 49]

Les architectes J. Vollmer et H. Jassoy furent chargés en 1898 de l'exécution du nouvel hôtel-de-Ville de Stuttgart sur la base de leur projet primé au concours de 1894; il est vrai que l'exécution montre un ensemble beaucoup plus étendu que le projet primitif. Au mois d'octobre 1901, on pouvait prendre possession de la partie postérieure du bâtiment, tandis que l'autre partie put être inaugurée le premier avril 1905 (Pl. 49).

214 [1906: 49]

An open competition held in 1894 for a design for a new Guild hall in Stuttgart resulted in the prize design of the architects J. Vollmer and H. Jassoy being chosen; it was commenced on a considerably enlarged site in 1898 and the back part of the building was ready for use in October 1901, while the remainder of the building was inaugurated on 1 April 1905 (see plate 49).

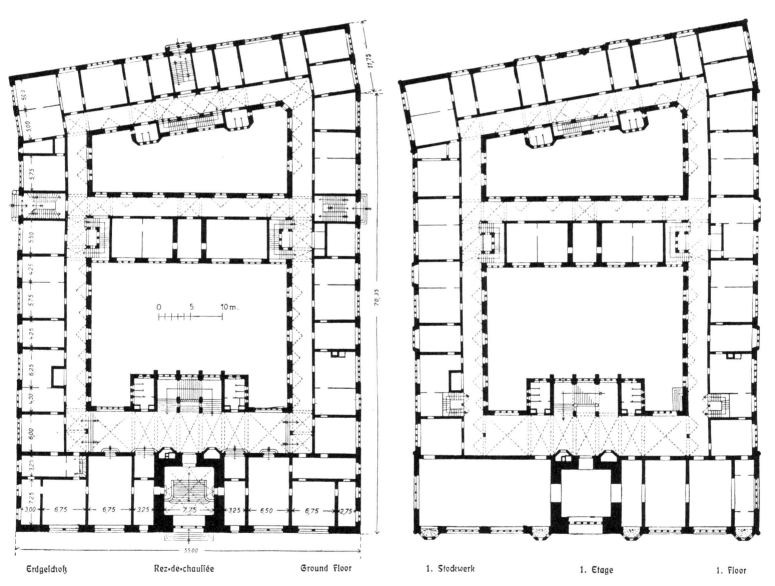

0   5   10m.

| Erdgeſchoß | Rez-de-chauſſée | Ground Floor | 1. Stockwerk | 1. Étage | 1. Floor |

Das ringsum freiliegende Gebäude umſchließt jetzt zwei Höfe; einen größeren Vorder- und einen kleineren Hinterhof. Das Erdgeſchoß wird außer von der Eingangshalle, den hell beleuchteten Flurgängen, der Haupt- und den Dienſttreppen durchweg von Bureauräumen eingenommen; im erſten Obergeſchoß liegen die Zimmer des Oberbürgermeiſters und der Gemeinderäte, ein kleinerer Sitzungsſaal und Bureaus; das zweite Obergeſchoß enthält den durch zwei Stockwerke gehenden

Le monument, libre de tous côtés, enferme deux cours; en avant une grande, en arrière une plus petite cour. Le rez-de-chaussée est occupé entièrement par des bureaux, outre la halle d'entrée, les corridors largement éclairés, l'escalier principal et les escaliers secondaires; au premier étage se trouvent les chambres du maire de la ville et des conseillers municipaux, une petite salle de conférences et des bureaux; le deuxième étage contient la grande salle de con-

The building stands open on all sides and surrounds two courtyards, the larger in front and smaller behind. The ground floor, with the exception of the space required by the entrance hall, the well-lighted corridors and the principal and secondary staircases, is entirely devoted to offices; on the first floor are the rooms of the mayor and the district councillors, a smaller committee room and some offices; the second floor contains the large Council Chamber extend-

großen Sißungsſaal, ſonſt wieder Bureaux; das dritte Obergeſchoß iſt ausſchließlich für Bureauzwecke ausgenußt. Im Souterrain an der Marktfront befindet ſich der Ratskeller. Sämtliche Decken ſind maſſiv hergeſtellt; das Dach iſt bis zum Kehlgebälk in Eiſen konſtruiert und mit Biberſchwänzen eingedeckt. Es iſt eine Niederdruckwaſſerheizung vorhanden, ebenſo eine Waſſerverſorgung ſowie eine Anlage für Gas- und elektriſche Beleuchtung.

Die Faſſaden ſind in ſpätgotiſcher Stilſaſſung aus württembergiſchen Keuperſandſtein hergeſtellt. Als beherrſchendes Hauptmotiv der Marktfaſſade erhebt ſich ein mächtiger, viereckiger Turm.

215 [1906; 60]

Das eingebaute Geſchäfts- und Wohnhaus, Badſtraße 60 in Berlin, umſchließt mit vier Flügeln einen geräumigen Hof. Die Anordnung der Grundriſſe erfolgte durch Architekt P. Keſten, während der Entwurf der Faſſaden von Architekt A. Zabel herrührt. Der Bau wurde etwa in elf Monaten bis zum Oktober 1905 zur Ausführung gebracht. Die Faſſaden ſind in Portlandzement mit einem Zuſatz von Romanzement gepußt, die Dächer mit glaſierten Marienburger Pfannen eingedeckt. Die Straßenfaſſade iſt durch vorgekragte Erker, offene Loggien und Balkons anſprechend belebt.

Das Erdgeſchoß enthält im Straßenflügel, außer dem zur Haupttreppe führenden Mitteleingange, mehrere Läden, ein Reſtaurations- und ein Banklokal. In den beiden Seiten- und dem hinteren Querflügel ſind vier Wohnungen mit beſonderen, vom Hofe zugänglichen Treppen eingerichtet. Die vier Obergeſchoſſe ſind zu je zehn Wohnungen, welche mit Küchen und Nebenräumen verſehen ſind, eingeteilt.

216 [1906; 50]

Die an drei ſtumpfwinklig zuſammenſtoßenden Straßenfluchten gelegene, einen geräumigen Hof umſchließende Häuſergruppe in Budapeſt, Szabadſag Ter 16, iſt von dem verſtorbenen Architekten Arthur Meinig entworfen und in etwa zwei Jahren für die Summe von 1500000 Kronen zur Ausführung gekommen. Es ſind zwei Häuſer zu einem Ganzen vereinigt, und jedes derſelben iſt mit einer bequem angeordneten Haupttreppe ausgeſtattet. Das Erdgeſchoß enthält an drei Fronten Läden; das erſte Obergeſchoß teilt ſich in zwei größere Wohnungen, während das zweite und dritte Obergeſchoß von je drei

férences montant de fond à travers deux étages; en outre, des bureaux; le troisième étage est exclusivement occupé par des bureaux. En sous-sol, du côté de la place du marché, se trouve le restaurant. Tous les plafonds sont de construction massive. Le toit est construit en fer jusqu'à la poutraison du milieu et recouvert en tuiles rouges. L'édifice est chauffé au moyen de calorifères à eau chaude à basse pression; il est pourvu de conduites d'eau, de gaz et d'électricité pour l'éclairage.

Les façades sont traitées dans le style du gothique tardif, elles sont construites en grès du Württemberg. Le motif principal de la façade sur la place du marché est une puissante tour carrée.

215 [1906; 60]

La maison mitoyenne de commerce et d'habitation Badstrasse 60 à Berlin entoure de ses quatre ailes une cour spacieuse. La disposition des plans est due à Monsieur P. Kesten architecte, tandis que l'architecte A. Zabel est l'auteur des façades. Le bâtiment fut élevé dans l'espace de onze mois environ, jusqu'au mois d'octobre 1905. Les façades sont crépies en ciment de Portland avec une mixture de ciment romain; les toits sont recouverts de tuiles émaillées de Marienbourg. La façade sur la rue est animée par des tourelles en saillie, des loggias ouvertes et des balcons.

Le rez-de-chaussée contient dans l'aile sur la rue outre l'entrée conduisant à l'escalier principal, plusieurs magasins et un comptoir de banque. Dans les deux ailes latérales et dans l'aile postérieure on a installé quatre logements avec escaliers spéciaux accessibles de la cour. Les quatre étages supérieurs contiennent chacun dix appartements pourvue de cuisines et de dépendances.

216 [1906; 50]

Le bloc de maisons situé à l'angle obtus formé par la rencontre de deux rues à Budapest, Szabadsag Ter 16 et entourant une grande cour a été construit d'après les plans de feu l'architecte Artur Meinig pour la somme de 1500000 Couronnes dans l'espace de deux ans environ. Ce bloc est composé de deux maisons réunies en une seule et chacune d'elles est pourvue d'un escalier commode. Le rez-de-chaussée contient des magasins sur trois fronts; le premier étage se divise en deux grands appartements, tandis que le second et le troisième étage sont chacun divisés en trois appartements. Entre le

ing upwards through two stories and some additional offices; the third story is occupied exclusively with offices. In the basement facing the market is the Guild hall restaurant. All the ceilings are massive; the roof is constructed of iron top beams and is covered with red flat tiles. Low pressure steam heating is used, warm water is every where laid on and lighting apparatus for gas and electricity is provided.

The facades are late Gothic in style, the material used being Württemberg Keuper sandstone; on the side facing the market is a massive square tower.

215 [1906; 60]

The business and dwelling house at Badstrasse 60 Berlin surrounds with its four wings a spacious yard. The ground plan is by the architect P. Kesten, the design of the facade is by the architect A. Zabel. The time occupied was about eleven months, it was finished in October 1905. The facades are of Portland cement with an addition of Roman cement, the roofs are of glazed Marienburg tiles. The street frontage is enriched by projecting bays, open loggias and balconies.

The ground floor contains on the street side several shops in addition to the entrance to the principal staircase; it contains also a restaurant and bank premises; in the two side wings and in the back wing are four lodgings with special entrances and staircases from the court yard. The four upper stories have each ten dwellings with kitchens and offices.

216 [1906; 50]

Three street frontages forming an obtuse angle have been chosen for the site of a group of houses at Szabadsag Ter 16, Budapest. They were designed by the deceased architect Arthur Meinig and occupied 2 years in building; the cost amounted to 1500000 Kronen. The houses are built round a spacious courtyard; two of them form one large house and each of them has a well constructed principal staircase. On the ground floor on three frontages are shops; the first upper story is

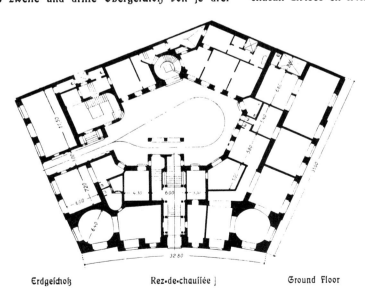

Erdgeſchoß   Rez-de-chauſſée

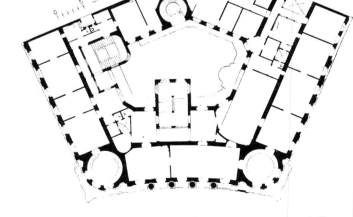

Ground Floor   1. Stockwerk   1. Étage   1. Floor

Wohnungen eingenommen werden. Zwiſchen Erdgeſchoß und erſtem Obergeſchoß iſt ein Mezzanin eingeſchoben (Taf. 50), das die Bureaux der Königlich Ungariſchen Seeſchiffahrts-Aktiengeſellſchaft „Adria" enthält.

rez-de-chaussée et le premier étage est installé un entresol contenant (Pl. 50) les bureaux de la société royale hongroise de navigation par actions, nommée „Adria".

Un caractère distinctif digne d'attention est

occupied by flats, on each two; the upper second and third stories have also flats, each story containing three. Between the ground and first floors an intermediate story has been built (see plate 50) for the bureaus of the Imperial

Als befondere Eigentümlichkeit der in Putzbau ausgeführten Faffaden ift das nach Wiener
Mufter erftrebte Zufammenfaffen des Ganzen
zu einer palaftartigen Wirkung hervorzuheben.
Namentlich tritt die für Gefchäfts- und Miets-
häufer ungewöhnliche Prachtentfaltung an der
leicht nach einwärts gekrümmten Vorderfaffade
hervor, welche durch turmartig ausgebildete,
runde, mit Kuppeldächern bekrönte Eckbauten
eingefaßt wird, mit einer durch beide Haupt-
gefchoffe reichenden, einen Balkon tragenden
korinthifchen Säulenftellung geziert ift und mit
einem großen gebogenen Giebel abfchließt. Bildhauerarbeiten, von Anton Szabó gefertigt, find
am Äußeren reichlich zur Verwendung gekommen.

la façon dont sont traitées les façades, elles
sont crépies, et d'après la mode viennoise, reliées
dans leur ensemble par une architecture de
palais. La façade principale frappe surtout par
le déploiement d'une somptuosité inusitée dans les
maisons de commerce et de rapport; cette façade
est de forme légèrement concave en plan, elle
est encadrée d'avant-corps en forme de tours
rondes, couronnées de toits au profil de coupoles,
elle est décorée d'une colonnade corinthienne
traversant les deux étages principaux et portant
un balcon, elle est terminée par un grand fronton
arrondi. La décoration plastique, œuvre du
sculpteur Antoine Szabó a été repandue à profusion à l'extérieur.

Hungarian "Seeschiffahrts - Aktiengesellschaft
Adria".

The facade is of plaster, with a harmonious
design after the Vienna style and which gives
the whole a palatial effect. A very magnificent
and unusual ornamentation is given to the
shops and dwelling house, with turrets and
gables and cupolas of various kinds; a balcony
on the principal front is supported by Corinthian
columns and crowned by a large arched gable.
The sculptural ornament which is very lavish,
is by Antony Szabó.

217 [1906: 51]

Ein Vorderhaus an der Straße und ein langer,
an einem Gartenhof gelegener Seitenflügel,
fowie eine im Sinne der Moderne durchgebildete
Putzfaffade bilden die bezeichnenden Merkmale
des Gefchäfts- und Wohnhaufes in Charlottenburg, Eofanderftraße 31, welches von
dem Architekten E. Linkenbach entworfen und
für die Baufumme von 210000 Mark in der
Zeit vom Mai 1905 bis April 1906 zur Ausführung gebracht wurde.

217 [1906: 51]

Une maison sur la rue et une longue aile
latérale située sur une cour en jardin, ainsi
que des façades en maçonnerie crépie, constituent
les éléments caractéristiques de la maison
de commerce et d'habitation Eosanderstrasse 31 à Charlottenbourg qui fut bâtie par
Monsieur E. Linkenbach architecte d'après ses
plans et pour la somme de 210000 Marks.

Le socle du rez-de-chaussée de la façade
sur la rue possède une assise inférieure de

217 [1906: 51]

The main features of the business and
dwelling house at Eosanderstrasse 31,
Charlottenburg are a modern plastered facade,
a front house facing the street and a long side
wing facing the garden. The architect was
E. Linkenbach and the cost of building
amounted to 210000 Marks.

The sockel of the ground floor on the street

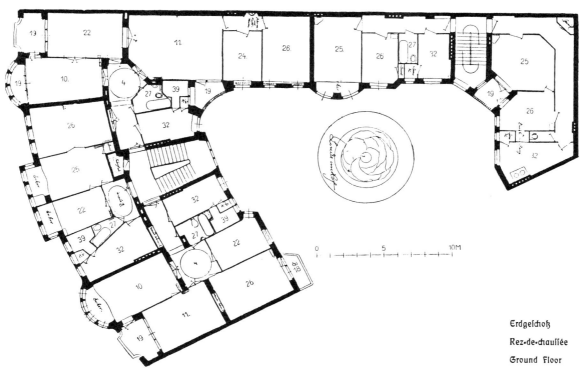

Erdgefchoß
Rez-de-chauffée
Ground Floor

Der Sockel des Erdgefchoffes der Straßen-
faffade zeigt eine untere Sandfteinfchicht und
blauglafierte Verblender; darüber folgt durch alle
Gefchoffe graugelber Förderftedter Kalkputz. Die
nächftfolgenden drei Obergefchoffe find mittelft
vertikaler, durch verfchiedenartig behandelte Putzflächen verzierte flache Wandftreifen gegliedert.
Der mittlere, viereckig vorfpringende und die
beiden feitlichen, halbrund vorgekragten Erker find
durch Balkons abgefchloffen, über denen fich noch
ein fünftes Obergefchoß erhebt. Die Begrenzung
der Faffade bilden beiderfeits offene Loggien.
Das Dach ift mit roten Ziegeln eingedeckt.

Das Erdgefchoß enthält Läden mit Wohnungen
und Gefchäftsräume, außerdem zwei Wohnungen
im Seitenflügel. Die übrigen Gefchoffe find in
Wohnungen von verfchiedener Größe eingeteilt.
Es ift eine Zentralheizung, eine Warmwaffer-
verforgung und elektrifche Beleuchtung eingerichtet.
Die Decken find nach dem Syftem Kohlmeß durch
leichte Gitterträger mit Formfteinummantelung
gebildet. Die fchwierigen Maurerarbeiten find
von Maurermeifter Gottlieb Tefch-Berlin ausgeführt.

pierre de taille et de briques émaillees bleues,
tous les étages au dessus sont en maçonnerie
crépie de mortier de chaux de Förderstedt. Les
trois étages situés au dessus du rez-de-chaussée
sont divisés en champs verticaux plats décorés
de surfaces ornementées de différentes façons.
La tourelle saillante, carrée du milieu ainsi que
les deux tourelles latérales se décrochant en
demi-cercle sont terminées par des balcons au
dessus des quels s'élève encore un cinquième
étage. La façade est terminée des deux côtés
par des loggias ouvertes. Le toit est recouvert
en tuiles rouges.

Le rez-de-chaussée contient des magasins
avec appartements et comptoirs et de plus, deux
appartements dans l'aile latérale. Les autres
étages sont divisés en logements de différentes
grandeurs. La maison est pourvue d'un chauffage
central, d'une conduite d'eau chaude, et d'éclairage électrique. Les plafonds sont construits
d'après le système Kohlmetz de légers sommiers en treillis revêtus de briques de formes
spéciales. La maçonnerie difficile est executée
par le maître-maçon Gottlieb Tesch à
Berlin.

side is of sandstone and blue glazed facings,
throughout the other storeys grey-yellow Förderstedt
lime plaster has been used. The three following
upper storeys have vertical articulations with
surfaces treated in various manners and ornamented in vertical stripes. The middle square
projecting bay, and the two semi-circular bays
at the side have all balconies over them, over
these a fifth story is built. On both sides of
the facade are open loggias.

The ground floor contains shops with dwellings attached, and two lodgings in the side
wings; the other storeys contain dwellings of
various sizes. The house is heated by hot
air, has warm water supply, and is lighted by
electric light. The ceilings are of the system
Kohlmetz, of light iron beams with Formstein
facings. The more difficult mason-work is
executed by Mr. Gottlieb Tesch-Berlin.

Von dem Albert Schumann-Theater in Frankfurt a. M., erbaut in den Jahren 1904/5 durch die Architekten Kristeller & Sonnenthal in Berlin, geben unsere Tafeln das Schaubild und den unteren Teil der Hauptfassade im größeren Maßstabe wieder.

Die in der Grundrißbildung zur Lösung gestellte Aufgabe betraf die Vereinigung eines Zirkus- mit einem Theatergebäude. Den Erfordernissen der Zirkusvorstellungen entspricht ein großer Rundraum A, während für Theaterzwecke ein besonderes Bühnenpodium B angeordnet ist. Das Theater ist derart konstruiert, daß die Parkettsitze C und das Orchester im zweiten Obergeschoß in zwei Tagen entfernt werden können, so daß eine Zirkusmanege und die umgebende amphitheatralische Sitzreihen zum Vorschein kommen. Das Vorderhaus enthält, außer den Eingängen D und Treppen, die Foyers E, an den Ecken eine Kaffeewirtschaft F und ein Weinrestaurant G; unter dem ganzen Gebäude ist ein Biertunnel angelegt. Unter der Manege befindet sich ein Wassergraben, der die Vorführung von Wasserpantomimen und das Emporsteigen eines Ballettkorps ermöglicht. Ebenfalls in der Tiefe sind die Stallungen angelegt, welche durch eine Luxferkonstruktion mit Tageslicht erhellt werden.

Die Baukosten für das ganze Gebäude betrugen 1 750 000 Mark.

Das in Mainsandstein ausgeführte Äußere des Zirkus- und Theatergebäudes bindet sich nicht an die Formen eines bestimmten historischen Stils, vielmehr geben die Fassaden eine in künstlerischer Eigenart frei erfundene Schöpfung. Der Charakter eines Theaters ist unverkennbar und wirkungsvoll zum Ausdruck gebracht. Über dem breiten Mitteleingange und den beiden Seitentüren öffnen sich in zwei Obergeschossen die Foyers, im ersten Geschoß in Verbindung mit einem Balkon, und treten in einen berechneten Gegensatz zu den geschlossenen Wänden des Zuschauerraumes. Die seitlichen Turmaufbauten der Hauptfront, wenn auch nicht aus dem inneren Bedürfnis hervorgegangen, erhöhen doch wesentlich die monumentale Gesamtwirkung.

218. 219 [1906: 53. 52]

Nos planches représentent la vue perspective et la partie inférieure de la façade à une plus grande échelle du théâtre Albert Schumann à Francfort sur le Mein; ce monument fut élevé dans les années 1904—1905 par les architectes Kristeller et Sonnenthal à Berlin.

Le problème posé dans la composition du plan était la combinaison d'un cirque et d'un bâtiment de théâtre. Pour les représentation de cirque, on a besoin d'un grand espace circulaire A, tandis que le théâtre exige une scène spéciale B. Le théâtre est construit de telle sorte, que les sièges de parquet C et l'orchestre au deuxième étage peuvent être enlevés en deux jours, de telle façon, qu'un manège de cirque et l'amphithéâtre des rangs d'alentour se présentent. La partie antérieure du bâtiment contient outre l'entrée D et les escaliers, les foyers E, dans les angles, un café F et un restaurant à vin G, sous tout le bâtiment on a disposé une cave à bière. Sous le manège se trouve une nappe d'eau qui perment l'exécution de naumachies et l'élévation d'un corps de ballet. Les écuries sont également disposées en sous sol, elles sont éclairées à jour grâce à l'emploi de constructions système Luxfer.

Les frais de construction pour tout l'édifice s'élevèrent à 1 750 000 Marks.

L'extérieur du théâtre exécuté en pierre du Mein ne se plie aux formes d'aucun style historique, mais les façades présentent plutôt l'exemple d'une création composée dans un esprit entièrement individuel. Le caractère du théâtre est exprimé d'une façon indubitable et frappant. Les foyers s'ouvrent dans les deux étages supérieurs, au dessus de la large entrée du milieu et des deux portes latérales, au premier étage, ils communiquent avec un balcon et ils forment un contraste bien étudié avec les murs fermés de la salle des spectateurs. Les couronnements latéraux de la façade principale en forme de tours, ne correspondent pas à une exigence du plan, mais ils contribuent puissamment à l'effet monumental de l'ensemble.

218. 219 [1906: 53. 52]

The Albert Schumann-theatre in Frankfort on Main was built in 1904 and 1905 by the architects Kristeller and Sonnenthal of Berlin. Our plates give an illustration of this, and of the lower part of the facade on an enlarged scale.

The problem given to the designer of the ground plan was the combination of a circus with a theatre. A circus requires a large amphitheatre (A), for theatre purposes a special stage-platform is constructed, (B). The theatre is so constructed that the Stalls (C) and the orchestra in the two upper story can be removed in two days, so that a circus equipment and an amphitheatre with rows of seats gradually ascending are arranged. The front building contains, in addition to the entrances, (D) and staircase the Foyers (E). At the corners are coffee saloons (F) and a wine restaurant (G). Under the whole building is a tunnel for beer-drinking. Under the stage is a water receptacle which admits of the equipment of water pantomimes, and also serves as a place from which the ballet corps can ascend. The stabling for the horses is also built in these underground premises which are lighted by the "Luxfer" construction of windows.

The cost of the entire building amounted to 1 750 000 Marks.

The exterior of the theatre, which is built of Main sandstone, does not keep strictly in style to any historical period, the facade is more an artistic free rendering of an individual style. It is however decidedly like a theatre, the style shows this unmistakeably. Over the wide middle entrance and the two side doors are the Foyers opening in two upper stories; on the first floor they are connected with a balcony, and are evidently intended to contrast with the enclosed walls of the auditorium. The side tower on the principal front, though not in any actual connec-

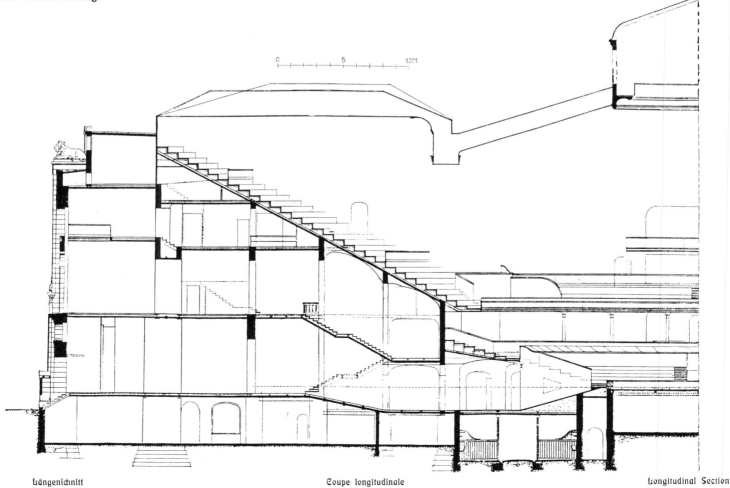

Längenschnitt   Coupe longitudinale   Longitudinal Section

Die zum Schmuck der Fassaden verwendeten figürlichen Skulpturen verdienen eine besondere Erwähnung. Professor Uphues lieferte die von Knodt in Kupfer getriebene Giebelgruppe des Rossebändigers in Gestalt eines römischen Soldaten, außerdem die fackeltragenden Gruppen von geschmiedeter Bronze zu beiden Seiten des Mitteleinganges. Bendorf hat die Figuren über den Fenstergesimsen des ersten Obergeschosses geschaffen.

Les statues servant à la décoration des façades méritent d'être spécialement mentionnées. Le professeur Uphues est l'auteur du modèle pour le groupe ornant le fronton; c'est un dompteur de chevaux sous la forme d'un soldat romain, ce groupe a été exécuté en cuivre repoussé par Knodt, Uphues a aussi composé les groupes de lampadaires de bronze forgé placés des deux côtés de l'entrée du milieu. Bendorf a modelé les figures placées au dessus des corniches de fenêtres du premier étage.

tion with the interior, is yet a decidedly effective finish.

The sculptural ornaments of the facade deserve special notice. They are designed by Professor Uphues, the gable group of the horse-tamer in the form of a Roman soldier has been hammered in copper by Knodt, as well as the torch bearing groups of wrought bronze on both sides of the middle entrance. Bendorf has designed the figures over the window mouldings of the first upper story.

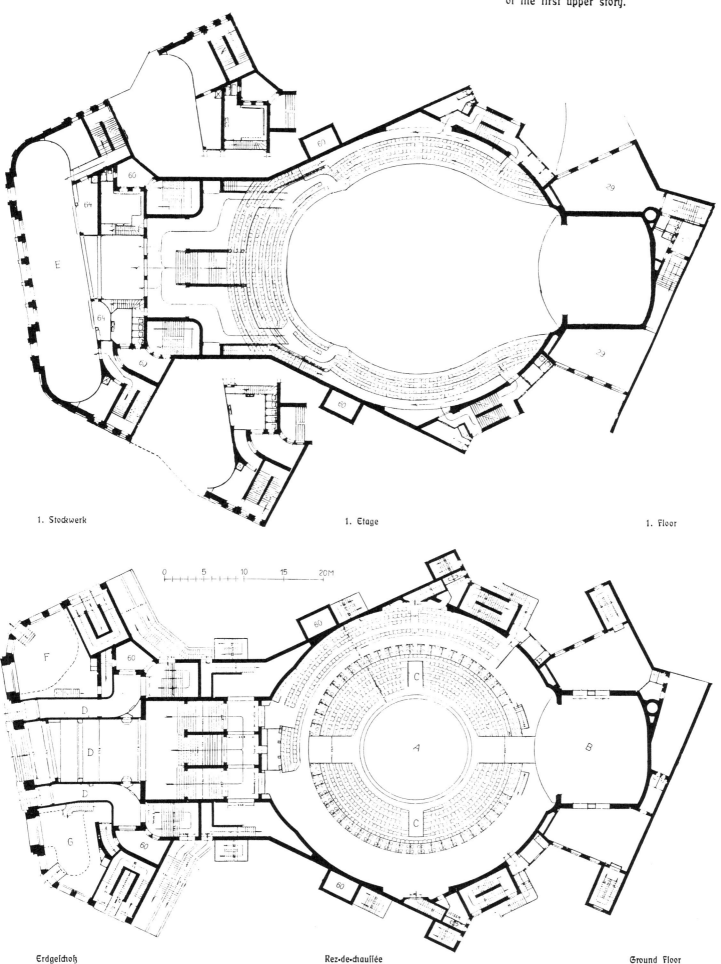

1. Stockwerk

1. Étage

1. Floor

Erdgeschoß

Rez-de-chaussée

Ground Floor

Das Reihenhaus in Koblenz, Friedrich-straße 50, deffen Faffade unfere Tafel wiedergibt, ift von dem Architekten C. Reich in Gemeinfchaft mit dem Bauingenieur C. Riffer für die Summe von 32000 Mark errichtet.

Es ift eine Pußfaffade, welche den im Sinne der Moderne umgebildeten Empireftil zeigt. Die Vertikalgliederung mittelft breiter Wandftreifen in den Obergefchoffen ift vorherrfchend und wird noch mehr durch den die Mittelachfe einnehmen-den, durch die Obergefchoffe reichenden, mit einem Dache für fich abgefchloffenen Erker hervorgehoben. Ein breiter, mittlerer Dachaufbau mit einem Giebeldach nebft anfchließenden Dach-fenftern bekrönen den mittleren Teil der Faffade, deren Verzierungsformen in flachem Relief ge-halten und in Mörtelpuß angetragen find.

La maison Friedrichstrasse 50 à Coblence dont notre planche donne la façade, est l'œuvre de l'architecte C. Reich, en collaboration avec l'ingenieur C. Riffer; cet immeuble a coûté 32000 Marks.

C'est une façade en maçonnerie crépie mon-trant les formes du style empire modifié dans le sens moderne. Le verticalisme est dominant, il est exprimé par de larges bandes dans les étages supérieurs, et encore accentué par une tourelle située dans l'axe principal, traversant les étages supérieurs et couronnée d'un toit spécial. Un large couronnement avec toit à fronton flanqué de lucarnes surmonte la partie centrale de la façade, dont les décorations sont exécutées en bas relief et modelées dans le mortier.

The house at Friedrichstrasse 50, Coblentz, the facade of which is given in our illustration, is by the architect C. Reich together with the engineer C. Riffer, and cost 32000 Marks.

The facade is of plaster, of the modern Empire style. The vertical articulation by means of broad belts is predominant, and this is emphasised by the bay in the centre, which reaches to the upper story, and is roofed by a separate roof. A broad middle roof erection ornaments the middle facade and has a gable roof with windows. The ornamentation is in flat relief with mortar plaster.

Das eingebaute Wohn- und Fabrikgebäude für Herrn C. G. T. Langenfcheidt in Schöne-berg-Berlin, Bahnftraße 29/30, umfchließt einen vollftändig unterkellerten Hofraum und wird an der Hinterfeite durch einen zweiten, gleichfalls unterkellerten Hof begrenzt. Die An-ordnung des Grundriffes fowie die 1904/05 er-folgte Ausführung find ein Werk des Architekten W. Gutzeit; den Entwurf für die Faffaden fertigte Architekt T. Welz. Die Baukoften be-trugen 560000 Mark. Die in Renaiffanceformen durchgebildete Straßenfront wird im mittleren Teile durch drei ausgekragte Erker und einen Giebelaufbau, in den Seitenteilen durch offene Loggien in Verbindung mit vorfpringenden Balkons

La maison d'habitation et de fabrique construite entre murs mitoyens pour M. M. C. G. T. Langenscheidt à Schöneberg près Berlin, Bahnstrasse 29/30, entoure une cour entièrement occupée par des caves et longe sur ses derrières une seconde cour également pour-vue de caves. La disposition du plan, ainsi que l'exécution du bâtiment qui eut lieu de 1904 à 1905 sont l'œuvre de Monsieur W. Gutzeit architecte; le projet pour les façades a été livré par Monsieur T. Welz architecte. Les frais de construction s'élevèrent à 560000 Marks. La façade sur la rue, traitée dans les formes de la Renaissance, est divisée dans sa partie centrale par trois tourelles saillantes et un couronnement avec fronton, dans les ailes latérales par des

Business premises, including a factory and dwelling house, have been built for Herrn C. G. T. Langenscheidt at Bahnstrasse 29 and 30, Schöneberg-Berlin. They comprise a yard with underground cellarage which is again repeated in a second courtyard at the extreme back of the house. The work was done in 1904 and 1905 and was designed by the architect W. Gutzeit; the facade was designed by the architect T. Welz. The cost amounted to 560000 Marks. The street frontage is in the Renaissance style, and is ornamented in the centre by three projecting bays and a gable erection; at the side are open loggias in connec-tion with projecting balconies. It is a plaster

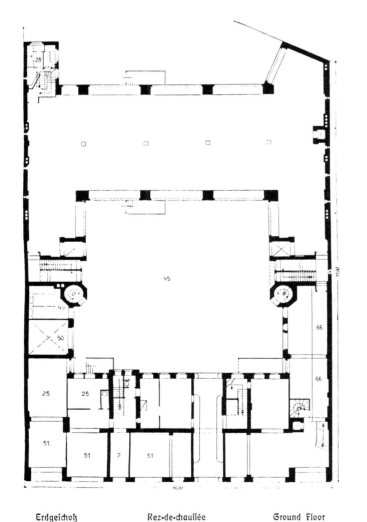
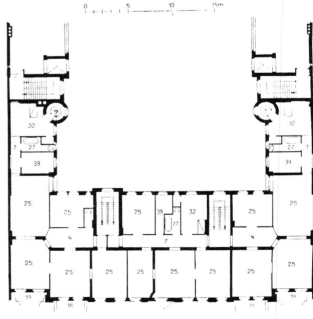

| Erdgefchoß | Rez-de-chauffée | Ground Floor | 1. Stockwerk | 1. Etage | 1. Floor |

gegliedert. Es ift ein Pußbau mit in Mörtel-ftuck angetragenen Verzierungen. Die Vorder-front des Fabrikflügels ift mit weißen und grünen Verblendern, die Hinterfront desfelben

loggias ouvertes communiquant avec des balcons en saillie. Le bâtiment est en maçonnerie crépie avec décorations modelées librement dans le mortier. La façade principale de l'aile de la

building with ornamentation in mortar stucco. The front part of the factory wing is faced with white and green tiles, the back walls with Rathenow tiles.

mit Rathenower Handstrichsteinen bekleidet. Das Erdgeschoß enthält an der Straßenfront Läden in Verbindung mit Wohnräumen; ein besonderer Eingang leitet zu einer Stockwerkstreppe, und eine Durchfahrt führt in den Hof und zugleich zu einer zweiten Treppe. Rückwärts an den Hof schließt sich das Fabrikgebäude an; die vier Obergeschosse sind im Vorderhause und in den Seitenflügeln zu Wohnungen, im Hintergebäude zu Fabriksälen eingerichtet.

fabrique est revêtue de briques blanches et vertes, la façade postérieure de cette même aile de briques à la main de Rathenow.

Le rez-de-chaussée contient sur la rue des magasins reliés à des appartements; une entrée spéciale conduit à l'escalier des étages, tandis qu'une porte cochère conduit dans la cour et en même temps à un second escalier. La fabrique se relie par derrière à la cour. Les quatre étages sont distribués en appartements dans le bâtiment de devant et dans les ailes, dans le bâtiment postérieur, en salles de fabrique.

The ground floor contains shops facing the street with dwelling rooms adjoining. A separate entrance leads to a staircase in connection with the various stories, and a thoroughfare through a gateway leads to the courtyard and thence to a second staircase. The factory is situated at the back of the courtyard. The four upper stories of the front house are arranged as dwellings, as are also the side wings. The back of the premises is entirely occupied with the factory.

222 [1906: 61]

Wie sehr geeignet das moderne Barock ist, um die monumentale Würde öffentlicher Gebäude auch am Äußeren zum Ausdruck zu bringen, beweist in hervorragender Weise der Neubau des Kriminalgerichtsgebäudes in Berlin-Moabit, Turmstraße 89—93, welcher in der Bauzeit von 1902 bis 1906 entstanden und von den Architekten Geh. Oberbaurat P. Thömer und Baurat C. Vohl entworfen ist.

Das ganz in Haustein ausgeführte Gebäude ist durch einen kräftig vorspringenden Mittelbau

222 [1906: 61]

Le bâtiment de la justice criminelle à Berlin-Moabit, Turmstrasse 89—93, construit de 1902 à 1906, prouve d'une manière saisissante, combien le style baroque moderne se prête à exprimer la dignité monumentale des édifices publics dans leurs façades. Ce monument es l'œuvre des architectes P. Thömer conseiller supérieur et C. Vohl conseiller.

Le bâtiment entièrement construit en pierre de taille est divisé par un corps central d'une forte saillie, par des tours couronnées de coupoles

222 [1906: 61]

The suitability of the barock style to give a monumental dignity to the exterior of public buildings may be seen in the new buildings of the "Kriminal-Gericht Gebäude" at Turmstrasse 89—93, Moabit-Berlin. The time occupied was 4 years from 1902 to 1906, and the design is by the architects Oberbaurat P. Thömer and Baurat C. Vohl.

The building is entirely of free-stone, has a massive projecting middle erection crowned with

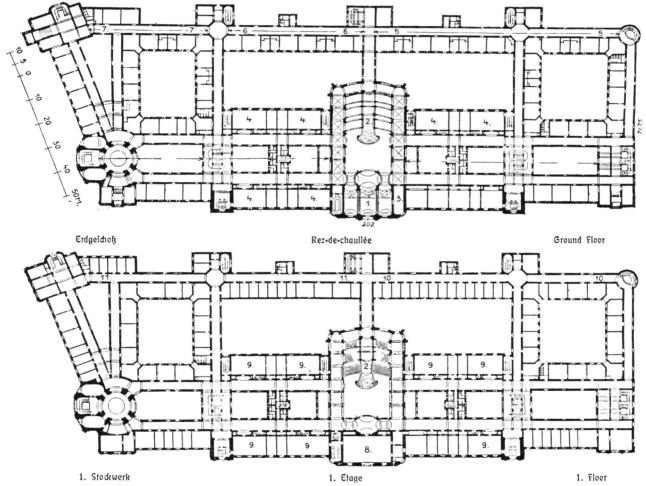

Erdgeschoß   Rez-de-chaussée   Ground Floor

1. Stockwerk   1. Étage   1. Floor

mit bekrönendem Flachgiebel, durch kuppelbedeckte Türme und Eckrisalite gegliedert. Über einem niedrigen Sockelgeschoß erheben sich durch zwei Geschosse reichende Pilaster, im Mittelbau von korinthischer, in den Rücklagen von ionischer Ordnung. In den zunächst an den Mittelbau anschließenden Flügeln ist noch ein drittes, durch Wandstreifen geteiltes Obergeschoß angeordnet. Das Prachtstück der Fassade an der Turmstraße bildet, ganz im Stile der älteren Barockbauten, das von übereckgestellten Säulen flankierte, mit einem vorgebauchten Rundbogen geschlossene und von einer ebenfalls vorgebauchten, durch beide Obergeschosse geführten Fenstergruppe überstiegene Portal. Über den flankierenden Säulen sind sitzende Figuren angebracht, auch die Fensterbekrönungen im ersten Stock sind besonders reich mit Gliederungen und Ornamentskulpturen bedacht.

et par des pavillons d'angle. Au dessus d'un socle bas s'élèvent des pilastres montant de fond à travers deux étages, ces pilastres sont d'ordre corinthien à l'avant-corps et ioniques dans les retraits. Un troisième étage divisé par des panneaux s'élève encore sur les ailes reliées directement à l'avant-corps. Un portail flanqué de colonnes placées sur la diagonale, recouvert d'un arc de plan curviligne, surmonté d'un groupe de fenêtres également de plan curviligne et embrassant deux étages forme la partie somptueuse de la façade sur la Turmstrasse tenue entièrement dans le style des anciens palais baroques. Des figures assises sont placées sur les colonnes flanquant le portail, les couronnements des fenêtres du premier étage sont aussi décorées d'une façon particulièrement riche au moyen de profils et d'ornements de sculpture.

a gable, and a tower crowned with a cupola; the corners have projecting ornaments. Over a low sockel storey are pillars reaching through two upper storeys, in the middle building are Corinthian pillars, in the back part Jonic. A wing joining the middle erection has a third storey separated from the others by mouldings. The most magnificent part of the facade is on the Turmstrasse, It is barock in style; the portal is flanked by pillars, finished off with a bulging arch, and by a group of windows also bulging and stretching through two storeys. Over the pillars are sitting sculptural figures; the window crowns of the first storey are too very richly articulated and ornamented with sculpture.

Die Villa Rohn in Mannheim, Mollstraße, ist ein Werk des Architekten Georg Freed daselbst. Für die Fassadenwirkung kommt wesentlich die gelungene Zusammenstellung verschiedenfarbigen Materials in Betracht. Für das Kellergeschoß ist rotvioletter Porphyr verwendet, für die Obergeschosse roter Pfälzer Sandstein mit Vergoldungen an den Giebeln der beiden Straßenfronten. Die Seitenfassaden haben blaugelb gefärbten Terranovaputz erhalten; das Holzwerk der oberen Teile der Straßen- und Gartenfronten zeigt einen bräunlichen Ton in Verbindung mit weißen Putzflächen; außerdem sind der große Fachwerksgiebel an der Straße sowie das obere Turmgeschoß wieder durch Vergoldungen belebt. Die Dächer sind mit Ziegeln eingedeckt.

Es sind zwei Wohnungen übereinander angeordnet, so daß im Untergeschoß und Dachgeschoß Küche und Schlafräume, im Erd- und Obergeschoß die eigentlichen Wohnräume liegen. Sämtliche Decken sind in Beton zwischen Eisenträgern hergestellt oder — wie die melonenförmigen Decken über den beiden achteckigen Räumen im Turm und die segmentförmigen Decken über den Speisezimmern — in eisenarmiertem Beton ausgeführt. Die gleichfalls in Eisenbeton konstruierte Haupttreppe hat eine Verkleidung von Eichenholz erhalten.

La villa Rohn à Mannheim, située Mollstrasse, est l'œuvre de l'architecte Georg Freed dans la même ville. L'emploi habile de matériaux de diverses couleurs contribue grandement à la belle apparence des façades. Pour le sous-sol, on a employé du porphyre d'un rouge violet, pour les étages supérieurs, de la pierre rouge du Palatinat avec dorures aux frontons des deux faces sur la rue. Les façades latérales ont été traitées en crépissage de Terra-Nova teinté en bleu jaune. Les surfaces en bois apparents des parties supérieures du côté de le rue et du jardin montrent un ton brunâtre pour les bois, se mariant avec le blanc ud crépissage; d'autre part, les grands frontons en pans de bois du côté de la rue ainsi que l'étage supérieur de la tour sont décorés de dorures. Les toits sont recouverts en tuiles.

On a disposé deux appartements l'un au dessus de l'autre, de façon que la cuisine et les chambres à coucher se trouvent en sous-sol et dans le toit, que les pièces d'habitation proprement dites occupent le rez-de-chaussée et le premier étage. Tous les plafonds sont construits en béton entre poutres en fer, ou en béton armé, comme cela a été le cas pour les plafonds en forme de côtés de melon au dessus des deux pièces octogonales dans la tour et pour les plafonds en forme de segment au dessus des salles à manger. L'escalier principal également construit en béton a été revêtu de bois de chêne.

The villa Rohn at Mollstrasse Mannheim was built by the architect George Freed. The good effect of the facade has been achieved by the successful combination of various materials. For the basement, red-violet porphyry has been used, the upper storeys are of red Palatinate sandstone, the gables of the two street frontages are gilded. The side facades have blue-yellow terranova plaster, the wood-work of the upper part of the street and garden frontages has a brownish tone in combination with white plastered surfaces; the large frame work gable on the street side as well as the upper tower storey are enlivened by gilding. The roofs are tiled.

The two lodgings are so arranged over each other that the basement and roof story contain kitchen and bedrooms, on the ground and first floors the actual dwelling rooms are arranged. The entire ceilings are of beton between iron girders, the melon-shaped ceilings over the two octagonal rooms in the tower and the segment-shaped ceiling of the dining room are also of iron and beton. The same construction has been used for the principal staircase which is however faced with oak wood work.

Die geschlossene Gesamtfront sowie der durchweg in rauhem Quaderwerk erfolgte Aufbau des Hauses der Landsmannschaft „Schottland" in Tübingen verleiht demselben einen wohl beabsichtigten burgartigen Charakter, selbstverständlich ohne daß eigentliche Befestigungsformen zur Anwendung gekommen sind. Architekt Arthur Müller in Stuttgart ist der Schöpfer des von August 1904 bis Juli 1905 mit einem Kostenaufwande von 50000 Mark ausgeführten Bauwerks. Die steilen Treppengiebel und ein kräftiger, viereckiger, mit einem abgewalmten Zeltdach bekrönter Eckturm verstärken den wehrhaften Gesamteindruck des Hauses. Ein im Obergeschoß vorspringender Sandsteinerker setzt sich in Holzkonstruktion als Dachaufbau mit seitlich angelehnten Dachfenstern fort.

Die Außenmauern bestehen aus Pfrondorfer Bruchsteinen von warmer, gelbbräunlicher Färbung, die Gliederungen aus Sandstein, während die

La façade sévère ainsi que la construction tout en bossages de la maison d'étudiants „Schottland" à Tubingue donnent à cet édifice le caractère bien cherché du reste, d'un château fort, sans que bien entendu, il ait été fait emploi de formes de fortification proprement dite. Monsieur Arthur Müller architecte à Stuttgart est l'auteur de cet édifice construit du mois d'août 1904 à celui de juillet 1905 pour la somme de 50000 Marks. Le haut fronton à degrés, ainsi qu'une forte tour carrée d'angle, couverte d'un toit à pans coupés augmentent l'impression générale de château fort que fait cette maison. Une tourelle en pierre saillante sur le premier étage se prolonge en construction de bois sur le toit et se relie à des lucarnes qui s'appuient sur elle.

Les façades sont en moellons de Pfrondorf d'une couleur jaune brunâtre très chaude, les membres d'architecture sont en pierre de taille, tandis que les parties visibles de bois de chêne

The house of the Landmannschaft "Schottland" in Tübingen shows on its entire frontage, and in its erection entirely of rough square stone work, that the design of the architect was to imitate a fortress, and this has been done without actually making a fortified castle of it. The architect is Arthur Müller of Stuttgart, the time occupied was from August 1904 to July 1905 and the cost was 50000 Marks. The steep staircase gable and an important square corner tower emphasise the castellated style of the whole. The projecting sandstone bay of the upper story is continued in the roof erection of wood which contains on the side the roof windows.

The outside walls are of Pfrondorf free stone of warm yellow brown colour, the articulations are of sandstone, while the visible

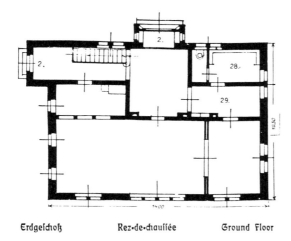

Erdgeschoß　　　Rez-de-chaussée　　　Ground Floor

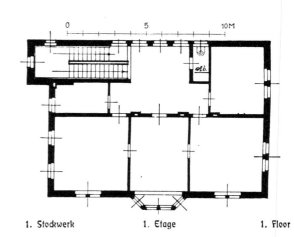

1. Stockwerk　　　1. Étage　　　1. Floor

sichtbaren Eichenholzteile grünlich lasiert sind. Das Haus enthält im Erdgeschoß einen größeren Fecht- und Kneipsaal. Das nicht mit der Kanalisation verbundene Grundstück wird mittelst Oberflächenberieselung entwässert.

Das Wappen im Bogenfelde des Hauptportals ist ein Werk des Bildhauers A. Schenk.

sont peintes en vert. L'immeuble contient au rez-de-chaussée une grande salle d'escrime et de fêtes. Le terrain qui n'est pas relié à la canalisation est pourvu d'un système d'irrigation de surface.

L'armoirie sculptée dans le tympan de la porte principale est l'œuvre du sculpteur A. Schenk.

woodwork is coloured green. In the basement is a large fencing and drinking saloon. The drainage is in connection with the town sewerage.

The coat of arms over the principal entrance is the work of the sculptor A. Schenk.

Als ein Bauwerk von vornehmem Charakter, welches in den Umfassungsmauern aus rauhem Quaderwerk von gelbem, pfälzischem Baustein ausgeführt und im Dachstock durch Marmorgewände mit Goldmosaik geschmückt ist, erscheint die Villa Fasig in Mannheim, Werderstraße 34, entworfen von dem Architekten A. Möller daselbst. Die Bauzeit hat etwa ein Jahr in Anspruch genommen; die Baukosten betrugen 300000 Mark. An den Fassaden hat der Autor den gelungenen Versuch gemacht, die Schmuckformen individuell im modernen Sinne zu gestalten. Der Erker im Mittelbau ist an der Brüstung des ersten Obergeschosses durch einen Figurenfries bereichert; außerdem findet sich im Felde des an den Ecken in große stilisierte Adlerköpfe auslaufenden, gebogenen Mittelgiebels der Hauptfront ein von Seitenfiguren begleitetes Wappen.

Die Verteilung der Räume auf das Erdgeschoß und die zwei Obergeschosse ist in der Weise bewirkt, daß im ersteren die um eine mittlere Diele gruppierten Wohnräume untergebracht sind, während im ersten Obergeschoß die wieder sämtlich von einer Diele zugänglichen Schlaf- und Kinderzimmer liegen, und endlich das Dachgeschoß von Gastzimmern, Räumen für Dienstpersonal und Trockenböden ausgefüllt wird.

Die Holzarbeiten im Innern der Villa sind aus der Königlich Bayerischen Hof-Fenster- und Türenfabrik des Bauherrn Anton Fasig hervorgegangen.

226 [1906: 67]

Auf einer gegen die Straße durch eine hohe Futtermauer abgeschlossenen Gartenterrasse erhebt sich die monumental wirkende Villa Steiner, Panoramastraße 15 in Stuttgart, entworfen und ausgeführt von den Architekten Lambert und Stahl daselbst. Die Errichtung des Gebäudes hat 1¼ Jahr in Anspruch genommen; die Baukosten betrugen 110000 Mark.

Der räumlich sehr entwickelte Grundriß zeigt im Erdgeschoß eine Halle mit frei aufsteigender Treppe, von der Halle zugänglich eine Flucht durch breite Schiebetüren miteinander verbundener Zimmer, außerdem die Küche und Nebenräume. Die Fassaden, aus blauem Sandstein hergestellt, zeigen mäßige Barockformen in moderner Auffassung. Auf einem Untergeschoß von bossiertem Quadermauerwerk erheben sich im Mittelrisalit ionische Pilaster, welche ein ununterbrochen durchgehendes Gebälk tragen. Über demselben setzt eine Attika mit Fenstern auf, und ein geradschenkliger Flachgiebel bekrönt den Aufbau. Die mit Schiefer eingedeckten Mansardendächer der Seitenteile sind durch Dachfenster belebt.

227 [1906: 75]

Das Äußere des in Grunewald, Ecke Beyme- und Hubertusbaderstraße gelegenen Landhauses läßt eine mannigfaltige Gruppierung bemerken. Außer einem starken, mit steilem, einmal durchbrochenem Pyramidendach bekrönten Eckturme sind ein Ausbau, mit einem Giebel schließend, dann ein zweiter Ausbau, der als Terrasse endigt, angeordnet, und zwischen beiden öffnet sich im Erdgeschoß eine Säulenloggia, welche im Obergeschoß einen Balkon trägt. Das Haus wurde von Architekt H. Meier in Grunewald für die Kostensumme von 200000 Mark ausgeführt.

Die Fassaden sind wesentlich in Putzbau, nur am Sockel und an einigen unteren Teilen in rauhem Sandsteinquaderwerk hergestellt. Das Erdgeschoß sowie das Obergeschoß umschließen je eine Wohnung mit Küche und Nebenräumen.

La villa Fasig à Mannheim Werderstrasse 34, construit par A. Möller architecte dans la même ville, nous apparaît comme édifice plein de noblesse, les façades en sont construites en pierres de taille jaune du Palatinat; dans l'étage du toit, les encadrements de fenêtres sont en marbre et les surfaces revêtues de mosaiques d'or. La construction a duré un an environ, les frais s'en élevèrent à 300000 Marks. Dans la décoration des façades, l'auteur a fait l'essai fort bien réussi de composer les ornements dans un style individuel et entièrement moderne. La tourelle du corps central est enrichie au contre-cœur du premier étage d'une frise de figures; d'autre part, nous voyons une armoirie accompagnée de figures latérales dans le tympan du fronton arrondi de la façade principale; les profils du fronton se terminent aux angles en grandes têtes d'aigles stylisés.

La distribution des pièces dans le rez-de-chaussée et les deux étages supérieurs est arrangée de telle sorte, que les chambres d'habitation sont groupés au rez-de-chaussée autour d'un hall, tandis que toutes les chambres à coucher et chambres d'enfants sont au premier étage groupées autour d'un vestibule et qu'enfin l'étage du toit est occupé par les chambres d'amis, les chambres pour le personnel de service et par l'étendage.

Les travaux de menuiserie de l'intérieur de la villa ont été livrés par la fabrique de fenêtres et de portes du propriétaire Monsieur Anton Fasig, fournisseur de la cour royale de Bavière.

226 [1906: 67]

Sur une terrasse de jardin portée par un haut mur de soutainement du côté de la rue, s'élève d'une façon monumentale la villa Steiner Panoramastrasse 15 à Stuttgart, projetée et exécutée par M. M. Lambert et Stahl architectes en cette ville. La construction de cette maison a exigé un an et un quart, les frais de construction s'élevèrent à 110000 Marks.

Le plan disposé d'une façon très spacieuse montre au rez-de-chaussée un hall avec grand escalier; du hall on pénètre dans une suite de pièces reliées entre elles par de larges portes à coulisse; cet étage contient en outre la cuisine et les dépendances. Les façades construites en pierre bleuâtre sont de formes d'un baroque sobre, traitées dans un esprit moderne. Sur un socle de bossages s'élèvent au corps central des pilastres ioniques portant un entablement non interrompu. Au dessus de cette corniche, s'élève une attique avec fenêtres; un fronton bas et droit surmonte ce couronnement. Le toit mansard est recouvert en ardoises, les côtés en sont interrompres par des lucarnes.

227 [1906: 75]

On remarque un groupement mouvementé à l'extérieur de la maison de campagne située à l'angle des rues Beyme- et Hubertusbaderstrasse à Grunewald. Outre une forte tour d'angle couronnée par un toit abrupt en forme de pyramide, interrompu sur un point nous voyons un avant-corps terminé par un fronton, puis un second avant-corps portant une terrasse, entre ces deux avant-corps s'ouvre au rez-de-chaussée une loggia à colonnes qui porte un balcon au premier étage. La maison a été bâtie par Monsieur H. Meier architecte à Grunewald pour la somme de 200000 Marks.

Les façades sont en majeure partie construites en maçonnerie crépie et dans quelques parties du bas, en bossages rustiqués. Le rez-de-chaussée et l'étage supérieur contiennent chacun un appartement avec cuisine et dépendances.

The villa Fasig, Werderstrasse 34, Mannheim, was designed by the architect A. Möller of that town. It has a distinguished appearance; the external walls are of rough square stones of yellow Palatinate lime stone, the upper story has marble walls ornamented with gold mosaic. The time occupied was about a year and the cost amounted to 300000 Marks. The architect has been very successful in giving the ornamental part of the facade an individual character, which is however distinctly modern. The balustrade of the bay in the middle part of the upper story is enriched by a sculptured frieze; the plain surfaces of the middle gable in the form of an eagle's head are further ornamented by sculptured ornaments, coat of arms etc.

The distribution of the apartments on the ground and two upper floors is such that the lower rooms are arranged round a central hall, in the upper story the nurseries and bed rooms lead too from a central hall. The upper story is occupied by spare bed rooms, servants' bed rooms and large garret for drying clothes.

The woodwork of the interior is from the Royal Bavarian window and door factory belonging to the owner of the villa Mr. Anton Fasig.

226 [1906: 67]

The villa Steiner, Panoramastrasse 15, Stuttgart, has a very effective site facing the street and flanked by a garden terrace. It was designed and executed by the architects Lambert and Stahl. The building occupied 1¼ years, and the cost amounted to 110000 Marks.

The very fully developed ground plan shows on the ground floor a hall with a free lying staircase; opening from the hall is a suite of rooms separated by sliding doors, as well as the kitchen and offices. The facade, of blue sandstone is of barock style, somewhat tempered by modern details. From the basement with its bassed square stone brick work rise Jonic columns which support a continuons entablature. Above this is an "Attic" with windows and a flat gable surmounts the erection. The mansard roofs, are covered with slate and on the side are enlivened by roof windows.

227 [1906: 75]

The house at the corner of the Beyme- and Hubertusbaderstrasse, Grunewald shows great variety in the grouping of the exterior. First is a corner tower with steep perforated pyramidal roof, then an erection finished off with a gable; a second erection ending in a terrace, and between the two on the ground floor is a pillared loggia over which is a balcony in the upper story. The house is the work of H. Meier of Grunewald and cost 200000 Marks.

The facades are principally of plaster, the base and other lower parts are of rough square sandstone work. The ground floor and each of the upper stories contains one dwelling with kitchen and offices.

Die romanischen Stilformen und die Ausführung in Sandsteinverblendung verleihen der äußeren Erscheinung des Landgerichtsgebäudes III in Berlin-Charlottenburg den Charakter einer einfachen, ernsten Monumentalität. Von mächtiger Wirkung ist der große Giebel des Mittelbaues, aus dessen Dach ein Türmchen emporsteigt. Die Grundrisse des Gebäudes sind von Geh. Oberbaurat P. Thömer, dem Landbauinspektor E. Petersen und dem Baurat P. Mönnich bearbeitet, während an der Gestaltung der Fassaden E. Petersen, Reg.-Baumeister H. Dernburg und Mönnich tätig waren. Die Bauzeit dauerte von 1901 bis 1906, und die Bausumme, einschließlich der Nebenkosten, betrug rund 1¹/₄ Millionen Mark.

Die Verblendung der Fassade ist aus rotbraunem Jerxheimer Roggenstein hergestellt, und zu den Gliederungen wurde grauer Kalkstein aus Rothenburg a. T. verwendet. Die hohen Dächer sind mit Ziegeln in der Form von Mönch und Nonne eingedeckt; einige Metalldächer haben Bleieindeckung erhalten. Alle Decken sind massiv ausgeführt, ebenso die meisten Gewölbe mit Einschluß der die große Halle überspannenden.

228 [1906: 77]

Les formes romantiques de son architecture, ainsi que le revêtement des murs de façade en plaques de pierre donnent au palais de justice III à Berlin-Charlottenburg le caractère d'une simple et sévère monumentalité. Le grand fronton du corps central dont le toit est surmonté d'une tourelle est d'un effet saisissant. Les plans de l'edifice ont été étudiés par le conseiller P. Thömer, l'inspecteur E. Petersen et le conseiller P. Mönnich, tandisque pour la composition des façades, M. M. E. Petersen, l'architecte du gouvernement H. Dernburg et Mönnich ont prêté leur concours. La construction dura de 1901 à 1906 et les frais, y compris les dépenses accessoires, s'élevèrent à un million et quart de Marks.

Le revêtement des façades fut exécuté en pierre rouge brune de Jerxheim, tandis-que pour les membres d'architecture on employa le calcaire gris de Rothenburg sur Tauber. Les hautes toitures sont recouvertes de tuiles de la forme dite moine et nonne; quelques toits métalliques furent recouverts en plomb. Tous les planchers sont de construction massive, ainsi que la plupart des voûtes, y compris celles qui couvrent la grand halle.

228 [1906: 77]

The "Landgericht III" building in Berlin-Charlottenburg, in the Romanesque style, and with facings of sandstone is a monumental edifice of severe simplicity. The great gable of the central portion, over the roof of which a small tower rises, is most effective. The ground plans are by the Geh. Oberbaurat P. Thömer, the Landbauinspektor E. Petersen and the Baurat P. Mönnich; the facades are by E. Petersen, Reg.-Baumeister H. Dernburg and Mönnich. The time occupied was from 1901 to 1906 and the cost, including incidental expenses was 1¹/₄ Millionen Marks.

The facing of the facade is of red-brown Jerxheimer Roggenstone, and for the articulations grey limestone from Rothenburg on the Tauber has been used. The high roofs are tiled with tiles in the form of monk and nun, some metal roofs are covered with lead. All the ceilings are solid, so are most of the vaulted roofs, including the one roofing the great hall.

Die Reihe der Privathäuser am Friedrichsplatz, Ecke der Augusta-Anlagen in Mannheim sollte nach Beschluß des Magistrats eine einheitliche Architektur im Sinne des dortigen Rosengartens erhalten. Professor Dr.-Ing. Bruno Schmitz in Charlottenburg wurde mit dem Entwurfe der Fassaden beauftragt und diese den Erstehern der Grundstücke mit der Verpflichtung zur Ausführung derselben übergeben. Obgleich mehrfach im einzelnen von den angelieferten Entwürfen abgewichen wurde, so kam doch im wesentlichen ein einheitliches Straßenbild zustande. Allerdings ist dasselbe bis jetzt noch nicht ganz in der projektierten Ausdehnung zur Vollendung gekommen.

Die Fassaden sind in rotem Sandstein verblendet, die Dächer sind mit grünen Falzziegeln und die Kuppel des Turms ist mit Kupfer eingedeckt. Eine im Erdgeschoß durchgeführte, mit Korbbögen überwölbte Arkadenstellung sowie ein über dieser herlaufender, offener Balkon verbinden sämtliche Häuser, welche durch giebelbekrönte Risalite und vorgebaute Erker in Barockformen gegliedert sind. Die Ecke der Häuserreihe ist durch einen breiteren, geschwungenen Giebel, über dem sich ein als durchbrochene Laterne gestalteter Kuppelturm erhebt, wirksam bezeichnet. Die Fenster der beiden Obergeschosse sind in senkrechter Richtung zu Gruppen zusammengezogen, außerdem sind die Fassaden durch reichen Skulpturenschmuck belebt.

229 [1906: 100]

Le bloc de maisons particulières au Friedrichsplatz à Mannheim, à l'angle du Park Augusta devait d'après décision de la municipalité être traité d'une façon architecturale uniforme, dans le genre du Rosengarten de la même ville. Monsieur le Professeur Docteur Bruno Schmitz à Charlottenburg fut chargé du projet des façades et ce projet fut remis aux premiers acquéreurs des terrains avec l'obligation de s'y conformer pour l'exécution des immeubles. Quoique dans bien des cas, on n'ait pas suivi le projet dans ses détails, on a cependant obtenu un effet d'ensemble uniforme. Il est vrai de dire que le groupe n'a pas encore été entièrement exécuté d'après le projet d'ensemble.

Les façades sont revêtues de pierre de grès rouge, les toits sont recouverts de tuiles à recouvrement vertes, la coupole de la tour est revêtue de cuivre. Une galerie à arcades en arcs à anse de panier établie au rez-de-chaussée ainsi qu'un balcon découvert la surmontant relient toutes les maisons qui sont divisées au moyen d'avant-corps couronnés de frontons et de tourelles saillantes de style baroque. L'angle du bloc de maisons est énergiquement indiqué par un large fronton de ligne ondulée au dessus du quel s'élève une tour à coupole traitée en lanterne ouverte. Les fenêtres des deux étages supérieurs sont reliées entre elles verticalement; les façades sont en entre richement décorées de sculptures.

229 [1906: 100]

According to a decision of the "magistrate" (town councillor) a row of private houses was to be built at the corner of the "Augusta-Anlagen" and the "Friedrichsplatz" at Mannheim in such a style as to harmonize with the "Rosengarten" lying there. Professor Dr.-Ing. Bruno Schmitz of Charlottenburg was entrusted with the design of the facade, and subsequently with the construction of the ground plan and the execution of the whole building. Although deviating in some respects from the design as first conceived it is still a harmonious street picture, as far as it is at present completed; there still remains a portion uncompleted.

The facades are faced with red sandstone, the roofs are of green tiles and the cupola of the tower is covered with copper. The ground floor has an oval-arched arcade extending along it, over this an open balcony connects all the houses; the centre erection is crowned by a gable and has projecting bags; the whole is of the barock style. The corner of the group has a curved gable of some breadth over which is a cupola of open stone work in the form of a lantern this is very effective. The windows of the two upper storeys are united into groups by perpendicular lines; the facades are richly ornamented with sculpture.

Zu den erfreulichen Erscheinungen auf dem Gebiete des neueren deutschen Architekturschaffens gehört die stetige Zunahme der Einzelfamilienhäuser, an denen individuelle Eigenart am besten zum Ausdruck kommen kann. Ein bemerkenswertes Beispiel dieser Gattung bietet die Villa G. Krauß in Pforzheim, Friedenstraße 30, erbaut von Architekt Th. Preckel B. D. A. Der Aufbau hat etwa zehn Monat in Anspruch genommen und 30000 Mark Kosten erfordert (Tafel 40). Die Wirtschaftsräume und die Küche sind in das Kellergeschoß verlegt, letztere ist durch einen Aufzug mit dem ersten Stock verbunden. Der erste Stock enthält die Wohnräume, sämtlich von einer geräumigen, durch das zweite Stockwerk reichenden Diele zugänglich, während im zweiten Stock die Schlaf- und Kinderzimmer liegen, welche eine über die Hälfte der Diele

230 [1906: 40]

La croissance continue de la création de maisons pour une seule famille est un des éléments les plus réjouissant dans le domaine de l'architecture moderne en Allemagne, et c'est aussi dans ce domaine que l'individualité et l'originalité peuvent le mieux se montrer. La villa G. Krauss à Pforzheim Friedenstrasse 30, construite par Monsieur Th. Preckel architecte offre un exemple remarquable de ce genre d'immeubles. La construction a duré à peu près dix mois et a absorbé une somme de 30000 Marks (Pl. 40). Les locaux de service et la cuisine ont été placés au sous-sol, cette dernière est reliée au premier étage par un monte-charges. Le premier étage contient les chambres d'habitation qui sont toutes groupées autour d'un hall spacieux montant de fond au deuxième étage et communiquant avec lui, tandis

230 [1906: 40]

One of the most welcome features of modern German architecture is the steady growth of the house adapted for one family, in which style of architecture individuality can best display itself. A good example of this is the villa G. Krauss in Pforzheim at Friedenstrasse 30 built by the architect Th. Preckel. The time occupied was about ten months and the cost was 30000 Marks (see plate 40). The domestic offices and kitchen are in the basement which has a lift to the next story. The first floor contains dwelling rooms arranged round a spacious square hall reaching upwards into the second story; the second floor contains bed rooms and

hinweggeführte Galerie verbindet; endlich ist noch das Dachgeschoß zu Zimmern ausgebaut. Das Wohnzimmer im ersten Stock ist durch einen polygonal vorspringenden Erker erweitert, der im zweiten Stock mit einem offenen Balkon und einspringender Fensternische abschließt. Das Speisezimmer steht mit einer Holzveranda in Verbindung, aus welcher eine Treppe in den Garten hinabführt.

Die Fassaden zeigen teilweise eine Verblendung mit rotem Sandstein, teilweise weiße Putzflächen, und einzelne Gliederungen sind durch Farbe in blau, schwarz und gold hervorgehoben. Sämtliche Dachflächen sind in Schiefer eingedeckt. Die mäßig verwendete Ornamentik des Äußeren trägt einen modernen Charakter, während die Einzelformen der Gliederungen an mittelalterliche Formgebung anklingen. Die Malereien am Äußern und besonders die an der Eichenholztäfelung der Dielendecken sind von dem Maler Scherberger ausgeführt.

231 [1906: 93]

Die stattliche Villa Schreib, auf einem Gartengrundstück in Charlottenburg, Fasanenstraße 86 errichtet, ist ein Werk des Architekten Felix Lindhorst. Die Bauzeit dauerte von April 1905 bis Februar 1906; die Baukosten betrugen 100 000 Mark. Die durchweg in Putzbau hergestellten Fassaden des zweistöckigen Baues, an der Straßenfront durch ein vorspringendes Mittelrisalit belebt, zeigen Formen des Empirestils in moderner gefälliger Auffassung. Das in den Steilflächen mit Dachfenstern ausgestattete Mansarddach ist mit Biberschwänzen eingedeckt.

232 [1906: 81]

Das Geschäfts- und Wohnhaus Zacherl in Wien, Bauernmarkt 5, ist nach dem Entwurfe des Architekten Josef Plecnik etwa im Laufe eines Jahres errichtet. Die Fassade ist in den oberen Geschossen mit geschliffenen, graublauen Granitplatten bekleidet. Die von Prof. Metzner modellierten Karyatiden unter dem Dachgesims sowie dieses selbst bestehen aus Steinzeug, während das Dach eine Bekleidung von Kupfer erhalten hat.

que les chambres à coucher et les chambres d'enfants sont situées au second étage; ces pièces sont reliées entre elles par une galerie conduisante au travers de la moitié du hall. Enfin le toit contient encore des chambres. La chambre d'habitation au premier étage est augmentée de la surface d'une tourelle polygonale en saillie; cette tourelle forme au second étage balcon découvert avec bow-window. La salle-à-manger est reliée à une veranda en bois qui communique avec le jardin par un escalier.

Les façades sont en partie revêtues de pierre rouge, en partie crépies en blanc: quelques détails sont rehaussés de couleur en bleu, noir et or. Toutes les surfaces du toit sont recouvertes en ardoises. La décoration extérieure, employée avec beaucoup de réserve est traitée dans un esprit moderne, tandis que le détail des différents motifs se rapproche du style du Moyenâge. Les peintures à l'extérieur ainsi que celles qui décorent le plafond en boiserie du hall sont dues au peintre Scherberger.

231 [1906: 93]

L'imposante villa Schreib construite dans un jardin à Charlottenburg, Fasanenstrasse 86 est une œuvre de l'architecte Felix Lindhorst. La construction dura du mois d'avril 1905 à celui de février 1906; les frais s'élevèrent à 100000 Marks. Les façades de cette maison comprenant deux étages sont entièrement construites en maçonnerie crépie, la façade sur la rue est agrémentée d'un corps central saillant, elles sont traitées dans les formes du style empire, dans un sentiment moderne très artistique. Le toit mansard pourvu de lucarnes dans sa partie abrupte est recouvert en tuiles.

232 [1906: 81]

La maison de commerce et d'habitation Zacherl à Vienne, Bauernmarkt 5, a été construite dans l'espace d'un an environ, d'après les plans de Monsieur Josef Plecnik architecte. La façade est aux étages supérieurs revêtue de plaques de granit gris-bleu polies. Les cariatides sous la corniche modelées par le professeur Metzner, ainsi que la corniche elle-même sont en pierre artificielle, tandis que le toit a été recouvert en cuivre.

nursery leading from a gallery going half round the hall; the roof story contains additional rooms. The drawing room on the first floor has a polygonal projecting bay, over which is a balcony leading from the second floor, open and finished off with projecting window niches. The dining room leads on to a wooden verandah from which steps lead into the garden.

The facades are partly faced with red sandstone and partly of white plastered surfaces, certain architectural articulations are of blue, black and gold colour. All the roofs are of slate. The moderately used ornament of the exterior is strictly modern in character, while many of the details are medieval in form. The painting of the exterior, and that of the oak panelling of the hall is by the painter Scherberger.

231 [1906: 93]

The stately villa Schreib, built on a garden site at Fasanenstrasse 86, Charlottenburg, is the work of the architect Felix Lindhorst. The time occupied was from April 1905 to February 1906 and the cost amounted to 100000 Marks. The villa consists of two storeys and is entirely of plaster; the facade on the street frontage is varied by a projecting middle risalit, the style is Empire with an agreeable modern modification. The steep roof is tiled with flat red tiles.

232 [1906: 81]

The business premises and dwelling house Zacherl at Bauernmarkt 5, Vienna have been built in the course of a year according to the design of the architect Josef Plecnik. The upper part of the facade is faced with carved grey-blue granite slabs. The Caryatides under the roof cornice, modelled by Professor Metzner, are as well as the cornice of stone; the roof has a covering of copper.

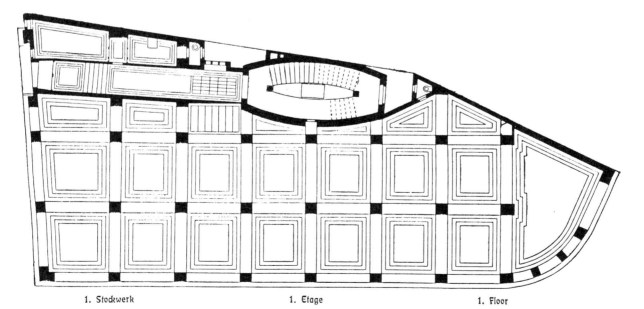

| 1. Stockwerk | 1. Étage | 1. Floor |

Erdgeschoß und Mezzanin sind ganz zu Geschäftszwecken eingerichtet und nur durch Pfeilerstellungen geteilt, dagegen sind die vier oberen Geschosse zu Wohnungen bestimmt. Sämtliche Pfeiler und Decken sind in Eisen und Beton hergestellt.

Le rez-de-chaussée et l'entresol ont été entièrement distribués en locaux de commerce et sont seulement divisés par des colonnes, par contre, les quatre étages supérieurs ont été arrangés en appartements. Tous les piliers et plafonds ont été construits en béton armé.

The ground floor and intermediate storey are used entirely for business purposes and are separated only by pillars; the upper storeys are arranged as dwellings. All the pillars and ceilings are of iron and beton.

Als allseitig freiliegender Renaissancebau von bedeutenden Abmessungen, mit vier Flügeln einen Hof umschließend, erscheint das Gebäude der Österreich-Ungarischen Bank in Budapest, welches von dem Architekten Ignacy Alpar entworfen und in einer Bauzeit von drei Jahren für die Kostensumme von 4500000 Kronen errichtet wurde.

Die in gelblichem Siebenbürgener Sandstein ausgeführten, reich mit Säulenstellungen und figürlichen Reliefs geschmückten, zweistöckigen Fassaden erheben sich über einem Sockel von bossiertem Quaderwerk und tragen noch eine in Friesform ausgebildete Halbetage. Die Bekrönung des ganz in Stein ausgeführten, 1,45 Meter ausladenden Hauptgesimses wird durch turmartige Aufbauten über den Eck- und Mittelrisaliten, welch letztere einen Giebel und in den Rücklagen Balustraden einschließen, gebildet. Die Figurenfriese sind von Bildhauer Karl Senyei, die Köpfe der Schlußsteine von Bildhauer Eduard Mayer gefertigt.

Das Erdgeschoß enthält in der Mitte des Vorderflügels den Haupteingang, welcher zu einem Vestibül und zu einer anschließenden geräumigen Vorhalle führt, aus welcher in der Mittelachse die Haupttreppe und seitwärts zwei Nebentreppen zu den Obergeschossen aufsteigen. An den Seitenfronten liegen die Einfahrt zum Hof und zwei Eingänge zu den Wohnungen, welche in einem der Seitenflügel und einem Teil des rückwärts gelegenen Flügels angeordnet sind. An den abgestumpften Ecke und im anderen Seitenflügel sind Kassenräume und Zimmer für die Verwaltung eingerichtet. Der Tresor, welcher rings mit einem Beobachtungsgange umgeben ist, bildet den mittleren Teil des rückwärts gelegenen Flügels. Der erste Stock wird, außer von einer

---

Le bâtiment de la banque austro-hongroise à Buda-Pest, bâtie dans l'espace de trois ans pour la somme de 4500000 couronnes, d'après les plans de l'architecte Ignacy Alpar se présente en monument de style Renaissance, de dimensions considérables, libre de tous côtés et composé de quatre ailes entourant une cour.

Les façades de deux étages exécutées en pierre jaune de Siebenburg, richement décorées d'ordres de colonnes et de sculptures en relief, se dressent sur un socle de pierres en bossage et portent un étage bas, traité en forme de frise. La corniche est entièrement construite en pierre, elle fait une saillie de 1,45 mètres, elle est couronnée de surélévations en forme de tours aux angles et au corps central, ce dernier est surmonté d'un fronton et de balustrades en retrait. La frise décorée de figures est l'œuvre du sculpteur Karl Senyei; le sculpteur Eduard Mayer a exécuté les têtes des clefs.

Le rez-de-chaussée contient au milieu de l'aile centrale, l'entrée principale qui conduit à un vestibule et à une vaste halle adjacente; à partie de cette dernière, s'élèvent dans l'axe central l'escalier principal et latéralement, deux escaliers secondaires qui conduisent aux étages supérieurs. Sur les faces latérales se trouvent la porte cochère conduisant dans la cour et deux entrées pour les appartements, lesquels sont distribués dans une des ailes latérales et dans une partie de l'aile située en arrière. Des chambres pour l'administration et des bureaux de caisse ont été disposés à l'angle coupé et dans l'autre aile latérale. Le trésor entouré d'un chemin de ronde forme la partie centrale de l'aile postérieure. Le premier étage est

---

The building of the "Österreich-Ungarischen Bank in Budapest" was designed by the architect Ignacy Alpar, occupied three years to build and cost 4500000 Kronen. It is a free-standing Renaiscence building of important dimensions consisting of four wings surrounding a courtyard.

The material is of yellowish Siebenbürgen sandstone, the facade, richly ornamented with pillars and sculptural figures, is two storeys high and rises from a sockel of bossed square stones. There is, in addition an intermediate storey of half the height. The upper part is crowned with a rich moulding, projecting 1,45 meters, over which are towerlike erections over the corner and middle building. The frieze is by the Sculptor Karl Senyei, the capitals of the Raystones by Eduard Mayer.

The ground floor contains in the centre of the front wing the principal entrance, which leads to a vestibule and to a spacious anteroom from which in the middle the principal staircase ascends, sidewards are two secondary staircases leading to the upper storeys. On the side frontages are the entrance to the courtyard and two entrances to the dwellings which occupy the side wings and part of the back building. On the corner and other side wings are rooms for the cash, and for the administration. The tresor which is surrounded by a gallery for constant watch is in the middle

---

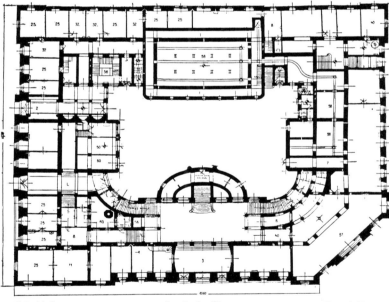

Erdgeschoß   Rez-de-chaussée   Ground Floor

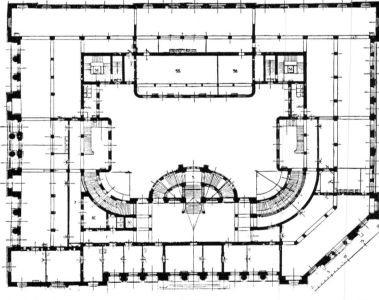

1. Stockwerk   1. Étage   1. Floor

---

in der Mittelachse des Vorderflügels sich über der unteren Halle wiederholenden größeren Vorhalle, ganz von den Geschäftsräumen der Bank eingenommen. Das Innere des Gebäudes zeigt eine vornehme Ausstattung sowie massiv überwölbte Gänge und Treppenläufe.

---

entièrement consacré aux locaux de la banque, à l'exception d'un grand vestibule situé dans l'axe du corps central, au dessus de la halle du bas. L'intérieur du bâtiment montre une décoration pleine de distinction, les corridors et les escaliers sont recouverts de voûtes massives.

---

part of the back wing. The whole of the first floor, except a large vestibule in the middle of the front over the lower vestibule, is occupied by the bank. The interior is handsomely fitted up and the stairs and vaulted corridors are all solid and massive.

Die Fassaden des Hauses der Kaufmannschaft in Wien, Lothringerstraße 10 und Schwarzenbergplatz 7, zeigen die Wiederaufnahme des flotten, altwienerischen Barockstils. Das Erdgeschoß und das nächstfolgende Stockwerk sind einfach gequadert; das zweite und dritte Stockwerk sind mittelst der Fensterarchitektur zusammengezogen, und die großen ionischen

---

Les façades de la maison de l'association de marchands à Vienne, Lothringerstrasse 10 et Schwarzenbergplatz 7 montrent la reprise de l'ancien baroque viennois, style hardiment décoratif. Le rez-de-chaussée et l'étage au dessus sont en simple bossage; le second et le troisième étages sont liés l'un à l'autre au moyen de l'architecture encadrant

---

The "Hauses der Kaufmannschaft" at Lothringerstrasse 10 and Schwarzenbergplatz 7 Vienna shows in its facade that a revival has taken place of the smart Old-Vienna Barock style. The ground-floor and the next storey are of simple square stones; the second and third storeys are united externally

---

Pilaſter des Mittelriſalits der Hauptfront durch-
ſeßen das zweite und dritte ſowie noch ein viertes
oberſtes Stockwerk und tragen über dem Hauptgeſims eine Attika, welche teils in geſchwungenen
Formen, teils als Baluſtrade ausgebildet iſt. In
derſelben Art wiederholt ſich die Attika über der
Seitenfront. Entwurf und Ausführung des Gebäudes ſind von dem Architekten Ernſt
von Gotthilf bewirkt; die Bauzeit erſtreckte
ſich durch zwei Jahre, und die Baukoſten betrugen
einſchließlich der Saaldekoration und der Bureau-
einrichtungen 580 000 Kronen.

les fenêtres, tandis que les grands pilastres
ioniques de l'avant-corps du centre de la façade
principale traversent le second, le troisième et
un quatrième étages et portent au dessus de la
corniche principale une attique; laquelle se
termine en lignes ondulées d'une part, en balustrade d'autre part. L'attique se répète sous la
même forme au dessus de la façade latérale.
Les plans et l'exécution sont l'œuvre de l'architecte Ernst de Gotthilf; la durée de la construction dura deux ans, les frais s'élevèrent
à 580 000 Couronnes, y compris la décoration
de la salle et l'installation des bureaux.

by the window architecture, and the large
Jonic pillars of the centre erection extend
through the second third and fourth storeys
and have, over the principal moulding an
"Attika" which is built out partly as a balustrade. In the same style is the "Attika" over
the side frontage. The design and execution
of the building are by the architect Ernst
von Gotthilf; the time occupied was two
years, and the cost of building including the
decoration of the hall and the bureau fittings
amounted to 580 000 Kronen.

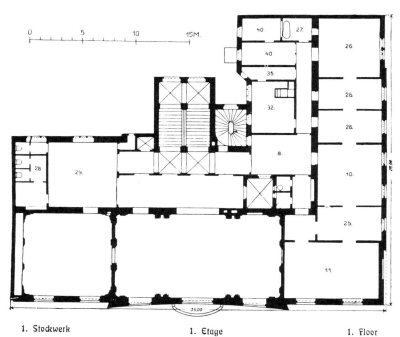

1. Stockwerk   1. Etage   1. Floor

Im erſten Stock, zu dem eine doppelarmige
Treppe emporführt, liegen der noch durch das
zweite Stockwerk reichende Feſtſaal (A), dann ein
Sißungsſaal (B), begleitet von einem Vorraum mit
anſchließender Garderobe, und außerdem eine
geräumige, von den Feſt- und Geſchäftsräumen
getrennte Wohnung. In den übrigen Stockwerken
ſind hauptſächlich Verwaltungsräume untergebracht.

Das Äußere des Gebäudes iſt durch ein ſäulen-
flankiertes Portal mit einem ſich darüber erhebenden Fenſterausbau und durch Figurengruppen und Vaſen, welche die Attika bekrönen,
ausgezeichnet.

Au premier étage, auquel conduit un escalier
à deux bras, se trouvent la salle des fêtes
montant de fond à travers le deuxième étage,
une salle de séances accompagnée d'un vestibule
et d'un vestiaire adjacent ainsi qu'un spacieuse
appartement séparé des locaux de fête et de
travail. Dans les autres étages on a surtout
disposé des locaux d'administration.

L'extérieur du monument se distingue par
un portail flanqué de colonnes surmonté d'un
avant-corps en bow-window ainsi que par une
décoration de groupes de figures et de vases
couronnant l'attique.

On the first floor, to which a double staircase
ascends, is the large banquetting hall reaching
through two storeys, next comes a committee
room with an ante room and cloak room adjoining, and in addition a spacions dwelling
quite separate from the rest of the business
and other rooms. In the other storeys are
principally the offices of the administration.

The exterior is further enhanced in dignity
by a pillared portal over which is an important
window, and by sculptural groups and vases
which crown the "Attika".

235 [1906; 78]

Ebenſo durch maleriſchen Aufbau wie durch
reiche Farbenwirkung des Äußern zeichnet
ſich die von dem Architekten Aladar Arkay
im modern ungariſchen Stile erbaute Villa in

235 [1906; 78]

La villa Andrassystrasse 127a à Buda-
Pest, construite en style moderne hongrois
par Monsieur Aladar Arkay, architecte, se
distingue autant par sa silhouette pittoresque que

235 [1906; 78]

The villa, built at Andrassystrasse 127a,
Budapest by the architect Aladar
Arkay is distinguished both by the pictu-
resque erection and by the effective colouring

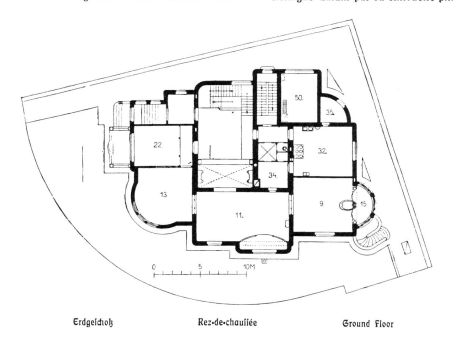

Erdgeſchoß   Rez-de-chauſſée   Ground Floor

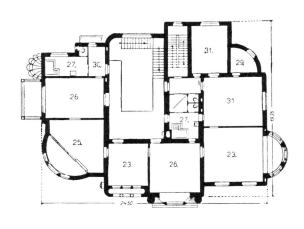

1. Stockwerk   1. Etage   1. Floor

Budapeſt, Andraſſyſtraße 127a aus. Der Bau wurde im Laufe eines Jahres unter der Spezialleitung des Architekten J. Spacel vollendet und koſtete 150000 Kronen, ohne Einrechnung der inneren Einrichtung und des Grundwertes.

Es iſt ein Backſteinbau mit gelbem Mörtelputz des Äußeren, in Glasmoſaik hergeſtellten Flachornamenten und aus Majolika gebildeten, blau, grün und weiß gehaltenen, teilweiſe vergoldeten Säulen, Pilaſtern, Logglabögen, Dachfenſtern und Firſtbekrönungen. Das Dach iſt mit Schiefer gedeckt, während Kuppel und Erkerdächer mit vergoldetem Kupferblech überzogen ſind.

Im Erdgeſchoß liegen die Empfangsräume, die Diele mit der Treppe, der Speiſeſaal mit gewölbter Decke, der Salon mit Wintergarten u. a. Im erſten Stockwerk ſind Wohn- und Schlafräume der Familie untergebracht, und das Dachgeſchoß iſt zu Bureauräumen ausgenutzt. Das Haus beſitzt eine Niederdruckdampfheizung und elektriſche Beleuchtung.

236 [1906: 99]

Die Anlage einer offenen, in leicht geſchwungener Linie ausgebogenen, dem zurückſpringenden mittleren Teil der Hauptfront vorgelegten Pfeilerhalle ſichert der von den Architekten Prof. Hackhofer und Rumpelmayer errichteten Villa des Dr. Marbach in Dornbach bei Wien eine vornehme Geſamtwirkung. Über der Pfeilerhalle, ihrer ganzen Ausdehnung nach, erſtreckt ſich eine offene Terraſſe. Das über der Mittelpartie der Vorderfront gegen die Dächer der vorſpringenden Eckbauten emporgehobene, überhängende Manſarddach gab Gelegenheit zur Anlage einer oberen Halbetage. Die Einzelformen der Villa zeigen eine freie Auffaſſung des Empireſtils.

237 [1906: 47]

Als ein individuell, wenn auch ohne beſonderen Aufwand ausgeſtalteter Wohnſitz zeigt ſich die Villa Heerdweg 101 in Darmſtadt, von Profeſſor H. Metzendorf in Bensheim entworfen und in einer Bauzeit von 1½ Jahren für 35000 Mark Baukoſten zur Ausführung gebracht. Die Wohnräume im Erdgeſchoß ſind von einer Diele zugänglich; der Salon iſt durch einen Erkerausbau erweitert, und an das Eßzimmer ſchließt ſich ein Wintergarten an. Das Obergeſchoß enthält die Schlafzimmer (Tafel 47).

par la riche coloration de son extérieur. Le bâtiment fut élevé dans l'espace d'un an, sous la direction spéciale de l'architecte, J. Spacel et coûta 150000 couronnes, sans compter les aménagements intérieurs et le terrain.

C'est une construction en maçonnerie de briques crépie en mortier jaune à l'extérieur, dont la décoration consiste principalement en ornements plats de mosaïque de verre et de faïence et en colonnes, pilastres, arcs de loggias lucarnes et crêtes de toits en partie dorés, en partie peints en bleu, vert et blanc.

Les salles de réception, le hall avec escalier, la salle à manger avec plafond voûté, le salon avec jardin d'hiver etc. se trouvent au rez-de-chaussée. Le premier étage contient les chambres à coucher et d'habitation, tandis que des comptoirs ont été installés sous le toit. La maison est pourvue d'un calorifère à vapeur à basse pression et de lumière électrique.

236 [1906: 99]

La disposition d'un portique ouvert, supporté par des piliers, légèrement cintré placé en avant de la partie du centre en retrait donne à la villa du Docteur Marbach à Dornbach près Vienne un grand caractère de distinction, cette villa a été construite par les architectes Professeur Hackhofer et Rumpelmayer. Au dessus du portique et sur toute sa longueur règne une terrasse découverte. Le toit mansard situé au dessus du corps central de la façade principale, et suspendu entre les toits des deux ailes latérales saillantes offrit l'occasion d'établir un étage bas. Le détail de la villa est traité dans l'esprit d'une interprétation libre du style Empire.

237 [1906: 47]

La villa Heerdweg 101 à Darmstadt a été construite par le Professeur H. Metzendorf de Bensheim et d'après ses plans, dans l'espace d'un an et demi, pour la somme de 35000 Marks. Cette construction montre beaucoup d'originalité malgré la dépense limitée. Les pièces d'habitation du rez-de-chaussée sont accessibles depuis hall; le salon est augmenté de la surface d'un bow-window et un jardin, d'hiver s'ajoute à la salle à manger. L'étage supérieur contient les chambres à coucher (Pl. 47).

of the exterior. It is in modern Hungarian style, occupied one year to build under the superintendence of the architect J. Spacel, and cost 150000 Kronen exclusive of interior fittings and the site.

It is a brick building, with yellow plaster for the exterior; the flat ornamentation is of blue, green and white glass mosaic and majolika; the pillars, pilasters, bays and roof gables are partly gilded. The roof is of slate, the cupola and roofs of the bays are of gilded copper.

The reception rooms are on the ground floor, as is too the square hall from which the staircase leads, the dining room with a vaulted roof the drawing room with conservatory etc. On the first floor are dwelling rooms and bed rooms, the roof storey is arranged as bureaus. The house has low pressure heating apparatus and electric light.

236 [1906: 99]

The architects Professor Hackhofer and Rumpelmayer have built a villa for Dr. Marbach at Dornbach near Vienna. The villa has on the principal front a pillared vestibule projecting in the middle of the building from the receding centre, this adds greatly to the distinction of its appearance. Over this pillared hall is an open terrace extending to its full length. The erection of the roof storey with the projecting corners has given the architect an opportunity for planing an upper intermediate story. The general style of the building is Empire.

237 [1906: 47]

The villa, Heerdweg 101, Darmstadt, built by Professor H. Metzendorf of Bensheim, although unpretentious in style is yet distinguished by a certain individuality. The time occupied was 1½ years and the cost amounted to 30000 Marks. The living rooms on the ground floor are arranged round a square hall, the drawing room is enlarged by a bay and the dining room has an entrance into the conservatory. The upper stories contain the bed rooms (see plate 47).

Erdgeſchoß   Rez-de-chauſſée   Ground floor

Die maleriſche Wirkung des Aufbaues wird durch einen polygonalen, turmartigen Dacherker, durch den offenen Altan und die Giebel an den beiden Hauptfronten bedingt. Die Umfaſſungs-

Le caractère pittoresque de l'ensemble est obtenu au moyen du couronnement d'une tourelle polygonale, au moyen d'une loggia ouverte et des pignons des deux faces principales. Les

The picturesque effect of the elevation is the result of the polygonal corner tower, and of the open balcony with the gables over the two principal frontages. The boundary wall of the

mauern des Keller- und Erdgeſchoſſes beſtehen aus Heigenbrücker Buntſandſtein; die Giebelwände ſind mit Ziegeln bekleidet und die Dächer mit roten Biberſchwänzen eingedeckt.

238 [1906; 7]

An der Friedrich Karlſtraße in Mannheim hat Carl Wittmann im Zeitraum eines Jahres eine Häuſergruppe erbaut, die er durch eine einheitliche Architektur zuſammengefaßt hat (Tafel 7). Mit Geſchick iſt er der Einförmigkeit der langgeſtreckten Faſſade durch Einſchaltung eines turmartigen Mittelbaues, durch Erker und der Betonung der Ecke durch einen halbrunden Ausbau begegnet. Das Erdgeſchoß enthält Geſchäftslokale und Läden, die oberen Geſchoſſe Mietwohnungen. Die Details der Faſſade, die in rotem Mainſandſtein ausgeführt iſt, ſchließen ſich an die ſüddeutſche Spätrenaiſſance an.

Die Baukoſten betrugen 260000 Mark.

239 [1906; 83]

An den Faſſaden des Wohn- und Geſchäftshauſes Windmühlengaſſe 24 in Wien hat der Architekt desſelben, K. K. Baurat O. Marmorek, den gelungenen Verſuch gemacht, die im Empireſtil gehaltenen Motive vom Mittelriſalit des früher an dieſer Stelle ſtehenden, zu Anfang des 19. Jahrhunderts von Hofbaumeiſter Jäger erbauten Hauſes wieder zu verwenden, und hat mit dieſem Vorgehen eine ganz modern anmutende Wirkung für den Neubau erzielt. Die Bauzeit nahm etwa acht Monate in Anſpruch, und die Baukoſten betrugen 160000 Kronen.

Für die ganz in Putzbau durchgeführten Faſſaden des fünfſtöckigen Hauſes ſind beſonders die flachrund vorſpringenden, durch drei Obergeſchoſſe reichenden Erker, dann der vor dem vierten Obergeſchoſſe durchlaufende Balkon und endlich die halbrunden Dachgiebel bezeichnend. Im Erdgeſchoß ſind Läden, in ſämtlichen Obergeſchoſſen Wohnungen angeordnet.

240 [1907; 2]

Das ausgedehnte, von zwei Straßen zugängliche, mehrere Höfe umſchließende Geſchäftshaus der Allgemeinen Elektrizitäts-Geſellſchaft in Berlin iſt von Architekt Profeſſor

---

murs des caves et du rez-de-chaussée sont en pierre de couleur de Heigenbrück; les façades des frontons sont revêtues en briques et les toits sont recouverts en tuiles rouges.

238 [1906; 7]

Monsieur Carl Wittmann, a bâti dans une année à la Friedrich Karlstrasse à Mannheim un groupe de maisons qu'il a reliées entre elles par une architecture uniforme (Planches 7). Il a évité avec une grande habileté la monotonie d'une longue façade, en l'interrompant par un corps central en forme de tour, par des tourelles et en accentuant l'angle au moyen d'un avant corps de forme arrondie. Le rez-de-chaussée contient des locaux de commerce et des magasins, les étages supérieurs des appartements à louer. Les détails des façades qui sont exécutées en pierre rouge du Main sont traités dans l'esprit de la renaissance tardive de l'Allemagne du Sud.

Les frais de construction s'élevèrent à 260000 Marks.

239 [1906; 83]

Monsieur O. Marmorek architecte conseiller imperial a fait pour les façades de la maison de commerce et d'habitation Windmühlengasse 24 à Vienne l'intéressante tentative d'employer dans la nouvelle construction le motif de l'avant-corps central de la maison autrefois située à cette place, cet immeuble de style empire avait été construite au commencement du 19me siècle par l'architecte de la cour Jäger. L'architecte a ainsi obtenu un charmant effet moderne dans sa composition. La construction exigea huit mois environ et absorba une somme de 160000 Couronnes.

Les tourelles en saillie de segment de cercle traversant trois étages, ainsi que les balcons régnant sur tout le front au quatrième étage et enfin le fronton demi circulaire sont les motifs caractéristiques des façades de cet édifice comprenant cinq étages et entièrement construit en maçonnerie crépie. Au rez-de-chaussée se trouvent des magasins, tandis que les étages supérieurs ont été distribués en appartements.

240 [1907; 2]

La vaste maison d'administration de la société générale d'électricité à Berlin, accessible de deux rues et entourant plusieurs cours a été composée par Monsieur le Professeur

---

basement and ground floor is of Heigenbrück coloured sandstone, the walls of the gables are faced with tiles and the roofs are covered with flat red tiles.

238 [1906; 7]

During one year Carl Wittmann has built a group of houses in the Friedrich Carlstrasse, Mannheim which form one harmonious building (see plate 7). He has cleverly avoided the monotony of a long facade by introducing a tower-like middle erection, and a half circular corner bay. The ground floor contains business premises and shops, the upper floors are let as flats. The style is late South German Renaissance; the facade is of red Main sandstone.

The cost of building amounted to 260000 Marks.

239 [1906; 83]

The dwelling and business house Windmühlengasse 24, Vienna, has been built by the Baurat O. Marmorek in a period of eight months, at a cost of 160000 Kronen. The architect set himself the task of utilizing the middle risalit of a house in Empire style which stood formerly on the same site, and which was built by the Court Baumeister Jäger at the beginning of the 19th century. He has been most successful, and the new building is an effective modern edifice.

The house is five storeys high, the facades are of plaster; specially effective are the half-round projecting bays extending through three storeys the balcony extending along the 4th storey and lastly, the half-round roof gable. The ground floor is arranged for shops, the upper storeys contain dwellings.

240 [1907; 2]

The premises of the Allgemeine Elektrizitäts-Gesellschaft at Berlin are very extensive, having entrances from two streets and containing several large courtyards. They were

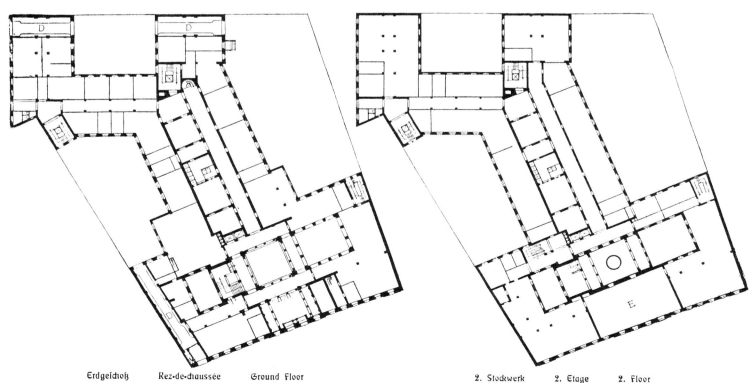

Erdgeſchoß   Rez-de-chaussée   Ground Floor   2. Stockwerk   2. Etage   2. Floor

H. Meffel entworfen und gelangte vom Oktober 1905 bis Oktober 1906 zur Ausführung. Die Bauptfront hat eine durch das Erdgeschoß und drei Obergeschosse gehende, kräftige Pfeilergliederung erhalten und ist in Bartershofener Kalkstein und Puß hergestellt. Die Fenster des ersten und zweiten Obergeschosses sind in senkrechter Richtung zusammengezogen. Das vorspringende Mittelrisalit ist mit einem Dreiecksgiebel bekrönt; ein viertes Geschoß wird durch einen schmalen Dachstreifen von den unteren Bauptgeschossen getrennt; über der Dachdurchschneidung erhebt sich ein Dachreitertürmchen in Tempelform. Die Fronten der Böfe sind in Cottaer Sandstein und Pußflächen ausgeführt.

Sämtliche Geschosse sind zu Geschäftsräumen verwendet; außerdem liegen im ersten Obergeschoß die Zimmer der Direktion und zwei Konferenzsäle; im zweiten Obergeschoß ist ein Sißungssaal (E) untergebracht. Der im Erdgeschoß inmitten der Bauptfront angeordneten Eingangshalle schließt sich unmittelbar ein Lichthof an, und seitwärts von diesem ein zweiter, durch eine Passage getrennter, während an der entgegengesetzten Seite die Bauptreppe aufsteigt. In den Flügeln sind noch mehrere Treppen sowie Aufzüge verteilt. Die Böfe sind mittelst Durchfahrten (D) zugänglich gemacht.

241, 242 [1907: 8, 9]

Auf einem Grundstück von geringer Tiefe, aber bedeutender Längenausdehnung erhebt sich das Wohnhaus „Zu den drei Lerchen" in Wien, Lerchengasse 3 und 5, welches nach dem Entwurfe des k. k. Baurats Osk. Marmorek in etwa sieben Monaten für die Kostensumme von 180000 Kronen erbaut wurde. Die Fassade ist in Pußbau ausgeführt und zeigt moderne, an den Empirestil anklingende Formenbildung. Die Pußflächen sind teils glatt durch Streifen gegliedert, teils tropfsteinartig oder in grober Körnung behandelt. Zwei flach viereckig vorspringende Erker durchsetzen die vier oberen Stockwerke und schließen einen flachrund aus-

H. Messel et fut exécutée du mois d'octobre 1905 à celui d'octobre 1906. La façade principale a été divisée par de vigoureux piliers traversant le rez-de-chaussée et les trois étages supérieurs, elle est exécutée en pierre calcaire de Hartershofen et en maçonnerie crépie. Les fenêtres du premier et du second étage sont reliées l'une à l'autre dans le sens vertical.

L'avant corps central saillant est couronné par un fronton triangulaire; un quatrième étage est séparé des étages principaux inférieurs, au moyen d'une bande de toit étroite; au dessus du point d'intersection des toits s'élève une petite tour en forme de temple. Les façades des cours sont en pierre de Cotta et en surfaces crépies. Tous les étages sont disposés en comptoirs; en outre les chambres de la direction et deux salles de conférences se trouvent au premier étage; au deuxième, une salle de séances (E). Une cour communique directement avec la halle d'entrée située au rez-de-chaussée au milieu de la façade principale; à côté de cette cour s'en ouvre une seconde séparée par un passage, tandis que du côté opposé l'escalier principale s'élève. Dans les ailes sont encore disposés plusieurs escaliers et ascenseurs. Les cours sont accessibles par des passages à voitures (D).

241, 242 [1907: 8, 9]

La maison d'habitation „aux trois alouettes", Lerchengasse 3 et 5 à Vienne, construite d'après les plans de l'architecte conseiller Oskar Marmorek, se trouve sur un terrain de largeur restreinte, mais d'une profondeur considérable; cet immeuble fut élevé dans l'espace de sept mois environ pour la somme de 180000 Couronnes. La façade est exécutée en maçonnerie crépie et montre une décoration moderne, inspirée du style empire. Les surfaces de crépissage sont en partie lisses et divisées en bandes, en partie traitées en stalactites ou en gros grain. Deux tourelles saillantes plates et carrées traversent

designed by the architect Professor H. Messel and occupied the time from October 1905 to October 1906 in building. The principal front is distinguished by massive pillars extending through the ground floor and the three upper floors; the material is Hartershofen limestone and plaster. The windows of the first and second upper storeys are drawn together in a perpendicular direction. The projecting middle risalit is crowned with a triangular gable; a fourth storey is separated by a small roof erection from the lower principal storeys; over the division in the roof is a tower erected in the form of a temple. The courtyard frontages are of Cotta sandstone and plaster.

Every floor is equipped as business premises; on the first floor is a room for the Board of Directors and two conference rooms; in the second storey is a committee room (E). The entrance hall is in the middle of the principal front and leads directly to a skylighted hall from this on the side, a second hall is reached through a passage; and on the other side the principal staircase ascends. In the side wings are several staircases and lifts. The courtyards are all accessible by thoroughfares (D) to the street.

241, 242 [1907: 8, 9]

The dwelling house "Zu den drei Lerchen", Lerchengasse 3 and 5 at Vienna is built on a site of inconsiderable depth, but of extensive length, according to the plan of the Imperial Baurat Oskar Marmorek. The house occupied seven months in building and cost 180000 Kronen. The facade is of plaster, and shows in its modern forms considerable resemblance to the Empire style. The plaster surfaces are partly smooth and articulated by stripes, or are coarsely grained to imitate stalactites. Two flat four-cornered projecting bays are continued through

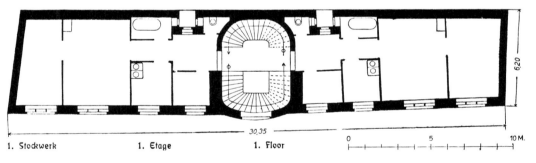

<table>
<tr><td>1. Stockwerk</td><td>1. Etage</td><td>1. Floor</td><td>30,35   629   0   5   10 M.</td></tr>
</table>

gebogenen, mittleren Fassadenteil zwischen sich ein. Die Erker sowohl, wie der flachrunde Vorsprung sind wagrecht durch ein Gesims abgeschlossen, und über ihnen biegt sich das Bauptgesims zu einem flachen Dreiecksgiebel auf.

Binter dem ausgeschwungenen Fassadenteil liegen das Vestibül und die mit Wendelstufen versehene einzige Treppe, leßtere die in jedem Geschosse vorhandenen, von Vorpläßen zugänglichen beiden Wohnungen trennend. Der geringen Tiefe des Grundstücks halber konnte nur eine Reihe von der Straßenfront aus beleuchteter Zimmer angeordnet werden, jedoch erhalten die Baderäume und Klosetts von den in ganzer Böhe des Gebäudes durchgeführten kleinen Lichthöfen aus Beleuchtung. Im ersten Stock ergeben sich zwei an der Binterseite des Treppenhauses gelegene fensterlose Räume.

243 [1907: 3]

Aus einer größeren Anzahl von Villenbauten, welche in der Villenkolonie „Klingenteich" in Beidelberg von den Architekten

les quatre étages supérieurs et encadrent entre eux un motif central de façade arrondi en forme de segment. Les tourelles, ainsi que la partie de façade en saillie circulaire sont terminées par une corniche horizontale: au-dessus, cette corniche se relève et forme un fronton triangulaire plat.

Le vestibule et le seul escalier de la maison, pourvu de marches tournantes se trouvent derrière la partie arrondie de la façade; cet escalier se retrouve à tous les étages, accessible des vestibules et séparant les deux appartements. Par suite du peu de largeur du terrain à bâtir, on n'a pu installer que peu de pièces recevant leur jour de la façade sur la rue; cependant, les chambres de bain et les water-closets sont éclairés et aérés par de petites cours percées sur toute la hauteur de l'édifice. Au premier étage se trouvent deux pièces situées en arrière de la cage d'escalier, non pourvues de fenêtres.

243 [1907: 3]

Nous allons publier ici deux exemples choisis entre un grand nombre de maisons de campagne que Messieurs Kumpf et Wolf architectes

four upper storeys and enclose a rounded centre part of the facade between them. The bays, as well as the rounded projection are finished off horizontally by a moulding, and over this, the principal moulding is curved upwards over a triangular flat gable.

Behind the projecting facade erection is the vestibule and the staircase which is made in a spiral form. From this staircase on each floor leads an entrance hall belonging to the separate dwellings. On account of the narrowness of the site, only one row of rooms lighted from the street could be built; the bath rooms and lavatories are however lighted by a skylight which is constructed through all the storeys. On the first floor are two window-less rooms lying at the back of the hall.

243 [1907: 3]

Out of a large number of villas, designed and built for the villa colony "Klingenteich" in Heidelberg by the architects Kumpf

Kumpf und Wolf dafelbft entworfen und ausgeführt find, werden hier zwei Beifpiele in Abbildungen vorgeführt.

Die Villa E. Wolf, Unter der Schanz 2, im Laufe eines Sommers für die Summe von 35 000 M., einfchließlich der Stützmauern, Einfriedigung und Gartenanlage, hergeftellt, zeichnet fich durch einfache, gefällige Gruppenbildung aus. Der Sockel befteht aus rotem, geflammtem Neckarftein in weißer Fugung; die oberen Sandfteingliederungen find in rotem, geflammtem Hetzbacher Odenwaldftein ausgeführt. Es ift am Äußern eine reiche Farbenwirkung angeftrebt, indem die eichenen Schindeln goldbraun lafiert, die Fachwerke und Dachüberftände dunkelolivengrün geftrichen find. Die Ortbretter haben weiße Färbung mit roten Einfaffungen erhalten; die Schnitzereien erfcheinen in rot und gelb. Fenfter und Blumengalerie im Giebel find weiß, die Läden dunkelrot mit weißen Füllungen und aufgemalten Rofenkränzen, Rinnen und Abfallröhren wieder weiß und die fchmiedeeifernen Gitter weißgrün gehalten. Die oberen Mauerflächen find weiß gepußt, während ein feitlicher Anbau teilweife befchindeltes Holzfachwerk zeigt.

à Heidelberg ont élevées dans la colonie de villas „Klingenteich" dans cette ville.

La villa E. Wolf, Unter der Schanz 2, construite dans l'espace d'un été pour la somme de 35 000 Marks, y compris le mur de soutenement, l'entourage et le jardin, se distingue par le groupement simple et agréable de ses parties. Le socle est construit en pierre rouge, flammée du Neckar jointroiées en blanc; les membres d'architecture du haut sont en pierre rouge flammée de l'Odenwald. On a obtenu un riche effet polychrome en teintant les bardeaux de chêne en ton brun d'or, les pans de bois et les saillier du toit en vert olive foncé. Les panneaux en planches ont été peints en blanc avec encadrements rouges. Les fenêtres et les balcons à fleurs du pignon sont blancs; les contrevents sont rouges foncés avec panneaux blancs et couronnes de roses peintes; les chêneaux et tuyaux de descente sont blancs; les balustrades de fer forgé vert clair. Les surfaces de maçonnerie du haut sont crépies en blanc, tandis qu'une annexe latérale ainsi que les pignons sont en partie en pans de bois avec recouvrement de bardeaux.

and Wolf, we have given the following two examples with illustrations.

The villa E. Wolf, "Unter der Schanz" 2, was built in the course of one summer for the sum of 35 000 Marks inclusive of supporting walls, boundary fence and arrangement of garden. The grouping is pleasing though simple. The sockel is of red Neckar stone with white pointings; the upper articulations of sandstone are carried out in red Hetzbach Odenwald stone. The exterior is a successful design in colour, the oaken shingles are stained gold-brown, the frame work and projection of the roof are of dark olive-green. The cross-cuts have white and red colouring, the carving is of red and yellow. The windows and flower receptacles in the gable are white, the shutters dark red with white mouldings and with stencilled rose-wreaths; the gutters and drain-pipes are white, and the wrought iron work is greenish-white. The upper surfaces are all plastered white, a side building as well as the gables are partly of shingled wood frame work. The projecting roof is covered with flat red tiles.

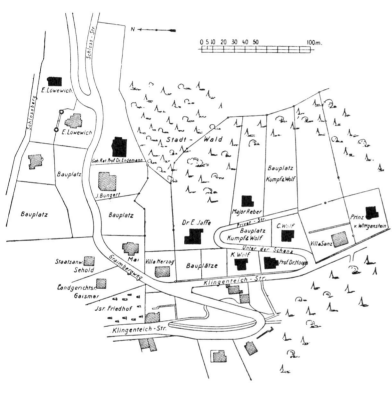

Erdgefchoß
Rez-de-chaussée
Ground Floor

1. Stockwerk
1. Etage
1. Floor

Villa Wolf.

Das Wohnzimmer im Erdgefchoß ift durch einen eingebauten Sitzplatz mit vorfpringendem Balkon, das Eßzimmer dafelbft durch einen Erkervorbau erweitert; außerdem liegt in demfelben Gefchoß die Küche mit Nebenräumen. Das ausgebaute Dachgefchoß enthält die Schlaf- und Fremdenzimmer.

La chambre d'habitation du rez-de-chaussée est agrandie au moyen d'une niche avec banc et balcon en saillie; la salle à manger, au moyen d'une tourelle également en saillie. Au même étage se trouve la cuisine avec ses dépendances. L'étage du toit contient les chambres à coucher et d'amis, dont une communique avec une loggia.

The living room on the ground-floor has a bay with a projecting balcony; the dining room is enlarged by a bay, and the kitchen and domestic offices lie on the same floor. The roof story is walled and timbered and contains the bed rooms and spare rooms one of which is in connection with a loggia.

244 [1907: 30]

Ein entfchiedenes, von Erfolg begleitetes Streben nach Erweiterung des architektonifchen Formenkreifes im modernen Sinne bekundet Profeffor Bruno Möhring in Berlin an dem von ihm entworfenen Haus Huesgen in Traben a. Mofel. Schon der kräftige Gegenfatz des in rauhem Feldfteinmauerwerk hergeftellten Sockelgefchoffes und der Terraffe in Verbindung mit der Einfriedigungsmauer zu den eigenartig behandelten Pußflächen der Obergefchoffe bringt eine ausdrucksvolle Befonderheit der Auffaffung zur Erfcheinung, welche noch durch die Reihung der Flächenornamentik, die Verzierungen der ausladenden Giebeleinfaffungen und die Abftufung der Dachflächen, deren unterer Teil gefchweift ift, verftärkt wird.

244 [1907: 30]

Monsieur le professeur Bruno Möhring architecte à Berlin témoigne dans la maison Huesgen à Traben sur Moselle, dont il a fait les plans, d'une tendance décidée, couronnée de succès, à élargir le cercle des formes architecturales dans l'esprit moderne. Le vigoureux contraste de la maçonnerie brute, de pierres non taillés dont sont construits le rez-de-chaussée et la terrasse, reliées au mur d'enceinte avec les surfaces originales des étages supérieurs montre à lui seul une façon particulière de composer. Cette manière est encore accentuée par le caractère des ornements des surfaces, les décorations des encadrements saillants des pignons, et par la disposition en degrés des toits, dont la partie inférieure est ondulée.

244 [1907: 30]

The architect Prof. Bruno Möhring of Berlin has designed the "Haus Huesgen" in Traben on the Moselle, and has been most successful in embodying the modern spirit in its widest sense in the architectural forms he has employed. A most effective contrast is gained by the employment of the rough stone formation for the lower storey and the boundary wall together with the terrace; and the uncommon execution of the plastering of the surfaces of the upper storey, an effect which is further heightened by the distinctive character of the flat ornamentation, by the decorations of the projecting gables and the formation of the roof, the under part of which is curved.

Um die Diele gruppieren lich die Gelellichafts-
räume und Ebzimmer, lebtere mit der ebenfalls
im Hochparterre gelegenen Küche in Verbindung
itehend; im Obergeichoß lind die Wohn- und
Schlafzimmer nebit Zubehör untergebracht. Die
innere Einrichtung iit bequem und zum Teil
reich ausgeitattet. Als Mitarbeiter lind tätig
geweien: die Firma W. Kümmel in Berlin für
Möbel, die Firma W. Knodt in Traben für die
übrigen Tilchlerarbeiten, O. Schulz in Berlin für
die Balkongitter, außerdem Bildhauer G. Roch
in Berlin und die Dekorationsmaler A. Eckhardt
in Berlin und E. Göße in Trarbach.

Les pièces de société et la salle à manger
sont groupées autour du hall, la salle à manger
est reliée à la cuisine qui se trouve également
au rez-de-chaussée. A l'étage supérieur se trouvent les chambres à coucher et d'habitation avec
dépendances. L'arrangement intérieur est commode et en partie riche. La maison W. Kümmel
à Berlin a livré les meubles, W. Knodt à Traben
les autres travaux de menuiserie O. Schulz
à Berlin a exécuté les balustrades des balcons.
Le sculpteur Roch de Berlin et les peintres
décorateurs A. Eckhardt à Berlin et E. Götze
à Trarbach ont aussi contribué à cette œuvre.

The reception rooms and dining room are
grouped round the square hall, the dining room
on the first storey is in connnection with the
kitchen on the same floor; on the upper floors
are dwelling and bed rooms with appertenances.
The equipment of the interior is distinguished
by great comfort and in some parts by luxury.
As coadjutors in the work may be mentioned
the firm W. Kümmel of Berlin for furniture,
the firm W. Knodt of Traben for joinery,
O. Schulz of Berlin for the iron railings of
the balcony; in addition the sculptor G. Roch,
the decorative painter A. Eckhardt both of
Berlin and the painter E. Götze of Trarbach.

245 [1907: 11]

Bemerkenswert in der Anlage der Villa
Lautenbacher in Schwabing-München,
Maria-Josefaltraße 11, iit die völlig durchgeführte Trennung von Wohnhaus und Stall-
betrieb, obgleich die betreffenden Gebäude zu-
lammenhängen. Das Äußere derielben zeichnet
lich durch wirkiame Silhouettenbildung, einfache,
aus dem Bedürfnis hervorgegangene Gruppierung
und der modernen Richtung entiprechende Bildung
der Einzelformen aus. Den Entwurf lieferte Prof.
Eman. v. Seidl in München; die Ausführung
durch das Baugeichäft E. Seidl & O. Steinbeis
erfolgte vom Februar 1905 bis April 1906; die
Baukoiten betrugen 215000 Kronen.
Die geiamte Baugruppe bildet einen Pubbau
mit reichlicher Verwendung von Betonquaderungen
und bildhauerilchen Ausichmückungen. Das Wohnhaus enthält im Erdgeichoß eine große Diele
mit der frei im Halbkreile aufiteigenden Treppe,
ferner eine Anzahl Zimmer, von denen das
Speiiezimmer mit einem Erkerausbau verlehen
iit, und das Herrenzimmer mit einer offenen Vorhalle und einer Terraile in Verbindung iteht.
Im Obergeichoß lind, von einem geräumigen Vor-
plab zugänglich, das Schlafzimmer mit Zubehör,
das Fremdenzimmer und einige Wirtichaftsräume
untergebracht, von denen einzelne wieder mit
Terraiien in Zuiammenhang gebracht lind.
Das an die Auffahrtshalle des Wohnhaules
itoßende Stallgebäude enthält im Erdgeichoß den
Pferdeitall mit Nebenräumen und den Wagen-
ichuppen, über lich ein als Speicher dienender
Dachraum befindet. Über dem Pferdeitall iit die
Kutichierwohnung angeordnet.

Ce qu'il y a de remarquable dans la disposition de la villa Lautenbacher à Schwabing-Munich, Maria-Josefastrasse 11, est
la séparation complète de l'habitation et du
service de l'écurie, quoique ces deux bâtiments
soient reliés entre eux. L'extérieur de ces immeubles se distingue par une silhouette simple
mais caractéristique, provenant du groupement
indiqué par les nécessités du service et de la
combinaison des différentes formes correspondent
à la tendance moderne. Le professeur Em-
manuel von Seidl architecte à Munich est
l'auteur des plans, l'exécution en fut confiée à la
maison E. Seidl et O. Steinbeis entrepreneurs,
elle dura de février 1905 jusqu'en avril 1906
les frais s'élevèrent à 215000 Couronnes.
Le groupe entier se compose d'une bâtisse en
maçonnerie crépie avec emploi abondant de blocs
de ciment et d'ornementation sculpturale. La
maison d'habitation contient au rez-de-chaussée
un grand hall avec un escalier s'élevant librement en demi-cercle, puis un certain nombre
de chambres dont la salle à manger est pourvue
d'une tourelle en saillie et la chambre de Monsieur avec une loggia ouverte et communiquant
avec une terrasse. A l'étage supérieur, se trouvent la chambre à coucher avec dépendances, la
chambre d'amis et quelques locaux de service, le
tout accessible d'un vestibule spacieux; quelques
unes des pièces ont été reliées à des terrasses.
La dépendance adjacente à la maison de maîtres
contient au rez-de-chaussée l'écurie avec locaux de
service et la remise, au-dessus de laquelle se
trouve une salle servant de grenier. Au-dessus de
l'écurie a été installé un appartement pour le cocher.

The erection of the villa Lautenbacher
in Schwabing-Munich, Maria
Josefastrasse 11 is chiefly remarkable
for the manner in which the villa and stabling are kept entirely separate although the
buildings are actually joining each other. The
exterior has been most successfully grouped
to form an effective silhouette, and the single
details are all of a decidedly modern style.
The design is by Prof. Eman. v. Seidl of
Munich, the execution of the design was placed
in the hands of E. Seidl and O. Steinbeis,
the time occupied was from February 1905 to
April 1906, and the cost of building amounted
to 215000 Kronen.
The entire group of buildings is of plaster
with a plentiful use of beton squares and
sculptural ornament. The dwelling house contains on the ground floor a square hall from
which a free semi-circular staircase ascends;
from the hall lead a number of rooms, the
dining room is enlarged by a bay, and the
smoking room by an open porch leading to
a terrace. On the upper storeys, and led to
by a spacious ante room, are bed rooms and
spare rooms and certain domestic offices, from
some of these rooms are entrances to the
terrace.
The stables, which lie near the carriage
entrance to the house contain on the ground
floor the horse boxes with necessary accommodation, and the carriage house; over this
latter are lofts for forage; over the stables is
the dwelling of the coachman.

246 [1907: 20]

Als ein Bauwerk von entichieden moderner Ausbildung, lowohl was die Formen des Äußern,
wie die inneren Anordnungen anbelangt, zeigt lich
die von Architekt Leop. Bauer in Wien ent-

La villa Schreibwaldstrasse 148 à Brünn,
située dans un jardin et libre de tous côtés
nous apparaît comme construction d'une composition absolument moderne, tant en ce qui

The architect Leopold Bauer of Vienna
has built a villa in Brünn, Schreibwaldstrasse 148. The house stands detached,
and surrounded by a garden; the exterior, as

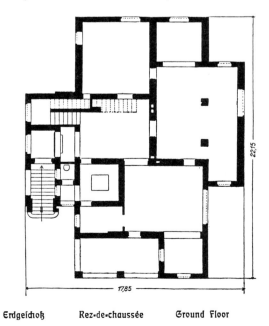

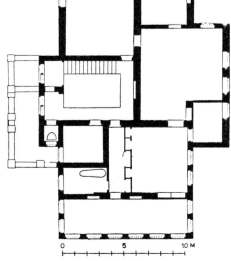

| Erdgeichoß | Rez-de-chaussée | Ground Floor | 1. Stockwerk | 1. Etage | 1. Floor |

worfene, ringsum frei in einem Garten gelegene Villa in Brünn, Schreibwaldstraße 148. Die Ausführung des Baues nahm etwa 1½ Jahre in Anspruch, die Baukosten betrugen, Grundwert und Einrichtung ausgeschlossen, 70000 Kronen.

Das Sockelgeschoß ist in den Umfassungen aus Bruchsteinmauerwerk hergestellt; die Wände des Hochparterre und des Obergeschosses sind mit weißem Putz überzogen, welcher in den oberen Teilen mit freihändig angetragenen Mörtelverzierungen geschmückt ist. Die einfache Gruppierung der Baumassen hat eine weitere Belebung durch Terrassenanlagen erhalten. Die abgewalmten, stark vorspringenden Dächer sind mit Falzziegeln eingedeckt.

Wohn- und Schlafzimmer sind auf das Hochparterre und den Oberstock verteilt und überall mit massiven Decken versehen. Es ist eine Warmwasser-Zentralheizung vorhanden; zugleich wurde eine Warmwasserversorgung für drei Badezimmer und sämtliche Waschtische eingerichtet. Außerdem ist für Gas zur Beleuchtung und Heizung, sowie für elektrische Anlagen gesorgt.

247 [1907: 80]

Von entschieden eigenartiger Wirkung erscheint die Villa Breuker in Traben a. d. M., von Architekt Prof. Br. Möhring entworfen. Es ist ein auf einer Terrasse gelegener zweistöckiger Putzbau mit weit ausladendem, flachem Dach, dessen Traufplatte durch langgestreckte Konsolen unterstützt wird und aus dessen Mitte ein turmartiges, mit steilem Walmdach überdecktes Obergeschoß herauswächst. Ein polygonal hervortretender Erker über der vorgelegten Terrasse ist in den Flächen mit Verblendziegeln bekleidet und trägt als Dachbekrönung einen mit Fenstern durchbrochenen runden Aufsatz. Unter dem Dachgesims zieht sich rings ein gleichfalls in Verblendziegeln ausgeführter breiter Fries hin, in welchen die gerade überdeckten Fenster des Obergeschosses einschneiden.

Im Erdgeschoß ist die Diele, der Salon, das Speise- und das Wohnzimmer nebst der Küche untergebracht, während das Obergeschoß die Schlafzimmer mit angrenzender Loggia, ein Arbeits- und zwei Fremdenzimmer enthält, welche Räume sämtlich wieder von einer mittleren Diele zugänglich sind.

248 [1907: 22]

In Jahrgang V, Heft 3, Tafel 75 der Architektur des XX. Jahrhunderts ist bereits eine Fassadenzeichnung des nach den Plänen des Architekten H. Müller-Erkelenz erbauten Geschäftshauses für die „Kölnische Zeitung" in Köln a. Rh., Breitestraße- und Langestraße-ecke veröffentlicht worden. Als Ergänzung dieser Mitteilung erfolgen hier noch zwei weitere Abbildungen der Fassaden desselben Bauwerks; die eine gibt die Eckansicht, die andere die Frontansicht mit dem Portal, dem darüber flach vorspringenden Fensterausbau und dem bekrönenden Rundgiebel. Die Fassaden sind in drei Geschossen aus grauem Lauterthaler Sandstein ausgeführt, während der Sockel aus poliertem Granit aus dem Fichtelgebirge besteht.

249 [1907: 24]

Das von Architekt Josef Müller entworfene, in einer Bauzeit von etwa 15 Monaten für die Summe von 100000 Kronen ausgeführte Wohnhaus in Brünn, Franz Josefstraße 12, erhält durch das in verschiedener Höhenlage angeordnete Hauptgesims und die in Türmchenform aufsteigenden Dachaufbauten ein eigenartiges Gepräge; außerdem wird die modern durchgebildete Fassade durch zwei polygonal vorspringende, durch zwei Obergeschosse geführte Erker

concerne l'extérieur que la disposition intérieure. C'est l'œuvre de Monsieur Leopold Bauer architecte à Vienne. L'exécution de l'immeuble prit près d'un an et demi; les frais de construction s'élevèrent à 70000 couronnes, non compris la valeur du terrain et les arrangements intérieurs.

L'étage du socle est construit en moellons dans les murs de façades. Les murs du rez-de-chaussée élevé et du premier étage sont crépis en blanc; le crépissage est décoré dans le haut d'ornements modelés à main libre. Le simple groupement des masses a été rehaussé par des terrasses. Les toits à grande saillie sont recouverts en tuiles à recouvrement.

Les chambres à coucher et d'habitation sont réparties au rez-de-chaussée et au premier étage et partout recouvertes de plafonds de construction massive. On a installé un chauffage central à eau chaude; en outre il existe une conduite d'eau chaude pour trois chambres de bain et tous les lavabos. L'installation du gaz pour éclairage et chauffage et celle de l'électricité ne font pas non plus défaut.

247 [1907: 80]

La villa Breuker à Traben s. Moselle, bâtie par Mr. le professeur Br. Möhring, architecte et d'un effet très particulier. C'est une construction à deux étages, crépie, située sur une terrasse avec toit plat à grande saillie, dont le cheneau est supporté par de longues consoles; au dessus de ce toit et dans son milieu, s'élève un étage en forme de tour couvert d'un toit abrupt. Une tourelle de forme polygonale fait saillie sur la terrasse, ses surfaces sont revêtues de briques et elle porte un couronnement arrondi, percé de fenêtres. Au dessous de la corniche règne une large frise également revêtue de briques, dans laquelle pénètrent les fenêtres à linteaux droits de l'étage supérieur.

Le rez-de-chaussée contient le hall, le salon, la salle à manger et la chambre d'habitation, ainsi que la cuisine, au premier étage se trouvent les chambres à coucher communiquant avec la loggia, les chambres de travail et d'amis; toutes ces pièces communiquent avec un vestibule central.

248 [1907: 22]

Nous avons déjà publié dans la cinquième année de l'architecture du XXme siècle, livraison 3me, Planche 75, un dessin de façade de la maison de commerce pour la „Gazette de Cologne" à Cologne sur Rhin, à l'angle des rues Breitestrasse et Langestrasse, maison construite par Monsieur H. Müller-Erkelenz architecte. Pour compléter la publication de cet édifice, nous faisons suivre encore deux nouvelles vues de façades; l'une d'elles rend la vue d'angle, l'autre la façade avec le portail, le bow-window saillant au-dessus, et le fronton circulaire formant couronnement. Les façades de trois étages sont construites en pierre grise de Lauterthal, tandis que le socle est en granit poli du Fichtelgebirge.

249 [1907: 24]

La maison d'habitation construite à Brünn, Franz Josefstrasse 12, par Monsieur Josef Müller dans l'espace de 15 mois, pour la somme de 100000 couronnes a un aspect particulier, grâce aux différentes hauteurs de la corniche et aux sur-élévations du toit qui se terminent en forme de tourelle; d'autre part, la façade traitée dans un esprit tout moderne est égayée par deux tourelles polygonales saillantes, traversant deux étages. Le crépissage des surfaces de maçonnerie est

well as the equipment and arrangement of the interior, is distinctly modern. The execution of the building occupied 1½ years, the cost, exclusive of site and interior fittings, amounted to 70000 Kronen.

The erection as far as the ground floor is of freestone, the walls of the upper storeys are faced with white plaster which in the upper part is decorated with freehand mortar ornament. The grouping of the various parts of the building is somewhat simple, but an enlivening effect is produced by the terraces leading to the garden. The curved, widely projecting roofs are covered with red tiles.

The dwelling rooms and bedrooms are all in the first and second storeys and all have solid ceilings. The house is heated by hot water, the apparatus serves too for the supply of three bathrooms and for the washing-stands in the various bedrooms. Gas and electric light are both used for lighting.

247 [1907: 80]

The villa Breuker at Traben a. d. M. by the architect Prof. Br. Möhring is a decidedly characteristic and effective erection. It is a two storied plaster building rising from a terrace with a widely projecting flat roof, the gutters being supported by widely extending consoles; out of the middle of the roof rises a turred-like upper storey with a steep curved roof. A polygonal projecting bay over the terrace is faced on the surfaces with tiles and carries as a roof crown a round erection furnished with windows. Under the roof moulding is a broad frieze carried out in tiles, and in this the windows of the upper storey are cut.

On the ground floor is the hall, the drawing room, the dining room and morning room; the upper storey contains a bed room with a loggia, a study, and two spare rooms, all these rooms are entered from a middle hall.

248 [1907: 22]

Volume V, number 3, plate 75 of the "Architektur des XX. Jahrhunderts" contains the drawing of a facade according to the design of the architect H. Müller-Erkelenz which was used for the building of the business premises of the "Kölnische Zeitung" at the corner of the Breite- and Langestrasse Cologne on Rhine. As a completion of this former publication are here given two additional illustrations of the facade of this building, one gives a corner view, the other a view of the front with the portal, the flat projecting window over it, and the round gable which crowns it. The facade, in three storeys is of grey Lauterthaler sandstone, the sockel is of polished granite from the Fichtelgebirge.

249 [1907: 24]

The house situated at Franz Josefstrasse 12, Brünn was designed by the architect Josef Müller, it occupied 15 months in building and cost 100000 Kronen. The principal moulding which is applied at different heights on the facade, and the ornamental towers which decorate the roof, give to the house a distinctive appearance. This is enhanced by two projecting polygonal bays carried through two upper storeys; the whole facade presenting

belebt. Der Flächenpuß besteht aus grauem Podoler Zementkalk, während zu den schmückenden Inkrustationen rötlichgraue Keramitplatten verwendet sind. Das Hauptgesims ist aus armiertem Zementstampfbeton hergestellt.

Im Erdgeschoß sowie im zweiten und dritten Obergeschoß sind je zwei Wohnungen eingerichtet, während die Räume des ersten Obergeschosses zu einer Wohnung zusammengefaßt sind. Die sämtliche Geschosse verbindende Treppe, deren Handgeländer vom Kunstschlosser V. Urbanovsky gefertigt wurde, hat ihre Stelle in der Mitte der Hinterfront gefunden.

en mortier de ciment gris de Podol, tandis que la décoration de ces surfaces consiste en incrustations de plaques céramiques, d'une couleur grise rougeâtre. La corniche est construite en ciment armé.

Au rez-de-chaussée, ainsi que dans les deuxième et troisième étages, on a installé deux logements, tandis que les pièces du premier étage ne forment qu'un grand appartement. Tous les étages sont réunis au moyen d'un escalier qui se trouve au milieu de la face postérieure; cet escalier est orné d'une balustrade en fer forgé exécutée par le serrurier d'art V. Urbanovsky.

a distinctly modern style. The surfaces are plastered with grey cement lime, the decorative incrustations are of reddish ceramic tiles. The principal moulding is strengthened and composed of cement-beton.

On the ground floor, and in the second and third storeys are respectively two flats, while the first floor is all in one and forms one flat. A staircase, situated at the middle of the front at the back of the house leads to all the floors and is furnished with an ornamental balustrade the work of the artistic iron worker V. Urbanovsky.

250 [1907: 25]

Als ein Pußbau von moderner Stilisierung erscheint das Wohn- und Geschäftshaus in Brünn, Franz Josefstraße 14/16, entworfen von dem Architekten Josef Müller und von demselben in etwa neun Monaten für die Summe von 160000 Kronen zur Ausführung gebracht. Die Fassade ist durch zwei ausgekragte, die drei oberen Stockwerke durchsießende Erkervorbauten gegliedert; und über dem mittleren Teil der Front verkröpft sich das Hauptgesims über einem Giebel mit abgestumpfter Spiße. Die Pußflächen sind in grauem Podoler Zementkalk hergestellt und durch rötlichgraue Keramitplattenverkleidung gemustert. Das weit ausladende Hauptgesims besteht aus armiertem Zementstampfbeton.

Das Erdgeschoß enthält an der Vorderfront Geschäftslokale, von denen die an den Ecken gelegenen mit je einem Wohnraume verbunden sind; an der Hinterfront sind zwei Wohnungen untergebracht. In den vier Obergeschossen sind je zwei durch das Stiegenhaus getrennte Wohnungen mit Zubehör angeordnet. Das Stiegengeländer stammt aus der Werkstatt des Kunstschlossers V. Urbanovsky.

250 [1907: 25]

La maison de commerce et d'habitation Franz Josefstrasse 14/16 à Brünn, construite par Monsieur Josef Müller et d'après ses plans, dans l'espace de neuf mois à peu près, pour la somme de 160000 couronnes est un immeuble de maçonnerie crépie traité en style moderne. La façade est divisée au moyen de deux tourelles saillantes traversant les deux étages supérieurs; la corniche principale se brise dans la partie centrale pour former un fronton avec angle tronqué dans le haut. Les surfaces crépies sont exécutées en mortier de ciment gris de Podol et agrémentées de plaques céramiques gris-rougeâtres. La corniche à grande saillie est construite en béton armé comprimé.

Le rez-de-chaussée contient des locaux de commerce, dont ceux qui sont situés aux angles ont chacun deux chambres d'habitation à leur disposition. Sur la façade de derrière on a aménagé deux appartements. Dans chacun des quatre étages supérieurs se trouvent deux appartements avec dépendances, séparés par la cage d'escalier. La balustrade de l'escalier sort des ateliers de serrurerie artistique de V. Urbanovsky.

250 [1907: 25]

The house at Franz Josefstrasse 14/16 in Brünn, built by the architect Josef Müller in nine months at a cost of 160000 Kronen, is a plastered building of a decidedly modern style. The facade is ornamented by projecting bays extending through three storeys. Over the centre of the facade the principal moulding is continued upwards to a gable ending with a blunt point. The plastered surfaces are of grey "Podol" cement lime, and are varied by designs in red-grey ceramic tiles. The principal moulding projects far out and is composed of cement-beton.

On the frontage facing the street are business premises; those at the corners have in addition to the shops a living room adjoining; on the back frontage two flats are arranged. The four upper storeys each contains two flats with domestic offices, separated by a general staircase. The ornamental iron balustrade is by the artist in iron work V. Urbanovsky.

251 [1907: 26]

Die moderne Wirkung der in Verpuß ausgeführten Fassade des Wohnhauses in Wien, Penzingerstraße 40, ist wesentlich durch den Gegensaß der glatten und rauhen Flächen, dann auch durch das absichtliche Vermeiden aller historisch hergebrachten Stilformen bedingt. Der Entwurf stammt von Architekt Karl Fischl. Die durch Schrägen nach oben begrenzten Sturze der Öffnungen im Erdgeschoß sind durch rauhen Verpuß und tafelförmige Einlagen hervorgehoben. Der mit einer mittleren Spiße hervortretende schmale Erker im ersten Stock ruht auf Konsolen, die wieder durch gebogene eiserne Streben unterstüßt werden, und schließt mit einer Altane, welche durch eine Loggia vertieft wird. Die durch Pfosten geteilten Fenster der beiden Obergeschosse sind in senkrechter Richtung zusammengezogen und werden von einem einspringenden Profil umrahmt. Unter dem weit vortretenden Dachgesims öffnet sich eine Reihe schmaler Schlißfenster, deren nischenartig durchbrochene Brüstungen sich nach außen vorschieben.

251 [1907: 26]

Le caractère moderne de la façade en maçonnerie crépie de la maison d'habitation Penzingerstrasse 40 à Vienne, est surtout exprimé par le contraste des surfaces lisses et rugueuses ainsi que par l'évitation intentionnelle de toute forme de style historique. Le projet est de Monsieur Karl Fischl architecte. Les linteaux des ouvertures du rez-de-chaussée sont bordées dans le haut par des lignes inclinées et décorés de panneaux en forme de plaques et de crépissage rugueux. La tourelle du premier étage, saillante, étroite, avec angle pointu au milieu repose sur des consoles supportées elles-mêmes par des fers recourbées, elle est terminée par une terrasse derrière laquelle s'ouvre une loggia. Les fenêtres des deux étages supérieurs, séparées par un meneau sont de lignes convergentes vers le haut en entourées d'un profil rentrant. Au dessus de la corniche à grande saillie s'ouvre une rangée de fenêtres étroites dont les contre-cœurs percés en forme de niches dépassent le nu du mur.

251 [1907: 26]

The dwelling house at Penzingerstrasse 40 Vienna has a facade of plaster and receives its characteristic modern appearance principally by the contrast between the smooth and rough surfaces and by the intentional avoidance of all historical and conventional architectural styles. The design is by the architect Karl Fischl. The lintels of the openings in the ground floor, bounded in the upper part by a slope, are of rough plaster with inlaid plates which gives them an effective appearance. The narrow projecting bay of the first storey has its foundations on pillars which are again supported by arched iron beams; above this is a terrace to which a loggia is joined. The windows of the two upper storeys are articulated by pillars and are joined perpendicularly by a projecting moulding. Under the widely projecting roof moulding are a row of narrow windows with a broken niche like balustrade.

252 [1907: 27]

Die in Formen des traditionellen Wiener Barocks durchgebildeten Fassaden des Gebäudes der k. k. Konsular-Akademie in Wien, Waisenhausgasse, sichern demselben das Gepräge echt monumentaler Würde. Architekt war Ludw. Baumann, k. k. Oberbaurat; die Bauzeit nahm zwei Jahre in Anspruch, und die Baukosten betrugen, einschließlich der Möblierung sämtlicher Räume, 1200000 Kronen.

Auf ein Hauptgebäude und zwei durch Durchfahrten von diesem abgetrennte Seitentrakte, leßtere zwischen Nachbargebäuden liegend, sind die Räume der Akademie verteilt, und an die

252 [1907: 27]

Les façades de l'académie consulaire royale et impériale à Vienne, Waisenhausgasse, sont traitées dans les formes traditionelles du Baroque viennois, qui lui donnent un caractère vraiment monumental. L'architecte de cet édifice est le conseiller Ludw. Baumann. La construction dura deux ans, et les frais s'élevèrent à 1 200 000 Couronnes, y compris le mobilier de toutes les salles.

Les localités de l'académie sont réparties entre le corps central et deux ailes séparées de ce dernier par deux portes cochères; ces ailes se trouvent entre des maisons voisines; une

252 [1907: 27]

The Imperial and Royal "Konsular-Akademie" at Waisenhausgasse Vienna is a building of great distinction, the facade is of the style of the traditional Vienna barock; the effect is one of monumental dignity. The architect was Ludwig Baumann, Oberbaurat, the time occupied was two years, and the cost, including the equipment and furnishing of the interior amounted to 1 200 000 Kronen.

The edifice is divided into a principal building and two side buildings, lying between neighbouring buildings, and separated from the

Hinterseite des Hauptgebäudes schließt sich ein großer Hof an. Die Vorderfront des Hauptgebäudes wird durch ein vorspringendes Mittelrisalit, welches den von Säulen flankierten Haupteingang enthält und mit einem Pavillondach abschließt, gegliedert. Die durch Pilasterarchitektur der beiden oberen Geschosse angedeuteten Eckrisalite sind durch Helmdächer in geschweiften Formen beendet. Über dem Hauptgesims zieht sich eine in bewegten Formen gehaltene Balustrade hin. Die Fassaden sind in Putzbau ausgeführt; nur zu einzelnen Teilen der Außenarchitektur sind andere Materialien verwendet: Mannersdorfer Stein für den Sockel, Marzana-Stein für das Portal, Kunstsandstein für Attika, Balustrade, Einfriedigung und Tore. Die figürlichen Bildhauerarbeiten hat Othm. Schimkowitz geliefert, die Kunstschlosserarbeiten Alex. Nahr.

Die vier Geschosse des Hauptgebäudes sowie das Tiefparterre desselben und die zweigeschossigen Seitentrakte enthalten Beamtenwohnungen, Diensträume, Hörsäle, Zimmer der Professoren und

grande cour s'étend derrière le corps principal. La façade de ce dernier est divisée par un avant corps central contenant l'entrée principale flanquée de colonnes et couronnée par un toit en pavillon. Les corps d'angle indiqués par l'architecture en pilastre des deux étages supérieurs sont surmontés de toits en forme de bonnets ondulés. Une balustrade de formes mouvementées décore la grande corniche. Les façades sont construites en maçonnerie crépie; d'autres matériaux ne sont employés que pour quelques parties de l'architecture extérieure, par exemple, de la pierre de Mannersdorf pour le socle; de la pierre de Marzana pour le portail, de la pierre artificielle pour l'attique, la balustrade, le mur d'enceinte et les portes. Le sculpteur Othm. Schimkowitz est l'auteur des figures décoratives; les fers forgés artistiques sont dûs à Alex. Nahr.

Les quatre étages du bâtiment principal, ainsi que le sous-sol et les deux étages des ailes contiennent des appartements d'employés, des localités de service, des amphithéâtres, des

main building by thoroughfares. At the back of the principal part is a large courtyard. The principal front has a centre projection which contains the chief entrance flanked by pillars and roofed with a pavilion balcony. The corner projections of the two upper storeys are ornamented with pilaster architecture and are crowned with helmets in a curved form. Over the principal moulding is a gracefully formed balustrade. The facades are of plaster, only a few parts of the exterior architecture show another material such as Mannersdorf stone for the sockel, Marzana stone for the portal, artificial sandstone for the attics, balustrades, walls surrounding the building and for the doorways. The sculptural work is by Othm. Schimkowitz, the artistic locks are by Alex. Nahr.

The four storeys of the principal building as well as the lower first floor and the two storeyed side buildings contain dwellings for the officials, rooms for the transaction of business,

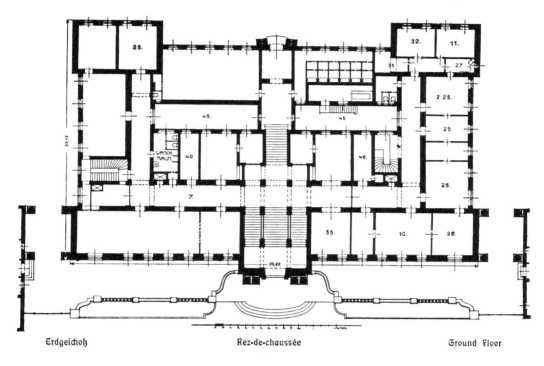

Erdgeschoß   Rez-de-chaussée   Ground Floor

Wohn- nebst Schlafräume für die Studierenden. Zwischen die nach rückwärts gewendeten Flügel des Hauptgebäudes ist die Turnhalle, mit einer Badeanlage verbunden, eingebaut. Die durch alle Geschosse des Hauptgebäudes führende dreiarmige Prachttreppe mündet auf die das ganze Gebäude durchschneidenden, von den Schmalseiten her beleuchteten Wandelgänge.

chambres de professeurs, et des chambres d'étude et à coucher pour les étudiants; entre les ailes du bâtiment principal qui s'étendent en arrière, on a bâti la salle de gymnastique, reliée à un établissement de bains. Le magnifique escalier à trois rampes qui traverse tous les étages du bâtiment principal aboutit aux corridors éclairés sur les faces latérales et traversant tout l'édifice.

lecture rooms, rooms for the professors, and dwelling and sleeping rooms for the students. Behind the principal building is a gymnasium connected with a bathing house. A magnificent staircase, of three flights leads upwards through the entire building and is in connection with corridors lighted from the narrow side and which extend through the whole building.

253 [1907: 33]

Für den Backsteinfugenbau in Verbindung mit Gliederungen aus Sandstein gibt das Gebäude der Bezirks-Krankenkasse in Brünn, Franz Josefstraße 24/26, entworfen von Architekt H. Geßner in Wien, ein bezeichnendes Beispiel moderner Auffassung der Formen. Die Baukosten betrugen 170000 Kronen. Über einem hohen Sockelgeschoß aus Sandstein erheben sich vier Geschosse in rotem Ziegelmauerwerk, durch die in Sandstein ausgeführten Sohlbänke und Stürze der Fenster, Auskragungsschichten und Abschlußbrüstungen der beiden seitlich polygonal vorspringenden Erker unterbrochen. Letztere durchsetzen zwei Obergeschosse, schließen je mit einer Altane und werden von flach eingebogenen Mauerflächen überstiegen. Der mittlere Teil der Fassade ist höher geführt als die Seitenteile, enthält eine breite Inschrifttafel und schließt mit einem stark vortretenden Dachgesims, hinter welchem das mit einem Aufbau bekrönte Walmdach aufsteigt.

253 [1907: 33]

Le bâtiment de l'hôpital de district de Brünn, Franz Josefstrasse 24/26 construit par Monsieur H. Gessner architecte à Vienne est un exemple de l'emploi de formes modernes pour une construction en briques apparentes jointoyées avec membres d'architecture en pierre. Les frais s'élevèrent à 170 000 couronnes. Au dessus d'un rez-de-chaussée en pierre s'élèvent quatre étages en maçonnerie de briques rouges, cette surface est interrompue par les linteaux et les appuis des fenêtres, les bandeaux et les contre-cœurs des deux tourelles saillantes polygonales en pierre de taille; les tourelles latérales traversent les deux étages supérieurs, elles portent des terrasses et sont surmontées de murs en forme de courbe surbaissée. La partie du centre de la façade est plus élevée que les parties latérales, elle contient une plaque avec inscription et est couronnée d'une corniche de grande saillie au dessus de la quelle se dresse une construction couronnée d'un toit tronqué.

253 [1907: 33]

The building of the district "Krankenkasse" in Brünn at Franz Josefstrasse 24—26 is the design of the architect H. Gessner of Vienna. It is a characteristic example of modern style; it is built of pointed bricks with articulations of sandstone. The cost amounted to 170000 Kronen. Over the high sockel of sandstone rise four storeys of red tile brickwork; these are varied by the sandstone used for the window sills and lintels, for the various projections, and for the balustrades of the two polygonal projecting bays at the side. These bays are continued upwards through two storeys, they finish each with a terrace and are crowned with flat arched constructions. The middle of the facade is higher than the side, contains a broad inscription plate and is finished by a widely projecting roof moulding behind which rises the vaulted roof crowned with an ornamental erection.

Eine durch plaſtiſche Gliederung reich belebte Faſſade zeichnet das Geſchäftshaus F. Lindner in Leipzig, Brühl 28, 30 aus. Entwurf und Ausführung des Gebäudes ſtammen von den Architekten Leopold und Alfr. Stenßler. Die Bauzeit dauerte von April bis Juli 1906, und die Baukoſten betrugen 90000 Mark.

Die in gelbem Portaer Sandſtein hergeſtellte Faſſade wird durch zwei ſchmale Eckriſalite flankiert, welche ſich nach oben zu Türmchen entwickeln und in den unteren drei Geſchoſſen breite Schaufenſter, in den oberen beiden Geſchoſſen durch ſchmale Pfeiler getrennte Fenſtergruppen zwiſchen ſich einſchließen. Die Eckriſalite treten in den oberen Teilen, vom zweiten Stock ab, mittelſt Auskragung ſtärker hervor, und die endigenden Türmchen ſind mit barockgeſchweiften Hauben bekrönt. Im vierten Geſchoſſe baut ſich vor dem mittleren, mit einem Segmentbogen abgeſchloſſenen Teile der Faſſade ein flachrunder Balkon auf Konſolen heraus. Die Schaufenſter im Erdgeſchoß ſind durch Gerüſte in Schmiedeeiſen, die in den oberen Geſchoſſen durch ſolche in Holz ausgefüllt. Die Firmentafeln haben eine dunkelrote Färbung erhalten; die Turmdächer ſind mit Kupfer, das Hauptdach iſt mit blauem Schiefer eingedeckt.

Das Gebäude umſchließt in allen vier Geſchoſſen ſowie im Dachgeſchoß einen ungeteilten,

Une façade richement décorée de motifs de sculpture distingue la maison de commerce F. Lindner, Brühl 28 et 30 à Leipzig. Le projet et l'exécution sont dus aux architectes Leopold et Alfred Stentzler. La construction dura d'avril à juillet 1906 et les frais s'élevèrent à 90000 Marcs.

La façade construite en grès jaune de Porta est flanquée par deux étroits avant-corps qui se terminent dans le haut par deux tourelles, et qui encadrent dans les trois étages inférieurs de larges devantures, dans les deux étages supérieurs, des fenêtres séparées entre elles par de minces piliers. Les avant-corps d'angle font saillie dans le haut, à partir du deuxième étage, au moyen de consoles, et les tourelles qui les surmontent se terminent en bonnets contournés de style baroque. Au quatrième étage, on voit saillir un balcon de forme arrondie porté sur des consoles et situé dans la partie de la façade terminée en forme de segment. Les devantures de magasin sont garnies au rez-de-chaussée de cadres en fer, dans les étages superieurs, de cadres en bois. Les enseignes commerciales sont peintes en rouge foncé. Les toits des tours sont recouverts en cuivre, celui de la maison, en ardoises bleues.

La maison entoure de ses quatre étages ainsi que du toit un espace libre, couvert d'un plafond

The business house of F. Lindner at Leipsic, Brühl 28 and 30 is distinguished by the richly ornamented facade with its sculptural articulations. The design and execution of the building are by the architects Leopold and Alfred Stentzler; the time occupied was from April to July 1906 and the cost of building amounted to 90000 Marks.

The facade is of yellow Porta sandstone, it is flanked by two small corner risalits which are carried up and are finished off at the roof with small towers, and which on the lower three storeys are formed into broad shop windows, these again on two storeys have the window groups articulated by slender pillars. The corner projections in the upper part, from the second storey upwards, are still more built out, and the small towers at the summit are crowned with helmets in the barock style. On the fourth floor, on the middle of the facade and enclosed by a segment arch is a flat rounded balcony resting on short consoles. The shop windows on the ground floor are strengthened by wrought iron construction, those of the upper storeys are strengthened by wood. The business plates for the names of the firms are dark red the roofs of the towers are of copper; the principal roof is covered with slate.

The building has on each of the four storeys

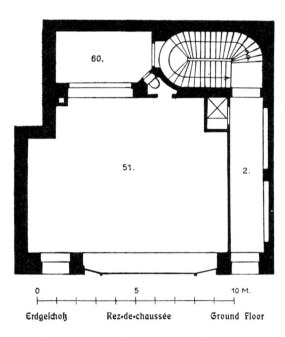

60.

51.

2.

0   5   10 M.

Erdgeſchoß   Rez-de-chaussée   Ground Floor

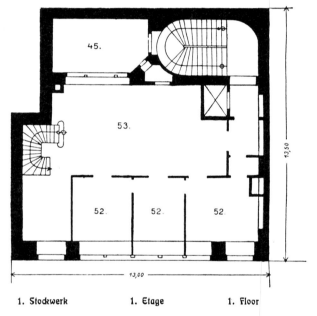

45.

53.

52.   52.   52.

13,00

13,50

1. Stockwerk   1. Etage   1. Floor

durch eine 9 Meter freitragende, aus Eiſenträgern und Hohlſteinen konſtruierte Decke überſpannten Raum, der durch leichte Zwiſchenwände beliebig geteilt werden kann. Die Modelle zu den in Stein ausgeführten Bildhauerarbeiten an der Faſſade lieferte Fr. Schmerſer.

de 9 mètres de portée, construit en poutres de fer et en hourdis. Cet espace peut être à volonté divisé au moyen de parois légères. Les modèles pour les travaux de sculpture de la façade exécutés en pierre ont été livrés par Fr. Schmerser.

as well as in the roof an unoccupied space 9 meters wide with a ceiling constructed of iron and stone which can at will be divided into various rooms by slight dividing walls. The models for the stone sculptural work on the facade were furnished by Fr. Schmerser.

Die vier untere Stockwerke durchſließenden, erſt im fünften Stockwerk durch die Horizontallinie einer Brüſtung unterbrochenen ſchlanken, breite Schaufenſter zwiſchen ſich einſchließenden Pfeiler geben der Faſſade des Geſchäftshauſes in Berlin, Gertraudtenſtraße 27, Ecke Roßſtraße, den einheitlichen Charakter, wie er der inneren Beſtimmung des Gebäudes entſpricht. Die langen unteren kannelierten Pfeiler ſind unter der, an der abgerundeten Ecke balkonartig vorſpringenden Brüſtung durch kräftige konſolenartige Voluten beendigt, während die oberen kurzen, gleichfalls kannelierten Pfeiler ein in die Unterglieder des Traufgeſimſes mittelſt Verkröpfungen übergehendes Kapitell tragen. Die abgerundete Ecke der Faſſade iſt durch einen turmartigen Aufſatz ausgezeichnet, der mit einer in doppelt

Les piliers élancés, traversant les quatre étages inférieurs, interrompus seulement au cinquième étage par la ligne horizontale d'un contre-cœur et encadrant les larges devantures donnent son caractère particulier à la façade de la maison de commerce située a l'angle des rues Gertraudtenstrasse 27 et Rossstrasse à Berlin; cette architecture correspond du reste à la distribution intérieure de l'édifice. Les longs piliers cannelés dans le bas sont terminés par de vigoureuses volutes en forme de consoles qui soutiennent des saillies arrondies du contre-cœur formant balcons, tandis que les courts piliers supérieurs également cannelés portent un chapiteau pénétrant grâce à un décrochement dans les moulures inférieures de la corniche. L'angle arrondé de la façade

The facade of the business house, Gertraudtenstrasse 27, corner of Rossstrasse Berlin, shows a harmonious uniformity corresponding to its interior requirements. This uniformity has been achieved by rows of long broad windows throughout four storeys, only interrupted at the fifth storey by the horizontal line of a moulding. The windows are separated by fluted pillars which are finished off at the top by massive spirals supporting a kind of balcony; the upper shorter pillars are also fluted, and end above en the roof moulding with a curved capital. The rounded corner of the facade is ornamented by a tower-like erection finished off with a curved

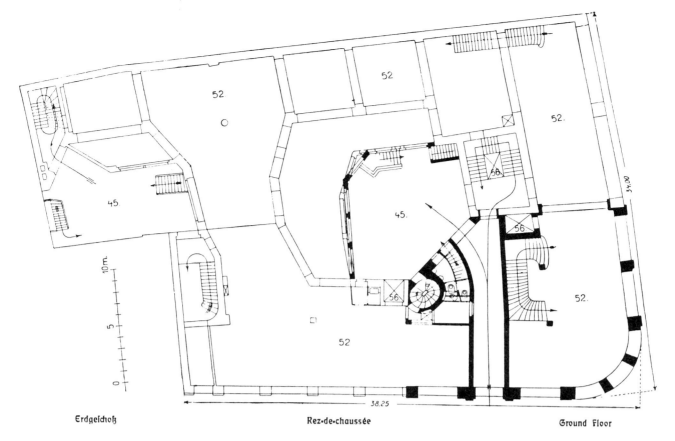

Erdgeſchoß   Rez-de-chaussée   Ground Floor

geſchwungener Linie gebildeten Kegelhaube ab-
ſchließt. Architekten des von Juni 1906 bis März
1907 für die Bauſumme von 320000 Mark ausgeführten Gebäudes ſind Amtsbaurat W. Gerbens
und P. Taeger. Die Faſſade beſteht aus
Warthauer Sandſtein, die Dächer ſind mit Biberſchwänzen eingedeckt.

Jedes der fünf Geſchoſſe iſt zu einem, nur
durch wenige Stützpfeiler unterbrochenen Geſchäfts-
raum ausgebildet; allein im Erdgeſchoß iſt eine
Durchfahrt abgetrennt. Die Geſchoſſe werden
untereinander durch Treppen und Aufzüge verbunden, außerdem führt eine beſondere, rauch-
und feuerſicher umſchloſſene, innerhalb des
Geſchäftsraumes liegende Treppe vom Erdgeſchoß
zum erſten Obergeſchoß empor. Das Dachgeſchoß
wird durch eine Freikonſtruktion in Eiſen gebildet.

est couronné d'une sorte de tour couverte d'un
toit en forme de quille d'un profil doublement
ondulé. Les architectes de cette construction
qui fut élevée pour la somme de 320 000 Marks
du mois de Juin 1906 à celui de mars 1907
sont Messieurs W. Gerbens conseiller et
P. Taeger. Les façades sont en pierre de
Warthau, les toits recouverts en tuiles.

Chacun des cinq étages consiste en un local
de commerce dont l'espace est seulement interrompu par quelques colonnes; au rez-de-
chaussée seulement, se trouve un passage.
Les étages sont reliés entre eux par des escaliers
et des ascenseurs, en outre, un escalier spécial,
isolé, à l'abri du feu et de la fumée, monte
à travers les bureaux, du rez-de-chaussée
à l'étage supérieur. Une construction en fer
forme l'étage du toit.

cone-shaped crown. The architects were "Amtsbaurat" W. Gerbens and P. Täger, the time
occupied was from June 1906 till March 1907
and the cost amounted to 320000 Marks. The
facade is of Warthau sandstone, the roof is of
flat red tiles.

Each of the five storeys consists of one large
hall only interrupted by a few supporting pillars,
on the ground floor an entrance goes through
to the back. All the floors are connected by
lifts and staircases; in addition there is a
special smoke-and fire-proof staircase inside the
business rooms, leading from the ground floor
to the first-floor. The roof storey is constructed
of iron framework.

256 [1907; 38]

D ie Geſamterſcheinung des von Architekt Prof.
H. Metzendorf entworfenen Landhauſes
in Bensheim, Ludwigſtraße 23, wird weſentlich von der die oberen Wandteile des Erdgeſchoſſes und ſämtliche Giebelflächen bedecken-
den Bretterverſchalung bedingt, während der
Sockel des Hauſes aus rotem Bruchſteinmauer-
werk, das Erdgeſchoß in rauhem Verputz mit
einzelnen Teilen aus Werkſtücken hergeſtellt iſt.
In der Hauptfront öffnet ſich einerſeits eine

256 [1907; 38]

L a physionomie de la maison de campagne
construite à Bensheim, Ernst Ludwigstrasse 23 par le professeur H. Metzendorf
est fortement influencée par les revêtements de
planches couvrant les parties supérieures des
murs du rez-de-chaussée et toutes les surfaces
des pignons. Le socle est en maçonnerie de
pierres rouges, le rez-de-chaussée en maçonnerie crépie, avec quelques pierres de taille.
Sur la façade principale s'ouvre d'un côté une

256 [1907; 38]

T he house built by Prof. H. Metzendorf
at Ernst Ludwigstrasse 23, Bensheim
has acquired its characteristic appearance from
the upper part of the wall of the ground floor,
and the whole of the surface of the gables
which are faced with wood, the sockel of the
house is of red freestone, and part of the ground
floor is of rough plaster. On one side of the
principal front is a spacious covered porch on

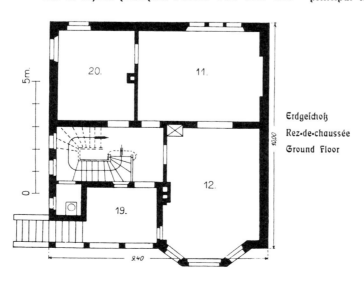

Erdgeſchoß
Rez-de-chaussée
Ground Floor

geräumige bedeckte Vorhalle auf Säulen, andererseits springt ein flach polygonaler Vorbau heraus. Im Dachgiebel befindet sich ein durch Schiebeladen verschließbares, mit einem vorgelegten Blumenbrett versehenes Fenster. Die weit ausladenden Dachflächen sind mit roten Biberschwänzen eingedeckt. Im Erdgeschoß gruppieren sich die Wohnzimmer um eine Diele mit freiliegender Treppe; andere Wohn- und Schlafräume befinden sich im ausgebauten Dachgeschoß.

halle spacieuse, couverte, portée par des colonnes, d'un autre côté un avant-corps polygonal fait saillie. Dans le fronton du toit, se trouve une fenêtre pourvue d'un volet à coulisse et d'un balcon pour fleurs. Les surfaces du toit à vaste saillie sont recouvertes en tuiles rouges. Les pièces d'habitation se groupent au rez-de-chaussée autour d'un hall, avec escalier, d'autres pièces et les chambres à coucher se trouvent dans l'étage du toit.

pillars, on the other side a flat polygonal entrance is built out. In the roof gable is a window furnished with shutters which can be closed and locked, and ornamented with flower boxes. The widely projecting roof is covered with flat red tiles. On the ground floor are grouped the dwelling rooms around a square hall with a free staircase, other rooms and bed rooms are situated in the roof storey.

257 [1907; 45]

Das in guten Verhältnissen unter gänzlicher Vermeidung ornamentalen Schmuckes erbaute Landhaus zu Köln a. Rh., Marienburg, Lindenallee 41, von dem Architekten Steph. Mattar in Köln entworfen, liegt allseitig frei und ist von einem Garten umgeben. Die Bauzeit dauerte von 1905 bis 1906. Die Baukosten betrugen rund 35000 Mark, mit Ausschluß des Grundstückwertes und der Kosten der Einfriedigung. Der mittlere, den Haupteingang enthaltende Teil der Front wird durch ein gemeinsames Dach mit dem von der einen Seite aufsteigenden Erker und dem an der anderen Seite vorspringenden niedrigen Flügelvorbau verbunden. Hinter dem

257 [1907; 45]

La maison de campagne Marienburg, Lindenallee 41 à Cologne s. R. construite par l'architecte Steph. Mattar de la même ville, est libre de tous côtés et entourée d'un jardin, ce bâtiment a de belles proportions et ne possède aucune décoration ornementale. La construction dura de 1905 à 1906. Les frais s'élevèrent à 35000 Marks en bloc, sans compter la valeur du terrain et la fermeture du jardin. La partie centrale de la façade, contenant l'entrée principale est reliée par un toit commun à la tourelle s'élevant d'un des côtés et à l'aile plus basse faisant saillie de l'autre côté. Derrière ce toit, s'élève la façade de l'étage supérieur, construit

257 [1907; 45]

The country house built by the architect Stephan Mattar at Lindenallee 41, Marienburg, Cologne on Rhine is distinguished by its correct proportions and by the absence of ornamental details. The house lies detached and is surrounded by a garden; the time occupied was from 1905 to 1906, and the cost of building (exclusive of site and the boundary wall enclosing the garden) amounted to 35000 Marks. The middle of the facade contains the principal entrance which is connected by a roof extending over a projecting bay on the one side, and with a low projecting wing on the other side. Over this roof and behind

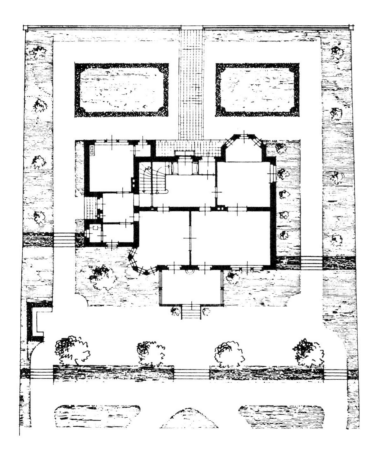

Erdgeschoß
Rez-de-chaussée
Ground Floor

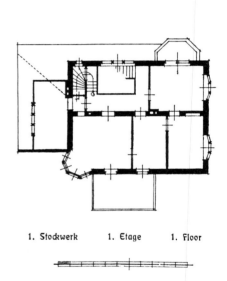

1. Stockwerk   1. Etage   1. Floor

erwähnten Dache steigt die in gerader Flucht durchgeführte Front des Oberstockes auf. Das weit ausladende Dachgesims hat über dem breiten Mittelfenster eine Aufbiegung erhalten. Die Fassaden sind in roten, weißgefugten Verblendziegeln, abwechselnd mit einzelnen Putzflächen ausgeführt. Das sichtbare eichene Holzwerk ist weiß lackiert. Die Dächer sind mit roten Biberschwänzen eingedeckt.

Bei Anordnung des Grundrisses ist auf die vorteilhafteste Lage der Räume nach den Himmelsrichtungen Bedacht genommen; die Küche liegt zu ebener Erde.

sur un alignement droit. L'avant-toit à grande saillie se relève en une courbe au dessus de la large fenêtre du milieu. Les façades sont exécutées en maçonnerie de briques apparentes jointoyées en blanc et alternant avec quelques surfaces crépies. Le bois de chêne apparent est peint en blanc. Les toits sont recouverts en tuiles rouges.

Pour la disposition du plan, on a eu égard à la situation la plus favorable par rapport à l'orientation; la cuisine est située au rez-de-chaussée.

it, rises the upper storey of the house. The widely projecting roof moulding is curved upwards in the centre over the broad middle window. The facade is of red tiles with white pointing, this is occasionally contrasted with plastered surfaces. The oak wood-work is visible and is painted white. The roofs are of flat red tiles.

The design of the ground plan shows that weight was laid on the position of the rooms as to the points of the compass; and the kitchen is conveniently placed on the same floor as the dining room.

258 [1907; 41]

Die in geschlossener Reihe nebeneinander gelegenen drei Einzelfamilienhäuser in Düsseldorf, Prinz Georgstraße 37, 39, 41, von Architekt Gottfr. Wehling daselbst ent-

258 [1907; 41]

Les trois maisons mitoyennes pour familles situées Prinz Georgstrasse 37, 39 et 41 à Dusseldorf, construites par Mr. Gottfr. Wehling, architecte en cette ville

258 [1907; 41]

The architect Gottfried Wehling has built at Prinz Georgstrasse 37, 39 and 41 in Düsseldorf a row of three houses each intended for the occupation of one family;

worfen und ausgeführt, find als Pußbauten in moderner Stilifierung durchgebildet. Die Fafaden der Häufer Nr. 37 und 39 find mit grau-gelblichem Puß verfehen; das Haus Nr. 41 zeigt in den Obergefchoffen dunkelgrauen Puß und im Erdgefchoß gefugtes, dunkelgraues Klinkermauerwerk; außerdem ift jedes der drei Häufer durch einen im Erdgefchoß vorfpringenden Erker ausgezeichnet, und das Haus Nr. 41 noch weiterhin durch einen fteilen, abgetreppten Giebel in ganzer Breite der Front. Die Baukoften betrugen für das Haus Nr. 37 24000 Mark, für die Häufer Nr. 39 und 41 je 27000 Mark.

In allen drei in der inneren Anordnung gleichmäßig angelegten Häufern find die Wohn- und Schlafzimmer für je eine Familie auf das Erdgefchoß und zwei Obergefchoffe verteilt, während das Kellergefchoß die Küche nebft den Wirtfchaftsräumen enthält.

et d'après ses plans sont traitées en stile moderne. Les façades des maisons No. 37 et 39 sont crépies d'une couleur grise jaunâtre; la maison No. 41 a aux étages supérieurs un crépissage brun foncé et au rez-de-chaussée une maçonnerie apparente jointoyée, d'un gris foncé. D'autre part, chacune des maisons est agrémentée d'une tourelle saillante au rez-de-chaussée, la maison No. 41 a de plus sur toute la largeur de la façade un fronton élevé et en gradins. Les frais de construction s'élevèrent pour la maison No. 37 à 24000 Marks, pour chacune des maisons 39 et 41 à 27000 Marks.

Dans chacune des trois maisons, la disposition intérieure est la même, les chambres d'habitation et à coucher pour une famille sont réparties entre le rez-de-chaussée et les deux étages supérieurs, tandis que le sous-sol contient la cuisine et les localités nécessaires au service.

they are plastered buildings in the modern style. The facades of the houses 37 and 39 are of yellowish grey plaster, the house 41 has in the upper storeys dark grey plaster, and on the ground floor dark grey rough brickwork; each of the houses has a projecting bay on the ground floor, and the house 41 has a steep graduated gable occupying the whole breadth of the front. The cost of building for the house 37 amounted to 24000 Marks, for the houses 39 and 41 each 27000 Marks.

The interior of all the houses is similar, the rooms for living and sleeping are arranged on the ground floor and the two upper floors, in the basement are the kitchens and other domestic offices.

259 [1907; 67]

Für die Außengliederung des Wohnhausbaues in Wien, Wickenburggaffe, Ecke Floriangaffe, kommen die an beiden Fronten vorfpringenden, durch drei Gefchoffe geführten, mit offenen Altanen endigenden Erker und die beiden breiten, das Dachgefims durchfchneidenden, in flach abgerundeten Konturen fchließenden Giebel in Betracht. Architekt des in etwa neun Monaten für die Baufumme von 350000 Kronen ausgeführten Gebäudes war der k. k. Baurat Osk. Marmorek in Wien. Die Fafaden find in chokoladenfarbigem Rauhpuß hergeftellt und mit in Mörtelftuck angetragenen pflanzlichen und rautenförmigen Verzierungen ausgeftattet. Die Auskragungen der Erker zeigen weiche, dem Pußftil entfprechende Formen. Das Hochparterre und die zwei unteren Gefchoffe find zu Bureauräumen für das Landwehr-Divifions-Kommando verwendet und find mit eigenem Eingang und befonderer Treppe verfehen; dagegen find die beiden oberen Gefchoffe zu Wohnungen eingerichtet.

259 [1907; 67]

Les deux façades de la maison d'habitation située à l'angle des rues Wickenburggasse et Floriangasse à Vienne, sont divisées au moyen de tourelles saillantes, traversant trois étages, couronnées de terrasses et de deux frontons interrompant la corniche et terminés par des contours de forme arrondie. L'architecte de l'édifice est le conseiller imperial et royal Osk. Marmorek, à Vienne qui l'exécuta pour la somme de 350000 couronnes. Les façades sont recouvertes d'un enduit brut de couleur chocolat, décoré d'ornements modelés en mortier, empruntes à la flore ou en forme de losanges. Les saillies des tourelles sont de formes molles, convenant à la technique du crépissage. Le rez-de-chaussée et les deux étages inférieurs sont destinés aux bureaux du commandement de la division de Landwehr et sont pourvus d'une entrée particulière et d'un escalier spécial. Par contre les deux étages supérieurs sont distribués en appartements.

259 [1907; 67]

The dwelling house built at the corner of the Wickenburg- and Floriangasse in Vienna is distinguished in its exterior architecture by a bay repeated in each of the three storeys and ending with an open gallery above, and by a broad gable cutting through the roof moulding and finished off with flat rounded forms. The architect was the Imperial Baurat Osk. Marmorek of Vienna, the time occupied was 9 months and the cost amounted to 350000 Kronen. The facades are of chocolate coloured rough plaster and are ornamented by an application in stucco of foliage and similar forms. The projections of the bay a gracefully ornamented with decorations suitable to be carried out in plaster. The first floor and two floors underneath it are occupied by offices for the "Landwehr-Divisions-Kommando" these have a separate entrance and staircase; the two upper storeys are arranged as dwellings.

260 [1907; 58]

In anfprechender Weife ift die Evang. Kirche in Köln a. Rh., Bayenthal-Marienburg, mit dem Pfarrhaufe zu einer gefchloffenen, von Gartenanlagen umgebenen Baugruppe vereinigt. Urheber des in etwa zwei Jahren für die Koftenfumme von 250000 Mark zur Ausführung gebrachten Bauwerks ift der Geh. Baurat Otto March in Charlottenburg. Dem nahezu quadratifchen, einfchiffigen Kirchenraum ift einerfeits in der Längsachfe die polygonal gefchloffene Altarnifche mit der feitwärts gelegenen Sakriftei, andererfeits der in ganzer Breite nach dem Kirchenfchiff geöffnete Konfirmandenfaal mit dem zugehörigen Vorfaal und der als Eckbau errichtete Turm, welcher zu ebener Erde den Haupteingang enthält, angefügt. Über dem Konfirmandenfaal ift die Orgelempore angeordnet und über dem Vorfaal die Orgelkammer. Der in romanifchen Stilformen durchgeführte Außenbau ift mit rauh bearbeiteten Tuffteinquadern verblendet, die Architekturgliederungen beftehen aus Pfälzer Sandftein. Das Kirchenfchiff ift mit einer fichtbaren Holzkonftruktion überdeckt, welche gefprengte rundbogige Binder und fchräge Deckenflächen zeigt; die Altarnifche hat ein Kappengewölbe erhalten. Die Dächer find mit Schiefer eingedeckt. Das Gefamtbild der Kirche wirkt malerifch durch die den Zentralbau andeutenden Seitengiebel des Schiffs, den frei entwickelten Turmbau mit der vorgelegten Eingangshalle und den Ausbau für die Emporentreppe, fowie durch das befondere Eingangsportal für den Vorraum des Konfirmandenfaals.

Das unmittelbar mit der Sakriftei in Ver-

260 [1907; 58]

L'église protestante à Cologne sur Rhin, Bayenthal-Marienburg forme avec la cure un groupe de bâtiments harmonieux entouré d'un jardin. L'auteur de ces constructions élevées dans l'espace d'environ deux ans pour la somme de 250000 Marks est le conseiller Otto March à Charlottenburg. La nef proprement dite de l'église est un espace à peu près carré sans bas côtés, il est entouré, d'une part, sur son grand axe, par une niche polygonale contenant l'autel avec la sacristie située à côté, d'autre part, par la salle de confirmation ouverte dans toute sa largeur sur la nef, elle est pourvue d'un vestibule et d'une tour formant angle et contenant l'entrée principale au rez-de-chaussée. Au dessus de la salle de confirmation se trouve la galerie des orgues et au dessus du vestibule, les soufflets. L'extérieur de l'édifice traité en formes de style roman est revêtu de tuf brut, les membres d'architecture sont en pierre du Palatinat. L'église est recouverte d'une construction de bois apparent dans laquelle on voit les fermes en forme d'arcs à plein cintre et les pans inclinés du plafond. La niche de l'autel a été fermée au moyen d'une voûte. Les toits sont recouverts en ardoises. L'ensemble de l'église produit un effet pittoresque, grâce aux frontons latéraux de la nef indiquant une disposition centrale, à la tour qui s'élève librement avec le porche en saillie et l'annexe contenant l'escalier des galeries, grâce aussi au portail conduisant au vestibule de la salle de confirmation.

La maison de la cure, reliée directement

260 [1907; 58]

The Evangelical Church at Bayenthal-Marienburg, Cologne on Rhine, together with parsonage house forms an attractive group surrounded by gardens. The designer is the Geheimer Baurat Otto March of Charlottenburg, the time occupied was about two years and the cost amounted to 250000 Marks. The space in the interior is nearly quadrilateral and is divided into two by the nave; on one side of the transept is the polygonal altar chancel which is in connection with the vestry; on the other side is a confirmation hall for the preparation of candidates, extending the whole breadth of the church; leading into this is an entrance hall, and at the corner is a tower, containing the principal entrance which is even with the ground. Over the confirmation hall is the organ gallery and over the entrance hall is the organ loft. The exterior is in Romanesque style; it is faced with rough square Tuff stones the architectural articulations being of sandstone from the Palatinate. The nave is roofed with wood, the construction being exposed to view and showing rounded arches and sloping roof surfaces; the altar niche has a Welsh vaulted roof. The roofs are of slate. The general effect of the building is picturesque, this is achieved by the side gable of the nave, the free standing tower with entrance porch and the projecting entrance to the gallery steps, as well as by the entrance to the confirmation hall.

bindung ſtehende, zum Teil zweigeſchoſſige Pfarrhaus iſt in den Außenfronten gleich der Kirche
mit rauhen Tuffiteinquadern bekleidet und hat
überhängende abgewalmte, in Schiefer eingedeckte Dachflächen erhalten, die durch einen
mit Schopf verſehenen Giebel und mehrere
Dachluken unterbrochen werden. Das Erdgeſchoß
enthält eine Anzahl Wohnzimmer, das Eßzimmer,
von dem eine Veranda zugänglich wird, die

à la sacristie, est ainsi que l'église revêtue de
pierres de tuf brutes, elle est en partie à deux
étages et porte un toit à saillie, en ardoises,
les surfaces de ce toit sont interrompues par
un fronton et plusieurs lucarnes. Le rez-de-
chaussée contient plusieurs chambres d'habitation,
la salle à manger, reliée à une veranda, la
cuisine et l'escalier conduisant à l'étage supé-

The parsonage is in immediate connection
with the vestry, it is partly two-storeyed, and
is faced, like the church with rough square
stones; it has too, curved roof projections
covered with slate and broken by several roof
openings and a hip-roofed gable. The ground
floor contains dwelling-rooms, the dining room
leading to a verandah, the kitchen and a stair-

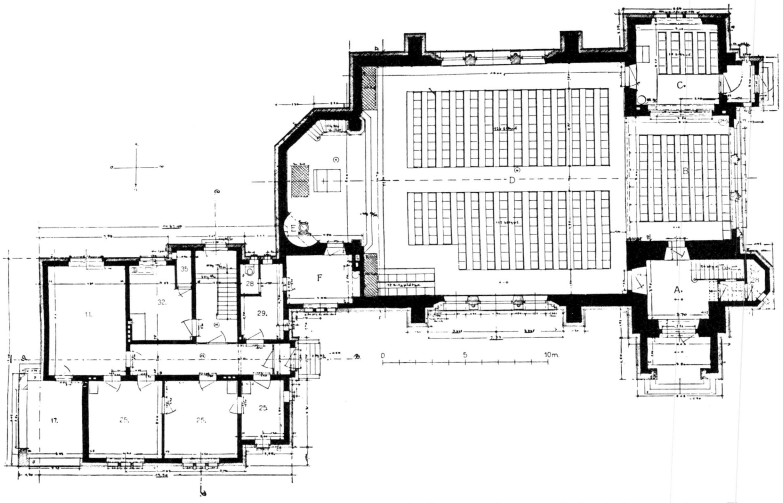

Küche und die zum Obergeſchoß führende Treppe.
Im Obergeſchoß ſind weiterhin Wohn- und Schlafzimmer, ein Baderaum und ein Balkon über der
unteren Veranda angeordnet. Die Moſaikarbeiten
in der Kirche ſind von Odorico-Berlin, die Glasmalereien von Hildebrandt-Berlin ausgeführt.

rieur. A cet étage sont situées d'autres chambres
d'habitation et à coucher, une chambre de bains
et un balcon au dessus de la veranda du rez-
de-chaussée. Les travaux en mosaïque dans
l'église sont de Odorico à Berlin, les vitraux
peints de Hildebrandt de la même ville.

case leading to the upper storey. The upper
storey contains bedrooms, bath-room and a balcony over the verandah. The mosaic work in
the church is by Odorico of Berlin, and the
stained glass windows are by Hildebrandt of
Berlin.

261 [1907: 100]

Die Villa György in Budapeſt, Iſtvan-
ut 79, zeigt Formen der nationalen
Renaiſſance untermiſcht mit orientaliſchen Anklängen. Es iſt ein zweiſtöckiger Putzbau in
maleriſcher Gruppierung, an welchem die
Gliederungen und Ecken, ſowie die Einfaſſungen
und Sturze der Öffnungen in, Sandſtein hergeſtellt ſind. An einer der Fronten ſpringt im
Erdgeſchoß ein mit einer Altane abſchließender
Erker hervor. Die Trauflinie des Daches ver-
birgt ſich teilweiſe hinter einer in gebrochenen
Linien ausgehenden Mauerüberhöhung, und wird
andererſeits durch Dachaufbauten, die mit Fenſtern
verſehen ſind, unterbrochen. Die ſteilen entweder
durch Giebel begrenzten oder abgewalmten
Dächer ſind mit Biberſchwänzen eingedeckt.

261 [1907: 100]

La villa György à Budapest, Istvan ut 79,
montre les formes de la renaissance
nationale mêlées de réminiscences orientales.
C'est une construction de maçonnerie crépie,
d'un groupement pittoresque, les membres d'architecture, les encadrements et les linteaux des
ouvertures sont en pierre de taille. Sur une
des faces du rez-de-chaussée, une tourelle surmontée d'un balcon fait saillie. Le chéneau est
en partie masqué derrière un mur surélevé et
terminé en ligne ondulée en partie interrompu
par des lucarnes. Les toits abrupts sont en
partie bordés par des pignons ou en forme de
comble à croupe, ils sont recouverts en tuiles.

261 [1907: 100]

The villa György, Istvan ut 79, Budapest, is designed according to the national
Renascence type with an admixture of orientalism.
It is a two-storeyed plaster building grouped in
a picturesque manner, all the architectural articulations as well as the bays, the framing and
supports of the various openings are of sandstone. On one of the frontages on the ground
floor is a bay above which is a terrace. The
highest line of the roof is partly hidden by a
brickwork erection in broken lines; this part is
further varied by roof erections containing windows. The steep roof, which has several gables,
is covered with flat red tiles.

262 [1907: 56]

In vornehmer Monumentalität, was die innere
Anlage und die äußeren Formen anbetrifft,
zeigt ſich das Gebäude der neuen Börſe in
Budapeſt, ein Werk des Architekten Ignácz
Alpár, welches in einer Bauzeit von etwa drei
Jahren für die Bauſumme von 4 300 000 Kronen,
die innere Einrichtung eingerechnet, entſtanden iſt.
Die mit großen Säulen beſetzte Hauptfront iſt in

262 [1907: 56]

La nouvelle Bourse de Budapest, œuvre
de l'architecte Ignáce Alpár, se présente,
tant dans sa disposition intérieure que dans ses
formes extérieures, comme un monument d'une
grande noblesse, sa construction dura environ
trois ans et exigea une somme de 4 300 000 Couronnes, y compris les aménagements intérieurs.
La façade principale, décorée de grandes colonnes,

262 [1907: 56]

The new Exchange at Budapest is
a monumental building of great distinction
both as to its interior arrangement and its
exterior grouping. It is a work of the architect
Ignácz Alpár, occupied three years in building and cost 4 300 000 Kronen. This cost is
inclusive of interior fittings and equipment. The
principal front is distinguished by a row of

der Mitte durch ein mächtiges, von Türmen flankiertes Portal unterbrochen und an den Ecken von breiten, mit Giebeln bekrönten Risaliten begrenzt, über denen sich noch attikenartige Aufbauten erheben. Die Säulen bestehen aus grauem Sandstein, die Flächen haben einen Zementverputz erhalten.

Aus dem Vestibül in der Mitte der Hauptfront gelangt man über eine breite Treppe zur Zentralhalle, an welche sich in der Längsachse beiderseits die Foyers anschließen, das eine zum Saal der Effektenbörse, das andere zum Saal der Warenbörse führend. Die großen Säle sind absichtlich an die Seitenfronten gerückt, um die Anlage von Oberlicht oder hohem Seitenlicht zu vermeiden, da beide Beleuchtungsarten namentlich für den Geschäftsbetrieb in der Getreidebörse unbrauchbar sein würden. Die letztere ist außerdem nach Norden verlegt, um auch jede Störung in der Getreidebewertung durch etwa eindringende Sonnenstrahlen fern zu halten. Die 18 m hohen Säle sind mit stark gegliederten Rabitz-Gewölbedecken überspannt. Die Garderoben wurden des bequemen Gebrauchs halber an beiden Seiten der Foyers angeordnet und erhalten wie diese das Licht von vier anstoßenden inneren Höfen. An den äußeren Längsfronten liegen, von Korridoren zugänglich, die Räume für den Post- und

est interrompue dans sa partie centrale par un portail puissant, flanqué de tours, elle est limitée aux angles par des avant-corps larges, couronnés de frontons, au dessus des quels s'élèvent encore des constructions en forme d'attiques. Les colonnes sont en pierre grise, les surfaces ont été crépies au ciment.

Du vestibule, situé au milieu de la façade principale, on atteint au moyen d'un large escalier le hall central avec lequel communiquent des deux côtés sur l'axe longitudinal les foyers, l'un donnant accès à la salle de la bourse des effets, l'autre à la salle de la bourse des marchandises. Les grandes salles sont intentionnellement reculées jusqu'aux façades latérales pour éviter l'éclairage du haut ou de fenêtres élevées, parceque ces deux genres d'éclairage seraient défectueux, particulièrement pour la marche des affaires de la bourse des céréales. Cette dernière est en outre orientée vers le nord, pour empêcher tout dérangement dans l'appréciation des céréales par la présence de rayons de soleil. Les salles hautes de 18 mètres sont recouvertes de voûtes, système Rabitz à fortes moulures. Les vestiaires ont été disposées des deux côtés des foyers pour la commodité du service, elles sont ainsi que les foyers, éclairées par quatre cours intérieures. Aux façades extérieures longitudinales se trouvent les bureaux

large pillars broken in the centre of the building by a magnificent portal flanked by towers; the corners of this centre are ornamented with broad spaces crowned with gables, and over these are ornamental attics. The pillars are of grey sandstone, the surfaces are of cement plaster.

From the vestibule in the middle of the principal front one reaches the central hall by means of a broad flight of steps; on this central hall are joined on each side "foyers" extending the length of the building; from one "foyer" are entrances to the "Effekten Börse" and from the other to the "Waren Börse". The large halls are placed purposely at the side fronts in order to avoid sky lights and high side lights, both of which are useless for the business of the corn exchange; the rooms for this exchange are supplied with north light in order to allow of a careful examination of the different kinds of grain uninfluenced by sunlight. The halls are 18 meters high and are roofed with firmly joined, wire and plaster vaulted ceilings "Rabitz-gewölbe". The wardrobe-rooms are placed for convenience on both sides of the foyers, and receive light, as do the foyers from four adjoining interior courtyards. At the end of the building, and extending the whole length with en-

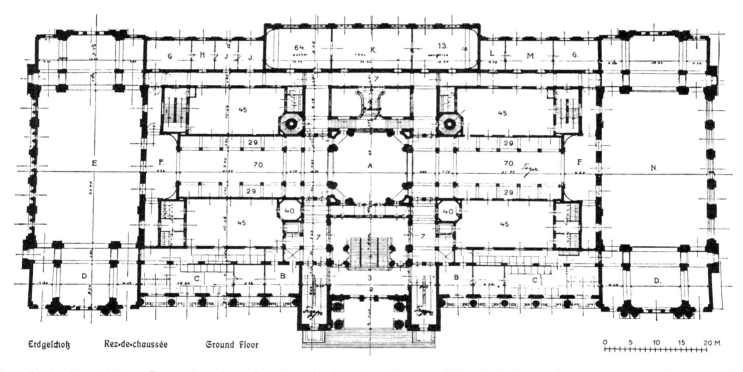

Erdgeschoß   Rez-de-chaussée   Ground Floor   0 5 10 15 20 M.

Telegraphendienst, verschiedene Bureauräume sowie das Konversationszimmer mit anschließendem Büffet und Rauchzimmer. Im Obergeschosse befinden sich außer mehreren Sitzungsälen die Räume des Börsengerichts, einer ausschließlich in Budapest eingeführten Einrichtung. Sämtliche Räume werden durch eine Niederdruck-Dampfheizung erwärmt.

de poste et de télégraphe, divers comptoirs, ainsi que les salles de conversation reliées à un buffet et fumoir, accessibles par des corridors. A l'étage supérieur se trouvent outre plusieurs salles de séances, les bureaux du tribunal de la bourse, une institution fonctionnant spécialement à Budapest. Toutes les localités sont chauffées au moyen d'un calorifère à vapeur à basse pression.

trances from corridors are the rooms for the post and telegraph service, various bureaus, a conversation room with refreshment room and smoking room adjoining. On the upper story, as well as several committee rooms are the rooms of the Court of the Exchange, a court which is peculiar to the Budapest Exchange. The entire building is heated by steam.

263 [1907: 62]

Der von dem k. k. Baurat Osk. Marmorek in Wien aufgestellte Entwurf eines Börsengebäudes für Czernowitz in der Bukowina ist nicht zur Ausführung gekommen. Die in Putzbau gedachte vordere Fassade zeigt im Erdgeschoß über der vorgelegten, durch eine Balustrade abgeschlossene Terrasse eine in Eisenkonstruktion auszuführende Vorhalle.

263 [1907: 62]

Le projet de bourse pour Czernowitz en Bukovine, par le conseiller impérial et royal Osk. Marmorek n'a pas été exécuté. La façade principale projetée en maçonnerie crépie montre au rez-de-chaussée, au dessus d'une terrasse située en avant et couronnée d'une balustrade, un vestibule qui aurait dû être exécuté en fer.

263 [1907: 62]

The design for an Exchange building for Czernowitz "in der Bukowina" by the Imperial and Royal Baurat Osk. Marmorek has not been put into execution. The front facade, intended to be carried out in plaster shows a vestibule in iron construction on the ground floor in connection with a terrace enclosed by a balustrade.

264 [1907: 63]

Das Gebäude der Pension Gibson in Partenkirchen, an einer Berglehne gelegen und in die waldige Umgebung, die in nächster Nähe der Baulichkeiten parkartig um-

264 [1907: 63]

Le bâtiment de la pension Gibson à Partenkirchen, appuyé au penchant d'une montagne, et entouré d'un parc est harmonieusement relié au paysage, il est composé d'une

264 [1907: 63]

The house "Pension Gibson" in Partenkirchen is situated on the slope of a mountain; the wooded sides are effectivly utilized to give the grounds a park-like appea-

geitaltet iit, geichickt hineinkomponiert, beiteht aus einem Neubau, der mit einem etwas höher gelegenen Umbau zu einer Gruppe verbunden iit. Der Neubau, von Architekt Ludw. C. Lutz in München von März bis Juli 1906 für die Koitenfumme von rund 85000 Mark errichtet, bildet einen Maffivbau in rauhem Kalkmörtelpuß der Flächen mit gleichfalls maffiv ausgeführten Loggien, die dem an der Hauptfront voripringenden Mittelbau vorgelegt find. Die außerdem am Mittelbau angebrachten überdeckten Balkone, fowie die an den Seitenflügeln find in Holzkonitruktion hergeitellt. Das Holzwerk iit weiß, die Feniterläden find graugrün geitrichen. Die überitehenden Dachflächen find mit roten Ziegeln eingedeckt und werden durch Dachaufbauten mit Feniteröffnungen unterbrochen.

construction neuve, reliée à l'ancienne maison transformée, située plus haut et forme avec elle un groupe pittoresque. Le nouveau bâtiment construit par Monsieur Ludw. C. Lutz à Munich, du mois de mars à celui de juillet 1906, pour la somme de 85000 Marks en bloc, est une construction massive de maçonnerie crépie avec des Loggias également massives, qui sont placées devant l'avant-corps central de la façade principale. Les balcons couverts décorant en outre l'avant-corps, ainsi que ceux des ailes latérales sont construits en bois. Le bois est blanc, les volets des fenêtres sont peints en vert-gris. Les surfaces du toit saillant sont recouvertes en tuiles rouges et sont interrompues par des lucarnes.

rance, and a new building joined to a somewhat higher older edifice forms a picturesque group. The new building was built from March till July 1906 by the architect Ludwig C. Lutz of Munich at a cost of 85000 Marks. It is of solid construction in rough plaster, with massive loggias on the principal front springing from the middle erection. Other covered balconies in the middle front as well as those on the side wings are of wood. The woodwork is white, the window shutters are greygreen. The projecting roof is covered with red tiles and is broken at intervals by attic windows.

265 [1907: 68]

Durch den Wechfel des für die Faffaden gewählten Materials: gefugtes Ziegelmauerwerk, welches nach oben in Bogenlinien abichließt, für das Erdgeichoß und Pußflächen für das Obergeichoß, erhält das Einzelfamilienhaus in Cöln a. Rh., Joeitraße 19, entworfen von dem Architekten M. G. Gradl in Stuttgart, ausgeführt von dem Architekten A. Riffart in Köln, feinen befonders charakteriitiichen Ausdruck. Der polygonale Erkervorbau inmitten der Front, im Erdgeichoß geichloffen, im Obergeichoß zwiichen Rundpfeilern geöffnet und eine Altane tragend, iit ebenfalls in fichtbarem Ziegelmauerwerk ausgeführt. Über dem Ausbau erhebt fich ein von geichwungenen Konturen begrenzter Giebel. Das iteile Dach iit mit Schiefer eingedeckt, ebenfo iit der obere Teil des Seitengiebels beichiefert. Die Wohn- und Schlafzimmer find auf beide Geichoffe verteilt und um eine mittlere Diele gruppiert.

265 [1907: 68]

La maison pour une famille construite à Cologne, Joestrasse 19, par Monsieur A. Riffart, architecte à Cologne, d'après les plans de Monsieur M. G. Gradl, architecte à Stuttgart, est caractérisée par la variété des matériaux employés pour les façades; maçonnerie de briques jointoyées, terminée dans le haut en lignes arquées pour le rez-de-chaussée et surfaces crépies pour l'étage supérieur. La tourelle saillante polygonale au milieu de la façade du rez-de-chaussée, ouverte entre des piliers au premier étage et portant une terrasse, est également exécutée en briques apparentes. Au dessus de l'avant-corps, s'élève un fronton aux contours arrondis. Le toit escarpé est recouvert en ardoises, ainsi que la partie supérieure du fronton latéral. Les chambres d'habitation et à coucher sont réparties dans les deux étages et groupées entour d'un hall central.

265 [1907: 68]

A house intended for one family has been built at Joestrasse 19, Cologne-on-Rhine, by the architect A. Riffart of Cologne according to the design of the architect M. G. Gradl of Stuttgart. The building has a characteristic appearance through the ingenious contrast of the materials chosen for the facade; pointed brickwork finished off above in arches for the ground floor and plastered surfaces for the upper storeys. A polygonal bay projection in the middle of the front is closed on the ground floor, but open on all the others and ornamented with round pillars; it is finished off above with a terrace and is built of pointed brick work. Above all is a gable with curved forms. The steep roof is covered with slate as well as the upper part of the side gable. The dwelling rooms and bedrooms are distributed on both floors, and are arranged round a square hall.

266 [1907: 82]

In einiger Anlehnung an den Typus des fränkiichen Bauernhaufes, obgleich in freier Behandlung der Einzelformen, zeigt fich das maleriich im Wald gelegene Landhaus in Heidelberg, Klingenteichitraße 15a, von den Architekten Kumpf & Wolf herrührend. Der Bau hat die Zeit von etwa dreiviertel Jahren in Anipruch genommen und iit mit einem Koitenaufwand von 30000 Mark hergeitellt. Das Untergeichoß beiteht aus rotem Bruchitein, das Erdgeichoß iit weiß verpußt, das Holzwerk des Giebels, die Bretterverichalung eines Teils der Fronten, fowie die Beichindelung des großen abgeichopften Giebels und des an der Front voripringenden Eckerkers find braun gefärbt. Die hölzernen Säulen der Feniergruppe im unteren Teile des Giebels, fowie auch das Holzwerk fämtlicher Feniter find weiß gehalten. Das weit überhängende Dach iit mit roten Biberichwänzen eingedeckt. Die Räume des Haufes find mit Möbeln im Bauernitil ausgeitattet.

266 [1907: 82]

La maison de campagne située d'une façon pittoresque dans la forêt Klingenteichstrasse 15a à Heidelberg, bâtie par les architectes Kumpf & Wolf, montre quelque parenté avec le type de la maison de paysans de la Franconie, quoique les formes soient traitées avec une entière liberté. La construction a duré à peu près trois quarts d'année et a coûté 30000 Marks. Le socle est en maçonnerie de moellons rouges; le rez-de-chaussée est crépi en clair, le bois apparent du fronton, le revêtement en planches d'une partie des façades, ainsi que les bardeaux du grand fronton et de la tourelle faisant saillie sur la façade sont peints en brun. Les colonnes en bois des groupes de fenêtres de la partie inférieure du fronton, ainsi que le bois de toutes les fenêtres sont peints en blanc. Le toit à grande saillie est recouvert en tuiles rouges. Les chambres sont garnies de meubles en style compagnard.

266 [1907: 82]

The house at Klingenteichstrasse 15a Heidelberg, by the architects Kumpf and Wolf is similar in type to the Frankish peasants farm house, although the separate details are somewhat freely handled. The villa is picturesque by situated in a wood. The time occupied was $^3/_4$ of a year, and the cost amounted to 30000 Marks. The basement is of red freestone, the ground floor of white plaster, the woodwork of the gables, the woodwork of part of the front as well as the shingle on the large gable and the corner bay built out on the front are all coloured brown. The wooden pillars of the group of windows in the lower part of the gable as well as the woodwork of the windows are always white. The widely projecting roof is covered with flat red tiles. The furniture of the house is in the same style of peasants farmhouse.

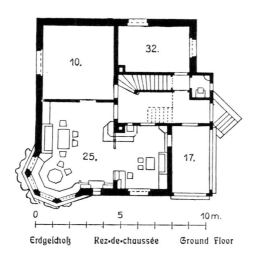

0   5   10 m.

Erdgeichoß   Rez-de-chaussée   Ground Floor

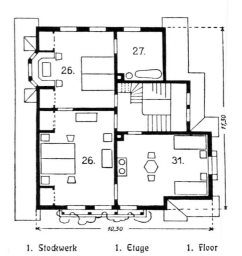

1. Stockwerk   1. Etage   1. Floor

Im Erdgeschoß liegen Wohn- und Herren-zimmer, ersteres durch den Eckerker erweitert, der einen Ausblick nach der Stadt gewährt, letzteres in Verbindung mit einer Veranda, dann der Salon, die Küche und die Diele, welche die

On the ground floor are drawing room and study, the first enlarged by a bay with a beauti-ful view of the town this bay leads to a ver-andah; then comes the drawing room, the kitchen, the hall (from which each room can be

Au rez-de-chaussée se trouvent les chambres d'habitation et de Monsieur, le première agrandie par la tourelle offrant un coup d'oeil sur la ville, la dernière reliée à une veranda; puis le salon, la cuisine et le vestibule qui donne

267 [1907: 69]

Die Fassaden des allseitig freiliegenden Doppel-Wohnhauses in Dresden, Nürnberger-straße 36/38, sind durch ausgekragte, die beiden Obergeschosse durchsetzende, überdeckte, durch Altane abgeschlossene Balkons und in den um ein Geschoß höher geführten, flach vorspringen-den, mit steilen Giebeln bekrönten Risaliten,

267 [1907: 69]

Les façades de la maison d'habitation double, libre de tous côtes, Nürnberger-strasse 36/38 à Dresde, sont caractérisées par des tourelles fermées, en saillie, traversant les deux étages supérieurs, surmontées de balcons découverts, et par d'autres balcons portés un des consoles en fer et appliqués sur

267 [1907: 69]

The double dwelling house at Nürn-bergerstrasse 36/38, Dresden lies free on all sides. The facades are enlivened and characterized by projecting balconies reaching through the two upper storeys; these balconies are covered and are finished off in the highest storey by a terrace-like erection, beyond this

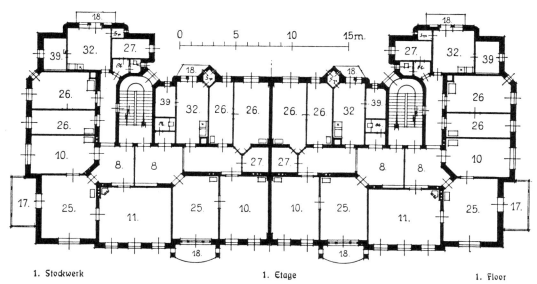

1. Stockwerk   1. Etage   1. Floor

durch offene, auf leichten, eisernen Konsolen ruhende Balkons belebt. Die Steilflächen der Mansardedächer werden mehrfach durch Dach-fenster unterbrochen. Die Architekten Linke & Leukert sind Urheber des in etwa sieben Monaten für die Kostensumme von rund 210000 Mark ausgeführten Gebäudes. Die durchaus in modernen Formen gehaltenen Fassaden haben eine Sandsteinverblendung erhalten, im Sockel-geschoß aus gelbem, im Erdgeschoß und oberen Stockwerken aus weißem Cottaer Stein bestehend. Die eisernen Brüstungsgeländer der oberen offenen Balkons sowie die Konsolen der-selben sind blau, die Fenster elfenbeinweiß ge-strichen; die Dächer sind mit rotglasierten Biber-schwänzen eingedeckt. In jedem Geschoß des Doppelhauses sind vier Wohnungen mit allem Zubehör untergebracht.

des avantcorps peu saillants surmontés de frontons abrupts. Les parties abruptes des toits mansards sont interrompues plusieurs fois par des lucarnes. Cette construction a été élevée dans l'espace de sept mois à peuprès pour la somme de 210 000 Marcs en bloc d'après les plans de M. M. Linke et Leukert architectes. Les façades entierement traitées en formes modernes ont été revêtues de pierre de Cotta jaune au socle, blanche au rez-de-chaussée et aux étages. Les appuis de fenêtres en fer des balcons superieurs, ainsi que leurs consoles sont bleus, les fenêtres sont peintes en blanc d'ivoire. Les toits sont recouverts en tuiles rouges. A chaque étage de la maison double, on a distribué quatre appartements avec toutes leurs dépendances.

are steep gables, the upper balconies resting on light iron pillars. The steep sides of the mansard roofs are frequently broken by win-dows. The building was designed by the archi-tects Linke and Leukert, it occupied seven months in building and cost about 210 000 Marks. The style of the facades is thoroughly modern, they are faced throughout with sandstone, the lower with yellow sandstone, and the upper with white Cotta stone. The iron balustrades of the upper balconies and the consoles on which they rest are painted blue, the windows are ivory white; the roofs are of red glazed flat tiles. In each of the storeys of the double house are four dwellings with appropriate domestic offices.

268 [1907: 70]

Die aufwändig mit Thüringer Sandstein ver-blendete Fassade des dreistöckigen Einzel-familienhauses in Düsseldorf, Prinz Georg-straße 122, zeigt im Erdgeschoß Quaderwerk mit eingeschnittenen Fugen und rundbogig ge-schlossenen Öffnungen des Einfahrtors und der breiten, durch Steinpfosten geteilten Fenster. Die beiden oberen Geschosse werden durch Pilaster mit modern aufgefaßten Kapitellen durchsetzt, welche gerade überdeckte Fenster zwischen sich einschließen und ein Gebälk samt Attika tragen. Der Bau ist von Architekt Leonh. Sandkaulen entworfen und ausgeführt.

Das Erdgeschoß enthält außer dem ärztlichen Warte- und Sprechzimmer des Besitzers, das Eß-zimmer in Verbindung mit einem Wintergarten, der Anrichte und dem zur Küche in das Keller-geschoß führenden Aufzug, sowie die von der Durchfahrt zugängliche Diele, aus welcher eine freiliegende Treppe bis zum ersten Obergeschoß emporführt. Über dem hinteren Teile der Durch-fahrt hat sich ein als Garderobe dienendes Zwischengeschoß ergeben, welches durch eine Wendeltreppe mit dem Erd- und Kellergeschoß in Verbindung gesetzt ist. Auf die beiden Ober-

268 [1907: 70]

La riche façade revêtue de pierre de Thuringe, de la maison pour une famille, Prinz Georgstrasse 122 à Dusseldorf est à trois étages, elle montre au rez-de-chaussée un appareil de pierres jointoyées et des ouvertures recouvertes d'arcs, telles que la porte-cochère et les fenêtres à meneaux de pierre. Les deux étages supérieurs sont divisés par des pilastres avec chapiteaux de composition moderne qui encadrent des fenêtres à linteaux droits et portent un entablement avec attique. Cette construction a été exécutée par l'architecte Leonh. Sandkaulen et d'après ses plans.

Le rez-de-chaussée contient, outre les chambres d'attente et de consultation du propriétaire, qui est médecin, la salle à manger reliée à un jardin d'hiver, l'office et un monte-charge conduisant à la cuisine et à la cave; au même étage se trouve le hall accessible depuis le passage, de ce hall, conduit un escalier au premier étage. Au dessus de la partie postérieure du passage, on a ménagé un entresol servant de vestiaire, lequel est relié au sous-sol et au rez-de-chaussée au moyen d'un escalier tournant. Les chambres

268 [1907: 70]

The house situated at Prinz Georg-strasse 122 Dusseldorf is intended for the use of one family; the facade of the building, which consists of three storeys, is faced with Thuringian sandstone; the ground floor is of pointed square stones, the entrance is arched, as are the windows, articulated by stone pillars. The two upper storeys are orna-mented with pilasters having capitals of modern design; these enclose covered windows between them and have a balcony and an attic. The building is designed by the architect Leonh. Sandkaulen who also carried the work out.

The ground floor contains the waiting and consulting rooms of the owner — a doctor; the dining room with a conservatory, a serving room connected by a lift with the kitchen, and a square hall from which a free staircase leads to the first floor. At the back part of the entrance an intermediate storey has been constructed containing cloak-rooms, this is in connection with the ground floor and basement by means of a spiral staircase. On the two

geichofie find die Gefellfchafts-, Wohn- und Schlafzimmer verteilt, während der Dachraum für die Waichküche, Kammern für Dienitboten und Crockenböden ausgenutzt ist.

269 [1907: 71]

Die Straßenfront des von den Architekten Hart & Lefier entworfenen, in den Jahren 1905 und 1906 für die Koftenfumme von rund 100000 Mark ausgeführten Geichäftshaufes in Berlin, Poftitraße 30, ist mit Sandstein verblendet und läßt in der Behandlung der Formen den einheitlichen, die Anlage von Wohnräumen ausichließenden Charakter des Gebäudes hervortreten. Das in Boffenquadern hergeitellte Erdgeichoß enthält die Eingänge mit ihren kleeblattförmig geftalteten Oberlichtöffnungen und ein breites im Korbbogen überwölbtes Schaufenfter. Die drei oberen Geichoffe werden durch flache, abgerundete Pfeiler zu einer Einheit verbunden. Die breitere Mittelachfe der Faffade ist im erften und zweiten Obergeichoß durch einen flachrund vorfpringenden, durch ichmale Pfeiler geteilten Fenitervorbau ausgefüllt, der mit einer Baluitrade abichließt. Hinter diefer, im dritten Obergeichoß, ipringt wieder ein als leichtes Eifengerüft ericheinendes, breites polygonales Fenfter vor, von der Trauflinie des Daches in derfelben Linie begleitet. Die rechtsfeitige Schmalachfe läßt durch die Form der ichräg anfteigenden Fenfter auf die dahinter liegende Treppe ichließen und endigt als Türmchen mit gebogenem Helmdach, während fich daneben ein breiter Dachaufbau mit Fenitern entwickelt.

In allen vier Geichoffen ift je ein großer ungeteilter Geichäftsraum angeordnet, welcher durch zwei Treppen, eine unmittelbar an die Straßenfront, die andere an die Hoffront anitoßend, fowie durch einen ebenfalls an der letzteren liegenden Aufzug zugänglich gemacht wird. Im Erdgeichoß ift ein befonderer Flurgang zur Verbindung des Straßeneingangs mit der hinteren Treppe abgetrennt. Der Hof ift unterkellert und mit Deckenöffnungen für Oberlicht verfehen.

270 [1907: 72]

Auf dem von der Markgrafenftraße bis zur Charlottenitraße durchgehenden Berliner Bauterrain ift eine Gruppe von vier einzeln für fich abgeichloffenen Geichäftshäufern von Oktober 1905 bis dahin 1906 durch den Architekten Regierungs-Baumeifter Joh. Hirte zur Ausführung gebracht worden. Die Faffade des Geichäftshaufes Union in Berlin, Markgrafenitraße 92/93, ift bis zum Gurtgefims im eriten Stock mit hellgrauem, ichwediichem Labradorgranit bekleidet, die oberen Stockwerke find in Ettringer Tuffitein ausgeführt, die Brüftungen und Dächer der beiden im zweiten und dritten Obergeichoffe vorfpringenden Erker, fowie die Abdeckungen und Abfallrohre find in Kupfer hergeftellt. Die Dächer find mit blaugrauen Biberichwänzen eingedeckt, Schaufenfter und Ladeneingänge beitehen aus Teakholz, die Frontfenfter aus Eichenholz. Das Haus ift in allen Teilen maffiv in Eifen und Stein konftruiert; dem im Keller angelegten Trefor werden Licht und Luft unmittelbar von der Straße zugeführt; die Täfelungen im Sitzungsfaal find in Bombay-Rosewood-Holz mit reichen Intarfien, die in den Sitzungszimmern in dunkelgebeiztem Eichenholz ausgeführt.

Das Erdgeichoß enthält Läden, die drei oberen Geichoffe find zu Geichäfts- und Bureauräumen eingerichtet, im vierten Stockwerk des Vorderhaufes find hohe bis in das Dachgeichoß reichende, mit Oberlicht verfehene Räume angeordnet, die zu Atelierzwecken benutzt werden können. Übrigens ift durch die Anlage mehrerer Höfe dafür geforgt, daß den Räumen genügend viel Licht zufließen kann. Die Faffade wurde

---

de réception, d'habitation et à coucher sont réparties sur les deux étages supérieurs, tandis que l'étage du toit contient la buanderie, les chambres de domestiques et le séchoir.

269 [1907: 71]

La façade sur rue de la maison de commerce, Poststrasse 30 à Berlin est revêtue de pierre de taille et permet, par la manière dont sont traitées les formes, de reconnaître le caractère d'unité et d'adaptation aux services. C'est l'œuvre des architectes Hart & Lesser, elle fut élevée dans les années 1905 et 1906, pour la somme ronde de 100000 Marks. Le rez-de-chaussée construit en bossages, contient les entrées avec leurs impostes en forme de feuille de trèfle et une large devanture de magasin recouverte d'une anse de panier. Les trois étages supérieurs sont reliés en une unité architectonique au moyen de piliers plats et arrondis. La large travée du milieu de la façade est au premier et au second étage garnie par un bow-window faisant saillie, en forme de segment et divisé par de minces piliers; une balustrade le couronne. Derrière cette balustrade, au troisième étage, une nouvelle fenêtre fait saillie, elle paraît être une légère construction en fer, large et de forme polygonale, elle se termine avec la ligne de la corniche. La travée étroite de droite, fait pressentir, grâce à la forme de ses fenêtres montant en biais, l'escalier qu'elle masque, elle se termine en tourelle avec un toit ondulé, tandis qu'à côté se développe une large lucarne.

Dans tous les quatre étages a été disposé un grand local de commerce non divisé, il est accessible au moyen de deux escaliers, l'un situé directement sur la façade, l'autre sur la cour, et d'un lift également situé sur la cour. Au rez-de-chaussée se trouve un vestibule spécial, etablissant la communication de l'entrée avec l'escalier postérieur. La cour est excavée et pourvue de vitrages pour l'éclairage de locaux souterrains.

270 [1907: 72]

Monsieur Joh. Hirte, architecte du gouvernement, a construit un bloc de quatre maisons de commerce séparées, sur le terrain s'étendant des rues Markgrafenstrasse à la Charlottenstrasse à Berlin, du mois d'octobre 1905 à celui d'octobre 1906. La façade de la maison de commerce „Union" à Berlin, Markgrafenstrasse 92/93 est revêtue jusqu'au bandeau du premier étage de granit suédois de Labrador, les étages supérieurs sont en tuf de Ettringen. Les contre-cœurs, et les toits des deux tourelles faisant saillie au second et au troisième étage, ainsi que les couvertes et les tuyaux de descente sont en cuivre. Les toits sont recouverts en tuiles bleu-grisâtres, les devantures et les entrées des magasins sont en bois de Teak, les fenêtres des façades en chêne. La maison est dans toutes ses parties construite massive en fer et en pierre; le trésor installé en sous-sol reçoit le jour et l'air directement de la rue; les boiseries de la salle des séances sont en bois de rose de Bombay avec de riches marquetteries, celles des chambres de conférences sont en bois de chêne ciré foncé.

Le rez-de-chaussée contient des magasins, les trois étages supérieurs sont disposés en locaux de commerce et en comptoirs, au quatrième étage de la maison de devant, se trouvent de hautes salles pénétrant dans l'étage du toit et éclairées par le haut, elles peuvent être utilisées comme ateliers. On a du reste eu soin de faire pénétrer partout une lumière abondante, grâce à la disposition de plusieurs cours. La façade a été exécutée par Ph. Holz-

---

upper storeys are reception rooms, dwelling rooms and bedrooms; in the roof storey are wash house, servants' rooms and a large attic for drying clothes.

269 [1907: 71]

The business premises at Poststrasse 30, Berlin was built during the years 1905 and 1906 at a cost of 100000 Marks according to the design of the architects Hart and Lesser. The facade facing the street is faced with sandstone; the style is throughout uniform, and shows the exclusive use of the building for business purposes. The ground floor is of bossed square stones, it contains the entrance which has a trefoil-formed skylight and a broad arched shop window. The upper storeys are all harmoniously ornamented with flat arched pillars. The broad middle erection of the facade is filled up in the first and second storeys by a flat rounded window projection, articulated by small pillars and finished off with a balustrade. Behind this, in the third storey, springs forward a light, broad, polygonal window with iron framework, placed in a line with the rain gutter of the roof. The narrow side on the right, by means of the sloping window, is in connection with the staircase at the back, and is finished off with a helmet-formed tower at the side of which a broad roof erection with windows is built.

On all four floors is one undivided business room, entrance to which is by two staircases one next to the street front, the other on the courtyard side; on this side too is the connection with the lifts. On the ground floor is a special entrance corridor to connect the front entrance with the back staircase. The courtyard is provided with cellarage, and is lighted by skylights.

270 [1907: 72]

A group of four single business houses has been built on a site extending from the Charlottenstrasse to the Markgrafenstrasse Berlin from October 1905 to October 1906 by the architect and Regierungs-Baumeister Joh. Hirte. The facade of the business premises "Union" a Berlin, Markgrafenstrasse 92 and 93, is faced up to the string-course of the first floor with light grey Swedish Labrador granite, the upper storeys are of Ettringer tuffstone, the balustrades and roofs of the projecting bays of the second and third upper storeys, as well as the small roofs and drain gutters are of copper. The roofs are covered with blue-grey flat tiles; shop windows and shop entrances are of teak-wood, the front windows have oak-wood frames. The house is in all parts solidly constructed of iron and stone; the safes in the cellars are provided with light and air by shafts in connection with the street; the panelling in the Board room is of Bombay rosewood richly inlaid, that of the Committee rooms is of darkly stained oakwood.

The ground floor contains shops, the three upper storeys are devoted to bureaus and business premises; on the fourth floor of the front house are high rooms, sky-lighted, reaching up to the roof, which are intended for artists' studios. The provision of several courtyards, well-lighted, serves to give the whole of the building sufficient light. The facade is the work

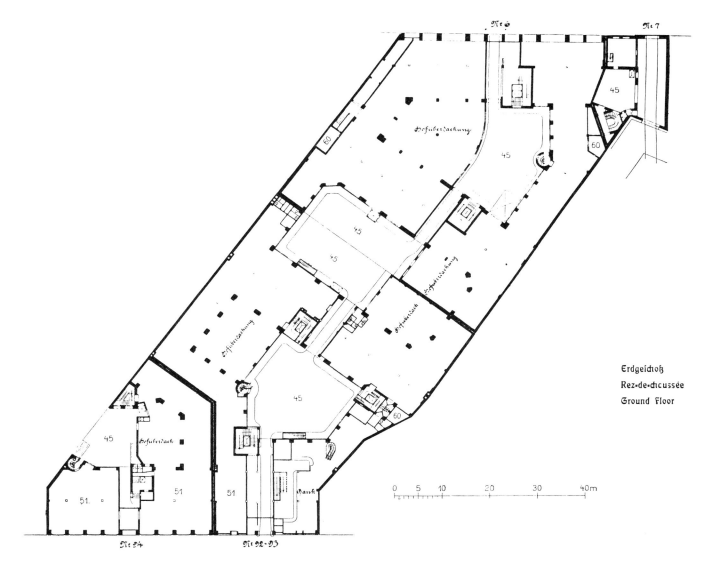

Erdgeſchoß
Rez-de-chcussée
Ground Floor

0 5 10   20   30   40m

Nr 6   Nr 7
Nr 94   Nr 92-93

---

von Ph. Holzmann & Co. ausgeführt, die Labradorarbeiten von Kolkmeyer, die Marmorarbeiten von O. L. Schneider, die Holzarbeiten von W. Kümmel. Die eiſernen Torwege lieferten Hillerſcheidt & Kasbaum, die feuerſichere Treſoranlage ſtammt von M. Fabian.

271 [1907: 75]

Das Wohnhaus in Köln a. Rh., Volksgartenſtraße 24, nach dem Entwurfe des Architekten H. Reitſamer ausgeführt, zeichnet ſich durch einen kuppelbekrönten, in drei Obergeſchoſſen mit Balkons ausgeſtatteten Eckbau aus. Dieſer wird beiderſeits durch vorſpringende, vom Boden aufſteigende, durch alle Geſchoſſe geführte Anbauten flankiert. Die Faſſaden ſind als Putzbau in modernen Formen geſtaltet. Jedes der vier Geſchoſſe enthält eine Wohnung; zur Verbindung der Geſchoſſe dient eine Treppe, welche ſtets auf einen beiderſeits eingebauten Flurgang mündet.

272, 273, 274 [1907: 76, 78, 79]

Der mächtige Bau des Stollwerckhauſes in Köln a. Rh., Hohe Straße, Straße am Hof und Wallrafplatz gelegen, nach dem Entwurfe des Architekten Reg.-Baumeiſter K. Moritz vom Juni 1906 bis April 1907 für die Grunderwerbs- und Baukoſten einſchließende Summe von rund 5 000 000 Mark errichtet, iſt beſtimmt, Kaufläden, größere Räume für Warenausſtellungen und Kontore in ſich aufzunehmen, und bringt dieſe Beſtimmung äußerlich durch die in den Faſſaden vorherrſchende wagerechte Schichtung der Stockwerke klar zum Ausdruck, im Gegenſatz zu den die innere Einheitlichkeit des Betriebes durch die äußere Vertikalgliederung betonenden Warenhäuſern. Maßgebend für die Grundrißgeſtaltung des Stollwerckhauſes war die Anlage einer von der Hohen Straße zum Platz am Hof führenden Paſſage, der Stollwerckshalle, an Stelle einer alten Verbindungsſtraße. Der Hauptbau erhebt ſich

---

mann & Co., les ouvrages en Labrador par Kolkmeyer, ceux de marbre par O. L. Schneider, la menuiserie est due à W. Kümmel. Les portes en fer ont été livrées par Hillerscheidt & Kasbaum, le trésor à l'abri du feu par M. Fabian.

271 [1907: 75]

La maison d'habitation Volksgartenstrasse 24 à Cologne, construite d'après le projet de l'architecte H. Reitsamer, se distingue par une construction d'angle, couronnée d'une coupole et pourvue de balcons à trois étages. Cette construction est flanquée des deux côtés de saillies montant de fond et traversant tous les étages. Les façades sont crépies et traitées dans les formes modernes. Chacun des quatre étages contient un appartement; un escalier relie les étages, il débouche à chacun d'eux sur un vestibule.

272, 273, 274 [1907: 76, 78, 79]

L'imposante construction de la maison de commerce Stollwerck, Hohe Strasse, Strasse am Hof et Wallrafplatz à Cologne sur Rhin, a été élevée d'après les plans de Mr. K. Moritz architecte du gouvernement, du mois de juin 1906 à celui d'avril 1907, les frais de construction et d'acquisition du terrain s'élevèrent à 5 000 000 Marks en bloc. Ce bâtiment est destiné à abriter des magasins, de grands locaux pour expositions de marchandises, et des comptoirs, cette disposition est exprimée en façade par la division horizontale très accentuée des étages, bien distincte de la division verticale des grands magasins qui correspond à une organisation intérieure uniforme. L'établissement d'un passage conduisant de la Hohe Strasse au Platz am Hof, nommé Stollwerckshalle et remplaçant une ancienne rue a été d'une grande influence sur la composition du plan de la

---

of Ph. Holzmann & Co.; the Labrador work is by Kolkmeyer, the marble work by O. L. Schneider, the wood work by W. Kümmel. The iron gates were provided by Hillerscheidt & Kasbaum, the fire-proof safe equipment is from the firm M. Fabian.

271 [1907: 75]

The dwelling house at Volksgartenstrasse 24, Cologne on Rhine, has been built according to the design of the architect H. Reitsamer. It has a corner erection containing balconies on three storeys and over these is a cupola. These balconies are flanked on either side by other projecting erections reaching from the ground floor to the roof. The facades are of plaster in modern forms. On each of the four storeys is one flat; the flats are reached by a staircase which has a corridor leading to each entrance.

272, 273, 274 [1907: 76, 78, 79]

The magnificent building of the Stollwerckhouse situated on a site bounded by the Hohe Strasse, Strasse am Hof and Wallrafplatz, Cologne on Rhine, is according to the design of the architect Reg.-Baumeister K. Moritz. It was built from June 1906 to April 1907 for the sum of 5 000 000 Marks inclusive of site and building expenditure. It is designed for large shops, for spacious accommodation for the exhibition of goods and for bureaus; this design is apparent at once from a view of the facade which brings the horizontal arrangement of the various divisions clearly to the eye; this is in sharp contrast to the architecture of the usual "Warenhaus" or bazaar which emphasizes the fact of the one purpose of the building by the exterior vertical articulation of the facade. The

nach der Straße am Hof zu nördlich der Halle, während südlich derselben der kleinere Nebenbau angeordnet ist; beide Bauteile sind durch brückenartige Übergänge an den Stirnwänden der durch ein gewölbtes Glasdach abgeschlossenen Halle untereinander verbunden.

Die in der Hauptsache aus fränkischem Muschelkalkstein hergestellten Fassaden — nur für die Pfeiler im Erdgeschoß, die Tafeln und Bänder zur Aufnahme der Firmennamen ist schwedischer Granit verwendet — sind in breite Schaufenster zwischen schmalen Pfeilern aufgelöst, welche über dem zweiten Obergeschoß durch Segmentbogen verbunden werden. Die abgerundeten Gebäudeecken zeigen eine engere Pfeilerstellung, ebenso sind die Fenster im dritten Obergeschoß durch Steinpfosten geteilt. Über dem kräftig bandartig vorspringenden, den ringsumlaufenden Altan begrenzenden Hauptgesims folgt das vierte, etwas zurückgesetzte Obergeschoß. Das abgewalmte Satteldach ist mit Kupfer eingedeckt, trägt große Dachfenster und einen Dachreiterturm mit achteckiger Laterne, der von dem Wahrzeichen des Hauses Stollwerck überragt wird. Der Haupteingang in der Hohen Straße ist rund vertieft und zeigt als plastischen Schmuck den Vater Rhein mit seinen Nebenflüssen, von Joseph Moest herrührend. Über dem Ausgange an der Straße

maison. Le bâtiment principal s'élève sur la rue Strasse am Hof au nord de la halle, tandis qu'au sud de cette dernière on a disposé la plus petite partie. Les deux parties sont reliées entre elles au moyen de communications en forme de ponts, fixées aux faces de la halle recouverte d'un vitrage voûté.

Les façades sont en général exécutées en pierre calcaire de Franconie, on n'a employé du granit de Suède que pour les piliers du rez-de-chaussée, les tableaux et rubans destinés à recevoir les enseignes. Ces façades sont divisées en larges fenêtres entre de minces piliers reliés entre eux par des arcs surbaissées au second étage. Les angles arrondis de la maison sont divisés en piliers plus rapprochés, les fenêtres du troisième étage sont divisées par des meneaux en pierre. Au dessus de la corniche à saillie vigoureuse en forme de bandeau, bordant le balcon régnant autour de l'édifice, s'élève le quatrième étage un peu en retrait. Le comble à croupe est recouvert en cuivre, Il porte des grandes lucarnes et un cavalier avec lanterne octogonale, surmontée de la marque de la maison Stollwerck. L'entrée principale sur la Hohe Strasse est situé dans un enfoncement circulaire et est décoré d'une œuvre plastique representant

groundplan was influenced by a passage leading from the Hohe Strasse to Platz am Hof, the "Stollwerckshalle" in the place of an old connecting street. The principal block rises towards the Strasse am Hof to the north of the "Halle", while towards the south extends the smaller auxiliary building; both buildings are connected by bridge-like passages forming a glass-roofed hall.

The facade is principally of Frankish Muschellime stone (for the pillars on the ground floor, for plates and spaces for the name of the firm Swedish granite has been used), and consists of broad shop windows divided by narrow pillars which over the second upper storey are united by segment arches. On the rounded corners of the building the pillars are more frequent; the windows on the third upper storey are divided by stone pilasters. A broad projecting band bounds the terrace running round the principal moulding, and over this cornes the fourth storey set somewhat backward. The curved roof is covered with copper, contains large roof windows, a roof tower with octagonal lantern, over which is the emblem of the house of Stollwerck. The principal entrance in the Hohe Strasse is round

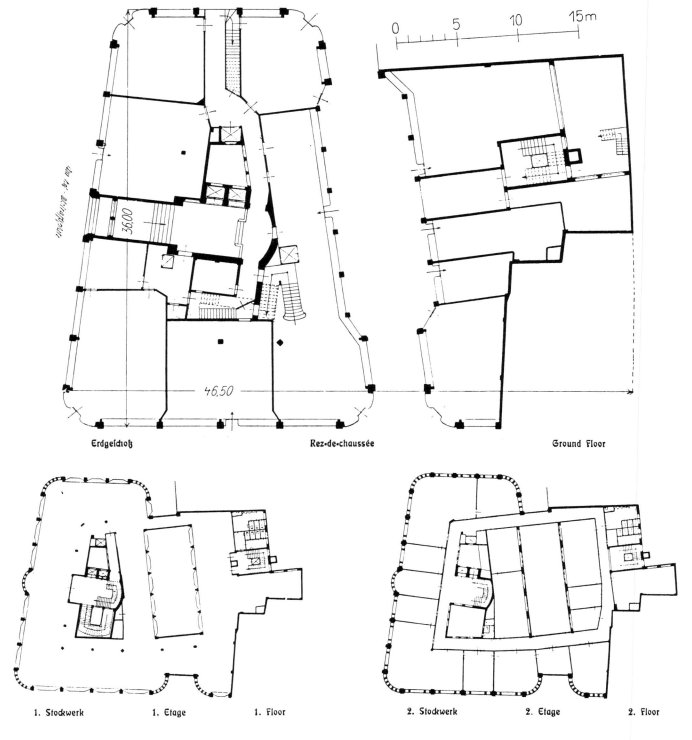

Erdgeschoß   Rez-de-chaussée   Ground Floor

1. Stockwerk   1. Etage   1. Floor   2. Stockwerk   2. Etage   2. Floor

am Hof thront die Figur einer Colonia mit dem Dombaumodell in der Hand, von Erwin Holler geschaffen. Von demselben sind die sechs Reliefs mit knieenden Arbeitergestalten über den Bogen der drei Ecken Am Hof gefertigt. Die Verzierungen der Friesbänder über dem Erdgeschoß und am Hauptgesims zeigen altgermanische Motive. Einen weiteren Schmuck der Fassaden bilden die an wagerechten Armen hängenden Kugeln der Preßgaslampen.

Das Erdgeschoß enthält Läden verschiedener Größe, das darüber liegende Zwischengeschoß ist für Großisten bestimmt und das folgende erste Hauptgeschoß, in größerer Höhenabmessung, als mächtiger Ausstellungsraum ausgebildet. Die beiden folgenden Obergeschosse sind für Bureauzwecke in kleinere Räume geteilt, im dritten befindet sich ein geräumiges Atelier. Über dem ausgebauten Mansardengeschoß dehnt sich der weite Dachraum aus. Es sind zwei Kellergeschosse übereinander angeordnet. Die Verbindung der Geschosse ist durch mehrere Treppen und Aufzüge hergestellt. Die Haupttreppe und die daneben liegenden beiden großen Personenaufzüge sind bis zum obersten Geschoß durchgeführt, zur Lastenbeförderung dient ein dritter, großer Aufzug, während zwei kleinere Aufzüge für den Verkehr vom Untergeschoß bis zum Zwischengeschoß bestimmt sind; Nebentreppen sind noch drei angelegt. Die Decken sind in Eisenbeton hergestellt; die Erwärmung sämtlicher Räume geschieht durch eine Niederdruck-Dampfheizung.

Die Vorhalle, sowie das anschließende Haupttreppenhaus sind an den Innenwänden mit Marmor bekleidet. Zwei Reliefs von F. Albermann schmücken die Eingangshalle. Der Haupteingang ist durch eine metallene Scheidewand geteilt, welche die bronzene Reiterfigur Karls des Großen, ein Werk Graseggers, trägt; in Stein gehauen stehen rechts und links Krieger des Kaisers und seinen Reitknecht. Die Stollwercks-halle ist durch den rötlichen Ton des Marmors an den Wänden und die Bronze der aus Durmametall bestehenden Fenster- und Türrahmen bezeichnet. An der inneren Stirnwand der Halle sind zwei von Albermann gefertigte Reliefs angebracht. Zwölf Kinderfiguren von R. Bosselt stellen als Pfeilerabschlüsse die verschiedenen Geschäftszweige in einem Reigen vor. Von der Stollwerckshalle führt ein besonderer Aufgang, in deutschrotem Marmor gehalten, zu dem Nebenbau hinüber.

le Rhine avec ses affluents, par Joseph Moest. Au dessus de l'entrée sur la Strasse am Hof trône la figure de la ville de Cologne avec le modèle du dôme dans la main, œuvre de Erwin Holler. C'est le même artiste qui a exécuté les six reliefs, représentant des ouvriers agenouilleés au dessus de l'arc des trois angles Am Hof. Les ornements des frises audessus du rez-de-chaussée et à la corniche montrent des motifs anciens germains. Les boules des lampes suspendues à des bras horizontaux concourent aussi à embellir la façade.

Le rez-de-chaussée contient des magasins de différentes grandeurs, l'entresol qui le surmonte est destiné à des commerces en gros, le premier étage d'une plus grande hauteur servira de vaste local d'éxposition. Les deux étages suivants sous disposés en plus petits locaux pour bureaux, au troisième étage se trouve un vaste atelier. Au dessus de l'étage mansardé se trouve un grand comble. Il ya deux étages de caves. La communication des étages entre eux est assurée au moyen de plusieurs escaliers et ascenseurs. L'escalier principal et les deux ascenseurs qui l'accompagnent conduisent jusqu'à l'étage supérieur. Pour le transport des marchandises sert un troisième grand ascenseur, tandis que deux plus petits ascenseurs assurent la communication du sous-sol à l'entresol. Il ya en outre trois escaliers secondaires. Les plafonds sont construits en béton armé; tous les locaux sont chauffés au moyen d'un calorifère à vapeur à basse préssion.

Le vestibule, ainsi que la cage d'escalier située à côté ont leurs parois intérieures revêtues de marbre. Deux reliefs de F. Albermann décorent la halle d'entrée. L'entrée principale est séparée par une paroi en métal portant la figure équestre de Charles-Magne, œuvre de Ms. Grasegger; à droite et à gauché, on voit des guerriers de l'empereur et son écuyer. La Stollwerckshalle est caractérisée par le ton rougeâtre du marbre des parois et le bronze des encadrements en métal de Durma des fenêtres et des portes, à la paroi intérieure de la halle se trouvent deux reliefs exécutés par Albermann. Douze figures d'enfants par R. Bosselt représentent dans une ronde, comme couronnements de piliers, les diverses branches du commerce. Un escalier spécial exécuté en marbre allemand rouge conduit de la Stollwerckshalle au bâtiment secondaire.

and deep and has a sculptural ornament of Father Rhine and his tributaries by Joseph Moest of Cologne. Over the exits on the Strasse am Hof is the figure of Colonia with a model of the Dome in her hand by Erwin Holler. From this artist are too the six reliefs with kneeling workmens' figures over the arches of the three corners "Am Hof". The ornaments of the frieze band over the ground floor and on the principal moulding have for their subject old German myths. A further ornamental detail of the facade is the illumination, consisting of balls for gas lamps hauging from a horizontal arm.

The ground floor contains shops of various size, that lying over the intermediate storey, is intended for wholesale merchants, and the floor above, of great height is intended for the exhibition of goods. The two following floors are arranged as bureaus and divided into small rooms, on the third floor is a spacious studio. Over the well built mansard storey is a spacious roof room. There are two basements arranged one over the other. The counection between the floors is by various staircases and lifts. The principal staircase and the two passenger lifts on each side, reach from the basement to the top of the building. For goods a third large lift is provided, while two smaller lifts are for conveyance to the intermediate storey; three secondary staircases are also constructed. The ceilings are of iron beton, the heating of all the building is by steam.

The entrance hall as well as the walls of the principal staircase are faced with marble. Two reliefs by F. Albermann ornament this hall. The principal entrance has a dividing metal wall displaying a bronze equestrian figure of Charles the Great, a work of Graseggers. Right and left are stone figures showing soldiers of the Emperor and his page. The "Stollwercks Halle" is shown by the red tone of the marble used and by the bronze out of Durma metal used for the door and window frames. On the upper part of the wall of the hall are two reliefs by Albermann. Twelve childrens' figures by R. Bosselt divided by pillars are used to designate the various branches of the manufacture. From the "Stollwerck's Halle" leads a special entrance, principally in German-red toned marble, to the side building.

275 [1907: 83]

Das Wohnhaus in Charlottenburg, Bismarckstraße 12, von Architekt Reg.-Baumeister L. Otte herrührend, bildet einen Putzbau in fünf Geschossen und einem teilweise ausgebauten Dachgeschoß. Die Architekturformen sind in modernem Barock gehalten. Zu beiden Seiten der Front im zweiten und dritten Obergeschoß springen überdeckte Balkons auf Konsolen vor, von denen die rechts belegenen durch logenartige Einbauten erweitert sind. Ein auf Figurenhermen ruhender offener Balkon im zweiten Obergeschoß nimmt die Mitte der Fassade ein, die von einem breiten, von Fenstern durchbrochenen geschweiften Dachgiebel abgeschlossen wird. Das gebrochene Dach ist mit Falzziegeln eingedeckt.

275 [1907: 83]

La maison d'habitation Bismarckstrasse 12 à Charlottenbourg construite par Mr. L. Otte architecte du gouvernement est un édifice de maçonnerie crépie, de cinq étages avec un toit en partie occupé par des appartements. Les formes d'architecture sont traitées en style baroque moderne. Des deux côtés de la façade on voit saillir des balcons couverts au second et au troisième étages; ceux de droite sont agrandis par des enfoncements en forme de loggias. Un balcon découvert au second étage, reposant sur des cariatides en forme d'hermes occupe le milieu de la façade, qui est couronnée par un large fronton ondulé, percé de fenêtres. Le toit de ligne brisée est recouvert de tuiles à recouvrement.

275 [1907: 83]

The dwelling house at Bismarckstrasse 12, Charlottenburg, designed by the architect L. Otte is a plaster building of five storeys and a roof storey partly arranged for dwellings. The style is modern barock. On each side of the front in the second and third storey are covered balconies resting on console supports; the balconies on the right are further enlarged by loggias. In the second upper storey, the middle of the facade is occupied by an open balcony supported by sculptured ornament; over this is a broad roof gable with a curved boundary line, and containing windows. The roof, which has a broken line, is covered with tiles.

276 [1907: 97]

Eine reich verzierte Fassade, an die Formen des Empirestils erinnernd, zeichnet das von Architekt Tony Müller entworfene Wohnhaus in Köln a. Rh., Moltkestraße 27, vorteilhaft aus. Das Erdgeschoß, die Eingänge enthaltend, sowie das erste Obergeschoß sind gequadert und werden durch ein über der mittleren Fenstergruppe ausgebauchtes Bandgesims nach oben

276 [1907: 97]

Une riche façade rappelant les formes du style empire distingue favorablement la maison d'habitation Moltkestrasse 27 à Cologne sur Rhine bâtie par Mr. Tony Müller, architecte. Le rez-de-chaussée auquel se trouvent les entrées, ainsi que le premier étage sont construits en bosses et sont couronnés dans le haut par un cordon faisant ressaut audessus

276 [1907: 97]

The dwelling house at Moltkestrasse 27, Cologne on Rhine, designed by the architect Tony Müller is advantageously distinguished by its richly ornamented facade, recalling many of the forms of the Empire style. The ground floor, containing the entrance, and the first floor, are of large square stones and

abgeſchloſſen. Das zweite und dritte Obergeſchoß ſind durch gepaarte mit eigenartig geformten joniſierenden Kapitellen und Gebälkſtücken bekrönte Säulen in eins zuſammengezogen. Die breitere Mittelachſe zwiſchen dieſen nimmt in beiden Obergeſchoſſen ein flachrund ausgebogener, durch ein flaches Kuppeldach abgeſchloſſener Fenſterausbau ein, während ſich in der einen Seitenachſe zwei Loggien übereinander, in der anderen Fenſter öffnen. Über dem Fenſterausbau erhebt ſich ein von gebrochener Rundlinie begrenzter Dachgiebel, in dem ſich eine Loge öffnet. Zu ſeiten des Giebels ſind Dachfenſter auf dem unteren Teile des gebrochenen Daches angeordnet. Die mittleren Säulenpaare werden durch vollrund modellierte Figurengruppen bekrönt, welche ebenſo wie die figürlichen Reliefs zwiſchen den Seitenfenſtern des zweiten und und dritten Obergeſchoſſes von dem Bildhauer J. Wolf herrühren.

Der Bau wurde etwa im Laufe eines Jahres für die Koſtenſumme von rund 220 000 Mark hergeſtellt. Der Sockel beſteht aus Niedermendiger Baſaltlava, das Portal aus Sandſtein, während die übrigen Faſſadenflächen in Verputz ausgeführt ſind. Der langgeſtreckte Grundriß zeigt im Vorderhauſe eine reich bemeſſene und ausgeſtattete Wohnung, im Hinterhauſe Atelier- und Bureauräume.

277 [1907: 88]

Das Amtsgebäude in München, Dachauerſtraße 8, iſt der An- und Umbau eines älteren Gebäudes, ausgeführt nach dem Entwurf des Architekten k. Bauamtaſſeſſors K. Beſtelmeyer. Es enthält ein Polizeiamt, eine Schutzmannſchaftſtation und außerdem eine Anzahl Dienſtwohnungen. Die Bauzeit nahm etwa fünf Monate in Anſpruch. Die mit einem Erkerausbau im dritten Obergeſchoß verſehene, ſonſt ungegliederte vierſtöckige Faſſade iſt in naturfarbenem Kalkmörtel verputzt und mit einem Biberſchwanzdach abgedeckt. Die Fenſterläden ſind hellgrün, die Einfahrtstore dunkelrot, die Fenſter weiß und die Fenſtergitter ſtumpfblau geſtrichen.

278 [1907: 91]

Das Haus Girardet, ſogenanntes „Feuerſchlößchen", in Honnef a. Rh., entworfen von Architekt W. v. Tettau, zeichnet ſich durch reiche Gruppenbildung am Äußeren, freie Behandlung der an das Empire erinnernden Einzelformen und großräumige Geſtaltung des Inneren vorteilhaft aus. Die Bauzeit nahm etwa ein und ein halbes Jahr in Anſpruch, die Baukoſten betrugen rund 450 000 Mark. Die Außenwände ſind aus Ettringer Tuff, der Sockel und die Einfaſſungen aus Kalkſtein hergeſtellt; das gebrochene mit Fenſterluken verſehene Hauptdach, das mit einem Schopf verſehene zeltartig abgewalmte Dach eines Vorbaues und die kuppelartig geſchwungenen Dächer zweier anderer Vorbauten ſind mit Schiefer eingedeckt.

Die Lichtöffnungen im Erdgeſchoß ſind rundbogig geſchloſſen, die Fenſter im Obergeſchoß der Hauptfront ſind mit Pilaſterſtreifen eingefaßt und durch Steinpfoſten geteilt, an dem derſelben Front vorgelegten vom Boden aus aufſteigenden Ausbau ſind im Obergeſchoß zwiſchen den Fenſtern vollrunde Figuren angebracht, darüber im Dachgeſchoß öffnet ſich eine Laube auf Säulen. Ein anderer durch beide Geſchoſſe gehender Vorbau trägt ebenfalls im Dachgeſchoß eine Laube. Der mittlere Teil des Erdgeſchoſſes iſt zu einer geräumigen Halle mit anſchließender Diele und freiliegender Treppe ausgebildet; Speiſe- und Wohnzimmer reihen ſich um den Mittelraum. Das Obergeſchoß enthält, wieder von einer Halle zugänglich, die Schlafzimmer, außerdem ſind im ausgebauten Dachgeſchoß eine Anzahl Zimmer für Fremde und Dienſtperſonal untergebracht.

des fenêtres du milieu. Le second et le troisième étages sont reliés entre eux par des colonnes accouplées avec de singuliers chapiteaux jonisant et surmontées de fragments d'entablement. L'axe du milieu entre ces colonnes est marqué aux deux étages supérieurs par un groupe de fenêtres faisant saillie en arc de cercle et recouvert d'un toit en forme de coupole plate; les axes latéraux sont marqués d'un côté par deux loggias situées l'une au dessus de l'autre; de l'autre côté, par des fenêtres. Au dessus du groupe de fenêtres saillant, s'élève un pignon inscrit dans une ligne arrondie et brisée dans lequel s'ouvre une loggia. Des deux côtés du pignon sont disposées des lucarnes dans la partie inférieure du toit mansard. Les colonnes accouplées du milieu sont couronnées de groupes d'enfants modelés en ronde bosse, lesquels, ainsi que les reliefs de figures situés entre les fenêtres du second et du troisième étages sont dûs au sculpteur J. Wolf.

La construction dura un an et coûta 220 000 Marks. Le socle est en basalt de lave de Niedermendig, le portail en pierre, tandis que les autres parties des façades sont en maçonnerie crépie. Le plan allongé montre dans la partie antérieure un appartement riche et spacieux; dans la maison de derrière sont des ateliers et des bureaux.

277 [1907: 88]

La mairie de la Dachauerstrasse 8 à Munich, est une transformation et une augmentation d'une bâtiment plus ancien construit d'après le projet de Mr. K. Bestelmeyer architecte et assesseur. Elle contient un bureau de police, une station d'agents et un certain nombre d'appartements de service. La construction dura environ cinq mois. La façade à quatre étages, sans divisions architecturales a une tourelle au troisième étage, elle est traitée en crépissage couleur naturelle et est couverte en tuiles. Les volets de fenêtres sont peints en vert clair, la porte cochère en rouge sombre, les fenêtres en blanc et les grilles des fenêtres en bleu foncé.

278 [1907: 91]

La maison Girardet, dite le Feuerschlösschen à Honnef sur le Rhin, bâtie d'après les plans de W. v. Tettau architecte, se distingue avantageusement par sa riche silhouette extérieure, la manière libre dont ont été traitées les formes rappelant celles du style empire, et la large distribution de l'intérieur. La durée de la construction fut d'àpeu près un an et demi, les frais s'élevèrent à 450 000 Marks. Les façades sont en tuffe de Ettringen, le socle et les encadrements en pierre calcaire. Le toit mansard, interrompu par des lucarnes; le toit en forme de tente couvrant un avant-corps et les toits ondulés, en forme de coupole recouvrant deux autres avant-corps sont recouverts en ardoises.

Les fenêtres du rez-de-chaussée sont couvertes en plein-cintre, celles du premier étage de la façade principale sont encadrées de pilastres et partagées par des meneaux en pierre; on a placé des figures en ronde-bosse entre les fenêtres du premier étage de l'avant-corps montant de front devant la même façade; au dessus, dans l'étage du toit, s'ouvre une loggia portée par des colonnes. Un autre avant-corps traversant les deux étages porte également une loggia dans le toit. La partie centrale du rez-de-chaussée est utilisée pour un hall spacieux, correspondant à un vestibule et à un escalier suspendu; le salon et la salle à manger communiquent à cette pièce centrale. L'étage supérieur contient les chambres à coucher qui communiquent ellesmêmes avec un hall. On a en outre disposé un certain nombre de chambres d'amis et de domestiques dans les mansardes.

are finished by a band of moulding over the middle window group. The second and third upper storey are united by pairs of characteristically designed pillars with Jonic capitals and ornaments. The broad middle erection between these is filled by a flat rounded window projection extending through two storeys and finished off with a cupola-formed roof; on the side, two loggias one over the other open towards the windows. Over the window projection is built a roof gable with a broken boundary line, from which a niche opens. On the side of the gables are roof windows arranged on the lower side of the roof. The middle group of pillars are crowned by fullsized sculptured figures; these as well as the figures in relief between the side windows of the second and third storey are by the sculptor J. Wolf.

The building occupied one year and cost about 220 000 Marks. The sockel is of "Niedermendiger" basalt lava, the portal is of sandstone, the remainting parts of the facade are of plaster. The ground plan of great length shows in the front house a spaciously designed and complete dwelling; the back house contains studios and offices.

277 [1907: 88]

The official building at Dachauerstrasse 8, Munich, consist of additions and alterations to an older building carried out according to the design of the architect K. Bestelmeyer. It contains a police office, a policemen's station, and a number of official dwellings. The time occupied in building was about 5 months. The third upper storey contains a bay, except this, the four storeyed facade is quite plain, is plastered with natural coloured lime plaster, and roofed with flat red tiles. The window shutters are light green, the entrance door dark red. The windows white and the window railings a dull blue.

278 [1907: 91]

The house Gerardet the so-called "Feuerschlöschen" at Honnef on Rhine was designed by the architect W. von Tettau. Its chief characteristic is a successful grouping of the exterior, together with the spacious arrangements of the interior; the style is in most details Empire. The time occupied was about 6 months the cost amounted to 450 000 Marks. The exterior walls are of Ettringer tuff stone, the sockel and the praming of lime stone; the principal roof has window niches, the roof of the projecting erection is rounded and has a tentlike ornament, other roofs are ornamented with cupolas. And the whole is covered with slate.

The windows of the ground floor have rounded aiches those of the upper storey in the principal front are articulated by stone pillars. In the front is an erection reaching upwards from the basement, the windows of which are ornamented with complete sculptural figures over this, in the roof storey, is an arbour on pillars. Another projecting erection contains too a balcony on pillars. The middle part of the ground floor is constructed to form a spacious hall opening into an interior hall which contains a free staircase, dining rooms and dwelling rooms are arranged round this interior hall. The upper storey contains the bedrooms, the roof storey contains spare rooms and servants' quarters.

Die auf einer Anhöhe inmitten eines Gartens gelegene Villa Sarre in Neubabelsberg, Kaiferstraße 39, ein Werk des Architekten Reg.-Baumeifters O. Sior, verrät fowohl in der Gruppenbildung wie in den Einzelformen den Einfluß der italienifchen Frührenaiffance. Der einen Front ift im Erdgefchoß eine geräumige, rundbogige, auf Säulen ruhende, mit einer Altane abfchließende Halle vorgelegt, die mit einer Terraffe in Verbindung fteht. Die rundbogig gefchloffenen zweigeteilten Fenfter des Erdgefchoffes erinnern an florentinifche Mufter, die Fenfter des Obergefchoffes find dagegen geradlinig überdeckt. Der eine Flügel des Gebäudes trägt ein zweites, von einer offenen, architravierten Säulenftellung umzogenes Gefchoß, welches von einem flachen abgewalmten Dach überdeckt ift. Ebenfo ift der höher geführte viereckige Ausfichtsturm mit einer oberen offenen architravierten Säulenhalle und einem darüber abfchließenden flachen Zeltdach ausgeftattet. Das Untergefchoß, die Gebäudeecken und einige Fenfterfturze find aus rauh bearbeiteten Quadern hergeftellt, während die Mauerflächen im Erd- und Obergefchoß verputzt find.

La villa Sarre à Neubabelsberg, Kaiserstrasse 39, œuvre de Mr. O. Sior architecte du gouvernement est située sur une élévation au milieu d'un jardin; elle accuse tant dans le groupement de ses parties que dans son détail, l'influence de la renaissance italienne primitive. Une halle arrondie, spacieuse, portée sur des colonnes, surmontée d'un balcon et communiquant avec une terrasse a été placée en avant d'une des façades au rez-de-chaussée. Les fenêtres doubles à plein-cintre du rez-de-chaussée rappellent un motif florentin tandis que les fenêtres du premier étage ont un l'inteau droit. Une des ailes de la maison porte un second étage entouré d'une colonnade architravée et ouverte elle est couverte d'un plat en forme de comble à croupe; de même, le belvédère carré et surélevé est couronné d'une colonnade ouverte architravée, couverte d'un toit plat. Le sous-sol les angles de la maison et quelques linteaux de fenêtres sont en pierre de taille brute, tandis que les surfaces de maçonnerie du rez-de-chaussée et de l'étage supérieur sont crépis.

The villa Sarre at Kaiserstrasse 39, Neubabelsberg, is a work of the architect Reg.-Baumeister O. Sior. It is situated on an eminence in the middle of a garden and shows both by its grouping as well as by the various details the style of the early Italian Renaissence. On one front is, on the ground floor, a spacious arched hall resting on pillars and finished off with a terrace. The arched two-sided windows of the ground floor are very similar to the Florentine style, the windows of the upper storeys are finished off with straight lines. One wing of the building has a second storey surrounded by an open row of pillars in architrave form, and covered with a flat, slightly curved roof. The same architecture has been used for the high square tower with an open pillared hall above, covered with a tent like roof. The lower storey, the corners of the building, and some window supports are of rough square stones, the walls of the ground and upper storeys are plastered.

Ein ergebnislofer Wettbewerb war bereits vorausgegangen, als man den Auftrag zur Auffteilung eines Entwurfs für den Bau des Neuen Kurhaufes in Wiesbaden an Profeffor Dr. Fr. von Thierfch erteilte. Nach deffen Plane wurde der Bau im Januar 1905 begonnen und konnte nach feiner Vollendung im Mai 1907 eingeweiht werden. Die Gefamtkoften der Bauausführung betrugen einfchließlich der künftlerifchen Arbeiten und der Mobiliarbefchaffung rd. 4 425 000 Mark. An der Ausarbeitung der Bauzeichnungen war Architekt H. Lömpel hervorragend beteiligt, während die örtliche Bauleitung dem Architekten K. Werz übertragen war.

Das Äußere des Gebäudes ift in den Formen der klaffifch-edeln Renaiffance gehalten und wird befonders wirkungsvoll durch den mächtigen Säulenportikus mit Giebeldreieck über der Zufahrtsrampe und den über der Wandelhalle fich erhebenden Kuppelbau ausgezeichnet. Die Sockelverkleidung des Unterbaues befteht aus Fichtelgebirgsgranit, die Faffadenflächen find mit weißgelbem Dürkheimer Sandftein bekleidet. Für Säulen und Gebälke des weftlichen Portalmittelbaues kam fchlefifcher Quarzfandftein zur Verwendung. Ein großer Teil der Dachkonftruktionen ift in Eifen ausgeführt, die Dacheindeckung befteht wefentlich aus Cauberfchiefer, mit Zuhilfenahme des Kupfers für Einzelheiten. Von figürlichen Bildhauerarbeiten für das Äußere kommen hauptfächlich in Betracht: Die Nifchenfiguren des Weftportikus von Ch. Jaeckle, die Flachreliefs an den Flügeln der Weftfront von Prof. R. v. Goffen und Prof. H. Kaufmann, die Einzelfiguren und Kindergruppen auf den Oftrifaliten von C. Bermann und L. Dafio.

Den Glanzpunkt des Innern bildet die große, den ganzen Querbau einnehmende Wandelhalle mit dem mittleren Kuppelraum und den oberen Galerien. Vor den Kuppelpfeilern haben vier Marmorfiguren, Kopien nach antiken Originalen Platz gefunden; die figürlichen Darftellungen am Tambour der Kuppel rühren von Prof. E. Pfeifer her, die Marmorfopraporten dafelbft von Prof. E. Hahn. Die Entwürfe zu den vier Mofaikmedaillons der Zwickel find von Prof. J. Diez gefertigt. Zu beiden Seiten der Halle fchließen fich in der Längenachfe die Konzertfäle an. Der große Konzertfaal, um welchen fich der Gürtel der Konverfations- und Lefezimmer legt, befitzt große Säulen von Naffauer Marmor, eine Marmorverkleidung der oberen Flächen und Pfeiler und im unteren Teile eine reiche Mahagonivertäfelung.

Un concours avait déjà eu lieu sans résultat, lorsque le Professeur, Docteur v. Thiersch reçut la commande de présenter des plans pour la nouvelle maison de réunion à Visbaden. D'après ces plans, la construction put être commencée en Janvier 1905 et inaugurée en Mai 1907, après son achèvement. Les frais de construction s'élevèrent, y compris le mobilier, à la somme en bloc de 4 425 000 Marks. Pour l'exécution des dessins, la collaboration de Mr. H. Lömpel doit être particulièrement mentionnée, la conduite des travaux sur place fut confiée à Mr. K. Werz architecte.

L'extérieur du monument est tenu dans les nobles formes de la Renaissance, et est particulièrement rehaussé par le puissant portique à colonnes avec fronton surmontant la rampe d'accès et la coupole couronnant le grand vestibule. Le revêtement du socle du rez-de-chaussée est en granit du Fichtelgebirge, les façades sont recouvertes de pierre blanche de Dürkheim. On employa de la pierre de quarz de Silèsie pour les colonnes et l'entablement du portique central ouest. Une grande partie des construction des toits est en fer, la couverture est en ardoises de Cauber avec quelques parties en cuivre. Il faut nommer les artistes suivants qui ont contribué à la décoration sculpturale de l'extérieur: Mr. Ch. Jaeckle pour les figures des niches du portique occidental, Mr. le professeur R. v. Gossen et Mr. le professeur H. Kaufmann pour les bas-reliefs, aux ailes de la façade occidentale, M. M. C. Bermann et L. Dasio pour les figures isolées et les groupes d'enfants.

Le grand hall occupant tout le bâtiment transversal, forme avec sa coupole centrale et ses galeries supérieures le point le plus brillant de l'intérieur. En avant des piliers de la coupole on a placé quatre statues en marbre, copies d'originaux antiques, les décorations figurales du tambour de la coupole sont du professeur E. Pfeiffer, les surportes du professeur E. Hahn. Mr. J. Diez Professeur est l'auteur des projets pour les quatre médaillons en mosaïque des pendentifs. Des deux côtés du hall, dans le sens de la longueur, s'étendent les salles de concert. La grande salle de concert entourée d'une ceinture de chambres de lecture et de conversation est décorée de grandes colonnes de marbre de Nassau, d'un revêtement de marbre des parties supérieures des piliers et d'une riche boiserie

An open competition for a design for a new "Kurhaus" in Wiesbaden had no successful result: Professor Dr. Fr. von Thiersch was therefore invited to send in a plan for the building. This plan was chosen and the "Kurhaus" was begun in January 1905, its completion and inauguration took place in May 1907. The entire cost, including all artistic work and the interior equipment amounted to 4 425 000 Marks. The most important coadjutor in the execution of the design was the architect H. Lömpel, the local superintendence was in the hands of the architect K. Werz.

The exterior is in the form of the nobly classic Renaissance and is made specially effective by a massive pillared portico with a triangular gable over the entrance drive and by a cupola which is erected over the "Wandelhalle" (promenade). The sockel of the basement storey is faced with granite from the Fichtelgebirge, the surfaces of the facade are covered with yellow-white Dürkheim sandstone. For the pillars and supports of the west central portal Silesian quarz sandstone has been used. The greater part of the roof construction is of iron, the tiling is mainly of Cauber slate, with the assistance of copper for certain details. The sculptural work for the exterior was principally in the hands of Ch. Jaeckle who designed the figures in the niches of the west portico, of Professor R. von Gossen and Professor H. Kaufmann who designed the reliefs on the west front, and of E. Hermann and L. Dasio who designed the single groups and childrens figures.

The most splendid feature of the interior is the spacious "Wandelhalle" which occupies the whole transverse of the building with the middle cupola hall and the upper galleries. The cupola pillars are ornamented by four marble figures copies of antique originals, the illustrative figures on the tambour of the cupola are by Professor E. Pfeifer, the marble work of the same is by Professor E. Hahn. The designs for the four mosaic medallions of the spandrel are by Professor J. Diez. On both sides of the hall extend longitudinally the concert saloons, the great concert hall, round which lies the zone of conversation and reading rooms, has large pillars of Nassau marble, marble facings on all the upper surfaces and pillars

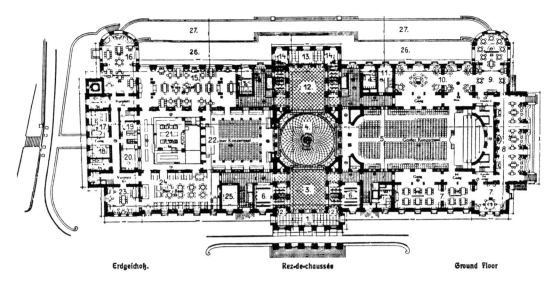

Erdgeſchoß.   Rez-de-chaussée   Ground Floor

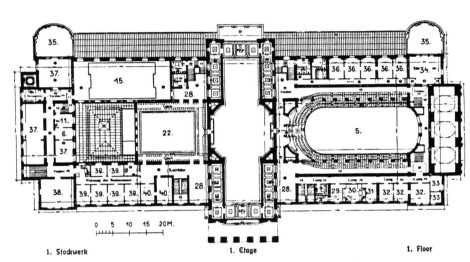

0 5 10 15 20M.

1. Stockwerk   1. Etage   1. Floor

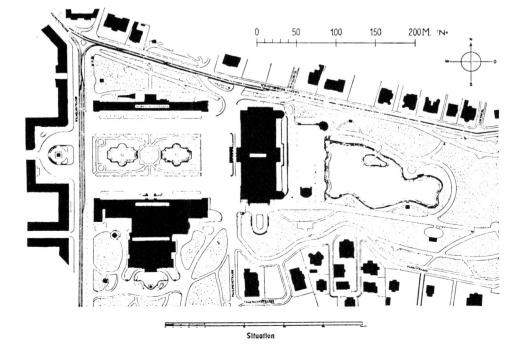

0   50   100   150   200M.

Situation

Erdgeschoß

1. Westlicher Windfang
2. Kasse
3. West-Vestibul
4. Zentralkuppel
5. Großer Konzertsaal
6. Garderobe
7. Lesezimmer
8. Gartenhalle
9. Spielzimmer
10. Konversationsaal
11. Servierraum
12. Ost-Vestibul
13. Östlicher Windfang
14. Büffet
15. Weinsaal
16. Kleiner Restaurationssaal
17. Weinstube
18. Amerikan. Baar
19. Spülküche
20. Anrichte
21. Küche
22. Kleiner Konzertsaal
23. Kleiner Biersaal
24. Biersaal
25. Portier
26. Obere Terrasse
27. Unter Terrasse

Obergeschoß

28. Foyer
29. Empfangszimmer
30. Arbeitszimmer des Kurdirektors
31. Ankleidezimmer
32. Zimmer der Kur-inspektion
33. Zimmer
34. Stimmzimmer
35. Terrasse
36. Künstlerzimmer
37. Gesellschaftszimmer
38. Billardzimmer
39. Wohnung des Restaurateurs
40. Buchhaltung und Kasse

Rez-de-chaussée

1. Tambour occidental
2. Caisse
3. Vestibule occidental
4. Coupole centrale
5. Grande salle de concert
6. Vestiaire
7. Cabinet de lecture
8. Salon sur jardin
9. Salle de restaurant
10. Salon
11. Pièce de service
12. Vestibule oriental
13. Tambour oriental
14. Buffet
15. Salle du bar à vin
16. Petite salle de restaurant
17. Bar à vin
18. Bar américain
19. Pièce de service
20. Office
21. Cuisine
22. Petite salle de concert
23. Petite salle du bar à bière
24. Salle du bar à bière
25. Portier
26. Terrasse supérieure
27. Terrasse inférieure

Etage

28. Hall
29. Salon
30. Bureau du directeur des thermes
31. Vestiaire
32. Bureau de l'inspection thermale
33. Bureau
34. Salle de musique
35. Terrasse
36. Bureau d'artiste
37. Salon
38. Salle de billard
39. Logement du restaurateur
40. Comptabilité et caisse

Ground Floor

1. West Porch
2. Cashier
3. West Vestibule
4. Central Dome
5. Large Concert Hall
6. Cloakroom
7. Reading Room
8. Garden Hall
9. Dining Room
10. Conversation Room
11. Serving Room
12. East Vestibule
13. East Porch
14. Buffet
15. Wine Hall
16. Small Restaurant
17. Wine Tavern
18. American Bar
19. Scullery
20. Pantry
21. Kitchen
22. Small Concert Hall
23. Small Beer Hall
24. Beer Hall
25. Porter
26. Upper Terrace
27. Lower Terrace

Upper Floor

28. Foyer
29. Reception Room
30. Director's Office
31. Dressing-Room
32. Spa Supervision
33. Room
34. Tuning Room
35. Terrace
36. Greenroom
37. Sitting-Room
38. Billiards Room
39. Apartment for Restaurant Owner
40. Accounting and Cashier

Ein Fries von Nereiden und Tritonen, von H. Storch ausgeführt, umzieht das mittlere Deckenfeld. Die Stuckreliefs in den Nischen des Saals, Apollo von den Musen umgeben und den Sonnengott auf dem Fünfgespann fahrend, find gleichfalls Werke des Vorgenannten. In den kleinen Konzertsaal find die Architekturteile des alten abgebrochenen Kurfaals wieder eingebaut worden. In die aus Kirfchbaumholz hergeftellte Täfelung des Weinfaals find Gemälde von Prof. Kirchbach und H. Weinberger eingelaffen.

Die Hauptküche ift als befonderes Glashaus in den großen Lichthof des Nordflügels eingebaut; die Kücheneinrichtung ift von F. Küpperbach & Söhne ausgeführt. Die Gewölbdecken der Räume find meift als maffive Backfteinkonftruktion durchgeführt, während die Flachdecken aus armiertem Beton zwifchen Eifenträgern beftehen. Die Beleuchtung erfolgt elektrifch von eigenen Kraftanlagen aus. Die Heizungsvorrichtung gliedert fich in Niederdruckdampf- und Dampfwarmwaffer-heizungsgruppen; zugleich find umfängliche Lüftungseinrichtungen fowie Waffererforgung und Ableitung der Abwäffer angeordnet.

282 [1908: 4]

Die Villa des Herrn Dr. Becker in Baden-Baden, von Architekt Prof. H. Metzendorf entworfen, zeigt fich in der Hauptanlage als einfacher, gefchloffener Baukörper mit fteilem Satteldach überdeckt, wird jedoch durch einen polygonalen, vom Boden auffteigenden, durch beide Obergefchoffe geführten, mit gefchweiftem Zeltdach abfchließenden Erker, durch eine vorfpringende Loggia, den das Eßzimmer erweiternden Ausbau und eine dem Erdgefchoß angefügte Laube hinreichend belebt. Außerdem trägt das Dach mehrere, mit gefchwungenen Giebeln bekrönte Fenfteraufbauten. Das Hauptgefchoß enthält, um eine mittlere Diele gruppiert, aus welcher die freiliegende Treppe auffteigt, die Wohn- und Gefellfchaftszimmer. Küche und Wirtfchaftsräume find im Untergefchoß untergebracht, während das Obergefchoß wefentlich für die Schlafzimmer in Anfpruch genommen ift. Am Zimmer der Frau liegt die Loggia und am Eß-zimmer der Wintergarten, ferner fteht das Mufik-zimmer mit dem Erkerausbau in Verbindung. Die Faffaden find im Unter- und Hauptgefchoß in boffiertem Quaderwerk, im oberen Gefchoß und den Giebeln in rauhem Mörtelpuß hergeftellt. Das Dach ift mit Biberfchwänzen eingedeckt und die Wandflächen der Dachaufbauten find befchiefert.

283 [1908: 20]

Die in romanifchen Stilformen erbaute Luther-kirche in Karlsruhe, am Melanchthon-plaß, trägt in der Hauptanordnung dem Charakter des neueren proteftantifchen Kirchenbaues Rechnung; fie erfcheint als Kreuzanlage mit feitlicher Turmftellung und gibt einen Zufammenfchluß von Kirche, Gemeinde-, Konfirmandenfaal und Pfarrhaus zu einer einheitlich verbundenen Baugruppe. Der Entwurf, von den Architekten Curjel & Mofer herrührend, ift aus einem engeren Wettbewerb hervorgegangen und wurde vom März 1905 bis zum Oktober 1907 zur Ausführung gebracht, und zwar unter der Spezialleitung des Architekten Jägel. Kirche und Pfarrhaus famt Orgel und Glocke kofteten rund 467 000 Mark.

Die freiftehende Kirche mit dem Konfirmanden- und Gemeindefaal, dem zurückgefchobenen Pfarr-haufe und dem vorliegenden Pfarrgarten bildet ein fchönes, mannigfaltig bewegtes Ganzes, welches durch die von Bildhauer Kiefer ausgeführte Koloffalrelieffatue Luthers am Turmfuß noch einen bedeutfamen Schmuck erhalten hat, außerdem find die vordere Vorhalle und das

---

d'acajou dans le bas. Une frise de néréides et de tritons, exécutée par Mr. H. Storch entoure le panneau central du plafond. Le même artiste a livré les reliefs de stuc, dans les niches de la salle, Apollon entouré des muses, et le dieu Soleil monté sur son char à six chevaux. Dans la petite salle de concert on a replacé quelques fragments de l'ancienne maison de réunion démolie. Dans la boiserie de bois de cerisier, sont enchassées des peintures de Mr. le professeur Kirchbach et de Mr. H. Weinberger.

La cuisine principale est une construction spéciale, vitrée, située dans la grande cour de l'aile nord. L'installation de la cuisine est de F. Küpperbach & Fils. Les voûtes des salles sont en général massives et construites en briques, tandis que les plafonds sont en béton armé entre sommiers en fer. L'éclairage électrique est fourni par une usine propre. Le chauffage central est produit par des calorifères combinés de vapeur à basse pression et d'eau chaude; l'établissement est en outre pourvu d'importantes installations pour ventilation, conduites d'eaux et canalisation.

282 [1908: 4]

La villa de Mr. le Dr. Becker à Baden-Baden est l'œuvre du professeur H. Metzendorf architecte; cette maison forme une masse simple couverte d'un grand toit à pente raide. Une tourelle polygonale, montant de fond, traversant les deux étages supérieurs et couronnée d'un toit ondulé, ainsi qu'une loggia en saillie, un bow-window de la salle à manger et une pergola appuyée au rez-de-chaussée suffisent à animer les façades. D'autre part, le toit est agrémenté de plusieurs lucarnes avec pignons ondulés. L'étage principal contient les pièces d'habitation et de société groupées autour d'un hall central duquel s'élève un escalier suspendu. La cuisine et les dépendances sont situées en sous-sol, tandis que l'étage supérieur contient les chambres à coucher. La chambre de madame communique avec la loggia et la salle à manger avec le jardin d'hiver, une loge en saillie augmente la surface de la chambre de musique. Les façades sont en bossages de pierre au rez-de-chaussée et au premier étage et en maçonnerie crépie à l'étage supérieur et aux pignons. Le toit est recouvert en tuiles et les surfaces des lucarnes sont recouvertes en ardoises.

283 [1908: 20]

L'église de Luther, Melanchtonplatz à Carlsruhe, construite en formes romanes, tient compte en général du caractère du temple protestant moderne; nous remarquons la disposition en forme de croix avec une tour latérale et la combinaison, de l'église, de la salle de confirmation, de la salle de paroisse, et de la cure en un groupe de bâtiments. M. M. Curjel et Moser architectes ont livré le projet qui doit son origine à un concours restreint, les plans furent exécutés du mois de mars 1905 à celui d'octobre 1907, sous la direction spéciale de M. Jägel architecte. L'église et la cure avec les orgues et les cloches ont coûté 467 000 Marks en bloc.

L'église libre de sous côtés, avec la salle de confirmation et la salle de paroisse, la cure placée en arrière et le jardin situé devant la cure, forme un bel ensemble très mouvementé, la statue colossale de Luther au pied de la tour, exécutée par le sculpteur Kiefer ajoute à la composition un intérêt particulier; en outre, le

---

and in the lower part a rich panelling of mahogany. A frieze of Nereids and Tritons by H. Storch is carried round the middle bay of the ceiling. The stucco reliefs in the niches of the hall, Apollo surrounded by the Muses, and the sun god on the fivehorsed chariot are the work of the same artist. The small concert hall contains the architectural parts of the old "Kurhaus". In the cherry-wood panelling of the wine saloon are pictures at in by Professor Kirchbach and H. Weinberger.

The principal kitchen is built as a glasshouse in the skylighted court yard of the north wing, the equipment of the kitchen is by F. Küpperbach & Sons. The vaulted ceilings of the building are principally of solid brick construction, the flat ceilings are of beton and iron. The lighting is by electricity, the building having its own power-house; the heating is in alternate groups of low pressure steam, and warm water apparatus, at the same time a most complete system of ventilation, water supply and drainage has been constructed.

282 [1908: 4]

The villa of Dr. Becker in Baden-Baden, designed by the architecte Prof. H. Metzendorff is a simple block of building with a steep King-post roof, the monotony of this, is however enlivened by a polygonal bay which extends upwards through all the storeys commencing at the ground floor, and finished off with a tent roof; it is further ornamented by a projecting loggia which enlarges the dining room and by a similar construction on the ground floor, the roof too, has several window erections with ornamental details. The principal floor contains a square hall from which a free staircase ascends, and round which are grouped the various living and reception rooms. The kitchen and domestic offices are in the basement, the bedrooms are all on the upper storey. From the morning room leads a loggia and from the dining room a conservatory, the music room is in connection with the bay. The facades of the basement and first floor are of bossed square stones, the upper floors and the gables are of rough plaster. The roof is of flat red tiles and the surfaces of the roof windows are slated.

283 [1908: 20]

The Luther church on the Melanchthon-platz in Carlsruhe is built in the Romanesque style, and resembles in character the greater number of modern Protestant churches. It is built in the form of a cross with a side tower, and includes in one architectural group the church, the vestry, the confirmation hall and parsonage house. The design, by the architects Curjel and Moser, was the result of a limited competition and was built from March 1905 to October 1907 under the special superintendence of the architect Jägel. The entire cost of church, parsonage and organ amounted to about 467 000 Marks.

The church, standing free, the meeting hall, the confirmation hall, the parsonage with its surrounding garden forms a pleasant and varied group, and has received an important ornamental appearance by the colossal relief statue of Luther (by sculptor Kiefer) which is placed at the foot of the tower. It is further ornamented by the

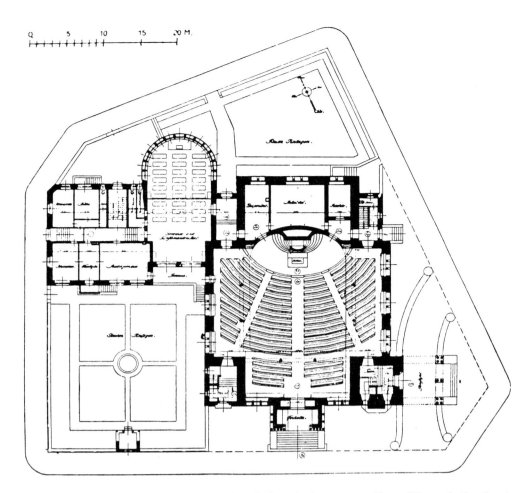

Glockengeschoß des Turmes durch Vergoldungen hervorgehoben. Die Außenwände der Kirche, der Saalbauten und des Pfarrhauses sind in bossiertem Quaderwerk hergestellt, die Dächer sind mit Schiefer eingedeckt. Das überwölbte, mit Emporen in den Kreuzflügeln und mit einer flachrund ausspringenden Altarnische ausgestattete Innere der Kirche ist einschließlich der Wandflächen mit einem silbergrauen Ton, teilweise mit dunkelgrauem und vergoldetem Ornament überzogen. Als Flächenschmuck treten die von Prof. Laeuger herrührenden Glasmalereien der Fenster in den Kreuzarmen und über der Orgelempore hervor. Die Kanzelwand schmückt die bildnerische Darstellung der Bergpredigt von Bildhauer Binz. Die große Glocke, vom Großherzog gestiftet, ist von Gebr. Bachert gegossen und trägt die Reliefbildnisse des Großherzoglichen Ehepaars.

porche et l'étage des cloches de la tour ont été enrichis de dorures. Les façades de l'église, des salles et de la cure sont en bossages; les toits sont recouverts en ardoises. L'intérieur voûté de l'église montre des galeries dans les transepts et une niche d'autel en forme de segment; il est, y compris les parois, recouvert d'un ton gris d'argent, recouvert en partie d'un ornement gris foncé et doré. Les vitraux peints des fenêtres des transepts et de celles au dessus de la tribune des orgues sont dus au professeur Laeuger. La paroi de la chaire est décorée d'une représentation plastique du sermon sur la montagne exécutée par Mr. Binz, sculpteur. La grande cloche donnée par le Grand-Duc et fondue par M. M. Bachert frères, porte en relief le portrait du couple grand-ducal.

gilding of the front porch and of the belfry. The walls of the church, the halls and the parsonage are faced with bossed square stones, the roofs are covered with slate. The interior is vaulted, has galleries in the side aisles and has a circular projecting chancel; the colouring of the whole of the interior is silver-grey with darker grey and gilded ornament. The stained glass windows ornamented the windows of the side aisles and the organ loft are by Professor Laeuger. The wall of the chancel is decorated by sculptural illustrations of the Sermon on the Mount by the sculptor Binz. The big bell, presented by the Grand Duke was cast by Brothers Bachert and has on it a relief portrait of the Grand ducal couple.

284 [1908; 12]

Durch die Zusammenstellung verschiedenfarbiger Baustoffe: weißen Rappuß der Flächen, gelben Muschelkalkstein des Sockels und hellgrünen englischen Schiefer der Dächer, welche den beherrschenden Farbenakkord: gelb, grün, weiß hervorbringen, gewinnt das Äußere der Villa O. Henkell in Wiesbaden einen besonderen Reiz, zu dessen Erhöhung die malerische Gruppierung des Bauwerks beiträgt. Der Entwurf der Fassaden stammt von dem Architekten H. B. Wieland und von diesem und dem Architekten J. Hötzel die Anordnung der Grundrisse. Die Bauzeit nahm ein und einviertel Jahr in Anspruch.

Den Hauptraum des Erdgeschosses bildet eine große Halle, welche durch eine Kaminnische besonders ausgezeichnet ist. Außerdem sind hier das Damenzimmer mit einem Erker und einer Arbeitsecke, das mit dem Billardzimmer im Kellergeschoß unmittelbar in Verbindung stehende Herrenzimmer, das mit zwei Anrichteräumen ausgestattete Eßzimmer, die geräumige, mit reichlichem Zubehör ausgestattete Küche und ferner Zimmer für Dienstboten angeordnet. Ein vorspringender Gebäudeflügel enthält den Automobilschuppen. Im ersten Obergeschoß liegen die

284 [1908; 12]

La villa O. Henkell à Wiesbaden a un charme particulier, grâce à la combinaison des différents matériaux de construction; crépissage blanc des surfaces, pierre calcaire jaune du socle et ardoise anglaise vert clair des toits; blanc, jaune et vert forment l'accord dominant, dont le groupement des masses augmente encore l'aspect pittoresque. Mr. H. B. Wieland architecte a fait le projet des façades, tandis que la disposition des plans est dûe à la fois à Mrs. Wieland et Hötzel architectes. La construction dura une année et quart.

Un grand hall forme la pièce principale du rez-de-chaussée, ce hall est décoré d'une niche avec cheminée. Le boudoir avec une tourelle et un angle séparé, le fumoir relié directement avec la salle de billard située en sous-sol, salle à manger pourvue de deux offices, la cuisine spacieuse accompagnée de toutes les dépendances nécessaires, et enfin la chambre pour les domestiques se trouvent également au rez-de-chaussée. Une aile en saillie contient le garage à automobiles. Au premier étage se trouvent les chambres à coucher de la famille avec leurs chambres de bains et toilettes, la

284 [1908; 12]

The exterior of the villa O. Henkell in Wiesbaden has been given a peculiar charm by the harmonious combination of various building materials; white rough plaster for the surfaces, yellow shell lime stone for the basement and light green English slate for the roofs emphasize the preponderating colour harmony viz: green, yellow and white — the picturesque grouping of the erection adding not a little to the general effect. The design of the facade is by the architect H. B. Wieland, the same artist together with the architect J. Hötzel constructed the ground plan, and the time occupied in building was 1¼ years.

The principal space on the ground floor is occupied by a spacious hall, in which the distinguishing feature is a large open fire-place. Round this hall are arranged the drawing room with a bay and cosy corner, the study and smoking room in connection with the billiard room in the basement, the dining room with two serving rooms adjoining, the spacious kitchen with complete domestic offices and the rooms for servants. A projecting wing of the building contains the automobile garage. On the first

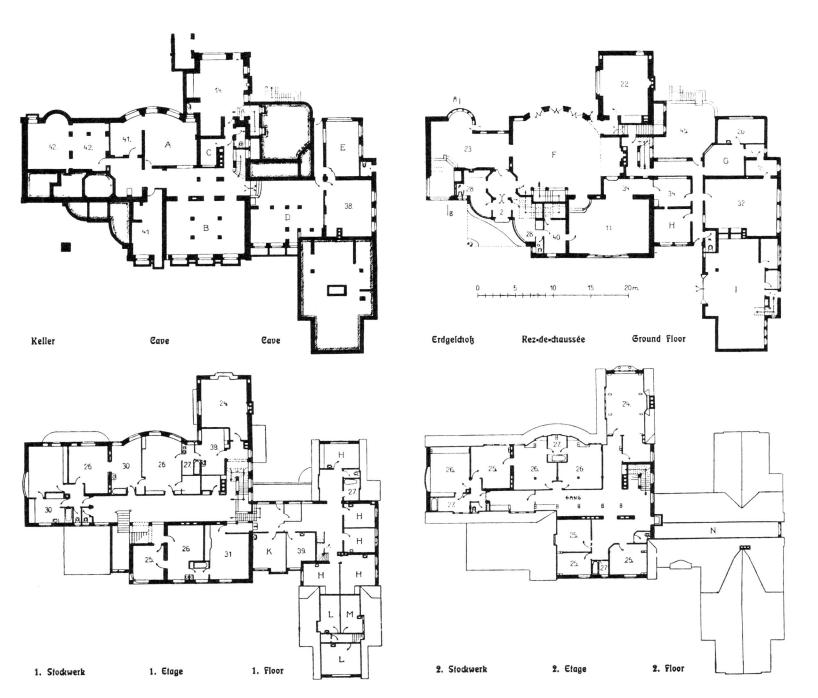

Keller	Cave	Cave

Erdgeíchoß	Rez-de-chaussée	Ground Floor

1. Stockwerk	1. Etage	1. Floor

2. Stockwerk	2. Etage	2. Floor

Schlafzimmer der Familie mit ihren Baderäumen und Toiletten, das Kinderzimmer neben dem Zimmer der Gouvernante und feitlich für fich abgetrennt eine Anzahl Wohn- und Schlafzimmer für das Bausperional, den Chauffeur und den Gärtner. Das ausgebaute Dachgeíchoß enthält noch mehrere Wohn- und Schlafzimmer, fowie das Kinderfpielzimmer. Im Kellergeíchoß find außer dem ídion erwähnten Billardzimmer die Waíchküche, das Bügelzimmer, fowie die Beiz- und Vorratsräume untergebracht.

Die Entwürfe zu fämtlichen Details und Zimmereinrichtungen lieferten die Architekten B. B. Wieland und J. Bötzel, unter Beihilfe von Fr. Geiger und J. Marídiall, mit Aus-nahme der Einrichtung von drei Schlafzimmern im erften Stock, die von Prof. A. Niemeyer in München herrührt.

chambre des enfants près de la chambre de la gouvernante, et à côté, séparées du reste de la maison, une suite de chambres à coucher et d'habitation pour le personnel, domestiques, le chauffeur et le jardinier. Dans les combles sont situées encore plusieurs chambres à coucher et d'habitation, ainsi que la chambre de jeu des enfants. En sous-sol on a aménagé outre la salle de billard déjà citée, la buanderie, la chambre à repasser, ainsi que les bûchers et le garde manger.

Les architectes H. B. Wieland et J. Hötzel, secondés par Fr. Geiger et J. Marschall livrèrent tous les détails pour l'ameublement des pièces, à l'exception des trois chambres à coucher au premier étage, dont le projet à été fait par le professeur A. Niemeyer à Munich.

upper storey are the bedrooms for the family, the bathrooms and lavatories, the nurseries and rooms for the governess. On the side and separated from the rest, are the living and sleeping rooms of the chauffeur and gardener. The roof storey contains several rooms, some bedrooms a day nursery &c. In the basement, in addition to the above mentioned billiard room are the wash house the laundry as well as the store rooms and heating apparatus.

The designs of the various details connected with the furniture and the interior equipment are by the architects H. B. Wieland and J. Hötzel with the assistance of Fr. Geiger and J. Marschall. The three bedrooms on the first floor were designed by Professor A. Niemeyer of Munich.

285 [1908; 7]

Der Entwurf zu dem Gebäude der Vik-torialchule, der höheren Mädchenschule in Frankfurt a. M. und des zugehörigen Dienst-wohnhauses, von Stadtbauinípektor, Reg.-Bau-meifter a. D. K. Wilde ftammend, war aus einem Wettbewerb hervorgegangen und mit dem erften Preife ausgezeichnet, und ift ohne wefentliche Abänderungen im Laufe von etwa zwei Jahren für die Baufumme von zufammen 586000 Mark, einíchließlich der Mobiliarbefchaffung zur Aus-führung gekommen. Es ift ein Putzbau, welcher

285 [1908; 7]

Les plans pour les bâtiments de l'école Victoria, école supérieure de jeunes filles à Frankfort sur le Main et de l'annexe pour logements, sont l'oeuvre de Mr. Wilde architecte de la ville; ce travail est le résultat d'un concours, dans lequel les plans de Mr. Wilde avaient reçu le premier prix, ils furent exécutés, sans changements importants, dans l'espace de deux ans pour la somme de 386000 Marks, y compris l'ameublement. L'édifice est en maçonnerie crépie, le socle, les encadrements

285 [1908; 7]

The Victoria School (Girls' High School) at Frankfort on Main, together with the official residence adjoining has been built according to the design of the Town Building Inspector "Reg. Baumeifter a. D." K. Wilde. The plan was distinguished by the first prize in an open competition and has been used without any material alteration; the time oc-cupied in building was two years and the cost was 586000 Marks including the interior fittings

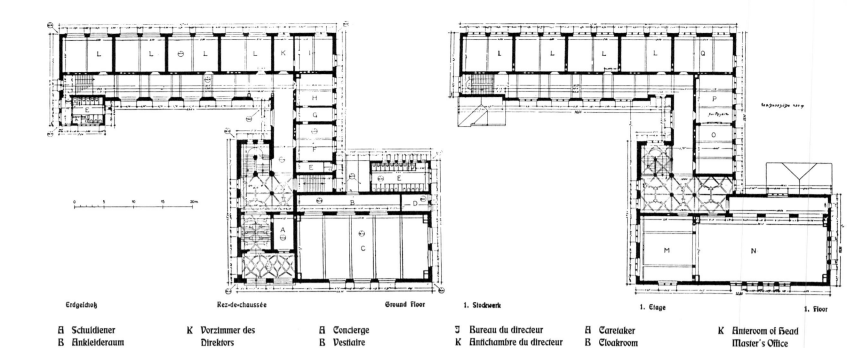

Erdgeſchoß		Rez-de-chaussée		Ground Floor	1. Stockwerk	1. Étage	1. Floor

eine Sockelverblendung, Einfaſſungen der Fenſter, Portale und Geſimſe aus rotem Mainſandſtein erhalten hat. Die ſteilen Dächer ſind mit Schiefer, eingedeckt. Ebenſo ſind die Giebel und oberen Teile der Stockwerkswände beſchiefert und treten deshalb in lebhaften Farbenkontraſt zu den hellen Putzflächen und den roten Sandſteingliederungen. Die Baumaſſen zeigen eine einfache aber doch wirkſame Gruppierung, deren Eindruck noch durch den über dem Haupttreppenhauſe aufſteigenden, mit einer doppelt abgeſetzten Zwiebelhaube bekrönten Turm erhöht wird. Die Einzelformen der Faſſade nähern ſich in ihrer ſtiliſtiſchen Auffaſſung, wenn auch frei behandelt, der dem Spätmittelalter naheſtehenden Deutſchrenaiſſance.

Das Erdgeſchoß enthält, außer der ſtattlichen Eingangshalle und der Haupttreppe, die Turnhalle und eine Anzahl von hellbeleuchteten, in dem Klaſſenflügel beſonders breit angelegten Korridoren zugänglichen Dienſt- und Klaſſenzimmer, ferner eine Nebentreppe und die Kloſetträume. Im erſten Obergeſchoß iſt über der Turnhalle, die durch zwei Geſchoſſe reichende, mit einer Empore verſehene Aula angeordnet, daneben der Singſaal, dann ſind eine Anzahl Klaſſenzimmer, ein Lehrſaal für Physik mit Apparatenzimmer und ein Konferenzzimmer vorhanden. Das zweite Obergeſchoß iſt vornehmlich zu Klaſſenzimmern eingerichtet und nimmt noch den Lehrſaal für Naturkunde und ein zugehöriges Zimmer für Apparate auf. Im dritten Obergeſchoß liegen Klaſſenräume, der Zeichenſaal mit Modellkammer, die Schülerinnenbibliothek und eine Dunkelkammer. Das Kellergeſchoß dient für Warmluftheizungs-, Kraft- und elektriſche Lichtanlagen und umſchließt noch die Milch- und Waſchküche, den Fahrradraum und Vorratskeller. Das Haupttreppenhaus iſt mit gemauerten Kreuzgewölben unter Verwendung profilierter Sandſteinrippen aus rotem Mainſandſtein überdeckt. Die Geſchoßdecken aller Nutzräume beſtehen aus eiſenarmiertem Beton.

Als Mitarbeiter ſind zu nennen: die Architekten Wellerdick und Gebauer für die Bearbeitung der Ausführungspläne, Architekt Schmitz für die Bauführung. Die Kunſtſchmiedarbeit und die Beleuchtungskörper lieferte Fr. Brechermacher, die Kunſtmalereien K. Lanz.

des fenêtres, les portes et profils sont revêtus de pierre rouge du main. Les toits à forte pente sont recouverts en ardoises. Les frontons et les parties supérieures sont également revêtus en ardoises et forment un contraste violent par leur coloration sombre avec les surfaces claires de la maçonnerie crépie et les moulures de pierre rouge. Le groupement des masses est simple mais d'un grand effet, l'impression est encore augmentée par le couronnement en forme de tour à double lobe de l'escalier principal. Le détail des façades rappelle, quoique traité librement, le caractère de la Renaissance allemande parente du Moyen-âge tardif.

Le rez-de-chaussée contient, à part une imposante halle d'entrée et l'escalier principal, la salle de gymnastique un certain nombre de salles d'école et de service grandes et claires, situées dans une aile spéciale et accessibles par de larges corridors, puis un escalier secondaire et les cabinets. A l'étage supérieur se trouve au dessus de la salle de gymnastique, l'aula occupant la hauteur de deux étages et pourvue de galeries; à coté, la salle de chant, puis plusieurs classes, un auditoire de physique avec salle pour les appareils et une salle de conférences. Le second étage qui est principalement réservé aux classes contient en outre une salle pour sciences naturelles et une chambre dépendante pour les appareils. Au troisième étage, nous trouvons les classes, la salle de dessin avec chambre à modèles, la bibliothèque des élèves et une chambre noire. Le sous-sol est occupé par les locaux destinés au chauffage central, et aux installations pour la force et la lumière électriques par les appareils de ventilation par la buanderie la laiterie, le garage des bicyclettes et le garde-manger. L'escalier principal est couvert d'une voûte avec arêtes profilées en pierre rouge du Main. Les planchers sont construits en béton armé.

Nommons comme collaborateurs, les architectes Wellerdick et Gebauer pour l'exécution des plans de construction, Mr. Schmitz architecte pour la conduite des travaux. Les fers forgés et les lampes ont été livrés par Fr. Brechermacher; les peintures artistiques sont dues à Mr. K. Lanz.

and equipment. It is a plaster building; the basement, the window frames, the portals and mouldings having a facing of red Main sandstone. The steep roofs are covered with slate; slate too has been used to face the gables and the upper part of the outside walls, this colouring forms an effective contrast to the light plaster and to the red articulations. The building is simply but effectively grouped, the impression of the whole being greatly enhanced by a tower rising from the centre entrance hall and crowned by an Imperial roof. The details of the facade are, although freely handled, reminiscent of the late medieval style nearly approaching the German Renascence.

The ground floor contains, as well as the stately entrance hall and principal staircase, a gymnasium and a flight of well-lighted corridors, those leading to the class rooms being specially broad, here too are lavatories and a secondary staircase. On the first floor over the entrance hall and reaching upward through two storeys is the great Hall or "Aula" which is furnished with a gallery; adjoining this is a singing room, a row of class rooms, a class room for instruction in physics with the necessary apparatus room and a conference room. The second upper storey is designed principally for class-rooms, here too is the class room for instruction in natural science with the room for apparatus. On the third storey are class rooms, the drawing school with a room for models, the scholars' Library and a dark room for photography. The basement contains the electric light and heating apparatus, a milk kitchen, a wash kitchen a room for cycles and a cellar for stores. The principal hall is vaulted and ceiled with an ornamental design in red sandstone; all the ceilings of the various floors are of beton and iron.

As coadjutors may be mentioned the architects Wellerdick and Gebauer for the plan of execution, architect Schmitz for the carrying out of the building. The artistic iron work and the chandeliers are by Fr. Brechermacher, the artistic colouring by K. Lanz.

Die nach den Plänen des Architekten Prof. Theodor Fischer in Stuttgart erbaute Max Josef-Brücke in München schwingt sich in weit gespanntem Segmentbogen über die Isar. Es ist ein Betonbau, wie sie in der letzten Zeit häufig zur Ausführung gekommen sind. Am Äußeren der Konstruktion ist der Steinschnitt angedeutet. Die Brückenbahn wird durch eine Reihe über der Hauptwölbung aufsetzender Bogen getragen. Ebenso sind die Uferanschlüsse durch bogenförmig geschlossene Öffnungen unterbrochen.

Le pont Max Josef à Munich, bâti d'après les plans de Mr. Theodor Fischer architecte, Stuttgart, franchit l'Isar d'un arc hardi en forme de segment de cercle. C'est une construction en béton, comme il en a été exécuté beaucoup ces derniers temps. L'appareil des pierres est indiqué à l'extérieur. Le tablier du pont est porté par une suite d'arcs posés sur la voûte principale. Les têtes du pont sont percées d'ouvertures en forme d'arc.

The Max Josef bridge in Munich is thrown in wide-spanned segment arches over the Isar. It was built according to the design of architect Theodor Fischer, Stuttgart. It is of beton construction as is now so frequently seen. The exterior is so built as to resemble cut stone; the bridge railway is carried on a row of arches supported by the principal vaulted arch, and the approaches on the river bank are broken by arched openings.

Ein ausgesprochen modernes, zugleich echt monumentales Gepräge trägt das Kunstausstellungsgebäude in Mannheim, entworfen von Architekt Prof. H. Billing und in

Le bâtiment d'exposition à Mannheim, œuvre du professeur H. Billing a un caractère très-moderne et très-monumental, il a été construit du mois d'octobre 1905 à celui

The building of the Art Exhibition in Mannheim designed by the architect Prof. H. Billing, is a decidedly modern creation, at the same time a monumental edifice. It was

Erdgeschoß — Rez-de-chaussée — Ground Floor — 1. Stockwerk — 1. Etage — 1. Floor

der Zeit vom Oktober 1905 bis April 1907 für die Kostensumme von 600000 M. zur Ausführung gekommen. Vor dem vorspringenden, stark einwärts gebogenen Mittelrisalit, welches den Eingang enthält, ist eine Freitreppe angeordnet, auf deren Wangen Sphinxfiguren lagern. Als Einfassung des Risalits dienen profilierte, schlank aufstrebende, von Figurenpaaren bekrönte Doppelpfeiler. Die zurückliegenden Fassadenflächen sind nur im unteren Teile von einer gekuppelten Reihe von Fenstern durchbrochen, mit Ausnahme der Eckrisalite und des mittleren, höher geführten Kuppelbaues, welche wieder nur oben Fenster enthalten. Die geschlossenen Wandteile sind durch Lisenen gegliedert. Die Fassadenverblendung besteht aus rotem Maintaler Sandstein. Das geschweifte, gebrochene Zeltdach der Kuppel des Mittelbaues ist in Kupfer eingedeckt.

Das Erdgeschoß des Mittelbaues enthält, auf das Vestibül folgend, die im Innern mit echtem Marmor bekleidete, durch beide Geschosse gehende Kuppelhalle und zu beiden Seiten derselben die zum Obergeschosse führenden geraden Treppenarme. Aus der Kuppelhalle tritt man in den großen Ausstellungssaal, an den sich zu beiden Seiten je zwei Flügelbauten mit Ausstellungsräumen anschließen. Die vorderen Flügel sind zweistöckig, die hinteren einstöckig ausgebildet. Im Obergeschoß wird der Kuppelraum rings von einer Pfeilerhalle umzogen, an die sich über dem Vestibül der Leseraum und an den übrigen drei Seiten weitere Ausstellungsräume anreihen.

d'avril 1907 pour la somme de 600000 Marks. Devant l'avant corps saillant et de plan fortement concave, formant entrée, s'élève un escalier sur les côtés duquel reposent des lions. Des piliers doubles, profilés et élancés, couronnés de deux figures, encadrent l'avant-corps. Les ailes de la façade ne sont pourvues de fenêtres qu'au rez-de-chaussée. Les pavillons d'angle et la partie centrale plus élevée, couronnée d'une coupole, n'ont des fenêtres que dans le haut. Les pleins du mur sont divisés par des profils verticaux. Le revêtement des façades est en pierre rouge du Main. La coupole à double courbe sur le corps central est recouverte en cuivre.

Le rez-de-chaussée du bâtiment centrale contient, après le vestibule, la halle à coupole revêtue de marbre, montant de fond à travers deux étages; dans cette halle se trouve l'escalier droit montant des deux côtés à l'étage supérieur. De cette halle on pénètre dans la grande salle d'exposition, à laquelle sont reliées de chaque côté deux ailes contenant des salles d'exposition. Les ailes de devant sont à deux étages, celles de derrière a un étage. A l'étage supérieur, la coupole est entourée d'une rangée de piliers, sur laquelle s'ouvrent au dessus du vestibule, la salle de lecture et sur les traisantes cotés, des salles d'exposition.

built from October 1905 to April 1907 and the cost amounted to 600000 Marks. The centre erection which contains the entrance projects and is arched sharply inwards; a free flight of steps flanked by figures of the sphinx leads to the entrance; the centre erection is defined and ornamented by tall slender pillars arranged in couples and crowned by sculptural figures. The retreating parts of the facade are only broken by a row of windows arranged in pairs exceptions to this are the corner projection and the middle cupola erection higher than the rest of the building — these have only windows above. The walls are articulated by pilaster strips. The facing of the facade is of red Main valley sandstone. The curved tent roof of the cupola of the middle erection is covered with copper.

The ground floor of the middle building contains an entrance vestibule which leads to a high centre hall roofed by the cupola and stretching upwards through two storeys, this is faced with marble and leads to a staircase on each side ascending to the upper floors. From this hall one proceeds into the great exhibition hall which is flanked by side galleries also used for exhibition purposes. The front galleries are two storeyed the back galleries have only one. On the upper storey the cupola gallery is surrounded by a pillared hall, over the vestibule is a reading room — the other sides of the gallery are used for exhibits.

Das durch monumentale Barockformen ausgezeichnete Kgl. bayer. Armeemuseum in München, am Ostende des Hofgartens gelegen, ist nach dem Entwurfe des Geh. Oberbaurats v. Mellinger unter Beihilfe des Baurats Kurz, des Bauamtmanns Maxon und des Architekten Rosenstock errichtet. Die Bauzeit

Le monumental Musée militaire royal bavarois à Munich, de style baroque a été construit dans la partie est des jardins royaux, d'après le projet de M. le conseiller von Mellinger avec le concours de messieurs les architectes Kurz, Maxon, Rosenstock. La durée de la construction a été de 4 ans et

The Royal Bavarian Army Museum in Munich situated on the Ostade of the Hofgarten, is a monumental building in Barock style. The design is by the Geh. Oberbaurat von Mellinger with the assistance of the Baurat Kurz, the building official Maxon and the architect Rosenstock. The time oc-

hat vier Jahre in Anspruch genommen; die Baukoften betrugen rund 2 250 000 Mark. Die vordere Front des durch einen vorspringenden Mittelbau und zwei die Rücklagen einfassende Eckbauten, von denen der links gelegene durch einen Flügelbau erweitert wird, gegliederten Gebäudes ist mit grauem fränkischem Sandstein verblendet, während die hintere Front als Pußbau erscheint. Der den Mittelbau bekrönenden, über einem Tambour auffteigenden, in Kupfer eingedeckten Halbkreiskuppel ist eine hohe ionische

les frais se sont élevés en chiffres ronds à 2250000 Marks. La façade de devant est en grès gris de Franconie. Elle se compose d'un bâtiment central en avancement et de deux bâtiments d'angles en retrait; le bâtiment d'angle de gauche se continue encore par une aile. La façade de derrière par contre est en maçonnerie crépie. Le bâtiment central est couronné par une coupole en forme de demi-sphère recouverte en cuivre et reposant sur un tambour; devant s'élève un haut péristyle ionien auquel on accède

cupied in building was four years, and the cost amounted to 2 250 000 Marks. The front facade is distinguished by a projecting middle erection flanked by two receding corners; that on the left is further enlarged by a side wing. The whole of the front is faced with grey Frankish sandstone, the back frontages are of plaster. The middle erection is crowned by a semicircular cupola, roofed with copper, and springing from a tambour or tholobate; in front of the building is a high hall with Ionic pillars

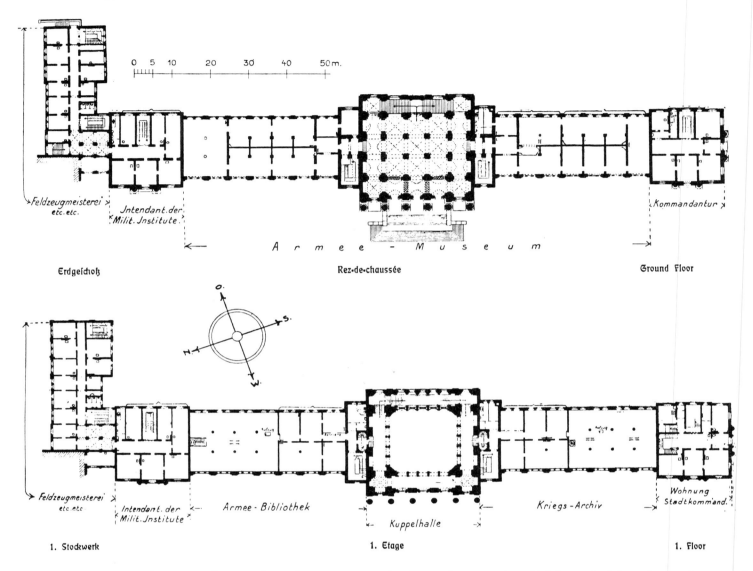

Erdgeschoß   Rez-de-chaussée   Ground Floor

1. Stockwerk   1. Étage   1. Floor

Säulenhalle vorgelegt, zu welcher vom Garten aus eine Freitreppe emporführt. Den oberen Abschluß der Halle bildet eine mit Figuren und Trophäen geschmückte Attika. Die Vorder- und Seitenfronten der Eckbauten sind ebenfalls durch vorgestellte, sämtliche Geschosse durchsetzende Säulen wirksam belebt und durch eine Attika beendigt. In den vorspringenden Teilen der Fronten sind die Fenster im Erdgeschoß rundbogig, im Hauptgeschoß geradlinig überdeckt, während die durch Pfeiler- oder Säulenstellungen geteilten Fenster in beiden Geschossen der Rücklagen an der Vorderfront zusammengezogen und in rundbogig geschlossene Blenden eingestellt sind.

Aus der Säulenvorhalle des Mittelbaues führen drei rundbogig überdeckte Türen in die gewölbte mittlere Pfeilerhalle, das Vestibül, das mit den Statuen bayerischer Herzoge ausgestattet ist; beiderseits schließen sich die Säle des Armeemuseums an. Im Hintergrunde der Pfeilerhalle führt eine doppelarmige Marmortreppe aufwärts zur Kuppelhalle des Obergeschosses, welches außerdem das Kriegsarchiv und die Armeebibliothek enthält. Der Eckbau rechts ist im Erdgeschoß für die Kommandantur, im Obergeschoß für die Wohnung des Stadtkommandanten benußt. Im Eckbau links liegt die Intendantur der Militärinstitute und die Feldzeugmeisterei.

du jardin par une escalier libre. Le sommet du péristyle représente une attique ornée de statues et de trophées. Les façades frontales et latérales sont également égayées par des colonnes occupant toute la hauteur des étages et terminées par une attique. Les fenêtres des parties de la façade en avancement sont au rez-de-chaussée voutées en plein cintre, celles du premier étage à linteaux droits tandis que les fenêtres des deux étages des parties rentrantes sont partagées par des piliers ou des colonnes, reliées entre elles et encadrées dans un tableau couronné d'un plein cintre.

Du péristyle du bâtiment central 3 portes en arceaux plein cintre conduisent dans un hall vouté soutenu par des piliers, le vestibule, qui est orné de statues des ducs bavarois; des deux cotés du vestibule s'ouvrent les deux portes du musée. Derrière le hall vouté, un escalier de marbre à double rampe conduit à l'intérieur de la coupole, l'étage supérieur qui contient les archives de la guerre et la bibliothéque militaire. Le bâtiment d'angle à droite sert au rez-de-chaussée aux bureaux du commandement, le 1er étage de demeure au commandant de place. Dans le bâtiment de gauche se trouve l'intendance militaire et le commandement de l'artillerie. La voute de la coupole ainsi que la lanterne et

which is reached from the garden grounds by broad steps lying free. The pillared hall is finished off above by a gallery ornamented with sculptural figures. The front and side facades of the corner erections are ornamented through each storey most effectively by rows of pillars ending in a gallery or "attika". The windows on the ground floor of the centre front are finished off with round arches, those on the principal storey have straight lines, while the windows of the receding erections have their various articulations joined under one rounded arch with which they are finished off.

From the pillared hall at the entrance, three arched doors lead to a vaulted pillared vestibule in which are placed sculptured figures of Bavarian dukes; on both sides of this vestibule are placed the halls of the army museum. At the back of the pillared hall, a double marble staircase leads to the cupola hall of the upper storey; here are the war archives and the military library. The right corner building on the ground floor is destined for the military "Kommandantur", the upper storey is devoted to the dwelling of the „Stadtkommandanten". In the left corner building is the administration

Die Kuppelwölbung mit Laterne und Tragpfeilern besteht aus Eisenbeton. Die Arkaden unter der Galerie des Kuppelraumes ruhen auf Säulen von rotem bayerischem Marmor, die vier Gewölbzwickel der Kuppel sind mit vier Ordensfiguren in Relief geschmückt, am Tambour sind Schlachtentafeln von allegorischen Figuren flankiert und über dem Hauptportal des Mittelbaues drei in Glasmosaik ausgeführte Bilder angebracht. Die Figuren an der Attika des Mittelbaues rühren von Prof. H. Kauffmann her, die Trophäen daselbst von Prof. Prusner. Die am Äußeren und im Inneren verwendeten figürlichen Reliefs sind von Prof. Pfeiffer und Bildhauer Burger geschaffen.

les piliers qui la supportent sont en béton armé. Les arcatures au dessous de la galerie de la coupole sont en marbre rouge de Bavière. Les quatre pendentifs de la coupole sont decorés de figures d'ordre en relief, au tambour de coupole se trouvent des plaques commémoratives de batailles, flanquées de figures allégoriques et au dessus de l'entrée principale du bâtiment central, trois tableaux exécutées en mosaïque de verre. Les figures de l'Attique du bâtiment central viennent du professeur H. Kauffmann, les trophées du professeur Prusner. Les figures en relief employées pour la décoration intérieure et extérieure, ont été faites par le professeur Pfeiffer et le sculpteur Burger.

of the military institute and of the apparatus for military equipment and implements. The vaulted cupola with its lantern and girders is all of iron beton. The arcades under the galleries of the cupola hall are of red Bavarian marble. One spandril of the cupola is ornamented by figures in relief, on the tambour are reliefs of battle fields flanked by allegorical figures, and over the principal portal of the centre building three pictures in glass mosaic. The figures on the gallery of the middle building are by Prof. H. Kauffmann, the trophies of the same are by Prof. Prusner. The sculptural reliefs of the interior and exterior are by Prof. Pfeiffer and the sculptor Burger.

289 [1908: 11]

Die Fassaden des Geschäftshauses Hettlage in Köln a. Rh., Schildergasse 38/42, sind zwar, der inneren Bestimmung des Gebäudes entsprechend, durch schlanke, im Erdgeschoß breite Schaufenster, in den oberen Geschossen durch Fenstergruppen mit Eisen- und Bronzeeinbauten oder Steinpfostenteilungen zwischen sich einschließende Pfeiler durchsetzt, jedoch erscheint gleichzeitig eine starke Betonung der Horizontale in den Brüstungen der Stockwerke. Architekt des in etwa 5 Monaten für die Kostensumme von 250 000 Mark ausgeführten Baues ist Reg.-Baumeister E. Moritz. Die Fassaden sind in hellem Sandstein verblendet und die mit Fledermausfenstern versehenen Dächer in Ziegel eingedeckt. Die Brüstungen über dem Erdgeschoß sind mit Pflanzenornamenten, die über dem ersten Oberstock mit figürlichen Reliefs ausgestattet.

Das Erdgeschoß bildet eine große, nur durch Pfeilerstellungen geteilte Verkaufshalle, welche einen mit Glas überdeckten Lichthof in sich einschließt. Ein besonderer Eingang führt zu einer seitwärts gelegenen Treppe, außerdem verbindet eine zweite freiliegende Treppe das Erdgeschoß mit dem ersten Obergeschoß, dessen Räume sich ebenfalls nach dem Lichthof hin öffnen. Die Decken sämtlicher Stockwerke sind aus Beton mit Eiseneinlagen hergestellt.

289 [1908: 11]

Les façades de la maison de commerce Hettlage à Cologne sur le Rhin, Schildergasse 38/42, sont, il est vrai, fortement divisées dans le sens vertical par des piliers encadrant, au rez-de-chaussée, de larges devantures, aux étages supérieurs des groupes de fenêtres partagées par des meneaux en pierre ou des divisions de fer et de bronze; cette disposition correspond à la destination du bâtiment. On a cependant eu soin d'exprimer fortement l'horizontale au moyen des contre-coeurs des étages. Mr. E. Moritz, architecte du gouvernement, est l'auteur de cet édifice élevé dans l'espace de 5 mois environ, pour la somme de 250000 Marks. Les façades sont revêtues de pierre claire, les toits percés de lucarnes, dites „chauve-souris" sont recouverts en tuiles. Les appuis de fenêtres au dessus du rez-de-chaussée sont décorés de plantes ornementales, ceux du premier étage de figures en relief.

Le rez-de-chaussée forme un grand magasin divisé seulement par des piliers, et entourant une cour vitrée. Une entrée spéciale conduit à un escalier latéral, un second escalier suspendu relie le rez-de-chaussée au premier étage, dont les locaux s'ouvrent également sur la cour vitrée. Les plafonds de tous les étages sont construits en béton armé.

289 [1908: 11]

The facades of the business house Hettlage at Cologne on Rhine, Schildergasse 38 to 42, are arranged to correspond with the interior of the building. On the ground floor are slender groups of windows with broad shop windows, on the upper floors are window groups with iron and bronze frames and set between pillars; at the same time the general breastwork of the facades is marked strongly by horizontal lines. The architect was the Reg.-Baumeister E. Moritz, the time occupied was 5 months and the cost amounted to 250000 Marks. The facades are faced with light sandstone and the roofs, which have "deadmanseye" windows, are covered with slate. The parapets over the ground floor are ornamented with foliage reliefs — those over the first floor with sculptural figures.

The ground floor consists of a large shop only divided by slender pillars, a skylighted court is in connection with this. A special entrance leads to a staircase at the side, a second free staircase leads from the ground floor to the first floor the rooms of which are also in connection with the skylighted court. The ceilings of the whole are of beton with iron girders.

290 [1908: 17]

Zur Gliederung der sechsstöckigen Fassade des Wohn- und Geschäftshauses in Wien, Graben 17, hat der Architekt desselben E. von Gotthilf die Formen des alten Wiener Barocks in moderner Wiedergabe benutzt. Die beiden unteren Ladengeschosse sind in Eisenfachwerk hergestellt und schließen mit einer in der ganzen Breite der Fassade durchlaufenden, balkonartig vorgekragten Brüstung ab. Darüber folgen Fenster zwischen Putzflächen, deren Bekrönungen Balkongitter tragen und welche mit den Fenstern des nächst höheren Stockwerkes in senkrechter Richtung zusammengezogen sind. Zwischen den Fenstern der drei oberen, ebenfalls verputzten Stockwerke steigen breite, unten mit abgesetzten Quaderungen, oben mit konsolartigen Vorsprüngen verzierte Pfeiler auf. Auf zwei dieser Auskragungen knien Atlantenfiguren, von Bildhauer R. Tautenhagen herrührend, welche das weit ausladende Dachgesims zu stützen scheinen. Zwei halbe geschweifte Giebel bilden beiderseits den oberen Abschluß der Fassade und fassen die steile Glasfläche des im Dachgeschosse angebrachten Atelierfensters zwischen sich ein. Die Bauausführung nahm etwa elf Monate in Anspruch. Die Baukosten betrugen 344 700 Kronen.

Das Erdgeschoß umfaßt ein ausgedehntes Geschäftslokal einschließlich eines glasüberdeckten Hofes und einen langgestreckten, zu einer im Oval um ein Auge geschwungenen Treppe führenden Flurgang. Ähnlich wie das Erdgeschoß ist das erste Obergeschoß eingerichtet, nur fehlt der Flur.

290 [1908: 17]

Mr. E. von Gotthilf, architecte de la maison de commerce Graben 17 à Vienne a choisi pour l'architecture des façades de cet immeuble à six étages, les formes de l'ancien style baroque viennois, dans une interprétation moderne. Les deux étages inférieurs occupés par des magasins sont en charpente métallique et sont couronnés par une balustrade saillant en forme de balcon sur toute la largeur de la façade. Au dessus s'élèvent les fenêtres encadrées de surfaces crépies, ces fenêtres ont des couronnements avec balustrades de balcon et sont reliées verticalement aux fenêtres de l'étage supérieur. Entre les fenêtres des trois étages du haut, lesquels sont également crépis, montent de larges piliers ornés de bossages dans le bas et de sallies en forme de consoles dans le haut. Sur deux de ces sallies sont agenouillés les Atlantes, qui semblent porter la grande saillie de la corniche; elles sont l'œuvre de Mr. R. Tautenhagen, sculpteur. Deux demi frontons aux lignes ondulées forment des deux côtés le couronnement de la façade et flanquent les surfaces vitrées des fenêtres d'atelier situé dans le toit. La construction dura environ onze mois. Les frais s'élevèrent à 344 700 Couronnes.

Le rez-de-chaussée contient un vaste local de commerce, une cour vitrée et un vestibule allongé, conduisant à un escalier construit sur un plan elliptique. Le premier étage ressemble au rez-de-chaussée, seulement le vestibule manque.

290 [1908: 17]

The dwelling and business house at Graben 17, Vienna is by the architect E. von Gotthilf who has chosen for the articulation the forms of the old Vienna barock with a modern modification. The two lower storeys, arranged as shops, are of iron framework and are finished off with a projecting balcony-like parapet which extends the whole length of the facade. Over this are windows in the plastered surfaces the crowns of which are built ont into balcony balustrades and which are joined perpendicularly with the windows of the next storey. Between the windows of the three upper storeys (which are also plastered) are broad pillars with square stones as pediment and with projecting capitals. On two of these projections are kneeling Atlas figures by the sculptor R. Tautenhagen, these support the widely projecting roof moulding. Two semicircular gables on each side form the upper finish to the facade and flank the steep glass surfaces of studio windows of an atelier which occupies the roof storey. The execution of the building lasted 11 months, and the cost amounted to 344 700 Kronen.

The ground floor contains spacious business premises including a glass-covered courtyard and a long corridor leading to a staircase winding round and lighted by a ground glass window. The upper storey is arranged like the ground

Die vier folgenden Obergeschosse enthalten je eine größere Vorder- und eine kleinere Hinterwohnung. Im Dachgeschosse ist im Vorderhause ein Atelier mit Wohnung und im Hinterhause ebenfalls ein solches angeordnet.

Les quatre étages suivants contiennent chacun un grand appartement sur le devant et un plus petit en arrière. Dans le toit se trouve un atelier avec appartement en avant et un autre en arrière.

floor without the entrance. The four upper storeys contain each a large front flat and a small back flat. In the front house is a studio on the roof storey with residence, the same is also arranged in the back house.

291 [1908; 51]

Das Gebäude der Kreditbank in Basel, Freiestraße 109, ist in einer Bauzeit von etwa fünfviertel Jahren für die Bausumme von rund 600 000 Mark und nach dem Entwurfe des Architekten E. Faesch zur Ausführung gekommen. Die in Kalkstein verblendete Fassade erhält durch senkrechte, die drei Geschosse zusammenfassende Pfeiler den streng einheitlichen Charakter eines Geschäftshauses. Auf den konsolartig ausgebauchten Einfassungen des Portals stehen Bronzefiguren, die von E. Zimmermann modelliert und von Brandstetter gegossen sind. Die rundbogig geschlossenen Fenster des Erdgeschosses sind mit kräftigen, als Kartuschen gestalteten Schlußsteinen versehen, die Fenster im ersten Obergeschoß sind geradlinig, die im zweiten im geschwungenen Flachbogen überdeckt. Die als Risalite schwach vortretenden Endachsen der Front tragen eine Attika über der stark ausladenden Trauf-

291 [1908; 51]

Le bâtiment de la banque de crédit, Freiestrasse 109 à Bâle, a été élevé dans l'espace d'environ un an et un quart pour la somme de 600000 Marks en bloc d'après les plans de Mr. E. Faesch architecte. La façade construite en pierre calcaire doit aux pillers verticaux, montant à travers trois étages, le caractère sévère et uniforme d'une maison de commerce. Sur les encadrements du portail traités en forme de consoles sont placées des figures de bronze modelées par E. Zimmermann et fondues par Brandstetter. Les fenêtres en plein-cintre du rez-de-chaussée sont pourvues de clefs vigoureuses ayant forme de cartouches; les fenêtres du premier étage sont à linteaux droits, ceux du deuxième étage couvertes d'un arc surbaissé et ondulé. Les ailes de la façade faisant légèrement saillie portent une attique au-dessus de la corniche très

291 [1908; 51]

The building of the Kredit Bank at Freiestrasse 109, Basel, was built in about a year and a quarter for the sum of 600000 Marks, according to the design of the architect E. Faesch. The facade, which is faced with lime stone, has the appearance of a business house, this effect is helped by the uniform design of pillars which extend through each of the three storeys. Bronze figures have been placed on the projecting moulding of the portal, these have been modelled by E. Zimmermann and cast by Brandstetter. The round arched windows of the ground floor have massive keystones in the shape of cartridges, the windows of the first upper storey are straight-lined, those of the second are arched. The slightly projecting ends of the front have a terrace over

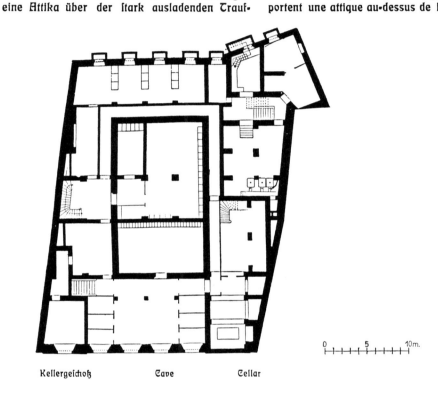

Kellergeschoß　　Cave　　Cellar

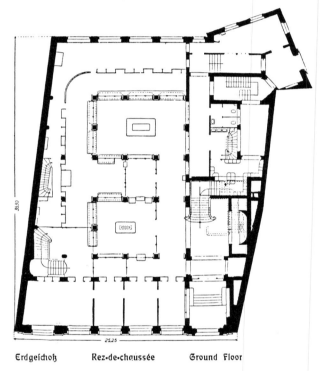

Erdgeschoß　Rez-de-chaussée　Ground Floor

platte, während in den Zwischenachsen steinerne Dachlucken angeordnet sind.

Der Haupteingang führt im Erdgeschoß zu der aus Marmor hergestellten Haupttreppe und zu dem mit einem Glasdach überspannten Kassenhofe, dessen monolithe Pfeiler wieder aus Marmor bestehen. Sämtliche innere Teilungs- und Lichthofswände sowie die Decken sind in Eisen konstruiert. Es sind noch mehrere Nebentreppen und ein Aufzug vorhanden. Das erste und zweite Obergeschoß enthalten, an den Fronten und um den mittleren Lichthof gelagert, die Direktorialzimmer und eine Anzahl Geschäftsräume. Im dritten Geschoß liegt noch ein Sitzungssaal an der Vorderfront, das übrige bildet den unausgebauten Dachraum. Das Kellergeschoß ist für den feuersicheren Tresor, für die Archivräume und die Heizungsanlage benutzt.

saillante, tandis que dans les parties rentrantes se trouvent des lucarnes en pierre.

L'entrée principale conduit au rez-de-chaussée à l'escalier principal construit en marbre et à la cour des guichets couverte d'un toit en verre; les piliers de cette cour sont formés de monolithes de marbre. Toutes les divisions intérieures et parois des cours, ainsi que les planchers sont construit en fer. Il existe encore plusieurs escaliers secondaires et un lift. Le premier et le second étages contiennent sur la façade et autours de la cour centrale, les chambres de la direction et plusieurs bureaux. Au troisième étage se trouve une salle de conférences sur le devant, le toit occupe le reste de la place. Le sous-sol contient un trésor à l'abri du fer, les pièces pour les archives et le calorifère.

the widely projecting eaves lead, between are stone framed windows in the roof.

The principal entrance leads through the ground floor to the principal staircase which is of marble and to the courtyard containing the rooms for the cash over which is a glass roof supported by monolith pillars. All the interior walls are of iron as are also the ceilings. There are several secondary staircases and a lift. On the first and second storeys, distributed along the front and over the skylighted courtyard are the directors' rooms and some business bureaus. On the third floor, in front is a committee room, the remainder is occupied by the roof storey which has been left as garrets. The basement is reserved for the fire-proof safes, for the archives and for the heating apparatus.

292 [1908; 53]

In einer Bauperiode von Oktober 1904 bis Januar 1907 ist der Neubau der „Münchner Neuesten Nachrichten" in München, Sendlingerstraße 80, nach dem Entwurfe der Architekten Heilmann & Littmann zur Vollendung

292 [1908; 53]

Le bâtiment des „Münchner Neuesten Nachrichten" Sendlingerstrasse 80 à Munich a été élevé du mois d'octobre 1904 à celui de janvier 1907, d'après le projet de M. M. Heilmann & Littmann architectes. Les frais

292 [1908; 53]

The new premises of the "Münchener Neuesten Nachrichten" at Sendlingerstrasse 80, Munich, was built from October 1904 to January 1907 according to the design of the architects Heilmann and Littmann;

gekommen. Die Baukoſten betrugen 950000 Mark. Die reich verzierte Faſſade iſt in Muſchel-kalkſtein hergeſtellt, Portale und Fenſter ſind in getriebener Bronze ausgeführt, die Dächer in roten Biberſchwänzen eingedeckt. Das Erdgeſchoß zeigt breite Rundbogenportale und ebenſolche Fenſter, der erſte Stock iſt zwiſchen den Erker-ausbauten mit einem durchlaufenden Balkon ab-geſchloſſen, der durch Einzel- und Doppelfiguren-pfeiler geſtützt wird. Die Eckausbauten ſetzen ſich bis zum Traufgeſims fort, die mittleren Aus-bauten endigen als polygonale Türmchen mit beſonderen Zeltdächern. Über den weit aus-ladenden Hauptdächern erheben ſich in den niedrigeren Seitenteilen zuſammenhängende Fenſteraufbauten, während der mittlere höhere Teil der Front über dem ausgeſchwungenen Trauf-geſims mit einem Walmdach bekrönt iſt.

Das Erdgeſchoß enthält hinter der Eingangs-halle den Expeditionsſaal, dem ein großer Hof-raum mit einer ſeitlichen Durchfahrt folgt, außer-dem befinden ſich an der Front noch mehrere Büreauräume, die Haupttreppe und die Aufzüge. Das erſte, zweite und dritte Obergeſchoß ſind durchweg zu Geſchäftsräumen beſtimmt, die Vor-plätze ſind ſeitlich von einem Lichthofe aus be-leuchtet. Im Dachgeſchoß befindet ſich der große Setzerſaal. Das Kellergeſchoß dient als Keſſel- und Kohlenraum ſowie als Lagerkeller.

Die Wände der Eingangshalle im Erdgeſchoß ſind mit Majolikafliesen bekleidet, ſämtliche Decken und der Dachſtuhl ſind in Eiſenbeton ausgeführt, die Gewölbe in Rabitzmanier. Als Mitarbeiter werden genannt: Architekt Goebel und die Bild-hauer J. Seidler und F. Enderle.

293 [1908: 16]

Im Geſamtbilde der Villa Leydhecker in Darmſtadt, Prinz Chriſtiansweg 11, treten die hohen Dächer mächtig hervor und verleihen dem Ganzen den Ausdruck traulichen Behagens. Das von Architekt Prof. F. Pützer herrührende Bauwerk erhebt ſich in verputzten Flächen über einem Quaderſockel. Die ſteilen, in ganzer Höhe oder im oberen Teile vorgekragten Giebel laſſen ſichtbaren Holzverband oder be-ſchindelte Flächen bemerken. An dem Giebel der Hauptfront tritt ein flachrunder, durch beide Geſchoſſe geführter Erker vor. Dem Haupteingang iſt eine geräumige, auf Säulen ruhende, für ſich mit einem Dache abgeſchloſſene Halle vorgelegt. Die Dächer ſind mit Biberſchwänzen eingedeckt und an der Vorderfront durch einen Fenſteraufbau unterbrochen.

s'élevèrent à 950000 Marks. La façade riche-ment décorée est en pierre calcaire, les portes et fenêtres en bronze, les toits sont recouverts en tuiles rouges. Le rez-de-chaussée a des portails et des fenêtres en plein-cintre; le premier étage est surmonté d'un balcon passant d'une tourelle à l'autre, il est supporté par des piliers formés de figures singles et doubles. Les tourelles d'angle montent jusqu'à la corniche, celles du milieu se terminent en tourelles poly-gonales avec des toits spéciaux en forme de tente. Au dessus des toits à grande saillie s'élèvent dans les parties plus basses des ailes des lucarnes reliées entre elles, tandis que la partie centrale plus élevée du corps central est terminée au dessus de la corniche contournée par un toit en forme de croupe.

Le rez-de-chaussée contient derrière la halle d'entrée la salle d'expédition, à laquelle une grande cour avec passage à voitures fait suite, plusieurs bureaux, l'escalier principal et les ascenseurs se trouvent en outre sur la façade. Le premier, le second et le troisième étages sont entièrement distribués en locaux de travail; les vestibules sont éclairés latéralement par une cour. Dans le toit se trouve une très grande salle pour compositeurs. Le sous-sol est disposé en local pour chaudières, en magasins à charbon et en cave.

Les parois de la halle d'entrée au rez-de-chaussée sont revêtues de plaques céramiques; tous les planchers et le toit sont construits en béton armé; les voûtes en construction dite Rabitz. Nommons comme collaborateurs l'archi-tecte Goebel et les sculpteurs J. Seidler et F. Enderle.

293 [1908: 16]

Dans l'aspect général de la villa Leydhecker à Darmstadt, Prinz Christiansweg 11, les toitures élevées jouent un rôle prépondérant et donnent à l'ensemble un caractère de chaude intimité. Ce bâtiment, œuvre de Mr. le pro-fesseur F. Pützer est en maçonnerie crépie. Il est supporté par un soubassement en pierre. Les hauts pignons, faisant saillie sur toute leur hauteur ou seulement dans leur partie supérieure, font voir des bois apparents ou des surfaces recouvertes de bardeaux. Une tourelle traversant deux étages, fait saillie en segment de cercle sur le fronton de la façade principale. Un hall spacieux, porté par des colonnes et couvert d'un toit spécial, forme porche devant l'entrée principale. Les toits sont recouverts en tuiles, et sont interrompus sur la face principale par une lucarne.

the cost amounted to 950000 Marks. The richly ornamented facade is of shell limestone, portals and windows are of hammered bronze, the roofs are covered with flat red tiles. The portals on the ground floor are crowned by round arches and the windows are also arched; on the first floor is a balcony running the whole lenght between the corner projecting bays; this balcony is supported by single and double figure groups in the form of pillars. The corner bays are continued upwards to the gutter moulding, the middle erections are finished off with small polygonal towers with separate tent roofs. Over the widely projecting principal roof, in the low side wings are a row window projections; the higher part of the front over the curved roof moulding is crowned by a vaulted roof.

The ground floor contains first the "Ex-pedition Hall" behind the entrance vestibule, this is followed by a large courtyard with a side entrance for vehicles; in the front are many bureaus the principal staircase and the lifts. All three upper storeys are arranged as business bureaus, the entrances are lighted at the side by skylights. In the roof is the spacious storey arranged as a compositor's room. The basement is used as store room and for the heating apparatus.

The walls of the entrance hall on the ground floor are faced with majolica, all ceilings and the roof supports are of iron beton, the vaulting is of the Rabitz system. As coadjutors are named architect Goebel and the sculptors J. Seidler and F. Enderle.

293 [1908: 16]

The villa Leydhecker, Prinz Christians-weg 11, Darmstadt, has an extremely home-like appearance which is enhanced by the high steep roofs, a very striking feature. It is by the architect Prof. F. Pützer, the sockel is of square stones and the upper part is plastered. The steep projecting gable has partly wood construction and is partly shingled. On the gable of the principal front is a round bay extending through two storeys. The principal entrance is a spacious hall resting on pillars and having a special roof; the roofs are covered with flat red tiles, and are broken on the front by a window erection.

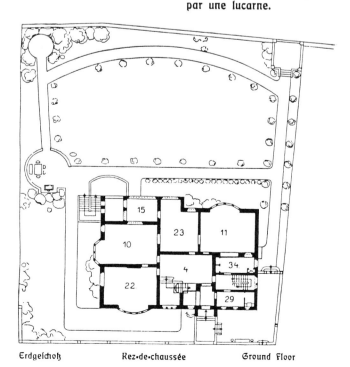

Erdgeſchoß   Rez-de-chaussée   Ground Floor

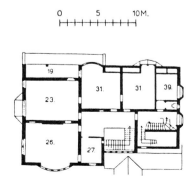

0   5   10M.

1. Stockwerk   1. Etage   1. Floor

Das Erdgeschoß enthält, um eine Diele mit freiliegender Treppe gruppiert, die hauptfächlichiten
Wohnräume, den Wintergarten mit anitoßender
Balle und einer nach dem Garten hinabführen-
den Treppe, fowie das Eßzimmer und die Anrichte, welche letztere durch einen Speifenaufzug
mit der im Untergeschoß liegenden Küche verbunden iit. Im Obergeschoß iit das Schlafzimmer, daneben das Bad, das mit einer Loggia
verbundene Boudoir, zwei Gaft- und ein Mädchenzimmer untergebracht. Im ausgebauten Dachgeschoß find noch weitere Gaftzimmer fowie
Räume für Dienftperfonal eingerichtet.

294 [1908; 19]

Es iit ein reizvoller Gruppenbau, den Architekt
F. L. Mayer in dem villenartigen Wohn-
haufe zu Karlsruhe, Richard Wagnerftraße,
Ecke Schubertftraße, geschaffen hat. Über
einem Untergeschoß aus rauhen Sandfteinquadern
erheben fich die in Verputz hergeftellten Fronten,
welche teilweife wieder mit rauhen Quadern an
den Ecken eingefaßt und mit Sandfteingliederungen
ausgeftattet find. Zwischen Haupt- und Flügel-
gebäude iit ein niedriger, mit einer Terraffe
endigender Bauteil eingeschoben. Die mit ver-
fchalten Überhängen verfehenen Giebel der in
Schiefer eingedeckten iteilen Dächer find im
oberen Teil abgeschopft und ebenfalls beschiefert.
Die Dachfläche wird durch ein breites Lukenfenster in fogenannter Fledermausform belebt.

295 [1908; 22]

Die von Architekt G. v. Mayenburg herrührende Villa in Dresden-Loschwitz,
Wunderlichftraße, iit von einem Garten umgeben und zeichnet fich durch eine wirkfame
Gruppierung der Baumaffen aus. Die Hauptfront löft fich in zwei polygonale Eckbauten auf,
die einen hohen Giebel flankieren. Die eine
Seitenfront enthält den in einem überdachten
Vorbau liegenden Eingang, einen breiten Fenfter-
aufbau im Dache und darüber nochmals Dach-
fenfter, an der anderen Seitenfront tritt am Erdgeschoß ein polygonaler Erker hervor, der mit
einer Plattform abfchließt und mit dem Garten
durch eine Treppe in Verbindung iteht. Die
iteilen, mehrfach gebrochenen Dächer überfpannen
ein ausgebautes Dachgeschoß und find mit Biberfchwänzen eingedeckt. Die Wandflächen des
Äußeren find in Verputz mit einigen angetragenen
Verzierungen ausgeführt.

296, 298 [1908; 49, 47]

Die in Abbildungen mitgeteilten Bauwerke
der Kolonie Merck in Darmftadt find
nach Entwürfen von Architekt Prof. F. Pützer
errichtet. Es find fämtlich Putzbauten, auf Sockeln
von Werkfteinen fich erhebend, mit hohen in
Biberfchwänzen eingedeckten Dächern verfehen
und in modern aufgefaßten Formen gehalten.
Das eine größere, im Mittelbau turmartig in
fechs Stockwerken auffteigende Gebäude mit den
angelehnten zweiftöckigen Flügelbauten, vor deren
Fronten fich im erften Stock Altane erftrecken,
iit mit gebrochenen abgewalmten Dächern überdeckt. Über dem Mittelbau erhebt fich ein mit

---

Le rez-de-chaussée contient les principales
pièces groupées autour d'un hall dans lequel
se trouve l'escalier suspendu; ce sont: le jardin
d'hiver communiquant avec un hall et un
escalier conduisant dans le jardin, la salle à
manger et l'office, cette dernière reliée par un
monte-plats avec la cuisine située dans le sous-
sol. A l'étage supérieur se trouvent la chambre à
coucher, à côté le bain, le boudoir communiquant
avec une loggia, deux chambres d'amis et une
chambre de domestique. Le toit contient encore
d'autres chambres d'amis et des chambres pour
le personnel.

294 [1908; 19]

La villa, Richard Wagnerstrasse, angle
Schubertstrasse, à Karlsruhe œuvre de
l'architecte F. L. Mayer est un bâtiment tres
interessant. Au dessus du sous-sol construit en
moellons de grès s'élevent en maçonnerie crépie
les façades ornées de moulures en grès et encadrées par des angles en pierres de taille.
L'édifice principal est relié à l'aile par un corps
de bâtiment plus bas et achevé a une terrasse.
Les frontons en pans de bois sur leurs parties
supérieures comme les pans du toit sont recouverts
d'ardoise. La pente du toit est agréablement au
orné par une fenêtre très large en forme appelé
chauve-souris.

295 [1908; 22]

La villa située Wunderlichstrasse à Dresde-
Loschwitz, œuvre de Mr. G. von Mayenburg architecte, est entourée d'un jardin, elle se
distingue par un groupement intéressant des
masses. La façade principale est décorée de
deux avant-corps polygonaux latéraux qui flanquent un haut fronton. Une des ailes contient
l'entrée précédée d'un auvent couvert, un large
bow-window dans le toit et des lucarnes au
dessus; dans l'autre aile on voit saillir un avant-
corps polygonal au rez-de-chaussée, il est couvert
d'une terrasse et relié au jardin par un escalier.
Les toits abrupts, plusieurs fois brisés contiennent
un appartement et sont recouverts en tuiles.
Les façades sont exécutées en maçonnerie crépie
avec quelques décorations modelées dans le
mortier.

296, 298 [1908; 49, 47]

Les constructions de la colonie Merck à
Darmstadt dont nous publions les illustrations ont été élevées d'après les projets de Mr.
F. Pützer architecte professeur. Ce sont toutes
des bâtisses crépies, elevées sur socles de pierre
avec de hauts toits recouverts en tuiles et tenues
dans des formes modernes. Une des maisons
est une construction avec un grand-corps central
de six étages -s'élevant en forme de tour et
flanqué d'ailes de deux étages, sur leur façade
s'étend au premier étage un balcon; la maison
est recouverte d'un toit brisé à croupe. Au
dessus du corps central s'élève une tourelle à

The ground floor contains, grouped round a
square hall, the free staircase, the principal
dwelling rooms, the winter garden with a hall
adjoining and a staircase leading to the garden,
the dining room and serving room, the latter in
connection with a dinner lift leading to the
kitchen. On the upper storey is a bedroom
with a bath room, a boudoir in connection with
a loggia, two spare bedrooms and a servants'
bedroom. In the roof storey are other spare
rooms and rooms for servants.

294 [1908; 19]

A most charming grouping of the various
parts has given a most picturesque effect
to the villa-like dwelling house built by the
architect F. L. Mayer at Richard Wagnerstrasse, corner of Schubertstrasse, Carlsruhe. Over a basement storey of rough square
sandstone is built the plastered upper storey;
this is partly cornered by sandstone square
stones, articulations are also of sandstone.
Between the principal building and the side
wings a low terraced erection has been constructed. The gables, part of which have overhanging projections, are of slate as are also the
steep roofs. The surface of the roof is lighted
by a broad low window, the so-called "dead-
mans-eye" window.

295 [1908; 22]

The villa in the Wunderlichstrasse,
Dresden-Loschwitz, is by the architect
G. v. Mayenburg; it is surrounded by a garden
and is most effectively grouped. The principal
front has two polygonal corner erections which
flank a high gable. The one side front contains the entrance which has a roofed projecting
portico, a broad window erection in the roof
and over that, other roof windows; the other
side front has on the ground floor a polygonal
bay finished off with a platform from which
steps lead into the garden. The steep roofs,
frequently broken, cover a well built roof storey
and are tiled with flat red tiles. The outside
walls are of plaster with occasional plastic ornament.

296, 298 [1908; 49, 47]

The buildings of the colony "Merck" in
Darmstadt, communicated to us by
illustrations, are the work of Prof. F. Pützer.
They are all plaster buildings erected on a
basement of freestone, they are all roofed with
flat red tiles and the style is throughout modern.
The middle erection of the larger building has
a tower, and is carried up to six storeys; it
has side wings of two storeys on the front of
which are placed galleries reaching along the
first storey; this has a curved roof with a
broken roof line. The middle erection is

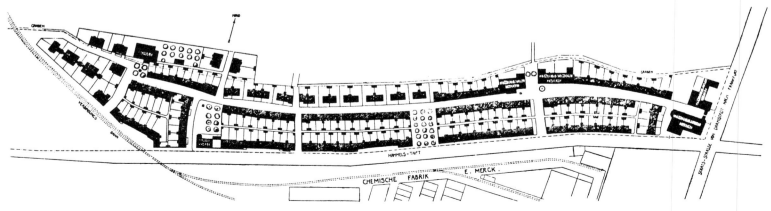

einer offenen Galerie umgebenes mit geschweifter Haube bekröntes Uhrtürmchen. Ein zweites größeres mit dem vorigen durch im Stichbogen überwölbte Durchfahrten verbundenes Gebäude ist zweistöckig und enthält noch ein ausgebautes Dachgeschoß in dem an der Hauptfront vorspringenden Mittelbau. In der Durchschneidung der abgewalmten oder mit Giebeln abschließenden Dächer steigt ein runder Turm auf, der mit einer Plattform endigt. Die meist einstöckigen, seltener zweistöckigen oder mit Giebelstuben versehenen Familienhäuser der Kolonie sind schlicht in den Formen gehalten und mit überhängenden Winkeldächern ausgestattet. Einzelne obere Wandteile, besonders Giebelflächen, sind mit Schindeln beschlagen, auch finden sich mehrfach durch Pfeiler unterstützte Lauben zu ebener Erde unter den vortretenden Giebeln angeordnet.

horloge entourée d'une galerie ouverte et couronnée d'un toit ondulé. Une seconde maison de grande dimention reliée à la précédente par une porte cochère couverte en arc surbaissé est de deux étages et possède encore un étage dans le toit du corps central faisant saillie sur la façade principale. Au point de rencontre des toits à croupe et des toits des pignons s'élève une tour ronde portant une plateforme. Les maisons de la colonie, pour la plupart à un étage, plus rarement à deux étages ou pourvues de chambres dans les pignons sont de formes modestes et couvertes de toits en saillie et très élevés, quelques parties supérieures des murs, surtout les surfaces des pignons sont recouvertes en bardeaux, on voit aussi souvent des colonnes supportées par des piliers disposés sur le sol et portant les pignons saillants.

crowned by a clock tower, surrounded by an open gallery and having a helmet-shaped roof. A second building, connected with the first by a throroughfare roofed by a depressed arch, is two-storeyed and contains a well-built roof storey in the projecting middle front. From the curved or gabled roof rises a round tower ending in a platform. The houses of the colony, intended for the habitation of one family, are mostly one-storeyed, seldom two-storeyed, and have sometimes rooms in the gabled roof. They are all simply constructed and have overhanging roofs. Many of the upper wall surfaces particularly those of the gables are covered with shingle, in some houses are verandahs on the ground floor supported by pillars reaching to the gables.

297 [1908: 1]

Die einfach gegliederte, in Dorlaer Kalkstein ausgeführte Straßenfront der Nationalbank für Deutschland in Berlin, Behrenstraße 68/69, wie das gesamte Bauwerk von Geh. Reg.-Rat, Prof. Dr.-Ing. A. Messel entworfen, bringt den Charakter des Zweckmäßigen, der Bestimmung des Gebäudes im Dienste des öffentlichen Verkehrs entsprechend, in bezeichnender Weise zum Ausdruck. Das Erdgeschoß zeigt rundbogig geschlossene Fenster, die beiden Obergeschosse werden durch breite Pfeilerstreifen zusammengehalten und die Steilfläche des ge-

297 [1908: 1]

Construite en pierre calcaire de Dorlaer, la simple façade de la banque nationale allemande à Berlin, Behrenstrasse 68/69, œuvre, comme l'édifice tout entier, de Mr. le Professeur Dr.-Ing. A. Messel, fait ressortir d'une façon marquée le but, l'emploi de l'édifice destiné au besoin du trafic public. Le rez-de-chaussée montre des fenêtres à arcs plein-cintre encadrées; les deux étages superieurs sont reliés par de larges piliers. La ligne brisée du toit est recouverte de tuiles rouges tandis que les deux pans du toit sont pourvus de lucarnes. Sur le

297 [1908: 1]

The National Bank for Deutschland, Behrenstrasse 68 and 69, Berlin is by Geh. Reg.-Rat Prof. Dr.-Ing. A. Messel. The simply articulated street frontage of Dorlaer limestone, as well as the entire building suggests at the first view that utility, the application of means to ends has been the first care of the architect. The ground floor has round arched windows, the two upper storeys are joined by broad pillared strips and the line of the steep red-tiled roof is broken by various roof windows. The entrance is in the middle projecting erection

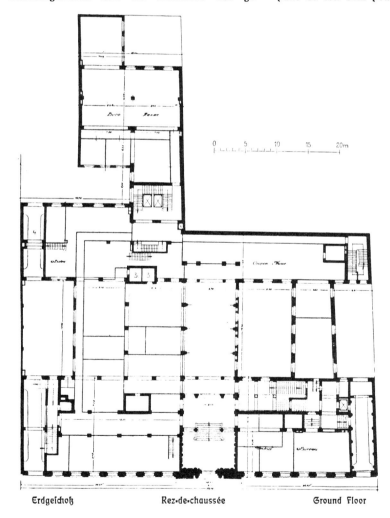

Erdgeschoß   Rez-de-chaussée   Ground Floor

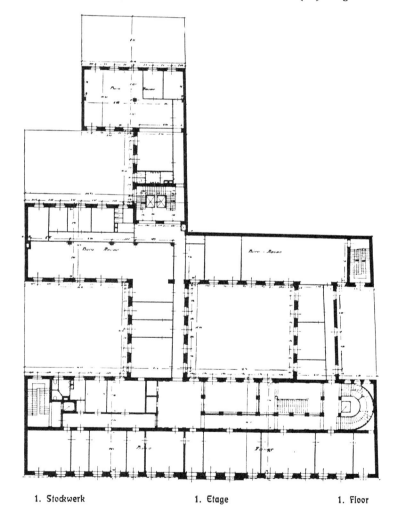

1. Stockwerk   1. Etage   1. Floor

brochenen, mit Biberschwänzen eingedeckten Daches ist mit Dachfenstern besetzt. Im Mittelrisalit öffnet sich der Haupteingang, der durch eingestellte dorische Säulen monumentale Würde erhält. Die oberen Fenster sind wagrecht geschlossen, durch Stürze mit Schlußsteinen und Sohlbänke ausgezeichnet, welche letztere unter den Fenstern des ersten Obergeschosses durch flach vorspringende Konsolen gestützt werden.

An das Vestibül im Erdgeschoß sind seitwärts die Haupttreppe, die Depositenkasse und das

milieu de la façade s'ouvre l'entrée principale qui, ornée de colonnes doriques, fait un effet grandiose; les fenêtres supérieures sont encadrées par la corniche decorée d'une clef de voute et par un rehard de fenêtre qui pour les fenêtres du premier étage sont soutenus par deux corniches en saillie.

A part le vestibule le rez-de-chaussée contient encore l'escalier principal, la caisse des dépôts et le bureau de change; dans l'axe du milieu se trouve le hall aux guichets, éclairé par un cour ouverte, ensuite à côté les caisses et bureaux

and is ornamented by Doric pillars giving the whole a monumental appearance. The upper windows close laterally and are ornamented by cap-pieces with keystones and with window sills; these last are on the first floor supported by projecting consoles.

By the vestibule on the ground floor at the side is the principal staircase leading to the deposit bureau and the exchange bureau. In the middle space is the chief Cash lighted by

Wechselbureau angeschlossen. In der Mittelachse folgt der Kassenhof, von einem offenen Hofe aus beleuchtet, dann die nebenliegenden Kassen- und Bureauräume. In einem Flügel ist die Couponkasse untergebracht, und ein hinterwärts sich erstreckender Flügelbau enthält noch weitere Bureauräume. Drei Nebenhöfe sind durch Durchfahrten zugänglich gemacht. Die Direktionsräume nehmen mit den Konferenzzimmern das gesamte erste Obergeschoß des Vordergebäudes ein, während der Sitzungssaal in das zweite Obergeschoß verlegt ist. Das Kellergeschoß ist zur Anlage der Tresorräume und Stahlkammern sowie der dazu gehörigen Nebenräume verwendet. Neben der Haupttreppe dienen drei weitere Treppen sowie vier elektrisch betriebene Aufzüge für den inneren Verkehr. Die Heizungs- und Kühlanlagen sind in den Hofunterkellerungen untergebracht.

Von den an der inneren Ausstattung beteiligten Firmen sind zu nennen: Die Saalburger Marmorwerke für Marmorarbeiten im Vestibül und Kassenhof, K. Teich für ebensolche im Haupttreppenhause, F. P. Krüger für die Bronzedecke im Kassenhof und Prof. Wrba für Ausführung der Modell- und Steinbildhauerarbeiten an der Fassade.

299 [1908: 72]

Ein Werk von entschieden monumentalem Gepräge ist in dem Gebäude des Erzbischöfl. Ordinariats in Freiburg i. Br. entstanden. Entworfen und ausgeführt ist dasselbe vom Architekten, Bauinspektor R. Jeblinger in einem Zeitraum von etwa drei Jahren und für die Baukostensumme von rund 900 000 Mark, so daß sich für den Kubikmeter umbauten Raum ein Kostenbetrag von 23,30 Mark ergibt. Die Fassaden sind in grobkörnigem, sattgelbem und rotgeflammtem Pfälzer Sandstein verblendet und in wuchtigen romanischen Stilformen gehalten. Das Mittelrisalit der Längsstraßenfront enthält das Portal mit einwärts abgetreppten Leibungen, darüber folgen in eine breite Blende gefaßte gekuppelte Fenster und seitlich lösen sich Rundtürmchen ab, welche den abschließenden steilen Giebel beiderseits einfassen. Die Fenster im Erdgeschoß der Rücklagen sind von tiefschattigen Arkaden begleitet, die Fenster im ersten Obergeschoß sind gekuppelt und liegen in viereckigen Blenden, die im zweiten Stock sind gleichfalls gekuppelt. Über der Traufkante des Daches erhebt sich eine Reihe von Giebelluken, die durch Zwischenmauern mit Durchbrechungen untereinander verbunden sind. Nahe an den Enden der Längsfront erheben sich mit steilen Zeltdächern abgeschlossene Türme, außerdem sind die Eckrisalite mit vorgekragten Erkern bereichert und endigen mit Giebeln. Die Herstellung des Bandornaments in den breiten Friesen, der Säulenkapitelle und sonstiger Schmuckformen wurde absichtlich den handwerklich gelernten Steinmetzen anvertraut.

Auch das Innere des Gebäudes ist wie das Äußere nach romanischen Motiven ausgestaltet. Im Mittelbau schließen sich die Arme der Haupttreppe beiderseits an die Eingangshalle und einen langen Flurgang an, in der einen Seitenfront öffnet sich ein zweiter Eingang und in der anderen eine Einfahrt zum Hof, beidemale in Verbindung mit Treppen stehend. Die Räume zu Verwaltungs-, Lehr- und Wohnzwecken sind auf drei Geschosse verteilt. Die Keller sind mit Betongewölben überspannt, die Räume in den oberen Geschossen mit Voutendecken, während die Stiegenhäuser mit Moniergewölben versehen sind.

300 [1908: 86]

Das aus einem Vorderbau und zwei Seitenflügeln bestehende Wohnhaus in Wilmersdorf-Berlin, Helmstedterstraße 2, nach dem Entwurfe der Architekten Siemering und

qui en dependent. Dans une aile se trouve la caisse des coupons, une aile de bâtiment se continuant derrière contient d'autres bureaux. Trois cours dependantes sont reliées par un passage. Les bureaux de la direction et la salle des conférences occupent tout le premier étage de l'édifice de devant, tandis que la salle des séances a été placée au deuxième étage. L'étage de cave a été employé pour l'aménagement des chambres de trésor, des coffres-forts ainsi que des dépendances. A part l'escalier principal l'on dispose encore de trois autres escaliers ainsi que de quatre ascenseurs pour le service intérieur. Les appareils de chauffage et de ventilation se trouvent dans la cour de l'étage inférieur des caves.

Parmi les maisons qui ont pris part à la décoration de l'intérieur nommons: die Saalburger Marmorwerken pour les Marmorarbeiten pour le vestibule et le hall au guichets, la maison K. Teich dans la même partie pour l'escalier principal, F. P. Krüger pour le plafond en bronze du hall aux guichets et M. le Professeur Wrba pour la conduite des travaux de sculpture de la façade.

299 [1908: 72]

Le palais de l'ordinariat de l'archevêché de Fribourg en Brisgau est une œuvre d'une monumentalité incontestable. Les plans et l'exécution sont de Mr. R. Jeblinger, architecte inspecteur la durée des travaux fut de trois ans, les frais s'élevèrent à 900 000 Marks en bloc, le mètre cube de construction coûte 23,30 Marks. Les façades sont revêtues de pierre du Palatinat jaune foncé et flammé de rouge et traitées dans le style roman lourd. L'avant-corps central de la façade sur la rue contient le portail avec embrasures profilées en dedans, au dessus se trouvent des fenêtres jumelles encadrées dans une large surface; sur les côtés se détachent des tourelles rondes qui encadrent à droite et à gauche le pignon élevé. Les fenêtres du rez-de-chaussée des arrières-corps sont entourées d'arcades profondes; les fenêtres du premier étage sont accouplées encadrées dans des cadres carrés, celles du second sont également accouplées. Au dessus de la corniche s'élève une suite de lucarnes à pignons reliées entre elles par des murs à jour. Près des extrémités de la façade principale se dressent, des tours couronnées de hauts toits; les ailes d'angle sont en outre enrichies de tourelles saillantes et couronnées de pignons. On confia intentionnellement l'exécution de l'ornement de la large frise, des chapiteaux de colonne et des autres décorations à des ouvriers tailleurs de pierre.

L'intérieur du monument comme son extérieur est traité dans le style roman. Dans le corps-central les bras de l'escalier principal se relient des deux côtés à la halle d'entrée et à un long corridor. Sur une des faces latérales s'ouvre une seconde entrée et sur l'autre un passage conduisant dans la cour; ces deux entrées communiquent avec des escaliers. Les pièces destinées à l'administration, à l'enseignement et à l'habitation sont réparties sur trois étages. Les caves sont recouvertes de voûtes en béton; les pièces des étages avec des voûtes plates; les cages d'escaliers sont pourvues de voûtes système Monier.

300 [1908: 86]

La maison d'habitation, Helmstedterstrasse 2 à Wilmersdorf-Berlin, consistant en un corps principal et deux ailes latérales a été élevée dans l'espace d'un été d'après les

a skylight, this is surrounded by the various cash and bureau rooms. In one wing is the coupon Cash, and a wing extending backwards contains various additional bureaus. Three secondary courtyards are all in connection with each other. The rooms of the administration together with the committee rooms occupy the whole of the first floor of the front building, the large hall for meetings is on the second floor. The basement is utilized for tresors, safes and the offices necessary for these. In addition to the principal staircase are three secondary staircases and four lifts worked electrically. The heating and cooling apparatus are in the cellars of the courtyard.

Of the firms employed in the interior equipment the following may be named. The Saalburger Marmorwerke for marble work in the vestibule and chief cash; K. Teich for the same on the principal staircase, F. P. Krüger for the bronze ceiling in the principal cash and Professor Wrba for the carrying out of the sculptural work of the facade.

299 [1908: 72]

A building of decidedly imposing appearance is the office of the archiepiscopate at Freiburg im Breisgau. The work has been designed and executed by the architect Baumeister R. Jeblinger. It occupied a period of about 3 years in building and cost about 900 000 Marks; this gives for each cubic metre of building a sum of 23,30 Mark. The facades are of coarse-grained, deep yellow and red-flamed Palatinate sandstone and are of massive proportions in the Romanesque style. The middle erection of the long street frontage contains the portal with an inside embrasure over this comes a broad row of windows; at the side are small round towers which finish off on both sides the steep gable. The windows on the ground floor of the recess have deeply shadowed arcades, those of the first floor are coupled and lie in square facings, those of the second floor are also coupled. Over the gutter corner of the roof are a row of gable windows joined by walls. Nearly at the end of the long frontage are towers with steep tent roofs; the corner erection is ornamented with projecting bays crowned with gables. The execution of the band ornaments of the broad frieze, the capitals of the pillars and the remaining ornamental parts were given expressly into the hands of technically trained stonemasons.

The interior of the building is, like the outside, in the Romanesque style. In the middle building the entrance hall and a long corridor lead on each side to the principal staircase; one side frontage contains a second entrance, and the other is a carriage entrance to the courtyard, each entrance is in connection with a staircase. The rooms for the administration, for instruction and for residences are arranged on three storeys. The basement has vaulted beton ceilings, the rooms of the upper storeys have Vouten ceilings, those of the staircase are vaulted Monier construction.

300 [1908: 86]

The house, situated at Helmstedterstrasse 2, Wilmersdorf-Berlin, consists of one front house and two side wings. It was built according to the design of the architects

C. Schmidt im Laufe eines Sommers ausgeführt, ist ein Putzbau in plastisch stark bewegter Fassadenbildung. Der Verputz ist dunkelgelb gefärbt; das mit Dachpfannen eingedeckte Dach zeigt zu beiden Seiten turmartig erhöhte geschweifte Zeltdächer. Die über dem Erdgeschoß vorgekragten Erkerausbauten sind im zweiten Obergeschoß zusammengewölbt und bilden eine Nische, in der im zweiten Obergeschoß ein Balkon vortritt. Die in der Flucht der Erker im dritten Obergeschoß durchlaufende Frontwand wird durch eine breite, hinter einer Säulenstellung sich öffnende Loggia unterbrochen. Der mittlere Teil der Front erhält über dem dritten Obergeschoß den Abschluß durch eine Galerie, hinter welcher ein zurücktretendes, wieder in der Mitte loggienartig geöffnetes viertes Obergeschoß aufsteigt. Das Dachgesims zeigt eine aufgebogene Linie. Zu beiden Seiten der Erkerausbauten sind in drei Obergeschossen polygonale Balkons ausgekragt, von denen der zu oberst gelegene mit einem besonderen Dache versehen ist.

Das von Säulen eingefaßte Eingangsportal führt unmittelbar zur Treppe, an welche sich in jedem Geschosse beiderseits die Flurgänge anschließen. Hinter der Haupttreppe ist ein Aufzug und eine zweite vom Hofe aus zugängliche Treppe angeordnet. Jedes der fünf Geschosse enthält zwei geräumige Wohnungen.

301 [1908; 30]

Das in gemischter Massiv-Holzbauweise ausgeführte, einfach gruppierte Landhaus in Petit-Saconnex bei Genf ist das Werk des Architekten M. Braillard, hat eine Bauzeit von 6 Monaten und einen Kostenaufwand von 16 500 Franks erfordert. Soweit die Umfassungswände massiv sind, bestehen sie aus gelben Schnittsteinen von Choiry und aus gelbem, rauhem Jurakalkstein mit breiten, ausgestrichenen Mörtelfugen. Das Fachwerk des in Holzbau ausgeführten Teils ist mit Backsteinen ausgemauert. Die mit vollem oder abgewalmtem Giebel abschließenden Dächer sind mit roten Ziegeln eingedeckt. Das Erdgeschoß enthält, außer dem Flur, der Küche und der Wäschekammer, den Salon und das mit einer Terrasse in Verbindung stehende Eßzimmer. Im ersten Stock sind noch mehrere Zimmer und ein Baderaum angeordnet. Sämtliche Wohnräume sind nach Süden gerichtet und haben die Aussicht nach dem Genfer See und dem Montblanc. Die gedeckte Vorhalle liegt an der Nordseite, um im heißen Sommer als Zufluchtsort zu dienen. Das Haus ist mit einer Zentralheizung versehen.

302 [1908; 38]

In ansprechenden, modernen Formen erhebt sich die Villa Georg Kaiser in Darmstadt, Mathildenhöhe, inmitten einer Gartenanlage. Der von Architekt Prof. H. Metzendorf entworfene zweistöckige Bau wurde im Laufe eines Jahres fertiggestellt. Es ist ein Putzbau in rauhgehaltenen Flächen, mit Einzelgliederungen in Werkstein ausgestattet. Der farbige Reiz des Äußeren wird noch durch die weiß gestrichenen Läden der Fenster des Obergeschosses und der Dachgiebel gehoben. An der der Straße zugekehrten Giebelfront werden durch das Zurücksetzen der Mauer im Obergeschosse zwei leicht vorspringende Fensterausbauten gebildet, welche für sich mit geschweiften Dächern abschließen. Der Haupt- sowie die Seitengiebel der steilen, mit Biberschwänzen eingedeckten Dächer sind von mehrfach gebrochenen, geschwungenen Konturen begrenzt. Das Erdgeschoß der Villa wird über einen Terrassengang zugänglich; an das Wohnzimmer schließt sich ein Wintergarten an, über dem eine Altane sich erstreckt und das Eßzimmer steht mit einer Veranda in Verbindung,

---

plans de M. M. Siemering et C. Schmidt architectes; c'est une construction en maçonnerie crépie avec des façades très mouvementées. Le crépissage est teint en jaune foncé, le toit couvert en tuiles montre des deux côtés, des pavillons élevés en forme de tours. Les tourelles faisant saillie au dessus du rez-de-chaussée sont reliés par une voûte au second étages et forment une niche, dans la quelle paraît un balcon au second étage. La façade du troisième étage se trouvant au nu des tourelles, est interrompue par une large loggia s'ouvrant derrière une colonnade. La partie centrale de la façade se termine au dessus du troisième étage, par une galerie, derrière laquelle s'élève un quatrième étage en retrait, s'ouvrant également au milieu en forme de loggia. La corniche se relève en arc. Des deux côtés des tourelles, des balcons de forme polygonale font saillie dans les trois étages supérieurs, ceux du haut sont couverts d'un toit spécial.

Le portail d'entrée encadré de colonnes conduit directement à l'escalier, avec lequel communiquent à chaque étage, les vestibules. Derrière l'escalier principal se trouve un lift et un second escalier accessible de la cour. Chacun des cinq étages contient deux appartements spacieux.

301 [1908; 30]

La maison de campagne au Petit-Saconnex près Genève, construite en partie massive, et en partie en bois est l'œuvre de M. Braillard architecte, la construction a duré 6 mois et a coûté 16 500 Frs. Les parties massives des façades sont en pierre jaunes de Choiry et en maçonnerie brute de pierre calcaire jaune du Jura avec de larges joints enduits de mortier. Les pans des parties construites en bois sont garnis de maçonnerie de briques. Les toits terminés par des pignons pleins ou en croupe sont recouverts en tuiles rouges. Le rez-de-chaussée contient, outre le vestibule, la cuisine et la buanderie, le salon et la salle à manger reliée à une terrasse. Au premier étage on a disposé plusieurs chambres et une salle de bain. Toutes les pièces sont orientées vers le sud et ont la vue sur le lac de Genève et le Mont-Blanc. Le porche couvert est situé au nord et offre un abri pendant les chaleurs de l'été. La maison est pourvue d'un chauffage central.

302 [1908; 38]

Au milieu d'un jardin s'élève la villa Georg Kaiser, Mathildenhöhe à Darmstadt, elle est tenue dans des formes modernes très élégantes. Cette maison à deux étages a été construite dans l'espace d'une année, d'après le projet de Mr. le professeur H. Metzendorf. La construction est en maçonnerie crépie grossièrement avec quelques moulures en pierre. Le charme de la couleur de l'extérieur est encore rehaussé par les volets des fenêtres de l'étage supérieur, peints en blanc et par les pignons du toit. Sur la façade à pignon donnant sur la rue, on a obtenu deux bowindows saillants légèrement en reculant le mur de l'étage supérieur; ces bowindows sont couronnés par des toits de profil ondulé. Le pignon principal et les pignons latéraux des toits abrupts recouverts en tuiles sont bordés de lignes ondulées, plusieurs fois brisées. Le rez-de-chaussée de la villa est accessible d'une terrasse; la chambre d'habitation communique avec un jardin d'hiver au dessus duquel s'étend un balcon; la salle à

Siemering and C. Schmidt in the course of one summer. It is a plaster building, with a facade ornamented with characteristic plastic of striking effect. The plaster is coloured dark yellow, the roof is tiled and has on both sides high towers with tent roofs. The corner bays projecting over the ground floor are brought together in the second upper storey and form a niche from which in the second storey a balcony projects. The front wall of the third storey in a line with the bay has a broad loggia with pillars in front; the middle part of the front has an effective termination in a gallery over the third upper storey from which a receding fourth storey with loggias rises. The roof moulding shows a curved line. On both sides of the bays, on three storeys, project polygonal balconies, over the upper of these a separate roof is constructed.

The entrance portal is flanked by pillars and leads directly to the staircase on which on either side the entrances are situated. Behind the principal staircase is a lift and from the courtyard ascends a second staircase. On each of the five storeys are two spacious flats.

301 [1908; 30]

A simply-grouped country house, a mixture of wood and stone, has been built at Petit-Saconnex near Geneva by the architect M. Braillard; the time occupied was 6 months and the cost amounted to 16 500 Francs. The stone work of the outside walls is of yellow stone from Choiry, and of rough yellow Jura limestone with broad mortar pointing. The frame work of the wooden part of the building is partly of brick. The roof is finished off with gables more or less curved and is covered with red tiles. The ground floor contains the hall, the kitchen, the washhouse, a drawing room and a dining room leading to a terrace. On the first floor are several rooms and a bath room. All of the rooms have a south aspect, and have a view of Mont-Blanc and the lake of Geneva. The covered entrance lies on the north side, and affords a cool refuge during the hot summer months. The house is heated all over by steam.

302 [1908; 38]

The villa Georg Kaiser at Mathildenhöhe, Darmstadt, is an attractive building in the modern style, standing in its own grounds. The two storeyed building is the work of Prof. H. Metzendorf, and occupied one year to build. It is a plaster building with rough surfaces and certain articulations of freestone. The charm of the colouring is further enhanced by the white window shutters of the upper storey and the roof gable. The gables fronting the street consist of two slightly projecting windows placed in the receding wall and finished off with curved roofs. The greater part of the steep roof, which is covered with flat red tiles, is variously ornamented and diversified by broken lines. The ground floor of the villa is entered by a terrace walk, the drawing room leads to a conservatory over which a terrace is erected; the dining room

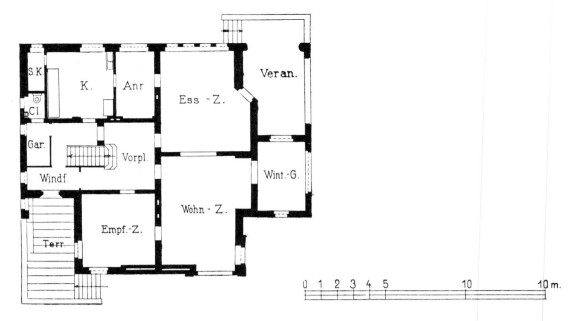

Erdgeſchoß   Rez-de-chaussée   Ground Floor

0 1 2 3 4 5   10   10 m.

von welcher man mittelſt einer Freitreppe in den Garten hinabſteigt. Die übrigen Zimmer ſind in dem Obergeſchoſſe und dem teilweiſe aus-gebauten Dachgeſchoß untergebracht.

303 [1908: 100]

Das von Architekt A. Bacher entworfene villen-artige Wohnhaus in Brünn, Schreit-waldſtraße 144, iſt in etwa 11 Monaten für die Summe von 80 000 Mark zur Ausführung gekommen. Es iſt ein Putzbau, der auf einem, im ſogenannten Zyklopenverband ausgeführten Steinſockel ruht. Das lebhaft gruppierte Äußere zeigt im Oberſtock an der Straßenfront rechts eine bedeckte Laube in Holzkonſtruktion, auf kräftigen Konſolen ausgekragt; links an der-ſelben Front tritt wieder im Obergeſchoß und auf Konſolen ruhend, ein Erkervorbau heraus, der von turmartig aufſtrebenden, die Dachlinie durchbrechenden Pfeilern flankiert wird. Eine der Seitenfronten iſt mit einem giebelbekrönten Riſalit ausgeſtattet. Das überhängende Dach, mit einer durch Konſolen geſtützten Traufplatte verſehen, iſt mit Falzziegeln eingedeckt. Über dem Eingangsflur iſt Oberlicht angeordnet und die Stufen der Treppe ſind teilweiſe aus Marmor oder Granit hergeſtellt.

304 [1908: 44]

Als Obſieger in einem engeren Wettbewerb wurde der Architekt Baurat Sig. v. Quittner mit der Aufſtellung der Pläne ſowie mit der Bau-leitung für das Gebäude der Lebensver-ſicherungs-Geſellſchaft The Gresham, in Budapeſt am Franz Joſefplatz gelegen, be-auftragt. Das umfängliche Bauwerk beſteht aus vier ſelbſtändigen Häuſern, von denen die drei vorderen im Erdgeſchoß durch eine innere Paſſage verbunden ſind. Die Bauzeit erſtreckte ſich auf drei Jahre, und die Baukoſten betrugen, aus-ſchließlich des Grunderwerbs, rund 300 000 Kronen. Die im reichen Barockſtil durchgeführte Haupt-front iſt durch ein breites, giebelbekröntes Mittel-riſalit und durch Ecktürme, welche in Aufſätzen mit Kuppeldächern endigen, gegliedert. Das oberſte Geſchoß zeigt in den Seitenteilen der Front eine Stellung kurzer gepaarter Säulen vor niſchenartigen Vertiefungen. Der Sockel der Faſſade iſt aus Granit hergeſtellt, die Ober-geſchoſſe ſind weſentlich aus Lockuber Sandſtein, und nur in einzelnen Teilen aus hartem Kalk-ſtein mit mäßiger Verwendung von Glasmoſaiken auf Goldgrund ausgeführt. Die Portale der Geſchäftslokale ſind aus Bronzeteilen gebildet, welche von Pfeilern aus ſchwediſchem Granit eingefaßt werden. Das Dach iſt mit engliſchem Schiefer, die beiden Türme ſind mit Kupfer einge-deckt.

manger est reliée à une veranda d'où l'on peut descendre au jardin par un escalier libre. Les autres pièces sont situées à l'étage supérieur et dans l'étage du toit.

303 [1908: 100]

La maison d'habitation à caractère de villa construite par Mr. A. Bacher, architecte, Schreitwaldstrasse 144 à Brünn dans l'es-pace d'environ 11 mois a coûté 80 000 Marks. C'est un bâtiment en maçonnerie crépie reposant sur un socle de pierre à appareil cyclopéen. L'extérieur d'un groupement pittoresque montre sur la façade principale à l'étage supérieur à droite, une pergola en bois couverte, portée par de vigoureuses consoles; à gauche, sur la même façade une tourelle portée également sur des consoles fait saillie au premier étage, elle est flanquée de piliers en forme de tours qui traversent la ligne du toit. Une des façades latérales est pourvue d'un avant-corps couronné d'un fronton. Le toit en saillie avec un larmier supporté par des consoles est recouvert en tuiles. Le vestibule est éclairé par le haut, les marches d'escalier sont en partie en marbre et en partie en granit.

304 [1908: 44]

Ayant remporté la victoire dans un concours restreint, Mr. Sig. v. Quittner architecte conseiller fut chargé des plans et de l'éxécution de la maison pour la société d'assurances pour la vie „The Gresham" Franz Joseph-platz à Budapest. Le vaste édifice se compose de quatre maisons distinctes, dont les trois de devant sont reliées entre elles au rez-de-chaussée par un passage intérieur. La construction dura trois ans et les frais s'élevèrent, non compris l'acquisition du terrain à 300 000 Couronnes en bloc. La façade principale en riche style baroque est divisée par un large avant-corps central surmonté d'un fronton et par des tours d'angle terminées par des toits en cuivre. L'étage supérieur est décoré sur les côtés de la façade par des colonnes accouplées, trapues avec des enfoncements en forme de niches. Le socle de la façade est en granit, les étages supérieurs sont en grande partie en pierre de Lobkub et en partie en pierre calcaire dure avec décoration de mosaïque de verre sur fond d'or. Les portails des bureaux sont en bronze, encadrés de granit de Suède. Le toit est recouvert en ardoise anglaise, les deux tours en cuivre.

Le rez-de-chaussée et l'entre-sol contiennent

leads on to a veranda, this has a staircase leading to the garden. The remaining rooms are contained in the first floor and in the roof storey.

303 [1908: 100]

The house at Schreitwaldstrasse 144, Brünn, by the architect A. Bacher is built in the villa style. It occupied 11 months to build and cost 80 000 Marks. It is a plaster building resting on a so-called "Cyclop" stone basement. The charmingly grouped exterior has on the first floor in the front a covered balcony of wooden construction projecting over massive consoles; on the same floor, to the left is a projecting bay also resting on consoles, and flanked by tower-like pillars which extend up-wards breaking the roof line. One of the side fronts has a middle projecting erection crowned by a gable. The projecting roof, which has a gutter supported by consoles, is covered with ridged tiles. Over the entrance hall is a skylight, and the steps of the staircase are partly of marble and granite.

304 [1908: 44]

As victor in an open competition, the archi-tect Baurat Sig. v. Quittner was en-trusted with the design and execution of the building for the Insurance Company "The Gresham" erected at Franz Josef Platz in Budapest. The spacious building consists of four independent houses, three of which in the front are connected on the ground floor by corridors. The time occupied in building was three years, and the cost amounted to 300 000 Kronen exclusive of site. The principal front is of richly ornamented barock style, it has a broad projecting middle erection crowned by gables and corner turrets ending in cupola roofs. The top storey, at the side of the front is ornamented by pairs of short pillars, the spaces between receding in the form of niches. The sockel of the facade is of granite, the upper storeys mostly of Lockuber sandstone; only in some places hard limestone has been used with a moderate use of glass mosaic on a gold ground. The portals of the business premises are of bronze set in pillars of Swedish granite. The roof is of English slate, and both towers are roofed with copper.

Erdgeſchoß und Mezzanine enthalten Läden und eine von der Zrinyigaſſe zur Mécleygaſſe durchgehende, mit einem Arm nach dem Franz Joſefquai abzweigende und mit einer Glasdecke verſehene Paſſage. Im erſten Stock befinden ſich die Bureauräume der Filiale der Gresham-Geſellſchaft und in den übrigen drei Obergeſchoſſen große, elegant ausgeſtattete Mietswohnungen, von denen in jedem Geſchoß je zwei in einer der vier Bauabteilungen angeordnet ſind. Das Gebäude beſitzt vier Haupt- und vier

des magasins et un passage vitré, traversant de la Zrinyigasse à la Mécleygasse avec une bifurcation du côté du Franz Josephquai. Au premier étage se trouvent les bureaux de la succursale de la société de Gresham, dans les trois étages supérieurs on a aménagé de grands appartements à louer élégamment distribués, il y en a deux dans chacune des quatre divisions. Le bâtiment possède quatre escaliers principaux et quatre escaliers de service, de plus quatre lifts électriques et quatre monte-charges. Tous

Ground floor and intermediate storey are dedicated to shops; a passage leads through from the Zrinyigasse to the Mécleygasse with one arm branching off to the Franz Josef Quay and covered with a glass roof. On the first floor are the premises of the branch business of the Gresham company, on the other floors are large, elegantly built flats; on each of the floors of the four houses are two flats. The building has four principal and four secondary

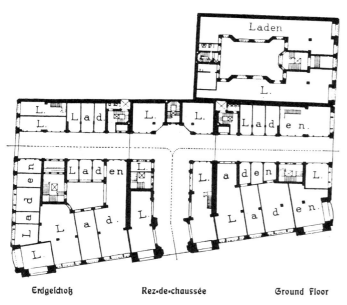
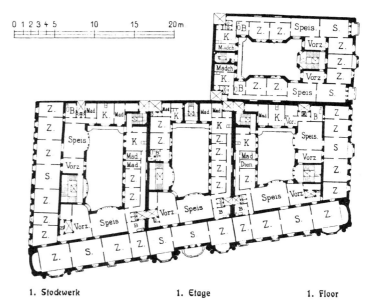

Erdgeſchoß   Rez-de-chaussée   Ground Floor   1. Stockwerk   1. Étage   1. Floor

Nebentreppen, ferner vier elektriſche Perſonen- und vier Laſtenaufzüge. Sämtliche Zwiſchendecken ſind in Ziegelgewölben zwiſchen Eiſenträgern ausgeführt. Die Erwärmung der Räume geſchieht durch eine Zentral-Dampf-Niederdruckheizung, außerdem iſt Warmwaſſerverſorgung für Bäder und Waſchtiſche vorgeſehen und die Beleuchtung erfolgt durch elektriſches und Gaslicht.

Der Figurenfries oberhalb der Fenſter des erſten Stocks iſt ein Werk des Bildhauers Prof. Maroti, während das Gresham-Porträt im Hauptgiebel ſowie die Figuren auf dem Mittelerker im erſten Stock von Bildhauer Telcs herrühren. Außerdem iſt die Faſſade mit Bildwerken von Ligeti, Marjó und Songrácz geſchmückt. Die Architekturgliederung der Paſſage iſt mit Tonplatten aus der Fabrik von Zſolnay in Fünfkirchen bekleidet, dieſelben werden von Bronzerahmen eingefaßt.

les planchers sont construits en voûtes de briques entre poutres de fer. Les locaux sont chauffés au moyen d'un chauffage central à vapeur à basse pression; il y a en outre un appareil à eau chaude pour bains et toilettes, l'éclairage est à l'électricité et au gaz.

La frise de personnages, au dessus des fenêtres du premier étage, est l'œuvre du sculpteur, professeur Maroti, tandis que le portrait de Gresham dans le fronton principal ainsi que les figures de la tourelle du milieu, au premier étage, sont du sculpteur Telcs. La façade est en outre décorée de sculptures de M. M. Ligeti, Marjó et Songrácz. Les divisions architecturales du passage sont revêtues de plaques de céramique de la fabrique de Zsolnay à Fünfkirchen, ces plaques sont enchassées dans des cadres de bronze.

staircases, four electric passenger lifts and four goods lifts. All the ceilings are of vaulted tiles between iron girders. The heating is steam low pressure system, warm water is laid in on all floors, and the lighting is by gas and electricity.

The frieze sculpture over the window of the first floor is the work of Prof. Maroti; the Gresham portrait in the principal gable as well as the figures of the middle bay in the first floor are by Prof. Telcs. The other ornaments of the facade are by Ligeti, Marjó and Songrácz. The architectural articulations of the passage are of tiles from the factory of Zsolnay from Fünfkirchen, these are enclosed in bronze framing.

305 [1908; 56]

Das Jügelhaus, das neue Auditoriengebäude der Akademie für Sozial- und Handelswiſſenſchaften zu Frankfurt a. M., Jordanſtraße, ein Werk des Architekten Baurat L. Neher, iſt im Laufe von etwa 2¼ Jahren zur Ausführung gekommen. Die ſpezielle Bauleitung fiel den Architekten S. Simon und R. Voltz zuteil. Der umbaute Kubikmeter, von der Kellerſohle bis zum Dachgeſims gemeſſen, hat 24,60 Mark gekoſtet und für die innere Ausſtattung ſind rund 210000 Mark aufgewendet. Die mächtigen, im Barockſtil gehaltenen Faſſaden ſind aus rotem Mainſandſtein, von einzelnen Putzflächen unterbrochen, hergeſtellt. Ebenſo iſt für Veſtibüle und Treppenhäuſer roter Mainſandſtein zur Verwendung gekommen. Das Hauptportal wird von Säulen flankiert und von einem gebrochenen Giebel, auf deſſen Schenkeln Figuren ſitzen, überſtiegen. Die beiden unteren Geſchoſſe ſind gequadert, das obere Geſchoß wird durch Pilaſterſtreifen gegliedert und zeigt halbrund geſchloſſene Fenſter und über dieſen kreisrunde Fenſter. Der obere Abſchluß der Faſſade wird durch eine Attika gebildet.

La maison Jügel, le nouveau bâtiment pour cours de l'académie des sciences sociales et commerciales à Frankfort s. M., Jordanstrasse, est l'œuvre de Mr. L. Neher architecte conseiller, la construction dura environ deux ans et un quart. Les architectes S. Simon et R. Voltz furent chargés de la direction spéciale des travaux. Le mètre cube de construction mesuré du sol des caves à la corniche a coûté 24,60 Marks, on a en outre dépensé 210000 Marks en bloc pour les installations intérieures. Les puissantes façades traitées en style baroque sont en pierre rouge du Main, dont les surfaces sont interrompues par quelques champs crépis. On a également employé la pierre rouge du Main pour les vestibules et les cages d'escaliers. Le portail principal est flanqué de colonnes et couronné d'un fronton brisé sur lequel reposent des figures. Les deux étages du bas sont traités en bossages; l'étage supérieur est divisé par des pilastres, les fenêtres sont recouvertes en plein-cintre, au dessus d'elles se trouvent des fenêtres rondes. La partie supérieure de la façade est formée par une attique.

305 [1908; 56]

The "Jügelhaus" a new building containing lecture halls connected with the Academy for "Social- und Handelswiſſenſchaften" at Frankfort on Main, Jordanstrasse, is the work of the architect Baurat L. Neher, and occupied about 2¼ years in building. The special superintendence was entrusted to the architects S. Simon and R. Voltz. The cubic meter of building from the cellar to the roof moulding amounted to 24,60 Marks; the cost of the interior equipment amounted to about 210000 Marks. The facades, which are of great size and distinction, are in the barock style, the material is red Main sandstone diversified occasionally by plastered surfaces. Red Main sandstone has too been chosen for the vestibule and staircases. The principal entrance is flanked by pillars and crowned by a gable with a broken line on the haunch of which are sculptured figures. Both of the lower storeys are of large square stones, the upper storeys are articulated by pillared stripes and have semicircular crowns to the windows; the windows of the top storey are circular. The summit of the facade is finished off by a attic.

Das Gebäude gliedert sich in einen Mittelbau und zwei Seitenflügel. Jedes Stockwerk des Mittelbaues enthält eine geräumige Wandelhalle, welche durch die beiderseits einmündenden Haupttreppen zugänglich ist und mit diesen zusammen eine bedeutende Raumwirkung erzielt, außerdem sind vier Hörsäle vorhanden. Im ersten Obergeschoß sind an der Vorderfront ein größerer und zwei kleinere Hörsäle angeordnet, nach hinten liegen der Sitzungssaal und ein Lesezimmer für die Dozenten, dann ein Lesesaal und ein Schreib-

Le bâtiment est divisé en un corps central et deux ailes latérales. Chaque étage du corps-central contient une halle spacieuse, bordée de chaque côté d'un grand escalier, le tout produit un imposant effet; quatre salles de cours sont en outre situées dans chacun de ces étages. Au premier étage sont disposées sur la façade une grande et deux petites salles de cours; en arrière se trouvent la salle des conférences, une salle de lecture pour les professeurs, une salle de lecture et de travail pour les élèves et une

The building is divided into a middle erection and two side wings. Each storey of the middle building contains a spacious covered promenade which is reached on both sides from the principal staircase, this whole arrangement gives an effective spaciousness which works very agreeably. There are on this floor four lecture rooms. On the first floor in the front is one large and two small lecture rooms, behind lie a committee room, a reading room for the lecturers, a reading room and writing

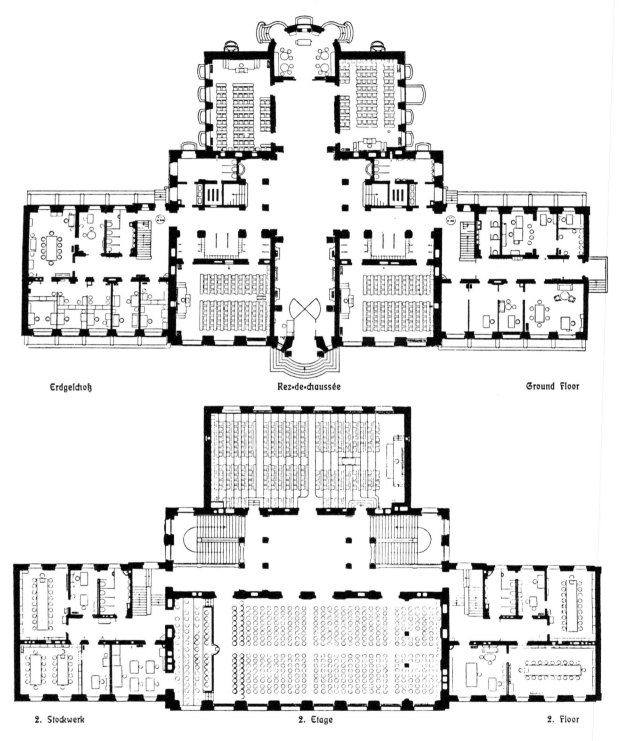

Erdgeschoß   Rez-de-chaussée   Ground Floor

2. Stockwerk   2. Étage   2. Floor

zimmer für Studierende, endlich der Empfangs- und Sitzungssaal der E. E. Jügelstiftung. Im zweiten Obergeschoß ist das Auditorium maximum und die Aula gelegen, im nächst höheren Stockwerk die Zentralbibliothek und mehrere Seminarzimmer. Die beiden Flügel sind für Seminare, das psychologische Institut und die technologische Abteilung benutzt. Das Untergeschoß enthält die Räume für die Niederdruckdampfheizung, die Lehrmittelsammlungen und anderes.

Die Portalfiguren rühren von Krüger her, die Figuren der Attika von Herold, die drei Bronze-Porträtreliefs an der Front von Bäumler. Die beiden Jügelmonumente an der Wand der Eingangshalle sind von Prof. Varnesi gefertigt.

salle de réception et de séances du comité E. E. Jügelstiftung. Au deuxième étage se trouvent la grande salle d'audition et la Aula; à l'étage au dessus, la bibliothèque centrale et plusieurs chambres du séminaire. Les deux ailes sont consacrées aux séminaires, à l'institut psychologique, et à la branche de technologie. Le sous-sol contient les localités destinées au chauffage à la vapeur à basse pression, aux collections d'enseignement etc.

Les figures du portail sont de Mr. Krüger, celles de l'attique de Herold; Bäumler est l'auteur des trois portraits reliefs en bronze de la façade. Les deux monuments de Jügel à la paroi de la halle d'entrée ont été exécutés par le professeur Varnesi.

room for the students, and a reception and committee room for the administration of the Jügel foundation. In the second storey are the large lecture hall and the "aula", on the next floor is the central library and several class rooms. The two side wings are reserved for class rooms, for the psychological institute and for the technological department. The basement contains the apparatus for the low pressure steam heating, the collection of teaching apparatus and other things.

The figures on the entrance portal are by Krüger, those on the terrace by Herold; the three bronze portrait reliefs on the front are by Bäumler. The two Jügel monuments on the wall of the entrance hall are by Prof. Varnesi.

Die Turnhalle des Turnvereins „Jahn" in München, Widenmayerstraße, unmittelbar am Ufer der Isar in nächster Nähe der Max Joseph-Brücke gelegen, ist ein Werk des Architekten H. Hartl. Die Baukosten betrugen 160000 Mark, die innere Einrichtung eingeschlossen. Das in Pußbau ausgeführte Giebelhaus mit seinen hohen roten Ziegeldächern zeichnet sich durch gelungene Gruppierung der Baumassen aus. An der einen Ecke springt ein runder als Turm endigender Ausbau vor und auf dem Dachfirst erhebt sich ein Ventilationstürmchen. Den Mittelpunkt des Gebäudes bildet die große, von beiden Schmalseiten beleuchtete, mit einem Rabitzgewölbe überspannte Turnhalle. Der Südanbau enthält im Erdgeschoß das Haupttreppenhaus, das Kneipzimmer, die Hausmeisterwohnung u. a., während sich darüber im ersten Stock der Damenturnsaal mit Zubehör befindet. Im Nordanbau liegt im Erdgeschoß unter anderen der Ankleideraum, im oberen Stockwerk daselbst ist der Ankleideraum für Zöglinge untergebracht, an den sich beiderseits Terrassen anschließen. Für sämtliche Räume ist eine Zentralheizung angelegt. An der Südfront ist in Stockwerkshöhe ein Relief, Ringkämpfer, Diskuswerfer und Steinstößer darstellend, angebracht.

La salle de gymnastique de la société "Jahn", Widenmayerstrasse à Munich, située directement au bord de l'Isar, près du pont de Max Joseph, est l'œuvre de Mr. H. Hartl architecte. Les frais de construction s'élevèrent à 160000 Marks, y compris les installations intérieures. Le bâtiment à pignon est construit en maçonnerie crépie, il est recouvert en tuiles rouges et se distingue par un groupement pittoresque des masses. Sur un des angles, on voit un avant-corps rond faire saille et se terminer en forme de tour, sur le faîte du toit s'élève une tourelle de ventilation. La grande halle de gymnastique, recouverte d'une voûte de système Rabitz, éclairée sur ses deux faces étroites, forme le centre de la composition. L'annexe sud contient au rez-de-chaussée l'escalier principal, la cantine, l'appartement du concierge et d'autres localités, tandis qu'au premier étage se trouve la salle de gymnastique des dames avec dépendances. L'aile du nord contient au rez-de-chaussée les vestiaires et au premier étage les chambres de toilette pour élèves; des deux côtés s'étendent des terrasses. Un chauffage central fonctionne pour toutes les localités. Un relief de la hauteur d'un étage, représentant des lutteurs, des discoboles et des athlètes jetant des pierres décore la façade méridionale.

The gymnasium of the Athletic Club "Jahn" at Widenmayerstrasse Munich, situated on the banks of the Isar near the Max Joseph Bridge, is the work of the architect H. Hartl. The cost of building amounted to 160000 Marks including the interior equipment. The gable house carried out in plaster with its high red tiled roofs is distinguished by the effective grouping of the various parts. On one corner projects a circular building ending in a tower, and the roof is diversified by small towers for ventilation. The middle part of the building is occupied by the gymnasium hall, lighted on the two sides and with a Rabitz vaulted roof. The south building contains on the ground floor the principal staircase, the drinking room, the lodging for the house steward etc.; over this on the first floor is a gymnasium for ladies with adjoining offices. On the north side on the ground floor is the dressing room; on the upper storey is a dressing room for scholars on both sides of which are terraces. All the rooms have central heating. On the south frontage is a relief illustrative of wrestlers, discus throwers and stone throwers.

In kräftigen Formen der Deutschrenaissance und reicher Gliederung der Massen erhebt sich die in gelbem Sandstein verblendete Villa Hoepfner in Karlsruhe, Rintheimerstraße 15. Der Entwurf stammt von den Architekten Curjel & Moser und die Ausführung erfolgte in etwa 1½ Jahren für die Baukostensumme von 180000 Mark. Charakteristisch für die Erscheinung des Äußeren sind die an drei Fronten aufsteigenden mächtigen, in mehrfach gebrochenen Konturen beendeten Giebel. An zwei Fronten sind dem Erdgeschoß geräumige, mit dem Garten in Verbindung stehende Terrassen vorgelegt, zugleich finden sich mehrere vom Boden aufsteigende, durch ein oder auch zwei Geschosse geführte, mit Altanen abgeschlossene Erker, außerdem sind noch polygonal vorspringende Fensterausbauten im Oberstock und ein Balkon im Dachgeschoß des einen Giebels angeordnet. Die zum Haupteingang führende Freitreppe wird durch einen bedeckten Vorbau aus Glas und Eisen geschützt. Das gebrochene, in Schiefer eingedeckte Dach trägt auf den unteren Steilflächen Dachfenster.

Im Erdgeschoß lagern sich die Zimmer um eine geräumige zentrale Diele mit freiliegender Treppe und in Verbindung mit einer Terrasse stehend. Die Küche nebst Nebenräumen ist gleichfalls im Erdgeschoß untergebracht. Den Mittelpunkt des Obergeschosses bildet wieder eine Diele, nach welcher sich ein Schrankraum öffnet und von der eine Anzahl Wohn- und Schlafzimmer sowie ein Badekabinett zugänglich sind. Das Dachgeschoß, in welches sich die Treppe von der Diele aus fortsetzt, ist ebenfalls zu Zimmern ausgebaut.

La villa Hoepfner à Carlsruhe, Rintheimerstrasse 15, est traitée en formes vigoureuses de la Renaissance allemande, avec groupement riche des masses. Le plan est de MM. Curjel & Moser, architectes, et les frais de la construction qui dura un an et demi s'élevèrent à 180000 Marks. De puissants pignons de ligne plusieurs fois brisées placès sur trois des façades sont caractéristiques pour l'aspect de cet édifice. Sur deux faces sont placées au rez-de-chaussée de spacieuses terrasses communiquant avec le jardin, d'autre part, la maison possède plusieurs tourelles montant de fond à travers un ou deux étages et couronnées de balcons, on voit en outre des bow windows de forme polygonale au premier étage et un balcon situé, dans un des pignons du toit. L'escalier libre conduisant à l'entrée principale est recouvert d'un avant-corps en fer et en verre. Le toit brisé, recouvert en ardoises est pourvu de lucarnes dans sa partie inférieure.

Au rez-de-chaussée les chambres se groupent autour d'un hall spacieux avec escalier suspendu et communiquant avec une terrasse. La cuisine et ses dépendances est également située au rez-de-chaussée. Un hall forme le centre du premier étage, sur le hall s'ouvre une chambre à armoires et plusieurs chambres d'habitation et à coucher avec une chambre de bain. L'étage du toit au quel monte l'escalier du hall est aussi distribué en chambres.

The villa Hoepfner at Rintheimerstrasse 15, Carlsruhe, shows the strong forms of the German Renascence; It is solidly and effectively grouped and is faced with yellow sandstone. The design is by the architects Curjel and Moser, the time occupied in building was 1½ years and the cost amounted to 180000 Marks. The facades have gained their characteristic appearance by the erection on three sides of enormous gables which are finished off in various architectural ways. On two sides, on the ground floor and in connection with the garden are spacious terraces; from the ground floor upwards rise several bays extending through one or two upper storeys and finishing off with a terrace; in addition are several polygonal projecting window erections in the upper storeys with a gable in the roof. A flight of steps lying free leads to the principal entrance which is protected from the weather by a roof of glass and iron. The roof line is variously broken, slate is used for roofing and the steep parts of the roof have windows.

On the ground floor all the rooms are arranged round a spacious central hall with a free staircase and having an outlet on to the terrace. The kitchen, with domestic offices, is also on the ground floor. The central point of the first upper storey is another square hall from which open a wardrobe room, several bed rooms with bathroom, and other rooms. A staircase leads from this hall to the roof storey where there are several more rooms.

Das in rot geflammtem Miltenberger Mainsandstein in einer Bauzeit von drei Jahren ausgeführte Landeshaus in Wiesbaden, Kaiser-Friedrich-Ring und Moritzstraße, zeigt barocke Stilformen in Annäherung an die Erscheinung der aus älterer Zeit stammenden öffentlichen Gebäude der Nassauischen Gegend. Der Entwurf, von den Architekten Friedrich W. Werz und Paul Huber herrührend, ist die Folge eines Wettbewerbes, in dem die genannten Architekten den ersten Preis davontrugen. In der Mitte der im stumpfen Winkel gebrochenen Hauptfront erhebt sich ein korinthischer, mit einem

Le palais du gouvernement Kaiser Friedrich-Ring et Moritzstrasse à Wiesbaden, bâti dans l'espace de trois ans en grès flammé rouge de Miltenberg est traité en style baroque, s'inspirant des monuments publics anciens de la contrée de Nassau. Le projet est des architectes Friedrich W. Werz et Paul Huber, il a remporté le premier prix dans un concours public. Au milieu de la façade principale brisée en angle obtus, s'élève un portique à colonnes corinthiennes couronné d'un fronton triangulaire orné de figures. Le rez-

The "Landeshaus" at Kaiser-Friedrich-Ring and Moritzstrasse Wiesbaden is of red flamed Miltenberg Main sandstone and occupied three years in building. The style is barock, with a strong likeness to old architecture still seen in public buildings in the Nassau district. The design, by the architects Friedrich W. Werz and Paul Huber was the result of an open competition in which these architects gained the first prize. In the middle of the principal frontage, the line of which is broken by an obtuse angle, rises a Corinthian pillared portico crowned by a trian-

figurengeschmückten Dreiecksgiebel bekrönter Säulenportikus. Das Erdgeschoß zeigt Bossenquader, im Hauptgeschoß wechseln reich eingefaßte und durch Segmentgiebel bekrönte Fenster mit einfacher behandelten, im Viereck geschnittenen, während die im zweiten Obergeschosse mit Flachbogen überdeckt sind. Die beiden Obergeschosse sind durch vertiefte Tafeln zwischen den Fenstern zu einer Einheit zusammengefaßt. Über dem Mittelbau der Vorderfront erhebt sich ein höheres, gebrochenes, pavillonartig abgewalmtes Dach; die niedrigeren, gleichfalls gebrochenen Dächer der Seitenflügel sind in den unteren Steilflächen mit einer Reihe von Fenstern besetzt. Die Dächer sind mit rheinischem Schiefer eingedeckt und das Holzwerk der Fenster hat weißen Anstrich erhalten.

de-chaussée est en bossages, à l'étage principal, des fenêtres richement encadrées et couronnées d'un fronton en segment alternent avec des simples fenêtres de forme carrée, tandis que celles du second étage sont couvertes d'un arc surbaissé. Les deux étages supérieurs sont reliés entre eux au moyen de panneaux rentrants placés entre les fenêtres. Au dessus du corps central de la façade principale s'élève un haut toit de ligne brisée, en croupe de comble, en forme de pavillon. Les toits plus bas, également brisés des ailes latérales, sont dans la partie inférieure pourvus d'une rangée de lucarnes. Les toits sont recouverts en ardoises rhénanes, le bois des fenêtres a été peint en blanc.

gular gable ornamented with figures. The ground floor walls are of bossed square stones, on the principal storey richly framed windows with segment gable crowns alternate with plain square-cut-windows; the windows on the second storey are crowned with flat arches. The two upper storeys have a certain uniformity, the spaces between all the windows having a panelled recess. Over the middle erection of the front rises a high pavilion-like hipped roof the line of which is broken, the low roofs of the side wings have also broken lines and have in their steep parts, rows of windows. The roofs are covered with Rhenish slate, and the woodwork of the windows is painted white.

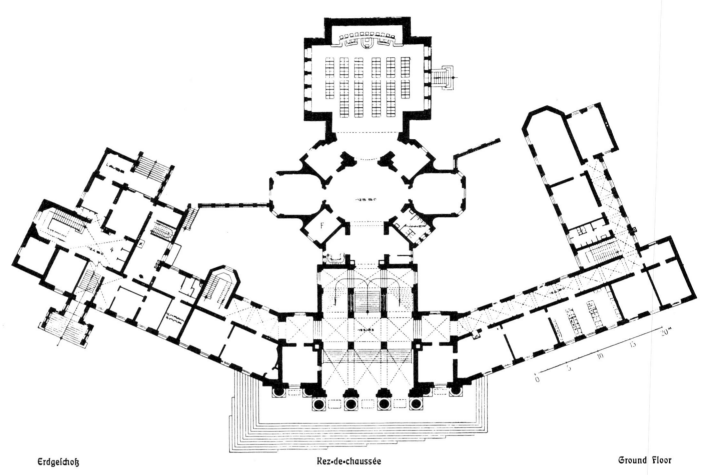

Erdgeschoß   Rez-de-chaussée   Ground Floor

In der Grundrißanlage ist die Trennung der für die Öffentlichkeit bestimmten Räume von den Arbeitsräumen und der Landeshauptmannswohnung derart durchgeführt, daß jede Abteilung gesondert erscheint. Im Erdgeschoß gelangt man über eine breite Freitreppe in die den Mittelbau einnehmende Eingangshalle und in das Haupttreppenhaus, an welches sich in beiden Flügelbauten die Arbeitsräume der Abteilungen und die Bureauräume angliedern. In halber Höhe des Erdgeschosses, von der Haupttreppe durch eine Vorhalle getrennt, liegt der Sitzungssaal für den Kommunallandtag, und von der Vorhalle zugänglich sind Räume für den Landtags-Vorsitzenden, den Regierungskommissar und Kommissionen angeordnet. Im ersten Stock des Mittelbaues ist der Landesausschuß-Sitzungssaal untergebracht, an den sich im rechten Flügel Verwaltungsräume anschließen. Der linksseitige Flügelbau gehört vornehmlich der im Erdgeschosse und im ersten Obergeschoß eingerichteten Landeshauptmannswohnung an. Die Sitzungssäle sowie mehrere Zimmer der Landeshauptmannswohnung haben eine vornehme Ausstattung erhalten. Die Haupttreppe ist aus poliertem Granit hergestellt, die Treppenhausfenster sind in Glasmalerei ausgeführt. Die Decken sind als Koenensche Voutendecken und die Dachbinder über dem Haupt- und Saalbau in Eisenkonstruktion hergestellt. Im

En plan on a obtenu une séparation des locaux destinés au public et des bureaux ainsi que de l'appartement du gouverneur; cette séparation est de nature à mettre chaque partie en évidence. Au rez-de-chaussée, on pénètre par un large escalier dans la halle d'entrée occupant le corps central; les bureaux des différents services se relient à cette halle dans les deux ailes. A demi hauteur du rez-de-chaussée, séparé de l'escalier principal par un vestibule, se trouve la salle de séances pour le gouvernement communal et du vestibule, on pénètre dans les salles du président, du commissaire du gouvernement et des commissions. Au premier étage du corps central est située la salle de séances du comité du Landtag auquel se joignent dans l'aile droite les bureaux d'administration. L'aile gauche est spécialement destinée à l'appartement du gouverneur réparti au rez-de-chaussée et au premier étage. Les salles de séances ainsi que plusieurs pièces de l'appartement du gouverneur ont été traitées avec luxe. L'escalier principal est en granit poli. Les fenêtres de cet escalier sont garnies de vitraux peints. Les plafonds sont construits en voûtes plates du système Koenen et les fermes du toit au dessus du corps de bâtiment principal et des salles sont

The ground plan shows that the separation between the rooms intended for the public, and those intended for work has been very thoroughly provided for, each department being perfectly independent of the other. On the ground floor, the entrance hall is approached by a broad flight of steps, the hall contains the principal staircase, on each side wing are arranged the rooms of the departments and various bureaus. In an intermediate storey above the ground floor and separated by an entrance hall lie the committee rooms of the Diet, those of the Presidents of the Diet, of the Government Commissioner and other committee rooms. On the first floor of the middle building is a committee room for the board of representatives, and this is followed by a number of rooms for the Administration. The left side wing belongs principally to the dwelling of the "Landeshauptmann" part of which is also contained in the ground floor and first storey. The rooms of this dwelling, as well as the various committee rooms have an interior equipment of much distinction. The principal staircase is of polished granite, the windows are of stained glass. The ceilings are of the "Koenen Vouten Plan" system and the roof binder over the roof of the great hall is constructed of iron.

Mittelbau des Sockelgeschosses find die Räume für die Zentralheizung angelegt.

Die Giebelgruppe ist vom Bildhauer Krüger modelliert, die Kapitelle der Säulen und die Fensterverzierungen find Arbeiten des Bildhauers Schill, der ornamentierte Fries unter dem Hauptgesims stammt vom Bildhauer Bierbrauer. Die Glasmalereien im Sitzungssaal find von K. Witthun vormals H. Lüthi ausgeführt.

309 [1908; 87]

Als Monumentalbau von bedeutenden Abmessungen, mit vier Flügeln einen glasüberdeckten Lichthof umschließend, erscheint das Museum der Senckenberg. Naturforschenden Gesellschaft in Frankfurt a. M., an der Viktoria-Allee gelegen, vom Kgl. Baurat Ludw. Neher entworfen und in einer Bauzeit von 2 Jahren 8 Monaten für die Kostensumme von 995 480 Mark, die innere feste Einrichtung eingeschlossen, zur Ausführung gebracht. Es würde sich hiernach für den Kubikmeter umbauten Raum, den Lichthof eingerechnet, ein Einheitspreis von 18,67 Mark ergeben. Für das Äußere sowie für das Innere des Lichthofes, der Vestibüle und des großen Treppenhauses ist roter Mainsandstein mit Putzflächen abwechselnd zur Verwendung gekommen. Die Formen find im Barockstil gehalten in absichtlicher Übereinstimmung mit dem Stil der alten Senckenbergischen Bauten. Das Museumsgebäude ist durch Arkadengänge

309 [1908; 87]

Le musée de la société d'histoire naturelle Senckenberg à Frankfort sur Main situé sur la Victoria-allee, apparaît comme monument de grandes dimensions; composé de quatre ailes entourant une cour vitrée; cet édifice a été élevé dans l'espace de deux ans et huit mois d'après les plans de Mr. Ludw. Neher, architecte conseiller. La construction, y compris les amenagements intérieurs fixes coûta 995 480 Marks. Cette somme représente un prix de 18,67 Marks pour le mètre cube d'espace construit, y compris la cour vitrée. Pour les façades ainsi que pour l'intérieur de la cour, des vestibules et du grand escalier, on a employé la pierre rouge du Main alternant avec des surfaces crépies. Les formes sont de style baroque avec l'intention d'harmoniser ainsi avec les anciennes constructions de la fondation Senckenberg. Le musée est relié au moyen de passages à arcades, d'une part avec

309 [1908; 87]

The Museum of the "Senckenberg. Naturforschenden Gesellschaft" built in the Viktoria Allee Frankfurt on Main is the design of the Royal Baurat Ludwig Neher; it occupied 2 years and 8 months in building and cost 995 480 Marks inclusive of the interior fittings. This gives a cost per cubic meter, including the skylighted court, of 18,67 Marks. It is a stately building with four wings and is of much architectural importance, the four wings enclose a glass-roofed courtyard. For the outside walls, the interior of the courtyard, the vestibule and the grand staircase red Main sandstone is used varied occasionally with plastered surfaces. The style is barock, purposely in keeping with the old Senckenberg buildings. The Museum itself is connected by arcades with the "Physikalischen Institut" on one side, and on the other with the library and lecture hall of the "Jügelstiftung". The ground floor is of

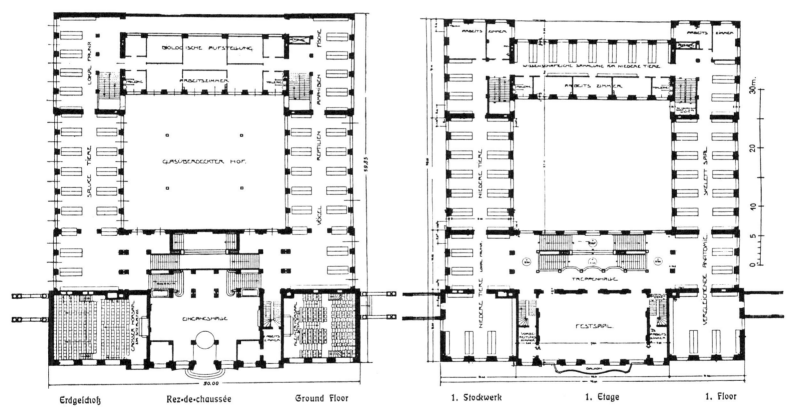

| Erdgeschoß | Rez-de-chaussée | Ground Floor | 1. Stockwerk | 1. Etage | 1. Floor |

einerseits mit dem Physikalischen Institut, andererseits mit dem Bibliothek- und Auditoriengebäude der Jügelstiftung in Verbindung gebracht. Das gequaderte Erdgeschoß zeigt Rundbogenfenster, über dem rundbogigen Portal erstreckt sich ein Balkon auf Konsolen, die Fenster der beiden Obergeschosse find flachbogig überdeckt und durch vertiefte Tafeln getrennt. Der Mittelbau der Hauptfront wird durch einen breiten geschwungenen, mit in Kupfer getriebenen Freifiguren und ein Relieffeld geschmückten Giebel bekrönt. Das Figürliche ist von Bildhauer J. Belz modelliert. Aus dem gebrochenen, in den Steilflächen mit Fensteraufbauten besetzten Dache erhebt sich ein mit umlaufender Galerie und über dieser aufsteigenden Laterne versehener Dachreiterturm.

Vor der großen Eingangshalle im Mittelbau ist ein geräumiger Windfang angeordnet, außer-

l'institut de physique, d'autre part avec la bibliothèque et les salles d'audition de la fondation Jügel. Les fenêtres du rez-de-chaussée en bossages sont à plein cintre, au dessus du portail fermé en arc, s'étend un balcon porté sur des consoles, les fenêtres des deux étages superieurs sont à arc surbaissé et séparées par des panneaux enfoncés. Le corps central de la façade principale est couronné par un large fronton courbé, orné de figures en cuivre repoussé et d'un champ en relief. La partie figurale a été modelée par Mr. J. Belz sculpteur. Au dessus du toit brisé et pourvu de lucarnes sur les côtés s'élève un cavalier avec galerie surmontée d'une lanterne.

Au devant de la grande halle d'entrée dans le corps-central on a disposé un tambour spacieux; en outre, des locaux pour le portier

square stones, and has round arched windows, over the portal, which is also arched, is a balcony resting on consoles, the windows of the two upper storeys have flat arched framing and are divided by receding panels. The middle erection of the principal front is crowned by a broadly curved gable ornamented with free-standing figures of worked copper and with reliefs of sculpture. The figures were modelled by the sculptor J. Belz. The roof line is broken, is varied in the steep parts by windows, and has a turret with a gallery running round it from which finishes it off.

Before the spacious entrance hall in the middle building is a large wind-screen, adjoining are rooms for door-keeper and for cloakrooms. On each side of the principal vestibule lie two large lecture halls extending from the ground

dem lind anlchließend Portier- und Garderoberäume vorgesehen. Zu beiden Seiten des Hauptvestibüls liegen die vom Untergeschoß in das Hauptgeschoß mit amphitheatralilchen Sitzreihen auflteigenden beiden Hörläle, die von den Arkaden der Nord- und Südleite zugänglich lind. Außerdem lind im Untergeschoß untergebracht: die Lehrlammlung neben dem kleinen Hörlaale, die Verwaltungsräume, die doppelläufige Haupttreppe zum Hauptgeschoß und weiter zum erlten Obergeschoß führend. Eine dreiteilige Halle mit breiter Freitreppe führt abwärts in das Untergeschoß zu dem für Ausltellungszwecke benußten bedeckten Hofe, dem lich mit offenen Hallen rechts das geologilche, links das mineralogilche und im Querbau das paläontologilche Muleum anreihen. An der Außenfront nach rückwärts liegen die Arbeitszimmer, die Hausmeilterwohnung und in einem Anbau der Präparationslaal mit Nebenräumen. Das Hauptgeschoß enthält noch an beiden Seiten des Hofes die Säle für Säugetiere und die Lokalfauna, für Vögel, Reptilien, Amphibien und Filche, und im Querflügel die gegen einen breiten Gang durch Glaswände lich öffnenden Kojen der biologilchen Schaultellung. Im erlten Obergeschoß liegt an der Vorderfront der durch zwei Stockwerke reichende Feltlaal, an den übrigen drei Seiten des Hofes ichließen lich die Säle für niedere Tiere, für vergleichende Anatomie und Skelettierung lowie eine Anzahl Arbeitszimmer an. Vier kleinere Treppen und ein Aufzug vermitteln die Verbindung mit lämtlichen oberen Geicholien. Im zweiten Obergeschoß lind zwei geräumige Laboratorien, fünf Arbeitszimmer, ein photographilches Atelier und lieben große Säle für willenlchaftliche Sammlungen untergebracht. Das dritte Obergeschoß, durch die Dachaufbauten des Vorderbaues gebildet, ilt zu Magazinräumen verwendet. Für die Beheizung des Gebäudes ilt Warmwal1erheizung und Niederdruckdampfheizung vorgelehen, die Kellelanlage ilt unter dem Eingangsveltibül eingebaut.

et pour le veltiaire se trouvent en communication avec la halle. Des deux côtés du vestibule principal se trouvent les deux salles de conférences montant en forme d'amphithéâtres du sous-sol au rez-de-chaussée; ces deux salles sont accessibles par les arcades des ailes du nord et du sud. On a en outre placé au sous-sol, la collection de l'enseignement avec les petites salles de cours, les bureaux de l'administration, l'escalier à double rampe conduisant aux étages supérieurs. Une halle à trois nefs avec large escalier suspendu conduit dans le sous-sol, à la cour couverte servant à des expositions; le musée minéralogique à droite et le musée paléontologique à gauche dans une aile transversale sont reliés à cette cour par des halles ouvertes. Sur la façade postérieure se trouvent les chambres de travail, l'appartement du concierge et dans une annexe, la salle de préparations avec dépendances. L'étage principal contient encore des deux côtés de la cour, les salles pour mammifères, et la faune locale, oiseaux, reptiles, amphibies et poissons, et niches pour représentations biologiques, placées dans une aile transversale, ouvertes sur un large corridor et pourvues de vitrages. Au premier étage se trouve sur le devant la salle des fêtes montant de fond à travers deux étages, sur les trois autres faces de la cour se relient des salles pour les animaux inférieurs, pour anatomie comparée, pour les squelettes ainsi qu'un certain nombre de chambres de travail. Quatre petits escaliers et un lift établissent la communication entre tous les étages supérieurs. Au second étage sont deux grand laboratoires, cinq chambres de travail, un atelier photographique et sept grandes salles pour collections scientifiques. Le troisième étage formé des lucarnes de l'avant corps est utilisé comme magasin. On a employé le chauffage à eau chaud et à vapeur à basse pression; les chaudières ont été placées au dessous du vestibule d'entrée.

floor to the principal storey with seats arranged in an amphitheatre; these halls can be entered too from the arcades at the sides on north and south. On the ground floor are also arranged: — the educational collection, a small lecture room, the rooms for the administration the principal double staircase leading to the principal storey and afterwards to the upper storeys. A hall with three divisions with a broad free staircase, leads downwards through the basement to the courtyard which is roofed with glass and which is used for exhibition purposes; on this join by means of open halls the geological museum on the right, the mineralogical museum on the left and in the transverse building the paleontological museum. At the back of the principal frontage lie the work-rooms and the house-stewards lodging; in an additional wing is the preparation room with surrounding apartments. On the principal floor on both sides of the court are the collections of mammalia and of the local fauna, for birds, reptiles, amphibia and fishes. In the transverse wing are glass protected receptacles for biological exhibits, approached by a broad gang way. On the next storey in the front is a large hall for various ceremonies extending upwards through two storeys, on the other three sides of the courtyard are the collections of the lower animals, for comparative anatomy and articulation, as well as work rooms and studies. Four secondary staircases with a lift lead to the upper storeys. In the second upper storey are two spacious laboratories, five studies, a photographic studio, and seven large halls for scientific collections. The third upper storey formed by the roof erection of the main building is used as a store magazine. The building is heated with warm water and low pressure steam heating, the apparatus is built under the entrance vestibule.

310, 311 [1908; 78, 79]

Als ein monumentales Bauwerk in deutlcher Frührenaillance, unter ltarker Anlehnung an lpätgotilche Formen, erlcheint das Rathaus in Recklinghaulen, ein Werk des Architekten Müller-Jena, dellen Entwurf in einer engeren

310, 311 [1908; 78, 79]

L'hôtel-de-ville de Recklinghausen, œuvre de Mr. Müller-Jena, architecte, a été exécuté du mois de juin 1904 à celui de juillet 1908 pour la somme de 1 100 000 Marks, d'après un plan sorti premier d'un concours

310, 311 [1908; 78, 79]

The Guildhall in Recklinghausen, a stately building in German early Renascence with a strong resemblance to the late Gothic, is the work of the architect Müller-Jena, and was built according to a design

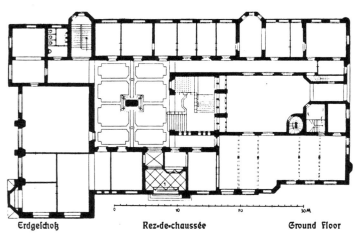

Erdgeichoß   Rez-de-chaussée   Ground Floor

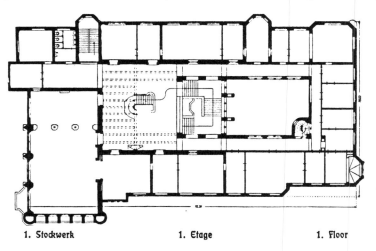

1. Stockwerk   1. Étage   1. Floor

Konkurrenz den 1. Preis erzielt hatte, ausgeführt in der Bauzeit vom Juni 1904 bis Juli 1908 für die Baukoltenlumme von 1 100 000 Mark. Örtliche Bauleiter waren Reg.-Baumeilter Heil und Bauführer Schmiß, als ltädtilcher Oberleiter fungierte Stadtbaurat Gronarz. Das in der Hauptlache dreiltöckige Gebäude zeigt gefällige Gruppierung und ilt reichlich mit Erkerausbauten, Balkonen, Giebeln und Türmchen ausgeltattet. Aus den lteilen Dächern wächlt ein mächtiger, viereckiger, mit mehrfach gebrochener Haube be-

restreint. Cet édifice est une construction monumentale, traitée dans le style de renaissance allemande primitive avec forte influence de formes gothiques tardives. La surveillance locale des travaux fut confiée à M. M. Heil architecte du gouvernement et Schmitz conducteur de travaux. Le conseiller architecte Gronarz fonctionnait comme délégué supérieur de la ville. Le bâtiment est en général à trois étages, il possède un groupement pittoresque et est abondamment pourvu d'avant-corps, de balcons,

which won the first prize in an open competition. It was built from June 1904 to July 1908 and cost 1 100 000 Mark. The local building superintendents were the Reg.-Baumeister Heil and the Bauführer Schmitz; as municipal upper superintendent the Town building councillor Gronarz was appointed. The principal building is three storeyed, is effectively grouped and is lavishly ornamented with bays, balconies, gables and towers. From the steep roofs rises a large square tower crowned

krönter Turm heraus. Das Material der Faſſaden beſteht aus rötlich-gelbem Eifelkalkſtein für die Flächen, Kaiſerſteinbruch Medarder Sandſtein für die Gliederungen und Baſalt für den Sockel. Die Dächer ſind in Schiefer, der Turm iſt in Kupfer eingedeckt. Die ſchwierige Fundamentierung in ſchwimmendem Fließſand und einer Hochmoorſchicht verurſachte allein einen Koſtenaufwand von 160 000 Mark. Die geſamte Unterkellerung iſt waſſerdicht in Eiſenbeton hergeſtellt.

Im Erdgeſchoß führt ein breites, rundbogiges Portal zu der überwölbten Eingangshalle und von da zu der geräumigen zentralen Diele, in deren Mitte ein mächtiger Pfeiler aufſteigt und der ſich das Haupttreppenhaus mit maſſiver Treppe in gebrochenen Läufen unmittelbar anſchließt, ſeitlich von dem durch eine Einfahrt zugänglichen Hofe aus erleuchtet. Außerdem enthält das Erdgeſchoß die Stadtkaſſe mit dem Treſor, das Meldeamt, die Sparkaſſe und weiter eine Anzahl Bureauräume. Den Mittelpunkt des erſten Obergeſchoſſes bildet wieder eine mit einem Rippengewölbe überdeckte Diele, entſprechend der unteren, in welcher die nach oben führende Treppe, um einen mittleren Pfeiler ſich windend und auf eine umlaufende Galerie mündend, aufſteigt. Im erſten Obergeſchoß liegen der große Stadtverordneten- und der Magiſtratsſitzungsſaal, die Amtszimmer der beiden Bürgermeiſter, das Standesamt nebſt verſchiedenen Bureauräumen. Die figürlichen Arbeiten am Äußeren ſtammen vom Bildhauer Graſſegger, die im Innern vom Bildhauer E. Haller. Die Malereien in den Sälen ſind vom Maler Heinſig ausgeführt.

de pignons et de tourelles. Au dessus des toits s'élève une puissante tour carrée, couronnée d'un toit à profil brisé. Les façades sont en pierre du Eifel jaune rougeâtre pour les surfaces, en pierre de Medard, Kaisersteinbruch pour les profils et en basalt pour le socle. Les toits sont recouverts en ardoises, la tour en cuivre. Des fondations difficiles dans du sable mouvant et une couche marécageuse occasionèrent une dépense de 160 000 Marks. Tout le dessous des caves est en béton armé imperméable.

Au rez-de-chaussée, un portail à plein cintre, large, conduit dans la halle d'entrée voûtée et de là, à une spacieuse halle centrale au milieu de laquelle s'élève un puissant pilier et qui communique directement avec un escalier massif à rampes brisées. Cette halle est éclairée latéralement par une cour avec porte cochère. Le rez-de-chaussée est en outre occupé par la caisse de la ville avec le trésor, le bureau de police, la caisse d'épargne et un certain nombre de bureaux. Une halle couverte d'une voûte d'arêtes, correspondant à celle du rez-de-chaussée, forme la partie centrale du premier étage; l'escalier conduisant au dessus s'enroule autour d'un pilier central et aboutit à une galerie entourant le local. Au premier étage, se trouvent la grande salle du conseil municipal et des séances, les chambres des deux maires, l'état civil et plusieurs bureaux. Les travaux de sculpture de l'extérieur sont de Mr. Grassegger sculpteur, ceux de l'intérieur de Mr. E. Haller. Le peintre Heinsig a exécuté les peintures dans les salles.

with richly ornamented cap. The material for the facades is reddish yellow Eifel limestone for the surfaces, Kaiser quarry Medard sandstone for the articulations, and basalt for the basement. The roofs are of slate and the tower is roofed with copper. The site on shifting sand and moor-land gave rise to great difficulties in the foundation which alone cost 160000 Mark. The entire cellarage is rendered water-proof by a construction of iron beton.

On the ground floor, a broad arched portal leads to a vaulted entrance hall, and that opens into a spacious central hall in the middle of which rises a massive pillar, from this hall ascends the principal staircase solidly built and divided into several flights; it is lighted on the side from a courtyard to which there is a separate entrance. The ground floor contains also, the municipal counting-house with safes; the Registry Office, the Savings Bank, and a number of bureaus. The central point of the upper storey is again a large square vaulted hall corresponding to that on the ground floor, in which the staircase winds upwards round a central pillar and opens on to a gallery running round the building. On the first floor are large rooms for the use of town councillors, a magistrates' committee room, the official rooms of two mayors, the marriage Registry office and several other bureaus. The sculptural ornament of the exterior is by the sculptor Grassegger, that of the interior by the sculptor E. Haller. The paintings in the various halls are by the painter Heinsig.

312, 313 [1909; 1, 2]

Das Wohnhaus Kretzer in Berlin, Bendlerſtraße 6, von Architekt Geh. Reg.-Rat Prof. A. Meſſel entworfen, zeigt eine Faſſade aus fränkiſchem Kalkſtein mit roſagrauen Naturputzflächen. Das Ebenerdgeſchoß und der erſte Oberſtock ſind durch kannelierte Wandſtreifen in eins zuſammengezogen und werden von einer Brüſtung bekrönt, hinter welcher ſich ein in der Front etwas zurückſpringendes zweites Obergeſchoß erhebt. Das gebrochene, mit Biberſchwänzen eingedeckte Dach iſt durch Dachfenſter belebt. Der Vorgarten iſt mit einem Sockel aus Kalkſtein mit Kalkſteinkugeln, die durch eine ſtarke Eiſenſtange gehalten werden, eingefriedigt. Der bildhaueriſche Schmuck der Faſſade ſtammt von Prof. Wrba, die Bauleitung beſorgte Reg.-Baumeiſter Mac Lean.

312, 313 [1909; 1, 2]

La maison d'habitation Kretzer à Berlin, Bendlerstrasse 6, a été construite par Mr. A. Messel, professeur, conseiller, elle montre une façade en pierre calcaire de Franconie avec surfaces crépies naturelles, d'un ton gris-rose. Le rez-de-chaussée et le premier étages sont reliés entre eux par des piliers cannelés et sont surmontés d'une balustrade, derrière laquelle s'élève le second étage en retrait sur la façade. Le toit mansard recouvert en tuiles, est interrompu par des lucarnes. Le jardin sur la rue est entouré d'un socle de pierre calcaire, décoré de boules en pierres fixées par une forte barre de fer. La décoration sculpturale est due au sculpteur, professeur Wrba; Mr. Mac Lean fut chargé de la conduite des travaux.

Le rez-de-chaussée contient un hall occupant

312, 313 [1909; 1, 2]

The house Kretzer at Bendlerstrasse 6, Berlin, was designed by the architect Professor A. Messel and shows a facade of Frankish limestone with rose-grey natural plastered surfaces. The ground-floor and the first floor are uniformly ornamented by fluted stripes extending through both storeys and are crowned by a balustrade, behind which in front rises a second upper storey somewhat receding. The roof line is broken and has several windows, the roofing is of flat red tiles. The front garden has a sockel of limestone and is surrounded by a fencing of limestone balls through which pass strong iron railings. The sculptural ornament is by Professor Wrba, the superintendence of the building operations was in the hands of Regierungsbaumeister Mc Lean.

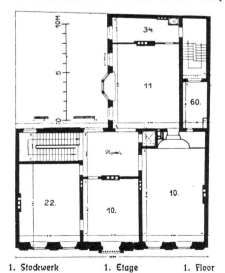

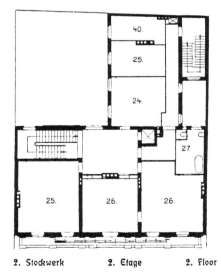

Erdgeſchoß   Rez-de-chaussée   Ground Floor   1. Stockwerk   1. Etage   1. Floor   2. Stockwerk   2. Etage   2. Floor

Das Erdgeſchoß enthält eine die ganze Tiefe des Vorderhauſes einnehmende Halle, welche mit einer Säulenſtellung aus Thüringer Kalkſtein und Terrakotten von Fr. Naager geſchmückt iſt. An die Halle ſchließt ſich das Haupttreppenhaus an. In jedem Stockwerk gruppieren ſich die Zimmer um einen Vorraum. Im Erdgeſchoß liegen noch

toute la profondeur de la maison, il est décoré d'une colonnade de pierre calcaire de Turinge et de céramiques de Mr. Fr. Naager. L'escalier principal communique avec la hall. A chaque étage, les chambres se groupent autour d'un vestibule. Au rez-de-chaussée se trouvent encore la cuisine, le vestiaire et les locaux du concierge.

The ground floor contains a hall extending the whole depth of the front house, and ornamented with pillars of Thuringian sandstone and terra-cotta by Professor Naager. From the hall leads the principal staircase. In each storey the rooms are grouped round an entrance

die Küche, Garderoben- und Portierräume. Die Hauptgesellschaftszimmer sind im ersten Oberstock untergebracht. Der zweite Oberstock und der ausgebaute Dachraum sind zur Anlage der Schlafzimmer, der Räume für die Dienerschaft, der Plätt-, Näh- und Schrankzimmer benutzt.

314 [1909; 3]

Das Rolandhaus in Bremen, ein Geschäftshaus mit Läden und großem Restaurant im Erdgeschoß und mit Kontorräumen in den vier Obergeschossen, hat die Hauptfront am Brill und die Hinterfront an der Langenstraße. Die Fassaden sind nach dem Entwurfe des Architekten W. H. Schacht, die Grundrisse nach dem des Architekten G. Schellenberger ausgeführt. Die Bauzeit nahm 7 Monate in Anspruch. Die Hauptfassade in gelbrötlicher Kunststeinmasse wurde zugleich mit der Eisenbetonkonstruktion in fester Schalung eingestampft und nach der Ausschalung bearbeitet. Dieselbe wird durch aufsteigende Pfeiler geteilt und ebenso sind die eingeschlossenen Fenstergruppen im ersten Obergeschosse durch Säulchen, in den übrigen Obergeschossen durch schmale Pfeiler geteilt. Die Schaufenster des gequaderten Erdgeschosses zeigen Korbbogen und schmiedeeiserne Rahmeneinsätze. Die Fenstergruppen im ersten Obergeschoß springen in flacher Rundung vor, tragen barock stilisierte Giebelbekrönungen und zwischen denselben sind von Bildhauer W. Mues gefertigte Figuren in Hochrelief angebracht. Sämtliche Fenster der Obergeschosse sind geradlinig geschlossen. Das mit Ziegeln eingedeckte Dach wird im unteren Teile durch eine halbstockartige Fensterflucht unterbrochen, ebenso trägt der obere Dachteil eine Reihe von Dachfenstern.

Der seitwärts liegende Haupteingang im Erdgeschoß steht mit der Treppe, den Aufzügen und einem offenen, von einer Einfahrt zugänglichen Hof in Verbindung. Ein zweiter Eingang zwischen den Läden führt zu dem mit Oberlicht versehenen Restaurationslokal und steht mittelst eines Lichthofs mit den Zimmern des hinteren Flügels in Verbindung. Die Kontorräume der Obergeschosse umschließen jedesmal einen Lichthof. Das Kellergeschoß enthält namentlich den Maschinen- und Zentralheizraum. Das ganze Gebäude ist in Eisenbetonkonstruktion hergestellt.

315 [1909; 12]

Das Geschäftshaus des General-Anzeigers in Düsseldorf, Ecke Grabenstraße und Königs-Allee, umschließt mit vier Flügeln einen offenen Hof und liegt an zwei Fronten frei. Der Entwurf stammt von dem Architekten Herm. vom Endt und ist in zwei Bauperioden vom Herbst 1905 bis zum Frühjahr 1908 zur Ausführung gekommen. Die vierstöckigen Straßenfronten sind ganz in eine von durchschließenden Pfeilern durchsetzte Fensterarchitektur aufgelöst und mehrfach durch erkerartig ausgekragte, das erste und zweite Obergeschoß einnehmende, mit Altanen beendigte Ausbauten belebt. Der Mittelbau der Front an der Königs-Allee trägt einen barocken, durch figürliche Skulptur verzierten Giebel. Über dem Dachfirst steigt ein mit einer Galerie abschließendes Dachreitertürmchen auf. Die Fassaden sind mit hellgrauem bayerischen Muschelkalkstein verblendet. Die Bildhauerarbeiten sind im figürlichen Teil von Bildhauer A. Pehle, im ornamentalen Teil von Bildhauer H. Stader gefertigt. Die Oberlichtfüllung über dem Haupteingang, das Vordach des Geschäftseingangs an der Ecke und die Uhr sind aus Bronze in der Bildgießerei von Bernh. Förster gegossen. Sämtliche Fensteröffnungen sind geradlinig überdeckt, die gebrochenen Dächer mit Biberschwänzen eingedeckt.

Les principales pièces de réception sont situées au premier étage. Le second étage et le toit mansard ont été disposés pour recevoir les chambres à coucher, les chambres des domestiques, les chambres de repassage, de lingerie et d'armoires.

314 [1909; 3]

La maison de commerce, Rolandhaus à Brême, ayant des magasins et un grand restaurant au rez-de-chaussée et de comptoirs aux quatre étages supérieurs, a sa façade principale sur le Brill et sa façade postérieure sur la Langenstrasse. Les façades sont exécutées d'après les dessins de Mr. W. H. Schacht architecte, tandis que Mr. G. Schellenberger est l'auteur des plans. La construction dura 7 mois. La façade principale en pierre artificielle rouge-jaunâtre fut moulée en même temps que les constructions de béton armé et fut travaillée après l'enlèvement de l'enveloppe. Cette façade est divisée par des piliers élancés, et les groupes de fenêtres qu'ils encadrent sont partagés au premier étage par des colonnettes, aux autres étages par des meneaux. Les devantures de magasins du rez-de-chaussée traité en bossages, montrent des arcs en anse de panier et des cadres en fer forgé. Les groupes de fenêtres du premier étage font saillie en forme de segment de cercle, ils portent des frontons ornés, de forme baroque, entre eux sont placées des figures en haut relief exécutées par Mr. W. Mues, sculpteur. Toutes les fenêtres des étages supérieurs sont à linteau droit. Le toit recouvert en tuiles est interrompu dans sa partie inférieure par une rangée de fenêtres formant un demi étage; la partie supérieure du toit porte aussi une rangée de lucarnes.

L'entrée principale, située de côté au rez-de-chaussée, communique avec l'escalier, les ascenseurs, et une cour ouverte accessible par une porte cochère. Une seconde entrée, entre les magasins conduit au restaurant éclairé par le haut et communique par une cour avec les chambres de l'aile postérieure. Les comptoirs des étages supérieurs entourent chaque fois une cour. Le sous-sol contient principalement les locaux pour les machines et le chauffage central. Tout l'immeuble est construit en béton armé.

315 [1909; 12]

La maison de commerce du General-Anzeiger à Düsseldorf, angle Grabenstrasse et Königs-Allée, entoure de ses quatre ailes une cour ouverte et a deux façades libres. Mr. Herm. vom Endt, architecte, est l'auteur du projet qui fut exécuté en deux périodes, de l'automne 1905 au printemps 1908. Les façades sont entièrement composées de piliers qui les divisent en fenêtres, elles sont animées par de nombreuses saillies traversant le premier et le second étage et terminées par un balcon. Le corps central de la façade sur la Königs-Allée porte un fronton de formes baroques, et décoré de figures sculptées. Au dessus du faîte s'élève une tourelle terminée par une galerie. Les façades sont revêtues de pierre calcaire gris claire de Bavière. Les travaux de sculpture sont dus, dans la partie figurale à Mr. A. Pehle, dans celle ornementale, à Mr. A. Stader sculpteur. Le jour d'enhaut audessus de l'entrée principale, l'avant-toit de l'entrée des magasins sur l'angle, et l'horloge sont en bronze fondu dans les ateliers de Bernh. Förster. Toutes les ouvertures de fenêtres sont à linteaux droits, les toits brisés sont recouverts en tuiles.

hall. On the ground floor are kitchens, cloak-rooms and a porter's lodging. The principal reception rooms are on the first upper storey; the second storey and the roof storey are used for bedrooms, rooms for the servants, a laundry, a sewing-room and a room for wardrobes.

314 [1909; 3]

The Roland house in Bremen has its principal front on the Brill and the back frontage on the Langenstrasse. It is a business house with shops and a large restaurant on the ground floor and bureaus on the four upper storeys. The facades are from the design of the architect W. H. Schacht, the ground plan was designed by the architect G. Schellenberger. The time occupied was 7 months. The principal facade is of yellow-red artificial stone; it was worked together with the iron beton construction. The facade is divided by pillars running throughout, the window groups are also articulated by small pillars on the first floor, and on the other floors by smaller ones. The shop windows of the ground floor have oval arches and are framed by wrought iron. The window groups of the first upper storey have flat curves and are crowned with gables in the barock style, between which are sculptured figures in high relief by the sculptor W. Mues. All the windows of the upper storey are finished off with straight lines. The roof, which is tiled, has in its lower part a row of windows for an intermediate storey, the upper part has also a row of windows.

The principal entrance lying at the side of the ground floor, is in connection with the staircase, the lifts and with a courtyard which has an entrance for vehicles. A second entrance between the shops leads to the restaurant which is lighted from above, and which, by means of a skylighted courtyard is in connection with a back wing of the building. The bureaus on the upper storeys have each a skylighted court. The basement contains the machine and central heating rooms. The whole building is of iron beton construction.

315 [1909; 12]

The business premises of the "General-Anzeiger", corner of Grabenstrasse and Königs-Allee, Düsseldorf, encloses an open courtyard with four wings, and is free on two street-frontages. The design is by the architect Herm. von Endt and was carried out in two periods between the autumn of 1905 and the spring of 1908. The four-storeyed street frontage shows a window construction of pillars which extend upwards through all the storeys without interruption, it is enlivened by numerous projecting bays which, erected on the first and second storeys, end in balconies and terraces. The middle erection on the Königs-Allee has a gable in the barock style and is crowned with sculptural figures. Over the roof ridge rises a tower with a gallery running round it. The facades are faced with light grey Bavarian shell limestone. The statuary is by the sculptor A. Pehle, the ornamental part by the sculptor H. Stader. The framing of the skylight over the principal entrance, the porch of the business entrance at the corner and the clock are of bronze and were cast at the foundry of Bernh. Förster. All the windows have straight-lined openings, the roofs are covered with flat-red tiles.

Die Räume für den Zeitungsbetrieb sind zweckmäßig auf die vier Geschosse verteilt; der in der Grabenstraße gelegene Gebäudeflügel wird vom Königlichen Amtsgericht benutzt. Im Erdgeschoß finden sich drei Eingänge und eine Durchfahrt, außerdem sind zwei Haupt- und zwei Nebentreppen vorhanden. Die Treppe an der Königs-Allee ist in graublauem pentelischem, die an der Grabenstraße in gelbem Comblanchien-Marmor teils geschliffen, teils poliert ausgeführt. Sämtliche Decken und innere Stützen bestehen aus Eisenbeton.

316, 317 [1909; 4, 5]

Das allseitig freiliegende, drei offene Höfe umschließende Verwaltungs- und Polizeigebäude am Ostertor in Bremen, ist auf unregelmäßig geformtem Baugrunde, so daß drei Fronten einen Knick erhalten mußten, in der Bauzeit vom Januar 1906 bis Oktober 1908 in Formen der deutschen Spätrenaissance errichtet. Die Baukosten betrugen etwa 1½ Millionen Mark. Die erste allgemeine Grundrißdisposition erfolgte durch die Hochbauinspektion in Bremen, die weitere Ausarbeitung der Grundrisse sowie der Entwurf der Fassaden ist ein Werk des Architekten C. Börnstein. Der Haupteingang öffnet sich rundbogig in der Front „Am Wall", wird von zwei hochstrebenden, mit reich verzierten Giebeln abschließenden Türmen eingefaßt und ist mit einem breiten ausgekragten Erker überbaut, über dessen Dache sich wieder ein Giebel erhebt. Hinter den Türmen steigt das mächtige, steile, mit Ziegeln eingedeckte Dach auf, welches mit einem Dachreitertürmchen bekrönt ist. Die Fassadenteile neben den Türmen sind im ersten Obergeschoß zurückgesetzt, so daß sich offene Altane bilden. Die Front an der Ostertorstraße wird durch einen ausgekragten, durch sämtliche Geschosse geführten Erker belebt. Die Fenster des Erdgeschosses sind rundbogig, sonst überall geradlinig geschlossen, nur die des zweiten Obergeschosses sind in Gruppen vereinigt und durch schmale Zwischenpfeiler getrennt. Die Giebelornamente, Fenstereinfassungen und sonstigen Gliederungen sind aus Sandstein; die Flächen der Türme und Erkerausbauten sowie die Rustikaquaderung sind aus Tuffstein hergestellt, die übrigen Flächen haben Verputz erhalten.

Im Untergeschoß sind außer verschiedenen Amtszimmern, Arrestzellen und Aktenzimmern,

les locaux pour l'administration du journal sont pratiques et répartis sur quatre étages; l'aile située sur la Grabenstrasse est occupée par le tribunal royal. Au rez-de-chaussée se trouvent trois entrées, une porte cochère et en outre, deux escaliers principaux et deux secondaires. L'escalier sur la Königs-Allee est en marbre gris, celui sur la Grabenstrasse en marbre jaune de Comblanchien, ils sont en partie polis, en partie bouchardés. Tous les planchers et supports intérieurs sont en béton armé.

316, 317 [1909; 4, 5]

Le bâtiment d'administration et de police au Ostertor à Brême est construit sur un terrain de forme irrégulière, de telle sorte que trois façades sont élevées sur une ligne brisée, il est libre de tous côtés et embrasse trois cours ouvertes. Cet édifice traité dans les formes de la Renaissance allemande tardive a été élevé du mois de janvier 1906 à celui d'octobre 1908; les frais s'élevèrent à 1½ million de Marks. La première esquisse de plan fut faite par le bureau de l'inspection des bâtiments de Brême, les études subséquentes des plans, ainsi que le projet des façades, sont l'œuvre de Mr. C. Börnstein architecte. L'entrée principale s'ouvre en arc de cercle sur la façade „Am Wall", elle est flanquée par deux tours élevées, couronnées de riches pignons et surmontée d'une large tourelle saillante, derrière le toit de laquelle s'élève encore un pignon. Derrière les tours, monte le toit puissant, abrupt, recouvert de tuiles et portant un cavalier. Les parties des façades près des tours sont en retrait au premier étage, de sorte qu'il se forme des terrasses ouvertes. La façade sur la Ostertorstrasse est ornée d'une tourelle en saillie, traversant tous les étages. Les fenêtres du rez-de-chaussée sont à plein cintre, toutes les autres sont à linteaux droits, seulement celles du second étage sont reliées par groupes et séparées par de petits piliers. Les ornements des pignons, les encadrements de fenêtres et tous les profils sont de pierre; les surfaces des tours et des tourelles ainsi que les refends sont en pierre de tuffe; les autres surfaces, en maçonnerie crépie.

Au sous-sol, on a disposé, outre differents locaux d'administration, les chambres d'arrêt, et les chambres d'actes, les localités pour le chauffage

The rooms for the business production of the paper are conveniently arranged on the four storeys; the wing lying on the Grabenstrasse is used by the Royal Court of Justice. On the ground floor are the three entrances and an entrance for vehicles, there are as well two principal and two secondary staircases. The staircase on the Königs-Allee is carried out in grey blue marble, that on the Grabenstrasse in yellow Comblanchien marble partly carved and partly polished. All the ceilings and interior supports are of iron beton.

316, 317 [1909; 4, 5]

The "Verwaltungs und Polizei" building at Ostertor in Bremen is a building lying on all sides free and containing three open courtyards. The site was of so irregular a formation that three of the frontages had to be erected with a break. The style is German Late Renascence; the time occupied in building was from Jan. 1906 to October 1908, and the cost amounted to 1½ Million Marks. The first general ground plan was made under the direction of the Building Municipal authorities of Bremen, the execution of this plan and the design for the facades are the work of the architect C. Börnstein. The principal entrance consisting of rounded arches is in the front "Am Wall"; it is flanked by two high towers crowned with highly ornamental gables; above it is a broad projecting bay over the roof of which is another gable. Behind the towers rises an imposing steep roof covered with tiles at the top of which is another roof ornament of small towers. The parts of the facade by the side of the towers recede in the upper storey to allow of the construction of balconies. The frontage on the Ostertor side is enlivened by projecting bays which are continued through each storey. The windows of the ground floor have rounded arches, those of the other floors are in all cases straight lined; on the second floor the windows are united into groups separated by slender pillars. The ornaments of the gables, the window framing, and other articulations are all of sandstone, the surfaces of the towers, of the bays as well as of the "rustica" square stones are of tuff stone, the other surfaces are plastered.

In the basement are various official apart-

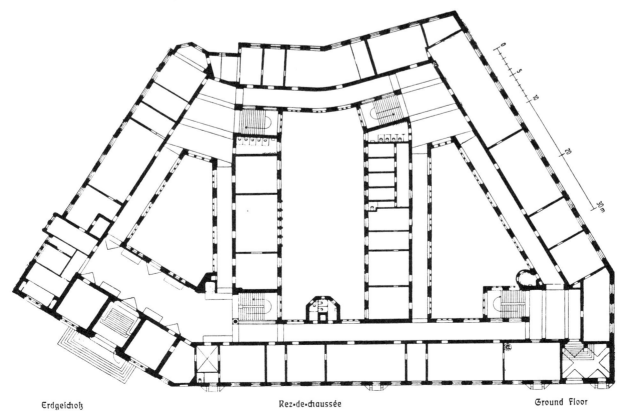

Erdgeschoß   Rez-de-chaussée   Ground Floor

Räume für die Beizung und Wohnungen für den Bausmeister und anderes Dienstperlonal untergebracht. Die Böfe sind von den Straßen und untereinander mittelst Durchfahrten zugänglich gemacht. Das Gebäude ist sowohl durch einen unterirdischen Gang als durch eine Straßenbrücke mit dem nebenstehendem Gerichtshaule verbunden, um die Überbringung von Polizeigefangenen zu vermitteln. Das Erdgeschoß enthält neben den Eingängen und Treppen die Amtszimmer der Polizeidirektion, das Zentralmeldeamt und anderes. Die indirekte Beleuchtung der Wandelgänge ist nach Möglichkeit vermieden. Im ersten Obergeschosse liegen die Räume für das Unfallverlicherungsamt, die Krankenkasen, das Invalidenverlicherungsamt, für den Gesundheitsrat und die Armenpflege. Das zweite Obergeschoß ist für das Kriminalamt und die Gewerbeinspektion ausgenutzt. Die Anlage von Aborten und Pissoirs sowie von Aufzügen ist für sämtliche Geschoße vorgesehen. Schließlich ist noch das Dachgeschoß teilweile zu Wohnungen und Aktenräumen ausgebaut.

318 [1909; 34]

Das Landhaus in München, Möhlstraße 45, zweistöckig und mit einem teilweile ausgebauten Dachgeschosse versehen, ist nach dem Entwurfe des verstorbenen Architekten Ludwig Steinmeß in elfmonatlicher Bauzeit errichtet. Die Baukosten betrugen ca. 70000 Mark. Es bildet einen Putzbau mit abgewalmtem, in Biberschwänzen eingedecktem Dach, welches von Dachsenstern und von einem Giebel unterbrochen wird. Der rundbogige Baupteingang liegt an einer Seitenfront, in einem mit Pultdach überdeckten, an einen Vorsprung sich anlehnenden Anbau, sonst sind die Fenster geradlinig geschlossen, mit Ausnahme der in dem schmalen Giebelfelde der Bauptfront befindlichen rundbogig überwölbten gepaarten Fenster. Der mit einem Giebel abschließenden Seitenfront ist im Erdgeschoß ein Anbau hinzugefügt, der im Obergeschoß eine geräumige Altane trägt.

Die Bauausführung lag in den Bänden des Baugeschäftes Bans Tax, die Bildhauerarbeiten erledigte Karl Fischer, beide in München.

319 [1909; 7]

Das zweistöckige, noch durch ein ausgebautes Dachgeschoß erweiterte Einzelfamilienhaus in Bremen, Blumenthalstraße 14, ist in allseitig freier Lage nach dem Entwurfe des Architekten W. Blanke etwa im Laufe eines Jahres errichtet worden. Die Bauptfront ist durch einen ausgekragten überdeckten Balkon im ersten Stock und durch einen steilen, von geschwungenen Konturen begrenzten Giebel ausgezeichnet; der an einer Seitenfront liegende Eingang ist mit einer Balle überbaut. Sämtliche Fronten sind in gewelltem Verputz ausgeführt, der Sockel ist mit dunkelblauen Glasuriteinen bekleidet, der Giebel der Balkonüberdeckung sowie einzelne obere Teile der Seitenfronten zeigen Fachwerk in Eichenholz, teilweile mit Schnitzereien verziert. Das gebrochene Dach ist mit Schiefer eingedeckt.

Das Erdgeschoß enthält eine Diele mit freiaufsteigender Treppe, Gesellschafts- und Wohnzimmer sowie das Speisezimmer nebst anschließender Terrasse und dem mit der Küche durch einen Aufzug in Verbindung stehenden Anrichteraum. Im ersten Obergeschoß liegen außer Wohn- und Kinderzimmern die Schlafräume nebst dem Bad. Im zweiten Ober- bzw. ausgebauten Dachgeschoß sind noch mehrere Wohn- und Schlafzimmer sowie ein zweites Bad eingerichtet. Das Kellergeschoß ist zur Anlage der Küchen, des Raumes für die Zentralheizung und sonstiger Wirtschaftsräume ausgenutzt. Das Innere des Bauses ist reich ausgestattet; Treppenhaus und Speisezimmer zeigen hohe Täfelungen in Eichenholz und die Treppe ist mit einem eichenen geschnitzten Geländer versehen.

et les logements pour le concierge et pour le personnel de service. Les cours sont reliées entre elles et avec les rues par des passages à voitures. Le bâtiment est rélié au palais de justice voisin par un passage souterrain et par un pont sur rue pour permettre le transfert des prisonniers. Le rez-de-chaussée contient, à part les entrées secondaires et les escaliers, les chambres de travail de la direction de police, le bureau de recensement et d'autres pièces. On a évité autant que possible l'éclairage indirect des corridors. Au premier étage se trouvent les bureaux pour l'assurance contre les accidents, contre la maladie et l'invalidité, pour le conseil de salubrité publique et pour les secours aux pauvres. Le deuxième étage est consacré aux bureaux de la police criminelle et de l'inspection des métiers. On a établi des cabinets d'aisance et des pissoirs ainsi que des lifts à tous les étages. Enfin, l'étage du toit a encore été en partie utilisé pour des appartements et des dépôts d'actes.

318 [1909; 34]

La maison de campagne Möhlstrasse 45 à Munich, construction à deux étages avec toit mansardé, a été construite dans l'espace de 11 mois d'après les plans de feu Mr. Ludwig Steinmetz architecte. Les frais s'élevèrent à 70000 Marks environ. La maison est une construction crépite avec toit à croupe recouvert en tuiles, ce dernier interrompu par des lucarnes et un pignon. L'entrée principale à plein cintre est située sur une façade latérale, elle s'appuie à un avant corps et est recouverte d'un toit en appentis. En général, les fenêtres sont droites, à l'exception fenêtres à plein cintre, ornées qui se trouvent dans le mince panneau de pignon de la façade principale. La façade latérale terminée par un pignon est ornée au rez-de-chaussée d'une annexe portant au premier un balcon spacieux.

La maison d'entreprise Hans Tax à Munich exécuta les travaux, Mr. Carl Fischer également à Munich se chargea de la sculpture.

319 [1909; 7]

La maison pour une famille Blumenthalstrasse 14 à Brême, construction à deux étages augmentée d'un étage mansardé, libre de tous côtés, a été élevée dans l'espace d'un an environ, d'après le projet de Mr. W. Blanke architecte. La façade principale se distingue par un balcon saillant et couvert au premier étage et par un pignon abrupt, aux contours ondulés. L'entrée principale située sur une face latérale est recouverte d'un porche. Toutes les façades sont crépies d'une manière ondulée; le socle est revêtu de briques émaillée bleues foncées. Le fronton de la couverture du balcon, ainsi que quelques parties des faces latérales sont traitées en pans de bois de chêne en partie sculptés. Le toit brisé est recouvert en ardoises.

Le rez-de-chaussée contient un hall avec escalier suspendu, pièces de réception et d'habitation, et salle à manger communiquant avec terrasse adjacente et avec l'office relié à la cuisine par un monte plats. Au premier étage se trouvent, outre les chambres d'enfants et d'habitation, les chambres à coucher avec bain. Au second étage ou étage mansardé, on a disposé encore plusieurs chambres à coucher et d'habitation et un second bain. Le sous-sol contient les cuisines, le local pour chauffage central et d'autres pièces de service. L'intérieur de la maison est richement traité, l'escalier et la salle à manger ont de hautes boiseries de chêne, la balustrade d'escalier est de bois sculpté.

ments, arrest cells and archive rooms; rooms for heating apparatus and lodgings for the house steward and other officials. The courtyards have all communication with each other and with the street, and the building is connected with the neighbouring Court House by a subterranean passage and by a bridge over the street in order to convey prisoners. The ground floor contains with the entrances and staircase, the official rooms of the police administration, the central application office and other offices. Any indirect lighting of the corridors has been avoided as far as possible. On the first floor are the rooms for the Accident Insurance office, the Sick Fund, the Invalid Insurance office, for the sanitary authorities and for those of the care of the poor. The second upper storey is for the Criminal court and for the accommodation of Trade Inspection. On each floor are lavatories and lifts. The roof storey is partly arranged for dwellings and for archives.

318 [1909; 34]

The country house at Möhlstrasse 45, Munich, is a two-storeyed building with a roof storey partly utilized for dwelling rooms. The design is by the deceased architect Ludwig Steinmeß, it occupied 11 months in building and cost 70000 Marks. It is a plaster building with a hipped roof covered with flat red tiles; the roof is interrupted in various places by windows and by a gable. The principal entrance has rounded arches and his on the side frontage, it has a projecting porch over which is a protecting roof. All other windows are straightlined with the exception of a round arched window grouped of two which is placed in the narrow strip of gable surface over the principal frontage. The side frontage is finished off with a gable, it has too on the ground floor a projecting bay over which is a balcony.

The execution of the building was placed in the hands of the building firm Hans Tax that of the sculptural work in the hands of Karl Fischer both Munich firms.

319 [1909; 7]

The house at Blumenthalstrasse 14, Bremen, is intended for the use of one family; it is two storeyed and additional accommodation has been won by arranging the roof storey, as dwelling rooms. The house is free on all sides; the architect was W. Blanke and the time occupied was one year. The principal front is distinguished by projecting covered balcony on the first floor, and by a steep gable with curved contours. The entrance lies at the side and is built with a covered hall. All the fronts are carried out in plaster work, the sockel is faced with dark blue glazed tiles, the gable over the covered balcony and certain upper parts of the side frontage are of oak frame work, this is variously ornamented with carving. The roof, which has a broken line, is covered with slate.

The ground floor contains a square hall with a free staircase, round it are reception and dwelling rooms, the dining room with terrace adjoining; and a serving room connected with the kitchen by a lift. On the first upper storey are sitting-rooms, the nurseries, bedrooms and bathroom; on the second, that is the roof storey, are several more rooms some bedrooms and another bathroom. The basement contains the kitchen, the room for the central heating and other domestic offices. The fittings and equipment of the interior are very luxurious, the staircase and dining room have a high panelling of oak, the balustrade of the staircase is of carved oak.

Das im Villenviertel liegende, mit Vorgarten versehene, durch malerischen Aufbau der Fronten ausgezeichnete vierstöckige Wohnhaus in Düsseldorf, Herderstraße 59, ist nach dem Entwurfe des Architekten W. May im Laufe eines Jahres für die Kostensumme von 187 000 Mark zustande gebracht. Die kürzere Front an der Ahnfeldstraße zeigt einen vom Boden aufgehende Vorbau, der sich im ersten Stock in einen Erker mit anstoßender Loggia auflöst und im zweiten Stock eine Altane sowie die Fortsetzung des Erkers trägt. Der vierte Stock zeigt im Mittel eine mit einem Flugdach abgedeckte Laube und unter dem bekrönenden überhängenden Giebel einen Fenstervorbau mit einem zweiten Flugdach. An einer Seite des Giebels schließt sich eine mit einem Zeltdach überdeckte Laube an, an der anderen Seite eine Fenstergruppe. Im Erdgeschoß des rechtsseitigen Fassadenteils führt eine Freitreppe zu einer Terrasse, und vor den Fenstern des ersten und zweiten Obergeschosses sind halbrunde Balkons ausgekragt. Die längere Front enthält ein stattlich ausgebildetes Portal und ist im Hauptteil mit einem überhängenden Giebel abgeschlossen, unter dem ein Fensterausbau hervortritt. Der Sockel besteht aus Niedermd. Basalt, darüber folgt eine Verblendung aus teils bossierten, teils glatt bearbeiteten Quadern aus gelbem geflammten Pfälzer Sandstein, dazwischen verteilt finden sich Putzflächen in Zement. Die Giebel zeigen Holzfachwerk mit teilweiser Beschieferung; die Dächer sind mit Biberschwänzen eingedeckt.

Die herrschaftlich ausgestatteten, je einen Wintergarten einschließenden Wohnungen im Erdgeschoß, im ersten und zweiten Stock sind mit Warmwasserheizung, Heißwasserleitung, Heiz- und Leuchtgas, sowie mit elektrischer Lichtanlage versehen.

321 [1909; 32]

Das Landhaus in Kopenhagen ist in gemischter Massiv-Holzbauweise nach dem Entwurfe des Architekten Jensen errichtet. Das massive verputzte Erdgeschoß trägt an der Eingangsfront ein durchgehendes Pultdach, hinter dem das Obergeschoß in ebenfalls verputztem Fachwerk aufsteigt. Die Eingangtür hat in Fortsetzung des Pultdaches ein Schutzdach erhalten. Die Fenster sind geradlinig geschlossen; der Seitenfront ist ein einstöckiger Anbau angefügt, der ein besonderes abgewalmtes Dach erhalten hat. Das ebenfalls abgewalmte, mit Dachfenstern besetzte Hauptdach ist wie die übrigen Dächer mit Ziegeln eingedeckt.

322 [1909; 9]

Die Kirche in Wyk, mit dem Pfarrhause zu einer malerisch wirksamen Gruppe verbunden, ein Werk der Architekten Curjel & Moser, ist im Laufe von 2 Jahren für die Baukostensumme von 338 000 Mark, Pfarrhaus und Konfirmandensaal eingeschlossen, errichtet. Die örtliche Bauleitung war an Architekt H. Hubmann übertragen. Die Stilformen sind spätgotisch; der Turm steigt viereckig in wuchtiger Masse, im Glockengeschoß leicht nach oben verjüngt, auf und ist mit einem geschweiften, in Metall eingedeckten Walmdach versehen, aus dem sich ein Dachreiter entwickelt, wieder mit einem geschweiften Helm bekrönt. Vor der Turmfront erstreckt sich eine überwölbte, rundbogige, von achteckigen Türmchen eingefaßte Vorhalle. Dem außen mit Strebepfeilern besetzten, von einem Pfannendach überdeckten Kirchenschiff ist eine niedrigere Altarnische angefügt, die sich nach innen rundbogig öffnet. Der einschiffige Kirchenraum enthält an der Turmseite eine Orgelempor und ist mit einem gesprengten Dachstuhl in sichtbarer Holzkonstruktion überdeckt. Das Material der Mauern besteht aus roten,

---

La maison d'habitation à quatre étages Herderstrasse 59 à Düsseldorf, construite d'après les plans de Mr. W. May, dans l'espace d'un an pour la somme de 187 000 Marks est située dans un quartier de villas, elle est précédée d'un jardin et se distingue par le groupement pittoresque de ses masses. La petite façade sur la Ahnfeldstrasse montre un avant-corps montant de fond, terminé au premier étage en tourelle avec loggia adjacente; au second étage, l'avant-corps porte un balcon et la continuation de la tourelle. Le quatrième étage est surmonté d'une pergola couverte d'un toit et d'un bow-window, également couvert d'un toit, au-dessus d'un pignon en saillie. Le pignon est bordé d'un côté par une pergola couverte, de l'autre côté, par une lucarne. Au rez-de-chaussée de l'aile droite de la façade, un escalier conduit à une terrasse, et des balcons en demi-cercle sont placés en avant des fenêtres du premier et du second étages. La grande façade possède un portail monumental et est dans sa partie principale, couronnée d'un pignon saillant audessus duquel un groupe de fenêtres fait saillie. Le socle est en basalt de Niedermd., audessus s'élève un revêtement de pierres jaunes flammées du Palatinat en partie brutes, en partie travaillées. Entre ces pierres sont disposées des surfaces crépies au ciment. Les pignons sont en pans de bois et en partie revêtus d'ardoises; les toits sont recouverts en tuiles.

Les appartements de maîtres au rez-de-chaussée, au premier et au second étages, comprenant chacun un jardin d'hiver, sont pourvus de chauffage à eau chaude, de conduite d'eau chaude, de gaz à chauffer et à éclairer, ainsi que de lumière électrique.

321 [1909; 32]

La maison de campagne à Copenhague est construite d'après les plans de Mr. Jensen architecte en bois et massif en pierre. Le rez-de-chaussée en maçonnerie crépie, derrière lequel s'élève le premier étage en pans de bois et maçonnerie crépie. La porte d'entrée est couverte d'un porche formé par la continuation d'un toit en appentis. Les fenêtres sont couvertes à linteaux droits; sur la façade latérale on a construit une annexe d'un étage couverte d'un toit spécial en forme de croupe. Le toit principal également en forme de croupe et portant des lucarnes est couvert en tuiles comme les autres toits.

322 [1909; 9]

L'église de Wyk formant avec la cure un groupe de bâtiments pittoresque a été construite dans l'espace de deux ans par MM. Curjel & Moser architectes pour la somme de 338 000 Marks, y compris la cure et la salle des cathécumènes. La conduite des travaux avait été confiée à Mr. H. Hubmann architecte. Les formes sont celles du gothique tardif, la tour s'élève, de proportions puissantes, s'amincissant légèrement à la hauteur de l'étage des cloches, elle est couronnée d'un toit ondulé en métal, sur lequel se dresse un cavalier surmonté lui même d'une flèche aux contours ondulés. Au devant de la tour s'étend un porche voûté en plein cintre, flanqué, de tourelles octogonales. A la nef de l'église, pourvue à l'extérieur de contreforts et couverte d'un toit en tuiles est adjointe une niche d'autel basse ouverte sur l'église en forme d'arc de cercle. L'intérieur composé d'une nef contient un chœur d'orgues du côté de la tour et est couvert d'une charpente en bois apparente. Les murs sont construits en briques

---

The four-storeyed dwelling house at Herderstrasse 59, Düsseldorf, lies in the villa quarter of the city, it has a front garden and a picturesque frontage to the facade. The design is by the architect W. May, it occupied one year in building and cost 187 000 Marks. The shorter frontage on the Ahnfeldstrasse shows a projection extending throughout the entire height, this on the first floor forms a bay with loggia adjoining, on the second floor is a continuation of the bay with a balcony. The fourth storey has in the centre an alcove with a tent roof, and under the overhanging gable which crowns the whole is a window projection with a second tent roof. On one side of the gable is a covered balcony with a tent roof, on the other side is a group of windows. On the ground floor of the right side of the facade a free flight of steps leads to a terrace, before the windows of the first and second upper storeys project semicircular balconies. The longer frontage contains a stately portal and is crowned by a projecting gable under which a window group projects. The sockel consists of Niedermd. basalt, then follows a facing of partly bossed partly smooth square stones of yellow flamed sandstone from the Palatinate, between are plastered surfaces in cement. The gables are of wood framework and are partly slated, the roofs are of flat red tiles.

The flats are of superior class, have each a conservatory and have warm water heating, warm water laid on, gas for cooking and for illumination as well as electric light.

321 [1909; 32]

The country house in Copenhagen is a mixture of solid with frame-work, it is from the design of the architect Jensen. The ground floor is solid and is plastered, it has on the entrance side a projecting roof, behind which an upper storey of plastered frame-work rises. The entrance door has a protecting roof, and the windows have all straight lines. On the side frontage a projecting erection has been built of one storey which has a separate hipped roof. The principal roof is also hipped, it is covered with tiles and has several windows.

322 [1909; 9]

The church in Wyk is built from the design of the architects Curjel and Moser. It is built with a parsonage and forms an effective and picturesque group. It occupied 2 years in building and cost 338 000 Marks including the parsonage and a hall for confirmation candidates. The local superintendence of the building was entrusted to the architect H. Hubmann. The style is late Gothic, the massive square tower rises with the belfry to an imposing height and is crowned with a hipped roof in metal; from this a roof erection rises which is again crowned by a helmet shaped cupola. In the front of the tower is a vaulted, round arched portico enclosed with two octagonal towers. The nave is roofed with flat tiles and set with buttresses, it is joined to a lower chancel which is rounded by arches in the interior. The church, which has only one aisle, has on the tower side an organ loft and is covered by a wood roofing which is visible. The material of the walls is

gefugten Handftrichziegeln in Kloiterformat, die auch an den inneren Wandflächen ohne Verputz geblieben find.

Die Fronten des zweitöckigen Pfarrhaufes find wie die der Kirche aus gefugten Handftrichziegeln hergeitellt. Das Gebäude enthält außer der Pfarrwohnung den Konfirmandenfaal und ift mit einem gebrochenen Pfannendach überdeckt.

Das Gebäude der Schillerfchule in Frankfurt a. M., Garten- und Morgenfternitraße, bildet einen langgeitreckten Gruppenbau mit durchweg frei liegenden Fronten in modern aufgefaßten Renaifanceformen. Der Entwurf itammt von dem Architekten H. Eberhardt, früher Stadtbaumeiiter in Frankfurt, jetzt Direktor der technifchen Lehranitalt in Offenbach a. M.; die Ausführung nahm etwa 2 Jahre in Anipruch und koitete rund 600 000 Mark gegen 644 000 Mark des Voranichlags. Das Erdgeichoß des Schulgebäudes zeigt Quaderarchitektur in rotem Sanditein und rundbogig überwölbte Feniter. Die Ecken, fowie die Einfaiungen und Teilungen der Feniter in den Obergeichoien find gleichfalls in rotem Sanditein ausgeführt, mit Ausnahme der Feniterpfeiler der Aula, die aus Eifenbeton beitehen. Die Flächen der Obergeichoie des Klaiengebäudes find mit grauem Putz verfehen. Die zweitöckige Direktorwohnung iit im Erdgeichoß mit Gliederungen und Sockel in Sanditein, fonit mit Putzflächen ausgeitattet, während das Obergeichoß eine Beichieferung erhalten hat und fich nach der Straßenfront mit einer breiten Loggia öffnet. Die teilweife abgewalmten, teilweife gebrochenen Dachflächen find durch Gruppen von Dachfenitern belebt und fämtlich mit Schiefer eingedeckt.

Das Klaiengebäude an der Gartenitraße erhält ein charakteriitifches Gepräge durch die hohen Feniter der die beiden Obergeichoie durchfetzenden Aula und iit mit Giebeln in geichwungenen Konturen eingefaßt. Über dem Dachfirit erhebt fich ein platt endigendes Dachreitertürmchen. Im Erdgeichoß des Trakts an der Gartenitraße liegen der Haupteingang, die Treppe,

rouges à la main, jointoyées, de format dit de cloître, ces briques sont aussi restées apparentes et sans crépissage aux surfaces de l'intérieur. Les façades de la maison de cure à deux étages, sont ainsi que l'église en briques à la main, jointoyées. Le bâtiment contient, outre l'appartement du pasteur, la salle des cathécumènes, il est couvert d'un toit mansard en tuiles.

L'école de Schiller à Francfort s. M., Garten- et Morgenfternstrasse, forme un groupe de constructions allongé, avec des façades entièrement dégagées, traitées dans les formes de la Renaissance modernisée. Le projet et dû à Mr. H. Eberhardt architecte, autrefois architecte de la ville de Francfort, maintenant directeur de l'école technique à Offenbach s. M. La construction dura environ deux ans et coûta 600 000 Marks en bloc, tandis que le devis était de 644 000 Marks. Le rez-de-chaussée du bâtiment est en bossages de pierre rouge avec fenêtres à plein cintre. Les angles, ainsi que les encadrements et les meneaux des fenêtres du premier étage sont également en pierre rouge, à l'exception des piliers des fenêtres de l'aula qui sont construits en béton armé. Les surfaces du premier étage du bâtiment des classes sont crépies en gris. Les deux étages de l'appartement du directeur sont traités au rez-de-chaussée et au socle en pierre et en surfaces crépies, tandis que le premier étage est revêtu d'ardoises et s'ouvre du côté de la rue en une large loggia. Les surfaces du toit soit en croupe, soit mansardés soit recouvertes d'ardoises et divisées par des groupes de lucarnes.

La maison d'école sur la Gartenstrasse est caractérisée par les hautes fenêtres de la aula qui traverse deux étages, elle est surmontée de pignons à contours ondulés. Au dessus du faîte s'élève une tourelle terminée en plate-forme. Au rez-de-chaussée de l'aile sur la Gartenstrasse, se trouvent l'entrée principale, l'escalier, plusieurs

red fluted tiling of "Cloister" form, the interior is of the same and is left without facing of other material.

The fronts of the two-storeyed parsonage are, like the church of red tiles, the building contains the Confirmation Hall and is roofed with flat tiles.

The building of the Schiller School at Garten- and Morgensternstrasse, Frankfort on Main, consists of a long extending group of buildings, lying on all sides free, in the Renascence style, but with modern touches. The design is by the architect H. Eberhardt formerly the municipal building master of Frankfort and now director of the technical school at Offenbach am Main; it occupied 2 years in building and cost about 600 000 Marks, the estimate being 644 000 Marks. The ground floor of the school buildings is of square stones of red sandstone, the windows having rounded arches; the corners, the framing and articulations of the windows in the upper storey are also carried out in red sandstone, with the exception of the window pillars of the Aula which are of iron beton. The surfaces of the upper storeys of the class rooms are of grey plaster. The two-storeyed dwelling of the Head Master has on the ground floor and basement articulations in sandstone, but has otherwise plastered surfaces, while the upper storey is faced with slate and has, on the street front, a broad loggia. The roof surfaces are partly hipped and partly with a broken line, they have various groups of windows and are covered with slate.

The class room building on the Gartenstrasse is characteristically distinguished by the high window of the Aula extending through two storeys and crowned by a gable with curved contours. Over the roof is a tower with a flat

A Eingang
B Schuldiener
C Sprechzimmer
D Direktor
E Bibliothek
F Lehrerzimmer
G Heizer
H Durchfahrt
J Geräte
K Turnhalle
L Bedürfnisanstalt
M Klasse
N Lehrerinnenzimmer
O Kombinierte Klasse

A Entrée
B Concierge
C Parloir
D Directeur
E Bibliothèque
F Salle des professeurs
G Chaufferie
H Passage
J Appareils
K Gymnase
L Cabinets d'aisances
M Salle de classe
N Salle des professeurs (femmes)
O Salle de classe polyvalente

A Entrance
B Caretaker
C Office
D Head Master
E Library
F Teachers' Room
G Furnaceman
H Carriageway
J Equipment Room
K Gymnasium
L Lavatories
M Classroom
N Women Teachers' Room
O Combined Classroom

Erdgeichoß
Rez-de-chaussée
Ground Floor

mehrere Amts- und übrigens Klassenzimmer. Der Flügel an der Morgensternstraße enthält eine zweite Treppe nebst Amts- und Klassenzimmern, daneben öffnet sich die Durchfahrt und weiterhin folgen die Bedürfnisanstalten und die Turnhalle. Die Decke und der Dachstuhl der Aula sind aus Eisenbeton hergestellt. Die Bildhauerarbeiten lieferten die Bildhauer W. Ohly und Seiler.

324 [1909; 46]

Die Gruppe von drei Wohnhäusern in Frankfurt-Sachsenhausen, Gartenstraße 51, 53 und 55, von Architekt G. A. Plaß entworfen, ist, die Ausgestaltung der Fronten anbelangend, einheitlich im Stil deutscher Spätrenaissance zusammen komponiert. Die Bauzeit dauerte etwa 9 Monate, und die Baukosten betrugen insgesamt 142 000 Mark. Das mittlere Haus Nr. 53, mit dem Eingang von der Gartenstraße, ist durch einen rechteckig, über einen durch Säulchen geteilten Fenstergruppe vorgekragten Erker im Oberstock und durch einen über die ganze Frontbreite sich erstreckenden, doppelt abgesetzten steilen Giebel ausgezeichnet. Im unteren Absatze des Giebels befinden sich zwei polygonal vorspringende Fensterausbauten. Das rechts von dem vorigen gelegene Haus Nr. 55 hat den mit einem Schutzdach versehenen Eingang an der wieder mit einem in zwei Absätzen aufsteigenden Giebel abgeschlossenen Seitenfront erhalten. Ein vorgebautes Fenster im Obergeschoß ist durch ein Blumenbrett geschmückt; die Steilfläche des Daches trägt breite Dachfenster. Fenster derselben Art unterbrechen die Dachfläche des links gelegenen Hauses Nr. 51, außerdem springt an der Ecke im Oberstock ein polygonaler Fronterker vor. Die Gliederungen sämtlicher Fassaden sind aus Muschelkalkstein, die Flächen in naturfarbenem Putz hergestellt. Die Absätze der Giebel sowie die gebrochenen Dächer sind mit Schiefer eingedeckt. Die Bildhauerarbeiten am Portal von Nr. 53 sind von Joh. Belz, die Kupferbeschläge der Tür von Fr. Brechenmacher hergestellt.

Das Haus Nr. 53 enthält im Erdgeschoß eine Wohnung mit dem an das Speisezimmer anschließenden Wintergarten, während die Küche im Keller untergebracht ist. Das Ober- und das Dachgeschoß sind zusammen für eine zweite Wohnung benutzt, welche wieder einen mit dem Speisezimmer in Verbindung stehenden Wintergarten zeigt und die im Obergeschoß angeordnete Küche enthält. Die Stockwerkstreppe hat ein Oberlicht erhalten. Die Decken des Hauses sind in Eisenbeton, die Zwischenwände massiv-freitragend in Lugino-Konstruktion hergestellt. Das Haus Nr. 55 enthält nur eine reichlich bemessene Wohnung mit auf Erd-, Ober- und Dachgeschoß verteilten Zimmern. Das Erdgeschoß ist mit einer Diele und einer an das Speisezimmer anstoßenden Terrasse ausgestattet und nimmt zugleich die Küche auf. Im Obergeschoß liegen die Schlafzimmer und das Bad, im Dachgeschoß noch andere Wohnräume und Kammern, während das Kellergeschoß unter anderm zur Anlage der Waschküche und des Plättraums benutzt ist.

325 [1909; 20]

Das fünfstöckige Geschäftshaus „Gertig" in Hamburg, Gr. Burstah 15—17, Ecke Bohnenstraße, ist im Laufe von zwei Jahren für die Baukostensumme von 450000 Mark zur Ausführung gekommen. Die Grundrisse sind gemeinschaftlich von den Architekten Freitag & Wurzbach und G. Radel bearbeitet, während die architektonische Formgebung speziell den Herren Freitag & Wurzbach anheimfiel. Die enge Fenterteilung der in roten Gresflamme Ullersdorfer Glasursteinen ausgeführten Fassade bietet den Vorzug der bequemen Teilbarkeit der Stockwerke in kleinere Einzelkontore. Die

---

classes et chambres d'administration. L'aile sur la Morgensternstrasse contient un second escalier ainsi que classes et chambres d'administration; tout à côté s'ouvre la porte cochère, plus loin suivent les cabinets et la halle de gymnastique. Les plafonds et la toiture de la Aula sont construits en béton armé. Les travaux de sculpture sont des sculpteurs W. Ohly et Seiler.

324 [1909; 46]

Le groupe de trois maisons d'habitation Gartenstrasse 51, 53 et 55 à Frankfort-Sachsenhausen, bâti par Mr. G. A. Platz, architecte, est quant au caractère des façades composé uniformément dans le style de renaissance allemande tardive. La construction dura environ neuf mois et coûta en tout 142 000 Marks. La maison du milieu, No. 53 avec son entrée sur la Gartenstrasse se distingue par une tourelle rectangulaire faisant saillie au premier étage au dessus d'un groupe de fenêtres divisé par des colonnettes et par un pignon haut s'élevant sur toute la largeur de la façade et divisé en deux dégrés. Dans le dégré inférieur se trouvent deux fenêtres saillantes de plan polygonal. La maison No. 55, à droite de la précédente, a une entrée protégée par un avant toit et une façade également surmontée d'un fronton à deux dégrés. Une fenêtre saillante à l'étage supérieur est ornée d'un balcon à fleurs, les faces latérales du toit portent de larges lucarnes. Des fenêtres de la même sorte interrompent la surface du toit de le maison de gauche No. 51, une tourelle polygonale s'avance en outre sur l'angle du premier étage. Les moulures de toutes les façades sont en pierre calcaire, les surfaces sont crépies en couleur naturelle. Les dégrés des pignons, ainsi que les toits brisés sont recouverts en ardoises. La sculpture du portail de le maison No. 53 sont de Mr. Joh. Belz, la serrurerie de cuivre des portes de Mr. Fr. Brechenmacher.

La maison No. 53 contient au rez-de-chaussée, un appartement avec un jardin d'hiver adjacent à la salle à manger, tandis que la cuisine est située au sous-sol. Le premier étage et l'étage du toit sont réunis en un second appartement, lequel a également une salle à manger communiquant avec un jardin d'hiver et une cuisine au premier. L'escalier principal est éclairé par le haut. Les planchers sont en béton armé, les parois massives, portant librement, sont construites d'après le système Lugino. La maison No. 55 contient un appartement spacieux avec chambres réparties sur le rez-de-chaussée, le premier et dans le toit. Le rez-de-chaussée a une salle à manger communiquant avec une terrasse et contient aussi la cuisine. Au premier se trouvent les chambres à coucher et le bain; dans le toit on a placé d'autres chambres d'habitation, et de domestiques, tandis que le sous-sol contient entre autres la buanderie et la chambre à repasser.

325 [1909; 20]

La maison de commerce à cinq étages „Gertig" à Hambourg, angle Gr. Burstah 15—17 et Bohnenstrasse, a été construite dans l'espace de deux ans pour la somme de 450000 Marks. Les plans ont été établis par les architectes Freitag & Wurzbach et G. Radel; la partie artistique, architecturale resta spécialement la part de MM. Freitag & Wurzbach. La division étroite des fenêtres dans la façade de briques émaillées de grès flammé de Ullersdorf, offre l'avantage d'un partage facile des étages en plusieurs comptoirs. Les contre-

---

top. In the ground floor of the section on the Gartenstrasse are the principal entrance, the steps, several official apartments and some classrooms, at the side is the courtyard entrance, the lavatories and the gymnasium. The ceilings and roof supports are of iron beton. The sculptural details are by Messro W. Ohly and Seiler.

324 [1909; 46]

A group of three dwelling houses at Gartenstrasse 51, 53 and 55, Frankfurt-Sachsenhausen, has been designed by the architect G. A. Platz. The style, as far as the facades are concerned, is composed from the German Late Renascence. The time occupied was about 9 months and the cost amounted to 142 000 Marks. The middle house No. 53 with the entrance towards the Gartenstrasse has for its distinguishing features a rectangular projecting bay in the upper storey, placed over a group of windows divided by small pillars, and a steep gable stretching over the whole breadth of the front with a double settle. On the lower settle of the gable are two polygonal window erections. The house No. 55, to the right of the house mentioned above, has the entrance protected by a projecting glass roof, and has on the side front a gable rising in a double settle. A window in the upper storey is ornamented by a flower receptacle; the steep surfaces of the roof are varied by broad roof windows. The same design of windows has been used to break the roof surfaces of the house No. 51 lying to the left; on this house at the corner projects in the upper storey a polygonal bay. The articulations of all the facades are of shell limestone, the surfaces are of natural coloured plaster. The settles of the gables as well as the broken roofs are covered with slate. The sculptural work on the portal of No. 53 is by Joh. Belz, the copper ornaments on the door are by Fr. Brechenmacher.

The house Nr. 53 contains on the ground floor a dwelling with a dining room opening into a conservatory, the kitchen is in the basement. The upper and roof storeys are combined to form another dwelling, this too has a dining room leading into a conservatory and has the kitchen in the roof storey. The staircase leading to the flats is lighted by a skylight. The ceilings of all houses are of iron beton, the dividing walls are massively built and of Lugino construction. The house No. 55 contains only one spacious dwelling, the apartments being distributed throughout the ground, upper and roof storeys. The ground floor has a square hall, a dining room leading to a terrace, and the kitchen. The upper floor contains bedrooms and bathroom the roof storey other dwelling rooms and attics and the basement has among other offices, the washhouse and laundry.

325 [1909; 20]

A five-storeyed business house has been built called "Gertig" at 15—17 Gr. Burstah, corner of Bohnenstrasse Hamburg. It occupied two years in building and cost 450 000 Marks. The ground-plan was the joint work of the architects Freitag and Wurzbach and G. Radel, the architectural erection was exclusively the work Herrn Freitag and Wurzbach. The narrow window apertures in the facade (which is of red Grèsflammes Ullersdorf glazed tiles) have the advantage of allowing a greater freedom in the construction of smaller details.

Brüstungen der Fenster sind reliefartig verziert; auch der obere Abschluß der an dem niedriger gehaltenen Eckbau vorspringenden Rundung ist durch eine weibliche geflügelte Figur ausgezeichnet. Über der nach innen geschweiften Vorderseite des Eckbaues erhebt sich ein breiter Dacherker. Eine niedriger gehaltene Achse der Fassade wiederholt sich über dem Eingange am Ende der Bohnenstraßenfront und wird gleichfalls von einem Dacherker bekrönt.

Aus der Eingangshalle gelangt man in das um einige Stufen höher liegende Treppenhaus mit der um ein Auge gewundenen Treppe. An das Treppenhaus schließt sich einerseits ein Lift, andererseits ein Durchgang nach dem Lichthofe, dann ein Paternoster-Fahrstuhl und der Raum für den Hauswart an. In dem mit einem Hebekrahn versehenen Hofe ist noch weiter ein Warenaufzug angebracht. Die sonst ungeteilten Räume sämtlicher Geschosse werden nur durch schmiedeeiserne Stützen unterbrochen und stehen durch einen Korridor mit dem Treppenhause, den Aufzügen und Toiletten in Verbindung. Das Erdgeschoß enthält Läden, das Hochparterre sowie die vier Obergeschosse sind für Musterlager und Kontorzwecke bestimmt und können durch Zwischenwände beliebig geteilt werden. Die Aktenräume im Dachboden werden nach Bedarf den einzelnen Kontoren zugewiesen.

Eintrittshalle, Treppenhaus und Treppe sind in Marmor ausgeführt, die Decken massiv in Hohlsteinen. Die zur Wasserversorgung, Gasleitung und für das elektrische Licht erforderlichen Anlagen sowie eine in jedem Lokal regulierbare Zentralheizung sind vorhanden.

326 [1909; 26]

Bezeichnend für die äußere Erscheinung des Geschäftshauses in Hamburg, Neuer Wall 27—29, ist die Herstellung der Fassaden in grünen Glasursteinen und die reiche Verzierung durch glasierte Terrakotten. Der Entwurf stammt von den Architekten Freytag & Wurzbach, die Ausführung nahm etwa ein Jahr in Anspruch und verursachte einen Kostenaufwand von 770 000 Mark. Die Modelle zu den Ornamenten der Fassade lieferte Bildhauer R. Kühn. Die beiden unteren Geschosse öffnen sich mit breiten Schaufenstern, die drei folgenden Obergeschosse sind durch senkrecht aufsteigende Pfeiler zusammengezogen, welche die Fenstergruppen zwischen sich einschließen. Die Lichtöffnungen sind geradlinig überdeckt, mit Ausnahme der oberen Schaufensteröffnung in der abgerundeten Ecke und der Fenster im dritten Obergeschoß, über denen flache, verzierte Rundbogen, an venetianische Fassadenabschlüsse anklingend, den Dachkranz bilden. Die Ecke wird durch einen in Absätzen aufsteigenden Kuppelturm bekrönt. Das Erdgeschoß enthält Läden und umschließt einen Lichthof; die vier Obergeschosse sind zu Kontorräumen unter möglichster Vermeidung von Zwischenwänden eingerichtet.

327 [1909; 27]

Der Neubau des Geschäftshauses in Hamburg, Neuer Wall 26—28, nach dem Entwurfe der Architekten Freytag & Wurzbach im Anschluß an das von denselben Architekten herrührende Geschäftshaus Neuer Wall 27—29 errichtet, hat ebenfalls wie dieses eine Fassadenbekleidung in grünen Glasursteinen in Verbindung mit Verzierungen in glasierter Terrakotta erhalten. Die Bauzeit nahm etwa ein Jahr in Anspruch und die Baukosten betrugen rund 700 000 Mark. Die Ausbildung der beiden unteren Geschosse ist durch die geforderte Anlage breiter Schaufensteröffnungen bedingt. Ein starkes Gurtglied trennt die drei durch aufstrebende Pfeiler zusammengezogenen Obergeschosse von den unteren. Die geradlinig über-

cœurs des fenêtres sont décorés en relief; le couronnement de la saillie arrondie des angles tenus plus bas que le reste, est formé d'une figure de femme ailée. Une large tourelle s'élève au dessus de la partie à courbe rentrante de l'angle. Une partie plus basse de la façade se répète au dessus de l'entrée, à l'extrémité de la façade sur la Bohnenstrasse et est également couronnée d'une tourelle.

De la halle d'entrée, on pénètre dans la cage d'escalier élevée de quelques marches et contenant un escalier tournant. La cage d'escalier communique d'une part, avec un lift, d'autre part avec un passage conduisant dans la cour, puis avec un ascenseur à marche continue et la loge du portier. Dans la cour pourvue d'une grue, se trouve encore un monte-charges. Les pièces de tous les étages sont libres de toutes divisions, elles ne sont interrompues que par des supports en fer et sont reliées par un corridor à l'escalier, aux ascenseurs et aux toilettes. Le rez-de-chaussée contient des magasins, l'entresol et les quatre étages sont organisés pour dépôts de marchandises et comptoirs et peuvent être divisés à volonté par des parois. Les pièces pour dépôts d'actes dans le toit sont louées à volonté avec les bureaux.

La halle d'entrée, la cage et l'escalier sont exécutés en marbre, les planchers sont massifs en hourdis creux. L'immeuble est pourvu d'eau, de gaz, de lumière électrique et d'un chauffage central pour tous les locaux.

326 [1909; 26]

Ce qu'il y a de caractéristique dans l'aspect extérieur de la maison de commerce Neuer Wall 27—29 à Hambourg, c'est l'emploi pour les façades de briques émaillées vertes et la riche décoration de terres cuites artistiques. Les plans sont de M. M. Freytag & Wurzbach, l'exécution dura un an environ et coûta 770 000 Marks. Mr. Kühn, sculpteur livra les modèles pour les ornements de la façade. Les deux étages inférieurs s'ouvrent en larges devantures de magasins, les trois étages supérieurs sont divisés en groupes de fenêtres encadrés par des piliers verticaux. Les ouvertures sont à linteaux droits, à l'exception de la fenêtre du haut de l'angle arrondi et des fenêtres du troisième étage, qui sont couvertes d'arcs surbaissés et ornés, rappelant le couronnement de façades vénitiennes et formant la corniche. L'angle est couronné d'une tour en forme de coupole montant par degrés. Le rez-de-chaussée contient des magasins et entoure une cour. Les quatre étages sont disposés pour comptoirs en évitant autant que possible les divisions.

327 [1909; 27]

Le nouveau bâtiment de commerce, Neuer Wall 26 et 28 à Hambourg construit d'après les plans de M. M. Freytag & Wurzbach, adjacent à la maison de commerce, Neuer Wall 27—29 due aux mêmes architectes a comme cette dernière une façade revêtue de plaques e'maillés vertes combinées avec des ornements en terracotta venie. La construction dura un an environ et les frais s'élevèrent à 700000 Marks. L'architecture des deux étages inférieurs est donnée par la disposition nécessaire de larges devantures de magasins. Un fort cordon sépare les étages inférieurs des trois supérieurs reliés entre eux par des piliers élancés. Les fenêtres droites remplissent

The breast-work of the windows have ornamental reliefs, the projecting curve of the somewhat low corner erection is distinguished on its upper part by a winged female statue. Over the front of the corner erection curving inwards is a broad projecting roof bay. The low-built axis of the facade is repeated over the entrance at the end of the Bohnenstrasse frontage and is also crowned by a roof bay.

From the entrance hall, one reaches by means of a few steps the hall with an open staircase winding round a circular window. On one side of the staircase is a lift, on the other a door to the skylighted court, then comes a Paternoster lift and the rooms for the house-steward. In the court yard is a lifting-crane and another lift for goods. The rooms of all the storeys are supported by wrought iron pillars, except these there is no partition; they are all in connection with a corridor leading to the staircase, with the lifts and with lavatories. The ground floor contains shops, the next storey as well as the four upper floors are designed for goods stores and samples, and for bureaus; these can be divided at will into separate rooms. The rooms in the attic for the storing of documents are added as required to the various bureaus.

The entrance hall, the staircase and stairs are all of marble, the ceilings are of stone and solid. The installations for water, for gas, for electric light and for central heating are all provided.

326 [1909; 26]

The exterior of the business house, Neuer Wall 27—29, Hamburg, is distinguished by its facade in green glazed tiles with a rich ornamentation of glazed terracotta. The design is by the architects Freytag and Wurzbach, it occupied about a year in building and cost 770 000 Marks. The models for the ornaments of the facade were by the sculptor R. Kühn. The two lower storeys open with broad shop windows; the three upper storeys are grouped by perpendicular pillars between which are the windows. The windows have straight frames except those of the shop windows in the rounded corner and those of the third storey over which are rounded ornamental arches, somewhat resembling Venetian facades and which form the roof moulding. The corner is crowned by a cupola tower which rises in successive platforms to the top. The ground floor contains shops and is arranged rouud a skylighted court, the four upper storeys are arranged as bureaus with the use of as few dividing walls as possible.

327 [1909; 27]

The new buildings of the business house, Neuer Wall 26—28, Hamburg, according to the design of the architects Freytag and Wurzbach, have been added to the original premises 27—29 which were also designed by the same architects. They have all the same facing of the facades in green glazed stone with ornaments of glazed terra-cotta. The time occupied was one year, and the cost amounted to Mk. 700 000. The erection of the two lower storeys favoured the construction of broad shop windows; a massive moulding separates these from the three storeys above them which are distinguished by pillars running through the whole height. The windows have straightlined

deckten Fenster füllen den Raum zwischen den Pfeilern. Der Dachkranz wird durch bogenartige Abschlußlinien gebildet, hinter denen noch Dachfenster aufsteigen. Das untere Geschoß enthält Läden, die ebensowohl wie die in den oberen Geschossen angeordneten, nur durch Pfeilerstützen geteilten Kontorräume einen größeren offenen Hof umschließen und mit Toiletten, die mit kleineren Lichthöfen und einem breiten Flurgang in Verbindung stehen, außerdem mit einer Treppe, einem Paternoster- und einem Warenaufzuge ausgestattet sind.

l'espace entre les piliers. La corniche est formée par une ligne en forme d'arcs; au dessus s'élèvent des lucarnes. Le rez-de-chaussée contient des magasins qui, comme les étages supérieurs entourent une grande cour, ces localités, sont disposées en comptoirs et contiennent des supports pour les étages superieurs il s'y trouve des toilettes éclairées par de petites cours et reliées à de larges corridors. La maison est en outre desservie par un escalier, un ascenseurs à mouvement continue et un monte-charges.

frames and occupy the spaces between the pillars. The roof moulding is formed by arched lines behind which are placed roof windows. The lower storey contains shops, these, as well as the bureau accommodation of the upper storeys, are only divided by pillar supports; the whole surrounds a spacious open courtyard in which are lavatories, these are in connection with a smaller skylighted court and a broad corridor, there are also secondary staircases a „Paternoster" lift and a goods lift.

328 [1909; 47]

Das Wohn- und Ladenhaus in Darmstadt, Schloßgartenstraße 5, bildet einen Doppelbau mit drei freiliegenden Außenfronten, getrennten Treppenhäusern und gemeinschaftlichem Hof. Der Entwurf ist ein Werk des Architekten R. Strecker, mußte jedoch infolge eines von dem Großherzogl. Ministerium neu aufgestellten Bebauungsplans von dem Autor umgearbeitet werden. Die Ausführung geschah durch die Firma Strecker & Münch, dauerte etwa 9 Monate und kostete rund 120 000 Mark. Die Hauptfront wird durch zwei runde, über dem Erdgeschoß ausgekragte Erkertürme eingefaßt, die den Dachkranz durchsetzen, mit glockenförmigen Helmen endigen und im ersten und zweiten Obergeschoß durch offene Balkons mit dem breiten, rechteckigen, in einer Altane abschließenden Mittelerker in Verbindung stehen. Ein zweiter Erker ist an der Seitenfront angebracht. Die Schaufensteröffnungen im Erdgeschoß sind im Korbbogen, die Fenster der drei Obergeschosse geradlinig geschlossen. Auf der gebrochenen, mit Schiefer eingedeckten Dachfläche erhebt sich über jeder Front ein giebelbekrönter Fensteraufbau, außerdem sind noch einzelne Dachfenster angeordnet. Das Erdgeschoß ist aus hellem Mainsandstein hergestellt, die oberen Fassadenflächen sind verputzt und mit ornamentalen Bildhauerarbeiten von Fried. Schleich geschmückt.

Das Erdgeschoß enthält außer den Läden eine Wohnung mit Küche, dann den Eingangsflur, die Durchfahrt zum Hof und zwei Stockwerkstreppen. Die drei Obergeschosse sowie das Dachgeschoß sind zu Wohnungen eingerichtet. Die erste Zwischendecke besteht aus einem Betongewölbe, für die Treppen fand das Moniersystem Anwendung, die beiden Ecktürme werden im Erdgeschoß durch Trägerkränze abgestützt.

328 [1909; 47]

La maison d'habitation et de magasins Schlossgartenstrasse 5 à Darmstadt forme un immeuble double avec trois façades, des escaliers séparés et une cour commune. Mr. R. Strecker architecte est l'auteur du plan qui dut être du reste remanié par suite d'un plan nouveau de construction élaboré par le ministère grand-ducal. L'exécution fut remise à M. M. Strecker & Münch, elle dura neuf mois et coûta 120 000 Marks. La façade principale est flanquée de deux tours rondes faisant saillie sur le rez-de-chaussée, elles traversent la corniche et se terminent par des toits en forme de cloches, elles sont reliées au premier et au second étages par des balcons découverts à la tourelle du milieu; cette dernière est large, de plan rectangulaire et est terminée par une terrasse. Une seconde tourelle a été adaptée à la façade latérale. Les devantures de magasin au rez-de-chaussée sont couvertes en anse de-panier, celles des trois étages supérieurs sont à linteaux droits. Sur le toit brisé, recouvert en ardoises s'élève sur chaque façade une lucarne couronnée d'un pignon, d'autres fenêtres sont en outre placées sur le toit. Le rez-de-chaussée est en pierre claire du Main, les surfaces des étages supérieurs sont crépies et décorées d'ornements de Mr. Fried. Schleich sculpteur.

Le rez-de-chaussée contient outre les magasins, un appartement avec cuisine, le vestibule d'entrée, le passage pour la cour et deux escaliers pour les étages. Les trois étages supérieurs ainsi que le toit sont disposés en appartements. Le premier plafond est formé par une voûte en béton, les escaliers sont construits d'après le système Monier. Les deux tours d'angle sont supportées par des cadres en fer.

328 [1909; 47]

The dwelling house with shops at Schlossgartenstrasse 5, Darmstadt, is a double building with three free outside frontages with separate staircases but a common courtyard. The design is by the architect R. Strecker, but this design was subject to revision on account of the new building plan arranged by the Grand Ducal Ministry. The execution was placed in the hands of the firm Strecker and Münch, it occupied 9 months in building and cost about 120 000 Marks. The principal front is flanked by two round corner towers projecting over the ground floor and rising over the roof line, these end in a bell-shaped roof and have on the first and second floors open balconies connected with the broad rectangular middle bay. A second bay projects on the side frontage. The shop windows on the ground floor are arched those of the upper storeys are straight-lined. The roof line is broken, and has on each frontage a gable window erection, other windows are also in the roof which is every where covered with slate. The ground floor is of light Main sandstone, the upper facades are plastered and have ornamental sculpture by Friedrich Schleich.

The ground floor contains as well as the shops a dwelling with kitchen, the entrance floor a thoroughfare to the courtyard and two staircases. The three upper storeys and the roof storey are arranged as dwellings. The first ceiling is of beton, for the staircases the Monier system has been used, the two corner towers are supported on the ground floor by girders.

329 [1909; 21]

Das fünfstöckige Kontorhaus in Hamburg, Alsterdamm 4/5, Ecke Brandsende, ein Werk der Architekten J. G. Rambatz und W. Jolasse, ist etwa im Laufe eines Jahres für die Baukostensumme von rund 400 000 Mark errichtet. Die Kosten für den Kubikmeter umbauten Raumes betragen danach 4,30 Mark. Die in gelbem Cottaer Sandstein verblendete Fassade zeigt antikisierende, jedoch modern aufgefaßte Formen. Das breite Mittelrisalit der Vorderfront, welches den Eingang enthält, wird durch Tragefiguren unter dem abschließenden Gurtgesims des ersten Stocks und durch vorgekragte Balkons im zweiten und dritten Obergeschoß belebt. Ein über den Eckpfeilern mit Figuren versehener Flachgiebel bekrönt das Risalit. Die zurückliegenden Seitenteile der Vorderfassade sind in schwach ausgebogene, durch schmale Pfeiler geteilte Fensterflächen aufgelöst. Das Dach ist in Kupfer eingedeckt. Die Portalfiguren in Sandstein, sowie die in Kupfer getriebenen Giebelfiguren sind Schöpfungen des Bildhauers Arth. Bock.

Die beiden im Erdgeschoß angeordneten Läden werden durch den Eingangsflur getrennt, an den sich das mit Oberlicht versehene Treppenhaus und seitwärts die Aufzüge sowie die Toiletten an-

329 [1909; 21]

La maison de comptoirs à cinq étages, angle de l'Alsterdamm 4/5 et de la Brandsende à Hambourg est l'œuvre des architectes J. G. Rambatz et W. Jolasse, elle fut construite dans l'espace d'un an à peu près pour la somme de 400 000 Marks. Le mètre cube d'espace construit coûta 4,30 Marks. La façade revêtue de pierre jaune de Cotta est de formes antiques, mais modernisées. Le large avant-corps de la façade principale, contenant l'entrée, est décoré de cariatides sous le cordon du premier étage et par des balcons au second et au troisième étages. Un fronton bas, orné de figures au dessus de piliers d'angle, couronne l'avant-corps. Les parties latérales en retrait sont divisées par des surfaces de fenêtres légèrement convexes et partagées par de minces meneaux. Le toit est recouvert en cuivre. Les figures du portail en pierre, ainsi que celles du fronton en cuivre repoussé, sont dues au sculpteur Arth. Bock.

Les deux magasins disposés au rez-de-chaussée sont séparés par la porte d'entrée à laquelle sont reliés, l'escalier avec lanterne vitrée et latéralement les lifts et les toilettes. Sur le derrière de la cour ouverte, se trouve un

329 [1909; 21]

The five-storeyed "Kontor Haus" in Hamburg, situated at Alster-Damm 4/5 corner of Brandsende is a work of the architects J. G. Rambatz and W. Jolasse, it occupied a year in building and cost about 400 000 Marks; the cost of each built cubic meter amounting to 4,30 Marks. The facade is faced with yellow Cotta sandstone, and though of antique form has yet many modern touches. The broad middle erection of the front which contains the entrance, is enlivened by Caryatides supporting the balustrade moulding of the first floor and by projecting balconies in the second and third upper storeys. Over the corner pillars of the centre erection is a flat gable crowned with statuary. The receding sides of the front facade have window surfaces divided by narrow pillars. The roof is of copper. The portal figures of sandstone as well as the gable figures of hammered copper are the work of the sculptor Arth. Bock.

The two shops on the ground floor are separated by the entrance hall which leads to a

ichließen. An der Rückfeite des offenen Hofes ift links eine Nebentreppe angeordnet. Die vier Obergeichoffe find zu Kontorräumen beitimmt und können nach Bedarf durch leichte Zwischenwände geteilt werden. Die Decken find durchweg maffiv, die Treppen in Stein und Eifen ausgeführt. Ein Paternoster-Fahrituhl, ein Knopfiteuerungs-Fahrituhl und ein Laitenaufzug im Hof verbinden fämtliche Geichoffe. Die Räume find mit einer regulierbaren Zentralheizung und einer elektrichen Lichtanlage ausgeitattet.

escalier secondaire. Les quatre étages supérieurs sont destinés à des bureaux et peuvent être divisés à volonté au moyen de parois légères. Les planchers sont massifs, les escaliers en pierre et en fer. Tous les étages sont reliés entre eux au moyen d'un ascenseur à marche continue, d'un lift électrique et d'un monte-charges dans la cour. Les localités sont pourvues d'un chauffage central et d'éclairage électrique.

skylighted staircase and sidewards to the lifts and the lavatories. At the back of the open courtyard is a secondary staircase. The four upper storeys are arranged as bureaus and can be divided as required. The ceilings are throughout solid, the stairs of stone and iron. All the floors are reached by a Paternoster lift, a lift for passengers and a goods lift in the courtyard. There is also electric light and central heating.

330 [1909; 23]

Das an drei Seiten freiliegende, mit einem Garten ausgeitattete Gebäude der Rhein.-Weitf. Diskontobank in Recklinghaufen, von dem Architekten Müller-Jena entworfen, kam in etwa 14 Monaten für die Baukoitenfumme von 300000 Mark zur Ausführung. Die dreiitöckige Faifade ift mit Sanditein aus dem Medarder Kaifer-Steinbruch verblendet und zeigt

La maison de la Rhein. Weitf. Diskontobank à Recklinghausen, libre de trois côtés et pourvue d'un jardin a été élevée d'après les plans de Mr. Müller, architecte à Jena; la construction dura 14 mois environ et coûta 300000 Marks. La façade de trois étages est revêtue de pierre des carrières de Medard et est traitée en formes d'un baroque discret; le

The Rhein-Westphalian Diskonto Bank in Recklinghausen was designed by the architect Müller-Jena. It is free on three sides and surrounded by a garden; the time occupied in building was 14 months and the cost amounted to 300 000 Marks. The three-storeyed facade is faced with sandstone from the "Medard Kaiser" Stone quarry and is slightly leaning to

A Eingang zu den Wohnungen
A¹ Eingang zur Bank
B Direktionsflur und Warteraum
C Publikum
D Sprechzimmer
E Direktion
F Privatbureau
G Korrespondenz
H Buchhalterei
J Kasse
K Effekten
L Treppe vom Effekten-Tresor
M Effekten-Sprechzimmer
N Lichthof
O Bleiche
P Kinder-Spielplatz
Q Laube
R Sitzplatz (unter a, b, c, d Tresor)

A Apartement Entrance
B Bank Entrance
C Vestibule and Waiting Room for Director's Office
D Conference Room
E Director's Office
F Private Room
G Secretary
H Accounting
J Teller's Counter

K Securities
L Stairs to Securities Strong-room
M Securities Office
N Patio
O Bleaching Ground
P Playground
Q Arbour
R Benches (Strong-box located under a, b, c, & d)

A Accès aux logements
A¹ Accès à la banque
B Couloir de la direction et salle d'attente
C Public
D Cabinet d'entretiens
E Direction
F Bureau privé
G Correspondance
H Comptabilité
J Caisse
K Effets
L Accès au coffre-fort
M Cabinet d'entretiens relatifs aux effets
N Cour vitrée
O Blanchisserie
P Terrain de jeux
Q Tonnelle
R Bancs (le coffre-fort se trouve sous a, b, c, d)

Erdgeichoß | Rez-de-chaussée | Ground Floor

mäßige Barockformen: das Erdgeichoß gequaderte Flächen, die beiden Obergeichoffe durchgehende Pfeiler und Säulen und über dem Mittelrifalit eine bekrönende Attika. Die Fenter des erien Obergeichoffes find geradlinig, die des zweiten im Stichbogen geichloffen und ebenfalls mittelit der Brüitungstafeln zufammengezogen. Über dem gebrochenen Dach wird die von einem Gitter umgebene Einfaffung des Oberlichtichachts fichtbar. Die Portalfiguren itammen vom Bildhauer Grasegger, mit der Bauleitung war Architekt W. Tietmann betraut.

Im Erdgeichoß öffnen lich an der Vorderfront zwei feitlich nebeneinander gelegene Eingänge, von denen der eine zu den oberen Wohnungen, der zweite zu den Geichäftsräumen der Bank führt. Die Mitte des Erdgeichoffes nimmt der geräumige, von oben beleuchtete Verkehrsraum für das Publikum ein, um den lich allieitig die Kaifen-, Effekten-, Direktorial- und fonitigen Verwaltungszimmer gruppieren. Die beiden Obergeichoffe enthalten die herrichaftlichen, mit einem Wintergarten ausgeitatteten Wohnungen für die Bankdirektoren. Die Treppe zu den Wohnungen wird von einem Lichthofe her beleuchtet. Die Decken find maifiv und der unter dem Mittelraum gelegene Tresor ift in Eifenbeton hergeitellt.

rez-de-chaussée est en refends, les deux étages supérieurs sont traversés par des pilastres et des colonnes; au dessus de l'avant-corps central s'élève une attique. Les fenêtres du premier sont à linteau droit, celles du second en arc de segment, elles sont reliées l'une à l'autre au moyen de panneaux de contre-cœur. On aperçoit au dessus du toit mansard l'ouverture de la cour entourée d'une balustrade. Les figures ornant le portail sont de Mr. Grasegger sculpteur, Mr. Tietmann architecte s'est chargé de la conduite des travaux.

Au rez-de-chaussée s'ouvrent, sur la face principale, deux entrées l'une à côté de l'autre, dont une conduit aux étages supérieurs, l'autre aux bureaux de la banque. Le milieu du rez-de-chaussée est occupé par le hall spacieux, éclairé en haut, destiné au public, autour du quel se groupent la caisse, les effets, ainsi que les chambres de la direction et de l'administration. Les deux étages supérieurs contiennent les appartements de maîtres, pourvus d'un jardin d'hiver pour les directeurs de l'établissement. L'escalier des appartements est éclairé par une cour. Les planchers sont de construction massive et le trésor situé au dessous de la pièce centrale est en béton armé.

the barock style; the ground floor has square-cut surfaces, the two upper storeys have pillars reaching throughout their height and over the centre projection is a gallery which crowns the erection. The windows of the first upper storey are straight-lined, those of the second are finished with segmental arches and joined together by the breast-moulding. Over the broken roof-line can be seen the skylight surrounded by a railing. The figures over the portal are by the sculptor Grasegger, the superintendence of the building was entrusted to the architect W. Tietmann.

On the ground floor in the front are two entrances placed next to each other, one of which leads to the dwellings on the upper storey, and the other to the business rooms of the bank. The whole centre of the ground floor is occupied by the spacious hall, lighted from above, for the use of the public; from this lead on all sides, the cash, the stock and share department the rooms for the directors and other administrative bureaus. The two upper storeys contain the well-appointed dwelling with a winter garden, for the use of the Bank Director. The staircase leading to the dwelling is lighted from above. The ceilings are all solid, and the strong-room under the centre hall is of iron beton.

Das Gebäude des Restaurant Fürstenhof in Kiel, in den drei Obergeschossen zu Wohnungen ausgebaut, ist von dem Architekten J. Theede entworfen. Die beiden Straßenfronten des Eckhauses zeigen in der Hauptsache eine kräftige, durch breite aufsteigende Pfeiler gegliederte gefugte Backsteinarchitektur, die von einzelnen ornamentierten Putzflächen unterbrochen wird. Nur der Sockel, der rundbogige Haupteingang, der abgerundete Eckbau, die vortretenden Erker, sowie einzelnes Figürliche an den Pfeilern zwischen den Fenstern im zweiten Oberstock sind in Schnittstein ausgeführt und teilweise wieder mit Putzflächen in Verbindung gesetzt. Der über dem mit einer Altane abschließenden Eckbau rund nach innen einspringende Fassadenteil trägt in der unteren Fläche des gebrochenen mit Hohlpfannen eingedeckten Daches ein breites giebelbekröntes Dachfenster. Die drei Gruppen von Dachfenstern über der Seitenfront sind mit besonderen steilen abgewalmten Dächern überdeckt.

La maison du restaurant Fürstenhof à Kiel, dans laquelle les trois étages supérieurs ont été disposés en appartements, a été bâtie d'après les plans de Mr. F. Theede architecte. Les deux façades sur rue de cet immeuble d'angle montrent une architecture vigoureuse du briques à joints apparents divisée par de larges piliers interrompus par des surfaces crépies et ornementées. Seuls, le socle, l'entrée à plein cintre, l'angle arrondi, la tourelle en saillie, ainsi que quelques figures appliquées sur les piliers entre les fenêtres du deuxième étage sont en pierre de taille et reliées en partie avec des surfaces crépies. La partie rentrante de la façade au dessus du motif d'angle surmonté d'un balcon porte une lucarne couronnée d'un large pignon dans la partie inférieure du toit mansard en tuiles. Les trois groupes de lucarnes au dessus de la façade latérale sont recouverts de toits spéciaux, abrupts et à croupe.

The building of the restaurant Fürstenhof in Kiel is arranged for dwellings in the three upper storeys and was designed by the architect J. Theede. Both street frontages of the corner house show as their principal feature a massive brick construction with broad pillars, broken occasionally by ornamented plaster surfaces. The sockel, the rounded arches of the principal entrance, the circular corner building, the projecting bay as well as some part of the statuary on the pillars between the windows on the second storey are of cut stone and in some parts of plaster. The part of the facade over the corner erection (which is crowned by a terrace) springs inwards and has in the lower part of the roof a broad window with a gable. The three groups of roof windows over the side frontage have special steep hipped roofs.

Das Warenhaus Jacobsen in Kiel, Ecke Holsten- und Rosenstraße, ist im Anschluß an einen älteren Gebäudeteil errichtet. Der Entwurf, von Architekt Fr. Brantzky herrührend, erhielt in einem Wettbewerb den ersten Preis. Es ist ein Putzbau mit gleichzeitiger Verwendung reicher Metallverzierung, besonders im Erdgeschoß. Der Haupteingang ist rundbogig geschlossen, die Ladenöffnungen im Erdgeschoß, sowie die Fenster der Obergeschosse sind geradlinig überdeckt, von Pfeilern geteilt und zwischen solchen, die ganze Fassadenhöhe durchsießenden, eingeschlossen. Einzelne Fenster im ersten Obergeschoß sind in flacher Rundung vorgekragt und zwischen den Eckrisaliten ergibt sich ein schmaler erkerartiger Fassadenteil. Über dem Dachgesims der Hauptfront erheben sich steile volutenbesetzte Treppengiebel, außerdem ist die Seitenfront im vierten Oberstock durch ein breites und hohes Fenster bezeichnet und ebenfalls durch einen abgetreppten Giebel abgeschlossen. Zu seiten des Haupteinganges sind Rundfiguren angebracht. Die steilen Dächer sind mit Ziegeln eingedeckt.

Le grand magasin Jacobsen à Kiel, angle de la Holsten- et de la Rosenstrasse, a été construit relié à un corp de bâtiment ancien. Le projet dû à Mr. Brantzky architecte reçut le premier prix dans un concours. C'est une construction de maçonnerie crépie avec emploi de riches décorations de métal, surtout au rez-de-chaussée. L'entrée principale est recouverte à plein cintre, les devantures de magasin au rez-de-chaussée, ainsi que les fenêtres des étages supérieurs sont à linteaux droits, séparées par des meneaux, et encadrées par des piliers traversant toute la hauteur de la façade. Quelques fenêtres au premier étage font saillie à plan de segment et entre les refends d'angle se trouve une mince partie de façade en forme de tourelle saillante. Au dessus de la corniche de la façade principale s'élèvent des pignons abrupt en forme d'escaliers, ornés de volutes; la façade latérale est en outre décorée au quatrième étage d'une haute et large fenêtre et terminée elle aussi par un pignon en escalier. Sur les côtés de l'entrée principale se trouvent des figures en ronde bosse. Les toits sont recouverts en tuiles.

The bazaar Jacobsen at the corner of Holsten and Rosenstrasse, Kiel, has been built on to an old building. The design is by the architect F. Brantzky and obtained the first prize at an open competition. It is a plaster building, but metal ornamentation has been largely used particularly on the ground floor. The principal entrance is enclosed by rounded arches, the openings to the shops on the ground floor, as well as the windows of the upper storey have horizontal lines, and are divided by pillars which extend through to the entire height of the facade. Some windows on the first upper storey have flat rounded projections and between the corner risalits is a small bay like erection of the facade. Over the roof moulding of the principal front rise steep pillar-like step gables; the side front of the fourth upper storey has a broad and high window, and is also finished off by a gable as above. At the side of the front entrance are sculptural figures. The steep roofs are covered with tiles.

Der Zusammenschluß der drei Wohnhäuser in Basel, Schützenmattstraße 49—53, zu einer Gruppe von einheitlichem Charakter ergibt sich aus der gleichmäßigen Behandlung der zweistöckigen Fassaden in moderner Ausgestaltung der Formen. Der Entwurf stammt von dem Architekten Baumeister B. Aichner. Die Fassaden sind verputzt und in Mörtel modellierten Ornamenten geschmückt. Die Eingänge sind sämtlich mit einem auf Säulen ruhenden Schutzdache versehen; die Steilflächen der gebrochenen, mit Schiefer eingedeckten Dächer sind mit Dachfenstern besetzt, die wieder von Säulchen eingefaßt werden, Fenster und Eingangstüren haben durchweg geradlinige Überdeckungen erhalten. Das links gelegene Haus zeichnet sich durch einen im Erdgeschoß vorspringenden Erker aus und durch den beschieferten, in geschwungenen Konturen begrenzten Giebel, der in der Mitte eine vorgebaute Fenstergruppe enthält. Ein Flugdach überdeckt sämtliche Fenster des Giebels. Das mittlere Haus zeigt wie das vorige einen vom Boden aufsteigenden Erker, der im Obergeschoß mit einer Altane abschließt. Die Dachfläche ist durch zwei breite Dachfenster belebt. Am rechtsgelegenen Hause durchbricht ein von Pfeilern eingefaßter Vorbau beide Geschosse und die Dachlinie, über dieser noch ein drittes Geschoß bildend und mit einem leicht geschwungenen Giebel schließend.

Le ralliement des trois maisons d'habitation Schützenmattstrasse 49 à 53, Basel, en un groupe de caractère uniforme a été obtenu par l'architecture égale des façades de deux étages dans un esprit moderne. Le projet est de Mr. B. Aichner architecte et entrepreneur. Les façades sont crépies et décorées d'ornements modelés dans le mortier. Toutes les entrées sont pourvues d'un avant-toit reposant sur des colonnes. Les surfaces du toit mansard recouvert d'ardoises sont interrompues par des lucarnes encadrées de colonnettes. Les fenêtres et les portes sont toutes à couverture droite. La maison de gauche se distingue par une tourelle faisant saillie au rez-de-chaussée et par un fronton de contours ondulés, revêtu d'ardoises et portant dans son milieu un groupe de fenêtres en saillie. Un toit leger recouvre toutes fenêtres du pignon. La maison du milieu, comme la précédente, montre une tourelle montant de fond, couronné à l'étage supérieur par une terrasse. La surface du toit est animée par deux larges lucarnes. A la maison de droite, on remarque un avant-corps encadrè de piliers traversant les deux étages et la corniche, au dessus de laquelle il forme un troisième étage, is est terminé par un pignon de conturs légèrement ondulés.

The three houses at Schützenmattstrasse 49—53, Basel, have been formed into one harmonious architectural group by the uniform treatment of the design for the facades which are two-storeyed and of quite modern style. The design is by the architect B. Aichner. The facades are of plaster with articulations of ornamental mortar. The entrances have pillars on which rest a roof for protection from the weather; the steep surfaces of the roof are covered with slate, the roof has a broken line and various windows ornamented with small pillars; the windows and doors are everywhere finished off with straight lines. The house on the left has a bay on the ground floor and a curved gable covered with slate, in the middle of this is a projecting group of windows all of which have a protecting roof. The middle house, like the above mentioned house has also a bay on the ground floor which is continued through the other storeys and finished off by a terrace. The roof has two broad roof windows. The house on the right is produced through a pillared entrance portico upwards through two storeys and the roof line over this forms another storey in which is a slightly curved gable.

Die durch eine gemeinschaftliche Brandmauer verbundenen beiden Wohnhäuser in Düsseldorf, Graf Adolphstraße 32/34, sind vom Architekten Wilh. May im Laufe eines Jahres errichtet und haben jedes rund 95 000 Mark Baukosten verursacht. Die Fassaden beider Häuser sind mit polygonalen, über dem Erdgeschosse ausgekragten, durch drei Obergeschosse geführten Erkerausbauten, außerdem vor den Seitenfenstern mit halbrund vortretenden Balkons versehen und durch steile etwa zwei Drittele der Fronten überdeckende Giebel bekrönt. Die Fassade des Hauses Nr. 32 ist in Dolomit und Pußflächen, die des Hauses Nr. 34 in Pfälzer Sandstein und Pußflächen hergestellt. Das Erdgeschoß ist durchweg zu Läden mit breiten Schaufenstern ausgebaut, die drei Obergeschosse enthalten im Vorderhause und den Flügelbauten je zwei hochherrschaftlich ausgestaltete Wohnungen, deren Räume einschließlich der Küchen mit Zubehör von einer Diele zugänglich sind. Jedes Haus enthält eine durch alle Geschosse führende Treppe und ist mit einer Zentral-Niederdruckwasserheizung versehen.

Les deux maisons d'habitation mitoyennes, Graf Adolphstrasse 32 et 34 à Dusseldorf, ont été construites en une année par Mr. Wilh. May, architecte, chacune d'elles a coûté en bloc 95 000 Marks. Les façades des deux maisons sont ornées des tourelles polygonales faisant saillie au dessus du rez-dechaussée et traversant trois étages et de balcons en arc de cercle au devant des fenêtres latérales, des frontons abrupts s'élèvent au dessus des deux tiers à peu près des façades. La façade du No. 32 est en pierre de dolomite et en maçonnerie crépie, celle du No. 34, en pierre du Palatinat et en surfaces crépies. Le rez-de-chaussée est entièrement occupé par des magasins avec larges devantures, les trois étages supérieurs contiennent chacun, dans la partie antérieure et les ailes, deux appartements de maîtres, dont les chambres et la cuisine avec dépendances sont accessibles d'un hall. Chaque maison a un escalier conduisant à tous les étages et est pourvue d'un calorifère à eau chaude à basse pression.

The two dwelling houses at Graf Adolphstrasse 32—34, Düsseldorf, are joined by a fire wall. They are built from the designs of the architect Wilh. May, the time occupied was about a year, and each cost about 95000 Marks. Both houses have polygonal projecting bays extending through three upper storeys; the side windows have semi-circular balconies before them, and are crowned by steep projecting gables. The facade of No. 32 is in dolomite and plastered surfaces, that of 34 in Pfalzsandstone and plaster. The ground floor is occupied entirely by shops with broad windows; the three upper storeys in the front building and in the side wings contain each two superior flats, so arranged that all the rooms with the kitchen and offices lie round a square hall. Each house has a stair-case leading throughout to each flat and is heated with central low-pressure steam apparatus.

Das vierstöckige Wohnhaus in München, Romanstraße 5, von Architekt H. Lettner entworfen und in etwa 8 Monaten für die Kostensumme von 75 000 Mark zur Ausführung gebracht, zeichnet sich durch moderne Auffassung der Formen des Äußeren aus. Die durch lange vertikale, schwach vortretende Streifen gegliederten Fassaden sind mit rauhem, abwechselnd gelb, grün und blaugrün getöntem Mörtelverputz versehen und die reichlich verwendeten Flächenornamente in Pflanzenformen sind vergoldet. Im zweiten Obergeschoß kragt ein Balkon heraus, dessen Brüstungsgitter ebenfalls Vergoldung zeigt. Die Risalite beider Fronten haben Abschlüsse im Flachbogen erhalten, und auf den Steilflächen des gebrochenen, mit Biberschwänzen eingedeckten Daches erheben sich Fensteraufbauten. Die vier Geschosse enthalten je zwei Wohnungen, außerdem sind im ausgebauten Dachgeschoß noch einige Zimmer eingerichtet.

La maison d'habitation à quatre étages, Romanstrasse 5, à Munich, bâtie dans l'espace de huit mois environ pour la somme de 75 000 Marks, d'après les plans de Mr. H. Lettner architecte, se distingue à l'extérieur par le modernisme de ses formes. Les façades divisées par de longs bandeaux verticaux, de peu de saillie sont décorées de panneaux crépis à gros grain, variant du jaune au vert et au vert-bleu; les nombreux ornements montrant des formes de plantes sont dorés. Au deuxième étage, un balcon fait saillie, ses balustrades sont également dorées. Les avant-corps des deux façades sont couronnées de frontons en arc de cercle, et des lucarnes s'élèvent sur les parties abruptes du toit mansard recouvert en tuiles. Les quatre étages contiennent chacun deux appartements, on a en outre disposé quelques chambres dans le toit.

The four storeyed house at Romanstrasse 5, Munich, was designed by the architect H. Lettner, occupied 8 months in building and cost 75 000 Marks. The style of the exterior is distinctly modern. The facades are of rough mortar plaster alternately yellow, green and blue green, and articulated by long vertical slightly marked stripes; the foliage ornamentation, rather lavishly used, is gilded. On the second upper storey projects a balcony, the balustrade of which is also gilded. The middle erections of both fronts are finished off by flat arches, and in the roof, which is covered with flat red tiles are several window groups. The four storeys contain each two flats; other rooms are built in the roof storey.

Das in sämtlichen Geschossen zu Verkaufszwecken dienende Kaufhaus „Hettlage" in Dortmund bringt diese Bestimmung gleichfalls in dem einheitlich behandelten Äußeren zum Ausdruck. Urheber des in etwa 7 Monaten für die Bausumme von 320 000 Mark errichteten Gebäudes ist Architekt O. Engler. Senkrecht vom Boden bis zum dritten Obergeschoß aufsteigende Pfeiler gliedern die Fassaden und schließen die Lichtöffnungen zwischen sich ein; diese erscheinen im Erdgeschoß als breite Schaufenster, in den beiden Obergeschossen als mehrfach geteilte, entweder in gerader Flucht liegende oder in schwacher Rundung ausgebogene Fenster-

La maison de commerce "Hettlage", à Dortmund, disposée dans tous ses étages en comptoirs, montre clairement cette disposition à l'extérieur, traité d'une façon uniforme. Mr. O. Engler, architecte, est l'auteur de cet édifice élevé en sept mois environ pour la somme de 320000 Marks. Des piliers verticaux, montant du sol jusqu'au troisième étage, partagent les façades et encadrent les fenêtres. Ces ouvertures sont au rez-de-chaussée de larges devantures, aux deux étages supérieurs, des groupes de fenêtres divisées plusieurs fois par des meneaux et couvertes en partie par des linteaux droits, en partie par des arcs surbaissés. La

The uniformity in the treatment of the facade of the Bazaar "Hettlage" in Dortmund shows the purpose for which the building was erected, every floor being devoted to shops. The designer was the architect O. Engler, the time occupied in building was 7 months and the cost amounted to 320000 Marks. From the basement upwards to the third storey rise perpendicular pillars enclosing between them the windows which on the ground floor are broad shop-windows; on the other floors however they are variously divided some being in straight rows and others in slightly arched groups. The

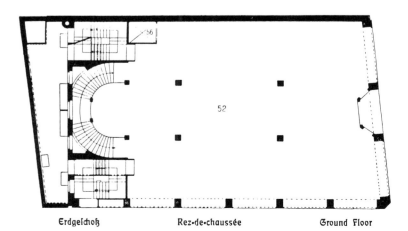

| Erdgeschoß | Rez-de-chaussée | Ground Floor |

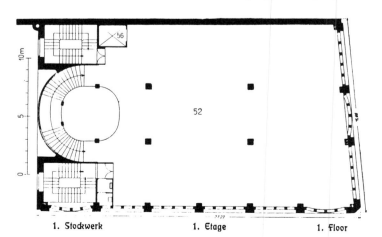

| 1. Stockwerk | 1. Étage | 1. Floor |

gruppen. Der obere Teil der durchgehenden Pfeiler ist mit figürlichen Reliefs geschmückt. Die Pendeltür des vertieft liegenden Eingangs ist samt dem Oberlicht in Bronze hergestellt. Über dem das zweite Obergeschoß abschließenden stark ausladenden Gesimse folgt das dritte wieder durch Pfeiler gegliederte und in Fenstergruppen aufgelöste Obergeschoß. Über der Eingangsfront erhebt sich ein mit geschwungenem Giebel abschließender Dachaufbau, und aus dem First des gebrochenen Daches steigt ein mit umlaufender Galerie versehener, noch ein zurückgesetztes mit gebrochener Kuppelhaube bekröntes Geschoß tragender Turm empor. Die Fronten sind mit fränkischem Muschelkalkstein bekleidet; im übrigen bestehen Wände und Pfeiler aus Eisenbeton, ebenso die massiven Decken. Das Dach ist mit grünglasierten Falzziegeln eingedeckt und der Turm, sowie die Dachfenster haben Kupferbedachung erhalten.

Die Verkaufsräume im Erdgeschoß und in den drei Obergeschossen sind nur durch Pfeiler geteilt und durch eine freiliegende, im Halbkreis geschwungene Haupttreppe, sowie durch zwei Nebentreppen und einen Aufzug miteinander in Verbindung gesetzt. In dem durch Dachfenster beleuchteten Dachgeschoß sind Lagerräume eingerichtet, ebenso im Keller, der außerdem die Zentral-Heizungsanlage enthält.

337 [1909: 31]

Die vier nebeneinander liegenden, durch gleichmäßige Gestaltung der Fassadenformen zu einer Gruppe zusammengeschlossenen Wohnhäuser in Charlottenburg, Kurfürstendamm 56 bis 59, sind nach den Entwürfen des Architekten Regierungsbaumeisters H. Toebelmann und des Architekten H. Groß im Laufe von 4 Jahren zur Ausführung gekommen. Die fünfstöckigen Häuser sind sämtlich durch breite, durch vier Geschosse reichende, mit Altanen abschließende, zum Teil mit Loggien und Balkons in Verbindung stehende und andere Ausbauten wirksam plastisch belebt. Das Eckhaus an der Wielandstraße trägt einen, die abgestumpfte Ecke an der Leibnizstraße drei kuppelartige, von Rundgiebeln flankierte Ecktürme. Die mittleren Häuser sind durch flachrunde, von Attiken bekrönte Vorsprünge ausgezeichnet, über denen sich abgewalmte, pavillonartig erhöhte Dächer erheben. Die Fassaden sind mit Putz in gelblich-brauner und Sandsteingliederungen in gelblich-grüner Färbung versehen. Die Kuppeln der Türme sind in Kupfer eingedeckt. Die plastische Ornamentik der Fassaden ist nach Bildhauer Rödel modelliert. Die Häuser Nr. 56, 57 und 59 enthalten in jedem Geschosse zwei Wohnungen, das Haus Nr. 58 je eine Wohnung; dieselben sind sämtlich herrschaftlich ausgestattet und mit Badezimmern und sonstigem Zubehör versehen.

338 [1909: 62]

Das Semperhaus in Hamburg, Spitalerstraße, bildet ein sechsstöckiges Geschäftshaus mit zwei freiliegenden Fronten und ist nach dem Entwurfe der Architekten Fr. Bach und Klosterburg im Laufe von 3 Jahren, von 1906 bis 1909, für die Baukostensumme von rund 600 000 Mark errichtet. Die Hauptfront ist durch ein breites Mittel- und zwei Eckrisalite gegliedert, aus deren in Pavillonform aufsteigenden Dächern polygonale Aufbauten hervorwachsen, die mit durchbrochenen kuppelüberdeckten Türmen bekrönt sind. Das Erdgeschoß öffnet sich zu Schaufenstern für Läden, die Fenster im ersten Obergeschoß sind geradlinig geschlossen und zeigen in den Rücklagen abgerundete Ecken. Die folgenden vier Obergeschosse sind mit einer durchgehenden Pfeiler- bzw. Säulenarchitektur gegliedert, welche die Fenster zwischen sich einschließt. Die Fassaden

partie supérieure des piliers est ornée de reliefs avec figures. La porte de l'entrée disposée en profondeur est en bronze, ainsi que l'imposte. Au dessus de la corniche très saillante qui couronne le deuxième étage, s'élève le troisième également divisé par des piliers encadrant des groupes de fenêtres. Au dessus de la façade d'entrée s'élève un corps de bâtiment couronné d'un pignon ondulé et sur le faîte du toit mansard se dresse une tour entourée d'une galerie, derrière laquelle, un étage en retrait porte un toit en forme de bonnet à jour. Les façades sont revêtues de pierre calcaire de Franconie; les parois et piliers sont en béton armé, ainsi que les plafonds. Le toit est recouvert en tuiles à recouvrement et la tour, ainsi que les lucarnes sont revêtues de cuivre.

Les locaux de vente au rez-de-chaussée et dans les trois étages supérieurs ne sont séparés que par des piliers et reliés entre eux par un escalier principal, suspendu, en demi-cercle, ainsi que par deux escaliers secondaires et un monte-charges. Dans la mansarde éclairée par des lucarnes se trouvent des entrepôts, ainsi que dans la cave qui contient en outre le chauffage central.

337 [1909: 31]

Les quatre maisons d'habitation situées l'une à côté de l'autre et reliées en un groupe par la conformité des façades, Kurfurstendamm 56 à 59 à Charlottenbourg ont été construites dans l'espace de quatre ans par M. M. H. Toebelmann, architecte du gouvernement et H. Gross, architecte. Les maisons à cinq étages sont toutes divisées par de larges avant-corps traversant quatre étages, surmontés de terrasses et reliées en partie entre eux par des loggias et des balcons. La maison d'angle sur la Wielandstrasse porte une tour flanquée de pignons arrondis, l'angle obtus sur la Leibnitzstrasse est décorée de trois tours du même genre. Les maisons du milieu sont décorées d'avant-corps arrondis, couronnés d'attiques au dessus desquels se dressent des toits à croupe, élevés en forme de pavillons. Les façades sont en maçonnerie crépie de couleur brune-jaunâtre avec moulures en pierre de couleur jaune-verte. Les coupoles des tours sont recouvertes en cuivre. L'ornementation plastique des façades a été modelée par le sculpteur Rödel. Les maisons No. 56, 57 et 59 contiennent deux appartements à chaque étage, la maison No. 58, un seul appartement par étage. Ces appartements sont installés avec luxe, pourvus de bains et des dépendances nécessaires.

338 [1909: 62]

La maison Semper à Hambourg, Spitalerstrasse est un immeuble de rapport de six étages avec deux façades libres; il a été élevé dans l'espace de trois ans, de 1906 à 1909 d'après les plans de M. M. Fr. Bach & Klosterburg architectes pour la somme en bloc de 600000 Marks. La façade principale est divisée par un large avant-corps central et deux ailes latérales au dessus des quelles s'élèvent des toit en forme de pavillons polygonaux, couronnés de tours à jour portant des coupoles. Le rez-de-chaussée est percé de devantures de magasins. Les fenêtres du premier étage sont à linteaux droits et ont les angles arrondis dans les parties en retrait. Les quatre étages suivants sont divisés par des piliers et colonnes qui les traversent et encadrent les fenêtres entre eux. Les façades

upper part of the pillars is ornamented with sculptural figures. The swinging door of the entrance, which lies in a deep recess, is of bronze as is also the skylight. The second storey is marked by widely projecting moulding, over this comes the third storey articulated by pillars and with broad flights of windows. Over the front entrance is a roof erection with a curved gable, and from the ridge of the roof rises a tower round which a gallery is erected and which is crowned by a cupola. The front facades are faced with Frankish shell limestone; walls and pillars are of iron beton, as are also the solid ceilings. The roof is of green glazed tiles, the tower and the roof windows have copper roofs.

The sale rooms on the ground floor, and on the three upper storeys are only separated by pillars, the various floors are reached by a free semi-circular principal staircase, by two secondary staircases and a lift. Warehouse rooms are arranged in the roof storey which is lighted by windows, more storage rooms are in the basement, where is also the machinery for the central heating.

337 [1909: 31]

Four houses standing together at Kurfürstendamm 56 to 59, Charlottenburg, form a harmonious group with facades all of the same design. They were built after the design of the architect Regierungsbaumeister H. Toebelmann and the architect H. Gross in the space of about four years. The houses have five storeys, they are all ornamented with effectively placed balconies and loggias which reach upwards through four storeys and are finished off with a terrace. The corner house at the Wielandstrasse has a corner tower flanked by rounded gables, the corner on the Leibnitzstrasse forming an obtuse angle. The middle houses have projections crowned with open balconies over which pavilion-like hipped roofs are constructed. The facades are of plaster of yellow-brown colour with sandstone articulations of yellowish green. The cupolas of the towers are roofed with copper. The plastic ornament of the facades is by sculptor Rödel. The houses 56, 57 and 59 contain on each floor two lodgings, the house 58 has only one dwelling on each floor; they are all equipped with bathrooms and every modern comfort in a superior style.

338 [1909: 62]

The Semper house Spitalerstrasse Hamburg is a six-storeyed business house with two free frontages built according to the design of the architects Fr. Bach and Klosterburg in the course of three years (1906—1909) for the sum of 600 000 Marks. The principal front is articulated by one broad middle projection and two corner projections; the pavilion-formed roofs of these are further ornamented with polygonal erections crowned with open-work cupola-covered towers. The ground floor opens into shops with broad windows, the windows in the upper storey are straight-lined and have in the recess rounded corners. The following four upper storeys are articulated with pillars extending upwards throughout between which the windows are grouped.

lind mit grauem Muſchelkalkſteln verblendet und an den Riſalten durch ſigürliche Hochreliefs und überdem durch ein von Prof. Semper ausgeführtes Monument für Gottfried Semper geſchmückt. Sämtliche Räume haben maſſiv-freitragende Decken erhalten.

sont revêtues de pierre calcaire grise, les ailes sont décorées de figures en haut relief, et d'un monument à Gottfried Semper exécuté par le professeur Semper. Tous les locaux ont été pourvus de planchers de construction massive.

The facades are faced with grey shell limestone, the projections have statuary in high relief; over this is a monument for Gottfried Semper executed by Professor Semper. All the rooms have solid suspended ceilings.

339 [1909; 83]

Der Stahlhof in Düſſeldorf, den Intereſſen des Stahlmarktes dienend, bringt ſeine ausſchließliche Beſtimmung zum Geſchäftsgebäude in den einheitlich gegliederten Fronten überzeugend zum Ausdruck. Der Entwurf ſtammt von Architekt Baurat Joh. Radke und iſt im Laufe von 2¼ Jahren für die Bauſumme von 2 000 000 Mark zur Ausführung gekommen. Die im großen durch Flügelanlagen und vorſpringende, mit Giebeln bekrönte Riſalite, im einzelnen durch aufſtrebende Pfeiler gegliederten Fronten erheben ſich im Mittel- und einem Flügelbau in zwei, ſonſt in drei Geſchoſſen und ſind durch eine galerieartige, vor den aufſteigenden Dachflächen durchbrochene Brüſtung nach oben abgeſchloſſen. Über derTraufkante folgen, außer den zwei Fenſterreihen übereinander zeigenden Hauptgiebeln, mehrere gleichfalls mit Giebeln beendete Fenſteraufbauten. Aus den ſich durchſchneidenden Dachfirſten des Mittelbaues ſtrebt ein ſchlanker Turm in zwei Abſätzen und durchbrochener Helmſpitze empor. Das Portal iſt rundbogig, in den oberen Geſchoſſen geradlinig, in den Giebeln wieder flachbogig überdeckt. Die Faſſaden zeigen eine Bekleidung mit Olsbrücker Sandſtein, die gebrochenen Dächer haben eine Eindeckung mit Biberſchwänzen erhalten. Die Bildhauerarbeiten an den Faſſaden ſind von A. Simatſchek ausgeführt.

339 [1909; 83]

Le bâtiment Stahlhof à Düsseldorf, servant aux intérêts du marché de l'acier, montre clairement dans ses façades traitées d'une façon uniforme, sa destination exclusivement commerciale. Le projet est de Mr. Joh. Radke conseiller architecte et a été exécuté dans l'espace de deux ans et demi pour la somme de 2 000 000 Marks. Les façades divisées par les ailes et des avant-corps surmontés de pignons et décorées de piliers, s'élèvent de deux étages au corps-central et à une aile, dans les autres parties elles en ont trois et sont couronnées par une balustrade à jour en forme de galerie interrompue par les parties de toit élevées. Au dessus de la corniche s'élèvent, à part les deux pignons principaux à deux étages de fenêtres, plusieurs lucarnes également couronnées de pignons. Au dessus du point où les faîtes du toit du corps central se croisent se dresse une tour élancée de deux étages avec un toit pointu et à jour. Le portail est à plein cintre, les fenêtres du rez-de-chaussée à arc surbaissé, celles des étages supérieurs sont à linteaux droits, celles des pignons à arc surbaissé. Les façades sont revêtues de pierre de Olsbruck; les toits brisés ont été recouverts en tuiles. Les travaux de sculpture des façades sont de Mr. Simatschek.

339 [1909; 83]

The "Stahlhof" in Dusseldorf, devoted to the interests of the steel market, is a building, the uniformity of whose frontage, is a sign of its being used exclusively for business purposes. The design is by the architect Baurat Joh. Radke, and was built in 2¼ years for the sum of 2 000 000 Marks. The spacious frontage is diversified by side wings and by projecting centre erections crowned with gables, these, articulated by lofty pillars rise in the middle and in one side wing to two storeys, in the other parts to three storeys and are finished off by a gallery surrounded by an open-work balustrade placed in front of the rising roof. Over the rain-gutter, in addition to the principal gables with their two rows of windows, follow several window erections all crowned with gables. From the roof ridge of the middle erection rises a slender tower in two steps, and crowned with a broken helmet shaped summit. The portal has rounded arches, the windows of the ground floor are flatly arched, on the upper storey straightlined and again on the gables flatly arched. The facades are faced with Olsbrück sandstone. The roofs are covered with flat red tiles. The sculptural work of the facade is by A. Simatschek.

340 [1909; 33]

Das Schulgebäude in München, Hohenzollernſtraße, aus einem Hauptgebäude und zwei anſchließenden Flügeln beſtehend, mit einem großen Hofe verbunden, der einerſeits von der offenen Turnhalle begrenzt wird und an einer Ecke das kleine Gebäude für den Kindergarten aufnimmt, iſt von Architekt Baurat R. Rehlen entworfen. Die Ausführung erfolgte etwa im Laufe von 1½ Jahren für die Geſamtkoſtenſumme von 656 700 Mark, wovon 44 700 Mark auf die innere Einrichtung entfallen, die zum Teil neu zu beſchaffen war. Die Hauptfront zeigt den um ein Geſchoß niedrigeren Mittelteil zwiſchen zwei Giebelfronten, der längere Flügel wird ebenfalls von Giebeln begrenzt. Der eine Haupteingang in der einſpringenden Ecke liegt in einem mit einer Altane abſchließenden Vorbau, der zweite Haupteingang iſt zwiſchen dem Flügelbau und der Turnhalle angeordnet. Die überall geradlinig überdeckten Fenſter ſind paarweiſe, durch einen ſchmalen Pfeiler getrennt, zuſammengeſchloſſen. Der Brunnen im Hofe und die Reliefs über den Eingängen ſind von Schülern unter der Leitung des Bildhauers Jobſt ausgeführt. Die Kellermauern bis zur Sockeloberkante beſtehen aus Beton, die oberen Backſteinmauern ſind verputzt und die ſteilen Dächer mit Biberſchwänzen eingedeckt.

340 [1909; 33]

La maison d'école, Hohenzollernstrasse à Munich, se composant d'un bâtiment principal et de deux ailes, reliées par une grande cour, a été bâtie d'après les plans de Mr. R. Rehlen, architecte conseiller. La cour est bordée d'un côté par la salle de gymnastique ouverte, elle contient d'autre part le petit bâtiment du jardin d'enfants. La construction dura environ un an et demi et les frais s'élevèrent à 656 700 Marks, dont 44 700 pour les aménagements intérieurs dont une partie fut créée à neuf. La façade principale consiste en une partie centrale plus basse d'un étage, flanquée de deux pignons; la plus longue des ailes est également encadrée de pignons. Une des entrées principales, dans l'angle rentrant, se trouve dans un avant-corps surmonté d'une terrasse, la seconde entrée est disposée entre l'aile et la gymnastique. Les fenêtres, toutes à linteaux droits, sont groupées deux par deux et séparées par un mince pilier. La fontaine dans la cour et les reliefs au dessus des entrées ont été exécutés par des élèves, sous la direction de Mr. Jobst sculpteur. Les murs de cave jusque sur le socle sont en béton, les murs supérieurs en maçonnerie de briques sont crépis, et les toits abrupts sont recouverts en tuiles.

340 [1909; 33]

The school buildings at Hohenzollern Strasse, Munich, consist of one principal building with two adjoining wings; all are enclosed in a large courtyard one side of which is bounded by an open gymnasium; at one corner is a smaller building for the Kindergarten. The architect is the Baurat R. Rehlen, the time occupied in building was 1½ years and the cost amounted to 656,700 Marks of which sum 44,700 Marks were spent on interior equipment and apparatus part of wich had to be newly provided. The principal front has a low middle erection between two gable fronts, the long wing is also ornamented with gables. One principal entrance in a corner recess opens into a porch over which is a balcony; the second principal entrance is placed between the side wing and the gymnasium. The windows are everywhere straight-lined and are in groups of two separated by narrow pillars. The fountain in the courtyard and the reliefs over the entrance are designed by pupils under the direction of sculptor Jobst. The basement walls up to the groundfloor moulding are of beton the upper storeys are of brick with plaster and the steep roofs are covered with flat red tiles.

341 [1909; 50]

Das umfängliche an zwei Fronten freiliegende, in vier Geſchoſſen aufſteigende Gebäude des Landes-Taubſtummen-Inſtituts in Budapeſt, Jſtvan-ut 95, iſt von den Architekten Baumgarten & Herzog entworfen. Die an orientaliſche Formgebung anklingenden Faſſaden ſind in Putzflächen mit Pfeilern, Geſimſen und Fenſtereinfaſſungen in gefugter Ziegelverblendung ausgeführt. Die ſteilen Dächer ſind mit Biberſchwänzen eingedeckt. Dem vorſpringenden, durch Pfeiler dreigeteilten Mittelbau der Hauptfront iſt eine Freitreppe mit Auffahrtsrampe

341 [1909; 50]

La maison à quatre étages du Asile des sourds-muets Stefan à Buda-Pest, Jstvan-ut 95, primitivement libre de deux côtés, est l'œuvre de M. M. Baumgarten & Herzog architectes. Les façades rappelant le style oriental sont exécutées en surfaces de maçonnerie crépie avec piliers, profils et encadrements de fenêtres en briques apparentes jointoyées. Les toits abrupts sont recouverts en tuiles. Au devant de l'avant-corps central de la façade principal, divisé par des piliers saillants, on a placé un escalier avec rampes d'accès pour les voitures.

341 [1909; 50]

The Deaf and Dumb asylum at Jstvanut 95, Budapest is a fourstoreyed building lying free on two sides. It was designed by the architects Baumgarten and Herzog. The facades are of oriental design, the surfaces are plastered, the pillars the mouldings and the window frames are faced with glazed tiles. The steep roofs are covered with flat red tiles. The middle erection projects, is divided by pillars into three parts, and has the principal entrance

vorgelegt. Die drei mittleren überwölbten Eingangstüren find mit' gleichfalls überwölbten Oberlichtfenstern verfehen; über denfelben öffnet fich eine große, zweifach geteilte, mit maßwerkartigen Formen durchfließte und mit folchen abfchließende Fenftergruppe. Über den gebogenen Linien des Dachgefimfes erheben fich Giebel in mehrfach gefchweiften in Akroterien ausblühenden Formen. Den Mittelbau überdeckt ein fteiles mit Ecktürmchen und durchbrochener Baluftrade bekröntes Pavillondach. Die freiliegende Seitenfront ift durch von Pfeilern eingefaßte Eck- und Mittelrifalite gegliedert, die in Giebeln oder Attiken endigen, hinter denen fich Pavillondächer erheben. Der Dachkranz zwischen den Vorlagen trägt durchweg eine von gefchwungenen Konturen begrenzte Attika. Die Fenfter find in gebrochenen Linien überwölbt. Jm oberften Gefchoffe des Mittelbaues find von Ornamenten umgebene Rundfenfter angeordnet.

Les trois portes d'entrée voûtées du milieu sont surmontées de fenêtres également voûtées. Au dessus se trouve un grand groupe de fenêtres partagé en deux, les fenêtres sont garnies de meneaux. Au dessus des lignes courbes de la corniche s'élèvent des pignons aux contours plusieurs fois ondulés et se terminant en acrotères. Un toit en forme de pavillon couronne le corps central, il est abrupt et surmonté de tourelles d'angle et d'une balustrade à jour. La façade latérale dégagée est partagée par des avantcorps d'angle et du centre, encadrés par des piliers et se terminant en pignons on en attiques derrière lesquels s'élèvent des toits en forme de pavillons. La corniche porte entre les avantcorps une attique de contours ondulés. Les fenêtres sont couvertes en ligne brisée. A l'étage supérieur du corps central on a disposé des fenêtres rondes entourées d'ornements.

approached by a free flight of steps. The three middle extrance doors have vaulted roofs and windows above. Over these is a large group of windows divided into two parts by masonry. Over the arched line of the roof moulding rise gables in various designs of ornament. The middle erection is crowned by a pavilion roof, this is steep, has corner towers and a balustrade. The free lying side frontage is articulated by corner and middle erections separated by pillars all of which are produced upwards and end in gables or terraces behind which rise pavilion roofs. The entire roof moulding forms a terrace with curved contours. The windows have broken lined framing, the upper storey of the middle building has an ornamented circular window.

342 [1909: 52]

Das Königl. Amtsgericht in Düffeldorf ift in dem an der Grabenftraße gelegenen Flügel des Gebäudes für den Düffeldorfer Generalanzeiger (Vgl. Heft 1, 1909, S. 6, Taf. 12—13 der Architekt. d. XX. Jahrh.) untergebracht. Architekt des gefamten Bauwerks war H. vom Endt B. D. A.; die Bauzeit nahm etwa 3 Jahre in Anfpruch. Die Faffade ift mit Mufchelkalkftein verblendet, das Dach ift mit braunroten Biberfchwänzen eingedeckt. Die figürlichen und ornamentalen Bildhauerarbeiten an der Faffade ftammen von A. Pehle und H. Stader. Übrigens ift alles bezüglich Ausbildung der Faffaden des Gebäudes für den Generalanzeiger gefagte auch für den hier zur Darftellung gelangten Flügel an der Grabenftraße zutreffend.

342 [1909: 52]

Le tribunal royal de Dusseldorf a été établi dans l'aile de la Grabenstrasse du bâtiment destiné au Dusseldorfer Generalanzeiger (voyez livraison 1, 1909, p. 6, Pl. 12—13, Architecture du XXième siècle). L'architecte de tout le bâtiment est Mr. H. vom Endt B. D. A. La construction dura environ trois ans. La façade est revêtue de pierre calcaire; le toit est recouvert de tuiles rouges brunes. Les décorations figurales et ornementales de la façade sont de M. M. A. Pehle et H. Stader. Du reste, tout ce qui a été dit au sujet de l'architecture des façades du Generalanzeiger est aussi valable pour l'aile de la Grabenstrasse représentée ici.

342 [1909: 52]

The Royal Law Courts building in Düsseldorf has been arranged in a wing of the premises of the Düsseldorf "General-Anzeiger" overlooking the Grabenstrasse (comp. No. 1, 1909, S. 6, Plate 12—13 of "Architect. d. XX. Jahrh."). The architect of the whole building was H. vom Endt B. D. A.; the time occupied in building was about 3 years. The facade is faced with shell-limestone, the roof is covered with red-brown tiles. The sculptural ornamentation of the facade is by A. Pehle and H. Stader. What has been already said respecting the facade of the building for the "General Anzeiger" applies also to this wing on the Grabenstrasse of which an illustration is here given.

343 [1909: 55]

Die Gefamtausführung des Gefchäftshaufes für die Neue Preußifche (Kreuz-) Zeitung in Berlin, Bernburgerftraße 24/25, erfolgte durch den Architekten, Jnhaber des Baugefchäftes C. Kühn, von dem auch der Grundriß des Gebäudes herrührt, während die Faffade von Architekt F. Lindhorft entworfen wurde. Die Ausführung dauerte etwa 10 Monate und koftete rund 475000 Mark. An der Faffade find über dem Erdgefchoß zwei viereckige, durch drei Obergefchoffe geführte Erker vorgekragt, deren fenkrecht zufammengezogenen Fenftergruppen in leichter Rundung vortreten. Die Seitenfenfter im erften Stock find mit Balkons ausgeftattet. Die beiden Portalöffnungen fowie die Fenfter im Erdgefchoß zeigen Korbbögen, fonft find alle übrigen Lichtöffnungen geradlinig überdeckt. Jm vierten Stockwerk treten die Seitenteile der Vorderfront etwas zurück, um die Möglichkeit zu geben, den Mittelbau höher ausführen zu können, als es fonft die Straßenbreite zugelaffen hätte. Die in hydraulifchem Mörtel verpußte Vorderfaffade fchmückt eine Statue der Boruffia; die Hinterfronten find mit glafierten Ziegeln verblendet.

Das ganze Gebäude, mit Ausnahme der im Quergebäude angeordneten, wegen des Gewichts der Druckereimafchinen mit Bulbeifendecken verfehenen Räume für die Druckerei, dient Bureauzwecken. Die Decken find fämtlich maffiv hergeftellt und zum Zwecke der Schalldämpfung mittelft eifengarnierter Korkplatten und Filzeinlagen ifoliert. Das Gebäude umfchließt einen ganz unterkellerten Mittel- und einen Hinterhof.

343 [1909: 55]

L'exécution de la maison du journal Neue Preussische (Kreuz-) Zeitung, Bernburgerstrasse 24/25 à Berlin fut confiée à Mr. C. Kühn architecte et entrepreneur qui en fit aussi le plan, tandis que la façade fut composée par Mr. F. Lindhorst architecte. La construction dura environ 10 mois et coûta 475000 Marks en bloc. Sur la façade, on voit audessus du rez-de-chaussée, deux tourelles saillantes, quadrangulaires, traversant trois étages et dont les fenêtres reliées entre elles verticalement font saillie en forme de segment. Les fenêtres de côté, au premier étage, sont pourvues de balcons. Les deux portes principales ainsi que les fenêtres du rez-de-chaussée sont couvertes en anse de panier, tandis que toutes les autres ouvertures sont à linteaux droits. Au quatrième étage, les ailes de la façade sont un peu en retrait pour permetre d'élever la partie centrale plus haut que cela n'aurait été possible par rapport à la largeur de la rue. La façade crépie en mortier hydraulique est ornée d'une statue de la Borussia; les façades postérieures sont revêtues de briques émaillées.

Tout le bâtiment, à l'exception des locaux destinés à l'imprimerie, disposés dans l'aile transversale et pourvus de planchers de fer de construction spéciale à cause du poids des machines est occupé par des bureaux. Tous les planchers sont de construction massive et pourvus d'isolations de plaques de liège garnies de fer et de feutre pour éviter la sonorité. Le bâtiment entoure une cour centrale couvrant des caves et une arrière-cour.

343 [1909: 55]

The business premises of the "Neue Preussische (Kreuz) Zeitung" at Bernburgerstrasse 24—25, Berlin, were designed by the builder, the architect C. Kühn who is also responsible for the ground plan; the facade is by the architect F. Lindhorst. The time occupied was about 10 months and the cost amounted to 475 000 Marks. The facade contains over the ground floor, two rectangular projecting bays which extend through three upper storeys; the windows, slightly projecting are arched. The side windows of the first floor have balconies. The two portals and the windows of the ground floor are arched, all other openings are straightlined. On the fourth storey the side parts of the frontage recede slightly in order to allow the middle erection to be carried up higher than is usually permitted for a street frontage. The front facade is of hydraulic mortar plaster and is ornamented by a statue of "Borussia", the back walls are faced with glazed tiles.

The whole building is occupied by the bureaus of the newspaper, except the side wings in which are the printing presses, these rooms have bulb-iron ceilings for greater strength. The ceilings are everywhere solid and, in order to isolate the sound and the vibration, are fitted with layers of cork and felt. The building surrounds a middle and back courtyard under both of which are basements.

344 [1909: 67]

Das Kaufmannshaus der Aktiengefellfchaft in Hamburg, Gr. Bleichen 31 und Bleichenbrücke 10, von drei Seiten freiliegend, nach dem Entwurfe der Architekten

344 [1909: 67]

La maison de commerce de la société par actions à Hambourg, Gr. Bleichen 31 et Bleichenbrücke 10, libre de trois côtés, a été élevée dans l'espace d'un an par les archi-

344 [1909: 67]

The "Kaufmannshaus der Aktiengesellschaft" at Gr. Bleichen 31 and Bleichenbrücke 10, Hamburg, lies on three sides free. It was built from the design of the architects

H. Stammann und G. Zinnow im Laufe eines Jahres ausgeführt, hat 2 116 000 Mark Baukoften verurfacht, fo daß auf den Kubikmeter umbauten Raum 21,6 Mark zu rechnen find. Die beiden Straßenfronten öffnen fich im Erdgefchoß zu breiten Schaufenftern, die drei nächftfolgenden Obergefchoffe find mittelft durchgehender Pfeiler in Felder geteilt, die durch Fensteröffnungen ganz ausgefüllt werden und im dritten Obergefchoß durch Korbbogen gefchloffen find, über denen ein kräftiges Gefims fortläuft. Die Fenfter im erften und zweiten Obergefchoß find erkerartig vorgebaut. Das über dem Gefims folgende, etwas zurücktretende Dachgefchoß ift mit kleineren, zu zweien gekuppelten Fenftern und in der Mitte jeder Straßenfront mit einem gefchweiften Giebelaufbau ausgeftattet. An zwei Ecken des Gebäudes erheben fich Turmauffäße, mit gefchweiften, im oberen Teil durchbrochenen Helmen bekrönt. Die Verblendung der Fronten befteht im Erdgefchoß der Straßenfronten und im Kellergefchoß der Wafferfront aus bayerifchem hellem Granit, in den Obergefchoffen aus weißen Laubaner Porzellanziegeln. Die Fenftererker find aus Schmiedeeifen hergeftellt.

Das Gebäude umfchließt einen inneren, in der Höhe des Erdgefchoffes mit Glas überdeckten Lichthof, zu dem der Haupteingang durch ein Veftibül führt. Ein zweiter Eingang verbindet mittelft eines langen Flurs die beiden Haupttreppen. Eine Einfahrt führt zu einem offenen Hofe an der Nachbarfeite. Das Kellergefchoß enthält ein Reftaurant an der Wafferfeite, die Räume für Heizung und die Mafchinen der vier elektrifchen Aufzüge fowie die zu den Läden gehörigen Lagerräume. Die vier oberen Stockwerke find zu Kontoren und Mufterlagern beftimmt, das Dachgefchoß ift zu Akten- und Arbeitsräumen eingerichtet. Für zwei Hauswärter find im vierten und im Dachgefchoß kleinere Wohnungen vorgefehen. Die Fundamentierung des Gebäudes gefchah auf einer Betonplatte mit Trägereinlage, teils auf vorhandenen Fundamenten, teils auf eingerammten Pfählen. Im Innern find gußeiferne Säulen als Stützen, Könenfche Voutendecken auf Trägern und Trennwände aus Schlackenbeton oder poröfen Ziegeln verwendet. Als Heizung dient eine Warmwaffer-Niederdruckheizung.

345 [1909; 85]

In einer Bauzeit vom Jahre 1906 bis 1909 ift der Anbau zum Grand Hôtel Royal in Stockholm mit einem Koftenaufwand von rund 1 800 000 Kronen nach dem Entwurfe des Architekten E. Stenhammer entftanden. An der Ecke des Erdgefchoffes öffnet fich nach beiden Fronten eine überwölbte Vorhalle, aus der man in das Veftibül und zur Haupttreppe gelangt. Der ausgekragte runde Eckerker im erften Stock

tectes H. Stammann & G. Zinnow pour la somme de 2 116 000 Marks: le mètre cube de construction coûte 21,6 Marks. Les deux façades sur rue s'ouvrent au rez-de-chaussée en larges devantures de magasin: les trois étages supérieurs sont divisés en panneaux par des piliers; ces panneaux sont entièrement occupés par des fenêtres et fermés dans le haut par des arcs en anse de panier, audessus desquels s'étend une vigoureuse corniche. Les fenêtres du premier et du second étages font légèrement saillie. L'étage du toit, audessus de la corniche est un peu en retrait, il est pourvu de petites fenêtres accouplées et au milieu d'un pignon de profil ondulé. Aux deux angles du bâtiment s'élèvent des tours avec des toits ondulés, à jour dans leur partie supérieure. Le revêtement des façades sur rue, au rez-de-chaussée, et du sous-sol du côté de l'eau consiste en granit clair de la Haute Bavière; aux étages supérieurs, en briques émaillées. Les fenêtres saillantes sont construites en fer forgé.

Le bâtiment entoure une cour intérieure vitrée à la hauteur du rez-de-chaussée: l'entrée principale y conduit par un vestibule. Une autre entrée relie les deux escaliers principaux au moyen d'un long corridor. Une porte cochère conduit à une cour ouverte sur le côté. Le sous-sol contient un restaurant du côté de l'eau, les locaux pour le chauffage et les machines des quatre lifts électriques, ainsi que les entrepôts pour les quatre magasins. Les quatre étages supérieurs sont disposés en comptoirs et magasins: le toit en dépôts d'actes et en bureaux. On a placé deux petits appartements pour gardiens au quatrième étage et dans le toit. Les fondations de l'édifice furent placées en partie sur une plaque de béton armée de sommiers, en partie sur d'anciens fondements et en partie sur pilotis. A l'intérieur se trouvent des colonnes en fonte, des voûtes système Könen sur poutres en fer, des cloisons en béton d'escarbilles ou de briques creuses. Un calorifère à eau chaude à basse pression livre la chaleur.

345 [1909; 85]

L'agrandissement du Grand Hôtel Royal à Stockholm a été construit de l'année 1906 à 1909 pour la somme de 1 800 000 Couronnes, d'après les plans de M. E. Stenhammer, architecte. Un porche voûté s'ouvre sur les deux faces, à l'angle du rez-de-chaussée, ce porche donne accès au vestibule et à l'escalier principal. La tourelle ronde, en saillie au premier étage et le balcon du même étage appartiennent

H. Stammann and G. Zinnow in the course of one year at a cost of 2 116 000 Marks, that is 21,6 Marks per cubic meter of built space. The two street frontages open on the ground floor on broad shop windows, the three following upper storeys are divided by pillars into panels which are quite filled up with windows and finished off in the third upper storey by arches over which is a massive moulding. The windows of the first and second upper storey have projecting bays. The roof storey over the moulding recedes a little and has small windows in groups of two, in the middle of each street frontage is a curved gable erection. On two corners of the building are towers with ornamented helmet shaped roofs. The facing of the façade is, on the ground floor of the street frontage and on the basement of the water front, of light Bavarian granite, on the upper storeys of white Lauban porcelain tiles. The window bays are of wrought iron.

The building extends round a skylighted courtyard roofed with glass of the same height as the ground floor, to this the principal entrance leads through a vestibule. A second entrance connects the two principal staircases by means of a long corridor. A waggon entrance leads to an open yard on the other side. The basement contains a restaurant on the water front, the rooms for heating apparatus and the machines for the four electric lifts; here too are storerooms for the various shops. The four upper storeys are set apart for bureaus and show rooms, the roof storey is reserved for archives and work-rooms. On the fourth floor and in the roof storey are small lodgings for the house porters. The foundation of the building is of beton with girders partly on an existing fundament and partly on piles. The interior is supported by cast iron pillars, has "Könen Vouten" ceilings on girders and separating walls of beton or porous bricks. The heating is warm water low pressure system.

345 [1909; 85]

The Grand Hotel Royal in Stockholm has received considerable additions and alterations which occupied a period from 1906 to 1909 at a cost of 1 800 000 Kronen. The design was by the architect E. Stenhammer. At the corner of the ground floor is a vaulted entrance portal opening on two frontages, this leads to the vestibule and the principal staircase.

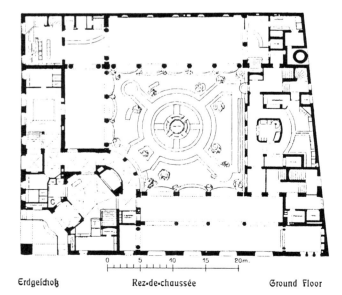

Erdgefchoß   Rez-de-chaussée   Ground Floor

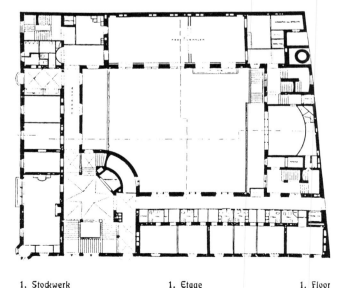

1. Stockwerk   1. Etage   1. Floor

und ein daselbst an der Front vortretender Balkon gehören zu einem Lesesaal. Die einfach gehaltenen Fassaden sind teils mit grauem Kalkstein, teils mit gelbem Verputz bekleidet; das Dach hat eine Metalleindeckung erhalten. Den Kern der inneren Anordnung der Hotelräume bildet der mit einem Glasdach überdeckte Wintergarten in zentraler Lage, nach dem sich im Erdgeschoß zwei Speisesäle und ein großer Cafésalon mit rundbogigen Säulenarkaden öffnen. Die Gastzimmer verteilen sich auf vier Obergeschosse. Die Wände des Wintergartens sind mit gelbrotem poliertem Stuckputz bedeckt; im übrigen bilden Eisen- und Betonkonstruktionen die Hauptbestandteile des Baues.

à une salle de lecture. Les façades traitées d'une façon réservée sont en partie en pierre grise, en partie en crépissage jaune; le toit est recouvert en métal. Le centre de la disposition intérieure des pièces de l'hôtel est formé par un jardin d'hiver vitré, sur lequel s'ouvrent au rez-de-chaussée deux salles à manger et un grand café-salon avec colonnes et arcades à plein cintre. Les chambres d'étrangers se répartissent sur les quatre étages supérieurs. Les parois du jardin d'hiver sont recouvertes de stuc poli rouge-jaune; le bâtiment est presque entièrement construit en fer et en béton.

The round projecting bay and balcony on the first floor open from the Reading room. The facades are simple in design, and are partly of grey limestone and partly of yellow plaster. The roof has a covering of metal. The centre of the interior of the hotel is a "winter garden" with a glass roof, skylighted; from this open on the ground floor two dining saloons, and a spacious café with arched pillars. The guest chambers are distributed over the four upper storeys. The walls of the winter garden are of yellowish-red polished plaster the remainder of the building is principally of beton and iron.

346 [1909: 56]

Das zweistöckige Landhaus in Charlottenburg-Westend, Plantanenallee 14, ist nach dem Entwurfe der Architekten Wolfg. Siemering und J. Habicht etwa im Laufe eines Jahres zur Ausführung gekommen. An den nahezu quadratischen Baukörper schließt sich an einer Front eine halbrunde geschlossene, mit Säulen besetzte Halle an, die sich über einer Terrasse erhebt und im Oberstock eine Altane trägt. Der Haupteingang führt in eine offene, vorspringende Halle und aus dieser in einen Vorraum, an welchen sich die zweigeschossige Diele mit freiliegender Treppe angliedert. Die Seitenfronten im Erdgeschoß sind einerseits durch einen ausgekragten Erker, andererseits durch einen rechteckigen Ausbau belebt. Die Fassaden sind gelb verputzt und zeigen im Obergeschoß eine ornamentale Musterung; die Fensterläden im oberen Geschoß sind grün gestrichen. Das mit roten Dachpfannen eingedeckte, allseitig abgewalmte Dach wird durch Fensteraufbauten und Luckenöffnungen unterbrochen. Im Erdgeschoß liegen die Wohnzimmer, das Speisezimmer und die Küche, während das Obergeschoß die Schlaf- und Fremdenzimmer enthält.

La maison de campagne à deux étages Plantanenallée 14 à Charlottenburg-Westend, a été construite d'après les plans de M. M. Wolfgang Siemering & J. Habicht dans le courant d'un an environ. Sur une des faces du bâtiment, à peu près carré, s'élève au dessus d'une terrasse, une halle fermée, demi-circulaire, entourée de colonnes et portant un balcon à l'étage supérieur. L'entrée principale conduit dans un porche ouvert et saillant et de ce dernier, dans un vestibule communiquant avec un hall à deux étages contenant l'escalier. Les faces latérales sont agrémentées au rez-de-chaussée, d'un côté par une tourelle saillante, de l'autre par un avant-corps quadrangulaire. Les façades sont crépies en jaune, et sont décorées d'ornements au premier étage; les volets sont peints en vert au premier étage. Le toit recouvert de tuiles rouges, construit en croupe de tous côtés, est interrompu par des lucarnes et de petites fenêtres. Au rez-de-chaussée se trouvent les chambres d'habitation, la salle-à-manger et la cuisine, tandis que le premier étage contient les chambres à coucher et d'amis.

The two storeyed country house at Plantanenallee 14, Charlottenburg-Westend, was designed by the architects Wolfgang Siemering and J. Habicht and was built in about a year. The house is nearly square, on one front is a semi-circular closed hall with pillars rising over a terrace, and over which on the upper storey is a balcony. The principal entrance leads to an open projecting hall and this to a vestibule leading to the square hall which extends upwards through two storeys with a free staircase. The side frontage of the basement is enlivened on one side by a projecting bay and on the other by a rectangular projection. The facades are of yellow plaster and on the upper storey are ornamented, the window shutters here are green. The roof is everywhere hipped, is covered with red pantiles and has windows and openings. The ground floor contains the dwelling rooms, dining room and kitchen, the upper rooms are bedrooms and spare-rooms.

347 [1909: 60]

In freier Lage und anmutiger Gruppierung erhebt sich das von Architekt Geh. Baurat Prof. G. Wickop entworfene, in einer Bauzeit von etwa einem Jahre ausgeführte Landhaus in Darmstadt, Roquetteweg 15. Das Wohnhaus einschließlich der Einfriedigung hat 132 800 Mark, das Stallgebäude 12 700 Mark Baukosten verursacht. Der Haupteingang liegt unter einer vorspringenden offenen Vorhalle, zu welcher Freitreppen emporführen. Ein zweiter Eingang mündet in den mit einer Rundung nach außen vortretenden Treppenturm; außerdem ist noch ein Aufgang zu einer Terrasse und ein Nebeneingang zur Küche angeordnet. Der flachrunde Ausbau des Salons im Erdgeschoß an der Rückseite trägt die durch einen Rücksprung verbreiterte Altane, und im Obergeschoß an der Seitenfront tritt ein flachrunder Erkerausbau hervor. Die Hauptfront ist durch einen breiten, geschwungenen Giebel ausgezeichnet, sonst sind die Dächer durch überhängende, steile Giebel abgeschlossen. Das Untergeschoß ist mit gelbgrauen Mainsandsteinquadern verblendet, die oberen Flächen zeigen Mörtelverputz, der einen zweiten gekörnten Auftrag erhalten hat. Die Hauptdächer sind mit Biberschwänzen, die des Vorbaues und des Turms mit Kupfer eingedeckt. Die Reliefs am Erker und Vorbau sind Arbeiten des Bildhauers Jobst, die Antragearbeiten sind von Bildhauer Scheich gefertigt.

Das hohe Erdgeschoß enthält eine Diele mit Windfang und von dieser zugänglich die Wohnzimmer, das Eßzimmer und die Küche. Im Obergeschoß liegen die Schlafzimmer, die Kinder- und Fremdenzimmer sowie die Mädchenkammer. Diele, Speisezimmer, Arbeits- und Musikzimmer

La maison de campagne, Roquetteweg 15 à Darmstadt forme un groupe pittoresque dans un site charmant, elle a été construite dans l'espace d'un an environ par le professeur G. Wickop, conseiller. La maison avec la clôture a coûté 132800 Marks, l'écurie 12700 Marks. L'entrée principale se trouve abritée sous un porche ouvert et saillant, auquel conduisent des escaliers. Une autre entrée aboutit à un escalier formant saillie arrondie sur le dehors, on a en outre disposé une montée sur une terrasse et une entrée secondaire pour la cuisine. La saillie en segment du salon sur la façade postérieure au rez-de-chaussée porte une terrasse augmentée d'une partie rentrante. Au premier étage d'une des faces latérales, on voit saillir une tourelle arrondie. La façade principale est décorée d'un large fronton de contours ondulés, les toits sont du reste terminés par des pignons saillants et abrupts. Le rez-de-chaussée est revêtu de pierre du Main grise-jaunâtre; les surfaces supérieures sont crépies et ensuite granulées. Les toits principaux sont recouverts en tuiles, ceux du porche et de la tour en cuivre. Les décorations en relief de la tourelle et de l'avant-corps sont dûs à Mr. Jobst sculpteur, Mr. Scheich sculpteur a exécuté le modelage des façades.

Le rez-de-chaussée élevé contient un hall avec tambour, la chambre d'habitation, la salle-à-manger et la cuisine donnent sur le hall. A l'étage supérieur se trouvent les chambres à coucher, d'enfants et d'amis ainsi que les chambres de bonnes. Le hall, la salle-à-manger, la chambre de travail et celle de musique, ainsi que le salon

The country house at Roquetteweg 15, Darmstadt, was designed by the architect Geh. Baurat Prof. E. Wickop and is distinguished by its free position and its effective grouping. The house, including boundary wall, cost 132 800 Marks; the stabling 12 700 Marks, the time occupied was about one year. The principal entrance lies under a projecting open portico, to which a free flight of steps leads; a second entrance is in a projecting circular tower with steps; another entrance leads from a terrace, and a kitchen entrance is also provided. The round bay of the drawing room on the ground floor has on one side a recess in which is built a broad balcony, on the side frontage of the upper storey a round projecting bay is placed. The principal front is crowned by a broad curved gable, the other parts of the roof are finished off by steep projecting gables. The lower part of the house is faced with yellow-grey Main sandstone square stones, the upper surfaces show mortar plaster with a second application of coarse-grained plaster. The principal roofs are covered with flat red tiles, the portico and the tower with copper. The reliefs on the bays and projections are by the sculptor Jobst, the stucco work by the sculptor Scheich.

The high ground floor contains a square hall, from this open all the sitting rooms, the dining room and the kitchen. On the upper storeys are the bedrooms, the nurseries and spare rooms, the servants' bedrooms. The hall, the dining room, the study and music room as

fowie der Salon find reich durch feine Holzarbeiten geichmückt. Es ift eine Warmwaffer-
heizung, eine Warmwafferleitung und eine Ent-
ftaubungsanlage eingerichtet.

sont richement décorés de fins travaux de menuiserie. La maison est pourvue d'un calorifère a
eau chaude, d'une conduite d'eau chaude et d'un
appareil de nettoyage.

well as the drawing room are richly ornamented
with beautiful wood-work. The house is heated
with warm water, and has a suction cleaning
apparatus.

348 [1909: 91]

Die Straßenfront des Landhaufes in Kopenhagen, Engskistevey 6, wird durch einen
die ganze Breite einnehmenden Giebel mit einwärts geichwungenen Konturen in eins zufammen-
gefaßt und ift mit einem vom Boden aufgehenden
polygonalen Erkeraufbau geichmückt, der mit
einer Altane abichließt. Die Spitze des Giebels
wird durch eine Sonnenuhr bekrönt. Urheber

348 [1909: 91]

La façade sur la rue de la maison de
campagne Engskistevey 6, à Copenhague, est entièrement couronnée d'un pignon
aux contours ondulés en dedans, elle est ornée
en outre d'un avant-corps polygonal montant de
fond et surmonté d'un balcon. Le sommet du
fronton est surmonté d'une horloge solaire. Mr.

348 [1909: 91]

The country house at Engskistevey 6,
Copenhagen, has on its whole breadth
a gable with a curved recess, and is ornamented
by a projecting bay extending upwards from the
ground floor, polygonal in form and ending in
an open terrace. The top of the gable is
crowned with a sun-dial. The house was

| Erdgeichoß | Rez-de-chaussée | Ground Floor | Schnitt | Coup | Section | 1. Stockwerk | 1. Etage | 1. Floor |

des im Laufe eines Jahres für die Koftenfumme
von 28000 Kronen errichteten Baues ift Architekt
Alb. Oppenheim. Die Faffaden find aus hand-
geftrichenen gefugten Ziegeln hergeftellt. Das
Erdgeichoß enthält die Diele mit freiliegender
Treppe, eine Anzahl Wohnzimmer, die Küche
mit befonderem Eingang von außen und eine
feitwärts an das Speifezimmer ftoßende Laube.
In dem ausgebauten Dachgeichoß liegen die
Schlafzimmer, feitwärts von den etwas gegen die
unteren Fronten zurückgeletzten Fenfterwänden
begrenzt. Im Kellergeichoß ift eine Zentralheizung mit Ventilationsanlage eingerichtet.

Alb. Oppenheim est l'architecte de cet édifice
construit dans le cours d'une année pour le
prix de 28000 couronnes. Les façades sont
en briques jointoyées. Le rez-de-chaussée
contient le hall avec escalier suspendu, un
certain nombre de chambres, la cuisine avec
entrée séparée et une veranda adjacente au
coté de la salle à manger. Dans le toit se
trouvent les chambres à coucher mansardées
par la paroi des fenêtres placée un peu en
retrait sur les murs de face. Au sous-sol on
a installé un chauffage central avec ventilation.

designed by the architect Alb. Oppenheim, it
occupied one year to build and cost 28000
Kronen. The facades are of brick, hand-pointed.
The ground-floor contains the hall with a free
staircase, a number of rooms, the kitchen with
a separate entrance from outside and a balcony
lying at the side in connection with the dining
room. In the roof storey lie the bedrooms,
the walls of which lie on the recess of the
front gable. In the basement is the central
heating apparatus with a ventilation arrangement.

349 [1909: 99]

Das in parkartiger Umgebung gelegene, zur
Aufnahme von Gäften eingerichtete Landhaus in Summerville, S. A., ift ein Werk der
Architekten Kenep & Wendel. Das lang-
geftreckte Gebäude ift reichlich mit offenen und
geichloffenen Hallen ausgeftattet, die mit Altanen
abichließen. Das Erdgeichoß ift als Putzbau ausgeführt mit einzelnen Teilen in gefugtem Ziegelmauerwerk. Das Obergeichoß ift im Dachraum
untergebracht und wird in den Fronten von den

349 [1909: 99]

La maison pension, en forme de villa, située
dans une sorte de parc à Summerville
S. A. est l'œuvre de M. M. Kenep & Wendel,
architectes. L'édifice allongé est abondamment
fourni de halles fermées et ouvertes couronnées
de terrasses. Le rez-de-chaussée est en
maçonnerie crépie, avec quelques parties de
briques jointoyées. L'étage supérieur est installé
dans le toit, et est bordé sur les façades par
les surfaces brisées du toit. Le pignon et le

349 [1909: 99]

The country house at Summerville, S. A.,
was designed by the architects Kenep and
Wendel. It has park like grounds and is intended for the accommodation of guests. The
long extendig building has numerous open balconies and various terraces. It is a plaster
building, with parts in pointed brick-work on the
upper storey (which is contained in the roof)
the walls are formed by the steep sides of the

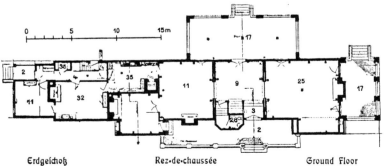

| Erdgeichoß | Rez-de-chaussée | Ground Floor | 1. Stockwerk | 1. Etage | 1. Floor |

Steilflächen des gebrochenen Daches begrenzt.
Die Giebel und die Dachflächen find beichiefert.
An die Eingangshalle im Erdgeichoß, die mit
Vorplatz und Treppe in Verbindung fteht, ichließen
fich an den Fronten eine offene Halle und eine
Terraffe an, fowie beiderfeits der Salon und
zwei Speifezimmer. Weiterhin folgen Küche,
Speifekammer und Dienereßzimmer. Das Ober-
geichoß enthält geräumige Schlafräume, meift
mit Ausgängen nach den Altanen verfehen.

toit sont recouverts en ardoises. Le porche d'entrée, au rez-de-chaussée, communiquant avec
le vestibule et l'escalier, s'ouvre en avant sur
une halle ouverte et une terrasse, des deux
côtes, sur le salon et deux salles-à-manger.
Ensuite viennent la cuisine, le garde-manger et
la chambre à manger des domestiques. L'étage
supérieur contient de grands chambres à coucher
ayant la plupart des sorties sur des balcons.

broken roof. The gables and roof surfaces are
slated. On the entrance hall on the ground
floor, which is in connection with the vestibule
and staircase, joins a long open hall and terrace,
this is repeated on the drawing room and the
two dining rooms. In the interior are kitchen
pantry and servants' hall. The upper storey
contains spacious bedrooms most of them leading
to terraces.

Das Geſchäftshaus in Berlin, Ritter-
ſtraße 77/78, von Architekt O. Kaufmann
entworfen, hat eine Bauzeit von 9 Monaten und
einen Koſtenaufwand von rd. 580 000 Mark erfordert. Die in thüringiſchem Muſchelkalkſtein
verblendete Faſſade wird durch die vom Erdgeſchoß bis in das dritte Obergeſchoß reichenden,
oben mittelſt einer bogenförmig geſchwungenen
Giebelarchitektur abgeſchloſſenen Pfeiler kräftig
zu einer Einheit verbunden. Im Erdgeſchoß
öffnen ſich außer der Einfahrt im Korbbogen
überwölbte, flachrund ausgebogene Schaufenſter-
öffnungen. In den drei Obergeſchoſſen treten
ſenkrecht zuſammengezogene Fenſterausbauten
hervor. Das vierte Obergeſchoß iſt in Fenſtergruppen mit hermenartigen Teilungspfeilern auf-
gelöſt. Die figuralen Bildhauerarbeiten der Faſſade
ſind von Frydag modelliert und die Malereien
der Einfahrt hat R. Rohland gefertigt. Das Dach
iſt mit grauen holländiſchen Pfannen eingedeckt.

Das einen mittleren und einen hinteren Hof
umſchließende Gebäude enthält im Erdgeſchoß
Läden, in den vier Obergeſchoſſen Geſchäftsräume.
Die Grundrißgeſtaltung wurde teilweiſe durch die
ſtehengebliebenen Reſte von zwei älteren Häuſern
bedingt, an deren Stelle der Neubau getreten iſt.

La maison de commerce, Ritterstrasse 77
et 78 à Berlin, elevée par Mr. O. Kaufmann architecte, a coûté 580 000 Marks en bloc,
la construction a duré 9 mois. La façade revêtue
de pierre calcaire de Thuringe est traitée d'une
façon uniforme, au moyen de piliers montant
du rez-de-chaussée au troisième étage et portant
une architecture de pignons à arcs ondulés.
Au rez-de-chaussée s'ouvrent, outre l'entrée en
anse de panier, des devantures de magasin à arc
surbaissé. Aux trois étages supérieurs, on voit
saillir des groupes de fenêtres reliées entre
elles verticalement. Le quatrième étage est
divisé en groupes de fenêtres avec meneaux en
forme d'hermes. Les décorations figurales de
la façade sont de Mr. Frydag sculpteur, tandis
que Mr. R. Rohland a exécuté les peintures
de l'entrée. Le toit est recouvert en tuiles grises
de Hollande.

Le bâtiment entourant une cour centrale et
une postérieure contient des magasins au rez-
de-chaussée, et dans les quatre étages supérieurs des comptoirs. La disposition du plan
fut en partie dictée par les restes de deux anciennes maisons que la nouvelle construction
a remplacées.

The business house at Ritterstrasse 77/78,
Berlin, was designed by the architect
O. Kaufmann. It occupied 9 months in building
and cost 580 000 Marks. The facade is faced
with Thuringian shell-limestone, from the ground
floor to the third upper storey it is brought by
the use of pillars into one harmonious design
and is finished off at the roof by an arched
architectural erection in the form of gables. On
the ground floor is a carriage entrance and
several shop-windows, vaulted and rounded, to
which doors also are added. On the three upper
storeys are window projections joined perpendicularly. On the fourth upper storey the pillars
dividing the window groups have sculptured heads
as capitals. The statuary of the facade is modelled
by Frydag, the painting over the entrance is
by R. Rohland. The roof is covered with grey
Dutch pantiles.

The building encloses one middle courtyard
and one back courtyard; it has on the ground
floor shops and on the upper storeys business
premises. The ground plan was so designed
as to make use of two old houses, parts of which
remained standing, on these the new building
has been erected.

Das Régierungsgebäude in Kristiania
bildet ein großes umſchloſſenes Viereck mit
an beiden Längsfronten vorſpringenden Flügelbauten und einer Anzahl größerer und kleinerer

Le palais du gouvernement, à Christiania
forme un grand carré fermé, avec ailes saillantes sur les deux côtés allongés, il contient
plusieurs cours de dimensions différentes. Mr.

The Government Official Building in
Christiania is a large enclosed square,
having on each of the two long frontages, projecting side wings and a number of large and

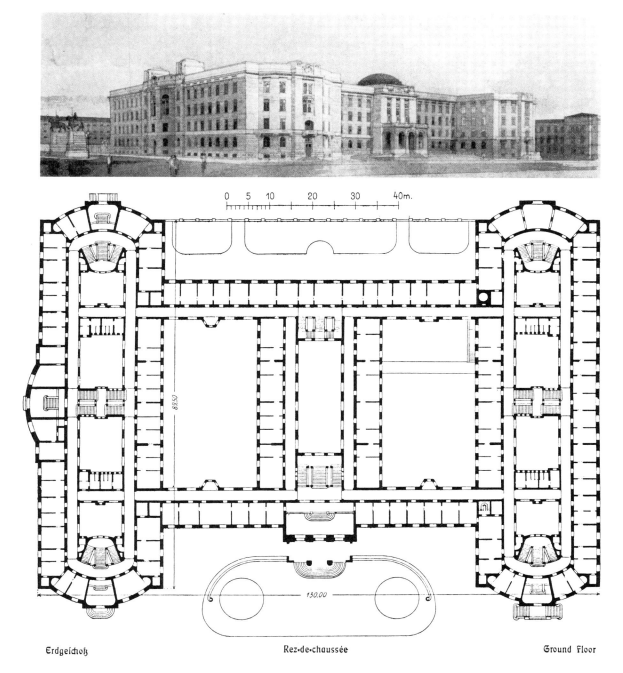

Erdgeſchoß · Rez-de-chaussée · Ground Floor

Innenhöfe. Architekt der Fassaden ist H. Bull, die Grundrisse sind von Architekt S. Lenschow entworfen. Die Bausumme ist insgesamt mit 1553000 Kronen veranschlagt. In der Bauzeit vom Jahre 1901 angefangen ist bis jetzt nur das südliche Dritteil des ganzen Gebäudes vollendet worden. Die Hauptfront wird durch den Mittelbau mit vorgelegter Unterfahrtshalle und die in flacher Rundung heraustretenden, noch durch ein Mittelrisalit geteilten Flügelbauten gegliedert. Die vier Geschosse und ein Untergeschoß enthaltenden Fronten sind mit rauhbossierten roten Granitquadern bekleidet, über dem Erdgeschoß von einem glatt bearbeiteten Gurt- und Brüstungsgesims unterbrochen und durch ein Hauptgesims mit glattem Fries, über dem sich eine Attika erhebt, abgeschlossen. Über dem Mittelbau tritt eine flache Kuppel hervor. Die eine Seitenfront ist wieder durch einen flachrund vortretenden Mittelbau mit flankierenden Türmen geteilt. Die Fenster des Erdgeschosses sind rundbogig, die des ersten und zweiten Obergeschosses geradlinig überdeckt, während die des dritten Obergeschosses über den gleichfalls geradlinigen Sturzen noch im Korbbogen gebildete Blenden zeigen. Die Stockwerke enthalten zahlreiche Amtszimmer, Bureaus und Sitzungssäle sowie eine Anzahl meist dreiarmiger Verbindungstreppen, die ebenso wie die Verbindungsgänge von den Höfen ausreichendes Licht erhalten.

H. Bull, architecte, a composé les façades, Mr. S. Lenschow, architecte, les plans. Le devis s'élève en tout à 1553000 Couronnes. Commencé en 1901, l'édifice n'est terminé aujourd'hui qu'au tiers de sa partie méridionale. La façade principale sera divisée par le corps central avec porche saillant et par les ailes de plan circulaire, partagées au milieu par un avant-corps. Les quatre étages et le rez-de-chaussée des façades sont revêtues de bossages de granit rouge; au dessus du rez-de-chaussée, s'étend un cordon poli, le tout est couronné d'une corniche à frise lisse au dessus de laquelle s'élève un attique. Au dessus du corps central se trouve une coupole plate. Une des façades latérales est décorée d'un avant-corps arrondi, flanqué de tours. Les fenêtres du rez-de-chaussée sont à plein cintre, celles du premier et du second étages sont droites, tandis que celles du troisième étage portent audessus de leur linteau droit un tympan formé d'un arc en anse de panier. Les étages contiennent de nombreux bureaux, chambres de travail et de conférences, ainsi que plusieurs escaliers, dont la plupart sont à trois rampes, ces escaliers, ainsi que les corridors reçoivent une abondante lumière des cours.

small interior courtyards. The architect of the facade is H. Bull, the ground plan is by the architect S. Lenschow. The cost estimate amounts to 1533000 Kronen. It was begun in 1901, and up to the present, only the south end of the building is completed, about a third of the whole. The principal front has a centre erection with a projecting carriage entrance and is further enlarged by side wings with circular projections. The four storeys and the basement are faced on their fronts with square bossed granite stones, over this is a flat moulding, and at the top a principal moulding with a flat frieze over which is a terrace. Over the middle erection is a cupola. The side frontage has again a slightly curved middle erection projecting, and is flanked by towers. The windows on the ground floor have rounded arches those of the first and second storeys are straight-lined, while those of the third upper storey over the straightlined lintels have slightly arched mouldings. On each storey are numerous offices, bureaus, committee rooms which are reached by various staircases most of them in three flights. All these as well as the corridors leading to the courtyard are well lighted.

352 [1909; 81]

Das Universitäts-Klubgebäude in Chicago, Ill., hat die Form eines sogenannten „Wolkenkratzers" und steigt in neun Stockwerken und einem ausgebauten Dachgeschoß auf. Der

352 [1909; 81]

Le batiment du club de l'Université à Chicago (Ill.) a la forme d'un "gratte nuages" et s'élève en neuf étages et un toit. Le projet est dû à M. M. Hollabird & Roche.

352 [1909; 81]

The University Club House at Chicago, is one of the so-called "skyscrapers" and rises to a height of nine storeys and a roof storey. The architects were Messrs Hollabird

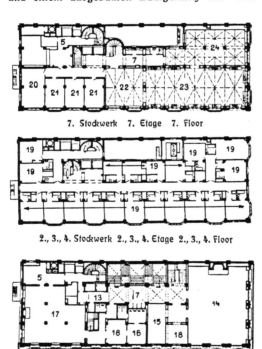

7. Stockwerk   7. Etage   7. Floor

2., 3., 4. Stockwerk   2., 3., 4. Etage   2., 3., 4. Floor

1. Stockwerk   1. Etage   1. Floor

Erdgeschoß   Rez-de-chaussée   Ground Floor

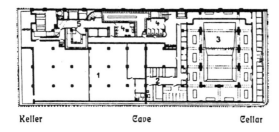

Keller   Cave   Cellar

8. Stockwerk   8. Etage   8. Floor

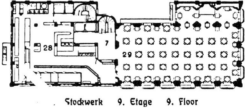

Stockwerk   9. Etage   9. Floor

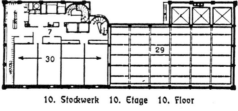

10. Stockwerk   10. Etage   10. Floor

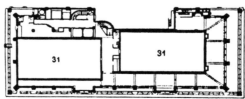

11. Stockwerk   11. Etage   11. Floor

0 5 10   20   50 m

1. Keller	17. Salle de restaurant pour dames
2. Türk. Bad	18. Cabinet de conversation
3. Schwimm- und Röm. Bad	19. Chambres à coucher
4. Toiletten	20. Bureau du directeur
5. Raum für die Angestellten	21. Salle de restaurant individuelle
6. Vestibül	22. Café
7. Halle	23. Salle de billard
8. Eingang für die Damen	24. Salle de restaurant
9. Läden	25. Salle de réunion
10. Bureau	26. Bibliothèque
11. Waschraum	27. Salon
12. Chekraum	28. Cuisine
13. Vorzimmer	29. Grande salle de restaurant
14. Frühstückszimmer	30. Salles de repos
15. Schreibzimmer	31. Terrains de jeu en terrasse
16. Damenzimmer	
17. Damen-Speisezimmer	1. Cellar
18. Konversationszimmer	2. Turkish Bath
19. Schlafzimmer	3. Swimming Pool and
20. Direktorzimmer	Roman Bath
21. Einzel-Speisezimmer	4. Lavatories
22. Café	5. Personnel
23. Billardzimmer	6. Vestibule
24. Spielzimmer	7. Hall
25. Versammlungszimmer	8. Women's Entrance
26. Bibliothek	9. Shops
27. Gesellschaftszimmer	10. Office
28. Küche	11. Wash Room
29. Großer Speisesaal	12. Check Room
30. Ruheräume	13. Anteroom
31. Dachspielplätze	14. Breakfast Room
	15. Study
1. Cave	16. Women's Sitting-Room
2. Bains turcs	17. Women's Dining Room
3. Piscine et bains romains	18. Sitting-Room
4. Cabinets	19. Bedroom
5. Salle de service	20. Director's Office
6. Vestibule	21. Individual Dining Rooms
7. Hall	22. Café
8. Entrée réservée aux dames	23. Billiards Room
9. Commerces	24. Dining Room
10. Bureau	25. Assembly Room
11. Lavabos	26. Library
12. Salle de service	27. Drawing-Room
13. Antichambre	28. Kitchen
14. Salle du petit déjeuner	29. Large Dining Hall
15. Salle d'écriture	30. Rest Rooms
16. Salon pour dames	31. Roof Courts

Entwurf ſtammt von den Architekten Holabird & Roche. Die in Hauſtein verblendeten Faſſaden sind in Formen engliſcher Gotik ausgebildet und mit einer Anzahl flach vorſpringender, durch mehrere Geſchoſſe geführter Erker und in den oberen Geſchoſſen mit vorgekragten Balkons ausgeſtattet. Das Dachgeſims, ebenſo die Erker, ſind mit einem Zinnenkranz bekrönt. Das Dachgeſchoß iſt mit ſeinen Fronten etwas gegen die unteren zurückgeſetzt und mit einem Giebeldache überdeckt, in welches einzelne Fenſteraufbauten einſchneiden. Das Untergeſchoß enthält Bäder und Heizanlagen, das Erdgeſchoß iſt teilweiſe zu Läden benutzt, auf die übrigen Geſchoſſe verteilen ſich Eßſäle, zahlreiche Wohn- und Schlafzimmer, Billard- und Spielſäle, Bibliothek- und Leſeräume. Das Dachgeſchoß endlich enthält große Spielräume. Die Stockwerke ſind durch Treppen und mehrere Aufzüge mit einander in Verbindung geſetzt.

353 [1910; 1]

Als umfängliche, mehrere Höfe einſchließende Baugruppe stellt sich das Cecilienhaus in Charlottenburg, Berlinerſtraße 137, dar. Das Gebäude ist von dem Vaterländiſchen Frauenverein in Charlottenburg unter weſentlicher Förderung durch den Schatzmeiſter des Vereins, Stadtverordneten Jachmann, und mit Unterſtützung der Stadt errichtet und dient der geſamten freien Wohlfahrtspflege Charlottenburgs. Der Entwurf ſtammt vom Architekten Stadtbauinſpektor W. Spickendorff. Als Mitarbeiter an der Entwurfsbearbeitung und Detaillierung war Architekt Stein tätig, die örtliche Bauleitung beſorgte Regierungsbauführer Böhringer. Als zeitweiliger Vertreter des Verfaſſers des Entwurfs fungierte Architekt Stadtbauinſpektor Walter, beſonders betreffs des inneren Ausbaues. Für die techniſchen Betriebseinrichtungen war Stadtbauinſpektor Meyer beirätig. Modelle zu den Bildhauerarbeiten, namentlich der Köpfe eines Kriegers und einer Schweſter an der Straßenfront, lieferten Breitkopf-Coſel, Latt und Hillmann & Heinemann. Die Bauzeit dauerte vom Februar 1907 bis April 1909, die Einweihung fand im Mai 1909 statt. Die Baukosten betrugen 1 230 000 Mark.

Die einſchließlich des Zwiſchengeſchoſſes fünfſtöckige Fassade in der Berlinerſtraße enthält im Erdgeſchoß die bis zum erſten Stock reichende Durchfahrt und zu beiden Seiten Läden; im fünften Geſchoß ist eine in ganzer Breite durchgehende auf Pfeilern ruhende Loggia vorgekragt, über der sich ein flacher Giebel in gebrochener Linie erhebt. Ein bekrönender Dachreiterturm dient als Wahrzeichen, um die Stätte der Nächſtenliebe für Hilfesuchende zu bezeichnen. Die Hoffronten sind zwar einfach, aber doch fassadenmäßig ausgeſtaltet. Über den Dienſtwohnungen, der Klinik und den Wohnräumen der Schwestern sind Dachgärten angelegt. Die Fassade an der Berlinerſtraße ist in hydrauliſchem, naturfarbigem Mörtel verputzt, unter mäßiger Verwendung von Hauſteinen für einzelne Gliederungen. Der Sockel besteht aus Niedermendiger Basaltlava, die sonstigen Hauſteinglieder sind aus Harzer Muſchelkalk hergestellt. Das hohe Dach ist mit holländiſchen Pfannen eingedeckt, der Dachreiter mit Kupfer. Die Durchfahrt ist mit Cadiner Flieſen bekleidet, die Decke derſelben mit Cadiner Majoliken. Die Hoffronten sind größtenteils in hydrauliſchem, naturfarbenem Mörtelputz hergestellt, die Sockel aus sächſiſchem Granit, die Hauſteingliederungen aus Ettringer Tuffstein. Die massiven Kohlmetzdecken tragen die Dachgärten und ein mit Rathenower Ziegeln ummauertes Wasserbassin.

Im Zwiſchengeſchoß an der vorderen Durchfahrt liegt die Pförtnerwohnung, im ersten und zweiten Stock je eine Wohnung für den Direktor und den Schriftleiter der Zeitſchrift „Das rote Kreuz", den dritten Stock nehmen die Räume für die Schweſterſchaft ein. An der Durchfahrt ist das Pförtnerzimmer untergebracht, ebenſo die Fürsorgeſtelle für Lungenkranke.

Am Hof 1 enthält das Zwiſchengeſchoß die Wohnung des Hausinſpektors, der erste Stock die Haus-

353 [1910; 1]

L'établissement „Cecilienhaus" situé à Berlin-Charlottenburg, Berlinerstraße 137, forme un vaste ensemble comprenant plusieurs cours. Le bâtiment fut construit par l'association patriotique des femmes de Charlottenburg avec le soutien actif de son trésorier, le conseiller municipal Jachmann, et la collaboration de la ville. Cette institution de bienfaisance assure soins et assistance aux habitants de Charlottenburg. Les plans furent exécutés par l'architecte W. Spickendorff, en collaboration avec l'architecte Stein. Le maître d'œuvre Böhringer fut chargé de la direction des travaux. L'architecte Walter assura le remplacement temporaire de l'initiateur des plans, en particulier pour l'aménagement intérieur. L'inspecteur municipal du bâtiment Meyer fut nommé responsable des installations techniques. Les modèles des ouvrages sculptés, en particulier la tête d'un guerrier ainsi qu'une infirmière ornant la façade sur rue, furent exécutés par Breitkopf-Cosel, Latt et Hillmann & Heinemann. Les travaux durèrent du mois de février 1907 au mois d'avril 1909 et coûtèrent la somme de 1 230 000 marks. L'inauguration eut lieu en mai 1909.

La façade de cinq étages, entresol compris, donnant sur la Berlinerstraße, comprend, au rez-de-chaussée, flanqué par deux commerces, un passage s'élevant jusqu'au premier étage. Une loggia, occupant toute la largeur de l'édifice et reposant sur des piliers, se dégage du cinquième étage. Un pignon plat aux lignes brisées coiffe l'ensemble. Un clocheton, symbole d'assistance et d'amour de son prochain, se détache du toit. Les façades sur cour, traitées simplement, s'harmonisent parfaitement avec le reste de l'édifice. Des jardins-terrasses sont aménagés au-dessus des logements de fonction et des pièces d'habitation des infirmières. La façade donnant sur la Berlinerstraße est enduite d'un crépi de mortier hydraulique naturel, certains ornements sont réalisés en pierres taillées. Le socle est en lave basaltique de Niedermendingen, les parements en coquillart du Harz. Le toit est recouvert de tuiles hollandaises, le clocheton porte une couverture de cuivre. Le passage est revêtu de dalles, la voûte de majolique. Les murs extérieurs sur cour présentent un crépi de mortier hydraulique naturel, les socles sont en granit de Saxe, les ornements en tuf d'Ettringen. Des planchers massifs portent les jardins-terrasses et un bassin en briques de Rathenow.

A l'entresol, contigu au passage, est aménagé le logement du concierge. Les premiers et deuxième étages abritent les appartements du directeur et du rédacteur en chef de la revue „Das rote Kreuz". Les pièces destinées aux infirmières se trouvent au troisième étage. La loge du concierge et le bureau d'assistance aux malades pulmonaires sont situés à l'entrée.

Sur la cour 1 sont aménagés le logement de l'inspecteur de l'établissement au rez-de-chaussée, l'administration au premier étage, la maison d'édition de la revue „Das rote Kreuz" au deuxième étage et les salles de cours et de conférences au troisième étage.

353 [1910; 1]

The "Cecilienhaus" in the Charlottenburg district of Berlin (Berlinerstrasse 137) represents an architectural complex of extensive dimensions encompassing a number of inner courtyards. Construction of this institution of welfare for the needy of Charlottenburg was sponsored by the Women's Club of the Fatherland and city councillor Jachmann, with additional funding from the city government. The building was designed by the municipal building inspector W. Spickendorff; secondary drafts and details were provided by the architect Stein. Local construction was directed by the municipal building supervisor Böhringer. The municipal building inspector Walter temporarily substituted for the original architects, especially with regard to the interior design. Advice concerning the technical installations was supplied by municipal building supervisor Meyer. Sculptural work, especially the busts of a warrior and a nurse on the street front, was conceived by Breitkopf-Cosel, Latt, and Hillmann § Heinemann. Construction lasted from February 1907 to April 1909, with the dedication ceremony taking place in May 1909. Building costs amounted to 1,230,000 Marks.

The five—storey façade on the Berlinerstrasse side of the building, which includes a mezzanine, has at the ground level a carriage—way rising to the height of the first storey, and shops to either side. The entire breadth of the fifth storey is occupied by a projecting loggia supported by pillars; above it is a low—pitched gable with broken lines. The crowning ridge turret serves as a landmark for those in need of the charitable service offered here. The fronts facing the inner courtyards, although plain in design, present an agreeable façade. Roof gardens have been laid out above the staff's living quarters, the clinic and the nurses' flats. The Berlinerstrasse frontage has been rendered in naturally—coloured plaster with hydraulic binding, and a modest amount of ashlar has been employed for its individual articulations. The socle consists of basalt lava from Niedermendingen, with other architectural ornamentation being made of shell limestone from the Harz region. The high—pitched roof is covered with Dutch pantiles, the ridge turret with copper. The gateway is furnished with tile from Cadin, and its ceiling with majolica from the same area. The courtyard fronts are largely faced with natural—coloured plaster using hydraulic binding, the socles with granite from Saxony and the principal articulations are of tufa from Ettringen. Massive shale floor slabs support the roof gardens and a water basin with a surrounding wall of Rathenow brick.

The mezzanine at the front gateway contains the living quarters of the porter, the first and second storey each contain a flat for the director and the editor of the journal "The Red Cross". The third storey is reserved for nurses' rooms. A room for the porter is located next to the gateway, as is the welfare centre for those with respiratory illnesses.

The mezzanine of courtyard 1 contains the

and Roche. The facades are faced with lime stone and are English Gothic in style; they are ornamented with a number of flat projecting bays extending through several storeys, these have on the upper storeys open balconies built on to them. The roof moulding, as well as the bays have battlement ornaments. The roof storey recedes slightly and is ornamented with gables in which are various window groups. The basement contains baths and heating apparatus, the ground floor is partly used as shops; the remaining floors contain dining rooms numerous dwelling and bed rooms, billiard rooms and card-rooms, library and reading rooms. In the roof storey are spacious card-rooms. The storeys are connected with each other by various lifts and staircases.

Les façades sont revêtues de pierre et composées dans le style gothique anglais, ells sont divisées par de nombreuses tourelles peu saillantes, traversant plusieurs étages, dans le haut on voit des balcons en saillie. La corniche, ainsi que les tourelles sont couronnées de créneaux. Les surfaces du toit sont un peu en retrait sur les façades, un pignon percé de quelques groupes de fenêtres les domine. Le sous-sol est occupé par des bains et les calorifères; le rez-de-chaussée contient en partie des magasins; dans les autres étages, sont réparties des salles-à-manger, de nombreuses chambres d'habitation et chambres à coucher, des salles de billard et de jeu, des bibliothèques et des salles de lecture. Le toit enfin est disposé en grandes salles de jeu. Les étages sont réunis entre eux par des escaliers et plusieurs ascenseurs.

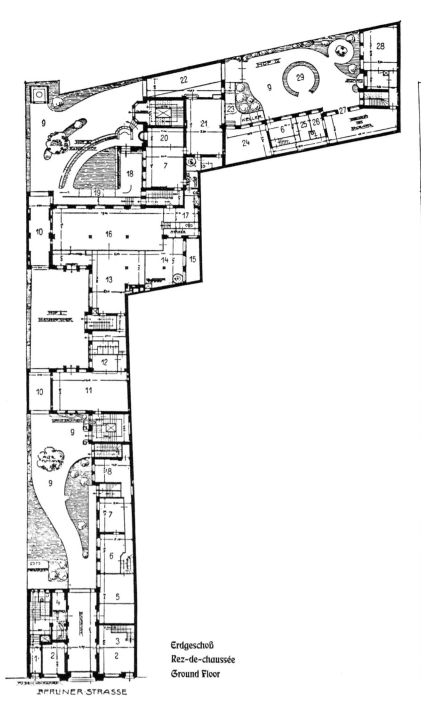

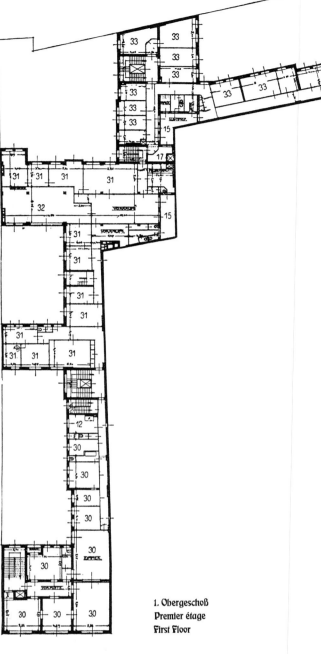

Erdgeschoß
Rez-de-chaussée
Ground Floor

BERLINER STRASSE

1. Obergeschoß
Premier étage
First Floor

1. Eingang zu den Wohnungen	1. Accès aux appartements	1. Apartment house entrance
2. Laden	2. Commerce	2. Shop
3. Einfahrt	3. Entrée	3. Carriage—way
4. Pförtner	4. Concierge	4. Porter
5. Warteraum für Lungenkranke	5. Salle d'attente pour les malades pulmonaires	5. Waiting Room for Lung—disease Patients
6. Aufnahmeraum	6. Bureau des admissions	6. Reception
7. Untersuchungsraum	7. Salle de consultations	7. Examination Room
8. Schwesternbureau	8. Bureau des infirmières	8. Nurses' Office
9. Hof	9. Cour	9. Courtyard
10. Durchfahrt	10. Passage	10. Gateway
11. Saal für Kaffeeküche	11. Cuisine secondaire	11. Coffee Room
12. Küche	12. Cuisine	12. Kitchen
13. Frauenspeisesaal der Volksküche	13. Réfectoire des femmes	13. Women's Dining Hall of the Public Kitchen
14. Speisenausgabe	14. Salle de distribution des repas	14. Serving Area
15. Lichthof	15. Cour vitrée	15. Patio
16. Männerspeisesaal der Volksküche	16. Réfectoire des hommes	16. Men's Dining Hall of the Public Kitchen
17. Wäsche	17. Lingerie	17. Laundry Room
18. Kleiderablage	18. Vestiaire	18. Cloakroom
19. Steigende Rampentreppe	19. Rampe d'accès	19. Ramp stairs
20. Arztzimmer	20. Cabinet du médecin	20. Physician's Room
21. Warteraum	21. Salle d'attente	21. Waiting Room
22. Raum für Kinderwagen	22. Remise pour les voitures d'enfants	22. Room for Perambulators
23. Rampe zum Keller	23. Rampe d'accès à la cave	23. Basement Ramp
24. Tageraum für Säuglinge	24. Salle des nourissons	24. Day Nursery for Infants
25. Bad	25. Lavabos-bains	25. Bath
26. Klosett	26. Water-closets	26. Water Closet
27. Tageraum für Spielkinder	27. Salle de jeux	27. Day Nursery for Children
28. Nachtraum für Kinder	28. Dortoir des enfants	28. Night Quarters for Children
29. Spielplatz	29. Terrain de jeux	29. Playground
30. Wohnräume	30. Pièces d'habitation	30. Living Quarters
31. Bureauräume	31. Salles de bureaux	31. Offices
32. Öffentliche Schreibstube	32. Salle d'écriture publique	32. Orderly Room
33. Krankenräume	33. Salles des malades	33. Patient's Rooms
34. Tageraum	34. Salle de réunions	34. Sitting—Room
35. Schwestern-Wohnräume	35. Pièces d'habitation des infirmières	35. Nurses' Living Quarters

verwaltung, der zweite Stock den Verlag für „Das rote Kreuz" u.a., der dritte Stock die Vortrags- und Unterrichtssäle. Am Hof II ist im Erdgeschoß die Volksküche eingerichtet, im Zwischengeschoß die Zentralküche, im ersten Stock Vereinsräume. Am Hof III enthält das Untergeschoß die Milchküche, das Zwischengeschoß das Arztzimmer und die Krankenküche, der erste und dritte Stock das Sanatorium, der vierte Stock die Dampfwaschküche, das Dachgeschoß das Röntgenkabinett. Am Hof IV befindet sich im Erdgeschoß die Krippe, in den oberen Geschossen sind Wohnungen für die Schwestern angeordnet.

Das Gebäude ist in allen Teilen mit Heißwasser-Zentralheizung, Warmwasserversorgung, Fahrstühlen, Staubsauge- und Gefrieranlage ausgestattet.

354 [1910; 17]

Das mehrfach durch Fassadenvorsprünge und Verwendung verschiedenartigen Materials belebte Wohnhaus in Berlin-Friedenau, Saarstraße 8, in der Bauzeit von 1908–1909 für die Baukostensumme von 140 000 Mark, das Grundstück nicht eingerechnet, hergestellt, ist in der Fassade von Architekt Alb. Weber, im Grudriß von Architekt C. Kremser entworfen. Die als Risalite vortretenden, durch alle Geschosse geführten seitlichen Fassadenteile werden noch durch Fensterausbauten gegliedert. Die beiden unteren Geschosse sind mit braunen gefugten Eisenklinkern verkleidet und durch Reihen von Dachpfannen von den oberen Geschossen geschieden. Der den Eingang enthaltende mittlere, rückliegende Fassadenteil wird durch Pfeiler gegliedert. Die beiden nächstfolgenden Obergeschosse zeigen gelben Flächenverputz, während das oberste fünfte in den Risaliten vorgekragte Geschoß wieder teilweise mit Dachpfannen bekleidet ist, die auch weiter zur Eindeckung des Daches verwendet sind. Die Fenster sind gradlinig oder im Korbbogen geschlossen.

In sämtlichen Geschossen sind Wohnungen eingerichtet.

355 [1910; 24]

Das im Erdgeschoß zu Läden, in den vier Obergeschossen zu Wohnungen eingerichtete Wohnhaus in Charlottenburg, Bismarckstraße 10, Ecke Neue Grolmanstraße, stammt in der Fassade von Architekt H. Lassen unter Mitwirkung von Architekt B. Taut, in der Grundrißanlage von Architekt A. Vogdt. Die Bauzeit dauerte 1 Jahr, die Baukosten betrugen insgesamt 520 000 Mark, danach für den Quadratmeter berechnet 650 Mark. Das Haus wird an beiden Fronten durch ausgekragte, drei Obergeschossen durchsetzende Erker belebt, als Altane endigend, die sich in balkonartigen Galerien fortsetzen; außerdem durchbricht ein Giebelaufbau die noch weiter mit Reihen von Dachfenstern besetzten Dachflächen. Erdgeschoß und Vorhalle sind in Rheinischem Basalt, die oberen Fassadenflächen in Terralitputz ausgeführt; die Abdeckungen der zum Teil in flacher Rundung vortretenden Fenstergruppen bestehen aus Kupfer, während die Dächer mit grauen holländischen Pfannen eingedeckt sind. Die plastischen Figuren an den Fassaden sind vom Bildhauer Ulr. Nitschke als handgeformte Terrakotten hergestellt; von demselben rühren die Deckenmalereien der Empfangshalle und der Halle im vierten Stock her.

Das gesamte Haus hat nur einen Haupteingang von der Bismarckstraße aus, folglich nur eine Haupttreppe erhalten, und kann die Bedienung der Ersparnis wegen von nur einem Fahrstuhl aus beschafft werden. Jedes der vier Obergeschosse enthält zwei geräumige, vornehm ausgestattete Wohnungen. Der Kinderspielsaal und der Turnsaal sind durch starke Korkestrichschichten von den darunter liegenden Räumen isoliert.

356 [1910; 5]

Die anmutig gruppierte Villa für Dr. Möller in Kopenhagen, Lundwangsvej, ein Werk des Architekten C. Brümmer, ist etwa im Laufe eines Jahres für die Baukostensumme von 45 000 Kronen in modernen

---

Sur la cour II sont installées, la cuisine populaire au rez-de-chaussée, la cuisine centrale à l'entresol et les salles des associations au premier étage. Sur la cour III se trouvent la laiterie au sous-sol, le cabinet médical et la cuisine destinée aux malades à l'entresol, le sanatorium aux premier et troisième étages, la buanderie au quatrième étage et la salle des examens radiographiques à l'étage des combles. Sur la cour IV se situent la crèche au rez-de-chaussée et des logements pour les infirmières dans les étages supérieurs.

L'ensemble de l'établissement est équipé d'un chauffage central à eau chaude, d'eau chaude, d'ascenseurs, d'installations réfrigérées et d'un système d'aspiration de la poussière.

354 [1910; 17]

Cet immeuble situé à Berlin-Friedenau, Saarstraße 8, se distingue par les nombreuses saillies de sa façade et par l'utilisation de matériaux très variés. Le bâtiment fut construit de 1908 à 1909 et coûta la somme de 140 000 marks, terrain non compris. La façade fut conçue par l'architecte Alb. Weber, les plans furent exécutés par l'architecte C. Kremser. Les avancées latérales de la façade sont assorties de bow-windows. Les deux étages inférieurs, revêtus de briques vitrifiées jointoyées de couleur brune, sont séparés des niveaux supérieurs par quelques rangées de tuiles creuses. Le corps de logis, situé en retrait et abritant l'entrée, est orné de piliers. Les deux étages suivants ont reçu un enduit jaune, le cinquième et dernier étage présente un revêtement de tuiles creuses, lesquelles recouvrent également les versants du toit. Les fenêtres sont droites ou surbaissées.

L'ensemble des étages est occupé par des logements.

355 [1910; 24]

Cet immeuble de rapport, situé à Berlin-Charlottenburg, à l'angle des rues Bismarckstraße et Neue Grolmanstraße, abrite des commerces au rez-de-chaussée et des logements dans les quatre étages supérieurs. La façade fut dessinée par l'architecte H. Lassen avec la collaboration de l'architecte B. Taut. Les plans furent exécutés par l'architecte A. Vogdt. La construction nécessita une année de travail et revint à 520 000 marks, soit un prix de 650 marks au mètre carré. Les deux façades de l'immeuble sont agrémentées d'oriels montant sur trois étages, se terminant en plates-formes et se prolongeant latéralement en galeries ayant des formes de balcons. Un pignon se détache des versants mansardés du toit. Le rez-de-chaussée et le porche sont réalisés en basalte du Rhin, les murs des étages supérieurs sont enduits d'un crépi. Le recouvrement des baies saillantes arrondies est en cuivre. Les toits portent une couverture de tuiles hollandaises grises. Les ornements en terre cuite des façades furent modelés manuellement par le sculpteur Ulr. Nitschke. Il exécuta également les peintures du plafond du hall d'entrée et du hall du quatrième étage.

L'immeuble ne possédant qu'une seule entrée sur la Bismarckstraße, c'est donc un unique escalier qui relie les étages entre eux. Par raison d'économie, le service ne peut être assuré que par l'ascenseur. Chacun des quatre étages est occupé par deux vastes logements élégamment aménagés. Le plancher de la salle de jeux des enfants tout comme celui de la salle de gymnastique sont isolés des pièces inférieures par d'épaisses couches de liège.

356 [1910; 5]

La villa du Dr. Möller à Copenhague, Lundwangsvej, fut construite sur les plans de l'architecte C. Brümmer. Il s'agit d'une propriété de style moderne à la composition audacieuse. Les travaux, réa-

---

caretaker's flat, the first floor is occupied by the caretaker's office. the second floor includes the editorial offices of "The Red Cross", the third floor is occupied by lecture halls and classrooms. Courtyard II has a public soup kitchen at its ground floor, the central kitchen on its mezzanine, and meeting rooms on the first floor. Courtyard III has the dairy on its ground floor, the physician's room and the patients' kitchen on the mezzanine, the sanatorium on the first and third floors, the steam laundry room on the fourth, and a X—ray room on the roof storey. Courtyard IV has the nursery on its ground floor, and living quarters for the hospital nurses on the upper floors.

All parts of the building are centrally heated with hotwater, supplied with hot & cold running water, lifts, vacuuming and freezing units.

354 [1910; 17]

The apartment building in the Friedenau district of Berlin (Saarstrasse 8) ist decorated by a number of projections in its façade and features a striking application of different building materials. It was constructed from 1908–1909 at a cost of 140,000 Marks (not including the price of the building site). The façade was designed by the architect Alb. Weber, the ground plan by architect C. Kremser. Two lateral projecting façades extend the full height of the building and also include bay windows. The two lower storeys are faced with brown clinker brickwork and separated from the upper storeys by rows of pantiles. The entrance is located in the recessed middle part of the façade, which is interrupted by pillars. The next two upper stories are rendered in yellow plaster, whilst the top fifth storey projects slightly over the side façades and is partially covered with roof pantiles, which are also employed for the roof itself. All windows are either straightlined or set in basket arches.

Flats have been laid out on all floors.

355 [1910; 24]

The four—storey apartment building with shops on the ground floor, in the Charlottenburg district of Berlin (Bismarckstrasse 10/corner of Neue Grolmanstrasse) was completed in one year at a cost of 520,000 Marks, calculated at 650 Marks per square metre. The façade was designed by the architect B. Lassen with assistance from the architect B. Taut; the ground plan was drafted by the architect A. Vogdt. Both fronts of the house are characterized by bays which run the height of the first three upper storeys and finish with a terrace adjoining a continuous gallery. In addition, a gabled structure breaks the line of the roof, which itself has rows of small windows. The ground floor and entry hall are faced with Rhine basalt, the upper façades are rendered in terrazzo plaster; the slightly rounded window projections are covered with copper, the roofs with grey Dutch pantiles. The terra—cotta figures of the façade are the work of the sculptor Ulr. Nitschke, who formed them by hand. He also created the frescos on the reception—hall ceiling as well as those located in the hall on the fourth floor.

The entire house has only one entrance, located on the Bismarckstrasse, and consequently, only one main staircase. Due to this thrifty measure, it can be serviced by only one lift. Each upper storey has two spacious flats furnished in an refined manner. The children's play—room as well as the gymnastics hall are insulated from the rooms below by thick cork panels.

356 [1910; 5]

The gracefully grouped villa built for Dr. Möller in Copenhagen (Lundvangsvej) is the work of the architect C. Brümmer. This house, with its attractive

Formen errichtet. Mit der Bauleitung war Architekt Wolf–Hansen beauftragt. An der Straßenfront springt die mit einem Schleppdach überdeckte Eingangshalle vor, die sich an den zweistöckigen, von geschweiften Giebeln begrenzten Flügelbau anlehnt. An der Seitenfront öffnen sich zwei Loggien, wieder beiderseits im Anschluß an ein höher geführtes, giebelbekröntes Risalit. Die Fassaden sind in gefugtem, rotem, handgestrichenem Backsteinmauerwerk hergestellt; die geschwungenen Dächer sind in roten Ziegeln eingedeckt.

Als Besonderheit der Grundrißanlage ist zu betrachten, daß die Schlafzimmer 1½ Elle über dem Niveau des Wohnzimmers und des Herrenzimmers erhöht liegen, und daß das Eßzimmer und die Küche unter den am höchsten gelegenen Zimmern im Kellergeschoß angeordnet sind.

lisés en une année, coûtèrent la somme de 45 000 couronnes. L'architecte Wolf–Hansen assura la conduite des travaux. Un porche abritant l'entrée, adossé à l'aile de deux étages coiffée d'un pignon aux contours ondulés, se détache de la façade sur rue. Deux loggias, s'ouvrant sur la façade latérale, flanquent un avant-corps couronné d'un pignon. Les murs de façade sont construits en briques jointoyées rouges. Les toits de forme infléchie sont recouverts de tuiles rouges.

Comme particularité des plans, il convient de remarquer que, d'une part, les chambres à coucher sont aménagées une aune et demie au-dessus du niveau de la salle de séjour et que d'autre part, la salle à manger ainsi que la cuisine, situées sous les pièces les plus en hauteur, sont installées au sous-sol.

modern lines, was completed in the course of one year at a cost of 45,000 Crowns. Construction was supervised by the architect Wolf–Hansen. The street front has a projecting entrance hall covered with a pent roof attached to the two–storey side wing with its curved gables. On the side front, two loggias open on both sides of a rising middle erection, which finishes in a curved gable. The façades are of hand–painted red brickwork; the roof is covered with red tile.

One special characteristic of the ground plan is worthy of note – the bedrooms lie 1½ ell above the level of the sitting–room and study. Furthermore, the dining–room and kitchen habe been placed as the structures's highest basement rooms.

357 [1910; 6]

Die aus drei zweistöckigen Wohnhäusern bestehende Baugruppe in Karlsruhe, Beethofenstraße 1–5, ist nach dem Entwurfe der Architekten Curjel & Moser etwa im Laufe eines Jahres ausgeführt. Die Baukosten für je eines der Häuser betrugen rund zwischen 55 000 bis 60 000 Mark. Die beiden nach außen gelegenen Häuser der Gruppe sind an der Straßenfront durch vorspringende Eckrisalite ausgezeichnet, während das mittlere Haus daselbst einen ausgekragten Balkon im Obergeschoß und einen über die ganze Breite sich erstreckenden Dachaufbau mit abschließendem Giebel zeigt. Die Fronten sind im Erdgeschoß

357 [1910; 6]

Ces maisons mitoyennes de deux étages, situées à Karlsruhe, Beethovenstraße 1–5, furent construites en l'espace d'une année sur les plans des architectes Curjel & Moser. Les coûts des travaux par maison se montèrent à une somme oscillant entre 55 000 et 60 000 marks. Les façades sur rue des deux maisons latérales sont assorties d'un avant-corps d'angle. La construction médiane présente, quant à elle, un balcon saillant à l'étage et une construction mansardée occupant toute la largeur de la façade. Au rez-de-chaussée, les murs extérieurs sont en partie

357 [1910; 6]

The group of three two–storey houses in Karlsruhe (Beethovenstrasse 1–5) was constructed according to the plans of the architects Curjel & Moser in the course of about one year, with the building costs of each house ranging from 55,000 to 60,000 Marks. The frontage of the two houses at either end of the group are characterized by their corner projections, whilst the middle house has a projecting balcony at its upper storey and a roof structure, which spans its entire breadth and ends in a straight gable. A large part of the ground floor front is faced with yellow

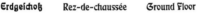

Erdgeschoß   Rez-de-chaussée   Ground Floor   Obergeschoß   Etage   Upper Floor

zum Teil aus gelben, rohbearbeiteten Sandsteinquadern, zum Teil in glattem und gemustertem Putz hergestellt. Das Obergeschoß und der Dachaufbau enthalten durchweg Putzflächen. Das gebrochene, mit Dachfenstern besetzte Dach ist mit Schiefer eingedeckt.

Das Mittelhaus hat den Eingang von der Straße, bei den Eckhäusern liegen die Eingänge an den Seitenfronten. Jedes der drei Häuser enthält eine auf Erd- und Obergeschoß verteilte Wohnung, außerdem eine Halle mit offener Treppe und Veranden in beiden Geschossen. Die Halle des mittleren Hauses ist mit Oberlicht ausgestattet.

réalisés en pierres de taille jaunes traitées en bossage brut et en partie enduits de crépi. Le premier étage ainsi que l'étage mansardé sont partiellement crépis. Le toit mansardé au comble brisé est recouvert d'ardoises.

L'accès à la maison médiane se fait par la façade sur rue. Les entrées des habitations latérales se trouvent sur les côtés. Chacune des trois maisons comprend un logement présentant un hall avec escalier et des vérandas aux deux niveaux. L'antichambre de la maison médiane est éclairé par une verrière.

sandstone rustication, other surfaces are rendered in smooth, patterned plasterwork. The fronts of the upper storey and roof structure are plastered throughout. The broken roof and its dormers are covered with shingles.

The middle house has its entrance facing the street, the entrances of both end houses are at the side. Each of the three houses has a flat occupying its ground and upper floors; in addition, a hallway with an open staircase and verandas located on both floors. The hall of the middle house is furnished with skylights.

358 [1910; 11]

Die ringsum freigelegene zweistöckige Villa „Guggenheim" in Worms, Röderstraße 8, ist von Architekt Prof. H. Metzendorf entworfen, wurde etwa im Laufe eines Jahres ausgeführt und verursachte rund 45 000 Mark Baukosten. Die Grundform des Hauses bildet im wesentlichen ein geschlossenes Viereck, abgesehen von den Anbauten der Seitenfronten, von denen der rechtsseitige den Eingangsflur und die Treppe in sich aufnimmt, der linksseitige im Erdgeschoß ein Zimmer bildet und im Obergeschoß mit einer Altane abschließt. An der Straßenfront tritt ein durch beide Geschosse geführter, flachrund vorspringender Fensterausbau heraus. Der Sockel ist in unregelmäßigem Schichtgemäuer aus graugrünem Sandstein hergestellt; aus demselben Material bestehen die Fenstereinfassungen und sonstigen Architekturteile beider

358 [1910; 11]

La villa „Guggenheim" à Worms, Röderstraße 8, est une construction isolée, construite en l'espace d'une année pour la somme de 45 000 marks. Les plans furent exécutés par l'architecte H. Metzendorf. La maison se présente comme un quadrilatère fermé, les avancées des façades latérales mises à part. L'avant-corps droit comprend le couloir d'entrée et l'escalier, le gauche abrite une pièce au rez-de-chaussée et se termine par une plate-forme au premier étage. Un bow-window légèrement convexe, s'élevant sur les deux niveaux, saillit de la façade sur rue. Le socle est réalisé en maçonnerie irrégulière composée de grès gris-vert. Les encadrements des fenêtres et les détails architecturaux sont exécutés avec le même matériau. Les

358 [1910; 11]

The free–standing, two–storey Guggenheim house in Worms (Röderstrasse 8) was designed by the architect Professor H. Metzendorf and completed within the course of one year at a cost of approximately 45,000 Marks. Apart from two side extensions, the basic plan of the structure is essentially that of a closed square. The extension on the right side of the villa contains the entry hall and outer steps, the one on the left has a room at ground level and is topped by a balcony. A slightly–rounded bay with windows runs the height of the street façade. The socle consists of irregularly–laid courses of grey-green sandstone; the same material is used for the window mouldings and other architectural ornamentation of both storeys. The

Geschosse. Die übrigen Wandflächen sind verputzt und mehrfach gemustert. Das gebrochene Dach trägt auf den Steilflächen eine Anzahl Dachfenster und ist mit Schiefer eingedeckt. Die auf zwei Geschosse verteilten Gesellschafts-, Wohn- und Schlafzimmer sind vornehm ausgestattet; im Erdgeschoß ist noch die Küche untergebracht.

359 [1910; 16]

Das ausnehmend reich mit Ausbauten und malerisch wirkenden Dachlösungen ausgestattete Wohnhaus in Hannover, Seelhorststraße 18, ist nach dem Entwurfe des Architekten Dr.-Ing. Ferd. Eichwede ausgeführt. Die Eingangsfront wird im Erdgeschoß durch einen halbrund vortretenden, mit einer Altane abschließenden Erkervorbau belebt, über dem sich eine loggienartig vertieft liegende, rundbogig überwölbte Fenstergruppe öffnet. Ein hoher Giebel bekrönt diesen Teil der Fassade, an den sich seitwärts im Obergeschoß eine in Holzkonstruktion hergestellte Laube und ein runder, turmartiger Aufbau anlehnen. Die anstoßende Straßenfront enthält wieder inmitten des Erdgeschosses einen leicht vorgekragten, in die Fläche des hohen überragenden Giebels einschneidenden Fensterausbau. Seitlich befindet sich als eine Art Loggia ein mit besonderem eine Altane umschließendem Dache versehener Anbau. Der Sockel, das Erdgeschoß, der Eckturm sowie die Gliederungen in den Obergeschossen sind aus Haustein, erstere in rauher, letztere in glatter Bearbeitung ausgeführt, die oberen Fassadenflächen zeigen Verputz. Der eine hohe gebogene Giebel der Straßenfront sowie sämtliche Dachflächen sind beschiefert. Die Gesellschafts- und Wohnzimmer sind im Erdgeschoß, den Obergeschossen und dem zum Teil ausgebauten Dachgeschosse untergebracht.

360 [1910; 26]

Die von Architekt Prof. Herm. Billing entworfene und zur Ausführung gebrachte Villa in Karlsruhe i. B., Moltkestraße 35, zeigt zwei Geschosse und ein teilweise ausgebautes Dachgeschoß und ist durch einen Vorgarten von der Straße getrennt. Die Straßenfront ist im Erdgeschoß mit einer Eingangshalle ausgestattet, die mit einem gebogenen, in Metall eingedeckten Dach abschließt. Das weit ausladende Traufgesims des Hauptdaches wird inmitten der Straßenfront durch einen Rundgiebel, in dem sich ein Halbkreisfenster öffnet, durchbrochen. Sonst sind Tür- und Fensteröffnungen geradlinig überdeckt. Das Erdgeschoß mit der Vorhalle und einzelne obere Gliederungen sind in Werkstein hergestellt; die oberen Fassadenflächen sind verputzt. Das gebrochene, abgewalmte, in den Steilflächen mit Fenstern besetzte Dach ist beschiefert.

361 [1910; 27]

Zu einem in Koblenz mit der Hauptfront am Kaiser-Wilhelm-Ring gelegenen Häuserblock gehört das Wohnhaus 4 derselben Straße, von Architekt Conr. Reich entworfen. Die dreistöckige Straßenfront wird durch einen viereckig vorspringenden, mit einer Altane endigenden Ausbau belebt, an welchen sich seitwärts eine ausgekragte, mit besonderem Dache bekrönte Loggia anschließt. Über dem Dachgesims, im mittleren Teil der Fassade, erhebt sich ein Fensterausbau, von einem in der Einfassung geschwungenen steilen Giebel überragt. Das mit Schiefer eingedeckte Dach trägt außerdem zwei gleichfalls mit geschwungenen Giebeln versehene Gruppenfenster. Das Erdgeschoß wird zu Geschäftsräumen benutzt, die beiden Obergeschosse sowie das ausgebaute Dachgeschoß enthalten Wohnungen.

362 [1910; 33]

Die beiden zu einer Baugruppe vereinigten, durch malerische Behandlung ausgezeichneten Wohnhäuser in Koblenz, Mainzerstraße 40/42, ein Werk der Architekten Gebr. Friedhofen, sind im Laufe eines Jahres errichtet. Die Baukosten betrugen für das Haus Nr. 40 rund 125 000 Mark, für das Haus Nr. 42 rund 45 000 Mark. Das letztere Haus ist an der Straßenfront mit einem im Erdgeschoß vorspringenden Erker

les surfaces des murs sont enduites d'un crépi et présentent de nombreux ornements. Le toit au comble brisé est recouvert d'ardoises. Le brisis est percé de nombreuses lucarnes. Les pièces de réceptions, les salles de séjour et les chambres à coucher, réparties sur les deux niveaux de la villa, sont élégamment aménagées. La cuisine est installée au sous-sol.

359 [1910; 16]

Cette villa située à Hanovre, Seelhorststraße 18, est caractérisée par son asymétrie et l'ensemble pittoresque formé par ses toits. Les plans furent exécutés par l'architecte Dr. Ferd. Eichwede. La façade abritant l'entrée est assortie, au rez-de-chaussée, d'un avant-corps arrondi supportant une plate-forme, au-dessus duquel s'ouvre, en retrait, un groupe de fenêtres cintrées aux allures de loggias. Un haut pignon, flanqué à l'étage d'une tonnelle de bois et d'une tourelle, coiffe cette partie de la façade. L'opposite reprend la même composition. Du centre du rez-de-chaussée se détache une avancée s'élevant au-delà de la corniche du toit. Latéralement se greffe une saillie, un genre de loggia, coiffée d'un toit particulier surmonté d'une plate-forme. Le socle, le rez-de-chaussée, la tour d'angle ainsi que les ornements des étages supérieurs sont réalisés en pierres de taille traitées de façon rustique ou lisse. Les surfaces supérieures des murs de façade présentent un crépi. Le haut pignon de la façade sur rue ainsi que l'ensemble des toits sont recouverts d'ardoises. Les salles de réception et les pièces d'habitation sont aménagées au rez-de-chaussée, dans les étages et sous les combles.

360 [1910; 26]

La villa située à Karlsruhe, Moltkestraße 35, construite par l'architecte Prof. Herm. Billing, s'élève sur deux étages dont un mansardé. La façade sur rue, agrémentée d'un jardin frontal, est assortie, au rez-de-chaussée, d'un porche recouvert d'un toit métallique. La corniche particulièrement saillante du toit est interrompue, dans la partie médiane de la façade, par un pignon arrondi, percé par une fenêtre en demi-cercle. Les ouvertures des portes et fenêtres sont à linteau droit. Le rez-de-chaussée et le porche ainsi que quelques ornements sont réalisés en pierres de taille. Les murs de façade supérieurs sont crépis. Le toit mansardé en croupe porte une toiture d'ardoises.

361 [1910; 27]

Cet immeuble de rapport, situé à Coblence, Kaiser-Wilhelm-Ring 4, appartient à un ensemble architectural, conçu par l'architecte Conr. Reich. La façade sur rue, haute de trois étages, est enrichie d'un avant-corps quadrangulaire, se terminant par une plate-forme, auquel s'adosse latéralement une loggia saillante couronnée d'un toit propre. Une construction mansardée, coiffée d'un pignon aux lignes ondulées, se détache du toit, dans la partie médiane de la façade. Le toit d'ardoises est, en outre, percé de deux groupes de fenêtres présentant chacun un pignon aux contours identiques. Le rez-de-chaussée est occupé par des locaux de commerce, les deux étages supérieurs et les combles mansardées abritent des logements.

362 [1910; 33]

Cet ensemble composé de deux constructions se singularise par son aspect pittoresque. Les maisons, situées à Coblence, Mainzerstraße 40/42, furent exécutées en l'espace d'une année, sur les plans des frères Friedhofen, architectes. Les travaux de la maison au no. 40 de la rue coûtèrent la somme de 125 000 marks, ceux la maison au no. 42, 45 000 marks. Cette

remaining exterior surfaces are faced with plaster and patterned in various ways. The steeper slope of the roof has a number of dormer windows; the entire roof is covered with shingles. Parlours, sitting—rooms and bedrooms are distributed throughout the two storeys of the villa, and are replete with elegant furnishings. The kitchen is located on the ground floor.

359 [1910; 16]

The villa—like residence in Hannover (Seelhorststrasse 18) is exceptionally ornate in its various groupings and picturesque roof structure. It was designed by the architectural engineer Dr. Ferd. Eichwede. The entrance front is decorated at the ground level by a semicircular bay topped by a balcony, above which opens a recessed loggia with a group of windows in round arches. A high—pitched gable crowns this section of the façade, which is flanked at the upper storey by a bower of wooden construction and a round tower—like projection. The middle of the adjoining street façade has a slightly projecting group of windows at the ground level, and a group of small bay windows cut into the high—pitched gable. To the side is a covered loggia—like extension whose roof is topped by a balcony. The socle, the ground floor and the articulations of the upper storeys are fronted with rough—hewn blocks of stone, those of the upper storey have been smoothed; the upper façades are faced with plaster. The high, curved gable at the street front as well as the entire roof are hung with shingles. Parlours and sitting—rooms are located on the ground floor, the upper floors and the roof floor.

360 [1910; 26]

The villa at Moltkestrasse 35 in Karlsruhe is a two—storey structure with an attic storey. Designed by the architect Professor Herm. Billing, the villa is separated from the street by a front garden. The street front has at the ground level an entrance hall with a roof covered in metal. The broad overhanging eaves of the main roof are broken at the middle of the street front by a round gable with a semi—circular window in the middle. All other windows and doors are straight—lined. The ground floor with its entrance hall as well as individual articulations in the upper storey are rendered in ashlar; the upper façade is of plaster. The hipped roof is covered with slate and has dormer windows in its steeper slope.

361 [1910; 27]

The architect Conr. Reich designed the apartment building Kaiser Wilhelm Ring 4 in Koblenz, which is part of a group of apartment buildings located in the same street. The three—storey street front is marked by a square—sided projection which ends in a terrace and has to its side a loggia with a separate roof. At the middle of the façade a window structure rises above the roof moulding, above that towers a high—pitched shaped gable. The slate roof also has two double—windowed dormers with curved gables. The ground floor is used for business purposes, the two upper floors as well as the furnished attic storey contain flats.

362 [1910; 33]

The two semi—detached houses at Mainzerstrasse 40/42 in Koblenz exhibit a high degree of artistic craftsmanship. Designed by the architect Gebr. Friedhofen, they were both completed in the course of one year, the house at No. 40 costing about 125,000 Marks, the one at No. 42 about 45,000 Marks. The

mit anschließender Loggia, über denen sich ein einerseits mit rundem Eckerker, andererseits mit einer Laube verbundener Giebel erhebt, ausgestattet. Das zweite Obergeschoß und der darüber folgende geschwungene Giebel sind in reich verziertem Holzfachwerk ausgeführt; die Fenster sind mit bemalten Läden versehen. An der Seitenfront befindet sich der mit einem Schutzdach überdeckte Eingang, und als Abschluß zeigt sich ein mit Flugdächern ausgestatteter, abgeschopfter, überhängender Giebel. Der Sockel sowie ein Teil des Erdgeschosses sind aus rauh bearbeitetem Sandstein hergestellt, die körnig behandelten Putzflächen haben rosa-violette Färbung erhalten.

Die stark übertretenden Dächer beider Häuser sind mit Schiefer eingedeckt und durch Dachluken unterbrochen. Sämtliche Geschosse des Hauses Nr. 42 werden von den Räumen einer Wohnung eingenommen, deren Küche im Erdgeschoß und deren Waschküche im Keller untergebracht ist.

363 [1910; 95]

Das nach dem Entwurfe der Architekten Curjel und Moser in einer 1½ Jahre dauernden Bauzeit, für die Kostensumme von 90 000 Mark ausgeführte Wohnhaus in Basel, Schützenmattstraße 55, erscheint als ein von zwei zusammenstoßenden, mit geschwungenen steilen Giebeln abgeschlossenen Flügeln gebildeter Eckbau. Die kürzere Vorderfront zeigt einen im Erd- und Obergeschoß halbrund vorspringenden, im Giebelgeschoß mit einer Altane endigenden Erkerbau; an der längeren Seitenfront befindet sich durch eine Vorhalle, mit Balkon im Obergeschoß, geschützte Eingang. Die Hinterfront ist mit einem Nebeneingang und einer breiteren, mittelst Freitreppe zugänglichen Loggia im Erdgeschoß ausgestattet. Der Sockel besteht aus Kalkstein, die oberen Teile der Fronten sind in rauhem, grau gefärbtem, durch Musterungen belebtem Verputz ausgeführt. Das gebrochene Dach ist mit Schiefer eingedeckt und trägt einen Fensteraufbau auf der unteren Steilfläche.

Das Erdgeschoß enthält eine Diele mit vorangehendem Windfang und freiliegender Treppe; die Anlage der Diele wiederholt sich im Obergeschoß. Wohn- und Schlafzimmer sind auf Erd- und Obergeschoß sowie auf das ausgebaute Dachgeschoß verteilt.

364 [1910; 30]

Das Geschäftshaus in Berlin, Friedrichstraße 184, ist nach dem Entwurfe der Architekten Curt Berndt und M. Lange ausgeführt. Die Bauzeit dauerte 9 Monate und die Baukosten betrugen 250 000 Mark. Die beiden unteren Geschosse öffnen sich nach der Straße mit breiten Schaufenstern, außerdem enthält das Erdgeschoß den Eingang und das nächstfolgende Geschoß in der Mitte einen besonders überdachten Erkervorbau. Die folgenden drei Obergeschosse sind einheitlich durch einen in den Laibungsflächen verzierten Rahmen zusammengehalten, der wieder durch zwei säulenartige, abgekantete, mit verzierten Feldern und Blätterkapitellen ausgestattete Pfeiler geteilt wird. Letztere tragen eine weit ausladende Gesimsplatte, auf welcher ein Ornamentaufsatz mit einer mittleren Figur ruht. Die Bildhauerarbeiten sind von Rob. Schirmer ausgeführt. Der obere Teil der Front baucht sich nischenartig aus und wird von einem geschwungenen Dachgesims begrenzt. Die Straßenfront besteht vom ersten Obergeschoß bis zum Dachgeschoß aus schlesischem Sandstein; die Erdgeschoßpfeiler sind mit Labradorgranit bekleidet. Die Laibungen des Hauseingangs haben eine Marmorbekleidung erhalten. Die Hoffassade ist mit Glasursteinen verblendet und durch Gliederungen in Zementputz belebt. Der Dachstuhl ist aus Holzsparren auf Eisenplatten und Eisenbindern hergestellt. Die steilen Dachflächen an der Vorderfront sind mit grauen Pfannen, die am Hofe mit Schiefer eingedeckt.

Das Erdgeschoß enthält zwei Läden, den Eingangsflur, die Haupttreppe mit dem Personenaufzug, außerdem eine Nebentreppe. Die oberen Geschosse sind als ungeteilte Geschäftsräume ausgebildet; der Hof ist unterkellert. Sämtliche Decken sind massiv mit

dernière est assortie, au rez-de-chaussée de la façade sur rue, d'un avant corps, englobant une loggia, surmonté par un pignon comprenant une logette d'angle arrondie et une tonnelle contiguë. Le deuxième étage ainsi que le pignon aux lignes ondulées présentent un colombage de bois richement décoré. Les fenêtres sont pourvues de volets peints. L'entrée, sur la façade latérale, est abritée par un porche coiffé d'un pignon saillant en croupe. Le socle ainsi qu'une partie du rez-de-chaussée offrent un appareil de pierres gréseuses traitées en bossage brut. Les murs rustiqués ont reçu un badigeon rose violet. Les toits particulièrement saillants sont recouverts d'ardoises et sont percés de lucarnes. Cette maison est conçue pour abriter un seul logement. La cuisine est aménagée au rez-de-chaussée, la buanderie est installée à la cave.

363 [1910; 95]

La maison bâloise, située dans la Schützenmattstraße au no. 55, fut construite sur les plans des architectes Curjel et Moser. Les travaux, qui durèrent un an et demi, coûtèrent la somme de 90 000 marks. Cette demeure apparaît comme une construction composée de deux ailes coiffées de pignons. La façade frontale, la plus étroite, présente une avancée arrondie montant de fond sur deux niveaux et se terminant par une plate-forme à l'étage des combles. L'entrée, placée sur la façade latérale, est abritée par un porche supportant un balcon. La façade postérieure est assortie, au rez-de-chaussée, d'une entrée secondaire et d'une vaste loggia accessible par un perron. Le socle est construit en castines, les murs extérieurs sont enduits d'un crépi rustique, de couleur grise, présentant des parements. Le toit au comble brisé est recouvert d'ardoises. Le brisis est troué d'une fenêtre mansardée.

Le rez-de-chaussée comprend un tambour s'ouvrant sur un hall d'entrée avec escalier attenant. La disposition du hall se répète à l'étage. Les pièces de séjour et les chambres à coucher sont réparties sur les trois niveaux de la maison.

364 [1910; 30]

L'immeuble à usage commercial, situé à Berlin, Friedrichstraße 184, fut conçu par les architectes Curt Berndt et M. Lange. La construction nécessita neuf mois de travail et coûta la somme de 250 000 marks. Les deux niveaux inférieurs sont troués par de larges devantures auxquelles s'ajoute un passage au rez-de-chaussée. Le premier étage est également assorti, en son centre, d'un bow-window portant toiture. Les trois étages suivants forment, de par l'encadrement décoré de la surface intérieure, un ensemble homogène. Cette surface est elle-même divisée par deux piliers chanfreinés, ornés de petits panneaux, aux chapiteaux à décor végétal, supportant une corniche saillante sur laquelle repose un ensemble sculpté. Les ornements plastiques sont l'œuvre de Rob. Schirmer. La partie supérieure de la façade s'incurve et se termine par une corniche aux lignes ondulées. Les murs extérieurs, donnant sur la rue, sont, du premier étage aux combles, réalisés en grès de Silésie. Les piliers du rez-de-chaussée sont revêtus de granit. Les intrados de l'entrée ont reçu un parement de marbre. La façade sur cour est revêtue de briques vernies et enrichie d'ornements dans le crépi de ciment. La charpente est à chevrons de bois associés à des plaques de fer et des poutres maîtresses de fer. Les versants pentus du toit sont recouverts, sur rue, de tuiles creuses grises, sur cour, d'ardoises.

Le rez-de-chaussée comprend deux commerces, le couloir d'entrée, l'escalier principal avec l'ascenseur ainsi qu'un escalier de service. Les étages supérieurs sont occupés par des salles de bureaux non-cloisonnées. Une cave se trouve sous la cour. L'ensemble des planchers sont massifs, constitués de pou-

frontage of the latter house has a bay at the ground level which ends with a loggia, above that is a gable connected to a round bay at one side and to a bower at the other. The second storey and the shaped gable above it have been rendered in richly—ornamented half—timber; the windows have painted shutters. A porch is located at the side front, which ends with an overhanging hipped gable with winged roofs. The socle as well as part of the ground storey are faced with rusticated sandstone, the rough—grained plastered surfaces are red—violet in colour. All levels of the house No. 42 are occupied by one apartment, with the kitchen being located on the ground floor and the laundry—room in the basement.

363 [1910; 95]

Constructed in 18 months according to the plans of the architects Curjel and Moser at a cost of 90,000 Marks, the apartment building in Basel (Schützenmattstrasse 55) gives the appearance of a corner structure consisting of two perpendicular wings with high—pitched, shaped gables. The narrower front has a rounded bay extending through the first storey and ending with a small terrace at the gabled storey. An entrance porch with a balcony at the first storey is located at the long side front. The back front has a side entrance and broad stairs leading to a loggia at the ground level. The socle is of limestone, the upper part of the façade is rendered in rough grey plaster with a decorative pattern. The slate roof exhibits a window structure in its lower, steeper part. The open stairs with a draught lobby at the ground floor leads to an entry hall. The arrangement around the hall is repeated on the first floor. Sitting—rooms and bedrooms are located on the ground and first floors, as well as on the attic floor.

364 [1910; 30]

The commercial building in Berlin (Friedrichstrasse 184) was designed by the architects Curt Berndt and M. Lange and erected in the space of 9 months at a cost of 250,000 Marks. Broad shop windows line the lower two storeys of the street front, which in addition has an entrance at the ground level and a covered bay in the middle of the first storey. The upper three storeys are framed by broad ornamented reveals and broken by two multi—faced columns with decorative panels and foliated capitals. The columns support an overhangig cornice slab with ornamental devices and a central figure. The sculptures are the work of Rob. Schirmer. The upper part of the principal front is concave and crowned by a gable of graceful curves. The frontage from the first storey upwards is rendered in Silesian sandstone; the pilasters of the ground floor are faced with Labrador granite. The reveal of the entrance is of marble. The courtyard façade is faced with glazed stonework and ornamented with concrete articulations. The roof framework consists of wooden rafters resting on iron plates and trusses. The steep pitch of the front roof is covered with pantiles, the courtyard side with slate.

The ground floor has two shops, an entry hall, the principal staircase with a lift, as well as a side staircase. The upper storeys consist of open office space; the courtyard has a basement. All floors have iron reinforcements placed between iron girders, are hung

Eiseneinlagen zwischen eisernen Trägern hergestellt, mit Rabitzdecken unterspannt und mit einer Betonschicht, welche einen Korkestrich und den Linoleumbelag aufnimmt, überdeckt. Das Dachgeschoß ist durch eine Rohrgewebe-Putzdecke auf hölzerner Unterlage abgeschlossen. Die Metalleinfassungen und Bekleidungen am Dach der Straßenfront und an der Vorderfassade bestehen aus Kupfer, die der übrigen Dachteile aus Zink. Die Keller sind mit weißen Glasursteinen verkleidet. Die Fenster im ersten Stock und dem Erker, die Schaufenster, die Ladentüren sowie die Eingangstür bestehen aus poliertem australischem Teakholz. Die Treppen sind aus Kunstsandstein hergestellt. Es ist eine zentrale Niederdruckdampfheizung eingerichtet, außerdem eine Gas- und elektrische Lichtanlage.

tres de fer renfermant une garniture de fer, recouverts d'un treillis puis d'une couche de béton à laquelle s'ajoutent une aire de liège et un revêtement de linoléum. L'étage des combles se termine par un plafond composé d'une couche de roseaux enduite sur une base de bois. Les encadrements métalliques et les revêtements du versant du toit et de la façade sur rue sont en cuivre, ceux de l'autre versant sont en zinc. Les caves sont parées de briques vernies blanches. Les fenêtres du premier étage, le bow-window, les devantures. Les portes du commerce ainsi que la porte d'entrée sont en teck australien poli. Les escaliers sont réalisés en grès artificiel. Un chauffage central à vapeur à basse pression et une installation d'éclairage au gaz et à l'électricité ont été aménagées.

with Rabitz suspended ceilings and covered by a concrete layer with a corkboard and linoleum exterior. The roof storey is finished off by reed lathing plaster supported by a wooden framework. The metal mouldings and surfaces of the roof on the front façade are of copper, those of the other parts of the roof are of zinc. The cellar is panelled with white glazed stonework. Polished Australian teak—wood has been used for the windows in the first—storey and bay, the shop windows and doors as well as the front door. The stairs are of imitation sandstone. Low—pressure steam heating has been installed, as well as a gas and electrical lighting system.

365 [1910; 36]

Das Kaufhaus der Firma C. M. Goldschmidt in Worms, Marktplatz 5 und 7, kam in achtmonatlicher Bauzeit nach dem Entwurfe und unter Leitung der Architekten Rindfüsser & Kühn für die Baukostensumme von 200 000 Mark zur Ausführung. In der

Le grand magasin des établissements C. M. Goldschmidt à Worms, Marktplatz 5 et 7, fut construit en huit mois sur les plans et sous la direction des architectes Rindfüller & Kühn. Les travaux coûtèrent la somme de 200 000 marks. Les architectes tinrent

The department store of the C. M. Goldschmidt firm in Worms (Marktplatz 5 und 7) was built over a period of eight months according to the plans of the architects Rindfüsser & Kühn, who also supervised the construction amounting to 200,000 Marks. Great care

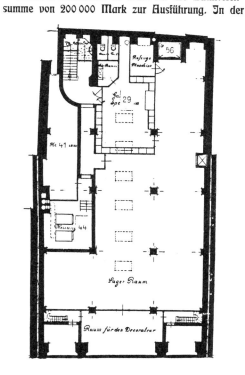

Keller   Sous-sol   Basement

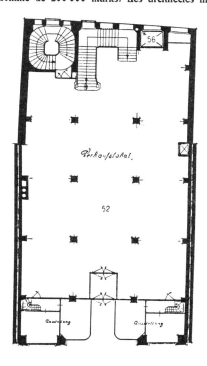

Erdgeschoß   Rez-de-chaussée   Ground Floor

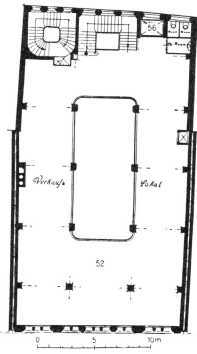

Obergeschoß   Etage   Upper Floor

Fassadengestaltung wurde auf die historische Umgebung des Platzes und besonders auf den naheliegenden Dom Rücksicht genommen. Zwischen durchgehenden Pfeilern öffnen sich im Erdgeschoß Schaufensteröffnungen und in den beiden Obergeschossen mehrfach durch schmälere Pfeiler geteilte Fenstergruppen. Über dem Dachgesims erhebt sich im mittleren Teil ein Fensteraufbau, der mit einem Flachgiebel abschließt. Die Fassaden sind in hellgeflammtem Maintalsandstein, in den unteren Teilen mit reicher Bildhauerarbeit hergestellt. Die Schaufenstereinrichtung besteht aus Bronze. Das gebrochene Dach ist mit Schiefer eingedeckt.

Die drei Geschosse enthalten große, nur durch Pfeiler getrennte Verkaufsräume und werden durch einen mittleren Lichthof mit ringslaufenden Galerien erleuchtet. An der Hinterfront führt eine geschlossene Brücke in Höhe des zweiten Obergeschosses über den anstoßenden Pariser Platz zu den Engroshäusern der Firma. An der Rücklage des Gebäudes befindet sich die Haupttreppe, die Nottreppe und der Personenaufzug. Die Ausstellungsräume hinter den Schaufenstern des Erdgeschosses sind mit dem Dekorationsmagazin im Kellergeschoß durch je eine Treppe verbunden. Der innere Ausbau wurde in armiertem Beton, die dekorative Ausstattung der Räume in hellem Eichenholz mit schwarzen Intarsien ausgeführt, mit Ausnahme des Modellsalons, der graues Ahorngetäfel mit Intarsien erhalten hat. Eine Zentralheizungs- sowie eine elektrische Lichtanlage sind eingerichtet.

compte de l'environnement historique de la place et de la proximité de la cathédrale dans la composition de la façade. Des piliers montant de fond encadrent des devantures, au rez-de-chaussée, et des groupes de fenêtres, eux-mêmes divisés par de petits piliers, dans les étages supérieurs. une construction mansardée coiffée d'un pignon en delta s'élève de la corniche du toit. Les murs de façade sont construits en grès clair flammé de la vallée du Main, les parties inférieures sont assorties de nombreux ouvrages sculptés. Les devantures sont en bronze. Le toit au comble brisé porte une toiture d'ardoises.

Les trois étages comprennent de vastes surfaces de vente non-cloisonnées, simplement divisées par une ordonnance de piliers et éclairées par une cour médiane vitrée, ceinte d'une galerie. Une passerelle fermée relie, au niveau du deuxième étage, la façade postérieure aux comptoirs de gros situés de l'autre côté de la place. L'escalier principal, l'escalier de secours et l'ascenseur sont situés au fond du magasin. Les surfaces d'exposition derrière les devantures du rez-de-chaussée sont chacune directement reliées par un escalier à la réserve de décorations installée au sous-sol. L'intérieur de l'édifice est réalisé en béton armé. L'aménagement décoratif des pièces est en chêne clair marqueté de noir, le salon de présentation est assorti de lambris d'érable gris marqueté. Le magasin est équipé d'un chauffage central et d'une installation d'éclairage électrique.

was taken in designing the façade, keeping it in harmony with the historical nature of the market square and especially the nearby cathedral. The pilasters running the entire length of the façade frame on the ground level shop windows, on the upper floors groups of windows broken up by narrower pilasters. The middle of the façade is dominated by a windowed superstructure above the roof moulding which supports a straight gable. The façades are rendered in lightly—mottled sandstone from the Main valley, and are richly sculptured in their lower parts. The mouldings of the shop windows are of bronze; the roof is covered with slate.

The three storeys of the store contain large open sales—rooms which are divided only by pillars and lighted by a central patio surrounded by a gallery. At the back side of the building, a covered bridge at the second storey crosses over the adjacent Pariser Platz, leading to the firm's wholesale departement. The principal staircase is located at the rear of the building, as are the fire escapes and lifts. Each of the two show—rooms behind the shop windows are connected to the window dresser's storage room in the basement by means of a staircase. The edifice's inner construction is of reinforced concrete, and the rooms are decoratively panelled in light oak with black marquetry, with exception of the fashions salon, which is decorated in grey maple with marquetry. Central heating and electric lighting have also been furnished.

Das in Berlin, Friedrichstraße 58 und Leipziger-straße 29 gelegene, einen Eckbau bildende Kaufhaus Mädler, nach dem Entwurfe des Architekten Reg.-Baumeister R. Leibnitz in der Bauzeit von Oktober 1908 bis Oktober 1909 zur Ausführung gekommen, hat eine Baukostensumme von 550 000 Mark erfordert. Das Erdgeschoß ist in Schaufensterflächen, zwischen denen sich der überwölbte, zugleich als Durchfahrt dienende Eingang befindet, aufgelöst und wird durch ein stark ausladendes Gurtgesims gegen die oberen Geschosse abgeschlossen. Das erste, zweite und dritte Obergeschoß sind mit durchgehenden Pfeilern gegliedert, die im Querschnitt nach außen verjüngt sind, um dem Licht möglichst freien Eintritt in das Innere zu gewähren. Die Pfeilerkapitelle tragen die Zeichen der zwölf Monate und an den Seitenflächen der Pfeiler sind die auf Diensten stehenden vierundzwanzig Figuren, Gewerbe und Handwerker darstellend, angebracht. Die zusammengezogenen Fenster des ersten und zweiten Obergeschosses sind mit Ausbauten versehen und rundbogig überdeckt; über dem Eingange springt erkerartig ein halbrunder, mit einer Altane endigender Vorbau heraus. Die Fassadenflächen im dritten Obergeschoß werden zwischen den Pfeilern ganz von Fenstergruppen ausgefüllt, die sich in gleicher Anordnung an dem über dem weit ausladenden, mit einer Balustrade versehenen Abschlußgesimse sich erhebenden vierten Obergeschoß wiederholen. Die Fassaden sind in grauem Tuffstein verblendet; das gebrochene, im unteren Teile geschweifte, im oberen mit Dachfenstern besetzte Dach ist mit Kupfer eingedeckt. Die Bildhauerarbeiten an der Fassade sind von Rich. Kühn gefertigt.

Das Erdgeschoß enthält eine Anzahl Ladenräume, außerdem den zu drei Stockwerkstreppen, zu dem Personen- und Lastenaufzug sowie zu dem teilweise überbauten Hofraum führenden Eingangsflur. Das erste und zweite Obergeschoß umschließen je einen ungeteilten Geschäftsraum; das dritte Obergeschoß ist zu Bureauräumen verwendet, ebenso das vierte Obergeschoß. Das ganze Gebäude einschließlich des Hofraums ist unterkellert. Sämtliche Decken sind massiv hergestellt, auch die Dachkonstruktion ist in Eisen mit massivem Zwischenboden ausgeführt. Das untere Dachgeschoß dient als Lagerraum.

Le grand magasin berlinois Mädler, situé à l'angle des rues Friedrichstraße et Leipzigerstraße, fut conçu par l'architecte R. Leibnitz. Les travaux, qui durèrent du mois d'octobre 1908 au mois d'octobre 1909, coûtèrent la somme de 550 000 marks. Le rez-de-chaussée, séparé des autres étages par un cordon saillant, se compose de devantures entre lesquelles s'ouvre une entrée voûtée servant également de passage. Les premier, deuxième et troisième étages présentent une ordonnance de piliers continus se rétrécissant vers l'extérieur afin de ne pas gêner la pénétration de la lumière. Les chapiteaux des piliers sont ornés des symboles des douze mois de l'année, leurs surfaces latérales offrent des colonnes dégagées portant vingt-quatre figures représentant différents corps de métier. Les ouvertures cintrées des premier et deuxième étages forment un ensemble et sont assorties d'oriels. Au-dessus de l'entrée se détache une avancée arrondie couronnée par un balcon. Au troisième étage, les surfaces comprises entre les piliers sont occupées par des fenêtres groupées. Le quatrième étage, s'élevant derrière une balustrade bordant une corniche très saillante, reprend cet alignement régulier des ouvertures. Les murs de façade sont revêtus de tuf gris. Le toit au comble brisé porte une couverture de cuivre. Les brisis sont légèrement incurvés, les terrasons sont percés de fenêtres. Les sculptures ornant la façade furent exécutées par Rich. Kühn.

Le rez-de-chaussée comprend des commerces ainsi que le couloir d'entrée menant aux trois escaliers, à l'ascenseur, au monte-charge et à la cour partiellement recouverte. Les premier et deuxième étages renferment chacun un local de commerce non-cloisonné. Les troisième et quatrième étages sont occupés par des bureaux. Un sous-sol s'étend sous toute la surface du bâtiment, cour comprise. L'ensemble des planchers est massif. La charpente est construite en fer avec des fonds intermédiaires massifs. L'étage mansardé inférieur sert d'entrepôt.

The Mädler office building in Berlin, located at the corner of Friedrichstrasse and Leipzigerstrasse, was designed by the government architect R. Leibnitz and completed from October 1908 to October 1909 at a cost of 550,000 Marks. The ground level is occupied by shop windows and an arched carriageway, and is separated from the upper storeys by a sharply overhanging string-course. The first to third storeys are articulated by a giant order of pillars which are tapered to allow a maximum amount of natural lighting to reach the interior. The capitals of the pillars bear the allegorical designs of the twelve months; the sides of the pillars are carved with twenty-four figures representing tradesmen and craftsmen at work. The vertical windows of the first and second storeys have been placed in bays with round arches. A semi-circular projection located over the entrance is topped by a small terrace. The third-storey façade is entirely occupied by groups of windows separated by pilasters; their arrangement is repeated on the storey above which has a balustrade supported by the overhanging cornice. The façades are faces with grey shell limestone; the lower part of the broken roof is covered with copper, the upper part with slate. The sculptures of the façade are the work of Rich. Kühn.

A number of shops are located on the ground floor, as is the vestibule bordered by three staircases leading to the upper floors, lifts and service elevators, and a partially covered courtyard. The first and second floors each contain an open office space; the third and fourth floors have been partitioned into smaller offices. A basement runs under the entire building, including the courtyard. All ceilings are of concrete; even the roof construction employs an iron framework with reinforced false ceilings. The lower roof storey serves as a storage area.

Das von den Architekten Eitel und Steigleder errichtete Schauspielhaus in Stuttgart zeigt an der Kleinen Königstraße ein Stück freiliegender Front und ist sonst umbaut oder von Höfen umgeben. Indes sind

Le théâtre de Stuttgart, construit sur les plans des architectes Eitel et Steigleder, est un édifice, serré entre des cours et des bâtiments, présentant sur la Kleine Königstraße un petit morceau de façade déga-

Designed by the architects Eitel and Steigleder, the theater in Stuttgart has a partially exposed front facing the Kleine Königstrasse, otherwise the edifice is surrounded by other buildings and courtyards. The

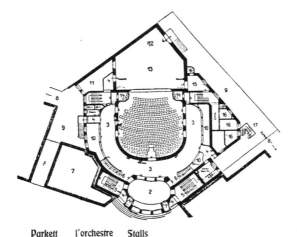

Parkett   l'orchestre   Stalls

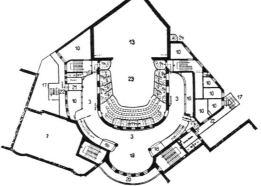

1. Rang   Premier balcon   Dress Circle

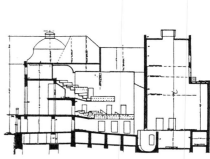

Längsschnitt   Coupe longitudinale   Longitudinal Section

1. Kasse	13. Bühne	
2. Kassenhalle	14. Loge	
3. Umgang	15. Konversat.	
4. Ausgang	16. Künstler-Garderobe	
5. Treppe z. 2. Rang	17. Nottreppe	
6. Treppe z. 1. Rang	18. Büfett	
7. Geschäftshaus	19. Foyer	
8. Durchfahrt	20. Balkon	
9. Hof	21. Notausgang	
10. Garderobe	22. Rettungspodest	
11. Requisiten	23. Zuschauerraum	
12. Hinterbühne	24. Bühnentreppe	

1. Caisse	13. Scène
2. Hall des caisses	14. Loge
3. Dégagement	15. Cabinet
4. Sortie	16. Loge des artistes
5. Escalier d'accès au deuxième balcon	17. Escalier de secours
6. Escalier d'accès au premier balcon	18. Buffet
7. Bureaux	19. Foyer
8. Passage	20. Balcon
9. Cour	21. Sortie de secours
10. Vestiaire	22. Palier de sécurité
11. Accessoires	23. Salle de théâtre
12. Arrière-scène	24. Escalier d'accès à la scène

1. Box-office	13. Stage
2. Box-office Hall	14. Loge
3. Passage	15. Box
4. Exit	16. Conversation-room
5. Stairs to Upper Circle	17. Emergency stairs
6. Stairs to Dress Circle	18. Buffet
7. Office Wing	19. Foyer
8. Carriageway	20. Terrace
9. Courtyard	21. Emergency exit
10. Cloak-room	22. Rescue Platform
11. Property-room	23. Spectator's Area
12. Back-stage	24. Stage Stairs

letztere mit Durchfahrten versehen, und es fehlt auch sonst nicht an Ausgängen. Der vortretende, kuppelbekrönte Rundbau an der Kleinen Königstraße enthält unten die Kassenhalle mit Eingängen und Schutzdach, darüber das durch zwei Geschosse gehende Foyer, dem ein Balkon vorgelegt ist; darüber folgt, in der Höhe des Amphitheaters, eine Garderobe. Das Parkett und die beiden Ränge des Zuschauerraums sind von breiten Umgängen umzogen, an welche sich nach außen Büfetts, Garderoben, Toiletten, Treppen und Ankleideräume für die Künstler, nebst Ausgängen zu den Höfen anschließen. Dem Bühnenhause sind beiderseits in Parketthöhe ein Requisitenraum und ein Konversationszimmer angegliedert.

368 [1910; 37]

Die zu einem Doppelhaus vereinigten beiden Wohnhäuser in Worms, Mozartstraße 4 und 6, sind im Laufe eines Jahres nach dem Entwurfe des Architekten Georg Metzendorf für insgesamt rund 45 000 Mark Baukosten zur Ausführung gekommen.

An der Straßenfront tritt ein breiter, an den Seitenfronten je ein schmalerer, die Dachlinie durchbrechender, mit halbrundem Giebel abgeschlossener Vorbau heraus, von denen der an der Seitenfront gelegene jedesmal den Eingang enthält. In den Seitenteilen der Straßenfassade wölben sich im ersten Stock flachrunde Balkons hervor. Die Tür- und Fensteröffnungen sind geradlinig abgedeckt, im Dachgeschoß des Vorbaues an der Straßenseite sind runde Fenster angebracht. An der Rückseite des Gebäudes zeigen sich im Erdgeschoß Veranden, über denen sich Balkons befinden. Die Fassadenflächen sind mit gekörntem Verputz versehen, die Pfeiler und sonstigen Architekturgliederungen sind aus rotem Pfälzer Sandstein hergestellt und zum Teil vergoldet. Jedes Haus enthält eine auf beide Geschosse verteilte Wohnung, deren Räume von einer Diele mit freiliegender Treppe zugänglich sind. Wohnzimmer, Speisezimmer und Küche sind im Erdgeschoß untergebracht, während das Obergeschoß hauptsächlich die Schlafzimmer und das Bad enthält.

369 [1910; 57]

Die beiden zu einer Gruppe vereinigten Wohnhäuser in Nürnberg, Prinzregentenufer 9, sind nach dem Entwurfe der Architekten Peringer und Rogler im Laufe des Jahres 1909 errichtet. An der Front des links gelegenen Hauses ist das Erdgeschoß mit dem Sockelgeschoß zu einem gemeinsamen Unterbau zusammengezogen und zeigt breite, durch scheitrechte Bogen vereinigte Pfeiler, welche die Fenstergruppen umfassen. Darüber folgen drei Obergeschosse, deren mittlerer Teil durch kräftige, in ganzer Höhe durchgehende, auf Konsolen stehende, mit Kapitellen bekrönte Halbsäulen, welche als Architrav eine mit Vasen besetzte Brüstung tragen, geteilt wird. Die gerade überdeckten, durch eine Umrahmung zusammengehaltenen Fenster in den Feldern zwischen den Säulen werden durch schmale Pfeiler getrennt. Von den Seitenteilen der Fassade enthält die eine im Erdgeschoß den Eingang; in beiden Teilen kragen sich im zweiten und dritten Obergeschoß Fensterausbauten vor. Das fünfte Geschoß tritt im mittleren Teile hinter die auf Säulen ruhende Brüstung zurück und wird durch das weit ausladende Dachgesims gedeckt, während sich über den Seitenteilen offene Loggien bilden. Das gequaderte Erdgeschoß sowie die Säulen bestehen aus rotem Mögeldorfer Sandstein; die oberen Fassadenflächen sind verputzt und der Sockel ist in gestocktem Beton hergestellt. Das Dach hat eine Ziegeleindeckung erhalten und die Rinnen bestehen aus Kupfer.

Beide Häuser umschließen in jedem Geschoß eine geräumige, mit Haupt- und Nebentreppe ausgestattete Wohnung. Die Gründung wurde auf Betonpfählen ausgeführt. Konstruktion und Berechnung der Gründung erfolgten durch Dyckerhoff & Wichmann A.-G.

370 [1910; 99]

Der von den Architekten Eitel und Steigleder errichtete Neubauteil des Warenhauses „Kaiserhof" in Stuttgart, Marienstr. 10, mußte mit dem bestehenden Hintergebäude in der Grundrißanlage in Einklang

---

gée. Des passages assurent l'accès aux cours. Les portes de sorties sont nombreuses. Le corps du bâtiment arrondi, saillant, couronné d'une coupole, comprend, au rez-de-chaussée, le hall des caisses ainsi que les entrées abritées par un auvent, puis au premier étage, un foyer s'élevant sur deux étages, assorti d'un balcon, et enfin un vestiaire. L'orchestre ainsi que les premiers rangs de la salle des spectacle sont ceints de larges dégagements permettant l'accès aux buffets, aux vestiaires, aux toilettes, aux escaliers, aux loges des artistes et aux sorties sur cour. La cage de scène est flanquée, au niveau de l'orchestre, de la salle des accessoires et d'un petit cabinet.

368 [1910; 37]

Ces deux maisons mitoyennes, situées à Worms, Mozartstraße 4 et 6, furent construites en l'espace d'une année pour la somme de 45 000 marks. Les plans furent exécutés par l'architecte Georg Metzendorf. La façade sur rue est assortie d'un large avant-corps s'élevant au-delà de la corniche du toit et se terminant par un pignon arrondi. Un avant-corps plus étroit, abritant l'entrée et présentant les mêmes caractéristiques que le précédent se dégage de chaque façade latérale. De part et d'autre de la façade frontale se détache un balcon en demi-cercle. Les ouvertures des portes et des fenêtres sont à linteau droit, des lucarnes percent le mur de façade de l'avancée frontale, au niveau de l'étage mansardé. Le rez-de-chaussée de la façade postérieure présente des vérandas surmontées de balcons. Les murs extérieurs sont rustiqués, les piliers et les autres éléments de décoration sont réalisés en grès rouge du Palatinat et en partie dorés. Chaque maison abrite un appartement agencé sur les deux niveaux. Les pièces sont accessibles par l'antichambre comprenant l'escalier. La salle de séjour, la salle à manger et la cuisine sont aménagées au rez-de-chaussée. L'étage est occupé par les chambres à coucher et la salle de bains.

369 [1910; 57]

Les deux immeubles de rapport mitoyens, situés à Munich, Prinzregentenufer 9, furent construits, sur les plans des architectes Peringer et Rogler, au cours de l'année 1909. Le rez-de-chaussée et l'entresol de l'immeuble de gauche forment un ensemble et présentent des piliers, réunis par des plates-bandes appareillées, encadrant des fenêtres groupées. Les trois étages suivants sont divisés, dans leur partie médiane, par de puissantes demi-colonnes continues, reposant sur des consoles, couronnées de chapiteaux et portant, comme architrave, une balustrades ornée de vases. Elles flanquent des fenêtres droites groupées, elles-mêmes divisées par d'étroits piliers. Les ailes, dont l'une abrite l'entrée au rez-de-chaussée, sont assorties, aux deuxième et troisième étages, de bow-windows. Le cinquième étage du corps de bâtiment, s'élevant en retrait derrière la balustrade reposant sur les colonnes, est recouvert par la corniche saillante du toit. De part et d'autre s'ouvrent des loggias. Le rez-de-chaussée ainsi que les colonnes sont construits en grès rouge de Mögeldorf. Les surfaces supérieures des murs de façade sont enduites d'un crépi, le socle est en béton bretelé. Le toit présente une couverture de tuiles, les gouttières sont en cuivre.

Les deux immeubles abritent à chaque étage un vaste appartement, équipé d'un escalier principal et d'un escalier de service. Les fondations furent réalisées sur des poteaux de béton. La construction et les calculs des fondations furent exécutés par les établissements Dyckerhoff & Wichmann.

370 [1910; 99]

Les architectes Eitel et Steigleder qui exécutèrent les plans du nouveau bâtiment du grand magasin „Kaiserhof" de Stuttgart, Marienstraße 10, durent tenir compte de l'edifice déjà existant pour créer un ensem-

---

latter contain carriageways and an abundance of exits. The projecting round structure at the Kleine Königstrasse is crowned with a cupola; on its ground floor are located the box—office hall, entrances and a covered porch, above that, a foyer extending through two storeys, and a terrace. Further up, at the level of the amphitheater, is a cloak—room. The stalls, dress circle and upper circle are encircled by broad passages having on their outer side buffets, cloak—rooms, lavatories, staircases and dressing—rooms for the performers, as well as exits leading to the courtyards. The stage—house is flanked by a property room and a conversation room.

368 [1910; 37]

The two houses which form an apartment building in Worms (Mozartstrasse 4 and 6) were built in the course of one year based on the plans of the architect Georg Metzendorf for a total of approximately 45,000 Marks.

The street front has a broad bay extending above the roof line and ending with a curved semi—circular gable. The side fronts have a similar structure, albeit narrower, each of which also contains an entrance. A slightly rounded balcony supported by an arched corbel projects from each side of the street front at the first storey. The doorways and windows are straight—lined; the attic storey of the front bay has round windows. The rear side of the house has verandas at the ground level covered by balconies at the first storey. The façades are rendered in granular plaster, the pilasters and other architectural ornaments are of red sandstone from the Palatinate and partially gilded. Each house has an apartment occupying both storeys, whose rooms are arranged round a hall with an open staircase. The sitting—room, dining—room and kitchen are on the ground floor, whilst the upper floor contains chiefly the bedrooms and bath.

369 [1910; 57]

Two apartment buildings in Nuremberg (Prinz-regentenufer 9) form a unified structure and were built according to the designs of Peringer and Rogler during the year 1909. The ground floor at the front of the house on the left is integrated with the basement floor in a common base structure with broad pilasters with camber arches over groups of windows. Three upper storeys rise above, with the entire height of the middle section of the façade being broken up by a giant order of massive engaged columns resting on consoles and ornamented with capitals. The latter form an architrave supporting a vase—lined balustrade. The straight—lined windows between the column are grouped by a moulding and separated by narrow pilasters. One side of the façade contains the ground—level entrance and both ends have oriel windows at the second and third storeys. The middle section of the fifth storey is recessed behind the column—supported balustrade and is covered by the overhanging roof cornice, whereas open loggias are located at either side. The ashlar facing of the ground level and the columns is of red sandstone from Mögeldorf; the upper façades are plastered and the socle is of bush—hammered concrete. The roof is covered in clay tile and has copper gutters.

Both houses have a spacious flat on each floor, with a principal and a side staircase. The foundation rests on concrete piers and was engineered by the firm of Dyckerhoff & Wichmann.

370 [1910; 99]

In their design of the new addition to the "Kaiserhof" department store in Stuttgart (Marienstrasse 40) the architects Eitel and Steigleder have successfully integrated it into the ground plan of

gebracht werden. Die Bauzeit dauerte 4 Monate, und die Kosten für Neu- und Umbau betrugen 250 000 Mark. Die in breite Schaufenster aufgelöste Fassade im Erdgeschoß und ersten Obergeschoß ist ganz in Eisenkonstruktion mit teilweiser Kupferverkleidung hergestellt. Im zweiten und dritten Obergeschoß bestehen die durchgehenden Pfeilervorlagen aus glasierten Verblendziegeln, die Einlagestreifen aus verzierten Tonplatten, und die Zwischenfelder sind gleichfalls mit bemusterten Tonplatten bekleidet. Über dem weit ausladenden Dachgesims erhebt sich eine Brüstung, die in der Mitte der Fassade durch ein flaches Giebelfeld unterbrochen wird. Sämtliche Geschosse enthalten zusammenhängende, nur durch Pfeilerreihen geteilte, durch Treppen und Aufzüge verbundene Verkaufsräume. Im Erdgeschoß führt eine Durchfahrt zu einem offenen Hofraume, außerdem ist noch ein kleiner Lichthof vorhanden.

ble harmonieux. Les travaux de construction et de transformation durèrent 4 mois, et revinrent à 250 000 marks. Le rez-de-chaussée et le premier étage présentent une façade percée de larges devantures, entièrement réalisée en fer et partiellement revêtue de cuivre. Les deuxième et troisième étages offrent une ordonnance de pilastres continus en briques de parement vernies. Les bandes de jointure ainsi que les pans de mur séparant les fenêtres sont parés de plaques de terre cuite ornementées. Une balustrade s'élevant sur la corniche très saillante est interrompue, en son centre, par un pignon en delta. L'ensemble des étages est composé de surfaces de vente non-cloisonnées, divisées par une ordonnance de piliers et communiquant par des escaliers et des ascenseurs. Le rez-de-chaussée est assorti d'un passage reliant la rue à la cour ouverte. Le bâtiment est également pourvu d'une petite cour vitrée.

the existing rear structure. Construction of the new building and the accompanying remodelling of the old one lasted 4 months at a cost of 250,000 Marks. The ground floor façade is carved up into broad shop windows and partially rendered in copper plates. Pilasters faced with glazed clay brick extend the height of the second and third storeys; the filler strips and metopes are rendered in ornamented clay tiles. A balustrade is located over the overhanging roof cornice and is broken in the middle of the façade by a low—pitched pediment. All floors of the building have open sales—rooms divided only by rows of pillars and connected to one another by stairs and lifts. A carriageway at the ground level leads to an open courtyard; in addition, there is also a small patio.

371, 372 [1910; 63, 64]

In hoher Lage, einen herrlichen Ausblick auf die Danziger Bucht gewährend, ist der Axthof, in Pelonken bei Oliva errichtet, und zwar in einer Bauzeit von etwa einem Jahre, für die Bausumme von 70 000 Mark, nach dem Entwurfe des Architekten Curt Hempel. Das zweistöckige, mit einem teilweise ausgebauten Dachgeschoß versehene Gebäude ist reichlich durch Ausbauten belebt. An der Hauptfront springt im Erdgeschoß ein Wintergarten in Form eines Flügelbaues vor, außerdem ein flachrund ausgebogener Fensterausbau und im Obergeschoß ein Balkon. Der einen Giebelfront ist eine Terrasse mit großer geschwungener Freitreppe vorgelegt; das Obergeschoß daselbst zeigt zwei vorgekragte Erker, welche einen offenen, sich zur Loggia erweiternden Balkon zwischen sich einschließen und von dem gleicherweise vorspringenden Giebel überdeckt werden. Die andere Giebelseite enthält den Haupteingang, in einem vorspringenden, mit einem Giebel schließenden Fassadenteil gelegen. Die hintere Front ist durch einen Verandenausbau mit oberer Altane und eine anschließende Terrasse ausgezeichnet. Das weit ausladende hohe Dach trägt über beiden Fronten ausgedehnte, an den Enden mit Zeltdächern bekrönte Fensteraufbauten. Die Fronten sind über einem Sockel aus Bruchsteinen in roter Ziegelverkleidung und teilweise in grüngrauem Fachwerk hergestellt. Das Dach ist mit Falzziegeln eingedeckt.

Das Erdgeschoß enthält die Diele mit freiliegender Treppe und anschließendem Wintergarten, dann das Wohnzimmer, das Speisezimmer in Verbindung mit einer Terrasse und den Salon, welcher sich nach der Veranda und einer daneben gelegenen Terrasse öffnet. Im Obergeschoß liegen die durch Erkerausbauten erweiterten Schlafzimmer mit Ausgängen nach dem Balkon, außerdem noch eine Anzahl Zimmer und das Bad. Das Kellergeschoß ist zur Anlage der Küche, der Waschküche mit Rollkammer, des Raums für die Heizung und der Gärtnerwohnung benutzt.

Cette propriété, construite sur les hauteurs de Pelonken, non loin d'Oliva, bénéficie d'une vue splendide sur la baie de Dantzig. La villa fut réalisée en une année, sur les plans de l'architecte Curt Hempel, pour la somme de 70 000 marks. Il s'agit d'une maison asymétrique de deux étages au toit partiellement mansardé. La façade principale est assortie, au rez-de-chaussée, d'un bow-window arrondi et d'une aile abritant un jardin d'hiver et, à l'étage, d'un balcon. La façade pignon est flanquée d'une terrasse accessible par un perron; du premier étage saillissent deux bow-windows encadrant un balcon-loggia, couvert par le pignon protubérant. L'entrée principale est située dans une avancée de la façade opposée. La façade postérieure est caractérisée par une véranda, surmontée d'un balcon, avec terrasse attenante. Le haut toit saillant est percé de fenêtres mansardées couronnées dans leurs extrémités par des toits en pavillon. Les murs de façade, revêtus de briques rouges, présentent partiellement des colombages vert gris. Le socle est réalisé en pierres de taille. Le toit est recouvert de tuiles à emboîtement.

Le rez-de-chaussée comprend l'antichambre, l'escalier et le jardin d'hiver contigu, puis la salle de séjour communiquant avec une terrasse et le salon, lui-même attenant à la véranda et à la terrasse. A l'étage sont aménagées les chambres à coucher, agrandies par les bow-windows et donnant sur le balcon, d'autres pièces et la salle de bains. La cuisine, la buanderie et la lingerie, la chaufferie ainsi que le logement du jardinier sont installés au sous-sol.

The Axthof county house in Pelonken near Oliva has been built on a elevated location affording a delightful view of Danzig Bay. Construction was carried out according to the plans of the architect Curt Hempel in the course of one year at a cost of 70,000 Marks. The attractive two—storey house with an attic storey is richly furnished with outbuildings and projections. A winter garden in the shape of an wing extension projects from the ground floor of the principal front, which also has a slightly—rounded bay with windows and a small balcony on the first floor. A terrace with sweeping stairs is located in front of one of the gabled fronts, which has at its first storey two cantilevered oriels flanking a loggia, which is covered by the overhanging gable and opens onto a balcony. The main entrance is located within the façade projection of the other gabled front. The rear front has a veranda which is topped by a balcony and opens out onto a terrace. The wide—span high—pitched roof has at both fronts windowed superstructures crowned by pyramidal roofs at both ends. The red—bricked fronts rest on a socle of rubble masonry; the gabled surfaces are rendered in green—grey half—timbering. The roof is covered with interlocking tiles.

Located on the ground floor are the hall with an open staircase and the winter garden, then the sitting— room, the dining—room, which opens onto the terrace, and the drawing—room which opens onto the veranda and its adjoining terrace. The upper storey contains bedrooms, which are enlarged by the corner oriels and have doors leading to the balcony, plus a number of other rooms, and the bath. The basement is used for the kitchen, laundry and heating facilities, and also contains the gardener's flat.

---

373 [1910; 50]

Das Pacific Building in San Francisco, von Architekt Ch. Whittlesey entworfen, gibt ein charakteristisches Beispiel von den in gewaltigen Abmessungen errichteten Neubauten, mit denen sich Jung-Francisco aus der durch die Erdbebenkatastrophe hervorgerufenen allgemeinen Verwüstung blitzschnell wieder erhoben hat. Das mit zwei Fronten freiliegende, neunstöckige Gebäude enthält in den unteren beiden, aus Quaderwerk hergestellten durch ein starkes Gurtgesims von dem oberen Teil der Fassaden abgetrennten Geschossen durchgehends Läden mit breiten Schaufenstern. Die oberen Geschosse werden über dem dritten Geschoß durch turmartige, über die Dachlinie hinausreichende Vorsprünge sowohl an der abgerundeten Ecke zwischen den Fronten als auch an den Endigungen derselben und durch die zwischen den Fenstern bis zum achten Geschoß aufsteigenden Pfeiler gegliedert. Die Fensteröffnungen des zweiten Ladengeschosses und des achten Obergeschosses sind mit stumpfen Spitzbögen überdeckt. Die übrigen Fensteröffnungen

Le Pacific Building de San Francisco, conçu par l'architecte Ch. Whittlesey, donne un exemple caractéristique des nouvelles constructions, aux proportions gigantesques, qui ont permis au jeune San-Francisco de se remettre aussi rapidement des ravages occasionnés par le tremblement de terre. Cet immeuble de neuf étages présente deux façades dégagées. Les deux niveaux inférieurs, réalisés en pierres de taille et séparés des autres étages par un cordon saillant, abritent des commerces pourvus de devantures. Les étages supérieurs sont assortis, au-dessus du troisième étage, d'avancées aux allures de tour, se détachant de l'angle arrondi des deux façades et de leurs extrémités et s'élevant au-delà de la corniche du toit, ainsi que de piliers montant entre les fenêtres jusqu'au huitième étage. Le deuxième étage des commerces et le huitième étage présentent des ouvertures en arcs en fiers-

San Francisco's Pacific Building, the product of architect Ch. Whittlesey, is typical of the many new structures of impressive dimensions currently being erected by the young city in its successful and lightning—fast recovery from the devastation caused by the catastrophic earthquake. The two lower floors of the nine—storey building with two exposed fronts are rendered in ashlar and set off from the upper stories by a prominent string—course; they are occupied by continuous rows of broad shop windows. The upper storeys are articulated by turret—like projections starting above the third storey and rising above the roof line. These projections are located on either side of the rounded corner of the building als well as at the end of both fronts. In addition, the upper façade is divided by pilasters extending to the eight storey, between which are located straight—lined windows. The windows of the two storefront storeys and the eighth storey are

sind geradlinig geschlossen. Unter dem neunten Geschoß zieht sich wieder ein starkes Gurtgesims hin; und das mit einer Balustrade bekrönte Abschlußgesims des flachen Daches ist mit einem Spitzbogenfries ausgestattet.

374 [1910; 72]

Das Wohnhaus in Nürnberg, Laufertorgraben 37, 39, ist ein Werk der Architekten Bieber und Vanwerden, ebenso das Haus 41, 43 derselben Straße. Die in Werksteinen verblendeten Fassaden zeichnen sich durch monumentales Gepräge aus. Die fünfstöckige Front des Hauses 37, 39 entwickelt sich der Breite nach dreigliedrig. Die Mitte nimmt ein breiter, vom Boden aufsteigender, viereckiger, durch zwei Obergeschosse reichender, eine Altane tragender Erkerausbau ein, über dem ein schmaler Dachstreif den Rücksprung der Fassade im vierten Obergeschoß vermittelt; die Seitenteile werden über dem Erdgeschoß und über dem dritten und vierten Obergeschoß durch Gurtgesimse geteilt und sind mit Giebeln in geschwungenen Konturen bekrönt. Das Quaderwerk des Erdgeschosses zeigt rauhe Bearbeitung oder aufgeschnittene Fugen, das der oberen Geschosse glatte, geschlossene Flächen, die sowohl am Erker als an den Giebeln durch Tafelpilaster und reliefierte Brüstungsfelder verziert sind. Der Haupteingang ist rundbogig, die Fenster sind sämtlich geradlinig überdeckt und die im Erdgeschoß mit abgerundeten Ecken versehen. Das übertretende Dach ist mit Biberschwänzen eingedeckt.

375 [1910; 74]

Das mit zwei Fronten freiliegende, dreistöckige Gebäude der Süddeutschen Diskonto-Gesellschaft in Mannheim, D 3 Nr. 15, wurde nach dem Entwurfe des Architekten Kgl. Baurat H. Ritter, unter Mitwirkung des Architekten E. Rückgauer von der Firma Ph. Holzmann & Co. ausgeführt, und zeigt im Äußeren die Formen des Stils Louis XVI. Die Bauzeit betrug 18 Monate. Die Fassaden sind im Erdgeschoß und ersten Obergeschoß mittelst durchgehender korinthischer Pilaster gegliedert und mit Architrav, Fries und Bekrönungsgesims abgeschlossen. Darüber erhebt sich das zweite Obergeschoß wieder durch Pilaster mit Ausnischungen, in denen Vasen stehen, geteilt und mit einer Balustrade bekrönt. Der Haupteingang liegt in der Straßenfront nach D 3 Nr. 15 und ist mit Säulen

point. Les autres fenêtres sont à linteau droit. Un cordon saillant orne la façade sous le neuvième étage. La corniche du toit plat, couronnée d'une balustrade, est parée d'une frise composée d'arcs en tiers-point.

374 [1910; 72]

Les immeubles construits à Nuremberg, Laufertorgraben 37, 39, 41, 43 sont l'œuvre des architectes Bieber et Vanwerden. Les murs de façade revêtus de pierres de taille se distinguent par leur aspect monumental. La façade, haute de cinq étages, de l'immeuble situé aux no. 37, 39 de la rue, est organisée, dans la largeur, en trois parties. Le centre est occupé par un large avant-corps quadrangulaire, montant de fond sur deux étages, supportant un balcon surmonté d'une étroite bande de toiture soulignant ainsi le quatrième étage en retrait. Les parties latérales sont divisées, au-dessus du rez-de-chaussée et des troisième et quatrième étages, par un cordon et sont respectivement coiffées d'un pignon aux contours ondulés. Le rez-de-chaussée est en pierres de taille traitées en bossage brut ou montrant des joints non-affleurants. Les murs supérieurs offrent des surfaces lisses et présentent, sur l'avant-corps et les pignons, des pilatres et des reliefs. L'entrée principale est en plein cintre, les fenêtres sont à linteau droit, celles du rez-de-chaussée sont assorties d'angles arrondis. Le toit saillant est revêtu de tuiles plates.

375 [1910; 74]

Le bâtiment du comptoir d'escompte, „Süddeutsche Diskonto-Gesellschaft", situé à Mannheim, D 3 nr. 15 fut construit sur les plans de l'architecte H. Ritter, en collaboration avec l'architecte E. Rückgauer de la société Ph. Holzmann & Co. Cet édifice de trois étages, offrant deux façades dégagées fut réalisé en style Louis XVI. Les travaux durèrent 18 mois. Les façades du rez-de-chaussée et du premier étage s'organisent autour de pilastres corinthiens continus, supportant architrave, frise et corniche de couronnement. Le deuxième étage, présentant des pilastres concaves renfermant des vases, est surmonté d'une balustrade. L'entrée principale, flanquée de colonnes, se trouve sur la façade sur rue. Les murs de façades portent un revêtement de grès clair. Le socle est en granit. Le toit

framed in obtuse pointed arches. A prominent string-course is again located at the ninth storey; the upper cornice is crowned by a balustrade, the flat roof has a frieze of pointed arches.

374 [1910; 72]

The apartment building in Nuremberg (Laufertorgraben 37, 39) as well as the houses at No. 41 and 43 in the same street is the work of the architects Bieber and Vanwerden. It owes its monumental appearance to the ashlar rendering of the façades. The five-storey front of the house at No. 37, 39 is divided up into three horizontal sections. The middle section features a broad square bay which runs from the ground level through the two upper storeys and ends in a balcony. The narrow roof strip above this marks the recessed façade of the fourth storey. The side sections are divided by string-courses over the ground level as well as over the third and fourth stories, and are crowned by shaped gables. The ashlar at the ground level has either rough or banded rustication, that of the upper stories has a smooth, unjointed surface. The ornamentation at the bay and gables consists of relief panels. The principal entrance is framed in a round arch, all windows are straight-lined except for those at the ground level, which have rounded corners. The overhanging roof is covered with flat red tiles.

375 [1910; 74]

The three-storey corner building of the German Discount Bank in Mannheim was designed by the royal architect H. Ritter, with additional plans provided by the architect E. Rückgauer of the firm Ph. Holzmann & Co. The two exposed fronts borrow heavily from the style of Louis XVI. Conctruction occupied 18 months. The façades of the ground and first floors are articulated by Corinthian pilasters with an architrave, frieze and crowning cornice. The second storey is again articulated by pilasters and niches containing vase figures, and is crowned by a balustrade. The principal entrance is located at No. 15 D–3 Street and is framed by columns. The fronts are faced with

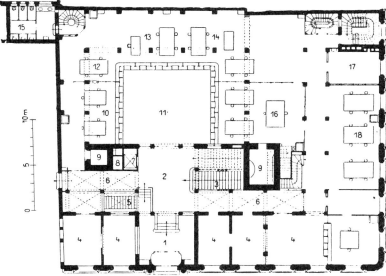

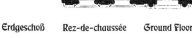

Erdgeschoß   Rez-de-chaussée   Ground Floor   2. Obergeschoß   2ème étage   Upper Floor

1. Vorhalle	15. Toiletten	1. Hall d'entrée
2. Vestibül	16. Effektenbureau	2. Vestibule
3. Haupttreppe	17. Vorstand des	3. Escalier principal
4. Zimmer	Wechselbureaus	4. Bureaux
5. Treppe zur Stahlkammer	18. Wechselbureau	5. Accès à la chambre forte
6. Gang		6. Couloir
7. Aufzug		7. Ascenseur
8. Frischluftschacht	30. Sitzungssaal	8. Conduit d'aération
9. Gewölbe	31. Oberlicht	9. Salle voûtée
10. Kasse	32. Bad	10. Caisse
11. Publikum	33. Buchhaltung	11. Public
12. Schecks	34. Küche	12. Chèques
13. Wechsel	35. Hof	13. Lettres de change
14. Kupons	36. Holzzementdach	14. Coupons

15. Toilettes	1. Porch	15. WC
16. Bureau des titres	2. Vestibule	16. Shares and Securities
17. Direction du bureau	3. Grand Staircase	17. Director's Room
des lettres de change	4. Room	for Exchange Office
18. Bureau des lettres de change	5. Stairs to Strong Room	18. Change Office
	6. Passage	
	7. Lift	
30. Salle de réunions	8. Fresh-air Ventilation Shaft	30. Meeting Room
31. Verrière	9. Vault	31. Sky-light
32. Salle de bains	10. Teller's Counter	32. Bath
33. Comptabilité	11. Public Area	33. Accounting
34. Cuisine	12. Cheques	34. Kitchen
35. Cour	13. Exchange	35. Courtyard
36. Toit en pâte de bois	14. Coupons	36. Häusler-type Roof Cladding

eingefaßt. Die Verblendung der Fronten besteht aus hellem Altleininger Sandstein, der Sockel ist in Granit hergestellt. Das Dach ist mit Schiefer eingedeckt. Die figürlichen Reliefs an den Fensterbrüstungen sind von Prof. A. Varnesi modelliert.

Das Erdgeschoß enthält das Vestibül, dem ein Windfang vorangeht, die Haupttreppe, mehrere Nebentreppen, den Aufzug und sonst die vorwiegend für den Verkehr mit dem Publikum bestimmten Räume: den großen Schalterraum mit Glasdach, die Wechselstube mit Sprechzimmern, die Kasse, die Treppe zur Stahlkammer und zwei kleinere Gewölbe. In das Sockelgeschoß sind die Stahlkammer, die Effekten- und Kupongewölbe eingebaut, außerdem sind hier, mit besonderem Eingang von der Kunststraße, die Garderobe, Toiletten und Waschräume, ferner die Heizungs-, Lüftungs-, Entstaubungs- und Rohrpostanlage untergebracht. Im ersten Obergeschoß liegen die Direktions-, Sitzungs- und Sprechzimmer, dann die Räume für das Sekretariat, die Korrespondenz, Registratur und Expedition. Das zweite Obergeschoß umschließt den großen Sitzungssaal mit Nebenräumen, die Buchhaltung und die Hausmeisterwohnung.

Die Direktionszimmer im ersten Obergeschoß sind im Barockstil, eine Anzahl anderer Räume im Stil Louis XVI. ausgestattet. Alle Räume werden mit Warmwasserheizung erwärmt und mit erwärmter Luft ventiliert.

376 [1910; 75]

Das Gebäude des Kaiserl. Postamts in Berlin, Linkstraße 5, ist nach dem Entwurfe des Architekten Kaiserl. Postbaurat Walter unter örtlicher Bauleitung des Architekten Kaiserl. Postbauinspektor Rahm ausgeführt. Die im mittleren Teile in vier, in den schmalen Seitenteilen in drei Geschossen aufsteigende Fassade läßt den Charakter des öffentlichen Gebäudes hervortreten. Das Erdgeschoß enthält im Korbbogen überwölbte Eingänge, Einfahrten und Fenster; im ersten und zweiten Obergeschoß sind Gruppenfenster mit geraden Sturzen angeordnet, das eine Mal durch Säulen, das andere Mal durch Pfeiler geteilt. Der mittlere Teil der Fassade wird beiderseits durch polygonale, im Erdgeschoß vorgekragte, bis zur Dachlinie fortgesetzte und mit Zeltdächern überdeckte, reich ornamentierte Erker begrenzt; über dem Dachgesimse folgt ein geschwungenes Giebelfeld mit dem Reichsadler. Die Fassade ist mit Werksteinen verblendet, und die Flächen sind durch einzelne rauh belassene Quadern belebt. Die Dächer haben Biberschwanzeindeckung erhalten und tragen in den unteren Seitenteilen Dachfenster mit Giebelabschluß.

377 [1910; 58]

Die zweistöckige, mit hohem, überhängendem Dach ausgestattete Villa Knudsen in Kopenhagen, Svanemöllevej 56, von Architekt Carl Brümmer entworfen, ist im Laufe eines Jahres für die Baukostensumme von rund 40 000 Kronen zur Ausführung gebracht. Die Straßenfront enthält den Haupteingang unter einem in geschwungener Form überdachten Vorbau; darüber öffnet sich ein durch beide Geschosse reichendes breites, in Bogenlinie schließendes Fenster, dem ein entsprechend geformter Dachgiebel folgt. Die Fenster neben dem Eingang sind als Vierpässe gebildet und von Rundbogennischen eingefaßt. Dem Erdgeschoß sind beiderseits niedrigere Anbauten mit besonderen Dächern angefügt. An der Gartenfront springen zwei flachrunde, Altane tragende Erkerausbauten vor, zwischen denen sich eine Terrasse mit Freitreppe befindet. Die Fronten sind in gefugten handgestrichenen Backsteinen hergestellt; das abgewalmte Dach ist mit roten Ziegeln eingedeckt. Die hölzernen Figuren am Haupteingang sind ein Werk des Bildhauers Th. Berentzen. Den Mittelpunkt des Erdgeschosses bildet die Halle, aus der die freiliegende Stockwerkstreppe aufsteigt und an welche sich die Zimmer anschließen. Speisezimmer und Salon sind durch die Erkerausbauten erweitert, das Gartenzimmer öffnet sich nach der Terrasse. Anrichte und Küche sind neben dem Speisezimmer angeordnet. Im Obergeschoß liegen die Schlafzimmer mit Ausgängen nach den Altanen, Kinder- und Mädchenzimmer sowie der Baderaum.

est recouvert d'ardoises. Les reliefs sculptés ornant le bandeau des fenêtres furent modelés par le professeur A. Varnell.

Le rez-de-chaussée comprend le vestibule, précédé par un tambour, l'escalier principal, de nombreux escaliers secondaires, l'ascenseur ainsi que des salles destinées à l'accueil du public, à savoir la grande salle des guichets recouverte d'une verrière, la salle des lettres de change et ses cabinets d'entretiens, la caisse, l'escalier menant à la chambre forte et deux petites salles voûtées. Les sous-sol abrite la chambre forte, les salles voûtées renfermant les titres et les coupons. Le vestiaire, les toilettes et les cabinets de toilette, la chaufferie, les installations d'aération, d'aspiration de la poussière ainsi que de la poste pneumatique, accessibles par la Kunststraße, y sont également installés. Le premier étage est occupé par les bureaux de la direction, la salle de réunions, les cabinets d'entretiens, les salles de bureaux destinées au secrétariat, à la correspondance, aux expéditions et aux registres. Au deuxième étage sont aménagés la grande salle de réunions et ses cabinets attenants, la comptabilité et le logement du concierge.

Le bureau de la direction offre une décoration de style baroque, un certain nombre de pièces sont meublées en style Louis XVI. L'ensemble des pièces sont chauffées par un chauffage central à eau chaude et sont ventilées avec de l'air chaud.

376 [1910; 75]

Le bâtiment du bureau de poste impérial de Berlin, Linkstrße 5, fut construit sur les plans de l'architecte Walter. La direction des travaux fut assurée par l'architecte Rahm. La composition de la façade, haute de quatre étages dans la partie centrale, de trois dans les parties latérales, souligne la vocation publique de l'édifice. Le rez-de-chaussée est percé d'entrées, de passages et de fenêtres surbaissées. Les deuxième et troisième étages présentent des groupes de fenêtres à linteau droit, divisées par des colonnes ou des piliers. La partie médiane de la façade est flanquée de logettes, richement décorées, couronnées de toits en pavillon, se dégageant du rez-de-chaussée et s'élevant jusqu'à la corniche du toit. Un pignon aux contours ondulés portant l'aigle, emblème de l'empire, coiffe la façade. Les murs extérieurs, revêtus de pierres de taille, présentent des moellons traités en bossage brut de décoration. Les toits recouverts de tuiles plates sont troués latéralement de fenêtres mansardées.

377 [1910; 58]

C'est à l'architecte Carl Brümmer que l'on doit la villa Knudsen, située à Copenhague, Svanemöllevej 56. Cette maison, haute de deux étages, coiffée d'un haut toit saillant, fut construite en l'espace d'une année pour la somme de 40 000 couronnes. L'entrée principale, sur la façade sur rue, est abritée par un porche, au-dessus duquel s'ouvre, montant sur les deux étages, une large baie aux lignes ondulées, elle-même surmontée d'un pignon présentant des contours identiques. Les fenêtres quadrilobées flanquant l'entrée s'inscrivent dans des niches cintrées. Le rez-de-chaussée est assorti de part et d'autre de constructions basses, recouvertes d'une toiture. De la façade sur jardin saillissent deux oriels arrondis, couronnés de balcons, encadrant une terrasse accessible par un perron. Les murs de façade sont construits en briques jointoyées, peintes à la main. Le toit en croupe est recouvert de tuiles rouges. Les sculptures de bois décorant l'entrée furent exécutées par le sculpteur Th. Berentzen. Le rez-de-chaussée, organisé autour de l'antichambre comprenant l'escalier, abrite le salon et la salle à manger agrandis par les oriels, la cuisine et l'office attenants et la pièce-jardin donnant sur la terrasse. A l'étage sont aménagées les chambres à coucher contiguës aux balcons, la chambre des enfants et celle des domestiques ainsi que la salle de bains.

light sandstone from Altleiningen, the socle is of granite and the roof is covered with slate. The relief sculptures are based on models created by Professor A. Varnesi.

Located on the ground floor are the vestibule preceded by a draught lobby, the grand staircase, a number of side stairs, the lift and rooms for the use of the bank's patrons: the spacious tellers' hall with a glass ceiling, the exchange room with its conference rooms, the tellers' hall, the steps to the strong room, and two smaller vaults. The basement contains the strong room, the shares and securities vault, as well as a special entrance facing the Kunststrasse, cloakrooms, lavatories and a wash—room. Installations for heating, ventilation and an air—carrier system are also located here. On the first floor are rooms for the director, conferences and consultations, then those for the secretaries, correspondence, registry and dispatching. The second story contains the large meeting room complete with side chambers, accountants' rooms and living quarters for the caretaker.

The rooms for the director on the first storey are furnished in a Baroque style, a number of other rooms are decorated in the style of Louis XVI. All rooms have hot water central heating and warmed—air ventilation.

376 [1910; 75]

The Imperial Post Office in Berlin (Linkstrasse 5) was designed by the Imperial Posts architect Walter, with construction carried out under the supervision of the Imperial Posts Inspector Rahm. The façade, with its middle part divided into four storeys and its narrower sides into three storeys, is characteristic of a public building. The ground floor entrances, carriageways and windows are framed in basket arches. The windows of the first and second storeys have straight—lined mouldings, the former divided by columns, the latter by pilasters. Both sides of the middle façade have richly—ornamented polygonal bays which are cantilevered at the first storey and extend to the roof line where they are crowned by pyramidal roofs. A shaped pediment rises above the roof moulding bearing the Imperial eagle. The façade is faced with ashlar and punctuated with rusticated stones. The roof is covered in flat red tiles, with gabled dormers in its steeper, lower section.

377 [1910; 58]

A work of the architect Carl Brümmer is the two—storey Villa Knudsen in Copenhagen (Svanemöllevej 56). This country house with a high—pitched overhanging roof was completed in one year at a cost of approximately 40,000 Crowns. The main entrance at the street front is covered by a gracefully—curving porch, above which opens a broad window culminating in an outline of an arch which follows the shape of the gable. To either side of the entrance are quatrefoil oculus windows set in round—arched niches. One-storey side—wings with lean—to roofs are located on each side of the house. Two slightly—rounded bays with balconies project at the garden front; located between them is a terrace with stairs leading into the garden. The fronts are of brick, the hipped roof is covered with red tile. The figures of wood at the main entrance are the work of the sculptor Th. Berentzen. The focal point of the ground floor is occupied by the hall which leads to the open staircase as well as to the other rooms. The dining room and the drawing—room occupy the bay area; the garden room opens onto the terrace. Pantries and kitchen are located next to the dining—room. Bedrooms with doors leading onto the balconies are located on the upper floor, as well as the nursery, maid's room, and bath.

Ein ovaler, etwas erhöhter Vorplatz, dem eine durch beide Geschosse der Front bis zum Dachgesims reichende Einbuchtung entspricht, geht dem rundbogigen, in einem Mauervorsprung eingeschlossenen Haupteingange des von einem Garten umgebenen Landhauses in Pullach bei München voran. Der zweistöckige Bau wurde nach dem Entwurfe der Architekten Gebrüder Rank im Laufe eines Jahres ausgeführt, und kostete, einschließlich der schwierigen Fundierungsarbeiten, 35000 Mark. An einer Seitenfront des sonst schlichten Hauses springt im Erdgeschoß ein Erker vor; und an der Hinterfront, gleichfalls im Erdgeschoß, ist eine Veranda sowie ein zweiter Ausbau vor einer loggienartigen Vertiefung angeordnet. Die Fronten haben rauhen Verputz in graugrüner Bemalung erhalten. Das abgewalmte, weit übertretende Dach ist mit Ziegeln eingedeckt. Der Garten ist mit einem teilweise offenen, in Holzkonstruktion hergestellten, mit einem Zeltdach überdeckten Gartenhäuschen ausgestattet. Als Fundament des Wohnhauses dient eine Eisenbetonplatte, um der Gefahr des Abrutschens am Isarabhange zu begegnen.

Das Erdgeschoß enthält, hinter einem Windfang liegend, die Diele mit offener Treppe, das Eßzimmer mit überwölbtem·Erkerausbau und dem Ausblicke auf die Veranda, dann zwei Wohnzimmer, die Küche und eine Kammer. Im Obergeschoß liegen das Atelier der Besitzerin, der Kunstmalerin Klara Walther, das Schlafzimmer, das Bad und eine Kammer.

Das mit drei Flügeln einen offenen Hofraum umschließende Gebäude der Wäschefabrik in Bielefeld, Feilenstraße 31, ist nach dem Entwurfe des Architekten Bernh. Kramer errichtet. Die Bauzeit nahm zwei Jahre in Anspruch und die Baukosten haben rund 400000 Mark betragen. Die Fassaden sind in gefugten hannöverischen Verblendziegeln, abwechselnd mit Flächen in Spritzguß und mit Fensterabwässerungen aus schlesischen, grünen Glasursteinen hergestellt. Über dem aus einer Rundbogennische mit Giebelabschluß in gebogener Linie gebildeten Portalbau, welcher das im Stichbogen überwölbte Einfahrtstor der Hauptfront einschließt, erhebt sich die quadratische, als Wasserreservoir dienende, mit geschwungenen Giebeln und einer in gebrochener Linie aufsteigenden Dachpyramide bekrönte Turm. Das Erdgeschoß der Front zeigt im Stichbogen geschlossene Fenster in schlichter Mauer, die drei Obergeschosse sind durch in ganzer Höhe aufsteigende Pfeiler gegliedert, welche die im ersten und zweiten Obergeschosse mittels einer Umrahmung zusammengezogenen Fenster, im ersten Obergeschoß gradlinig, im zweiten im Korbbogen überdeckt, zwischen sich einschließen. Die Fenster im dritten Obergeschoß sind paarweise gekuppelt und mit geraden Sturzen versehen. Das eine Ende des Vorderflügels ist durch einen höher geführten, eine zweite Durchfahrt enthaltenden Bauteil bezeichnet. Die Dächer sind flach gehalten, mit Ausnahme der in Ziegeln eingedeckten Turmpyramide.

Das Erdgeschoß umschließt in zwei Flügeln Beamtenwohnungen, die Räume für Lager, Ausgabe, Versand und Packerei, sowie in einem dritten Flügel die Wäscherei. Im ersten und zweiten Obergeschoß sind die Kontore, der Tresor, die Räume für Versand, Abnahme, Näherei, Zuschneiderei und Plätterei untergebracht. Das über dem Vorderflügel sich erstreckende Dachgeschoß ist zu Lagerräumen benutzt. Im Keller liegen wieder Lagerräume, außerdem die Kartonnagefabrik, die Heizung und der Speisesaal. Sämtliche Decken sind massiv zwischen Trägern hergestellt.

Inmitten eines symmetrisch angelegten Gartens, auf einer durch eine Stützmauer begrenzten, mit Freitreppen verbundenen Terrasse erhebt sich in gleichfalls streng symmetrischer Anlage das Haus Müller-Renner in Winterthur, Rychenbergstraße 9. Der Entwurf des im Laufe zweier Jahre erbauten Hauses mit seinen Nebengebäuden, Stall, Gewächshaus und Automobilschuppen, stammt von den Architekten

Un palier ovale, quelque peu surélevé, en symétrie avec la découpe de la façade, précède l'entrée cintrée, enchâssée dans une saillie de maçonnerie, de cette villa de campagne de Pullach, non loin de Munich. Cette maison de deux étages fut réalisée en l'espace d'une année sur les plans des frères Rank, architectes. Les travaux, compliqués par les problèmes de fondations, coûterent la somme de 35000 marks. La maison aux lignes sobres présente un bow-window au rez-de-chaussée d'une des façades latérales. Le rez-de-chaussée de la façade postérieure est assorti d'une véranda et d'une avancée contiguë à un renfoncement en forme de loggia. Les murs de façade rustiqués ont reçu un badigeon vert gris. Le toit en croupe saillant est recouvert de tuiles. Un petit pavillon de bois, partiellement ouvert, recouvert d'un toit en bâtière est aménagé dans le jardin. Pour pallier les dangers de glissement de terrain sur ce versant de la vallée de l'Isar, les fondations furent remplacées par une plaque de béton.

Le rez-de-chaussée comprend le hall d'entrée et l'escalier attenant, sur lesquels s'ouvre le tambour, la salle à manger et son bow-window voûté avec véranda attenante, puis deux salles de séjour, la cuisine, et un débarras. L'étage est occupé par l'atelier de la propriétaire, le peintre Klara Walther, la chambre à coucher, la salle de bains et un débarras.

L'édifice de la manufacture de linge de Bielefeld, Feilenstraße 31, fut conçu par l'architecte Bernh. Kramer. Il s'agit d'un bâtiment composé de trois ailes ceignant une cour ouverte. Les travaux durèrent deux années et coûterent la somme de 400000 marks. Les façades présentent un revêtement de briques hanovriennes jointoyées alternant avec un crépi enduit au pistolet, les fenêtres sont assorties de bandeaux inclinés pour assurer le ruissellement des eaux réalisés en briques vernies vertes de Silésie. Le portail d'entrée surbaissé s'inscrit dans un ensemble formé par une niche en plein cintre coiffée d'un pignon. Il est surmonté d'une tour quadrangulaire, ornée d'un pignon et couronnée d'un toit en pyramide aux lignes brisées, faisant fonction de réservoir d'eau. Des fenêtres surbaissées trouent le mur sobre du rez-de-chaussée. Les trois étages supérieurs offrent une ordonnance à piliers continus, encadrant les ouvertures. Les fenêtres droites du premier étage et celles surbaissées du deuxième étage forment un ensemble. Les fenêtres du troisième étage, regroupées par paires, sont à linteau droit. L'extrémité d'une aile frontale se distingue par une construction plus élevée renfermant un deuxième passage. Les toits sont plats, exception faite de la pyramide recouverte de tuiles coiffant la tour.

Le rez-de-chaussée est occupé par des logements d'employés, par des pièces destinées à l'entrepôt, à la distribution, aux expéditions et au conditionnement, ainsi que par la buanderie dans une troisième aile. Aux premier et deuxième étages sont aménagés les comptoirs, le coffre-fort, les pièces abritant les expéditions et la réception, les ateliers de couture, de coupe et de repassage. L'étage des combles de l'aile frontale sert d'entrepôt. Au sous-sol sont installés des entrepôts, la cartonnerie, la chaufferie et le réfectoire. Les planchers sont composés de solives garnies de hourdis massifs.

C'est sur une terrasse bordée par un mur de soutènement et accessible par un perron, au milieu d'un jardin à la française que se dresse la propriété Müller-Renner à Winterthur, Rychenbergstraße 9. Cette demeure aux lignes sévèrement symétriques fut conçue et réalisée par les architects A. Rittmeyer & Furrer. La construction de la villa et de ses dépendances, écurie, serre, et garage-automobile nécessita

A raised, oval forecourt, which reflects the shape of the recess extending through both storeys of the front, leads to the arched entrance of the country house in Pullach near Munich. The two—storey edifice was completed in the course of one year according to the plans of the Rank Brothers architectural firm. Total costs, including the arduous foundation work, amounted to 35,000 Marks. One side front of the otherwise plain construction has a bay at the ground level; at the back of the house, also at the ground level, is a veranda as well as a second projecting structure located in front of a loggia—like depression. The fronts are of rough plaster and painted a grey—green colour. The overhanging hipped roof is covered with clay tile. The garden is graced by an open—sided garden cottage constructed of wood and covered by a pyramidal roof. The entire dwelling rests on a foundation of reinforced concrete to prevent any danger of shifting towards the nearby slope.

The ground floor has a draught lobby leading to the main hall with an open staircase, a dining—room with an arched bay and a view of the veranda, then two sitting—rooms, the kitchen and a closet. The atelier of the owner, the painter Klara Walther, is located on the upper floor, as are the bedrooms, bath and a closet.

Construction of the clothing manufacturing factory in Bielefeld (Feilenstrasse 31), designed by the architect Bernh. Kramer, occupied two years and amounted to about 400,000 Marks. The three wings of the building encompass an open courtyard. The façades are alternately rendered in clay brick facing from Hannover and machine—applied plaster. The window coping is of green glazed tile from Silesia. The portal erection is ornamented at the principal front by a round—arched niche covered with a shaped gable and an entrance gate framed in an segmental arch. A square tower with shaped gables and a broken pyramid roof dominates the building's profile. The tower serves as a water reservoir. The ground floor of the front has windows in segmental arches and unadorned walls; the three upper storeys are articulated with pilasters running to the roof line which frame vertical windows in the second and third storeys; those at the first storey are straight—lined, those of the second are framed in round arches. The windows of the third storey are paired between the pilasters, and have straight lintels. One end of the front wing consists of a higher structure which contains a second carriage—way. All roofs are flat except for the tile—covered pyramid roof of the tower.

Two wings of the ground floor contain living quarters for state officials, rooms for storage, distribution, dispatch and packing; the laundry is located in the third wing. The first and second floors contain offices, the strong room, plus rooms for dispatch, receiving, sewing, tailoring and ironing. The roof storey of the front wing is used for storage, as is also the basement. Here, too, is where cardboard containers are produced, and where the heating installation and dining hall are located. All ceilings are of concrete and supported by girders.

Rising from the middle of symmetrically laid—out gardens with a front terrace and retaining wall is the Renner—Müller house in Winterthur (Rychenbergstrasse 9). Its strictly symmetrical design, which reflects its environs, is the work of the architects Rittmeyer & Furrer, members of the Association of Swiss Architects, who also supervised the two—year construction of the house and its outlying structures: stall,

B. S. A. Rittmeyer & Furrer, denen auch die Ausführung zuteil fällt. Die Baukosten betrugen 48 Fr. für den Kubikmeter umbauten Raumes. Der von zwei turmartig entwickelten, durch sämtliche Geschosse bis zur Dachlinie geführten polygonalen Eckerkern eingefaßten Hauptfront ist wieder eine Terrasse mit anschließenden Freitreppen vorgelegt. Der mittlere Teil der Front zeigt im Erdgeschoß die durch Säulen eingefaßten Eingänge zur Halle, über dem ersten Stock einen Balkon und als obere Endigung einen flachrundbegrenzten Giebel. Von der vorderen Terrasse führen Freitreppen zu den mit Altanen abschließenden Veranden der Seitenfronten. Vor dem Eingange an der Hinterfront ist eine mit besonderem Dach überdeckte offene Halle angeordnet und seitwärts im Obergeschoß eine Altane, von dem steilen Giebel des vorspringenden Flügelbaues überragt. Die Fassaden sind mit gelbem Kalkstein verblendet; die Treppen bestehen aus Granit. Die teilweise abgewalmten hohen Dächer sind mit roten Biberschwänzen eingedeckt.

Den Mittelpunkt des Erdgeschosses bildet die geräumige Halle, aus der die freiliegende Haupttreppe emporsteigt. Die Täfelung der Halle und die Treppe sind aus Birnbaumholz, Heizkörpermantel und Holzkamin mit der anschließenden Wand aus Marmor hergestellt. Das Eßzimmer ist in Eichenholz, das Rauchzimmer in Zitronenholz ausgeführt. Außerdem enthält das Erdgeschoß den Salon, das Dienstbotenzimmer, die Garderobe und die Küche mit Nebenräumen. Das Obergeschoß, in dem sich die Anlage der zentralen Halle wiederholt, ist hauptsächlich zu Schlafzimmern eingerichtet; ferner sind hier die Kinderzimmer, das Gastzimmer und das Badezimmer untergebracht. Das Haus ist teilweise doppelt unterkellert.

381 [1910; 87]

Das durch vortretende, pavillonartige Eckbauten und eine nach auswärts geschwungener Linie geführten Mittelbau gegliederte Gebäude der Gutenbergschule in Erfurt, Gutenbergstraße, ein Werk des Architekten Stadtbaurat P. Peters, ist etwa im Laufe eines Jahres für die Bausumme von 443 000 Mark zur Ausführung gekommen. Der Haupteingang liegt in der Mitte eines eingeschossigen Vorbaues; die den Mittelbau der Vorderfront einfassenden Risalite sind im zweiten Obergeschoß mit runden, ausgekragten Eckerkern versehen; die Giebel der Risalite und Eckbauten sowie der des Mittelbaues sind sowohl an der Vorderwie Hinterfront in geschwungenen Linien nach oben abgeschlossen. Die Fenster der viergeschossigen Fronten sind meist in Gruppen zusammengezogen. Die Sockelflächen bestehen aus gelbem Seeberger Sandstein; die Gliederungen der oberen Geschosse sind aus hellgrauem Mainsandstein hergestellt und die Flächen in grauem hydraulichen Kalkmörtel verputzt. Die hohen Dächer sind mit roten Sömmerdaer Biberschwänzen eingedeckt.

Der in allen Geschossen durchgehende breite Flurgang wird beiderseits von Räumen eingefaßt und erhält an beiden Schmalenden Licht von den dort angeordneten Treppen. Das Erdgeschoß enthält in der Mittelachse, von zwei Nebentreppen begleitet, das Konferenzzimmer; links vom Eingangsflur liegen die Zimmer des Rektors und Klassenräume, rechts davon die Kastellanwohnung und weitere Klassenräume. Die Decken sind durchweg massiv nach dem System Kleine ausgeführt.

382 [1910; 88]

Das vierstöckige Geschäftshaus in München, „Café Odeon", Briennerstraße 56, ist nach dem Entwurfe der Architekten Heilmann & Littmann im Laufe eines Jahres errichtet. Das Erdgeschoß, an der Front mit breiten rundbogigen Eingängen und Fenstern ausgestattet, ist einschließlich des darüber sich hinziehenden Balkons aus gelbem Bamberger Sandstein hergestellt. Das erste und zweite Obergeschoß sind mittelst umrahmter Tafeln zu einer Einheit zusammengezogen und durch ein Gesims mit plastisch verziertem Fries abgeschlossen. Darüber folgt das dritte Obergeschoß mit verzierten Feldern zwischen den Fenstern und kräftig ausladendem Dachgesims. Die oberen Fassa-

---

deux années de travail. Les coûts de construction se montèrent à 48 francs par mètre cube de volume construit. La façade principale, flanquée de part et d'autre d'une avancée polygonale aux allures de tour, montant de fond sur tous les étages jusqu'à la corniche du toit, est pourvue d'une terrasse accessible par un perron. La partie centrale de la façade est assortie, au rez-de-chaussée, d'entrées encadrées de colonnes conduisant au hall, puis, d'un balcon au-dessus du premier étage, et enfin d'un pignon arrondi. Des escaliers mènent de la terrasse frontale aux vérandas couronnées de plate-formes des façades latérales. L'entrée sur la façade postérieure est abritée par un porche hypostyle ouvert et couvert d'un toit. Au premier étage, un balcon est protégé par le pignon pentu de l'aile saillante. Les murs de façade sont revêtus de grès jaune. Les escaliers sont en granit. Les toits hauts, partiellement en croupe, sont recouverts de tuiles plates.

Le rez-de-chaussée est agencé autour du grand hall comprenant l'escalier principal. Le hall et la cage d'escalier présentent des lambris réalisés en poirier, les cache-radiateurs, la cheminée et le mur attenant sont en marbre. La salle à manger est en hêtre, le fumoir en bois de citronnier. Le rez-de-chaussée comprend en outre le salon, la chambre des domestiques, la garde-robe, la cuisine et l'office. A l'étage, qui reprend la disposition des pièces autour du hall, sont aménagées, les chambres à coucher, les chambres des enfants, la chambre d'amis et la salle de bains. La maison est équipée d'une cave, en partie sur deux niveaux.

381 [1910; 87]

Le bâtiment de l'école Gutenberg d'Erfurt, Gutenbergstraße, fut conçu par l'architecte P. Peters. Les travaux durèrent une année et coûtèrent la somme de 443 000 marks. Cet édifice se compose de deux ailes aux allures de pavillons et d'un corps de bâtiment légèrement convexe. L'entrée principale se trouve au centre d'une avancée haute d'un étage. Les avantcorps flanquant la façade principale du corps de logis sont assortis, au deuxième étage, de logettes rondes saillantes. Les pignons des avant-corps, des ailes ainsi que ceux du corps de bâtiment présentent des contours ondulés. Les façades de quatre étages sont percées de fenêtres essentiellement groupées. Le socle est construit en grès jaune de Seeberg. Les ornements des étages supérieurs sont réalisés en grès du Main gris clair. Les mur extérieurs présentent un crépi de mortier hydraulique gris. Les toits portent une couverture de tuiles plates rouges.

Le large couloir, continu à tous les étages, est bordé de salles et est éclairé aux extrémités par les cages d'escalier. Le centre du rez-de-chaussée est occupé par la salle de conférences flanquée de deux escaliers secondaires. A gauche de l'escalier d'entrée se trouvent les bureaux du directeur ainsi que des salles de classe, à droite le logement de l'intendant et d'autres salles de classe. Les planchers massifs sont construits selon la méthode Kleine.

382 [1910; 88]

Cet immeuble munichois de quatre étages, le „Café Odeon", situé dans la Briennerstraße au no. 56, fut construit en l'espace d'une année d'après les plans exécutés par les architectes Heilmann & Littmann. Le rez-de-chaussée, percé de larges ouvertures cintrées, et le balcon le surmontant sont réalisés en grès jaune de Bamberg. Les premier et deuxième étages forment, de par les encadrements, un ensemble, achevé par un cordon orné de sculptures. Le troisième étage présente, entre les fenêtres, des pans de murs très décorés ainsi qu'une corniche extrêmement saillante. Les murs de façade sont garnis d'un mortier de chaux non-lissé. Les façades

---

greenhouse and motor—car shed. Building costs amounted to 48 Francs per square metre of developed land. A terrace with open stairs has been placed in front of the principal façade, which is flanked by two tower—like polygonal bays extending through all storeys to the roof line. At the ground level of the middle section of the front are columned entrances leading to the main hall; a balcony is located over the first storey, and a rounded gable above that. Stairs lead from the front terrace to verandas at both side fronts which culminate in balconies. An open hall covered by a projecting roof is located at the entrance on the rear front, which has a side balcony on its upper level covered by the steep gable of the projecting wing structure. The façades are faced with yellow limestone; the stairs are of granite. The steep, half—hipped roofs are covered with flat red tile. The focal point of the ground floor is the spacious entry hall with an open staircase. The hall and stairs are furnished in pearwood wainscotting. Radiator covers and the fireplace with its adjacent wall are covered in marble. The dining—room has oak panelling, the smoking—room is furnished in lemonwood. In addition, the ground floor contains the drawing—room, a servant's room, the cloak—room and the kitchen and its side rooms. The upper floor, where the arrangement of the central hall is repeated, is mainly occupied by bedrooms; the nursery, guest room and bath are also located here. The house is partially furnished with a double basement.

381 [1910; 87]

Prominent, pavilion—like corner structures and a sweeping middle erection are the two striking architectural characteristics of the Gutenberg School in Erfurt, a work of the municipal architect P. Peters. The edifice was constructed in approximately one year at a cost of 443,000 Marks. The main entrance lies in the middle of a one—storey forebuilding. The middle erection of the principal front is framed by projections with round corner bays at the second storey. The gables of the projections and corner structures on both sides of the building are curved. Most of the windows in the four—storey fronts are arranged in groups. The socle surface consists of yellow sandstone from Seeberg; the articulations of the upper storeys are of light grey Main sandstone, with the flat surfaces being faced with grey hydraulic—bound lime mortar. The high—pitched roofs are covered with flat red tile from Sömmerdaer.

The broad corridor running the length of the building is flanked on both sides by rooms and is lit by natural light from the stairways located at both ends of the building. At the central axis of the ground floor is the conference room, which is flanked by two side stairs; to the left of the entrance hall are the rooms of the headmaster as well as classrooms, to the right are more classrooms and the living quarters of the caretaker. The massive floors have been constructed according to the Kleine system of hollow floors slabs.

382 [1910; 88]

The four—storey "Odeon Café" in Munich (Briennerstrasse 56) was built according to the plans of the architects Heilmann & Littmann in the course of a single year. The ground floor front, with its broad entrances and windows framed in round arches, and the overhanging balcony at the first floor are both of yellow sandstone from Bamberg. The first and second floors are joined by a panel façade and finished off by a cornice with a sculptured frieze. The third storey has ornamented panels between the windows and the overhanging roof moulding. The upper façades are faced with lime mortar plaster and their ornamentations are

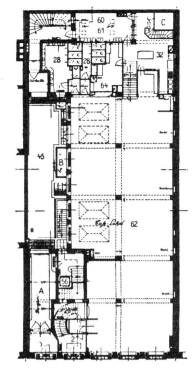
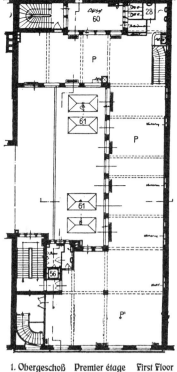
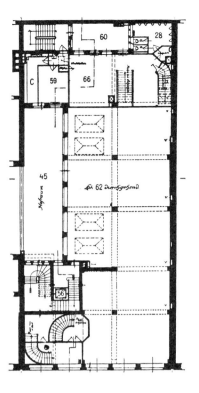
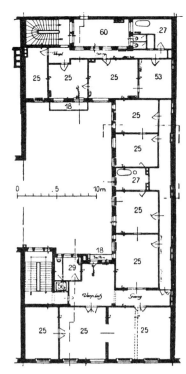

Erdgeschoß	Rez-de-chaussée	Ground Floor	1. Obergeschoß	Premier étage	First Floor

A Durchfahrt B Lichtschacht C Magazin P Billardsaal

A Passage B Puits au jour C Réserve P Salle de billard

A. Carriageway B. Light Well C. Store D. Billiard Hall

---

denflächen zeigen rauhen Kalkmörtelputz und Ornamente in Zementguß. Das Dach trägt eine Reihe mit Rundgiebeln abgeschlossene Dachfenster.

Im Erdgeschoß befindet sich ein großes Kaffeelokal, von der Straße und dem seitlich gelegenen Hofraume aus, außerdem durch Oberlicht beleuchtet. Zur Seite liegen die mit dem Hofraum in Verbindung stehende Durchfahrt, die zu den Obergeschossen führenden Treppen und der Personenaufzug. An der Rückfront sind um einen Lichthof die Toiletten, das Büfett, die Kaffeeküche, die zur Galerie über vorgenannten Räumen, sowie eine zweite zu den Obergeschossen führende Treppe angeordnet. Neben der Galerie liegen ein Bureau- und ein Magazinraum und zur Seite des Lichthofs eine Toilette. Das erste Obergeschoß wird von einem Saal für 20 Billards eingenommen, der durch mehrere Treppen vom Erdgeschoß aus zugänglich ist. Das zweite und dritte Obergeschoß sind zur Anlage je einer größeren Vorder- und einer Hofwohnung benutzt. Das Kellergeschoß enthält die zum Betriebe der Kaffeewirtschaft erforderlichen Backräume, den Heizraum, das Dienstbotenzimmer und anderes, außerdem die zu den Wohnungen gehörenden Kellerräume. Pfeiler, Unterzüge und Decken sind in Eisenbeton ausgeführt. Die Wand- und Plafondbemalung des Kaffeelokals lieferte Maler Mössl.

383 [1911; 1]

Das in der Kaufingerstraße 11 und 12 und in der Fürstenfelderstraße 4 und 5 gelegene, zwischen beiden Straßen sich erstreckende Haus „Zum Paulanerbräu" in München ist ein Werk der Architekten Heilmann & Littmann und wurde in einer Bauzeit von etwa 5 Monaten zur Ausführung gebracht. Die Front an der Kaufingerstraße zeigt im Erdgeschoß die Eingänge zur Stockwerkstreppe, zum Ladengeschäft, zwischen den Schaufenstern gelegen und zu dem Restaurationslokal; darüber folgen drei Obergeschosse und ein teilweise zurückgesetztes, teilweise in dem geschwungenen abschließenden Giebel des durch sämtliche Geschosse geführten Fassadenvorsprungs gelegenes viertes Obergeschoß. Vor dem Zurücksprunge der Fassade zieht sich eine mit Vasen bekrönte Brüstung hin, und über dem Dachgesims erheben sich turmartige Fensteraufbauten. Erdgeschoß und erstes Stockwerk der Fassade sind in Marktbreiter Muschelkalk, die übrigen Geschosse in Bamberger Sandstein ausgeführt. Das Dach oberhalb des ersten Stocks als Risalitabschluß, wie auch die Laterne sind in Kupfer hergestellt.

Im Erdgeschoß liegen die Restaurationslokalitäten des Paulanerbräu samt den Räumen des zugehöri-

les ornements sont en béton moulé. Le toit porte une série de fenêtres mansardées coiffées d'un pignon arrondi.

Le rez-de-chaussée abrite un vaste café, recevant un éclairage donné par la rue, la cour latérale et une verrière. Latéralement se trouvent le passage reliant la cour à la rue ainsi que l'ascenseur et l'escalier conduisant aux étages supérieurs. Les toilettes, le comptoir, une petite cuisine, un escalier menant à la galerie, jeté au-dessus des pièces précédemment citées et un deuxième escalier assurant l'accès aux étages supérieurs sont aménagés à l'arrière, autour d'une cour vitrée. A côté de la galerie sont installés un bureau, une réserve et des toilettes. Le premier étage est occupé par une salle contenant 20 billards, accessible du rez-de-chaussée par de nombreux escaliers. Les deuxième et troisième étages comprennent respectivement deux grands logements donnant l'un sur rue, l'autre sur cour. Le sous-sol renferme, entre autres, les cuisines du café, la chaufferie, la chambre des domestiques et les caves des logements. Les piliers, les solives et les planchers sont réalisés en béton armé. Les peintures murales du café furent exécutées par le peintre Mössl.

383 [1911; 1]

L'immeuble munichois „Zum Paulanerbräu", dont la surface s'étend entre deux rues, présente deux façades s'ouvrant respectivement sur la Kaufingerstraße et la Fürstenfelderstraße. Ce bâtiment, conçu par les architectes Heilmann & Littmann, fut exécuté en quelque cinq mois. La façade donnant sur la Kaufingerstraße est composée, au rez-de-chaussée, de trois entrées menant, l'une à la cage d'escalier, l'autre, située entre les devantures, au local de commerce, et la troisième à la salle de restaurant. L'immeuble comprend trois étages, puis un quatrième situé en partie en retrait et en partie dans le pignon aux lignes ondulés qui coiffe la saillie de la façade. Une balustrade couronnée de vases orne le renfoncement de la façade. Des fenêtres mansardées, aux allures de tourelles, se dressent de la corniche du toit. Les murs de façade du rez-de-chaussée et du premier étage sont en coquillart, les étages suivants sont réalisés en grès de Bamberg. Le toit de la saillie, au niveau du premier étage, ainsi que les lanternes sont réalisés en cuivre.

Au rez-de-chaussée se trouvent les salles de restaurant de la brasserie ainsi que les cuisines, un com-

of cement. The roof has a number of dormers framed in round gables.

The large café is located on the ground floor and accessible from the street as well as from the side courtyards; it is also supplied with roof lighting. At one side of the ground floor is a carriageway connected to the courtyard, a stairway leading to the upper floors, and a lift. A patio at the rear elevation is surrounded by public conveniences, the buffet, the coffee kitchen and a staircase leading to the gallery located above the aforementioned rooms. An office and store—room are located next to the gallery, and a lavatory is located to one side of the patio. The first floor is occupied by a large hall with 20 billiard tables and is connected to the ground floor by a number of staircases. The second and third floors each have two large fronts, one at the front of the building and one overlooking the courtyard. The basement is furnished with the bakery ovens used by the café establishment, and also includes a heating room, a staff room, and basement rooms for the buildings's tenants. Piers, joists and ceilings are of reinforced concrete. The murals and ceiling frescos are the work of the artist Mössl.

383 [1911; 1]

The commercial building "Zum Paulanerbräu" in Munich is bordered by the Kaufingerstraae 11—12 at the front and the Fürstenfelderstrasse 4—5 at the rear. Designed by Heilann and Littman, the edifice was constructed over the course of about 5 years. The ground level of its front façade on the Kaufingerstrasse exhibits doorways placed between the shop windows which lead to stairways, shops, and the restaurant. Three storeys are located above the ground floor, with the fourth set back at the sides. The middle section of the fourth floor is covered by a shaped gable, which finishes the projection running the whole length of the façade. A balustrade decorated with vases extends along the upper recesses of the façade, and turret—like superstructures with windows rise above the roof moulding. The façade at the ground level and first—storey is rendered in shell limestone from Markbreit; the upper stories are faced with sandstone from Bamberg. The projecting roof above the first storey and the lanterns are made of copper.

On the ground floor are located the brewery—sponsored restaurants and the accompanying kitchen

gen Küchenbetriebs, ein größerer Ladenraum und die Stockwerkstreppen, von denen die eine mit einem Personenaufzug verbunden ist. Das erste Obergeschoß ist zu Geschäfts- und Wirtschaftsräumen eingerichtet. Alle Geschosse sind mit massiven Decken ausgestattet. Als Mitarbeiter sind zu nennen: Bildhauer J. Seidler und Glasmaler Viglmann.

merce assez vaste et les cages d'escalier. Un ascenseur relie les étages entre eux. Le premier étage est occupé par des bureaux et des locaux de service. Tous les étages sont équipés de planchers massifs. Le sculpteur J. Seidler et le peintre sur verre Viglmann participèrent à l'élaboration des lieux.

space, a spacious storage room and stairways to the upper floors, one of which leads to a lift. The first floor has been designed for offices and conference rooms. All floors are provided with solid—construction ceilings. Recognition should also be given to the sculptor J. Seidler and the glass painter Viglmann.

384 [1911; 6]

Die reich in Formen des Barockstils ausgestatteten fünfstöckigen Fronten des Gebäudes der Ungar. Commerzialbank in Budapest umschließen einen Eckbau von bedeutenden Abmessungen. Die Ausführung erfolgte nach dem Entwurfe des Architekten Baurat Sigmund v. Quittner in einer etwa 2 Jahre dauernden Bauzeit für die Kostensumme von rund 4 000 000 Kronen. Das Erdgeschoß sowie das Zwischengeschoß, letzteres mit im Korbbogen geschlossenen Öffnungen, sind zu einer Einheit zusammengezogen und werden

384 [1911; 6]

The richly—ornamented Baroque façades of the five—storey Hungarian Commerce Bank grace a corner building of considerable size. Construction lasting a period of approximately 2 years was carried out according to the plans of the architect and senior government building officer Sigm. v. Quittner at a cost of about 4,000,000 Crowns. The ground floor and mezzanine – the latter exhibiting openings framed in basket arches – form a unified whole topped by a project-

384 [1911; 6]

La banque hongroise de Budapest est un bâtiment de cinq étages, aux formes imposantes, présentant de riches formes baroques. Cet édifice à pan coupé fut conçu par l'architecte Sigm. von Quittner. La construction dura près de deux années et coûta 4 000 000 couronnes. Le rez-de-chaussée et l'entresol, ce dernier présentant des ouvertures surbaissées, forment un ensemble terminé par un balcon saillant courant le long de la façade. Les trois étages supérieurs offrent une

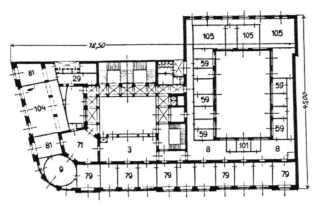

Erdgeschoß und 1. Stock	Rez-de-chaussée et premier étage	Ground Floor and First Floor

durch einen umlaufenden, ausgekragten Balkon abgeschlossen. Die oberen drei Geschosse sind mittelst einer durchgehenden Pilaster- und vorgestellten Säulenordnung gegliedert und haben über dem Hauptgesims ein teilweise hinter einer Balustrade zurückgesetztes Dachgeschoß erhalten. Die Fenster des ersten Obergeschosses sind rundbogig, die des zweiten und dritten Obergeschosses geradlinig überdeckt und im Eckbau mit Balkons ausgestattet. Die abgerundete, durch angelehnte Säulen ausgezeichnete freie Ecke wird durch schmale, turmartige Aufsätze tragende Risalite eingefaßt und durch einen rund aufsteigenden Kuppelbau bekrönt. Die Seitenfronten, von denen die längere durch einen Mittelrisalit mit Rundgiebel unterbrochen wird, sind wieder durch schmale Eckrisalite mit Aufsätzen beendet. Sockel und Portale sind in rotem, geschliffenem und poliertem Granit, die Fassaden in gelbgrauem Kalkstein hergestellt. Die Figurengruppe ist von Bildhauer Margó, das große Wappen mit Genien und die ornamentalen Bildhauerarbeiten sind von Maroti geschaffen.

Im Erdgeschoß liegen die vom Vestibül zugängliche Halle, der große, von Schaltern umgebene Kassensaal für den Verkehr des Publikums, die Hauptkasse und eine Anzahl Geschäftsräume. Der erste Stock enthält die Zimmer der Direktion, den Sitzungssaal, die Konferenzzimmer und zahlreiche Bureauräume. Vestibül, Halle, Haupttreppe und Kassensaal sind mit teils weißen, teils farbigen Platten aus ungarischem Marmor verkleidet.

ordonnance de pilatres et de colonnes saillantes continus et sont surmontés d'un étage mansardé, s'élevant partiellement en retrait derrière une balustrade. Les fenêtres du premier étage sont en plein cintre, celles des deuxième et troisième étages sont à linteau droit et, dans l'angle, pourvues de balcons. Le pan coupé arrondi, assorti de colonnes, est encadré d'avancées supportant des couronnements aux allures d'étroites tourelles. L'ensemble est dominé par un dôme. Les façades sont flanquées, dans leurs extrémités, d'étroites avancées portant couronnement. La façade la plus longue présente, en son centre, un avant-corps coiffé d'un pignon arrondi. Le socle et les encadrements des portails sont en granit rouge poli, les murs extérieurs sont réalisés en grès jaune gris. Les statues de la coupole furent réalisées par le sculpteur Margó, le blason et ses génies ainsi que les ouvrages plastiques ornementaux furent exécutés par le sculpteur Maroti.

Le rez-de-chaussée comprend le hall accessible par un vestibule, la grande salle des guichets destinée au public, la caisse centrale ainsi que des bureaux. Au premier étage sont installés les bureaux de la direction, la salle de réunion, les salles de conférences et de nombreux bureaux. Le vestibule, le hall, l'escalier principal et la salle des caisses sont revêtus de plaques de marbre hongrois polychromes et blanches.

ing balcony running along all sides. The upper three storeys are articulated by continuous pilasters and engaged columns. The recessed top storey above the main cornice is partially hidden by a balustrade. The windows of the first storey are framed in round arches, those above in straight frames, and those of the corner section have balconies. The slightly rounded center corner with engaged columns is framed by projections which terminate in narrow, turret—like superstructures. A domed structure rises above the corner. The side fronts, of which the longer of the two is divided by a center projection topped by a round gable, also terminate in narrow, turreted corner projections. The socle and portal are of smooth red polished granite, the façade of yellow—grey limestone. The group of figures at the cupola was created by the sculptor Margó; other sculptural ornamentation, including the large coat—of—arms with allegorical figures, is the work of Maroti.

The ground floor contains the vestibule and entry hall, the large main hall lined by wickets for public commerce, the main teller's window and numerous offices. The first floor contains the director's offices, the session—room, conference rooms and numerous offices. The vestibule, hall, main staircase and main hall are panelled in either white or coloured Hungarian marble.

385 [1911; 8]

Das Gebäude der Banque Populaire in Genf, Quai des Bergues, bildet einen Eckbau mit drei freiliegenden Fronten und ist nach dem Entwurfe der Architekten Maurette und Henchoz in einer Frist von etwa 2 Jahren für die Baukostensumme von rund 650 000 Frcs. einschl. der Inneneinrichtung zur Ausführung gebracht. Das Erdgeschoß zeigt rauhes Quaderwerk und im Korbbogen überwölbte Tür- und Lichtöffnungen, die folgenden Obergeschosse sind mit einer vorgestellten, durchgehenden ionischen Säulenstellung ausgestattet, welche die der Höhe nach zusammengezogenen, mit vorgelegten Balkons versehenen, geradlinig überdeckten Fenster zwischen sich einschließt. Über dem reichen Hauptgesims der Fronten erhebt sich

385 [1911; 8]

La banque populaire de Genève, quai des Bergues, est abritée dans un édifice, à pan coupé, présentant deux façades dégagées. Réalisé en l'espace d'une année, sur les plans des architectes Maurette et Henchoz, ce bâtiment revint à 650 000 francs, aménagement intérieur compris. Le rez-de-chaussée offre des bossages rustiques et des ouvertures surbaissées. Les étages supérieurs sont organisés autour de colonnes ioniques continues, encadrant des fenêtres en tribune à linteau droit. Sur l'entablement richement travaillé s'élève, en retrait derrière une balustrade, un quatrième étage, coiffé d'un toit en forme de pavillon. Le

385 [1911; 8]

The Banque Populaire building in Geneva (Quai des Bergues) comprises a corner edifice with exposed fronts. It was erected according to the plans of the architects Maurette and Henchoz within a period of approximately 2 years. Construction costs, including the interior design, amounted to about 650,000 Francs. Its ground floor front displays rustication and basket arches for the entrances and windows. The upper storeys feature projected Ionic columns framing straight—lined windows which are fronted by balconies. A forth storey topped by a pavilion—style roof and set back behind a balustrade rises above the

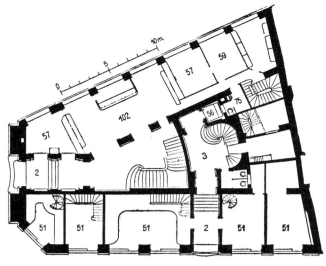
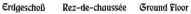

Erdgeschoß   Rez-de-chaussée   Ground Floor

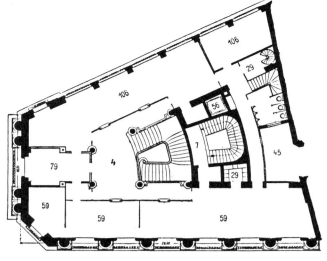

Zwischengeschoß   Entresol   Mezzanine

ein hinter einer Balustrade zurückspringendes, mit einem pavillonartig geformten Dach abgeschlossenes viertes Obergeschoß. Die Front der stumpfen Ecke trägt ein vierseitiges Kuppeldach mit bekrönender durchbrochener Laterne. An der Vorderseite der Kuppel schneidet ein Rundgiebel über einer Fenstergruppe ein. Der Unterbau der im Wettbewerb mit dem 1. Preise ausgezeichneten Fassaden besteht aus gelblichem Sandstein von Villete, die Obergeschosse sind in gelblichem Savonnières Kalkstein ausgeführt. Die Bildhauerarbeiten der Fassade rühren von Fasanino her, die Zinkornamente von V. Brolliet. Die Dächer sind mit Schiefer eingedeckt.

Das Erdgeschoß enthält den zu einer Treppe führenden Eingang zu den Geschäftsräumen der Bank, während an einer Seitenfront der zweite Eingang zu einem Vestibül mit Aufzug und der zu den Wohnungen der oberen Geschosse führenden Treppe, außerdem Läden mit großen Schaufenstern liegen. An der Hinterfront ist die Wohnung für den Hauswart, über der sich ein offener Hof erstreckt, angebracht. Im Entresol sind die Zimmer der Direktion und die Bureauräume der Bank untergebracht.

Die oberen Geschosse enthalten Wohnungen. Die Decken der Räume sind in armiertem Beton zwischen Eisenträgern hergestellt.

386 [1911: 19]

Der Wilhelmsbau in Stuttgart, das an der Königs- und Marienstraße sowie an der Passage gelegene Eckgebäude der Wilhelmsbau-Aktiengesellschaft, Königsstraße 78, Marienstraße 1 B und Kleine Königsstraße 8, von den Architekten Heim und Früh, etwa im

pan coupé porte un toit en coupole à quatre versants, couronné d'une lanterne. Un pignon arrondi, surmontant un groupe de fenêtres, coupe le versant frontal de la coupole. Le socle de l'édifice, pour lequel les architectes avaient obtenu le premier prix lors du concours, est construit en grès jaunâtre de Villette, les murs extérieurs des étages supérieurs sont en castines jaunâtres. Les travaux de sculpture des façades furent réalisés par monieur Fasanino, les ornements de zinc sont l'œuvre de V. Brolliet. Les toits sont recouverts d'ardoises.

Le rez-de-chaussée comprend l'entrée des bureaux de la banque, donnant sur un escalier, ainsi qu'une deuxième entrée, située sur une des façades latérales, conduisant à un vestibule avec ascenseur et à l'escalier desservant les logements des étages supérieurs, et enfin des commerces, assortis de larges devantures. Le logement du gardien, surmonté d'une cour ouverte, est situé à l'arrière du bâtiment. Les bureaux de la direction ainsi que les salles de bureau de la banque sont installés à l'entresol.

Les étages supérieurs abritent des logements. Les planchers des pièces sont composés de poutres de fer garnies de béton armé.

386 [1911: 19]

Le bâtiment d'angle de la société anonyme „Wilhelmsbau" de Stuttgart, situé aux no. 78 de la Wilhelmstraße, no. 1B de la Marienstraße et no. 8 de la kleine Königstraße fut construit en l'espace d'une année par les architectes Heim et Früh pour la somme

elaborate cornice. The front of the obtuse corner supports a four—sided cupola, which is crowned by an open—worked lantern. The front side of the cupola is occupied by a round gable set over a group of windows. The lower section of this award-winning façade is of yellowish Villette sandstone, the upper storeys of yellowish Savonnières limestone. The sculptural details of the façade were created by Fasanino, the zinc ornamentation by V. Brolliet. The roofs are covered with slate.

At the main entrance on the ground floor is a staircase leading to the offices of the bank, while a side entrance leads to a vestibule with a lift and stairs leading to living quarters located in the upper stories. In addition, the side front contains shops with large windows. Living quarters for the house caretaker are attached at the back of the building and covered by an open courtyard. The mezzanine contains the offices for administration and accounting.

Living quarters are located on the upper floors. The ceilings of the rooms are constructed of reinforced concrete cast between iron trusses.

386 [1911: 19]

The "Wilhelmsbau" commercial building in Stuttgart (Königstrasse 78) is a corner edifice owned by the Wilhelmsbau Co. Bordered by the Königstrasse and Marienstrasse, as well as a side passageway, it was erected in the course of one year from the plans of

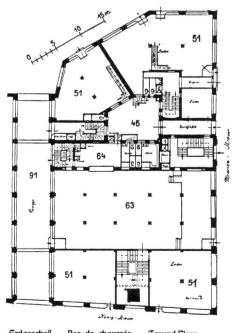

Erdgeschoß   Rez-de-chaussée   Ground Floor

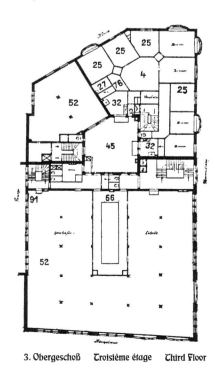

3. Obergeschoß   Troisième étage   Third Floor

Laufe eines Jahres von rund 1 500 000 Mark errichtet, ist im Erdgeschoß für Läden und ein Restaurant, im ersten Obergeschoß für ein Café und in den folgenden drei bzw. vier Obergeschossen ausschließlich für Geschäfts- und Bureauzwecke bestimmt. Die Fassaden sind in gelbem Klingemünster Sandstein ausgeführt; die architektonische Gliederung derselben ist besonders darauf berechnet, der Königstraße einen monumentalen Abschluß zu geben. Mit Rücksicht hierauf erhebt sich an der Ecke der Königs- und Marienstraße neben einem hohen Giebelaufbau ein massiger viereckiger, eine offene Galerie und einen zurückgesetzten, mit geschweiftem Dach abschließenden Aufsatz tragender Turm. Das mit Biberschwänzen eingedeckte Dach zeigt eine doppelt gebrochene Linie.

Im Erdgeschoß liegen zwei Läden und die Räume für den Betrieb eines großen Restaurants. Von der Königstraße führt eine breite Freitreppe in die Räume des ersten Stocks, die samt einem langgestreckten, weit ausladenden Balkon zu einem Café eingerichtet sind. Der Aufgang zu den durch drei Obergeschosse gehenden Geschäfts- und Bureauräumen liegt, getrennt von den Eingängen zur Restauration und zum Café, an der Marienstraße und ist mit einem Paternosteraufzug ausgestattet. Die Heizung sämtlicher Räume geschieht mittelst einer Niederdruck-Dampfanlage. Eine Wasserspülung, Einrichtungen für Nutz- und Leuchtgas sowie für elektrisches Licht, außerdem die erforderlichen Warenaufzüge sind überall vorhanden. Der ganze Gebäudekörper ist als Eisenbetonbau ohne Zwischenwände konstruiert, so daß Räume in jeder Größe abgeteilt werden können.

Die Innenräume von Restaurant und Café haben eine feinere künstlerische Ausbildung erfahren.

387 [1911; 2]

Die zweistöckige, freiliegende Villa Bally in Bern, Elfenstraße 16, ist nach dem Entwurfe des Architekten Max Hans Kühne, jetzt Mitinhaber der Firma Prof. William Lossow und Max Hans Kühne, Dresden, in einer Bauzeit von 9 Monaten für die Baukostensumme von 225 000 Frcs. errichtet. Die Eingangsfront zeigt eine durch beide Geschosse gehendes, über der Dachlinie mit einem geschweiften Giebel abschließendes Mittelrisalit und an jeder Seite desselben eine flachrunde Ausbuchtung der Fassade, von denen die eine, zur Nebentreppe gehörend, den Nebeneingang enthält. Über dem von Pfeilern eingefaßten, zum Vorraum führenden Haupteingang ist im Obergeschoß ein Balkon ausgekragt. An der einen Seitenfront tritt ein bis zur Dachlinie gehender Ausbau hervor, an der anderen Seitenfront schließt sich der Wintergarten mit darüberliegender Altane an, daneben erstreckt sich eine Terrasse vor einem überdeckten polygonalen Erker und weiterhin die rund vorspringende Erweiterung des Speisezimmers. Die Fassaden sind in hellem Verputz mit Verwendung einzelner Sandsteingliederungen gehalten. Das gebrochene, abgewalmte Dach ist mit Biberschwänzen eingedeckt und trägt eine Anzahl Dachfenster.

Im Erdgeschoß liegen um eine Diele mit offener Haupttreppe das Wohn- und das Speisezimmer, der Salon in Verbindung mit dem Wintergarten, die Küche nebst Nebenräumen und die Nebentreppe mit Wendelstufen. Das Obergeschoß enthält wieder um eine als Frühstücksplatz ausgebildete Diele gruppiert, von einem Umgange zugänglich, vornehmlich die Schlafzimmer, das Bad und außerdem einige Wohnzimmer.

388 [1911; 3]

Das zweistöckige, mit teilweise ausgebautem Dachgeschoß versehene Gebäude der Uto-Garage A.-G. in Zürich, Seefeldquai 1, die Automobil-Garage mit Reparaturwerkstätten, Bureaus und Lagerräumen enthaltend, ist erstmalig nach den Plänen der Architekten Froté Westermann & Co. im Laufe eines Jahres errichtet und wieder im Laufe eines Jahres nach dem Entwurfe des Architekten Rob. Angst umgebaut. Die Baukosten der Ausführung Froté Westermann haben 130 000 Frcs., die des Umbaues Angst 210 000 Frcs. betragen. Die verputzten Fronten sind einfach in den Formen gehalten, zeigen im Erdgeschoß

---

de 1 500 000 marks. Cet édifice abrite des commerces et un restaurant au rez-de-chaussée, un salon de thé au premier étage, ainsi que des bureaux et des locaux de commerces dans les trois voire quatre étages restants. Les murs de façade sont réalisés en grès jaune de Klingenmünster. Leurs ornements architecturaux furent conçus pour apporter une touche monumentale à la fin de la rue. C'est dans cette optique que s'élève, au coin de la Königstraße et de la Marienstraße, contiguë à un haut pignon, une tour massive portant une galerie ouverte derrière laquelle se dresse en retrait un couronnement coiffé d'un toit aux pans incurvés. Le toit recouvert de tuiles plates présente une double ligne de bris.

Au rez-de-chaussée sont aménagés deux commerces et les pièces nécessaires à l'exploitation d'un grand restaurant. Un grand escalier, donnant sur la Königstraße, conduit au premier étage, occupé, ainsi que son large balcon, par un salon de thé. L'accès aux étages supérieurs, séparé des entrées du restaurant et du café, s'effectue par la Marienstraße. Cette entrée est pourvue d'un pater-noster. Des bureaux et des locaux de commerce sont installés dans les trois étages supérieurs.

Un chauffage à vapeur à basse pression assure le chauffage de l'ensemble des pièces. L'immeuble est équipé de chasse d'eau, d'installations de gaz utilitaire, de gaz d'éclairage et d'éclairage électrique, ainsi que de remonte-charges. Le bâtiment est construit en béton armé sans cloison pour assurer une libre ordonnance des pièces.

Les salles intérieures du restaurant et du café offrent une composition particulièrement élaborée.

387 [1911; 2]

La villa Bally de Berne, Elfenstraße 16, est une construction dégagée s'élevant sur deux étages. Les plans furent exécutés par l'architecte Max Hans Kühne, maintenant co-propriétaire du bureau „Prof. William Lossow". La maison, construite en neuf mois, coûta la somme des 225 000 francs. La façade principale offre une avancée médiane montant de fond, coiffée d'un pignon aux contours ondulés se dégageant de la ligne du toit. Cette avancée est flanquée de saillies convexes dont l'une renferme l'escalier et l'entrée de service. Le premier étage est assorti d'un balcon soutenu par les piliers encadrant l'entrée principale donnant sur le hall. D'une des façades latérales se détache un avant-corps montant jusqu'à la ligne du toit. La façade opposée présente un jardin d'hiver surmonté d'un balcon. Ensuite se trouvent une terrasse s'étendant devant un bow-window polygonal couvert puis l'avancée arrondie de la salle à manger. Les murs de façade, crépis de couleur grise, sont parementés de grès en quelque endroit. Le toit en croupe, au comble brisé, est recouvert de tuiles plates et percé de fenêtres mansardées.

Au rez-de-chaussée s'ordonnent, autour d'un hall comprenant l'escalier principal, la salle de séjour, la salle à manger, le salon relié au jardin d'hiver, la cuisine et les dépendances, ainsi que l'escalier de service en colimaçon. L'étage, reprenant l'ordonnance des pièces autour du hall, transformé en salle du petit déjeuner, comprend les chambres à coucher élégamment aménagées, la salle de bains et d'autres pièces de séjour.

388 [1911; 3]

Le bâtiment du Uto-Garage A. G de Zurich, Seefeldquai 1, abrite un garage-automobile avec ateliers de réparations, des bureaux et des entrepôts. Cet édifice de deux étages, portant un toit partiellement mansardé, fut d'abord construit sur les plans des architectes Frote Westermann & Co. La réalisation de l'ouvrage se fit en l'espace d'une année et coûta la somme des 130 000 francs. Le bâtiment fut ensuite modifié par l'architecte Rob. Angst. La seconde partie des travaux dura une année et revint à 210 000 francs. Les façades crépies sont traitées simplement. Les murs

---

the architects Heim and Früh and cost approximately 1,500,000 Marks. The ground floor has been designed to accommodate shops and a restaurant, the first floor a café, while the remaining upper stories have been set aside exclusively for office and business functions. The façades, which are rendered in yellow sandstone from Klingenmünster, are designed to lend a monumental effect to this end of the Königstrasse. This effect is particularly enhanced by the massive square corner tower with an open gallery and recessed superstructure covered by a curved roof, as well as by the high-pitched gable of the side front. The building has a tiled Mansard roof.

The ground floor is furnished with two shops and all the rooms needed for the operation of a large restaurant. A wide, open staircase on the Königstrasse side leads to rooms in the first floor which comprise the café, together with a long balcony. The Marienstrasse entrance, which leads to offices and business room on the three upper stories, is separate from the entrances to the restaurant and the café, and has a paternoster lift.

All rooms are heated by low-pressure steam heating. The premises are also furnished with a flushing cistern system, a supply of natural gas for lighting and utilities, electric lighting, as well as lifts necessary for transporting goods. The entire structure is constructed of reinforced concrete with no intervening walls, so that the available space may be divided up into rooms of all sizes.

The interiors of the restaurant and café have been fashioned in a refined and artistic manner.

387 [1911; 2]

The Villa Bally in Bern, Switzerland (Elfenstrasse 16) was constructed from the plans of architect Max Hans Kühne (now of the offices of Prof. William Lossow and Max Hans Kühne, Dresden). Completed over a period of 9 months, the construction costs of this two-storey, free-standing villa amounted to 225,000 Francs. Its entrance front has a centre projection running the height of both storeys and terminates in a curved gable located slightly above the roof line. The front is flanked on both sides by a slightly rounded projections, one of which contains the staircase and side entrance. A balcony at the upper level juts out over the main entrance, which is framed in columns and leads into the waiting-room. An extension of one of the villa's side fronts reaches the roof line while the other side incorporates a winter-garden topped by a gallery, a terrace located in front of a polygonal bay-window, as well as a rounded extension of the dining room. All façades are covered in lightly-colored plaster and have sandstone articulations. The hipped roof is covered with flat tiles and features a number of dormer windows.

The ground floor hall containing the open main staircase is surrounded by the living and dining rooms, a drawing-room connected to the winter-garden, the kitchen with its side rooms, and the auxiliary spiral staircase. Similarly, the upper floor contains a hall serving as a breakfast area, which is connected by a circular passage to the surrounding bedrooms, bath and several sitting-rooms.

388 [1911; 3]

The two-storeyed automobile garage, with furnished space in the attic, of the Uto Garage AG in Zürich (Seefeldquai 1) is a complex of repair shops, offices and storage rooms. Originally constructed over several years according to the plans of the architect office of Froté Westermann & Co., it later underwent a one-year reconstruction based on the plans of architect Rob. Angst. Construction costs of the Westerman design amounted to 130,000 Francs, those of the Angst remodelling 210,000 Francs. The plastered fronts are simple in design, with a number of ground level car-

Erdgeschoß   Rez-de-chaussée   Ground Floor

1. Stock   Premier étage   First Floor

mehrere im Korbbogen geschlossene Einfahrtstore, in beiden Geschossen geradlinig überdeckte Fenstergruppen und über der vortretenden Dachkante eine Anzahl, zum Teil durch Fensterreihen verbundene, mit gebrochenen Giebeln abschließende Dachaufbauten. Die Dächer sind mit Biberschwänzen eingedeckt und das Hauptdach wird im First durch ein Oberlicht unterbrochen.

Erdgeschoß und erster Stock enthalten die Räume zur Unterbringung der Automobile und sind durch zwei elektrische Aufzüge, einer für Wagen nach allen Stockwerken, ein zweiter für Personen nach dem ersten und zweiten Stock führend, von Wüst & Co. ausgeführt, verbunden. Die starken Eisenbetonkonstruktionen der Decken und Stützen sind nach den Plänen und Berechnungen des Ingenieurs Zipke, die Dachkonstruktionen mit Eisenbindern von F. Gauger und die Ventilationsanlagen für alle Stockwerke von E. Kündig-Honeger hergestellt. Die Decken der Räume werden durch ein System von Balken, auf Unterzügen und Pfeilern ruhend, gebildet. Die Belastung aller Stockwerke ist auf 750 bis 1000 kg für den Quadratmeter bemessen. Im ersten Stock sind noch die Direktions- und Konferenzzimmer, Bureaus und Magazine, außerdem eine Wohnung untergebracht.

sont percés, au rez-de-chaussée , de plusieurs portails surbaissés et de fenêtres droites dans les étages supérieurs. L'étage des combles présente des fenêtres mansardées, coiffées de pignons brisés. Les toits saillants sont recouverts de tuiles plates. Le toit principal porte un lanterneau sur son faîte.

Le rez-de-chaussée et le premier étage sont occupés par les salles destinées au rangement des voitures. Deux lifts électriques installés par Wüst & Co. relient les étages entre eux, l'un pour les voitures, montant à tous les étages, l'autre pour les personnes, desservant les premier et deuxième étages. Les solides constructions en béton armé des planchers et des piliers de support furent réalisées d'après les plans et calculs de l'ingénieur Zipke. Les charpentes aux poutres maîtresses de fer furent exécutées par F. Gauger. E. Kündig-Honeger se chargea des installations de ventilation pour l'ensemble des étages. Les planchers sont construits selon un système de poutres reposant sur des sous-poutres et des piliers. La capacité de charge des étages a été calculée pour osciller entre 750 et 1000 kg par mètre carré. Le premier étage abrite les bureaux de la direction, les salles de réunion, des bureaux, des magasins ainsi qu'un appartement.

riageways framed in basket arches. Groups of straight—lined windows open at both levels. Above the projecting end of the roof are a number of roof superstructures partially connected by rows of windows which terminate in broken gables. The entire roof is covered with flat tiles, and the top ridge of the main roof has been replaced with a sky—light.

Space for automobiles is located on the ground floor and the first floor, which are connected by two electric lifts – the one for autos services all levels, the other one for personnel the first and second floors – which were constructed by Wüst & Co. The solid construction of the ceilings and supports in reinforced concrete was designed and supervised by the engineer Zipke, the iron trusses of the roof are the work of F. Gauger, and the ventilation installation for all floors were produced by E. Kündig—Honeger. The ceilings comprise a system of beams resting on cross girders and trusses. The total stress of all stories has been gauged at 750—1,000 kilogrammes per square metre. The first floor also contains administrative offices, conference rooms, offices and storage space, as well as living quarters.

389 [1911; 5]

Als Bauwerk von ausgesprochen monumentalem Charakter und bedeutenden Abmessungen, in antikisierenden, modern aufgefaßten Formen erscheint das ringsum freiliegende Kunsthaus in Zürich, nach dem Entwurfe der Architekten Curjel & Moser in einer Bauzeit von 2½ Jahren für die Baukostensumme von 1 000 000 Frcs. ausgeführt. Als Bauführer waren die Architekten Eckardt, Barth und Markwalder tätig. An einen dreistöckigen Baukörper schließt sich ein zweistöckiger, langgestreckter Flügelbau an. Der vorderen Schmalfront des höher geführten Gebäudeteils ist im Erdgeschoß eine Vorhalle vorgelegt, welche den Haupteingang enthält und mit einem Glasdach abschließt; die hintere Schmalfront zeigt ein breites Gruppenfenster, die Seitenfront geradlinig überdeckte Fenster. Im ersten Obergeschoß sind auf beiden Schmalseiten durch Säulen geteilte Fenstergruppen und auf der Längsseite einzelne Fenster angebracht, sämtlich wieder geradlinig überdeckt. Das zweite Obergeschoß ist ganz fensterlos, durch Rahmenprofile und flach vorspringende Tafeln gegliedert und über dem Dachgesims mit einem flachen abgewalmten Glasdach abgeschlossen. – Der zweistöckige Flügelbau hat abgestumpfte Ecken mit einem Nebeneingang in einer derselben erhalten und zeigt im Erdgeschoß an allen Seiten Fenster. Die Fronten im Obergeschoß sind durch eine Stellung von dorisierenden Doppelsäulen, welche Nischen zwischen sich einschließen und mit Architrav und Kranzgesims bekrönt sind, ausgezeichnet. Nur die nach der Straße gekehrte längere Front hat breite Fenster zwischen den Säulen aufzuweisen, die anderen Fronten sind fensterlos geblieben; den oberen Abschluß bildet wieder ein flaches abge-

389 [1911; 5]

Le musée des beaux arts de Zurich se présente comme un vaste édifice de caractère résolument monumental. Cette construction dégagée, de forme classique mais traitée dans un esprit moderne, fut exécutée sur les plans des architectes Curjel & Moser. Les travaux furent réalisés en deux années et demie pour la somme de 1 000 000 francs. Les architectes Eckardt, Barth & Markwalder furent chargés de la conduite des travaux. Le corps de bâtiment, haut de trois étages, est joint d'une aile allongée, montant sur deux étages. L'étroite façade frontale du corps de logis présente, au rez-de-chaussée, un porche, recouvert d'une toiture de verre, abritant l'entrée principale. L'opposite est percé d'une large baie, la façade latérale de fenêtres à linteau droit. Les deux façades étroites offrent au premier étage des fenêtres droites, groupées, divisées par des colonnes. Les quelques ouvertures de la façade la plus longue sont toutes à linteau droit. Le second étage, aveugle, orné de reliefs d'encadrements et de plaques faiblement saillantes, est coiffé d'une verrière légèrement en croupe. L'aile de deux étages présente des pans coupés dont l'un renferme l'entrée secondaire. Le rez-de-chaussée est pourvu de fenêtres de tous les côtés. Les façades du premier étage offrent une ordonnance de doubles colonnes doriques, encadrant des niches, et surmontée d'une architrave et d'une corniche. Seule la façade sur rue présente de larges fenêtres entre les colonnes. Les autres faces du bâtiment sont aveugles. Une verrière plate, en croupe couvre cette partie de l'édifice. Le

389 [1911; 5]

The Art museum in Zurich is a construction of decidedly monumental character and impressive size, in which the Classic style has been infused with modern forms. Designed by the architects Curjel & Moser, this free—standing structure was completed over a period of 2½ years and cost 1,000,000 Francs. Construction was supervised by the architects Eckardt, Barth and Markwalder. A three—storey edifice is connected to a longer two—storey wing. A glass—roofed entry hall containing the main entrance projects from the narrower front of the taller building; on the side opposite is a broad group of windows, while the wider side front has straight—lined windows. The first storey of both narrow sides has groups of windows broken up by columns; that of the long side has individual windows, again all of which are straight—lined. The second storey is completely without windows, articulated by slightly projecting framed flat panels and finished off above the roof moulding by a hipped roof of glass. – The two—storeyed side wing has truncated corners. The side entrance is located in one of these, and there are windows throughout entire ground floor. The fronts of the upper level are ornamented by coupled Doric columns with intervening niches, and are crowned by an architrave and cornice. Only the front facing the street contains broad windows, the other fronts lack fenestration. The upper part of the building is also topped by a low—pitched hipped roof of glass. The

Blick ins Treppenhaus   Vue de la cage d'escalier   View of the Staircase

Bronzetür   Porte en bronze   Bronze Door

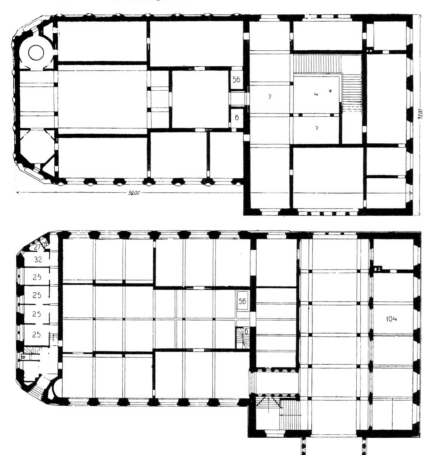

1. Obergeschoß   Premier étage   First Floor
Erdgeschoß   Rez-de-chaussée   Ground Floor

Halle   Hall   Hall

walmtes Glasdach. Der Gebäudesockel ist aus Urner Granit hergestellt, die oberen Fassaden sind aus blaugrauem Züricher Sandstein gebildet. Die Dachbedekkung besteht ausschließlich aus Drahtglastafeln, kittlos verlegt auf einer eisernen Sprossenkonstruktion.

Das Erdgeschoß des höheren Gebäudekörpers enthält inmitten eine der ganzen Länge nach durchgehende dreischiffige Halle, an welche sich einerseits der Sitzungssaal und eine Anzahl Räume, andererseits der Aufgang zur Stockwerkstreppe und weitere Räume anschließen.

Im Flügelbau sind im Erdgeschoß an allen drei Fronten fensterbeleuchtete Räume angeordnet, welche einen mittleren fensterlosen Raum umgeben. Das erste Obergeschoß zeigt inmitten die mit Oberlicht versehene Treppenhalle, einerseits an einen breiten Wandelgang anschließend, an den drei übrigen Seiten von Räumen mit Seitenfenstern umgeben. Im Obergeschoß des Flügelbaues liegen an einer Längsseite Räume mit

socle est en granit. Les murs de façade sont en grès zurichois bleu gris. La couverture du toit est exclusivement composée de plaques de verre filé, assemblées sans joint sur une construction de croisillons de fer.

Le rez-de-chaussée du corps de bâtiment comprend en son centre un large hall continu à trois nefs, flanquant, d'une part la salle de réunions ainsi que quelques autres salles, et d'autre part l'accès à l'escalier et un certain nombre de salles. Le rez-de-chaussée de l'aile est occupé par des salles, agencées autour d'une pièce centrale aveugle, et ordonnées le long des trois fronts, bénéficiant ainsi de la lumière naturelle. Au premier étage, la cage d'escalier, située au centre, reçoit un éclairage par le haut. Elle est encadrée, sur un côté par un large promenoir, et sur les trois autres côtés pr des salles pourvues de fenêtres. Le premier étage de l'aile comprend, sur le long côté, des salles

socle is of granite from Uri, the upper façades are faced with blue—grey sandstone from Zurich. The roofing is made exclusively of wire—glass panels set without putty in an iron rung construction.

A three—aisle hall runs the entire length of the ground floor, one side of which is flanked by the session—room and a number of various other rooms, the other side by more rooms and a staircase leading to the upper floors. Arranged around the perimeter of the ground floor of the side wing are well—lit rooms surrounding a central windowless room. A staircase illuminated by sky—lights leads to the middle of the upper floor which has on one side a flight of stairs and on the other three sides rooms with side windows. On the long side of the side wing are rooms with lighting

Seitenlicht, sonst sind sämtliche an den Fronten und in der Mittelachse untergebrachten Räume durch Oberlicht beleuchtet. Das zweite Obergeschoß des höheren Gebäudeteils enthält, die Treppenhalle umgebend, durchweg Oberlichtsäle. Eine Tür sowie die Fenstergitter sind in Bronze ausgeführt. Die mehrere Räume schmückenden Bildwerke sind von den Bildhauern Burkhardt, Kieser, Haller, Hünerwadel, Oswald und Dr. Kißling geschaffen.

390 [1911: 16]

Das einen stark modernen Zug in der Fassadengestaltung aufweisende Empfangsgebäude auf dem Bahnhof Mülheim a. Rh., ein Werk der Architekten Baurat Mettegang und Regierungsbaumeister Müller, ist für die Baukostensumme von 430 000 Mark zur Ausführung gekommen. Der höher geführte Mittelbau des Gebäudes, dem ein flaches Schutzdach über dem unteren Teil der Fassade vorgelegt ist, zeigt im oberen Teil derselben eine Auflösung in breite Pfeiler, welche die mehrfach eng geteilten hohen Fenster zwischen sich einschließen. In das übertretende, steile, gebrochene, in den unteren Fächern geschweifte Dach ist die Uhr in einem nach oben abgerundeten Vorsprung eingebaut. Die Flügelbauten rechts und links des Mittelbaues sind niedriger als dieser gehalten, zeigen indes eine ähnliche Fassaden- und Dachausbildung. Dem rechten Flügel, der sich nach der Hinterseite zweistöckig fortsetzt, ist in der Höhe des Untergeschosses ein Anbau angefügt. An Materialien für die Fassade sind Tuffstein und Kalkstein zur Verwendung gekommen; Die Dächer haben eine Schiefereindeckung erhalten.

Der Mittelbau enthält in den niedrigen Einbauten an der Außenfront die mit Windfängen versehenen Eingänge zur großen Eintrittshalle. Ebenso sind in den Einbauten an der Eingangsfront Räume für den Pförtner, die Fahrpläne, die Polizei, das Handgepäck und den Fernsprecher vorgesehen.

Im Hintergrund der Halle liegen um einen Hofraum die Fahrkartenausgabe, eine Anzahl Diensträume und die Toiletten. Links von der Eintrittshalle sind die Wartesäle und der Schänkraum mit Küche und Waschküche angeordnet, rechtsseitig die Gepäckabfertigung und wieder eine Anzahl Diensträume.

391, 392 [1911: 10, 11]

Die St. Antoniuskirche des kath. Kultusvereins in Zürich, eine dreischiffige Basilika in streng romanischen Formen, mit Ausnahme des Turms, der in der Gestaltung selbständig moderne Auffassung bemerken läßt, ist ein Werk der Architekten Curjel und Moser und wurde in einer Bauzeit von 2½ Jahren für die Bausumme von rund 550 000 Frcs. zur Ausführung gebracht. Die Westfront mit dem erhöht liegenden, von einer Freitreppe zugänglichen, zunächst in eine Vorhalle führenden, von Säulen eingefaßten, rundbogigen Hauptportal wird einerseits von dem hohen, ohne Absätze bis zum Glockengeschoß fensterlos aufsteigenden, mit dem durch Säulenstellungen geöffneten und einer undurchbrochenen Steinpyramide bekrönten Turm, dem seitlich eine offene, auf Säulen ruhende Vorhalle vorgelegt ist, flankiert; andererseits durch eine Erweiterung des Seitenschiffs begrenzt. Über den niedrigen, mit Rundbogenfenstern versehenen Mauern der durch Strebepfeiler getrennten Joche der Seitenschiffe steigen die Oberwände des Mittelschiffs auf und sind durch rundbogige Gruppenfenster, von denen das mittlere überhöht ist, durchbrochen. Der im gedrückten Kreisbogen vorspringende Chor erhebt sich ganz fensterlos in der Höhe des Mittelschiffs und wird an einer Seite von dem Anbau der Sakristei, an der anderen Seite von dem Anbau eines Betsaales eingefaßt. Der nördliche Seiteneingang ist durch kurze Säulchen mit nebenliegenden schmalen Fenstern verbunden, während der südliche Seiteneingang, rundbogig wie der vorige, einfacher gehalten ist. Sämtliche Außenwände sind aus Steinquadern mit rauhen Bossen hergestellt; die flachen Dächer sind mit Biberschwänzen eingedeckt.

Das hohe Mittelschiff des vierjochigen Langhauses, der Chor, sowie die durch Rundbogenarkaden auf

390 [1911: 16]

La gare de Mülheim-sur-le-Rhin fut conçue par les architectes Mettegang et Müller, sa réalisation revint à 430 000 marks. La conception de la façade du hall d'accueil atteste d'une grande modernité. Le corps de bâtiment, plus élevé assorti d'un auvent plat au-dessus de la partie inférieure de la façade, présente, dans sa partie supérieure, une ordonnance de larges piliers, encadrant de hautes fenêtres , elles-mêmes divisées par des meneaux verticaux. Le brisis légèrement concave du toit saillant et pentu est troué par une horloge, encastrée dans une avancée arrondie vers le haut. Les ailes plus basses, situées à gauche et à droite du corps de logis, offrent une composition identique des toits et des façades. Une construction annexe d'un étage s'adosse latéralement à l'aile droite, qui se prolonge en une construction de deux étages sur sa partie postérieure. Les murs de façade sont réalisés en tuf et en castine. Les toits sont recouverts d'ardoises.

Le corps de bâtiment abrite, dans l'avant-corps bas de la façade frontale, précédées par des tambours, les entrées donnant sur le grand hall. La loge du portier, le bureau de police, le guichet des bagages à main, les tableaux indicateurs ainsi qu'une cabine de téléphone se trouvent dans cet avant-corps.

Les guichets, quelques locaux de service et les toilettes sont répartis autour d'une cour, au fond du hall. A gauche du hall d'entrée sont aménagés les salles d'attente, le buffet de la gare avec la cuisine et l'office, à droite sont installés le guichet de l'enregistrement des bagages ainsi que quelques locaux de service.

391, 392 [1911: 10, 11]

L'église Saint Antoine de Zurich est une basilique catholique à trois nefs, présentant des formes de style strictement roman, exception faite du clocher, qui seul relève d'une conception moderne. Réalisée en deux années et demie, cette église, conçue par les architectes Curjel et Moser, coûta la somme de 550 000 francs. La façade occidentale présente un portail en plein cintre, flanqué de colonnes, légèrement surélevé et accessible par quelques marches menant d'abord au porche. Cette façade est, d'une part assortie du clocher, auquel s'adosse latéralement un porche ouvert, reposant sur des colonnes, et d'autre part limitée par l'extension de la nef latérale. La tour du clocher, traitée sobrement, sans ouverture, jusqu'aux cloches où elle offre alors une ordonnance de colonnes, est couronnée par une pyramide de pierre. Sur les murs bas, troués de fenêtres cintrées, des travées des nefs latérales, elles-mêmes divisées par des contreforts, se dressent les murs supérieurs de la nef centrale, percés de fenêtres groupées en plein cintre, l'ouverture centrale étant la plus haute. Le chœur en arc de cercle surbaissé, s'élevant sans ouverture à la hauteur de la nef centrale, est encadré d'une part par la sacristie, et d'autre part par une salle de prières. L'entrée latérale nord est reliée par de courtes colonnettes aux étroites fenêtres contiguës alors que l'entrée médionale, en plein cintre comme la précédente, offre un aspect simple. Les toits plats portent une couverture de tuiles plates.

Le haut vaisseau de la longue nef aux quatre travées, le chœur ainsi que les nefs latérales, séparées

390 [1911: 16]

Façades of strikingly modern design are the prominent feature of the Mühlheim—on—Rhine railway station, a work of the architect Baurat Mettegang and government architect Müller, which cost 430,000 Marks. The building's taller middle erection, which has a flat canopy under its façade, is articulated by groups of narrow windows located between broad pilasters. A clock has been set in a slightly rounded projection at the lower part of the steep overhanging roof, which has a curved lower section. The side wings to the left and right are lower in profile yet display a façade and roof design similar to that of the middle structure. The right wing, whose rear front continues as a two—storeyed edifice, is attached to an annex structure extending the height of its first storey. The façades are of tufa and limestone; the roof is covered in slate.

The low projection of the middle erection contains the draught lobby leading to the spacious entry hall, as well as rooms for porters, timetables, police, luggage and loudspeaker systems.

An open area at the back of the hall is surrounded by ticket counters, a number of service—rooms and washrooms. To the left of the entry hall are waiting—rooms and a cupboard room leading to the kitchen and washroom. To the right are rooms for luggage transport and other services.

391, 392 [1911: 10, 11]

St. Anthony's Church of the Zurich Catholic community, a three—aisle basilica which, apart from the singularly modern style of the tower, strictly adheres to Romanesque forms, is the work of the architects Curjel & Moser and was completed within 2½ years at a cost of about 550,000 Francs. The elevated principal portal in the west front has a round arch flanked by pillars and a perron leading onto a porch. The portal is flanked on one side by a non—stepped high tower with a pyramidal roof, whose only windows are set between columns in the belfry. An open porch resting on columns skirts the north side of the tower. The other side of the principal portal is bordered by an extension of the side aisle. Rising above the low walls of the side aisles, whose bays contain arched windows separated by flying buttresses, are the upper walls of the nave. They open with groups of three windows each, the middle window projecting above the other two. The oval—shaped chancel rises to the height of the nave and is windowless. It is flanked on one side by an extension of the sacristy and on the other by an extension of the prayer—hall. The entrance on the north side is connected to the adjacent narrow windows by short columns, while the entrance on the south side, although also decorated with round arches, is simpler in design. Each outer wall is faced with bossed ashlar, the roofs are covered with flat red tile.

Cross vaulting covers the high nave of the four—bayed long house, the chancel, as well as the side aisles, which are separated from the nave by arcades

Ansicht nach dem Altar   Vue de l'autel   View of the Altar

Ansicht nach der Empore   Vue de la galerie   View of the Gallery

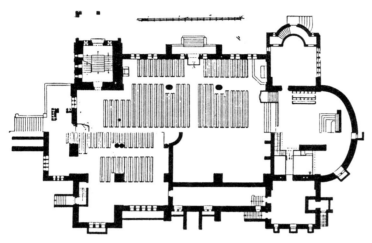

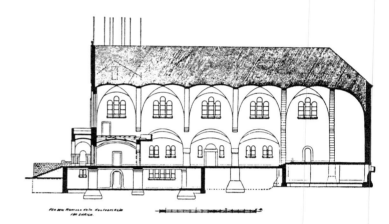

Halbgrundriß vom Erdgeschoß und der Empore   Plan du rez-de-chaussée et de la galerie

Halb Plan of the Ground Floor and Gallery

Längsschnitt   Coupe longitudinale   Longitudinal Section

Säulen von oblongem Grundriß abgetrennten Seitenschiffe, sind durch Kreuzgewölbe, die letzteren mit nach den Arkaden ansteigenden Kappen, überdeckt. An der Eingangsseite, dem Chor gegenüber, ist die Orgelempore eingebaut. Unter der westlichen Vorhalle und den anstoßenden zwei Jochen des Langhauses, mit Einschluß der Seitenschiffe, erstreckt sich eine Unterkirche, auch der Chor mit seinen Anbauten und das südliche Seitenschiff sind unterkellert.

393 [1911; 91]

Der Erweiterungsbau des Bureaugebäudes der Firma W. Brügmann & Sohn in Dortmund, Ardeystraße, durch Umformung des älteren eingeschossigen Flügels und einen mehrgeschossigen neuen Anbau, ist im Laufe eines Jahres durch die Architekten Schmidtmann und Klemp zur Ausführung gekommen. Die Baukosten betrugen 183 000 Mark. Der eingeschossige Bauteil wurde mit einer Brüstung und zwei kleinen Dachgiebeln an der Front versehen. Der neue zweigeschossige, teilweise durch ein ausgebautes Dachgeschoß erweiterte Neubau zeigt an beiden freiliegenden Fronten je einen Giebel mit geschwungenen Konturen und im Erdgeschoß einen Eckturm, von einem spitzen Kegeldach bekrönt. Die Fassaden sind mit Tuffstein bekleidet und die Dächer mit Falzziegeln eingedeckt.

Im Erdgeschoß befinden sich Geschäftsräume; der große Saal im eingeschossigen Bauteil dient zur Buchhalterei. Der Neubau enthält im Erdgeschoß die Wohnung für den Prokuristen und wird sonst in seiner Gesamtheit zu Bureauzwecken benutzt.

394 [1911; 17]

Eine Bauanlage von ungewöhnlich großen Abmessungen wird durch das Lagerhaus in Köln a. Rh., am Agrippina-Ufer gelegen, gebildet. Urheber des Entwurfs zu Grundrissen und Fassaden ist der Architekt, Stadtbauinspektor Verbeek; die Bauzeit fällt in die Jahre 1909 und 1910, und die Baukosten betragen rund 15000 000 Mark, einschließlich der Bureauge-

par des arcades en plein cintre reposant sur des colonnes de forme oblongue, sont couverts de voûtes d'ogives. L'orgue est aménagé, face au chœur, au-dessus de l'entrée. Sous le porche occidental et sous les deux travées adjacentes du vaisseau se trouve une crypte. Cet espace souterrain s'étend sous le chœur, la sacristie et les salles de prières ainsi que sous la nef latérale sud.

393 [1911; 91]

Les travaux d'agrandissement du bâtiment de bureaux de la compagnie W. Brügmann & Sohn à Dortmund, Ardeystraße, furent réalisés en l'espace d'une année pour la somme de 183 000 marks. Les plans furent exécutés par les architectes Schmidtmann et Klemp. Il s'agissait de restructurer l'ancienne aile à un étage et d'y adjoindre un nouveau corps de bâtiment de plusieurs étages. La façade de l'ancien bâtiment fut assortie d'un entablement et de deux petits pignons. Le nouveau corps de logis, au toit partiellement mansardé, présente un pignon aux lignes ondulées sur chacune des deux façades ainsi qu'une tour d'angle, coiffée d'un toit en poivrière, au niveau du rez-de-chaussée. Les murs extérieurs portent un revêtement de tuf. Les toits sont recouverts de tuiles à emboîtement.

Le rez-de-chaussée abrite des bureaux. La comptabilité à été aménagée dans la grande salle de l'ancienne aile. Le rez-de-chaussée du nouveau bâtiment est occupé par le logement du fondé de pouvoir. Des bureaux sont installés dans la surface restante.

394 [1911; 17]

L'entrepôt de Cologne, sur la rive Agrippina, est un édifice aux proportions étonnamment vastes. Les plans furent exécutés par l'architecte Verbeek. Les travaux de construction, réalisés en 1909 et 1910, revinrent à 1 500 000 marks, bâtiment des bureaux, systèmes de transport des céréales et grues compris. La façade sur rue est flanquée, sur l'aile, du bâtiment des

of round arches resting on oblong pillars. The severies of the side aisles are placed above the arcades. The choir is located at the entrance side opposite the chancel. A basement church is located under the west porch, the adjacent two bays of the basilica, and the side aisles. A cellar has also been dug under the chancel and its extensions, as well as the south side aisle.

393 [1911; 91]

The office building of the firm W. Brügmann & Son in Dortmund (Ardeystrasse) has been enlarged by the remodelling of the existing one—storey wing and the addition of a new corner building with several storeys. Completion of the design by architects Schmidtmann and Klemp occupied one year and cost 183,00 Marks. The frontage of one—storey section was given a parapet and two small roof gables. The new two—storey annexe with a roof storey has a shaped gable on each of its two exposed fronts and a corner tower with a conical roof at the ground floor level. The façades are of tufa and the roof is covered with interlocking tile.

Offices are located on the ground floor; the large hall in the one—storey wing is used for book—keeping. On the ground floor of the new building are living quarters for the managing clerk. All other rooms are designated for the exclusive use of business.

394 [1911; 17]

The warehouse located on the Agrippina quay on the Rhine river in Cologne is a construction of remarkably large dimensions. The blueprint of the ground plan and façades was created by the municipal architect Verbeek. Construction of the storehouse, including the office building, grain transport installations and cranes, was carried out over the years 1909 and

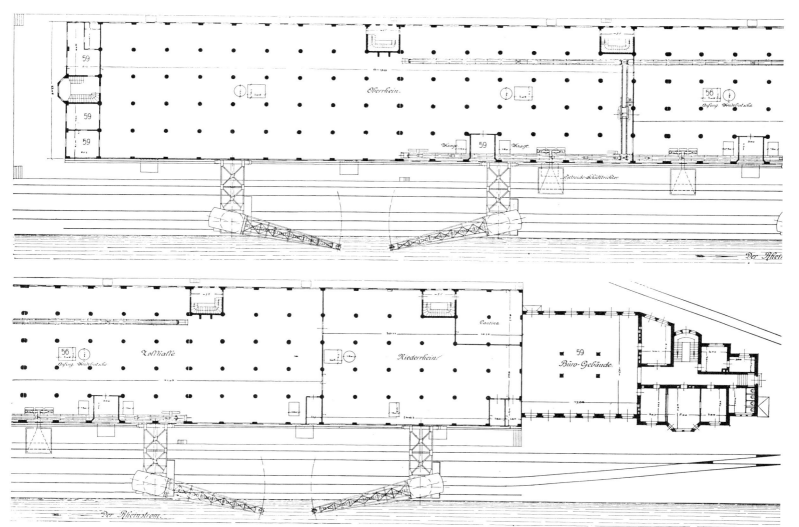

Grundriß vom Erdgeschoß   Plan du rez-de-chaussée   Plan of Ground Floor

bäude, der Getreidetransporteinrichtungen und Krahnen. Die Straßenansicht des Gebäudes zeigt an einem Flügel das zweistöckige, mit einem ausgebauten Dachgeschoß und Turm versehene Bureaugebäude. Die anschließende Fassade der teils fünf-, teils siebenstöckigen, in den oberen drei Geschossen abgetreppten und mit Pultdächern über den Abtreppungen versehenen Lagerhäuser, wird durch sieben, den Querbauten entsprechende, steile Giebel, außerdem durch zwei den mittleren höheren Gebäudeteil einfassende Türme unterbrochen. Die Rheinansicht hat eine ähnliche Gestaltung wie die vorige aufzuweisen, enthält jedoch im Erdgeschoß eine Anzahl Ladetüren, über denen sich ein durch Konsolen unterstütztes Schutzdach hinzieht und in den Stockwerken der Giebel übereinander liegende Ladeluken. Die Außenflächen der in Eisenbeton hergestellten Umfassungswände sind in einfachen Formen gehalten, abgeputzt und gelblich abgetönt. Türen und Lichtöffnungen haben keinerlei Gliederungen aufzuweisen. Die ebenfalls in Eisenbeton ausgeführten Dächer haben eine Eindeckung von Schiefer erhalten.

Das Bureaugebäude enthält eine Anzahl Diensträume, außerdem sind noch mehrere Bureauzimmer über das Gebäude verteilt. Die große Lagerhalle gliedert sich in zwei Abteilungen, eine für den Oberrhein, eine für den Niederrhein; und zwischen beiden liegt die Zollhalle. Mehrere Treppen, Aufzüge und Wendelrutschen verbinden die Geschosse. Die inneren Freistützen bestehen aus Eisenbeton, ebenso ist die Fundierung auf Eisenbetonpfählen erfolgt. Berechnung und Ausführung der Eisenbetonarbeiten sind durch Weirich & Reinken in Kiel und Köln geliefert.

bureaux, haut de deux étages, assorti d'un toit mansardé et d'une tour. La façade attenante des entrepôts est coupée par sept pignons, correspondant aux bâtiments latéraux, et par deux tours encadrant la partie médiane de l'édifice, la plus élevée. L'entrepôt s'élève sur cinq voire sept étages, les trois étages supérieurs sont en escalier et coiffés de toits en appentis. La façade sur le Rhin est semblable à la précédente. Elle présente, en outre, au rez-de-chaussée, de nombreuses portes de chargement surmontées par un auvent en encorbellement, ainsi que, dans les étages des pignons, des lucarnes de chargement disposées les unes sous les autres. Les murs extérieurs en béton armé, enduits d'un crépi jaunâtre, offrent des formes simples. Les ouvertures des portes et des fenêtres sont traitées tout à fait sobrement.

Le bâtiment des bureaux abrite de nombreux locaux de service et des salles de travail. La grande halle est divisée en deux départements, un pour le Bas-Rhin, l'autre pour le Haut-Rhin. Entre les deux se situe la douane. De nombreux escaliers, ascenseurs et toboggans en colimaçon assurent la communication entre les étages. Les piliers de support intérieurs sont en béton armé, les fondations sont réalisées sur des poteaux en béton armé. Les travaux de béton armé furent calculés et exécutés par Weirich & Reinken à Kiel et à Cologne.

1910 at a cost of about 1,500,000 Marks. The street front of the edifice has on one wing a two—storey office building with a roof storey and tower. The adjoining façade of the part five—storey, part seven—storey storehouse is broken up by seven high-pitched gables, whose articulations match those of the longitudinal sections, as well as by two towers framing the higher middle section of the building. The upper three stories of the storehouse are stepped, with each step being covered by shed roofs. The Rhine front is similar in appearance. However, its ground level has a number of loading ports covered by a cantilevered canopy, while the gabled storeys have been provided with cargo hatches placed one above the other. The exterior surfaces of the enclosing walls of reinforced concrete are simple in form, rough—cast and dull—yellow in color. The doors and light openings lack ornamentation. All roofs, whose structure is again of reinforced concrete, are covered with slate.

The office building has a number of bureaus. The large hall of the storehouse is divided into two departments, one for the Upper Rhine, and one for the Lower Rhine; both are separated by a Customs Hall. All floors are connected by a number of staircases, lifts and spiral slideways. The freestanding supports of the interior are of reinforced concrete; in addition, the foundation rests on reinforced concrete piers. The engineering and construction of the reinforced concrete framework was carried out by Weirich & Reinken in Kiel and Cologne.

395 [1911; 41]

In ganz freier Lage erhebt sich der Gruppenbau des Städtischen Hallenschwimmbades in Darmstadt, mit der Hauptfront an der Mühlstraße gelegen. Nach einem ohne Endergebnis verlaufenem Wettbewerbe wurde der zur Ausführung bestimmte Entwurf von Architekt Stadtbaurat Aug. Buxbaum aufgestellt. An den Ausführungszeichnungen waren die Architek-

395 [1911; 41]

L'ensemble formé par les bâtiments de la piscine municipale de Darmstadt bénéficie d'une situation dégagée. La façade principale donne sur la Mühlstraße. Ce projet ayant fait l'objet d'un concours qui resta sans résultat, ce fut la conception de l'architecte Aug. Buxbaum qui fut finalement choisie. Les architectes Mink, Schnatz et Minner participèrent à l'éla-

395 [1911; 41]

The Municipal Baths complex in Darmstadt is set in spacious surroundings, with its principal front overlooking the Mühlstrasse. Since the architectural competition produced no satisfactory design, construction proceeded according to a blueprint by the Municipal Architect Aug. Buxbaum. The architects Mink, Schnatz and Minner also participated in drawing up

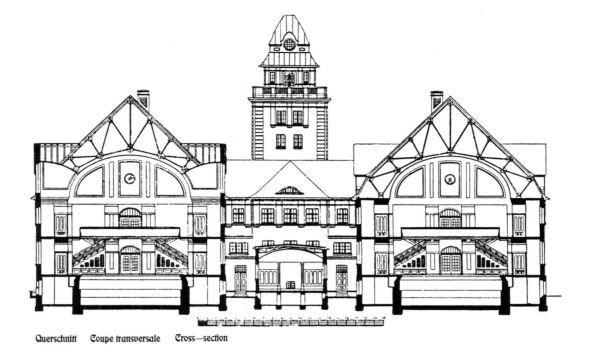

Querschnitt   Coupe transversale   Cross—section

ten Mink, Schnatz und Minner beteiligt, die örtliche Bauleitung besorgte Oesterling. Im Verlaufe von 3 Jahren wurde der Bau zur Vollendung gebracht und verursachte einen Kostenaufwand von 968 000 Mark. Die zweistöckige Hauptfront, in deren Mitte sich der Haupteingang öffnet, wird von zwei Flügelbauten eingefaßt und ist mit einem mächtigen quadratischen Wasserturm bekrönt, der mit einer Brüstung und einem hinter dieser zurückgesetzten, in zwei mit Zeltdächern versehenen Absätzen aufsteigenden Aufbau abschließt. Die äußere Architektur ist in hellgrauem Verputz unter Verwendung von weißgelbem Flonheimer Sandstein in einfachen Formen ausgeführt. Nur das Portal hat einen reicheren bildnerischen Schmuck nach Modellen des Bildhauers H. Jobst erfahren. Die beschieferten, über den Seitenflügeln gebrochenen, zum Teil mit Fensteraufbauten besetzten Dächer sind mit hölzernen, übertretenden Traufgesimsen ausgestattet.

Die Turmkrone ist mit Kupfer eingedeckt.

An den Schmalseiten des Vorgartens liegen die Wartehalle und die Bedürfnisanstalt. Die Badeanstalt enthält ein Schwimmbad für Männer, eines für Frauen, das russisch-römische Bad, Wannenbäder, Brausezellen und eine Abteilung für Heil- und Sonnenbäder. Der Vorraum zeigt an den Wänden Tonreliefs nach Modellen von Jobst. Die Kassenhalle trennt die Abteilungen für Männer und Frauen; zwei Treppen führen nach den Wannenbädern im Obergeschloß. Das Kesselhaus ist in einem besonderen Gebäude untergebracht. Die Heizung geschieht in allen Räumen mit Dampf, die Beleuchtung mit elektrischem Licht, die Belüftung durch erwärmte Druckluft. Für den Betriebsleiter ist ein Wohnhaus dem Hauptgebäude angegliedert. Die Decken bestehen aus Eisenbeton; die Tonnengewölbe der Schwimmhallen sind nach dem Moniersystem hergestellt.

boration des plans. La direction locale des travaux fut assurée par monsieur Oesterling. La construction fut réalisée en trois années pour la somme de 968 000 marks. La façade principale comprend deux étages et est flanquée de deux ailes. L'entrée principale, située dans la partie médiane, est surmontée d'un massif château d'eau carré, couronné d'une balustrade, derrière laquelle s'élève, en retrait, une tour en recoupement, pourvue de deux toitures en bâtière. Enduite d'un crépi gris clair, la façade, traitée sobrement, offre quelques éléments en grès de Flonheim. Le portail présente une riche ornementation réalisée d'après les modèles du sculpteur H. Jobst. Les toits, aux combles brisés au-dessus des ailes, ont reçu une toiture d'ardoises. Partiellement troués de fenêtres mansardées, ils sont assortis de larmiers de bois saillants.

La tour est recouverte de plaques de cuivre.

Le hall d'attente et les cabinets d'aisances sont situés dans les étroites façades donnant sur le jardin frontal. L'établissement se compose d'un bassin pour les hommes, d'un pour les femmes, d'un bain russoromain, de baignoires, de cabines de douche, de bains thermaux et d'un solarium. Les murs du hall sont décorés de reliefs en terre cuite exécutés d'après des modèles du sculpteur Jobst. Le hall aux causses sépare le département homme de celui des femmes. Deux escaliers, contigus aux baignoires, conduisent à l'étage. La chaufferie est aménagée dans un bâtiment particulier. L'établissement est équipé d'un chauffage à vapeur, d'éclairage électrique et d'un système d'aération par air chauffé. La maison d'habitation du directeur jouxte le bâtiment principal. Les planchers sont en béton armé. Les voûtes en berceau des salles des bassins furent réalisées d'après le système Monier.

the plans, and local construction was supervised by Oesterling. Construction was completed in the course of 3 years at a cost of 968,000 Marks. The two—storey principal front, in whose middle the main entrance is located, is flanked by two wings and crowned by a mighty water tower square in shape. The tower is finished off by a parapet behind which rises a two—stepped superstructure with a pyramidal roof. The façace of the exterior is faced with light—grey plaster mixed with sandstone from Flonheim, and is modest in design. Only the portal exhibits an artistic degree of ornamentation, which is based on models created by the sculptor H. Jobst. The slate roof, which has broken lines at the side wings, contains Dormer windows and has overhanging wooden eaves. The tower dome is covered with copper.

The waiting hall and public conveniences are bordered by the narrow side of the front garden. Bathing facilities include a swimming pool for men, another one for women, a Russian—Roman bath, tub baths, showering compartments, and a separate area for medicinal baths and sun bathing. The walls of the entry hall are decorated with clay reliefs based on the models of Jobst. The bathing areas for men and women are separated by the cash—office hall; two staircases lead to the tub baths on the upper floor. The boiler house is located in a separate building. All rooms are steam—heated, illuminated by electric light, and ventilated by warmed compressed air. Living quarters for the director are located in an annexe of the main building. The ceilings are of reinforced concrete; the barrel—vault construction of the indoor pools is based on the Monier system.

396 [1911; 64]

Einer dieser Amerika eigentümlichen, durch die Knappheit und die hohen Kosten für den Erwerb des Baugrundes hervorgerufenen „Wolkenkratzer" erscheint in dem 19 Geschosse umfassenden Downtown Building, Knickerbocker Trust Company, New York, ein Werk der Architekten Mc Kim, Mead & White. Die drei unteren Geschosse sind mit durchgehenden Pilastern ausgestattet, der Eingang ist mit korinthischen Säulen eingefaßt. Zwischen Architrav und Kranzgesims der Säulenstellung ist ein weiteres Geschoß eingefügt. Die Fenster der folgenden 14 Obergeschosse sind einfach viereckig gestaltet, ohne Einfassung und Bekrönung. Erst das oberste über einem Gurtgesims aufsteigende Geschoß zeigt wieder reichere architektonische Gliederung durch Pfeiler, Rundbogenfenster zwischen Säulen, Fries mit Fenstern, Bekrönungsgesims und Brüstung mit abschlie-

396 [1911; 64]

Le gratte-ciel de 19 étages de la Knickerbocker Trust Company, conçu par les architectes Mc Kim, Mead & White, est une de ces constructions propres à l'Amérique, nées de la pénurie et de la cherté des terrains. Les trois étages inférieurs sont assortis de pilastres montant de fond. L'entrée est flanquée de colonnes corinthiennes. Un étage a été inséré dans l'entablement des colonnes, entre l'architrave et la corniche. Les ouvertures des 14 étages suivants offrent une structure rectangulaire toute simple. Ce n'est qu'avec le dernier étage, s'élevant sur un cordon, que réapparaissent de riches ornements architectoniques, sous la forme de piliers, fenêtres en plein cintre encadrées de colonnes, frise percée de fenêtres, corniche et balustrade surmontées d'une plate-forme. Le plan du

396 [1911; 64]

The Knickerbocker Trust Building in New York is typical of that type of construction peculiar to America called the "sky—scraper", a design dictated by the limited supply, and high cost, of building sites. The 19—storey Downtown Building is the work of the architects McKim, Mead & White. Pilasters run the height of the first three storeys, and the entrance is framed by Corinthian columns. An additional floor is located between the architrave and the cornices of the columns. The windows of the next 14 storeys are of simple rectangular form, with no moulding or crowning. A rich array of architectural ornamentation is only to be found again at the uppermost storey above the string—course: pillars, windows with round arches between columns, a frieze containing windows, a crowning cornice and a top platform with a balustrade.

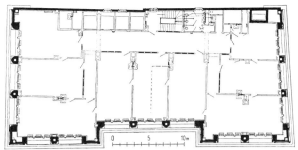

Grundriß des 19. Obergeschosses   Plan du 19ème étage

Plan of the 19th Floor

Detail der oberen Geschosse   Détail des étages supérieurs

Details of the Upper Storeys

Eingang   Entrée   Entrance

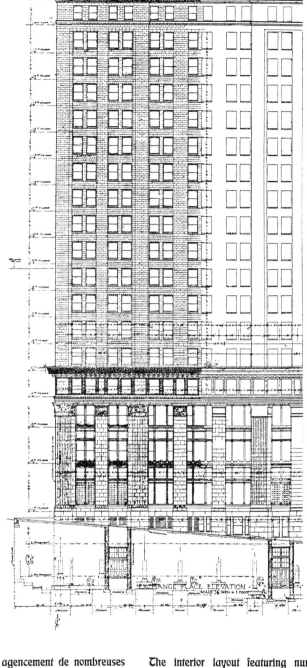

Bender Plattform. Der Grundriß des 19. Geschosses läßt eine Teilung in eine Anzahl zusammenhängender Räume bemerken, im Anschluß an die Treppe und mehrere Elevatoren.

397 [1911: 27]

Die Erweiterungsbauten der Technischen Hochschule in Darmstadt, die Maschinenhalle, dann das Hauptgebäude, sind im Laufe von 6 Jahren, abschließend nach den Entwürfen des Architekten, Geh. Baurat Prof. G. Wickop, zur Vollendung gebracht. Die Fassade des neuen Westflügels ist in der Formensprache eines persönlich aufgefaßten, kräftig wirkenden Barocks behandelt. Das Erdgeschoß zeigt bossierte Quaderschichten und viereckige Fenster; im ersten und zweiten Obergeschoß sind die Fenster der Höhe nach zusammengezogen und mit Bekrönungen in Form gebogener Giebel versehen. Die paarweise gekuppelten Fenster des dritten Obergeschosses haben geraden Abschluß erhalten. In der Mitte der Front tritt über dem ersten Obergeschoß ein flachrunder Erkerausbau hervor, der über die Dachlinie hinausführt, mit einer Plattform endigt; der Eingang liegt seitwärts. Die obe-

19ème étage présente un agencement de nombreuses pièces communiquantes, accessibles par un escalier et des ascenseurs.

397 [1911: 27]

Les agrandissements de l'université technique de Darmstadt, soit la halle aux machines et un bâtiment principal, furent réalisés en l'espace de six années sur les plans de l'architecte prof. G. Wickop. La façade de l'aile occidentale est traitée selon une interprétation personnelle d'un style profondément baroque. Le rez-de-chaussée présente des moellons en bossage et des fenêtres rectangulaires. Les ouvertures des premier et deuxième étages forment un ensemble et offrent des couronnements en forme de pignons arqués. Les fenêtres du troisième étage, regroupées en paires, sont à linteau droit. La partie médiane de la façade est assortie d'une avancée arrondie, se détachant au-dessus du rez-de-chaussée, s'élevant au-delà de la ligne du toit et se terminant par une plate-forme. L'entrée est située latéralement. Les murs extérieurs des étages

The interior layout featuring numerous connecting rooms is exemplified in the plan of the 19th floor, which also shows the position of the staircase and a number of lifts.

397 [1911: 27]

The new additions to the Technical University in Darmstadt, which commenced with the machinery room and then proceeded to the main building, were completed in the course of six years, with the final designs being provided by the senior architect Professor G. Wickop. The façade of the new west wing is developed in an distinctly personal, yet strongly expressive Baroque manner. The ground floor is faced with layers of bossed ashlar and square windows; the windows of the first and second storeys are rectangular and crowned with curved gables. The coupled windows of the third storey are straight—lined. An oriel at the center of the front extends from the first storey through the roof line, where it ends in a platform. The entrance is at the side. The upper façades are of

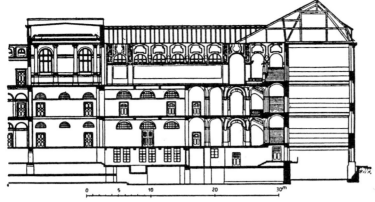

Schnitt durch den Mittelbau des Hauptgebäudes   Coupe du corps médian du bâtiment principal   Maschinenhalle   Halle aux machines   Machinery Hall
Profile of the Middle Erection of the Main Building

ren Geschosse sind in den Außenflächen verputzt, unter gleichzeitiger Verwendung von Hausteingliederungen. Das gebrochene beschieferte Dach trägt eine Anzahl von Fensteraufbauten.

Nach Vollendung der Erweiterungsbauten ergab sich für das Ganze ein rings geschlossener, um zwei große Innenhöfe gruppierter Bau. Der alte Westflügel an der Hochschulstraße erhielt durch Einschaltung eines neuen Treppenhauses eine bedeutende Verlängerung mittelst eines selbständigen Baukörpers, an den sich nach hinten am Hofe noch ein eingeschossiges Bauwerk anschließt, das die Haupträume der Material-Prüfungsanstalt und des Maschinen-Laboratoriums III aufnimmt. Das Kraftwerk besteht aus einem mächtigen Hallenbau, mit der Längsfront an der Magdalenstraße liegend. Das Äußere der Kraftzentrale zeigt wuchtige moderne Formen. Die Verteilung der übrigen Räume ist aus den Grundrissen ersichtlich. Sämtliche Decken in den neuen Bauteilen wurden aus Beton hergestellt, in letzterer Weise auch die Treppen.

supérieurs, enduits d'un crépi, ont reçu quelques ornements en pierres taillées. Le toit d'ardoises, au comble brisé, est percé de fenêtres mansardées.

Les travaux d'agrandissement terminés, il résulta un ensemble fermé, groupé autour de deux cours intérieures. L'ancienne aile occidentale, donnant sur la rue, bénéficia, par l'ajout d'une cage d'escalier, d'un prolongement important de par un corps de bâtiment indépendant, auquel se rattache, par derrière, sur la cour, une construction d'un étage, abritant les pièces principales du contrôle des matériaux et du laboratoire des machines III. La centrale est aménagée dans une vaste halle, dont le côté le plus long s'ouvre sur la Magdalenstraße. Les plans donnent un clair aperçu de la disposition des autres salles. L'ensemble des planchers des nouvelles constructions furent exécutés en béton et partiellement en béton armé, c'est dans ce dernier matériau que furent réalisés les escaliers.

plaster with cut stone articulations. The slate roof has a number of dormers.

The new construction resulted in an edifice closed on all sides and grouped round two large inner courtyards. The old west wing was noticeably lengthened by the addition of a new stairwell housed in a structure of its own. This is attached to an one—storey building at the courtyard side. The latter houses the principal rooms of the material testing institute and machine laboratory Nr. 3. The power station consists of an imposing hall whose long frontage faces the Magdalenstrasse. The exterior of the power station displays a solid modern character. The distribution of the other rooms can be seen in the floor plans. All ceilings of the newly—added buildings are of concrete, some are of reinforced concrete, which was also used for the staircases.

398 [1911; 34]

Das monumental ausgebildete Museum für historische und moderne Kunstwerke der Stadt Genf, an der Esplanade de l'Observatoire, der rue des Casemattes, de Monnetier und dem Boulevard Helvétique gelegen, ein Werk des Architekten Marc Camoletti, ist in einer Bauzeit von 6 Jahren zur Ausführung gekommen und hat 3½ Millionen Frcs. an Baukosten erfordert. Die Hauptfront an der Esplanade de l'Observatoire, im Mittelrisalit das Portal enthaltend, mit Eckrisaliten abschließend, ist durch ionische Halbsäulen und an den Risaliten durch frei vorgestellte Säulen gegliedert. Den Abschluß der Front nach oben bildet ein Gebälk mit Hauptgesims und darauffolgender Attika. Die große Figurengruppe über dem Mittelrisalit sowie die Gruppen über den Eckrisaliten sind von Bildhauer P. Arnlehn geschaffen. Die Fenster sind rundbogig geschlossen und werden an den Seitenfronten durch Pfeiler eingerahmt. Die Fenster des Erdgeschosses sind an der Hauptfront geradlinig, an den Seitenfronten im Stichbogen geschlossen. Die Fassaden sind aus verschiedenen Materialien, am Äußeren aus helltönigem Savonnière-Kalkstein, auf dem sich die Tafeln von Cipolin antique de Valais mit den Namen berühmter Künstler abheben, dargestellt.

Das freiliegende Gebäude umschließt mit vier Flügeln einen offenen, mit Gartenanlagen ausgestatteten Hof. Aus dem Vestibül im Erdgeschoß, von zwei großen Sälen eingeschlossen, gelangt man zu der doppelläufigen Treppe, die sich im Hauptgeschoß fortsetzt. Das Erdgeschoß enthält außerdem eine Anzahl Säle für historische und moderne Kunstwerke, namentlich auch für Rüstungen. Im Hauptgeschoß sind die Säle und Kabinette für Malwerke untergebracht, während das Entresol-Geschoß die Räume für Tonzeug und Münzen aufnimmt. Die Säle im Hauptgeschoß haben Glasdecken erhalten. Vestibül und Treppenhaus sind in Stein von Montpaon und die Balustraden

398 [1911; 34]

Le monumental musée d'art ancien et moderne de la ville de Genève, donnant sur l'esplanade de l'observatoire, la rue des casemattes, la rue de Monnetier et le boulevard helvétique, est l'œuvre de l'architecte Marc Camoletti. Construit en six années, il nécessita la somme de 3½ millions de frcs. La façade principale sur l'esplanade de l'observatoire, est assortie d'une avancée centrale, abritant le portail d'entrée, et de deux avancées flanquant les extrémités. Elle présente une ordonnance de demi-colonnes ioniques et de colonnes dégagées dans les avancées d'angle et est couronnée par un entablement surmonté d'un attique. Les sculptures portées par l'avancée centrale ainsi que celles ornant les avancées d'angle furent exécutées par P. Arlehn. Les fenêtres en plein cintre sont encadrées de piliers sur les façades latérales. Les ouvertures perçant le rez-de-chaussée sont droites sur la façade principale et surbaissées sur les façades latérales. Les murs extérieurs sont réalisés en différents matériaux. Des plaques de Cipolin antique de Valais, portant les noms d'artistes fameux, se détachent de la façade en castine claire.

Cet édifice dégagé ceint, de ses quatre ailes, une cour ouverte aménagée en jardin. Le vestibule du rez-de-chaussée, flanqué de deux grandes salles, donne sur l'escalier à deux volées qui se prolonge jusqu'à l'étage supérieur. Le rez-de-chaussée est occupé par les salles réservées aux œuvres anciennes et modernes ainsi qu'aux armures. A l'étage sont aménagés les salles et les cabinets de peinture. Les pièces de poterie et les collections numismatiques sont exposées à l'entresol. Les salles situées à l'étage sont pourvues de plafonds de verre. Le vestibule et la cage d'escalier sont en pierres de Montpaon, les balustrades en pierres de Tavel. Les façades sur cour ont reçu un

398 [1911; 34]

The monumentally styled museum for classical and modern art in the city of Geneva (located at the Eiplanade de l'Observatoire, the rue des Casemattes, de Monnetier and the Boulevard Velevétique) is the work of the architect Marc Camoleti. It was completed in 6 years and cost 3½ million Francs. The principal front facing the Eiplanade de l'Observatoire has a middle projection in which the main entrance is located, and is bordered by corner projections. Ionic half—columns line the principal front, and its projections are articulated by freely—projecting pillars. The front is finished off at the top by an entablature with the principal cornice and followed by an parapet. The large groups of figures over the middle and corner projections were created by the sculptor P. Arnlehn. The windows have round arches, and those on the side fronts are framed by pillars. The ground floor windows are straight—lined on the principal front, those on the sides are set in segmental arches. The façades are rendered with various materials, the exterior layer is of lightly—coloured limestone from Savonnière which is ornamented with tablets of cipolin engraved with the names of famous artists.

The four wings of the free—standing edifice encompass a courtyard with its gardens. Flanked on both sides by two large halls, the ground floor vestibule opens onto a double—flight staircase which leads to the main floor. In addition, the ground floor contains a number of halls for classical and modern art, in particular for collections of armour. The halls and galleries for paintings are located on the main floor, while the mezzanine is reserved for pottery and coin collections. The halls of the main floor have glass ceilings. The vestibule and staircase are furnished in stonework from Montpaon, and the balustrades in stonework from

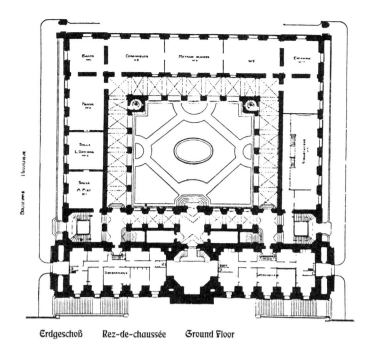

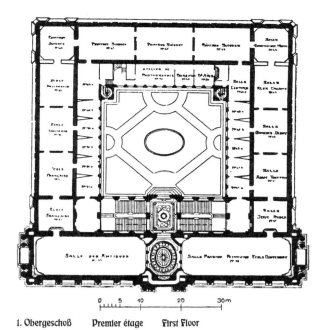

Erdgeschoß	Rez-de-chaussée	Ground Floor

1. Obergeschoß	Premier étage	First Floor

in Stein von Tavel ausgeführt. Die Hoffassaden sind mit Stein von Euville verblendet. Die Gerüste der mit Oberlicht versehenen Dächer bestehen aus Eisen.

Das Untergeschoß ist für die Hofeinfahrt und zur Anlage von Ateliers, Magazinen, Ventilations- und Heizanlagen benutzt. Es ist eine Niederdruck-Dampfheizung mit automatischer Regelung vorgesehen, die gleiche Einrichtung ist für die Ventilationsanlage getroffen.

399 [1911; 30]

Das Landhaus Hannig in Berlin-Dahlem, Friedenthalstraße 4, ist nach dem Entwurfe des Architekten B. D. A. O. Berlich in einer Bauzeit von 7 Monaten für die Kostensumme von 40 000 Mark zur Ausführung gekommen. Es ist ein Erdgeschoß und ein zum Teil im ausgebauten Dachgeschoß untergebrachtes Obergeschoß vorhanden. An den seitwärts gelegenen überbauten Eingang schließt sich das rund vorspringende Treppenhaus für die zum Maleratelier führende Wendeltreppe, weiter ein Erkerausbau im Erdgeschoß und der zweistöckige Gebäudeteil an. Das überhängende gebrochene Dach des einstöckigen Gebäudeteils trägt auf der unteren gebogenen Fläche einen in gebogener Linie abschließenden breiten Fensteraufbau. Der Sockel ist in gefugten Rathenower Ziegeln hergestellt, die oberen Flächen der Fronten sind in hydraulischem Mörtel verputzt. Das Dach ist mit holländischen Pfannen eingedeckt und die Giebelflächen sind mit Schindeln beschlagen.

Das Erdgeschoß enthält das Atelier des Besitzers, des Bildhauers Hannig, mit dem erhöhten Erkersitz und die Wohnzimmer, sämtlich von der Diele mit offener Treppe zugänglich. Das Speisezimmer ist mit einem Fensterausbau, der Salon mit anstoßendem Wintergarten versehen. Außerdem liegt hier die Küche.

Im Obergeschoß ist ein Maleratelier mit Nebenzimmer eingerichtet, und abgetrennt von diesen sind die Schlaf- und Kinderzimmer sowie das Bad untergebracht.

400 [1911; 61]

Das Landhaus in Nürnberg, Liebigstraße 3, bildet einen geschlossenen, nahezu quadratischen, im Aufbau zweistöckigen Baukörper, der mit einem gebrochenen, zeltartig abgewalmten, auf den unteren Flächen Lukenfenster tragenden Dache überdeckt ist. Urheber des Entwurfs ist Architekt P. L. Troost. Dem Eingange ist eine auf Säulen ruhende, halbkreisförmig überdeckte Vorhalle vorgelegt, die sich zwischen einer als Veranda ausgebildeten Einfriedungsmauer öffnet. An der einen Seitenfront des Hauses springt im Erdgeschoß ein polygonaler, mit einer Altane abschließender Vorbau heraus, dessen Fenstertüren auf eine beiderseits sich erstreckende, durch eine Freitreppe zugängliche, figurengeschmückte Terrasse münden. Außer-

revêtement de pierres d'Euville. Les charpentes des toits assortis de verrières sont en fer.

Le sous-sol abrite le passage assurant l'accès à la cour, des ateliers, des magasins ainsi que les dispositifs de ventilation et de chauffage. Un chauffage à vapeur à basse pression à réglage automatique ainsi qu'un équipement identique pour la ventilation sont prévus.

399 [1911; 30]

La villa Hannig de Berlin-Dahlem, Friedenthalstraße 4, est l'œuvre de l'architecte O. Berlich. Sa construction dura sept mois et coûta 40 000 marks. Elle se compose d'un rez-de-chaussée et d'un étage, situé en partie dans un toit mansard. L'entrée latérale, abritée sous un porche, jouxte la saillie arrondie formée par l'escalier en colimaçon conduisant à l'atelier de peinture, puis se trouvent l'avant-corps du rez-de-chaussée et enfin le corps de deux étages. Le toit saillant, en croupe, de la partie à un étage, présente, dans le brisis incurvé, une large fenêtre mansardée s'arrondissant vers le haut. Le socle est construit en briques de Rathenow jointoyées, les surfaces supérieures sont enduites d'un crépi de mortier hydraulique. Le toit est recouvert de tuiles hollandaises creuses. Les surfaces des pignons sont revêtues de bardeaux.

Le rez-de-chaussée abrite l'atelier du propriétaire, le sculpteur Hannig, ainsi que la salle de séjour, accessible par l'antichambre comprenant un escalier, la salle de séjour assortie d'un bow-window, le salon attenant au jardin d'hiver et enfin la cuisine.

À l'étage sont installés d'une part un atelier de peinture et ses dépendances, formant un ensemble indépendant, et d'autre part les chambres à coucher, la chambre des enfants et la salle de bains.

400 [1911; 61]

Cette villa de Nuremberg, Liebigstraße 3, est une construction fermée, presque carrée, montant sur deux étages et recouverte d'un toit en croupe, percé de lucarnes. Les plans furent exécutés par l'architecte P. L. Troost. L'entrée est abritée par un porche hypostyle en demi-cercle, donnant sur un mur de clôture transformé en pergola. Une des façades latérales est assortie, au rez-de-chaussée, d'une avancée polygonale, couronnée par une plate-forme. Les portes-fenêtres de cet oriel s'ouvrent sur une terrasse ornée de sculptures, accessible par un perron. Les fenêtres inférieures de cette façade sont légèrement bombées. La

Tavel. The façades of the courtyard are of Euville ashlar. The framework of the skylight roof is of iron.

The basement level is used as an entrance to the courtyard and is where the ateliers, storage rooms, ventilation and heating installations are located. The building ist heated with low—pressure steam heating with thermostats, ventilation is carried out in the same manner.

399 [1911; 30]

The Hannig residence in the Dahlem suburb of Berlin (Friedenthalstrasse 4) was built according to the plan of the architect O. Berlich, member of the Association of German Architects, in a period of 7 months at a cost of 40,000 Marks. The building consists of a ground floor and an upper floor, the latter being partially expanded to include a roof storey. The covered side entrance is abutted by a round projecting stairwell with spiral stairs leading to the painter's atelier, as well as by a bay at the ground level, and the two—storeyed part of the house. The overhanging broken roof of the one—storeyed section of the house has a group of three windows projecting under a slightly curved gable. The foundations are of bonded Rathenow brick, the upper surfaces of the fronts are plastered with hydraulic mortar. The roof is covered with pantiles, and the gabled fronts are hung with shingles.

The ground floor is occupied by the atelier of the owner, the sculptor Hannig, with its oriel seat, and the sitting—room. Both lead to the entry hall with an open staircase. The dining—room features a window projection and the salon opens onto a winter garden. The kitchen is also located on the ground floor.

The upper floor consists of a painter's atelier, and separate from this, the bedrooms and children's rooms, as well as a bathroom.

400 [1911; 61]

The private residence in Nuremberg (Liebigstrasse 3) is a two—storey building almost completely square in structure and composition. It is covered by a pyramidal hipped roof with dormers in its lower slope. The design was conceived by the architect P. L. Troost. The entrance is covered by a semi—circular canopy resting on columns and opens onto a veranda enclosed by two walls. A polygonal bay at one of the side fronts has a balcony on top and French doors opening onto a terrace. The terrace, which is also accessible by a perron, stretches along the side of the house and is ornamented with statuary. The win-

dem sind die unteren Gruppenfenster derselben Front leicht nach außen gebogen. Die Rückfront ist wieder im Erdgeschoß mit einem flachrund heraustretenden Fensterausbau gegliedert. Das Ganze bildet einen Putzbau mit äußeren Muschelkalkgliederungen und inneren Betondecken. Das Dach ist mit Falzziegeln eingedeckt.

Die auf Erd- und Obergeschoß verteilten Wohn- und Schlafzimmer liegen um eine mittlere Halle, von der seitwärts die Treppe aufsteigt. Das Erdgeschoß enthält noch die Anrichte mit dem Speisenaufzug; im Obergeschoß ist das geräumige Bad neben dem Toilettenzimmer untergebracht.

401 [1911; 39]

Die in Gartenanlagen eingebettete Villa Frizzoni in Bergamo, Rue Victor Emanuel, ein Werk des Architekten Professor Giov. Barboglio, ist in zwei Baujahren für die Kostensumme von 150 000 Frcs. zur Ausführung gekommen. Der dreistöckige Aufbau zeigt an der Eingangsfront eine rundbogige, von Säulen gestützte, eine als Laube ausgebildete Altane tragende Halle und breite, mehrfach geteilte, von Rundbogen umrahmte Fenster. Der seitwärts liegende Eingangs- und Treppenflur ist im ersten Obergeschoß mit einer offenen, durch einen*vorspringenden Balkon erweiterten, im zweiten Obergeschoß mit einer als Altane endigenden Halle ausgestattet. Von den vorspringenden Bauteilen der einen Seitenfront ist der an der Eingangsfront im vierten Obergeschoß als Loggia ausgebildet. Einzelne Fenster im ersten Obergeschoß sind gruppiert und in einer flachbogigen, von Säulen flankierten Umrahmung zusammengefaßt, einem dieser Fenster ist ein Balkon vorgelegt. Die übrigen Fenster sind geradlinig überdeckt. Unter den weit überhängenden, die Holzkonstruktion zeigenden, von hölzernen Konsolen gestützten Dachkanten, dem südlichen Charakter der Anlage entsprechend, zieht sich ein fein gemalter Blumenfries hin. Die Verblendung des Erdgeschosses sowie die Architekturgliederungen sind in Kunstsandstein hergestellt, die Putzflächen sind gelb gefärbt.

Das Erdgeschoß enthält das Wohn- und das Spielzimmer der Kinder, Küche, Waschküche und Dienerzimmer. Im ersten Stock liegen die Salons, das Speisezimmer, die Bibliothek, das Dienerzimmer, die Garderobe und die Haupt- und Nebentreppe. Das zweite Obergeschoß ist zur Anlage von Wohn- und Schlafzimmern sowie des Baderaumes benutzt.

402 [1911; 40]

Die zweistöckige Villa Gonella in Turin, Via Silvio Pellico 31, ein Werk des Architekten Ing. Giov. Chevalley, zeigt in der Ecke zwischen den mit flachen Giebeln abschließenden Flügelbauten einen durch beide Geschosse geführten, im Obergeschoß als Loggia ausgebildeten, mit einer Terrasse abschließenden Ausbau. Im Erdgeschoß des einen Flügels öffnet sich eine überwölbte Halle; übrigens sind die Fenster teils im Flachbogen, teil geradlinig geschlossen. Der Eingang liegt an der Seitenfront und wird von einem vorgekragten Balkon überragt. Die Fronten sind im Sockel und in den Gliederungen aus Haustein, in den Flächen in Backsteinmauerwerk ausgeführt. Die flachen Dächer sind mit Ziegeln eingedeckt.

403 [1911; 51]

Über einem hohen, von Terrassen gebildeten Unterbau erhebt sich die in gemischter Massiv-Holzbauweise ausgeführte, wirkungsvoll gruppierte Villa in Freiburg i. Br., Mercystraße 26. Der Bau wurde nach dem Entwurfe des Architekten B. D. A. Professor H. Eberhard im Verlaufe eines Jahres mit einem Kostenaufwand von 147 000 Mark, die Terrassenanlage sowie die Inneneinrichtung mit den Möbeln eingerechnet, errichtet. An der Straßenfront springen zwei Eckflügelbauten vor, zwischen sich eine auf der Terrasse liegende Gartenhalle einschließend. An einer Seitenfront ist der von einer Vorhalle überdeckte, mittels einer Freitreppe zugängliche, mit einer Terrassenlaube in Verbindung stehende Eingang angeordnet; an der anderen Seitenfront springt ein runder, durch

401 [1911; 39]

La villa Frizzoni, située à Bergame, via Vittorio Emanuele, se dresse au milieu d'un grand jardin. Conçue par l'architecte prof. Giov. Barboglio, la propriété fut construite en deux ans pour la somme de 150 000 frcs. Cette villa de trois étages, aux toits plats, offre, sur la façade principale, de larges fenêtres à meneaux dans des embrasures en arcades ainsi qu'un portique dont les colonnes supportent une plate-forme aménagée en tonnelle. Le hall d'entrée comprenant l'escalier, situé latéralement, est assorti d'un balcon saillant au premier étage et d'un portique couronné d'une plate-forme au deuxième étage. Un des avant-corps d'une des façades latérales est troué d'une loggia, au niveau du quatrième étage de la façade principale. Les fenêtres groupées du premier étage sont insérées dans des encadrements surbaissés, flanqués de colonnes. Une de ces ouvertures présente un balcon. Les fenêtres restantes sont droites. Une délicate frise de fleurs peintes court le long de la corniche du toit. Le toit très saillant, laissant apparaître une partie de la charpente de bois, révèle un encorbellement en bois, typique des régions méridionales. Le revêtement du rez-de-chaussée ainsi que les ornements architecturaux sont en grès artificiel. Les murs ont reçu un crépi jaune.

Le rez-de-chaussée abrite la salle à manger, la chambre de jeu des enfants, la cuisine, la buanderie et la chambre des domestiques. Au premier étage sont aménagés les salons, la salle à manger, le cabinet de lecture, la chambre des domestiques, la garde-robe ainsi que l'escalier principal et l'escalier de service. Le deuxième étage est occupé par les pièces de séjour, les chambres à coucher et la salle de bains.

402 [1911; 40]

La villa Gonella de Turin, via Silvio Pellico 31, est l'œuvre de l'architecte Giov. Chevalley. La maison est assortie, dans l'angle, entre les deux ailes à pignon plat, d'une avancée montant sur deux étages, aménagée en loggia au premier étage et se terminant en terrasse. Un hall voûté s'ouvre au rez-de-chaussée d'une des ailes. Les façades offrent des ouvertures droites ou surbaissées. L'entrée, située sur la façade latérale, est surmontée d'un balcon saillant. Le socle et les ornements sont en pierres taillées, les murs présentent une maçonnerie de briques. Les toits plats sont recouverts de tuiles.

403 [1911; 51]

Cette impressionnante villa, située à Fribourg, Mercystrasse 26, fut construite dans un appareil de bois et de pierres, sur une base en terrasses. Les travaux, effectués sur les plans de l'architecte prof. H. Eberhard, furent réalisés en une année pour la somme de 147 000 marks, terrasse, aménagement intérieur et mobilier compris. Deux ailes d'angle, encadrant un jardin couvert aménagé sur la terrasse, se détachent de la façade sur rue. Située sur une façade latérale et contiguë à une terrasse, l'entrée, protégée par un porche, est accessible par un perron. La façade opposée est assortie d'une saillie ronde, montant sur deux étages. Le socle est réalisé en maçonnerie de

façade postérieure présente, au rez-de-chaussée, un bow-window de forme convexe. Les murs de façade crépis offrent des ornements en coquillart. Les planchers sont en béton. Le toit porte une couverture de tuiles plates.

Les pièces de séjour et les chambres à coucher du rez-de-chaussée et de l'étage sont agencées autour d'un hall central, attenant à l'escalier. Au rez-de-chaussée se trouvent l'office et un monte-plats. La vaste salle de bains et les cabinets d'aisance attenants sont à l'étage.

401 [1911; 39]

Nestled amongst hilly gardens in Bergamo, the Villa Frizzoni (Rue Victor Emanuel) is the work of the architect Professor Giov—Barboglio. Construction was completed in two years at a cost of 150,000 Francs. The entrance front of the flat—roofed three—storey edifice has an arched porch whose columns support a balcony designed as a bower. Its broad windows are set in curved arches and divided by a number of individual frames. The perron at the side leads to an open projecting balcony on the first floor, and continues up to a terrace on the second floor which represents a continuation of the hall. A loggia at the fourth storey of the entrance front is formed by the projections of the side front. Several groups of windows on the first floor are framed by a flatly—arched moulding and columns, one of these windows has a balcony. The other windows are straight—lined. In keeping with the Southern character of the site, a delicate frieze of flowers has been painted below the overhangig wooden eaves supported by wooden brackets. The facing of the ground floor and the architectural ornamentation are of artificial sandstone. The plastered surfaces are uniformly yellow in colour.

Located on the ground floor are the sitting—room and children's playroom, kitchen, washroom, and servants' rooms. The drawing room, dining room, library, a servant's room, wardrobe as well as the main and side staircases are located on the first floor. The second floor contains sitting—rooms, bedrooms, and a bath.

402 [1911; 40]

The two—storey Villa Gonella in Turin (Via Silvio Pellico 31) is the work of the certified architect Giov. Chevalley. Extending between two wings of the house, which have straight gables, is a projection with a loggia at the first storey and a terrace on top. A vaulted hall opens at the ground floor of one wing; the window frames are either slightly arched or straight—lined. The entrance at the side front is covered by a projecting balcony. The socle and articulations of the fronts are of ashlar, the walls are of brick. The saddle-back roofs are covered with tile.

403 [1911; 51]

The Bubat country house in Freiburg (Mercy-strasse 26) is impressively situated on an elevated foundation of terraces. Its solid—wood construction scheme was designed by Professor H. Eberhard, member of the Association of German Architects. Construction was carried out over the course of one year at a cost of 147,000 Marks, including the terraces and interior furnishings. The street front is marked by two corner wing projections which enclose a garden porch located on the terrace. The covered entrance on the side front opens onto a terrace bower and is reached by stairs leading from the lower terraces. The other side front has a rounded projection running the height of the

beide Geschosse geführter Ausbau vor. Der Sockel der Fronten besteht aus rauhem Kalksteinmauerwerk, die Flächen im Erdgeschoß sind graugelb verputzt, die des Obergeschosses mit karbolisierten Schindeln beschlagen. Die überhängenden Dächer, im mittleren Teile der Straßenfront von einer Fenstergruppe unterbrochen, haben eine Eindeckung mit dunkelroten Biberschwänzen erhalten. Die verwendeten Bildhauerarbeiten sind von K. Huber gefertigt.

Im Erdgeschoß ist die Wohndiele mit anstoßendem Erkersitzplatz, das Billardzimmer, das Herrenzimmer mit darunterliegender Trinkstube, das Speisezimmer, die Küche nebst Anrichte und die von dem Vorraume und der Diele zugängliche Stockwerkstreppe angeordnet. Das Obergeschoß enthält die Schlafzimmer mit dem Baderaum, das Fräuleinzimmer und mehrere offene Balkons in Verbindung mit den Zimmern.

404 [1911; 60]

Das fünfstöckige, noch ein ausgebautes Dachgeschoß umfassende, durch Vorgärten von der Straße getrennte Wohnhaus in Zürich II, Eisenbahnstraße 12, Ecke Splügenstraße, ein Werk des Architekten B. S. A. H. Müller, kam im Laufe von zwei Jahren zur Ausführung. An der abgestumpften Ecke ist, über dem Erdgeschoß beginnend, ein polygonaler, durch sämtliche Obergeschosse geführter, den übertretenden Dachkranz tragender, im vierten Obergeschoß von Säulen umstellter Erker ausgekragt. An der längeren Front erhebt sich ein Giebel, in geschwungenen Konturen endigend und in der Spitze eine offene Loggia zeigend. An derselben Front befindet sich ein über dem ersten Obergeschoß ausgekragter, im obersten Geschoß wieder mit Säulen umstellter und über den vortretenden Dachkranz hinausgeführter Erker. Außerdem springen vor den Fenstern beider Fronten eine Anzahl verschieden gestalteter Balkons vor. Die überhängenden gebrochenen Dächer sind mit Lukenfenstern besetzt und mit Schiefer eingedeckt. Die Fassadenflächen sind mit Terranova-Verputz versehen, unten grau, oben olivengrün gefärbt und an mehreren Stellen ornamental gemustert. Ein Teil der Architekturgliederungen ist aus Sandstein hergestellt.

405 [1911; 77]

Von einem Garten umgeben, wie alle anderen Wohnbauten des Geländes, ringsum freiliegend, erhebt sich das Landhaus Schröder in Hagen i. W., Gartenvorstadt Eppenhausen, Haßleyerstraße 37. Das zweistöckige Gebäude ist in etwa 14 Monaten nach dem Entwurfe des Architekten Professor Peter Behrens für die Kostensumme von rund 80 000 Mark errichtet. Der Eingang ist an einer schmalen Seitenfront angeordnet; an der einen Längsfront springt ein durch beide Geschosse gehender mit einem geschweiften Giebel abschließender Ausbau hervor; der anderen Längsfront ist im Erdgeschoß eine offene Halle, von einer Freitreppe zugänglich und eine Altane tragend, vorgelegt. Einfriedung, Sockel sowie einzelne der oberen Frontwände sind aus am Ort gefundenem dunklem Bruchstein hergestellt, während die übrigen Flächen mit Terranovaputz und teilweise mit weißem Kunstsandstein bedeckt sind. Das abgewalmte Dach ist mit Schiefer eingedeckt.

Das Erdgeschoß enthält den mit einem Windfang versehenen Eingangsflur, von dem aus Wohn-, Empfangs- und Eßzimmer zugänglich sind; außerdem sind Küche mit Speisekammer und Anrichte, sowie eine Garderobe vorhanden. Im Obergeschoß sind die Schlafzimmer, das Ankleidezimmer und das Bad untergebracht.

406 [1911; 54]

Das zweistöckige, mit teilweise ausgebautem Dachgeschoß versehene Einfamilienhaus in Düsseldorf, Lindemannstraße 34, ein Werk der Architekten Reg.-Baumeister Carl Moritz und Werner Stahl, ist in einer Bauzeit von etwa 10 Monaten für die Kostensumme von 120 000 Mark zur Ausführung gekommen. Die durch einen Vorgarten von der Straße getrennte, mit vorgelegter Terrasse ausgestattete Fassade wird

castines brutes. Les murs du rez-de-chaussée sont enduits d'un crépi gris jaune, ceux des étages supérieurs sont revêtus de bardeaux carbolisés. Les toits saillants, percés dans leur partie médiane d'un groupe de fenêtres mansardées, sont recouverts de tuiles plates rouge foncé. Les travaux de sculpture furent exécutés par K. Huber.

Le rez-de-chaussée comprend la salle de séjour, la salle de billard, le cabinet de travail, au-dessous duquel se trouve le bar, la salle à manger, la cuisine, l'office et la cage d'escalier accessible par le vestibule et l'antichambre. L'étage est occupé par les chambres à coucher, la salle de bains, la chambre de mademoiselle ainsi que de nombreux balcons attenants aux chambres.

404 [1911; 60]

Cet immeuble zurichois, situé à l'angle des Eisenbahnstraße et Splügenstraße, conçu par l'architecte H. Müller, fut réalisé en l'espace de deux années. Il s'agit d'un bâtiment de cinq étages, étage mansardé non compris, séparé de la rue par un jardin frontal. Dans l'angle, au-dessus du premier étage, se dégage un avant-corps polygonal, s'élevant jusqu'au toit et assorti de colonnes au quatrième étage. Un pignon aux contours ondulés, enchâssant une loggia ouverte, se détache de la façade la plus longue. Cette façade présente une avancée se dégageant au-dessus du deuxième étage et montant jusqu'au toit. Elle est ornée de colonnes au quatrième étage. Des balcons saillants, de formes différentes, parent certaines fenêtres des façades. Les toits d'ardoises, aux combles brisés sont percés de lucarnes. Les murs extérieurs ont reçu un crépi de couleur grise dans leur partie inférieure, de couleur vert olive dans leur partie supérieure, offrant par endroit un décor. Les ornements architecturaux sont en partie réalisés en grès.

405 [1911; 77]

La propriété Schröder, située aux environs de Hagen, dans la cité-ardin d'Eppenhausen, se dresse dans un jardin clos. Réalisée en quelque 14 mois sur les plans de l'architecte Peter Behrens, elle côuta la somme de 80 000 marks. L'entrée se situe sur l'étroite façade latérale. Une des façade frontale est assortie d'un avant-corps, montant sur les deux étages et coiffé d'un pignon ondulé. Au rez-de-chaussée, la façade opposée présente, accessible par un perron, un portique dont les colonnes supportent une plate-forme. Les murs de clôture, le socle ainsi que la partie supérieure des murs extérieurs sont construits en pierres de taille locales, de couleur brune. Les surfaces restantes sont enduites d'un crépi et partiellement revêtues de grès blanc. Le toit en croupe porte une couverture d'ardoises.

Le rez-de-chaussée comprend la salle de séjour, l'antichambre et la salle à manger, accessibles par un couloir d'entrée équipé d'un tambour, ainsi que la cuisine avec son garde-manger et son office, et enfin une garde-robe. A l'étage sont aménagés les chambres à coucher, la garde-robe et la salle de bains.

406 [1911; 54]

Cet hôtel particulier, situé à Düsseldorf, Lindemannstraße 34, est l'œuvre des architectes Carl Moritz et Werner Stahl. Les travaux furent effectués en quelque dix mois pour la somme de 120 000 marks. Il s'agit d'une construction s'élevant sur deux étages, pourvue d'un toit en partie mansardé et séparée de la rue par un jardin frontal. La façade, assortie d'une

two stories. The socle of the fronts consists of limestone ashlar, the surfaces of the ground floor front consist of grey–yellow plaster and the upper storey is paneled with tar shingles. The overhanging roof, which in the middle section of the street front is broken by a group of windows, is covered with flat red tiles. Sculptural work was carried out by K. Huber.

The ground floor contains the living room with an adjoining bay sitting–room, the billiard–room, a study with its sunken refreshment parlour, the dining–room, the kitchen and pantries, as well as the main staircase, which is accessible from the hall and anterooms. Bedrooms and a bath are located on the upper floor, as is the maid's room. Many of the rooms open onto balconies.

404 [1911; 60]

The five–storey apartment building with an additional roof storey in Zurich (Eisenbahnstrasse 12) is separated from the street by a small front garden and is the work of H. Müller, member of the Swiss Association of Architects. Completed in 2 years, it features a polygonal bay running from the ground floor to the fourth storey, where it is decorated with columns and covered by an overhanging roof cornice. The long frontage is dominated by a curved gable with a loggia at the top. The same front also has an oriel extending from the first through the fourth storey, where it is also adorned with columns and crowned by the cornice. In addition, the windows of both fronts have balconies of various designs. The overhanging roof has skylights and is covered with slate. The façades are faced with terranova plaster, grey below and olive green above, and ornamented at many places. Parts of the architectural ornamentation are of sandstone.

405 [1911; 77]

The two–storey Schröder house in the Eppenhausen suburb of Hagen (Hassleyerstrasse 37), like all other residences in the area, is surrounded by a spacious garden. Designed by the architect Professor Peter Behrens, this freestanding house was completed in about 14 months at a cost of 80,000 Marks. The entrance is located at one of the narrow side fronts; a projection topped by a curved gable runs through the two storeys of one long front. A porch with a perron is situated at the ground level of the other long front and it is covered by a balcony. The garden walls, socle and parts of the frontage walls are of dark rubble masonry from the near vicinity while the remaining surfaces are covered with Terranova plaster and articulated with white artificial sandstone. The hipped roof is covered with slate.

The porch leads to the living room, parlour, and dining room. The ground floor also contains the kitchen with dressers and pantry, and a wardrobe. Bedrooms, a dressing–room and a bath are located on the upper floor.

406 [1911; 54]

The apartment building at Lindemannstrasse 34 in Düsseldorf, a work of the architect Carl Moritz, was completed in approximately 10 months at a cost of 120,000 Marks. The two–storey house with a partial roof floor is separated from the street by a front garden and adjoining terrace. The front façade is framed by two corner projections, one of which contains the en-

durch schmale Eckrisalite eingefaßt, von denen das links gelegene den Eingang enthält. In dem zurückliegenden Teil der Front steigen kräftige dorische, beide Geschosse durchsetzende Säulen auf, welche die geradlinig überdeckten, im Obergeschoß mit Balkons versehenen Fenster zwischen sich einschließen und den die ganze Breite des Rücksprungs überragenden Dachkranz tragen. Über den Eckrisaliten sowie über der Mitte der Front erheben sich breite Fensteraufbauten, die Steilfläche des Daches einnehmend. Die Fassade ist mit hellgrauem und gelbem Dürkheimer Sandstein bekleidet; das gebrochene Dach hat eine Eindeckung von Biberschwänzen erhalten. Die figürlichen Bildwerke an der Fassade sind von Bildhauer C. Neuhaus geschaffen.

Das Erdgeschoß enthält einen ovalen zur Diele mit freiliegender Treppe führenden Eingangsflur, außerdem eine Reihe Zimmer, den Wintergarten, die Küche und die um einen kleinen Lichthof gelegenen Nebenräume. Wintergarten und Speisezimmer zeigen flachrunde Fensterausbauten in Verbindung mit einer Terrasse. Im Obergeschoß wiederholt sich die Anlage der Diele, um welche sich die Wohn- und Schlafzimmer, sowie das durch Oberlicht beleuchtete Badezimmer gruppieren.

407 [1911: 94]

Das vierstöckige Geschäftshaus in Lübeck, Johannisstraße, Ecke Breitestraße, ist ein Werk der Architekten Schötz, Schötz & Redelstorff. Die in Sandstein verblendeten Fassaden werden durch vom Boden bis zum Dachgesims durchgehende Pfeiler, welche die Fenstergruppen zwischen sich einschließen, geteilt. Die Ladenöffnungen im Erdgeschoß sowie die Fenster im ersten und zweiten Obergeschoß sind geradlinig geschlossen, während die drei Portalöffnungen im Mittelrisalit der Hauptfront rundbogig überwölbt sind. Die Fenster des dritten Obergeschosses sind flachbogig überdeckt und mit ovalen Oberlichtern versehen. Das Mittelrisalit sowie ein Erkerrisalit schließen mit Dreiecksgiebeln ab. Das Dach zeigt eine zusammenhängende Reihe von Fenstern und ist mit Ziegeln eingedeckt. Das Erdgeschoß ist zu Läden ausgebaut, die drei Obergeschosse enthalten Geschäftsräume.

408 [1911: 57]

Die zu einem einheitlichen, monumental wirkenden Architekturbilde zusammengeschmolzene Gruppe von fünf Wohnhäusern in Basel, Spalenring-Ahornstraße, im Entwurf von Architekt Rud. Linder herrührend, kam in den Jahren 1909–1910 zur Ausführung. Die Häuser liegen an zwei Fronten und der gebrochenen Ecke frei und sind an der Ahornstraße um einen nach der Straßenseite offenen Hof mit abgerundeten Ecken gelagert. Ein innerer Hof an der geschlossenen Seite zeigt ebenfalls die Rundform. Der vierstöckige

terrasse, est flanquée de part et d'autre d'étroits avant-corps, dont le gauche abrite l'entrée. Le renfoncement de la façade présente de puissantes colonnes doriques, continues sur deux étages, encadrant des fenêtres droites, en tribune au premier étage, et soutenant l'avancée du toit. Le brisis est percé, dans toute sa largeur, de fenêtres mansardées. Les murs de façade sont revêtus de grès de Türkheim gris clair et jaune. Le toit au comble brisé porte une couverture de tuiles plates. Les ornements plastiques de la façade furent exécutés par le sculpteur C. Neuhaus.

Le rez-de-chaussée abrite un couloir d'entrée ovale, menant à une antichambre comprenant l'escalier, ainsi que des pièces, le jardin d'hiver, la cuisine, et des dépendances ordonnées autour d'une petite cour vitrée. Le jardin d'hiver et la salle à manger présentent des bow-windows convexes donnant sur une terrasse. L'agencement des pièces autour du hall est repris à l'étage qui comprend la salle de séjour, les chambres à coucher ainsi qu'une salle de bains éclairée par un toit vitré.

407 [1911: 94]

L'immeuble à usage commercial de quatre étages, situé à Lübeck, à l'angle des Johannisstraße et Breitestraße, est l'œuvre des architectes Schöß, Schöß & Redelstorff. Les façades, revêtues de grès, présentent des piliers montant de fond jusqu'à la corniche du toit, encadrant des fenêtres groupées. Les devantures des commerces ainsi que les fenêtres du premier et deuxième étages sont à linteau droit. Les ouvertures des trois passages de l'avancée médiane sont en plein cintre. Les fenêtres du troisième étage sont surbaissées et sont assorties d'ouvertures ovales. L'avancée médiane ainsi que l'avancée d'angle sont coiffées de pignons en delta. Le toit mansardé est recouvert de tuiles. Le rez-de-chaussée est occupé par des commerces, les trois étages supérieurs abritent des bureaux.

408 [1911: 57]

Ce monumental ensemble architectural bâlois, comprenant cinq immeubles de rapport, donne sur les Spalenringstraße et Ahornstraße. Conçu par l'architecte Rud. Linder, il fut construit dans les années 1909 et 1910. L'ensemble présente deux façades et un pan coupé dégagé. Sur l'Ahornstraße, les immeubles sont groupés autour d'une cour, aux angles arrondis, ouverte sur la rue. Une cour intérieure, donnant sur un mur aveugle offre une même forme ronde. La cour

trance. The recessed part of the façade has Doric columns running the height of the two storeys which frame straight—lined windows, of which those on the upper floor are fronted by balconies. The recessed front is entirely covered by an overhanging roof moulding. Windowed structures have been built into the lower slope of the roof above both corner projections and the middle erection. The façade is faced with light—green and yellow sandstone from Dürkheim; the roof is covered with flat red tiling. The reliefs of the façade are the work of the sculptor C. Neuhaus.

The ground floor has an oval entry hall with an open staircase. The entry hall leads to the central hall, plus a number of rooms, a winter—garden, the kitchen, and side rooms grouped round a small patio. The winter—garden and kitchen have bay windows overlooking the terrace. The central hall arrangement is repeated on the upper floor, being surrounded by bedrooms, sitting—rooms and a bath with roof lights.

407 [1911: 94]

The four—storey office building in Lübeck (corner of Johannisstrasse & Breitestrasse) is the work of the architects Schöss, Schöss & Redelstorff. The sandstone—faced façades are divided by continuous pillars running from the ground floor to the roof moulding, with groups of windows between them. Openings in the façade for shops on the ground level as well as the windows of the first and second floors are straight—lined, whereas the three portals of the middle erection have round arches. The windows of the third floor are ornamented with flat arches and oval sky—lights. The middle structure as well as one corner projection are crowned by straight—sided pediments. The roof contains a continuous row of windows and is covered with tile. Shops are located on the ground floor, and the three upper floors are reserved for offices.

408 [1911: 57]

A monumental and unified architectural form has been achieved by the integration of 5 apartment buildings into a single complex located in the city of Basel (Spalenring—Ahornstrasse). Based on the design of the architect Rud. Linder, this impressive edifice was completed in the years 1909–1910. The houses are exposed on two fronts and a obtuse corner; those facing the Ahornstrasse are grouped round a courtyard with rounded corners, which opens onto the

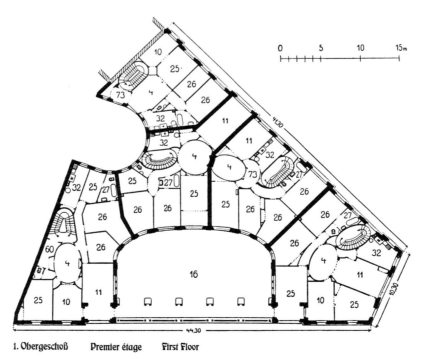

0   5   10   15m

1. Obergeschoß   Premier étage   First Floor

Aufbau an der Ahornstraße zeigt den durch einen Bogengang mit oberer Terrasse nach vorn begrenzten Hof seitlich von pavillonartigen Eckbauten eingeschlossen. In der Mitte der zurückliegenden Front erhebt sich ein die Dachlinie durchbrechender, überhängender Giebel in geschweiften Formen. Den Eckpavillons schließen sich an der Hofseite im vierten Stock Altane an, und vor den Fenstern desselben Geschosses erstrecken sich galerieartig verlaufende Balkons.

Die Fassaden sind in gelbem und weißem Terranovaputz hergestellt; die gebrochenen, in den Steilflächen mit Lukenfenstern besetzten Dächer sind mit Biberschwänzen eingedeckt.

In jedem Stockwerk der fünf durch Brandmauern getrennten Häuser ist eine um eine Halle gruppierte, von einer Treppe zugängliche Wohnung eingerichtet, welche außer dem Eß- und Wohnzimmer, die Schlafzimmer, die Küche und das Bad enthält.

409 [1911; 71]

Das in sechs Geschossen aufsteigende Geschäfts- und Wohnhaus in Genf, Avenue Pictet de Rochemont 2, ein Werk des Architekten Ed. Chevallaz, ist im Laufe eines Jahres für die Bausumme von 450 000 Frcs. zur Ausführung gekommen. Die abgerundete Ecke ist mit einem Turm bekrönt, der ein kegelförmiges, mit Luken ausgestattetes Spitzdach trägt. Die Ladenöffnungen im Erdgeschoß sowie die Fenster des ersten Obergeschosses sind flachbogig überwölbt. Die folgenden drei Geschosse, von dem unteren durch eine umlaufende, vorgekragte, offene Galerie geschieden, zeigen der Höhe nach zusammengezogene, mit Balkons versehene Fenster, die im zweiten und dritten Obergeschoß geradlinig, im vierten rundbogig geschlossen sind. Das fünfte Obergeschoß wächst wieder über einer umlaufenden, vorgekragten Galerie empor, deren von der Brüstung aufsteigende Pfeiler den weit ausladenden Dachkranz tragen. Die Steilfläche des Daches ist mit Fensterluken besetzt, die von überhängenden abgestumpften Giebeln eingefaßt sind. Die Fronten sind in gefugtem Ziegelmauerwerk mit Gliederungen in weißem Sandstein ausgeführt, während die beiden unteren Geschosse eine Bekleidung mit Quadern von Roche de Villette zeigen.

Die Dachflächen, einschließlich der Spitze des Eckturms, haben Biberschwanz-Eindeckung erhalten.

Im Erdgeschoß befinden sich Läden und der Haupteingang; in jedem der fünf Obergeschosse sind zwei getrennte, von einer gemeinschaftlichen Treppe zugängliche Wohnungen eingerichtet, Salon, Wohn- und Eßzimmer, sowie Schlafzimmer, Dienerzimmer, Baderaum und Küche enthaltend.

410 [1911; 90]

Das Geschäfts- und Wohnhaus „Posthof" in Dortmund, Hiltropwall, bildet einen fünfstöckigen Eckbau und ist im Laufe eines Jahres nach dem Entwurfe der Architekten Schmidtmann und Klemp errichtet. Die Baukosten betrugen rund 450 000 Mark bei 745 qm bebauter Fläche. Das Erdgeschoß öffnet sich zu den Schaufenstern der Läden. Die abgerundete Ecke, im Erdgeschoß durch eine Säulenstellung ausgezeichnet, wird in drei Obergeschossen durch Balkons belebt und trägt im fünften Stock eine offene Loggia, wieder mit einer Säulenstellung. An beiden Fronten springen ausgekragte Erker vor, die durch drei Obergeschosse geführt sind und mit Altanen abschließen, über denen sich ein die Dachlinie durchbrechender Giebel aufbaut. Die Fassaden sind in hellgrauem Horner Nahtesandstein hergestellt; die Pfeiler zwischen den Schaufenstern sind mit rotem schwedischen Virbogranit bekleidet. Das mit einer Fensterreihe besetzte Dach hat eine Eindeckung mit grauen Biberschwänzen erhalten.

Das Erdgeschoß enthält durchweg Ladenlokale, während in den den Obergeschossen je zwei große Wohnungen mit getrennten Eingängen und Treppenhäusern eingerichtet sind. Letztere sind an den Wänden mit Marmor verkleidet. Im Treppenhaus am Hiltropwall ist ein Personenaufzug angelegt. Die Fundamentierung des Gebäudes geschah auf Zementpfeilern, und das Konstruktionsgerippe wurde in Eisenbeton ausgeführt.

s'ouvrant sur la Ahornstraße est flanquée de constructions d'angle aux allures de pavillons et délimitée par des arcades surmontées d'une terrasse. Un pignon aux lignes ondulées s'élève du renfoncement de la façade, coupant ainsi la ligne du toit. Les pavillons d'angle sont assortis de plates-formes au quatrième étage de la façade sur cour. Un balcon circulaire orne les fenêtres de cet étage.

Les murs de façade ont reçu un enduit jaune et blanc. Les toits aux combles brisés, percés de fenêtres sont recouverts de tuiles plates.

Les immeubles hauts de cinq étages sont séparés par des murs mitoyens. Les étages offrent une disposition identique, soit un logement aménagé autour d'une antichambre, accessible par un escalier, comprenant la salle de séjour, la salle à manger, les chambres à coucher, la cuisine et la salle de bains.

409 [1911; 71]

L'immeuble de six étages, situé à Genève, 2 avenue Pictet de Rochemond, est l'œuvre de l'architecte Ed. Chevallaz. Il fut construit en une année et coûta la somme de 450 000 frcs. Le pan coupé est couronné d'une tour coiffée d'un toit pointu en poivrière, percé de lucarnes. Le rez-de-chaussée ainsi que le premier étage présentent des ouvertures surbaissées. Les trois étages suivants, séparés des niveaux inférieurs par un balcon en galerie, offrent un ensemble homogène. Les fenêtres en tribune, régulièrement alignées, sont à linteau droit aux deuxième et troisième étages et en plein cintre au quatrième niveau. Le cinquième étage s'élève derrière une galerie saillante dont les balustres supportent l'avancée du toit. Les lucarnes sont assorties de pignons arrondis et saillants. Les façades, réalisées en briques jointoyées, présentent des ornements de grès. Les étages inférieurs portent un revêtement de moellons de Roche de Villette.

Les surfaces des toits ainsi que la pointe de la tour d'angle sont recouvertes de tuiles plates.

Le rez-de-chaussée abrite des commerces et l'entrée principale. Chacun des étages supérieurs renferme deux logements séparés et accessibles par un escalier commun. Les logements comprennent salon, salle de séjour, salle à manger, chambres à coucher, chambre des domestiques, salle de bains et cuisine.

410 [1911; 90]

L'immeuble „Posthof" de Dortmund, Hiltropwall, fut érigé en l'espace d'une année sur les plans des architectes Schmidtmann et Klemp. Les travaux revinrent à 450 000 marks pour 745 mètres cubes de volume construit. Le rez-de-chaussée est percé de devantures. Le pan coupé, souligné au rez-de-chaussée par des colonnes, présente des balcons sur trois étages et une loggia assortie de colonnes au dernier niveau. Des bow-windows montant sur trois étages, se terminant en balcons et coiffés de pignons en delta saillissent des façades. Les murs de façade sont en grès. Les piliers encadrant les devantures offrent un parement de granit suédois rouge. Le toit mansardé est recouvert de tuiles plates grises.

Le rez-de-chaussée est occupé par des commerces. Chaque étage abrite deux grands appartments accessibles par des entrées et des escaliers séparés. Les murs des cages d'escaliers sont revêtus de marbre. L'entrée donnant sur le Hiltropwall est équipée d'un ascenseur. Les fondations de l'immeuble furent réalisées sur des piliers en ciment, l'ossature est en béton armé.

street. The inner courtyard on the closed side of the complex is also round in form. The courtyard of the four-storey front facing the Ahornstrasse is bordered by an arcade at street level and a terrace above that, and is flanked by two pavilion-like corner erections. A curved gable at the middle of the front rises above the roof line. The corner edifices have balconies on the fourth floor, and the same floor has a continuous balcony running along its exterior gallery.

The façades are of yellow and white terranova plaster, the roof is covered with flat red tiles and is broken up by gabled windows.

The five houses are separated from each other by a fire wall; each floor has flats grouped round a central hall leading to a staircase. The flats are furnished with a dining and sitting-room, as well as bedrooms, kitchen and bath.

409 [1911; 71]

The six-storey apartment building in Geneva (Avenue Pictet de Rochemont 2) was designed by the architect Ed. Chevallaz and completed in the course of one year at a cost of 450,000 Francs. The rounded corner of the structure is crowned by a tower which supports a pointed roof with roof lights. Entrances to the shops on the ground floor as well as the windows of the first storey are slightly arched. The three stories above, the lower of which has a continuous projecting gallery, have rectangular windows with balconies; the windows of the second and third stories are straight-lined, those of the fourth storey are framed in round arches. Another projecting gallery runs along the fifth storey, with pillars on the parapet supporting the overhanging roof cornice. The inclined section of the roof has roof lights framed in overhanging, truncated gables. The fronts are of bonded brick with articulations of white sandstone; the ground and first floors are faced with Roche de Villette ashlar.

Flat red tiles cover the roof and the top of the corner tower.

The ground floor contains shops and the main entrance; each of the other floors has two flats separated by a common staircase. Each flat has a drawing-room, sitting-room, dining-room, as well as bedrooms, servant's room, bath and kitchen.

410 [1911; 90]

The apartment building "Posthof" in Dortmund (Hiltropwall) is a corner house designed by the architects Schmidtmann and Klemp. This edifice encompassing 745 square metres was completed in the course of one year at a cost of 450,000 Marks. The ground floor opens with shop windows. The rounded corner of the building is decorated by a group of columns at ground level and has balconies on the three upper storeys; it supports a fourth-storey loggia with columns. Both fronts have bays extending the height of three stories which are topped by a balcony and a straight gable rising above the roof line. The façades are of light grey sandstone from Horn; the pillars between the shop windows are faced with diorite granite. A row of windows runs along the roof, which is covered with flat grey tiles.

The ground floor comprises only shops, while each of the upper floors contains two spacious flats with separate entrances and staircases, the latter having marble panelling. The Hiltropwall staircase is equipped with a lift. The building's foundations rest on concrete piers and has a reinforced concrete framework.

Das Geschäfts- und Wohnhaus in München, Sonnenstraße 5, im Besitz des Baumeisters Gerstenecker, bildet einen fünfstöckigen, mit teilweise ausgebautem Dachstock versehenen Eckbau. Die Hauptfront wird durch flache, sämtliche Geschosse durchsetzende Pfeilervorlagen, außerdem durch zwei viereckige, über dem ersten Obergeschoß ausgekragte, bis zur Dachkante durchgeführte erkerartige Vorlagen gegliedert. Sämtliche Lichtöffnungen sind geradlinig überdeckt. Der obere Teil der Pfeilervorlagen ist mit figürlichen Reliefs geschmückt. Die Giebel der Hauptfront sowie der an der Seitenfront schließen mit geschwungenen Konturen; der eine Giebel der Hauptfront zeigt eine von Säulen geteilte Fenstergruppe und wird seitlich von Löwenfiguren begleitet.

Die Fassaden sind verputzt und mehrfach mit plastischen Verzierungen ausgestattet. Das Erdgeschoß ist zu Läden ausgebaut, die Obergeschosse enthalten Wohnungen.

412, 413 [1911; 78, 79]

Das zweistöckige Landhaus Cuno in der Gartenvorstadt Eppenhausen bei Hagen i. W., Haßleyerstraße gelegen, von Gärten umgeben, wie auch die sämtlichen übrigen auf dem Gelände errichteten Wohnbauten, ist ein Werk des Architekten Professor Peter Behrens, in etwa 7 Monaten für die Bausumme von 95 000 Mark zur Ausführung gebracht. Die Eingangsfront wird durch ein mittleres, abgerundetes, in einem Rücksprung liegendes, durch Fenster, die beide Geschosse zusammenziehen, gegliedertes, die Dachlinie durchbrechendes Risalit geteilt. Die ebenfalls abgerundete, abgestumpfte Ecke enthält den Eingang zum Vestibül. Die Rückfront zeigt eine Terrasse zwischen zwei im Erdgeschoß vorspringenden Ausbauten. Auch die eine Seitenfront ist mit einem Ausbau im Erdgeschoß versehen, der mit einer Altane abschließt. Über dem Dachgesims erhebt sich eine geschlossene Brüstung, hinter welcher das flache, mit Schiefer eingedeckte Dach aufsteigt. Die Einfriedung sowie die Frontmauern des Erdgeschosses sind aus am Ort gefundenen dunklem Bruchstein hergestellt, die oberen Fassadenteile zeigen weißen Kunststeinputz und einzelne Gliederungen aus Kunststein. Die Eckpfeiler der Einfriedung erhalten Plastiken von Höxger.

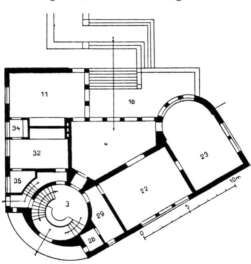

Erdgeschoß   Rez-de-chaussée   Ground Floor

Im Erdgeschoß liegen die Eingangshalle mit der gewundenen, um ein Auge geführten Treppe, dahinter folgen die Diele, vor welcher sich eine Terrasse mit Freitreppe erstreckt, Damen-, Herren- und Speisezimmer, sowie die Küche mit Speisekammer und Anrichte. Das Obergeschoß enthält die Schlafzimmer, in Verbindung mit einer Altane, das Fremdenzimmer, das Mädchenzimmer und den Baderaum.

414 [1911; 80]

Haus Rump in Hagen, Eppenhausenstraße 151, in 5 Monaten für die Kostensumme von 40 000 Mark nach dem Entwurfe der Architekten B. D. A. Gebrüder Ludwigs errichtet, ist zweistöckig und besitzt ein ausgebautes Dachgeschoß. An der Vorderfront springt im

L'immeuble munichois, situé au no 5 de la Sonnenstraße, est la propriété de l'architecte Gerstenecker. Il s'agit d'un bâtiment d'angle de cinq étages, au toit partiellement mansardé. La façade principale présente une ordonnance de pilastres continus ainsi que deux avancées quadrangulaires, se détachant audessus du premier étage et montant jusqu'à la corniche du toit. Toutes les ouvertures sont à linteau droit. La partie supérieure des pilastres offre un décor sculpté. Les pignons ont des contours ondulés. Le pignon de la façade principale, percé de fenêtres flanquées de colonnes, est encadré de lions sculptés.

Les murs de façade, enduits d'un crépi, sont assortis d'ornements plastiques. Le rez-de-chaussée abrite des commerces. Des logements sont aménagés dans les étages.

412, 413 [1911; 78, 79]

La propriété Cuno, située dans la cité-jardin d'Eppenhausen, non loin de Hagen, fut conçue par l'architecte Peter Behrens. Il s'agit d'une villa de deux étages, assortie d'un jardin comme les autres construction de ce quartier. Construite en 7 mois, la maison revint à 95 000 marks. La façade principale est flanquée, dans un renfoncement de sa partie médiane, d'un avant-corps arrondi. Percé de fenêtres, il s'élève sur les deux étages et dépasse la ligne du toit. Un appendice arrondi abrite l'entrée conduisant au vestibule. La façade postérieure présente, au niveau du rez-de-chaussée, une terrasse entre deux avancées. Une des façades latérales offre, elle aussi, au rez-dechaussée, une saillie supportant une plate-forme. Un entablement continu, s'élevant sur la corniche, supporte le toit d'ardoises. Les murs de clôture ainsi que le socle de la villa sont en pierres de taille locales de couleur brune, les murs de façade, enduits d'un crépi artificiel blanc, offrent quelques ornements en pierres artificielles. Les piliers d'angle des murs de clôture sont ornés de sculptures de l'artiste Höxger.

Beleuchtungskörper   Luminaire   Illuminator

Le rez-de-chaussée abrite l'entrée comprenant l'escalier en spirale sur poteau central, puis le hall donnant sur une terrasse accessible par un perron, le boudoir, le cabinet de travail, la salle à manger ainsi que la cuisine avec son garde-manger et son office. L'étage comprend les chambres à coucher contiguës à un balcon, la chambre d'amis, la chambre des domestiques et la salle de bains.

414 [1911; 80]

La propriété Rump, située à Hagen, Eppenhausenstraße 151, est l'œuvre des frères Ludwig, architectes. La villa de deux étages, coiffée d'un toit mansard, fut réalisée en cinq mois pour la somme de 40 000 marks. La partie médiane de la façade princi-

The corner apartment building in Munich (Sonnenstrasse 5) is owned by the master architect Gerstenecker and has five storeys and a partial roof storey. The principal front is decorated with flat pilasters running through five storeys, plus two rectangular baylike projections extending from the top of the first floor to the roof moulding. All windows are straight-lined. The tops of the pilasters are ornamented with figural reliefs. The gables of the principal front and that of the side front end in graceful curves; one of the gables on the principal front has a group of windows separated by columns, and is flanked by two lion figures.

The plastered façades are richly ornamented. The ground floor contains shops, the upper storeys flats.

412, 413 [1911; 78, 79]

The two-storey Cuno house in Eppenhausen near Hagen in Westphalia (Hassleyerstrasse) is, like all other residences in this countrified suburb, surrounded by gardens. Designed by the architect Professor Peter Behrens, it was completed in approximately 7 months at a cost of 95,000 Marks. Recessed in the middle of the entrance front is a rounded middle erection rising from the ground floor and breaking the roof line; it contains windows between its arrangement of pillars. The truncated corner is also rounded off and contains the entrance and vestibule. The rear front has a terrace located between two ground-floor projections. One of the side fronts also has a bay by a balcony. A closed parapet rises above the roof moulding; the low-pitched roof is covered with tile. The garden walls as well as the front walls of the ground floor are of local dark ashlar; the upper façades are plastered white with individual articulations of imitation stone. The corner pillars of the garden wall are decorated with statues by the sculptor Höxger.

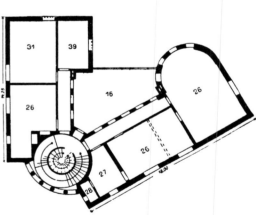

Obergeschoß   Étage   Upper Floor

The ground floor contains the entry hall with a spiral staircase, behind which are the main hall, which connects to a terrace with a perron, sitting-rooms and drawing rooms, the dining room as well as the kitchen and pantries. The upper floor contains bedrooms leading onto the balcony, a guest-room, the maid's room and bath.

414 [1911; 80]

The Rump house in Hagen (Eppenhausenstrasse 151) was constructed in 5 months at a cost of 40,000 Marks. The two-storey house with a roof storey was designed by the Ludwig brothers, members of the Association of German Architects. The ground

Erdgeschoß eine halbrunde, auf Säulen ruhende offene Halle vor, die eine Altane trägt, und über der sich im Obergeschoß ein halbrunder, die Dachlinie durchbrechender, mit einem Dachgeschoß gekrönter Aufbau erhebt. Die Außenflächen des Hauses sind in Terranova verputzt und im oberen Teile mit Schieferbekleidung versehen. Das Dach ist mit Schiefer eingedeckt. Der Eingang liegt an einer Seitenfront. Die Gesellschafts-, Wohn- und Wirtschaftsräume verteilen sich auf beide Geschosse sowie auf das Dachgeschoß.

415 [1911; 81]

Das im Aufbau mehrfach gruppierte, zweistöckige Haus Rath in Hagen, Eppenhauserstraße 155, in 5 Monaten für die Kostensumme von 60 000 Mark errichtet, ist ein Werk des Architekten B. D. A. Gebrüder Ludwigs. Der Eingang an der Vorderfront, in einem vorspringenden, mit einem gebrochenen Giebel abschließenden Flügelbau gelegen, bildet eine offene, mit besonderem Dach versehene Halle. Dem Erdgeschoß der Seitenfront ist ein breiter, in der Mitte zu einer Loggia sich öffnender Ausbau vorgelegt, der eine Altane trägt. Im Obergeschoß bildet sich eine halbrund einspringende Nische, darüber erhebt sich ein gebrochener Giebel. Der Sockel ist aus Dolomitstein hergestellt, die oberen Flächen zeigen Terranovaputz. Die überhängenden gebrochenen Dächer sind mit Schiefer eingedeckt. Die Gesellschafts-, Wohn- und Wirtschaftsräume liegen in beiden Geschossen und im teilweise ausgebauten Dachgeschoß verteilt.

416 [1911; 21]

Das Gebäude der Württ. Vereinsbank, Depositenkasse in Stuttgart, Königsstraße 72, bildet einen sechsstöckigen Eckbau und ist nach dem Entwurfe des Architekten Baurat K. Hengerer und des Architekten Rich. Katz, unter spezieller Bauleitung des ersteren in 4 Monaten für die Bausumme von 130 000 Mark zur Ausführung gekommen. Die beiden unteren Geschosse sind mittelst starker Pfeiler zusammengezogen, welche den in der abgerundeten Ecke liegenden Eingang zum Banklokal, die Schaufenster und sonstigen Lichtöffnungen zwischen sich einschließen. Die Ecke der Fronten ist durch einen mächtigen, über dem ersten Stock ausgekragten, rund vorspringenden, als Turm mit Kuppelabschluß über das Dach hinausragenden Erker ausgezeichnet. Das sechste Geschoß öffnet sich an einer Frontseite zu einer von Säulen getragenen Loggia. Die Fassaden sind in weißem Mainsandstein verkleidet; die Decken und die Erkerentlastung sind in Eisenbeton ausgeführt. – Im Erdgeschoß liegen die Lokalitäten der Bank, ein Laden und der zur Treppe sowie zum Personenaufzug führende Eingangsflur; letzterer ist von einem Lichthof aus beleuchtet. Die oberen Geschosse enthalten ungeteilte Geschäftsräume.

417 [1911; 59]

Das in sämtlichen fünf Geschossen zu Verkaufszwecken eingerichtete Geschäfts- und Ladenhaus in Berlin, Zimmerstraße 14/15, läßt diese Bestimmung auch in der einheitlichen Gestaltung des Äußeren erkennen. Der Entwurf, vom Architekten Dipl.-Ing. Alex. Weiß stammend, ist vom April 1910 bis zum April 1911 für die Baukostensumme von 320 000 Mark zur Ausführung gekommen. Im Erdgeschoß zeigt die Fassade eine Anzahl von Korbbogen überwölbter Ladenöffnungen neben dem geradlinig überdeckten Eingang. Das erste Obergeschoß ist im mittleren Teile durch eine Stellung von Doppelsäulen gegliedert, die auf Auskragungen ruhen und eine mit Figuren bekrönte Brüstung tragen. Die Fenster desselben Geschosses sind durch schmale Pfeiler geteilt, ebenso sind die der Höhe nach zusammengezogen, mit Bekrönungsgesimsen versehenen Fenster des zweiten und dritten Obergeschosses gebildet. Über einem durchgehenden Brüstungsgesims setzen die Fenster des vierten Obergeschosses mit gleicher Pfeilerteilung wie die der unteren Geschosse an. Auf der Dachfläche sind nach oben flach angeordnete Fenster angeordnet. Die Bekleidung der Fassade besteht aus grauem fränkischem Muschelkalk; die figürlichen Bildhauerarbeiten an derselben sind von M. Bauer ausgeführt.

pale est assortie, au rez-de-chaussée, d'une avancée arrondie, ouverte, flanquée de colonnes et couronnée d'une plate-forme, sur laquelle s'élève une saillie arrondie, coiffée d'un toit mansardé. Les murs de façade sont enduits d'un crépi, les surfaces supérieures ainsi que le toit portent un revêtement d'ardoises. L'entrée se situe sur une façade latérale. Les salles de réception, les pièces de séjour et les pièces de service sont aménagées sur les deux étages et sur l'étage mansardé.

415 [1911; 81]

La villa Rath, à Hagen, Eppenhausenstraße 155, fut construite en 5 mois pour la somme de 60 000 marks. Les frères Ludwig, architectes, conçurent cette maison de deux étages de composition asymétrique. L'entrée, située sur la façade principale, est abritée par un porche, inséré dans un avant-corps coiffé d'un pignon aux lignes brisées. Le rez-de-chaussée de la façade latérale est assorti d'une large avancée portant balcon, s'ouvrant sur une loggia. Le premier étage présente une niche concave surmontée d'un pignon aux lignes brisées. Le socle est en pierres des Dolomites, les murs sont crépis. Les toits saillants aux combles brisés portent une couverture d'ardoises. L'ordonnance des pièces de réception, de séjour et de service s'effectue sur les deux étages et sur l'étage mansard.

416 [1911; 21]

L'immeuble abritant la banque wurtembourgeoise de Stuttgart, Königstraße 72, est un bâtiment d'angle de six étages, conçu par les architectes K. Hengerer et Rich. Katz. Les travaux, conduits par le premier cité, furent réalisés en quatre mois pour la somme de 130 000 marks. Les deux étages inférieurs, organisés autour de forts piliers encadrant l'entrée de la banque située dans l'angle, les devantures et autres ouvertures, forment un ensemble. L'angle des deux façades est assorti, au-dessus du premier étage, d'une avancée massive, ronde et saillante, surmontée d'une tourelle, coiffée d'une coupole, s'élevant au-delà du toit. Le sixième étage présente, sur une des façades, une loggia reposant sur des colonnes. Les murs extérieurs sont revêtus de grès blanc du Main. Les planchers et les allèges de l'avancée sont en béton armé. Le rez-de-chaussée est occupé par les locaux de la banque, un commerce ainsi qu'un couloir d'entrée menant à l'escalier et à l'ascenseur. Le couloir est éclairé par une cour vitrée. Les étages supérieurs présentent des locaux non-cloisonnés.

417 [1911; 59]

Ce bâtiment berlinois de cinq étages, situé aux no. 14 et 15 de la Zimmerstraße, fut uniquement conçu à des fins commerciales. La conception homogène de la façade atteste de cette vocation. L'immeuble fut réalisé sur les plans de l'architecte Alex. Weiß. La construction dura du mois d'avril 1910 au mois d'avril 1911 et revint à 320 000 marks. La façade présente, au rez-de-chaussée, des devantures surbaissées ainsi qu'une entrée à linteau droit. La partie médiane du premier étage offre une ordonnance de double colonnes en encorbellement, portant une balustrade surmontée de sculptures. Les fenêtres des étages sont divisées par d'étroits piliers. Les ouvertures des deuxième et troisième niveaux forment un ensemble terminé par une corniche de couronnement. Les fenêtres du quatrième étage, situées au-dessus d'un bandeau continu, présente la même structure homogène. Les versants du toit sont percés de lucarnes. Les murs de façade ont reçu un revêtement de coquillart gris de Franconie. Les sculptures sont l'œuvre de M. Bauer.

floor of the front of the house has a semi–circular projecting veranda resting on columns and crowned by a balcony. Above this on the first floor is a smaller concentric projection rising above the roof line and topped by part of the roof storey. The outer surfaces of the house are of terranova plaster, and its upper section is hung with shingles; the roof is covered with tiles. The entrance is located at one side. Rooms for dining, sleeping and entertaining are distributed throughout the two floors as well as the roof storey.

415 [1911; 81]

The Rath house, a two–storey residence with a roof storey and multiple architectural groupings can be seen in Hagen, Westphalia (Eppenhausenstrasse 155). Designed by the Ludwig brothers, members of the Association of German Architects, it was completed in five months at a cost of 60,000 Marks. The porch on the front is covered by a separate roof, which is integrated into the façade's broken–base gable. At the ground level of the side front is a broad bay which opens out onto a terrace and is covered by a balcony. The storey above has a recessed semi–circular niche covered by a broken gable. The socle is of dolomitic ashlar, the exterior surfaces are rendered in terranova plaster. The overhanging roof is covered with slate. Rooms for dining, sleeping and entertaining are distributed throughout the two floors as well as the roof storey.

416 [1911; 21]

The branch office of the Württemberg Vereinsbank in Stuttgart (Königsstrasse 72) was designed according to the plans drawn up by the government architect K. Hengerer, who acted as special supervisor during the four months of construction, and the architect Rich. Katz. This six–storey corner building cost 100,000 Marks to build. The two lower storeys are joined by massive pillars, which frame the bank's entrance located in the rounded corner of the building, the shop windows and other openings in the façade. The corner of the fronts is dominated by a rounded oriel starting above the first floor and ending in a tower whose dome rises above the roof ridge. The front side of the sixth storey opens onto a loggia with columns. The façades are faced with white sandstone from the Main; the ceilings and the bay stress reliefs are of reinforced concrete. – The ground floor contains bank rooms, a shop and the entry hall which leads to both the staircase and the lift. The entry hall is lit by an open courtyard. The upper floors contain open office space.

417 [1911; 59]

All five floors of the commercial building in Berlin (Zimmerstrasse 14/15) are devoted to business purposes, a fact which is reflected in its unified exterior design. Based on the plans of the architectural engineer Alex. Weiß, construction was carried out from Arpil 1910 to April 1911 at a cost of 320,000 Marks. The ground–floor façade has a number of carriageways framed in basket arches, and a straight–lined entrance. The middle section of the first storey is ornamented with a row of coupled columns which rest on base projections and support a baulstrade crowned with figures. The windows of this storey are separated by narrow pilasters, as are the narrow rectangular windows of the second and third storeys, which are topped by an architrave. The windows of the fourth storey are located above the parapet moulding and are divided by the same arrangement of pilasters as the lower storeys. The roof has flatly arched dormer windows. The façade is rendered in grey Franconian shell limestone; its sculptured figures are the work of M. Bauer.

Einfahrt   Passage   Entrance

Treppenaufgang   Cage d'escalier   Staircase

Das Erdgeschoß wird von einem nur durch Pfeiler geteilten Geschäftsraum eingenommen, an den sich rückwärts ein mit Glas überdeckter Hof, zwei Treppen und ein Fahrstuhl, seitwärts ein mit Steinplatten an den Wänden bekleideter, mit einer Balkendecke versehener Eingangsflur anschließen. Der Flur führt einmal zum Haupttreppenhause, dessen Wände im unteren Teile mit Marmor bekleidet sind, dann zu dem offenen Hofe. Die oberen Geschosse, von der Haupttreppe und zwei Nebentreppen zugänglich, enthalten je einen wieder nur durch Pfeiler geteilten, mit Aufzügen ausgestatteten Raum.

418 [1911; 65]

Das nach dem Entwurfe der Architekten B. D. A. Beutinger und Steiner im Verlaufe zweier Jahre mit einem Kostenaufwand von 65 000 Mark errichtete Geschäfts- und Wohnhaus in Heilbronn a. N., Kaiserstraße 46, zeigt eine in gelblichweißem, geflammtem Sandstein von Klingenmünster verblendete Fassade. Im Erdgeschoß öffnen sich Schaufenster neben einem Durchfahrtstor. Das zweite Obergeschoß ist durch eine Stellung von Doppelsäulen gegliedert, zwischen denen breite, mit vorgekragten Balkons versehene Fenster angebracht sind. Die durch schmale Pfeiler geteilten Doppelfenster im dritten und vierten Obergeschoß sind zum Teil mit Balkons ausgestattet und haben nach außen ausladende Sturze erhalten. Durchgehende Pfeiler teilen die Außenflächen des dritten und vierten Obergeschosses sowie des steilen, in geschwungenen Konturen endigenden Giebels. Das Dach ist mit Biberschwänzen eingedeckt.

Das Erdgeschoß nimmt einen einheitlichen Ladenraum und die seitlich danebenliegende Durchfahrt auf. Die Gestaltung der an der Rückfront erweiterten Durchfahrt war durch besondere Verhältnisse geboten. Die Obergeschosse enthalten je eine mit Küche und Bad versehene Wohnung. Die Fundamentierung des Hauses mußte unter schwierigen Verhältnissen erfolgen.

419 [1911; 67]

Das fünfstöckige, mit einem ausgebauten Dachgeschoß versehene Geschäftshaus der Württembergischen Metallwarenfabrik in Stuttgart, Königstraße 31 B, entworfen von Architekt Alb. Eitel, ist im Laufe eines Jahres für die Kostensumme von rund 400 000 Mark zur Ausführung gekommen.

Die Fassade, aus grauem Muschelkalkstein hergestellt, zeigt in den beiden unteren Geschossen Schaufenster, im Erdgeschoß geradlinig, im Zwischengeschoß mit Korbbogen überdeckt. Die folgenden

La surface du rez-de-chaussée est occupée par un local de commerce non-cloisonné, divisé par des piliers, donnant à l'arrière sur une cour vitrée, deux escaliers, un ascenseur et latéralement sur un couloir d'entrée aux murs revêtus de dalles de pierres et au plafond à poutres. Le couloir conduit à la cage d'escalier, dont la partie inférieure des murs est habillée de marbre, puis à la cour ouverte. Les étages supérieurs, accessibles par un escalier principal, deux escaliers de service et des ascenseurs, abritent une seule pièce divisée par une ordonnance de piliers.

418 [1911; 65]

L'immeuble, situé à Heilbronn, Kaiserstraße 46, fut construit en l'espace de deux années sur les plans des architectes Beutinger et Steiner. Les travaux coutèrent la somme de 65 000 marks. La façade porte un revêtement de grès flammé blanc jaunâtre de Klingenmünster. Le rez-de-chaussée présente des devantures et une porte cochère. Le deuxième étage offre une ordonnance de colonnes doubles, encadrant de larges fenêtres en tribune. Les fenêtres des troisième et quatrième étages, divisées par d'étroits meneaux, sont partiellement assorties de balcons et sont pourvues de linteaux saillants. Des piliers continus, montant du troisième étage jusqu'au pignon, ornent la façade supérieure. Le toit est recouvert de tuiles plates.

Le rez-de-chaussée abrite des locaux de commerce et une porte cochère. L'élargissement du passage sur la façade postérieure fut rendu possible grâce à certaines circonstances. Chaque étage est respectivement occupé par un logement, équipé d'une cuisine et d'une salle de bains. Les travaux de fondations de l'immeuble s'effectuèrent dans des conditions particulièrement difficiles.

419 [1911; 67]

L'immeuble de la „Württembergische Metallwarenfabrik", situé à Stuttgart, Königstraße 31b, fut conçu par l'architecte Alb. Eitel. Les travaux de construction de ce bâtiment de cinq étages coiffé d'un toit mansard, réalisés en l'espace d'une année, revinrent à 400 000 marks.

Les murs de façade, en coquillart gris, présentent des devantures sur les deux étages inférieurs; il s'agit de devantures droites au rez-de-chaussée et de devantures surbaissées à l'entresol. Les trois étages sui-

The ground floor comprises one room divided only by pillars; this is bordered at the back by a glass—covered courtyard, two staircases and a lift. To the side is an entry hall with a beamed ceiling and stone slab walls which leads to the main staircase, whose walls are panelled in marble in their lower half, and then to the open courtyard. Each of the upper storeys, which are reached by the main staircase and two side stairs, also contains a large open room divided by pillars and furnished with lifts.

418 [1911; 65]

Built in the course of two years according to the plans of the architects Beutinger and Steiner, members of the Association of German Architects, and at a cost of 65,000 Marks, the apartment building in Heilbronn—on—Neckar is faced with yellow—white grained sandstone from Klingenmünster. Shop windows are on the ground floor next to a gateway. The second storey façade has an arrangement of coupled columns framing broad windows with projecting balconies. The double windows of the third and fourth stories are divided by narrow pilasters and have projecting lintels; some of the windows have balconies. The exterior surfaces of the third and fourth storeys, as well as the high—pitched contoured gable, are articulated by continuous pilasters. The roof is covered with flat red tile.

The ground floor contains a unified shop space and carriageway at one side. The design of the carriageway, which widens at the rear of the building, was favoured by special conditions. Each of the upper storeys contains one flat with kitchen and bath. The foundations of the house were laid under particularly difficult conditions.

419 [1911; 67]

The office building of the Württemberg Metal Goods Co. in Stuttgart (Königstrasse 31 B), a five—story edifice with a roof storey, was designed by the architect Alb. Eitel and completed in the course of one year at a cost of about 400,000 Marks.

The façade of grey shell limestone has shop windows on its ground and first floors, those on the ground floor are straight—lined, those of the first floor in basket arches. Continuous pilasters run through the upper

frei Obergeschosse sind mittelst durchlaufender Pfeiler zusammengezogen, die die leicht ausgebogenen, geradlinig geschlossenen Fenstergruppen zwischen sich einschließen. Den oberen Abschluß bildet eine Brüstung, hinter welcher das Dachgeschoß, der mittlere höhere Teil mit Korbbogenfenstern versehen, aufsteigt. Die Dächer sind mit Dachpfannen eingedeckt. Die Modelle zu den Figuren an der Fassade lieferte Professor Wrba, die Steinausführung derselben erfolgte durch die Bildhauer Göhle, Rieble und Wüst.

Das Erdgeschoß enthält, teilweise durch Oberlicht erhellt, in Verbindung mit dem Eingangsflur die Haupttreppe, den Personenaufzug und hinterliegenden Lichthof, sowie die Nebentreppe mit Warenaufzug. Im Zwischengeschoß sind Verkaufs-, Ankleide-, Bureau- und Atelierräume, einen Lichthof umschließend, untergebracht. Das erste, zweite und dritte Obergeschoß sind zur Anlage von Bureauräumen benutzt. Die Decken und Stützen sind bis zum Erdgeschoß in Eisenbeton, die der darüberliegenden Geschosse in Eisenkonstruktion ausgeführt.

420 [1912: 1]

Die in vier Stockwerken über einem Sockelgeschoß aufsteigende, mit einem Dachaufbau bekrönte Fassade des Geschäftshauses Caan & Heumann in Köln a. Rh., Apostelnkloster 5, bringt die einheitliche Bestimmung des Inneren durch die vorgelegten, sämtliche Geschosse vom Sockel bis zum übertretenden Dachgesims durchsetzenden Pfeiler zum Ausdruck. Das Gebäude kam nach dem Entwurfe des Architekten Peter Gaertner, unter Mitarbeit des Architekten J. Bernd, in einer Bauzeit von 9 Monaten für die Kostensumme von 150 000 Mark zur Ausführung. Der rundbogig überwölbten Einfahrt im Erdgeschoß einerseits entspricht andererseits ein rundbogiges Fenster; sonst sind die der Höhe nach zusammengezogenen, in der Mittelachse in leichter Rundung ausgebauchten Fenster geradlinig überdeckt. Der Dachausbau wird wieder von Pfeilern eingefaßt, die eine Loggia einschließen, und trägt ein zeltförmiges Dach. Die Verblendung der Fassade besteht aus hellem Pfälzer Sandstein, die des Sockels aus Dolomit. Das Dach ist mit tiefroten Mönch- und Nonnenziegeln eingedeckt.

Die überwölbte Durchfahrt führt zur Haupttreppe und weiter zu dem offenen Hof. Somit wird das Erdgeschoß ganz von zusammenhängenden, teilweise durch Oberlicht erhellten Geschäftsräumen eingenommen, aus denen wieder eine Treppe emporführt, und von denen an der Straßenfront zwei Privatbureaus abgetrennt sind. Die oberen Geschosse enthalten gleichfalls ungeteilte Geschäftsräume.

421 [1912: 2]

Das vierstöckige Wohn- und Geschäftshaus in Wiesbaden, Ecke Wilhelm- und Friedrichstraße, nimmt die Filiale der Deutschen Bank nebst einer Anzahl Wohnungen auf, und ist nach dem Entwurfe der Architektenfirma Ph. Holzmann & Co. unter Mitarbeit des Architekten Rückgauer in einer Bauzeit von etwa 11 Monaten errichtet. Das Erdgeschoß enthält die flach überwölbten Eingänge und schließt mit durchgehenden vorgekragten Balkons nach oben ab. Die zwischen durchgehenden Pfeilern eingeschlossenen, im ersten und zweiten Obergerschoß zusammengezogenen Fenster sind in den mittleren Achsen flach nach außen gerundet und wieder mit vorgekragten Balkons abgeschlossen. Das dritte, ebenfalls durch Pfeiler gegliederte Obergeschoß trägt den weit übertretenden Dachkranz, über dem sich auf der Steilfläche des gebrochenen Daches eine Reihe Fenster erhebt. Die Fassaden sind mit hellgelbem Keininger (Pfälzer) Sandstein verblendet; die Dachdeckung besteht aus rheinischem Schiefer.

Die Stahlkammer sowie das Gewölbe für Effekten und Coupons im Kellergeschoß sind von einem Kontrollgang umgeben, dem sich ein Raum für das Publikum anschließt. Außerdem sind Räume für das Archiv, die Heizung und für den Bedarf der Wohnungen vorhanden. Im Erdgeschoß liegt an der Ecke der Verkehrsraum für das Publikum mit doppelten Eingängen, an diesen Raum schließen sich die Bureaus für Effek-

vants, traités de façon homogène, sont organisés autour de piliers continus, flanquant des fenêtres à meneaux droites, et légèrement convexes. L'étage mansardé, dont la partie médiane est percée de fenêtres surbaissées, s'élève derrière une balustrade. Les toits sont recouverts de tuiles flammandes. Les modèles des sculptures de la façade furent exécutés par le professeur Wrba, leur réalisation fut l'œuvre des sculpteurs Göhle, Rieble et Wüst.

Le rez-de-chaussée, en partie éclairé par une toiture vitrée, abrite l'escalier de service, le montecharges et l'escalier principal communiquant avec le couloir d'entrée, l'ascenseur et l'arrière cour vitrée. L'entresol est occupé par les locaux de vente, le vestiaire, les bureaux et les ateliers aménagés autour d'une cour vitrée. Les premier, deuxième et troisième étages sont utilisés comme bureaux. Les planchers et les supports sont en béton armé jusqu'au rez-de-chaussée et en fer dans les étages suivants.

420 [1912: 1]

L'immeuble Caan & Heumann de Cologne, Apostelnkloster 5, est un édifice de quatre étages, équipé d'un sous-sol et coiffé d'un toit mansard. La façade présente une ordonnance à piliers saillants, montant du socle jusqu'à la corniche, soulignant ainsi la vocation commerciale du bâtiment. Les plans furent exécutés par l'architecte Peter Gaertner en coopération avec l'architecte J. Bernd. Les travaux de construction, qui durèrent 9 mois, revinrent à 150 000 marks. Le rez-de-chaussée présente deux ouvertures cintrées symétriques, un passage d'un côté et une fenêtres de l'autre. Les fenêtres, régulièrement alignées, sont à linteau droit, celles de la partie médiane sont légèrement convexes. Une construction mansardée, flanquée de deux piliers et couverte d'un toit en pavillon abrite une loggia. La façade est revêtue de grès clair du Palatinat, le socle de grès des Dolomites. Le toit porte une couverture de tuiles romaines rouge foncé.

Le passage voûté conduit au grand escalier puis à la cour ouverte. Le rez-de-chaussée comprend deux bureaux indépendants, aménagés sur la rue, ainsi que des locaux non-cloisonnés, partiellement éclairés par des verrières et équipés d'un escalier. Les étages supérieurs sont également occupés par des locaux non-cloisonnés.

421 [1912: 2]

Cet immeuble de Wiesbaden, situé à l'angle des rues Wilhelm et Friedrichstraße, abrite une filiale de la „Deutsche Bank" ainsi que de nombreux logements. La construction ce ce bâtiment de quatre étages nécessita onze mois de travail. Les plans furent réalisés par le bureau d'architecture Ph. Holzmann & Co. en collaboration avec l'architecte Rückgauer. Le rez-de-chaussée présente des entrées surbaissées et s'achève par des balcons saillants courant le long de la façade. Flanquées de piliers continus, de forme convexe dans la partie centrale de la façade, les fenêtres en tribune du premier et deuxième étages forment un ensemble homogène. Le troisième étage présente une composition identique aux deux niveaux inférieurs. Le toit s'élève sur une corniche saillante et présente une série de fenêtres mansardées trouant le brisis. Les façades sont revêtues de grès jaune clair du Palatinat. Le toit porte une couverture d'ardoises de la région du Rhin.

Le sous-sol abrite la chambre forte ainsi que la salle voûtée renfermant les titres et les coupons d'intérêt, entourées d'un couloir de contrôle auquel se greffe une salle pour le public, ainsi que les archives, la chaufferie et les caves des logements. Le rez-de-chaussée comprend, dans l'angle, accessible par une double entrée, une salle destinée au public, sur laquelle donnent les bureaux des titres et des lettres de change ainsi que la caisse. Une entrée indépendante

three storeys, between which groups of straight—ined windows curve slightly outward. The pilasters end in an overhanging balustrade behind which rises the roof storey with its higher middle erection with windows framed in basket arches. The roof is covered with pantiles. The figures of the façade are based on models created by Professor Wrba, and completed by the sculptors Göhle, Rieble and Wüst.

The entrance to the ground floor, which is partially lit by skylights, leads to main staircase, lift and a courtyard at the rear, as well as to the side staircase and a lift for goods. On the mezzanine, sales rooms, dressing—rooms, offices and ateliers are grouped round a central patio. The first, second and third storeys are reserved for office space. All ceilings and ground floor piers are of reinforced concrete; the floors above are supported by an iron framework.

420 [1912: 1]

The singular purpose of the Caan and Heumann commercial building in Cologne (Apostelnkloster 5) is expressed in the unified design of its four—storey façade with engaged pillars running from the base to the overhanging roof moulding. The building, which also contains a basement and a roof storey, was constructed according to the plans of the architect Peter Gaertner, with the cooperation of the architect J. Bernd, over the course of 9 months at a cost of 150,000 Marks. The arched carriageway at one side is balanced by the arched window at the other; otherwise, the horizontal, slightly concave windows of the façade are straight—lined. The roof superstructure is again flanked by pillars, with a loggia in its centre, and supports a pyramidal roof. The façade is faced with light sandstone from the Palatinate, the socle is of dolomite. The roof is covered with scarlet ridzed tiles.

The arched carriageway leads to the principal staircase and, farther along, to an open courtyard. Otherwise, the ground floor ist entirely occupied by connected office rooms partially lit by skylights. The offices are bordered by a stairway leading to the upper floors and by two private offices on the street front of the building. The upper storeys also contain undivided office space.

421 [1912: 2]

The four—storey commercial and residential building in Wiesbaden (corner of Wilhelmstrasse and Friedrichstrasse) is occupied by a branch of the German Bank, as well as by a number of flats. Designed by the architectural firm of Ph. Holzmann & Co. with the cooperation of the architect Rückgauer, the building was completed in approximately 11 months. The entrances at the ground floor are framed by flat arches, and a projecting balcony runs the width of both façades at the level of the first storey. The windows of the first and second storeys are framed between continuous pilasters, have a slightly protruding central axis, and also end in balconies. The third storey is articulated by pilasters, and ends in an overhanging roof moulding; a row of windows are placed in the steeper slope of the roof. The façades are faced with light—yellow sandstone from the Palatinate; the roof is covered with slate.

The strong room as well as the vault for securities and coupons are enclosed by a security corridor on the basement, which leads to a room for the bank's patrons. Also located here are archive offices, heating chambers, and service rooms for the use of the flat occupants. The public hall with its double entrances is located at one corner of the ground floor. This room leads to offices for securities, exchange and tellers. A

ten, Wechsel und Kasse an. Ein besonderer Eingang führt zu den Treppen und dem dahinter liegenden Hof. Das erste Obergeschoß enthält Diensträume der Bank, Vorstandszimmer, Säle für Buchhaltung und Korrespondenz. Das zweite und dritte Obergeschoß sind zu größeren Wohnungen eingerichtet. Im Dachgeschoß befindet sich die Hausmeisterwohnung. Sämtliche Konstruktionen sind feuersicher hergestellt.

422 [1912; 4]

Das Geschäftshaus der Versicherungs-Gesellschaft Rhenania in Köln a. Rh., Wörtherstraße 10, eine geschlossene Baugruppe mit dem Direktorwohnhause bildend, ist von den Architekten B. D. A. Schreiterer und Below entworfen, und in 11 bzw. 12 Monaten zur Ausführung gekommen. Die Baukosten des Verwaltungsgebäudes betrugen 225 000 Mark, die des Direktorwohnhauses 145 000 Mark. Die über dem Sokkelgeschoß zweigeschossig aufsteigenden, mit einem ausgebauten Dachgeschoß versehenen Fassaden des Geschäftshauses zeigen einfache der inneren Bestimmung entsprechende Formgebung. Die Mittelrisalite an beiden Fronten durchbrechen die Dachlinien und sind im Erd- und Obergeschoß durch Pilasterstreifen zusammengezogen, ebenso die geradlinig überdeckten Fenster beider Geschosse. Die steilen Flächen des gebrochenen, mit Schiefer eingedeckten Daches sind mit einer Reihe von Fenstern besetzt. Das zweigeschossige, gleichfalls mit einem gebrochenen Schieferdach überdeckte Direktorwohnhaus ist mehrfach gruppiert und schließt sich dem Geschäftshause unmittelbar an. Der Sockel ist durchweg aus Muschelkalkstein hergestellt, die oberen Geschosse der Straßenfronten aus Kenzittuff, die Hof- und Gartenfronten sind in silbergrauem Terrasit verputzt.

422 [1912; 4]

Les locaux de la compagnie d'assurances Rhenania de Cologne, Wörtherstraße 10, forment, avec la maison du directeur, un ensemble groupé. Les travaux, effectués d'après les plans des architectes Schreiterer et Below, furent terminés en l'espace d'une année. Il en coûta 225 000 marks pour réaliser le bâtiment administratif et 145 000 pour la maison du directeur. Le bâtiment administratif, qui s'élève sur deux niveaux au-dessus d'un étage en sous-sol, est assorti d'un étage mansardé. Les façades aux lignes pures attestent de la vocation des lieux. Elles présentent des avancées montant au-delà de la ligne du toit, offrant des striures saillantes. Les fenêtres droites du rez-de-chaussée et du premier étage sont flanquées de pilatres continus de façon à former un ensemble homogène. Le brisis du toit en ardoises est troué de fenêtres mansardées. La maison du directeur jouxte les locaux administratifs. Il s'agit d'une construction asymétrique de deux étages, coiffée d'un toit en ardoises au comble brisé. Le socle est en coquillart, les murs extérieurs donnant sur la rue sont en tuf, ceux donnant sur la cour et le jardin sont enduits d'un crépi gris argenté.

422 [1912; 4]

The office building of the Rhenania Insurance Association in Cologne (Wörtherstrasse 10), a self-contained group of buildings which includes the director's residence, is the work of the architects Schreiterer and Below, members of the Association of German Architects. The administration building was completed in 11 months at a cost of 225,000 Marks, the director's residence in 12 months for 145,000 Marks. Reflecting the purpose of the interior, the front façade of the two-storey office building with basement and roof storey is simple in design. Middle projections at both fronts rise above the roof line and are flanked at the first and second storeys by pilaster strips, as are the straight-lined windows of both storeys. The steep section of the slate roof has dormer windows and a group of straight-lined windows in the upper part of the middle projection. The two-storey director's house also has a slate roof and is arranged in multiple architectural groupings which directly adjoin the office building. Its socle is made entirely of shell limestone, the upper storeys facing the street are of tufa, the courtyard and garden fronts are plastered with silver-grey terrazzo.

Erdgeschoß   Rez-de-chaussée   Ground Floor

Obergeschoß   Étage   First Floor

Das Sockelgeschoß des Geschäftshauses enthält das Archiv, die Räume für Akten und Beamtengarderobe, außerdem die Wohnung des Hausmeisters und den Eingangsflur mit Treppenaufgang. Im Erdgeschoß sind die Zimmer der Direktion, des Aufsichtsrats, die Kasse, eine Anzahl Bureauräume sowie die Haupt- und Nebentreppe untergebracht. Im Obergeschoß sind weitere Bureauräume, die Zimmer für Direktor, Arzt und Justiziar angeordnet. Die reichlich bemessenen Wohn-, Gesellschafts- und Wirtschaftsräume des Direktorwohnhauses verteilen sich auf drei Geschosse. Sämtliche Decken sind aus Eisenbeton, die Treppen in Kunstsandstein hergestellt. Die Bildhauerarbeiten rühren von E. Haller her.

423 [1912; 22]

Wie der Grundriß ergibt, wurde das Gebäude der Frankfurter Transport-, Unfall- und Glasversicherungs-Aktien-Gesellschaft in Frankfurt a. M., Guiolettstraße 2, als Anbau an das ältere durch Architekt von Hoven erbaute Hauptgebäude errichtet. Der neue Anbau kam nach dem Entwurfe der Architekten Rindsfüßer und Kühn in einer Bauzeit von 9 Monaten für die Baukostensumme von 450 000 Mark zur Ausführung. Die im Hauptteil vierstöckige, mit gebrochenem Dach abschließende Fassade ist durch aufsteigende Pfeiler geteilt und hat einen risalitartigen,

Les archives, les salles des dossiers, le vestiaire des employés, le logement du concierge, le couloir d'entrée et la cage d'escalier sont aménagés à l'étage en sous-sol. Le rez-de-chaussée abrite les bureaux de la direction, ceux du conseil d'administration, la caisse, de nombreuses salles de bureau, le grand escalier et l'escalier de service. Au premier étage sont installés d'autres locaux ainsi que les bureaux du directeur, du médecin et du justicier. Les trois niveaux de la maison du directeur sont occupés par de vastes pièces de séjour, de réception et de service. Les planchers sont en béton armé, les escaliers en grès artificiel. Les travaux de sculpture furent exécutés par E. Haller.

423 [1912; 22]

Comme on peut le constater d'après les plans, le bâtiment de la compagnie d'assurances francfortoise, situé au no. 2 de la Guiolettstraße, fut greffé à un ouvrage déjà existant, construit en son temps par l'architecte von Hoven. Conçu par les architectes Rindsfüßer et Kühn, le nouvel édifice fut réalisé en neuf mois pour la somme de 450 000 marks. La façade de quatre étages est harmonieusement divisée de pilastres. Elle présente, au niveau des deux étages infé-

The basement of the office building contains archives, rooms for documents, and cloak-rooms. The caretaker's living quarters and the entry hall with stairs are also located here. On the ground floor are the director's office, board rooms, the cashier's office, a number of other offices as well as the main staircase and side stairs. More offices are located on the first floor, which also contains rooms for the director, physician and justiciary. The spacious sitting-rooms, conference rooms and living quarters of the director's house are distributed throughout three storeys. All ceilings are of reinforced concrete; the stairs are of imitation sandstone. The sculptural ornamentation is by E. Haller.

423 [1912; 22]

The building of the Frankfurt Transport, Accident and Glass Joint-Stock Insurance Company in Frankfurt-on-Main (Guiolettstrasse 2) was designed by the architects Rindsfüsser and Kühn as a new addition to the older structure, the work of the architect von Hoven. Construction of the new building occupied 9 months and cost 450,000 Marks. Its principal section has a four-storey façade ending in a broken-line roof, the façade is divided by pilasters and features a middle projection in the first and second

durch das erste und zweite Obergeschoß geführten, mit Figuren gezierten Vorsprung aufzuweisen. Das rundbogige Portal trägt einen Figurenfries. Die auf Versicherung bezughabenden Figuren sind von Bildhauer E. W. Ohly modelliert und durch die Bildhauer Fr. Scheuing und E. Warmuth in Stein ausgeführt. Ebenso lieferte Ohly die Modelle für die Steinverzierungen und keramischen Arbeiten im Vestibül. Das Tor wurde in Bronze hergestellt. Portal und Sockelgeschoß der Fassade bestehen aus fränkischem Muschelkalkstein, die Sandsteinarbeiten aus gelbgeflammtem Lichtensteiner Maintalsandstein. Das mit Schiefer eingedeckte Dach ist mit Dachfenstern ausgestattet.

In Eingang und Vestibül sind die Wände mit Keramik aus der Großherzogl. Keramischen Manufaktur zu Darmstadt ausgestattet, die Treppen sind mit Marmor belegt. Decken und Wände sind in Mörteltechnik in künstlerischer Ausführung durch Hofdekorationsmaler J. Hembus hergestellt. Die Geschäftsräume schließen einen Hof ein. Die innere Konstruktion nebst Dach ist in armiertem Eisenbeton mit Hohldecken ausgeführt. Die Decken sind durchweg mit Krebschem Rohrzellengewebe verputzt, um Isolierung und Schallsicherung zu erlangen.

424 [1912; 5]

Der Gartenplan für die Landhausbesiedlung in Schönberger Tal bei Bensheim a. B., von Heinrich E. Klein aufgestellt, zeigt eine Anzahl Wohnhäuser, freiliegend zwischen Baumgruppen und Gartenplätzen, und bietet das Bild einer wirklichen Gartenstadt.

Die Wohnhäuser, nach den Entwürfen des Architekten Professor Heinrich Metzendorf im Laufe etwa eines Jahres errichtet, sind meist in malerischen Formen des gemischten Massiv-Holzbaustils gehalten.

Haus Nr. 1 zeigt rotes Sockelmauerwerk, darüber schwarzes und braunes Ziegelmauerwerk mit verschmierten Mörtelfugen, im Obergeschoß Bretterverschalung und weiße Anstriche der Fensterrahmen und Läden. An einer Ecke springt ein runder Erkervorbau vor, mit einer Altane abschließend. Das weit übertretende abgewalmte Dach ist mit Ziegeln eingedeckt. Das Erdgeschoß enthält die Diele mit frei aufsteigender Treppe, Salon, Wohnzimmer, Eßzimmer in Verbindung mit dem Wintergarten und die Küche.

Haus Nr. 4, zweistöckig wie das vorige, ist im Erdgeschoß mit einer vorgekragten, eine Altane tragenden, in Holzkonstruktion ausgeführten Laube ausgestattet. An einer Ecke springt ein polygonaler Erker vor. Der Eingang an der Seitenfront mündet in einen einstöckigen Flügelbau. Der Sockel ist in rotem Bruchsteinmauerwerk hergestellt; die oberen Frontmauern sind grau verputzt. Der abgeschopfte Giebel ist mit Brettern verschalt. Einzelne Holzteile sind weiß gestrichen. Das Dach ist mit roten Ziegeln eingedeckt. Im Erdgeschoß liegen der Vorraum mit offener Treppe, der Salon, das Eßzimmer in Verbindung mit dem Erkerausbau und dem Wintergarten und die Küche.

rieurs, une avancée ornée de plastiques. Le portail en plein cintre est surmonté d'une frise sculptée. Les ornements, traités sur le thème des assurances, furent modelés par le sculpteur E. W. Ohly et exécutés en pierre par les sculpteurs Fr. Scheuing et E. Warmuth. Monsieur Ohly fournit également les modèles des décors de pierre et de céramique du vestibule. Le portail est en bronze. L'encadrement du portail ainsi que le socle sont réalisés en coquillart franconien, les ouvrages de pierre sont en grès flammé jaune de la vallée du Main. Le toit mansard a reçu une couverture d'ardoises.

Les murs de l'entrée et du vestibule offrent des ornements de céramique de la manufacture de Darmstadt. Les escaliers sont habillés de marbre. Les plafonds et les murs furent superbement réalisés en technique de mortier par le peintre décorateur à la cour J. Hembus. Les bureaux donnent sur une cour. L'ossature de l'immeuble ainsi que le toit sont en béton armé. Les faux plafonds sont insonorisés et isolés par un revêtement anti-cancéreux.

424 [1912; 5]

Le plan du lotissement de la vallée de Schönberg, non loin de Bensheim-en-Brisgau, exécuté par l'architecte Heinrich E. Klein, présente de nombreuses constructions dégagées, entourées d'arbres et de jardins, offrant l'image d'une véritable cité-jardin.

Les maisons, construites sur les plans de l'architecte Heinrich Metzendorf, furent réalisées en une année. Elles ont l'aspect pittoresque des constructions de pierres et de bois.

La maison no. 1 présente un socle de maçonnerie rouge sur lequel s'élèvent des murs de briques brunes et noires jointoyées. L'étage porte un revêtement de lattes de bois. Les cadres des fenêtres ainsi que les volets sont peints en blanc. Un avant-corps arrondi supportant un balcon se détache d'un angle de la façade. Le toit saillant en croupe est recouvert de tuiles. Le rez-de-chaussée abrite le hall comprenant l'escalier, le salon, la salle de séjour, la salle à manger communiquant avec le jardin d'hiver et la cuisine.

La maison no. 4 s'élève sur deux étages comme la précédente. Elle est assortie, au rez-de-chaussée, d'une loge en bois, couronnée d'un balcon. Un bow-window polygonal saillit d'un angle. Le socle est en pierres de taille rouges. Les murs extérieurs ont reçu un enduit gris. Le pignon à croupe faîtière est habillé de lattes de bois. Quelques éléments de bois sont peints en blanc. Le toit porte une couverture de tuiles rouges. Au rez-de-chaussée sont aménagés le salon, la salle à manger donnant sur le jardin d'hiver, la cuisine ainsi que le hall et l'escalier.

storeys which is ornamented by standing figures. The portal is framed in a round arch and crowned by a frieze of figures carved in stone which illustrate the insurance trade, a work designed by the sculptor E. W. Ohly and sculpted by Fr. Scheing and E. Warmuth. Mr. Ohly also provided the models for the stone and ceramic ornamentation in the vestibule. The gate is cast in bronze. The portal and the basement façade consist of shell limestone from Franconia, the sandstone workings employs light-grained sandstone from the Main. The slate roof has dormer windows.

The walls of the entrance and vestibule are tiled in ceramic from the Grand-Ducal Ceramic Works at Darmstadt, the stairs are laid in marble. The court decorateur J. Hembus has ornamented the ceilings and walls using artistic mortar techniques. Various offices are arranged around a central courtyard. The structural framework and the roof supports are constructed with reinforced concrete and concrete hollow floors. All ceilings are plastered with reed lathing in unburned lime, so as to provide adequate heating and acoustic insulation.

424 [1912; 5]

Drafted by Heinrich E. Klein, the site plan of the country housing estate in the Schönberg Valley near Bensheim, which shows a number of free-standing houses located between groups of trees and garden landscapes, represents an ideal garden town.

Most of the houses designed by the architect Professor Heinrich Metzendorf and constructed in the course of approximately one year have been built in picturesque styles using a mixed timber and stone construction.

House No. 1 has red socle masonry, plus brown and black brickwork with grouted mortar joints. The upper storey is covered with board formwork, with the window frames and shutters painted white. A round bay covered by a balcony projects from one side of the front. The wide, overhanging roof is covered with clay tiles. The ground floor contains the entry hall with an open staircase, the drawing-room, a sitting-room, and a dining room leading to the winter garden and to the kitchen.

House Nr. 4, like No. 1, is two-storeyed. The ground level front of the house has a projecting wooden bower covered by a balcony. A polygonal bay is located at one corner. The entrance at the side front leads to a single-storeyed wing structure. The socle is of red rubble masonry, the upper fronts are faced with grey plaster. The half-tipped gable is covered with planking, and the wooden ornamentation is painted in white. The roof is covered with red clay tile. On the ground floor are the entry hall with open stairs, the drawing-room, the dining room leading to the bay-room and the winter garden, and the kitchen.

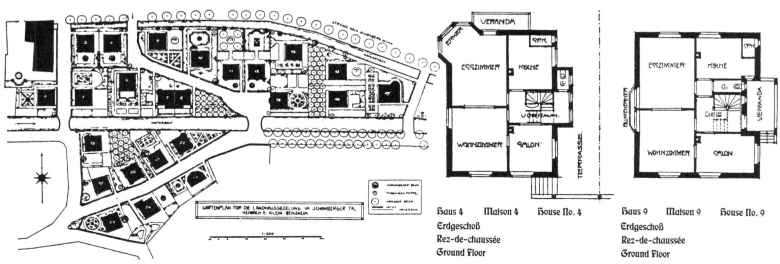

Haus 4   Maison 4   House No. 4
Erdgeschoß
Rez-de-chaussée
Ground Floor

Haus 9   Maison 9   House No. 9
Erdgeschoß
Rez-de-chaussée
Ground Floor

Gartenplan für die Landhaussiedlung im Schönberger Tal   Plan du lotissement de la vallée de Schönberg   Site plan of the country housing estate in the Schönberg Valley

Haus Nr. 9 stimmt in der inneren Einrichtung in der Hauptsache mit den vorgenannten Häusern überein. Das Sockelmauerwerk besteht aus grauen und gelben Bruchsteinen, Erd- und Obergeschoßmauern aus schwarzen und braunen Backsteinen. Das Dach ist mit Ziegeln eingedeckt. In der Mitte der Straßenfront springt eine offene Halle vor, die im oberen Geschoß eine Altane trägt. Dieselbe wird von zwei mit Brettern verschalten geschwungenen Giebeln flankiert. Das Dach ist mit Ziegeln eingedeckt.

Haus Nr. 24 zeigt rotes Sockelmauerwerk, darüber Mauerwerk der Fronten aus rotem Sauerbruchstein. Das übertretende Ziegeldach ist gebrochen. Die mit besonderem Dach versehene Eingangshalle an der Giebelfront führt zu Vorraum und Treppe. Sonst entspricht die Einrichtung des Grundrisses der für die übrigen Häuser angewendeten.

425 [1912; 18]

Das Bahnhofsgebäude in Godesberg, ein Werk des Architekten Baurat Mettegang, schließt sich in den Formen des Aufbaues der mittelrheinischen Bauweise an. Das Äußere erscheint in lebhafter Gruppierung und ist mit hohen, gebrochenen, übertretenden Dächern überdeckt, die durch Giebel, teilweise mit Abschopfung versehen, begrenzt sind. Der äußere Haupteingang zum Vestibül ist mit einer besonders überdachten Vorhalle versehen; ebenso erhebt sich an der einen Schmalseite eine geräumige, wieder mit besonderem Dach ausgestattete Veranda. An der anderen Schmalseite ist im Oberstock ein Balkon mit hinterliegender Loggia vorgekragt, die unter der geschweiften Dachfläche endigt; an der Ecke der Front erhebt sich eine polygonaler, von einer in Absätzen geschweiften Haube bekrönter Uhrturm. Das Gebäude bildet einen Putzbau über einem aus Bruchsteinen hergestellten Sockel. Die mit Schiefer eingedeckten Dächer tragen eine Anzahl Fensteraufbauten.

Im Innern zeichnet sich das Vestibül durch große Abmessungen und dekorative Ausbildung der Wandflächen aus. Der untere Teil der Wände mit den Eingängen zu den Wartesälen besteht aus gefugtem Ziegelmauerwerk, während der obere Teil bemalt ist und sich mit einer flachen Voute der Decke anschließt.

Die Bahnbrücke, von Bauinspektor Müller erbaut, spannt sich in flacher, geknickter Bogenlinie über den Weg und zeigt Mauerwerk aus unbehauenen Bruchsteinen mit vortretenden Bossen.

426 [1912; 14]

Die zweistöckige, in den Ausbauten dreistöckige, außerdem mit einem ausgebauten Dachgeschoß versehene Villa Osthaus in Hagen i. W., Kreishausstraße 5, von Architekt Professor Fr. Schumacher, Hamburg, entworfen, ist in einer Bauzeit von etwa einem Jahre für die Bausumme von 113 000 Mark, einschließlich der Gartenanlagen, zur Ausführung gekommen. Die Straßenfront öffnet sich im Erd- und Obergeschoß durch Loggien, die zwischen vorspringenden Ausbauten liegen. Der Eingang in der Seitenfront mündet in eine vorspringende offene Halle, über der sich das Ober- und das Dachgeschoß erheben; letzteres in pavillonartiger Form. Der Haupteingang führt zu dem Vorraum in einem einstöckigen Seitenflü-

La maison no. 9 correspond, dans son aménagement intérieur, aux maisons évoquées ci-dessus. Le socle est en pierres de taille grises et jaunes, les murs du rez-de-chaussée et de l'étage sont en briques noires et brunes. Le toit est recouvert de tuiles. Du centre de la façade sur rue se dégage une loge ouverte portant balcon, lequel est flanqué de deux pignons aux lignes ondulées, parés de lattes de bois. La couverture du toit est en tuiles.

La maison no. 24 présente un socle en maçonnerie rouge et des murs en pierres de taille rouges. Le toit saillant au comble brisé est recouvert de tuiles. L'entrée, abritée par un porche coiffé d'un toit, donne sur le hall et l'escalier. L'aménagement intérieur correspond à celui des autres maisons.

425 [1912; 18]

La gare de Godesberg, conçue par l'architecte Mettegang, atteste, de par sa structure, du style de construction de la région du Rhin. La façade variée et asymétrique, agrémentée de pignons est coiffée d'un haut toit saillant au comble brisé. L'entrée principale, menant au hall, est assortie d'un porche. Une des façades latérales est flanquée d'une vaste véranda recouverte d'un toit. La façade opposite présente, au niveau du premier étage, une loggia abritée sous un toit de forme concave et pourvue d'un balcon saillant. La tour polygonale de l'horloge, surmontée d'une calotte en trois parties, s'élève dans l'angle de la façade. Le socle du bâtiment est en pierres de taille, les murs extérieurs sont crépis. Les toits, recouverts d'ardoises, sont percés de fenêtres mansardées.

A l'intérieur, le hall se distingue par ses vastes proportions et la décoration de ses murs. La partie inférieure des murs, trouée par les entrées menant aux salles d'attente, est réalisée en briques apparentes jointoyées. La partie supérieure a reçu un badigeon. Le plafond offre une légère voûte.

Le pont de chemin de fer, construit par l'inspecteur du bâtiment Müller, présente une arche surbaissée brisée, supportée par des murs de pierres brutes traitées en bossage.

426 [1912; 14]

La villa Osthaus, située à Hagen, Kreishausstraße 5, fut conçue par l'architecte hambourgeois Fr. Schumacher. Réalisée en une année, la propriété revint à 113 000 marks, aménagement du jardin compris. Il s'agit d'une villa de trois voire quatre étages, coiffée d'un toit mansardé. La façade sur rue est assortie, au rez-de-chaussée et à l'étage, de loggias encadrées par deux bow-windows. L'entrée sur la façade latérale donne sur un hall ouvert et saillant au-dessus duquel s'élèvent les étages supérieurs. L'entrée principale, aménagée dans une aile d'un étage, conduit à une antichambre. La façade postérieure pré-

The interior arrangement of House No. 9 is basically very similar to that of the houses just described. The socle consists of grey and yellow rubble masonry, the first and second floors of black and brown brick. The roof is clay—tiled. An open porch juts from the middle of the street front, with a balcony at the first storey. Above the balcony are two timbered gables with clay tile roofs.

House No. 24 has red basement walls, and the fronts above are of red rubble masonry. The overhanging tiled roof has broken lines. The covered porch at the gabled front leads to the entry hall and stairs. In all other respects, the plan of this house corresponds to that of the others discussed here.

425 [1912; 18]

The design of the Bad Godesberg railway station, a work of the municipal architect Mettegang, conforms to the architectural form popularly employed in the Middle Rhine region. The exterior is grouped in an engaging manner and covered with high—pitched overhanging roofs marked by gables, some of which are half—hipped. The principal entrance to the vestibule has a porch with a separate overhanging roof; a veranda is located at the first storey of one side front, again covered by a separate roof. The other side of the building has a projecting balcony at one upper floor with a recessed loggia covered by shaped section of the roof. A polygonal clock tower rises at one corner, which is crowned by a stepped, dome—shaped roof. The building is covered with plaster and rests on a foundation of rubble masonry. The slate roofs have a number of window structures.

The interior hall is noticeable in its large dimensions and the rich ornamentation of its walls. The lower half of the walls are of bonded brickwork, while the upper half is painted, culminating in the inclined haunch of the ceiling.

The railway bridge, built by the building inspector Müller, spans the passageway in a flat, segmented arch; its masonry is of unhewn ashlar with protruding rustication.

426 [1912; 14]

The Villa Osthaus in Hagen, Westphalia (Kreishausstrasse 5) was designed by the architect Professor Fr. Schumacher of Hamburg and completed in about one year at a cost of 113,000 Marks, including landscaping work. The two—storey house has three—storeyed extensions and a attic storey. The street front opens at the ground and first storey onto loggias flanked by two bays. The entrance at the side leads to an open hall surmounted by the upper and attic storeys, the latter having a pavilion—like design. The main entrance leads to an entrance hall in the single—storeyed side wing. The rear elevation has a

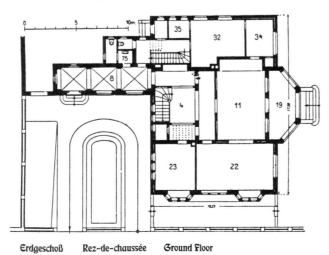

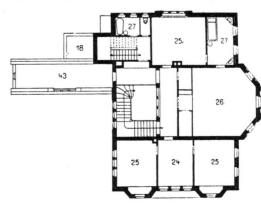

Erdgeschoß   Rez-de-chaussée   Ground Floor   Obergeschoß   Etage   Upper Floor

gel. Die Rückfront besitzt einen im Obergeschoß schwach vortretenden, die Dachlinie durchschneidenden Ausbau. Die Fronten sind in Terranova verputzt und mit einzelnen Sandsteingliederungen ausgestattet. Das gebrochene, Dachfenster tragende Dach hat eine Eindeckung von Biberschwänzen erhalten.

Das Erdgeschoß enthält die mit einem Vorraum versehene Diele mit der offen liegenden Haupttreppe, das Herren- und das Damenzimmer, das mit der Loggia in Verbindung stehende Speisezimmer, die Küche mit Nebenräumen und die Nebentreppe. Im Obergeschoß liegen das Schlafzimmer des Besitzers mit anschließenden Garderoben, das Wohnzimmer, das Ankleidezimmer mit Bad, ein zweites Badezimmer und die Kinderzimmer.

427 [1912: 15]

Das villenartige Wohnhaus Fischer in Siegen a. d. S., Giersbergstraße 17, ist in einer Bauzeit von 12 Monaten nach dem Entwurfe des Architekten Gg. Metzendorf zur Ausführung gekommen. Das Erdgeschoß besitzt eine überbaute Eingangshalle an der Vorderfront und an der Rückfront eine Veranda, die mit einem offenen Balkon vor einer Loggia abschließt. Im Obergeschoß der Vorderfront, bereits im Dachraum gelegen, befinden sich zwei ausspringende Fensterbauten, die unter dem vorgekragten Giebel endigen. An einer Seitenfront erhebt sich aus der Dachfläche ein mit geschwungenem Giebel bekrönter Ausbau. Das sichtbare Mauerwerk des Erdgeschosses ist in weiß gefugtem Schieferstein ausgeführt; das Obergeschoß zeigt Fachwerk mit braun gebeizter Holzschindlung und weißen Gesimsen. Das steile Dach ist mit Schiefer eingedeckt.

Im Erdgeschoß liegt die mit einer Holzbalkendecke ausgestattete Diele, aus welcher die Stockwerkstreppe frei aufsteigt. Außerdem enthält das Erdgeschoß das Empfangs-, das Wohn- und Eßzimmer, letzteres mit anschließender Veranda, endlich die Küche mit Nebenräumen. Im Obergeschoß sind das Schlafzimmer, in Verbindung mit der Loggia, das Ankleidezimmer, das Bad, das Zimmer der Tochter und zwei Fremdenzimmer, um die Diele gruppiert, untergebracht.

428 [1912: 16]

Inmitten eines Gartens, auf hoher Terrasse erhebt sich das Haus Gontermann in Siegen a. d. S., nach dem Entwurfe des Architekten Gg. Metzendorf in etwa 16 Monaten errichtet. Über der mächtigen, aus Bruchsteinen hergestellten, mit massiver Brüstung bekrönten Terrassenmauer steigt die mit jonischen Säulen ausgestattete, von einer Freitreppe zugängliche, eine Altane tragende, offene Halle in der Mitte der Gartenfront auf. Zu beiden Seiten springen mit jonischen Pilastern gezierte Eckrisalite vor, und über der Halle erhebt sich ein das gebrochene Dach durchschneidender Aufbau, mit einem geschwungenen Giebel endigend. An der Eingangsfront zeigt sich ein halbrund vorspringender Hallenvorbau, in dem sich die Eingangstür befindet. Dem zweigeschossigen mit übertretendem Schieferdach versehenen Hauptgebäude ist ein eingeschossiger durch ein Dachgeschoss bereicherter, ebenfalls von einem gebrochenen Dach überdeckter Küchenanbau angefügt. Die Fronten sind in gelbem Flonheimer Sandstein mit gelbem Putz der Flächen ausgeführt.

Die Diele im Erdgeschoß, von der Eingangshalle zugänglich, enthält die freiliegende Haupttreppe. Um die Diele lagern sich der Salon, das Speisezimmer, das Wohnzimmer, das Herrenzimmer; im Anbau ist die Küche mit besonderem Nebeneingang angelegt. Im Obergeschoß geht ein geräumiger Vorraum dem Frühstückszimmer, den Zimmern der Söhne, dem Schlafzimmer der Eltern und dem im Dachgeschoß des Anbaues untergebrachten Ankleide- und Badezimmer voran.

429 [1912: 29]

Die dreigeschossige, im Aufbau malerisch wirkende Villa Karlsbrunn in Bad Nauheim, von Architekt B. D. A. Leonh. Kraft als vornehmes Ärzthaus entworfen, ist in einer Bauzeit von etwa 6 Monaten zur Ausführung gekommen und hat 60 000 Mark Baukosten verursacht, wobei die Mobiliarbeschaffung ein-

sente, au premier étage, une avancée légèrement saillante. Les murs de façade crépis offrent quelques ornements en grès. Le toit mansardé au comble brisé porte une couverture de tuiles plates.

Le rez-de-chaussée abrite l'antichambre avec l'escalier principal, le cabinet de travail, le boudoir, la salle à manger communiquant avec la loggia, la cuisine et ses dépendances ainsi que l'escalier de service. Au premier étage sont aménagées la chambre à coucher du propriétaire et sa garde-robe attenante, la salle de séjour, la garde-robe avec bain, une deuxième salle de bains et la chambre des enfants.

427 [1912: 15]

Cette maison aux allures de villa, située à Siegen-en-Westphalie, Giesbergstraße 17, fut construite en 12 mois d'après les plans de l'architecte Eg. Metzendorf. Le rez-de-chaussée présente, sur la façade principale, un porche abritant l'entrée, et, sur l'opposite, une véranda supportant un balcon assortissant une loggia. Le premier étage de la façade principale, aménagé en fait dans les combles, est assorti de deux bow-windows surmontés d'un pignon saillant. Une construction mansardée, coiffée d'un pignon aux lignes concaves, s'élève du toit de la façade latérale. Le rez-de-chaussée offre une maçonnerie apparente, composée de pierres schisteuses jointoyées de blanc. L'étage est revêtu de bardeaux de couleur brune. Les encadrements sont blancs. Le toit pentu porte une couverture d'ardoises.

Au rez-de-chaussée sont aménagés le hall d'entrée, pourvu d'un plafond aux poutres apparentes ainsi que l'escalier, le salon, la salle de séjour, la salle à manger communiquant avec la véranda, la cuisine et l'office. À l'étage, groupés autour d'une antichambre, s'agencent la chambre à coucher avec loggia attenante, la garde-robe, la salle de bains, la chambre de mademoiselle et deux chambres d'amis.

428 [1912: 16]

Entourée d'un jardin, appuyée sur une haute terrasse en pierres de taille, la villa Gontermann domine la ville de Siegen-en-Westphalie. Construite sur les plans de l'architecte Eg. Metzendorf, elle fut achevée en 16 mois. La façade sur jardin est assortie d'une terrasse bordée d'une balustrade massive et accessible par un perron. De la terrasse se dégage, flanqué par deux avancées ornées de pilatres ioniques, un portique dont les colonnes ioniques supportent un balcon au-dessus duquel s'élève un avant-corps coiffé d'un pignon aux lignes ondulées. Une avancée semi-circulaire abrite l'entrée sur la façade principale. Au corps de bâtiment de deux étages, portant une toiture d'ardoises saillante, se greffe une aile d'un étage, aux combles aménagés, dans laquelle a été installée la cuisine. Les murs extérieurs, enduits d'un crépi jaune, présentent quelques éléments en grès jaune de Flonheim.

Le rez-de-chaussée comprend l'antichambre avec l'escalier principal accessible par le hall d'entrée, autour de laquelle s'agencent le salon, la salle à manger, la salle de séjour et le cabinet de travail. La cuisine et une entrée de service sont situées dans l'aile. La salle du petit déjeuner, les chambres des fils et la chambre à coucher des parents sont disposées autour d'un grand hall au premier étage. La salle de bains et la garde-robe se trouvent dans l'étage mansardé de l'aile.

429 [1912: 29]

La villa Karlsbrunn de Bad Nauheim est l'œuvre de l'architecte Leonh. Kraft. Conçue comme maison de notable, cette pittoresque villa de trois étages, fut construite en six mois pour la somme de 60 000 marks, mobilier compris. Un large avant-corps de deux étages, orné en son centre d'une saillie arrondie,

slightly projecting oriel extending from the upper floor and ending above the roof line. The fronts are faced with terranova plaster with sandstone articulations. The broken roof has dormers and is covered with flat red tile.

On the ground floor are the lobby leading to the hall with the open main staircase, the study and boudoir, the dining room leading to the loggia, the kitchen and its side rooms as well as the side stairs. The owner's bedroom and cloak—room are located on the upper floor, as are the sitting—room, dressing—room with bath, a second bath and the children's rooms.

427 [1912: 15]

The villa—like Fischer house in Siegen in Westphalia (Gierbergstrasse 17) was constructed in about 17 months according to the plans of the architect G. Metzendorf. The ground floor has a covered entry hall at the front of the house and a veranda at the rear which is finished off by an open balcony located in front of a loggia. At the upper part of the front façade, which is covered by the roof, are two bay windows located under the projecting gable. A middle erection at the side front is crowned by a curbed gable. The visible masonry of the basement is of slate with white penciling. The upper storey has half—timbering with hung shingles stained brown.

The main hall on the ground floor has a ceiling of wooden beams and leads to the open staircase. The drawing—room, sitting—room, dinging room—which leads out onto the veranda—kitchen and its side rooms are also located on the ground floor. Leading from the hall on the upper floor are the bedrooms connected to the loggia, the dressing—room, the bath, the daughter's room and two guest rooms.

428 [1912: 16]

Situated above elevated terraces and surrounded by a garden, the Gontermann house in Siegen was designed by the architect Gg. Metzendorf and built in approximately 16 months. In the middle of the garden front, above the massive rough—hewn walls of the terrace with its solid balustrade, is an open hall lined with Jonic columns. It has open stairs and is covered by a balcony. The hall is flanked by corner projections with Jonic pilasters. A middle erection rises above the roof line and is topped by a shaped gable. A semi—circular porch containing the entrance is located at the other side of the house. The two—storey house with an overhanging slate roof has a one—storey kitchen wing with an attic storey and a roof with broken lines. The fronts are faced with a mixture of yellow sandstone from Flonheim and plaster of the same colour.

The entrance leads to the ground floor hall with an open staircase. Surrounding the hall are the drawing—room, the dining room, the sitting—room, and the study. The kitchen annexe has its own entrance. The upper floor contains a spacious entry room with a brakfast—niche, the son's rooms, the parents's bedroom and, on the attic floor of the annexe, dressing— room and bath.

429 [1912: 29]

The three—story Villa Darlsbrunn in Bad Nauheim has been built in a particularly picturesque manner based on the design of the architect Leonh. Kraft, member of the Association of German Architects. Construction of the doctor's elegant residence occupied approximately 6 months and cost 60,000 Marks, includ-

geschlossen ist. An der Eingangsfront erhebt sich ein breites, durch zwei Geschosse gehendes Risalit, in dessen Mitte ein halbrunder Vorbau hervorspringt. Im zweiten Obergeschoß sind über den Ecken der Front runde turmartige Erker ausgekragt; das Dach ist abgewalmt. Der Sockel besteht aus Wetterauquarzit, die Stufen der äußeren Terrassentreppen sind aus Vogelsberger Basalt gebildet, die Fensterbänke aus gelbweißem Sandstein. Die Flächen der Fronten sind mit feinkörnigem, blaugrauem Porphyrputz versehen. Das Dach zeigt eine Eindeckung mit Mühlacker Segmentbiberschwänzen. Die Ecktürme und der Eingangsvorbau sind mit Kupfer gedeckt; die Fenster weiß gestrichen und die Terrassen mit roten Steinzeugplatten gedeckt. Auf der Ostfront des Hauses befindet sich ein Glasmosaik von Puhl & Wagner und im Eßzimmer ein Wandbrunnen von Prof. Läuger.

Die durch zwei Geschosse geführte Halle im Erdgeschoß, der ein Windfang vorausgeht, soll als Ergänzung des anschließenden Wartezimmers dienen und enthält die frei aufsteigende Treppe. Außerdem liegen im Erdgeschoß das Sprech- und Untersuchungszimmer sowie das Speisezimmer mit Anrichte und Aufzug. Das erste und zweite Obergeschoß enthalten Wohnzimmer, Salon, Schlafzimmer, Arbeits-, Fremden- und Mädchenzimmer sowie das Bad. Küche, Spülküche, Bügelstube, Heizraum und mehrere Wirtschaftsräume sind im Keller untergebracht.

430 [1912: 33]

Das durch mehrfache malerische Gruppierung belebte, zweigeschossige, freistehende Einfamilienhaus Botzong in Heidelberg-Neuenheim, Bergstraße 107, ein Werk des Architekten E. Th. Merz, ist im Laufe eines Sommers errichtet und hat 25 000 Mark Baukosten verursacht.

Die an beiden Straßenfluchten gelegene Ecke des Hauses ist durch einen, durch beide Geschosse geführten, im Obergeschoß eine Altane mit offener Säulenhalle tragenden Vorbau ausgezeichnet. Der seitwärts liegende Hauseingang ist mit einer überdachten Vorhalle überbaut. Das übertretende, abgewalmte Hauptdach wird durch größere Dachfenster unterbrochen und ist mit Biberschwänzen eingedeckt. Sockel und Gliederungen der Fronten bestehen aus weißem Sandstein, die Flächen haben Verputz erhalten.

Das Erdgeschoß enthält, von einer Diele mit freiliegender Treppe zugänglich, das Empfangs- und das Wohnzimmer, außerdem die Küche. Im Obergeschoß sind weitere Zimmer und das Bad angeordnet.

431 [1912: 23]

Das Geschäftshaus Diehl in Köln a. Rh., bildet einen Eckbau, an der Hohestraße und der Minoritenstraße gelegen, nach dem Richartzplatz durchgehend. Der Entwurf ist von dem Architekten Müller-Erkelenz aufgestellt. Die Fassadenbildung entspricht der inneren einheitlichen Bestimmung des Gebäudes als Geschäftshaus. Das Erdgeschoß zeigt außer den Eingängen breite Schaufenster; die Fenster des ersten und zweiten Obergeschosses gruppiert und der Höhe nach zusammengezogen, schließen nach oben im flachen Bogen und werden von Pfeilern eingefaßt, die durch sämtliche Geschosse geführt sind. Der runde Eckbau ist mit Figuren geschmückt, hat über dem ersten Obergeschoß einen umlaufenden Balkon aufzuweisen und wird durch einen kuppelförmig überdeckten, hinter einer Galerie aufsteigenden Turmaufsatz bekrönt. An der Fassade nach der Hohestraße hin springen über dem Erdgeschoß zwei polygonale Erkerausbauten vor, die im ersten Obergeschoß durch einen Balkon verbunden sind, im dritten Obergeschoß eine Loggia zwischen sich einschließen und über den Dachlinien mit Kuppeldächern endigen. Der Erkerausbau an der anderen, sich der vorigen anschließenden Fassade geht durch das erste und zweite Obergeschoß und trägt eine Altane.

Die Fassaden sind in Werksteinen verblendet; das Dach ist mit Schiefer eingedeckt und wird durch eine Anzahl Dachluken unterbrochen.

se dégage de la façade principale. Deux tourelles d'angle saillissent de part et d'autre de la façade du deuxième étage. Le socle est réalisé en quartzite, les marches du perron sont en basalte de Vogelsberg, les rebords des fenêtres en grès crème. Les murs de façade sont enduits d'un crépi de porphyre bleu gris à grains fins. Le toit en croupe est recouvert de tuiles plates de Mühlacker. Les tourelles ainsi que le porche ont reçu une toiture en cuivre. Les fenêtres sont peintes en blanc, les terrasses sont revêtues de dalles de grès rouge. La façade orientale est assortie d'une mosaïque de verre exécutée par Puhl & Wagner, la salle à manger présente une fontaine murale réalisée par le professeur Läuger.

Précédé d'un tambour, le hall du rez-de-chaussée qui s'élève sur deux étages, est prévu comme complément de la salle d'attente attenante et comprend l'escalier. Au rez-de-chaussée sont aménagés le cabinet du médecin et la salle de consultation ainsi que la salle à manger, l'office et l'ascenseur. La salle de séjour, le salon, les chambres à coucher, le cabinet de travail, la chambre d'amis, la chambre des domestiques ainsi que la salle de bains sont installés aux premier et deuxième étages. La cuisine, la dépense, la lingerie, la chaufferie ainsi que d'autres pièces de service se trouvent au sous-sol.

430 [1912: 33]

La propriété Botzong, construction dégagée de deux étages, située à Heidelberg-Neuenheim, Bergstraße 107, fut conçue par l'architecte E. Th. Merz. Cette pittoresque maison, de composition asymétrique, fut construite en l'espace d'un été pour la somme de 25 000 marks. L'emplacement de la maison, à l'angle de deux rues, est souligné par une avancée cornière de la façade, supportant une loggia ornée de colonnes au premier étage. L'entrée, placée sur une façade latérale, est assortie d'un porche. Le toit en croupe saillant, percé de grosses fenêtres, est recouvert de tuiles plates. Le socle ainsi que les ornements de la façade sont en grès blanc, les murs extérieurs présentent un crépi.

Au rez-de-chaussée sont aménagés le salon, la salle de séjour et la cuisine accessibles par l'antichambre comprenant l'escalier. Le premier étage abrite d'autres pièces ainsi que la salle de bains.

431 [1912: 23]

Œuvre de l'architecte Müller-Erkelenz, l'immeuble Diehl de Cologne donne sur les Hohestraße, Minoritenstraße et la Richartzplatz. La composition de la façade atteste de la vocation commerciale des lieux. La façade du rez-de-chaussée est percée par les larges ouvertures des devantures et des entrées. Les fenêtres groupées et régulièrement alignées des deux étages inférieurs forment des ensembles se terminant en arc surbaissé. Des pilastres s'élevant sur toute la hauteur de la façade encadrent les fenêtres. La tour d'angle, ornée de sculptures et ceinte d'un balcon saillant circulaire au niveau du premier étage, est surmontée d'une tourelle en coupole. La façade donnant sur la Hohestraße est assortie, au-dessus du rez-de-chaussée, de deux avancées polygonales, reliées par un balcon au niveau du premier étage, enchâssant une loggia au troisième étage et coiffées de toits en coupole. L'avant-corps de la façade contiguë monte sur deux étages et est couronné d'un balcon.

Les murs de façade sont revêtus de pierres de taille. Le toit recouvert d'ardoises présente de nombreuses lucarnes.

ing the interior furnishings. A broad projection at the entrance front runs the height of two storeys, in the middle of which is a protruding semi-circular porch. Round, turret-like bays decorate the corners of the front at the second storey; the roof is hipped. The socle consists of quartzite, the steps of the outer terrace are of basalt from Vogelsberg, and the window sills are of light-yellow sandstone. The surface of the fronts is covered with finegrained, blue-grey porphyric plaster. The roof is covered with segmental red tile from Mühlacker. The corner turrets and the entry porch are roofed with copper. The windows are painted white, and the terraces are covered with red stoneware tile. The east side of the house is decorated by a glass mosaic from Puhl & Wagner, and there is a wall-fixed fountain in the dining room.

The ground floor entry hall, which extends to the height of two storeys and is preceded by a draught lobby, was designed to complement the adjacent waiting-room. An open staircase is also located here. The ground floor also contains the office room and the examination room, as well as the dining room, pantry, and lift. The first and second floors contain sitting-rooms, a drawing-room, bedrooms, a study, a guest room, the maid's room and the bath. The kitchen, laundry room, ironing closet, heating room and other service rooms are located in the basement.

430 [1912: 33]

The one-family house in Heidelberg Neuenheim (Bergstrasse 107) shows in its design a multiple grouping of picturesque architectural elements. The two-storey residence is the work of the architect E. Th. Merz and was built in the course of a summer at a cost of 25,000 Marks.

The corner of the house aligned with the road has a projecting structure running the height of both storeys and culminating in an open columnated gallery. The house entrance at the side has a covered porch. The overhanging hipped roof has large roof windows and is covered with flat red tile. The socle and façade articulations are of white sandstone, the other surfaces are plastered.

The entry hall on the ground floor has an open staircase and leads to the drawing-room and the sitting-room, as well as to the kitchen. Other rooms are located on the upper floor, including the bath.

431 [1912: 23]

The Diehl office building in Cologne, a corner edifice located at Hohestrasse and Minoritenstrasse and bordering Richartplatz, was designed by the architect Müller-Erkelenz. The façade of the building reflects the unified purpose of its interior as a business establishment. The frontage at the ground level has, besides the entryways, rows of broad shop windows; the grouped windows of the first and second storeys, which are divided by pilasters running the height of the façade , are vertical and culminate at the top in flat arches. The round corner structure is ornamented with sculptured figures and has a balcony running around it between the first and second storeys. The structure is crowned by a domed turret with an encompassing gallery. The front facing the Hohestrasse has two polygonal bays, connected to each other at the first floor by a balcony, which flank a third-floor loggia and culminate above the roof moulding with dome-shaped roofs. The bay projection on the adjoining frontage extends through the first and second storey and supports a balcony.

The façades are faced with ashlar; the roof is covered with slate and has a number of windows.

Das ausschließlich Verkaufszwecken gewidmete Geschäftshaus Gebr. Alsberg in Hagen i. W., Elberfelderstraße 14, läßt diese Bestimmung bereits in dem einheitlichen Aufbau der Fassade erkennen. Der Entwurf rührt von dem Architekten Fritz Niebel her; die Bauzeit betrug 6 Monate, die Baukosten beliefen sich auf 400 000 Mark. Die Fassade ist im Erdgeschoß sowie dem ersten und zweiten Obergeschoß durch vorspringende, durchgehende Pfeiler gegliedert, welche die unteren Schaufenster und die oberen, mehrfach geteilten Gruppenfenster zwischen sich einschließen. Das dritte Obergeschoß enthält ebenfalls Fenstergruppen, die von dem Dachgesims und einer Brüstung überragt werden, hinter der sich das zurückgesetzte Dachgeschoß mit rundbogig abgeschlossenen Fenstern erhebt. Die Fassade ist samt den Figuren an den Pfeilern über dem Erdgeschoß in gelblichem Sandstein ausgeführt; das Dach ist mit Hohlziegeln eingedeckt.

Das Erdgeschoß enthält eine seitliche Durchfahrt zum Hof mit nebenliegender Treppe und einen großen, nur durch Pfeiler geteilten Ladenraum. An der Hoffront liegt die Haupttreppe, einen Personenaufzug umschließend, die Nebentreppe und ein Lastenaufzug. Die ungeteilten Ladenräume im ersten und zweiten Obergeschoß schließen einen mittleren Lichthof ein und sind durch Treppen und Aufzüge mit den unteren Stockwerken verbunden. Im Kellergeschoß sind die Lagerräume untergebracht, neben denen sich Gänge hinziehen, die zu dem Koch- und Heizraum, der Garderobe und den Bureauräumen führen. Sämtliche Trägerkonstruktionen sind in Eisenbeton hergestellt.

La façade, traitée de façon régulière, de l'immeuble des frères Alsberg à Hagen, Elberfeldstraße 14, correspond parfaitement à la vocation strictement commerciale de cet édifice. Conçu par l'architecte Fritz Niebel, le bâtiment fut construit en six mois pour la somme de 400 000 marks. La façade est rythmée par des piliers saillants, montant de fond jusqu'au deuxième étage, encadrant ainsi les devantures inférieures et les fenêtres à meneaux des niveaux supérieurs. Le troisième étage présente des ouvertures identiques, surmontées par une corniche et un entablement derrière lequel s'élève l'étage des combles assorti de fenêtres cintrées. Les murs de façade ainsi que les sculptures ornant les piliers sont réalisées en grès jaunâtre. Le toit est recouvert de tuiles creuses.

Le rez-de-chaussée comprend un passage latéral donnant sur la cour ainsi qu'un escalier contigu et une grande surface commerciale simplement divisée par une ordonnance de piliers. Le grand escalier avec l'ascenseur, l'escalier de service et un monte-charge sont situés côté cour. Les surfaces commerciales non-cloisonnées du premier et deuxième étage sont percées en leur centre par une cour à toiture de verre. Escaliers et ascenseurs assurent la communication avec les étages inférieurs. Au sous-sol sont installés les entrepôts. Des couloirs conduisent à la cuisine, à la chaufferie, au vestiaire et à des bureaux. L'ossature du bâtiment est en béton armé.

The commercial building in Hagen in Westphalia (Elberfelderstrasse 47) is completely devoted to sales purposes, which is reflected in the unified style of its façade. The design was drafted by the architect Fritz Niebel, with construction occupying 6 months and costing 400,000 Marks. The façade is articulated by pilasters extending from the ground to the third storey which frame the ground floor shop windows and the windows of the upper storey, which are further divided by narrower pilasters. The third storey façade is also broken up by groups of windows placed under the roof cornice and parapet, behind which lies the recessed attic storey with windows framed in round arches. The entire façade, including the sculptured figures on the pilasters, is of yellow sandstone; the roof is covered with wooden tiles.

The ground floor contains a side carriageway leading to the rear courtyard, an adjacent stairway, and a large sales room divided only by rows of pillars. At the courtyard side of the building are the principal staircase, which encompasses the lift, a side staircase, and a goods lift. The open sales rooms on the first and second floors are situated round a central patio and connected to the lower floors by means of lifts and stairways. Store rooms are located in the basement, from which corridors lead to the boiler and heating rooms, the cloak—room and offices. The supporting structural framework is made entirely of reinforced concrete.

Das dreistöckige Gebäude des Café Palant in Köln a. Rh., Hohestraße, Ecke Minoritenstraße, in der Fassade von Architekt Philipp Fritz, in den Grundrissen von Architekt Rob. Perthel entworfen und unter Bauleitung des letzteren in etwa 8 Monaten ausgeführt, hat rund 250 000 Mark an Baukosten verursacht. Im Erdgeschoß und ersten Obergeschoß sind breite Schaufensteröffnungen zwischen durchgehenden Pfeilern angelegt; im zweiten Obergeschoß zeigen sich mehrfach geteilte Fenstergruppen. Auf der Dachfläche erheben sich eine Anzahl Fensteraufbauten. Die Fassaden sind aus weißem Mainsandstein hergestellt; das Dach ist mit Moselschiefer eingedeckt. Die drei Figurengruppen an der Fassade rühren von Bildhauer Schreiner her, die musizierenden Putten an den Schlußsteinen von Bildhauer Rothe. Das Cafélokal im Erdgeschoß hat an den Pfeilerköpfen schmückende Reliefs erhalten.

Das Erdgeschoß und der überdachte Hof, sowie das ganze erste Obergeschoß dienen für Zwecke des Cafés, das zweite Obergeschoß nimmt die Küchenanlage und die Wohnung auf. Die Geschosse sind durch eine Haupttreppe verbunden, ein Seitengang im Erdgeschoß führt zur Nebentreppe. Im Dachgeschoß und im Keller sind Räume für das Personal, die Wirtschaft, für Heizung und Toiletten vorgesehen. Die Schaufenster sind versenkbar, eine Ventilationsanlage mit vorgewärmter Luftzuführung und Ozonmischung ist eingerichtet.

L'immeuble de trois étages du café Palant à Cologne, situé à l'angle des rues Hohestraße et Minoritenstraße, fut construit en huit mois pour la somme de 250 000 marks. Les façades sont l'œuvre de l'architecte Philipp Fritz, les plans furent exécutés par l'architecte Rob. Perthel à qui fut confiée la conduite des travaux. De larges baies flanquées de piliers percent la façade du rez-de-chaussée et du premier étage. Le deuxième étage présente des fenêtres à meneaux. Les murs extérieurs sont revêtus de grès blanc de la vallée du Main. Le toit mansardé porte une toiture d'ardoises de la Moselle. Les trois motifs sculptés de la façade furent réalisés par le sculpteur Schreiner, les angelots musiciens ornant les clés de voûte sont du sculpteur Rothe. Les chapiteaux des piliers offrent des reliefs ornementaux.

Le rez-de-chaussée, la cour ouverte ainsi que la surface du premier étage sont occupés par le café. Le deuxième étage abrite les cuisines et un logement. Un grand escalier ainsi qu'un escalier de service auquel on accède par le couloir latéral du rez-de-chaussée assurent la communication entre les étages. L'étage des combles et le sous-sol comprennent les pièces destinées au personnel, les dépendances du café, la chaufferie et les cabinets d'aisance. Le café est équipé de baies escamotables et d'un système de ventilation à air chaud mélangé à de l'ozone.

The three—storey Café Palant in Cologne (corner of Hohestrasse – Minoritenstrasse), whose façade was designed by the architect Philipp Fritz and ground plan by the architect Rob. Perthel, was constructed under the supervision of the latter in about 8 months, with costs running to approximately 250,000 Marks. Broad showcase windows have been placed at the ground floor and first storey between continuous pillars. At the second storey are groups of multiple windows, and a number of windowed superstructures have been placed in the lower part of the roof. The façades are of white Main sandstone; the roof is covered with slate from the Mosel region. The three groups of figures on the façade are the work of the sculptor Schreiner, the music—making puttons at the keystones are by the sculptor Rothe. The capitals of the pillars in the coffee—house are ornamented with reliefs.

The ground floor and the covered courtyard, as well as the entire first floor are occupied by café rooms. On the second floor are the kitchen facilities and the living quarters. All floors are connected by a main staircase; a side entrance at the ground level leads to the side stairs. The attic storey and basement contain rooms for the staff, service and heating rooms, and public conveniences. The showcase windows can be dropped; a system of ventilation with pre—warmed air intake and ozone supply has also been installed.

Das Geschäftshaus „Zeilpalast" in Frankfurt a. M., Zeil-, Ecke Liebfrauenstraße, ist nach dem Entwurfe der Architekten Rindsfüßer und Kühn, in einer Bauzeit von etwa 9 Monaten mit einem Kostenaufwand von 600 000 Mark errichtet. Das Gebäude bildet einen fünfgeschossigen Eckbau mit drei freiliegenden Fronten und abgerundeten Ecken. Das Erdgeschoß enthält Schaufensteröffnungen; die oberen vier Geschosse sind mittelst durchgehender Pfeiler gegliedert, welche die gruppierten Fenster zwischen sich einschließen. Das steile, überhängende, abgewalmte Dach trägt Dachaufbauten mit Fenstern und zeigt über der First einen viereckigen Aufbau, den ein offenes mit einer Kuppel überdecktes Türmchen bekrönt. Die Fassaden sind im Erdgeschoß mit keramischen Platten aus der Großherzogl. Manufaktur zu Darmstadt verblen-

L'immeuble francfortois „Zeilpalast" situé à l'angle des rues Zeil et Liebfrauenstraße, fut construit sur les plans des architectes Rindsfüßer et Kühn. Les travaux menés à bien en neuf mois revinrent à 600 000 marks. Cet immeuble d'angle de cinq étages offre trois façades dégagées. La façade du rez-de-chaussée est percée de devantures. Des piliers continus à tous les étages encadrent des fenêtres groupées. Le toit en croupe pentu et saillant présente des fenêtres mansardées. Un chapiteau quadrangulaire, surmonté d'une tourelle coiffée d'une coupole, se dresse sur le faîte du toit. Les murs de façade sont revêtus, au rez-de-chaussée, de dalles de céramique de la manufacture de Darmstadt. Les armatures des vitrines et des devantures sont en bronze. Les murs de façade sont en

The commercial building "Zeilpalast" in Frankfurt—on—Main (corner of Liebfrauenstrasse) was designed by the architects Rindsfüsser and Kühn and constructed in approximately 9 months at a cost of 600,000 Marks. The five—storey corner structure has three exposed fronts and rounded corners. Shop windows are placed at the ground floor, the upper storeys are articulated by continuous pilasters between which are arranged groups of windows. The steep, overhanging hipped roof has windowed superstructures and a square erection at its ridge, upon which an open domed tower has been placed. The ground floor façade is covered with ceramic tile from the Grand—Ducal Ceramic Works at Darmstadt. Shop windows and dis-

det; Schaufenster und Schaukästen sind in Bronze hergestellt. Die oberen vier Geschosse der Fassaden sind in gelbweißem, geflammtem Pfälzer Sandstein ausgeführt. Das Dach ist mit grünlich patinierten Ziegeln eingedeckt. Die Modelle der Bildhauerarbeiten an der Fassade rührten von Bildhauer Ohly her.

Das ganze Haus dient als Geschäftshaus und ist einschließlich der Erdgeschoßpfeiler und des Daches in Eisenbeton konstruiert. Eingangsflur, Vestibül und Treppenhaus sind mit Marmor bekleidet. Im Erdgeschoß befinden sich Ladenlokale und der zur Stockwerkstreppe und den Aufzügen führende Flurgang; die oberen Geschosse enthalten Kontorräume, die sich um einen Lichthof gruppieren.

435 [1912; 25]

Der im Laufe eines Jahres zur Ausführung gekommene Westflügel des Verwaltungsgebäudes Siemens & Halske A.-G. in Charlottenburg, Nonnendamm-Allee, ist in der Fassade von Architekt

grès crème flammé du Palatinat. Le toit est recouvert de tuiles verdâtres patinées. Les modèles des décors sculptés furent exécutés par le sculpteur Ohly.

L'immeuble, construit uniquement à des fins commerciales, est réalisé en béton armé, y compris le toit et les piliers du rez-de-chaussée. Les murs du couloir d'entrée, du vestibule ainsi que de la cage d'escalier sont parés de marbre. Le rez-de-chaussée est occupé par des commerces et par le couloir conduisant à l'escalier et aux ascenseurs. Des bureaux, agencés autour d'une cour vitrée, sont installés dans les étages supérieurs.

435 [1912; 25]

L'aile occidentale du bâtiment administratif de la société berlinoise Siemens & Halske, située à Charlottenburg sur la Nonnendamm-Allee, fut construite en une année. Les plans furent exécutés par

play cases are of bronze. The upper four storeys of façades are covered with yellow—white mottled sandstone from the Palatinate, and the roof is covered with green pantiles. The façade sculptures were designed by the sculptor Ohly.

The entire building is used for commercial purposes. Its structural framework, including the ground floor pillars and roof, is of reinforced concrete. The entry hall, vestibule and staircase are panelled in marble. The ground floor contains shops and a corridor leading to the stairway and lifts; the upper floors have offices grouped around a patio.

435 [1912; 25]

Erected in the course of one year, the west wing of the Siemens & Halske administration building in the Charlottenburg district of Berlin (Nonnendamm Allee) is the work of the architects Fr. Blume, who

Gesamtansicht   Vue d'ensemble   Overall View

Fassadendetail   Détail de la façade   Detail of Façade

Vestibül   Vestibule   Vestibule

Fr. Blume, in den Grundrissen von Architekt, Regierungsbaumeister Janisch entworfen. Die im Erdgeschoß mit flachbogig überdeckten Fenstern versehene, in den drei Obergeschossen mittels durchgehender Pfeiler gegliederte, mit einem Mittelrisalit ausgestattete und durch Eckrisalite begrenzte Fassade wird von einem gebrochenen, eine Reihe Dachfenster tragenden Dache überdeckt. Dem Haupteingang im Mittelrisalit ist eine offene, einen Balkon tragende Säulenhalle vorgelegt. Die Fassade ist mit mattroten Freienwalder Verblendziegeln und mit Gliederungen in sächsischem Sandstein hergestellt. Das Dach ist mit Falzziegeln eingedeckt.

Der langgestreckte Grundriß, einerseits und im Mittelbau mit Flügelbauten versehen, enthält im Erdgeschoß die Haupttreppe, zwei Nebentreppen und Aufzüge, sowie eine größere Anzahl an einen durchgehenden Flurgang beiderseits aufgereihte Geschäfts-

l'architecte Janisch, les façades sont l'œuvre de l'architecte Fr. Blume. La façade s'organise autour d'une avancée centrale et de deux avant-corps d'angle. Les ouvertures du rez-de-chaussée présentent des arcs surbaissés, celles des étages supérieurs sont flanquées de piliers continus. L'entrée principale, située dans l'avant-corps central, est assortie d'un porche ouvert dont les colonnes portent un balcon. Les murs extérieurs sont parés de briques rouge mat de Freienwald, les ornements sont en grès de Saxe. Le toit mansard est percé des fenêtres et porte une couverture de tuiles à emboîtement.

Le corps de bâtiment, assorti d'une aile latérale et d'une aile médiane, comprend, au rez-de-chaussée, le grand escalier, deux escaliers secondaires, des ascenseurs ainsi que des salles et des bureaux, amé-

designed the façade, and the government architect Fr. Blume, who drafted the ground plan. The façade has straight—lined windows at the ground level, is divided by pilasters continuing from the first to third storeys, and is articulated by slightly projecting erections at its middle and at both corners. The roof has a broken line and supports rows of dormers. The main entrance in the middle erection is fronted by a porch with columns supporting an overhead balcony. The façade has a clay brick facing with dulled red colouring from Freienwald, and its articulations are of sandstone from Saxony.

The rectangular ground plan of the building, with wings in the middle and at one end, has on the ground floor the principal staircase, two side stairs and lifts, as well as a considerable number of business rooms, conference rooms and offices located to either side of the corridor running the entire length of the building. The

räume, Säle und Bureauzimmer. Der Tresor, ebenfalls im Erdgeschoß gelegen, ist von massiven Wänden umschlossen.

Das Vestibül zeigt die im Rundbogen überdeckten Eingänge zu den Fluchten der Haupttreppe.

436 [1912; 31]

Das durch mächtige Vertikalgliederung der Fassaden, als einheitlich einem Zwecke dienend, charakterisierte Kaufhaus S. Wronker & Co. in Frankfurt a. M., Zeil 33, 35, 37 und Holzgraben 6, 8, 10, ist vom Architekten B. D. A. Otto Engler entworfen und in zwei Bauabschnitten für die Baukostensumme von rund 1 800 000 Mark zur Ausführung gekommen. Die Front an der Zeil zeigt fünf Geschosse und ein ausgebautes Dachgeschoß. Die vier unteren Geschosse sind mittelst durchgehender Pfeiler zu einer Einheit verbunden und werden durch ein starkes Gurtgesims nach oben abgeschlossen; das fünfte Geschoß ist gleichfalls durch Pfeiler zwischen den gruppierten Fenstern geteilt. Es folgt das mit seinen giebelbekrönten Aufbauten in die Dachfläche einschneidende Dachgeschoß. Die breiten Lichtöffnungen und Eingänge des Erdgeschosses sind im Korbbogen überdeckt; die Gruppenfenster der nächstfolgenden drei Obergeschosse zeigen in gebrochener Linie geformte Sturze. Das mittlere Hauptportal ist mit Figuren bekrönt; ebenso ist figürlicher Schmuck an den Pfeilern der Eckrisalite angebracht. Die Fassade am Holzgraben ist mehrfach durch Risalite gegliedert, von denen einige langgestreckte Fenster enthalten und mit gebrochenen Dachhauben und seitlich emporwachsenden Türmchen abschließen. Das mittelste Risalit trägt einen Giebel in geschwungenen Barockformen. Die Front an der Zeil ist mit Muschelkalkstein, die am Holzgraben mit Mainsandstein verblendet.

Sämtliche Geschosse enthalten je einen großen, nur durch Pfeilerstellungen geteilten Verkaufsraum; die Räume sind durch vier Treppen mit geraden Läufen und zwei gebogenen Treppen, außerdem durch eine Anzahl Aufzüge miteinander in Verbindung gesetzt. In der breiten Mittelachse der Räume bilden sich zwei bis zum fünften Geschoß durchgeführte, glasüberdeckte Höfe. Das Dachgeschoß enthält an der Zeil einen großen durchgehenden Lagerraum. Der Keller ist in zwei Geschossen angelegt; im oberen Geschoß sind Lagerräume, Garderoben, Räume für Transformatoren, Auszeichnen und Expedition, ferner eine Kantine, der Kühlraum und die Räume für Heizung und Kohlen angeordnet; das untere Kellergeschoß ist zur Anlage von Lagerräumen und Räumen für die Aufzugmaschinen benutzt, ein Teil ist nicht unterkellert geblieben. Decken und Stützen sind in Eisenbeton ausgeführt.

437 [1912; 100]

Das Geschäftshaus in Wien, Fleischmarkt 1 (Residenzpalast), nach dem Entwurfe des Dipl.-Architekten Arthur Baron errichtet, gliedert sich in zwei Hauptteile, in ein großes, dreifrontiges Eckhaus gegen die Rotenturmstraße und ein Mittelhaus gegen den Fleischmarkt; zwischen beiden liegt ein zur Beleuchtung der Treppen dienender Hof. Das Vestibül ist vom Fleischmarkt zugänglich und steht in Verbindung mit der halbrunden Haupttreppe, in deren Spindel ein Personenaufzug sich befindet. Der Gebäudeteil gegen die Rotenturmstraße umschließt wieder einen Hof, der zu einer, durch drei Geschosse gehende, glasbedeckten Halle ausgebaut ist. In den Souterraingeschossen sind Säle untergebracht, ein Theatersaal und ein Kinosaal.

Dem Erdgeschoß und den beiden folgenden Geschossen wurde ein aus Schmiedeeisen hergestelltes und im unteren Teile mit Bronze überzogenes Portal vorgelegt, welches zum Teil durch Pfeiler aus poliertem Granit unterbrochen wird. Die übrigen Geschosse erhielten eine keramische Verblendung der Fassade aus wetterbeständigen Kacheln. Die vertikalen Dachteile sind mit profiliertem Kupferblech überzogen. Außer den Nachbar- und Treppenhausmauern sind sämtliche Mauern in Eisenbetonpfeiler mit darüber

---

nagés de part et d'autre d'un long couloir. Le trésor, à l'abri derrière des murs massifs, est également installé au rez-de-chaussée.

Le vestibule offre des entrées en plein cintre donnant sur le grand escalier.

436 [1912; 31]

Caractérisé par l'ordonnance à colonnes de sa façade, le grand magasin francfortois S. Wronker & Co., Zeil 33, 35, 37, Holzgraben 6, 8, 10, fut conçu par l'architecte Otto Engler. Les travaux, qui se déroulèrent en deux phases, coûtèrent la somme de 1 800 000 marks. La façade sur le Zeil se compose de cinq étages et d'un étage mansardé. Les quatre étages inférieurs, verticalement divisés par des piliers montant de fond, forment une unité terminée par un cordon saillant. Le cinquième étage présente une composition identique. L'étage des combles est assorti de fenêtres mansardées à pignon. Le rez-de-chaussée est percé de larges ouvertures surbaissées. Les fenêtres groupées des trois étages supérieurs présentent des linteaux brisés. Le portail central ainsi que les piliers des avancées d'angle sont ornés de sculptures. La façade donnant sur le Holzgraben est ponctuée de nombreux avant-corps, certains troués par de longues et étroites fenêtres, coiffés de calottes brisées et bordés latéralement de tourelles. L'avant-corps central est couronné d'un pignon aux formes baroques. Côté Zeil, les murs de façade sont en coquillart, côté Holzgraben, ils sont revêtus de grès du Main.

Chaque étage comprend une grande salle de vente non-cloisonnée, divisée par une ordonnance de piliers. Quatre escaliers à volées droites, deux grands escaliers tournants ainsi que de nombreux ascenseurs assurent la communication entre les étages. Deux cours à toiture de verre percent les étages en leur centre et sur toute leur hauteur. Les combles donnant sur le Zeil servent de dépôt. Le sous-sol est aménagé sur deux niveaux. Le niveau supérieur est occupé par les magasins, les vestiaires, les locaux destinés aux transformateurs, à l'étiquetage et aux expéditions, ainsi qu'une cantine, la chambre froide, la chaufferie et le dépôt de combustibles. Le niveau inférieur est utilisé comme entrepôt et abrite également la machinerie. Le sous-sol ne s'étend que sous une partie de l'edifice. L'ossature intérieure est en béton armé.

437 [1912; 100]

L'immeuble (Residenzpalast) situé à Vienne, Fleischmarkt 1, fut réalisé sur les plans de l'architecte Arthur Baron. Il se compose de deux corps de bâtiment, l'un en angle présentant trois façades donnant sur la Rotenturmstraße et l'autre faisant face à la place Fleischmarkt. Une cour vitrée destinée à éclairer l'escalier relie les deux parties. Le vestibule accessible par la place Fleischmarkt, communique avec le grand escalier semi-circulaire, renfermant en son centre un ascenseur. Le bâtiment côté Rotenturmstraße comprend une cour vitrée montant sur trois étages. Les sous-sols sont occupés par une salle de théâtre et une salle de cinéma.

Un portail en fer forgé, paré de bronze dans sa partie inférieure et assorti de piliers de granit poli, s'élève du rez-de-chaussée au deuxième étage. Les murs de façade ont reçu un revêtement de carreaux de céramique traitée pour résister aux intempéries. Les versants verticaux du toit portent une couverture de tôle de cuivre. Hormis les murs mitoyens et ceux de la cage d'escalier, l'ensemble des murs se compose de piliers de béton armé supportant des sous-poutres transversales. Le toit de l'immeuble est en béton armé.

---

strong room is also located on the ground floor and enclosed by massive walls.

The vestibule has entrances framed in round arches which lead to the flight of stairs from the principal staircase.

436 [1912; 31]

The Wronker department Store in Frankfurt—on—Main (Zeil & Holzgraben) is characterised by the prominent vertical division of its façades, which highlights the singular function of the building. It was designed by the architect Otto Engler, member of the Association of German Architects, and completed in two stages of construction amounting to approximately 1,800,000 Marks. The Zeil frontage has five storeys and a roof storey. The four lower storeys are unified by a series of continuous pillars which culminate at a projecting stringcourse. The fifth storey is again articulated by pillars located between its window groupings. Above that follows the roof storey, which is punctuated with superstructures crowned by gables. The broad fenestration and entrances of the ground level are framed in basket arches; the groups of windows in the next three storeys have a broken line of curved lintels. The main portal in the middle is crowned with figures, and sculptured ornamentation is also to be seen at the corner projections. The Holzgraben façade is divided by multiple projections, some of which contain vertical windows and are finished with broken roof domes and lateral towers. The projection closest to the middle bears a gable shaped in a Baroque manner. The Zeil façade is covered with shell limestone, that facing the Holzgraben with Main sandstone.

Each floor contains an open sales hall divided only by an arrangement of pillars; the floors are connected by four straight stairs and two curved stairs, and, in addition, a number of lifts. At the broad middle axis of the second to fifth floors are continuous, glass—covered patios. The roof storey has a large connecting storage room at the Zeil side of the building. The basement consists of two levels. The upper level contains storage rooms, cloak—rooms, rooms for transformers, labelling, and forwarding, as well as the cafeteria, cooling chamber, and rooms for heating and coal. The lower level of the basement is used for storage and lift machinery; a portion of it has not been dug out. All supports and flooring are of reinforced concrete.

437 [1912; 100]

The commercial building in Vienna (Fleischmarkt 1), constructed according to the plans of the certified architect Arthur Baron, is divided into two main parts: a larger corner edifice with three exposed fronts on the Rotenturmstrasse, and a central building facing the Fleischmarkt. A courtyard is located between the two buildings so as to provide adequate lighting for the stairwell. The vestibule has its entrance at the Fleischmarkt and is connected to the semi—circular main staircase, with a lift in its newel. The structure on the Rotenturmstrasse again encompasses a courtyard, which expands into a three—storey, glass—covered hall. The basement contains various halls, a cinema and a theatre.

A portal of wrought iron with bronze furnishings on its lower half decorates the ground floor and the first two storeys. It is partially articulated by pillars of polished granite. The façades of the other storeys are faced with weather—resistant ceramic tiles. The vertical surfaces of the roof are covered with formed copper sheets. Apart from the neighboring walls and the stairwell, all walls are of reinforced concrete piers with joists at the top. The roof of the building is made of

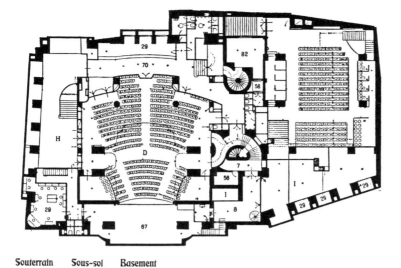

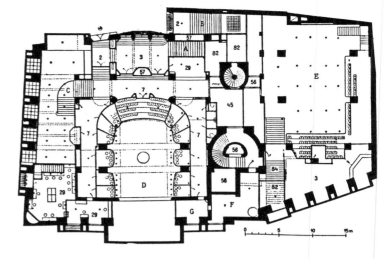

Souterrain   Sous-sol   Basement

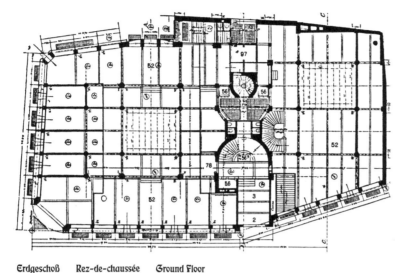

Erdgeschoß   Rez-de-chaussée   Ground Floor

Erklärungen zu den Grundrissen des Souterrains	Légende du plan du sous-sol	Key to (Plan of Stalls)
A Abgang zur Singspielhalle	A Accès à la salle de spectacle	A. Exit to Singspiel Hall
B Abgang zum Kinosaal	B Accès à la salle de cinéma	B. Exit to Cinema
C Abgang in das Souterrain	C Accès au sous-sol	C. Exit to Basement
D Singspielhalle	D Salle de spectacle	D. Singspiel Hall
E Kinosaal	E Salle de cinéma	E. Cinema
F Konversationszimmer	F Cabinet	F. Lounge
G Inspektionsarzt	G Médecin	G. Doctor's Room
H Speisesaal	H Salle de restaurant	H. Dining Hall
J Requisiten	J Accessoires	J. Stage Property

liegenden Unterzügen aufgelöst. Das Dach des Hauses ist in Eisenbeton konstruiert; die Dachräume dienen als Werkstätten und Ateliers. Es ist eine Niederdruckdampfheizung eingerichtet und außerdem eine elektrisch betriebene Ventilationsanlage.

Les pièces mansardées sont utilisées comme ateliers et comme salles de travail. L'édifice est équipé d'un chauffage à vapeur à basse pression ainsi que d'un système de ventilation électrique.

reinforced concrete; the rooms therein serve as workshops and ateliers. Low—pressure steam heating has been installed, as well as an electrically—driven ventilation system.

438 [1912; 37]

Von Gartenanlagen umgeben, bildet die zweistöckige Villa Bahls in Karlsruhe i. B., Moltkestraße 33, einen mehrfach gruppierten Eckbau. Oberbaurat Prof. Dr. H. Billing ist der Urheber des Entwurfs, der im Laufe eines Jahres für die Baukostensumme von 110 000 Mark zur Ausführung gebracht wurde. Das Eingangsportal öffnet sich in einem dem Erdgeschoß vorgelegten Anbau der Seitenfront, der mit einem Metalldach abschließt. Über dem Portal befindet sich, in einer Muschel stehend, die von den Bildhauern Gebr. Merger geschaffene Figur einer Flora. Die Kunstschmiedearbeiten sind hier von Fr. Lang ausgeführt. Der breit entwickelte Ausbau im Erdgeschoß einer Straßenfront trägt eine Altane, ebenso der halbrunde Ausbau der anderen Straßenfront. Noch andere Bauteile sind gleichfalls im Obergeschoß als Altane ausgebildet. Die Fronten sind mit Gliederungen in hellgelbem Pfälzer Sandstein ausgestattet, während die Flächen silbergrauen Terranovaputz zeigen. Auf den Steilflächen des gebrochenen, mit Schiefer eingedeckten Daches, unter dessen Dachgesims sich ein verzierter Fries hinzieht, erheben sich Aufbauten mit gruppierten oder vereinzelten Fenstern.

Im Erdgeschoß liegt eine geräumige Diele, in Verbindung mit dem Eingangsflur und der Stockwerkstreppe, außerdem sind hier der Salon, das Herrenzimmer, die Bibliothek, das Speisezimmer, die Küche und die Anrichte angeordnet. Das Obergeschoß enthält mehrere Wohnzimmer, das Schlafzimmer mit anstoßendem Ankleidezimmer und Bad, sowie das Billardzimmer.

438 [1912; 37]

La villa Bahls se dresse dans un jardin à Karlsruhe, Moltkestraße 33. Conçue par l'architecte prof. H. Billing, cette demeure asymétrique fut réalisée en l'espace d'une année pour la somme de 110 000 marks. L'entrée, sur une façade latérale, est abritée par un porche au toit métallique au-dessus duquel se trouve une sculpture de la déesse Flore, exécutée par les frères Merger, sculpteurs. Les ouvrages de fer forgé furent réalisés par Fr. Lang. Le large avant-corps se détachant au rez-de-chaussée de la façade sur rue est couronné d'une plate-forme. L'avancée arrondie de l'autre façade sur rue présente la même caractéristique et il en est de même pour les autres saillies. Les ornements des façades sont en grès jaune clair du Palatinat, les murs extérieurs sont enduits d'un crépi gris clair. Des fenêtres mansardées percent le brisis du toit en ardoises. Une frise ornementale court le long de la corniche.

Une grande antichambre communiquant avec le couloir d'entrée et l'escalier ainsi que le cabinet de travail de monsieur, la bibliothèque, la salle à manger, la cuisine et l'office sont installés au rez-de-chaussée. Le premier étage abrite deux salles de séjour, la chambre à coucher avec garde-robe et salle de bains attenantes, et la salle de billard.

438 [1912; 37]

Surrounded by gardens, the two—storey Bahls residence in Karlsruhe (Moltkestrasse 33) has a ground plan of multiple groupings designed by Chief Architect Professor Dr. H. Billing. Construction of the villa was completed within one year at a cost of 110,000 Marks. The entrance portal at the side front is located in a projecting structure covered by metal roofing. Above the portal is a sculptured figure of a flora standing in a shell, a work of the Merger Brothers. The wrought ironwork was created by Fr. Lang. The broad side structure at the ground level of the street front has a balcony on top, as does the semi—circular extension of the other street front. Other balconies are also located at the upper storey. The façades are articulated with light yellow sandstone from the Palatinate, and faced with silver—grey Terranova plaster. A ornamental frieze runs under the roof moulding, above which superstructures of individual or grouped windows have been placed in the lower part of the roof.

The ground floor contains a spacious hall connected to the entry hall and the stairs leading to the upper floor; the drawing—room, study, library, dining—room, kitchen and pantries are also located here. The upper floor has a number of sitting—rooms, the bedroom with adjoining dressing—room and bath, as well as a billiards room.

439 [1912: 38]

Jn bedeutenden Abmessungen zweistöckig, teilweise dreistöckig, erhebt sich die von Oberbaurat Prof. Dr. H. Billing in den Fassaden, von Architekt W. Vittali in den Grundrissen entworfene Doppelvilla in Karlsruhe i. B., Weberstraße 1 und 3. Die Bauzeit nahm ¾ Jahre in Anspruch, die Baukosten betrugen 240 000 Mark. Über der einen Ecke, die durch einen beide Geschosse umschließenden, flach vorspringenden Ausbau bereichert ist, erhebt sich ein drittes Geschoß; der anderen Ecke ist seitwärts ein als Altane endigender Ausbau mit anschließendem Hauseingang vorgelegt, über dem sich im dritten Geschoß eine Loggia öffnet. An einer Seitenfront springt ein Ausbau hervor, in dem der mit einer Vorhalle ausgezeichnete Hauseingang mündet. Auf den Steilflächen des gebrochenen Daches erheben sich im Rundbogen überwölbte Fensteraufbauten. Die Fenster beider Geschosse sind durch die verzierten Brüstungen zusammengezogen. Die Bekleidung der Frontwände besteht aus hellgelbem Pfälzer Sandstein. Das Dach mit seinen Fensteraufbauten ist mit Schiefer eingedeckt, während der pavillonartige Aufbau der einen Ecke ein Metalldach trägt. Die Bildhauerarbeiten fertigte Ad. Stadinger, die Kunstschlosserarbeiten E. Blum.

Beide Villen sind durch eine Brandmauer geschieden. Im Erdgeschoß befindet sich beiderseits eine Halle in Verbindung mit der Stockwerkstreppe, der Musiksalon, das Wohnzimmer, das Speisezimmer mit Ausgang nach einer Terrasse, die Küche mit Nebenräumen. Im Obergeschosse liegen, wieder um eine Halle gruppiert, die Schlafzimmer, sich nach Loggien öffnend, die Kinderzimmer, die Toilettenzimmer mit Bad und mehrere Wohnzimmer.

440 [1912: 39]

Die eine geschlossene Reihe bildenden, durch Brandmauern geschiedenen Einfamilienhäuser in Bern, Hallwylstraße 36–42, sind nach dem Entwurfe der Architekten F. u. H. Konitzer errichtet. Die Bauzeit nahm 8 Monate in Anspruch und die Baukosten für die Häuser Nr. 42, 40 und 38 betrugen je 33 000 Franks, für das Haus Nr. 36 50 000 Franks. Die im Aufbau zweistöckigen, teilweise dreistöckigen und mit ausgebautem Dachgeschoß versehenen Häuser sind an den Fronten in hellgelbem, rauhem Verputz hergestellt und mit blauem Schiefer eingedeckt. Das am Äußeren zur Ansicht kommende Holzwerk ist braunrot gefärbt. Die Fassaden sind mehrfach durch vom Boden aufgehende Vorsprünge belebt, die überdachte Altane tragen und öfter mit überkragten und abgeschopften, Dächer einschneidenden Giebeln abschließen. Die übertretenden Dächer sind mit einzelnen und gruppierten Fenstern ausgestattet.

439 [1912: 38]

Cette villa mitoyenne de deux voire trois étages présente des proportions importantes. Elle fut construite en l'espace de quinze mois pour une somme de 240 000 marks. Les façades et les plans sont respectivement l'œuvre des architectes H. Billing et W. Vitalli. Un des angles est assorti d'une avancée, haute de deux étages, au-dessus de laquelle s'élève un troisième étage. L'autre angle présente latéralement, contigu à l'entrée, un avant-corps couronné, au troisième étage, d'un balcon sur lequel s'ouvre une loggia. Une des entrées, située sur une façade latérale, est abritée par un porche. Des fenêtres mansardées cintrées percent le brisis du toit. Les fenêtres régulièrement alignées des deux étages sont séparées verticalement par des reliefs ornementaux. La façade principale a reçu un revêtement de grès crème du Palatinat. Le toit et les fenêtres mansardées sont recouverts d'ardoises. L'avant-corps cornier aux allures de pavillon est coiffé, quant à lui, d'un toit en métal. Les sculptures furent réalisées par Ad. Stadinger, E. Blum exécuta les ouvrages de serrurerie.

Un mur mitoyen sépare les deux villas. Au rez-de-chaussée de chaque demeure se trouvent une antichambre donnant sur l'escalier, le salon de musique, la salle de séjour, la salle à manger communiquant avec une terrasse, la cuisine et l'office. Les chambres à coucher avec loggia attenante, les chambres des enfants, la garde-robe, la salle de bains et des pieces de séjour sont agencées à l'étage, autour d'une antichambre.

440 [1912: 39]

Ces habitations individuelles juxtaposées, séparées par des murs mitoyens, situées à Berne, Hallwylstraße 36–42, furent conçues par les architectes F. & H. Konitzer. Les travaux de construction durèrent 8 mois. Les maisons aux no 42, 40 et 38 coûtèrent chacune 33 000 frcs, la maison au no 36 revint à 50 000 frcs. Les façades des habitations de deux voire trois étages, assorties de toits mansardés, sont revêtues d'un crépi grossier de couleur crème. Les toits portent une couverture d'ardoises bleues. Les boiseries apparentes ont reçu un badigeon rouge brun. Les façades présentent des avant-corps montant de fond, portant des balcons couverts et coiffés pour certains de pignons à croupe faîtière. Les toits saillants sont percés de fenêtres mansardées.

439 [1912: 38]

An edifice of notable proportions is the two–storey, pa2t.25ially three–storey apartment building in Karlsruhe (Weberstrasse 1 & 3). Construction of the building, whose façades were designed by Chief Architect Professor Dr. H. Billing and the ground plan drafted by the architect W. Vittali, occupied 15 months, with costs amounting to 240,000 Marks. A third storey rises above one corner containing a flat projection running the height of two storeys. To the side of the other corner is another projection ending with a balcony and a loggia set back at the third storey; an entrance to the house is located adjacent to this projection. At the other side of the house is a porched entrance located in an projecting structure. Dormer windows in round arches are located at the lower, steeper part of the roof. Ornamented aprons have been placed between the windows of the first and second stories. The walls of the front are faced with light–yellow sandstone from the Palatinate. The roof and dormers are covered with slate, whereas the pavilon–like superstructure at one corner has a metal roof. Sculptural work was done by Ad. Stadinger, the artistic locksmith's work by E. Blum.

Two residences are separated by a compartment wall. At each end of the ground floor is an entry hall connected to a stairway leading to the upper floor, a music salon, the sitting–room, the dining room leading out into the terrace, and the kitchen and pantries. On the upper floor, again placed around the central hall, are the bedrooms opening out onto loggias, the nursery, water–closet with bath and more sitting–rooms.

440 [1912: 39]

The self–contained group of terraced one–family houses—each separated from the other by a compartment wall—located in Bern (Hallwylstrasse 36–42) was designed by the architects F. and H. Konitzer. Construction occupied 8 months and the building costs of houses No. 42, 40 and 38 amounted to 33,000 Francs each, and 50,000 Francs for house No. 36. The fronts of the two–storey and three–storey houses with attic storeys are faced with rough plaster and their roofs are of slate. The exterior timbered surfaces have a rust–coloured stain. The fronts are articulated by a number of projections starting at ground level and ending with a covered balcony; many have projecting hipped gables cut into the roof. The overhanging roofs have separate as well as grouped windows.

Erdgeschoß Rez-de-chaussée Ground Floor
Obergeschoß Etage Upper Floor

Die Haupteingänge der Häuser führen aus den vor der Straßenfront sich hinziehenden Vorgärten zu den Dielen und den Stockwerkstreppen, an der Rückfront zu offenen Veranden. Sämtliche Häuser enthalten im Erdgeschoß Wohnzimmer, Eßzimmer und Küche im Anschluß an die Veranden; im Hause Nr. 36 ist außerdem noch ein Salon und ein Bureauzimmer vorhanden. Im Oberstock und im Dachstock liegen Schlafzimmer, Bad und weitere Wohnräume. Im Keller sind die Waschküchen und die Räume für Zentralheizung untergebracht.

L'accès aux entrées des maisons se fait par des jardins frontaux. Les entrées donnent sur un hall et sur la cage d'escalier. L'entrée postérieure débouche sur une véranda ouverte, attenante à la salle de séjour, à la salle à manger et à la cuisine. La maison située au no 36 de la rue comprend en outre un salon et un cabinet de travail. Au premier étage et sous les combles sont aménagées les chambres à coucher, la salle de bains et les pièces de séjour. La buanderie et la chaufferie sont au sous-sol.

A front garden extends along the street side of the houses. The main entrance of each house leads to an entry hall with stairs to the upper floor, and to an open veranda at the rear. A sitting–room is also located on the ground floor, as are a dining room and kitchen, the latter also leads to the veranda. House No. 6 also has a drawing–room and office room on the ground floor. The upper floor of all houses contains bedrooms, bath and other sitting–rooms. A laundry–room and rooms for central heating are located in the basements.

441 [1912: 42]

Die großzügig angelegte, mit künstlerischem Aufwand durchgebildete Sektkellerei Henkell & Co. in Biebrich a. Rh. ist nach dem aus einem engeren Wettbewerb hervorgegangenen Entwurfe des Architek-

441 [1912: 42]

Les bâtiments de la maison Henkell & Co, négociant en vins mousseux à Biebrich, furent réalisés en l'espace de deux années C'est à la suite d'un concours très serré que furent choisis les plans de

441 [1912: 42]

The Henkell & Co. champagne cellars in Biebrich–on–Rhine has been built on a generous scale and decorated in an artistic manner. Based on the design of the certified architect Professor

ten B. D. A. Professor P. Bonatz im Laufe von 2 Jahren zur Ausführung gekommen. Das Hauptgebäude, die Empfangshalle, den Konferenzsaal, den Empfangsraum, die privaten und technischen Bureauräume und die Eingänge zu den Kellern enthaltend, welche sämtlich in vornehmer schmuckvoller Ausstattung ausgeführt sind, zeigt in zwei Geschossen der Fassade eine Pfeilergliederung, die zusammengezogenen Fenster zwischen sich einschließend. Das mittlere Risalit der Hauptfront ist mit einem flachen Dreiecksgiebel bekrönt. Die Fronten sind mit deutschem Tra-

l'architecte prof. P. Bonatz. Les bâtiments forment un ensemble de grande envergure, aux ambitions artistiques très réussies. Le corps de logis abrite, sur deux étages, le hall d'accueil, la salle de conférences, la réception, les bureaux privés, les salles de travail et les accès aux caves. L'ensemble des pièces est aménagé avec beaucoup de raffinement. La façade présente une ordonnance à pilastres, encadrant des fenêtres régulièrement alignées. L'avant-corps central de la façade principale est coiffé d'un pignon en delta.

P. Bonatz, which won first prize in the demanding competition, construction was completed in the course of two years. The principal building contains the entrance hall, the conference hall, the reception room, private and technical offices and the entrances to the cellars, all of which are furnished in an elegant and tasteful style. The front of the principal building is articulated by pilasters running the height of the second storey, with vertical windows placed between them. The middle projection is crowned by a low-pitched straight gable. The façades are covered with

Gesamtansicht   Vue d'ensemble   General View

Große Halle mit der Freitreppe   Grand hall et escalier   Great Hall with Staircase

Eingang zur Empfangshalle   Accès au hall d'accueil
Entrance to Reception Hall

vertin aus Langensalza bekleidet. Decken und Stützen sind in Eisenbeton, teilweise in Marmor hergestellt; der Dachstuhl ist in Eisenkonstruktion ausgeführt, und das Dach ist mit Kupfer eingedeckt. Die an das Hauptgebäude anschließenden einstöckigen Flügelbauten sind zu Beamtenwohnungen eingerichtet und gleichfalls mit Kupfer eingedeckt. Der Ehrenhof ist an drei Seiten mit offenen gewölbten Säulenhallen umgeben, die sich vor dem Hauptgebäude und den beiden Flügelbauten erstrecken. Der Eingang zu großen, durch beide Geschosse geführten, mit einer umlaufenden Galerie und einer zu dieser emporführenden offenen Treppe ausgestatteten Empfangshalle ist im Korbbogen geschlossen. Die Bildhauerarbeiten sind von Prof. Behn geschaffen.

442, 443 [1912; 48, 49]

Die nach einheitlichem Plane angeordneten, symmetrisch den langgestreckten Sprudelhof und die Quellen mit Wandelhallen beiderseits umfassenden Neubauten der Badeanlage Bad Nauheim sind unter Oberleitung der Ministerial-Abteilung für Bauwesen in Darmstadt von der Neubaubehörde Bad Nauheim nach dem Gesamtentwurf des Architekten Bauinspektor Jost, unter Mitwirkung der Architekten Regierungsbaumeister von Heemskerck, Pfeiffer, Sehrt, Dogny, Petry, Hieronymi und Dr. Lipp im Verlaufe von 5

Les murs extérieurs portent un revêtement de travertin allemand. Les plafonds et les poutres maîtresses sont en béton armé ou en marbre. La charpente, réalisée en fer, soutient un toit recouvert de cuivre. Les ailes attenantes au corps de bâtiment, hautes d'un étage, sont occupées par les logements des employés. Elles offrent une toiture de cuivre. La cour d'honneur est ceinte, sur trois côtés, d'arcades assortissant les façades du corps de logis et des ailes. Le grand hall, accessible par une entrée surbaissée, monte sur deux niveaux. Une galerie circulaire, à laquelle conduit un grand escalier d'honneur, borde le hall. Les ouvrages sculptés furent exécutés par le professeur Behn.

442, 443 [1912; 48, 49]

Les bâtiments des établissements de bains de Bad-Nauheim furent construits par la ville de Nauheim, sous la direction du département ministériel à la construction de Darmstadt. Les plans furent exécutés par l'inspecteur du bâtiment Jost, en collaboration avec les architectes von Heemskerck, Pfeiffer, Sehrt, Dogny, Petry, Hieronymi et Lipp. Les travaux, qui durèrent cinq ans, coûtèrent la somme de 2 200 000 marks. Cet ensemble fut édifié autour d'une cour centrale agrémentée de sources jaillissantes.

German travertine. Ceilings and supports are of reinforced concrete, and partially clad in marble. The roof structure has an iron framework, with copper roofing. The one-storey wings to either side of the principal building are occupied by living quarters for public servants, and are also covered with copper. The Court of Honour is lined on three sides by a arched colonnade running in front of the principal building and the two side wings. The main entrance is framed in a basket arch and leads to the spacious entrance hall occupying both storeys, which is enclosed by a gallery on the upper floor. An open staircase leads to the gallery. The sculptured figures are the work of Professor Behn.

442, 443 [1912; 48, 49]

The new additions to the Bad Nauheim Baths have been symmetrically erected around both sides of the rectangular spa courtyard and its mineral springs in a unified design emphasized by a continuous colonnade. Based on the general plan of the municipal architect Jost, with assistance from the government architect von Heemskerck, and the architects Pfeiffer, Sehrt, Dogny, Petry, Hieronymi and Dr. Lipp, the five-year construction period was carried out under the auspices of the Head Direction of the Civil Con-

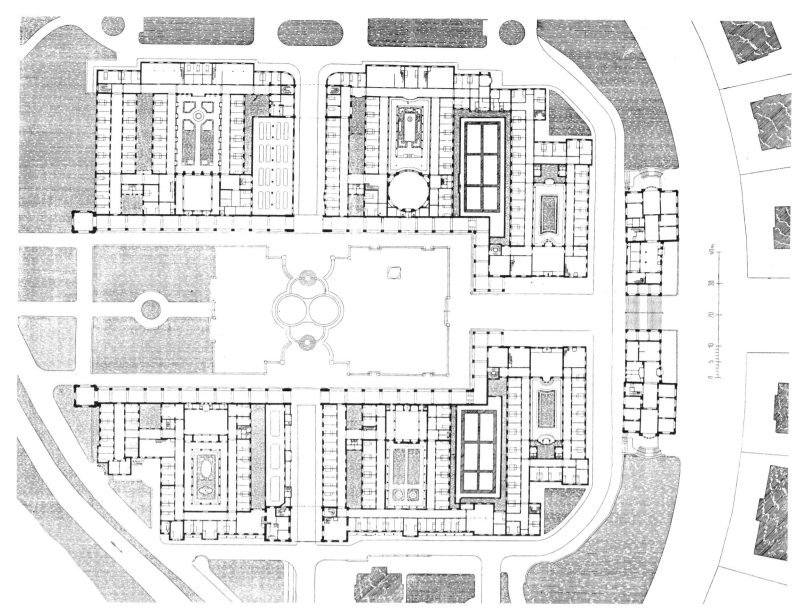

Jahren für die Kostensumme von rund 2 200 000 Mark zur Ausführung gekommen.

An dem von Hallen umgebenen Sprudelhof liegen 6 Badehäuser, in denen zusammen 265 Badewannen untergebracht sind. Jedes der Badehäuser umschließt einen reizvoll durchgebildeten inneren Schmuckhof, der in Verbindung mit einem Wartesaal steht und von den die Badezellen enthaltenden Flügelbauten begleitet ist. Die Außenfronten sämtlicher Baulichkeiten sind mit rauhem Verputz und Gliederungen aus Muschelkalkstein versehen. Die gebrochenen Dächer sind mit Ziegeln eingedeckt.

Der Schmuckhof des Badehauses 2 ist mit graublau glasierten Ziegeln und orangegelben Terrakotten verblendet. Wandplastik und Brunnen sind von Bildhauer Professor H. Jobst geschaffen. Auch das mächtige, von Seelöwenfiguren getragene Becken des Ernst-Ludwig-Sprudels ist nach dem Entwurfe des Professor H. Jobst ausgeführt.

Der Schmuckhof des Badehauses 6 zeigt plastische Arbeiten von Bildhauer Belz. Die Terrakottenfiguren und Ornamente stammen aus der Großherzogl. Keramischen Manufaktur in Darmstadt nach Modellen des Bildhauers Huber in Offenbach. Die Malerei in zwei Wartesälen ist von Professor Kleukens, eine der vier Fürstenzellen ist nach dem Entwurf von Professor Alb. Müller ausgeführt.

Die Badehäuser 4 und 5 sind je durch eine dem Erdgeschoß vorgelegte eine Altane tragende Bogenhalle, außerdem durch einen giebelbekrönten Dachaufbau, über dem sich ein Dachreitertürmchen erhebt, ausgezeichnet.

Die Badehäuser 6 und 7 (eine im Korbbogen überwölbte Straßenüberbauung einschließend) zeigen im zweiten Obergeschoß eine offene Säulenhalle.

Die Verwaltungsgebäude, der Bahnhofsallee gegenüber, bilden den querliegenden Abschluß der Badeanlage.

Six unités thermales, comprenant en tout 265 baignoires, donnent sur une cour bordée d'arcades. Chacune de ces unités thermales comprend une ravissante cour intérieure communiquant avec une salle d'attente contiguë aux ailes abritant les cabines de bains. Les murs de façade sont enduits d'un crépi et présentent des décors en coquillart. Les toits aux combles brisés sont recouverts d'ardoises.

La cour de l'unité thermale II offre un revêtement de tuiles vernies gris bleu et de terre cuite jaune orangé. Les sculptures murales ainsi que les fontaines sont l'œuvre du sculpteur H. Jobst. C'est à lui que l'on doit aussi la grande vasque supportée par des otaries de la source jaillissante Ernst-Ludwig.

La cour de l'unité VI présente des ouvrages façonnés par le sculpteur Belz. Les figures de terre cuite et les ornements furent réalisés par la manufacture de céramique de Darmstadt d'après les modèles du sculpteur Huber d'Offenbach. Les peintures de deux salles d'attente sont l'œuvre du professeur Kleukens, une des quatre cabines princières fut conçue par le professeur Alb. Müller.

Les unités thermales IV et V sont caractérisées par une avancée, au niveau du rez-de-chaussée, dont les arcades supportent un balcon et par un pignon couronnant un comble mansardé au-dessus duquel s'élève un lanterneau.

Les unités thermales VI et VII (comprenant un passage voûté) sont assorties, au deuxième étage, d'une saillie ouverte, pourvue de colonnes. Les combles des toits de ces unités sont partiellement brisés.

Les bâtiments administratifs, faisant face à l'allée de la gare, achèvent l'ensemble de par leur position perpendiculaire.

struction Ministry at Darmstadt by the Department of Civil Works in Bad Nauheim at a cost of approximately 2,220,000 Marks.

Behind the colonnade surrounding the spa's courtyard are 6 bath houses containing a total of 268 separate bathing tubs. Each bath house is built around a charmingly designed, ornamented courtyard which is connected to a waiting lobby and bordered by side wings containing the bathing cabins. The exterior façades of all buildings are faced with roughed plaster and articulations of shell limestone. The broken roofs are covered with clay tile.

The ornamental courtyard of bath house 2 is faced with grey—blue glazed tile and orange—yellow terracotta work. The wall ornamentation and the fountain are the work of the sculptor Professor H. Jobst, who also completed the mighty spring basin supported by sculptured sea lions.

The ornamental courtyard of bath house 6 shows plastic ornamentation completed by the sculptor Belz. The terracotta figures and ornaments were produced by the Grand—Ducal Ceramic Works at Darmstadt according to models supplied by the sculptor Huber of Offenbach. The murals decorating two waiting lobbys were created by Professor Kleukens, and one of the four princely bathing chambers was designed by Professor Alb. Müller.

Each of the bath houses 4 and 5 have at their fronts an arcade topped by a balcony, and in addition, a gabled roof erection with a ridge turret.

Bath houses 6 and 7 (which encompass a round—arched street covering) show an open terrace of columns at the second storey. The roofs of the houses are partially broken.

The administration building, located opposite the station boulevard, borders one end of the bathing complex.

Das vierstöckige, mit einem ausgebauten Dachgeschoß versehene Wohn- und Geschäftshaus C. Schirp in Köln a. Rh., Neumarkt 31, ist von Architekt B. D. A. Wilh. Kurth entworfen und im Laufe von 2 Jahren für die Baukostensumme von 330 000 Mark ausgeführt. Die Straßenfront zeigt im Erdgeschoß ein breites Schaufenster neben dem zu den oberen Wohnungen führenden Portal. Ein vorgekragter Erker durchsetzt die oberen drei Geschosse und trägt unter dem überhängenden, abgeschopften Giebel einen Loggienausbau. Die Fenstergruppe neben dem Erker im zweiten Obergeschoß tritt in flacher Rundung hervor. Das Erdgeschoß ist in schwedischem Granit, die Außenwände der oberen Geschosse sind in rotem Pfälzer Sandstein ausgeführt. Portal und Schaufenster bestehen aus Bronze, ebenso Teile des Erkers und der Dachhaube. Die Bronzen stammen aus der Kunstgießerei Vorwärts in Köln-Melaten. Die Dachdeckung ist von mattgrünen Biberschwänzen hergestellt.

Das Erdgeschoß enthält Ausstellungs-, Bureau- und Arbeitsräume, sowie die Diele mit anschließender Stockwerkstreppe und Personenaufzug. In den oberen Geschossen sind Wohnungen eingerichtet mit Küche und Zubehör, einen Lichthof umschließend. Der rückwärtsliegende Flügel enthält Arbeitsräume. Sämtliche Decken sind in Eisenkonstruktion mit Hohlkörperdecken ausgeführt.

In vier Geschossen und einem Dachgeschoß aufsteigend zeigt sich das Geschäftshaus Schraepler in Leipzig, Brühl 14/16. Das Gebäude ist von Architekt Walter Heßling entworfen, etwa in 7 Monaten zur Ausführung gekommen und hat 114 000 Mark an Baukosten, 197 000 Mark für Grunderwerb und 14 000 Mark für Nebenausgaben, also insgesamt 325 000 Mark Kosten erfordert. Über dem Erdgeschoß, den mittleren Eingang und zwei Schaufenster enthaltend, steigen das erste und zweite Obergeschoß mit breiten Fensteröffnungen und einem mittleren ausgekragten, in einen Balkon endigenden Erker versehen, empor. Ein mit Ziegeln eingedecktes Band trennt das dritte Obergeschoß von den unteren ab. Über dem mittleren Teil der Fassade erhebt sich ein steiler Giebel in geschweiften Umrissen, zu dessen Seiten sich das Dach einschneidende Fenster öffnen. Die Fassade ist mit grauem Kunstkalksteinputz überzogen. Die Modelle zu den Bildhauerarbeiten an der Fassade lieferte F. Pfeifer.

Das Erdgeschoß nimmt zu beiden Seiten des zur Stockwerkstreppe und zum Hof führenden Flurs je einen Laden auf; der links liegende steht in Verbindung mit einer Weinstube. Das erste und zweite Obergeschoß enthalten je einen großen ungeteilten Geschäftsraum; das dritte und vierte Obergeschoß Wohnräume. Das Haus ist mit allem neuzeitlichem Komfort ausgestattet: Fahrstuhl, Entstäubungsanlage, Einrichtungen für Gas- und elektrische Beleuchtung.

Das Geschäfts- und Wohnhaus Josef Fischer in Dortmund, Ostenhellweg, ist nach dem Entwurfe der Architekten Schmidtmann und Klemp im Laufe eines Jahres errichtet. Die Baukosten betrugen 525 000 Mark. Das Erdgeschoß der Fassade wird von dem in Bronze ausgeführten Schaufenstern und dem ebenfalls in Bronze hergestellten mächtigen Bogen über dem vertieft liegenden Eingange eingenommen. Die Schaufensterpfeiler erhielten Granitverkleidung. Die oberen drei Geschosse der Fassade sind mittelst durchgehender, vorspringender Pfeiler gegliedert, zwischen denen sich die paarweise zusammengefaßten, im ersten und zweiten Obergeschosse vereinigten Fenster einordnen. Über dem mittleren Teil der Fassade erhebt sich ein mit Fenstern und einem Balkon ausgestatteter, flachrund und mit einem Aufsatz schließender Giebel. Die oberen Geschosse der Fassade und der Giebel sind in rotem Mainsandstein ausgeführt. Das Dach ist mit Ziegeln eingedeckt. – Das große Ladenlokal im Erdgeschoß, sowie das im ersten Oberschoß gelegene, einen Lichthof umschließend, dienen allein Verkaufs-

L'immeuble C. Schirp de Cologne, Neumarkt 31, fut conçu par l'architecte Wilh. Kurt. Les travaux, menés à bien en deux années, revinrent à 330 000 marks. Il s'agit d'un immeuble de rapport de quatre étages à toit mansardé, au rez-de-chaussée duquel est installé un commerce. La façade principale est occupée, au rez-de-chaussée, par une large devanture et par un portail conduisant aux habitations supérieures. Les trois étages inférieurs sont assortis d'un avant-corps, supportant, au quatrième étage, une loggia coiffée d'un pignon éboulé. Les fenêtres du deuxième étage, contiguës à l'avant-corps, présentent une forme convexe. Le rez-de-chaussée est réalisé en granit suédois, les façades des étages supérieurs sont en grès rouge du Palatinat. Le portail, les devantures ainsi que certains éléments de l'avant-corps et de la calotte du toit sont en bronze. Ils furent exécutés par l'atelier de moulage Vorwärts de Cologne. Le toit est recouvert de tuiles plates vert foncé.

Le rez-de-chaussée abrite les pièces d'exposition, les bureaux, les cabinets de travail ainsi que le hall, la cage d'escalier et l'ascenseur. Les logements aménagés dans les étages sont agencés autour d'une cour vitrée. L'aile, située sur la façade postérieure, est occupée par des bureaux. L'ensemble des plafonds présente une ossature de fer garnie d'hourdis creux.

L'immeuble Schraepler de Leipzig, Brühl 14/16, se compose de quatre étages et d'un étage mansardé. Conçu par l'architecte Walter Heßling, il fut érigé en sept mois. Les coûts de construction se montèrent à 114 000 marks, 197 000 marks furent dépensés pour le terrain, à cela s'ajoutèrent 14 000 marks de frais annexes, soit une dépense totale de 325 000 marks. L'entrée, flanquée de deux devantures, occupe le rez-de-chaussée. La façade du premier et deuxième étages, percée de larges baies, présente, dans sa partie médiane, une avancée se terminant par un balcon. Un cordon saillant, habillé de tuiles, sépare le troisième étage des étages inférieurs. Un haut pignon aux lignes ondulées, assorti de part et d'autre d'une fenêtre mansardée, prolonge la partie centrale de la façade. Les murs extérieurs ont reçu un crépi gris. Les modèles des ouvrages sculptés furent exécutés par F. Pfeifer.

Deux commerces, séparés par un couloir donnant sur l'escalier et la cour, occupent la surface du rez-de-chaussée. Le commerce de gauche communique avec un débit de boissons. Les premier et deuxième étages abritent chacun une grande surface non-cloisonnée réservée à des fins commerciales. Aux troisième et quatrième étages sont installés des logements. Un ascenseur, un système d'absorption de la poussière ainsi qu'une installation d'éclairage électrique et au gaz garantissent un confort moderne.

Le bâtiment Josef Fischer de Dortmund, Ostenhellweg, est un immeuble de rapport abritant un commerce au rez-de-chaussée. Conçu par les architectes Schmidtmann et Klemp, cet immeuble fut réalisé en l'espace d'une année pour la somme de 525 000 marks. Le rez-de-chaussée de la façade est complètement occupé par les devantures de bronze et l'arc monumental, en bronze lui aussi, abritant l'entrée. Les piliers encadrant les devantures sont revêtus de granit. La façade est rythmée par des piliers montant sur trois étages qui encadrent les fenêtres groupées par paire. Un pignon arrondi, assorti de fenêtres et d'un balcon, et coiffé d'un chapiteau se détache de la partie médiane de la façade. Les étages ainsi que le pignon sont réalisés en grès rouge de la vallée du Main. Le toit porte une couverture de tuiles.

Le rez-de-chaussée et le premier étage ne sont utilisés qu'à des fins commerciales, le sous-sol sert de

The C. Schirp building located in Cologne (Neumarkt 31) was designed by the architect Wilh. Kurth, member of the Association of German Architects. Construction of the four–storey commercial building with a roof storey occupied 2 years and amounted to 330,000 Marks. The ground–level front has a broad shop window located next to the portal leading to the living quarters above. A cantilevered bay runs the height of the upper three storeys, and has at its top a loggia under the overhanging half–hipped roof. At the second storey, next to the bay, is a slightly curved oriel window. The ground front is faced with Swedish granite, the upper storeys with red sandstone from the Palatinate. The portal and shop window are of bronze, as are parts of the bay and roof dome. The bronze was produced at the Vorwärts Art Foundry in Cologne. Roofing consists of pale–green flat tile.

The ground floor contains showrooms, offices and work rooms, as well as the hall with adjoining stairs to the upper floors, and a lift. Located on the upper floors around a patio are living quarters with a kitchen and sundries. The rear wing contains offices. All ceilings are of reinforced concrete with hollow concrete blocks.

The Schraepler building in Leipzig (Brühl 14/16) is a commercial building consisting of four storeys and a roof storey. Designed by the architect Walter Hessling, it was completed in approximately 7 months. Construction costs were 114,000 Marks, the land acquisition a further 14,000 Marks and 197,000 Marks were spent for additional expenses, amounting to a total of 325,000 Marks. Rising above the ground floor, which has an entrance flanked by two shop windows, are the second and third storeys with broad windows and a projecting bay ending in a balcony. A broad string–course with clay tiles separates the third storey from the lower ones. Above the middle of the façade is a high–pitched shaped gable flanked by dormer windows bisecting the roof line. The façade is plastered in grey limestone; the sculptured ornamentation is based on models created by F. Pfeifer.

The ground floor is occupied by an entry hall leading to the stairs and to the rear courtyard, and which has a shop to either side. The shop to the left is connected to a wine tavern. The first and second floors each contain a large open office room; the third and fourth floor are occupied with living quarters. The house is furnished with all modern conveniences: lift, de–dusting ventilation system, and installations for electrical and gas lighting.

The Josef Fisher building in Dortmund (Ostenhellweg) was designed by the architects Schmidtmann and Klemp, and built in the course of one year at a cost of 525,000 Marks. The façade at the ground level is occupied by showcases worked in bronze, as well as a monumental arch, also in bronze, which covers the recessed entrance. The pilasters separating the showcases are rendered in granite. The upper three storeys of the front are articulated by continuous projecting pillars, between which are located pairs of windows; the windows at the first and second storeys run unbroken. A flat–round gable with windows, balcony and superstructure crowns the middle section of the façade. The upper storeys and the gable are rendered in red Main sandstone. The roof is covered with clay tile.

The large store on the ground floor as well the store on the first floor, which is situated round a patio, are used exclusively for commercial purposes. The

zwecken, während der Keller als Lagerraum benutzt wird. Die Treppen an der Front des Gebäudes sind derart angelegt, daß sie keinen Teil der Schaufenster beanspruchen. Der Garten an der Rückfront am Bruderweg ist mit einer Einfahrt versehen. Das zweite und dritte Obergeschoß sind zu Wohnungszwecken nutzbar gemacht, so daß zwei Wohnungen geschaffen wurden, die im zweiten Obergeschoß die Wohnräume und durch eine besondere Dielentreppe verbunden, im dritten Obergeschoß die Schlafräume enthalten. Außerdem sind Werkstatträume an der Rückfront und Dachgärten zu beiden Seiten des Lichthofs angelegt. Das ganze Konstruktionsgerippe ist in Eisen, die Decken sind in Eisenbeton hergestellt.

447 [1912: 78]

Von Gärten umgeben erhebt sich die zweigeschossige Villa Müller in Darmstadt, Nicolaiweg 16, nach dem Entwurfe des Eigentümers, Architekt Professor Albin Müller, Mitglied der Künstlerkolonie Darmstadt, im Laufe eines Jahres errichtet. Das Erdgeschoß zeigt an der Straßenfront einen breiten, mit einer Altane nach oben abschließenden Fensterausbau und seitwärts die von einer Freitreppe zugängliche Eingangshalle. Dem Seitenflügel ist eine Terrasse vorgelegt. Die Fassaden sind mit gelbgrauem Naturputz versehen; das Obergeschoß des Hauptbaues ist mit violettgrauen Ziegeln verblendet. Das abgewalmte Dach des Hauptbaues ist mit violettgrauen Biberschwanzziegeln eingedeckt und mit Dachfenstern ausgestattet. Der Seitenflügel trägt im Obergeschoß eine Plattform.

Im Erdgeschoß liegen Empfangszimmer, Damen- und Herrenzimmer, Eßzimmer, Anrichte, Küche und Speisekammer von einem Vorraum zugänglich, an den sich die Stockwerkstreppe anschließt. Das Obergeschoß enthält die Schlafzimmer für Familie und Kinder, das Kinderspielzimmer, das Ankleidezimmer, das Bad und die Nähstube. Die Plattform über dem Seitenflügel ist zu einem seitlich von Lauben eingefaßten Licht- und Sonnenbade eingerichtet.

448 [1912: 84]

Inmitten von Gartenanlagen erhebt sich die Villa Bahner in Bensheim, Roonstraße 5, einstöckig, ein ausgebautes Dachgeschoß enthaltend, als Werk des Architekten Professor H. Metzendorf, im Laufe zweier Baujahre für die Baukostensumme von 15 000 Mark zur Ausführung gebracht. Das einfache Gebäude zeigt auf beiden Giebelfronten im Erdgeschoß je einen Erker, an der einen Front viereckig, an der anderen polygonal hervortretend. Der letztere Erker trägt einen Fensterausbau mit besonderem Dach im Giebel. Auf der Fläche des überhängenden steilen gebrochenen Daches erhebt sich ein viereckiger beschieferter Aufbau, das Atelier des Eigentümers Kunstmaler Bahner umschließend, oben mit einer Glashalle zwischen massiven Pfeilern bekrönt. Die Giebel sind im oberen Teil abgeschopft. Die Fronten zeigen rotes Sockelmauerwerk, darüber graue Putzflächen. Das Ziegeldach ist rot, die Anstriche der Fenster und Läden sind weiß.

Im Erdgeschoß liegen um eine Diele mit Windfang und frei aufsteigender Treppe gereiht, der Salon, das Wohnzimmer und die Küche.

449 [1912: 82]

Das an drei Fronten freiliegende, in vier Geschossen aufsteigende Wohn- und Geschäftshaus der Städte-Feuer-Sozietät der Provinz Sachsen in Magdeburg, Breiteweg 110, ist nach dem Entwurfe des Architekten Alb. Schütze im Laufe von zwei Baujahren für die Bausumme von 250 000 Mark errichtet. Die Fassade enthält im Erdgeschoß neben den Eingängen Schaufensteröffnungen; die oberen drei Geschosse sind durch flache Pilaster zu einer Einheit zusammengezogen. Die eine der beiden abgerundeten Ecken trägt im zweiten Obergeschoß einen auf Konsolen ausgekragten Balkon, und ist über dem Dachgesims durch einen Ziergiebel mit dem Wappenadler in Relief ausgezeichnet. Die Fensterbrüstungen im dritten Obergeschoß enthalten figürliche Reliefs, ebenso sind figürliche Darstellungen und Masken unter den Konsolen des Balkons und an den Kapitellen der Wandpi-

---

dépôt. Les escaliers ont été installés latéralement de sorte à ne pas entamer l'espace réservé aux devantures. Le jardin postérieur donnant sur le Bruderweg est équipé d'un accès. Les deuxième et troisième étages abritent des logements agencés sur deux niveaux. Les pièces de séjour sont au deuxième étage, les chambres à coucher au troisième. Un escalier installé dans l'antichambre relie les deux niveaux entre eux. Des ateliers de travail se trouvent sur la façade postérieure. Des jardins-terrasses ont été aménagés de part et d'autre de la cour vitrée. L'ossature de l'immeuble est en fer, les planchers sont en béton armé.

447 [1912: 78]

La villa „Müller", située à Darmstadt, Nicolaiweg 16, fut construite en une année sur les plans de son propriétaire, l'architecte Albin Müller, membre de la colonie des artistes de Darmstadt. Cette villa de deux étages, bordée de jardins, présente, sur la façade sur rue, un large bow-window supportant un balcon, ainsi qu'un porche latéral accessible par un perron. L'aile est assortie d'une terrasse. Les façades sont enduites d'un crépi gris jaune. L'étage du corps de bâtiment est revêtu de briques gris mauve. Des tuiles plates gris mauve recouvrent le toit en croupe percé de fenêtres mansardées. L'aile est couronnée au premier étage d'une plate-forme.

Le rez-de-chaussée comprend le salon, le boudoir, le cabinet de travail, la salle à manger, l'office, la cuisine et le garde-manger; toutes ces pièces sont accessibles par un hall attenant à la cage d'escalier. Le premier étage abrite les chambres à coucher des parents et des enfants, la salle de jeu, la garde-robe, la salle de bains et le cabinet de couture. La plate-forme, située sur l'aile, bordée par une tonnelle, a été aménagée en solarium.

448 [1912: 84]

La villa Bahner, assortie d'un jardin enclos, à Bensheim, Roonstraße 5, fut construite sur les plans de l'architecte H. Metzendorf. Les travaux furent réalisés en deux années et coûtèrent la somme de 15 000 marks. Il s'agit d'une maison toute simple, portant un toit mansardé et présentant, sur chaque façade pignon, une saillie, l'une quadrangulaire, l'autre polygonale. La saillie polygonale supporte un bow-window abrité par une bande de toiture. Une construction mansardée quadrangulaire, recouverte d'ardoises, et abritant l'atelier du propriétaire, le peintre Bahner, se détache d'un versant pentu du toit au comble brisé. Cette construction porte un toit en verrière, flanquée de deux piliers massifs. Les pignons sont éboutés. Le socle de la façade est en maçonnerie rouge, les murs sont enduits d'un crépi gris. Le toit de tuiles est rouge, les fenêtres et les volets ont reçu un badigeon blanc.

Le salon, la salle de séjour et la cuisine sont aménagés au rez-de-chaussée autour d'un hall assorti d'un tambour et d'un escalier.

449 [1912: 82]

L'immeuble des services communaux contre l'incendie de la province de Saxe à Magdebourg, Breiteweg 110, fut construit en deux années pour la somme de 250 000 marks. Les plans furent exécutés par l'architecte Alb. Schütze. Il s'agit d'un immeuble de quatre étages offrant trois façades dégagées. La façade du rez-de-chaussée est percée par les ouvertures des entrées et des devantures. Les trois étages supérieurs, présentant une ordonnance à pilastres, forment un ensemble. Un des deux angles arrondis est assorti, au deuxième étage, d'un balcon en encorbellement et, au-dessus de la corniche du toit, d'un blason en relief portant l'aigle. Les bandeaux des fenêtres du troisième étage, les corbeaux supportant les consoles du balcon ainsi que les chapiteaux des pilas-

---

stairs at the front of the building have been placed in such a way as to not interfere with the showcases. The garden to the rear, located at the Bruderweg, has a carriage—way. The second and third floors have been designed to accomodate living quarters, and so two flats now occupy the second floor, where the sitting—rooms and a separate connecting hall stairs are located, as well as the third floor, where the bedrooms are situated. In addition, workshops are located at the rear of the building, and a roof garden is placed to both sides of the patio. The building's structural framework is of iron, the floors are of reinforced concrete.

447 [1912: 78]

Situated in a country setting surrounded by gardens, the Müller residence in Darmstadt (Nicolaiweg 16), which was constructed in the course of one year, was designed by the owner, the architect Professor Ablin Müller, who is also a member of the Darmstadt Artists' Colony. The ground level front shows a broad bay of windows which finishes with a balcony at the first storey; the stairs from the street lead to the porched entrance at one side of the front. A terrace is located in front of the side wing. The façades are of yellow—grey plaster; the upper storey of the principal structure has been faced with purple—grey clay tile. The hipped roof is covered with purple—grey flat tile and contains dormer windows. A platform is situated on the top of the side wing.

The entry hall on the ground floor leads to the drawing—room, boudoir and study, dining room, pantry and kitchen facilities. The staircase to the side of the entry hall leads to the upper floor, which contains the bedrooms for the family and children, nursery, dressing—room, bath and sewing—room. The platform on the side wing has been decorated with a bower and sunbath.

448 [1912: 84]

Placed in a garden setting, the Bahner house in Bensheim (Roonstrasse 5) was designed by the architect Professor H. Metzendorf and built in the course of two years at a cost of 15,000 Marks. The one—storey house with a attic storey is simple in design, with a bay projecting from each of the gabled sides: one bay is polygonal, the other square in form. The latter bay is topped with its own roof located within the gable. A square superstructure rises from one side of the steep, overhanging roof, containing the atelier of the owner, the painter Bahner, and is crowned by a glass hall located between two massive pillars. The gable is hipped in its upper part. The villa is faced with a red basement masonry, with grey plaster surfaces above that. The tiled roof is red, and the shutters and frames of the windows are painted white.

The ground floor contains an entrance hall with a draught lobby and open stairs, the drawing—room, living room and kitchen.

449 [1912: 82]

The four—storey commercial building of the Saxony Municipal Fire Society in Magdeburg (Breiteweg 10) was designed by the architect Alb. Schütze and built in the course of two years for 250,000 Marks. The three exposed fronts of the building have shop windows at the ground level, while the upper floors are unified by continuous pilasters. One of the two rounded corners of the edifice has at the second storey a projecting balcony resting on consoles, and is ornamented by a decorative pediment above the roof moulding showing a relief of a heraldic eagle. The window aprons of the third storey contain figures in relief, and other figures and decorative masks have been placed under the consoles of the balcony and at the capitals of the wall pilasters. The font at the ground level is made of

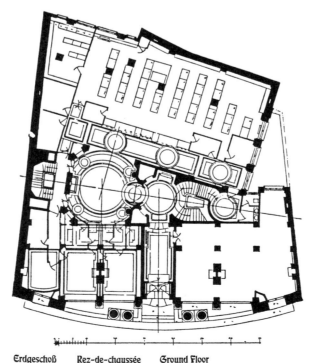

Hofeingang   Entrée sur cour   Back—Door

1. Obergeschoß   1er étage   Upper Floor

laster angebracht. Das Erdgeschoß ist in poliertem Kossainer Granit mit teilweiser Verwendung von Bronzen hergestellt; die oberen Geschosse haben grauen Terranovaputz erhalten. Das steile, über den Ecken pavillonartig ausgebildete Dach ist mit Kupfer eingedeckt und trägt mehrere Dachfenster. Die elliptische freitragende Haupttreppe, die Nebentreppe, sowie die größeren Unterzüge sind in Eisenbeton hergestellt; sämtliche Decken sind als trägerlose Hohlsteindecken, nach System Westphal, zur Ausführung gebracht.

450 [1912; 90]

Die General Buildings, Aldwych, London, ein Gebäude, zur Aufnahme der General-Unfall-, Feuer- und Lebensversicherungs-Korporation bestimmt, ist nach dem Plane des Architekten J. J. Burnet errichtet. Die Straßenfront ist flachrund ausgebogen, das Erdgeschoß und die Mezzanine sind durch eine Säulenstellung ausgezeichnet; über dem ersten Obergeschoß zieht sich ein durchlaufender Balkon hin, über dem sich in der Mittelachse eine Fensterarchitektur mit einfassenden Säulen und bekrönenden Figuren erhebt. Über dem umlaufenden Gesims, mit dem das vierte Obergeschoß abschließt, bildet sich ein Umgang, hinter dem das Dachgeschoß aufsteigt. Die Fassade ist in Portlandsandstein mit Verwendung von Granit für die unteren Teile ausgeführt. Die Kapitelle der Granitsäulen der Vorhalle bestehen aus schwarzem Marmor, die dahinter liegende Fassadengliederung ist wieder aus Marmor, die über den Säulen

tres sont ornés de reliefs ornementaux. Le rez-de-chaussée, réalisé en granit poli, présente certains éléments en bronze. Les étages supérieurs ont reçu un crépi gris. Le toit pentu, en pavillon au-dessus des angles, est percé de fenêtres mansardées. Le grand escalier hélicoïdal, l'escalier de service ainsi que les sous-poutres les plus importantes sont en béton armé. L'immeuble est équipé de faux plafonds construits sur le système Westphal.

450 [1912; 90]

L'immeuble londonien de la compagnie d'assurances générales fut construit sur les plans de l'architecte J. J. Burnet. L'édifice offre une façade sur rue légèrement convexe, assortie de colonnes au rez-de-chaussée et à l'entresol. Un balcon, derrière lequel se détache une fenêtre flanquée de colonnes et surmontée de sculptures, court sur toute la largeur de la façade, au dessus du premier étage. Le quatrième étage se termine par une corniche couronnée d'une galerie. Un toit mansardé, recouvert d'ardoises, coiffe l'ensemble. Les murs de façade sont en grès de Portland et présentent des éléments de granit dans les parties inférieures. Les chapiteaux des colonnes de granit ainsi que les ornements de la façade du rez-de-

polished granite from Kossain with bronze articulations; the upper storeys have been plastered with grey terranova. The steep roof, pavilon—like at the corners, is covered with copper and has numerous dormers. The elliptical, self—supporting main staircase, the side stairs, as well as the larger joists are constructed of reinforced concrete. All floors have been constructed as girderless hollow block floors using the Westphalian system.

450 [1912; 90]

The general building in Aldwych, London, to be occupied by the General Accident Fire and Life Assurance Corporation, was designed by the architect J. J. Burnet. The frontage is slightly convex, with the ground level and mezzanine divided by columns. A continuous balcony runs above the first floor, above that at the middle axis of the front is an ornamented window framed by columns crowned by sculptured figures. Above the running cornice located above the fourth floor is an ambulatory located in front of the roof storey. The façades are faced with Portland sandstone, and granite has also been employed for the lower sections. The capitals of the granite porch columns are of black marble, the articulations of the façade behind these are again of marble, and the allegorical figures

Erdgeschoß   Rez-de-chaussée   Ground Floor

Mezzanin   Entresol   Mezzanine

stehenden allegorischen Figuren sind aus Metall hergestellt. Das Dach ist mit Schiefer eingedeckt.

Im Erdgeschoß führt der Eingangsflur zu einem Vestibül und weiter zu einer mit Kuppel und Oberlicht ausgestatteten Wartehalle für das Publikum; seitwärts und hinterwärts schließen sich Bureauräume an. Ein zweites Vestibül mit seitlichem Eingang steht mit der Haupttreppe und dem Aufzug in Verbindung. Das Mezzaningeschoß enthält einen größeren Saal, ein anstoßendes Speisezimmer und eine Anzahl Bureauräume. In den oberen Geschossen sind größere, durch Pfeilerstellungen geteilte Geschäftsräume untergebracht.

451 [1912: 93]

Durch eine im steilen Ovalbogen geschlossene Nische der Straßenfront sind sämtliche Geschosse des Kaufhauses in Budapest, Andrássy ut 39, einheitlich zusammengefaßt. Der Entwurf stammt vom Architekten Sigmund Sziklai, ist im Laufe von 2 Jahren zur Ausführung gekommen und hat 1 450 000 Kronen an Baukosten verursacht. Von einem älteren Kasinogebäude ist der an der Mohrengassenfront gelegene Konzertsaal mit den Freskogemälden von Lotz erhalten; und über demselben im vierten Stock wurde ein Buffetraum eingerichtet. Der unter dem Lotzsaal liegende Raum ist mit den Erdgeschoßräumen in Verbindung gebracht, so daß der Eintretende die ganze Tiefe des Hauses überblickt. Das Erdgeschoß der Fassade weist eine breite mittlere Öffnung auf, die durch ein Eisenbetonsprengwerk überbrückt ist. Auf diesem ruhen der vordere Teil der Erdgeschoßdecke und zwei aufsteigende Pfeiler der Front, welche die Decken der oberen Geschosse tragen. Der Sockel der Fassade besteht aus rotem schwedischem Granit, während der obere Teil derselben aus gelblichem Lóskuter Sandstein und rötlichgelbem Pyrogranit hergestellt ist. Die bis zum vierten Stock führende, im ersten Stock fünfarmige, in den oberen Geschossen dreiarmige, aus Eisenbeton freitragend konstruierte, den inneren Lichthof überbrückende Haupttreppe hat einen Stufenbelag von Marmor erhalten. Die rückwärts gelegene Not- und Nebentreppe ruht großenteils auf einem Pfeiler. Im Büffetraum befindet sich an einem Ende die Küche, am anderen Ende der Orchesterraum. Sämtliche Dekken, Treppen, Dächer und Pfeiler sind aus Eisenbeton hergestellt. Die Dächer sind als hängende Gärten ausgebildet. Im Kellergeschoß sind die elektrischen Motoren unter dem Lichthof aufgestellt.

452 [1912: 94]

Einen Eckbau bildend, in vier Geschossen, einem Halbgeschoß und einer Mansarde aufsteigend, ist das Warenhaus Simon Fischer & Co. in Budapest, Bécsi-utcza und Erzsébet-tér Ecke, nach dem Entwurfe der Architekten Aladar Karman und Julius von Ullmann im Laufe eines Jahres errichtet und hat 1 200 000 Kronen Baukosten erfordert, einschließlich der Geschäftseinrichtung, jedoch ausschließlich der Kosten des Grunderwerbs. Die Eingangsfront ist durch die mittlere Bogennische im Halbgeschoß und durch zwei im ersten Obergeschoß ausgekragte, viereckig vorspringende, durch drei Geschosse gehende Erkerausbauten gegliedert, die durch Balkons verbunden sind. Die Gebäudeecken sowie die Seitenfront zeigen in den oberen drei Geschossen durchgehende Pfeiler, außerdem sind die Fenster derselben Front im zweiten und dritten Obergeschoß zusammengezogen und werden durch Pfeiler geteilt, die zum Teil mit Kannelierungen versehen sind. Das Erdgeschoß enthält Ladenöffnungen, in Eisenkonstruktion mit in Kupfer getriebenen Verzierungen hergestellt. Die Säulen zwischen den Fenstern des Halbgeschosses bestehen aus rosafarbigem Marmor. Die oberhalb durchgehende Verdachung ist aus getriebenem Kupferblech mit stark vergoldeter Untersicht ausgeführt. Die oberen Fassadenflächen sind verputzt; das stark vorspringende Hauptgesims, aus Eisenbeton bestehend, ist plastisch verziert und reich vergoldet. Das gebrochene, Dachfenster tragende Dach ist mit Ziegeln eingedeckt. Als Mitarbeiter werden genannt: Baumeister Alexander und Julius Willisch und Bildhauer Manó Rakos.

---

chaussée sont en marbre. Les figures allégoriques surmontant les colonnes sont en métal.

Au rez-de-chaussée, le couloir d'entrée conduit à un vestibule puis à une salle d'attente publique éclairée par une verrière. Des bureaux sont installés sur l'arrière et les côtés. Un second vestibule avec accès latéral donne sur le grand escalier et sur l'ascenseur. L'entresol comprend une grande salle, une salle à manger attenante et de nombreuses salles de bureau. Les étages supérieurs sont occupés par de vastes bureaux divisés par des ordonnances de piliers.

451 [1912: 93]

Les étages du grand magasin de Budapest, Andrássy ut 39, sont regroupés dans une niche pratiquée dans l'arcade ovale de la façade frontale. Conçu par l'architecte Sigmund Sziklai, cet édifice, construit en deux années, coûta la somme de 1 450 000 couronnes. De l'ancien casino a été conservée la salle de concert décorée de fresques exécutées par Lotz, donnant sur la Mohrengasse. Au-dessus, au quatrième étage, a été aménagé un salon de thé. La salle située sous la salle Lotz communique avec le rez-de-chaussée afin que les clients aient une vue d'ensemble des lieux. La façade du rez-de-chaussée présente, dans son centre, une large ouverture traversée par une ferme à contre-fiches en béton armé. Ces contre-fiches soutiennent la partie avant du plafond du rez-de-chaussée ainsi que les piliers de la façade, eux-mêmes porteurs des planchers des étages supérieurs. Le socle de la façade est en granit suédois rouge, les murs sont en grès jaunâtre et en granit rouge jaune. Le grand escalier continu à tous les étages, jeté sur la cour vitrée, présente cinq volées au premier étage et trois dans les étages supérieurs. L'escalier est construit en béton armé, les marches portent un revêtement de marbre. L'escalier de service et escalier de secours à la fois, placé au fond du magasin, repose pratiquement sur un unique pilier. Le salon de thé est flanqué d'une part de la cuisine et d'autre part de la salle d'orchestre. L'ensemble des plafonds, des escaliers, des toits et des piliers est réalisé en béton armé. Des jardins suspendus ont été aménagés sur les toits. La machinerie électrique est installée au sous-sol, sous la cour vitrée.

452 [1912: 94]

Le grand magasin Simon Fischer & Co. de Budapest, situé à l'angle des rues Bécsi-utcza et Erzsébet-tér, fut conçu par les architectes Aladar Karman et Julius von Ullmann. Construit en l'espace d'une année, cet immeuble d'angle de quatre étages, assorti d'un entresol et d'un étage mansardé, coûta, sans le terrain, la somme de 1 200 000 couronnes, aménagement du magasin compris. La façade principale s'organise autour d'une niche médiane cintrée, au niveau de l'entresol, et de deux saillies quadrangulaires montant sur trois étages et reliées par des balcons. Les angles du bâtiment ainsi que la façade latérale présentent des piliers continus aux trois étages superieurs. Cette façade présente aux deuxième et troisième étages des fenêtres groupées par paires et divisées par des piliers partiellement cannelés. Le rez-de-chaussée est percé de devantures dont les armatures sont en fer avec des ornements de cuivre martelé. Les fenêtres de l'entresol sont abritées par une bande de toiture continue en tôle de cuivre martelée dont la partie inférieure, visible de la chaussée, a reçu un revêtement doré. Les colonnes séparant les ouvertures de l'entresol sont en marbre. Les surfaces supérieures de la façade sont crépies. Richement sculptée et dorée, la corniche très saillante est en béton armé. Le toit mansardé au comble brisé est recouvert de tuiles. Les architectes Alexander et Julius Willisch ainsi que le sculpteur Manó Rakos participèrent à l'élaboration de cet édifice.

---

above the columns are made of metal. The roof is covered with slate.

The entrance hall on the ground floor leads to a vestibule and, further on, to a waiting hall for the public, which has a cupola and sky—lights; offices are located to the side and back. A second vestibule from the side entrance is connected to the main staircase and lifts. The mezzanine contains a rather large hall which borders a dining room and a number of offices. Large, open offices with pillars are located on the upper floors.

451 [1912: 93]

An eccentric elipse—shaped arch frames a niche running the height of all storeys of the department store in Budapest (Andrassy ut. 39). Designed by the architect Sigmund Sziklai, the building was constructed over a period of 2 years and cost 1,450,000 Crowns. At the Mohrengassen front is a concert hall, decorated with frescos painted by Lotz, which is contained within an older casino; a buffet room has been furnished above on the fourth floor. The room under the Lotz hall is connected to other rooms on the ground floor, thus affording a person entering the building with a survey of the entire depth of the building. The façade at the ground level has a large opening in its centre which is bridged by a strutted frame of reinforced concrete. This supports the front part of the ground floor ceiling and two pillars, which in turn support the ceilings of the upper floors. The façades socle consists of red Swedish granite, whilst the upper part of the façade is of yellow sandstone from Lóskut and red—yellow pyrogranite. The main staircase, constructed of reinforced concrete as a self—supporting structure, leads up to the fourth floor; it is a five—flight stair at the first floor and triple—flight at the upper floors. The stairs span the inner patio and have steps of marble. The emergency side stairs are located at the back of the building and are chiefly supported by one pillar. The kitchen is located at one end of the buffet room, an orchestra floor at the other. All floors, steps, roofs and piers are constructed of reinforced concrete. The roofs have been designed as hanging gardens. Electric motors have been installed in the basement under the patio.

452 [1912: 94]

The four—storey corner building, with a mezzanine and mansard, of the Simon Fischer Co. in Budapest (corner of Bécsi ut. and Erzsébet tér) was designed by the architects Aladar Karman and Julius von Ullmann and constructed in the course of one year at a cost of 1,200,000 Crowns, including the interior office and store furnishings, but not, however, the price of the land acquisition. The middle of the entrance front is decorated by a arched niche at the mezzanine, and by two cantilevered square bays rising from the first to the fourth storey, where they conclude in balconys. The corners of the building as well as a side front have continuous pillars at their upper three storeys, in addition, the windows at the second and third storeys of the side front are united by pilasters, which divides them into groups. The pilasters are partially fluted. Shop windows are located at the ground level, constructed of iron and have incised decorations of copper. The columns between the windows of the mezzanine are of pink marble. The continuous projecting cover overhead is of incised copper sheets with a prominently gilded underside. The surfaces of the upper façade have been plastered, the widely—overhanging principal cornice of reinforced concrete is richly ornamented and gilded. The two—pitched roof is covered with clay tile. Main assistance in the building's construction was provided by the building supervisors Alexander and Julius Willisch and the sculptor Manó Rakos.

Das Erdgeschoß umschließt einen großen, durch Pfeiler geteilten Geschäftsraum, in dem eine freiliegende, dreiarmige Treppe, ein Aufzug und eine Nebentreppe aufsteigen. Der seitliche Eingangsflur führt zur Stockwerkstreppe und zu zwei Nebentreppen. Das Halbgeschoß zeigt die ähnliche Anordnung wie das Erdgeschoß. Die drei Obergeschosse sind durch Geschäftsräume ausgefüllt, die sich um einen inneren Lichthof gruppieren. Das Mansardengeschoß und der Keller sind zur Anlage von Magazinen und Heizräumen benutzt. Im Keller, Erdgeschoß und Halbstock sind Eisenständer-Auswechslungen verwendet, die meistens mit genieteten Kastenträgern überdeckt sind.

453 [1912; 87]

Das auf einer Terrasse sich erhebende, zweistöckige Einfamilienhaus in Wien, Sternwartestraße 62, 64, nach dem Entwurfe des Architekten M. D. G., D. W. B. Robert Örley etwa im Laufe eines Jahres unter Mitwirkung des Besitzers Prof. F. Schmutzer errichtet, hat rund 270 800 Kronen Baukosten verursacht. An der Straßenfront und ebenso an einer Seitenfront zieht sich über dem Untergeschoß eine mittelst Freitreppen zugängliche Terrasse hin. Der leicht ausgebogene Mittelteil der Straßenfront trägt über dem Erdgeschoß eine durchgehende Altane und wird von einstöckigen Flügelbauten mit übertretenden gebrochenen Dächern eingefaßt. Im Obergeschoß des Mittelbaues derselben Front setzt sich die Ausbiegung bis zum Dachgesims fort. Die Fassaden sind verputzt und die Fensteraufbauten tragenden Dächer mit Ziegeln eingedeckt.

Das Hochparterre enthält die mittlere Halle, um welche sich Salon, Speisezimmer mit Erkerausbau, Wohnzimmer mit Veranda, zwei Schlafzimmer, Kinderzimmer und Fremdenzimmer lagern. Im Dachgeschoß liegt ein größerer und ein kleinerer Atelierraum. Außerdem sind hier die Arbeitsräume des Besitzers untergebracht. Das Untergeschoß ist zur Anlage der Küche, der Waschküche, des Dienerzimmers, der Wohnung des Hauswarts, der Heizung und eines größeren Gesellschaftszimmers benutzt.

454 [1912; 97]

Die Wohnhäuser für Beamte und Arbeiter in Frechen bei Köln a. Rh., Zeche Wachtberg I, sind im Laufe zweier Jahre nach den Entwürfen des Architekten Professor Georg Metzendorf zur Ausführung gekommen.

Das zweistöckige Wohnhaus des Grubeninspektors besteht aus zwei rechtwinklig aufeinanderstoßenden Flügeln. Die steilen Dächer sind durch überhängende Giebel begrenzt. Das Erdgeschoß enthält außer dem Flur, der Stockwerkstreppe und den Wohnzimmern, die Küche und die Spülküche. Im Obergeschoß liegen die Schlafzimmer und der Baderaum.

Das Haus des Betriebsführers ist zweistöckig; die Fronten sind durch flache Pfeilervorlagen gegliedert, welche die Fenster zwischen sich einschließen. Das übertretende, in den Flächen eingebogene Dach ist mit Fensteraufbauten besetzt. Das Haus enthält zwei durch eine Brandmauer getrennte Wohnungen mit besonderen Eingängen. Im Erdgeschoß liegen je ein Flur, ein Zimmer, die Wohnküche und die Spülküche. Das Obergeschoß umfaßt noch drei Zimmer.

Die zweistöckigen Arbeiterhäuser sind dreimal durch Brandmauern geteilt, so daß jedes Haus vier Wohnungen enthält. Die Eingänge an der Straßenfront sind von vorgelegten Terrassen und Freitreppen zugänglich. An der Rückfront schließen sich dem Hauptbau einstöckige Flügelanbauten an. Die überhängenden Dächer sind mit Dachfenstern besetzt. Jede Wohnung besteht im Erdgeschoß aus dem Flur mit Treppe, einem Zimmer, der Wohnküche und der im Anbau liegenden Waschküche. Im Obergeschoß sind noch zwei Zimmer angeordnet. Die Keller erstrecken sich nur unter einen Teile des Erdgeschosses.

Die Bruchsteinsockel sämtlicher Häuser sind gefugt. Die Fassaden haben Verputz erhalten. Die Fenster sind weiß gestrichen und die Dächer mit schwarzen Hohlpfannen eingedeckt.

Le rez-de-chaussée comprend une grande surface de vente, divisée par une ordonnance de piliers. Un escalier à trois volées, un ascenseur et un escalier de service assurent la communication entre les étages. Le couloir d'entrée latéral conduit à la cage d'escalier et aux escaliers de service. L'entresol présente les mêmes caractéristiques que le rez-de-chaussée. Les trois étages supérieurs sont occupés par des bureaux agencés autour d'une cour intérieure vitrée. L'étage mansardé ainsi que la cave servent d'entrepôt et de chaufferie. Des supports de fer enchevêtrés, couverts pour la plupart d'encaissements rivetés, furent utilisés pour la construction de la cave, du rez-de-chaussée et de l'entresol.

453 [1912; 87]

Cette villa viennoise, située aux n°62, 64 de la Sternwartestraße, fut érigée en une année sur les plans de l'architecte Robert Örley en collaboration avec le propriétaire prof. F. Schmutzer. Les coûts de construction se montèrent à 270 800 couronnes. Il s'agit d'une maison particulière de deux étages, appuyée sur une terrasse. Accessible par un perron, la terrasse, qui s'étend au-dessus du sous-sol, ceint les façades latérale et frontale de la maison. La façade principale présente une saillie convexe, flanquée de deux ailes d'un étage, coiffées de toits saillants aux combles brisés. Cette saillie montant jusqu'à la corniche du toit est coupée, au niveau du premier étage, par un balcon. Les murs de façade sont crépis, les toits mansardés ont reçu une couverture de tuiles.

Le rez-de-chaussée surélevé comprend un hall central autour duquel se répartissent le salon, la salle à manger et son bow-window, la salle de séjour attenante à la véranda, deux chambres à coucher, la chambre des enfants et la chambre d'amis. L'étage mansardé abrite deux ateliers de taille différente ainsi que les cabinets de travail du propriétaire. Le sous-sol est occupé par la cuisine et son office, la buanderie, la chambre des domestiques, le logement du gardien, la chaufferie ainsi qu'un grand salon.

454 [1912; 97]

Ces maisons situées à Frechen non loin de Cologne, Zeche Wachtberg I, furent conçues comme maisons d'habitation d'employés. Érigées sur les plans de l'architecte prof. Georg Metzendorf, elles furent menées à bien en deux années.

La maison de deux étages de l'inspecteur des mines se compose de deux ailes en équerre présentant des façades pignon et portant et toit aux versants pentus. Le rez-de-chaussée comprend le couloir, l'escalier, la salle de séjour, la cuisine et l'office. La salle de bains et les chambres sont aménagées à l'étage.

La maison du chef d'exploitation comporte deux étages. La façade est ponctuée de pilastres encadrant les fenêtres. Les versants légèrement concaves du toit saillant sont percés de fenêtres mansardées. La maison abrite deux logements, séparés par un mur mitoyen, ayant chacun une entrée particulière. Le rez-de-chaussée est occupé par le couloir, une pièce, la cuisine-salle à manger et l'office. A l'étage se trouvent trois autres pièces.

Les maisons à deux étages des ouvriers, divisées par trois murs mitoyens, offrent quatre logements. Les entrées, situées sur les façades sur rue, sont accessibles par des perrons. Des avant-corps d'un étage se greffent à la façade postérieure du corps de logis. Les toits saillants sont troués de fenêtres mansardées. Chaque logement se compose, au rez-de-chaussée, d'un couloir d'entrée renfermant l'escalier, d'une cuisine-salle à manger et d'un office installé dans l'aile. Deux pièces sont aménagées à l'étage. Les caves n'occupent qu'une partie de la surface construite.

Les socles des maisons sont réalisés en pierre de taille jointoyées. Les murs de façade sont enduits de crépi. Les encadrements des fenêtres ont reçu un badigeon blanc. Les toits portent une couverture de tuiles creuses noires.

The ground floor is occupied by a large room of the department store which is divided by pillars and contains the free—standing triple—flight staircase, a lift and a side stair. The entrance lobby to the side leads to the stair for the upper floors and to two side stairs. The plan of the mezzanine is similar to that of the ground floor. The three upper floors are occupied by offices grouped around a central patio. The mansard floor and the basement are used for storage and heating purposes. The basement, ground floor and mezzanine are framed with iron posts which are mostly covered by riveted hollow—web girders.

453 [1912; 87]

Rising from an elevated terrace, the one—family house in Vienna (Sternwartestrasse 62, 64) was designed by the certified architect Robert Örley. The owner, Professor F. Schmutzer, also assisted in the construction of the two—storey villa, which occupied approximately one year and amounted to a cost of about 270,000 Crowns. Terraces accessible by stairs have been arranged at the front and at one side. The slightly convex middle erection of the frontage has a continous balcony at the first storey which is framed by one—storey bays with overhanging double—pitched roofs. The middle erection of this front ends at the roof moulding. The façades are rendered in plaster and the roof with its window openings is covered with clay tile.

The raised ground floor contains the central hall surrounded by the drawing—room, the dining room extending into the bay, the sitting—room with veranda, two bedrooms, nursery and guest room. The attic floor is occupied by one larger and one smaller atelier. In addition, the work rooms of the owner are located here. In the basement are the kitchen facilities, the laundry room, the servant's room, living quarters for the caretaker, heating facilities and a spacious parlour.

454 [1912; 97]

New houses for workers an public officials have been completed in Cologne at the Wachtberg I mines. Construction was carried out over the course of two years based on the plans of the architect Professor Georg Metzendorf.

The two—storey house of the mine inspector consists of two wings which join at a right angle. Their steep roofs have overhanging gables. In addition to the entry hall, the stairway to the upper floor and sitting—rooms, the ground floor contains the kitchen and the scullery. Located on the upper floor are the bedrooms and the bathroom.

The works manager's house is two—storeyed. Its fronts are articulated by pilasters which have windows between them. Window erections have been placed in the overhanging roof, which curves inwards along its surface. The house contains two flats which are separated by a compartment wall and which have their own entrance. Each flat has an entry hall on the ground floor, as well as a separate room, a dwelling kitchen and a scullery. Another three rooms are located on the upper floor.

Each of the two—storey workers' houses has been built with three compartment walls, thus dividing each house into four flats. The entrances at the street front are accessible by exterior stairs leading to a front terrace. One—storey wing annexes project from the rear front of the house. The overhanging roofs have dormer windows. The ground floor of each flat contains an entry hall with stairs, a room, a dwelling kitchen and a laundry, which is located in the rear annexe. The upper floor contains another three rooms. The basement extends under only a part of the ground floor.

All dwellings have a socle of bonded rubble masonry. The façades are plastered, and the roofs are covered with black clipboard.

Die Entwürfe zu den Häusern der Wohnhausgruppe in Breslau, Menzelstraße, stammen von Architekt Professor H. Poelzig. Das Mittelhaus, Menzelstraße 87, steigt in vier Geschossen auf. Der mittlere Teil der Straßenfront bildet einen Rücksprung, vor dem sich in den drei Obergeschossen Balkons erstrecken. Durch sämtliche Geschosse geführte Pfeilervorlagen gliedern die mit gefärbtem Verputz versehene Fassade. Das übertretende, abgewalmte, mit Biberschwanzziegeln eingedeckte Dach ist mit einem großen, in geschwun-

Cet ensemble d'immeubles de Breslau fut conçu par l'architecte H. Poelzig. Le bâtiment central, au no 87 de la Menzelstraße, s'élève sur quatre étages. Un renfoncement, dans la partie médiane de la façade, enchâsse un balcon à chacun des trois étages. La façade enduite d'un crépi coloré, présente des pilastres montant de fond. Le toit en croupe saillant, recouvert de tuiles plates, est percé d'une grande fenêtre arrondie. Chacun des quatre étages de l'immeuble abrite un

The plans for the apartment complex in the Menzelstrasse in Breslau were drawn up by the architect Professor H. Poelzig. The house at Menzelstrasse 87 has four storeys and a middle section forming a rebound in which balconies are placed at the upper three storeys. Pilasters run the entire height of the plastered façade. The overhanging hipped roof is covered with flat red tile and has a prominent roof window outlined in curved lines. On each of the four floors is a

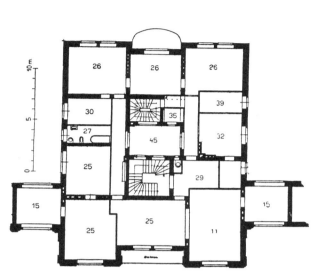

Menzelstraße 87   1. Obergeschoß   1er étage   First Floor

Menzel-/Wölflstraße   1. Obergeschoß   1er étage   First Floor

gener Linie begrenzten Dachfenster besetzt. Jedes der vier Geschosse des Hauses umfaßt eine größere, einen inneren Hof umschließende Wohnung, bestehend aus drei Wohnzimmern, dem Speisezimmer, drei Schlafzimmern, dem Ankleidezimmer mit nebenliegendem Bad, der Küche mit Anrichte und dem Mädchenzimmer. Eine Haupt- und eine Nebentreppe verbinden die Geschosse. Das Speisezimmer sowie eines der Wohnzimmer stehen mit Wintergärten in Verbindung, die in Seitenflügeln angeordnet sind. Vor dem mittleren Schlafzimmer an der Rückfront befindet sich ein Balkon.

Das Haus an der Ecke der Menzel- und Wölfl-straße besitzt wie das vorige vier Geschosse, und ist an der Front nach der Menzelstraße mit einem breit vorspringenden Bauteil versehen. Die mit Verputz ausgestattete Fassade zeigt gequaderte Ecken und mittlere Pfeiler. Das gebrochene Dach trägt Dachfenster. In sämtlichen Geschossen sind je zwei Wohnungen eingerichtet, einen inneren Hof und einen Lichthof umschließend. Jede Wohnung besteht aus einer Halle, fünf beziehungsweise vier Wohnzimmern, dem Speisezimmer, dem Mädchenzimmer, dem Bad, der Küche nebst Anrichte. Die gemeinschaftliche Haupt- sowie die Nebentreppe und die Hallen sind vom Innenhofe aus beleuchtet.

vaste appartement, agencé autour d'une cour, comprenant trois pièces de séjour, une salle à manger, trois chambres à coucher, une garde-robe avec salle de bains attenante, une cuisine avec office ainsi qu'une chambre des domestiques. Un grand escalier et un escalier de service relient les étages entre eux. La salle à manger ainsi qu'une des pièces de séjour communiquent avec le jardin d'hiver situé dans une aile. Une des chambres à coucher dispose d'un balcon.

Le bâtiment à l'angle des rues Menzel et Wölfl-straße comprend quatre étages comme le précédent. La façade sur la Menzelstraße est assortie d'un large avant-corps. La façade est agrémentée de pilastres et d'angles en pierres de tailles. Des fenêtres mansardées trouent le toit au comble brisé. Deux appartements, organisés autour d'une cour intérieure et d'une cour vitrée, sont aménagés à chaque étage. Chaque logement comporte une antichambre, quatre voire cinq pièces de séjour, une salle à manger, une chambre de domestiques, une salle de bains, une cuisine avec office. Le grand escalier commun, l'escalier de service ainsi que les antichambres sont éclairés par la cour intérieure.

flat arranged around an inner courtyard which consists of three sitting–rooms, a dining room, three bedrooms, a dressing–room with adjoining bathroom, a kitchen with pantry, and a maid's room. The floors are connected by a principal and side staircase. The dining room as well as one of the sitting–rooms are connected to winter gardens, each of which forms a side wing. A balcony has been placed outside the bedroom at the middle of the back front.

Similarly, the house at the corner of Menzel-strasse and Wölflstrasse has four storeys and has a broad, projecting erection facing the Menzelstrasse. The plastered façade is ornamented with rusticated corners and central pilasters. The broken–lined roof has dormer windows. Each floor is occupied by two flats encompassing an inner courtyard and a patio. Each flat consists of an entry hall, four or five sitting–rooms, a dining room, a maid's room, a bath, and a kitchen with pantry. The corridors, common principal staircase as well as the side stairs are lighted from the inner courtyard.

Das zweistöckige, in einem Garten liegende Landhaus in Charlottenburg-Westend, Lindenallee 5, ist in einer Bauzeit von 8 Monaten für die Baukostensumme von 70 000 Mark zur Ausführung gekommen. Der Entwurf stammt von Architekt Paul Zimmerreimer. Der an einer Seitenfront angeordnete überdeckte Haupteingang lehnt sich an einen polygonalen, durch beide Geschosse gehenden, mit einer Dachhaube abschließenden Vorbau. An der Straßenfront springt im Erdgeschoß ein viereckiger Erker hervor, der im Obergeschoß eine offene, mit Säulen ausgestattete, seitlich von Figuren begleitete, von besonderem Dach überdeckte Laube trägt. Die andere Seitenfront ist wieder durch einen in flacher Rundung heraustretenden, auf Konsolen ruhenden Erker gegliedert.

Der Eingang vom Garten an der Rückfront führt zu einer überdeckten, mit einer Altane abschließenden

La villa berlinoise, située à Charlottenburg dans la Lindenallee au no 5, fut construite en huit mois pour la somme de 70 000 marks. Les plans de cette maison de deux étages assortie d'un jardin furent exécutés par l'architecte Paul Zimmerreimer. Le porche, abritant l'entrée de la façade latérale, s'adosse à un avant-corps polygonal, coiffé d'une calotte, montant sur deux étages. Un bow-window portant balcon saillit de la façade sur rue. Flanqué de deux sculptures, le balcon est couvert par un toit supporté par des colonnes. L'autre façade latérale présente un oriel légèrement convexe en encorbellement.

L'entrée côté jardin donne sur une véranda surmontée d'un balcon. Les mur extérieurs sont enduits de crépi. Les ornements de la façade furent réalisés par le sculpteur Fritus. Le toit au comble brisé, percé de

Surrounded by a garden, the two–storey private residence in Charlottenburg-Westend (Lindenallee 5) was completed in 8 months at a cost of 70,000 Marks. The house was designed by the architect Paul Zimmerreimer. The covered main entrance at the side of the house abuts upon a polygonal projection which runs the height of both storeys and is crowned by a domeshaped roof. A square bay protrudes at the ground level of the street front and has at the upper storey an open loggia with columns, two flanking figures, and separate roofing. The other side façade also has a flatly–rounded oriel supported by consoles.

The rear entrance facing the garden leads to a covered veranda with a balcony on the top. The ornamental figures of the plastered façades are the work of the sculptor Fritus. The roof with broken lines is

Veranda. Die Fassaden sind in Putzbau hergestellt. Die Figuren an der Fassade fertigte Bildhauer Fritus. Das gebrochene Dach ist mit Biberschwänzen eingedeckt und mit Dachfenstern in Fledermausform besetzt.

Um die Diele mit anschließender Stockwerkstreppe liegen im Erdgeschoß Salon, Herrenzimmer, Wohnzimmer und Speisezimmer, nach dem sich die Veranda öffnet. Im Obergeschoß sind die Schlafzimmer nebst Bad und Toilette und die Fremdenzimmer angeordnet. Die Küchen und Wirtschaftsräume liegen im Kellergeschoß.

458 [1912; 99]

Das vierstöckige, durch ein ausgebautes Dachgeschoß erweiterte Wohnhaus in Breslau, Hohenzollernstraße 115/117, ist nach dem Entwurfe des Architekten Professor H. Poelzig errichtet. Die mit einem Vorgarten ausgestattete Straßenfront enthält die seitwärts gelegene, mit einem Korbbogen überdeckte Durchfahrt. Zwischen den beiden Eckrisaliten bilden sich zwei rundbogig geschlossene, durch zwei Obergeschosse gehende, die Fenster einschließende Nischen. Über dem zweiten Obergeschoß folgt zwischen den Eckbauten eine Altane, hinter welcher die Front des vierten Geschosses zurücktritt. Die Fassade ist mit gefärbtem Verputz versehen. Das gebrochene Dach trägt auf den unteren und oberen Flächen Dachfenster und ist mit Biberschwänzen eingedeckt. Die Bildhauerarbeiten an der Fassade lieferte Professor von Gosen.

Das Erdgeschoß enthält Bureauräume; im ersten Obergeschoß liegen, um eine Diele mit freiliegender Treppe geordnet, das Wohnzimmer, der Wintergarten, das Bibliothekzimmer, das Kinderzimmer in Verbindung mit einem Balkon an der Rückfront, die Küche nebst Anrichte, das Mädchenzimmer, die Nebentreppe sowie zwei Lichthöfe. Das zweite Obergeschoß enthält die Schlafräume.

459 [1912; 35]

Das villenartig ausgebildete, ringsum freiliegende, zweistöckige Einfamilienhaus Bunte in Karlsruhe i. B., Kriegstraße 64d, ist nach dem Entwurfe des Architekten Prof. Eugen Beck in 10½ Monaten für die Baukostensumme von 72 000 Mark zur Ausführung gekommen. Die Straßenfront ist durch Pilaster gegliedert, welche beide Geschosse zusammenfassen; vor dem mittleren Rücksprunge der Fassade erhebt sich im Erdgeschoß eine säulengetragene, mit einer Altane abschließende runde Halle. Im Obergeschoß wird der Rücksprung hinter der Altane durch das in ungebrochener Linie durchgeführte, überall vortretende Dachgesims überdeckt. Auf der Steilfläche des Daches steigt im Mittel der Straßenfront eine ausgebogene, mit einem Giebel bekrönte Fenstergruppe empor; auch die übrigen Dachseiten sind mit ähnlich geformten Fensteraufbauten versehen. Die eine Seitenfront zeigt im Erdgeschoß einen Fensterausbau, an den sich der von Säulen eingefaßte Hauseingang anschließt. Die Gliederungen der Fronten bestehen aus weißgelbem Klingenmünster Sandstein; die Flächen tragen rauhen, gekämmten Weißkalkputz von silbergrauer Farbe. Das gebrochene Dach ist mit deutschem Schiefer eingedeckt, ebenso sind die Dachaufbauten mit Schiefer beschlagen.

Das Erdgeschoß enthält, von einem Vorplatz zugänglich, das Herrenzimmer, den Salon, das Speisezimmer in Verbindung mit einer Terrasse, ferner die Küche mit Anrichte und die Stockwerkstreppe. Im Obergeschoß liegen, wieder um einen Vorplatz gruppiert, zwei Schlafzimmer mit Garderoben, das eine mit Ausgang nach dem Balkon und das Bad.

460 [1913; 1]

Einen Eckbau bildend, an zwei Straßen gelegen, erhebt sich das Geschäftshaus in Berlin, Lindenstraße 32/34, Ecke Feilnerstraße 13/15, nach Entwurf und Bauleitung ein Werk des Architekten Curt Leschnitzer. Die Ausführung erfolgte von Oktober 1911 bis Oktober 1912 und kostete rund 700 000 Mark. Erdgeschoß und erstes Obergeschoß sind durch einen skulpturengeschmückten Brüstungsfries nach oben begrenzt und öffnen sich mit breiten Schaufenstern und im Erdgeschoß durch das Eingangsportal und die Durchfahrt.

lucarnes à tabatière, a reçu une couverture de tuiles plates.

Le rez-de-chaussée comprend, agencés autour d'une antichambre contiguë à l'escalier, le salon, le cabinet de travail de monsieur, la salle de séjour ainsi que la salle à manger attenante à la véranda. L'étage est occupé par les chambres à coucher, la chambre d'amis, la salle de bains et le cabinet d'aisances. La cuisine et les pièces de service sont aménagées au sous-sol.

458 [1912; 99]

L'architecte H. Poelzig réalisa les plans de cet immeuble de quatre étages situé à Breslau, Hohenzollernstraße 115/117. La façade sur rue, assortie d'un jardin frontal, est percée latéralement d'un passage surbaissé. La partie médiane de la façade, composée de deux niches cintrées enchâssant des fenêtres et portant un balcon, est flanquée de deux avancées cornières. Le troisième étage s'élève en retrait derrière le balcon. La façade est revêtue d'un crépi coloré. Le toit au comble brisé présente une double rangée de fenêtres mansardées. Les ornements sculptés de la façade sont l'œuvre du professeur von Gosen.

Le rez-de-chaussée abrite des bureaux. Au premier étage, autour d'un hall renfermant l'escalier, sont aménagés la salle de séjour, le jardin d'hiver, la bibliothèque, la chambre des enfants donnant sur un balcon de la façade postérieure, la cuisine, l'office, la chambre des domestiques, l'escalier de service ainsi que deux cours vitrées. Le deuxième étage est occupé par les chambres à coucher.

459 [1912; 35]

La propriété Bunte, située à Karlsruhe, Kriegstraße 64d, fut érigée en dix mois et demi pour la somme de 72 000 marks. Il s'agit d'une construction dégagée de deux étages aux allures de villa. Les plans furent exécutés par l'architecte prof. Eugen Beck. La façade principale est ornée de pilastres sur toute sa hauteur. Au rez-de-chaussée, un perron arrondi, assorti de colonnes supportant un balcon, orne le renfoncement médian de la façade, surmonté au premier étage par la corniche saillante du toit. Un groupe convexe de fenêtres, coiffé d'un pignon, se détache du versant pentu du toit dominant la façade principale. Les autres versants sont eux aussi percés de fenêtres mansardées. Une des façades latérales présente, au rez-de-chaussée, un bow-window attenant à l'entrée flanquée de colonnes. Les ornements de la façade sont en grès de Klingenmünster, les murs extérieurs sont revêtus d'un crépi à la chaux de couleur gris argent. Le toit au comble brisé ainsi que les fenêtres mansardées portent une couverture d'ardoises.

Le rez-de-chaussée abrite un vestibule par lequel on accède au cabinet de travail de monsieur, au salon, à la salle à manger attenante à une terrasse, à la cuisine et à son office et à la cage d'escalier. Au premier étage sont aménagées, autour d'une antichambre, deux chambres à coucher avec leurs garderobe et une salle de bains.

460 [1913; 1]

Cet immeuble à usage commercial, situé à Berlin, à l'angle de la Lindenstraße et de la Feilnerstraße, fut construit par l'architecte Curt Leschnitzer. Les travaux durèrent du mois d'octobre 1911 au mois d'octobre 1912 et coûtèrent la somme de 700 000 marks. Le rez-de-chaussée et le premier étage sont séparés du reste du bâtiment par une corniche ornée. La façade des deux niveaux est percée par de larges devantures ainsi que par un passage et un portail d'entrée au rez-de-chaussée. La façade des trois derniers étages est

covered with flat red tile and has windows in the form of oval lutherns.

The ground floor entry hall contains the main staircase and is encompassed by the drawing-room, study, sitting-room and dining room, which opens out into the veranda. The upper floor contains the bedrooms as well as the bath, water closet, and guest room. The kitchen and service rooms are located in the basement.

458 [1912; 99]

The apartment building with four storeys and an additional roof storey in Breslau (Hohenzollernstrasse 115/117) was designed by the architect Professor H. Poelzig. To the left of the front garden is a carriageway set in a basket arch. The front façade has two round-arched niches in its centre which run the height of two storeys and which are flanked by two bays. The niches contain windows. A balcony is located between the side projections above the third storey, and behind that the recessed front of the third storey. The façades are faced with coloured plaster. Both slopes of the red tiled roof have windows. The ornamental sculptures on the façade are the work of Professor von Gosen.

The ground floor contains offices. Arranged around the hall on the first floor are an open stair, the sitting-room, the winter garden, library, the nursery leading onto the rear balcony, the kitchen and pantry, maid's room, side stairs, as well as two patios. The second floor is occupied by bedrooms.

459 [1912; 35]

The villa-like Bunte house in Karlsruhe (Kriegstrasse 64d), a free-standing structure with two storeys, was designed by the architect Professor Eugen Beck. The one-family house was completed in 10½ months with construction costs amounting to 72,000 Marks. The front façade is divided by pilasters running its entire height. A round porch with columns supporting a balcony projects in front of the returned centre section of the façade. The return behind the balcony at the first storey is covered by the unbroken, overhanging roof moulding. A gable with slightly convex windows is located in the steeper roof slope at the front of the house. At the ground level of one side front is a window bay connected to the main entrance, which is framed in columns. The articulations of the façades consist of light yellow sandstone from Klingenmünster; the surfaces are faced with rough, combed high-calcium lime plaster of silver-grey colour. The roof is covered with German slate, as are the roof superstructures.

The ground floor contains a hall bordered by a study, drawing-room, the dining room leading to one of the terraces, plus the kitchen with its pantries, and the staircase leading to the upper floor. Contained on the upper floor, and again grouped round the hall, are two bedrooms with cloak-rooms, one of which leads out onto the balcony, and a bath.

460 [1913; 1]

Located on the corner of Lindenstrasse and Feilnerstrasse in Berlin, the "Merkur" commercial building is the work of the architect Curt Leschnitzer, who also supervised the construction. This was carried out from October 1911 through October 1912 and cost approximately 700,000 Marks. The ground and first storeys are bordered at the top by a parapet frieze of sculptured ornamentation, and open with broad shop windows. The entrance and a carriageway are also located at the ground level. The upper three storeys

Die folgenden drei Obergeschosse sind durch aufsteigende breite und die Fenster trennende schmale Pfeiler zu einer Einheit zusammengezogen. Die an der Lindenstraße fünfstöckige, an der Feilnerstraße dreistöckige Fassade ist mit grauem Kirchheimer Muschelkalk bekleidet. Das abgewalmte, Dachfenster tragende Dach ist mit Ziegeln eingedeckt. Das Erdgeschoß enthält an der Lindenstraße den zur Haupttreppe und dem Paternosteraufzuge führenden Eingangsflur, die seitliche Einfahrt zum Hof und zwei Verkaufsräume. An der Feilnerstraße schließen sich Bureauräume, Nebentreppe und eine Durchfahrt zum zweiten Hofe an. Das erste und zweite Obergeschoß sind von je einem, nur durch Pfeilerstellungen geteilten Verkaufsraume eingenommen. Das dritte Obergeschoß ist zu Bureauräumen, das vierte Obergeschoß zu Bureau- und Atelierräumen eingerichtet. Im Kellergeschoß sind neben umfänglichen Lagerräumen die Zentralheizung und die Motorräume untergebracht.

Der gesamte Bau mit Decken, Stützen, Dachhaut und Dachkonstruktion ist in Beton ausgeführt.

461 [1913; 18]

Das im Erdgeschoß zu Läden, in den Obergeschossen zu Geschäfts- und Bureauräumen eingerichtete Geschäftshaus in Dresden, Pragerstraße 54, ist in 6 Monaten zur Ausführung gekommen und wurde im Baubureau des Erbauers E. Meißner von dem Architekten Martin Socke in Grundrissen und Fassaden entworfen. Die Baukosten betrugen 400 000 Mark. Das mit Einschluß des Dachgeschosses fünfstöckige Gebäude enthält im Erdgeschoß das rundbogige Portal und breite Schaufenster. Die oberen Geschosse der Straßenfront sind mit durchgehenden Pfeilern versehen und teilen sich in einen breiten Mittelbau und zwei schmale Seitenteile. In der Mittelachse kragt ein polygonaler, durch drei Obergeschosse geführter Erker vor, während im zweiten und dritten Obergeschosse der Seitenteile sich mit Brüstungsgittern versehene Loggien öffnen. Über dem dritten Obergeschosse zieht sich ein Gurtgesims und im mittleren Teile eine Altane hin, hinter welcher die Frontwand zurücktritt. Das vortretende Dachgesims trägt im Mittel einen größeren, mit einem Giebel abschließenden Dachaufbau. Die Straßenfront ist mit gelbem Cottaer Sandstein bekleidet, Erdgeschoß und erstes Obergeschoß enthalten eiserne Säulen, und die Einfassung der Schaufenster besteht aus Stahlblech. Die Hinterfront des Gebäudes ist in weißer Verblendung in Verbindung mit Edelputz hergestellt. Die Bildhauerarbeiten an der Fassade sind in der Werkstatt von Fleck & Jllmèrt nach Angabe des Architekten Fr. O. Hartmann ausgeführt.

Im Erdgeschoß, dem sich an der Hofseite zwei einstöckige Flügelbauten anschließen, befinden sich vier große Läden; in den vier Obergeschossen sind Bureauräume und Sprechzimmer für Ärzte geschaffen. Außer der Haupttreppe vermittelt ein elektrischer Personenaufzug den Verkehr zwischen sämtlichen Geschossen. Im Kellergeschoß sind große Räume für den Bedarf der Bodega und eine Niederdruck-Dampfheizung angelegt. Die Fundamente sind in Zementbeton, die Decken in Eisenbeton hergestellt.

462 [1913; 12]

Mit allen Fronten freiliegend, erhebt sich in vier Geschossen und einem ausgebauten Dachgeschoß das Gebäude des Wiener Bankvereins in Wien, am Schottenring. Der Entwurf stammt von dem Architekten K. K. Baurat E. von Gotthilf und dem Architekten Alex. Neumann. Die Ausführung nahm 2½ Jahre in Anspruch und verursachte rund 500 000 Kronen an Baukosten. Die Fronten am Schottenring und an der Schottengasse sind durch vorspringende Mittelrisalite gegliedert. Das gequaderte Erdgeschoß enthält die Portale; die am Schottenring und an der Schottengasse sich öffnenden sind von Säulen flankiert; ein drittes Portal liegt an der Schottenbastei. Die oberen drei Geschosse sind durch aufsteigende Pfeiler geteilt, welche die zum Teile geradlinig, im zweiten Obergeschosse rundbogig überdeckten Fenster zwischen sich einschließen. Die Mittelrisalite tragen ein viertes Obergeschoß und sind über dem vortretenden Dachkranz mit

---

traitée de façon homogène. De larges piliers encadrent, sur toute la hauteur, des groupes de fenêtres, elles-mêmes divisées par d'étroits piliers continus. La façade de cinq étages sur la Lindenstraße et celle de trois étages sur la Feilnerstraße sont revêtues de coquillart gris de Kirchheim. Le toit en croupe mansardé est recouvert de tuiles. Le rez-de-chaussée comprend, sur la Lindenstraße, un couloir d'entrée conduisant à l'escalier principal et au pater-noster, un passage latéral menant à la cour et deux locaux de commerce, sur la Feilnerstraße, des bureaux, un escalier secondaire et un passage donnant sur la deuxième cour. Les premier et deuxième étages sont occupés par une surface de vente divisée par des piliers. Le troisième étage abrite des bureaux, le quatrième est aménagé en bureaux et en ateliers. Le chauffage central, les salles des machines ainsi que de vastes entrepôts sont installés au sous-sol. L'ensemble du bâtiment, sont les planchers, les supports, la couverture et la charpente, sont en béton.

461 [1913; 18]

Cet immeuble de Dresdes, situé dans la Prager-straße 54, fut construit en l'espace de six mois par l'entrepreneur E. Meißner sur les plans de l'architecte Martin Socke. Les travaux coûtèrent la somme de 400 000 marks. Ce bâtiment de cinq étages dont un mansardé abrite des commerces au rez-de-chaussée et des bureaux dans les étages supérieurs. Le rez-de-chaussée est percé d'un passage en plein cintre et de larges devantures. La façade des étages supérieurs, ornée de piliers continus, s'organise autour d'un large corps médian et de deux parties latérales étroites. Une logette en saillie polygonale se détache du centre et s'élève sur trois étages. Elle est couronnée par une plate-forme derrière laquelle s'élève en retrait la façade du quatrième étage. Les parties latérales des deuxième et troisième étages sont assorties de loggias. Un cordon sépare les trois étages inférieurs du reste du bâtiment. La corniche saillante du toit supporte en son centre un groupe de lucarnes mansardées. La façade sur rue est revêtue de grès jaune de Cotta, le rez-de-chaussée ainsi que le premier étage présentent des colonnes de fer, l'encadrement des devantures est en tôle d'acier. La façade postérieure a reçu en partie un badigeon blanc, le reste est crépi. Les décors sculptés de la façade furent réalisés par l'atelier Fleck & Jllmèrt d'après les plans de l'architecte Fr. O. Hartmann.

Le rez-de-chaussée, prolongé sur la façade sur cour par deux ailes d'un étage, abrite quatre grands commerces. Des bureaux et des cabinets médicaux sont aménagés dans les quatre étages supérieurs. Un escalier et un ascenseur électrique assurent la communication entre les étages. Au sous-sol sont installés de vastes celliers ainsi qu'un chauffage central à vapeur à basse pression. Les fondations sont en béton de ciment, les planchers en béton armé.

462 [1913; 12]

La banque de Vienne, sur le Schottenring, est abritée dans un édifice dégagé de cinq étages dont un mansardé. Conçu par les architectes E. von Gotthilf et Alex. Neumann, ce bâtiment fut construit en deux années et demie et coûta la somme de 500 000 couronnes. Les façades sur les Schottenring et Schottengasse sont ornées d'avant-corps médians. Les murs en pierres de taille du rez-de-chaussée sont percés par les entrées. Celles-ci, donnant sur les Schottenring et Schottengasse, sont flanquées de colonnes. Une troisième entrée est située sur la Schottenbastei. Les trois étages supérieurs sont régulièrement divisés par des piliers encadrant les fenêtres en plein cintre du deuxième étage et celles à linteau droit des premier et troisième niveaux. Les avant-corps médians supportent un quatrième étage et se terminent en attique au-dessus d'une cor-

---

are joined by broad pillars as well as by narrower ones located between the windows. The façade, which on the Lindenstrasse is five-storeyed, on the Feilnerstrasse three-storeyed, is faced with shell limestone from Kirchheim. The hipped roof with dormers is covered with clay tile. The ground floor on the Lindenstrasse side contains an entrance hall leading to the principal staircase and paternoster lift, a carriageway at the side leading to the courtyard, and two sales rooms. At the Feilnerstrasse side are offices, side stairs and a carriageway to a second courtyard. The first and seconds floors each contain an open sales room broken up by pillars. The third floor contains offices, and the fourth floor is occupied by more offices and ateliers. The basement contains expansive store-rooms, as well as the central heating facilities and motor chambers.

The floors, supports, roofing skin and roof structure of the entire building are cast in concrete.

461 [1913;18]

The commercial building in Dresden (Pragerstrasse 54), with shops on its ground floor and offices ab2ve, was built in 6 months according to the plans and façade details drafted by the architect Martin Socke of the architect's office of E. Meissner. Construction costs amounted to 400,000 Marks. The five-storey edifice (including the roof storey) has at its ground level broad shop windows and a portal framed in a round arch. The upper storeys of the frontage have continuous pilasters and are grouped into a broad middle section and two narrower side sections. A polygonal oriel projects at the centre axis and extends the height of three storeys, while the two side sections have loggias at the second and third storeys ornamented with balustrade grilles. A string-course runs along the top of the third storey and supports a balcony in the middle section, where the façade is set back. At the middle of the overhanging roof moulding is a large roof structure with gables. The frontage is faced with yellow sandstone from Cotta; iron pillars have been placed at the ground level and first storey, and the windows have steel-plate working. The rear front of the building has white facing combined with premixed coloured external rendering. The sculptural ornamentation of the façade were produced by the studios of Fleck & Jllmert according to models supplied by the architect Fr. O. Hartmann.

The ground floor, which has two one-storey wings adjoining the courtyard, is occupied by four large shops; the four upper floors contain offices and consulting rooms for physicians. Access between the building's floors is provided by the principal staircase, as well as by an electric lift. The basement contains service rooms for the wine shop and a low-pressure heating installation. Foundations are of concrete, the ceilings of reinforced concrete.

462 [1913; 12]

The Wiener Bankverein building on the Schottenring in Vienna was designed by the Imperial and Royal architect E. von Gotthilf and the architect Alex. Neumann. Construction of the bank, whose fronts are exposed on all sides, occupied 2½ years. The fronts facing the Schottenring and the Schottengasse have a projecting middle structure. The ashlar-faced ground level contains portals; those opening onto the Schottenring and the Schottengasse are flanked by columns; a third portal is located at the Schottenbastel front. The upper three storeys are articulated by continuous pilasters which frame straight-lined and, on the second storey, round-arched, windows. The middle erections have a fourth storey and end with a terrace placed above the roof cornice. The steeper part of the roof contains dormers. At the top of the corner projec-

Vestibül   Vestibule   Vestibule   Kassenraum   Salle des caisses   Tellers' Hall

einer Attika beendet, während die Steilflächen des gebrochenen Daches mit Dachfenstern besetzt sind. Die Eckvorsprünge der Seitenfronten sind mit figurenbekrönten Dreiecksgiebeln versehen. Die Fassaden sind mit Arena-Marmor aus Pola bekleidet; das Dach ist mit Metallplatten eingedeckt.

Das Vestibül am Schottenring führt zur Haupttreppe und weiter in den mit Säulen ausgestatteten, mit einer Oberlichtkuppel überdeckten Kassensaal, in den ebenfalls die anderen Vestibüle münden. An den Kuppelraum schließen sich beiderseits die Verkehrssäle für das Publikum an. Ringsum liegend sind die zahlreichen, das Erdgeschoß füllenden, meist durch Pfeilerstellungen unterbrochenen Kassenräume, sowie Nebentreppen und der Personenaufzug angeordnet. Decken und Stützpfeiler sind in Eisenbeton hergestellt.

niche saillante. Les versants pentus du toit à comble brisé sont troués de fenêtres mansardées. Les avancées d'angle des façades latérales sont coiffées de pignons en delta couronnés de sculptures. Les murs de façade sont revêtus de marbre, le toit est recouvert de plaques métalliques.

Le vestibule sur le Schottenring conduit à l'escalier principal puis à la salle des caisses ornée de colonnes et surmontée d'une coupole de verre sur laquelle convergent les autres vestibules. De part et d'autre de la salle des caisses se greffent les salles destinées au public. Des guichets ainsi que les escaliers secondaires et l'ascenseur occupent l'espace restant.

tions of the side fronts are pediments crowned with ornamental figures. The façades are rendered in arena marble from Pola; the roof is covered with metal sheets.

The vestibule on the Schottenring side leads to the grand staircase and to the tellers' hall, which is lined with columns and covered by a domed rooflight. Other vestibules also lead into the tellers' hall. Both sides of the domed room are flanked by counter halls. The rest of the ground floor is filled up by an encircling array of cashiers' offices which are divided by various arrangements of pillars. The ground floor also contains secondary stairs and a lift. All ceilings and piers are cast in reinforced cement.

463 [1913; 19]

Das viergeschossige, mit ausgebautem Dachgeschoß versehene Geschäftshaus des Deutschen Creditvereins in Berlin, Köthenerstraße 44, ist nach dem Entwurfe des Architekten Paul Zimmerreiner im Laufe von 12 Monaten für die Kostensumme von 360 000 Mark errichtet. Das Erdgeschoß der Straßenfront ist durch eine vorgesetzte Säulenstellung ausgezeichnet und enthält das Portal; das erste und zweite Obergeschoß zeigen durch Pfeiler eingefaßte, mit Giebeln bekrönte seitliche Fenstervorbauten, ebenso sind die Fenster zwischen diesen durch Pfeiler eingefaßt und mit Giebeln abgeschlossen. Die übrigen Fenster im zweiten Obergeschoß sowie die paarweise zusammengefaßten im dritten Obergeschoß sind rundbogig überdeckt. Über dem weit übertretenden, durch Konsolen unterstützten Dachkranz erheben sich mit Flachgiebeln abgeschlossene Dachaufbauten. Die Front ist in rotem Mainsandstein ausgeführt.

Im Erdgeschoß führt das Vestibül zur Haupttreppe und anschließendem Aufzug und zu dem mit Oberlicht versehenen Verkehrsraum für das Publikum. Von diesem aus sind die Kassenräume zugänglich, an welche sich zwei Nebentreppen und ein Flurgang anschließen. Das erste Obergeschoß enthält, um den Lichthof gelagert, das Direktor- und das Konferenzzimmer, das Wartezimmer und die Registratur. Das zweite Obergeschoß ist zur Anlage vermietbarer Bureauräume benutzt. Das dritte Obergeschoß und das Dachgeschoß bergen gleichfalls vermietbare Bureauräume. Das Kellergeschoß enthält den Tresor, die Stahlkammer mit den Safes, Aktenräume und die Heizung.

463 [1913; 19]

L'immeuble de quatre étages dont un mansardé abritant l'institut de crédit de Berlin, Köthenerstraße 44, fut construit en douze mois pour la somme de 360 000 marks. Les plans furent réalisés par l'architecte Paul Zimmerreiner. Le rez-de-chaussée de la façade sur rue est caractérisé par un alignement de colonnes où un passage destiné à l'entrée a été aménagé. Aux premier et deuxième étages, les fenêtres latérales, flanquées de piliers saillants et couronnées d'un pignon, encadrent des ouvertures présentant la même structure. Les autres fenêtres du deuxième étage ainsi que celles du troisième étage sont en plein cintre. Au-dessus de la corniche en encorbellement se détachent des lucarnes mansardées. Le mur de façade est en grès rouge du Main.

Au rez-de-chaussée, le vestibule conduit à l'escalier principal contigu à l'ascenseur et au hall destiné au public. C'est par celui-ci, éclairé par une verrière, que se fait l'accès aux guichets. Deux escaliers secondaires et un couloir sont attenants. Au premier étage sont installés, agencés autour d'une cour vitrée, le bureau du directeur, la salle de conférences, la salle d'attente ainsi que les registres. Les deuxième, troisième étages ainsi que l'étage mansardé sont occupés par des bureaux en location. Le trésor, la chambre forte comprenant le coffre fort, les archives et la chaufferie sont aménagés au sous-sol.

463 [1913; 19]

The German Credit Union building in Berlin (Köthenerstrasse 44) is a four-storey structure with an additional roof storey. Designed by the architect Paul Zimmerreiner, it was completed over the course of 12 months at a cost of 360,000 Marks. The ground level of the frontage shows a row of slightly elevated columns, and the portico. The first and second storeys have to either side windowed projections crowned by a pediment and framed by pilasters. The intervening windows are also separated by pilasters and finished by pediments. The other windows of the second storey, as well as the coupled windows of the third, are framed in round arches. Windowed superstructures with flat gables are set above the wide eaves, which are suported by corbels. The façade is faced with red Main sandstone.

The ground floor vestibule leads to the principal staircase and the adjoining lift. It continues into the counter hall, which is illuminated by a roof light. This hall leads tho the teller's hall, which is bordered by two side stairs and a corridor. Arranged round the patio on the first floor are rooms for the director and a conference room, a waiting-room and the registry. The second floor has leased office space, as do the third floor and roof floor. The safe is located in the basement strong room, where there are also rooms for securities as well as for the heating installations.

464 [1913; 23]

Das an zwei Straßen liegende Geschäftshaus Bernh. Kaß in Berlin, Kaiser Wilhelmstraße 38 und Rosenstraße 9–13, ein Werk des Architekten Reg.-Baumeisters Paul Nathansohn, ist in einer Bauzeit von 22 Monaten errichtet und hat rund 1 000 000 M. Kosten verursacht. Die kürzere Front an der Kaiser Wilhelmstraße zeigt schwere, die vier Obergeschosse

464 [1923; 23]

L'immeuble Bernh. Katz de Berlin donne sur les rues Kaiser Wilhelmstraße et Rosenstraße. Conçu par l'architecte Paul Nathansohn, il nécessita onze mois de construction et coûta lala somme de 1 000 000 marks. La façade sur la Wilhelmstraße, présente audessus d'un rez-de-chaussée en pierres de taille percé

464 [1913; 23]

Facing both the Kaiser Wilhelm Strasse and the Rosenstrasse, the Katz building in Berlin was designed by the government architect Paul Nathansohn and completed in 11 months at a cost of about 1,000,000 Marks. The shorter front facing the Kaiser Wilhelm Strasse has massive columns extending from the first

durchsetzende Säulen über einem gequaderten, von flachbogig überwölbten Schaufenstern durchbrochenen Erdgeschoß. Der Hauptteil der Fassade, aus drei Zwischenweiten bestehend, ist einheitlich zusammengefaßt und von einem Zeltdach mit Mansarden bekrönt. Die Fenster der drei ersten Obergeschosse sind der Höhe nach zusammengezogen, die des etwas zurückgesetzten vierten Obergeschosses sind durch einen Dachstreif abgetrennt. Der seitliche Teil der Fassade trägt über dem dritten Obergeschosse einen Balkon und enthält im Erdgeschoß das im Flachbogen überwölbte Portal. Die Front an der Kaiser Wilhelmstraße ist mit Kirchheimer Muschelkalk bekleidet. Der bildhauerische Schmuck derselben, aus spielenden Putten und Kränzen am Sockel der Säulen und dem Schlußstein des Portals bestehend, ist von Bildhauer Rich. Knöhl geschaffen. Die Front an der Rosenstraße ist entsprechend der an der Kaiser Wilhelmstraße, aber einfacher gegliedert, zeigt eine Verblendung von Ettringer Tuffstein und wird ebenfalls von einem Mansardendach aus grauen holländischen Pfannen bekrönt.

Der seitliche Eingang an der Kaiser Wilhelmstraße führt zur Stockwerkstreppe mit dem Personenaufzug und weiterhin zu den beiden mittelst einer Durchfahrt verbundenen Höfen, deren Fronten Verblendziegel mit farbigen Einlagen zeigen. Aus dem zweiten Hofe führt eine Durchfahrt nach der Rosenstraße. Im Vestibül sind über dem Paneel aus Kirchheimer Muschelkalkplatten fünf Reliefs angebracht, die aus dem Abbruche des Hauses Rosenstraße 17 stammen. Das Geschäftshaus enthält in fünf Geschossen, durch Eisenstützen geteilte, mit Treppen und Aufzügen ausgestattete Räume, ein Keller- und zwei Dachgeschosse, ferner zwei Glashallen auf den Höfen. Im Dachgeschoß ist eine Kantine nebst Küche und Dachgarten eingerichtet.

Sämtliche Decken sind massiv auf Bulbeisen mit Eisenbetonvoute hergestellt.

465 [1913: 25]

Als Eckbau mit zwei Straßenfronten erhebt sich das Börsengebäude in Duisburg, nach dem Entwurfe der Architekten Bielenberg und Moser, denen in einem Wettbewerbe der zweite Preis erteilt wurde, im Laufe zweier Jahre für die Kostensumme von 660 000 Mark unter örtlicher Bauleitung des Architekten Walter errichtet. Die vierstöckige, außerdem mit einem Zwischengeschoß versehene Fassade wurd durch aufstrebende Pfeiler zu einer Einheit zusammengefaßt. Die Fenster der unteren Geschosse sind zu leicht vorgebogenen, durch schmale Pfeiler geteilten Gruppen zusammengefaßt, die über dem zweiten Obergeschoß mit Altanen vor den rundbogig geschlossenen Fenstern des dritten Obergeschosses endigen. Das vierte Obergeschoß enthält gleichfalls zu Gruppen vereinigte Fenster. Die schmalere Front enthält den Haupteingang und ist durch vorgestellte Säulen ausgezeichnet, über denen sich ein Balkon erstreckt. Der Sockel der Fassaden besteht aus Niedermendiger Basalt, die oberen Geschosse sind mit Ettriger Tuffstein bekleidet.

Im Untergeschoß liegen die Eingangshalle, die in den oberen Geschossen zweiarmige, kreisförmig geführte Haupttreppe, das Restaurant mit besonderem Eingang von der Seitenfront aus, die zugehörigen Nebenräume und die Kochküche. Das Erdgeschoß enthält den großen, durch Pfeilerstellungen geteilten Börsensaal, die Geschäftszimmer, das Telegraphen- und Telephonzimmer, ein Bierbüffet und mehrere Nebentreppen. Die drei über dem Saal folgenden Decken sind an den Dachbindern aufgehängt. Börsensaal und Restaurant haben eine Täfelung von Eichenholz erhalten. Im Zwischengeschoß sind die Sitzungssäle und die Musiktribünen für den Börsensaal untergebracht. Die folgenden Obergeschosse enthalten Bureauräume und im ersten Obergeschoß eine nach der Hofseite gekehrte Terrasse.

466 [1913: 30]

Das umfängliche, in vier Geschossen und einem ausgebauten Dachgeschoß aufsteigende Kontorhaus Reifenberg & Co. in Köln a. Rh., Zeppelinstraße 5–7, ist ein gemeinsames Werk der Architekten Prof. P. Bonatz, C. Schön und des Regierungsbaumeisters

---

par des devantures en plein cintre, de massives colonnes montant sur quatre étages. Le corps de bâtiment, composé de façon homogène, comprend trois largeurs intermédiaires et est couronné d'un toit en pavillon mansardé. Les fenêtres des trois étages inférieurs sont régulièrement alignées, celles du quatrième étage, légèrement en retrait, sont séparées des autres ouvertures par une bande de toiture. Le troisième étage de la partie latérale est surmonté d'une balustrade, au rez-de-chaussée, la façade est trouée par un passage surbaissé. La façade sur la Kaiser Wilhelmstraße est revêtue de coquillart de Kirchheim. Les ornements sculptés, les angelots, les couronnes sur les socles des colonnes et sur la clé de voûte du passage sont l'œuvre du sculpteur Rich. Knöhl. La façade sur la Rosenstraße s'harmonise avec la précédente. Elle est néanmoins traitée plus sobrement. Les murs sont revêtus de tuf d'Ettingen, le toit mansardé est recouvert de tuiles hollandaises grises.

L'entrée latérale sur la Wilhelmstraße conduit à la cage d'escalier et à l'ascenseur, puis aux deux cours reliées par un passage dont les murs ont reçu une couverture de briques polychromes. La deuxième cour communique par un passage avec la Rosenstraße. Dans le vestibule, cinq reliefs, récupérés lors de la destruction d'une maison située au no. 17 de la rue, ont été apposés au-dessus des lambris de coquillart. L'immeuble se compose de cinq étages, de deux étages mansardés, d'un sous-sol et de deux cours vitrées. Escaliers et ascenseurs assurent la communication entre les étages. Une cantine, attenante à la cuisine et au jardin-terrasse, est aménagée dans les combles.

L'ensemble des planchers sont massifs et couverts d'une voûte en béton armé.

465 [1913: 25]

La bourse de Duisbourg est abritée dans un bâtiment d'angle ayant deux façades sur rue. Cet édifice, ayant fait l'objet d'un concours, ce fut au deuxième prix, remporté par les architectes Bielenberg et Moser, que revint le contrat de construction. Les travaux qui durèrent deux années furent réalisés pour la somme de 660 000 marks. La façade de ce bâtiment de quatre étages, comprenant un entresol, est conçue autour de piliers montants. Les fenêtres des deux étages inférieurs, regroupées par quatre et séparées par d'étroits piliers, forment des ensembles convexes surmontés par des balcons, lesquels ornent les fenêtres cintrées du troisième étage. Le quatrième étage présente également des ouvertures groupées. La façade étroite, comprenant l'entrée principale, est caractérisée par un portique supportant un balcon. Le socle de la façade est en basalte de Niedermendigen, les étages sont revêtus de tuf d'Ettringen.

Le sous-sol comprend le hall d'entrée, l'escalier principal à deux volées dans les étages supérieurs, le restaurant ayant son entrée particulière sur la façade latérale, avec ses salles attenantes et sa cuisine. Le rez-de-chaussée abrite la corbeille divisée par des piliers, des bureaux, le télégraphe et le téléphone, un bar et de nombreux escaliers de dégagement. Les trois planchers, situés au-dessus de la corbeille, sont suspendus à la ferme. La corbeille ainsi que le restaurant sont lambrissés de chêne. Les salles de réunion et la tribune de musique destinées à la corbeille sont installées à l'entresol. Les étages supérieurs sont occupés par des bureaux. Une terrasse sur cour est aménagée au premier étage.

466 [1913: 30]

L'établissement commercial Reifenberg & Co. à Cologne, Zeppelinstraße 5–7, vaste bâtiment de cinq étages dont un mansardé, est l'œuvre de P. Bonath, C. Schön et Erberich. Il fut mené à bien en

---

through the fourth storeys. The ground level opens with flat arches, which are framed in banded rustication. The main part of the façade, which consists of three horizontal interfaces, has a uniform design and is covered by a pyramidal roof with mansards. The windows of the first three storeys are vertical in form, those of the fourth storey are somewhat recessed and covered by the overhanging roof moulding. A balcony is placed at one side of the façade at the fourth storey; an arched portal is placed directly below this at the ground level. The front facing the Kaiser Wilhelm Strasse is faced with shell limestone from Kirchheim. The sculptured ornamentation at the base of the columns and at the keystone of the portal depicts frolicking puttos and wreaths. These were created by the sculptor Rich. Knöhl. The front facing the Rosenstrasse is similar, yet more modest is appearance. It is faced with tufa from Ettringen and is also covered by a mansard roof with Dutch pantiles.

The entrance at the Kaiser Wilhelm Strasse leads to the staircase for the upper floors and the lift, and connects with the two courtyards joined by a carriageway. The courtyards have clay brick facing with coloured insertions. A carriageway leads from the second courtyard to the Rosenstrasse. Over the vestibule's wainscotting of Kirschheim shell limestone are five reliefs saved from the torn-down house at Rosenstrasse 17. The rooms of the five-storey commercial building are separated by iron supports; there are also a number of stairs and lifts, as well as a basement, two roof storeys and two glassed halls at the courtyards. A cafeteria with kitchen facilities is located on the roof floor, as is the rooftop garden.

All floors have an iron framework construction with inclined haunches of reinforced concrete.

465 [1913: 25]

The Stock Exchange in Duisburg, a corner building with two exposed fronts, is based on the design by the architects Bielenberg and Moser which took second place in the architectural competition. The two-year construction of the four-storey building with a mezzanine was supervised by the architect Walter, and cost 660,000 Marks. The unified appearance of the façade is created by a series of continuous pillars. The groups of slightly-protruding windows of the lower storeys are divided by narrow pilasters ending at balconies located in front of the third-storey windows, which are framed in rounded arches. The fourth storey also has groups of windows. The main entrance is at the short front and is framed by elevated columns supporting a balcony. The socle of the façade consists of Niedermendingen basalt; the upper storeys are faced with Ettringen tufa.

The basement contains the entry hall, a two-flight circular staircase, a restaurant with a separate entrance at the side front, service rooms and a kitchen. Located on the ground floor are the large Stock Exchange hall, which is divided by rows of pillars, offices, telephone and telegraph rooms, a beer buffet, as well as a number of side stairs. The three successive ceilings over the hall are supported by roof frames. The Stock Exchange hall and the restaurant are panelled in oak. The mezzanine contains meeting rooms and a musicians' gallery overlooking the Exchange hall. The floors above contain offices; the first floor has a terrace overlooking the courtyard.

466 [1913: 30]

The Reifenberg & Co. office building, a four-storey structure with an additional roof storey, has an long frontage at Zeppelinstrasse 5 and 7 in Cologne. It is the result of a design drafted by the architects

Erberich und ist im Laufe eines Jahres zur Ausführung gekommen. Die Fassaden sind in den unteren beiden Geschossen mit dorischen Halbsäulen besetzt; das Erdgeschoß zeigt Schaufensteröffnungen; der Eingang sowie die Fenstergruppen im ersten Obergeschoß sind leicht ausgebaucht. Das zweite Obergeschoß enthält geradlinig geschlossene Fenstergruppen und hat in der Mittelachse einen ausgekragten Balkon. Das mit weit ausladendem Dachgesims abschließende dritte Obergeschoß ist ganz in Fensteröffnungen aufgelöst. Über der Mitte der Front erhebt sich ein Dachaufbau mit steilem Giebel bekrönt, und beiderseits schließen sich Dachfenster an. Die Fassaden sind im unteren Teil in Muschelkalk, darüber in Tuffstein hergestellt. Die Dächer sind beschiefert. Der bildhauerische Schmuck der Fassaden rührt von Prof. Jansen her.

Dem durch Säulen ausgezeichneten Eingang in der Mitte der Straßenfront folgt die Halle mit offenliegender Treppe, beiderseits schließen sich Läden mit besonderen Treppen und hinterliegenden Lichtschächten an.

Der an der Olivengasse liegende Gebäudeteil enthält den Packraum, die Expedition und den Materialraum für Buchbinder. Die seitlichen Höfe sind durch Einfahrten zugänglich. Das erste Obergeschoß wird durch Lager-, Verkaufs-, Kontor- und Kassenräume eingenommen. Im zweiten und dritten Obergeschoß sind große, durch Pfeiler und Zwischenwände geteilte Räume angeordnet.

467, 468 [1913; 2, 4]

Die nebeneinander auf einem Gartengrundstück liegenden Villen Kempin und Stockhausen in Darmstadt, Christiansweg 23/25 sind nach dem Entwurfe des Architekten Prof. Heinr. Metzendorf im Laufe eines Jahres errichtet. Die Baukosten betrugen 19 000 Mark für die Villa Kempin und 34 000 Mark für die Villa Stockhausen.

Die Villa Kempin, Christiansweg 25, ist im Erdgeschoß mit einer überdeckten, offenen, auf Säulen ruhenden Halle ausgestattet, von welcher aus eine Tür zum Eingangsflur führt. An der einen Giebelfront befindet sich ein mit besonderem Dach versehener Erkervorbau. Das beiderseits mit überhangenden Giebeln abschließende, steile, weit vortretende Dach trägt auf den Flächen größere Fensteraufbauten. Im Erdgeschoß liegen Empfangszimmer, Eßzimmer, Küche und Stockwerkstreppe, während im Dachgeschoß ein großer Atelierraum und die Schlafzimmer untergebracht sind.

Der Gebäudesockel besteht aus Flonheimer buntem Sandstein, die oberen Fassadenflächen tragen grauen Putz, und der Giebel an der Wetterseite ist mit Brettern verschalt. Das Dach ist mit Biberschwänzen eingedeckt.

Die zweigeschossige, mit teilweise ausgebautem Dachgeschoß versehene Villa Stockhausen, Christiansweg 23, zeigt im Erdgeschoß an der einen Längsfront einen mit besonderem Dach abschließenden Vorbau, den Haupteingang enthaltend; an der gegenüber liegenden Front springt ein Erker vor, der eine Altane trägt. An der gegen die Straße gekehrten Giebelfront erhebt sich ein durch beide Geschosse geführter Eckerker, während die gegenüber liegende Front durch zwei Erkervorsprünge gegliedert ist, die einen überdeckten Sitzplatz zwischen sich einschließen. Der Sockel besteht wieder aus Flonheimer Sandstein, die oberen Frontwände sind grau verputzt, und der Wettergiebel ist mit eichenen Schindeln beschlagen. Das steile, mit Biberschwänzen eingedeckte Dach ist mit Fensteraufbauten besetzt. Das Erdgeschoß enthält die Wohnzimmer in Verbindung mit dem Wintergarten, das Eßzimmer und die Küche; im Obergeschosse sind die Schlafzimmer angeordnet.

469 [1913; 26]

Von einem Garten umgeben, in geschlossener, oblonger Form, zweigeschossig aufstrebend, mit einem ausgebauten Mansardendach abschließend, erscheint die Villa in München, Schönbergstraße 9, ein Werk des Architekten Otto Heinrich Riemerschmid, im Laufe von 7 Monaten errichtet. Inmitten der Straßen-

l'espace d'une année. Les façades des deux étages inférieurs sont assorties de demi-colonnes doriques. Le rez-de-chaussée est percé de larges ouvertures. L'entrée ainsi que les groupes de fenêtres du premier étage sont légèrement convexes. Les fenêtres du deuxième étage sont à linteau droit, l'une d'entre elles, au centre de la façade, est ornée d'un balcon en saillie. Le troisième étage, surmonté d'une corniche saillante, est constitué par un alignement d'ouvertures. Une construction mansardée, couronnée d'un pignon pentu, et flanquée de lucarnes s'élève de la partie médiane de la façade. La partie inférieure des murs de façade est réalisée en coquillart, le reste est en tuf. Les toits sont recouverts d'ardoises. Les ornements sculptés de la façade sont l'œuvre du professeur Jansen.

A l'entrée, marquée par deux colonnes au centre de la façade, succèdent le hall et l'escalier, encadrés de commerces équipés d'escaliers particuliers et de cours intérieures attenantes.

L'aile donnant sur la Olivengasse comprend la salle de conditionnement, les expéditions ainsi que la salle du matériel de reliure. Les cours latérales sont accessibles par des passages. Au premier étage sont aménagés magasins, salles de vente, comptoirs et caisses. Les deuxième et troisième étages sont occupés par de vastes salles divisées par des piliers et cloisons.

467, 468 [1913; 2, 4]

Bâties sur un même terrain, les villas Kempin et Stockhausen, situées à Darmstadt, Christiansweg 23/25, furent construites d'après les plans de l'architecte Heinr. Metzendorf. Les travaux furent achevés en l'espace d'une année et coûtèrent 19 000 marks pour la villa Kempin et 34 000 mark pour la villa Stockhausen.

La villa Kempin, au no 25 de la rue, est assortie, au rez-de-chaussée, d'une galerie ouverte à colonnes permettant l'accès à l'entrée. Un avant-corps coiffé d'une toiture particulière se détache de la façade pignon. Le toit pentu et saillant est percé de grandes fenêtres mansardées. Le salon, la salle à manger, la cuisine et l'escalier sont aménagés au rez-de-chaussée. L'étage est occupé par un vaste atelier et des chambres à coucher.

Le socle de la maison est en grès polychrome de Flonheim, les murs de façade sont revêtus d'un crépi gris. Le pignon de la façade occidentale est habillé de lattes de bois, le toit est recouvert de tuiles plates.

La villa Stockhausen, au no 23 de la rue, est une demeure de deux étages au toit mansardé. Le long côté présente un porche abritant l'entrée. L'opposite est assorti d'un avant-corps surmonté d'un balcon. Une avancée d'angle s'élevant sur deux étages se dégage de la façade pignon. La façade opposée s'organise autour de deux avancées encadrant une terrasse couverte. Le socle est également en grès de Flonheim, les murs crépis sont gris, le pignon occidental est protégé par des bardeaux de chêne. Le toit pentu, mansardé est recouvert de tuiles plates. Le rez-de-chaussée comprend la salle de séjour et le jardin d'hiver adjacent, la salle à manger et la cuisine. L'étage abrite les chambres à coucher.

469 [1913; 26]

Cette villa, située à Munich, Schönbergstraße 9, est l'œuvre de l'architecte Otto Heinrich Riemerschmid. Construite en sept mois, cette maison de forme oblongue s'élève sur deux étages et est coiffée d'un toit mansardé. De la partie médiane de la façade

Professor P. Bonatz and the government architect Erberich, and was constructed in the course of one year. The façades of the lower two storeys have Doric demi-columns, and broad windows open at the ground level. The entrance as well as the groups of windows at the first storey are slightly convex in form. The windows at the second floor are straight—lined, and there is a cantilevered balcony at the middle of the front. The third storey, which ends with the overhanging roof, is completely occupied by windows. A roof structure with steep gables is located at the middle of the front, with dormers to either side. The lower façades are of shell limestone, the upper surfaces are faced with tufa. The roofs are of slate. The ornamental sculptures of the façade are the work of Professor Jansen.

The columned entryway at the middle of the frontage leads to a hall with open stairs; shops are located at both sides, with light wells at the rear.

The part of the building bordering the Olivengasse contains rooms for dispatching and a storage room for bookbinders. The side courtyards are accessible by carriageways. The first floor is occupied by storage rooms, salesrooms, offices and cashier. The second and third floors have large rooms with dividing walls and pillars.

467, 468 [1913; 2, 4]

The two neighbouring houses located on a garden plot in Darmstadt were designed by the architect Professor Heinr. Metzendorf and constructed over the course of one year. The Kempin residence, Christiansweg 25, cost 19,000 Marks, the Stockhausen residence 34,000 Marks.

The Kempin residence has at the ground level a covered porch lined with columns which leads through a door to the entry hall. A bay with its own lean—to roof is located at one of the gabled fronts. Large roof superstructures with windows have been cut into the steep, projecting roof with overhanging gables. The ground floor contains a sitting—room, a dining room, kitchen and stairs. Situated on the upper floor are the bedrooms and a large atelier.

The socle of the house consists of coloured sandstone from Flonheim, the upper façades are faced with grey plaster, and the weather side of the gables are planked with boards. The roof is covered with red tile.

The two—storey Stockhausen residence also has an attic floor. The entrance is located within a roofed porch at the ground level of the longer front, the opposite front features a bay crowned by a balcony. The gabled front facing the street has a corner bay extending the height of the two storeys, while the opposing front is articulated by two bays with a seat located between them. The socle is again made of sandstone from Flonheim, the upper walls of the front are of grey plaster, and the weather gable is hung with oak shingles. The steep roof has windowed projections and is covered with flat red tile. The ground floor contains sitting—rooms which adjoin the winter garden, the dining room, and kitchen. Bedrooms occupy the upper floor.

469 [1913; 26]

Surrounded by a garden and assuming a closed, oblong shape, the two—storey house in Munich (Schönbergstrasse 9) was designed by the architect Otto Heinrich Riemerschmid and completed in the course of 7 months. A two—storey bay with an arched

front springt ein mit gewölbtem Dach bekröntes Risalit vor, dem im Erdgeschoß eine den Haupteingang enthaltende, eine Altane tragende Säulenhalle vorgelegt ist. An einer Seitenfront erhebt sich im Erdgeschoß ein Anbau, und die Rückfront ist wieder durch ein vorspringendes Risalit und seitwärts anschließende Terrassen belebt. Die Fenster im Erdgeschoß sind rundbogig, die im Obergeschoß geradlinig geschlossen. Die Fassaden sind in ockergelbem Verputz hergestellt; das Dach, in Blech gedeckt und schwarz gestrichen, trägt eine Reihe Dachfenster.

Das achteckige gewölbte Vestibül im Erdgeschoß umschließt in der Mitte einen Brunnen, anschließend folgen die Bibliothek, das Speisezimmer mit Anrichte, das Musikzimmer, das Atelier mit einem Aufgange zur Galerie. Das Obergeschoß enthält das Billardzimmer, zwei Wohnzimmer, das Gastzimmer, das Badezimmer sowie die Schlafzimmer der Eltern und Kinder. Im Dachgeschoß liegen noch zwei Zimmer, außerdem die Waschküche und andere Wirtschaftsräume. Das Kellergeschoß ist zur Anlage der Küche, des Dienerzimmers, des Heizraums und mehrerer Wirtschaftsräume benutzt.

470 [1913; 10]

Die geschlossene Gruppe von drei Landhäusern in München, Mauerkircherstraße 39, 41 und 43, ist nach dem Entwurfe des Architekten Paul Böhmer im Laufe eines Jahres errichtet. Die durch Brandmauern geschiedenen zweistöckigen Bauten sind durch Ausbauten gegliedert. Das links gelegene Eckhaus besitzt an der Straßenfront sowie an der freien Seitenfront vom Boden aufsteigende, mit einer Altane abschließende, halbrund vorspringende Erkerausbauten. Über der Altane an der Seitenfront öffnet sich eine Loggia. Das rechts gelegene Eckhaus und das mittlere Haus sind ebenfalls mit Erkervorbauten im Erdgeschoß versehen. Die Haupteingänge der Häuser sind an der Straßenfront angeordnet. Die Fronten sind verputzt und die übertretenden, über den Eckhäusern abgewalmten und gebrochenen Dächer sind mit Schiefer eingedeckt. Jedes der drei Häuser enthält eine auf beide Geschosse verteilte, um eine Diele mit freiliegender Treppe gruppierte Wohnung.

471 [1913; 35]

Das an drei Fronten freiliegende, vierstöckige Wohnhaus in München, Kufsteinerplatz 1, ist von Architekt, Königl. Hofoberbaurat Eugen Drollinger entworfen. Der mit einem Halbkreisgiebel abschließende Mittelbau der Hauptfront wird im zweiten Obergeschoß durch eine Altane unterbrochen, hinter welcher die obere Front zurücktritt. An den Ecken springen Risalite vor, die über dem zweiten Obergeschosse Dachstreifen tragen. Das Erdgeschoß der in Putzbau ausgeführten Fassaden ist gequadert, die oberen Geschosse sind durch flache Lisenen gegliedert. Im Erdgeschoß springt eine Nische vor, die mit einer Figur geziert ist. Das mit Ziegeln eingedeckte, abgewalmte Dach trägt auf dem First ein rundes Belvedere.

In den Geschossen sind je zwei Wohnungen mit Küche, Bad und Nebenräumen untergebracht.

472 [1913; 14]

Die in romanischen Stilformen errichtete Johanniskirche in Breslau, Hohenzollernstraße 86, ist mit dem Pfarr- und Gemeindehaus zu einer Baugruppe zusammengeschlossen. Der Entwurf stammt von den Architekten Gaze und Böttcher; der Auftrag zur Ausführung wurde den vorgenannten auf Grund eines öffentlichen Wettbewerbs übertragen. Die Bauzeit nahm 2 Jahre in Anspruch; die Baukosten der Kirche betrugen 600 000 Mark, die des Pfarr- und Gemeindehauses 170 000 Mark.

Die Johanniskirche stellt sich als ein Zentralbau mit zwei Kreuzarmen dar, einerseits mit der Vorhalle und den Treppen zu den Emporen und andererseits mit dem halbrunden Chor, der sich radial anschließenden Kapellen- und Sakristeianlagen ausgestattet. Der Turm steigt über der wieder von Türmchen flankierten Vierung empor und ist in der Höhe des Glockengeschosses von schlanken Türmchen eingefaßt,

sur rue se détache un avant-corps couronné d'un toit en coupole. L'entrée est assortie d'un porche dont les colonnes supportent une plate-forme. Une des façades latérales présente une avancée, la façade postérieure est agrémentée d'un avant-corps avec terrasse attenante. Les fenêtres du rez-de-chaussée sont en plein cintre, celles du premier étage à linteau droit. Les murs de façade ont reçu un crépi ocre jaune, le toit mansardé est recouvert de tôle peinte en noir.

Le rez-de-chaussée comprend le vestibule octogonal orné d'une fontaine, puis la bibliothèque, la salle à manger et l'office, le salon de musique, l'atelier avec accès à la galerie. L'étage est occupé par la salle de billard, deux salles de séjour, la chambre d'amis, la salle de bains ainsi que les chambres à coucher des parents et des enfants. À l'étage des combles sont aménagés deux autres pièces, la buanderie et des pièces de service. La cuisine, la chambre des domestiques, la chaufferie et des débarras sont installés au sous-sol.

470 [1913; 10]

Les trois maisons mitoyennes, situées à Munich, Mauerkircherstraße 39, 41 et 45, furent construites en l'espace d'une année sur les plans de l'architecte Paul Böhmer. Séparées par des murs mitoyens, ces habitations de deux étages sont agrémentées d'avancées. La maison d'angle, à gauche, est assortie, sur ses façades sur rue et latérale, de bow-windows arrondis, surmontés d'un balcon. Ces mêmes bow-windows ornent les rez-de-chaussée des deux autres maisons. Les entrées des habitations sont situées sur la façade sur rue. Les murs sont crépis. Les toits saillants sont recouverts d'ardoises. Des toits en croupe, aux combles brisés coiffent les maisons d'angle. Chacune des constructions abrite un logement, dont les pièces, réparties sur les deux niveaux, sont agencées autour d'un hall et d'un escalier.

471 [1913; 35]

L'immeuble de rapport, situé à Munich, Kufsteinerplatz 1, fut conçu par l'architecte à la cour, Eugen Drollinger. Il s'agit d'une construction de quatre étages, dégagée sur trois côtés. La partie médiane du corps de logis, couronnée par un pignon semi-circulaire, est interrompue, au niveau du second étage, par une plate-forme derrière laquelle s'élèvent en retrait les étages supérieurs. Des avancées hautes de deux étages et coiffées d'une bande de toiture se détachent des angles de l'immeuble. Le rez-de-chaussée de la façade crépie est en pierres de taille, les étages supérieurs sont ornés de bandes lombardes. Une niche faisant saillie et renfermant une sculpture pare le rez-de-chaussée. Un belvédère arrondi couronne le faîte du toit en croupe recouvert de tuiles.

Deux logements comprenant cuisine, bain et pièces de service sont aménagés à chaque étage.

472 [1913; 14]

L'église Saint Jean de Breslau, Hohenzollernstraße 86, fut l'objet d'un concours public que remportèrent les architectes Gaze et Böttcher. Conçue dans un style romantique, elle forme un ensemble avec le presbytère et la maison paroissiale. Les travaux durèrent deux années. L'édification de l'église coûta la somme de 600 00 marks, la construction de la cure et de la maison paroissiale revint à 170 000 marks.

L'église Saint Jean présente une structure fort simple en forme de croix. Les deux bras de la croix comprennent l'un, le narthex et l'escalier menant à la galerie, l'autre, le chœur semi-circulaire ainsi que les chapelles et sacristie attenantes. Au-dessus de la croisée des transepts flanquée de petites tours s'élève le clocher, lui-même encadré par des tourelles au niveau

roof projects from the middle of the frontage, at the base of which stands a porch whose columns support a balcony. A one-storey projection is located at the ground level of one side front, and the rear front is again articulated by a projection with an adjoining terrace. The ground level windows are famed in round arches, those of the upper storey are straight—lined. The façades are faced with yellow—ocre plaster. The mansard roof is covered with metal sheet roofing, which is painted black, and has a number of dormers.

The octagonal, vaulted vestibule on the ground floor has a fountain at its centre, and leads to the library, the dining room and its side rooms, the music room, and the atelier with stairs leading to a gallery. The upper floor contains a billiards room, two sitting—rooms, a guest room as well as bedrooms for the parents and children. Two additional room are located on the attic floor, as are the laundry—room and other service rooms. Kitchen facilities, the servant's room, heating and other utility rooms are located in the basement.

470 [1913; 10]

The semi—detached group of three apartments in Munich (Mauerkircherstrasse 39—43) was designed by the architect Paul Böhmer and constructed within one year. The two—storey structures are separated from one another by compartment masonry walls and exhibit a number of projections. Both the street front and the exposed side front of the left corner house have semi—circular cantilevered bays crowned by a balcony. A loggia opens above the side balcony. The right corner house and the middle house have bays at the ground level as well. The main entrances of all houses face the street. The façades are of plaster; the overhanging roof, which is hipped at the corner structures, is covered with slate. Each one of the three houses contains apartment with rooms on both floors arranged round an entry hall with open stairs.

471 [1913; 35]

The four—storey apartment building in Munich (Kufsteiner Platz), which is exposed on three sides, was built from the plans of the Imperial Court architect Eugen Drollinger. The middle erection of the principal front, which is crowned by a semi—circular gable, has a recess starting behind the second storey terrace. A roof strip runs above the second storey of the corner projections. The ground level of the plastered building is rendered in banded rustication, the upper storeys are articulated by flat pilaster—strips. A protruding niche at the ground level is ornamented with a sculptured figure. The hipped roof is covered with clay tile and has on its ridge a round look—out tower.

Each floor contains two flats with kitchen, bath and other rooms.

472 [1913; 14]

St. John's Church in Breslau (Hohenzollernstrasse 36), with its rectory and parish hall, forms a unified structure in the Romanesque style. Plans were drafted by the architects Gaze and Böttcher, who were given the contract on the basis of their award—winning design. Construction occupied 2 years, at a cost of 600,000 Marks for the church, and 170,000 Marks for the rectory and parish hall.

The basic structure of St. John's church represents a central structure with two cross arms. At one end is the porch and stairs leading to the choir, at the other the semi—circular chancel with its radiating chapels and sacristies. The church spire rises from the crossing, which itself is flanked by four turrets, and is accompanied by four slender turrets which reach the lower half of its pyramidal roof. The main entrance

Blick nach dem Altar   Vue de l'autel   View of the Altar
Blick nach der Empore   Vue de la galerie   View of the Choir

welche neben der schlanken Dachpyramide sich erheben. Der Haupteingang führt durch die Vorhalle in den vorderen Kreuzarm; die Nebeneingänge zu den Emporentreppen sind neben den Kreuzarmen angeordnet. Der Chor mit den umkreisenden Anlagen der Taufkapelle und der Sakristei bildet eine malerisch wirkende Gruppe. In den Kreuzarmen befinden sich Emporen. Das Innere der Kirche ist mit rundbogigen massiven Gewölben überspannt, die Vierung mit einer Kuppel. Die Außenfronten der Kirche sind teils in Rackwitzer, teils in Heuscheuer Sandstein ausgeführt. Die Dächer sowie der Turmhelm sind in Holzkonstruktion hergestellt. Bildhauer Schipke hat die figürlichen und ornamentalen Arbeiten am Äußeren des Gebäudes geschaffen; die Kartons zu den großen Glasfenstern rühren von Professor Engels her, die Ausführung der Fenster von C. Uhle. Bronzetüren und Treibarbeiten der Einzelfiguren am Hauptportal lieferte G. Kind.

Das mit der Kirche durch eine den Pfarrgarten abschließende Mauer verbundene, teils zwei-, teils dreistöckige Pfarr- und Gemeindehaus schließt sich in mehrfacher Gruppenbildung stilistisch den Formen des Kirchenbaues an. Der Eingang erfolgt durch eine offene Halle mit oberer Altane. An einer Ecke der Straßenfront springen an beiden Fronten zwei ausgekragte, unter dem Überhang des Giebels endigende Erkerausbauten vor; außerdem erhebt sich an der Seitenfront ein Runderker. Der Sockel besteht aus Sandstein, darüber folgt Mörtelputz. Die steilen Dächer sind mit Dachpfannen eingedeckt. Das Erdgeschoß enthält, um eine Diele gelagert, eine größere Wohnung mit Küche, ferner die Konfirmandensäle, das Zimmer des Rendanten und das des Küsters.

473 [1913; 89]

In monumentaler Ausprägung der Fassadenformen erscheint das vierstöckige Wohnhaus in Budapest, Fehervari-ut 49, ein Werk der Architekten Fischer & Döttl. In dem mit Sandsteinbossenquadern bekleideten Erdgeschoß öffnet sich das rundbogige Portal, über dem sich ein vorgekragter Balkon erstreckt. Die Fenster des Erdgeschosses sind flachbogig überwölbt, die im ersten Obergeschoß sind rundbogig geschlossen und werden von Säulchen flankiert. Die Fenster im zweiten Obergeschoß sind paarweise zusammengefaßt und sind ebenso wie die einfachen Fenster im dritten Obergeschoß mit Rundbogen überdeckt. Ein über dem Erd-

du beffroi. Le porche donne sur le narthex puis sur le bras antérieur. Les accès aux escaliers des galeries sont contigus. Le chœur forme avec le baptistère et la sacristie un ensemble aux proportions parfaites. L'intérieur de l'édifice est couvert par une voûte en berceau, la croisée des transepts par une coupole. Les murs extérieurs de l'église offrent un appareil associant le grès de Rackwith à celui de Heuscheu. La charpente des toits et de la flèche est en bois. Les ornements plastiques extérieurs sont l'œuvre du sculpteur Schipke. Les vitraux conçus par le professeur Engels furent réalisés par C. Uhle. Les portes en bronze ainsi que le bosselage des figures du portail furent exécutés par G. Kind.

L'édifice asymétrique de deux voire trois étages que forment le presbytère et la maison paroissiale s'harmonise parfaitement avec le style de l'église. L'entrée est abritée sous un porche supportant une plate-forme. A l'angle de la façade sur rue se détachent, sur chacun des murs, une avancée couronnée d'un pignon. Un avant-corps arrondi orne la façade latérale. Le socle est en grès, les murs sont crépis à la chaux. Les toits pentus sont recouverts de tuiles flammandes. Le rez-de-chaussée comprend, agencés autour d'un Hall, un vaste logement avec cuisine, le bureau de l'intendant et les salles de catéchisme.

473 [1913; 89]

L'immeuble de rapport, situé à Budapest, Ferhévári-ut 49, conçu par les architectes Fischer & Döttl, se distingue par la composition monumentale de sa façade. Le rez-de-chaussée , revêtu de pierres de taille traitées en bossage, est percé par une entrée cintrée surmontée d'un balcon saillant. Les fenêtres du rez-de-chaussée sont surbaissées, celles du premier étage sont cintrées et flanquées de colonnettes. Groupées par paire au deuxième étage, elles sont cintrées tout comme les simples ouvertures du troisième étage.

leads through the porch in the front cross arm; entrances to the choir stairs are located to the side of the cross arms. The chancel with its adjoining baptistery and sacristy form an picturesque ensemble. Choirs are located in the cross arms. The interior of the church is spanned by monolithic tunnel vaults, and the cupola rises above the crossing. The façades of the church are rendered in sandstone from Rackwitz and Heuscheu. The roofs as well as the polygonal spire are constructed of wood. The figures and ornamentation of the exterior are the work of the sculptor Schipke. The decoration of the large glass windows was designed by Professor Engels ands executed by C. Uhle. The bronze doors and the incised bronze ornamentation for the figures at the main portal were provided by G. Kind.

The rectory and parish hall are connected to the church by a wall which borders the rectory garden, and represent a two – and three—storey structural grouping arranged in the same style as that of the church. The entrance leads through an open hall covered by a balcony. One corner of the street front is flanked by two oriels which end under the overhanging gables. In addition, a round oriel projects from the side front. The socle is of sandstone covered by mortar plaster. The steep roofs are covered with pantiles. Arranged around the ground floor hall are a large flat with kitchen, plus the hall for confirmees, and rooms for the registrar and sexton.

473 [1913; 89]

A façade of monumental forms can be seen at the four—storey apartment building in Budapest (Fehérvári ut. 49), a work of the architects Fischer & Döttl. A round—arched portal is located at the ground level, which is rendered in bossed sandstone rustication, and is covered by a cantilevered balcony. The windows at the ground level are framed in flat arches, those of the first storey are set in round arches and flanked by colonnettes. The paired windows of the second storey are round—arched, as are the more

geschoß ausgekragter polygonaler Erker geht im ersten Obergeschoß in eine viereckige mit einer Säulenstellung geöffnete Loggia über, die eine Altane trägt. Ein steiler Giebel, in dem ein Wappenfeld angebracht ist, schließt den betreffenden, den Erker enthaltenden, in den Gliederungen mit Sandstein verblendeten Fassadenteil ab. Sonst sind die oberen Fassadenflächen in Verputz hergestellt. Das Dach ist mit Biberschwanzziegeln eingedeckt.

474 [1913; 27]

Das Zirkusgebäude Stosch-Sarrasani in Dresden-Neustadt liegt mit der Portalfront gegen den Königin-Carola-Platz und ist von drei Straßen umschlossen. Der Entwurf stammt von der Architektenfirma Heilmann und Littmann, unter Mitarbeit der Architekten A. Siegel, E. Goebel und A. Müller. Die Ausfüh-

Une logette polygonale se détache au-dessus du rez-de-chaussée, se transformant, au deuxième étage, en une loggia quadrangulaire dont les colonnes supportent un balcon au niveau du troisième étage. Un pignon pentu, orné d'un blason, coiffe cette partie de la façade partiellement revêtue de grès. Les surfaces supérieures des murs extérieurs sont enduites d'un crépi. Le toit est recouvert de tuiles plates.

474 [1913; 27]

Le bâtiment du cirque Sosch-Sarrasani de Dresdes-Neustadt fut conçu par le bureau d'architecture Heilann & Littmann en collaboration avec les architectes A. Siegel, E. Goebel, et A. Müller. Les travaux, conduits par les architectes A. Möller et

plainer ones of the third storey. A polygonal oriel above the ground floor becomes rectangular above the first floor, culminating in a loggia with columns at the second floor and a balcony at the third. A steep gable with a coat of arms finishes this part of the façade, which, together with its articulations, is rendered in sandstone. The other upper façades are faced in plaster. The roof is covered with flat red tile.

474 [1913; 27]

The Stosch—Sarrasani circus building in Dresden is situated with its portal front facing the Königin Carola Platz and is bordered by three streets. The plans for the structure were drawn up by the architect's office of Heilmann and Littmann, with assistance being provided by the architects A. Siegel, E. Goebel and

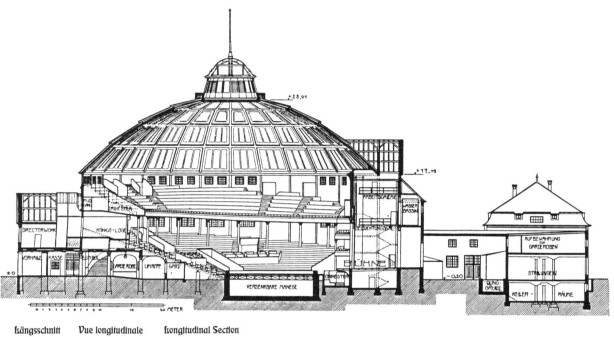

Längsschnitt   Vue longitudinale   Longitudinal Section

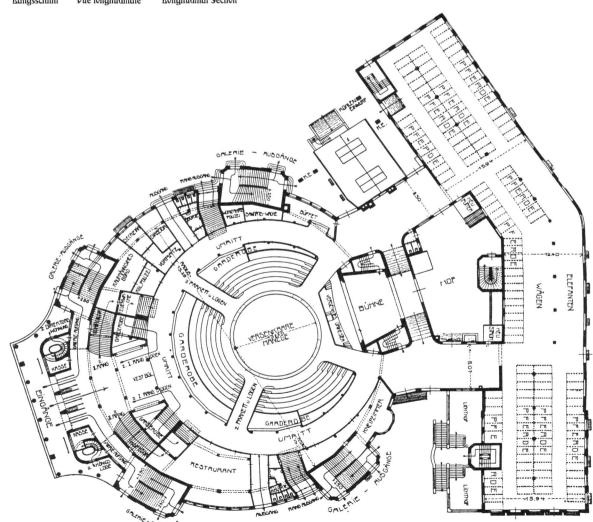

Erdgeschoß   Rez-de-chaussée   Ground Floor

Innenraum von der Bühne aus gegen die Königsloge gesehen   Vue de la scène sur la loge royale   Vestibül am Königin Carola-Platz   Vestibule donnant sur la place Königin Carola
View of the Imperial Box from the Stage   Vestibule at the Königin Carola Platz

rung erfolgte im Laufe zweier Jahre und war bis September 1912 beendet. Die Bauleitung besorgten Architekt A. Möller und Baumeister C. Winkler. Die äußere Erscheinung des Zirkusgebäudes ergibt sich aus der Zweckbestimmung des Innern. Sämtliche Fassaden sind in altdeutschem Verputz hergestellt, in verschiedener Behandlung der Flächen. Das Gebäude ist bis zur Kuppelspitze in Eisen konstruiert, wobei das Eisenfachwerk der Umfassungswände mit Backsteinen ausgemauert, mit Rabitz überspannt und beiderseitig überputzt ist. Die Galerietreppenhäuser, das Bühnenhaus, der Portalvorbau mit der Direktorwohnung und die Stallungsanlagen sind massiv in Backsteinen ausgeführt; die große Kuppelwölbung über dem Zirkusraum ist in Voltzmasse hergestellt.

Das Gebäude soll zwar in erster Linie zirzensischen Spielen dienen, ist jedoch zugleich für Varieté- und Musikaufführungen, sowie für Massenversammlungen geplant. Die Manege, die Bühne und das versenkte Orchester sind in exzentrischer Lage zur Rotunde des Zuschauerraums angeordnet; und der Bühne gegenüber befindet sich das Vestibül, an das sich beiderseits die Treppenhäuser anschließen. Vor dem Vestibül erhebt sich eine säulengetragene Vorhalle, darüber liegt im 1. Stock des Portalbaues die Direktorwohnung, während auf der rechten Seite des Portalvorbaues sich der Eingang zur Königsloge befindet. In der Vorhalle öffnen sich die Kassenräume und die Garderoben für Parkett- und Rangsitze. Ausgänge für das Publikum sind auf beiden Straßenfronten 24 vorhanden. Es sind Sitz- und Stehplätze für 3860 Personen eingerichtet. Die Kuppel mit einer lichten Höhe von 28,95 m ist nach System Schwedler mit anschließendem Tragring freitragend konstruiert. Das Bassin der versenkbaren Manege kann mit Wasser gefüllt werden, um pantomimische Wasserspiele zu ermöglichen. Mit der Manege hängt die ausgedehnte Stallungsanlage zusammen. In Verbindung mit dem Zuschauerraum, auf gleicher Höhe mit dem Parkett liegt ein Bier- und Weinrestaurant, in gleicher Lage befindet sich ein Büffet für kalte Speisen und Getränke. Das Maschinenhaus mit den Kesselanlagen für die Zentralheizung ist unter dem Hofe an der Briestestraße eingebaut.

475, 476 [1913; 38, 39]

Die nach dem Entwurfe des Architekten Jul. Goldschläger ausgeführten Wohnhäuser in Wien, Prinz Eugenstraße 30 bis 34 und 32a, zeichnen sich durch aufwandvolle Fassadenbildungen aus.

Die Wohnhausgruppe 30 bis 34 besteht aus zwei neben einem Gartenhof liegenden, durch einen überbauten Torbogen verbundenen Gebäuden. Die fünfstöckigen, im reichen Barockstil gehaltenen Fassaden sind in den drei ersten Obergeschossen durch Erker und vorgekragte Balkons gegliedert. Das vierte Obergeschoß erhebt sich über einem mit einer Galerie versehenen Gurtgesims und ist in den mittleren Teilen

C. Winkler, durèrent deux années et se terminèrent en septembre 1912. Le cirque est ceint de trois rues. L'entrée s'effectue par la place Königin Carola. L'aspect extérieur du bâtiment correspond à la vocation de l'intérieur. L'ensemble des façades sont crépies de façon traditionnelle avec traitements différents des surfaces. L'édifice est construit en fer jusqu'à l'extrémité de la coupole. Les colombages en fer des murs d'enceinte sont garnis de briques, recouverts d'un treillis puis crépis des deux côtés. Les escaliers des galeries, la cage de la scène, l'avant-corps comprenant l'entrée et le logement du directeur, les écuries présentent une construction massive de briques.

Le bâtiment, conçu en première ligne pour les jeux du cirque, accueille également des représentations de variétés, des spectacles de musique ainsi que des réunions de masse. Dans la salle de spectacle, le manège, la scène et l'orchestre, situé dans la trappe, sont excentrés. Le vestibule, faisant face à la scène, est flanqué d'escaliers. L'entrée, les salles des caisses ainsi que les vestiaires de l'orchestre et des galeries sont abrités par une avancée reposant sur des colonnes, occupée au premier étage par le logement du directeur. Sur le côté droit se trouve l'accès à la loge royale. 24 sorties sur les deux rues assurent le mouvement des spectateurs. Des places assises et debout ont été aménagées pour accueillir 3860 personnes. La coupole d'une hauteur libre de 28,95 mètres est construite d'après la méthode Schwedler. Le bassin du manège escamotable peut être rempli d'eau pour organiser des jeux aquatiques. Le manège est attenant aux écuries. Un restaurant et un café communiquent avec la salle de spectacle, à la hauteur de l'orchestre. La salle des machines et la chaudière pour le chauffage central sont installées sous la cour donnant sur la Briestestraße.

475, 476 [1913; 38, 39]

Les immeubles situés à Vienne, Prinz Eugenstraße 30 à 34 et 32a, furent construits sur les plans de l'architecte Jul. Goldschläger. Leur originalité réside dans la riche décoration des façades. L'ensemble d'habitation, aux no. 30 à 34, se compose de deux bâtiments de cinq étages, attenants à une cour avec jardin, joints par un passage cintré. Oriels et balcons saillants ornent les trois étages inférieurs des façades conçues dans un style très baroque. Le quatrième étage s'élève derrière une galerie prenant appui sur un

A. Müller. Construction occupied two years and was finally completed in September 1912. Supervising the construction were the architect A. Möller and the master builder C. Winkler. The outer appearance of the circus building conforms to the interior's intended purpose. The façades have been plastered in the old German style, with its surfaces being rendered in many different ways. The structural framework of the building, apart from the pointed cupola, is of iron, while the iron truss girders of the perimeter walls have been filled in with brick masonry, spanned with Rabitz type casing and plastered over on both sides. The stair wells of the galleries, the stage and backstage, the portal forebuilding containing the director's residence, and the animal quarters are solidly constructed of masonry brick. The expansive cupola vault over the circus arena is constructed of mass concrete.

Although the purpose of the building is primarily that of staging circus entertainment, it will also be used as a venue for variety shows and concerts, as well as mass public gatherings. The arena, stage and the orchestra pit have been eccentrically arranged relative to the position of the rotunda of the spectators' area. The vestibule is situated opposite the stage and is flanked by stairwells. In front of the vestibule is a porch with columns supporting the first floor of the director's residence. The entrance to the Imperial box is to the right of the porch. The porch opens to the box office and cloak—rooms for the stalls and dress and upper circles. 24 exits are located in two street fronts. There is a total of 3860 seats and standing—room places. The floor to ceiling height at the cupola is 28.95 metres; the self—supporting Schwedler's cupola has connecting binders. The basin of the sunken arena can be filled with water, thus allowing the performance of water pantomimes. The arena is connected to the stalls for circus animals. Bordering the spectators' area at the level of the stalls is a bar serving beer and wine; a buffet for cold dishes and refreshments is also located on this level. A machinery building with boiler rooms and the central heating installation has been constructed under the courtyard facing the Briestestrasse.

475, 476 [1913; 38, 39]

The apartment complex in Vienna (Prinz Eugenstrasse 30—34), designed by the architect Jul. Goldschläger, immediately strikes the observer by the splendour of its façades.

The complex consists of two houses situated next to a garden court and connected by a arched gateway. The five—storey façades are richly ornamented in the Baroque style. Those of the first three storeys are articulated by oriels and cantilevered balconies. The fourth storey is skirted by a string—course with a bal-

durch Giebel abgeschlossen. Die Fassaden sind in Putzbau hergestellt, mit einzelnen Gliederungen in Sandstein, die abgewalmten Dächer sind mit Schiefer eingedeckt. Die seitlichen Haupteingänge führen zu den Vestibülen und den hinterliegenden Stockwerkstreppen und Aufzügen. In jedem Stockwerk beider Häuser ist je eine größere Wohnung mit Küche und Nebenräumen eingerichtet.

Das zweistöckige, durch ein ausgebautes Dachgeschoß erweiterte Wohnhaus 32a ist durch einen vorspringenden Mittelbau ausgezeichnet, der im Erdgeschoß einen Brunnen einschließt, im Obergeschoß einen Balkon trägt und von einem Giebelaufbau bekrönt wird. Das abgewalmte Mansardendach ist mit Ziegeln eingedeckt. An den Mittelbau, den Salon, das Herrenzimmer, das Musikzimmer und den Wintergarten aufnehmend, schließen sich Flügelbauten an, von denen der eine das Speisezimmer mit vorgelegter Terrasse, der andere Waschküche, Trockenkammer und Dienerzimmer enthält.

477 [1913; 47]

Das Michaelerhaus in Wien, am Michaelerplatz gelegen, ein Geschäfts- und Wohnhaus von einfachen Formen, steigt als Eckbau in sechs Geschossen auf und ist nach dem Entwurfe des Architekten Adolf Loos im Laufe eines Jahres für die Baukostensumme von 1 Million Kronen errichtet. Geschäfts- und Wohnräume sind in der äußeren Erscheinung streng unterschieden; erstere in Erdgeschoß und Mezzanin sind mit größerem Reichtum ausgestattet, während die Wohnungen der oberen Geschosse, abgesehen von den Blumenkörben vor den Fenstern, ganz schmucklos erscheinen. An der stumpfen Ecke öffnet sich im Erdgeschoß eine Säulenhalle. Die Fassaden sind bis zum Gurtgesims über dem Mezzanin mit Marmor von Euböa, grün, dunkelgrau und weiß gestreift, bekleidet, die oberen Geschosse sind verputzt. Aufschriften, Beleuchtungskörper, Wappen, Säulenbasen und Kapitelle, Blumenkörbe vor den Fenstern und die Eindeckung des abgewalmten Daches bestehen aus Kupfer, die Fenster in den Stockwerken aus poliertem Mahagoni.

Das Erdgeschoß wird zum großen Teil von den Räumen des Herrenmodegeschäfts Goldmann & Salatsch eingenommen. Das Mezzaningeschoß enthält den großen Mittelraum mit der Buchhaltung und freiliegenden Treppen, außerdem für die Schneiderei das Stoffzimmer, die Probierkabinen, den Arbeitsraum und das Bügelzimmer. Innere Säulen und Decken bestehen aus Eisenbeton, die Zwischenwände der Wohnungen aus Gipsdielen. Ein Teil des Mezzanins besitzt ein Zwischengeschoß.

478 [1913; 41]

Als mächtiger Eckbau, von einem Kuppeltürmchen über der Eckrundung überragt, erhebt sich in sechs Geschossen und einem ausgebauten Dachgeschoß das Wohn- und Geschäftshaus in Budapest, Maria Valeria utcza 11, eine Schöpfung der Architekten Aladar Kármán und Julius Ullmann, in 15 Monaten für die Baukostensumme von 12000000 Kronen errichtet. Über Erdgeschoß und folgendem Halbgeschoß sowie über dem ersten Obergeschoß erstrecken sich außen umlaufende ausgekragte Galerien, durch Ausbauten unterbrochen, die im zweiten Obergeschoß endigen und durch Schiffsschnäbel, von seitlichen Figuren begleitet, verziert sind. Die drei folgenden Obergeschosse sind durch flache Pilaster gegliedert. Der Eckturm zeigt in der Höhe der seitwärts anschließenden, mit Fenstern versehenen Attika einen figürlichen Relieffries. Die Fassaden sind im Erdgeschoß und Halbgeschoß darüber mit geschliffenen Karstplatten bekleidet, die Säulen der Eingangshalle bestehen aus Kalkstein, die oberen Geschosse sind in Sandsteinmörtel verputzt. Das gebrochene Dach ist in Metall eingedeckt.

Das Gebäude umschließt mit vier Flügeln einen Hof. Die Eingangshalle an der Ecke führt mittels eines Flurganges zu der mit gebogenen Armen aufsteigenden Haupttreppe. Zu beiden Seiten schließen sich Flurgänge an, welche den Zugang zu den Zimmerreihen vermitteln. Außerdem enthält das Erdgeschoß ei-

---

cordon. Il est surmonté, dans sa partie médiane, d'un pignon en delta. Les murs de façade sont crépis et présentent quelques décors en grès. Les toits en croupe sont recouverts d'ardoises. Les entrées latérales conduisent aux vestibules, aux cages d'escalier et aux ascenseurs. Chaque étage comprend un vaste appartement équipé d'une cuisine et de pièces de service.

L'immeuble au no. 32a est un édifice s'élevant sur deux étages, caractérisé par un corps de logis saillant, enchâssant une fontaine au rez-de-chaussée, assorti d'un balcon à l'étage et couronné d'une construction à pignon. Le toit en croupe mansardé est recouvert de tuiles. Le corps de logis, occupé par le cabinet de travail de monsieur, le salon de musique et le jardin d'hiver, est flanqué par deux ailes abritant, l'une la salle à manger avec terrasse attenante, l'autre la buanderie, le séchoir et la chambre des domestiques.

477 [1913; 47]

L'immeuble à usage d'habitation et de commerce, situé sur la Michelerplatz à Vienne fut construit sur les plans de l'architecte Adolf Loos en l'espace d'une année pour la somme d'un million de couronnes. Il s'agit d'un immeuble à pan coupé de six étages aux lignes sobres. Sa structure extérieure témoigne de la double vocation des lieux. La façade richement ornée des rez-de-chaussée et mezzanine se distingue du reste du bâtiment dépouillé de tout décoration, hormis les corbeilles de fleurs aux fenêtres. Un des côtés est assorti d'un péristyle. Jusqu'au cordon, les façades sont revêtues de marbre vert, strié de gris foncé et blanc. Les étages supérieurs sont enduits d'un crépi. Les inscriptions, les luminaires, les blasons, la base des colonnes et leurs chapiteaux, les corbeilles aux fenêtres ainsi que la couverture du toit sont en cuivre, les chambranles des fenêtres des étages sont en acajou poli.

Le rez-de-chaussée est occupé, dans sa plus grande part, par la boutique d'articles de mode masculine Goldmann & Salatsch. La mezzanine abrite une grande pièce destinée à la comptabilité avec escalier, la salle des étoffes pour les tailleurs, les cabines d'essayage, l'atelier et la salle de repassage. Les colonnes intérieures ainsi que les planchers sont en béton armé, les cloisons des appartements sont en planches de plâtre. Un entresol a été aménagé dans une partie de la mezzanine.

478 [1913; 41]

Cet imposant immeuble de Budapest, Maria Valeria utcza 11, fut conçu par les architectes Aladar Kármán et Julius Ullmann. Les travaux, qui durèrent quinze mois, coûtèrent la somme de 1 200 000 couronnes. Il s'agit d'un immeuble à pan coupé, s'élevant sur sept étages dont un mansardé, surmonté dans l'angle d'une tourelle en coupole. La façade est assortie, au-dessus des deux étages inférieurs, de galeries saillantes interrompues par des oriels ornés de rostres flanqués de figures sculptées. Les trois étages suivants présentent une ordonnance de pilastres. La tour d'angle est ornée d'un relief sculpté, à la hauteur de l'étage en attique. Les murs de façade du rez-de-chaussée et de l'entresol sont revêtus de dalles de parement karstiques, les colonnes de l'entrée sont en castine, les étages supérieurs sont enduits au mortier gréseux. Le toit au comble brisé est recouvert de plaques de métal.

Les quatre ailes de l'immeuble closent une cour. L'entrée principale, située dans l'angle, conduit, par un corridor, à l'escalier principal à deux volées flanqué de couloirs permettant l'accès aux pièces en enfilade. Le rez-de-chaussée est également pourvu d'une

---

cony running along it, with its middle section culminating in gables. The façades are faced with plaster and sandstone ornamentation; the hipped roofs are covered with slate. The main entrances at the side of the frontage lead to vestibules and, at the back of the building, to staircases and lifts. Each floor of both houses contains a spacious flat with kitchen and other rooms.

The two-storey apartment building at No. 32a is marked by a projecting middle structure which encompasses a fountain at the ground level. A balcony is located directly above at the first storey and the entire middle section is crowned by a gabled superstructure. The hipped mansard roof is covered with clay tile. The middle structure, in which the drawing-room, study, music room and the winter garden are located, is flanked by side wings which contain the dining room leading onto a terrace, the laundry-room, drying room and servant's room.

477 [1913; 47]

Located at the corner of Michaelerplatz in Vienna, the Michaelerhaus office building is a six-storey edifice of simple design. Drafted by the architect Adolf Loos, it was constructed in the course of one year at a cost of 1 million Crowns. In addition to offices, the building also contains apartments, whose unadorned façades—save for the flower pots at the window sills—contrast sharply to the opulently-ornamented façades of the ground floor and mezzanine. A porch with columns opens at the obtuse corner of the building. The façades below the mezzanine string-course are rendered in marble with a combination of green, dark green and white patterns; the upper façades are of plaster. Lettering, lighting fixtures, coat-of-arms, as well as the base and capitals of the columns, window flower baskets and the roof cladding of the hipped roof are all of copper. The window frames of the upper floors are of polished mahogany.

The ground floor is chiefly occupied by the Goldmann & Salatsch establishment for gentlemen's fashions. The mezzanine contains a large central room for accounting, as well as the open stairs, a room for the tailor's materials, changing cabinets, a workshop and the ironing room. Piers and ceilings are of reinforced concrete; the walls dividing the flats are of gypsum plank. One section of the mezzanine contains a substorey.

478 [1913; 41]

The apartment building in Budapest (Maria Valeria utcza 11) is an imposing corner structure with a domed turret rising above its rounded corner. The six-storey edifice with a roof storey was created by the architects Aladar Kármán and Julius Ullmann and constructed in 15 months at a cost of 1,200,000 Crowns. Both the ground level mezzanine and the first storey are covered by continuous, cantilevered galleries, which are occasional broken by projections ending at the second storey of the façade, and which are ornamented with rostrums flanked by carved figures. The upper three storeys are joined by flat pilasters. The corner tower is decorated with a figural relief frieze situated at the level of the two lateral terraces with windows. The façades at the level of the ground floor and first storey are faced with polished karst panels, the entrance columns are of sandstone, and the upper storeys are rendered in sandstone mortar. The roof is covered with metal roof sheeting.

The four wings of the edifice encompass a courtyard. The entry hall at the corner leads along a corridor to the principal staircase of curved flights. Corridors at either side of the staircase lead past rows of rooms. Furthermore, the ground floor contains a side

nen seitlichen Eingang, der wieder mit einer Treppe in Verbindung steht, sowie mehrere Nebentreppen und Aufzüge. Die oberen Geschosse wiederholen im wesentlichen die Raumteilung des Erdgeschosses. Die Zimmer im ersten und zweiten Obergeschoß besitzen Ausgänge nach den außen umlaufenden Galerien. Decken, Pfeiler und die Konstruktionen der Mansarde sind in Eisenbeton ausgeführt. Die Stiegenanlage für die Räume der Königl. Fluß- und Seeschiffahrtsgesellschaft ist ebenfalls in Eisenbeton hergestellt und mit weißem ungarischen Marmor belegt.

479 [1913; 48]

Es sind drei zu einer Gruppe vereinigte, durch Brandmauern geschiedene Geschäfts- und Wohnhäuser in Heidelberg, Sophienstraße 7 bis 7b, die im Verlaufe von 2 Jahren nach den Entwürfen der Architekten Kumpf und Wolf zur Ausführung gekommen sind. Im Erdgeschoß der Häuser öffnen sich Schaufenster. Vor jedem Hause erhebt sich ein vorgekragter, durch drei Obergeschosse geführter, im dritten Obergeschosse loggienartig geöffneter, im Dachgeschoß mit einer Altane endigender Erkerausbau, dem sich seitwärts im ersten und zweiten Obergeschoß ausgekragte Balkons anschließen. Über der Dachlinie erhebt sich jedesmal ein Aufbau mit Giebel, daneben stehen Dachfenster auf der Steilfläche der Mansardendächer. Die Fassaden sind in gelbem Pfälzer Sandstein ausgeführt, die Dächer sind mit deutscher Beschieferung versehen.

Im Erdgeschoß sind sämtliche Häuser zu Läden ausgebaut; die oberen Geschosse enthalten je eine Wohnung mit Diele, eine Anzahl Wohn- und Schlafzimmer, Küche und Baderaum.

480 [1913; 54]

In reicher Gruppierung, mit malerisch wirkenden Dachformen ausgestattet, bildet das Park-Sanatorium in Budapest, Arena-utcza, ein Bauwerk von bedeutendem Umfang und einer Höhenentwicklung von vier Geschossen, die noch durch mannigfaltige Dachaufbauten bereichert ist. Der Entwurf stammt von den Architekten Komor und Jakob. Der mittlere abgerundete Teil der Hauptfront, gegen die beiden Eckflügelbauten zurücktretend, enthält den rundbogig überdeckten, von einer Freitreppe zugänglichen Eingang, über dem sich Fenstergruppen in drei Geschossen öffnen, und schließt nach oben mit einer durch ein Gitter geschützten Plattform ab. Die Flügelbauten tragen im vierten Stock an den Ecken Galerien, hinter denen sich polygonale, pavillonartige, mit Kuppeldächern bekrönte Fensteraufbauten erheben, außerdem treten seitlich vom Mittelbau viereckige Türmchen mit Zeltdächern hervor. Im mittleren Teile der Flügelbauten wird das gebrochene Dach durch Aufbauten unterbrochen. Die Fassaden sind mit verschieden gefärbtem Naturputz überzogen, die Dächer sind mit Biberschwänzen eingedeckt.

481 [1913; 61]

In fünf Geschossen erhebt sich das Wohnhaus in Wilmersdorf-Berlin, Bregenzerstraße 12, durch eine kräftig gegliederte Fassade ausgezeichnet. Der Entwurf stammt von den Architekten A. Klingenberg und Fr. Beyer und wurde im Verlaufe eines Jahres zur Ausführung gebracht. Die Straßenfront weist zwei über dem Erdgeschoß durch drei Obergeschosse geführte, mit Plattformen abschließende Erker auf, die im zweiten Obergeschosse durch einen gleichfalls ausgekragten Balkon verbunden werden und einen mit senkrecht aufsteigenden verzierten Lisenen gegliederten, oben abgerundeten Giebel zwischen sich einschließen. Die Eingangstür ist mit einem Volutengiebel bekrönt; an einem Seitenteile der Fassade öffnen sich Loggien in sämtlichen Geschossen. Die Fassade ist mit doppeltem Kiesputz überzogen, die seitlichen Flächen der beiden oberen Geschosse zeigen einen Behang von Ziegeln.

Jedes der Geschosse ist in zwei Wohnungen geteilt, die durch eine Haupt- und eine Nebentreppe verbunden sind. Jede Wohnung enthält, von einer Diele zugänglich, eine Anzahl Zimmer, von denen einige mit den Balkons und Loggien in Verbindung stehen, außerdem die Küche mit Nebenräumen. Die Hinterfront des Hauses stößt an einen Garten.

---

entrée secondaire latérale, donnant sur un escalier, des escaliers de service et ascenseurs. Les étages supérieurs reprennent la distribution des pièces du rez-de-chaussée. Les pièces des premier et deuxième étages communiquent avec les galeries. Les planchers, les piliers ainsi que l'ossature des mansardes sont réalisés en béton armé. L'escalier menant aux locaux de la société royale de navigation est en béton armé revêtu de dalles de marbre blanc de Hongrie.

479 [1913; 48]

Cet ensemble formé de trois immeubles séparés par des murs mitoyens, situé à Heidelberg, Sophienstrasse 7 à 7b, fut construit en l'espace de deux années, sur les plans des architectes Kumpf & Wolf. Des devantures percent les façades du rez-de-chaussée . Des façades de chaque immeuble se détachent des oriels flanqués de balcons saillants aux deux étages inférieurs, se transformant en loggias au troisième étage et se terminant en plates-formes à l'étage des combles. Les toits mansardés sont ornés de pignons. Les murs de façade ont été réalisés en grès jaune du Palatinat, les toits sont recouverts d'ardoises.

Les rez-de-chaussée abritent des commerces. Les étages supérieurs sont occupés chacun par un logement comprenant une antichambre, des salles de séjour et chambres à coucher, une cuisine et une salle des bains.

480 [1913; 54]

Le sanatorium de Budapest, Arena-utcza, œuvre intéressante des architectes Komor et Jakob est une vaste construction de quatre étages, dont le toit aux lignes variées apporte une note toute particulière à l'ensemble de l'édifice. Un perron donnant sur un passage cintré permet l'accès à l'entrée, abritée dans la partie centrale arrondie du corps de bâtiment. Celle-ci, flanquée de deux ailes légèrement protubérantes, est percée sur trois étages de fenêtres groupées et se termine par une plate-forme protégée par une rambarde. Les angles des ailes sont assortis, au niveau du quatrième étage, de galeries derrière lesquelles s'élèvent de grandes baies polygonales aux allures de pavillons, couronnées de toits en coupole. De part et d'autre du corps de bâtiment se dressent des tourelles quadrangulaires coiffées de toits en bâtière. Les toits aux combles brisés des ailes sont interrompus par des lucarnes mansardées. Les façades sont revêtues d'un enduit polychrome. Les toits sont recouverts de tuiles plates.

481 [1913; 61]

Cet immeuble de rapport de cinq étages, situé à Berlin-Wilmersdorf, Bregenzerstrasse 12, est caractérisé par la vigoureuse composition de sa façade. Conçu par les architectes A. Klingenberg et Fr. Beyer, il fut réalisé en l'espace d'une année. La façade sur rue est assortie de deux logettes faisant saillie au-dessus du rez-de-chaussée , s'élevant sur trois étages et se terminant par une plate-forme. Elles sont reliées au niveau du deuxième étage par un balcon saillant et encadrent un pignon arrondi orné de bandes lombardes verticales. L'entrée est coiffée d'un pignon à volutes. Sur un des côtés de la façade s'ouvrent des loggias à tous les étages. La façade est enduite d'un double crépi, les surfaces latérales des deux étages supérieurs sont revêtues de tuiles.

Chacun des étage abrite deux logements accessibles par un escalier principal et un escalier de service. Chaque logement comprend une cuisine, des pièces de service ainsi que plusieurs pièces, dont certaines attenantes à des balcons ou loggias, agencées autour d'une antichambre. La façade postérieure de l'immeuble donne sur un jardin.

---

entrance, which also connects to the staircase, as well a number of side stairs and lifts. This arrangement is essentially repeated in the plans of the upper floors. Rooms on the first and second floors have doors leading to the outer galleries. Ceilings, piers and mansards are constructed of reinforced concrete. The stair well for the rooms of the Royal Society of Inland Waters and Ocean Navigation is also built of reinforced concrete and finished with white Hungarian marble.

479 [1913; 48]

Three apartment houses, divided by compartment walls, form a unified architectural group in the Sophienstrasse 7 to 7b in Heidelberg. Construction was carried out over the course of 2 years according to plans drawn up by the architects Kumpf and Wolf. Shop windows open at the ground level of the houses. Projecting at the front of each house are oriels which extend from the first storey through the third storey, where they open in a loggia—like fashion, and finish at the roof storey as balconies. Adjoining the oriels are cantilevered balconies at the first and second stories. A gabled superstructure rises above the roof moulding of each house. The lower slope of the mansard roof contains dormers. The façades are rendered in yellow sandstone from the Palatinate; the roofs are covered with slate in the German style.

The ground floor of all houses is occupied by shops. Each of the upper floors contains a flat with entry hall, a number of bedrooms and sitting—rooms, kitchen and bath.

480 [1913; 54]

The Park Sanatorium in Budapest (Arena utcza) is an abundantly grouped structure of impressive dimensions. Designed by the architects Komor and Jakob, it reaches the height of four storeys and is graced by diverse superstructures and picturesque roofs. The rounded middle erection of the principal front, which is set back from the corner wings, has a round—arched portal with a perron. Groups of windows open in the three storeys above, and the middle of the façade is crowned by a platform with a latticed railing. Galleries are located at the corners of the side wings at the fourth storey, behind which are polygonal, pavilion—linke windowed structures with domed roofs. In addition, the middle erection is flanked by turrets with pyramidal roofs. The roof over the middle section of the side wings is topped by a superstructure. The façades are faced with natural plaster of various colours; the roofs are covered with flat red tile.

481 [1913; 61]

The five—storey apartment building in Berlin (Bregenzerstrasse 12) has a remarkably articulated façade. Designed by the architects A. Klingenberg and R. Beyer, it was completed over the course of one year. The frontage displays two oriels which project over the ground level and extend the height of three storeys. They are crowned by platforms and joined at the second storey by a similarly projecting balcony. Between the two oriels rises a curved gable ornamented with vertical lesenes. The entrance is crowned by a voluted gable; one side of the façade has loggias opening at all storeys. The façade is rendered in double—layered gravel plaster; the side façade at the upper storeys is hung with clay tile.

Each floor is occupied by two flats connected by both a main staircase and side stairs. Each flat contains a central hall leading to a number of rooms, some of which are connected to the balconies and loggias, plus the kitchen and side rooms. A garden is located behind the building.

Das mit einem Kuppelturm über der Ecke wirkungsvoll bekrönte Geschäfts- und Wohnhaus in Wien, Weihburggasse 9, in sechs Geschossen aufsteigend, ist nach dem Entwurfe des Architekten Ignaz

Cet immeuble de six étages, situé à Vienne, Weihburggasse 9, dont l'angle est coiffé d'une tourelle en coupole, fut construit sur les plans de l'architecte Ignaz Reiser. De larges baies trouent la façade des

Impressively crowned by a domed turret at one corner, the six—storey commercial building in Vienna (Weihburggasse 9), whose upper floors contain flats, was designed by the architect Ignatz Reiser.

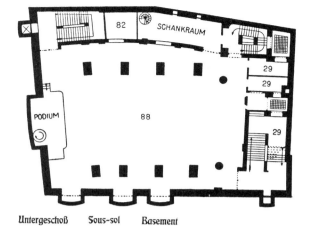

Untergeschoß Sous-sol Basement

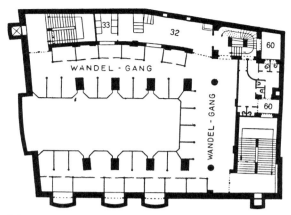

Galerie im Untergeschoß Salle et galeries dans le sous-sol
Upper Gallery in the basement

Reiser errichtet, Erdgeschoß, Mezzanin und das folgende Geschoß sind mit breiten Schaufenstern ausgestattet und werden durch vorgekragte Balkons nach oben abgeschlossen. An den Eckpfeilern sind Figuren angebracht. Die oberen drei Geschosse sind durch in flacher Rundung vortretende Fensterausbauten gegliedert, die sich bis zum Dachkranz fortsetzen. Die Fronten sind in Putzbau hergestellt; die Kuppel des Eckturms ist mit Metallplatten bekleidet. Das Untergeschoß wird von einem großen Saal mit oberer Galerie eingenommen. Das Erdgeschoß sowie die Mezzanine und das folgende Geschoß enthalten eine Anzahl Läden und Verkaufsräume. Das Erdgeschoß enthält das Vestibül und die Haupttreppe, die zum Untergeschoß führenden Treppen und die Wohnung des Hausbesorgers mit Küche. In den drei oberen Geschossen sind je zwei größere Wohnungen mit Küche und Badezimmer eingerichtet. Die Decken sämtlicher Räume sind in Eisenbeton hergestellt.

rez-de-chaussée , de l'entresol et de l'étage suivant. Les niveaux inférieurs, voués au négoce, sont séparés du reste de l'édifice par des balcons saillants. Des sculptures ornent les piliers d'angle. Les trois étages supérieurs sont assortis, jusqu'à la corniche du toit, de bow-windows légèrement convexes. Les murs de façade sont enduits d'un crépi, la coupole de la tourelle d'angle est revêtue de plaques metalliques. Le sous-sol est occupé par une grande salle surplombée de galeries. Le rez-de-chaussée ainsi que l'entresol et l'étage suivant abritent de nombreux commerces. Le rez-de-chaussée comprend le vestibule, l'escalier principal, l'escalier menant au sous-sol et le logement du gardien équipé d'une cuisine. Deux vastes appartements avec cuisine et salle de bains sont aménagés dans chacun des trois étages supérieurs. Les planchers de l'ensemble des pièces sont en béton armé.

Broad shop windows line the ground level, mezzanine and first storey. These are finished off by balconies projecting from the second storey. The corner pilasters are ornamented with figures. The upper three storeys are articulated by slightly rounded window oriels which extend to the roof moulding. The façades are faced with plaster; the dome of the corner turret is covered with metal plates. The basement contains a large hall with an upper gallery. The ground floor, as well as the mezzanine and first floor, are occupied by a number of shops and salesrooms. Located on the ground floor are also the vestibule and main staircase, side stairs leading to the basement and the caretaker's flat with kitchen. Each of the three upper floors contain two spacious flats with kitchen and bath. The ceilings of all floors are constructed of reinforced concrete.

Die in einfacher Fassadengliederung mit je vier Geschossen aufsteigenden beiden Wohnhäuser in Breslau, Hohenzollernstraße 111/112, sind nach dem Entwurfe des Architekten Professor Hans Poelzig errichtet.

An den vorspringenden Teil der Front schließen sich in drei Geschossen ausgekragte Balkons an. Über dem Dachgesims erheben sich Fenster in halbrunder Umrahmung. Die Fassade ist in gefärbtem Verputz hergestellt; das Dach ist mit Ziegeln eingedeckt.

Jedes Geschoß enthält eine um die Diele gruppierte Wohnung mit Küche und Nebenräumen, außerdem die Stockwerks- und die Nebentreppe. Es sind zwei Lichthöfe angeordnet.

Nebenstehend den Grundriß von Nr. 112, der Grundriß von Nr. 111 ist das Spiegelbild dieses Grundrisses.

Les deux immeubles de rapport situés à Breslau, Hohenzollernstraße 111/112, furent construits sur les plans de l'architecte Hans Poelzig. Il s'agit de deux édifices de quatre étages, sobres dans la composition des façades.

La façade est assortie d'un avant-corps flanqué sur trois étages de balcons saillants. Le toit est percé de lucarnes semi-circulaires. Les murs de façade sont revêtus d'un enduit coloré. Le toit est couvert de tuiles.

Chaque étage, accessible par un escalier principal et un escalier de service, abrite un logement agencé autour d'une antichambre et de deux cours vitrées, équipé d'une cuisine et de pièces de service.

Ci-joint le plan du no. 112. Le plan du no. 111 est identique à celui-ci.

Each of the two apartment houses in Breslau (Hohenzollernstrasse 111—112) have four storeys and façades of clear lines and simple ornamentation. Both were designed by the architect Professor Hans Poelzig.

Attached to the projecting section of the front are balconies at the three upper storeys. Semicircular roof windows rise above the roof moulding. The façade is faced in coloured rendering, and the roof is covered with clay tile.

Each floor contains a flat whose rooms are arranged round the entry hall, including a kitchen and side rooms, as well as a staircase and side stairs. Two patios are also located on each floor.

The floor plan illustrated here is that of No. 112. The plan of No. 111 is a mirror image of it.

Das zweistöckige, in gemischter Massiv-Holzbauweise errichtete Einfamilienhaus in Wien, Türkenschanz 23, ein Werk des Architekten M. D. G., D. W. B. Robert Orley, hat eine Bauzeit von 8 Monaten und einen Kostenaufwand von 74 274 Kronen erfordert. Die Straßenfront zeigt im Erdgeschoß einen Erkerausbau und schließt mit überhängendem, steilem, in der Spitze durch eine Verkragung unterbrochenem Giebel. Der Haupteingang ist an der Seitenfront angeordnet. Der Sockel der Fassaden besteht aus Donaukieseln, das Erdgeschoß trägt weißen Dolomitsandputz. Das Gebälk des Obergeschosses zeigt ultramarinblauen Anstrich, die überkragenden Seitenfronten sind beschiefert, die Fensterrahmen sind weiß gestrichen.

Im Erdgeschoß liegen der Vorflur, der Salon, das Speisezimmer mit der Anrichte, die Küche, das Dienstbotenzimmer und die Stockwerkstreppe. Das

Cette maison particulière située à Vienne, Türkenschanz 23, fut réalisée en huit mois pour la somme de 74 274 couronnes. Il s'agit d'une construction en bois et pierres de deux étages, conçue par l'architecte Robert Orley. La façade sur rue est assortie d'une logette au rez-de-chaussée et se termine par un pignon faisant saillie. L'entrée principale se trouve sur la façade latérale. Le socle de la façade est construit en galets du Danube, le rez-de-chaussée est revêtu d'un crépi de sable des Dolomites. La poutre de l'étage est enduite d'un badigeon bleu outremer, les façades latérales saillantes présentent une protection d'ardoises, les volets sont peints en blanc.

Au rez-de-chaussée sont aménagés le hall, le salon, la salle à manger et l'office, la chambre des domestiques ainsi que l'escalier. L'étage comprend les

The one—family house in Vienna (Türkenschanze 23) has two storeys and was built using a mixed solid—wood construction method. It is the work of the certified architect Robert Orley and was completed in 8 months at a cost of 74,274 Crowns. The front façade has bay windows at the ground—level, and finishes with an steep, overhanging gable with a cantilevered peak. The main entrance is located at the side of the house. The socle of the façade consists of Danube gravel; the ground level is faced with white dolomitic sand plaster. The timberwork of the upper storey is painted blue ultramarine, the projecting side fronts is covered with slate and the window frames are painted white.

On the ground floor lie an entry hall, the drawning—room, the dining room and pantries, the kitchen,

Obergeschoß enthält die Schlafzimmer, die Garderobe und das Badezimmer. Das Dachgeschoß ist zur Anlage der Waschküche und des Bügelzimmers benutzt, während im Kellergeschoß der Turnsaal mit Vorraum, die Wohnung des Hausbesorgers und der Heizraum untergebracht sind.

485 [1913; 81]

Als ein Werk des Architekten Wilhelm Koban erhebt sich die einstöckige, durch ein ausgebautes Dachgeschoß erweiterte Villa in Darmstadt, Hohler Weg 45. Die Bauzeit verteilte sich auf 2 Jahre. Die Baukosten betrugen 45 000 Mark. Der Haupteingang ist mit einem auf Konsolen ruhenden Balkon überbaut, über dem sich ein Dachaufbau erhebt. Der Rückfront ist eine offene Halle vorgelegt, die einen Altan trägt; darauf folgt wieder ein Dachaufbau mit abschließendem Giebel. Die Fronten tragen gelben Naturputz. Der Sockel ist mit Bruchsteinen verblendet und das gebrochene, beiderseits abgeschopfte Dach ist mit Handstrichziegeln eingedeckt.

Im Erdgeschoß befinden sich die Wohndiele mit nebenliegendem Treppenraum und vorgelegter, offener Halle, das Speisezimmer, die Bibliothek, das Empfangszimmer, die Küche und die Nebentreppe. Im Obergeschoß sind die Schlafzimmer für Eltern und Kinder, das Bad, das Atelier und das Schneiderzimmer angeordnet.

486, 487 [1913; 66, 68]

Das Landhaus in Pine Lake, Wisconsin, entworfen von Architekt F. R. Liebert, in mehreren Geschossen und reichlicher Gruppierung sich aufbauend, ist in gemischter Massiv-Holzbauweise errichtet. Die Fronten des Erdgeschosses sind mit Bruchsteinmauerwerk verblendet, die oberen Geschosse sind in Holzfachwerk hergestellt und mit roten Ziegeln ausgemauert. Die Baukosten betrugen 30 000 Doll. Im oberen Geschosse öffnen sich Galerien an allen Fronten. Das Erdgeschoß enthält das Vestibül, an welches die Halle sich anschließt, außerdem sind hier die Wohn- und Speisezimmer sowie die Küche untergebracht. Im Obergeschosse liegen die Schlafzimmer, die Zimmer der Kinder und das Bad. Die Zimmer sind mehrfach mit den offenen Galerien und Altanen in Verbindung gesetzt.

488 [1913; 90]

Das fünfstöckige Geschäftshaus in Breslau, Schweidnitzerstraße 28 und Zwingerplatz 8 bildet einen Eckbau mit zwei Fronten und abgerundeten Ecken, und ist im Laufe von 2 Baujahren für die Baukostensumme von 380 000 Mark nach dem Entwurfe der Architekten, Regierungsbaumeister a. D. R. und D. Ehrlich errichtet. Das Erdgeschoß öffnet sich mit Schaufenstern; das Eingangsportal ist im Korbbogen überwölbt, wird von Knabenfiguren tragenden Pfeilern eingefaßt, zeigt einen figürlich verzierten Schlußstein und über dem Deckgesims eine runde Balustrade für

---

chambres à coucher, la garde-robe et la salle de bains. L'étage des combles est occupé par la buanderie et la lingerie. Au sous-sol sont installés la salle de gymnastique et son hall, le logement du gardien et la chaufferie.

485 [1913; 81]

Conçue par l'architecte Wilhelm Koban, cette villa de Darmstadt, Hohlen Weg 45, fut réalisée en deux années pour la somme de 45 000 mark. Il s'agit d'une demeure s'élevant sur deux étages dont un mansardé. L'entrée se situe sous un balcon en encorbellement assortissant une fenêtre mansardée. La façade postérieure est flanquée d'une galerie ouverte supportant une plate-forme, derrière laquelle s'élève une avancée mansardée couronnée d'un pignon. Les murs de façade sont enduits d'un crépi jaune. Le socle est revêtu de pierres de taille de parement. Le toit en croupe au comble brisé est recouvert de tuiles artisanales.

Le rez-de-chaussée est occupé par une antichambre avec escalier attenant, communiquant avec la galerie ouverte, la salle à manger, le cabinet de lecture, le salon, la cuisine et l'escalier de service. L'étage comprend les chambres à coucher des parents et des enfants, la salle de bains, l'atelier et le salon de couture.

486, 487 [1913; 66, 68]

Cette propriété de campagne de Pine Lake, Wisconsin, fut conçue par l'architecte F. R. Liebert. Construite de pierres et de bois, s'élevant sur plusieurs étages, la villa forme un ensemble remarquable. Les murs de façade du rez-de-chaussée sont revêtus de pierres de taille jointoyées, ceux des étages supérieurs sont à colombages garnis de briques rouges. Les coûts de construction se montèrent à 30 000 dollars. Des galeries ornent l'ensemble des murs de façade au premier étage. Le rez-de-chaussée comprend le vestibule attenant à l'antichambre, la salle de séjour, la salle à manger ainsi que la cuisine . A l'étage supérieur sont aménagées les chambres à coucher, les chambres des enfants et la salle de bains. Les pièces communiquent avec les galeries et les balcons.

488 [1913; 90]

Cet immeuble à usage commercial, situé à Breslau, à l'angle de la Schweidnitzerstraße et de la Zwingerplatz fut construit en l'espace de deux années sur les plans des architectes R. et D. Ehrlich. Les travaux coûtèrent la somme de 380 000 marks. Il s'agit d'un édifice à pan coupé dont les deux façades s'élèvent sur cinq étages. La façade du rez-de-chaussée est percée de devantures. Le portail d'entrée, en arc en anse de panier, flanqué de piliers porteurs de sculptures de jeunes garçons et surmonté d'une balustrade arrondie

---

servant's room and staircase. The upper floor contains bedrooms, the cloak-room and bath. The attic floor is used for laundry and ironing, while the gymnastics room and its anteroom, the caretaker's living quarters, and the furnace room are located in the basement.

485 [1913; 81]

Designed by the architect Wilhelm Koban, the one-storey villa in Darmstadt (Hohler Weg 45), which also has a expanded attic storey, was completed over the course of 2 years, with costs amounting to 45,000 Marks. The main entrance is covered by a balcony resting on consoles, above which rises a roof projection. The back front has an open porch covered by a balcony, above which a gabled roof projection also rises. The fronts are covered with natural yellow plaster. The socle is faced with rubble masonry, and the hipped roof is covered with handmoulded tile.

Situated on the ground floor are the sitting room-entrance hall with the stairs and an open detached hall, the dining room, library, drawing-room, kitchen and the side stairs. The bedrooms for the parents and children, bath, the atelier and the sewing room are located on the upper floor.

486, 487 [1913; 66, 68]

The Adolf Finkler house in Pine Lake, Wisconsin, designed by the architect F. R. Liebert, is a multi-storeyed building of mixed solid-wood construction rich in architectural groupings. The ground level fronts are faced with rubble masonry; the upper storeys have a timber framework and filled in with red brick. Construction costs amounted to 30,000 Dollars. Upper galleries open at all sides of the house. The ground floor contains the vestibule connected to the hall; located on this floor are also sitting and dining rooms, as well as the kichten. The upper floor is occupied by bedrooms, a nursery, and the bath. The rooms lead out onto both the balconies and open galleries.

488 [1913; 90]

The five-storey commercial building in Breslau (Schweidnitzerstrasse 28) is a corner structure with two exposed fronts and rounded corners. Construction occupied 2 years and cost 380,000 Marks; the design is the work of the retired government architects R. and D. Ehrlich. Shop windows open at the ground level of both fronts. The entrance portal is framed in a basket arch and flanked by pillars supporting figures of young boys. The keystone of the portal is ornamented by figures. Above the cornice is a rounded balustrade for ornamental plants. The first,

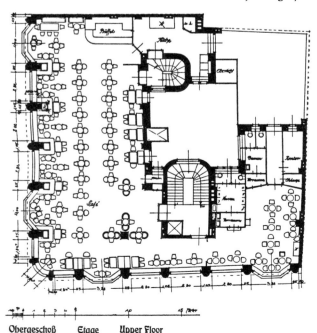

Obergeschoß   Etage   Upper Floor

Pflanzenschmuck. Die Fronten des ersten, zweiten und dritten Obergeschosses sind durch Halbsäulen, von denen einzelne Figuren tragen, sowie durch mehrere eckenartig vorspringende Fensterausbauten gegliedert. Das vierte, durch ein Quergesims abgetrennte Obergeschoß wird durch Pfeiler geteilt. Die Fassaden sind in rotem Sandstein verblendet; das steile Dach ist mit Ziegeln eingedeckt. Sämtliche Bildhauerarbeiten rühren von Bildhauer Schipke her.

Das Erdgeschoß enthält neben dem Eingangsflur mit der Stockwerkstreppe und dem Aufzug eine Anzahl Läden; an den im Erdgeschoß ringsumbauten Hof schließen sich eine Nebentreppe und ein zweiter Aufzug an. Das erste Obergeschoß ist zur Anlage eines großen, vornehm ausgestatteten Kaffeelokals mit Küche und Nebenräumen benutzt. Die folgenden Obergeschosse sind wieder zu Geschäftsräumen eingerichtet. Eisenbetonstützen, zum Teil in Rahmenkonstruktion, zum Teil in umschnürtem Beton hergestellt, durchsetzen sämtliche Geschosse. Die trägerlosen Hohlsteindecken sind nach dem System Dr. Holländer ausgeführt.

489 [1913; 94]

Das nach dem Entwurfe der Architekten Schilling & Gräbner errichtete Geschäfts- und Wohnhaus in Dresden, an der Kreuzkirche 8, erhebt sich in vier Geschossen und einem Dachgeschoß. Die Straßenfront wird durch zurückspringende schmale Seitenteile verlängert und enthält im Erdgeschoß eine Reihe im Korbbogen überdeckter Schaufenster, außerdem den von Halbsäulen eingefaßten, einen Balkon tragenden rundbogigen Haupteingang. An einer Seite der Front springt ein viereckiger ausgekragter, durch erstes und zweites Obergeschoß geführter, mit einer Altane im dritten Obergeschoß abschließender Erker hervor, an der anderen Seite öffnen sich im zurückliegenden Teile der Front in den drei Obergeschossen Loggien, denen Balkons vorgelegt sind. Das Erdgeschoß ist mit Sandstein bekleidet, die oberen Fassadenflächen sind verputzt. Das gebrochene mit Biberschwänzen eingedeckte Dach wird fast ganz von dem Aufbau des fünften Geschosses eingenommen und ist außerdem noch mit Dachfenstern besetzt.

490 [1913; 76]

Das Gebäude der Unfall-Versicherungs-Aktiengesellschaft und das Haus des Generaldirektors der Gesellschaft in Köln, Oppenheimerstraße, Ecke Kaiser Friedrich-Ufer, bilden eine durch einen niedrigeren Querbau verbundene mit Vorgärten ausgestattete Baugruppe. Die beiden nahezu gleichartig ausgebildeten zweistöckigen, mit gebrochenen abgewalmten, Dachaufbauten tragenden Dächern überdeckten Gebäude sind an den Fassaden mit Sandstein verblendet; die Dächer sind mit Schiefer eingedeckt. Der Entwurf, nach dem die Ausführung erfolgte, stammt vom Architekten Müller-Jena. Die Fronten beider Gebäude sind durch Pilasterstreifen gegliedert, der Verbindungsbau ist mit Halbsäulen versehen. Über dem Erdgeschoß des Versicherungsgebäudes, sowohl an der Straßenfront als an der freien, ein Mittelrisalit mit dem Eingang und einen breiten Dachaufbau mit Fenstern enthaltenden Seitenfront sind Knabenfiguren angebracht. Das Haus des Direktors zeigt an der Straßenfront einen mittleren durch eine Altane abgeschlossenen Erkerausbau und darüber einen breiten Dachaufbau mit flachrund schließendem Giebel. An der einen Seitenfront springt im mittleren mit einem Giebel die Dachlinie durchbrechenden Teile ein ausgekragter Balkon vor; an der anderen den Eingang enthaltenden langen Seitenfront erhebt sich ein durch beide Geschosse gehendes Risalit.

491 [1913; 99]

Das an zwei Fronten freiliegende, mit abgerundeter Ecke versehene, vierstöckige Warenhaus Petersdorff in Königsberg i. Pr., Krämerbrücke, Wassergasse, ist nach dem Entwurfe des Architekten Heitmann errichtet. Das jetzt stehende Gebäude bildet nur einen Teil des beabsichtigten umfänglichen Neubaues, für welchen der Entwurf bereits aufgestellt ist. Das mit breiten Schaufenstern ausgestattete Erdgeschoß enthält an der abgerundeten Ecke den rundbogig über-

à usage floral, présente une clé de voûte décorée. Les façades des trois étages inférieurs sont ornées de bow-windows et de demi-colonnes, certaines portant des sculptures. Le quatrième étage, séparé du reste du bâtiment par une corniche, présente une ordonnance régulière de piliers. Les murs extérieurs sont revêtus de grès rouge. Le toit pentu est recouvert de tuiles. Les ouvrages plastiques sont l'œuvre du sculpteur Schipke.

Le rez-de-chaussée comprend le hall d'entrée avec la cage d'escalier et l'ascenseur ainsi que quelques commerces. Un escalier secondaire et un deuxième ascenseur communiquent avec une cour intérieure. Le premier étage abrite un vaste et élégant salon de thé, équipé d'une cuisine et de pièces de service. Les étages suivants sont occupés par des locaux de commerce. Des supports de béton armé s'élèvent sur toute la hauteur de l'édifice. Les planchers creux sont réalisés d'après la méthode Holländer.

489 [1913; 94]

L'immeuble de rapport de cinq étages dont un mansardé, situé à Dresde, an der Kreuzkirche 8, fut construit sur les plans élaborés par les architectes Schilling & Gräbner. La façade sur rue est prolongée, en retrait, par une aile étroite. Elle est percée au rez-de-chaussée de devantures surbaissées et d'une entrée en plein cintre, flanquée de demi-colonnes supportant un balcon. A l'une des extrémités du bâtiment, se détache de la façade une logette quadrangulaire s'élevant sur deux étages et se terminant par une plate-forme au niveau du troisième étage. De l'autre côté, sur la façade en retrait, s'ouvrent, sur les trois étages, des loggias assorties de balcons saillants. Le rez-de-chaussée est revêtu de grès, les surfaces supérieures sont enduites d'un crépi. Le toit au comble brisé, recouvert de tuiles plates est percé de fenêtres. Son volume est quasiment absorbé par le cinquième étage.

490 [1913; 76]

L'édifice de la compagnie d'assurances ainsi que la maison de son directeur, situés à Cologne, à l'angle de l'Oppenheimerstraße et du quai Kaiser Friedrich, furent conçus par l'architecte Müller-Jena. Ces deux bâtiments de deux étages, reliés par une construction basse, forment un ensemble assorti d'un jardin frontal. Très semblables dans leur composition, ils sont coiffés de toits mansardés en croupe aux combles brisés et recouverts d'ardoises. Les murs de façade sont revêtus de dalles de parement gréseux. Les façades des deux édifices sont ornées de stries de pilastres, le bâtiment bas de demi-colonnes. Les façades sur rue et latérale du bâtiment de la compagnie d'assurances sont décorées, dans leur partie inférieure, de sculptures de jeunes garçons. Un avant-corps médian abritant l'entrée et coiffé d'une large baie mansardée se détache de la façade latérale. La maison du directeur présente, sur la façade sur rue, une avancée se terminant par une plate-forme surmontée d'un pignon arrondi. Un balcon saillant se dégage de la partie médiane, couronnée d'un pignon, d'une des façades latérales. L'autre, abritant l'entrée, est agrémentée d'un avant-corps s'élevant sur deux étages.

491 [1913; 99]

Le grand magasin Petersdorff de Königsberg, donnant sur les rues Krämerbrücke et Wassergasse, est un bâtiment de quatre étages, présentant deux façades dégagées et un angle arrondi. Il fut construit sur les plans de l'architecte Heitmann. L'édifice présent s'inscrit dans un vaste projet, dont les autres bâtiments, conçus sur plans, ne sont pas encore réa-

second and third storeys are articulated by demi-columns, some of which are topped by figures, and a number of windowed bays. The fourth floor, which is separated from the lower storeys by a transverse cornice, is divided by pillars. The façades are faced with red sandstone, and the steep roof is covered with tile. The ornamental figures are the work of the sculptor Schipke.

In addition to the entrance hall containing the staircase and lift, the ground floor is occupied by a number of shops. The enclosed courtyard on the ground floor is connected to a side stair and a second lift. The first floor has been designed for an elegant coffee-house of considerable size and also includes the kitchen and other service rooms. The remaining upper floors are planned for offices. All floors are supported by reinforced concrete piers, which are either of frame construction or have helical binding. The girderless hollow block floor is constructed according to the Holländer system.

489 [1913; 94]

Designed by the architects Schilling & Gräbner, the apartment building in Dresden (An der Kreuzkirche 8) has four-storeys and one roof storey. The frontage is extended by means of a returned narrow side structure, and contains a number of shop windows in basket arches. The round-arched main entrance is framed by demi-columns and covered by a balcony. A rectangular-shaped oriel extends form the first through the second storey at one side of the façade, and is topped by a balcony at the third storey. Loggias with balconies are located at the three upper storeys of the set-back section of the façade. The ground level is faced with sandstone, the upper façades are of plaster. The broken-lined roof, which is covered with flat red tile, is almost completely occupied by the fifth-storey superstructure; it also has a number of dormers.

490 [1913; 76]

The office building of the Accident Insurance Company in Cologne (corner of Oppenheimstrasse and Kaiser Friedrich Ufer) and the adjoining house of the company director form an architectural group connected by a lower cross building and front garden. Almost identical in design, both buildings have two storeys, hipped slate roofs with broken lines and superstructures, and façades of sandstone. Construction was based on the design of the architect Müller-Jena. The fronts of both edifices are articulated with pilaster strips, those of the connecting building with demi-columns. The two fronts of the insurance building are decorated by sculptured figures located over the ground level. Its exposed front contains a middle erection, which encloses the main entrance and finishes with a broad superstructure with windows. The director's house has at the middle of its street front an oriel topped by a balcony; above that is a superstructure with a curved gable. The middle of one of the side fronts has a gable rising above the roof line and a projecting balcony. The entrance is located at the other longer side front, which has a projection running through both storeys.

491 [1913; 99]

The four-storey commercial building housing the Petersdorff department store in Königsberg, Prussia has two exposed fronts and was designed by the architect Heitman. The existing structure represents only one part of a more extensive complex whose plans have recently been completed. The main entrance at the ground level, which is lined with broad shop win-

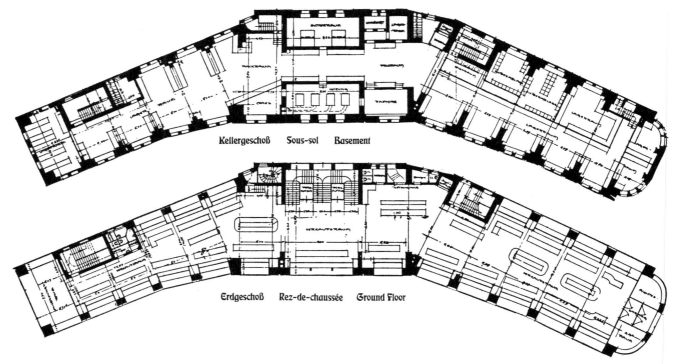

Kellergeschoß   Sous-sol   Basement

Erdgeschoß   Rez-de-chaussée   Ground Floor

deckten, durch ein weit ausladendes Vordach geschützten Haupteingang. Die oberen drei Geschosse sind einheitlich mit durchgehenden Pfeilern gegliedert, welche die der Höhe nach zusammen gezogenen, geradlinig überdeckten Fenstergruppen zwischen sich einschließen. Die den Charakter des Geschäftshauses ausdrückenden Fassaden sind mit Sandstein bekleidet. Das abgewalmte, mit Biberschwänzen eingedeckte steile Dach trägt sowohl über der Eckrundung wie an den Seitenfronten mehrfach ausgedehnte mit Giebeln abschließende Fensteraufbauten.

492 [1913: 86]

Das mächtige in vier Geschossen und einem ausgebauten Dachgeschoß sich erhebende, mit zwei Fronten freiliegende Gebäude der Königl. Eisenbahn-Direktion in Köln a. Rh., Kaiser Friedrich-Ufer, ist in den Fassaden mit einer sämtliche Geschosse durchsetzenden Pilastergliederung versehen. Der Mittelbau der Hauptfront zeigt eine Reihe freistehender jonischer Säulen, die über dem Dachgesims durch einen Aufsatz mit einer Folge von Fenstern bekrönt sind. Die geradlinig überdeckten Fenster aller Geschosse sind der Höhe nach zusammengezogen. Die Fassaden sind mit Sandstein bekleidet; das gebrochene, abgewalmte in den Steilflächen mit Dachfenstern besetzte Dach ist mit Schiefer eingedeckt.

493 [1913: 7]

Das Hungaria Fürdö (Bad) in Budapest, Dohany-utcza 44, bildet eine umfängliche, mit reichlichen Bequemlichkeiten für die 1 600 000 jährlichen Besucher ausgestattete Baulichkeit. Architekt der im Laufe zweier Jahre mit einem Kostenaufwand von 2 000 000 Kronen errichteten Anlage ist Emil Agoston. Die hochaufstrebende Straßenfront enthält das mehrfach mit figürlichen Gruppen Badender geschmückte Portal und zu beiden Seiten flach vorgebaute, durch sämtliche Geschosse gehende, von unteren vorgekragten Balkons aus ansetzende Fenstervorlagen. Die breite Fenstergruppe inmitten der Fassade ist gleichfalls mit einer vorspringenden Bank zur Aufstellung von Blumen versehen. Das weit ausladende Dach trägt im mittleren Teil einen flachen Giebel und ist zu beiden Seiten mit turmartigen Aufbauten bekrönt. Die Fassade ist mit Sandstein bekleidet und das Eingangstor in Bronze ausgeführt. Die Figurengruppen am Portal sind von Bildhauer K. Sandor geschaffen, die Glasmalereien von E. Roth.

Im Erdgeschoß liegen außer dem Vestibül und den Treppen die Schwimmbassins, die auch die oberen Stockwerke durchsetzen. Angeordnet sind noch ein Erfrischungsraum mit anschließendem Büffet, ein Frisiersaal und ein Verkaufsraum. Im Hofe ist ein Sonnenbad mit einer Anzahl Liegebetten eingerichtet. Die Baukonstruktionen sind in Eisenbeton hergestellt. Das Bassin von 70 m Länge und 18 m Breite hat eine

lisés. La façade du rez-de-chaussée, trouée de larges devantures, comprend, dans l'angle arrondi, l'entrée cintrée, abritée sous un porche. Une ordonnance à piliers, encadrant des fenêtres groupées à linteau droit régulièrement alignées, organise la façade des trois étages supérieurs. Les murs extérieurs sont revêtus de grès, soulignant ainsi la vocation commerciale des lieux. Le toit pentu en croupe, recouvert de tuiles plates est percé de nombreuses lucarnes.

492 [1913: 86]

Cet édifice imposant, haut de cinq étages dont un mansardé, abrite la direction des chemins de fer royaux à Cologne, Kaiser-Friedrich-Ufer. La façade présente une ordonnance à pilastres s'élevant sur toute la hauteur des murs. Le corps intermédiaire de la façade principale est assorti d'une série de colonnes ioniques couronnées de fenêtres au-dessus de la corniche du toit. Les fenêtres droites des étages sont régulièrement alignées. Les murs de façade sont revêtus de grès. Le toit en croupe au comble brisé est percé de fenêtres mansardées et porte une couverture d'ardoises.

493 [1913: 7]

Les établissements de bain de Budapest „Hungaria Fürdö", Dohanyutcza 44, proposent aux nombreux visiteurs (1 600 000 par an) un important ensemble richement aménagé. Le portail d'entrée, hautement décoré de figures de baigneurs sculptées, est encadré d'oriels en encorbellement s'élevant sur toute la façade. Le large ensemble de fenêtres, au centre de la façade, est assorti d'un rebord saillant destiné à l'arrangement de pots de fleurs. Le toit saillant, flanqué de deux tourelles, est pourvu, en son centre, d'un pignon plat. La façade est revêtue de grès, le portail est en bronze. Les ornements plastiques sont l'œuvre du sculpteur K. Sandor, la peinture sur verre fut réalisée par E. Roth.

Le rez-de-chaussée comprend le vestibule et l'escalier ainsi que les bassins de natation qui englobent les étages supérieurs, un café, un salon de coiffure et un commerce. Un solarium équipé de nombreuses chaises longues est aménagé dans la cour. L'ossature du bâtiment est en béton armé. Le bassin d'une longueur de 70 m, d'une largeur de 18 m et d'une profondeur variant de 1,50 à 3 m est couvert

dows, is placed in the rounded corner and is covered by an overhanging canopy. The upper three storeys are uniformly broken up by continuous pillars which frame rows of vertical straight—lined windows. The façades are characteristic of a commercial building and are faced with sandstone. The hipped roof is covered with flat red tile and has a number of windowed gables over the side fronts as well as the rounded corner.

492 [1913: 86]

The free—standing building of the head offices of the Royal Railway impressively rises to a height of four storeys and a large roof storey. Pilasters run the entire height of the two exposed façades. The middle erection of the principal front has a row of free—standing Jonic columns crowned above the cornice by a superstructure with a row of windows. All storeys have vertical straight—lined windows. The fronts are faced with sandstone; the slate roof is hipped and has dormers in its lower slope.

493 [1913: 7]

The Hungaria Fürdö (Baths) in Budapest (Dohany utcza 44) is an expansive structure which offers its 1,600,000 annual visitors a wealth of amenities. Constructed over the course of 2 years for 2,000,000 Crowns, the bathing establishment is the product of the architect Emil Agoston. The tall street front contains a portal ornamented with groups of bathers. To either side of the portal are window projections starting at cantilevered balconies and extending to the top of the façade. The broad group of windows at the centre of the façade is also decorated with a projecting ledge for flower boxes. The overhanging roof has a flat gable at its middle section and is crowned at both sides by turret—like superstructures. The façade is rendered in sandstone, the entrance door in bronze. The group of figures over the portal are the work of the sculptor K. Sandor. The glass paintings are by E. Roth.

Apart from the vestibule and stairs, the ground floor is occupied by the pools, whose walls extend through the upper floors, as well as a refreshment room and connecting buffet, a hairdresser's salon and a salesroom. A sun bath with a number of reclining chairs is located in the courtyard. The structural framework is made of reinforced concrete. The pool is 70 metres long and 18 metres wide, and has a depth

A Kasse für die Männerabteilung   A. Cashier for Men's Baths
B Kasse für die Frauenabteilung   B. Cashier for Women's Baths
C Schwimmbassin   C. Swimming Pool
D Pater Noster   D. Pater Noster
E warmes Bassin   E. Warm Bath
F Dampfkammer   F. Steam Room
G lauwarmes Bassin   G. Luke—warm Bath
H Lichtbad   H. Sun Bath
J Salzwasserbassin   J. Salt—water Bath
K Trockenraum   K. Drying—off Room
L Auskleideraum   L. Changing Room
M Herren-Frisier- und Pedikureraum   M. Barber's Shop and Pedicure
N Eingang zum Bassin   N. Entrance to Pool
O Damen-Frisiersalon   O. Hairdresser's salon
P warme Luft   P. Warm Air
Q kaltes Bassin   Q. Cold Bath
R Dusche   R. Douche

A caisse de la partie réservée aux hommes
B caisse de la partie réservée aux femmes
C bassin de natation
D pater-noster
E bassin d'eau chaude
F bain turc
G bassin d'eau tiède
H solarium
J bassin d'eau salée
K salle de repos
L vestiaire
M salon de coiffure pour hommes et soins pédicures
N accès au bassin
O salon de coiffure pour dames
P étuve sèche
Q bassin d'eau froide
R douches

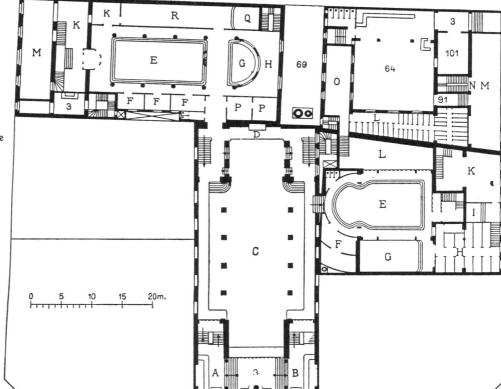

0 5 10 15 20m.

Erdgeschoß   Rez-de-chaussee   Ground Floor

Friseursaal   Salon de coiffure   Hairdresser's Salon

Schwimmbad   Bassin de natation   Swimming Pool

Wasserhöhe von 1,50–3,00 m, ist unterkellert und mit einem zum Teil verstellbaren Dachgerüst überdeckt. Die Innenbekleidung der Räume besteht meist aus weißem Marmor.

494 [1913; 95]

Das ringsum freiliegende mit drei Flügeln einen Hof umfassende Gebäude der Städtischen Schule in Budapest I, Fehérvári-ut, zählt im Hauptbau vier, in den Flügeln fünf Geschosse. Der Entwurf stammt von den Architekten Professoren Julius Sándy und Franz Orbán, die Ausführung lag in den Händen der Architekten David und Sohn. Die Bauzeit nahm 2 Jahre in Anspruch, die Baukosten betrugen 850 000 Kronen und, die innere Einrichtung eingerechnet, 972 000 Kronen. Die Hauptfront enthält zwei mit Quadermauerwerk eingefaßte Eingänge und einen über dem Mittelteil sich erhebenden geschweiften Giebel. Die Ecken der Front zeigen Altane als Abschluß über dem dritten Geschoß. Auf dem Dache in der Mittelachse der Hauptfront ist ein mit einer Galerie umgebener, kuppelbekrönter Dachreiterturm angeordnet. Die Seitenfronten werden durch schmale Eckrisalite begrenzt, die mit geschweiften Giebeln abschließen. Der Sockel sowie einzelne Fassadengliederungen sind in rotgelbem Sandstein hergestellt; die oberen Fassadenflächen tragen grauen Zementputz. Die gebrochenen Dächer sind

d'une toiture en partie mobile. Un sous-sol a été construit sous la piscine. Les salles sont revêtues en majeure partie de marbre blanc.

494 [1913; 95]

L'ensemble scolaire municipal de Budapest, Fehérvári-ut, se compose d'un corps de bâtiment de quatre étages et de trois ailes de cinq étages ceignant une cour. Les plans furent élaborés par les architectes Julius Sády et Franz Orbán. La direction des travaux releva de l'autorité des architectes David & fils. La construction nécessita deux années et coûta 850 000 couronnes. La somme se monta à 972 000 couronnes avec l'aménagement intérieur. La façade principale est assortie de deux entrées, comprises dans des avancées en pierres de taille traitées en bossage, et d'un pignon aux contours ondulés coiffant la partie médiane. Les angles de la façade se terminent par des plate-formes. Une tourelle couronnée d'une coupole et ceinte d'une galerie s'élève du centre du toit. Les façades latérales sont flanquées d'avancées étroites se terminant par un pignon aux contours ondulés. Le socle ainsi que les ornements de la façade sont en grès rouge-jaune. Les surfaces supérieures des murs extérieurs sont enduites d'un crépi cimenté gris. Les toits aux combles brisés sont recouverts de tuiles rouges, la

494 [1913; 95]

The free—standing New School in Budapest (Fehérvári ut.), with three wings bordering a courtyard, has a four—storey principal section, and five—storey wings. The plan is the work of the architects Professors Julius Sándy and Franz Orbán, and the final design was put into the hands of the architects David and Sohn. Construction lasted two years at a sum of 972,00 Crowns, including the interior furnishings. The main front has two entryways framed in ashlar and a shaped gable at the top of its middle section. The corners of the front have terraces which top the third storey. A domed ridge turret is placed at the central axis of the front. The side fronts have narrow corner projections ending in shaped gables. The socle as well as the façade ornamentation is of red—yellow sandstone. The upper façades are faced with grey concrete plaster. The roofs are covered with red tile, and the turret with copper. The window frames

mit roten Ziegeln, der Turm ist mit Kupfer eingedeckt. Die Fensterrahmen sind grün gestrichen. Fenstersturze und Teilungen der Treppenhausfenster sind in Eisenbeton ausgeführt.

Das Gebäude umfaßt die Volksschule für Knaben und Mädchen, die Bürgerschule für Mädchen, die Haushaltungsschule für Mädchen, die Kinderbewahranstalt, insgesamt 66 Schulsäle und Nebenräume, außerdem die Direktorwohnungen und 2 Turnsäle. Aula und Turnsaal liegen im dritten Stock in der Mitte.

495 [1913; 75]

Durch monumentale Ausbildung der Fassade ausgezeichnet, erhebt sich in fünf Geschossen das Gebäude der Asowschen Bank in St. Petersburg, Morskaja 5. Der Bau ist nach dem Entwurfe des Architekten Fedor Jwan Lidwall im Laufe von 2 Jahren

tourelle est revêtue d'une couverture de cuivre. Les chambranles des fenêtres sont peints en vert. Les appuis ainsi qui les meneaux des ouvertures de la cage d'escalier sont en béton armé.

L'établissement comprend l'école primaire de filles et de garçons, le cours élémentaire de filles, l'école de filles d'enseignement ménager, soit un total de 66 salles de classe et locaux dépendants, ainsi que les logements des directeurs et deux gymnases. La grande salle de réunion et la salle de gymnastique sont situées au centre du troisième étage.

495 [1913; 75]

Ce bâtiment de cinq étages, situé à Saint-Pétersbourg, Morskaja 5, abrite une banque. Caractérisé par sa façade monumentale, cet édifice, conçu par l'architecte Fedor Jwan Lidwall, fut construit en l'es-

are painted green. The window lintels and the mullions of the windows in the stair well are of reinforced concrete.

The building houses a elementary school for boys and girls, a girls' school, a domestic science school for girls, and a day-nursery. There are a total of 66 classrooms and other rooms, plus the director's flat and 2 gymnasiums. The auditorium and a gymnasium are located at the centre of the third floor.

495 [1913; 75]

The Asovian Bank in St. Petersburg (Morskaya 5) is a five-storey edifice with a façade of monumental design. The building was designed by the architect Fedor Jwan Lidwall and constructed over the

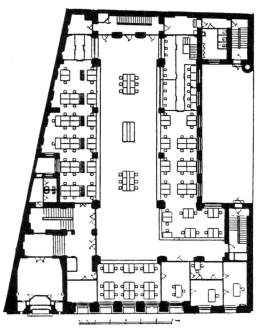

Erdgeschoß   Rez-de-chaussée   Ground Floor

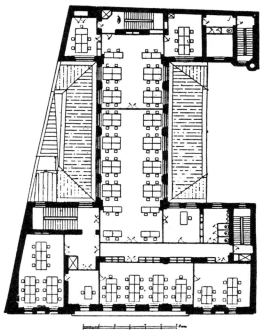

Obergeschoß   Premier étage   Upper Floor

errichtet. Der mittlere Teil der Straßenfront wird von einer die drei unteren Geschosse durchsetzenden, über dem Abschlußgesims Balkons tragenden Stellung jonischer Säulen eingenommen. Über dieser folgt ein Halbkreisfenster, von einem kleinen ausgekragten Balkon in der Mitte durchbrochen und als Abschluß des Fassadenteils ein überragender flacher Dreiecksgiebel. Der Eingang ist in einem Seitenteil der Fassade angeordnet; über dem Erdgeschoß beider Seitenteile erstreckt sich ein galerieartiger Balkon. Die figürlichen Reliefs an den Pfeilern des Erdgeschosses sowie die Figuren der Medaillons im vierten Stock des Mittelbaues sind Arbeiten des Bildhauers W. Kujnezoff. Die Fassade ist in grauem ostfinnischem Granit ausgeführt.

Das Erdgeschoß enthält eine große mittlere Halle für den Verkehr des Publikums, an welche sich beiderseits die mit einem Erdgeschoß abschließenden Kassen- und Bureauräume sowie Eingangshalle und Stockwerkstreppen anreihen. Die oberen Geschosse sind durchweg zur Anlage von Bureauräumen benutzt.

496 [1913; 84]

Das zwei freie Fronten zeigende, an der abgerundeten Ecke durch einen Turmaufbau ausgezeichnete Geschäfts- und Wohnhaus in Wien, Graben 16, ist als ein Werk des Architekten Pietro Palumbo im Laufe eines Jahres für die Baukostensumme von rund 1 000 000 Kronen zur Ausführung gekommen. Das Erdgeschoß und das darüber folgende Zwischengeschoß sind ebenso wie das Mezzaningeschoß mit breiten Schaufenstern versehen. Letzteres mit dem Unterschiede, daß eine Anzahl vorgebauter Fensterkasten angeordnet sind. Die Fenster der drei oberen Geschosse sind der Höhe nach zusammengezogen; vor den Fenstern des dritten Obergeschosses erstrecken sich galerieartige Balkons; ebenso sind die rundbogig

pace de deux années. La partie médiane de la façade sur rue est assortie de colonnes ioniques, supportant des fenêtres en tribune au quatrième étage, suivies, au cinquième étage, d'une baie en demi-cercle ornée en son milieu d'un petit balcon saillant. La façade s'achève par un pignon en delta. L'entrée se trouve sur une des ailes. Le rez-de-chaussée des deux ailes est surmonté d'un balcon aux allures de galerie. Les reliefs ornant les piliers du rez-de-chaussée ainsi que les ouvrages sculptés des médaillons du quatrième étage du corps central sont l'œuvre du sculpteur W. Kujnezoff. La façade est en granit finlandais gris.

Le rez-de-chaussée comprend l'entrée, l'escalier menant aux étages supérieurs ainsi que le grand hall central réservé au public, encadré de guichets et de bureaux. Les étages supérieurs sont occupés par des bureaux.

496 [1913; 84]

Cet immeuble, aux deux façades dégagées, situé à Vienne, Graben 16, se singularise par la tourelle coiffant le pan coupé. Œuvre de l'architecte Pietro Palumbo, cet édifice fut érigé en l'espace de deux années pour la somme de 1 000 000 couronnes. Le rez-de-chaussée, l'entresol et la mezzanine sont troués par de larges devantures. La mezzanine est en outre assortie de bow-windows. Les fenêtres des trois étages supérieurs sont régulièrement alignées. Un balcon continu, formant un genre de galerie, pare les ouvertures du troisième étage. Les fenêtres cintrées du

course of 2 years. At the centre of the frontage is a colonnade of Jonic columns running the height of the three lower storeys, with a balcony above the entablature. This is followed by a small cantilevered balcony set before a semi-circular window, and the façade finishes with an protruding triangular gable. The entrance is located at one side section of the façade. Both side sections have a gallery-like balcony running above the ground level. The figural reliefs on the ground level pillars as well as the medallion reliefs at the fourth storey of the middle section are the work of the sculptor W. Kuinetsoff. The façade is rendered in grey granite from Eastern Finland.

The ground floor of the bank contains a large central hall for public commerce which is lined on both sides by teller's counters and offices, whose ceilings are two storeys high, and the entry lobby and staircase. The entire floor space of the upper storeys is designated for offices.

496 [1913; 84]

The two exposed fronts of the apartment building in Vienna (Graben 16) are joined by a rounded corner with a turreted tower. Designed by the architect Pietro Palumbo, construction of the building, which also contains shops, was completed in one year at a cost of 1,000,000 Crowns. The ground level as well as the ground storey and the mezzanine above that are all lined with broad shop windows, the latter storey having a number of projecting window bays. The windows of the upper storeys are vertical; gallery-like balconies run along the windows of the third storey, whereas

geschlossenen Fenster im sechsten Obergeschoß einzeln mit vorgelegten Balkons versehen. Die Fassaden schließen nach oben mit einem kräftig ausladenden Dachgesims ab. Der Eckturm trägt ein mit Säulen umgebenes, von einer Kuppel bekröntes Belvedere. Am Ende der einen Front zeigt sich ein über die Dachlinie hinausgehender Aufbau. Im Erdgeschoß, dem Zwischengeschoß und der Mezzanine sind die Fronten mit Plauener Granit und schwedischem Labrador bekleidet, während die oberen Teile der Fassade aus Savonière-Kalkstein hergestellt sind. Die Mosaikverzierungen der Fassaden stammen aus der Werkstatt von Leop. Förstner. Das Dach ist in den Steilflächen teils mit Glas teils mit Schiefer eingedeckt.

Das Erdgeschoß ist zu Geschäftslokalen, zum Eingangsflur, zur Haupt- und Nebentreppe sowie zum Aufzug ausgebaut. Gleichfalls sind Zwischengeschoß und Mezzanine zu Geschäftsräumen eingerichtet. Die drei oberen Geschosse enthalten je eine größere Wohnung mit Küche, Bad und Zubehör, nur durch die Haupttreppe verbunden. Im Dachboden sind Ateliers untergebracht, im Souterrain und Kellergeschoß Magazine, Vorratskeller und der Heizraum. Die Dachkonstruktionen sind in Eisenbeton hergestellt, ebenso sämtliche Decken und Tragepfeiler bis zum Mezzanin. Die Portale der Geschäftsräume bestehen aus Tomback.

497 [1914: 2]

Das freiliegende in fünf Geschossen und einem ausgebauten Dachgeschoß aufsteigende Geschäftshaus der Leipziger Feuerversicherungs-Anstalt in Leipzig, am Thomasring und dem Fleischerplatz gelegen, ist nach dem Entwurfe der Architekten Geheimer Baurat Prof. Dr.-Ing. Hugo Licht und der Kgl. Bauräte G. Weidenbach und R. Tschammer errichtet. Die Bauzeit dauerte 1½ Jahre bis April 1913, die Baukosten betrugen 1 775 000 Mark ohne Architektenhonorar und ohne örtliche Bauleitung. Die Hauptfront ist durch zwei breite giebelbekrönte Risalite gegliedert. Die abgerundete zurückspringende Ecke enthält den Haupteingang, darüber eine Altane und schließt über dem vierten Geschoß wieder mit einer Altane ab. Die Seitenfront wird gleichfalls durch ein Risalit mit Giebel unterbrochen. Auf dem First der Dächer erheben sich drei kuppelbekrönte Türmchen. Die Straßenfronten sind in weißgelbem Bunzlauer und Rackwitzer Sandstein hergestellt, die Hinterfront ist verputzt. Die gebrochenen Dächer sind mit roten Biberschwänzen eingedeckt. An den Malerarbeiten war R. Hesse, an den Bildhauerarbeiten Professor Hartmann, W. und B. Wollstädter und Fr. Stellmacher als Ausführende beteiligt.

Das Gebäude besteht aus zwei durch eine Brandmauer geschiedenen Teilen, die nur einen Lichthof gemeinsam haben. Der linke Gebäudeteil enthält im Erd-, im ersten und zweiten Obergeschoß die Geschäftsräume der Leipziger Feuerversicherung, während das dritte und vierte Obergeschoß von der Thüringischen Gasgesellschaft benutzt werden. Der Zugang liegt an der runden Ecke, wo auch die Haupttreppe angeordnet ist. Eine Nebentreppe führt zu den im Dachgeschoß gelegenen kleinen Dienstwohnungen.

sixième étage sont assorties chacune d'un balcon. Une corniche très saillante achève la façade. La tour d'angle supporte un belvédère ceint de colonnes et couronné d'une coupole. A l'une des extrémités du bâtiment, la façade se prolonge au-delà de la ligne du toit. Le rez-de-chaussée, l'entresol et la mezzanine sont revêtus de granit de Plauen et de labrador suédois. Les murs supérieurs de façade sont construits en pierres à chaux. Les décors de mosaïque sur les façades sont l'oeuvre de Leop. Förstner. Les versants pentus du toit sont recouverts de verre ou d'ardoises.

Le rez-de-chaussée comprend le hall d'entrée, les escaliers principal et secondaire, l'ascenseur ainsi que des locaux de commerce. L'entresol et la mezzanine abritent également des commerce. Dans chacun des étages supérieurs est aménagé un vaste appartement avec cuisine, salle de bains et pieces de service, accessibles par l'escalier principal. A l'étage des combles sont installés des ateliers. Le sous-sol est occupé par les magasins, les caves à provisions et la chaufferie. La charpente du toit est réalisée en béton armé ainsi que l'ensemble des planchers et des piliers de support jusqu'à la mezzanine. Les portes des locaux de commerce sont en tombac.

497 [1914: 2]

Le bâtiment de la compagnie d'assurances leipzigoise contre l'incendie, haut de cinq étages, étage des combles non compris, situé à l'angle des Thomasring et Fleischerplatz, fut édifié d'après les plans des architectes prof. Hugo Licht, G. Weidenbach et R. Tschammer. Sa construction dura un an et demi (jusqu'en avril 1913) et revint à 1 775 000 marks, honoraires des architectes et frais de direction locale des travaux non compris. La façade principale est divisée par deux larges avant-corps couronnés d'un pignon. L'angle arrondi, en retrait, comprend l'entrée principale surmontée d'un balcon et se termine, au quatrième étage, par un balcon. La façade latérale présente également une avancée à pignon. Sur le faîte des toits se dressent trois tourelles coiffées de coupoles. Les façades sur rue sont construites en grès crème de Bunzlau et de Rackwitz, la façade postérieure est crépie. Les toits aux combles brisés sont recouverts de tuiles plates rouges. Les peintures furent exécutées par R. Hesse; le professeur Hartmann, W. et B. Wollstädler et Fr. Stellmacher se chargèrent des sculptures.

Le bâtiment se compose de deux parties, séparées par un mur mitoyen, ayant en commun une cour intérieure. L'aile de gauche abrite, au rez-de-chaussée ainsi qu'aux premier et deuxième étages, les bureaux de la compagnie d'assurances leipzigoise contre l'incendie. Les troisième et quatrième étages sont occupés par la compagnie de gaz thuringienne. L'entrée se trouve dans l'angle arrondi et donne sur le grand escalier. Un escalier de service conduit aux logements des employés situés sous les combles. L'aile de droite comprend, au rez-de-chaussée , des salles d'exposi-

individual balconies have been placed in front of the round—arched windows of the sixth storey. The façades finish at the top with a prominent roof moulding. The corner tower has a domed belvedere flanked by columns. The end of one front has a bay extending above the roof line. The fronts at the ground level, the ground storey and mezzanine are faced with Savonière limestone. The ornamental mosaics of the façades come from the studios of Leop. Förstner. The covering of the steeper slope of the roof is part glass, part slate.

The ground floor is designed for shops and has an entrance hall, a main staircase and side stairs, as well as a lift. Similarly, the ground storey and mezzanine are also taken up by shops. Each of the three upper floors contain a spacious flat with kitchen, bath and related rooms, and are connected by the main staircase only. Ateliers are to be found on the roof storey; the basement and cellar contain store rooms and the furnace room. The roof structure is of reinforced concrete, as are all ceilings and supporting piers below the mezzanine. The shop portals are made of tombac.

497 [1914: 2]

The free—standing building containing the head offices of the Leipzig Fire Insurance Company has five storeys and a roof storey. Located in Leipzig (corner of Thomasring and Fleischermarkt), the edifice was designed by privy architect Professor Dr. Hugo Licht and the royal architects G. Weidenbach and R. Tschammer. Construction occupied 1½ years and was completed in April 1913. Building costs amounted to 1,775,000 Marks, not including the architects' honorarium and local supervision. The principal front is articulated by two broad projections with gables. The entrance is located in the rounded, returned corner, which has balconies at the first and fourth storeys. The side front is also divided by a middle projection crowned by a gable. The roof ridge has three domed turrets. The frontage is rendered in yellow—white sandstone from Bunzlau and Rackwitz, the rear front is plastered. The roof is covered with flat red tile. The decorative paintings are the work of R. Hesse, and the sculptured ornamentation was carried out by Professor Hartmann, W. and B. Wollstädter and Fr. Stellmacher.

The building consists of two main sections divided by a compartment wall which are grouped round a single courtyard. The ground level, first and second floors of the left section are occupied by offices of the Leipzig Fire Insurance Company, while the third and fourth floors are taken up by the Thuringia Gas Company. The entrance is located at the rounded corner, as is the main staircase. A side stairway leads to a small company flat on the roof floor. The right wing contains

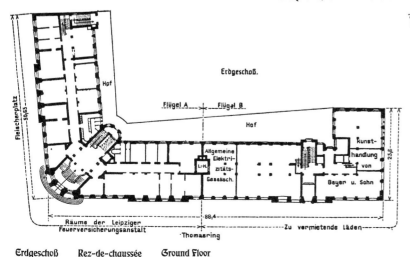

Erdgeschoß   Rez-de-chaussée   Ground Floor

Obergeschoß   Etage   Upper Floor

Der rechte Flügel enthält im Erdgeschoß Ausstellungs-räume und Läden. Im ersten Obergeschoß liegen die Räume der Allgem. Elektrizitäts-Gesellschaft, in den Geschossen darüber Geschäfts- und Lagerräume und im Dachgeschoß kleine Wohnungen. Der Eingang zur Verbindungstreppe liegt an der Hauptfront. Die Heiz-anlage des Hauses und die Kohlenaufzüge werden vom Hofe aus bedient. Es ist eine Niederdruckdampf-heizung vorgesehen.

498 [1914; 8]

Das Geschäftshaus „Markgrafeneck" in Berlin, Ecke Markgrafen- und Schützenstraße, in 5 Ge-schossen aufsteigend, ist nach dem Entwurfe des Ar-chitekten Regierungsbaumstr. a. D. Walter Schilbach im Laufe des Jahres 1913 errichtet. Die Eingangsfront enthält ein breites, mit einem Rundgiebel abschließendes mittleres Risalit; die anstoßende Front ist gleich-falls mit einem Risalit ausgestattet, das einen sämtliche Obergeschosse durchsetzenden polygonalen Erker ein-schließt und mit einem gebogenen Giebel endigt. Beide Fronten sind durch aufstrebende Pfeiler gegliedert, welche die bis zum dritten Obergeschosse zusam-mengezogenen Fenstergruppen zwischen sich ein-schließen. Das Erdgeschoß öffnet sich mit Schaufen-stern. Die Fenster im dritten Obergeschoß sind flach-bogig überdeckt, die im vierten Obergeschoß sind wie-der zu Gruppen vereinigt. Die Fassaden sind in Wert-heimer Jura-Muschelkalk hergestellt; das Dach ist mit Ziegeln eingedeckt und wird durch Oberlichter un-terbrochen. An den Bildhauerarbeiten der Front waren beteiligt: Professor E. Seger, die Bildhauer Westphal und Rauschart.

Das Erdgeschoß wird ganz von Läden eingenom-men; in den oberen Geschossen sind Räume für En-grosgeschäfte: Arbeits- und Expeditionssäle, sowie Kontore und Empfangszimmer untergebracht. Die Haupttreppe an der Front und eine zweite vom Hofe zugängliche Treppe sind mit Personenaufzügen ver-bunden. Außerdem sind noch 2 Lastenaufzüge und eine Nebentreppe vorhanden.

499, 500 [1914; 3, 4]

Das umfangreiche, freiliegende, in fünf Geschossen aufsteigende Bureaugebäude der Mannesmann-werke in Düsseldorf ist nach dem Entwurfe des Archi-tekten Professor Peter Behrens errichtet. Die Vorder-front enthält im Erdgeschoß den Haupteingang. Die Fassaden zeigen im Erdgeschoß bossiertes Quader-werk, im ersten Obergeschoß Pfeiler, welche die Fen-ster zwischen sich einschließen. Das zweite und dritte Obergeschoß sind durch aufstrebende schmale Pfeiler zu einer Einheit zusammengezogen, wieder die Fenster zwischen sich einschließend. Das vierte Obergeschoß enthält gruppierte Fenster. Die Hinterfront wird durch ein die Dachlinie durchbrechendes Risalit gegliedert. Die Fassadenflächen tragen eine Sandsteinbekleidung; die abgewalmten Dächer sind mit Biberschwänzen eingedeckt.

501 [1914; 7]

Die nach dem Entwurfe des Architekten Emanuel von Seidl errichtete Villa H. von Rath in Bonn, Coblenzerstraße 42, zeigt zwei Geschosse und ist mit einem gebrochenen abgewalmten Dach, dessen untere Flächen gebogen sind, überdeckt. Die Bausumme be-trug 245 000 Mark ohne Innenausstattung, diese ko-stete 75 000 Mark. Inmitten der Straßenfront springt ein polygonaler Ausbau vor, der sich durch beide Ge-schosse und über die Dachlinie hinaus turmartig fort-setzt. An einer Seitenfront ist der hinter einer Säulen-halle liegende, von Säulen eingefaßte, zurückgesetzte Haupteingang angeordnet, neben dem sich ein Anbau erhebt. An der anderen Seitenfront befindet sich ein flachrunder mit einer Altane abschließender Ausbau, und an der Rückfront eine Terrasse, zu der eine Frei-treppe emporführt. Der Sockel bis zum ersten Stock ist in gelbgeädertem Sandstein ausgeführt, die oberen Fassadenflächen sind verputzt. Die Läden sind blau-grün mit weiß gestrichen; das Dach ist mit grauen Ziegeln eingedeckt.

Das Innere der Villa enthält im Erdgeschoß eine Halle mit freiliegender Treppe und eine Anzahl auf-

---

tion et des commerce. Au premier étage sont aménagés les bureaux de la compagnie générale d'électricité, aux étages suivants des bureaux et des entrepôts, sous les combles de petits logements. L'accès à l'escalier de communication s'effectue sur la façade principale. Le chauffage de l'immeuble et les monte-charges pour le charbon sont commandés depuis la cour. Il est prévu un chauffage par vapeur à basse pression.

498 [1914; 8]

L'immeuble berlinois „Markgrafeneck", situé à l'angle des rues Markgrafenstraße et Schützen-straße, fut construit d'après les plans de l'architecte Walter Schilbach au cours de l'année 1913. La façade principale est assortie d'un large avant-corps terminé par un pignon en plein cintre. La façade contiguë présente une avancée comprenant un bow-window po-lygonal montant sur tous les étages et se terminant par un pignon arqué. Les deux façades sont rythmées de pilastres, lesquels encadrent, jusqu'au troisième étage, des ensembles de fenêtres. Le rez-de-chaussée est percé de devantures. Les fenêtres du troisième étage sont surbaissées, celles du quatrième sont groupées. Les murs de façades sont construits en coquillart juras-sique de Wertheim. Le toit est recouvert de tuiles et percé de lucarnes. Les ouvrages sculptés de la façade furent exécutés par le professeur E. Seger et les sculp-teurs Westphal et Rauschart.

Le rez-de-chaussée est entièrement occupé par des commerces. Dans les étages sont aménagés des commerces de gros avec leurs salles de manutention et d'expédition ainsi que des bureaux et des salles d'ac-cueil. Le grand escalier sur la façade principale ainsi qu'un second escalier accessible par la cour renferment en leur centre des ascenseurs. L'immeuble est en outre équipé d'un monte-charge et d'un escalier de service.

499, 500 [1914; 3, 4]

Les bureaux de la maison Mannesmann de Düssel-dorf sont abrités dans un vaste bâtiment dégagé, montant sur cinq étages, édifié sur les plans de l'archi-tecte prof. Peter Behrens. La façade principale com-prend l'entrée principale au rez-de-chaussée. A ce même niveau, les façades présentent des bossages, au premier étage des piliers engagés encadrant des fenê-tres. Les premier et deuxième étages forment un en-semble grâce à une ordonnance à étroits piliers conti-nus, flanquant les ouvertures. Le quatrième étage offre des fenêtres groupées. La façade postérieure est assor-tie d'un avant-corps coupant la ligne du toit. Les murs de façades sont revêtus de grès. Les toits en croupe portent une toiture de tuiles plates.

501 [1914; 7]

La villa H. von Rath, située à Bonn, Coblenzer-straße 42, fut construite sur les plans de l'archi-tecte Emanuel von Seidl. Elle comprend deux étages et est recouverte d'un toit en croupe au comble brisé dont les versants inférieurs sont incurvés. Les frais de cons-truction s'élevèrent à 245 000 marks, 75 000 marks furent dépensés pour l'aménagement intérieur. De la partie médiane de la façade saillit une avancée poly-gonale aux allures de tour, montant sur les deux étages et s'élevant au-delà de la ligne du toit. La façade latérale présente un porche hypostyle abritant l'entrée flanquée de colonnes, située en retrait. A côté se dresse un avant-corps. La façade opposée est as-sortie d'un bow-window convexe, surmonté d'un bal-con. La façade postérieure offre une terrasse accessible par un perron. Le socle montant jusqu'au premier étage est réalisé en grès veiné de jaune. Les surfaces supérieures des façades sont crépies. Les volets sont peints en vert bleu et rayés de blanc. Le toit porte une couverture de tuiles grises.

La villa abrite, au rez-de-chaussée, une anti-chambre comprenant l'escalier, ainsi que quelques

---

exhibition rooms and offices on its ground level; located on the first floor are the offices of the General Electric-ity Board. The floors above contain offices and store rooms, and the roof floor consists of small flats. The entrance to the connecting stairs is located at the main front. The heating facilities and coal lifts are accessible from the courtyard. Heating is provided by a low-pressure steam system.

498 [1914; 8]

The "Markgrafeneck" commercial building, located in Berlin at the corner of Markgrafenstrasse and Schützenstrasse, is the work of the retired government architect Walter Schilbach and was completed in the year 1913. The entrance front of the five-storey build-ing has a broad middle erection crowned by a rounded gable. The adjoining front also has a middle projec-tion, which encompasses a polygonal oriel extending through all upper storeys and ending in a rounded gable. Both fronts are articulated by continuous pilas-ters which frame gorups of windows running to the third storey. Shop windows line the ground level. The third storey windows are framed in flat arches, those of the fourth storey are again arranged in groups. The façades are rendered in Jurassic shell limestone from Wertheim; the roof is tiled and has skylights. The sculptural ornamentation of the façade is the work of Professor E. Seger and the sculptors Westphal and Rauschart.

The ground floor is completely taken up by shops. The upper floors contain rooms used by a wholesale firm: work and dispatch rooms, as well as offices and reception rooms. The main staircase at the front as well as two stairs at the courtyard are connected to lifts. Furthermore, there are two goods lifts and a side stair.

499, 500 [1914; 3, 4]

The expansively designed Mannesmann adminis-tration building in Düsseldorf is the work of the architect Peter Behrens. The principal front of the five-storey edifice contains the main entrance at the ground level, whose façades are rendered in bossed ashlar. The façade at the first storey is articulated by pillars between its windows. The second and third storeys are united by continuous pillars which again are separated by windows. The fourth storey is marked by grouped windows. The back front has a projection rising above the roof line. The façades are covered with sandstone, and the hipped roofs with flat tile.

501 [1914; 7]

Based on the plans of the architect Emanuel von Seidl, the H. von Rath house in Bonn (Coblen-zerstrasse 42) has two storeys and a hipped roof with curving lower slopes. Construction costs were 245,000 Marks, not including the interior furnishings, which amounted to 75,000 Marks. A polygonal bay projects at the middle of the street front and ends above the roof line in the shape of a turret. The recessed entrance is placed at the side front behind an arcade and is framed by columns. A bay is located next to the entrance. At the other side front is a projection with slightly rounded contours and a balcony on the top. A elevated terrace with open steps is laid out at the rear of the villa. The socle, which extends to the first storey, is of sandstone with yellow veining; the upper façades are faced with plaster. The shutters are painted bluish—green and white, and the roof is covered with grey tile. The interior of the house has a hall at the ground floor with

wandvoll mit Holztäfelungen ausgestatteter Räume: das Herren- und das Damenzimmer, die Garderobe, den Salon, das Speisezimmer, die Küche mit Anrichte, die Nebentreppe und einen Zierbrunnen in Porzellan. Im Obergeschoß liegen, um die Halle gruppiert, das Damenzimmer, die Garderobe, das Schlafzimmer, die Kinderzimmer, das Fremdenzimmer, das Speisezimmer und zwei Baderäume. Einzelne Zimmer stehen in Verbindung mit Altanen, von denen die eine überdeckt ist.

502 [1914; 5]

Die umfängliche, aus dem Hauptgebäude mit Seitenflügeln und dem anschließenden Gewächshause bestehende, von Garten-Anlagen umgebene Baugruppe der Rose Livingston Damenstiftung und Nellini Stift, in Frankfurt a. M., Cronstettenstraße, ist nach dem Entwurfe des Architekten Professor Bruno Paul in den Baujahren 1912 und 1913 errichtet. Die Straßenfront des zweistöckigen mit einem gebrochenen Dach überdeckten Hauptgebäudes zeigt ein mittleres Risalit mit Giebel, dem im Erdgeschoß die von einer Altane überragte Eingangshalle vorgelegt ist.

Die Seitenflügel sind durch Balkons ausgezeichnet. Auf dem Dache erhebt sich ein Türmchen mit glockenförmiger Haube. Die Steilflächen des Daches tragen Fenster. Die Gartenfront enthält im mittleren zurückspringenden Teile einen halbrunden mit einer Altane bekrönten Vorbau und im Dache einen Fensteraufbau mit Giebel. An die Innenseite der Flügelbauten lehnen sich Anbauten, die im Obergeschoß Altane tragen. Die Hauptarchitekturteile der Fassaden sind in fränkischem Muschelkalkstein hergestellt. Die Flächen sind in der Farbe des Werksteins verputzt. Die Läden sind grün, die Fenster weiß, die Eisengitter schwarz gestrichen. Die abgewalmten Dächer sind mit Ziegeln eingedeckt.

Das Gebäude bietet ein Heim für etwa 25 Damen. Der Grundriß zeigt ein gut ausgebildetes Vestibül und Haupttreppenhaus, helle Flure, behagliche Einzelräume mit Schlafnischen oder Schlafkabinetten. Zentral gelegen sind die Wohnräume und Wohnzimmer, Bibliothek, Eßzimmer und Büro. Es sind helle geräumige Küchen mit besonderem Küchenhof angeordnet; außerdem große Veranden und Balkons an der Südost- und Südwestseite. Ein vielseitig angelegter Park mit Lauben, Bassin, Springbrunnen und Gewächshäuser schließt das Gebäude ein. Die Malerarbeiten sind von Hembus ausgeführt.

503 [1914; 11]

Die zweistöckig aufsteigende Doppelvilla in Mannheim, Villa Dorrinck, Gutenbergstraße 27 und Villa Stotz, Otto Beckstraße 49, ist von den Architekten Dipl.-Ing. Detert und Ballenstedt entworfen und in einer Bauzeit von 2 Jahren ausgeführt. Die Baukosten betrugen, ohne Hinzurechnung des Grunderwerbs, 50 000 Mark für Villa Dorrinck und 60 000 Mark für Villa Stotz. Nach den von Stadtbauinspektor Dipl.-Ing. Ehlgötz herrührenden Erläuterungen gibt der Doppelbau eine bemerkenswert geschickte Bebauung einer Straßenecke. Durch den Farbengegensatz zwischen grauem Terranovaputz der Flächen und hellem Sandstein zu den Sockeln, Portalgruppen und Fensterverdachungen wird der äußere Reiz der Anlage erhöht. Die Villa an der Otto Beckstraße zeigt an der Straßenfront die vorspringende Eingangshalle mit Säulen, die einen Altan tragen. Die abgewalmten mit Fensteraufbauten versehenen Dächer sind mit Schiefer eingedeckt.

Der Höhenunterschied zwischen Garten und Straße gestattete eine zweckmäßige Ausnutzung der Untergeschosse zu Wirtschaftsräumen und Garagen. Die Küchen liegen im Erdgeschoß. Um die Dielen gruppieren sich die Gesellschaftsräume, die Wohn- und Schlafzimmer, während die Dienstbotengelasse im Dachgeschoß untergebracht sind.

504 [1914; 16]

Freiliegend, von Gartenanlagen umgeben, in reicher Gruppierung erscheint die Villa Lindgens in Köln a. Rh., Oberländerufer 130, in zwei Geschossen und einem ausgebauten Dachgeschoß aufsteigend.

502 [1914; 5]

Le vaste ensemble de bâtiments formé par la fondation Rose Livingston et le foyer Nellini, situé à Francfort-sur-le-Main, Cronstettenstraße, fut édifié dans les années 1912 et 1913 sur les plans de l'architecte prof. Bruno Paul. Il se compose d'un corps de logis flanqué de deux ailes, d'une serre et de jardins. La façade frontale du corps de bâtiment, haut de deux étages et recouvert d'un toit au comble brisé, présente un avant-corps médian surmonté d'un pignon et assorti, au rez-de-chaussée, d'un porche portant balcon. Sur les ailes saillissent des balcons. Une tourelle coiffée d'une calotte en forme de cloche se détache du toit. Les versants pentus du toit sont percés de fenêtres. Côté jardin, une avancée arrondie surmontée d'un balcon fait saillie du renfoncement de la façade. Une mansarde à pignon se dégage du toit. Des constructions annexes, couronnées de balcons, s'adossent aux côtés intérieurs des ailes. Les principaux éléments architecturaux des façades sont réalisés en coquillart franconien. Les murs sont crépis dans la couleur des pierres de taille. Les volets sont peints en vert, les fenêtres en blanc, les grilles de fer en noir. Les toits aux combles brisés sont recouverts de tuiles.

Le bâtiment offre un foyer à environ 25 femmes. Le plan développe un beau vestibule, le hall du grand escalier, des couloirs clairs, de confortables chambres individuelles avec alcôves. Au centre se trouvent les pièces communes et la salle de séjour, la bibliothèque, la salle à manger et le bureau. L'édifice est équipé de grandes cuisines claires avec cour attenante. De grandes vérandas ainsi que des balcons agrémentent les façades sud-est et sud-ouest. Un parc varié, comprenant tonnelles, bassin, jet d'eau et serres, entoure le bâtiment. Les travaux de peinture furent exécutés par Hembus.

503 [1914; 11]

Cette villa mitoyenne de deux étages, située à Mannheim, fut conçue par les architectes Detert et Ballenstedt et réalisée en deux ans. Elle se compose de la villa Dorrinck au no. 27 de la Gutenbergstraße et de la villa Stotz au no. 49 de la Otto Beckstraße. Sans compter le prix d'achat du terrain, la villa Dorrinck coûta 50 000 marks et la villa Stotz 60 000 marks. D'après les explications de l'ingénieur des travaux publics Ehlgötz, la villa mitoyenne offre un exemple remarquable de la construction optimale d'un angle de deux rues. Le charme de l'ensemble est accentué par le contraste des couleurs, entre le crépi gris des murs et le grès clair des socles, des portails et des moulures à rejéteaux. La villa Stotz présente, côté rue, un porche flanqué de colonnes et surmonté d'un balcon. Les toits en croupe mansardés sont recouverts d'ardoises.

La différence de niveau entre le jardin et la rue permit une utilisation pratique du sous-sol en garages et pièces de service. Les cuisines sont au rez-de-chaussée. Autour des antichambres s'ordonnent les salons, les salles de séjour et les chambres à coucher. Les chambres des domestiques se trouvent sous les toits.

504 [1914; 16]

Isolée au milieu d'un jardin, la villa Lindgens à Cologne-sur-le-Rhin, Oberländerufer 130, nous apparaît comme un riche ensemble de deux étages, auxquels s'ajoute l'étage des combles.

an open staircase and a number of rooms extravagantly furnished with wood panelling: the study and salon, the cloak-room, drawing-room, dining room, kitchen and pantries, the side stairs and a porcelain fountain. Arranged around the hall of the upper floor are the boudoir, a dressing-roomm and two baths. Many rooms are connected to the balconies, one of which is covered.

502 [1914; 5]

The extensive architectural complex of the Rose Livingston Ladies Foundation and Nellini Endowment in Frankfurt-on-Main (Cronstettenstrasse) consists of a principal building with side wings and an adjacent green-house, all of which are surrounded by gardens. Construction took place during the years 1912 and 1913 and was based on the plans of the architect Professor Bruno Paul. The street front of the principal building has a gabled middle erection above the porched main entrance, which is covered by a balcony at the first storey.

Balconies are also located at the side fronts. The roof is crowned by a ridge turret with a bell-shaped dome. Dormer windows are located in the steeper slope of the roof. A round bay topped by a balcony projects from the middle recessed part of the garden front, which has a windowed gable. Bays abut from the courtyard side of the wings and have balconies at the upper storey. The façades' main architectural components are of Franconian shell limestone. The surfaces of the façades are rendered in plaster, whose colour matches that of the rubble masonry. Green shutters flank the windows, which are painted white, and the iron grilles are painted black. The hipped roof is covered with tile.

The building serves as a home for approximately 25 women. The floor plan shows a proportioned vestibule and main stairwell, well-lit corridors and comfortable rooms with either sleeping niches or cabins. Living room and sitting rooms, the library, diningroom and office are arranged in a central location. The kitchens are spacious and airy, and situated round a kitchen court. In addition, large verandas and balconies are located at the south-west and south-east sides of the building. Bordering the house is a landscaped park with bowers, basins, a fountain and greenhouse. The painting work was carried out by von Hembus.

503 [1914; 11]

The two-storey double villa in Mannheim (Villa Dorrinck-Gutenbergstrasse 27, Villa Stotz-Otto Beckstrasse 49) was designed by the certified architects Detert and Ballenstedt and completed over the course of two years. Construction costs, which exclude the price of the building plot, amounted to 50,000 Marks for the Villa Dorrinck, and 60,000 Marks for the Villa Stotz. According to the commentary given by municipal architect Ehlgötz, this double house represents a remarkably adroit development of a street corner. The contrasting colours of grey terranova plaster used for the façade and the light sandstone used for the socle, porticos and window canopies highlight the villa's exterior in a delightful way. The villa situated in the Otto Beckstrasse has a projecting colonnaded porch at its side front with a balcony on top. The hipped slate roof has gables with windows.

The lower elevation of the garden relative to the street favoured a design of the basement floors which incorporates utility rooms and garages. The kitchens are located on the ground floor. Arranged round the central hall are drawing-rooms, sitting-rooms and bedrooms. The servant's quarters are located on the attic floor.

504 [1914; 16]

The Lindgens house on Cologne (Oberländerufer 130), a two-storey residence rich in architectural detail, has an attic storey and is surrounded by gardens. The free-standing structure was designed by

Der Entwurf rührt von den Architekten B. D. A. Schreiterer und Below her; die Ausführungszeit erstreckte sich über drei Jahre; die Baukosten betrugen 320 000 Mark, so daß 1 cbm umbauter Raum auf 42 Mark zu stehen kam. Die Hauptfront erhebt sich hinter einer Terrasse und zeigt im mittleren Teile die säulengetragene Eingangshalle, daneben zwei kleinere Ausbauten, die im Obergeschoß mit einer Altane schließen. Über dem Dachkranz folgt ein breiter Fensteraufbau mit Dreiecksgiebel. Die Rückfront ist mit einer den Garteneingang bildenden, eine Altane tragenden Säulenhalle ausgestattet, im Anschluß an den Wintergarten. Der Zugang zum Vestibül liegt an der Seitenfront. Der Sockel besteht aus Basaltlava, die Fassaden sind aus weißem Mainsandstein mit gelblicher Aderung hergestellt, das gebrochene abgewalmte mit Schiefer eingedeckte Dach trägt Dachfenster. Bildhauer Joh. Degen war für die Außenarbeiten, Jul. Seidler für die Innenarbeiten beschäftigt.

Das Erdgeschoß enthält eine mittlere Halle im Anschluß an das Vestibül und die Haupttreppe, das Herren- und das Damenzimmer, das Empfangszimmer, das Speisezimmer, das Sprechzimmer und den Wintergarten, außerdem die Küche, das Leutezimmer und die runde Nebentreppe.

Im Obergeschoß liegen, um die Halle gereiht, Wohnzimmer, Schlafzimmer, 2 Baderäume, das Ankleidezimmer und die Räume für die Dienerschaft. Das Sockelgeschoß ist zur Anlage einer Kegelbahn und des Turnsaals benutzt. Sämtliche Decken bestehen aus Eisenbeton und tragen eine Lage von Korkholz.

505 [1914; 12]

In strengen Formen, dreigeschossig, frei in der Landschaft liegend, mit drei Flügeln einen Hof umspannend, zeigt sich das Stadthaus in Lahtis, ein Werk des Architekten Eliel-Saarinen. Die Bauzeit nahm 2 Jahre in Anspruch; die Baukosten betrugen 375 000 finnische Mark (Francs). Zu dem rundbogig überwölbten Haupteingang im Vorderbau führt eine Freitreppe empor; über dem Eingang steigen drei polygonal vortretende, die Obergeschosse durchsetzende, bis zum Dachrand reichende Fensteraufbauten empor. Die Seitenfront wird durch einen Vorbau gegliedert, über dem sich ein in Absätzen emporsteigender von Eckbauten eingefaßter, mit einer Plattform schließender Turm erhebt. Die Fassaden sind im Untergeschoß mit Sandstein bekleidet, die oberen Geschosse sind in Ziegelfugenbau ausgeführt. Die abgewalmten, an der Seitenfront einen Giebel zeigenden Dächer sind mit Ziegeln eingedeckt.

Im Erdgeschoß des Vorderflügels liegt die zur Haupttreppe führende Eingangshalle mit seitlich anschließenden Hallen, außerdem eine Anzahl Diensträume. Der lange Seitenflügel enthält die Sitzungssäle und drei Nebentreppen. Im rückwärtsliegenden Flügelbau sind wieder Diensträume und zwei Nebentreppen angeordnet.

506 [1914; 21]

Das hauptsächlich zu Bureauzwecken dienende Ludwig Loewe Haus in Düsseldorf, am Wilhelmplatz gelegen, Eigentum der Firma Ludw. Loewe & Co. A.-G., im Laufe von zwei Baujahren errichtet, ist ein Werk des Architekten Richard Bauer und hat ohne das Grundstück 975 000 Mark an Baukosten verursacht. Das vierstöckige mit einem ausgebauten, in der Front etwas zurückgesetzten Dachgeschoß versehene, an zwei Fronten freiliegende mit vier Flügeln einen größeren Hof umschließende Gebäude ist durchweg in Eisenbeton ausgeführt, ebenso die Dächer und Treppen. Die Fassaden sind mit gemischtem Vorsatzbeton gleich mit dem Eisenbeton zusammengestampft und entsprechend behauen. Das Erdgeschoß öffnet sich zu Schaufenstern der Läden und zu rundbogigen Eingängen. Sowohl die Haupt- als die Seitenfront sind durch breite Mittelrisalte, die mit spitzbogigen Giebeln abschließen, mittels durchgehender Pfeiler und polygoner durch das dritte und vierte Obergeschoß geführter Erker gegliedert. Die Ecke zwischen den freiliegenden Fronten ist durch ein Kuppeltürmchen ausgezeichnet; und andere Türmchen mit Kuppeldächern erheben sich über den mit Biberschwänzen eingedeckten Dächern.

Les plans furent exécutés par les architectes Schreiterer et Below. Les travaux durèrent plus de trois ans et coûtèrent la somme des 320 000 marks, soit 42 marks par mètre cube de volume construit. La façade principale s'élève derrière une terrasse et présente, dans sa partie médiane, un portique flanqué de deux bow-windows portant un balcon à l'étage supérieur. Au dessus de l'arête du toit se dresse une large construction mansardée à pignon triangulaire. La façade postérieure est assortie d'un portique à colonnes, surmonté d'une plate-forme, s'ouvrant sur le jardin et communiquant avec le jardin d'hiver. L'accès au vestibule se fait par la façade latérale. Le socle se compose de basalte, les murs de façade sont en grès blanc du Main, veiné de jaune. Le toit en croupe au comble brisé, recouvert d'ardoises, est percé de fenêtres mansardées. Le sculpteur Joh. Degen s'occupa du travail extérieur, Jul. Seidler du travail intérieur.

Le rez-de-chaussée comprend le vestibule et le grand escalier donnant sur une antichambre médiane, le cabinet de travail de monsieur, le boudoir de madame, la salle de réception, la salle à manger, le salon et le jardin d'hiver ainsi que la cuisine, la salle des domestiques et l'escalier de service circulaire.

La salle de séjour, la chambre à coucher, deux salles de bains, la garde-robe et les chambres des domestiques s'ordonnent autour d'une antichambre au premier étage. Le sous-sol est occupé par un bowling et une salle de gymnastique. Tous les planchers sont en béton armé et garnis d'une couche de liège.

505 [1914; 12]

L'hôtel de ville de Lahtis fut conçu par l'architecte Eliel-Saarinen. Cet édifice isolé, haut de trois étages, offre des formes sévères. Sa construction dura deux ans et coûta la somme de 375 000 marks finlandais (francs). Un perron conduit à l'entrée principale cintrée et voûtée, située sur le bâtiment frontal. Au dessus de laquelle saillissent trois bow-windows polygonaux, continus jusqu'à l'arête du toit. La façade latérale est assortie d'un avant-corps, surmonté d'une tour à recoupements, flanquée de constructions d'angle et terminée par une plate-forme. Le socle des façades est paramenté de grès, les étages supérieurs offrent un briquetage jointoyé. Les toits en croupe, présentant un pignon sur la façade latérale, sont recouverts de tuiles.

Le rez-de-chaussée de l'aile frontale abrite le hall d'entrée donnant sur l'escalier principal et contigu latéralement à des salles, ainsi que des locaux de service. L'aile la plus longue comprend les salles de conférences et trois escaliers de service. Dans l'aile postérieure sont situées de nouveau des locaux de service et deux escaliers secondaires.

506 [1914; 21]

L'immeuble Ludwig Loewe, situé à Düsseldorf, Wilhelmplatz, abrite essentiellement des bureaux. Propriété de l'entreprise Ludwig Loewe & Co. A.-G, l'édifice fut conçu par l'architecte Richard Bauer et réalisé en deux années pour la somme de 975 000 marks, terrain non compris. Ce bâtiment, haut de quatre étages, présente un étage des combles en retrait et deux façades dégagées. Il se compose de quatre ailes entourant une grande cour et est totalement construit en béton armé, de même les toits et les escaliers. Les façades, réalisées en agrégats et en béton armé, ont été travaillées en conséquence. Au rez-de-chaussée s'ouvrent des devantures de commerces et des entrées cintrées. La façade principale, comme la façade latérale, est assortie d'une large avancée couronnée d'un pignon en tiers-point, de piliers montant de fond et de bow-windows polygonaux continus aux deuxième et troisième étages. L'angle des deux façades sur rue se caractérise par une tourelle à dôme; d'autres tourelles à dôme se dressent sur les toits recouverts de tuiles

---

the architects Schreiterer and Below, members of the Association of German Architects. Construction lasted over three years and cost 320,000 Marks, or, calculated in terms of developed space, 42 Marks per cubic metre. The principal façade is located behind a front terrace and has a colonnaded entry porch in its middle section, which is flanked by two smaller bays with upper balconies. A windowed superstructure with a triangular gable rises above the roof line. The garden entrance at the back front is covered by a colonnaded porch topped by a balcony; the winter garden borders this side of the house. The entrance to the entry hall is at the side front. The socle consists of basalt lava; the façades are rendered in white Main sandstone with yellow veining. The slate roof is hipped and has dormers. The sculptor Joh. Degen was commissioned for the exterior ornamentation, and Jul. Seidler was responsible for decorating the house's interior.

The ground floor contains a central hall connected to the entry hall and the main staircase, the study, boudoir, drawing-room, dining room, sitting-room and the winter garden. The kitchen, personnel room, and the spiral side stair are also located on the ground floor.

Lined along the hall of the upper floor are sitting-rooms, bedrooms, two baths, the dressing-room, and rooms for the servants. The basement is used for playing skittle-alley and gymnastics. All ceilings are constructed of reinforced concrete and layered with cork.

505 [1914; 12]

The Lahtis Town Hall in Finland, a free-standing structure of austere design, comprises three wings bordering a courtyard. Construction of the three-storey building based on the plans of the architects Eliel-Saarinen occupied 2 years and cost 375,000 Finnish Marks (Francs). The porch steps lead up to the round-arched main entrance. Three groups of oriel windows located above the entrance extend through the upper storeys and end at the edge of the roof. The side is articulated by a bay, which is surmounted by a stepped tower. Square corner projections flank the tower, which ends in a platform. The lower façades are faced with sandstone, those of the upper storey are of bonded brick. The tiled roof is hipped and has a gable at the side front.

The ground floor of the front wing contains the entrance hall, which leads to the main staircase, and two connecting halls at either side. In addition, a numer of service rooms are located here. The long side wing contains the assembly rooms and three side stairs. The rear wing is occupied by service rooms and two side stairs.

506 [1914; 21]

The principal function of the Ludwig Loewe building in Düsseldorf (Wilhelmplatz) is that of an office building. Owned by the Ludwig Loewe Company, it was completed in two years and was designed by the architect Richard Bauer. Construction costs, excluding the price of the building site, amounted to 975,000 Marks. The four-storey edifice with a slightly returned roof storey has two exposed sides and four wings which enclose a central courtyard. The entire structure, including the roofs and stairs, is of reinforced concrete. The façades consist of facing concrete tamped onto the reinforced concrete and then hewn to a finish. The ground floor opens with shop windows and entryways framed by round arches. Middle projections at both the main and side fronts end in gables with pointed arches. Both fronts are also articulated by continuous pilasters and polygonal oriels extending from the second through the third storey. A domed turret is situated at the corner of the two fronts; other dome-shaped turrets rise from the roof of flat red tile. The sculptor August Bauer created the ornamen-

Für den bildnerischen Schmuck der Fassaden wurde das Wahrzeichen der Firma „der schreitende Löwe" vom Bildhauer August Bauer ausgeführt, gewählt.

Vom Haupteingang gelangt man in den Vorraum, in dem sich Granittafeln mit dem Firmen-Verzeichnis der Hausbewohner angebracht finden. Auf den Vorraum folgt das Hauptvestibül, das mit dem Gemälde des Malers Hohenstein Adolf, einen Hochofen im Betriebe darstellend, geschmückt ist und ein hohes farbiges Marmorpaneel zeigt. Zu beiden Seiten führen Treppen zum ersten Obergeschoß, rechts befinden sich die Personenaufzüge.

In der Kassettendecke des Vestibüls sind als Beleuchtungskörper bronzeverzierte Kristallschalen angebracht. Die Ausbildung der Hoffronten, ist der der Straßenfronten angepaßt, außerdem ziert den Hof eine freistehende Brunnenschale. Ein Paternosterwerk und ein Stecklift führen zu den oberen Geschossen, überdem sind zwei Kastenaufzüge vorhanden. Für Heizung und Lüftung ist in ausreichender Weise gesorgt. Sämtliche Räume sind elektrisch beleuchtet.

507 [1914; 22]

Das Hôtel Dressel in Berlin, zugleich Geschäftshaus der Daimler Motoren-Gesellschaft, Unter den Linden 50—51, macht sich durch die in den Obergeschossen mit einer Säulenstellung geschmückte Fassade Unter den Linden bemerkbar. Urheber des im Laufe eines Jahres für die Kostensumme von 173 000

plates. Comme ornement de la façade, fut choisi l'emblème de l'entreprise „le lion qui marche", exécuté par le sculpteur August Bauer.

L'entrée principale donne sur un hall où sont apposées des plaques de granit indiquant la liste des entreprises établies dans l'immeuble. Suit le vestibule principal, orné d'un haut panneau de marbre polychrome et d'un tableau du peintre Hohenstein Adolf, représentant un haut fourneau en service. De part et d'autre se trouvent des escaliers menant au premier étage, à droite sont aménagés les ascenseurs.

Des coupes en cristal enjolivées de bronze sont installées comme luminaires au plafond à caissons. Le revêtement des façades sur cour s'harmonise à celui des façade sur rue. Une fontaine orne la cour. L'immeuble est équipé d'un pater-noster, d'un ascenseur et de deux monte-charges. Les installations de chauffage et d'aération sont suffisantes. L'ensemble des pièces sont éclairées à l'électricité.

507 [1914; 22]

L'hôtel Dressel de Berlin, Unter den Linden 50—51, se caractérise par sa façade ornée de colonnes aux étages supérieurs. Ce bâtiment qui abrite également les bureaux de la société des moteurs Daimler fut construit en une année sur les plans des architectes

tal figures of the façades, which were chosen to illustrate the company's emblem of "the striding lion".

The principal entrance leads to the foyer, which displays granite slabs into which the names of the firms occupying the building have been carved. The foyer is followed by the main vestibule, which has a high panel of coloured marble, and which is also decorated with a painting by the artist Hohenstein Adolf depicting a blast furnace in operation. Stairs at both ends of the vestibule lead to the first floor; lifts are located to the right.

Dish—shaped crystal lighting fixtures with bronze ornamentation have been installed in the coffer ceiling of the vestibule. The design of the courtyard façades conforms to that of the street frontage, and a free—standing fountain basin graces the courtyard. A paternoster and a side lift lead to the upper floors; there are also two service lifts present. Adequate provisions have been made for heating and ventilation. All rooms are illuminated with electric lighting.

507 [1914; 22]

The façade of Hotel Dressel in Berlin (Unter den Linden 50—51), which also serves as business premises for the Daimler Motor Co., catches the eye with its colonnade extending through the upper storeys. The building was designed by the architects Alfred

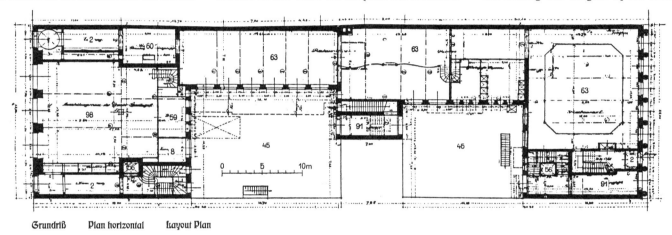

Grundriß   Plan horizontal   Layout Plan

Mark ausgeführten Entwurfs sind die Architekten Alfred Klingenberg und Fr. Beyer. Das Erdgeschoß öffnet sich mit drei rundbogigen Schaufenstern und zwei seitlichen Eingängen. Die drei Obergeschosse sind durch vorgestellte jonische Säulen zusammengezogen, welche die im zweiten und dritten Obergeschoß mit vorgelegten Balkons versehenen Fenstergruppen zwischen sich umschließen. Über der Säulenstellung folgt ein verzierter Fries und das Hauptgesims, weiter oben ein viertes Obergeschoß, das wieder mit einem von Rundbogenfenstern durchbrochenen mit einem bekrönenden Giebel ausgestattetes Dachgeschoß abschließt. Die Fassade ist in Muschelkalkstein hergestellt; die Bildhauerarbeiten an derselben, die Reliefs unter den Seitenfenstern der Obergeschosse, der verzierte Fries unter dem Hauptgesims sowie die freistehenden Figuren am Dachaufbau rühren von Jul. Wolf her.

Das Erdgeschoß enthält den Eingangsflur und den anschließenden Lichthof zugänglich, die an zwei mittelst einer Durchfahrt verbundenen Höfe und an der Mittelstraße liegenden Restaurations- und Wirtschaftsräume.

Neben der von der Mittelstraße her zum Innenhof führenden Durchfahrt liegt ein zweiter Eingang zum Restaurant und die Haupttreppe. Ein besonderer Eingang von der Front Unter den Linden her führt zu den Ausstellungsräumen der Daimler Motoren-Gesellschaft und zu einer mit einem Aufzug verbundenen Treppe.

508 [1914; 44]

Das einen Innenhof umschließende in vier Geschossen aufsteigende Bankhaus von der Heydt & Co. (Kleisthaus) in Berlin, Mauerstraße 53, ist nach dem Entwurf des Architekten Professor Bodo Ebhardt im Laufe eines Jahres errichtet. Die Fassade

Alfred Klingenberg et Fr. Beyer. Les travaux s'élevèrent à 173 000 marks. Trois devantures cintrées et deux entrées latérales s'ouvrent au rez-de-chaussée. Les trois étages supérieurs forment un ensemble grâce aux colonnes ioniques saillantes qui encadrent des fenêtres groupées, assorties de balcons aux deuxième et troisième étages. Les colonnes sont surmontées d'une frise décorée puis d'une corniche saillante sur laquelle s'élèvent le quatrième étage et l'étage des combles, percé de fenêtres cintrées et coiffé d'un pignon. La façade est en coquillart. Les sculptures, les reliefs sous les fenêtres latérales des étages supérieurs, la frise décorée ainsi que les statues du toit sont l'œuvre de Jul. Wolf.

Le rez-de-chaussée comprend le restaurant et les cuisines qui donnent sur la Mittelstraße et sur deux cours reliées par un passage. L'accès se fait par le couloir d'entrée et la cour intérieure adjacente.

Un deuxième accès au restaurant ainsi qu'un grand escalier sont contigus au passage reliant la rue à la cour intérieure. Les salles d'exposition de la société des moteurs daimler sont accessibles par une entrée située sur l'avenue Unter den Linden, entrée équipée d'un escalier et d'un ascenseur.

508 [1914; 44]

Le bâtiment de la banque Heydt & Co. (maison de Kleist) de Berlin, Mauerstraße 53, fut construit en un an d'après les plans de l'architecte prof. Bodo Ebhardt. Cet édifice, haut de quatre étages, comprend une cour intérieure. Au rez-de-chaussée, la façade

Klingenberg and Fr. Beyer and constructed in the course of one year at a cost of 173,000 Marks. The ground level opens with three round—arched showcase windows and two entrances at either side. The three upper storeys are joined by engaged Jonic columns, which frame balconies at the second and third storeys. The columns finish with an ornamented frieze and the main cornice. Above that is the fourth storey, which ends in the roof storey crowned by a gable with windows in round arches. The façade is faced with shell limestone. The sculptured ornamentation of the façade, the reliefs under the side windows of the upper storeys and the ornamental frieze under the principal cornice are the work of Jul. Wolf.

The ground floor contains the entry hall and an adjoining atrium which lead to two courtyards connected to one another by a carriageway. A restaurant and service rooms are located at the Mittelstrasse side of the ground floor.

A second entrance to the restaurant and the main staircase are located at the Mittelstrasse next to the carriageway leading to the inner courtyard. A separate entrance at the Unter den Linden front leads to the exhibition rooms of the Daimler Motor Company, and to stairs with a lift.

508 [1914; 44]

The Heydt & Co. bank building in Berlin (Mauerstrasse 53), a four—storey structure encompassing an inner courtyard, was designed by the architect Professor Bodo Ebhard and built in the course of one year. The façades at the ground level are of bossed ashlar.

zeigt im Erdgeschoß Bossenquaderung. Das erste und zweite Obergeschoß sind im vorspringenden Mittelbau durch jonische Pilaster gegliedert; über dem dritten Obergeschoß bildet ein Dreiecksgiebel den Abschluß. Der Sockel der Front besteht aus schlesischem Granit. Die oberen Fassadenflächen sind in Muschelkalkstein hergestellt. Die Hoffronten sind mit weißglasierten Verblendziegeln bekleidet. In dem alten, jetzt abgebrochenen Hause hatte Kleist gewohnt, und ist deshalb an der Front des Neubaues eine Relieftafel mit dem Bildnis des Dichters und der Pentesilea, modelliert von Bildhauer Kolbe, angebracht.

Das Erdgeschoß enthält den Eingangsflur mit der Stockwerkstreppe und die neben dem mit einer Luxferprismen-Glasbedachung versehenen Höfe gelegenen Geschäftsräume der Bank. Das erste Obergeschoß ist zur Anlage von Bureaus und Geschäftsräumen benutzt; im zweiten und dritten Obergeschosse sind außerdem Wohnräume untergebracht. An der Rückseite des Höfes ist eine zweite Stockwerkstreppe angeordnet. Die Zentralheizungs-, Warmwasserversorgungs-, Lüftungs-, Be- und Entwässerungs-, sowie Schmutzwasserhebeanlagen sind eingerichtet, ebenso elektrische Licht- und Kraftleitungen, Personen- und Aktenaufzüge. Im Kellergeschoß befindet sich der Tresor.

509 [1914: 23]

Das städtische Kurbadehaus „Kaiser-Friedrichs-Bad" in Wiesbaden erhebt sich am Fuße des alten Römerkastells Massiacum, anschließend an die historische Römermauer, an zwei Straßenzügen und an einem großen gärtnerischen Vorplatz gelegen, in drei Geschossen und einem ausgebauten Dachgeschoß. Die

présente des pierres de taille traitées en bossage. Les premier et deuxième étages offrent, dans leur partie médiane, une ordonnance à pilastres ioniques. Un pignon en delta, s'élevant au-dessus du troisième étage, couronne l'ensemble. Le socle de la façade est réalisé en granit de Silésie. Les surfaces supérieures sont en coquillart. Les façades sur cour sont habillées de briques de parement blanches vernissées. Kleist ayant vécu dans l'ancienne maison maintenant démolie, on apposa à la façade du nouvel édifice un bas-relief, modelé par le sculpteur Kolbe, avec le portrait du poète et le Penthésilée. Le rez-de-chaussée abrite le couloir d'entrée avec la cage d'escalier ainsi que les bureaux de la banque attenants à une cour couverte d'une verrière à prismes en verre à réflexion. Le premier étage est occupé par des bureaux et des locaux de travail. Des logements sont aménagés aux deuxième et troisième étages. Un deuxième escalier se trouve à l'arrière de la cour. Le bâtiment est équipé d'un chauffage central, d'une installation d'eau chaude, d'un système de ventilation, d'eau courante, d'un égout, d'une installation d'éclairage électrique, de conduites électriques, d'ascenseurs et de monte-documents. Le coffre-fort est installé au sous-sol.

509 [1914: 23]

L'établissement thermal „Kaiser-Friedrichs-Bad" de Wiesbaden est situé au pied de l'ancienne citadelle romaine „Massiacum", le long de deux rues et d'une esplanade aménagée en jardin. Il comprend trois étages et des combles aménagés. La supervision du projet fut confiée au maire Petri et au conseiller

The second and third storeys of the middle projections are joined by Ionic pilasters, and the third storey is crowned by a pediment. The socle of the front consists of Silesian granite; the upper façades are faced with shell limestone. The fronts facing the courtyard are faced with white glazed tile. Kleist once lived in the house torn down for the construction of the new building, which therefore has at its front a relief plaque created by the sculptor Kolbe which is dedicated to the writer and his main opus Pentesilea.

The ground floor contains the entry hall with stairs leading to the upper floors, and bank offices, which are adjacent to the courtyard covered with prismatic glass. The first floor is designated for offices; the second and third floors also include living quarters. A second stair leading to the upper floors is located at the courtyard side of the building. The premises are furnished with central heating, warm running water, as well as the necessary installations for ventilation, plumbing, and sewage. Electric lighting and power for the lifts and service lifts are also provided. The strong room is located in the basement.

509 [1914: 23]

The Municipal „Kaiser Friedrichs" Baths in Wiesbaden have been erected at the foot of the ancient Roman castellum of Massiacum, and are bordered by historic Roman walls, two streets lined with houses and a large landscaped square. Construction was put under

Ansicht   Vue d'ensemble   General View

Einfahrt   Entrée   Entrance Drive

Oberleitung war in den Händen des Bürgermeisters Petri und des Stadtbaurats Grün; Entwurf und Ausführung stammen von Architekt städt. Baurat A. O. Pauly. Die Ausführung dauerte von Oktober 1910 bis April 1913, die Baukosten betrugen 2,4 Millionen ohne, 3 Millionen Mark mit Bauplatz, so daß 1 cbm umbauter Raum mit Einrichtung 42,5 Mark gekostet hat. Die Eingangshalle vor der Hauptfront wird durch eine Stellung von Doppelsäulen gebildet und trägt eine Altane. Das Untergeschoß zeigt Rustikaquaderung, die beiden Obergeschosse sind mit durchgehenden Pfeilern gegliedert. An einer Seitenfront springen im ersten und zweiten Obergeschoß übereinander liegende Balkons vor, und über dem Dachgesims erhebt sich ein breiter Fensteraufbau mit einem Dreiecksgiebel abschließend. Für die Fassaden ist neben Putz Muschelkalk und gelblicher Tuffstein, für das gebrochene mit Dachfenstern besetzte Dach Schiefer verwandt. An der Hauptfassade heben sich neun von Bildhauer W. v. Heider geschaffene figürliche Reliefs hervor; außerdem waren die Bildhauer E. und W. Ohly, die Maler Völker, Wolf-Malm und Kaltwasser an der Ausschmückung des Inneren beteiligt.

An die Eingangshalle schließt sich die mit Marmorbekleidung reich ausgestattete Hauptwartehalle an, die mit dem von Völker gemalten Figurenfries geschmückt ist. Rechts von der Wartehalle liegt die Ab-

municipal Grün. L'architecte municipal A. O. Pauly exécuta les plans et fut chargé de leur réalisation. Les travaux durèrent du mois d'octobre 1910 au mois d'octobre 1913. Les frais de construction s'élevèrent à 2,4 millions de marks, auxquels s'ajouta le prix du terrain, soit une dépense totale de 3 millions de marks. Un mètre cube de volume construit revint ainsi à 42,5 marks, aménagement intérieur compris. L'entrée est assortie d'un portique formé par une rangée de colonnes géminées, surmonté d'une plate-forme. Le rez-de-chaussée présente des pierres de taille traitées en bossage rustique. Des pilastres rythment les deux étages suivants. Sur l'une des façade latérales saillissent, des premier et deuxième étages, des balcons régulièrement alignés. Une large construction mansardée, coiffée d'un pignon en delta, se détache du toit. Les murs de façade sont réalisés en crépi, en coquillart et en tuf jaunâtre. Le toit mansard au comble brisé porte une toiture d'ardoises. La façade principale offre neuf reliefs ornementaux exécutés par le sculpteur W. v. Heider. Les sculpteurs E. et W. Ohly, les peintres Völker, Wolf-Malm et Kaltwasser participèrent à la décoration de l'intérieur.

L'entrée donne sur la salle d'attente principale, richement décorée de marbre et ornée d'une frise peinte par Völker. To the right of the waiting

the general supervision of the Lord Mayor Petri and the municipal architect Grün; its plans and local supervision were carried out by the municipal architect A. O. Pauly. Construction lasted from October 1910 to April 1913 and costs, including 600,000 Marks for the building site, amounted to a total of 3 million Marks; or, in terms of developed space, 42.50 Marks per cubic metre. One side front has two balconies at the first and second storey placed on top of each other, and a windowed superstructure with a triangular gable projecting above the roof moulding. In addition to plaster, the façades are rendered in shell limestone and yellow tufa. The slate roof has a regular pattern of dormers. The principal façade is ornamented with nine figural reliefs created by the sculptor W. v. Heider. In addition, the sculptors E. and W. Ohly, and the painters Völker, Wolf-Malm and Kaltwasser contributed to the ornamentation of the interior.

The entry hall leads to the main waiting hall, which is clad in marble and decorated with a figural frieze painted by Völker. To the right of the waiting

teilung für Einatmen, links das Empfangszimmer für die Ärzte und Verwaltungsräume. Personenaufzüge sowie eine Treppe führen nach den oberen Geschossen. Rechts vom Hauptflur ist das römisch-russische Bad angeordnet. Die Räume dieser Abteilung reihen sich um eine durch zwei Geschosse gehende Halle, welche das Schwimmbad und das warme Sprudelbad enthält. Die Wandbilder sind durch Wolf-Malm ausgeführt. Außerdem enthält das Erdgeschoß noch eine Reihe von Thermalbädern, die Moorbäder und das Sandbad. Die Haupttreppe endigt im ersten Obergeschoß vor einer Wartehalle. An diese grenzt ein Erfrischungsraum. Von der Wartehalle gelangt man in die Wasserbehandlungsräume für Herren. Im zweiten Obergeschoß liegt wieder ein Warteraum, von dem aus die Wasserbehandlungsräume für Damen zugänglich sind.

510 [1914: 27]

Als mächtiger Eckbau in sechs Geschossen und einem ausgebauten Dachgeschoß aufsteigend, zeigt sich das von Architekt D. W. B. Fr. Höger entworfene, in den Jahren 1912 und 1913 ausgeführte Geschäftshaus Rappolt und Söhne in Hamburg, Mönkebergstraße und Barkhof. Die Baukosten betrugen rund 3 000 000 Mark. Das Erdgeschoß durch Schaufenster geöffnet und das folgende Zwischengeschoß mit im Stichbogen überdachten Fenstern sind durch eine Abschrägung in der Fassade von den 4 Obergeschossen abgetrennt. In der Mitte der durch Pfeilervorlagen gegliederten Längsfront springt eine ausgekragte breite durch 3 Geschosse geführte mit einer Altane abschließende Vorlage heraus. Die Ecke zwischen beiden Fronten wird durch einen abgerundeten über dem Zwischengeschoß mit einer Altane endigenden, mit Figuren bekrönten Zwischenbau ausgefüllt. Die Längsfront trägt auf dem gebrochenen, mit Schiefer eingedeckten Dache 4 mit geschwungenen Giebeln ausgestattete Fensteraufbauten. Über dem mit Altane abschließenden Ausbau der Schmalfront erhebt sich ein geschwungener mit einem Fenstervorbau versehener Giebel. Die Verblendung der Fassaden besteht aus violetten Bockhorneklinkern, unter Mitverwendung von Mühlhauser Travertin.

Hinter der Vorhalle im Erdgeschoß folgt die an einen Lichthof grenzende Haupttreppenhalle, der sich mehrere Aufzüge und ein Notausgang anschließen. Hauptsächlich wird das Erdgeschoß von Läden mit innerer Pfeilerstellung und einem Packraum einge-

peinte par Völker. A droite se trouvent les pièces réservées aux inhalations, à gauche le cabinet de consultations des médecins et les bureaux administratifs. Des ascenseurs ainsi qu'un escalier conduisent aux étages supérieurs. A droite du couloir principal est situé le bain russo-romain. Ses pièces s'agencent autour d'un hall montant sur deux étages, abritant la piscine et le bassin bouillonnant chaud. Les fresques sont l'œuvre du peintre Wolf-Malm. Le rez-de-chaussée comprend outre les bains thermaux, les bains de boue et un bain de sable. Le grand escalier aboutit au premier étage devant une salle d'attente attenante à une buvette. De la salle d'attente, on accède aux salles d'hydrothérapie réservées aux hommes. Au deuxième étage se trouvent les salles d'hydrothérapie réservées aux femmes accessibles par une salle d'attente.

510 [1914: 27]

C'est sous la forme d'un puissant bâtiment d'angle de six étages surmonté d'un étage mansardé que se présente l'établissement commercial hambourgeois „Rappolt und Söhne", situé sur les Mönkebergstraße et Barkhof. Il fut conçu par l'architecte Fr. Höger et construit dans les années 1912 et 1913. Les frais de construction s'élevèrent à environ 3 000 000 marks. Au-dessus du rez-de-chaussée, percé de devantures, et de l'entresol aux fenêtres couronnées d'arcs ciselés, se dressent en retrait les quatre étages supérieurs. La façade la plus longue, ponctuée de pilastres, présente, en son centre, une avancée montant sur trois étages et s'achevant par un balcon. L'angle formé entre les deux façades est occupé par une construction arrondie se terminant au-dessus de l'entresol par une plate-forme couronnée de statues. Quatre constructions mansardées, coiffées de pignons aux lignes ondulées, se détachent du toit recouvert d'ardoises. La façade latérale offre un avant-corps surmonté d'une plate-forme au-dessus duquel se dresse un pignon aux contours ondulés, assorti d'un bow-window. Les murs extérieurs sont parementés de briques hollandaises violettes et de travertin de Mühlhausen.

Le hall d'entrée s'ouvre sur la cage du grand escalier, contiguë à une cour vitrée et communiquant avec plusieurs ascenseurs et une sortie de secours. Le rez-de-chaussée est occupé principalement par des commerces, divisés par des piliers, et par une salle de

hall is the inhalation department, to the left the physician's waiting room and offices for the administration. Lifts and stairs lead to the upper floors. A Roman—Russian bath is located to the right of the main corridor. The rooms of this section run along a two—storey hall, which contains the swimming pool and the warm mineral baths. The murals here are the work of Wolf—Malm. The ground floor also has a number of thermal baths, mud baths, and the sand bath. The main stairs lead to a waiting hall on the first floor, which is located next to the refreshments buffet. The waiting hall leads to the water therapy rooms for men. The second floor also contains a waiting room, which leads to the water therapy rooms for women.

510 [1914: 27]

The Rappolt & Sons commercial building in Hamburg (corner of Mönkebergstrasse and Barkhof) is an imposing corner structure of six storeys and a roof storey. Designed by the head architect Fr. Höger, it was constructed during the years 1912 and 1913 at a cost of approximately 3,000,000 Marks. Both the ground level, which opens with shop windows, and the following storey, with its windows in segmental arches, are clearly delineated from the upper storeys by a beveled façade strip. The long front, which is articulated by pilasters, has at its middle section a broad cantilevered projection extending through three storeys and ending with a balcony. The corner between the two fronts is occupied by a rounded bay, which ends at the mezzanine level with a balcony and ornamental figures. Four shaped gables with windows extend through the slate roof of the long front. Another shaped gable with a rounded window oriel rises above the projection in the narrower front, which is also covered by a balcony. The facing of the façades consists of a combination of violet cement clinkers and travertine from Mühlhausen.

The ground floor portico leads to the main staircase hall and atrium, which contains a number of lifts and an emergency exit. The ground floor consists mainly of shops divided by interior pillars, and a

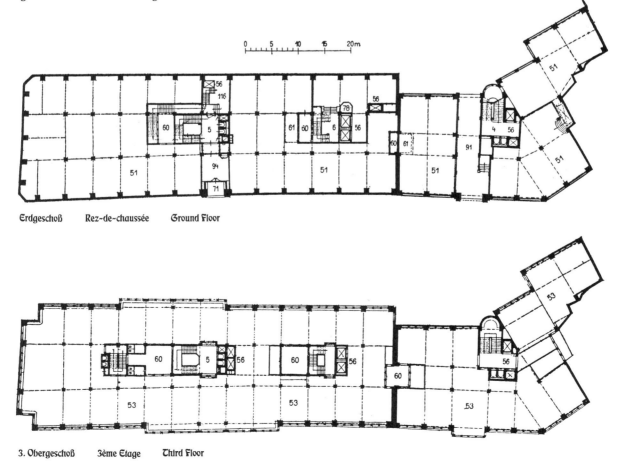

0 5 10 15 20m

Erdgeschoß   Rez-de-chaussée   Ground Floor

3. Obergeschoß   3ème Etage   Third Floor

nommen. Ein Ladenraum umschließt eine Arbeitertreppe mit einem Lichthof und zwei Lastenaufzügen verbunden. Ein Durchgang, die Jakobitwite, teilt die vermietbaren, mit besonderer Treppenhalle und Aufzügen versehenen Läden ab. Die Obergeschosse, durch Treppen und Aufzüge, enthalten Lager-, Fabrikations- und Bureauräume. Die Innenstruktur des Hauses besteht aus genieteter Eisenkonstruktion, die Decken sind aus Eisenbeton mit Weißschen Rohrgeweben hergestellt.

conditionnement. Un local de commerce s'agence autour d'un escalier réservé aux ouvriers, attenant à une cour vitrée et à deux monte-charges. Un passage, le Jakobitwite, sépare les locaux destinés à la location, équipés d'un escalier particulier et d'ascenseurs. Les étages supérieurs, accessibles par des escaliers et des ascenseurs, abritent des entrepôts, des salles de fabrication et des bureaux. L'ossature intérieure de l'édifice se compose d'une construction métallique rivetée. Les plafonds sont en béton armé, garni de lattis.

packing room. The service stairs are located in the loading room. The loading area has a service stair, which leads to a patio, and two service lifts. A passageway borders the shops to be let and their separate stair hall and lifts. The upper floors are connected by stairs and lifts, and contain rooms for storage, manufacturing, and a number of offices. The building has a riveted iron structural framework with reinforced concrete floors with reed lathing in the Weiss technique.

511, 524 [1914; 83, 85]

Die Häusergruppe am Kleberplatz in Straßburg i. El. umfaßt das Kaufhaus Modern, entworfen von den Architekten Berninger und Krafft, von 1912 bis 1914 zur Ausführung gekommen, links davon das Geschäfts- und Wohnhaus, entworfen von Architekt Paul Horn und rechts davon das Geschäfts- und Wohnhaus, entworfen von Architekt Grünwald.

Das in fünf Geschossen aufsteigende Kaufhaus Modern zeichnet sich durch einen beide Fronten verbindenden, in den Obergeschossen mit vorgestellten Säulen versehenen von turmartigen Aufbauten flankierten abgerundeten Eckbau aus. Das Erdgeschoß enthält die Eingänge und übrigens Schaufenster ringsum von einem Glasdach überragt. In den drei nächstfolgenden Obergeschossen sind die Fenster der Höhe nach zusammengezogen und von durchgehenden Pfeilern eingefaßt. Im vierten Obergeschoß liegen die gepaarten Fenster zwischen Konsolen, die das Dachgesims und die den Abschluß bildende Balustrade stützen. Zwischen den Fenstern im vierten Obergeschoß des Eckbaues sind Figuren angebracht. Die Bildhauerarbeiten sind von Alb. Schmitz und Stanly ausgeführt. Der Sockel der Fassade ist in graurötlichem Vogesengranit, die oberen Teile derselben sind in rotgrauem Vogesensandstein hergestellt. Die inneren Pfeiler und Deckengebälke bestehen aus Eisenbeton, die Fassadenpfeiler aus Vogesensandstein mit Backsteinhintermauerung.

Das Erdgeschoß zeigt den Haupteingang in der Rundung des Eckbaues und 2 Nebeneingänge in den flankierenden Türmchen und enthält einen großen ungeteilten mit Pfeilerstellungen versehenen Geschäftsraum, in dem die freiliegende von Aufzügen begleitete Haupttreppe aufsteigt. Es sind noch mehrere Stockwerkstreppen und Aufzüge angeordnet; ein weiterer Eingang liegt an der Helenengasse. Die Obergeschosse sind durch zwei Lichthöfe unterbrochen und enthalten gleichfalls ungeteilte Geschäftsräume.

Das links vom Kaufhause liegende Gebäude wird im Erdgeschoß an beiden Fronten von einer offenen Arkadenhalle umgeben, über der sich ringsum eine ausgekragte Gallerie erstreckt, und enthält unter anderem ein Kaffeehaus. Das erste Obergeschoß ist zu Geschäftszwecken bestimmt, die folgenden drei Obergeschosse sind teils zu Wohnungen teils zu Geschäftsräumen eingerichtet. Das rechts gelegene Gebäude im Erdgeschoß und dem darüber liegenden Geschoß als

511, 524 [1914; 83, 85]

Le groupe d'immeubles de la place Kléber de Strasbourg se compose du grand magasin Modern et de deux immeubles de rapport. Le grand magasin, œuvre des architectes Berninger et Krafft, fut réalisé de 1912 à 1914. Il est encadré, à gauche, par l'immeuble réalisé par l'architecte Paul Horn et, à droite, par celui conçu par l'architecte Grünwald.

Le grand magasin Modern, qui s'élève sur cinq étages, se caractérise par un avant-corps arrondi reliant les deux façades. Il est flanqué d'avancées aux allures de tours et orné, aux étages supérieurs, de colonnes saillantes. Le rez-de-chaussée est percé par les ouvertures des entrées et des devantures abritées sous un auvent de verre. Les fenêtres du quatrième étage, réunies par paire, sont encadrées des corbeaux qui soutiennent la corniche et la balustrade terminale. Les fenêtres du quatrième étage de l'avant-corps sont assorties de statues. Alb. Schmitz et Stanly exécutèrent les sculptures. Le socle de la façade est réalisé en granit gris rougeâtre des Vosges, les surfaces supérieures sont en grès rouge gris des Vosges. Les piliers intérieurs ainsi que le poutrage des plafonds sont en béton armé, les piliers des façades sont construits en grès des Vosges garnis d'un hourdis de briques.

Le rez-de-chaussée abrite l'entrée principale dans l'arrondi de l'avant-corps ainsi que deux entrées secondaires dans les saillies aux allures de tours. Il comprend une grande surface de vente d'un seul tenant, divisée par des piliers, ainsi qu'un grand escalier et des ascenseurs. L'accès aux étages est assuré d'autres escaliers et ascenseurs. Une troisième entrée est située la rue Sainte Hélène. Les étages supérieurs, coupés par des cours intérieures, abritent des surfaces de vente non-cloisonnées.

Le bâtiment situé à gauche du grand magasin est ceint, au rez-de-chaussée, d'arcades surmontées d'un balcon en galerie saillant. Un salon de thé y est, entre autres, installé. Le premier étage est réservé aux affaires, les trois étages suivants et l'étage des combles sont aménagés en logements et en bureaux. Le bâtiment de droite est occupé, aux rez-de-chaussée et

511, 524 [1914; 83, 85]

The group of buildings located at Kleberplatz in Strassburg comprises the Modern department store—designed by the architects Berninger and Krafft and built between 1914 and 1916—to the left a commercial building with apartments—designed by the architect Paul Horn—and to the right another commercial building with apartments, designed by the architect Grünwald.

The two wings of the five-storey Modern department store are joined by a rounded corner structure with engaged columns at its upper stories and two turret-like superstructures to either side. Entrances and showcases line the ground level, which is covered by a glass canopy running along the entire building. The windows of the following three storeys are arranged vertically and divided by continuous pillars. The paired windows of the fourth floor are set between consoles which support the roof cornice and balustrade. The fourth-storey windows of the corner structure are also ornamented with figures created by the sculptor Alb. Schmitz and Stanly. The socle of the façade is of grey-red granite from the Vosges mountains, and the upper portion of the façade is faced with red-grey Vosges sandstone. The inner pillars and the floor binders and joists are cast in reinforced concrete. The façade's pilasters are of Vosges sandstone with brick masonry backing.

The ground floor has a main entrance located in the rounded corner structure, and a side entrance in each of the flanking turreted projections. It contains a large open salesroom with pillars, and the main staircase with lifts. There are additional stairs and lifts in the building, plus another entrance at the Helenengasse. The upper floors enclose two patios and also contain open salesrooms.

The building to the left of the department store has an arcade running along its two fronts which is covered by a projecting gallery. Part of the ground floor is occupied by a coffee-house. The first floor is designated for business purposes; the upper three floors and the roof storey contain both flats and offices.

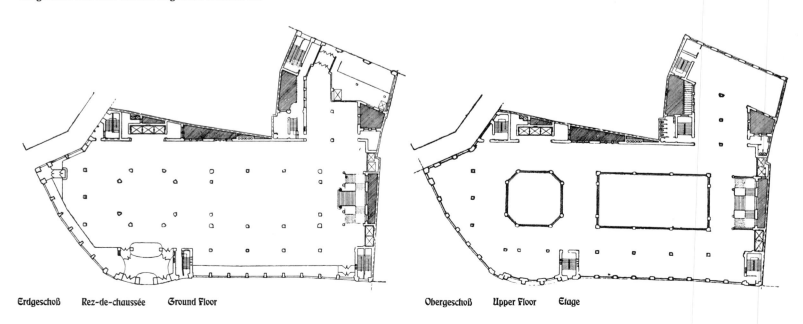

Erdgeschoß   Rez-de-chaussée   Ground Floor

Obergeschoß   Upper Floor   Etage

Geschäftsräume ausgebildet und mit einer darüberliegenden Gallerie abgeschlossen, enthält in den drei folgenden Obergeschossen und dem Dachgeschoß wieder teils Wohnungen teils Geschäftsräume.

512 [1914: 32]

An zwei Straßenfronten freiliegend, erheben sich die vierstöckigen, durch einen einstöckigen Mittelbau mit abgerundeter Ecke verbundenen Flügel des Geschäftshauses des Barmer Bankvereins in Düsseldorf. Urheber des in 18 Monaten für die Kostensumme von 1 000 000 Mark ausgeführten Gebäudes ist Architekt Kgl. Baurat Carl Moritz. Die Flügelbauten sind durch aufstrebende Pfeiler, die einstöckigen Verbindungsbauten durch Pilaster gegliedert. Der runde Eckbau trägt einen gleichfalls runden von Säulen umstellten, mit einer Kuppel bekrönten Turmbau. Die Fassaden sind in Muschelkalkstein ausgeführt, das abgewalmte Dach ist mit Schiefer, die Kuppel mit Aluminium eingedeckt. Die Bildhauer Grasegger und Moest haben den figürlichen Schmuck der Fassaden geliefert.

premier étage surmontés d'un balcon en galerie, par des bureaux. Des logements et des locaux de commerce se trouvent aux trois derniers étages et à l'étage des combles.

512 [1914: 32]

C'est à l'angle de deux rues que se dresse l'établissement bancaire „Barmer Bankverein" de Düsseldorf. Il se compose de deux ailes de quatre étages, reliées par un bâtiment d'un étage à angle arrondi. L'auteur de cet édifice, dont la réalisation dura 18 mois et qui coûta 1 000 000 marks, est l'architecte Carl Moritz. Les ailes présentent une ordonnance à piliers montant de fond, les bâtiments de jonction sont ponctués de pilastres. L'angle arrondi porte une tour ronde, entourée de colonnes et couronnée d'une coupole. Les façades sont réalisées en coquillart. Le toit en croupe est recouvert d'ardoises, la coupole d'aluminium. Les sculpteurs Grasegger et Moest exécutèrent l'ornementation des façades.

The building to the right of the departmental store has offices on its ground and first floors, with a gallery running above the latter. Again, the upper three floors contain both flats and offices.

512 [1914: 32]

The Barmer Bank in Düsseldorf consists of two four—storeyed wings joined at the corner by a rounded single—storeyed structure. The building has two exposed street fronts and was built according to plans drawn up by the Imperial architect Carl Moritz in the course of 18 months at a cost of 1,000,000 Marks. The wing structures are articulated by continuous pillars, the connecting structure by pilasters. The latter is topped by a round tower, which is encircled by columns and culminates in a dome. The façades are rendered in shell limestone, the hipped roof is covered with slate, and the dome is covered with aluminium sheeting. The ornamental figures on the façades are the work of the sculptors Grasegger and Mowar.

Erdgeschoß   Rez-de-chaussée   Ground Floor

Eingangshalle   Hall d'entrée   Entry Hall

Die Eingangshalle verbindet sich mit einem Vorraum, der zu der mit roter Marmorbekleidung der Wände und Täfelung in Eichenholz ausgestatteten Kassenhalle führt. Außerdem enthält das Erdgeschoß die Zimmer der Direktoren, die Sprechzimmer, die Kassenräume, die Buchhalterei und drei Treppenhäuser.

Le hall d'entrée débouche sur un vestibule qui conduit à la salle des guichets, dont les murs sont parés de marbre rouge et de lambris de chêne. Le rez-de-chaussée comprend, en outre, les bureaux des directeurs, les cabinets d'entretiens, les guichets, le bureau de la comptabilité et trois cages d'escaliers.

The entry hall is connected to a lobby, which in turn leads to the teller's hall. The walls of the latter are finished in red marble and oak wood wainscotting. The ground floor also contains the directors' rooms, conference rooms, cashiers' rooms, accounting offices and three stairwells.

513 [1914: 35]

Die Hauptfront des Gebäudes der Dresdner Bank in Leipzig, Goethestraße 3–5, ist durch eine jonische Säulenstellung monumental ausgezeichnet. Die Bauzeit nahm 1¼ Jahr in Anspruch; die Baukosten betrugen 1 100 000 Mark. Die Ausarbeitung der Baupläne, bei der Architekt Regierungsbaumeister Schütte mitwirkte, war vom Ministerium des Kultus und öffentlichen Unterrichts zu Dresden dem Architekten Geh. Hofrat Professor Dr. Ing. Martin Dülfer übertragen worden. Die Bauleitung übernahm Architekt Bau- und Finanzrat C. Sachse. Das gequaderte Erdgeschoß der Hauptfront öffnet sich mit rundbogigen Eingängen und Fenstern; die Säulenstellung im ersten und zweiten Obergeschoß schließt im mittleren Teil der Fassade Fenstervorbauten zwischen sich ein und wird durch ein Gebälk abgeschlossen. Über diesem erhebt sich das dritte Obergeschoß mit einem Giebel über der Mitte und Kindergruppen an den Pfeilern zwischen den Fenstern. Die mit Biberschwänzen eingedeckte Dachfläche wird durch einen Uhrturm bekrönt. Das ganze Gebäude ist in Eisenbeton hergestellt; die Fassade ist in Portaer Sandstein verblendet. Die gesamten Bildhauerarbeiten sind von W. & B. Wollstädter geliefert.

513 [1914: 35]

La façade principale du bâtiment de la „Dresdner Bank" de Leipzig, Goethestraße 3/5, se distingue par une ordonnance à colonnes ioniques. La construction nécessita un an et trois mois et coûta 1 100 000 marks. L'élaboration des plans, à laquelle participa l'architecte Schütte, fut confiée par le ministère de la culture et de l'éducation de Dresde à l'architecte prof. Martin Dülfer. L'architecte et conseiller financier C. Sachse prit en main la direction des travaux. Le rez-de-chaussée de la façade principale, en pierres de taille, est percé d'ouvertures en plein cintre. La partie médiane de la façade des premier et deuxième étages présente des colonnes encadrant des bow-windows et se terminant par un entablement. Suit le troisième étage dont les piliers, flanquant les fenêtres, sont ornés de sculptures d'enfants. Un pignon coiffe le centre de la façade. Une tour d'horloge se détache du toit recouvert de tuiles plates. Le bâtiment est construit en béton armé. Les murs extérieurs sont revêtus de grès. Les sculptures furent exécutées par W. et B. Wollstädter.

513 [1914: 35]

The principal front of the Dresden Bank in Leipzig (Goethestrasse 3–5) attains its monumental style through the use of Jonic columns. Construction of the building lasted 18 months and amounted to 1,100,000 Marks. The Ministry of Culture and Public Education at Dresden commissioned the architect and privy councillor Professor Dr. Martin Dülfer for drawing up the plans; he was assisted in this regard by the government architect Schütte. Construction was supervised by the architect and financial councillor C. Sachse. The ground level is rendered in banded rustication and opens with windows and entrances framed in round arches. The columns at the first and second stories have windows placed between them and end with an entablature. The third storey is located above with a gable at its middle and figures of children at the pillars between the windows. The roof of flat tile is crowned by a clock tower. The entire structure of the building is of reinforced concrete; the façade is faced with sandstone from Porta. All of the ornamental sculptures are the work of W. & B. Wollstädter.

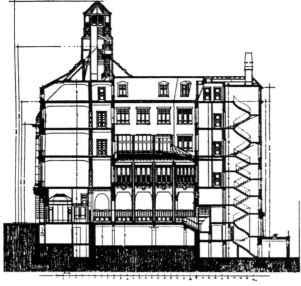

Querschnitt	Coupe transversale	Cross Section

Erdgeschoß u. Lageplan   Rez-de-chaussée et plan d'ensemble   Ground Floor and Site Plan

Im Sockelgeschoß liegen die Stahlkammer, der Tresorvorraum, ein großer Geschäftsraum, eine Anzahl Bureaus, durch mehrere Treppen und Aufzüge zugänglich, dann die Kleiderablage und die Toiletten, das Botenzimmer und der Apparatenraum. Das Erdgeschoß umschließt in der Mitte die Kassenhalle, welche mit einem Vorraum versehen ist, und mit den umgebenden Räumen für Beamte und der Banktreppe in unmittelbarer Verbindung steht. Ein zweiter Eingang in der Front führt zur Haupttreppe und der Portierloge. Den übrigen Raum nehmen das Direktorenzimmer, die Sprechzimmer und die Nebentreppen ein. Die eine Seite des Grundplans ist zur Anlage eines Ladens mit besonderer Stockwerkstreppe und Aufzug benutzt. Die Rippen des Oberlichts im Kassenraum sind in Eisenbeton gebildet und umrahmen die Luxferprismen der Glasdecke. Die weiteren Deckenträger sind gleichfalls in Eisenbeton hergestellt und mit Hartstuck verputzt. Die Verkleidung im unteren Drittel des Raumes sowie die Ausbildung der Portale und Türrahmen erfolgte in Marmor. Im ersten Obergeschoß nimmt ein Lichthof den Raum über der Kassenhalle ein, daneben liegen die Buchbinderei und der Korrespondenzsaal, außerdem sind Zimmer für die Buchhalterei, die Prokuristen und ein Sprechzimmer vorgesehen. Über dem Laden ist ein Geschäftsraum angeordnet. Das zweite und dritte Obergeschoß sind durch Geschäftsräume ausgefüllt. Im Dachgeschoß liegen Archivräume und 2 Wohnungen mit Küche und Zubehör. Das Kellergeschoß ist durch Kessel- und Motorenräume in Anspruch genommen.

514 [1914: 39]

Das einen Hof umschließende, vierstöckige, mit einem ausgebauten Dachgeschoß versehene Gebäude der Sibirischen Bank in St. Petersburg, Newski Pr. 44, ist nach dem Entwurfe des Architekten Boris Girschowitsch im Laufe von 2 Jahren für die Kostensumme von 1 000 000 Rubel zur Ausführung gekommen. Das Erdgeschoß enthält an der Front 3 Eingänge, einen rundbogigen mit einem Balkon überbauten und zwei gradlinig geschlossene. Die von 2 Eckrisaliten eingefaßte Front wird in 3 Obergeschossen durch korinthische Pilaster gegliedert. Die Fenster der Eckrisalite sind im zweiten Obergeschoß mit Balkons versehen. Über dem abschließenden Hauptgesims des mittleren Teils der Front folgt ein viertes Obergeschoß mit einer Attika und einem eingerahmten von Figuren begleiteten Mittelfenster. Das Material der Fassade besteht aus bronzefarbenem Granit; die Bildhauerarbeiten an derselben sind von Kuzelzow und Winkler ausgeführt.

Das Erdgeschoß zeigt die Durchfahrt zu dem Innenhofe, dann die Eingänge zur Haupttreppe und den Räumen der Bank. Das Vestibül ist mit Marmor bekleidet, der langgestreckte Kassenraum ist mit einem Glasdach überdeckt. Es sind noch mehrere Nebentreppen angeordnet, eine derselben führt zu der Stahlkammer im Kellergeschoß.

Au sous-sol se trouvent la chambre-forte, l'antichambre des coffres, une grande salle de travail, des bureaux accessibles par plusieurs escaliers et ascenseurs, puis le vestiaire et les cabinets d'aisances, la chambre des domestiques et la machinerie. Au centre du rez-de-chaussée est située la salle des guichets, assortie d'un hall, qui communique directement avec les pièces attenantes réservées aux employés et avec l'escalier de la banque. La façade offre une deuxième entrée donnant sur le grand escalier et la loge du portier. L'espace restant est occupé par le bureau du directeur, les cabinets d'entretiens et les escaliers de service. Un commerce et un escalier sont aménagés latéralement. La verrière de la salle des guichets se compose de nervures en béton armé encadrant des prismes en verre à réflexion. Les autres poutres du plafond sont en béton armé enduit de stuc. Le tiers inférieur de la salle ainsi que l'encadrement des portails et des portes sont parés de marbre. Au premier étage, une cour intérieure vitrée occupe l'espace situé au-dessus de la salle des guichets. A côté se trouvent l'atelier de reliure, la salle du courrier, la comptabilité, les bureaux des procuristes et un cabinet d'entretiens. Une salle de travail est aménagée au-dessus du commerce. Les deuxième et troisième étages comprennent des bureaux. Sous les combles sont installés les salles des archives ainsi que deux logements équipés d'une cuisine et de toilettes. La cave abrite la chaufferie et la machinerie.

514 [1914: 39]

Le bâtiment de la banque sibérienne de Saint Pétersbourg, Newski Pr. 44, fut construit en deux ans, sur les plans de l'architecte Boris Girschowitsch, pour la somme de 1 000 000 roubles. Il comprend quatre étages, un étage des combles et une cour intérieure. La façade du rez-de-chaussée compte trois entrées, une en plein cintre surmontée d'un balcon et deux terminées par un linteau droit. La façade principale, bordée de deux avant-corps, offre, sur trois étages, une ordonnance à pilastres corinthiens. Les fenêtres des avant-corps sont assorties de balcons au deuxième étage. A la corniche de la partie médiane de la façade succède un quatrième étage en attique présentant une fenêtre médiane flanquée de statues. Les murs extérieurs sont en granit de couleur bronze. Les sculptures sont l'œuvre de Kurzelzow et Winkler.

Le rez-de-chaussée est percé par le passage menant à la cour intérieure et par les entrées donnant sur le grand escalier et les différentes pièces de la banque. Le vestibule est revêtu de marbre. La salle des guichets, de forme oblongue, est recouverte d'une verrière. Le bâtiment est équipé de plusieurs escaliers de service, dont l'un conduit à la chambre-forte au sous-sol.

The basement contains the strong room and its anteroom, a large office and a number of smaller ones which are reached by several stairs and lifts. Cloak—rooms, lavatories, a message—room and the telephone room are also located here. The ground floor contains the counter hall at its centre, which is preceded by a lobby and directly connected to the surrounding rooms for officials and to the stairs of the bank. A second entrance at the front leads to the main staircase and the porter's lodge. The remaining space is taken up by the director's office, the conference room and the side stairs. One side of the ground plan is designated for a shop with separate stairs and lift. The ribs of the roof light in the teller's hall are constructed of reinforced concrete and support the prismatic panels of the glass ceiling. The other floor girders are also cast in reinforced concrete and plastered with granolithic concrete overlay. The lower third portion of the room, as well as the moulding of the portal and door frames, are faced with marble. The area above the teller's hall on the first floor is occupied by a patio. The adjoining rooms are used for the book binder's and secretaries' offices; other rooms are designated for accounting, managing clerks and reception. Additional office space is located above the shop. The second and third floors are taken up by offices. Archive rooms and two flats with a kitchen and other facilities are located on the roof floor. The basement is divided into boiler and motor chambers.

514 [1914: 39]

The Siberian Bank in St. Petersburg (Newskii Prospekt 44), a four—storey structure with an additional roof storey, is built round an inner courtyard. It was designed by the architect Boris Girshovich and completed over the course of two years at a cost of 1,000,000 Rubels. Three entrances open at the ground level front; one is framed in a round arch and covered by a balcony, the other two have straight frames. The front is flanked by corner projections and articulated by Corinthian pilasters running the height of three storyes. Small balconies are placed in front of the windows at the third storey of the corner projections. Located above the principal cornice of the front's middle section is a fourth storey with a terrace and a central window framed by ornamental figures. Bronze—coloured granite was used for the façade; its ornamental figures are the work of the sculptor Kuzelzoff and Winkler.

The ground floor contains a carriageway to the inner courtyard, then the entrances leading to the main staircase and the bank's interior. The vestibule is panelled with marble, the long rectangular counter hall is covered by a glass ceiling. A number of side stairs are also present, one of these leads to the strong room in the basement.

Das der Bavariahaus A.-G. gehörige Bavariahaus, Friedrich- Ecke Taubenstraße, ist nach
dem Entwurfe des Architekten Dipl.-Jng. Moritz Ernst
Lesser errichtet, unter Mitarbeit des Architekten
Th. Karsten. Die Bauzeit dauerte 9 Monate, die
Baukosten betrugen 1200 000 Mark. Das Gebäude
steigt in 4 Geschossen auf; der Haupteingang liegt in
einem Einsprung der Fassade, der im vierten Geschoß
durch einen Erkerausbau ausgefüllt wird. Das Erdgeschoß wird an der Friedrichstraße von Schaufenstern
eingenommen; an der Taubenstraße öffnet sich ein
zweiter Einsprung der Fassade als Hof. An einem
vortretenden Gebäudeteile erhebt sich ein durch drei
Obergeschosse geführter ausgekragter abgerundeter
Ausbau. Sämtliche Obergeschosse sind durch flache,
oben durch Rundbogen verbundene, im vierten Geschoß Balkons einschließende Lisenen zu einer Einheit
zusammengezogen. Die Fassade ist mit Platten aus
poliertem hellen norwegischen Labrador Granit und
mit Platten und Perfilen aus hellgrauem Cottaer Sandstein verkleidet; für die Bekleidung der Eingangsni-
sche und der Erker ist grauer geflammter Hohenberger
Marmor verwendet. Dasselbe Material kehrt in der
Verkleidung der Eingangshalle und des Kinotreppen-
hauses wieder. Die Gitter der Balkons sind vergoldet.
Die Reklameschilder der Fensterbrüstungen sind in
dunkelrotem Glasmosaik hergestellt, ebenso die Un-
terflächen der Erker und Balkons. Das abgewalmte
Dach ist mit grauen holländischen Ziegeln eingedeckt.

L'immeuble à Berlin, propriété de la société
anonyme „Bavariahaus", située au coin des
Friedrichstraße et Taubenstraße, fut construit en neuf
mois d'après les plans de l'architecte Moritz Ernst
Lesser avec la participation de l'architecte Th. Karsten. Les frais de construction s'élevèrent à 1200 000
marks. Le bâtiment monte sur quatre étages. L'entrée
principale se trouve dans un renfoncement de la façade, garni au quatrième étage par un bow-window.
Côté Friedrichstraße, le rez-de-chaussée est percé de
devantures, côté Taubenstraße, un deuxième renfoncement s'ouvre dans la façade et forme une cour. Une
partie en saillie de l'immeuble est assortie d'un avant-
corps convexe montant sur trois étages. Les étages,
traités en une unité, présentent des bandes lombardes,
reliées en haut par des arcs cintrés et encadrant des
fenêtres en tribune au quatrième étage. Les murs de
façade sont habillés de dalles de granit de labrador
norvégien poli et de dalles de grès gris clair. Le parement de l'encadrement de l'entrée et du bow-window
est en marbre gris flammé. Le même matériau fut
utilisé pour le revêtement des murs du hall d'entrée et
de la cage d'escalier du cinéma. Les grilles du balcon
sont dorées. Les inscriptions sur le bandeau des fenêtres ainsi que les surfaces sous le bow-window et sous
les balcons sont en mosaïque de verre rouge foncé. Le
toit en croupe est recouvert de tuiles hollandaises
grises.

The Bavaria Haus, owned by the Bavariahaus Co,
in Berlin (corner of Friedrichstrasse and Taubenstrasse) was constructed according to the plans to the
certified architect Moritz Ernst Lesser, with assistance
provided by the architect Th. Karsten. Construction of
the nine—storey building occupied 9 months at a cost
of 1,200,000 Marks. The main entrance is located in a
recess of the façade, which is filled out by a bay at the
fourth storey. Another recess in the Taubenstrasse front
forms a street courtyard. One side projection of the
building has a rounded cantilevered oriel extending
through three storeys. The upper storeys are unified by
flat lesenes arched at the top, with balconies located
between them at the fourth storey. The façade is faced
with slabs of light polished Norwegian Labrador granite, as well as with plates of light—grey Cotta sandstone. The niches of the entryway and the oriel are
made of grey mottled marble from Hohenberg; the
same material is used for the panelling of the entry hall
and the stairwell of the cinema. The balcony grilles are
gilded. The advertisement signs at the window aprons
are made of dark red glass mosaics, as are the under-
sides of the oriel and balconies. The hipped roof is
covered with grey Dutch pantiles.

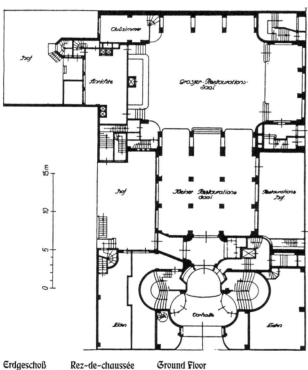

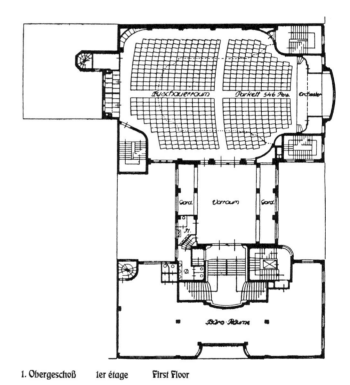

Erdgeschoß   Rez-de-chaussée   Ground Floor   1. Obergeschoß   1er étage   First Floor

Das Haus enthält im Erdgeschoß an der Friedrichstraße Läden, nach der Taubenstraße und nach
hinten zu ein großes Restaurant mit zwei Höfen und
umfänglichen Küchenanlagen; im ersten und zweiten
Stock liegt im mittleren und hinteren Gebäudeteil das
Kino des Uniontheaters; die vorderen Räume dieser
Geschosse, sowie die oberen Geschosse sind zu Bureauräumen bestimmt. Der ganze Bau ist in Eisenbe-
tonfachwerk konstruiert (Kahneisensystem). Für die
großen Räume sind Rahmenkonstruktionen gewählt;
im hinteren Bauteil befinden sich übereinander der
Rahmen für den großen Restaurationssaal ohne mitt-
lere Stützen, der für den Kinosaal mit zugehörigem
Rang, wieder ohne Stützen und das Fachwerk für zwei
Geschosse um einen Lichthof. Die Dachbinder sind in
Eisenkonstruktion ausgeführt.

L'immeuble abrite des commerces au rez-de-
chaussée de la Friedrichstraße. Un grand restaurant
avec deux cours et des cuisines spacieuses est installé
à l'arrière et sur la Taubenstraße. Le cinéma du théâtre de l'union est aménagé aux premier et deuxième
étages, dans la partie médiane et postérieure du bâtiment . Les pièces frontales de ces étages ainsi que
celles des étages suivants sont destinées à des bureaux. Le bâtiment est construit en colombages de
béton armé. Des stuctures à portiques furent choisies
pour les grandes salles. Dans la partie arrière de
l'immeuble se trouvent, l'un au-dessus de l'autre, le
portique de la grande salle de restauration sans pilier
central puis celui de la salle de cinéma, de nouveau
sans pilier, et enfin le colombage des deux étages
autour d'une cour intérieure. Les poutres maîtresses
sont en fer.

The ground floor of the building contains shops
along the Friedrichstrasse; the Taubenstrasse side and
the rear of the ground floor are occupied by a restaurant and its roomy kitchen facilities. At the middle and
rear of the first and second floor is the Union Theatre
cinema. The front rooms of this floor and the entire
space of the floors above it are designated for offices.
The building's framework consists of truss girders of
reinforced concrete (viz. the Kahn system of iron
trusses). The larger rooms are supported by frame
construction. Placed over one another at the back of
the building are the frame for the large restaurant
dining hall with no central supports, the frame for the
cinema and its upper circle, again without supports,
and finally the framework for two floors and a patio.
The roof frames are constructed of iron.

Das Junior'sche Einfamilienhaus in Frankfurt
a. M., Schaumainkai 43 a, ist im Verlaufe von 2
Baujahren von Architekt B. D. A. Geldmacher für die
Baukostensumme von 130 000 Mark errichtet. Die

La villa Junior, Schaumainkai 43a, à Francfort-
sur-le-Main, fut construite en deux ans, par l'architecte Geldmacher, pour la somme de 130 000
marks. La maison comprend deux étages s'élevant au-

The Junior House, a one—family residence located
in Frankfurt—on—Main (Schaumainkai 43a),
was designed by the architect Geldmacher, member of
the Association of German Architects, and built over

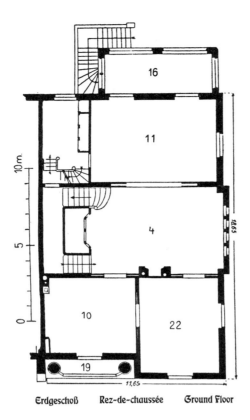

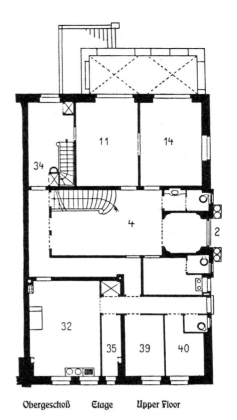

Erdgeschoß   Rez-de-chaussée   Ground Floor   Obergeschoß   Étage   Upper Floor

Straßenfront des über einem Untergeschoß sich zwei-stöckig erhebenden, mit ausgebautem Dachgeschoß versehenen Gebäudes zeigt einen mittleren, eine Ter-rasse bildenden, mit ionischen Säulen besetzten Rück-sprung. Die Fenster des Obergeschosses zwischen den Säulen sind mit Balkons versehen. Über dem Dachge-sims folgt eine von Fenstern durchbrochene Attika. Die Fassaden sind in Muschenkalkstein und Terranova-putz hergestellt. Das abgewalmte Dach ist mit Hohl-ziegeln eingedeckt.

Das Untergeschoß enthält in der Seitenfront den Haupteingang, der zu einem Vorplatz und weiter zu einer Halle mit freiliegender Treppe führt. Der Neben-eingang führt zur Küche und den seitwärts angeordne-ten Leutezimmern. Das Speise- und das Billardzimmer stehen in Verbindung mit einer Laube. Dem Salon ist eine Loggia vorgelegt, daneben liegt das Herren-zimmer. Das Speisezimmer mündet auf die Terrasse und hat neben sich den Anrichteraum. Im Oberge-schoß sind die Schlafräume untergebracht. Eine Warmwasserheizung und eine Warmwasserversorgung ist eingerichtet. Diele und Eßzimmer sind in Eichen-holz, das Herrenzimmer in Nußbaum ausgeführt.

dessus d'un étage en sous-sol ainsi que des combles aménagés. La façade principale présente une partie médiane en retrait formant une terrasse ornée de co-lonnes ioniques. Les fenêtres des étages supérieurs, situées entre les colonnes, sont dotées de balcons. Un attique, percé de fenêtres, succède à la corniche du toit. Les murs de façade, enduits de crépi, présentent des éléments en coquillart. Le toit en croupe est recou-vert de tuiles creuses.

L'entrée principale, qui se trouve sur la façade latérale au niveau de l'étage en sous-sol, donne sur un vestibule puis sur une antichambre comprenant un es-calier. L'entrée de service mène à la cuisine et aux chambres des domestiques aménagées sur le côte. La salle à manger et la salle de billard communiquent avec une tonnelle. Le salon, précédé d'une loggia, est attenant au cabinet de travail. La salle à manger, contiguë à l'office, débouche sur la terrasse. Les chambres à coucher se trouvent à l'étage supérieur. La villa est équipée d'un chauffage à eau chaude ainsi que d'une alimentation en eau chaude. Le vestibule et la salle à manger présentent un revêtement de bois de chêne, le cabinet de travail de bois de noyer.

the course of two years at a cost of 130,000 Marks. The two-storeys house has a basement and roof storeys. Its front shows a middle return with a terrace and Ionic columns. Balconies are placed at the upper storey windows between the columns. A roof parapet rises above the cornice and contains windows. The façades are faced with shell limestone and terranova plaster. The hipped roof is covered with curved tile.

The ground floor contains the main stairs at the side front which leads to a lobby and then to a hall with open stairs. The side entrance leads into the kitchen and the sitting-rooms to the side. The dining room and the billiards room are connected to a bower. A loggia is located in front of the drawing-room, which borders the study. The dining room opens onto the terrace and has a pantry located next to it. Bedrooms are situated on the upper floor. The house is supplied with warm running water and hot water central heat-ing. The entry hall and dining room are panelled in oak, the study in walnut.

517 [1914; 52]

Die Villa Herxheimer in Wiesbaden, Rösselstraße 35, mit durchgehender Diele, vorgelegtem Garten mit Terrasse, Küchen- und Nebenräumen im vertieften Küchenhof an der Hinterseite und ausgebautem Dach-geschoß, ein Werk des Architekten Professor Bruno Paul, ist im Verlauf von 2 Jahren zur Ausführung gekommen. Die Vorderfront besitzt einen halbrunden, mit Säulen umstellten, über einer Terrasse aufsteigen-den, im Obergeschoß eine Altane tragenden Ausbau, über dem die Fenster einfassenden Pilaster sich erhe-ben. Der gleichfalls von Pilastern eingefaßte Haupt-eingang liegt an einer Seitenfront, an der gegenüber-liegenden springt wieder ein mit einer Altane beende-ter Ausbau hervor. Die Rückfront ist durch zwei Flü-gelansätze gegliedert. Die Fassaden zeigen grauen Verputz mit Muschelkalksteinverwendung, grüne Lä-den, weiße Fenster und Dachgesimse sowie schwarze Eingangstür. Auf den geschweiften Steilflächen des gebrochenen, mit Biberschwänzen eingedeckten Da-ches erheben sich eine Anzahl Dachfenster mit vorge-legten Blumenkästen.

Im Erdgeschoß liegt die durch beide Geschosse gehende Wohndiele mit anschließendem Vorraum und nebengelegter Stockwerkstreppe, dann Herren- und Damenzimmer, Speisezimmer, Anrichte, Garderobe und Dienerzimmer.

517 [1914; 52]

La villa Herxheimer, située à Wiesbaden, Rössel-straße 35, fut réalisée en deux ans sur les plans de l'architecte Bruno Paul. Assortie d'un jardin et d'une terrasse, elle comprend une antichambre s'élevant sur deux niveaux, une cuisine et son office situées au sous-sol et donnant sur une arrière-cour ainsi qu'un étage mansardé. La façade principale présente une avancée arrondie, ornée de colonnes, qui s'élève au-dessus d'une terrasse et supporte un balcon à l'étage supé-rieur dont les fenêtres sont flanquées de pilastres. L'entrée principale, encadrée de pilastres, se trouve sur une façade latérale. De la façade opposée se dé-tache un avant-corps terminé par un balcon. La fa-çade postérieure comprend deux ailes. Les murs exté-rieurs, enduits d'un crépi gris, offrent des éléments en coquillart. Les volets sont verts, les fenêtres et la cor-niche blanches, la porte d'entrée noire. Le brisis légè-rement convexe du toit, recouvert de tuiles plates, est percé de fenêtres mansardées ornées de bacs à fleurs.

Le rez-de-chaussée comprend l'antichambre montant sur deux niveaux puis, contigu au hall d'en-trée, l'escalier, enfin le cabinet de travail de monsieur, le boudoir de madame, la salle à manger, la garde-robe et la chambre des domestiques.

517 [1914; 52]

The Herxheimer house in Wiesbaden (Rösselstrasse 35) is set back behind a front garden with terrace, and contains an entry hall extending to the back of the house, a kitchen and pantries located in a sunken kitchen court at the back, and an additional attic storey. Designed by the architect Professor Bruno Paul, it was built in two years. The front features a semicircular projection above the terrace which is lined with columns and supports a balcony. The windows above this are framed by pilasters in the façade. The main entrance at the side front is also framed by pilas-ters; the other side front has a projection which ends in a balcony. The rear façade is articulated by two wing projections. The façades are faced with grey plaster mixed with shell limestone. The shutters are painted green, the windows and the roof moulding white, and the entrance door is black. A number of dormers with flower boxes are placed in the steeper, curving section of the flat tile roof.

The living room-entrance hall on the ground floor extends through the first floor, and is bordered by an anteroom and the staircase, which leads to the study and boudoir, dining room, pantries, cloak-room and servant's room

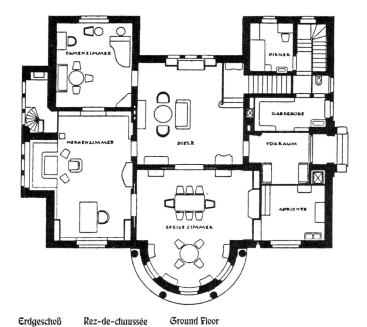

Erdgeschoß   Rez-de-chaussée   Ground Floor

Obergeschoß   Étage   Upper Floor

Das Obergeschoß enthält das Frühstückszimmer, die Schlafzimmer im Zusammenhang mit Ankleidezimmer und Bad, sowie die Fremdenzimmer, wieder mit einem Bad verbunden.

518 [1914: 38]

In malerischer Gruppierung, inmitten eines Parks auf einer Terrasse gelegen, erhebt sich das Landhaus O. H. Story, Chesunt Hill bei Boston, ein Werk des Architekten Chapman & Frazer. Der Eingangs-

Le premier étage est occupé par la salle du petit déjeuner, les chambres à coucher avec salle de bains et garde-robe attenantes ainsi que les chambres d'amis communiquant également avec une salle de bains.

518 [1914: 38]

Œuvre des architectes Chapman & Frazer, le manoir O. H. Story, à Chesunt Hill près de Boston, se dresse au milieu d'un parc, sur une terrasse et forme un ensemble pittoresque. La façade principale

The upper floor contains the breakfast room, bedrooms connected to the dressing—room and bath, as well as a guest—room, which again is connected to a bath.

518 [1914: 38]

Arranged in picturesque architectural groupings and located amidst a park—like setting, the Storey country house in Chestnut Hill near Boston is the work of the architects Chapman & Frazer. A porch

Halle, Blick von oben   L'antichambre vue d'en haut   Hall, view from above

Billardraum   La salle de billard   Billiard Room

front ist eine Halle vorgebaut, die eine Altane trägt und in der sich das in normanischem Bogen überwölbte Eingangstor öffnet. Daneben springt ein durch beide Geschosse geführter polygonaler Erker vor in Anlehnung an den mit einem Giebel schließenden Eckbau. Gegenüber diesem ist ein dreigeschossiger mit einer Plattform endigender turmartiger Bau angeordnet. Die Gartenfront zeigt über der Terrasse zwei mit Giebeln schließende Eckbauten, denen überdeckte Veranden vorgelegt sind, im zurückspringenden Teil der Front erhebt sich ein polygonaler Eckerker. Die Fassaden sind in Ziegelfugenbau von modern normanischer Stilisierung hergestellt. Die Wohnräume verteilen sich auf Erd- und Obergeschoß und auf ein teilweise ausgebautes Dachgeschoß.

519 [1914: 33]

Das Wohn- und Geschäftshaus „J. Stenc" in Prag, nach dem Entwurfe des Architekten Otakar Novotny im Laufe eines Jahres für die Bausumme von rund 480 000 Kronen errichtet, enthält 4 Geschosse und ein als Glashalle ausgebildetes Dachgeschoß. Die Front zeigt im Erdgeschoß den Eingang und zwischen Pfeilern in Nischen eingeschlossene Fenster. Die im

est assortie d'un porche, percé d'une entrée voûtée en arc normand et surmonté d'une plate-forme. Latéralement saillit une avancée polygonale, montant sur deux étages et s'adossant à l'aile cornière à pignon. De l'autre côté s'ordonne une construction en forme de tour, haute de trois étages et terminée par une plateforme. La façade côté jardin présente, au dessus de la terrasse, deux ailes cornières à pignons dont les vérandas font saillie. Un bow-window polygonal se détache du renfoncement de la façade. Les murs extérieurs sont construits en briques jointoyées, dans un style normand moderne. Les pièces habitables se répartissent sur le rez-de-chaussée , l'étage supérieur ainsi que sous les combles en partie aménagés.

519 [1914: 33]

L'immeuble „J. Stenc" de Prague fut construit en une année pour une somme d'environ 480 000 couronnes. Ce bâtiment, conçu par l'architecte Otakar Novotory, comprend quatre étages et un étage mansardé vitré. Au rez-de-chaussée, la façade présente des ouvertures abritées dans des niches et flanquées de

with balcony is situated at the front and covers the main entrance, which is set in a Norman arch. A polygonal bay to one side extends through two storeys and abuts against the gabled corner structure. At the opposite end of the front is a three—storey tower—like structure ending with a platform. Overlooking the terrace at the garden front are two gabled corner structures with covered verandas. An polygonal bay extrudes at the recessed part of the garden front. The façades are faced with bonded brickwork in a modern adaption of the Norman style. Living quarters are distributed throughout the ground and upper floors, as well as on the attic floor.

519 [1914: 33]

The J. Stenc building in Prague, an apartment building with shops, was designed by the architect Otakar Novotny and constructed in the course of one year at a cost of about 480,000 Crowns. It has four storeys and a glass—hall roof storey. The front at the ground level contains the entrance and windows in niches which are framed by pillars. A group of win-

zweiten Obergeschoß seitlich gelegene Fenstergruppe ist mit Brüstungsgittern versehen; über denselben ist ein Balkon ausgekragt. Der gefugte Backsteinbau der Fassade ist im Erdgeschoß aus weißen, in den Obergeschossen aus roten geschlemmten Ziegeln ausgeführt. Über dem Dachgesims folgt ein Glasdach in gebogener Form.

Im Erdgeschoß und in sämtlichen Obergeschossen sind Geschäfts- und Wohnräume, insbesondere ein großes photographisches Atelier mit zugehörigen Nebenräumen untergebracht. Die Verbindung zwischen den Geschossen wird durch 2 Haupt- und mehrere Nebentreppen bewirkt. Die Folge der Räume wird mehrmals durch Lichthöfe unterbrochen.

520 [1914: 40]

Das Einküchenhaus in Friedenau-Berlin, Wilhelmshöherstraße 18–19, der Einküchengesellschaft m. b. H. gehörig, ein Freibau von 4 Geschossen nebst Keller- und ausgebautem Dachgeschoß, ist nach dem Entwurfe des Architekten Albert Gessner, unter Bauleitung des Architekten Carl Bredow, im Verlaufe von 3 Jahren errichtet. Die mehrfach durch vortretende Flügel, Erkerausbauten und offene Loggien im ersten und zweiten Obergeschoß gegliederten Fronten sind mit teilweise überdachten Dachgärten bekrönt. Im Erdgeschoß ist eine große überdeckte Gartenhalle angelegt. Das Mauerwerk der Fronten besteht aus Kalksandsteinen mit rauhem graublau gefärbten Kunstputz überzogen. Die Rücklagen und Loggiaflächen sind mattheligelb, Holzwerk, Läden und Jalousien schwarzblau mit weißen Verzierungen gestrichen. Die abgewalmten Dächer haben eine Eindeckung mit holländischen Pfannen erhalten.

Die zu einer Baugruppe zusammengeschlossenen Häuser umschließen einen Lichthof, sind mit 4 Dielen, anschließenden Baderäumen und 2 Haupttreppen ausgestattet. Als Neuheit der Anlage ist die Einrichtung von 9 Speiseaufzügen zur Versorgung sämtlicher Wohnungen von der einzigen Zentralküche im Keller her anzuführen. Ein großer teilweise überdachter Dachgarten ist mittels Personenaufzug von unten erreichbar und ist zugleich durch Speisenaufzug an die Küche angeschlossen. Das Haus ist mit Dampfheizung und elektrischen Leitungen versehen.

521 [1914: 49]

Die in einem Mittel- und zwei Seitenteile gegliederte Fassade des dreistöckigen durch ein Unter- und ein ausgebautes Dachgeschoß erweiterten, nach dem Entwurfe des Architekten Kgl. Baurats Carl Moritz errichteten Geschäftshauses des Barmer Bankvereins in Köln a. Rh. ist mit Muschelkalkstein bekleidet. Das Gebäude wurde in einer Bauzeit von 15 Monaten vollendet und erforderte 876 000 Mark an Baukosten, einschließlich der inneren Einrichtung. Das rundbogige Portal, von Säulen und Eckpfeilern eingefaßt, trägt einen durch freistehende Figuren gezierten Balkon. Die Fenster der Seitenteile sind im ersten Obergeschosse mit Balkons versehen. Das durch ein Quergesims abgetrennte zweite Obergeschoß zeigt in den Nischen zwischen den Fenstern figürlichen in Bronze

piliers. Le groupe de fenêtres du deuxième étage, au-dessus duquel un balcon fait saillie, est assorti de grilles d'appui. Les murs de façade sont réalisés en briques jointoyées de couleur blanche au rez-de-chaussée et rouge dans les étages supérieurs. Une verrière de forme convexe s'élève au-dessus de la corniche du toit.

Le rez-de-chaussée et les étages abritent des commerces et des logements, en particulier un grand atelier de photographie et ses pièces annexes. Les étages sont accessibles par deux grands escaliers et plusieurs escaliers de service. Les pièces s'ordonnent autour de plusieurs cours vitrées.

520 [1914: 40]

Le foyer berlinois, situé Wilhelmshöherstraße 18–19, à Friedenau, appartient à la société des foyers. Il s'agit d'un bâtiment de quatre étages comprenant un sous-sol et un étage mansardé. Ce foyer, conçu par l'architecte Albert Gessner, fut réalisé en trois années sous la direction de l'architecte Carl Bredow. Les façades présentent, aux premier et second étages, des ailes en saillie, des bow-windows et des loggias et sont couronnées de jardins-terrasses en partie couverts. Une grande serre a été aménagée au rez-de-chaussée. Les murs de façade sont réalisés en castines et enduits d'un grossier crépi artificiel bleu gris. Les façades postérieures et les murs des loggias ont reçu un badigeon jaune mat, les boiseries, les volets et les jalousies sont peints en bleu noir et décorés de blanc. Les toits en croupe portent une couverture de tuiles hollandaises.

Les bâtiments se regroupent autour d'une cour intérieure et sont assortis de quatre vestibules, de salles de bains contiguës et de deux grands escaliers. Comme nouveauté, il convient de signaler l'installation de neuf monte-plats qui ravitaillent les appartements depuis l'unique cuisine centrale située au sous-sol. Un jardin-terrasse, partiellement couvert, est accessible depuis le bas par un ascenseur et communique avec la cuisine grâce à un monte-plat. Le bâtiment est équipé d'un chauffage à vapeur et de conduites électriques.

521 [1914: 49]

Le bâtiment de l'établissement bancaire „Barmer Bankverein" de Cologne présente une façade revêtue de coquillart, se composant d'une partie médiane et de deux parties latérales. L'édifice comprend trois étages, un sous-sol et un étage mansardé. Il fut érigé d'après les plans de l'architecte Carl Moritz. Sa construction dura quinze mois et coûta 876 000 marks, aménagement intérieur compris. Le portail cintré, flanqué de colonnes et de piliers d'angle, porte un balcon décoré de statues. Les parties latérales du premier étage sont assorties de fenêtres en tribune. Le deuxième étage, séparé du premier par une corniche transversale, présente, dans les niches situées entre les fenêtres, des figures ornementales en bronze. La porte

dows at one end of the second—storey have an apron grille and are covered by a cantilevered balcony at the third floor. The bonded brick masonry of the façade consists of white diluvial brick at the ground level, and red diluvial brick at the upper storeys. A curved glass roof rises over the roof moulding.

Offices and private living quarters are located on the ground floor and all upper floors. Of special note is the large photographer's studio with adjoining side rooms. Each floor is connected by 2 main staircases and a number of side stairs. The layout of the rooms is broken up by several patios.

520 [1914: 40]

The one—kitchen apartment building in the Friedenau district of Berlin (Wilhelmshöherstrasse 19–19), owned by the Einküchengesellschaft m.b.H., was designed by the architect Albert Gessner. Construction was carried out over three years and supervised by the architect Carl Bredow. The fronts are arranged into a number of projecting wings, oriels and open loggias at the first and second storeys. The façades end in partially covered roof gardens. Located at the ground floor is a large, covered garden terrace. The masonry work of the front was done in lime cemented sandstone and covered with bluish—grey rough imitation plaster. The surfaces of the loggias and returned sections of the structure are flat light yellow. The woodwork, shutters and slatted blinds are painted blackish-blue with white trimmings. The hipped roofs are covered with pantiles.

The houses which make up the complex are arranged as a unit around a patio and contain 4 halls with connecting baths, and two main staircases. It should also be mentioned that the latest addition to the apartment house was the installation of 9 food lifts to service all flats from the central kitchen in the basement. The spacious, partially covered roof garden can be reached by lift, and it too is serviced by the kitchen food lift. The house is furnished with steam heating and electricity.

521 [1914: 49]

The Barmer Bank building in Cologne, whose shell limestone façade is arranged into a middle and two side sections, is a three—storey structure with a basement and an additional roof storey. Designed by the royal architect Carl Moritz, the building was completed in 15 months at a cost of 876,000 Marks, including the interior furnishings. The round—arched portal, which is flanked by columns and corner pillars, is covered by a balcony decorated with free—standing figures. The windows in the first storey of the side section are provided with balconies. Separated from the lower façade by a transverse cornice, the second storey is ornamented with bronze figural reliefs placed

Inneres der Schalterhalle   Intérieur de la salle des guichets   Interior of the Counter Hall

ausgeführten Schmuck; die Eingangstür ist gleichfalls in Bronze ausgeführt. Die Bildhauerarbeiten rühren von Grasegger und Jos. Moest her. Die in Kupfer eingedeckte geschweifte Reibfläche des Daches ist mit Dachfenstern besetzt.

Das Erdgeschoß enthält die Eingangshalle nebst der neben der Haupttreppe liegenden Vorhalle. Der mittlere große Saal für den Verkehr des Publikums und die anschließenden Kassenräume sind mit einer ovalen kuppelförmigen Decke überspannt. Das Holzwerk besteht aus Mahagoni, Wände und Säulen sind in Marmor ausgeführt. Die übrigen Räume des Erdgeschosses sind zu Geschäfts- und Direktionszimmern sowie zur Anlage von zwei neben einem Lichthof angeordneten Nebentreppen benutzt.

522 [1914: 56]

Das mit Vorder- und Flügelbauten mehrere Höfe umschließende, an zwei Straßen grenzende Handelshaus Mauritiushof in Köln a. Rh., Mauritiussteinweg 77/79, in vier Geschossen und einem teilweise ausgebauten Dachgeschoß aufstrebend, ist nach dem Entwurf des Architekten Königl. Baurat Carl Moritz in zehn Monaten für die Baukostensumme von 510 000 Mark zur Ausführung gekommen. Das Erdgeschoß zeigt an der Hauptfront eine Reihe Rundbogenfenster zwischen zwei seitlichen, gleichfalls rundbogigen Eingängen. Das erste und zweite Obergeschoß sind durch verzierte, die Fenstergruppen umschließende Umrahmungen zusammengezogen; das dritte Obergeschoß ist in Fenstergruppen zwischen Pfeilerstellungen aufgelöst. Die Dachfenster sind mit Rundgiebeln abgeschlossen. Die Fassade ist in Westerwälder Trachyt ausgeführt, das Dach ist mit Ziegeln eingedeckt.

Ein Zugang an der Hauptfront führt zu einer Halle, an die sich zwei Stockwerkstreppen anschließen, daneben sind Bureau- und Konferenzzimmer angeordnet. Ein großer Lichthof, beiderseits von Geschäfts- und Lagerräumen begleitet, durchzieht das ganze Vordergebäude. Der zweite Seiteneingang dient als Durchfahrt zum offenen Hof. Die hinteren Flügelbauten, wieder an zwei Höfen liegend, sind zu Lagerräumen eingerichtet. Die Gesamtausführung des Gebäudes geschah in Eisenbeton.

523 [1914: 53]

Das einen Eckbau bildende, einen Innenhof umschließende, in 3 Geschossen über einem Untergeschoß aufsteigende mit einem teilweise ausgebauten Dachgeschoß versehene Museumsgebäude für ostasiatische Kunst in Köln a. Rh. Gereonswall und Bremerstraße, ist nach dem Entwurfe des Architekten B. D. A. Franz Brantzky im Laufe eines Jahres für die Bausumme von 250 000 Mark errichtet. Erdgeschoß und erstes Obergeschoß sind vom zweiten Obergeschoß durch ein starkes Gurtgesims getrennt und durch flache Pfeilervorlagen gegliedert. An der den Eingang enthaltenden Front am Gereonswall springt im Erdgeschoß ein mit besonderem Dach abschließender Fensterausbau hervor. Ein zweiter Eingang liegt in der Front an der Bremerstraße. Der hier mit einem Vorsprung beendete Hauptflügel schließt mit 2 verbundenen, übergekragten, spitzen Giebeln ab; an der Ecke zeigt sich im Erdgeschoß ein eine Altane tragender Ausbau. Die Fronten sind mit Tuffen und Sandstein bekleidet. Die mit Dachfenstern besetzten Dächer sind mit Schiefer eingedeckt.

Das Erdgeschoß enthält Vestibül, Eingangsflur und Haupttreppe, einen Saal für Skulpturen, das Direktorzimmer mit Vorplatz und eine Anzahl Ausstellungsräume. Das erste Obergeschoß ist wieder zur Anlage von Museumsräumen, namentlich für Gemälde benutzt.

524 [1914: 85] siehe 511

525 [1914: 58]

Das langgestreckte, durch Flügelbauten und einen mittleren in den Hof vorspringenden Ausbau erweiterte Amtsgebäude der Arbeiter Unfallversicherungsanstalt für Mähren und Schlesien in Brünn umfaßt außer einem Untergeschoß und einer Mazzarina vier Geschosse. Die Fassade, als Ergebnis eines Wett-

d'entrée est également réalisée en bronze. Les sculptures sont l'œuvre de Grasegger et de J. Moest. Le toit présente une surface frottante soudée, recouverte de cuivre et percée de fenêtres mansardées.

Le rez-de-chaussée comprend le hall d'entrée ainsi que le vestibule situé près de l'escalier principal. La grande salle centrale ouverte au public et les salles de guichet contiguës sont recouvertes d'un plafond ovale en forme de coupole. Les boiseries sont en acajou, les murs et les colonnes en marbre. Les autres pièces du rez-de-chaussée sont occupées par des salles de travail, les bureaux de la direction ainsi que par deux escaliers secondaires attenants à une cour intérieure.

522 [1914: 56]

La maison de commerce „Mauritiushof", située à Cologne, Mauritiussteinweg 77/79, fut réalisée en dix mois d'après les plans de l'architecte Carl Moritz, pour la somme des 510 000 marks. Il s'agit d'un ensemble composé d'un corps de bâtiment et de deux ailes insérant plusieurs cours. La construction s'élève sur quatre étages et sur un étage partiellement mansardé. La façade principale présente, au rez-de-chaussée, un alignement de fenêtres cintrées, comprises entre deux entrées également cintrées. Le premier et le deuxième étage forment un ensemble harmonieux grâce à l'encadrement décoratif des groupes de fenêtres. Le troisième étage est percé de fenêtres groupées, flanquées de pilastres. Les mansardés se terminent par des pignons arrondis. La façade est réalisée en trachyte de Westerwald, le toit est recouvert de tuiles.

Un accès latéral, aménagé sur la façade principale, donne sur un hall qui communique avec deux escaliers. A côté se trouvent des bureaux et des salles de conférences. Une grande cour intérieure, contiguë aux salles de travail et aux entrepôts, s'élève sur toute la hauteur du corps de bâtiment. La deuxième entrée assure le passage vers la cour intérieure couverte. Les deux ailes, comprenant des cours intérieures, sont occupées par des dépôts. L'ensemble du bâtiment fut réalisé en béton armé.

523 [1914: 53]

Le musée d'art asiatique de Cologne, situé sur les Gereonswall et Bremerstraße, fut construit en l'espace d'une année pour la somme de 250 000 marks. Ce bâtiment d'angle, assorti d'une cour, fut conçu par l'architecte Franz Brantzky. Le musée s'élève sur trois niveaux au-dessus d'un étage en sous-sol; les combles sont partiellement aménagés. Le rez-de-chaussée et le premier étage, rythmés de pilastres, sont séparés du deuxième étage par un fort bandeau. La façade donnant sur le Gereonswall et abritant l'entrée présente, au rez-de-chaussée, un bow-window recouvert d'un toit. Une deuxième entrée se trouve sur la Bremerstraße. L'aile principale, terminée par un avant-corps, est couronnée d'un ensemble de deux pignons pointus et saillants. Une avancée cornière, surmontée d'un balcon, saillit du rez-de-chaussée. Les murs de façades sont revêtus de tuf et de grès. Les toits mansardés sont recouverts d'ardoises.

Le rez-de-chaussée comprend le vestibule, le couloir avec le grand escalier, une salle consacrée aux sculptures et maintes salles d'exposition. Le premier étage est occupé par les salles du musée destinées notamment aux peintures.

524 [1914: 85] voir 511

525 [1914: 58]

L'ensemble administratif des assurances accidents pour travailleurs de Silésie et de Moravie de Brünn se compose d'un long corps de bâtiment assorti de deux ailes et d'un avant-corps s'avançant dans la cour. Il comprend quatre étages, un étage en sous-sol et une mezzanine. La façade, ayant fait l'objet d'un

between its windows; the entrance door is also cast in bronze. Sculptural work is by von Grasegger und Jos. Moest. The lower curved slope of the roof has dormers and is covered with copper.

The ground floor contains the entry hall together with the vestibule located next to the main staircase. The large central hall and the adjoining teller's counters are covered with an oval, dome-shaped ceiling. The woodwork is of mahogany, and the walls and columns are finished in marble. The remaining ground floor space is taken up by offices and directors' rooms, as well as by two side stairs bordering the courtyard.

522 [1914: 56]

Consisting of a forebuilding and two wings which encircle a courtyard, the building of Mauritiushof business firm was designed by the royal architect Carl Moritz and completed in 10 months at a cost of 510,000 Marks. The structure rises to a height of four storeys, with an aditional roof storey, and is bordered by two streets. A row of round-arched windows at the ground level of the main front are located between two entrances, which are also framed in round arches. The first two storeys and their groups of windows are framed in an ornamental moulding. The windows of the third story are separated by pilasters, and the roof windows end in round gables. The façade is rendered in trachyte from the Westerwald, and the roof is covered with tile.

One entrance at the side of the main front leads to a hall containing two staircases, adjoining offices and conference rooms. The large court traversing the entire forebuilding is flanked by offices and storage rooms. The other entrance serves as a carriageway to the open courtyard. The rear wing, which also adjoins the two courtyards, is occupied by storage rooms. The framework of the entire building is cast in reinforced concrete.

523 [1914: 53]

The new building of the Museum of East Asian Art in Cologne (corner of Gereonswall and Bremerstrasse) has three storeys, a partial roof storey, and a basement. The corner building, which surrounds an inner courtyard, was designed by Franz Brantzky, member of the Association of German Architects, and built in one year at a cost of 250,000 Marks. The ground level and first floor are separated from the second storey by a prominent string-course, and are articulated by pilasters. One entrance is located at the Gereonswall front, which has at its ground level a bay covered by a separate roof. A second entrance is situated at the Bremerstrasse front. The main wing here ends in an projection, and is crowned by two joined gables, which are cantilevered and high-pitched. A projecting structure topped by a balcony is located at the corner of the ground level. The façades are faced with tufa and sandstone. The roof contains dormers and is covered with slate.

The ground floor contains the vestibule, an entry hall and main staircase, a sculpture hall, the director's room with an anteroom, and a number of exhibition rooms. The first floor is also designed for museum rooms, particularly for the exhibition of paintings.

524 [1914: 85] see 511

525 [1914: 58]

The Brünn offices of the Workmen's Insurance Company of Moravia and Silesia are housed in a long main structure with wings and an extension projecting onto the centre courtyard at the back. In addition to the basement and the mezzanine, the building contains four storeys. The award-winning façade de-

Erdgeschoß   Rez-de-chaussée   Ground Floor

Portal   Portail   Portal   Eingang   Entrée   Entrance

bewerbs, ist von dem Preisträger Architekt Gottfried F. E. Czermak, der Grundriß von Architekt Baumeister Josef Fialla bei Stadtbaumeister Josef Jellinek entworfen. Die Bauzeit nahm 16 Monate in Anspruch, die Baukosten betrugen 800 000 Kronen. Der dreifach geteilte Eingang liegt in dem mittleren Vorsprung der Hauptfront; die Ecken derselben sind gleichfalls durch Risaliten vortretende Brüstung von den oberen Geschossen getrennt. Die Fenster des ersten Geschosses im Mittelrisalit der Front sind rundbogig, die übrigen Fenster geradlinig geschlossen. Über dem mittleren und den beiden Eckrisaliten erheben sich abgetrezzte, mit flachgewölbten Dächern schließende Dachaufbauten, welche die gebrochenen Dächer der Zwischenteile einschließen. Der Fassadenputz ist in lichtgelber Terranova hergestellt, der Sockel besteht aus Kunstsandstein, der Figurenfries an der Attika des Mittelrisalits ist ein Werk des Bildhauers Alfred Dreßler. Die Bauleitung besorgte Baumeister Josef Müller.

Das Erdgeschoß enthält im Vorderhause das Vestibül, das dahinterliegende Foyer mit den anschließenden Korridoren und die mit einem Lift verbundene Haupttreppe, außerdem eine Wohnung mit Küche, die Portierloge und eine Anzahl Büros. Im linken Seitenflügel liegen zwei Dienerwohnungen mit Küchen, im rechten Seitenflügel die Warteräume für Männer und Frauen, sowie die Zimmer des Chefarztes. In der Mezzanine sind die Kanzleiräume und die Registraturen untergebracht; das erste Obergeschoß enthält die Zimmer für Direktor und Präsidenten, den großen und den kleinen Sitzungssaal, Buchhaltung- und Kassenräume, Kanzlei und Garderobenzimmer. Das zweite Obergeschoß ist zur Anlage weiterer Kanzleizimmer und Registraturen benutzt, ebenso das dritte Obergeschoß. Als Zwischendecken wurden Rohrzellendecken von der Firma Donath & Co. hergestellt, welche auch sämtliche Beton-Tragkonstruktionen ausführte.

526 [1914: 81]

Der Personenbahnhof in Karlsruhe, Aufnahmegebäude, ist in den Fassaden, der Halle, den Warte-, Speise- und Hinterräumen von Architekt Baurat Professor A. Stürzenacker entworfen; die Gestaltung der Grundrisse sowie die Bauleitung fielen der Generaldirektion der Bad. Staatsbahnen anheim.

concours, fut conçue par l'architecte lauréat Gottfried F. E. Czermak. Les plans furent exécutés par l'architecte Josef Fialla travaillant pour l'architecte municipal Josef Jellinek. Les travaux de construction durèrent seize mois et coûtèrent 800 000 couronnes. L'entrée, divisée en trois parties, est située dans l'avant-corps médian de la façade principale. Les trois étages inférieurs sont séparés des trois étages supérieurs par le bandeau saillant de l'avant-corps. Les fenêtres du premier étage de l'avant-corps médian sont cintrées, les autres se terminent par un linteau droit. Les avant-corps latéraux et médian sont surmontés de constructions mansardées coiffées de toits surbaissés, encadrant ainsi les toits aux combles brisés des parties intermédiaires. Les façades sont enduites d'un crépi jaune clair, le socle est réalisé en grès artificiel. La frise ornementale sur l'attique de l'avant-corps médian est l'œuvre du sculpteur Alfred Dretzler. Josef Müller fut chargé de la conduite des travaux.

Le rez-de-chaussée du corps de bâtiment comprend le vestibule, le foyer et les corridors contigus, l'escalier principal auquel s'ajoute un ascenseur, ainsi qu'un logement avec cuisine, la loge du concierge et plusieurs bureaux. Dans l'aile de gauche sont aménagés deux logements avec cuisine destinés au personnel, dans l'aile de droite se trouvent les salles d'attente pour hommes et femmes ainsi que les bureaux du médecin-chef. La mezzanine est occupée par les secrétariats et les registres. Le premier étage abrite les bureaux du directeur et des présidents, la grande et la petite salle de conférences, la comptabilité, les guichets, le secrétariat et le vestiaire. Aux deuxième et troisième étages sont installés des secrétariats et des fichiers. Pour les faux-plafonds furent utilisés des hourdis fabriqués par l'entreprise Donath & Co., laquelle réalisa aussi l'ossature en béton.

526 [1914: 81]

Les façades, le hall, la salle d'attente, le restaurant et les arrière-salles de la gare de Karlsruhe furent conçus par l'architecte professeur A. Stürzenacker. L'élaboration du plan ainsi que la direction des travaux échurent à la direction générale des chemins de fer badois. La construction dura cinq ans et coûta

sign was created by the architect Gottfried F. E. Czermak; the ground plan is the work of the senior architect Josef Fialla in the service of the municipal architect Josef Jellinek. Construction was carried out over 16 months at a cost of 800,000 Crowns. The tripartite entrance is located in the middle projection of the main front, whose corners also form projections. The three lower storeys are separated from the upper part of the façade by a parapet moulding. The windows of first storey of the middle projection are framed in round arches; all others are straight—lined. The middle projection as well as the corner projections are crowned by stepped roof structures with flatly arched roofs. Between these are the lower roofs of the intervening sections. The façade is faced with light terranova plaster, and the socle consists of artificial sandstone. The figural frieze at the roof parapet of the middle projection is the work of the sculptor Alfred Dressler. Master builder Josef Müller supervised the construction.

The ground floor of the front building contains the vestibule, the foyer to the rear with its connecting corridors, the main staircase and the adjacent lift, as well as a flat with a kitchen, the porter's lodge, and a number of offices. The left wing is occupied by two servant's flats; the right wing by waiting rooms for men and women, and the office of the senior physician. Offices and registries are located on the mezzanine; the first floor contains rooms for the director and president, a small conference room and another larger one, offices for accounting and the cashier, as well as other offices and a cloak—room. The second floor is used for offices and registries, as is the third floor. The false ceilings of reed lathing were produced by the firm of Donath & Co., which also engineered the entire framework of concrete girders.

526 [1914: 81]

Construction of the Karlsruhe Railway Station lasted 5 years at a cost of approximately 2 million Marks. The municipal architect Professor A. Stürzenacker was responsible for the design of the façades, waiting rooms, restaurants and back rooms. The floor plan was drafted by the offices of the Baden State

Die Bauzeit nahm 5 Jahre in Anspruch. Die Baukosten betrugen rund 2 Millionen Mark. Den Haupteingang zur Schalterhalle bezeichnet ein einstöckiger Windfang, dem ein Schutzdach vorangeht, und der beiderseits von höher geführten Eingangshallen eingefaßt wird. Hinter diesen Vorbauten erhebt sich die Front der Schalterhalle mit großen Fenstern und mit einem gebrochenen Giebel abschließend. Die zu beiden Seiten des Mittelhaus sich anschließenden langen Fronten der Flügelbauten zeigen 2 Geschosse und über der Dachkante eine Reihe von Fenstern. Das Material der Fronten ist grüngelber Eppinger Sandstein, der Sockel besteht aus Schwagenwalder Granit, das Dach ist mit Schiefer eingedeckt. Die Bildhauerarbeiten stammen von Taudrer und Sabitscher, die dekorativen Malereien von Ernst, Haberstok und Wenenheuk.

Die Schalterhalle von teils 16 teils 18 m Spannweite ist in Eisenbeton ausgeführt, ebenso sind größtenteils die Dachstühle über dem Hauptbau in Eisenbeton hergestellt. Der untere Teil der Schalterhalle besteht in der Höhe von 3,50 m aus poliertem Vorsatzbeton, der übrige Teil aus gespitztem Vorsatzbeton. Die Flügelbauten, jedesmal einen Innenhof umschließend, enthalten die Wartesäle mit zugehörigen Wirtschaftsräumen, die Gepäckhalle, die Expreßgepäckhalle und außerdem eine Anzahl Geschäftsräume. Im Obergeschoß der Flügelbauten liegen die Fürstenzimmer, die Küchenräume, eine zweite Halle mit Wartesälen, sowie eine Anzahl Kassen- und Bureauräume. Das Dachgeschoß ist für die Wohnung des Wirts, zu Speicher und Büreauräumen ausgebaut.

527 [1914: 60]

Das in drei Teile gegliederte zweistöckige Wohnhaus Pott in Köln-Marienburg, am Südpark 51, Ecke Schillingrotter Platz, ist im Verlauf von zwei Jahren nach dem Entwurf des Architekten D. W. B. und B. D. A. Paul Pott errichtet. Die Baukosten betragen 80 000 Mark für Wohnhaus, Garage, Verbindungs- und Büroflügel, Gartenanlage und Einfriedigung. Das Wohnhaus mit dem Haupteingang an der Seitenfront zeigt eine abgerundete, über dem Obergeschoß mit einem Kuppeldach überdeckte Ecke, dann einen Fenstervorbau an der anschließenden Front mit besonderem Dach abschließend, über dem ein steiler Giebel aufsteigt. Die mit Säulen ausgestattete Veranda vor der Ausstellungshalle verbindet das Wohnhaus mit dem Bürohause, welches den Eingang in der Seitenfront erhalten hat und dessen Erdgeschoß durch einen breiten Dachstreifen vom Obergeschoß getrennt ist. Die Fassaden sind mit rauhem und feinem Terranovaputz überzogen, das Holzwerk der Fensterumrahmungen, die Gesimse und die Beschindelung der Giebel sind grün gestrichen. Die Dächer sind mit roten Biberschwänzen, die Kuppeldach ist mit Kupfer eingedeckt. Das Eisenwerk ist schwarz, die Zementsäulen sind weiß gestrichen; die äußeren Stufen bestehen aus Kunstgranit.

Das Wohnhaus enthält im Erdgeschoß die Halle, die angrenzende Treppe und den Kaminplatz, außerdem Empfangs- Speise- und Arbeitszimmer, sowie die Garage. Die Wirtschaftsräume sind im Kellergeschoß untergebracht. Im Obergeschoß liegen die Schlafzimmer und das Bad. Der Verbindungsflügel enthält im Erdgeschoß die Ausstellungshalle und im Obergeschoß das Atelier. Das Bürohaus ist in beiden Geschossen zu Büroräumen eingerichtet.

528 [1914: 89]

Das an zwei Straßenfronten freiliegende in 6 Geschossen aufsteigende Kauf- und Wohnhaus Modern und Breitner in Budapest wurde von den Architekten Révész und Kollár in einer Bauzeit von 1½ Jahren für die Kostensumme von 1300 000 Kronen errichtet. Erdgeschoß und Mezzaningeschosse zeigen Schaufenster; sämtliche Geschosse sind durch aufsteigende Pfeiler gegliedert. Der Eckbau ist durch einen Turm ausgezeichnet, der mit einem Kuppeldach abschließt. Die eine Front hat einen halbrunden Giebel bekrönt, die andere ist mit einem Glasdach versehen. Der Bau besteht größtenteils aus Eisenbeton, die Fassaden sind mit Porphiritputz bekleidet, der als

---

environ 2 millions de marks. Un tambour d'un étage, protégé par un auvent, et flanqué par des halls d'entrée d'une plus grande hauteur, caractérise l'entrée principale menant à la salle des guichets. Derrière ces constructions en saillie s'élève la façade de la salle des guichets, ornée de grandes fenêtres et d'un pignon aux lignes brisées. Les longues façades des ailes, encadrant la construction médiane, présentent deux étages et une rangée de fenêtres au-dessus de l'arête du toit. Les murs des façades sont en grès vert jaune d'Eppingen, le socle est en granit de Schwagenwald, le toit est recouvert d'ardoises. Les sculptures furent exécutées par messieurs Taudrer et Sabitscher, les peintures décoratives par messieurs Ernst, Haberstok et Wenenheuk.

La salle des guichets, d'une envergure de 16 voire 18 mètres, est réalisée en béton armé, de même que les charpentes des combles du bâtiment principal. La partie inférieure de la salle des guichets, est composée, sur 3,50 mètres, de béton de parement poli, le reste est réalisé en béton de parement appliqué au pistolet. Les ailes, insérant chacune une cour, abritent les salles d'attente et leurs salles annexes, la consigne, le service des colis express ainsi que des bureaux. A l'étage supérieur se trouvent les pièces princières, les cuisines, un deuxième hall avec unse salle d'attente, ainsi que des bureaux et des guichets. L'étage des combles est occupé par le logement du restaurateur, le grenier et des bureaux.

527 [1914: 60]

The Pott house in Cologne-Marienburg is a two-storey residence divided into three main parts. Designed by the certified architect Paul Pott, member of the Association of German Architects, it was built over a period of two years. Construction of the house, garage, the connecting and office wings, as well as the landscaping resulted in costs amounting to 80,000 Marks. The main house, whose entrance is located at the side, has a rounded corner covered by a domed roof above the upper storey. Bay windows covered by a separate roof project at the front, which is crowned by a high-pitched gable. The veranda in front of the exhibition room is lined with columns, and connects the main house and the office wing. The latter has a side entrance and a broad roof strip separating the ground level from the upper storey. The façades are faced with both rough and smooth terranova plaster; the wooden windows frames, mouldings and the gable shingles are painted green. The roof is covered with flat red tile, and the corner dome with copper sheeting. The wrought ironwork is painted black, the concrete columns white. The exterior stairs are of artificial granite.

The ground floor of the house contains the entry hall and adjoining stairs, a sitting-room with a fireplace, as well as a reception room, dining room and study, plus the garage. The kitchen and service room are located in the basement. The upper floor is occupied by bedrooms and the bath. The connecting wing has the exhibition room on the ground floor and a studio on the upper floor. The front wing is occupied solely by offices.

528 [1914: 89]

Le grand magasin Modern & Breitner de Budapest fut édifié par les architectes Révész et Kollár en un an et demi pour la somme de 1300 000 couronnes. Le bâtiment, haut de six étages, présente deux façades sur rue. Au rez-de-chaussée et à l'étage de la mezzanine s'ouvrent des devantures. La façade offre une ordonnance de pilastres. Le pan coupé se distingue par une tour qui se termine un toit en coupole. L'une des façades est couronnée d'un pignon arrondi, l'autre porte un toit en verrière. L'immeuble est construit, en grande partie, en béton armé. Les façades, revêtues d'un crépi porphyrique, présentent des éléments en grès artificiel. Le socle se compose de granit rouge, le

---

Railways, who also supervised the construction. A single-storey draught lobby is placed at the main entrance, which is covered by a wide canopy and flanked by taller entry halls. The front of the ticket counter hall is placed directly behind the entrance halls. It contains large windows and terminates in a broken gable. The long flanking wing fronts have two-storeys and a row of windows above the roof line. The fronts consist of greenish-yellow sandstone from Eppingen, the socle is of Schwagenwald granite, and the roof is covered with slate. The sculptural ornamentation is the work of von Taudrer and Sabitscher, and the decorative painting was done by Ernst Haberstok and Wenenheuk.

The booking hall, with spans of 16 and 18 metres, is constructed of reinforced concrete, as are large portions of the roof framework above the main structure. The lower 3,50 meters of the booking hall are made of polished facing concrete, the remaining areas are of pointed facing concrete. The side wings, each of which encloses an inner courtyard, contain the waiting rooms and station restaurants, luggage and express-luggage rooms, and a number of offices. the upper level of the wings contain the Prince's rooms, kitchens, an additional hall with waiting rooms, as well as a number of cashier's and accounting offices. The roof storey is occupied by the innkeeper's flat, storage areas and offices.

527 [1914: 60]

La villa Pott, située à Cologne, à l'angle des Schillingsrotterplatz et Südpark, fut réalisée d'après les plans de l'architecte Paul Pott. Il s'agit d'une maison de deux étages, se composant de trois parties. Les frais de construction de l'habitation, du garage, de l'aile intermédiaire, de l'aile des bureaux, de l'aménagement du jardin et du mur de clôture s'élevèrent à 80 000 marks. La maison d'habitation, dont l'entrée se trouve sur la façade latérale, présente un avant-corps arrondi, coiffé, au-dessus du premier étage, d'un toit en coupole. La façade adjacente est assortie d'un bow-window surmonté par un toit au-dessus duquel s'élève un pignon pentu. La véranda, ornée de colonnes, située devant la salle d'exposition, relie la maison d'habitation à l'aile des bureaux dont l'entrée se trouve sur la façade latérale et dont le rez-de-chaussée est séparé de l'étage supérieur par une large bande de toiture. Les murs de façade sont enduits de crépi grossier et fin, les châssis des fenêtres, les corniches et les bardeaux du pignon ont reçu un badigeon vert. Les toits sont recouverts de tuiles plates, le toit en coupole porte une couverture de cuivre. Les éléments métalliques sont noirs, les colonnes en ciment blanches. Les marches extérieures sont en granit artificiel.

La maison d'habitation comprend, au rez-de-chaussée, le hall, l'escalier contigu et la cheminée, le salon, la salle à manger, le cabinet de travail ainsi que le garage. Les pièces de service sont au sous-sol. Au premier étage sont aménagées les chambres à coucher et la salle de bains. L'aile intermédiaire abrite la salle d'exposition au rez-de-chaussée et l'atelier au premier étage. Les deux étages de l'aile des bureaux sont occupés par des salles de travail.

528 [1914: 89]

The Modern & Breitner department store in Budapest is a six-storey edifice with two exposed street fronts. Designed by the architects Révész and Kollár, it was completed in 1½ years at a cost of 1,3000,000 Crowns. Shop windows open at the ground level and mezzanine, and pillars extend through all storeys. The corner of the building is crowned by a tower with a dome-shaped roof. A shaped gable graces the top of one front; the other finishes with a glass roof. The structure consists chiefly of reinforced concrete, the façades are rendered in porphyric plaster which is finished with a layer of artificial sandstone. The socle

Kunstsandstein überarbeitet ist. Der Sockel besteht aus rotem Granit, die Portale aus Schmiedebronze. Der große Lichthof ist mit doppelter Verglasung versehen, oben in Glaseisenbeton, unten plastisch in elektrolitischer Fassung. Die Bildhauerarbeiten sind von K. Fleischl ausgeführt.

Das Gebäude ist für ein Engrosgeschäft in Tuch- und Futterwaren bestimmt. Längs der Front am Deákplatze sind die Räume des Kaufhauses angeordnet. Im Erdgeschoß, Hochparterre und Mezzanin liegen die Bedienungsräume, im ersten Obergeschoß Bureaus, im ersten Untergeschoß die Räume der Strazza, im zweiten Untergeschoß die Expedition. Zur Verbindung der Stockwerke dienen die große Freitreppe und 2 Aufzüge. Der mittlere Teil des Gebäudes wird durch einen glasüberdeckten Lichthof eingenommen, der durch sämtliche Geschosse bis zum Untergeschosse reicht. An der Hoffassade ist eine Nottreppe errichtet. Die anderen Teile des Erdgeschosses, des Hochparterre und der Mezzanine sind an einzelne Firmen vermietet. In den oberen Geschossen sind Mietswohnungen eingerichtet, die durch einen gesonderten Treppenaufgang und durch Aufzüge zu erreichen sind.

portail est en bronze forgé. La grande cour intérieure est pourvue d'un double vitrage dont l'extrados se compose de verre et de béton armé et l'intrados de verre et de nervures apparentes traitées par électrolyse. K. Fleischl exécuta les sculptures.

Le bâtiment est destiné à abriter un commerce de gros d'étoffes et de doublures. Le long de la façade, qui donne sur la place Deák, se trouvent les salles du grand magasin. Au rez-de-chaussée, à l'entresol et à la mezzanine sont aménagées les surfaces de vente, au premier étage les bureaux, au premier sous-sol les salles des mains courantes, au deuxième sous-sol celles de l'expédition. Les étages communiquent entre eux par un grand escalier et deux ascenseurs. La partie médiane du bâtiment est occupée par une cour intérieure vitrée descendant jusqu'au sous-sol. Un escalier de secours est installé sur un des côtes de la cour. Les autres parties du rez-de-chaussée, de l'entresol et de la mezzanine sont louées à des entreprises. Les étages supérieurs abritent des appartements de rapport, accessibles par un escalier indépendant et par des ascenseurs.

consists of red granite, the portals of wrought bronze. The large courtyard is furnished with double glazing framed at the upper floor in reinforced concrete, at the ground level in galvanised metal. The sculptural ornamentation is the work of K. Fleischl.

The building has been designed for a wholesale firm dealing in cloth and lining materials. The rooms of the department store line the side of the building facing Deák Square. Salesroom are located on the two ground floors and mezzanine, and the first floor contains offices. The first basement floor is occupied by waste-book rooms, while dispatch rooms are located on the second basement level. Floors are connected by a large open staircase and two lifts. The centre of the floor plan is taken up by a glass-covered courtyard, which extends through all floors to the basement. Fire stairs are located at the courtyard front. The remaining areas of the ground floors and mezzanine have been leased to other firms. The upper floor contain flats which are reached by a separate staircase and by lifts.

529 [1914: 97]

Das an zwei Straßen gelegene vierstöckige mit teilweise ausgebautem Dachgeschoß versehene Wohnhaus in Amsterdam Johannes Vermeerplein, ist ein Werk des Architekten de Klerk. Die schmalere Front zeigt einen doppelten von Pilastern eingefaßten Eingang. Über dem Erdgeschoß zieht sich eine auf Konsolen ruhende ringsum laufende Galerie hin. An den Ecken der längeren Front springen über dem Erdgeschoß zwei viereckige Erker hervor, die im dritten Obergeschoß durch gebrochene Dächer abgeschlossen werden. Der Mittelbau derselben Front ist durch Lisenen gegliedert, die oben mit dachartigen Vorsprüngen endigen. Das mit Dachpfannen eingedeckte abgewalmte Dach wird an den Ecken der Langseite durch Einsprünge unterbrochen. Über der Dachfläche erheben sich Schornsteinaufbauten in beträchtlicher Höhe. Die Fassaden sind in gefugtem Backsteinmauerwerk hergestellt. Die Brüstung der Galerie über dem Erdgeschoß besteht aus Ziegeln.

529 [1914: 97]

L'immeuble d'Amsterdam, situé Johannes Vermeerplein, est l'œuvre de l'architecte de Klerk. Il s'agit d'un bâtiment de quatre étages donnant sur deux rues. La façade la plus étroite offre une double entrée flanquée de pilastres. Une galerie en encorbellement, surmontant le rez-de-chaussée, court sur les façades. La façade la plus longue est assortie de deux avancées cornières se dégageant au-dessus du rez-de-chaussée et montant jusqu'au troisième étage où elles se terminent par des toits aux lignes brisées. La partie médiane de la même façade est ornée de lésènes surmontées de saillies en forme de toit. Le toit en croupe, recouvert de tuiles flamandes, présente des retraits dans les angles de la façade la plus longue. De hautes cheminées s'élèvent des toits. Les murs de façade sont réalisés en briques jointoyées. La balustrade de la galerie couronnant le rez-de-chaussée est en briques.

529 [1914: 97]

The apartment building in Amsterdam (Johannes Vermeerplein), with four storeys and a partial roof storey, has two exposed fronts and is the work of architect de Klerk. The narrow front has a double entrance framed in pilasters. A gallery supported by consoles runs along both sides above the ground level. At the corners of the long front are two oriels with broken roofs at the third storey. The middle section of this front is articulated by lesenes which finish at the top in roof-like projections. The hipped roof is covered with pantiles and is returned at the corners of the long front. Chimneys of noticeable height rise above the roof. The façades are rendered in brick masonry, and the gallery parapet is made of clay brick.

530 [1914: 86]

Das malerisch gruppierte F. B. Carters Landhaus in Evanston, Illinois, steigt in zwei Geschossen auf und ist von einem Park umgeben. Urheber des Entwurfs ist der Architekt Walter Barley Griffin. Beiden Fronten sind im Erdgeschoß ausgedehnte bedeckte Hallen vorgelegt. Das obere Geschoß tritt mit Auskragungen über das Erdgeschoß hervor und ist an den Seitenfronten mit Altanen ausgestattet, über denen sich vorspringende Dachteile erstrecken. Das Baumaterial für die Fassaden besteht im Erdgeschoß aus gefugtem Backsteinmauerwerk, im oberen Geschosse aus Fachwerk. Das weit überstehende flache Dach ist mit Ziegeln eingedeckt und wird an den Giebeln und Traufkanten durch Bretterverschalungen abgeschlossen.

530 [1914: 86]

La propriété de campagne de F. B. Carter à Evanston, en Illinois, forme un ensemble pittoresque entouré d'un grand parc. Cette villa de deux étages de composition asymétrique fut conçue par l'architecte Walter Barley Griffin. De larges galeries s'adossent au rez-de-chaussée des deux façades. L'étage supérieur fait saillie au-dessus du rez-de-chaussée et est assorti, sur les façades latérales, de balcons que surplombent les avant-toits. Le rez-de-chaussée est réalisé en briques jointoyées, les étages offrent des colombages. Le toit saillant est recouvert de tuiles. Les pignons et les larmiers portent un revêtement de lattes de bois.

530 [1914: 86]

The F. B. Carter house in Evanston, Illinois is a picturesque two-storey residence surrounded by a park. Plans were created by the architect Walter Barley Griffin. Both fronts of the house have covered porches. The upper storey protrudes over the ground level with cantilevers, and has side balconies covered by projecting extensions of the roof. The façades of the ground floor are made of bonded brick masonry, those of the upper storey are half-timbered. The broad overhanging roof is covered with tile and has boarded gables and eaves.

Ortsregister

Nomenclature des Localités

List of Places

1   [1901; 1] R. Moennich, O. Schmalz; Berlin · Königliches Land- und Amtsgericht I · Palais de justice · Law Courts

2 [1901; 4] Schilling & Graebner; Dresden · Dresden (Waisenhausstraße 13): Sächsische
Handelsbank, Hauptfront · Banque commerciale saxonne, façade principale · Saxon
commercial bank, facade

3 [1901; 5] Schilling & Graebner; Dresden · Dresde (Johannisallee 12): Sächsische
Handelsbank · Banque commerciale saxonne · Saxon commercial bank

4 [1901; 15] A.L. van Gendt en Zonen; Amsterdam (Spuistraat 140): Bankgebäude · Banque ·
Bank

5 [1901; 18] M. Macarthy; London · Londres (167 Queen's Gate s.w.): Wohnhaus · Immeuble
de rapport · Apartment building

6   [1901; 8] B. Sehring, K. Lachmann; Berlin (Leipziger Straße): Kaufhaus Tietz · Hauptfassade · Grand magasin Tietz, façade principale · Tietz department Store, façade

7 [1901; 14] R. Binet; Paris · Weltausstellung 1900, Hauptportal · Exposition universelle 1900, entrée principale · International Exhibition 1900, main entrance

8 [1901; 37] H. vom Endt; Düsseldorf · Düsseldorf: Apollotheater · Théâtre Apollon · Apollo Theater

4

[1901: 20] A. Messel: Berlin-Grunewald (Siemensstraße 4) · Villa Wertheim · Propriété de W. Wertheim · Wertheim house

[1901: 23] Eisenlohr & Weigle; Stuttgart (Rotebühlstraße 70): · Villa Simolin, Südansicht · Villa de Simolin, façade méridionale · Simolin house, south façade

11   [1901; 21] H.P. Berlage; Amsterdam (Damrak 75): Versicherungsgesellschaft · Compagnie d'assurances · Insurance company building

2   [1901; 29] Ch. Harrison Townsend: London · Londres (Bishopsgate): Volksbibliothek
Bibliothèque publique · Public library

13   [1901; 42] K. Hofmann: Worms: Neue Rheinbrücke · Pont nouveau du Rhin · New Rhine bridge

4   [1901; 41] F. Brantzky: Köln · Cologne (Hansaring): Kunstgewerbemuseum · Musée des Arts décoratifs · Museum of Decorative Arts

15 [1901; 43] Cambon, Durey & Galeron; Paris: · Hippodrome

16 [1901; 52] K. Hocheder; München · Munich: Neues Volksbad · Etablissement de bains publics · Public baths

17 [1901: 44] E. Cuypers: Amsterdam (Heerengracht 579–599): Bankgebäude · Banque · Bank

18 [1901: 54] A. Messel: Berlin (Vossstraße): Kaufhaus Wertheim · Grand magasin Wertheim · Wertheim department store

19 [1901: 56] Ch. Plumet: Paris (Avenue du Bois de Boulogne): Wohnhaus · Immeuble de rapport · Apartment building

9

20   [1901; 58] F.R. Voretzsch; Dresden · Dresde (Bürgerwiese 20): Wohnhaus · Immeuble de rapport · Apartment building

21   [1901; 63] H.P. Berlage, H. Bonda; Amsterdam (Raadhuisstraat 30, 32, 34): Wohn- und Geschäftshaus · Immeuble de rapport · Apartment building with shops

22   [1901; 66] G. Wehling; Düsseldorf · Düsseldorf (Schadowstraße 34): Wohn- und Geschäftshaus · Immeuble de rapport · Apartment building with shops

23   [1901; 94] J. Lavirotte; Paris (12, Rue Sédillot): Einfamilienhaus · Hôtel particulier · One-family house

24 [1901; 99] Schilling & Graebner; Dresden · Dresde (Hähnelstraße 13): Villa · Town house   25 [1901; 98] Schilling & Graebner; Dresden · Dresde (Hähnelstraße 13): Villa · Town house

[1901; 62] G. Kegel; Kassel · Cassel (Wilhelmshöhe): Stationsgebäude der Straßenbahn · Gare de tramway · Streetcar station building

27　[1901; 88] M. Dülfer; München · Munich (Bayerstraße 57–59): Wohn- und Geschäftshaus · Immeuble · Apartment building with shops

28 [1901; 67] L. Levy; Straßburg · Strasbourg · Strassburg: Neue Synagoge · Nouvelle Synagogue · New Synagogue

29 [1901; 68] L. Levy; Strassburg · Strasbourg · Straßburg: Neue Synagoge, Innenansicht · Nouvelle Synagogue, rue intérieure · New Synagogue, interior

30 [1901; 95] J. Lavirotte; Paris (3, Square Rapp): Wohnhaus · Immeuble de rapport · Apartment building

31 [1901; 10] A. Eitel; Stuttgart (Humboldtstraße 8): Villa Eitel · Eitel house

13

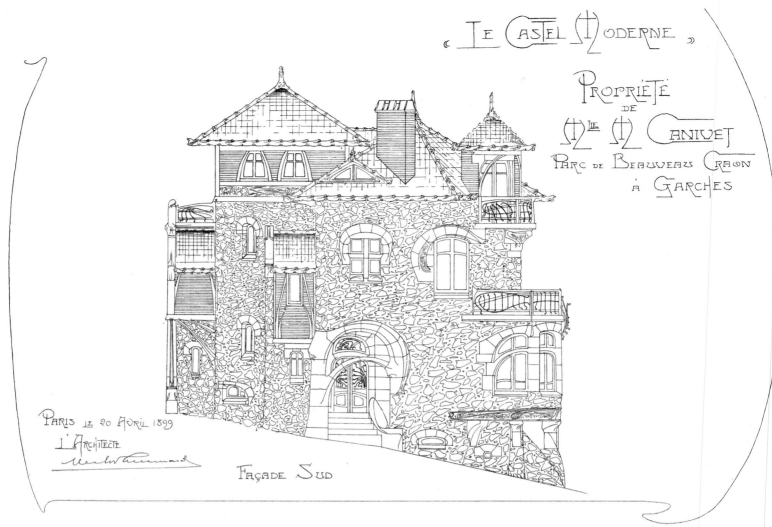

« Le Castel Moderne »

Propriété
de
Mᴸᴱ M. Canivet
Parc de Beauveau Craon
à Garches

Paris le 20 Avril 1899
L'Architecte

Façade Sud

32   [1901; 96] H. Guimard; Castel Beauveau-Craon

Propriété de M Mirand-Devos
à Versailles

Élévation de la Façade sur Rue

« Castel Eclipse »

L'Architecte

33   [1901; 97] H. Guimard; Castel Beauveau-Craon

[1902; 19] Berninger & Krafft: Straßburg · Strasbourg · Strassburg (Ruprechtsauer Allee 76): Villa Schützenberger · Propriété d'O. Schützenberger · Schützenberger house

35 [1902; 1] F. von Hoven; Frankfurt/Main · Francfort-sur-le-Main · Frankfurt-on-Main (Caunusanlage 18): Versicherungsgesellschaft · Compagnie d'assurances · Insurance company building

36 [1902; 9] F. Dehm, F. Olbricht; Wien · Vienne · Vienna (Althanplatz 4): Wohn- und Geschäftshaus · Immeuble · Apartment house with shops

37 [1902; 6] W. Martens; Berlin (Behrenstraße 46): Berliner Bank · Banque · Bank

[1902; 5] Beers, Clay & Dutton; Chicago: „Medinah Temple", Geschäftshaus · Palais commercial · Commercial building

39   [1902; 7] Curjel & Moser; Basel · Bâle: Pauluskirche · Eglise Saint Paul · St. Paul's Church

40   [1902; 44] Curjel & Moser; Karlsruhe (Hoffstraße 2): Wohnhaus · Immeuble de rapport Apartment building

41   [1902; 58] C.H. Peters; Amsterdam: Post- und Telegraphengebäude · Hôtel des Postes · Main Post Office

22 [1902; 10] M. Fabiani; Wien · Vienne · Vienna (Starhemberggasse 47): Wohn- und Geschäftshaus · Immeuble · Apartment building

43 [1902; 12] Curjel & Moser; Karlsruhe (Karlstraße/Akademiestraße): Bankhaus Homburger · Banque · Bank

44 [1902; 15] L. Lefranc; Paris (7—9, Boulevard du Temple): Wohn- und Geschäftshaus · Immeuble de rapport Apartment building with shops

45 [1902; 13] H. Walder; Karlsruhe (Kaiserstraße/Karlstraße): „Zum Monninger" · Immeuble · Apartment building with shops

46 [1902; 14] Berninger & Krafft; Straßburg · Strasbourg (Place Broglie): Wohn- und Geschäftshaus · Immeuble de rapport · Apartment building with shops

20

47　[1902; 17] A. Koch; Zürich · Zurich: Villa Ruegg-Honegger · Propriété de M. Ruegg-Honegger · Ruegg-Honegger house

48　[1902; 29] C.W. Stephens; London · Londres (Herbert Crescent, 11–14 Hans Place, Chelsea s.w.): Wohnhäusergruppe · Ensemble d'immeubles · Apartment complex

49　[1902; 30] A.H. Kersey; London · Londres (2–10 Parkstreet, Hyde Park): Wohnhäusergruppe · Ensemble d'immeubles · Apartment complex

50 [1902; 21] A. Kármán, J. von Ullmann; Budapest (Franzensplatz): „Königsbazar" · Etablissement commercial · Shop fronts

51 [1902; 22] A. Kármán, J. von Ullmann; Budapest (Franzensplatz): „Königsbazar" · Etablissement commercial · Commercial building

52 [1902; 23] M. Dülfer; München · Munich (Wolfrathshauser Straße 31½): Villa · Private residence

53 [1902; 41] E.T. Hapgood; Hartford, Connecticut (Farmington Avenue): Einfamilienhaus · Propriété · One-family house

54 [1902; 27] P. Thömer, A. Rüdell; Danzig · Dantzig: Hauptbahnhof · Gare centrale · Central Railway Station

55 [1902; 28] P. Thömer, A. Rüdell; Danzig · Dantzig: Hauptbahnhof, Schalterhalle · Gare centrale, halle aux guichets · Central Railway Station, passenger hall

56 [1902; 39] Schmohl & Staehelin; Stuttgart (Neckarstraße 56): Restaurant „Stuttgarter Bürgerhalle" · Brasserie · Restaurant

57 [1902; 36] W. Gebhardt; Berlin (Prinzenstraße 42): Wohn- und Geschäftshaus · Immeuble de rapport · Apartment building with shops

58 [1902; 38] Schmohl & Stähelin; Stuttgart (Neckarstraße 56): „Stuttgarter Bürgerhalle" · Immeuble de rapport et brasserie · Apartment building with restaurant

25

59 [1902; 33] Pfleghardt & Häfeli; Zürich · Zurich (Bahnhofstraße 69): Wohn- und Geschäftshaus · Immeuble de rapport · Apartment building with shops

60 [1902; 34] Pfleghardt & Häfeli; Zürich · Zurich (Bahnhofstraße 69): Wohn- und Geschäftshaus · Immeuble de rapport · Apartment building with shops

61 [1902; 42] F.R. Voretzsch; Dresden · Dresde (Reichenbachstraße 57): Wohnhaus · Immeuble de rapport · Apartment building

62 [1902; 50] G. Rathenau; Berlin (Leipziger Straße 92): Geschäftshaus · Immeuble à usage commercial · Commercial building

63   [1902; 47] A. Reimann; Berlin-Grunewald (Fontanestraße 8—10): Villa Heil

64   [1902; 52] Solf & Wichards; Berlin (Taubenstraße 16, 17, 18): Versicherungsgesellschaft
„Wilhelma" · Compagnie d'assurances · Insurance company building

65   [1902; 53] F. Ohmann, A. Dryack, F. Bendelmeyer; Prag · Prague (Hybernergasse 17):
Hotel Central · Hôtel · Hotel

27

66 [1902; 59] K. Holzmann; Wien · Vienne · Vienna (Alois-Drasche-Park 5): Wohnhaus · Immeuble de rapport · Apartment building

67 [1902; 72] A. Kármán, J. von Ullmann; Budapest (Szabadsay-tér 12, 11, 10): Wohnhäusergruppe Ensemble d'immeubles · Apartment building

68 [1902; 67] G. Gull; Zürich · Zurich: Stadthaus · Hôtel de ville · Town Hall

69 [1902: 73] E. Cuypers: Amsterdam (Jan Luykenstraat 2): Wohnhaus · Immeuble · Apartment building

70 [1902: 64] —: London · Londres: „Millais Buildings", Arbeiterwohnhäuser · Habitations ouvrières · Subsidized worker housing

71   [1902; 74] Ḧ. Ritter; Frankfurt/Main · Francfort-sur-le-Main · Frankfurt-on-Main (Taunusanlage 20): Versicherungsgesellschaft · Compagnie d'assurances · Insurance company building

72   [1902; 77] Billing & Mallebrein; Karlsruhe (Stephanienstraße 66): Wohnhaus und
Privatklinik · Hôtel particulier et clinique · Apartment building with private hospital

73   [1902; 78] Billing & Mallebrein; Karlsruhe (Stephanienstraße 66): Wohnhaus,
Halle · Hôtel particulier, vestibule · Apartment building, entrance hall

74 [1902; 76] V. Dylewski; Berlin (Schleswiger Ufer 9): „13. Realschule" · Ecole · School

75 [1902; 82] E. Blérot; Brüssel · Bruxelles · Brussels (34, Rue du Monastère): Wohnhaus · Hôtel particulier Apartment building

76 [1902; 88] Rindsfüsser & Kühn; Frankfurt/Main · Francfort-sur-le-Main · Frankfurt-on-Main (Roßmarkt 15–17): Wohn- und Geschäftshaus · Immeuble de rapport · Apartment building with shops

77 [1902; 92] G. Oberthür; Straßburg · Strasbourg · Strassburg (Am Hohen Steg): Kaufhaus „Kleine Metzig" · Grand magasin „Kleine Metzig" · Kleine Metzig department store

78   [1902; 90] O. Nebel; Koblenz · Coblence (Mainzer Straße 70): Villa Siebel

79   [1902; 97] H.F. Faulkner, Read & Macdonald; London-Hampstead · Londres-Hampstead (Elsworthy Road): Landhäuser · Maisons de campagne · Private residences

[1902; 99] R. d'Aronco; Turin: Erste internationale Ausstellung für dekorative Kunst, Eingang · La première exposition internationale d'art décoratif, l'entrée · First International Exhibition for Modern Decorative Art, entrance

[1902; 100] R. d'Aronco; Turin: Erste internationale Ausstellung für dekorative Kunst, Große Halle des Hauptgebäudes · La première exposition internationale d'art décoratif, le bâtiment principal; la grande halle First International Exhibition for Modern Decorative Art, Principal Building; main hall

82 [1903; 5] Th. Fischer; München-Schwabing · Munich-Schwabing: Evangelische Erlöserkirche · Eglise protestante · Protestant church

83 [1903; 9] F. Radke; Düsseldorf · Dusseldorf: Restaurant Düsselschlößchen

84 [1903; 100] F. Schulek; Budapest: Aufgang zur St. Matthiaskirche · Grand escalier et parvis de l'église Saint-Matthieu · Stairs to St. Matthias' Church

5   [1903; 14] M. Dülfer; München · Munich (Kaulbachstraße 22a): Wohnhaus · Immeuble de rapport · Apartment building

86   [1903; 21] O. Delisle; München · Munich (Herzog-Wilhelm-Straße 19): Zinshaus · Immeuble de rapport · Apartment building

7   [1903; 24] Gebr. Schauppmeyer; Köln · Cologne (Deutscher Ring 42): Wohnhaus Immeuble de rapport · Apartment building

88   [1903; 46] Weinreb & Spiegel; Budapest (Vaczi-körut 61): Wohn- und Geschäftshaus · Immeuble de rapport · Apartment building with shops

89 [1903; 20] R. Bislich: Berlin-Grunewald (Dunkerstraße 4): Landhaus Will · Propriété · Private residence

90 [1903; 30] K. Stief: Karlsruhe (Eisenlohrstraße 27): Einfamilienhaus · Maison individuelle · One-family house

91 [1903; 42] A. Stürzenacker: Karlsruhe (Am Rheinhafen): Wohnhaus des Hafendirektors · Maison du directeur du port · Residence of the harbor director

92 [1903; 56] Schilling & Graebner: Dresden-Blasewitz · Dresde-Blasewitz (Emser Allee 38): Villa Doehn · Propriété de M. Doehn · Doehn house

93 [1903; 38] K. Diestel; Dresden · Dresde (Wiener Straße 13): Geschäftshaus · Immeuble à usage commercial · Commercial building

94 [1903; 39] D. Joseph; London · Londres (Fitz James Avenue, w.): Wohnhäusergruppe Ensemble d'immeubles · Apartment complex

95 [1903; 55] H.P. Berlage; Leipzig (Augustusplatz 8): Versicherungsgebäude · Compagnie d'assurances · Insurance company building

96 [1903; 13] M. Dülfer; München · Munich (Kaulbachstraße 22a, 24, 26): Wohnhäusergruppe Ensemble d'immeubles · Apartment buildings

97 [1903; 63] O. Nebel; Koblenz-Oberwerth · Coblence-Oberwerth: Haus Castenholz · Hôtel Castenholz Castenholz house

98 [1903; 80] Lossow & Viehweger; Dresden · Dresde (Tiergartenstraße 52): Villa Lossow · Villa de W. Lossow · Lossow house

99 [1903; 3] M. Dülfer; Riederau/Ammersee: Landhaus Curry · Maison de campagne Curry · Curry residence

100 [1903; 94] F. Trump; München · Munich (Franz-Josef-Straße 34): Wohnhaus · Immeuble de rapport · Apartment building

101 [1903; 98] F.R. Voretzsch; Dresden · Dresde (Lindengasse 14): Wohnhaus · Immeuble de rapport · Apartment building

102 [1903; 61] F.B. Wade; London · Londres: 54 Mount Street/Palais des Lord Windsor · La résidence du Lord Windsor · The residence of Lord Windsor

103 [1903; 15] Hart & Lesser; Berlin (Kronenstraße 10): Geschäftshaus · Immeuble à usage commercial · Commercial building

39

104   [1903; 37] M. Fabiani; Wien · Vienne · Vienna (Ungarstraße 51–53): Geschäftshaus · Immeuble à usage commercial · Commercial building

105   [1903; 27] F. Schwechten; Potsdam (Am Brauhausberge): Königliche Kriegsschule · Ecole militaire royale · Military academy

106   [1903; 75] A. Stürzenacker; Karlsruhe (Rheinhafen): Werfthalle · Installation de construction navale · Harbor buildings

107   [1903; 74] A. Stürzenacker; Karlsruhe: Städtisches Elektrizitätswerk · Services municipaux d'électricité · Municipal power plant

108   [1903; 66] Erdmann & Spindler; Seifersdorf/Sorau: Fabrikgebäude · Bâtiment industriel · Factory building

109 [1903; 82] O. Heussner; Frankfurt/Main · Francfort-sur-le-Main · Frankfurt-on-Main: Hotel Fürstenhof · Hôtel · Hotel

110 [1903; 91] Th. Fischer; München · Munich (Elisabethplatz): Schule · Ecole · School

43

111   [1903; 25] Temper, Lossow & Viehweger; Dresden · Dresde (Theaterplatz): Staatliches Fernheiz- und Elektrizitätswerk · Services communaux de chauffage et d'électricité · State power and heating plant

42   [1903; 36] J. L. Cochran: Chicago (Lake Forrest): Landhäuser · Maisons de campagne · Private residences

113   [1903; 99] P. Jatzow: Berlin (Friedrichstraße 231): Geschäftshaus · Immeuble de rapport · Commercial building

114　[1903; 33] S.S. Beman; Chicago (Castle Square): v.l.n.r.: 1/2. Hotel-Auditorium mit Annex; 3. Studebaker-Building (Geschäftshaus und Theater); 4. Chicago-Clubhaus · De gauche à droite: 1/2. Hôtel et théâtre, auditorium et annexe; 3. Immeuble Studebaker (théâtre et bureaux); 4. Club de Chicago · From left: 1/2. Hotel and theater, auditorium and annex; 3. Studebaker Building (theater and office building); 4. Chicago Club House

115　[1903; 69] Eisenlohr & Weigle; Stuttgart: Kaufhaus E. Breuninger · Grand magasin E. Breuninger · Breuninger department store

116   [1903; 1] A. Messel; Berlin-Schöneberg (Victoria-Luise-Platz): Vereinshaus · Siège d'une association · Club house

117   [1903; 2] A. Messel; Berlin-Schöneberg (Victoria-Luise-Platz): Vereinshaus, Hoffront · Siège d'une association, cour · Club house, courtyard

118   [1903; 77] Reinhardt & Süssenguth; Dessau: Rathaus · Hôtel de ville · Town Hall

119   [1903; 78] M. Dülfer; München · Munich (Bayerstraße 43): Hotel Terminus · Hôtel Terminus · Terminus Hotel

120　[1904; 3] J.F. Bentley; London · Londres: Römisch-katholische Westminster-Kathedrale, Ansicht von Süden · La cathédrale catholique romaine de Westminster, vue du sud · Roman Catholic Cathedral of Westminster, south view

121　[1904; 2] J.F. Bentley; London · Londres: Römisch-Katholische Westminster-Kathedrale, Ansicht von Norden · La cathédrale catholique romaine de Westminster, vue du nord · Roman Catholic Cathedral of Westminster, north view

122   [1904; 4] H. P. Berlage; Amsterdam: Börse · La bourse · Stock Exchange

123 [1904; 5] H.P. Berlage; Amsterdam: Börse · La bourse · Stock Exchange

124 [1904; 6] H.P. Berlage; Amsterdam: Börse, Innenansicht · La bourse, vue intérieure · Stock Exchange, interior

125 [1904; 7] Cremer & Wolffenstein; Berlin (Jerusalemer Straße 46−47): Geschäftshaus.
Etablissement commercial · Commercial building

126 [1904; 13] A.F.M. Lange, K. Berndt; Berlin (Lindenstraße 3): „Industriepalast" · Immeuble de
rapport · Apartment building with shops

127 [1904; 50] W. Walther; Berlin (Alte Jakobstraße 130−132): Versicherungsgesellschaft „Victoria"
Compagnie d'assurances „Victoria" · Victoria insurance company

128 [1904; 45] A.F.M. Lange, K. Berndt; Berlin (Lindenstraße 69): Geschäftshaus · Grand
magasin · Department store

129 [1904; 10] O. Marmorek: Wien · Vienne · Vienna (Wienstraße 28): Wohn- und Geschäftshaus · Immeuble de rapport · Apartment building with restaurant

130   [1904; 27] Ҕ. Seeling; Frankfurt/Main · Francfort-sur-le-Main · Frankfurt-on-Main: Städtisches Schauspielhaus · Théâtre municipal · Municipal Theater

131   [1904; 28] Ҕ. Seeling; Frankfurt/Main · Francfort-sur-le-Main · Frankfurt-on-Main: Städtisches
Schauspielhaus, Foyer · Théâtre municipal, foyer · Municipal Theater, foyer

132   [1904; 30] Ҕ. Seeling; Gera: Fürstliches Theater, Theatersaal · Théâtre princier, salle de spectacle
Court Theater, auditorium

133　[1904; 29] H. Seeling; Gera: Fürstliches Theater · Théâtre princier · Court Theater

134　[1904; 31] H. Seeling; Gera: Fürstliches Theater, Konzertsaal · Théâtre princier, salle de concert · Court Theater, auditorium

135 [1904; 60] Ö. Lechner; Budapest (Hold-utcza): Königlich-Ungarische Postsparkasse · Caisse d'épargne · Savings bank

136 [1904; 17] H. Kármán, J. von Ullmann; Budapest (Leopoldring 12): Wohn- und Geschäftshaus Immeuble de rapport · Apartment building with shops

137 [1904; 79] H. Gessner; Berlin-Charlottenburg (Mommsenstraße 6): Wohnhaus · Immeuble de rapport · Apartment building

138 [1904; 80] E. Seidl; München · Munich (Maximiliansplatz 3): Wohn- und Geschäftshaus Immeuble de rapport · Commercial building with apartments

139 [1904; 61] K. Engel; Berlin (Spandauer Straße 26–30): Kaufhaus N. Israel · Grand magasin N. Israel · N. Israel department store

140 [1904; 84] F.R. Voretzsch, K. Voigt; Dresden · Dresde (Lindengasse 2, 4, 6): Wohnhäusergruppe · Ensemble d'immeubles · Apartment complex

141 [1904; 14] H. Billing; Karlsruhe (Baischstraße 2): Einfamilienhaus · Maison individuelle One-family house

142 [1904; 69] Lambert & Stahl; Stuttgart (Birkenwaldstraße 97a): Villa · Private residence

143 [1904; 57] Lundt & Kallmorgen; Hamburg · Hambourg (Ferdinandstraße 38–40): Geschäftshaus · Immeuble à usage commercial · Commercial building

144 [1904; 76] H. Billing; Karlsruhe (Stephanienstraße 94–96): Wohnhäuser · Ensemble d'immeubles · Apartment complex

145 [1904; 81] M. Dülfer; München · Munich (Franz-Josef-Straße 7, 9, 11): Wohnhäusergruppe Ensemble d'immeubles · Apartment complex

146 [1904; 83] M. Dülfer; München · Munich (Franz-Josef-Str. 9, 11): Wohnhaus Immeuble · Apartment building

147   [1904; 43] Curjel & Moser: Karlsruhe (Bachstraße 2–4): Doppelvilla · Villa mitoyenne · Two-family house

148   [1904; 32] O. March: Koblenz · Coblence (Mainzer Straße 54): Villa Timme · Propriété de M. Timme · Timme house

149   [1904; 64] C. Vohl: Berlin-Grunewald (Parkstraße): Villa Gerstenberg

150   [1904; 48] F. Bolte, O. Welsch: Köln · Cologne (Stadtgarten): Musikpavillon · Kiosque à musique · Bandstand

51   [1904; 20] C.R. Ashbee: London · Londres (75 Cheyne Walk): Einfamilienhaus · Maison individuelle · One-family house

152   [1904; 21] W. Kromhout, H.G. Jansen; Amsterdam: American Hotel · Hôtel américain · American Hotel

[1904: 24] J. Deininger: Wien · Vienne · Vienna (Matzlindorfer Straße 6): Wohn- und Geschäftshaus · Immeuble de rapport · Apartment building with shops

HELP U ZELVE

154 [1904; 25] J. van Aspersen: Antwerpen · Anvers · Antwerp (Rue du Peuple): Versammlungshaus der Genossenschaft „Help U Zelve" · Foyer de la coopérative „Help U Zelve" · Headquarters of the „Help U Zelve" association

5 [1904; 42] E. Guy Dawber, E. Boevey; Copsetiam, Surrey: Gärtnerwohnhaus · Maison du jardinier · Gardener's cottage

6 [1904; 89] M. Littmann; München-Bogenhausen · Munich-Bogenhausen (Höchlstraße 2): Lindenhof, Villa · Propriété · Private residence

157   [1905; 1] A. Messel; Berlin (Leipziger Straße 132, 137): Warenhaus · Grand magasin · Department store

158   [1905; 2] M. Dülfer, München · Munich (Gedonstraße 6): Doppelwohnhaus · Immeuble mitoyen · Apartment building

159   [1905; 18] R. Schmid; Freiburg/Breisgau · Fribourg-en-Brisgau (Studtstraße 21a): Villa · One-family house

67

160 [1905; 6] R. Moennich, O. Schmalz; Berlin: Königliches Land- und Amtsgericht 1 Palais de justice · Law Courts

161 [1905; 10] Wehling & Ludwig; Köln · Cologne (Deutscher Ring 31): Villa Bestgen

162 [1905; 7] E. von Gotthilf; Wien · Vienne · Vienna (Krugerstraße 3): Stiftungshaus der Wiener Kaufmannschaft · Immeuble de rapport (Fondation de l'association de marchands de Vienne) Headquarters of the commercial union of Vienna

163 [1905; 11] Heilmann & Littmann; München · Munich (Theatinerstraße 38–39): Geschäfts- und Wohnhaus · Immeuble · Apartment building with shops

164 [1905; 12] —; Sundridge Park, England · Angleterre: Landhaus · Manoir · Country house

165   [1905; 19] Hart & Lesser; Berlin (Kurfürstendamm 8): Wohnhaus · Immeuble de rapport Apartment building

166   [1905; 22] B. Möhring; Traben/Mosel · Traben-sur-Moselle · Traben-on-Mosel: Hotel Clauss-Feist Hôtel · Hotel

167   [1905; 23] M. Dülfer; Dortmund: Stadttheater · Théâtre municipal · Municipal Theater

168   [1905; 25] Hofmann; Worms: Nibelungenschule · École · School

169   [1905; 58] Hüter; Cochem/Mosel · Cochem-sur-Moselle · Cochem-on-Mosel: Bahnhof · Gare · Railway station

170   [1905; 33] Coolidge & Carlson; Chestnut Hill, Massachusetts: Landhaus · Propriété · Country cottage

171   [1905; 49] Heilmann & Littmann: München · Munich (Möhlstraße 27): Villa Schneider

172 [1905; 62] Lambert & Stahl; Stuttgart (Lessingstraße 12): Villa · Private residence

173 [1905; 96] E. Bierot; Brüssel · Bruxelles · Brussels (Rue de la Vallée): Wohnhaus
Immeuble de rapport · Apartment building

4 [1905; 86] G. Serrurier; Lüttich · Liège (2, Avenue de Cointe): Einfamilienhaus · Hôtel particulier · Private residence

175　[1905; 37] G. Sommaruga; Mailand · Milan: Palazzo Castiglioni · Palais Castiglioni · Castiglioni Palace

[1905; 44] Hoeniger & Sedelmeier; Berlin (Kronenstraße/Markgrafenstraße): Geschäftshaus · Immeuble à usage commercial · Commercial building

177   [1905; 50] Korb & Giergl; Budapest (Kigyo-tér 1): Wohn- und Geschäftshaus · Immeuble de rapport · Apartment building with shops

178   [1905; 54] H. Billing; Pforzheim (Am Markt 4): Wohnhaus · Immeuble de rapport · Apartment building

179   [1905; 52] A. Greifzu; Mainz · Mayence (Kaiserstraße 76–78): Wohnhaus · Immeuble de rappo Apartment building

180   [1905; 51] Ḡ. vom Endt; Düsseldorf · Dusseldorf (Kasernenstraße 67 A): Wohnhaus Immeuble de rapport · Apartment building with shops

181   [1905; 53] R. Bauer; Düsseldorf · Dusseldorf (Steinstraße 13 D): Wohnhaus · Immeuble de rapport · Apartment building

182   [1905; 64] Ḡ. vom Endt; Düsseldorf · Dusseldorf (Königsallee 25): Wohn- und Geschäftshaus, neue Fassade · Immeuble, façade · Shop front

183   [1905; 56] Friesé, Brion & Haug: Straßburg · Strasbourg · Strassburg (Alter Weinmarkt 24): Wohn- und Geschäftshaus · Immeuble de rapport · Commercial building with apartments

184   [1905; 65] Th. Trautmann, Curjel & Moser: Karlsruhe (Waldstraße 13): Wohn- und Geschäftshaus · Immeuble de rapport · Apartment building with shops

185   [1905; 81] V. Horta: Brüssel · Bruxelles · Brussels (111, Rue Neuve): Geschäftshaus Grand magasin · Department store

186   [1905; 88] Gebr. Friedhofen: Koblenz · Coblence: Bristol-Hotel · Hôtel Bristol · Bristol Hotel

187   [1905; 82] A. Biberfeld; Berlin-Schlachtensee: Sanatorium

188   [1905; 83] A. Biberfeld; Berlin-Schlachtensee: Sanatorium

189   [1905; 67] G. von Bezold: Nürnberg · Nuremberg: Germanisches Nationalmuseum Musée · Museum

190   [1905; 90] B. Schmitz: Köln · Cologne: „Bismarckburg" · Villa · Private residence

[1905; 66] Fellner & Helmer; Wien · Vienne · Vienna (Mariahilfer Hauptstraße 42—44): Warenhaus · Grand magasin · Department store

192 [1906; 2] M. Dülfer; Bensheim/Bergstraße: Rathaus · Hôtel de ville · Town Hall

193 [1906; 3] M. Dülfer; Bensheim/Bergstraße: Rathaus, Innenansicht · Hôtel de ville, vue intérieure
Town Hall, interior

194 [1906; 4] M. Dülfer; Bensheim/Bergstraße: Rathaus, Innenansicht · Hôtel de ville, vue intérieure
Town Hall, interior

195 [1906; 5] A. Biberfeld; Berlin-Wilmersdorf (Nachodstraße 30): Wohnhaus · Immeuble de rapport · Apartment building

196 [1906; 14] Hart & Lesser; Berlin-Charlottenburg (Berliner Straße 146): Wohnhaus Immeuble de rapport · Apartment building

197 [1906; 18] Gebr. Friedhofen; Koblenz · Coblence (Kaiser-Wilhelm-Ring 48): Wohnhaus Immeuble de rapport · Apartment building

198 [1906; 46] Gebr. Friedhofen; Koblenz · Coblence (Kaiser-Wilhelm-Ring 50): Wohnhaus Immeuble de rapport · Apartment building

199   [1906; 8] Curjel & Moser; Mannheim; St. Johanniskirche · Eglise Saint-Jean · St. John's Church

200   [1906; 88] Schilling & Graebner; Strehlen, bei Dresden · environs de Dresde · near Dresden: Kirche · Eglise · Church

201   [1906; 89] Schilling & Graebner, Strehlen, bei Dresden · environs de Dresde · near Dresden: Kirche · Eglise · Church

202 [1906; 15] P. Saintenoy: Brüssel · Bruxelles · Brussels: Warenhaus „Old England" · Grand magasin „Old England" · Old England department store

85

203   [1906; 22] Hüter; Traben-Trarbach: Bahnhof · Gare · Railway station

204   [1906; 36] P. Tischmeyer; Lüttich · Liège (3–5, Avenue des Ormes): Doppelvilla · Villa mitoyenne
Two family house

205   [1906; 42] Schilling & Graebner; Freiburg/Breisgau · Fribourg-en-Brisgau (Turmseestraße 72):
Doppelvilla · Villa mitoyenne · Two-family house

206 [1906; 27] Erdmann & Spindler; Bad Godesberg (Kaiserstraße 5a): Villa Düren

207 [1906; 48] R. Weber; Berlin (Lindenstraße 86): Geschäftshaus · Immeuble à usage commercial · Commercial building

208 [1906; 33] E.G. Dawber; Stow-on-the-Wold, England · Angleterre: „Nether Swell Manor", Landsitz · Manoir · Nether Swell Manor

87

209   [1906; 34] J. Durm; Freiburg/Breisgau · Fribourg-en-Brisgau: Das neue Friedrichsgymnasium · Le gymnase Friedrich · Friedrich Gymnasium

210   [1906; 37] A. Langheinrich; Mannheim: Turnhalle · Salle de gymnastique · Gymnasium

[1906; 41] J. Durm; Heidelberg: Universitätsbibliothek · Bibliothèque universitaire · University library

212   [1906; 44] H. Billing; Karlsruhe (Kriegsstraße 188): Wirtshaus „Zur roten Taube" · Restaurant

213   [1906; 45] H. Billing; Karlsruhe (Kriegsstraße 188): Wirtshaus „Zur roten Taube" · Restaurant

4 [1906; 49] J. Vollmer, H. Jassoy; Stuttgart: Rathaus · Hôtel de ville · Town Hall   215   [1906; 60] A. Zabel; Berlin (Badstraße 60): Wohnhaus · Immeuble de rapport · Apartment building

[1906; 50] A. Meinig; Budapest (Szabadsag Ter 16): Wohn- und Geschäftshaus · Immeuble · Commercial building with apartments

217 [1906; 51] E. Linkenbach; Berlin-Charlottenburg (Eosanderstraße 31): Wohnhaus · Immeuble de rapport · Apartment building

218 [1906; 53] Kristeller & Sonnenthal; Frankfurt/Main · Francfort-sur-le-Main · Frankfurt-on-Main; Albert-Schumann-Theater · Théâtre · Theater

219 [1906; 52] Kristeller & Sonnenthal; Frankfurt/Main · Francfort-sur-le-Main · Frankfurt-on-Main: Albert-Schumann-Theater · Théâtre · Theater

220 [1906; 56] C. Reich, C. Riffer; Koblenz · Coblence (Friedrichstraße 50): Wohnhaus
Immeuble de rapport · Apartment building

221 [1906; 70] J. Welz; Berlin-Schöneberg (Bahnstraße 29/30): Wohn- und Geschäftshaus
Immeuble de rapport · Apartment building with shops

222 [1906; 61] P. Thömer, C. Vohl; Berlin-Moabit (Turmstraße 89—93): Kriminalgerichtsgebäude · Tribunal criminel · Criminal Court

223   [1906; 57] G. Freed; Mannheim (Mollstraße 58): Wohnhaus · Hôtel particulier · Private residence

224   [1906; 73] A. Müller; Tübingen · Tubingue: Haus der Landsmannschaft „Schottland" · Maison d´étudiants · Fraternity house

225   [1906; 59] A. Möller; Mannheim (Werderstraße 34): Villa Fasig · Propriété d´A. Fasig · Fasig house

226 [1906; 67] Lambert & Stahl; Stuttgart (Panoramastraße 15): Villa Steiner

227 [1906; 75] H. Meier; Berlin-Grunewald (Beymestraße/Hubertus-Bader-Straße):
Privathaus · Hôtel particulier · Private residence

228 [1906; 77] R. Mönnich, H. Dernburg, E. Petersen; Berlin-Charlottenburg; Neubau des Landgerichts 3 · Palais de justice · Law Courts

229   [1906; 100] B. Schmitz; Mannheim (Friedrichsplatz/Augustaanlage): Wohn- und Geschäftshaus · Immeuble · Apartment building with shops

230   [1906; 40] Th. Preckel; Pforzheim (Friedenstraße 30): Einfamilienhaus · Hôtel particulier
Private residence

231   [1906; 93] F. Lindhorst; Berlin-Charlottenburg (Fasenanstraße 86): Villa Schreib

232   [1906; 81] J. Plečnik: Wien · Vienne · Vienna (Bauernmarkt 5): Geschäfts- und Wohnhaus · Immeuble · Commercial building with apartments

233   [1906; 91] J. Alpár; Budapest: Österreichisch-Ungarische Bank · Banque · Bank

234   [1906; 87] E. von Gotthilf; Wien · Vienne · Vienna (Lothringer Straße 10): Haus der Kaufmannschaft · Maison de l'association de marchands · Merchants' guild hall

235   [1906; 78] A. Arkay; Budapest (Andrassystraße 127a): Villa · Private residence

236   [1906; 99] J. Hackhofer, F. Rumpelmayer; Wien · Vienne · Vienna (Neuwaldegg): Villa Marbach · Propriété de M. Marbach · Marbach house

99

237   [1906; 47] Ꜧ. Metzendorf; Darmstadt (Ꜧeerdweg 101): Villa · Private residence

238   [1906; 7] C. Wittmann; Mannheim (Friedrich-Carl-Straße 2–4): Wohnhausgruppe · Ensemble
d'immeubles · Apartment complex

239   [1906; 83] O. Mamorek; Wien · Vienne · Vienna (Windmühlgasse 24): Wohn- und
Geschäftshaus · Immeuble de rapport · Commercial building with apartments

240   [1907; 2] A. Messel; Berlin (Friedrich-Karl-Uier 2—4) Verwaltungsgebäude der AEG · Bâtiment administratif · AEG administration building

241   [1907; 8] O. Marmorek; Wien · Vienne · Vienna (Lerchengasse 3—5): Wohnhaus
Immeuble de rapport · Apartment building

242   [1907; 9] O. Marmorek; Wien · Vienne · Vienna (Lerchengasse 5): Wohnhaus · Immeuble
de rapport · Apartment building

243　[1907; 3] —; Heidelberg (Unter der Schanze): Wohnhäuser · Propriétés · Country houses

244　[1907; 30] B. Möhring; Traben/Mosel · Traben-sur-Moselle · Traben-on-Mosel: Haus Adolph Huesgen · Propriété de Adolph Huesgen · Adolph Huesgen house

245　[1907; 11] E. Seidl; München · Munich (Maria-Josepha-Straße 11): Villa Lautenbacher

246   [1907; 20] L. Bauer; Brünn (Schreibwaldstraße 148): Villa · Private residence

247   [1907; 80] B. Möhring; Traben/Mosel · Traben-sur-Moselle · Traben-on-Mosel: Villa Breuker

248   [1907; 22] H. Müller-Erkelenz; Köln · Cologne (Breitestraße/Langestraße): Geschäftshaus der Kölnischen Zeitung · Maison du journal Kölnische Zeitung · Office building of the Kölnische Zeitung

249   [1907; 24] J. Müller; Brünn (Franz-Josef-Straße 12): Wohnhaus · Immeuble de rapport · Apartment building

250   [1907; 25] J. Müller; Brünn (Franz-Josef-Straße 15—16): Wohnhaus · Immeuble de rapport Apartment building

251   [1907; 26] K. Fischl; Wien · Vienne · Vienna (Penzingerstraße 40): Wohnhaus · Immeuble de rapport · Apartment building

252   [1907; 27] L. Baumann; Wien · Vienne · Vienna (Waisenhausgasse): K.u.K. Konsularakademie l'académie consulaire royale et impériale · Imperial consular academy

253   [1907; 33] H. Gessner; Brünn (Franz-Josef-Straße 24—26): Gebäude der Bezirkskrankenkasse Caisse d'assurance-maladie · Medical insurance building

254   [1907; 34] L. Stentzler, A. Stentzler; Leipzig (Brühl 28—30): Geschäftshaus · Immeuble à usage commercial · Commercial building

255   [1907; 61] W. Gerbens, P. Taeger; Berlin (Gertraudtenstraße/Roßstraße): Warenhaus Peek & Cloppenburg · Grand magasin Peek & Cloppenburg · Peek & Cloppenburg department store

256 [1907; 38] Ħ. Metzendorf; Bensheim/Bergstraße (Ernst-Ludwig-Straße 23): Villa · Private residence

257 [1907; 45] St. Mattar; Köln-Marienburg · Cologne-Marienbourg (Lindenallee 41): Villa · Private residence

258 [1907; 41] G. Wehling; Düsseldorf · Dusseldorf (Prinz-Georg-Straße 37, 39, 41): Einfamilienhäuser Maisons mitoyennes · Apartment buildings

259 [1907; 67] O. Marmorek; Wien · Vienne · Vienna (Wickenburggasse/Floriangasse): Wohnhaus Immeuble de rapport · Apartment building

260 [1907; 58] O. March; Köln · Cologne (Bayenthal-Marienburg): Evangelische Kirche · L'église protestante · Protestant church

261 [1907; 100] —, Budapest (Istvan-ut 79): Villa · Private residence

262 [1907; 56] J. Alpár; Budapest (Freiheitsplatz): Börse · La bourse · Stock Exchange

BÖRSE FÜR CZERNOWITZ

263   [1907; 62] O. Marmorek; Czernowitz, Bukowina · Bukovine: Börsengebäude, Entwurf · Le projet de bourse · Design for the Stock Exchange Building

54 [1907; 63] K.T. Lutz; Partenkirchen: Pension Gibson · Hôtel · Hotel

5 [1907; 68] M.G. Gradl, A. Riffart; Köln · Cologne (Fürst-Pückler-Straße/Joeststraße): Villa · Private residence

266 [1907; 82] Kumpf & Wolf; Heidelberg (Klingenteichstraße 15a): Villa · Private residence

109

267　[1907; 69] Linke & Leukert; Dresden · Dresde (Nürnberger Straße 36/38): Wohnhaus · Immeuble de rapport · Apartment building

268　[1907; 70] L. Sandkaulen; Düsseldorf · Dusseldorf (Prinz-Georg-Straße 122): Wohnhaus
Immeuble de rapport · Apartment building

269　[1907; 71] Hart & Lesser; Berlin (Poststraße 30): Geschäftshaus · Immeuble à usage
commercial · Commercial building

270   [1907; 72] J. Hirte: Berlin (Markgrafenstraße 92/93): Geschäftshaus Unionbau · Maison de commerce Unionbau · Unionbau, commercial building

271 [1907; 75] H. Reitsamer; Köln · Cologne (Volksgartenstraße 24): Wohnhaus · Immeuble de rapport · Apartment building

272 [1907; 76] K. Moritz; Köln · Cologne (Wallrafplatz): „Stollwerckhaus" · Maison de commerce Stollwerckhaus · Stollwerckhaus, commercial building

273 [1907; 78] K. Moritz; Köln · Cologne (Straße am Hof): „Stollwerckhaus" · Maison de commerce Stollwerckhaus · Stollwerckhaus, commercial building

274 [1907; 79] K. Moritz; Köln · Cologne: „Stollwerckhaus", Durchgang · Passage · Galleria

275   [1907: 83] L. Otte; Berlin-Charlottenburg (Bismarckstraße 12): Wohnhaus · Immeuble de rapport · Apartment building

276   [1907: 97] T. Müller; Köln · Cologne (Moltkestraße 27): Wohnhaus · Immeuble de rapport · Apartment building

277   [1907: 88] K. Bestelmeyer; München · Munich (Dachauer Straße 8): Wohnhaus · Immeuble de rapport · Apartment building

278 [1907; 91] W. Frhr. von Tettau; Honnef: „Feuerschloß" · Villa · Private residence

279 [1907; 99] O. Stor; Berlin-Neubabelsberg (Kaiserstraße 39); Villa · Private residence

280   [1908; 2] Fr. von Thiersch; Wiesbaden: Kurhaus · Maison de cure · Spa hotel

281   [1908; 3] Fr. von Thiersch; Wiesbaden: Kurhaus · Maison de cure · Spa hotel

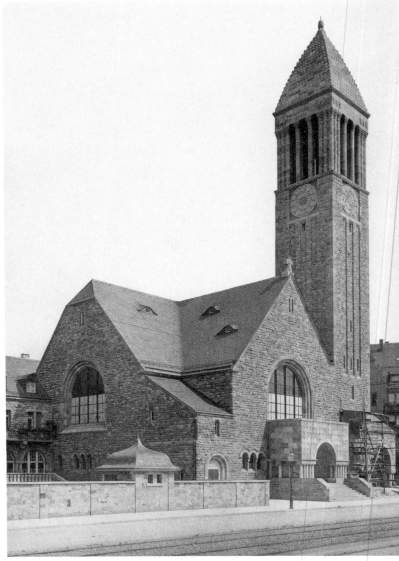

282   [1908; 4] H. Metzendorf; Baden-Baden: Villa Becker · Propriété de M. Becker · Becker house

283   [1908; 20] Curjel & Moser; Karlsruhe (Melanchthonplatz): Lutherkirche · L'église Luther Lutheran church

284   [1908; 12] H.B. Wieland; Wiesbaden: Villa Henkell · Propriété d'O. Henkell · Henkell house

285   [1908: 7] K. Wilde: Frankfurt/Main · Francfort-sur-le-Main · Frankfurt-on-Main: Victoriaschule · Ecole Victoria · Victoria School

286   [1908: 97] Th. Fischer: München · Munich: Max-Josef-Brücke · Le pont Max Josef · Max Josef Bridge

287 [1908; 10] Ḥ. Billing; Mannheim: Kunstausstellungsgebäude · Bâtiment d'exposition · Art Exhibition Building

288 [1908; 45] von Mellinger, Kurz, Maxon & Rosenstock; München · Munich: Königliches Bayerisches Armee-Museum · Musée militaire royal bavarois · Royal Bavarian Army Museum

289   [1908; 11] K. Moritz: Köln · Cologne (Schildergasse 38/42): Geschäftshaus Hettlage
Maison de commerce Hettlage · Hettlage commercial building

290   [1908; 17] E. von Gotthilf: Wien · Vienne · Vienna (Graben 17): Wohn- und Geschäftshaus
Immeuble de rapport · Apartment building with shops

291   [1908; 51] E. Faesch: Basel · Bâle (Freiestraße 109): Schweizer Kreditbank
Banque · Bank

292   [1908; 53] Heilmann & Littmann: München · Munich (Sendlingerstraße 80): Geschäftshaus der
Münchner Neuesten Nachrichten · Maison d'un journal · Office building of a journal

293   [1908; 16] F. Pützer; Darmstadt (Prinz-Christian-Weg 11): Villa · Private residence

294   [1908; 19] F. L. Mayer; Karlsruhe (Richard-Wagner-Straße/Schubertstraße): Villa · Private résidence

95 [1908; 22] G. von Mayenburg: Dresden-Loschwitz · Dresde-Loschwitz (Wunderlichstraße): Villa · Private residence

6 [1908; 49] F. Pützer: Darmstadt: Arbeiterkolonie E. Merck, Beamten- und Arbeiterwohnhäuser · Le lotissement E. Merck, habitations ouvrières · The E. Merck Colony, workers' houses

297　[1908; 1] A. Messel; Berlin: Nationalbank für Deutschland · Banque nationale allemande
The German National Bank

298　[1908; 47] F. Pützer; Darmstadt: Arbeiterkolonie E. Merck, Verwaltungsgebäude · Le
lotissement E. Merck, le bâtiment administratif · The E. Merck Colony, administration building

299　[1908; 72] R. Jeblinger; Freiburg/Breisgau · Fribourg-en-Brisgau: Erzbischöfliches
Ordinariat · Bâtiment administratif de l'archiépiscopat · Archepiscopal office building

300　[1908; 86] C. Schmidt; Berlin-Wilmersdorf (Helmstedter Straße 2): Wohnhaus · Immeuble
de rapport · Apartment building

301   [1908; 30] M. Braillard; Juragebirge, Kanton Bern · Le Jura, canton de Berne · The Jura
Mountains, canton Bern: Schulhaus · Ecole · School

302   [1908; 38] H. Metzendorf; Darmstadt (Alexandraweg 6): Villa · Private residence

3   [1908; 100] A. Bacher; Brünn (Schreitwaldstraße 144): Villa · Private residence

304   [1908; 44] S. von Quittner; Budapest (Franz-Josef-Platz): Lebensversicherungsgesellschaft „The Gresham" · Compagnie d'assurances „The Gresham" · Gresham life insurance building

305   [1908; 56] L. Neher, S. Simon, R. Voltz; Frankfurt/Main · Francfort-sur-le-Main · Frankfurt-on-Main (Jordanstraße): Auditoriengebäude der Akademie für Sozial- und Handelswissenschaften · Bâtiment de l'Université des Sciences Economiques et Sociales · The lecture hall building of the Academy for Sociology and Economics

306 [1908; 70] H. Hartl: München (Widenmayerstraße): Turnhalle des Turnvereins Jahn · Etablissement de gymnastique · Gymnasium

307 [1908; 95] Curjel & Moser: Karlsruhe (Rintheimerstraße 15): Villa Hoepfner

125

308   [1908; 76] F.W. Werz, P. Huber; Wiesbaden (Kaiser-Friedrich-Ring/Moritzstraße): Landeshaus · Palais du gouvernement · Government building

309   [1908; 87] K. Neher; Frankfurt/Main · Francfort-sur-le-Main · Frankfurt-on-Main (Victoria-Allee): Museum Senckenberg · Musée · Museum

310   [1908; 78] Müller-Jena B.D.A. Köln; Recklinghausen: Rathaus · Hôtel de ville · Town Hall

311   [1908; 79] Müller-Jena B.D.A. Köln; Recklinghausen: Rathaus; Treppenhaus · Hôtel de ville, cage d'escalier · Town Hall, staircase

312   [1909; 1] A. Messel; Berlin (Bendlerstraße 6): Wohnhaus · Maison · Apartment building

313   [1909; 2] A. Messel; Berlin (Bendlerstraße 6): Wohnhaus, Eingang · Maison, entrée · Apartment building, entrance

314   [1909; 3] W.H. Schacht; Bremen · Bréme (Am Brill): „Rolandhaus" · Immeuble à usage commercial · Commercial building

315   [1909; 12] H. vom Endt; Düsseldorf · Dusseldorf: Geschäftshaus des General-Anzeiger · Maison du journal General-Anzeiger · Office building of the General-Anzeiger

316   [1909; 4] C. Börnstein; Bremen · Brême (Am Ostertor): Verwaltungs- und Polizeigebäude · Bâtiment d'administration et de police · Administration and police office building

317   [1909; 5] C. Börnstein; Bremen · Brême (Am Ostertor): Verwaltungs- und Polizeigebäude · Bâtiment d'administration et de police · Administration and police office building

318   [1909; 34] k. Steinmetz; München · Munich (Möhlstraße 45): Wohnhaus · Maison · Apartment building

129

319   [1909; 7] W. Blanke; Bremen · Brême (Blumenthalstraße 14): Wohnhaus · Hôtel particulier · One-family house

320   [1909; 58] W. May; Düsseldorf · Dusseldorf (Herderstraße 59): Wohnhaus · Immeuble de rapport Apartment building

321   [1909; 32] Jensen; Kopenhagen · Copenhague · Copenhagen: Landhaus · Maison de campagne · Private residence

323 [1909; 17] H. Eberhardt; Frankfurt/Main · Francfort-sur-le-Main · Frankfurt-on-Main (Morgensternstraße): Schillerschule · Ecole Schiller · Schiller School

324 [1909; 46] G.H. Platz; Frankfurt/Main · Francfort-sur-le-Main · Frankfurt-on-Main (Sachsenhausen, Gartenstraße 51, 53, 55): Wohnhäusergruppe · Maisons mitoyennes · Apartment complex

325 [1909; 20] G. Radel, Freytag & Wurzbach; Hamburg · Hambourg (Großer Burstah 15—17):
Geschäftshaus Gertig · Maison de commerce Gertig · Gertig commercial building

326 [1909; 26] Freytag & Wurzbach; Hamburg · Hambourg (Neuer Wall 27—29): Geschäftshaus
Immeuble à usage commercial · Commercial building

327 [1909; 27] Freytag & Wurzbach; Hamburg · Hambourg (Neuer Wall 26—28):
Geschäftshaus · Immeuble à usage commercial · Commercial building

328 [1909; 47] R. Strecker; Darmstadt (Schloßgartenstraße 5): Wohn- und Geschäftshaus · Immeuble de rapport
Apartment building with shops

329 [1909; 21] J.G. Rambatz, W. Jolosse; Hamburg · Hambourg (Alsterdam 4/5): Kontorhaus
Immeuble à usage commercial · Commercial building

330 [1909; 23] Müller-Jena B.D.A., Köln; Recklinghausen: Rheinisch-Westfälische
Discontogesellschaft · Banque · Bank

331 [1909; 24] J. Theede; Kiel: Restaurant Fürstenhof

332 [1909; 25] F. Brantzky; Kiel: Kaufhaus W. Jacobsen · Grand magasin W. Jacobsen
W. Jacobsen department store

333　[1909; 28] B. Aichner; Basel · Bâle (Schützenmattstraße 39–53): Wohnhäusergruppe · Maisons mitoyennes · Apartment buildings

334　[1909; 86] W. May; Düsseldorf · Dusseldorf (Graf-Adolph-Straße 32/34): Doppelwohnhaus · Maison mitoyenne · Apartment building

335　[1909; 89] H. Lettner; München · Munich (Romanstraße 5): Wohnhaus · Immeuble de rapport · Apartment building

336　[1909; 87] O. Engler; Dortmund: Kaufhaus Hettlage · Grand magasin Hettlage · Hettlage department store

337　[1909; 31] H. Toebelmann, H. Groß; Berlin-Charlottenburg (Kurfürstendam 56–59): Wohnhäusergruppe · Ensemble d'immeubles · Apartment complex

338　[1909; 62] F. Bach; Hamburg · Hambourg (Spitalerstraße): „Semperhaus" · Immeuble à usage commercial · Commercial building

339 [1909; 83] J. Radke; Düsseldorf, Dusseldorf: Stahlhof · Immeuble à usage commercial · Commercial building

340 [1909; 33] R. Rehlen; München · Munich (Hohenzollernstraße): Schule · Ecole · School

341   [1909; 50] S. Baumgarten, S. Herzog; Budapest (Istvan-ut 95): Landestaubstummeninstitut · Etablissement pour des sourds-muets · Institute for the deaf and dumb

342 [1909; 52] H. vom Endt; Düsseldorf · Dusseldorf (Grabenstraße): Königliches Amtsgericht Tribunal royal · Royal Law Courts building

343 [1909; 55] C. Kühn, F. Lindhorst; Berlin (Bernburgerstraße 24–25): Geschäftshaus der Neuen Preußischen (Kreuz-) Zeitung · Maison du journal Neue Preußische (Kreuz-) Zeitung · Office building of the Neue Preußische (Kreuz-) Zeitung

44 [1909; 67] H. Stammann, G. Zinnow; Hamburg · Hambourg (Große Bleichen 31/ Bleichen-Brücke 10): Kaufmannshaus · Immeuble · Commercial building

345 [1909; 85] E. Stenhammer; Stockholm: Grand Hôtel Royal · Royal Grand Hotel

139

346   [1909; 56] W. Stemering, J. Habicht; Berlin-Charlottenburg-Westend (Platanenallee 14): Landhaus · Maison de campagne · Country house

347   [1909; 60] G. Wickop; Darmstadt (Roquetteweg 15): Villa · Private residence

140

48   [1909; 91] A. Oppenheim; Kopenhagen · Copenhague · Copenhagen (Engskistevej 6): Landhaus · Maison de campagne · Private residence

49   [1909; 98] Kenep & Wendel; Summerville, Georgia: Landhaus von F.H. Denny · Maison de campagne de F.H. Denny · F.H. Denny Country House

350 [1909; 71] O. Kaufmann; Berlin (Ritterstraße 78): Geschäftshaus · Immeuble à usage commercial · Commercial building

51   [1909; 80] H. Bull; Christiana/Oslo: Regierungsgebäude · Palais du gouvernement · Government building

352 [1909; 81] Holabird & Roche; Chicago: Universitäts-Clubgebäude · Bâtiment du club de l'université · University Club

353 [1910; 1] W. Spickendorff: Berlin-Charlottenburg (Berliner Straße 137): „Cecilienhaus"
Bureaux · Office building

354 [1910; 17] A. Weber: Berlin-Friedenau (Saarstraße 8): Wohnhaus · Immeuble de rapport
Apartment building

355 [1910; 24] H. Lassen, B. Taut: Berlin-Charlottenburg (Bismarckstraße 10): Wohnhaus · Immeuble de rapport · Apartment building

356   [1910; 5] C. Brümmer; Kopenhagen · Copenhague · Copenhagen (Lundvangsvej 12): Landhaus Dr. Möller · Propriété de campagne · Private residence

357   [1910; 6] Curjel & Moser; Karlsruhe (Beethovenstraße 1–5): Wohnhäusergruppe · Maisons mitoyennes · Apartment building

358 [1910; 11] H. Metzendorf; Worms (Röderstraße 8): Villa Guggenheim

359 [1910; 16] F. Eichwede; Hannover · Hanovre (Seelhorststraße 18): Villa · Private residence

147

360　[1910; 26] H. Billing; Karlsruhe (Moltkestraße 35): Villa · Private residence

361　[1910; 27] C. Reich; Koblenz · Coblence (Kaiser-Wilhelm-Ring 4): Wohnhaus · Immeuble de rapport · Apartment building

362　[1910; 33] Gebr. Friedhofen; Koblenz · Coblence (Mainzer Straße 42): Wohnhaus Maison · Apartment building

363　[1910; 95] Curjel & Moser; Basel · Bâle (Schützenmattstraße 55): Wohnhaus · Maison · Apartment building

364   [1910; 30] A.F.M. Lange, C. Berndt; Berlin (Friedrichstraße 181): Geschäftshaus
Immeuble à usage commercial · Commercial building

365   [1910; 36] Rindsfüsser & Kühn; Worms (Marktplatz 5–7): Kaufhaus C.M. Goldschmidt · Grand magasin
C. M. Goldschmidt · C.M. Goldschmidt department store

366   [1910; 38] R. Leibnitz; Berlin (Leipziger Straße 24/Friedrichstraße 58): Geschäftshaus Mädler
Grand magasin Mädler · Mädler office building

367   [1910; 79] Eitel & Steigleder; Stuttgart (Kleine Königstraße 7): Schauspielhaus · Théâtre · Theater

149

368 [1910; 37] G. Metzendorf; Worms (Mozartstraße 4–6): Doppelwohnhaus · Maison mitoyenne · Apartment building

369 [1910; 57] Peringer & Rogler; Nürnberg · Nuremberg (Prinzregentenufer 9): Wohnhaus Immeuble de rapport · Apartment building

370 [1910; 99] Eitel & Steigleder; Stuttgart (Marienstraße 10): Warenhaus Kaiserhof · Grand magasin Kaiserhof · Kaiserhof department store

371   [1910; 64] C. Hempel; Pelonken, bei Oliva/Danzig · environs d'Oliva/Dantzig · near Oliva/Danzig: „Axthof" · Propriété de campagne · Country house

372   [1910; 63] C. Hempel; Pelonken, bei Oliva/Danzig · environs d'Oliva/Dantzig · near Oliva/Danzig: „Axthof" · Propriété de campagne · Country house

373   [1910; 50] Ch. Whittlesey; San Francisco: „Pacific Building", Geschäftshaus · Immeuble à usage commercial · Pacific Building

374   [1910; 72] Bieber & Vanwerden; Nürnberg · Nuremberg (Laufentorgraben 37, 39, 41, 43): Wohnhäusergruppe · Ensemble d'immeubles · Apartment complex

375 [1910; 74] H. Ritter, E. Rückgauer; Mannheim: Deutsche Diskonto-Gesellschaft · Banque · Bank

376 [1910; 75] Walter & Rahm; Berlin (Linkstraße 4–5): Kaiserliches Postamt 9 · Bureau de poste · Post office

377   [1910; 58] C. Brümmer; Kopenhagen · Copenhague · Copenhagen (Stanmöllevej 56): Landhaus · Maison de campagne · Country house

378   [1910; 91] Gebr. Rank; München · Munich (Pullach): Landhaus der Kunstmalerin Klara Walther · Maison de campagne · Country house

379   [1910; 76] B. Kramer; Bielefeld (Feilenstraße 31): Fabrikgebäude · Bâtiment industriel · Factory building

380   [1910; 85] Rittmeyer & Fürrer B.S.A.; Winterthur: Landhaus des Herrn Müller-Renner · Propriété de campagne · Country house

381   [1910; 87] P. Peters; Erfurt: Gutenbergschule · Ecole Gutenberg · Gutenberg School

382 [1910; 88] Heilmann & Littmann; München · Munich (Briennerstraße 56): Café Odeon · Odeon Café

157

383 [1911; 1] Heilmann & Littmann; München · Munich (Kaufingerstraße 11/12): Geschäftshaus
Immeuble · Commercial building

384 [1911; 6] S. von Quittner; Budapest: Kommerzialbank · Banque · Bank

385 [1911; 8] J.A. Maurette, A.Heuchoz; Genf · Genève · Geneva: Banque Populaire Suisse · Bank

386 [1911; 19] Heim & Früh; Stuttgart (Königstraße 78): Geschäftshaus Wilhelmbau · Immeuble à
usage commercial · Commercial building

387 [1911; 2] M.H. Kühne; Bern · Berne (Elfenstraße 16): Villa · Private residence

388 [1911; 3] Froté Westermann & Co., R. Angst; Zürich · Zurich (Seefeldquai 1): Uto-Garage · Garage-automobile · Automobile garage

389   [1911; 5] Curjel & Moser; Zürich · Zürich: Kunsthaus · Musée des beaux-arts · Art museum

390   [1911; 16] Mettegang & Müller; Mühlheim/Rhein · Mühlheim-sur-le-Rhin · Mühlheim-on-Rhine: Bahnhof · Gare · Railway station

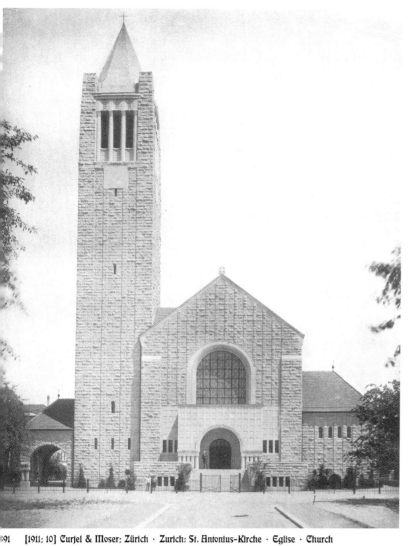

391   [1911; 10] Curjel & Moser; Zürich · Zurich: St. Antonius-Kirche · Eglise · Church   392   [1911; 11] Curjel & Moser; Zürich · Zurich: St. Antonius-Kirche · Eglise · Church

393   [1911; 91] Schmidtmann & Klemp; Dortmund (Ardeystraße 36): Bürogebäude · Bureaux · Office building

394   [1911; 17] Verbeek; Köln · Cologne (Agrippina-Ufer): Lagerhaus · Entrepôt · Warehouse

395   [1911; 41] A. Buxbaum; Darmstadt: Städtisches Schwimmbad · Bains municipaux · Municipal baths

396   [1911; 64] McKim, Mead & White; New York: „Downtown Building" · Gratte-ciel · Downtown Building, Knickerbocker Trust Company

397　[1911; 27] G. Wickop; Darmstadt: Technische Hochschule · École supérieure d'enseignement technique · Technical University

398　[1911; 34] M. Camoletti; Genf · Genève · Geneva: Museum · Musée · Museum

399 [1911; 30] O. Berlich; Berlin-Dahlem (Friedenthalstraße 4): Villa · Private residence

400 [1911; 61] P.L. Troost; Nürnberg · Nuremberg (Liebigstraße 3/Prinzregentenufer): Haus Chillingworth · Villa · Private residence

401 [1911; 39] G. Barbogli; Bergamo · Bergame (Via Vittorio Emmanuele): Villa Fricconi

402 [1911; 40] G. Chevalley; Turin (Via Silvio Pelligo 31): Villa Gonella

403　[1911; 51] H. Eberhardt; Freiburg/Breisgau · Fribourg-en-Brisgau (Mercystraße 26):
Landhaus · Propriété de campagne · Country house

404　[1911; 60] H. Müller; Zürich · Zurich (Eisenbahnstraße 12): Wohnhaus · Immeuble de rapport
Apartment building

405　[1911; 77] P. Behrens; Hagen-Eppenhausen (Haßleyerstraße 37): Landhaus Schröder · Propriété de campagne · Schröder house

406 [1911; 54] K. Moritz, W. Stahl; Düsseldorf · Dusseldorf (Lindemannstraße 34): Wohnhaus · Hôtel
particulier · Apartment building

407 [1911; 94] Schöß & Redelstorff; Lübeck (Johannisstraße/Breitenstraße): Geschäftshaus
Immeuble à usage commercial · Office building

408 [1911; 57] R. Linder; Basel · Bâle (Spalenring/Ahornstraße): Wohnhausgruppe · Ensemble d'immeubles · Apartment building

409   [1911; 71] E. Chevallaz; Genf · Genève · Geneva (2, Avenue Pictet de Rochemont):
Wohnhaus · Immeuble de rapport · Apartment building

410   [1911; 90] Schmidtmann & Klemp; Dortmund (Hiltroppwall/Hohestraße): „Posthof", Geschäfts- und Wohnhaus
Immeuble de rapport · Apartment building with shops

411   [1911; 89] Gerstenecker; München · Munich (Sonnenstraße 5): Wohn- und Geschäftshaus · Immeuble de rapport · Apartment building with shops

412 [1911; 78] P. Behrens; Hagen-Eppenhausen (Haßleyerstraße): Landhäuser Cuno und Schröder · Villas de MM. Cuno et Schröder · Cuno and Schröder houses

413 [1911; 79] P. Behrens; Hagen-Eppenhausen (Haßleyerstraße): Landhaus Cuno · Villa de M. Cuno · Cuno house

414   [1911; 80] Gebr. Ludwigs; Hagen-Eppenhausen (Eppenhausener Straße 151): Villa · Private residence

415   [1911; 81] Gebr. Ludwigs; Hagen-Eppenhausen (Eppenhausener Straße 155): Villa · Private residence

416   [1911; 21] K. Hengerer; Stuttgart (Königstraße 72): Württembergische Vereinsbank · Banque Bank

417   [1911; 59] A. Weiß; Berlin (Zimmerstraße 14/15): Geschäftshaus · Immeuble à usage commercial · Commercial building

418   [1911; 65] Beutinger & Steiner; Heilbronn (Kaiserstraße 46): Wohnhaus Immeuble de rapport · Apartment building

419   [1911; 67] A. Eitel; Stuttgart (Königstraße 318): Geschäftshaus · Grand magasin · Office building

420 [1912; 1] P. Gaertner, J. Bernd; Köln · Cologne (Apostelnkloster 5): Geschäftshaus · Immeuble à usage commercial · Commercial building

421 [1912; 2] Ph. Holzmann & Co., Rückgauer; Wiesbaden: Filiale der Deutschen Bank · Banque · The German Bank

422 [1912; 4] Schreiterer & Below B.D.A.; Köln · Cologne (Wörtherstraße 10): Bürogebäude · Immeuble de bureaux · Office building

423 [1912; 22] Rindsfüsser & Kühn; Frankfurt/Main · Francfort-sur-le-Main · Frankfurt-on-Main (Guiollettstraße 2): Versicherungsgebäude · Société d'assurances · Insurance company building

424　[1912; 5] H. Metzendorf; Bensheim: Eingang zur Landhaussiedlung Schönberger Tal · Entrée du lotissement „Schönberger Tal" · Entrance to country housing estate Schönberger Tal

425　[1912; 18] Mettegang; Bad Godesberg: Bahnhof · Gare · Railway station

426   [1912; 14] F. Schumacher; Hagen (Kreishausstraße 5): Villa H.E. Osthaus · Villa · Private residence

427   [1912; 15] G. Metzendorf; Siegen (Giersbergstraße 17): Landhaus Fischer · Maison de campagne · Private residence

428   [1912; 16] G. Metzendorf; Siegen: Landhaus H. Gontermann · Propriété de campagne · Private residence

429   [1912; 29] L. Kraft; Bad Nauheim (Karlstraße): Villa Karlsbrunn · Villa · Private residence

430   [1912; 33] C.Th. Merz; Heidelberg-Neuenheim (Bergstraße 107): Einfamilienhaus · Maison particulière · One-family house

431   [1912; 23] H. Müller-Erkelenz; Köln · Cologne: Haus Diehl, Büro- und Geschäftshaus
Immeuble à usage commercial · Office building

432   [1912; 55] F. Niebel; Hagen (Elberfelder Straße 47): Geschäftshaus · Immeuble à usage
commercial · Commercial building

433   [1912; 59] Ph. Fritz; Köln · Cologne (Hohestraße/Minoritenstraße): Café Palant · Palant Café

434   [1912; 76] Rindsfüsser & Kühn; Frankfurt/Main · Francfort-sur-le-Main · Frankfurt-on-Main
(Zeil/Liebfrauenstraße): Geschäftshaus Zeilpalast · Immeuble à usage commercial · Commercial
building

435 [1912; 25] F. Blume; Berlin-Charlottenburg: Verwaltungsgebäude Siemens & Halske AG · Bâtiment administratif de Siemens & Halske · Siemens & Halske administration building

436 [1912; 31] O. Engler; Frankfurt/Main · Francfort-sur-le-Main · Frankfurt-on-Main: Kaufhaus S. Wronker & Co. · Grand magasin Wronker & Co. · Wronker & Co. department store

437 [1912; 100] A. Baron; Wien · Vienne · Vienna (Fleischmarkt/Rotenturmstraße): Geschäfts- und Wohnhaus · Immeuble · Commercial building with apartments

438 [1912; 37] H. Billing; Karlsruhe (Moltkestraße 33): Villa · Private residence

439 [1912; 38] H. Billing; Karlsruhe (Weberstraße 1–3): Doppelwohnhaus · Maison mitoyenne · Apartment building

440 [1912; 39] F. & H. Konitzer; Bern · Berne (Hallwylstraße 42, 40, 38): Einfamilienhäuser · Habitations individuelles · One-family houses

441 [1912; 42] P. Bonatz; Biebrich/Rhein · Biebrich-sur-le-Rhin · Biebrich-on-Rhine: Sektkellerei Henkell & Co., Ehrenhof · Maison Henkell & Co., négociant en vins mousseux, cour d'honneur Henkell Trocken wine cellars and courtyard

442   [1912; 48] W. Jost, H. Jobst; Bad Nauheim: Badeanlage, Badehaus 4 und Verwaltungsgebäude · Etablissement de bains, unité thermale n° 4 et bâtiment administratif · Spa courtyard with bath house 4 and administration building

443   [1912; 49] W. Jost, H. Jobst; Bad Nauheim: Badeanlage, Schmuckhof von Badehaus 2 · Etablissement de bains, cour intérieure de l'unité thermale n° 2 · Spa courtyard of bath house 2

444 [1912; 62] W. Kurth; Köln · Cologne (Neumarkt 31): Haus Carl Schirp · Immeuble
Commercial building

445 [1912; 74] W. Hessling; Leipzig (Brühl 14/16): Geschäftshaus · Immeuble
Commercial building

446 [1912; 73] Schmidtmann & Klemp; Dortmund (Ostenhellweg): Kaufhaus · Grand magasin · Commercial building

447 [1912; 78] A. Müller; Darmstadt (Nicolaiweg 16): Villa · Private residence

448 [1912; 84] H. Metzendorf; Bensheim (Roonstraße 5): Villa des Kunstmalers Bahner · Villa · Country house

449 [1912; 82] A. Schütze; Magdeburg · Magdebourg (Breiteweg 110): Geschäfts- und Wohnhaus Immeuble · Apartment building with shops

450 [1912; 90] J.J. Burnet; London · Londres (Aldwych): Versicherungsgesellschaft · Compagnie d'assurances · Insurance company building

451 [1912; 93] S. Sziklai; Budapest (Andrássy-ut 39): Kaufhaus · Grand magasin Department store

452 [1912; 94] A. Kármán, J. von Ullmann; Budapest (Bécsi-utcza/Erzsébet-tér): Geschäfts- und Wohnhaus Immeuble de rapport · Apartment building with shops

453 [1912; 87] R. Orley; Wien · Vienne · Vienna (Sternwartestraße 62—64): Villa · Private residence

454 [1912; 97] G. Metzendorf; Frechen (Zeche Wachtberg 1): Arbeiterhäuser · Habitations ouvrières · Workers' houses

455   [1912; 91] H. Poelzig; Breslau (Menzelstraße 87); Menzelstraße/Wölflstraße); Wohnhausgruppe · Ensemble d'immeubles · Apartment buildings

456   [1912; 92] H. Poelzig; Breslau (Menzelstraße 87); Wohnhaus · Immeuble · Apartment building

457 [1912; 95] P. Zimmerreimer; Berlin-Charlottenburg (Westend; Lindenallee 5): Villa · Private residence

458 [1912; 99] H. Poelzig; Breslau (Hohenzollernstraße 115/117): Wohnhaus · Immeuble Apartment building

459 [1912; 35] E. Beck; Karlsruhe (Kriegstraße 64d): Einfamilienhaus · Maison individuelle · One-family house

187

460 [1913; 1] E. Leschnitzer; Berlin (Lindenstraße/Feilnerstraße): Geschäftshaus · Immeuble à usage commercial · Commercial building

461 [1913; 18] E. Meissner, M. Socke; Dresden · Dresde (Prager Straße 54): Geschäftshaus Immeuble à usage commercial · Commercial building

462 [1913; 12] E. von Gotthilf, A. Neumann; Wien · Vienne · Vienna (Am Schottenring): Geschäftshaus des Wiener Bankvereins · Banque · Bank

463 [1913; 19] P. Zimmerreimer; Berlin (Köthenerstraße 44): Geschäfts- und Bürohaus „Deutscher Credit-Verein" · Institut de crédit · Offices of the German Credit Union

464 [1913; 23] P. Nathansohn; Berlin (Kaiser-Wilhelm-Straße 38): Geschäftshaus Immeuble à usage commercial · Commercial building

465 [1913; 25] Bielenberg & Moser; Duisburg · Duisbourg: Börse · La bourse · Stock Exchange

466 [1913; 30] P. Bonatz, C. Schöne; Köln · Cologne (Zeppelinstraße 5—7): Geschäftshaus Etablissement commercial · Office building

189

467 [1913; 2] G. Metzendorf; Darmstadt (Prinz-Christian-Weg 25): Villa · Private residence

468 [1913; 4] G. Metzendorf; Darmstadt (Prinz-Christian-Weg 23): Villa · Private residence

469 [1913; 26] O.G. Riemerschmid; München · Munich (Schönbergstraße 9): Villa · Private residence

470   [1913; 10] P. Böhmer; München · Munich (Mauerkircherstraße 39, 41, 43): Wohnhausgruppe · Maisons mitoyennes · Apartment building

471   [1913; 35] E. Drollinger; München · Munich (Kufsteiner Platz 1): Wohnhaus · Immeuble de rapport · Apartment building

472　[1913; 14] Gaze & Böttcher; Breslau (Hohenzollernstraße 86): Johanniskirche · Eglise Saint-Jean
St. John's Church

473　[1913; 89] Fischer & Dörtl; Budapest (Fehervári-utcza 49): Wohnhaus · Immeuble de rapport
Apartment building

474　[1913; 27] Heilmann & Littmann; Dresden · Dresde (Königin-Carola-Platz): Zirkus Stosch-Sarasani · Cirque · Circus

475   [1913; 38] J. Goldschläger; Wien · Vienne · Vienna (Prinz-Eugen-Straße 32): Wohnhaus · Immeuble de rapport · Apartment building

476   [1913; 39] J. Goldschläger; Wien · Vienne · Vienna (Prinz-Eugen-Straße 30—34): Wohnhausgruppe · Immeubles de rapport · Apartment complex

477   [1913; 47] A. Loos; Wien · Vienne · Vienna (Michaelerplatz): Geschäfts- und Bürohaus · Immeuble · Office building

478 [1913; 41] A. Karmán, J. von Ullmann; Budapest (Maria Valeria utcza 11): Wohn- und Geschäftshaus · Immeuble de rapport · Apartment building with offices

479 [1913; 48] Kumpf & Wolf; Heidelberg (Sophienstraße 7/7b): Wohn- und Geschäftshaus Immeuble de rapport · Apartment building with shops

480 [1913; 54] Komor & Jakob; Budapest (Arena-utcza): Park-Sanatorium · Sanatorium

481   [1913; 61] A. Klingenberg, F. Beyer; Berlin (Bregenzer Straße 12): Wohnhaus · Immeuble de rapport · Apartment building

482   [1913; 62] J. Reiser; Wien · Vienne · Vienna (Weihburggasse 9): Geschäfts- und Wohnhaus Immeuble de rapport · Commercial building with apartments

483   [1913; 67] H. Poelzig; Breslau (Hohenzollernstraße 111–112): Wohnhaus · Immeuble de rapport · Apartment building

484 [1913; 56] R. Orley, Wien · Vienne · Vienna (Türkenschanzstraße 23): Villa · One-family house

485 [1913; 81] W. Koban; Darmstadt (Hohler Weg 45): Villa · Private residence

486 [1913; 68] F.R. Liebert; Pine Lake, Wisconsin: Landsitz Adolf Finkler · Propriété de campagne · Adolf Finkler Estate

196

487   [1913; 66] F.R. Liebert; Pine Lake, Wisconsin: Landsitz Adolf Finkler · *Propriété de campagne* · Adolf Finkler Estate

488 [1913; 90] R. Ehrlich, D. Ehrlich; Breslau (Schweidnitzer Straße 28/Zwingerplatz 8): Geschäftshaus · Immeuble à usage commercial · Commercial building

489 [1913; 94] Schilling & Graebner; Dresden · Dresde (An der Kreuzkirche 8): Geschäfts- und Wohnhaus · Immeuble de rapport · Apartment building with shops

490 [1913; 76] Müller-Jena; Köln · Cologne (Oppenheimerstraße/Kaiser-Friedrich-Ufer): Geschäftshaus · Compagnie d´assurances · Office building

491 [1913; 99] Heitmann; Königsberg (Krämerbrücke/Wassergasse): Kaufhaus · Grand magasin Commercial building

492 [1913; 86] –, Köln · Cologne (Kaiser-Friedrich-Ufer): Geschäftshaus der Königlichen Eisenbahndirektion · Direction des chemins de fer royaux · Office building of the Royal Railway Board

493   [1913; 7] E. Agoston; Budapest (Dohany-utcza 44): Ungaria-Bad · Etablissement de bains · Municipal baths

494   [1913; 95] J. Sándy, F. Orbán; Budapest (Fehérvári-utcza): Neue Schule · Ecole nouvelle · New School

495   [1913; 75] F.J. Lidwall; St. Petersburg · Saint-Pétersbourg (Morskaja 5): Asowsche Bank · Banque Bank

496   [1913; 84] P. Palumbo; Wien · Vienne · Vienna (Graben 16): Geschäfts- und Wohnhaus · Immeuble de rapport · Apartment building with shops

497   [1914; 2] H. Licht, G. Weidenbach, R. Tschammer; Leipzig: Feuerversicherungsverwaltungsgebäude · Compagnie d'assurances · Fire insurance administration building

498   [1914; 8] W. Schilbach; Berlin (Markgrafenstraße 25): Geschäftshaus · Immeuble à usage commercial · Commercial building

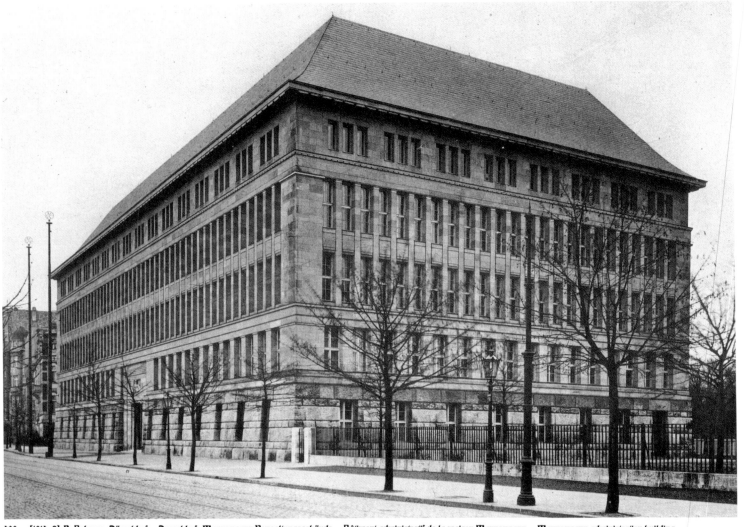

499   [1914; 3] P. Behrens; Düsseldorf · Dusseldorf: Mannesmann Verwaltungsgebäude · Bâtiment administratif de la maison Mannesmann · Mannesmann administration building

500   [1914; 4] P. Behrens; Düsseldorf · Dusseldorf: Mannesmann Verwaltungsgebäude · Bâtiment administratif de la maison Mannesmann · Mannesmann administration building

501   [1914; 7] E. von Seidl; Bonn (Koblenzer Straße 42): Haus Hermann von Rath · Villa de M. Hermann von Rath · Hermann von Rath house

502   [1914; 5] B. Paul; Frankfurt/Main · Francfort-sur-le-Main · Frankfurt-on-Main: Rose-Livingston-Damenstiftung, Nellini-Stift · Fondation Rose Livingston, Foyer Nellini · Rose Livingston's Foundation: Nellini endowment building

503   [1914; 11] Detert & Ballenstedt; Mannheim (Otto-Beck-Straße/Gutenbergstraße): Doppelvilla Stotz/Dorrinck · Villa mitoyenne · Private residence

504   [1914; 16] Schreiterer & Below; Köln · Cologne (Oberländer Ufer 130): Haus Adolf Lindgens · Villa · Private residence

505   [1914: 12] E. Saarinen; Lahtis, Finnland · Finlande · Finland: Stadthaus · Hôtel de ville · Town Hall

506   [1914: 21] R. Bauer; Düsseldorf · Dusseldorf (Wilhelmplatz/Immermannstraße): Ludwig-Loewe-Haus · Immeuble à usage commercial · Office building

507 [1914: 22] H. Klingenberg, F. Beyer; Berlin (Unter den Linden 24): Hotel Dressel · Hôtel · Hotel

508 [1914: 44] B. Ebhardt; Berlin (Mauerstraße 53): Bankhaus „Kleisthaus" · Banque · Bank

509 [1914: 23] H. O. Pauly; Wiesbaden (Coulinstraße): Städtisches Kaiser-Friedrich-Bad · Etablissement de bains · Municipal baths

510   [1914; 27] F. Höger; Hamburg · Hambourg: Rappolthaus · Etablissement commercial · Commercial building

511   [1914; 83] Berninger & Krafft; Straßburg · Strasbourg · Strassburg: Kaufhaus Modern · Grand magasin „Modern" · Modern department store

512   [1914; 32] K. Moritz; Düsseldorf · Dusseldorf: Gebäude des Barmer Bankvereins · Banque · Bank

513   [1914; 35] M. Dülfer; Leipzig: Gebäude der Dresdner Bank · Banque · Bank

208

514   [1914; 39] B. Girschowitsch; St. Petersburg · Saint Pétersbourg (Newski Prospekt 44): Sibirische Bank · Banque de Sibérie · Siberian Bank

515   [1914; 47] M. E. Lesser, Th. Karsten; Berlin (Friedrichstraße/Taubenstraße): Bavariahaus · Immeuble à usage commercial · Bavaria commercial building

516 [1914; 37] F.A. Geldmacher; Frankfurt/Main · Francfort-sur-le-Main · Frankfurt-on-Main (Schaumainkai 43/43a): Einfamilienhäuser · Villa mitoyenne · One-family house

517 [1914; 52] B. Paul; Wiesbaden (Rösselstraße 35): Villa · Private residence

210

518   [1914; 38] Chapman & Frazer; Chesunt Hill/Boston, Massachusetts: Landhaus O.H. Story · Manoir · Country house

519   [1914; 33] O. Novotny; Prag · Prague: Geschäfts- und Wohnhaus J. Stenc · Immeuble
Apartment building with shops

520   [1914; 40] A. Gessner, C. Bredow; Berlin-Friedenau (Wilhelmshoher Straße 18/19): Wohnheim · Foyer
Apartment building

521   [1914; 49] K. Moritz; Köln · Cologne: Gebäude des Barmer Bankvereins · Banque · Bank

522   [1914; 56] K. Moritz; Köln · Cologne (Mauritiusweg 77–79): Handelshaus Mauritiushof · Maison
de commerce Mauritiushof · Mauritiushof commercial building

523　[1914; 53] F. Brantzky; Köln · Cologne: Museum für ostasiatische Kunst · Musée d'art asiatique · Museum of East Asian Art

524　[1914; 85] P. Horn; Straßburg · Strasbourg · Strassburg (Place Kléber): Geschäftshaus · Maison à usage commercial · Commercial building

525 [1914; 58] G.F.E. Czermak; Brünn: Arbeiterunfallversicherungsanstalt · Bâtiment administratif · Workmen's insurance building

526 [1914; 81] A. Stürzenacker; Karlsruhe: Bahnhof · Gare · Railway station

527 [1914; 60] P. Pott; Köln-Marienburg · Cologne-Marienbourg (Am Südpark 51): Wohnhaus Pott · Propriété · Pott house

528 [1914; 89] Révész & Kollár; Budapest: Kauf- und Wohnhaus Modern & Breitner · Grand magasin
Department store with apartments

529 [1914; 97] M. de Klerk; Amsterdam (Johannes-Vermeerplein): Wohnhaus · Immeuble de rapport
Apartment building

530 [1914: 86] W.B. Griffin; Evanston, Jllinois: Landhaus F.B. Carter · Propriété de F.B. Carter · F.B. Carter residence